Nineteenth-Century
Literature Criticism

Guide to Gale Literary Criticism Series

When you need to review criticism of literary works, these are the Gale series to use:

If the author's death date is:

You should turn to:

After Dec. 31, 1959
(or author is still living)

CONTEMPORARY LITERARY CRITICISM

for example: Jorge Luis Borges, Anthony Burgess,
William Faulkner, Mary Gordon,
Ernest Hemingway, Iris Murdoch

1900 through 1959

TWENTIETH-CENTURY LITERARY CRITICISM

for example: Willa Cather, F. Scott Fitzgerald,
Henry James, Mark Twain, Virginia Woolf

1800 through 1899

NINETEENTH-CENTURY LITERATURE CRITICISM

for example: Fedor Dostoevski, Nathaniel Hawthorne,
George Sand, William Wordsworth

1400 through 1799

LITERATURE CRITICISM FROM 1400 TO 1800
(excluding Shakespeare)

for example: Anne Bradstreet, Daniel Defoe,
Alexander Pope, François Rabelais,
Jonathan Swift, Phillis Wheatley

SHAKESPEAREAN CRITICISM

Shakespeare's plays and poetry

Antiquity through 1399

CLASSICAL AND MEDIEVAL LITERATURE CRITICISM

for example: Dante, Homer, Plato, Sophocles, Vergil,
the Beowulf Poet

Gale also publishes related criticism series:

CHILDREN'S LITERATURE REVIEW

This series covers authors of all eras who have written for
the preschool through high school audience.

SHORT STORY CRITICISM

This series covers the major short fiction writers of all nationalities
and periods of literary history.

ISSN 0732-1864

Volume 22

Nineteenth-Century Literature Criticism

Excerpts from Criticism of the
Works of Novelists, Poets, Playwrights,
Short Story Writers, Philosophers, and Other
Creative Writers Who Died between 1800
and 1899, from the First Published Critical
Appraisals to Current Evaluations

Janet Mullane
Robert Thomas Wilson

Editors

Robin DuBlanc

Associate Editor

 **Gale Research Inc.**
Book Tower • Detroit, Michigan 48226

38250

STAFF

Janet Mullane, Robert Thomas Wilson, *Editors*

Robin DuBlanc, *Associate Editor*

Rachel Carlson, *Senior Assistant Editor*

Grace Jeromski, Ronald S. Nixon, *Assistant Editors*

Cherie D. Abbey, *Contributing Editor*
Denise Michlewicz Broderick, Melissa Reiff Hug, *Contributing Assistant Editors*

Jeanne A. Gough, *Permissions & Production Manager*
Linda M. Pugliese, *Production Supervisor*
Christine A. Galbraith, David G. Oblender, Linda M. Ross, *Editorial Assistants*
Suzanne Powers, Maureen A. Puhl, Lee Ann Welsh, *Senior Manuscript Assistants*
Donna Craft, Jennifer E. Gale, *Manuscript Assistants*

Victoria B. Cariappa, *Research Supervisor*
Maureen R. Richards, *Research Coordinator*
Mary D. Wise, *Senior Research Assistant*
Rogene M. Fisher, Kevin B. Hillstrom, Karen D. Kaus, Eric Priehs,
Filomena Sgambati, *Research Assistants*

Sandra C. Davis, *Text Permissions Supervisor*
Kathy Grell, Josephine M. Keene, *Text Permissions Coordinators*
Kimberly F. Smilay, *Senior Permissions Assistant*
H. Diane Cooper, *Permissions Assistant*
Maria L. Franklin, Lisa M. Lantz, Camille Robinson, Shalice Shah, Denise M. Singleton, *Permissions Clerks*

Patricia A. Seefelt, *Picture Permissions Supervisor*
Margaret A. Chamberlain, *Picture Permissions Coordinator*
Pamela A. Hayes, *Permissions Assistant*
Lillian Quickley, *Permissions Clerk*

Mary Beth Trimper, *Production Manager*
Marilyn Jackman, *External Production Assistant*

Arthur Chartow, *Art Director*
C. J. Jonik, *Keyliner*

Laura Bryant, *Production Supervisor*
Louise Gagné, *Internal Production Associate*
Shelly Andrews, *Internal Production Assistant*

Copyright © 1989 by Gale Research Inc.

Library of Congress Catalog Card Number 84-643008
ISBN 0-8103-5822-0
ISSN 0732-1864

Computerized photocomposition by
Typographics, Incorporated
Kansas City, Missouri

Printed in the United States of America

Contents

Preface

The nineteenth century was a time of tremendous growth in human endeavor: in science, in social history, and particularly in literature. The era saw the development of the novel, witnessed radical changes from classicism to romanticism to realism, and fostered intellectual and artistic ideas that continue to inspire authors of our own century. The importance of the writers of the nineteenth century is twofold, for they provide insight into their own time as well as into the universal nature of human experience.

The literary criticism of an era can also give us insight into the moral and intellectual atmosphere of the past because the criteria by which a work of art is judged reflect current philosophical and social attitudes. Literary criticism takes many forms: the traditional essay, the book or play review, even the parodic poem. Criticism can also be of several types: normative, descriptive, interpretive, textual, appreciative, generic. Collectively, the range of critical response helps us to understand a work of art, an author, an era.

Scope of the Series

Nineteenth-Century Literature Criticism (NCLC) is designed to serve as an introduction for the student of nineteenth-century literature to the authors of that period and to the most significant commentators on these authors. Since the analysis of this literature spans almost two hundred years, a vast amount of critical material confronts the student. For that reason, *NCLC* presents significant passages from published criticism to aid students in the location and selection of commentaries on authors who died between 1800 and 1899. The need for *NCLC* was suggested by the usefulness of the Gale series *Twentieth-Century Literary Criticism (TCLC)* and *Contemporary Literary Criticism (CLC)*, which excerpt criticism of creative writing of the twentieth century. For further information about *TCLC, CLC*, and Gale's other criticism series, users should consult the Guide to Gale Literary Criticism Series preceding the title page in this volume.

Each volume of *NCLC* is carefully compiled to include authors who represent a variety of genres and nationalities and who are currently regarded as the most important writers of their era. In addition to major authors who have attained worldwide renown, *NCLC* also presents criticism on lesser-known figures, many from non-English-speaking countries, whose significant contributions to literary history are important to the study of nineteenth-century literature. These authors are important artists in their own right and often enjoy such an immense popularity in their original language that English-speaking readers could benefit from a knowledge of their work.

Author entries in *NCLC* are intended to be definitive overviews. In order to devote more attention to each writer, approximately ten to fifteen authors are included in each 600-page volume, compared with about forty authors in a *CLC* volume of similar size. The length of each author entry is intended to reflect the amount of attention the author has received from critics writing in English and from foreign critics in translation. Articles and books that have not been translated into English are excluded. However, since many of the major foreign studies have been translated into English and are excerpted in *NCLC*, author entries reflect the viewpoints of many nationalities. Each author entry represents a historical overview of critical reaction to the author's work: early criticism is presented to indicate initial responses, later selections represent any rise or decline in the author's literary reputation, and current analyses provide students with a modern perspective. In each entry, we have attempted to identify and include excerpts from all seminal essays of criticism.

An author may appear more than once in the series because of the great quantity of critical material available or because of a resurgence of criticism generated by events such as an author's centennial or anniversary celebration, the republication or posthumous publication of an author's works, or the publication of a newly translated work. Usually, one or more author entries in each volume of *NCLC* are devoted to individual works or groups of works by major authors who have appeared previously in the series. Only those works that have been the subjects of extensive criticism and are widely studied in literature courses are selected for this in-depth treatment. Johann Wolfgang von Goethe's *Die Leiden des jungen Werthers (The Sorrows of Werter)* and William Makepeace Thackeray's *The History of Henry Esmond* are the subjects of such entries in *NCLC*, Volume 22.

Organization of the Book

An author entry consists of the following elements: author heading, biographical and critical introduction, principal works, excerpts of criticism (each preceded by explanatory notes and followed by a bibliographical citation), and an additional bibliography for further reading.

- The *author heading* consists of the author's full name, followed by birth and death dates. The unbracketed portion of the name denotes the form under which the author most commonly wrote. If an author wrote consistently under a pseudonym, the pseudonym will be listed in the author heading and the real name given in parentheses on the first line of the biographical and critical introduction. Also located at the beginning of the introduction are any name variations under which an author wrote, including transliterated forms for authors whose languages use nonroman alphabets. Uncertainty as to a birth or death date is indicated by a question mark.

- A *portrait* of the author is included when available. Many entries also feature illustrations of materials pertinent to an author's career, including manuscript pages, letters, book illustrations, and representations of important people, places, and events in an author's life.

- The *biographical and critical introduction* contains background information that introduces the reader to an author and to the critical debate surrounding his or her work. When applicable, biographical and critical introductions are followed by references to additional entries on the author in other literary reference series published by Gale Research Inc., including *Dictionary of Literary Biography, Children's Literature Review,* and *Something about the Author.*

- The list of *principal works* is chronological by date of first book publication and identifies the genre of each work. In those instances where the first publication was in a language other than English, the title and date of the first English-language edition are given in brackets. Unless otherwise indicated, dramas are dated by the first performance, rather than first publication.

- *Criticism* is arranged chronologically in each author entry to provide a useful perspective on changes in critical evaluation over the years. All titles by the author featured in the critical entry are printed in boldface type to enable the user to ascertain without difficulty the works being discussed. Also for purposes of easier identification, the critic's name and the publication date of the essay are given at the beginning of each piece of criticism. Unsigned criticism is preceded by the title of the journal in which it appeared. When an anonymous essay is later attributed to a critic, the critic's name appears in brackets at the beginning of the excerpt and in the bibliographical citation. Publication information (such as publisher names and book prices) and parenthetical numerical references (such as footnotes or page and line references to specific editions of works) have been deleted at the editor's discretion to provide smoother reading of the text.

- Critical essays are prefaced with *explanatory notes* as an additional aid to students using *NCLC*. The explanatory notes provide several types of useful information, including the reputation of the critic; the importance of a work of criticism; a synopsis of the essay; the specific approach of the critic (biographical, psychoanalytic, structuralist, etc.); and the growth of critical controversy or changes in critical trends regarding an author's work. In some cases, these notes include cross-references to related criticism in the author's entry or in the additional bibliography. Dates in parentheses within the explanatory notes refer to the year of a book publication when they follow a book title and to the date of an excerpt included in the entry when they follow a critic's name.

- A complete *bibliographical citation* designed to facilitate the location of the original essay or book follows each piece of criticism.

- The *additional bibliography* appearing at the end of each author entry suggests further reading on the author. In some cases it includes essays for which the editors could not obtain reprint rights.

The acknowledgments section lists the copyright holders who have granted permission to reprint material in this volume of *NCLC*. It does not, however, list every book or periodical reprinted or consulted for the volume.

Cumulative Indexes

Each volume of *NCLC* includes a cumulative index listing all the authors who have appeared in *Contemporary Literary Criticism, Twentieth-Century Literary Criticism, Nineteenth-Century Literature Criticism, Literature*

Criticism from 1400 to 1800, Classical and Medieval Literature Criticism, and *Short Story Criticism,* along with cross-references to the Gale series *Children's Literature Review, Authors in the News, Contemporary Authors, Contemporary Authors Autobiography Series, Dictionary of Literary Biography, Concise Dictionary of American Literary Biography, Something about the Author, Something about the Author Autobiography Series,* and *Yesterday's Authors of Books for Children.* Readers will welcome this cumulated author index as a useful tool for locating an author within the various series. The index, which lists birth and death dates when available, will be particularly valuable for those authors who are identified with a certain period but whose death dates cause them to be placed in another, or for those authors whose careers span two periods. For example, Fedor Dostoevski is found in *NCLC,* yet Leo Tolstoy, another major nineteenth-century Russian novelist, is found in *TCLC* because he died after 1899.

Each volume of *NCLC* also includes a cumulative nationality index to authors. Authors are listed alphabetically by nationality, followed by the volume numbers in which they appear.

Title Index

An important feature of *NCLC* is a cumulative title index, an alphabetical listing of the literary works discussed in the series since its inception. Each title listing includes the corresponding volume and page numbers where criticism may be located. Foreign language titles may be followed by the titles of English translations of these works or by English-language equivalents of these titles provided by critics. Page numbers following these translation titles refer to all pages on which any form of the title, either foreign language or translation, appears. Titles of novels, dramas, nonfiction books, and poetry, short story, or essay collections are printed in italics, while all individual poems, short stories, and essays are printed in roman type within quotation marks. In cases where the same title is used by different authors, the author's surname is given in parentheses after the title, e.g., *Poems* (Wordsworth) and *Poems* (Coleridge).

Suggestions Are Welcome

In response to various suggestions, several features have been added to *NCLC* since the series began, including: explanatory notes to excerpted criticism that provide important information regarding critics and their work; a cumulative author index listing authors in all Gale literary criticism series; entries devoted to criticism on a single work by a major author; more extensive illustrations; and a cumulative title index listing all the literary works discussed in the series.

The editors welcome additional comments and suggestions for expanding the coverage and enhancing the usefulness of the series.

Acknowledgments

The editors wish to thank the copyright holders of the excerpted criticism included in this volume, the permissions managers of many book and magazine publishing companies for assisting us in securing reprint rights, and Anthony Bogucki for assistance with copyright research. We are also grateful to the staffs of the Detroit Public Library, the Library of Congress, the University of Detroit Library, the University of Michigan Library, and the Wayne State University Library for making their resources available to us. Following is a list of the copyright holders who have granted us permission to reprint material in this volume of *NCLC*. Every effort has been made to trace copyright, but if omissions have been made, please let us know.

COPYRIGHTED EXCERPTS IN *NCLC,* VOLUME 22, WERE REPRINTED FROM THE FOLLOWING PERIODICALS:

American Literature, v. XXXV, November, 1963; v. XLII, March, 1970; v. XLIV, January, 1973. Copyright © 1963, 1970, 1973 Duke University Press, Durham, NC. All reprinted with permission of the publisher.—*American Quarterly,* v. IX, Winter, 1957 for "Adventures of the Young Man: An Approach to Charles Brockden Brown" by Warner Berthoff. Copyright 1957, renewed 1985, American Studies Association. Reprinted by permission of the publisher and the author.—*Essays in Literature,* v. 5, Spring, 1978. Copyright 1978 by Western Illinois University. Reprinted by permission of the publisher.—*Italica,* v. XXXVII, March, 1960. Reprinted by permission of the publisher.—*Kansas Quarterly,* v. 1, Summer, 1969 for "The Satiric Novels of Thomas Love Peacock" by Philip Pinkus. © copyright 1969 by the *Kansas Quarterly.* Reprinted by permission of the publisher and the author.—*The New York Times Book Review,* January 5, 1958. Copyright © 1958 by The New York Times Company. Reprinted by permission of the publisher.—*Nineteenth-Century Fiction,* v. 15, March, 1961 for "The Unity of 'Henry Esmond'" by George J. Worth. © by The Regents of the University of California. Reprinted by permission of The Regents and the author.—*Nineteenth-Century Fiction,* v. 27, December, 1972 for " 'Bankruptcy of His Heart': The Unfulfilled Life of Henry Esmond" by John Hagan; v. 29, December, 1974 for "Brockden Brown's Other Novels: 'Clara Howard' and 'Jane Talbot' " by Paul Witherington. © 1972, 1974 by The Regents of the University of California. Both reprinted by permission of The Regents and the respective authors.—*PMLA,* v. LXXV, March, 1960; v. LXXVII, March, 1962. Copyright © 1960, 1962 by the Modern Language Association of America. Both reprinted by permission of the Modern Language Association of America.—*Quarterly Review of Literature,* v. VIII, 1955 for "Giacomo Leopardi: Pioneer Among Exiles" by Theodore Weiss. © *Quarterly Review of Literature,* 1955. Renewed 1983 by the author. Reprinted by permission of the publisher.—*Research Studies,* v. 42, December, 1974 for "Geraldine Jewsbury and the Woman Question" by Meredith Cary; v. 51, June, 1983 for "New Sources on Geraldine Jewsbury and the Woman Question" by Monica Correa Fryckstedt. Both reprinted by permission of the respective authors.—*Revue des langues vivantes,* v. 27, 1961.—*The Victorian Newsletter,* n. 17, Spring, 1960. Reprinted by permission of *The Victorian Newsletter.*—*Women's Studies International Quarterly,* v. 2, 1979. Copyright © 1979 Pergamon Press Inc. Reprinted by permission of the publisher.

COPYRIGHTED EXCERPTS IN *NCLC,* VOLUME 22, WERE REPRINTED FROM THE FOLLOWING BOOKS:

Adams, Robert Martin. From *Nil: Episodes in the Literary Conquest of Void During the Nineteenth Century.* Oxford University Press, 1966. Copyright © 1966 by Robert Martin Adams. Reprinted by permission of Oxford University Press, Inc.—Auden, W. H. From a foreword to *"The Sorrows of Young Werther" and "Novella."* By Johann Wolfgang von Goethe, translated by Elizabeth Mayer, Louise Bogan, and W. H. Auden. Random House, 1971. Copyright © 1971 by Random House, Inc. All rights reserved. Reprinted by permission of the publisher.—Axelrod, Alan. From *Charles Brockden Brown: An American Tale.* University of Texas Press, 1983. Copyright © 1983 by the University of Texas Press. All rights reserved. Reprinted by permission of the publisher and the author.—Barricelli, Jean-Pierre. From an introduction to *Poems.* By Giacomo Leopardi, translated by Jean-Pierre Barricelli. Las Americas Publishing Company, 1963. Copyright © 1963 by Las Americas Publishing Company. All rights reserved. Reprinted by permission of the publisher.—Ben-Israel, Hedva. From *English Historians on the French Press Revolution.* Cambridge at the University Press, 1968. © Cambridge University Press 1968. Reprinted with the permission of the publisher and the author.—Blackall, Eric A. From *Goethe and the Novel.* Cornell University Press, 1976. Copyright © 1976 by Cornell University. All rights reserved. Used by permission of the publisher, Cornell University Press.—Burns, Bryan. From *The Novels of Thomas Love Peacock.* Croom Helm, 1985. © 1985 Bryan Burns. Reprinted by permission of the publisher.—Bush, Douglas. From *Mythology and the Romantic Tradition in English Poetry.* Cambridge, Mass.: Harvard University Press, 1937. Copyright 1937 by the President and Fellows of Harvard College. Renewed © 1964 by

Authors to Be Featured in Upcoming Volumes

Georg (Karl) Büchner (German dramatist)—An exponent of radical socialism who emphasized fatalism and despair in his view of the human condition, Büchner is noted for dramas that anticipate twentieth-century styles and themes, particularly those associated with naturalism. *Dantons Tod (Danton's Death),* a piercing study of the French Revolution, and his unfinished masterpiece *Woyzeck,* a portrait of the isolated, exploited, helpless Everyman, express with Büchner's celebrated poetic facility his austerely pessimistic vision.

George Eliot (English novelist, essayist, poet, editor, short story writer, and translator)—*NCLC* will present a critical entry on *Daniel Deronda,* Eliot's final novel. In the interrelated stories of its two principal characters—the self-confident yet unhappy Gwendolen Harleth and the mysterious, compelling Zionist Deronda—the novel reveals the hallmarks of Eliot's fiction: penetrating psychological analysis and insight into human character.

Stephen Collins Foster (American songwriter)—Foster was the composer of such perenially popular folk classics as "My Old Kentucky Home," "Camptown Races," and "Oh! Susanna."

Nathaniel Hawthorne (American novelist, short story writer, and essayist)—Considered one of the greatest American authors, Hawthorne is known for his exploration of spiritual and moral themes in the milieu of American Puritanism. *NCLC* will devote an entry to criticism of *The Marble Faun,* a novel unusual among Hawthorne's work in its Italian setting, but characteristic in its probing of the mysterious nature of sin and guilt.

William Hazlitt (English critic and essayist)—Hazlitt was one of the most important and influential commentators during the Romantic age in England. In his literary criticism and miscellaneous prose he combined discerning judgment with strongly stated personal opinion, producing essays noted for their discursive style, evocative descriptions, and urbane wit.

Charles-Marie-René Leconte de Lisle (French poet)—Leconte de Lisle was the leader of the Parnassians, a school of French poets that rejected the tenets of Romanticism in favor of emotional restraint, clarity of expression, and attention to artistic form. Inspired by the civilizations of ancient Greece, Scandinavia, and India, as well as by his love of nature, Leconte de Lisle's poetry has been described as impassive and pessimistic yet sensitive and acutely attuned to beauty.

George Henry Lewes (English philosopher, critic, journalist, novelist, and dramatist)—The longtime lover of novelist George Eliot and a significant influence on the development of her fiction, Lewes was a prolific and versatile man of letters in his own right. He wrote philosophical works, scientific studies, dramatic and literary criticism, plays, and novels, and served as editor of two influential periodicals, the *Leader* and the *Fortnightly Review*.

Herman Melville (American novelist, novella and short story writer, and poet)—A major figure in American literature, Melville is recognized for his exploration of complex metaphysical and moral themes in his novels and short fiction. *NCLC* will devote an entry to his novella *Billy Budd,* a symbolic inquiry into the nature of good and evil, innocence and guilt.

John Henry Newman (English theologian and writer)—An influential theologian, Newman was a key figure in the Oxford movement, whose adherents advocated the independence of the Church of England from the state and sought to establish a doctrinal basis for Anglicanism in the Church's evolution from Catholicism. Newman's subsequent conversion to Roman Catholicism inspired his best-known work, *Apologia pro vita sua,* an eloquent spiritual autobiography tracing the development of his beliefs.

Dmitry Ivanovich Pisarev (Russian critic and essayist)—Pisarev was the most militant of the Russian Civic Critics, an influential group of mid-nineteenth-century literary commentators who evaluated literature primarily on the basis of its social and political content. He is remembered for his controversial assault on the aesthetics and art of Alexander Pushkin as well as for his essays calling for radical social and political reform.

Stendhal (French novelist, novella writer, autobiographer, and critic)—Stendhal played an important role in the development of the modern psychological novel. In works that combine elements of both realism and romanticism, Stendhal produced subtle analyses of characters alienated from, yet intimately connected with, their society.

Charles Brockden Brown

1771-1810

American novelist, essayist, and short story writer.

Widely considered an important, if minor, American novelist, Brown is remembered for pioneering works of intellectual and psychological exploration influenced by the Gothic and sentimental literary traditions as well as by eighteenth-century rational philosophy and radical political theory. Brown is known today for his first four published novels, *Wieland, Ormond, Arthur Mervyn,* and *Edgar Huntly,* yet he also produced a number of other works, including two later novels, short stories, a fictional dialogue, essays, and political pamphlets. Although critics generally agree that Brown's major novels contain serious structural and stylistic flaws, many assert that their powerful, morally ambiguous themes and the intensity of Brown's imaginative vision compensate for these defects. Brown is also recognized as one of the first Americans to gain a significant audience abroad and to attempt to support himself by his literary endeavors; for these reasons he has often been called the first professional writer in America.

Born in Philadelphia to Quaker parents, Brown showed an early interest in intellectual pursuits, reading widely, especially in architecture and geography. In spite of poor health, Brown attended the Friends' Latin School in Philadelphia from age eleven to sixteen; at the end of this time, he became apprenticed to a lawyer instead of attending college, which was frowned upon by the Quaker religion. The study of law had no appeal for Brown, however, as he objected to the tedium of the work and the necessity of defending clients he believed to be guilty. His interests lay in literature, and, while still employed at the law office, he joined the Belles Lettres Club, a society dedicated to philosophical and political discussion, where he was exposed to radical doctrines that influenced much of his subsequent literary work. As Brown grew increasingly dissatisfied with his legal career prior to abandoning it in 1792, he devoted more and more of his time to literary endeavors. In 1789 he published a series of essays entitled *The Rhapsodist* in the *Columbian Magazine.* Here he questioned the effectiveness of the government formed after the American Revolution and demonstrated his growing interest in radical social and political ideas. Brown subsequently read Mary Wollstonecraft's *A Vindication of the Rights of Woman* (1792) and William Godwin's *An Enquiry concerning Political Justice* (1793), two works that profoundly influenced the course of his political thought. It was also around this time that friends became aware of Brown's deep emotional difficulties. Biographers speculate that chronic ill health was partially responsible for the debilitating periods of depression he suffered and note that Brown, through his own experience, was intimately familiar with the aberrant psychological states he was to portray in his novels.

In 1797, Brown completed his first novel, *Sky-Walk,* a work that was never published in its entirety. The following year, he entered a period of extraordinary literary activity with the publication of *Alcuin,* a fictional dialogue on the rights of women, and *Wieland,* his first important novel. In 1799, *Ormond,* the first part of *Arthur Mervyn,* and *Edgar Huntly* all appeared in rapid succession. Finding it difficult to support himself on the proceeds from his writing, Brown joined his

family's mercantile business in 1800. After the publication of the second part of *Arthur Mervyn* in the same year, and the appearance of *Clara Howard* and *Jane Talbot* in 1801, Brown turned away from writing novels, concentrating instead on producing a series of political pamphlets and editing and writing for the *Literary Magazine and American Register.* Brown married in 1804, and after the family business was dissolved in 1806, he relied largely on his editorial work to support his wife and children. In 1807 he became associated with the *American Register; or, General Repository of History, Politics, and Science.* Brown spent the last years of his life editing this periodical as well as composing political pamphlets and a geography. After contracting tuberculosis, Brown died in 1810.

Brown's lesser works—his essays, short stories, political pamphlets, and *Alcuin*—have been of relatively little interest to critics, who have for the most part singled out his first four published novels for analysis. *Alcuin,* the most frequently discussed of Brown's minor works, is a dialogue between a man and woman concerning women's rights. It contains arguments both for and against political and educational equality of the sexes and explores an imaginary society wherein these conditions exist. Throughout his writing career Brown remained concerned with these issues, as evidenced in the strong female characters in his novels. Like his shorter works, Brown's last two novels, *Clara Howard* and *Jane Talbot,* are of relatively little critical importance, although scholars consider them of interest in analyzing his artistic development. These two works are sentimental novels of the vicissitudes of love that have more conventional, less imaginative plot structures than his major works. Some commentators contend that the more conservative nature of these novels reflects a compromise between the intellectual and moral questioning present in Brown's earlier works and his later acceptance of the necessity of traditional religious and social values.

Scholars largely agree that Brown's most important works are his early novels, *Wieland, Ormond, Arthur Mervyn,* and *Edgar Huntly*. In these he incorporates, in varied combinations, pseudoscientific and realistic detail, elements of Gothic horror, the ideas of radical philosophers, his own moral, psychological, and epistemological speculations, and the eighteenth-century motif of sentimental seduction, which features a heroine struggling to retain her virtue. The convoluted plots of the novels, often illogical and unresolved, focus mainly on the inner world of Brown's complex, intellectual characters, examining both their sophisticated reasoning processes and deviant mental states and suggesting the existence of hidden psychological motives that determine the course of human action. Accordingly, although an outside world is evident in the works, Brown's main concern is with intellectual issues raised by the interaction of character and incident. Such subjects as educational theory, benevolent and utopian philosophy, religion, and Godwinian rationalism are explored in depth, while a recurring topic throughout the novels is the concept of appearance versus reality, particularly the moral dilemma that the dichotomy between them presents. This last theme is enhanced by Brown's frequent use of first person narrators whose credibility may be questioned. In *Wieland,* the first of the novels, the plot involves spontaneous combustion, mass murder, seduction, and ventriloquism. As the story unfolds, these elements are combined with Gothic symbolism and Brown's exploration of his characters' inner lives to create an atmosphere of psychological horror. On one level, *Wieland* is an exposé of the pitfalls of religious fanaticism. On another, however, it questions, like all of Brown's major novels, the veracity of humankind's knowledge of itself and the external world—in this case through the portrayal of unexplained events described by an unreliable narrator. Of the other novels, *Edgar Huntly* is similar to *Wieland* in its illustration of Huntly's mental turmoil through Gothic symbolism and in its use of a strange natural phenomenon (here, sleepwalking) as an indication of humankind's inability to understand reality by sense experience alone. The truth of the narrator's version of his experiences, as in *Wieland,* is suspect. In *Ormond,* Brown unites the theme of seduction with radical social theories concerning the education of women. Here, although the reliability of the narrator is undoubted, that of the protagonist is ambiguous. *Arthur Mervyn* explores the theme of appearance versus reality through the adventures of a seemingly innocent narrator who becomes incriminated in murder and theft, but whose declaration of benevolent intentions contradicts his actions.

Contemporary reviews of Brown's works often praised his clear and forceful style and his knowledge of the human heart while maintaining that his stories were improbable and that his use of detail and his narrative technique interfered with plot movement. In the late nineteenth and early twentieth centuries, critics focused on the importance of Brown's contribution to American letters. For his use of realistic details of American life, particularly his portrayal of native Americans and the wilder-

ness in *Edgar Huntly,* and for his role in initiating the American literary preoccupation with psychological horror, Brown was acclaimed as a pioneer in fiction and the father of American literature. In addition, his influence was traced in the works of Edgar Allan Poe, Nathaniel Hawthorne, and Herman Melville. Many scholars also lauded his imaginative powers, psychological subtlety, and well-drawn characters. Critics who viewed his contribution as mainly historical, however, censured his overblown style, illogical plots, and unreal characters. From the mid-twentieth century on, critics have generally found that the connection between Brown's various thematic concerns is sometimes tenuous. Commentators have also consistently agreed that the novels display plot discrepancies and a style that is marred, at times, by poor word choice and sentence structure, difficulties often attributed to the haste with which Brown wrote. Brown's characters, however, have generally been viewed as more successful. Among the most frequently discussed are the villains portrayed in *Wieland* and *Ormond* and the complicated protagonists of *Arthur Mervyn* and *Edgar Huntly,* who unwittingly harbor villainy within themselves. Many of Brown's female characters have also been praised for their intelligence and the level of their educational attainments. Some recent critics have examined the complexities that point of view presents in *Wieland, Edgar Huntly,* and *Arthur Mervyn*. Others have isolated Brown's themes and the origins of his philosophical ideas in an attempt to explore his purpose in writing the novels. Still others have concentrated on such specific topics as the relationship of Brown's fiction to the Gothic and sentimental literary traditions, the melodramatic aspects of the novels, and the presence of psychological symbolism in his writing. Despite the flaws of his works, Brown continues, because of his imaginative vision and the psychological and intellectual complexity of his fiction, to be regarded as an influential and innovative novelist in the history of American literature.

(See also *Dictionary of Literary Biography,* Vol. 37: *American Writers of the Early Republic;* Vol. 59: *American Literary Critics and Scholars, 1800-1850;* Vol. 73: *American Magazine Journalists, 1741-1850;* and *Concise Dictionary of American Literary Biography: Colonization to the American Renaissance, 1640-1865.*)

PRINCIPAL WORKS

Alcuin: A Dialogue   (fictional dialogue)   1798
Wieland; or, The Transformation   (novel)   1798
Arthur Mervyn; or, Memoirs of the Year 1793. 2 vols.
   (novel)   1799-1800
Edgar Huntly; or, Memoirs of a Sleep-Walker   (novel)
   1799
Ormond; or, The Secret Witness   (novel)   1799
Clara Howard   (novel)   1801; also published as *Philip
   Stanley; or, The Enthusiasm of Love,* 1807
Jane Talbot   (novel)   1801
*Carwin, the Biloquist, and Other American Tales and
   Pieces*. 3 vols.   (unfinished novel and short stories)
   1822
The Novels of Charles Brockden Brown. 7 vols.   (novels)
   1827
The Rhapsodist, and Other Uncollected Writings   (essays
   and novel fragment)   1943
The Novels and Related Works of Charles Brockden Brown.
   6 vols.   (novels and unfinished novels)   1977-87
Memoirs of Stephen Calvert   (unfinished novel)   1978

Carwin, the Biloquist and *Memoirs of Stephen Calvert* were published earlier in William Dunlap's *The Life of Charles Brockden Brown; Together with Selections from the Rarest of His Printed Works, from His Original Letters, and from His Manuscripts Before Unpublished*, 1815.

CHARLES BROCKDEN BROWN   (essay date 1798)

[*In the following excerpt from a letter to the editor of the* Weekly Magazine, *Brown announces plans for his forthcoming novel* Sky-Walk, *and advocates an American fiction designed to appeal to both intellectual and popular audiences. His remarks were first published on 17 March 1798.*]

To the story-telling moralist the United States is a new and untrodden field. He who shall examine objects with his own eyes, who shall employ the European models merely for the improvement of his taste, and adapt his fiction to all that is genuine and peculiar in the scenes before him, will be entitled at least to the praise of originality.

Here, as elsewhere, every man is engaged in the gratification of some passion. Some pleasure, intellectual or corporeal, or the grand instrument of all kinds of pleasure, money, constitutes the scope of every one's pursuit; but our ecclesiastical and political system, our domestic and social maxims, are, in many respects, entirely our own. He, therefore, who paints, not from books, but from nature, who introduces those lines and hues in which we differ, rather than those in which we resemble our kindred nations beyond the ocean, may lay some claim to the patronage of his countrymen.

The value of such works lies without doubt in their moral tendency. The popular tales have their merit, but there is one thing in which they are deficient. They are generally adapted to one class of readers only. By a string of well-connected incidents, they amuse the idle and thoughtless; but are spurned at by those who are satisfied with nothing but strains of lofty eloquence, by the exhibition of powerful motives, and a sort of audaciousness of character. The world is governed, not by the simpleton, but by the man of soaring passions and intellectual energy. By the display of such only can we hope to enchain the attention and ravish the souls of those who study and reflect. To gain their homage it is not needful to forego the approbation of those whose circumstances have hindered them from making the same progress. A contexture of facts capable of suspending the faculties of every soul in curiosity, may be joined with depth of views into human nature and all the subtleties of reasoning. Whether these properties be wedded in the present performance, the impartial reader must judge. (pp. 135-36)

> *Charles Brockden Brown, "Advertisement for 'Sky Walk'," in his* The Rhapsodist, and Other Uncollected Writings, *edited by Harry R. Warfel, Scholars' Facsimiles & Reprints, 1943, pp. 135-36.*

CHARLES BROCKDEN BROWN   (essay date 1799)

[*Brown stresses his unique use of native American detail in this excerpt from his preface to* Edgar Huntly, *first published in 1799.*]

The flattering reception that has been given, by the public, to **Arthur Mervyn,** has prompted the writer to solicit a continuance of the same favour, and to offer to the world a new performance [*Edgar Huntly*].

America has opened new views to the naturalist and politician, but has seldom furnished themes to the moral painter. That new springs of action and new motives to curiosity should operate, that the field of investigation, opened to us by our own country, should differ essentially from those which exist in Europe, may be readily conceived. The sources of amusement to the fancy and instruction to the heart, that are peculiar to ourselves, are equally numerous and inexhaustible. It is the purpose of this work to profit by some of these sources; to exhibit a series of adventures, growing out of the condition of our country, and connected with one of the most common and most wonderful diseases or affections of the human frame.

One merit the writer may at least claim: that of calling forth the passions and engaging the sympathy of the reader by means hitherto unemployed by preceding authors. Puerile superstition and exploded manners, Gothic castles and chimeras, are the materials usually employed for this end. The incidents of Indian hostility, and the perils of the Western wilderness, are far more suitable; and for a native of America to overlook these would admit of no apology. These, therefore, are, in part, the ingredients of this tale, and these he has been ambitious of depicting in vivid and faithful colours. The success of his efforts must be estimated by the liberal and candid reader.

> *Charles Brockden Brown, in a preface to his* Edgar Huntly; or, Memoirs of a Sleep-Walker, *edited by David Lee Clark, The Macmillan Company, 1928, p. xxiii.*

THE ANTI-JACOBIN REVIEW AND MAGAZINE   (essay date 1800)

[*In the following review, the critic condemns numerous aspects of* Ormond.]

This performance [*Ormond; or the Secret Witness*], though consisting of only one volume, from the smallness and closeness of its typography, contains nearly as much as three volumes printed in the usual manner. This may, perhaps, be an inducement to purchase it to those who are fond of "*a cheap pennyworth.*"

"*Ormond,*" says the author, "will, perhaps, appear to you a contradictory, or unintelligible being. I pretend not to the infallibility of inspiration. He is not a creature of fancy."—This *may* be true; but, from our study and knowledge of human nature, we are convinced that, if he be "not a creature of fancy," he must have been engendered in the brain of phrenzy. He is a "monster which the world never saw." From much disgusting and pernicious nonsense contained in the work before us, we extract the following palliation, or rather *vindication*, of the crime of suicide when compared with that of drunkenness.

> The pressure of grief is sometimes such as to prompt us to seek a refuge in voluntary death. *We must lay aside the burthen which we cannot sustain.* If thought degenerate into a vehicle of pain, *what remains but to destroy that vehicle?* For this end, death is the obvious, but not the only, or morally speaking, the worst means. There is one method of obtaining the bliss of forgetfulness, in comparison with which *suicide is innocent.*

Are these the deductions of a mind imbued with the powers of ratiocination?—No! They are the effusions of a pragmatic enthusiast! a mad-headed metaphysician! Such, indeed, is the whole of the performance, excepting the space which is occupied by a dry and prolix detail of the progress of the yellow fever.

We shall ony add, that, *if* a want of perspicuity, *if* a want of elegance in style, *if* a want of imagination, *if* a want of nature in the delineation of character, *if* a want of incident, *if* a want of plot and connection, and, finally, *if* a want of *common sense*, be excellencies in a novel, the author of *Ormond, Wieland, Arthur Mervyn,* &c. &c. has a fair claim to the laurel of pre-eminence in "the temple of Minerva."

> *A review of "Ormond; or, The Secret Witness," in*
> The Anti-Jacobin Review and Magazine, *Vol. VI,*
> *No. XXVI, August, 1800, p. 451.*

THE AMERICAN REVIEW, AND LITERARY JOURNAL (essay date 1802)

[*In the following excerpt from a review of* Wieland, *the anonymous critic discusses such elements of the novel as style, narrative technique, and characterization.*]

It will imply some commendation of the author's powers of narration, when we say, that having begun the perusal of [*Wieland*], we were irresistibly led on to the conclusion of the tale. The style is clear, forcible and correct. Passages of great elegance might be selected, and others which breathe a strain of lively and impassioned eloquence.

It is impossible not to sympathise in the terror and distress of the sister of Wieland. Persons of lively sensibility and active imaginations may, probably, think that some of the scenes are too shocking and painful to be endured even in fiction.

The soliloquies of some of the characters are unreasonably long, and the attention is wearied in listening to the conjectures, the reasonings, the hopes and fears which are successively formed and rejected, at a moment when expectation is already strained to its highest pitch. These intellectual conflicts and processes of the imagination show fertility of conception, and the art of the narrator; but this art is too often exercised in suspending the course of action so as to render the reader restless and impatient. The generality of readers love rather to be borne along by a rapid narrative, and to be roused to attention by the quick succession of new and unexpected incidents.

The characters which are introduced are not numerous; nor are they such as may be easily found in the walks of common life. Carwin is an extraordinary being, and, in some degree, incomprehensible. If his prototype is not in nature, he must be acknowledged the creature of a vigorous fancy, fitted to excite curiosity and expectation. The author seems to have intended to exhibit him more fully to view; but not having finished the portrait, or doubtful of the effect of the exhibition, has reserved him for some future occasion, when he may be made the hero of his own story. The consequences produced by the exercise of the powers imputed to him were not foreseen, and were beyond the reach of his controul. Their exertion was from the impulse of caprice, or for a momentary self-gratification. He is the author of the most dreadful calamities, without any malicious or evil intention.—The reader sees the misery and ruin of an amiable family, by ignorant and deluded beings, undeserving the severity of punishment.—The endowments of such a being as Carwin, if they can possibly exist to the extent here

imagined, are without advantage to the possessor, and can be of no benefit to mankind. This seems to be the principal lesson taught by the delineation of such a character.

Wieland and his family, in retirement, devoted to contemplation and study, and mixing little in the varied scenes of enlarged society, furnish few of those instructive facts and situations which may be supposed to occur in the usual progress of life. The even tenor of their existence is not broken by the stronger impulses of social feeling, or agitated by the conflict of violent passions. Their repose is disturbed, and their imaginations excited, by unknown and invisible agents. Comparisons, therefore, with the actual or probable situation of the reader, are not often suggested, nor are many precepts of instruction to be derived from examples too rare for general application. Against the freaks of a *ventriloquist,* or the illusions of a madman, no rules can be prescribed for our protection. No prudence or foresight can guard us against evils which are to flow from such causes. The example of Wieland may teach us, indeed, the necessity of placing due restraints on the imagination; the folly of that presumptuous desire which seeks for gratifications inconsistent with the laws of existence and the ordinary course of nature; and to be content with the light which is set before us in the path of our moral and religious duties, without seeking for new illuminations. From the exhibition, however, of an infatuated being, deluded by the suggestions of a disturbed intellect, into the commission of acts the most unnatural and horrid, it is doubtful whether any real good is to be derived. But whether benefit or harm, or how much of either is to be received from tales of this kind, we are not prepared to decide, and they are questions not easily solved. The good or ill effect of a book, in most cases, depends on the previous disposition and character of the reader.

The author has certainly contrived a narration deeply interesting; and whatever may be its faults, and some we have ventured to remark, *Wieland,* as a work of imagination, may be ranked high among the productions of the age. (pp. 36-8)

> *A review of "Wieland; or, The Transformation," in*
> The American Review, and Literary Journal, *Vol. 2,*
> *No. 1, January-March, 1802, pp. 28-38.*

THE CRITICAL REVIEW AND ANNALS OF LITERATURE (essay date 1803)

[*This critic enthusiastically praises* Arthur Mervyn.]

There is no inconsiderable degree of praise due to the author of [*Arthur Mervyn*] for the spirit and force of his diction, as well as the knowledge of the human heart displayed throughout. . . . The miseries suffered by the unhappy subjects of the yellow-fever in Philadelphia are very feelingly depicted; but perhaps so great a number of pages as are employed in the description of this malady, would better have become any other species of publication than a novel. If we were inclined to find fault, we might say that Mr. Brown has been frequently too minute in his relation of trivial occurrences, sometimes almost to garrulity; but we have been too much pleased, on the whole, to notice blemishes like these.

> *A review of "Arthur Mervyn: A Tale," in* The Critical
> Review and Annals of Literature, *Vol. XXXIX, September, 1803, p. 119.*

THE LITERARY JOURNAL (essay date 1804)

[*This anonymous critic censures* Jane Talbot.]

This novel [*Jane Talbot*] purports to have been written by the author of *Arthur Mervyn* and *Edgar Huntley,* but certainly this could scarcely have been collected from the perusal of the work itself. It is indeed something in his style and manner, but so very inferior in point of nervous language and vigour of imagination, that one can scarcely help suspecting that this is an awkward imitation by some other hand, and that he lent his name only. This author, we mean Mr. Browne, delights in pourtraying singular characters, but when these are well drawn and consistent with human nature, having the shades only strongly heightened, we generally read them with pleasure, and even with profit. The author appears to be friendly to the interests of religion and morality. But as to the present silly publication, we again assert that it can scarcely have been the work of the author whose name it bears.

A review of "Jane Talbot," in The Literary Journal, *Vol. III, No. VIII, May 1, 1804, p. 492.*

THE CRITICAL REVIEW, LONDON (essay date 1804)

[*In a review of* Edgar Huntly, *this critic comments on the believability of the novel and the ambiguous nature of Clithero's character.*]

The scene, through the greater part of [*Edgar Huntley*], is laid in America; and, on the whole, American scenes and manners are not inaccurately described. The numerous 'hair-breadth 'scapes,' however, and the strange sleep-walking adventures, are, scarcely within the bounds of probability; though the attention is kept so much alive by the changes of fortune, that we can seldom stay to examine the means by which they are produced. In the character of Clithero, there is something so gloomily savage, so extravagantly harsh, that we often shudder in contemplating him. He is artfully, also, kept at a distance; so that we can scarcely fix any distinct feature in our minds: the bad and good are so intimately blended, that we cannot ascertain the real hue at any one period. The author, too, leaves us in uncertainty; and, seemingly unable otherwise to dispose of him, drowns him, when the work has reached its destined conclusion.

A review of "Edgar Huntley; or, The Memoirs of a Sleep-Walker," in The Critical Review, London, n.s. *Vol. III, No. III, November, 1804, p. 360.*

THE BRITISH CRITIC (essay date 1811)

[*An anonymous critic offers a mixed assessment of* Wieland.]

[*Wieland*] is one of the most extraordinary compositions of the kind which have of late come before us, and to which we certainly cannot deny the praise of ingenious contrivance. They who delight in the marvellous, may here be gratified even to satiety. Yet amidst all the triumphs which are here recorded of artifice and fraud, over simplicity and innocence, it is made to appear, that the sufferers had to blame themselves for an excess of credulity, and a want of proper reflection on the consequences of their actions. This we presume is the moral which the writer intended to inculcate, but it is with so much intricacy enfolded in tales and incidents of wonder, that it requires great pains and patience to disentangle it. Many of the deceptions represented as practised successfully on various unsuspecting objects of both sexes, are effected by ventrilocution. We doubt, however, whether it could ever be carried to the extent which is here depictured.

A review of "Wieland; or, The Transformation," in The British Critic, *Vol. XXXVII, January, 1811, p. 70.*

THE GENTLEMAN'S MAGAZINE AND HISTORICAL CHRONICLE (essay date 1811)

[*This reviewer provides a brief but decidedly harsh review of* Wieland.]

[*Wieland* is a] most improbable and horrid tale; and evidently written by one whose talents might have been better employed.

A review of "Wieland; or, The Transformation," in The Gentleman's Magazine and Historical Chronicle, *Vol. LXXXI, April, 1811, p. 364.*

THE NORTH AMERICAN REVIEW AND MISCELLANEOUS JOURNAL (essay date 1819)

[*In the following excerpt from a review of William Dunlap's* The Life of Charles Brockden Brown *(see Additional Bibliography), the critic analyzes structure, characterization, and style in Brown's works.*]

Brown's mind is distinguished for strong, intense conception. If his thoughts are vast, he is still always master of them. He works with the greatest ease, as if his mind were fully possessed of his subject, and could not but suggest thoughts with freedom and rapidity. In the most monstrous and shocking narrative, he writes with the utmost sincerity, as if he laboured under a delusion which acted with a mischievous but uncontrollable power. He never, indeed, shews a desire to complete a story, nor draws a character so much for what it is to effect in the end, as for the development of mind. The present incident is perhaps fine in itself, and answers the author's purpose, and gives room for the display of great strength; but it has little or no connexion with others. With the greatest solicitude to tell us everything that passes in the mind before a purpose is formed, he is very careless as to any continuity or dependence in the events which lead to or flow from that purpose. He sometimes crowds more into one day than we should have expected in many, and at others leaps over so large an interval as to make the narrative improbable to all who are not in the secret. His characters cannot be relied upon: notwithstanding their strength and apparently stubborn singularities, they accommodate themselves readily to the author, sometimes losing all the importance with which they were at first invested, and at others accomplishing something beyond or opposite to what was expected, and almost what we can believe to be within the compass of human power in the agent or weakness in the sufferer. This incompleteness of views and inconsistency of characters is not owing to carelessness or haste in the writer; he had never determined how things should end, nor proposed to himself any prevailing object when he began, nor discovered one as he advanced. We generally close a story with a belief that as much more might be said. He was engrossed by single, separate scenes, such as invention suggested from time to time; and while we can account from this fact for our feeling little solicitude about the story as a whole, we must at the same time form a high estimate of an author's power, who can carry us through almost disconnected scenes without any considerable failure of interest. He seems fond of exciting and vexing curiosity, but when he fails of satisfying it, it is more, we believe, from forgetfulness than design.

There is very little variety in his writings; at least in those where his genius is most clearly discerned. He loves unusual, lawless characters, and extraordinary and tragic incident. There should not be a moment of calm brightness in the world, unless as it may serve to heighten the effect of approaching gloom and tempest. The innocent are doomed to suffer, as if virtue were best capable of enduring and shone most conspicuously in trial, or at least drew the largest sympathy. This suffering is of the mind; bodily pain and death appear but moderate and vulgar evils, and rather a refuge than punishment for the triumphant criminal, who has rioted in mischief till he is weary, and willing to die for repose since his work is ended. In these sad views of life, which make society worse than the wilderness and men's sympathy and promises little better than a mockery, there is no apparent design to mislead the world, or covertly condemn its opinions and awards, but merely to take a firm hold of the heart, by appeals to its pity, terror, indignation or wonder. He wants the universality and justice of a fair observer of the world. He thinks too much in one way, and that a narrow one. His views are of one kind, and shew that he thought more than he observed.

His style is clear, simple and nervous, with very little peculiarity, and not the slightest affectation or even consciousness of manner; rarely varying to suit the subject, or to distinguish conversation from narrative or description. It uniformly bears marks of a serious, thoughtful mind, remembering its excitement and suffering rather than experiencing them. There are, now and then, some attempts at playfulness and humour, but they are wholly unsuccessful, and sometimes ludicrous and offensive. There are few striking sentences which the reader would unconsciously retain for the beauty of their structure, or any peculiar terms; we have the thought without the expression. We should not pronounce Brown a man of genius, nor deny him that distinction, from his style. It might have been acquired by care and study, but it is the result only and never betrays the process. There is no attempt at what is too vaguely called fine writing; no needless ornament, no sacrifice of spirit and energy from a weak ambition of harmony or finish, no use of a strictly poetical term to excite the imagination, when another and a simpler one will convey the meaning more definitely. He uses words merely to express his own thoughts, and not to multiply our associations. He never allows them to outstrip, or, which is nearly the same thing, to take the place of feeling and truth. He appears to be above the common temptation to exhibit tokens of more passion than is felt, merely on account of 'the imaginary gracefulness of passion,' or to decorate scenes with borrowed beauties till they have lost every thing which could distinguish them, or even persuade us that we were in our own world.

It has been our object in these remarks, to point out some of Brown's prominent defects and excellences. We never intended to make an abstract of his stories; and such extracts as we could admit would do little justice to the author.—His readers will observe every-where that he was an ardent admirer of Godwin, though not his slave. Godwin himself has pronounced him a writer of distinguished genius and acknowledged himself in his debt.—The uses and evils of criticism can no longer be felt by him; the dead are beyond our judgment. It is for the living that their opinions and genius should be inquired into; and it is hardly less dishonourable to let the grave bury their worth than consecrate their errors. (pp. 75-7)

A review of "The Life of Charles Brockden Brown," in The North American Review and Miscellaneous Journal, *Vol. XXIV, June, 1819, pp. 58-77.*

JOHN KEATS (letter date 1819)

[*Keats is considered a key figure in the English Romantic movement and one of the major poets in the English language. Critics note that though his creative career spanned only four years, he achieved remarkable intellectual and artistic development. His poems, notably those contained in the collection* Lamia, Isabella, The Eve of St. Agnes, and Other Poems, *are valued not only for their sensuous imagery, simplicity, and passionate tone, but also for the insight they provide into aesthetic and human concerns, particularly the conflict between art and life. In an excerpt from a letter to a friend, Keats evaluates Brown's novel* Wieland, *comparing it with the works of Johann Christoph Friedrich von Schiller and William Godwin.*]

Ask [Reynolds] if he has read any of the American Brown's novels that Hazlitt speaks so much of. I have read one call'd **Wieland**—very powerful—something like Godwin. Between Schiller and Godwin. A Domestic prototype of S[c]hiller's Armenian. More clever in plot and incident than Godwin. A strange American scion of the German trunk. Powerful genius—accomplish'd horrors—I shall proceed tomorrow. (p. 424)

John Keats, in a letter to Richard Woodhouse on September 21, 1819, in The Letters of John Keats, *Vol. II, edited by Maurice Buxton Forman, Oxford University Press, London, 1931, pp. 420-27.*

[JOHN NEAL] (essay date 1824)

[*A novelist and essayist, Neal was one of the first Americans to contribute sketches and reviews of American literary figures to British periodicals. In the following excerpt from a two-part review of American writers, Neal provides a critique of language, subject matter, style, and plot in Brown's novels.*]

One is continually hearing, more or less, about American literature, of late, as if there were any such thing in the world as American literature; or any such thing in the United States of North America, as a body of native literature—the production of native writers—bearing any sort of national character, either of wisdom or beauty—heavy or light—*or* having any established authority, even among the people of the United States. And go where one will, since the apparition of one American writer among us, (of whom a word or two more by and by,) some half-a-dozen stories and storybooks; a little good poetry, (with some very bad poems;) four or five respectable, and as many more trumpery novels—with a book or two about theology—one is pretty sure to hear the most ridiculous and exaggerated misrepresentations, one way or the other, for or against *American* authorship, as if American authorship (so far as it goes) were anything different from English, or Scotch, or Irish authorship; as if there were any decided nationality in the style or manner of a book-maker in America—who writes English, or endeavours to write English—to set him apart, or distinguish him from a book-maker in the United Kingdom, who is engaged in the same business.

With two exceptions, or at the most three, there is no American writer who would not pass just as readily for an English writer, as for an American, whatever were the subject upon which he was writing; and these three are Paulding, Neal, and Charles Brockden Brown. . . . (pp. 304-05)

• • • • •

[Brown] was a good fellow; a sound, hearty specimen of Trans-Atlantic stuff. Brown was an American to the back-bone—without knowing it. He was a novelist; an imitator of Godwin, whose *Caleb Williams* made him. He had no poetry; no pathos; no wit; no humour; no pleasantry; no playfulness; no passion; little or no eloquence; no imagination—and, except where panthers were concerned, a most penurious and bony invention—meagre as death,—and yet—lacking all these natural powers—and working away, in a style with nothing remarkable in it—except a sort of absolute sincerity, like that of a man, who is altogether in earnest, and believes every word of his own story—he was able to secure the attention of extraordinary men, as other people (who write better) would that of children;—to impress his pictures upon the human heart, with such unexampled vivacity, that no time can obliterate them: and, withal, to fasten himself, with such tremendous power, upon a common incident, as to hold the spectator breathless.

His language was downright prose—the natural diction of the man himself—earnest—full of substantial good sense, clearness, and simplicity;—very sober and very plain, so as to leave only the *meaning* upon the mind. Nobody ever remembered the words of Charles Brockden Brown; nobody ever thought of the arrangement; yet nobody ever forgot what they conveyed. You feel, after he has described a thing—and you have just been poring over the description, not as if you had been reading about it; but, as if you, yourself, had seen it; or, at least,—as if you had just parted with a man who *had* seen it—a man, whose word had never been doubted; and who had been telling you of it—with his face flushed. He wrote in this peculiar style, not from choice; not because he understood the value or beauty of it, when seriously and wisely employed—but from necessity. He wrote after his peculiar fashion, because he was unable to write otherwise. There was no self-denial in it; no strong judgment; no sense of propriety; no perception of what is the true source of dramatic power (distinctness—vividness.) While hunting for a subject, he had the good luck to stumble upon one or two (having had the good luck before, to have the yellow fever) that suited his turn of expression, while he was imbued, heart and soul, with Godwin's thoughtful and exploring manner: and these one or two, he wore to death. The very incidents, which were often common-place, are tossed up, over and over again—with a tiresome circumstantiality, when he is not upon these particular subjects.—He discovered, at last perhaps, as many wiser men have done—when there was no use in the discovery—that it is much easier to suit the subject to the style, than the style to the subject;—no easy matter to change your language, or cast off your identity—your individuality—but 'mighty easy,' as a Virginian would say, to change your theme.

Brown was one of the only three or four professional authors, that America has ever produced. He was the first. He began, as all do, by writing for the newspapers—where that splendour of diction, for which the Southern Americans are so famous—is always in blast: He was thought little or nothing of, by his countrymen; *rose,* gradually, from the newspapers to the magazines, and circulating libraries; lived miserably poor; died, *as* he lived, miserably poor; and went into his grave with a broken heart. (pp. 421-22)

By great good luck, surprising perseverance, and munificent patronage—for America—poor Brown succeeded—(much, as the Poly-glott Bible maker succeeded, whose preface always brings the tears into our eyes—in burying all his friends—

outliving all confidence in himself—wasting fortune after fortune—breaking his legs, and wearing out his life, in deplorable slavery, without even knowing it.)—Even so, poor Brown succeeded—in getting out—by piece-meal, a small, miserable, *first* edition—on miserable paper (even for *that* country)—a *first* volume of one or two of his works—the second *volume* following, at an interval—perhaps of years—the second *edition* never—never, even to this hour.—Yet will these people talk of their *native* literature.

There has never been; or, as the *Quarterly* would have it—there has *not ever* been, any second edition, of anything that Brown ever wrote—in America, we mean. (pp. 422-23)

Brown wrote ***Arthur Mervyn; Edgar Huntly; Clara Howard; Wieland; Jane Talbot; Ormond;*** and some papers, which have since been collected, and called the ***Biloquist.***

Clara Howard and ***Jane Talbot*** are mere newspaper novels; sleepy, dull common-sense—very absolute prose—nothing more.

Arthur Mervyn is remarkably well managed, on many accounts; and miserably in others. It was the first, the germ of all his future productions. Welbeck was *himself*—he never equalled him, afterwards—though he did play him off, with a new name and a new dress, in every new piece. Explanations were designed—half-given, but never finished: machinery, half disclosed—and then forgotten, or abandoned.—Brown intended, at some future day, to explain the schoolmaster, that seduced the sister of Mervyn, into Welbeck:—Incidents are introduced, with great emphasis, which lead nowhere—to nothing; and, yet, are repeated in successive works.—Thus—(we speak only from recollection—and have not seen one of the books for many a year)—in ***Arthur Mervyn, Edgar Huntly,*** and, perhaps, in ***Jane Talbot,*** a sum of money comes into the possession of ''another person''—who converts it, under strong temptation, to his own use.—Let us pass on.

Edgar Huntly was the second essay—***Ormond,*** the last. About ***Wieland*** we are not very certain. These three are unfinished, irregular, surprising affairs. All are remarkable for vividness, circumstantiality, and startling disclosures, here and there: yet all are full of perplexity—incoherence—and contradiction. Sometimes, you are ready to believe that Brown had made up the whole stories, in his own mind, before he had put his pen to the paper; at others, you would swear that he had either never seen, or forgotten, the beginning, before he came to the end, of his own story. You never know, for example, in ***Edgar Huntly,*** whether—an Irishman, whose name we forget—a principal character, is, or is *not,* a murderer. Brown, himself, seems never to have made up his own mind on that point. So—in ***Wieland***—you never know whether Brown is, or is not, in earnest—whether Wieland was, or was not, supernaturally made away with. So—in ***Ormond***—who *was* the secret witness?—to what purpose?—What a miserable catastrophe it is—Quite enough to make anybody sick of puling explanations.—Now, all this mystery is well enough, when you understand the author's *intention.* Byron leaves a broken chain—for us to guess by—when his Corsair is gone. We *see* that he scorns to explain. Byron is mysterious—Brown only perplexing. Why?—Because Brown undertakes to explain; and fails. Brown might have refused as Byron did. We should have liked him, if he had, all the better for it; as we do Byron. But we shall never forgive him, or any other man, dead or alive, who skulks out of any undertaking, with an air—as if not he, but other people are to be pitied.—We have our eye on a case, in point; but—no matter now.

Brown wanted material. What little he found, though it had all the tenuity of pure gold, he drew out, by one contrivance and another, till it disappeared in his own hands. So long as it would bear its own weight, he would never let go of it; and, when it broke—he would leave off spinning, for a time, as if his heart had broken with it. He would seem to have always taken up a new piece before he had thrown off the old one (we do not mean that Old One, whom it is rather difficult for any author to throw off, after he has once given himself up to, the harlotry of the imagination)—to have clung, always, to one or two favourite ideas—the Ventriloquist—and the yellow fever—as if they were his nest-eggs: one might have written, with as much propriety, at the *end* of any story that he ever wrote, as in almost any part of it—after the fashion of Magazines—"TO BE CONTINUED." This grew, of course, out of a system which prevailed, then—and is now taking a new shape in the twopenny publication of costly works, by the number. He was a storyteller by profession. Like ****** He knew, very well—as did Hajji Baba—that nobody will pay for a joke, if he can help it; that, lunging point foremost, with an epigram—is like running hilt first with a small sword; that no man likes working for a dead horse; that, if you want your pay for a fat story, you must go round with your hat, before you have come to the knob. He was a magazine writer; and rather 'cute. There was no stealing *his* bait. If you nibbled, you were in, for the whole—like a woman in love—hook, trap, and all. Money-lenders; gamblers; and subscribers to a story—which is *"to be continued,"* nobody knows how long, are all in the same pickle. They must lend more; play higher; and shell out, again—or all that has been done, goes for nothing. You must have the last part of a story—or the first, is of no use to you: (this very article, now, is a pretty illustration)—our author knew this. He never let go of more than one end of a story; at a time—even when he had sold out. It is amusing to see how entirely he would forget where his own traps lay—while he was forging bait; his own hooks, while he was counterfeiting the flies. The curious box—broken to pieces, at night, so mysteriously (in **The Sleep Walker**) is in point. We could cite fifty more cases. **The Secret Witness** is hardly anything else, but a similar box—knocked apart, in a mysterious manner—the Lord knows wherefore. So with **Wieland:** In every case, you leave off, in a tease—a sort of uncomfortable, fidgetting, angry perplexity—ashamed of the concern, that you have shewn—and quite in a huff with him—very much as if you had been running yourself to death—in a hot wind—after a catastrophe—with the tail soaped.

Yet, our conclusion respecting Charles Brockden Brown, is this. He was the Godwin of America. Had he lived here—or anywhere, but in America—he would have been one of the most capital story-tellers—in a serious way, that ever lived. As it is, there is no one story of his, which will be remembered or read, after his countrymen shall have done justice to the genius that is really among them. They have enough of it—and of the right sort—if they will only give it fair play. Let them remember that no man will be great, unless he work hard; that no man will work hard, unless he is obliged—and that those who do so work, cannot afford to work for nothing, and find themselves. It would be well for his countrymen to profit by—not imitate—we despise imitation even of what is excellent—it would be well for them to profit by his example. We want once more, before we die, to look upon the face of a real North American. God send that we may! (pp. 424-25)

[*John Neal*], *"American Writers"* and *"American Writers No. II,"* in Blackwood's Edinburgh Maga-

zine, *Vol. XVI, Nos. XCII and XCIII, September and October, 1824, pp. 304-11; 415-28.*

[RICHARD HENRY DANA, SR.]   (essay date 1827)

[*Dana was an American poet, journalist, and editor during the early nineteenth century. In the following excerpt from a review of the 1827 edition of Brown's novels, he underscores the uniformity of Brown's subject matter and the power of his characterization.*]

Twenty odd years have been allowed to pass before even an imperfect edition of the works of fiction of our long unrivalled novelist is given to the public [**The Novels of Charles Brockden Brown,** (1827)]. Yet nearly the whole of that time Brown has been alone; for no one approached the height he rested on, till the author of the *Pioneers* and *Pilot* appeared. Like his own Clithero, he lay stretched in moody solitude, the waters of the noisy world rolling blindly on around him, and a wide chasm open between him and his fellow men. In 1815, Mr. Dunlap gave us a life of him; an ill arranged and bulky work, yet too meagre where it should be particular and full [see Additional Bibliography]. To this, however, we are indebted for all we know of Brown's life; and we owe to it also an article on Brown, which appeared in the *North American Review* for 1819; an article which, we fear, has left us little to say [see excerpt above]. (p. 321)

To the speculative mind, it is a curious fact that a man like Brown should of a sudden make his appearance in a new country, in which almost every individual was taken up in the eager pursuit of riches, or the hot and noisy contests of party politics; when every man of talent, who sought out distinction, went into one of the professions; when to make literature one's main employment, was held little better than being a drone; when almost the only men who wrote with force and simplicity were some of the leaders amongst our active politicians; when a man might look over our wide and busy territory, and see only here and there some self-deluded being dabbling in a dull, shallow stream, which he fancied running clear and strong to the brim with the waters of Helicon.

Did not the fact that Brown produced such works at such a time show clearly the power of genius over circumstances, we might be inclined to attribute to his loneliness of situation something of the solitariness, mysteriousness, and gloom, which surround all he wrote. But these come not of outward things. The energies of his soul were melancholy powers, and their path lay along the dusky dwelling-places of superstition, and fear, and death, and woe. The soul of such a man takes not its character from the world, but takes out from the world what suits its nature and passes the rest by; and what more it needs, and what it cannot find abroad, it turns for inward, and finds or creates it there. "My existence," says Brown, "is a series of thoughts, rather than of motions. Ratiocination and deduction leave my senses unemployed. The fulness of my fancy renders my eye vacant and inactive. Sensations do not precede and suggest, but follow and are secondary to the acts of my mind." So strong was this cast of his mind, and so single was it in its purpose, that of all men of imagination we know of none who appear from their writings to have looked so little at nature, or to have been so little open to its influences. With the exception of Mervyn's return to Hadwin's, and his last journey thence, and the opening of **Carwin,** with one or two more slight instances, he seldom attempts a description of natural scenery, or, where he labors it most, is confused and indistinct, as, for instance, in *Edgar Huntly*. It is amidst shut-up houses, still, deserted streets, noisome smells, and pestilence, and death, and near the slow, black hearse, and the dead man's grave, that his calling lies; and he has no time to turn aside to breathe the fresh, clear air of the country. He seems, in fiction, as intent upon his purpose as Howard ever was in real life; he who could spare no time from hospitals and prisons, for palaces and statues and pictures. This may be thought a serious deficiency in Brown's genius; yet it is curious to see how sometimes a defect takes somewhat the appearance of an advantage. This very want of variety has given such an air of truth to what he is about, showing such an earnest singleness of purpose, that perhaps no writer ever made his readers so completely forget that they were not reading a statement of some serious matter of fact; and so strong is this impression, that we even become half reconciled to improbabilities, which so vex us in fiction, though often happening in daily life. This enables us to bear, too, better with his style; for, along with something like a conviction that the man who had vivacity of genius enough for such inventions, could never have delivered himself with such dull poverty and pedantry of phrase, we at last are almost driven to the conclusion that however extraordinary it may be, it is nevertheless a fact; for the man "never could have made it," and that things must have happened pretty much as he tells us they did.

If Brown was remarkable for having appeared amongst a people whose pursuits and tastes had, at the time, little or no sympathy with his own, and in a country in which all was new, and partook of the alacrity of hope, and where no old remembrances made the mind contemplative and sad, nor old superstitions conjured up forms of undefined awe; he is scarcely less striking for standing apart, in the character of his mind, from almost every other man of high genius. He is more like Godwin than like any other; but differs from him in making so many of his characters live, and act, and perish, as if they were the slaves of supernatural powers, and the victims of a vague and dreadful fatality. Even here his character for truth is maintained; and his invisible agencies mingle with the commonest characters, and in the most ordinary scenes of life. It is true that these mysterious agencies are all explained away; yet such a hold do they take upon our minds, that we cannot shake off the mystical influence they have gained over us; and even those who have practised the deceptions, seem to have done it not so much from a love of deception as from a hankering after something resembling the supernatural, and an insane sort of delight in watching its strange and dreadful force over others; both he that is wrought upon, and he that works, seem, the one to suffer and the other to act, as under some resistless fate. Brown's fatal power is unsparing, and never stops; his griefs and sufferings are not of that kind which draws tears and softens the heart; it wears out the heart and takes away the strength of our spirits, so that we lie helpless under it. A power of this kind holds no associations with nature; for in the gloomiest, and the wildest, and barrenest scenes of nature, there is something enlarging, and elevating, something that tells us there is an end to our unmixed sorrow, something that lifts us above life, and breathes into us immortality—God is there! No! it is surrounded by man and the works of man—man in his ills, and sins, and feebleness; it is there alone that we can feel what is the bitterness and weariness of unmixed helplessness and woe.

So much was gloominess the character of Brown's genius, that he does not, like other authors, begin his story in a state of cheerfulness or quiet, and gradually lead on to disappointment

and affliction. Some one writes a letter to a friend who has asked him for an account of his suffering life. It hints at mysteries, and sorrows, and remorse—sorrows and remorse to which there can be no end, but in the rest of the grave. He has already passed through years of miseries, and we come in and go on with him to the end of his story; but they have not ended there; and we leave him praying that death may at last bring peace to his sick and worn heart. There is woe behind us, and woe before us. The spirit cries, with the Apocalyptic angel, seen flying through the midst of heaven, in vision by John, "Woe, woe, woe, to the inhabiters of the earth!" (pp. 322-25)

We have said that even the want of variety, and the defects of style in Brown have in some measure helped to the impression of the truth of his stories. But he makes this impression in a better way also, by his circumstantiality, his careful mention of a thousand little particulars. His personages, too, before undertaking the simplest act, go through a process of reasoning; we have all the *pros* and *cons* that can be started; and though the reasoning has too often more of show than substance, still, this being the way in which the larger part of the world reasons, we are more and more convinced of the truth of his relations. He certainly has this striking characteristic of genius, the power of making his characters living and breathing men, acting in situations which are distinctly and vividly presented to our minds. (p. 328)

Brown's style is rather remarkable. The structure of his sentences is for the most part simple, but his words! they remind one of the witty M. P.'s reply, when asked what was doing in the house; "Lord Castlereagh is airing his vocabulary this morning, that's all." To use the happy phrase of that lord, "the fundamental feature" of the style is a most pains-taking avoidance of the Saxon, wherever it is possible, and a use of words of Latin origin in such combinations as they were never put into before. Dudley's leaving New York is spoken of as "this evasion." "Her decay was eminently gradual." Constantia scarcely "retrieving her composure." "Retrieved reflection;" "extenuate the danger;" "extenuate both these species of merit;" "preclude the necessity;" "exclude from my countenance;" "resume her ancient country;" "immersed in perplexity;" "obvious to suppose;" "obvious to conclude;" "unavoidable to conclude;" "copious epistle;" "copiously interrogated;" "copious and elegant accommodation;" "my departure was easy and commodious;" "the barrier that severs her from Welbeck must be as high as heaven and insuperable as necessity;" "a few passengers likewise occurred, whose hasty," &c. No one who has once read the description of Carwin as he is first introduced, can ever forget it. Yet we are told, "shoulders broad and square, breast sunken, his head drooping, his body of uniform breadth, supported by long and lank legs, were the *ingredients* of his frame." The ingredients of a pudding!

Brown is much more remarkable for putting his thoughts into the form of questions than Godwin ever was, yet *to ask* and *to question* are scarcely to be met with through the whole six volumes, but instead of these, we have *interrogated, interrogations*, and even *interrogatories*. It is true that the kind of writing we speak of does not show itself equally in all his stories; some few of them are tolerably free from it.

This perverted taste is much to be regretted; for after the excitement of a first reading (when less attention is paid to the style of a powerful story), we are perpetually feeling the incongruity between the strong characters and passions and terrific scenes, and the language in which they are presented to us. The distinguished novelists of this day must by and by suffer from defect in style, while the beauty and truth of language of our old dramatists will help to the increased pleasure they give the more they are studied. Brown himself has beautifully said, ''The language of man is the 'intercourse of spirits,' the perfect and involuntary picture of every fixed or transient emotion to which his mind is subject.'' We wish he had remembered this, and left his passions and thoughts to speak their own tongue. (pp. 329-30)

It may be thought that we have dwelt too long upon the faults of Brown, and that we are of an ungracious temper for so doing. We have taken no delight in this part of our work, for we reverence his genius and feel an affection for so kind and good a man. If we speak with all our hearts of what is excellent in a great man, we shall do him little harm by pointing out his defects, while at the same time we are doing good to multitudes. We are not of those who would pull down a stone upon the head of him who is but just raising a structure for his own fame; nor of those who are glad to see the barren sands drifting over the foundation which another was beginning to lay. Brown has built up his eternal pyramid, and laid him down to rest in it. (pp. 332-33)

[Richard Henry Dana, Sr.], in a review of ''The Novels of Charles Brockden Brown,'' in The United States Review and Literary Gazette, *Vol. II, No. 5, August, 1827, pp. 321-33.*

WILLIAM HAZLITT   (essay date 1829)

[One of the most important commentators during the Romantic age, Hazlitt was an English critic and journalist. He is best known for his descriptive criticism in which he stressed that no motives beyond judgment and analysis are necessary on the part of the critic. Though he wrote on many diverse subjects, Hazlitt's most important critical achievements are his typically Romantic interpretation of characters from William Shakespeare's plays, influenced by the German critic August Wilhelm Schlegel, and his revival of interest in such Elizabethan dramatists as John Webster, Thomas Heywood, and Thomas Dekker. In the following excerpt from an essay originally published in the Edinburgh Review for October 1829, Hazlitt appraises Brown's works, focusing on the American characteristics of his imagination.]

Mr. Brown, who preceded [Washington Irving], and was the author of several novels which made some noise in this country, was a writer of a different stamp. Instead of hesitating before a scruple, and aspiring to avoid a fault, he braved criticism, and aimed only at effect. He was an inventor, but without materials. His strength and his efforts are convulsive throes—his works are a banquet of horrors. The hint of some of them is taken from *Caleb Williams* and *St. Leon,* but infinitely exaggerated, and carried to disgust and outrage. They are full (to disease) of imagination,—but it is forced, violent, and shocking. This is to be expected, we apprehend, in attempts of this kind in a country like America, where there is, generally speaking, no *natural imagination.* The mind must be excited by overstraining, by pulleys and levers. Mr. Brown was a man of genius, of strong passion, and active fancy; but his genius was not seconded by early habit, or by surrounding sympathy. His story and his interests are not wrought out, therefore, in the ordinary course of nature; but are, like the monster in Frankenstein, a man made by art and determined will. For instance, it may be said of him, as of Gawin Douglas, 'Of Brownies and Bogilis full is his Buik.' But no ghost, we will venture to say, was ever seen in North America. They do not

walk in broad day; and the night of ignorance and superstition which favours their appearance, was long past before the United States lifted up their head beyond the Atlantic wave. The inspired poet's tongue must have an echo in the state of public feeling, or of involuntary belief, or it soon grows harsh or mute. In America, they are 'so well policied,' so exempt from the knowledge of fraud or force, so free from the assaults of *the flesh and the devil,* that in pure hardness of belief they hoot the *Beggar's Opera* from the stage: with them, poverty and crime, pickpockets and highwaymen, the lock-up-house and the gallows, are things incredible to sense! In this orderly and undramatic state of security and freedom from natural foes, Mr. Brown has provided one of his heroes with a demon to torment him, and fixed him at his back;—but what is to keep him there? Not any prejudice or lurking superstition on the part of the American reader: for the lack of such, the writer is obliged to make up by incessant rodomontade, and face-making. The want of genuine imagination is always proved by caricature: monsters are the growth, not of passion, but of the attempt forcibly to stimulate it. In our own unrivalled Novelist, and the great exemplar of this kind of writing, we see how ease and strength are united. Tradition and invention meet half way; and nature scarce knows how to distinguish them. The reason is, there is here an old and solid ground in previous manners and opinion for imagination to rest upon. The air of this bleak northern clime is filled with legendary lore: not a castle without the stain of blood upon its floor or winding steps: not a glen without its ambush or its feat of arms: not a lake without its Lady! But the map of America is not historical; and, therefore, works of fiction do not take root in it; for the fiction, to be good for any thing, must not be in the author's mind, but belong to the age or country in which he lives. The genius of America is essentially mechanical and modern. (pp. 319-20)

William Hazlitt, ''American Literature—Dr. Channing,'' in The Complete Works of William Hazlitt, *Vol. 16, edited by P. P. Howe, J. M. Dent and Sons, Ltd., 1933, pp. 318-38.*

AMERICAN QUARTERLY REVIEW   (essay date 1830)

[This review provides an admiring survey of Brown's novels, discussing their originality, imaginative power, and characterization.]

It is [the] unfortunate propensity to prolixity in the philosophical novelist, together with his frequent and inevitable lapses into mysticism and obscurity, which renders his productions, despite of whatever talents they may display, less readable, and therefore less popular than those of the describer in fiction, although, in most cases, the performances of the latter are the result of mechanical tact rather than intellectual pre-eminence. There is, at least, one descriptive novelist of this country, whose peculiar powers consist in grouping and arranging, sometimes with considerable effect, but frequently with wearisome minuteness, and always with the square-and-rule exactness and measured precision of a *working man,*—those appearances of external nature with which he is familiar, rather than in displaying them with the bold, free, concise and vivid pictorial touches of a forcible and animated writer. Yet the novels of this descriptive writer are much more popular than those of the philosophical Brown, because his descriptions, long-winded and tediously minute as they often are, display to us the appearances of real, not of fanciful nature, and what is more to the purpose, they are always blended with a sufficiency of historical, or at least, probable events, to keep alive curiosity and render the reader anxious to learn the result of the tale.

The novels of Brown, on the contrary, are so glutted, if we may use the expression, with philosophical reflections, springing from the inexhuastible fertility of his superior intellect, that there is little room left in them for the admission of incidents. These are, therefore, comparatively few, and compressed into bounds so small, that it is with difficulty the reader can trace them. He, consequently, becomes tired of the search, his curiosity cools, he frets at being kept by the never-ending exhibitions of the author's powers of subtilizing, from the main object for which he took up the book, namely, to become acquainted with the fortunes or misfortunes of its characters. He, therefore, throws it aside, no doubt, fully convinced of the author's talents, but with no disposition ever to resume its perusal. (pp. 318-19)

Some of [Brown's] novels, however, abstract and metaphysical as they are, possess, in no slight degree, the power of entertaining. Desultory and superficial readers, it is true, such as chiefly resort to the circulating libraries for entertainment, will not derive much enjoyment from any of them. They will not have patience to go through the long but masterly discussions of the principles of duty, or investigations of the motives of action, with which they abound. Such are best pleased with sprightly dialogue, or hurried and animated narrative. But there are minds differently constituted; tastes differently formed. There are the serious and the reflecting, who read for the purpose of study rather than amusement, or rather the amusement most acceptable to them, is that which awakens in their minds, contemplations on the nature and dispositions of man, and on the duties and designs of existence. To those who relish such studies; who wish to animadvert upon theories and doctrines, and to see the positions of right and wrong illustrated by portraits drawn from human characters, and examples from the occurrences of human life, the works of Brown will afford a mental repast, rich and noble, which can be excelled by none with which we are acquainted, in the whole regions of fictitious literature.

As novels, therefore, although these works may not be so universally attractive as if they were of a lighter and more narrative cast, yet they have not been written in vain. They fill up a chasm or vacancy in a department of literature, which had not been before occupied, or occupied but in a very partial manner by one or two of Godwin's works. It has been said, that Godwin, in his *Saint Leon* and *Caleb Williams*, set the example to Brown of this style of writing. It may have been so, if affording a hint can be called setting an example. But Brown, if he took the hint from Godwin, has greatly improved on it. He has carried it to an extent, and raised it to a height much beyond any thing to be found in Godwin; and may justly be placed at the head of the school, if he may not be considered its founder. The existence of such a school of novel-writing, although it should not be so extensively popular as some others, is a matter, which, by increasing the varieties of this department of literature, must afford satisfaction to literary men; and, inasmuch as it addresses itself to the peculiar taste of some readers, it supplies a desideratum in letters which entitles its founders to gratitude and praise. The question of its popularity apart, it must be admitted to be a school of romance highly magnificent and instructive, and requiring greater powers of mind to excel in it than any other. By Americans it ought to be regarded with peculiar favour, for by an American it has been brought to the highest point it has yet attained.

On this account, Brown ought, in justice, to be considered the chief ornament of our national literature. In no other department of authorship, except that in which he has so greatly excelled, can we claim any superiority over other countries. Nor is excellence in the philosophical romance so slight a matter, that we should not be proud of it. It is a most difficult species of composition. To excel in it, requires a mind of the first rate order, fertile in ideas; choice, accurate, and flowing in expression; inventive, acute, and gifted with an almost intuitive skill in the nature, passions, and general pursuits of man, together with the obligations imposed on him by his various circumstances and positions in society. In short, the same powers of mind and knowledge of human nature, which enabled Brown to write *Wieland,* and *Arthur Mervyn,* would have enabled him to excel in any species of mental exertion to which he might have chosen to apply his faculties.

These novels, indeed, taken as a whole, appear to us a phenomenon in literature; and we are persuaded, that by every reflective mind, that studies them properly,—for to understand their worth, and appreciate their importance, requires much study—will consider them such. We have mentioned the opinion which several critics have advanced, that Brown was a follower of Godwin's school of romance. We now state explicitly, that we think such an opinion erroneous. That he took the hint of his peculiar manner of scrutinizing motives from Godwin, we will not controvert. But if he did, it was all he took from him. In nothing else does he resemble him; and, even in this, there is a peculiarity about Brown which sufficiently distinguishes him from his alleged model, and gives him, in our opinion, solid claims to originality in the only point in which it has ever been denied him. Godwin's strain is connected, deductive, argumentative. Brown's is abrupt, concise, and sententious. The one deduces and demonstrates; the other investigates and analyses; the one is expansive and profound; the other is close, pointed, and elucidative; the one is vehement and passionate; the other is intense and pathetic. In fact, except in their propensity to dwell on the operations of the mind, these two great writers have as little in common as any other fabricators of tales; and even moralizing, the topic which is so alluring to both, is approached by each in a manner so different, as to entitle him to the full credit of thinking for himself.

Having thus, as we hope, established for our countryman a sufficient claim to originality in the line of literature which he adopted,—for it is not pretended, that he, in any degree, resembles any other writer than Godwin—we will now go farther, and say, that we consider his novels much superior to those of his philosophical rival, in the demonstration which they afford of intellectual power. Godwin has produced no work so unique—so deeply philosophical, so awfully mysterious, and so overwhelmingly pathetic as *Wieland;* or so full of strange and impressive incidents, and just, yet novel reflections, as *Arthur Mervyn.* Godwin's knowledge of existing manners, appears to be more extensive than that which was possessed by Brown. He has drawn, therefore, more accurate pictures of his contemporaries, and his incidents seem to correspond more with the ordinary practices of life. But Brown excelled in the knowledge of our general nature. Man, in the abstract, seems to have been his favourite study. He delighted to contemplate him in reference to the universe, as a being forming an important link in the chain of creation, subject to certain laws and destinies which he cannot control, and liable, at the same time, to mutations of condition, powerfully affecting his well-being, which are greatly influenced by the results of his own volition. Godwin's personages are, in general, the artificial men and women of the world, whose fortunes and characters are operated upon, and very much modified, by the institutions of society. Brown's heroes and heroines, it is true, are also of this world, for they are human beings; but their conduct and fortunes seem to flow more from their natural condition and internal impulses, than from the operation of institutions, the influence of fashion, or the collisions of worldly competition.

But the great characteristic by which the novels of Brown are distinguished from all others, is the profound rationality of his personages, and their perpetual proneness to weigh the results of their actions before they are committed. Notwithstanding this habit of prudential calculation, his works do not contain a greater proportion of discreet and well-conducted personages than are to be found in productions which represent the transactions as resulting from less premeditation. The villains of Brown's creation are the most finished of all villains—deliberating ones. They are seldom driven by the irresistible agency of external circumstances to the commission of evil. They deliberate as if they had the free choice of action; they investigate and compare results, and at length, from determined preference—not from sudden impulse—they adopt the course which is criminal. On the other hand, his virtuous characters are doubly so, on account of their adhering rigidly to what is right, despite of every inconvenience and hardship to which they may be thereby exposed, and of which their premeditating habits have sufficiently apprized them.

We have thus far descanted on the general character of these remarkable novels. We shall now approach them more closely, and speak of each in reference to its peculiar merits—for, although there never was a series of fictitious works more similar in their leading features and prominent outlines, yet each is founded on a special basis, and unfolds events and characters peculiar to itself. The series consists of six different works—*Wieland, Arthur Mervyn, Edgar Huntly, Ormond, Jane Talbot,* and *Clara Howard,* neither of which is extended beyond one moderate duodecimo volume, except *Arthur Mervyn,* which consists of two. We have here arranged them in the order of their enumeration in the edition before us; and we believe, that in the same order their respective merits may be justly estimated.

Wieland, the first of the series, is undoubtedly the most singular and magnificent of them all. We know, indeed, of no narrative more powerfully conceived, and more impressively written than this. A tone of awful solemnity pervades it, which in some places arises to a degree of terrible intensity, sufficient to agitate the firmest nerves. It is, also, wonderfully original. We know of no model after which it might have been constructed. To neither its plot, its characters, nor its design, are we aware of any prototype. It relates disasters and sufferings of the wildest and most heart-rending description that can befall humanity. Its design, as well as its execution, is remote from every thing trite or common-place. It would seem almost impossible, at this age of the world, to discover any fresh topic of moral instruction. But the lesson taught in this work, if not absolutely new, has so rarely been made the subject of moral inculcation, that it possesses all the air and effect of originality. The delusions of mind which sometimes arise from the impression of unaccountable sights and sounds, are painted in such strong colours, and the calamities which they produce are illustrated by such awful examples, that a lesson is given against their indulgence, which must be felt and remembered by every reader.

The scenes of the story are in the neighbourhood of Philadelphia. Indeed all these novels are truly American in their localities. With the exception of a small portion, or rather epi-

sode, of *Edgar Huntly,* the scenes of which are in Ireland, all the events narrated in these works, take place on American soil. No exotic scenery, nor borrowed imagery in the descriptions of external nature, is introduced. Brown drew all his illustrations, as he drew his characters and his reflections, from the stores of his own mind. He borrowed nothing from books. He needed not to borrow. The abundance of his own resources is so apparent in every page, that it may be safely conjectured, that it would have cost him more trouble to either borrow or imitate, than to write in his own peculiar way, from his immediate impulses and reflections. (pp. 319-23)

[*Wieland*] is a production, which no human being can read without feeling deep interest; and no one of ordinary sensibility, without sympathizing almost to agony with the sufferers. Nor is there any adequate judge of the intellectual powers of man, but will admire their extraordinary display in the vivid conceptions and forcible delineations of incidents and characters contained in this work. Yet let us not be hyperbolical in our praise. Let not our admiration of the powers exhibited, render us blind to the faults that exist. This work has one great blemish, which notwithstanding its innumerable and unique beauties, must strike the most superficial reader. The explanation of the mysterious occurrences is altogether unsatisfactory. The faculty of ventriloquism possessed by Carwin, is insufficient to account for the visual deceptions—the luminous appearances, and apparition of faces—not to mention the explosion in the temple, and the violent blow inflicted on the elder Wieland, which occasioned his death.

Moreover, the character of Carwin is not only too improbable, but is utterly inconsistent with itself. Had he been represented as a perfectly malicious demon, delighting in the bloodshed and horrors which he occasioned, we might have overlooked or forgiven the improbability of such a sheer fiend, as he would then have been, existing in human shape. But he is represented as free from malice, and intending no evil. In his confession to the sister of Wieland, he says, that he acted merely for amusement, without anticipating the possibility of the evils which ensued. In reply to her accusations, "I am not this villain," he exclaims; "I have slain no one; I have prompted none to slay; I have handled a tool of wonderful efficacy, without malignant intentions, but without caution; ample will be the punishment of my temerity, if my conduct has contributed to this evil." How can this be reconciled with his commendation of Wieland for having slain his wife, and his diabolic injunction to complete the sacrifice by the destruction of his children? And after they were destroyed, to order Clara and Pleyel to be added to the list of victims, could not surely comport with harmless intentions. Yet an effort seems to be made by the author to excuse or palliate the agency of Carwin, and to throw on the credulity and weak-mindedness of Wieland, the whole guilt of these horrible transactions.

We shall not urge the charge which has been often made against this work, that the whole story is too improbable, and the actors in it too unlike human beings, to admit of even the transient credibility which should attach to a novel. We think that this charge is not altogether just. The incidents are certainly extraordinary; they were intended to be so. The characters were also intended to be extraordinary. In effecting these intentions, the very charge proves the author's success. If the transactions had been more conformable to worldly experience, and the personages more like the ordinary classes of mankind, the work would certainly have been more natural, and, no doubt, would have been to many readers more attractive. But it would have been less remarkable for those bold demonstrations of genius it now possesses in its wild originality, the force and grandeur of its delineations, its combinations of awfulness and pathos, and the singular scope and nature of its contemplations and reasonings.

Arthur Mervyn, in point of importance, as well as of arrangement, is the next novel of the series contained in the edition before us. It is much the longest, and by far the most diversified in its characters and details. It is inferior to *Wieland* in grandeur of conception and pathetic effect. But, if we may use the expression, it possesses more common-place interest; it belongs more to this world, and is therefore better calculated to win favour from the generality of readers. On commencing its perusal, after having passed through the sublimely agitating scenes of *Wieland,* we felt as if we were descending from the region of supernatural beings to the residence and society of men. In *Wieland,* our faculties were strained to a height of sublime terror, and our feelings agitated with preternatural horrors, from which we were partially relieved by engaging in the more earthly story of Arthur Mervyn.

The scenes of this work are laid in Philadelphia, during the pestilential season of 1793, when the population of this city suffered such dreadful calamities from the ravages of the yellow fever. The design of writing it is stated by the author in his preface, to have been to snatch from oblivion some of the instances of fortitude and constancy which were exhibited, and to transmit to posterity a faithful picture of the condition of this city, during that fatal period. Brown has thus tried his descriptive powers on an awful subject, which had already occupied the attention, and called forth the talents of some of the greatest masters of literary delineation in both ancient and modern times. (pp. 328-30)

We must observe . . . that the character of Welbeck in this production, is that of one of the most original and effectively drawn villains to be found in romance. There is nothing in these novels which so forcibly proves, that their author possessed, in an eminent degree, the rare faculty of imparting to characters of the same class, an individuality of features sufficient to show, that the conception of each was a totally separate and distinct operation of the mind. Each of his novels contains a villain, who makes a prominent figure in the work; but no two of these villains have the least resemblance to each other. Carwin is the villain of *Wieland;* for, in spite of all the softening down of his conduct in the explanatory portion of the work, he is still a villain—and one, too, worthy of all detestation. He is a mysterious demon, who, from unseen positions, wantonly and remorselessly launches the bolts of destruction upon the peaceful and the virtuous, from no other motive than a diabolical propensity to do mischief.

Welbeck, the *villain* of *Arthur Mervyn,* has nothing of the mystical demon about him. He is a downright scoundrel, actuated by the usual feelings and impulses of human depravity. He is a man of the world. He is a cheat, a hypocrite, a debauchee, a seducer of female innocence,—a coward, and a murderer. The author does not, as in the case of Carwin, make any attempt to palliate the enormities of this man. He does not invest him with a single redeeming quality. He endows him with no splendid atrocity—no amiable weakness. All his actions are mean, selfish, degrading, profligate, ungenerous, and inhuman. In fact, the whole man is utterly execrable. His fate, too, severe as it is, excites contempt instead of pity. We rejoice at the detection of his schemes—at the exposure of his de-

pravity; and when he dies, loathsomely, of a putrid fever, within the walls of a prison, we cannot spare him a sigh.

How much more is Brown to be commended for giving to this highly-finished portrait of a villain, a colouring and a fate so dismal and forbidding, than the far-trumpeted author who has attempted to give attraction to the wickedness of Paul Clifford? Brown's mind was too pure—he was too sincerely a lover of integrity and good morals, to render vice captivating by meretricious decorations. His great genius was never prostituted, like that of some of our more recent writers of unworthy celebrity, for the purpose of undermining virtuous principles, or of bringing into contempt the most useful and most sacred institutions of society.

The novel of *Edgar Huntly* now claims our attention. It is the wildest in its scenery, and perhaps the most romantic in its incidents, of any of the series. The author, in his preface [see excerpt dated 1799], professes to have written it with the intention of producing a novel exclusively American. He observes,—

> The field of investigation opened to us by our own country, differs essentially from those which exist in Europe. The sources of amusement to the fancy, and instruction to the heart, that are peculiar to ourselves, are equally numerous and inexhaustible. It is the purpose of this work to profit by some of these sources; to exhibit a series of adventures, growing out of the condition of our country, and connected with one of the most common and most wonderful diseases or affections of the human frame.

The disease referred to is that of sleep-walking, certainly a wonderful, and, we believe, not a common affection. In these *Memoirs of a Sleep-Walker,* for such is the secondary title of the work, his actions, during the paroxysm, are, we fear, carried beyond the point of credibility; and have a tendency, by their extravagance, to weaken the interest of the reader in the story, by destroying the illusion of the narrative, and reminding him too forcibly that he is perusing fiction. In every respect, indeed, this is an inferior performance to either of those on which we have been commenting. It has neither the awful and mysterious magnificence which characterizes *Wieland,* nor the animating variety of incidents and characters to be found in *Arthur Mervyn.* We are at a loss to know which of its characters is the hero of the work. It cannot be Edgar Huntly, although he lends it his name; for his adventures constitute but a very small portion of the performance, and are brought to no conclusion. He is the narrator of the tale, which he relates in an epistolary form to a Miss Waldegrave, for whom, it would appear, from some passages, that he has a kind of platonic love, mingled with some prudential attachment to the sum of seven or eight thousand dollars of which she had become possessed by the death of her brother. This brother was murdered by some unknown person, and from some unknown motive, for he is said to have had no enemy, and it was only by the discovery of documents among his papers after his death, that he was found to have possessed the money we have mentioned, which was lodged, in his name, in one of the Philadelphia banks. He was supposed to have died poor, his only apparent dependence having been upon the emoluments of a country-school. That this money was his, there was sufficient evidence in the credit he had on the bank-books; but how he became its owner, was as mysterious and unknown as the motive and author of his murder.

The mystery in relation to this money, however, was soon explained by the claim made upon it by a seafaring gentleman, supported by circumstantial proofs sufficient to satisfy any conscientious mind. The claimant admits that he has no legal proofs, and relies for justice solely upon the integrity and convictions, as to the validity of his claim, of Miss Waldegrave, the present possessor of his property. Edgar assures him that this lady will do him justice. Indeed, whenever he speaks of either her or himself, he represents both as immoveably upright. The restoration of the money is therefore naturally expected. But we do not hear that it ever took place. There is no more said of the seafaring man. The affairs of Miss Waldegrave, too, are consigned to neglect. The most probable inference from this silence of her lover, Edgar, is, that she gave up the money, and that he, in consequence, gave up the design of making her his wife. These are the two personages whom the author seems to have intended for the hero and heroine of his work. If the reader thinks proper to take them as such, we have no objection; but, for ourselves, we must repudiate them from such a dignified station, for they possess no attribute either of interest or moment, that can entitle them to it.

The most interesting female in the performance, is a pretty Irish girl, named Clarice. She captivates a young countryman of her own, called Clithero, which, by the way, is rather an odd name for an Irishman. From the days of king Heremon to those of William IV., we believe no son of Erin ever bore such an appellation. Now we conceive it very injudicious in an author to apply inappropriate names to his personages. What would we think of Sir Walter Scott, if he had given to his Scotch peasants Italian names, or Russian titles to his English nobles? Would we not at once feel the incongruity, and condemn its absurdity? What renders the misnomer in relation to this Irish youth, the more observable, is, that he performs by far the most important part among the dramatis personae of this work. In fact, the whole interest of it revolves around him. Were he absent from it, insipidity and insignificance would be its only qualities, and it would be totally unworthy of emanating from the same mind that produced **Wieland** and **Arthur Mervyn**. The remarkable character and singular adventures of Clithero, however, elevate this work to a high place in the scale of romance-writing, and entitle it to a fair participation in the applause which justice will for ever accord to the extraordinary series of fictions of which it forms a part. The virtues, the misfortunes, the enthusiasm, the remorse, and the singular malady of this youth, are depicted with all the force and fervour of the genius of Brown. His sorrows and his despair are not, perhaps, raised to the sublime and awful altitude of Wieland's, but they are conceived in the same spirit of intensity, and exhibited with the same masterly command over the imaginations and feelings of men. A delusive idea, proceeding from erroneous notions of duty, similar to what actuated Wieland, impels him to the commission of crime. This produces remorse, and a succession of the most dreadful sufferings, which, at length, terminate, like those of Wieland, in the commission of suicide.

We now come to the novel of **Ormond,** which is distinguished by containing a most attractive portrait of female loveliness, virtue, and fortitude. In the character of *Constantia Dudley,* there is something so endearing, so pathetic, and beautiful, while, at the same time, every thing is so apparently probable, so genuinely natural, that we could never weary in contemplating it. Her unshaken fortitude amidst all reverses, her untiring filial affection under the most trying circumstances, and the triumphant heroism she displayed in her last desperate and bloody struggle in defence of her honour, render her character

altogether, not only one which we must admire, but which we could worship. She is no puritan, but she has a due sense of her duty to Heaven. She is not free from all human weakness and error, for she is only a woman, but this renders her the more dear to our affections.

The character of Ormond is more in the style of Godwin than any other throughout these volumes. He is one of those metaphysical geniuses engendered by that fruitful mother of hair-brained speculative monsters, the *first* French Revolution, the great ambition of whom was to new-model society by abolishing all established institutions, and substituting their own extravagant systems in their stead. Ormond is just such a conception as we might suppose would naturally flow from the brain of the author of *Political Justice.* He is a wealthy and mysterious plotter against the existing religion and governments of Christendom. But he is a libertine, and his libertinism occasions his sudden and premature destruction by the hand of Constantia. His political schemes, therefore, whatever they were, for we are left altogether in the dark as to their precise nature and objects, are baffled, and we receive no more information respecting them. . . . [We consider **Ormond**] the best adapted of any of the series, to afford that diversified entertainment to the every-day reader which is most likely to acquire general popularity. (pp. 334-37)

[**Jane Talbot** and **Clara Howard**] are both inferior to either of those on which we have commented. Still they are works of merit, displaying in their composition the ability of a deep thinker as well as of a practised writer. They could not, indeed, be otherwise, for Brown is their author; and nothing could proceed from the mint of his rich intellect, without having upon it the stamp of genius and high literary merit. (p. 337)

A review of "The Novels of Charles Brockden Brown,"
in American Quarterly Review, *Vol. VIII, No. 16,*
December, 1830, pp. 312-37.

MARGARET FULLER (essay date 1846)

[*A distinguished critic and early feminist, Fuller played an important role in the developing cultural life of the United States during the first half of the nineteenth century. As a founding editor of the Transcendentalist journal, the* Dial, *and later as a contributor to Horace Greeley's* New York Tribune, *she was influential in introducing European art and literature to the United States. She wrote social, art, and music criticism, but she is most acclaimed as a literary critic; many rank her with Edgar Allan Poe as the finest in her era. Her* Woman in the Nineteenth Century *(1845) is now recognized as the first full-length American feminist treatise. In the following excerpt from an essay originally published in her* Papers on Literature and Art *in 1846, Fuller discusses Brown's portrayal of the individual soul and the differences between his male and female characters.*]

We rejoice to see these reprints of Brown's novels [**Ormond** and **Wieland**], as we have long been ashamed that one who ought to be the pride of the country, and who is in the higher qualities of the mind so far in advance of our other novelists, should have become almost inaccessible to the public.

It has been the custom to liken Brown to Godwin. But there was no imitation, no second-hand in the matter. They were congenial natures, and whichever had come first might have lent an impulse to the other. Either mind might have been conscious of the possession of that peculiar vein of ore without thinking of working it for the mint of the world, till the other, led by accident or overflow of feeling, showed him how easy it was to put the reveries of his solitary hours into words and upon paper for the benefit of his fellow-men.

My mind to me a kingdom is.

Such a man as Brown or Godwin has a right to say that. It is no scanty turbid rill, requiring to be daily fed from a thousand others or from the clouds! Its plenteous source rushes from a high mountain between bulwarks of stone. Its course, even and full, keeps ever green its banks and affords the means of life and joy to a million gliding shapes that fill its deep waters and twinkle above its golden sands.

Life and joy! Yes, joy! These two have been called the dark masters because they disclose the twilight recesses of the human heart. Yet their gravest page is joy compared with the mixed, shallow, uncertain pleasures of vulgar minds. Joy, because they were all alive and fulfilled the purposes of being. No sham, no imitation, no convention deformed or veiled their native lineaments, checked the use of their natural force. All alive themselves, they understood that there is no joy without truth, no perception of joy without real life. Unlike most men, existence was to them not a tissue of words and seemings, but a substantial possession.

Born Hegelians without the pretensions of science, they sought God in their own consciousness and found him. The heart, because it saw itself so fearfully and wonderfully made, did not disown its Maker. With the highest idea of the dignity, power, and beauty of which human nature is capable, they had courage to see by what an oblique course it proceeds, yet never lose faith that it would reach its destined aim. Thus their darkest disclosures are not hobgoblin shows, but precious revelations.

Brown is great as ever human writer was in showing the self-sustaining force of which a lonely mind is capable. He takes one person, makes him brood like the bee and extract from the common life before him all its sweetness, its bitterness, and its nourishment.

We say makes *him,* but it increases our own interest in Brown that, a prophet in this respect of a better era, he has usually placed this thinking, royal mind in the body of a woman. This personage too is always feminine, both in her character and circumstances, but a conclusive proof that the term "feminine" is not a synonym for "weak." Constantia, Clara Wieland, have loving hearts, graceful and plastic natures, but they have also noble thinking minds, full of resource, constancy, courage. The Marguerite of Godwin no less is all refinement, and the purest tenderness, but she is also the soul of honor, capable of deep discernment and of acting in conformity with the inferences she draws. The man of Brown and Godwin has not eaten of the fruit of the tree of knowledge and been driven to sustain himself by sweat of his brow for nothing, but has learned the structure and laws of things, and become a being rational, benignant, various, and desirous of supplying the loss of innocence by the attainment of virtue. So his woman need not be quite so weak as Eve, the slave of feeling or of flattery: she also has learned to guide her helm amid the storm across the troubled waters.

The horrors which mysteriously beset these persons, and against which, so far as outward facts go, they often strive in vain, are but a representation of those powers permitted to work in the same way throughout the affairs of this world. Their demoniacal attributes only represent a morbid state of the intellect, gone to excess from want of balance with the other powers. There is an intellectual as well as a physical drunkenness, and which no less impels to crime. Carwin, urged on to use his

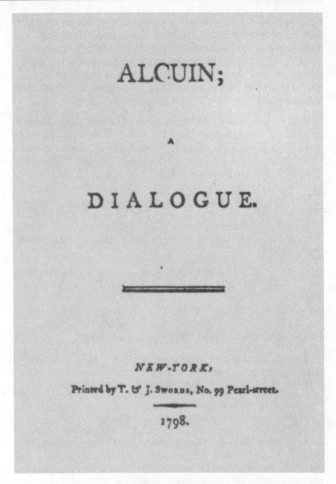

Title page to the first edition of Alcuin.

ventriloquism till the presence of such a strange agent wakened the seeds of fanaticism in the breast of Wieland, is in a state no more foreign to nature than that of the wretch executed last week, who felt himself drawn as by a spell to murder his victim because he had thought of her money and the pleasures it might bring him, till the feeling possessed his brain that hurls the gamester to ruin. The victims of such agency are like the soldier of the Rio Grande who, both legs shot off and his lifeblood rushing out with every pulse, replied serenely to his pitying comrades that "he had now that for which the soldier enlisted." The end of the drama is not in this world, and the fiction which rounds off the whole to harmony and felicity before the curtain falls sins against truth and deludes the reader. The Nelsons of the human race are all the more exposed to the assaults of fate that they are decorated with the badges of well-earned glory. Who but feels as they fall in death or rise again to a mutilated existence, that the end is not yet? Who that thinks, but must feel that the recompense is where Brown places it, in the accumulation of mental treasure, in the severe assay by fire that leaves the gold pure to be used sometime—somewhere.

Brown, man of the brooding eye, the teeming brain, the deep and fervent heart, if thy country prize thee not and has almost lost thee out of sight, it is that her heart is made shallow and cold, her eye dim, by the pomp of circumstance, the love of gross outward gain. She cannot long continue thus, for it takes a great deal of soul to keep a huge body from disease and dissolution. As there is more soul thou wilt be more sought, and many will yet sit down with thy Constantia to the meal and water on which she sustained her full and thoughtful existence, who could not endure the ennui of aldermanic dinners, or find any relish in the imitation of French cookery. Today many will read the words, and some have a cup large enough to receive the spirit before it is lost in the sand on which their feet are planted.

Brown's high standard of the delights of intellectual communion and of friendship correspond with the fondest hopes of early days. But in the relations of real life at present there is rarely more than one of the parties ready for such intercourse as he describes. On the one side there will be dryness, want of perception or variety, a stupidity unable to appreciate life's richest boon when offered to its grasp; and the finer nature is doomed to retrace its steps, unhappy as those who having force to raise a spirit cannot retain or make it substantial, and stretch out their arms only to bring them back empty to the breast. (pp. 377-80)

> *Margaret Fuller, ''Criticism,'' in her* The Writings of Margaret Fuller, *edited by Mason Wade, The Viking Press, 1941, pp. 219-404.*

JOHN GREENLEAF WHITTIER   (essay date 1866)

[*A noted American poet, abolitionist, journalist, and critic, Whittier encouraged the idea of American literary nationalism. His works are known for their moral content, simple sentiment, and humanitarianism. In the following excerpt from an essay first published in 1866, Whittier praises* Wieland *for its portrayal of the dangers of overzealous and misguided religious faith.*]

Alas for man when he turns from the light of reason and from the simple and clearly defined duties of the present life, and undertakes to pry into the mysteries of the future, bewildering himself with uncertain and vague prophecies, Oriental imagery, and obscure Hebrew texts! Simple, cheerful faith in God as our great and good Father, and love of His children as our brethren, acted out in all relations and duties, is certainly best for this world, and we believe also the best preparation for that to come. Once possessed by the falsity that God's design is that man should be wretched and gloomy here in order to obtain rest and happiness hereafter; that the mental agonies and bodily tortures of His creatures are pleasant to Him; that, after bestowing upon us reason for our guidance, He makes it of no avail by interposing contradictory revelations and arbitrary commands,—there is nothing to prevent one of a melancholic and excitable temperament from excesses so horrible as almost to justify the old belief in demoniac obsession.

Charles Brockden Brown, a writer whose merits have not yet been sufficiently acknowledged, has given a powerful and philosophical analysis of this morbid state of mind—this diseased conscientiousness, obeying the mad suggestions of a disordered brain as the injunctions of Divinity—in his remarkable story of **Wieland**. The hero of this strange and solemn romance, inheriting a melancholy and superstitious mental constitution, becomes in middle age the victim of a deep, and tranquil because deep, fanaticism. A demon in human form, perceiving his state of mind, wantonly experiments upon it, deepening and intensifying it by a fearful series of illusions of sight and sound. Tricks of jugglery and ventriloquism seem to his feverish fancies miracles and omens—the eye and the voice of the Almighty piercing the atmosphere of supernatural mystery in which he has long dwelt. He believes that he is called upon to sacrifice the beloved wife of his bosom as a testimony of the entire subjugation of his carnal reason and earthly affections to the Divine will. In the entire range of English literature there is no more thrilling passage than that which describes the execution of this baleful suggestion. The coloring of the picture is an intermingling of the lights of heaven and hell,—soft shades of tenderest pity and warm tints of unextinguishable love contrasting with the terrible outlines of an insane and cruel purpose, traced with the blood of murder. The masters of the old Greek tragedy have scarcely exceeded the sublime horror of this scene from the American novelist. The murderer confronted with his gentle and loving victim in her chamber; her anxious solicitude for his health and quiet; her affectionate caress of welcome; his own relentings and natural shrinking from his dreadful purpose; and the terrible strength which he supposes is lent him of Heaven, by which he puts down the promptings and yearnings of his human heart, and is enabled to execute the mandate of an inexorable Being,—are described with an intensity which almost stops the heart of the reader. (pp. 391-93)

Wieland is not a pleasant book. In one respect it resembles the modern tale of *Wuthering Heights:* it has great strength and power, but no beauty. Unlike that, however, it has an important and salutary moral. It is a warning to all who tamper with the mind and rashly experiment upon its religious element. As such, its perusal by the sectarian zealots of all classes would perhaps be quite as profitable as much of their present studies. (p. 395)

> *John Greenleaf Whittier, ''Fanaticism,'' in his* The Writings of John Greenleaf Whittier, Vol. VII, *Houghton, Mifflin and Company, 1889, pp. 391-95.*

GEORGE BARNETT SMITH   (essay date 1878)

[*Smith assesses the merit of Brown's novels, exploring such topics as imaginative power, plot, narrative technique, and style.*]

It is no affront to our readers to assume that to most of them the name at the head of this paper is wholly unfamiliar. Brockden Brown, as an American critic has remarked, ''is rarely spoken of but by those who have an habitual curiosity about everything literary, and a becoming pride in all good writing which appears amongst ourselves [Americans].'' His works ''have not met with the usual success of leaders in matters of taste, since with all their admiration they have not been able to extend his celebrity much beyond themselves.'' Some of his novels have been republished in this country, but copies of these it is now difficult to meet with. Yet a public which so liberally admires Hawthorne, ought to know something about a writer of kindred and more potent genius. If Hoffmann's *Night-pieces* and *Fancy Pieces after the manner of Jacques Callot* must rank first in the literature of the Weird, Brockden Brown comes second, and he adds to the weird such elements of psychological subtlety as give him a place to which Hoffman had no claim in the literature of spiritual analysis.

To a daring imagination—the most singular and flexible, perhaps, yet witnessed amongst American writers—Charles Brockden Brown united a placid temperament and a contemplative intellect. Such a combination of seemingly discordant, and yet sharply defined qualities, is almost unique. Deep-rooted melancholy, and the pathos of an apparently disordered mind, distinguish the works of this author, and yet few men were happier in their lives, or more profoundly enjoyed the simple fact of existence. He coveted no complex pleasures or recreations; his greatest solace was Nature; and he extracted happiness from those commonplace pursuits which by most men of genius would have been deemed monotonous and insupportable. His creations are dire, astounding, terrible—his life was sedate, tranquil, serene. (p. 399)

[The] one abiding impression left upon the mind after a perusal of his novels is that of a singular and abnormal imagination. We remember nothing exactly like them, either amongst English or American writers, and upon a first reflection they seem utterly out of harmony with the nature and disposition of the author himself. There is a fulness and spontaneity of eloquence in some of these romances which can only be matched by Shelley in poetry; and between these two minds there was not a little in common. Had Shelley written novels, we can well imagine that they would have been after the same type as Brown's—distinguished for a grand picturesqueness, and a bold and vivid imagination. One who knew Shelley well is reported to have said that "nothing so blended itself with the structure of his interior mind, as the creations of Brown." Much has been said of the similarity that exists between Godwin and Brockden Brown, and yet they present as many points of difference as of concord. Undoubtedly, Brown was a close reader of the author of *Political Justice,* but the cast of mind and disposition of the two varied considerably. The English philosopher was to a great extent cold, calculating, precise, and diplomatic. Brown was the very reverse of all these; he was calm and placid, not from lack of sympathy, of which he had abundance, but from his soft and childlike disposition. Then, too, he had moments of high poetic exaltation to which Godwin was a stranger. He has left on record, nevertheless, his sense of "the transcendent merits of *Caleb Williams,*" a work which impressed him so profoundly as to cause him the deepest dissatisfaction with his own early literary efforts. But the one protracted horror of *Caleb Williams* differs altogether from the fearful and ghostly situations in Brown's best novels. Indeed there is another work by Godwin which must have remained upon Brown's memory as clearly as, if not more so than, the masterpiece of fiction just named. It is in *St. Leon* that we see a nearer approach to the class of mysterious and apparently supernatural incidents in which Brown revelled. Passion was finely and terribly depicted in *Caleb Williams,* but it was in *St. Leon* that Godwin endeavoured to "mix human passions and feelings with incredible situations," to use his own language. The hero, St. Leon, becomes the depository of the two mighty secrets, the Philosopher's Stone and the Elixir Vitae. He becomes endowed with boundless wealth, and enjoys complete immunity from disease, weakness, and death. This strange romance, saturated with improbability, must have exercised, equally with its predecessor, a wonderful influence over Brown. Accordingly, as the first important result of his traffic with the mysterious phenomena of nature, we have the novel of *Wieland: or, The Ventriloquist.* This title, however, conveys no notion of the exact character of the romance. To a reader of an unsympathetic or unimaginative mind, it must always appear a very unsatisfactory work. The invention is so bizarre, the machinery so fantastic and unexpected. The author claims that the incidents occurred between the conclusion of the French and the beginning of the Revolutionary war; but the opinion of the reader will be that the age of miracles has indeed returned, if he be called upon to affirm his belief in the extraordinary events recorded in *Wieland.* We do not now refer to the conduct of the younger Wieland, for no deeds can be more strange, more cruel, or more revolting than those sometimes committed under the pressure of religious hallucination. The experience of Wieland in this direction is enough to appal the stoutest heart. (pp. 409-10)

What was the author's object in this story, which is a veritable *tour de force* of passion, misery, and terror? Some may object that the exceptional manifestations of Nature are not legitimate groundwork for the purposes of fiction; but there is no reason why that which is apparently beyond Nature, as well as that which in humanity strikes us with horror and awe, should not be taken by the artist whose genius has a special susceptibility in that direction. Brown used these things, and practically conveyed an indelible lesson against all superstition. Man is rebuked for his proneness to believe that he is worked upon by supernatural powers, and the crimes of Wieland are a protest against those hysterical religious feelings which may not always result in such dire calamities, but which—when cherished and brooded over—inevitably lead to the dethronement of reason. In the hands of a tiro, the materials of which **Wieland** is composed would have resulted in a melodrama of the commonest and most pinchbeck order; but being infused by the spirit and power of genius, they are transformed into a gloomy and awful tragedy, in which the reader forgets for a time the incredibility of the incidents and the impossibility of the situations.

Wieland, upon the whole, deservedly ranks as Brown's completest work of fiction. There is method in its composition, order in its development, and naturalness in its termination. In many of the author's efforts he appears to have devoted himself to the manipulation of particular phases of passion with an energy that has not served him throughout the work. Hence the fragmentary and unequal character of some of his novels. The great charge against him is that he has departed from the realities of every-day life. Griswold defends him by affirming that "the most incredible of his incidents had parallels in true history, and the metaphysical unity and consistency of his novels are apparent to all readers familiar with psychological phenomena. Griswold appears to have accepted Brown's own statements of the alleged facts upon which his novels were based. Even his warmest defender admits that he disregarded rules and cared little for criticism. This attitude of superiority to the laws which are supposed to govern fiction has in several cases marred the effect of what is otherwise really fine and remarkable work. The plain truth is that all this talk about probabilities and possibilities is wholly beside the mark. It is senseless to criticise a fairy tale by the standard of the morning paper, and it is just as senseless and perverse to insist on cramping invention within the arbitrary limits of commonplace realities as seen through commonplace vision.

In **Ormond,** Brown again devotes himself to the development of individual character. All his strength is spent upon the delineation of the hero of the novel, who in some respects appears more diabolical than Wieland. An affinity has been traced between Ormond and Falkland, the hero of Godwin's celebrated romance. In the outset this affinity appears real and substantial, but as Ormond gradually unfolds himself, it is perceived that the affinity is only superficial. Both characters are conceived originally in the most amiable colours; they are the paragons of benevolence and moral excellence—but lines of divergence quickly appear. Falkland has been drawn into the commission of a solitary act which haunts him with fatalistic power; but his real sentiments are what they first appear to be. Ormond, on the contrary, is one of those beings who place before themselves supreme objects of good, and are prepared to commit wholesale crimes to compass these objects. He is an angel of light to Constantia Dudley at the very moment when he is plotting her ruin, and overwhelming her with obligations the more readily to lead to the accomplishment of his desires. Failing in all, he endeavours to force her virtue, after having removed her father from his path. (pp. 413-15)

This combination of Moloch and Belial was never the character of Godwin's Falkland. Yet both romances have the common object of demonstrating the Fatalistic tendency of a master-passion. From the smouldering fire rises a Vesuvius of destruction. In the case of Ormond the ruin which he works is of a complete and devastating nature. There is no villainy so hateful, and yet at the same time so cruel and powerful for evil, as that which fashions and matures its purposes under the cloak of virtue and benevolence.

In the first part of *Arthur Mervyn, or Memoirs of the Year 1793,* Brown depicts the horrors of pestilence as witnessed in the city of Philadelphia. As he observed in the preface to his work, it is scarcely possible for such visitations to pass away without giving rise in thoughtful and humanitarian minds to schemes of reformation and improvement in the future, which, if they cannot wholly avert such visitations, may at least mitigate their effects. In the autumn of 1793 Philadelphia presented scenes of terror, and yet at the same time of fortitude and constancy, whose parallel must be sought for in the plague-stricken cities of the ancient world. "He that depicts," says the author, "in lively colours, the evils of disease and poverty, performs an eminent service to the sufferers, by calling forth benevolence in those who are able to afford relief; and he who pourtrays examples of disinterestedness and intrepidity, confers on virtue the notoriety and homage that are due to it, and rouses in the spectators the spirit of salutary emulation." (pp. 415-16)

This novel abounds in improbabilities and contradictions, and it is almost impossible to trace its complicated plot. Episodes are introduced which have no connection whatever with what has gone before, and as little to do with that which comes after them. In fact, the whole romance is an *olla podrida* of startling events. But there are passages in it which for beauty and eloquence have never been excelled by the author. The incidents are exceedingly dramatic, and the descriptions singularly graphic and picturesque. The novelist has defied the probabilities, but has succeeded in producing a brilliant series of rhetorical effects. (p. 417)

The descriptions of the plague in Philadelphia given in the first part of *Arthur Mervyn* have been ranked by some with Boccaccio's narrative of the *Plague of Florence* and Defoe's *History of the Plague of London;* and, undoubtedly, they possess all the force and vigour of the latter work. The second part of *Arthur Mervyn* need not detain us, for, while it contains isolated chapters of great excellence, it exceeds its predecessor in the inconsequence and unnecessarily complicated character of its incidents.

Brown's power of exciting breathless apprehension was never more strikingly shown than in *Edgar Huntly.* Events giving rise to wonder and suspense follow each other in rapid succession. We forget to discuss whether the characters are natural or not, and lose ourselves in their astounding experiences. It has been said of the description in this novel of the encounter between the hero and a panther, that to find a parallel for it we must go to the scene under the cliffs in *The Antiquary,* or that between the two ladies and the panthers in *The Pioneers.* Again has the author fallen back upon an abnormal human manifestation for the groundwork of his romance. Somnambulism has been called into requisition to produce startling and ingenious effects. Nor is this all; for there has been pressed into service the immitigable hostility which existed—and still

in part exists—between European settlers in the States and the Indian tribes. Conflicts between the whites and the indigenous Indians are detailed with realistic power, and opportunity is also given for the delineation of the magnificent scenery which abounds in the western portion of the American continent. We shall not attempt an analysis of this novel; but merely remark that it is a story told by the hero to the sister of his friend, Waldegrave, who has been mysteriously murdered under the boughs of an elm in the midst of a private road in a wild and romantic district of Pennsylvania. Huntly finds the sleep-walker, Clithero, at the murdered man's grave, and instinctively connects him with the crime. Clithero leads him a long and dangerous circuit through mountain fastnesses and over precipices, until the former plunges into a cavern and disappears. The scenes which ensue are of the most extraordinary description, and the imagination which conceived them may be justly called portentous. The life-long misery of Clithero, which assumed a maniacal form, had been caused by the supposed death of his patroness, with whose death he had always charged himself. After a series of adventures which it would be difficult to match out of our author's own works, it is shown that the lady is still alive. Clithero has become a hopeless madman, however, and commits suicide. This singular being, who towers through the novel like the spectre of the Brocken, is one of the most vivid portraitures of a class peculiar to Brown. Half man, half demon, he excites in the reader the most conflicting emotions—commiseration giving way to terror, terror to disgust, and disgust once more, and finally, to pity.

The novel of *Clara Howard* in some respects follows the lines of the work we have been discussing; but it lacks originality; and as Brown's chief merit lies neither in plot nor in individuality of character, but in the eloquence and romantic character of his narrative, when these fail him (as they do to a great extent in this later novel) he is not likely to retain the attention of the reader. Told in the form of letters, the history of Clara Howard is related with a method and perspicuity absent from Brown's other works; but what he gains in straightforward narrative and orderly plan, he loses in passion, force, intensity, genius. He has written with aquafortis before, but in *Clara Howard* he descends to the ordinary ink, shed in such immense quantities by the general purveyors of fiction.

But if (as we have already implied) Brown's novels must not be turned to for studies of character—save chiefly as concerns individuals under the control of strange or abnormal impulses—one exception certainly demands to be made in favour of the heroine of *Ormond.* Constantia Dudley—natural and attractive in the highest degree from the human point of view—is such a character as our leading English novelists need not have been ashamed to conceive. Shelley, who had a great distaste for novels as such, was greatly enamoured of this character, and expressed his strong admiration of the author's skill in her delineation. The daughter of an immensely wealthy American citizen, she is gradually reduced, by the reverses of fortune, to the deepest poverty. But trouble proves the true alembic for testing the depth and tenderness of her nature. When she is sixteen, the storm of adversity bursts in its full force upon her father's house. Her beauty, and the graces of her mind, attract a thousand admirers; but she resists them all to minister to the comfort of her father, who becomes blind, and falls into premature decay. The fever breaks out in the city; its ravages are terrible; but, surrounded by poverty and disease, Constantia pursues a charmed life, animated by a noble virtue and a splendid heroism. Highly educated and refined, and accustomed to all the luxuries which unbounded wealth can supply, she is compelled to descend, by stages which are the result of machination and villainy, to a condition of life which is a very lazar-house of poverty and disease. Yet through all she preserves the same sublime attitude of resignation and endurance, and attracts the admiration of even an Ormond, who loves her with all the passion of which such a nature is capable. She resists his attempts to entrap her affections, and when at length he endeavours to subject her to vileness and pollution, with Spartan courage and resolution she resists him to the death. There is nothing vague and shadowy in the character of Constantia Dudley, as is the case with so many of the novelist's *dramatis personae;* she gives one the impression of being a representation from life: she is a true woman, of a high and pure, but not an impossible type.

In one passage of **Clara Howard,** Brown shows that he was fully alive to the influence which Europe still wielded over both the literature and the character of the American people. Edward Hartley, the hero of the story, exclaims—

> Our books are almost wholly the productions of Europe, and the prejudices which infect us are derived chiefly from this source. These prejudices may be somewhat rectified by age and by converse with the world, but they flourish in full vigour in youthful minds, reared in seclusion and privacy, and undisciplined by intercourse with various classes of mankind. In me they possessed an unusual degree of strength. My words were selected and defined according to foreign usages, and my notions of dignity were modelled on a scale which the Revolution has completely taken away. I could never forget that my condition was that of a *peasant,* and in spite of reflection, I was the slave of those sentiments of self-contempt and humiliation which pertain to that condition elsewhere, though chimerical and visionary on the western side of the Atlantic.

The sensitive mind of Brown, and his pride as an American citizen, revolted from European manners and customs. There is no peasantry, as such, in the United States; hence, between the freeholder, however poor, and the richest citizen, there existed none of those sharp class distinctions which pertain to English society. Brown longed for the time when, just as America had triumphantly thrown off English tyranny, she would be able to throw off English customs and the prejudices derived from English literature.

The question, how it comes to pass that with all his power and originality, Charles Brockden Brown has never enjoyed the distinction of a popular writer, is not readily answered. It may, indeed, be said that the link between his creations and humanity in general is missing; there is no accord between them; and, moreover, he is an utter stranger to the humorous faculty. Much also might be said with regard to his deficiencies in the construction of plot; but, on the other hand, there must be set against these the varied charms of his style—its eloquence, its clearness, and its nervousness.

In Brown we not only behold a pioneer in the world of fiction, but one of the earliest of those writers who have endeavoured to give a native tone and character to American literature. Cut off at an age when he had only just begun to gauge his own powers, and to subjugate an imagination which had hitherto revelled in its wild luxuriance and growth, he has left behind him a surprising indication of possible achievements, rather than work accomplished of that full and compact nature of which he was capable. Like the great nation of which he formed a part, he was struggling with a youth of noble potentialities.

Hawthorne, Cooper, and others have since done more perfect work, but in none was there evidence of precisely the same latent original power. He was the intellectual product of a people as yet in its nonage, and which stepped forth amidst the nations of the world with all the hope and elasticity of youth, yet lacking the stronger fibre of manhood. To circumscribe the nature and extent of Brockden Brown's literary labours, however, had the Fates been propitious and his life been prolonged, would have been hazardous. But he passed away ere he had reached those greater heights to which he aspired, and which seemed accessible enough to such uncommon talents, such restless energy, and such powerful inspiration. (pp. 418-21)

George Barnett Smith, ''Brockden Brown,'' in The Fortnightly Review, *n.s. Vol. XXIV, July 1-December 1, 1878, pp. 399-421.*

HENRY A. BEERS   (essay date 1887)

[*Beers was a prominent American educator and essayist during the late nineteenth and early twentieth centuries. In the following excerpt, Beers attempts to classify Brown's fiction, offering a negative assessment of his plot development, characterization, and narrative technique.*]

Charles Brockden Brown, the first American novelist of any note, was also the first professional man of letters in this country who supported himself entirely by his pen. . . . Brown was an invalid and something of a recluse, with a relish for the ghastly in incident and the morbid in character. He was in some points a prophecy of Poe and Hawthorne, though his art was greatly inferior to Poe's, and almost infinitely so to Hawthorne's. His books belong more properly to the contemporary school of fiction in England which preceded the *Waverley Novels*—to the class that includes Beckford's *Vathek,* Godwin's *Caleb Williams* and *St. Leon,* Mrs. Shelley's *Frankenstein,* and such ''Gothic'' romances as Lewis's *Monk,* Walpole's *Castle of Otranto,* and Mrs. Radcliffe's *Mysteries of Udolpho.* A distinguishing characteristic of this whole school is what we may call the clumsy-horrible. Brown's romances are not wanting in inventive power, in occasional situations that are intensely thrilling, and in subtle analysis of character; but they are fatally defective in art. The narrative is by turns abrupt and tiresomely prolix, proceeding not so much by dialogue as by elaborate dissection and discussion of motives and states of mind, interspersed with the author's reflections. The wild improbabilities of plot and the unnatural and even monstrous developments of character are in startling contrast with the old-fashioned preciseness of the language; the conversations, when there are any, being conducted in that insipid dialect in which a fine woman was called an ''elegant female.'' (pp. 79-81)

Brown frequently raises a superstructure of mystery on a basis ludicrously weak. Thus the hero of his first novel, **Wieland** (whose father anticipates ''Nemo,'' in Dickens's *Bleak House,* by dying of spontaneous combustion), is led on by what he mistakes for spiritual voices to kill his wife and children; and the voices turn out to be produced by the ventriloquism of one Carwin, the villain of the story. Similarly in **Edgar Huntley,** the plot turns upon the phenomena of sleep-walking. Brown had the good sense to place the scene of his romances in his own country, and the only passages in them which have now a living interest are his descriptions of wilderness scenery in **Edgar Huntly,** and his graphic account in **Arthur Mervyn** of the yellow-fever epidemic in Philadelphia in 1793. Shelley was an admirer of Brown, and his experiments in prose fiction, such as *Zastrozzi* and *St. Irvyne the Rosicrucian,* are of the same abnormal and speculative type. (p. 82)

Henry A. Beers, "The Revolutionary Period: 1765-1815," in his An Outline Sketch of American Literature, *Chautauqua Press, 1887, pp. 51-85.*

JO. S. McCOWAN   (essay date 1896)

[*McCowan examines Brown's importance in the history of American literature.*]

Brown's novels, for the most part, possess chiefly an historical interest, from the fact that he was the first to write purely American fiction. He was the first to break away from the beaten paths followed by foreign writers, and to seek his characters and scenes in the unbroken wildernesses of the new world. He believed it to be the part of an American to use those "sources of amusement to the fancy and instruction to the heart that are peculiar to ourselves," and are, as he declared, "equally numerous and inexhaustible." He sought for truth in local color, and in the facts of sciene. This is shown especially in *Edgar Huntley, or the Adventures of a Sleepwalker,* in which, to use his own words [see excerpt dated 1799], he tried to "exhibit a series of adventures growing out of the conditions of our country, and connected with one of the most wonderful diseases or afflictions of the human frame." That he believed himself to be an innovator, may be seen from the following description of his "one merit—that of calling forth the passions and engaging the sympathy of the reader by means hitherto unemployed by preceding authors. Puerile superstitions and exploded manners, Gothic castles and chimeras are the materials usually employed for this end." He was going to deal with facts; to be, in short, a realist. But although he did not use the material spoken of in the preceding sentence, he used some means just as wildly imaginative. There is but little difference between the writings of Brown and those of acknowledged romanticists, for his novels are filled with flights of the wildest fancy and imagination. He differs from the British school in that he deals with American manners and customs. One critic has said that the heroines of Brown's writings differ from those of the old romance writers, only in the fact that they are a little more like sticks. While this is hardly true, we should yet never recognize his characters as walking our streets, working our fields, or visiting our homes. (pp. 175-76)

The incidents of Brown's plots are strung together with very little conection, but he was undoubtedly led into this defect by the haste of his composition. Three of his romances were completed in one year. One was begun before the other was finished, and all of them before a definite, well-formed plan was devised for their execution. (p. 178)

In marked contrast to . . . the evident rapidity of his composition, Brown has an elaborate, factitious style. Influenced by Godwin, he forced himself to write with unnatural vigor and condensation, resorting to pedantic epithets and elliptical forms of expression at the expense of simplicity and nature. But although he thus avails himself of every opportunity of telling the truth as he sees it in a roundabout way, there yet are many passages of undeniable eloquence and rhetorical beauty to be found scattered through his writings. As to his matter and thought, it is but natural that work done between the ages of twenty and thirty, should show to some extent the effects of maturity, but it is probable that a longer experience would have corrected such faults. It is impossible to predict what he might

have been. Some have said that he is greater than Cooper, but with this verdict the mass of readers has not agreed and is not likely to agree. Others have even claimed that he surpasses Hawthorne, but this is a bizarre judgment, for surely he never approximated the sublimity of thought and theme that Hawthorne achieved. But although we cannot say that he is the greatest American novelist, we can yet give him praise that is high enough for any man; he was the first in the field, the first native novelist to write American novels, the first to write of American scenery, of American customs, and American character. He was the founder of American romantic literature, and his name should be held in the highest honor by all Americans who are interested in their country's literature. (pp. 179-80)

Jo. S. McCowan, "Our First Novelist," in The Sewanee Review, *Vol. IV, No. 1, Winter, 1896, pp. 174-80.*

BARRETT WENDELL   (essay date 1900)

[*Wendell was a prominent Harvard educator during the late nineteenth and early twentieth centuries. In the following excerpt, he identifies the elements of Brown's novels that distinguish his works from those of contemporary English writers, citing Brown's style, his creation of an atmosphere of horror, and his use of realistic detail.*]

Beyond doubt one's first impression is that the novels of Brown are merely imitative.

After a while, however, one begins to feel, beneath his conscientious imitative effort, a touch of something individual. In that epoch-making *Wieland,* the hero is a gentleman of Philadelphia, who in the midst of almost ideal happiness is suddenly accosted by a mysterious voice which orders him to put to death his superhumanly perfect wife and children. The mysterious voice, which pursues him through increasing moods of horror, declares itself to be that of God. At last, driven to madness by this appalling command, Wieland obeys it and murders his family. To this point, in spite of confusion and turgidity, the story has power. The end is ludicrously weak; the voice of God turns out to have been merely the trick of a malignant ventriloquist. The triviality of this catastrophe tends to make you feel as if all the preceding horrors had been equally trivial. Really this is not the case. The chapters in which the mind of Wieland is gradually possessed by delusion could have been written only by one who had genuinely felt a sense of what hideously mysterious things may lie beyond human ken. Some such sense as this, in terribly serious form, haunted the imagination of Puritans. In a meretricious form it appears in the work of Poe. In a form alive with beauty it reveals itself throughout the melancholy romances of Hawthorne. In Poe's work and in Hawthorne's, it is handled with something like mastery, and few men of letters have been much further from mastery of their art than Charles Brockden Brown; but the sense of horror which Brown expressed in *Wieland* is genuine. To feel its power you need only compare it with the similar feeling expressed in Lewis's *Monk,* in the *Mysteries of Udolpho,* or even in *Caleb Williams* itself.

In two of Brown's later novels, *Ormond* and *Arthur Mervyn,* there are touches more directly from life which show another kind of power. Among his most poignant personal experiences was the terrible fact of epidemic yellow fever. During a visitation of this scourge Brown was in New York, where he was on intimate terms with one Dr. Smith, a young physician of about his own age. An Italian gentleman, arriving in town with an introduction to Dr. Smith, was taken with the plague and refused lodging in any respectable hotel. Smith found him, terribly ill, in a cheap lodging-house, whence he took him home. There the Italian died; and Smith, who contracted the disease, died too. Brockden Brown was with them all the while; he came to know the pestilence appallingly well. In both *Ormond* and *Arthur Mervyn* there are descriptions of epidemic yellow fever almost as powerful as Defoe's descriptions of the London plague. (pp. 162-64)

The power . . . of setting his scenes in a vividly real background again distinguishes Brown from his English contemporaries. His characters, meanwhile, are lifelessly conventional. In *Ormond,* for example, the villanous seducer who out-Lovelaces Lovelace in a literal Philadelphia is irretrievably "make believe;" and so is the incredibly spotless Constantia Dudley, who, oddly enough, is said to have impressed Shelley as the most perfect creature of human imagination. There is a funny touch in *Ormond,* which brings out as clearly as anything the contrast between Brown's true backgrounds and his tritely fictitious characters. Constantia Dudley, with a blind father on her hands, in the midst of epidemic yellow fever, is persecuted by her seducer at a moment when the total resources of the family amount to about five dollars. Old Mr. Dudley—who incidentally and for no reason has once been a drunkard, but has now recovered every paternal excellence—has travelled all over the world. In the course of his journeys in Italy he has remarked that the people of that country live very well on *polenta,* which is nothing but a mixture of Indian meal and water, resembling the Hasty Pudding so dear to the heart of Joel Barlow. In Philadelphia at that time Indian meal could be purchased very cheaply. With about two dollars and three quarters, then, Constantia procures meal enough to preserve the lives of her father, herself, and their devoted servant for something like three months, thereby triumphantly protecting her virtue from the assaults of wealthy persecution. Now, it is said that these facts concerning the price and the nutritive qualities of Indian meal are as true as were the horrors of yellow fever. Constantia and her father, meanwhile, and the wicked seducer, whose careers were so affected by these statistics, are rather less like anything human than are such marionettes as doubtless delighted the Italian travels of Mr. Dudley.

The veracity of Brown's backgrounds appears again in *Edgar Huntley.* The incidents of this story are unimportant, except as they carry a somnambulist into the woods and caves of the Pennsylvanian country. These, despite some theatrically conventional touches, are almost as real as the somnambulist is not. Such incongruities cannot blend harmoniously; Brown's incessant combination of reality in nature with unreality in character produces an effect of bewildering confusion.

Nor is this confusion in Brown's novels wholly a matter of conception. Few writers anywhere seem at first more hopelessly to lack constructive power. Take *Arthur Mervyn,* for example: the story begins in the first person; the narrator meets somebody in whose past history he is interested; thereupon the second personage begins to narrate his own past, also in the first person; in the course of this narrative a third character appears, who soon proceeds to begin a third autobiography; and so on. As one who is bewildered by this confusion, however, pauses to unravel it or to wonder what it means, a significant fact presents itself. Whoever tries to write fiction must soon discover one of his most difficult problems to be the choice and maintenance of a definite point of view. To secure one, this device of assuming the first person is as old as the *Odyssey,*

where Odysseus narrates so many memorable experiences to the king of the Phaeacians. In brief, a resort to this world-old device generally indicates a conscious effort to get material into manageable form. Paradoxical as it seems, then, these inextricable tangles of autobiography, which make Brockden Brown's construction appear so formless, probably arose from an impotent sense that form ought to be striven for; and, indeed, when any one of his autobiographic episodes is taken by itself, it will generally be found pretty satisfactory.

When we come to the technical question of style, too, the simple test of reading aloud will show that Brockden Brown's sense of form was unusual. Of course his work shows many of the careless faults inevitable when men write with undue haste; and his vocabulary is certainly turgid; and consciously trying to write effectively, he often wrote absurdly; but the man's ear was true. In reading any page of his aloud, you will find your voice dwelling where the sense requires it to dwell. Critics have remarked that if you wish to distinguish between the style of Addison and that of Steele, all you need do is to apply a vocal test. Addison's ear was so delicate that you require little art to bring out the emphasis of his periods; Steele wrote more for the eye. In other words, Steele comparatively lacked a trait which Addison and Brockden Brown possessed— an instinctive sense of formal phrasing.

If we regard Brockden Brown only as an imitator,—and as such he is perhaps most significant,—we may instructively remark that the literature of America begins exactly where the pure literature of a normally developed language is apt to leave off. A great literature, originating from the heart of the people, declares itself first in spontaneous songs and ballads and legends; it is apt to end in prose fiction. With laboured prose fiction our American literature begins. The laboured prose fiction of Brown has traits, however, which distinguish it from similar work in England. To begin with, the sense of horror which permeates it is not conventional but genuine. Brockden Brown could instinctively feel, more deeply than almost any native Englishman since the days of Elizabeth, what mystery may lurk just beyond human ken. In the second place, Brown's work, for all its apparent confusion, proves confused chiefly by impotent, futile attempt to assure his point of view by autobiographic device. In the third place he reveals on almost every page an instinctive sense of rhythmical form.

Brown's six novels are rather long, and all hastily written; and in his short, invalid life he never attempted any other form of fiction. As one considers his work, however, one may well incline to guess that if he had confined his attempts to single episodes,—if he had had the originality, in short, to invent the short story,—he might have done work favourably comparable with that of Irving or Poe or even Hawthorne. Brockden Brown, in brief, never stumbled on the one literary form which he might have mastered; pretty clearly that literary form was the sort of romantic short story whose motive is mysterious; and since his time that kind of short story has proved itself the most characteristic phase of native American fiction. (pp. 164-68)

Barrett Wendell, "Literature in the Middle States from 1798 to 1857," in his A Literary History of America, *Charles Scribner's Sons, 1900, pp. 157-232.*

WARREN BARTON BLAKE (essay date 1910)

[*Blake discusses Brown's role in the transition between eighteenth- and nineteenth-century literature in England and America.*]

Brockden Brown was, above all, a transitional figure. The phrase, "born out of his time," has by misapplication been rendered almost meaningless; but if so to be born is to miss the advantages of an earlier or later advent, it belongs to Brown. Coming earlier, his eccentric imagination would have won him wider recognition if not more lasting currency; coming later, he might have avoided the extravagances which blot his novels. In every one of his works there are given glimpses—glimpses too often teasingly furtive—of the Philadelphia of his day, and the outlying countryside. In *Edgar Huntley,* a wider and wilder vista opens before the reader: the scene remains Pennsylvania, to be sure, but a Pennsylvania of mountains, caves, wild-cats. Thus is another side of the novelist revealed to us: we see in him now one who staked out a claim on what was to be Fenimore Cooper's hunting ground—one who anticipated the more familiar novelist by a score of years. And even after the rise of Cooper, it was long before some judges acknowledged him as Brown's superior.

To-day, it is scarcely enough to study Brown in relation to his American successors. It is even decidedly worth while to recognize his kinship with English predecessors. And here it is important to examine what is, it seems to me, the basic principle of Professor Barrett Wendell's *Literary History* of these United States [see excerpt dated 1900]. That principle is, that American literature took its point of departure, not from contemporary English letters, but from those of the century before. Thus American literature has lagged some hundred years behind the product of the mother-country. This ingenious idea fits the case of Irving, but not Brown's. In living among his own people and writing tales about them, the second of these writers conceived his literary labors in what must to-day be recognized as a spirit wholly modern. To its age, his execution was modern in no less degree. Professor Wendell's generalization remains strikingly true, applied to Washington Irving. There was a writer whom an English essayist could tartly accuse of only transcribing the works of Addison and Fielding in another handwriting. But it is a far cry from the Geoffrey Crayon of the *Sketch Book* to the chronicler of 1793. Irving is only incidentally the creator of Rip Van Winkle, and Brown could justly claim the merit of arousing interest, not, like his English predecessors, by "puerile superstition and exploded manners, Gothic castles and chimeras," but by "the incidents of Indian hostility, and the perils of the Western Wilderness.... For a native of America to overlook these would admit of no apology." Without losing sight of the highly-colored—even morbid—imaginativeness of Brown (suggested in the sub-title of the *Edgar Huntley: Memoirs of a Sleepwalker*) honor is due him as the painter of American scenes, the chronicler of American manners. (pp. 432-33)

The statement that Brockden Brown is a transitional figure has been hazarded. Obviously he bridges, as the first American who may fairly be called a novelist, the wide gap between earlier English fiction and that of the new country. More definitely, he brings into unwelcome association the tawdry "Gothic romances" of the eighteenth century and the stories of Poe and Hawthorne. The first of Brown's novels to be completed and published—he had five novels in progress at once, and this explains many of their deficiencies—is, as it happens, rather the best of them all; and it suggests at once the sorry expedients of what we may call the make-shift school of mystery, and the noble methods of Brown's greater followers. Impressed by the "thrilling melancholy" of his *Wieland,* we may hesitate to find, with Richard Henry Stoddard, that Brown was "Poe's master in prose." And yet, however crude in comparison with

later and immeasurably more delicate romance, there is that in the pioneer's work which he caught neither from the mystery-mongering novels of eighteenth century England, nor from German Gothicism. I do not know whether the partial parallel between Schiller in his *Geisterseher* and Brown in *Wieland* has publicly been pointed out; if not, there is a subject for some doctor's thesis—learned and very dull. Schiller's story appeared in English, in an abridged translation, three years before the appearance of *Wieland;* it is interesting to add that another version of the German story was published in *Magnolia,* a Southern magazine printed at Savannah in 1841, just four years before Lowell printed his poem of the same name in the *Broadway Journal.* As for the correspondence between Schiller and Brown, all that seems significant is the fact that Schiller may have borne to the American something of the relation which a later German, Hoffmann, bore to Poe; or Tieck bore, possibly, to Hawthorne. The debt was slight enough, rest assured; yet there is pregnancy in the suggestion that even the forerunner of both Poe and Hawthorne seems to have taken a kind of starting point in Germany; ushering in, if one cares to word it so, the German influence upon our literature. It is easy to exaggerate all this; although the German influence upon our thought, and, specifically, upon our education, is another matter. It is worth noting this much, at least: that Brown looked not altogether to the past—he served to introduce a newer age.

His books, if they seem to us the crude expression of youth, are the expression of a literature's youth no less than an author's. In workmanship he is far from inefficient, for all his paired adjectives and overbalanced clauses. His language seems to us prolix and pretentious only if we go to it direct, instead of from the reading of his British predecessors. The "penalty" that he paid as citizen of a youthful democracy was more than compensated for: whatever one may think of the British critic's sneer, apropos of Poe, that "Americans are never safe from the pitfalls of a language that is older than their nation." Moreover, Brockden Brown was found remarkable—even in his day and generation—for writing in a style that is nervously instinct with repressed energy. His sentences are short—at times, like most modern writer's, monotonously so; but experiment, even literary experiment, is better than stagnation. And yet, immensely inferior to Poe and Hawthorne as artist—a circumstance that might almost be taken for granted—he is inferior to all great story tellers in his sacrifice of universal truth to the situation, the moment. His weird tales never transcend the plausible without always attaining even that quality. What Hawthorne wrote of *Twice Told Tales*—"instead of passion there is sentiment"—applies much more appropriately to *Wieland* and *Mervyn.* Finally, his skilfully presented illusions once explained away, we are left little more than a sordidly mundane reality. In luridness, however, this reality is all-sufficient.

Some parts of *Edgar Huntley* answer all the demands of modern melodrama, and cheapen the Indian-killer of the penny-dreadful. "I sat upon the ground," he makes Huntley tell us:—

> I sat upon the ground, supporting my head with my
> left hand, and resting on my knee the stock of a heavy
> musket. My countenance was wan and haggard, my
> neck and bosom were dyed in blood, and my limbs,
> almost stripped by the brambles of their slender cov-
> ering, were lacerated by a thousand wounds. Three
> savages, two of whom were steeped in gore, lay at
> a small distance, with the traces of recent life on their
> visages. Hard by was the girl, venting her anguish
> in the deepest groans.

In reading such a passage, we must be charitable enough to remember that Brockden Brown was at least an innovator.

One cannot approach Brown's stories without being persistently reminded of their literary background. (pp. 434-36)

The Castle of Otranto [by Horace Walpole] had its English and its German influence; German expressions of this *bas romantisme* were to react on England and to hasten the coming of what we may call the romanticism of the *Lyrical Ballads* and of Walter Scott. Thus both Scott and Brockden Brown derive, in some sort, from Horace Walpole—who smiled as he wrote *Otranto* and the *Mysterious Mother,* and smiled again when the world took his gingerbread conceits with perfect seriousness. Even had these stories of violence, portents, trapdoors, and shrieking women never been displaced by something rather better, the historical novel, they would none the less have had their *coup de grâce* in the altogether charming form of Jane Austen's *Northanger Abbey.* As it was, while Jane Austen was busily burlesquing the vulgar machinery of horror, and Scott was raising the novel out of the depths of sensibility to which it had been reduced, Brockden Brown stood on the borderland of the modern novel, and cast a look back to the lachrymose age he was leaving behind. Thus one of his heroes confesses himself to be ''a woman as regards tears.'' The tearfulness of Brown's too hysteric heroes is of a piece with their susceptibility to such an influence as 'biloquism' and their proneness to sleep-walking; their openness to hallucination.

Brown's place with reference to novelists who loomed large on the contemporary literary stage need not be argued here. If Brown himself had been asked to whom among writers of fiction he owed most, he would unfalteringly have answered, To William Godwin, author of *Caleb Williams, or Things as They Are.* ''When a mental comparison is made between this and the mass of novels, I am inclined to be pleased with my product,'' he wrote, somewhat pompously, of an uncompleted romance. ''But when the objects of comparison are changed, and I revolve the transcendant merits of *Caleb Williams,* my pleasure is diminished.'' Brown was not alone, even among American novelists, in paying tribute to the powers of Godwin. In 1820 the young Hawthorne wrote to his sister that he had almost given up writing poetry. He wrote, too, that he had bought the *Lord of the Isles,*—

> and I intend either to send it or to bring it to you. I like it as well as any of Scott's other poems. I have read Hogg's *Tales, Caleb Williams, St. Leon,* and *Mandeville.* I admire Godwin's novels, and intend to read them all. I shall read the *Abbot,* by the author of *Waverley,* as soon as I can hire it. I have read all Scott's novels except that. I wish I had not, that I might have the pleasure of reading them again. Next to these I like *Caleb Williams.*

No very hard and fast line was drawn, you see, between the tales of Godwin and Sir Walter's. Here, by the side of Brown's humble confession, and Hawthorne's words, is the place to set down Godwin's acknowledgment that, ''in a story-book called **Wieland,**'' written by ''a person, certainly of distinguished genius, who, I believe, was born and died in the province of Pennsylvania, in the United States of North America, and who called himself C. B. Brown,'' he had himself found the inspiration of his *Mandeville.* And *Mandeville,* be it noted, was one of the novels that Hawthorne placed next to the Scottish series. The circle is complete. ''Whichever had come first,'' wrote Margaret Fuller of those *Twin Hegelians,* Godwin and Brown, ''must have been an inspiration to the other'' [see

excerpt dated 1846]. It fell out, we have seen, that each *was* such an inspiration.

Nothing is less fruitful than the generality of *rapprochements* in literary characterization. Let pass, then, the character-correspondences: it is enough that Brown did not hesitate to imitate within reasonable limits. Somewhat unfortunately, he imitated himself more often than any other author. And Brown's books are, like Godwin's *Caleb Williams,* distinguished by a preoccupation with crime and a morbid sensibility. In powers of narration and description, perhaps the American is in advance of his master: though he, too, put his language to unusual strains and revealed, in the obviousness of his rhetorical devices, the ill effects of following a stilted and ungraceful guide. As for Godwin, his coldness, his general insufficiency of emotion, are the more remarkable for the warmth that he too often aims at. ''Emily,'' he writes of his heroine, ''was far from being entitled to the appellation of a beauty. Her person was petite and trivial; her complexion savoured of the brunette; and her face was marked with the small-pox, sufficiently to destroy its evenness and polish, though not enough to annihilate its expression.'' Small wonder if Hazlitt, who found *Caleb Williams* ''one of the most powerful novels in the English language,'' confessed that its author is, all the same, like an eight-day clock that must be wound up a long time before it will strike!

The relation between Brown and Godwin is more than a matter of style. That the American was, as had been asserted, fully abreast of the currents of British literature and British thought, is nowhere better illustrated than in his adopting the principles that disgraced Shelley; the principles that for a time at least made Godwin's name the most frequently cited of any in all England. In the dialogue of **Alcuin,** the son of respectable Philadelphia Quakers undertook to explain the ''new thought'' of those troubled days. His biographer of 1815 tells us that Brown was always fond of analysis, and even in early life took no opinion on trust. ''Much of his reading tended to confirm his predisposition to scepticism.'' And so we find him indulging in Utopian visions of a land where men and women dress alike; where they share equally in all occupations, and enjoy the same educational system. In the course of a dialogue the Godwinian objections to marriage as an institution are rehearsed as faithfully as they are stated in *Political Justice and Its Influence on Morals and Happiness.* Finally, after the American had safely passed through this quite natural phase, he turned it to account in the last of his novels, **Jane Talbot.** The hero, Henry Colden, had come under the spell of Godwin's masterpiece—described as a ''most fascinating book.'' Jane Talbot loves him, notwithstanding his heterodoxy, for—to drop into the rhetoric of the piece—though his understanding dissents, his heart is on the side of virtue. Earlier she had believed, with good people in general, that ''none but a sensualist could disbelieve; unbelief was a mere suggestion . . . to palliate or to reconcile us to the unlimited indulgence of our appetites.'' In this novel, which, like his **Clara Howard,** follows the letter-form, Brockden Brown all but opened up a new field; fell just short of establishing himself in a new reputation, sounder than his first. Certainly I know of no earlier story where the conflict lies so uniquely in ideas; where it is a question of faith and practise, of love and abstract duty. As it is, the novelist throws out a hint, and that is all. Since his era, novels dealing with religious doubt have made their stir—witness *Robert Elsmere*—and have been forgotten by a public which, reading more novels than the earlier generations, approaches fiction with less patience and less seriousness.

It is probable that Brown, like his Colden, remained a sceptic of a passive and unproselytizing kind. His faith was left in the unfinished condition of many of his writings. He had, ultimately, to live down an unorthodox reputation. When he returned to Philadelphia for all time, to found *The Literary Magazine and American Register,* he deemed it wise to declare himself "the ardent friend and the willing champion of the Christian religion." But one is more interested in Brown the analyist than in Brown the believer or the sceptic: for it was as analyist, we have seen, that he most closely resembles the Godwin of *Caleb Williams.* Each novelist is fonder of setting his heroes to pondering over past performances, sentiments, hopes, than of finding them springs of action, and launching them in full career. In the words of one of Brown's brooding heroes is expressed what the writer might justly have said of himself: "I cannot be satisfied with telling you that I am not well; but I must be searching with these careful eyes into causes." Of course his circumstantiality is easily justified; was it not one of Brown's contemporaries who described his product as "a concatenation of events which taken separately will be worthy of belief?" As for the painstaking analyist's preferences in subject matter, once more one may quote the words he lends to one of his heroes: "There is no book in which I read with more pleasure than the face of woman."—So might Richardson have written after one of his tea-drinkings at North End.

Yes, in Brockden Brown we see a romancer to be associated with Godwin, less as humanitarian than as psychologue. The latest comer among his causal critics writes that he was a terrorist by fashion only; by nature, a realist. Certainly his was an imagination more nimble, even more daring, than most of the terror school could boast. Nor was he a mere imitator: if only the wildness of his imaginings had been subjected to some sort of discipline, if only his compositions had been duly weighed and reviewed before their utterance (at least sufficiently to put them into order and consistency within themselves), he might be widely read with pleasure even to-day. The undisciplined quality of Brown's imagination is, after all, the one fact of which every hand-book of American literature informs the reader seeking knowledge in regard to him; one need not linger over it. What must not be lost sight of is that natural causes fascinated him, along with seemingly unnatural effects. He sought to rationalize mystery. That he never made the most of his talents, however, one must feel even in reading *Wieland:* his first novel and his best. Wieland is the victim of a ventriloquist who uses the voice of God, and other voices, more familiar to his victim. Led on by his voices, Wieland murders his wife and children; wakened at last to the cruel realities, he becomes a wilder maniac than ever. There are thrills in *Wieland,* there are thrills and purple patches in all the novels, but they are ragged, and, as we read more and more, increasingly disappointing. They suffer from the circumstance that their author kept several of them going at the same time, confused them among themselves, "lost his place" as completely as the most careless of his readers. We feel too—unjustly, perhaps, when all the conditions are regarded—that his gift has been prostituted. It is because he only toyed with his powers that so much of his work was left unfinished—that his *Edgar Huntley* has come down to us all at loose ends: two stories, not dove-tailed, but spliced. In another novel the interval between the publication of the volumes was interruption enough to change his hero's character and sentiments. Worse yet, the novelist completely forgot to bring to the altar or to the death-bed, that is the prequisite of romantic heroines, the fascinating Italian lady whom Mervyn had rescued from a thousand perils, but in the end left stranded. The novel itself—*Mervyn,* that is,—is pseudo-picaresque, with a well-meaning sentimentalist striving to fill the place of cheerful knave.

A contributor to *Blackwood's* wrote, almost a hundred years ago, that there were only two American authors "whose genius has reason to complain of British neglect:" Charles Brockden Brown and Washington Irving. Irving has long since won recognition for all that his countrymen may claim for him of talent. The same might be true of Brockden Brown had he acted on the principle that art is properly either representative or symbolical. He knew lesser truths: that it is not enough for fiction to be true—that it must *seem* true; that the appearance is often of more importance than the fact. He introduced footnotes referring to scientific works, and called attention to well-authenticated cases parallel to some of his own incidents (all of which was, at least, a charmingly naïve performance); he further 'documented' his stories in elaborating detail, leading always toward verisimilitude. Above all, he stood on the boundary line between the old-fashioned and the modern novel; between the light-hearted Walpole with his heavy-handed imitators, on the one hand, and the stories of Poe and Hawthorne on the other; between the sentimentalism of Richardson and Godwin, and the naturalism of the nineteenth century. He was, finally, a writer who dealt, not with *things* alone, nor with sensations, but with ideas. And yet, for reasons which I have tried to suggest, his novels appealed, in 1820, chiefly to subscribers to circulating libraries; they were not recognized as 'standard' works. Their attraction to-day is not as full-bodied literature, commended to the many, but to the student, the lover of old-fashioned favorites, the friend of the fantastic. (pp. 437-43)

> Warren Barton Blake, "Brockden Brown and the Novel," in The Sewanee Review, Vol. XVIII, No. 4, Autumn, 1910, pp. 431-43.

FRED LEWIS PATTEE   (essay date 1926)

[*An American literary historian, critic, poet, and novelist, Pattee was a pioneer in the study of American literature. He believed that literature is the popular expression of the people, rather than the work of an elite. In the following excerpt, he identifies rational, sentimental, and Gothic strains in* Wieland, *appraises its style and structure, and evaluates Brown's contribution to American letters.*]

The term "Father of American literature" belongs unquestionably to Charles Brockden Brown. To him belong also the first two decades of our republican literary history. He was an innovator in a revolutionary age, a literary genius in a land barren of literary men, a pioneer with courage to stand against even his own family and the ideals of his own generation. Says Dunlap, his earliest biographer, writing with contemporary knowledge: "To become exclusively an author was at that time a novelty in the United States, and if we except the editors of newspapers, no one had relied solely upon the support of his talents, and deliberately chosen this station in society." But what is even more significant, Brown chose for his profession *fiction,* a literary form almost untried in America, and one attacked by prejudice, denounced in every pulpit, and thundered against by all the moralists. (pp. ix-x)

The strongest of Brown's romances, the most noteworthy piece of fiction produced in America during the first generation of the republic, is unquestionably *Wieland, or the Transformation.* Built around a terror *motif,* with the unexplained and supernatural always in the foreground, it was nevertheless intended by its author to be a veiled sermon. "His purpose," he declared in his preface, "is neither selfish nor temporary, but aims at the illustration of some important branches of the moral constitution of man." The novel ends like a fable of Æsop with a carefully formulated moral.

To secure his Gothic effects in a new land bare of castles and utterly free from ghosts called for materials startlingly unusual and yet materials, in the opinion of his readers, not impossible. "The incidents related are extraordinary and rare," he announced in his preface. "Some of them, perhaps, approach as nearly to the nature of miracles as can be done by that which is not truly miraculous," yet he is sure they "will be found to correspond with the known principles of human nature."

His terror-compelling devices are three in number: the spontaneous combustion of the father of the two main characters, the ventriloquism of Carwin, and the religious mania of Wieland that drove him to sacrifice his entire family. (pp. xxviii-xxix)

The influence of *Caleb Williams* upon *Wieland* has been overstressed by critics. Godwin's theories concerning fiction undoubtedly had their effect upon Brown, and undoubtedly they set the key not only of *Wieland* but of *Ormond* and *Arthur Mervyn*. Godwin had sounded a new note in fiction. In the original preface to *Caleb Williams* he had written, "The question now afloat in the world respecting things as they are is the most interesting that can be presented to the human mind." The novelist, he contended, must dominate his reader, hold him by a very powerful interest, even terrorize him. The novel must have a moral purpose and the reader must be changed because of his reading. It must be a tale "that shall constitute an epoch in the mind of the reader, that no one, after he has read it, shall ever be exactly the same man that he was before." And yet, though woven of the most amazing and horrible and uncommon of materials, the novel must move at every point "within the laws and established course of nature as she operates in the planet we inhabit." It was his task as a novelist, he contended, "to mix human feelings and passions with incredible situations, and thus render them impressive and interesting."

The style of Godwin—headlong, intense—had undoubtedly its effect upon Brown, as did also Godwin's humanitarian objectives and his obvious moralizing. *Wieland* is spiced thickly with apothegms and axioms of the Godwin variety:

> The law is a system of expense, delay, and uncertainty.

> Self-denial, seasonably exercised, is one means of enhancing our gratifications.

> Those sentiments which we ought not to disclose it is criminal to harbor.

> There are no devils but those which are begotten upon selfishness and reared by cunning.

> Let that man who shall purpose to assign motives to the actions of another blush at his folly and forbear.

> The most perfect being must owe his exemption from vice to the absence of temptation. No human virtue is secure from degeneracy.

Moreover, the rough first sketch of Carwin presented in the novel is of *Caleb Williams* texture. Despite seeming monstrous crimes, Carwin is defended. He is "an unfortunate man," a thing to be pitied, a victim in the hands of an unscrupulous master who attempts to make him his cat's-paw, and he is also, like Williams, the victim of an uncontrollable curiosity.

The romance is braided of three other strands. The second, and by far the most conspicuous, may be called Richardsonian. The book is to be classed with the seduction novels so popular at the close of the eighteenth century—a book of the *Clarissa Harlowe* type. The tale is told in the first person, and "addressed," as the author carefully explains in his preface, "in the epistolary form, by the lady whose story it contains, to a small number of friends." The heroine is of the Richardson type, incredibly beautiful, "a being after whom sages may model their transcendent intelligence and painters their ideal beauty. Here is exemplified that union between intellect and form which has hitherto existed only in the conceptions of the poet." She is of sensibility all compact, living in a world that contains only the superlative degree. Five times during the progress of the tale, she faints, she sinks "into a fit," she falls "upon the floor lifeless" "into the sleep of death"; she shrieks— "while I had breath I shrieked"; and she languishes for weeks in the "rage of fever and the effusions of delirium." When not at this extreme she is at the other—she treads upon the clouds in ecstasy. She believes her lover is about to propose; Clarissa herself was never more dithyrambic:

> The moon will rise at eleven, and at that hour we shall wind along this bank. Possibly that hour will decide my fate. If suitable encouragement be given Pleyel will reveal his soul to me; and I, ere I reach this threshold, will be made the happiest of beings.

> And is this good to be mine? Add wings to thy speed, sweet evening; and thou, moon, I charge thee, shroud thy beams at the moment when my Pleyel whispers love. I would not for the world that the burning blushes and the mounting raptures of that moment should be visible.

In the midst of her happiness the villain appears, the seducer, the first sight of whom sends her into spasms of she knows not what. "This face, seen for a moment, continued for hours to occupy my fancy, to the exclusion of almost every other image." With feverish hand she makes a sketch of the face from memory and sits half the night and all the next day contemplating it with growing horror. The man soon justifies her blackest fears, pursues her through half the volume like another Lovelace, with weapons never before used in warfare against weak woman. Seduction, despite her utmost exertions, seems inevitable, and to her "The gulf that separates man from insects is not wider than that which severs the polluted from the chaste among women." Carwin has read Godwin evidently: he has no such prejudices. He hides in her closet and appears at her bedside at midnight advancing the cool argument: "Even if I execute my purpose, what injury is done? Your prejudices will call it by that name, but it merits it not." Then follows a new phase of the seduction *motif:* the seducer declares himself restrained by an unseen benignant personality whose voice could be heard but with no visible evidence of his presence in the room. "But for him I should long ere now have borne away the spoils of your honor."

There is another Richardsonian element: The heroine is constantly analyzing her own emotions. She pauses at dramatic moments when the reader is eager to be on with the story, to count the links in the chain of circumstances leading to the situation, to introspect and classify her sensations, and to tell in minutest detail all the reactions physical and psychological produced by the adventure. Hearing a shriek in her closet at midnight, she stands for five minutes and studies her sensations. She makes a psychological dissection at wearisome length when the reader is anxious to know what caused the fearful shriek "beyond the compass of human vocal organs." The method became a mannerism with Brown; he was almost a forerunner of Henry James. "An accurate history," he once wrote, "of the thoughts and feelings of any man, for one hour, is more valuable for some minds than a system of geography; and you, you tell me, are one of those who would rather travel into the mind of a ploughman than into the interior of Africa. I confess myself of your way of thinking." Brown was, records Dunlap, "ever fond of analysis."

The third strand is the Radcliffe element. *Wieland* is a tale of terror not unlike *The Mysteries of Udolpho*. Carwin is a man of horror closely akin to Mrs. Radcliffe's Italian. Compare the two men. This is Carwin:

> His cheeks were pallid and lank, his eyes sunken, his forehead overshadowed by coarse, straggling hairs, his teeth large and irregular, though sound and brilliantly white, and his chin discolored by a tetter. . . . And yet his forehead, so far as shaggy locks would allow it to be seen, his eyes lustrously black, and possessing, in the midst of haggardness, a radiance inexpressibly serene and potent, and something in the rest of his features which it would be in vain to describe, but which served to betoken a mind of the highest order, were essential ingredients in the portrait.

And this is the villain Schedoni described in *The Italian:*

> There was something terrible in his air, something almost superhuman. His cowl, too, as it threw a shade over the livid paleness of his face, increased its severe character, and gave an effect to his large melancholy eye which approached to horror. . . . There was something in his physiognomy extremely singular, and that cannot easily be defined. It bore the traces of many passions, which seemed to have fixed the features they no longer animated. An habitual gloom and austerity prevailed over the deep lines of his countenance, and his eyes were so piercing that they seemed to penetrate at a single glance into the hearts of men, and to read their most secret thoughts.

Carwin's eyes, it will be remembered, had a like power: "His eyes wandered from one object to another. When these powerful organs were fixed upon me, I shrunk into myself."

Mrs. Radcliffe leads her character to spectacles that freeze their blood, but she keeps the nature of the horrible object carefully from the reader until the final general unveiling. Emily in *The Mysteries of Udolpho* lifts the curtain from what she believes to be a picture—but "What it concealed was no picture, and, before she could leave the chamber, she dropped senseless to the floor." Not until near the end of the book is the reader enlightened as to what she saw. This device became characteristic of Brown: he is far more suggestive than even Mrs. Radcliffe. The reader is lured on and on irresistibly by mysteries that he feels soon are to be explained, and, as in *The Mysteries of Udolpho,* at last all the ghosts and supernatural machinery are carefully brought out and exhibited as mere natural phenomena—to the modern reader's disgust.

The final strand, the real soul of the romance, however, was of Brown's own creation. Despite the fact that Clara and Carwin dominate the first half of the book to the almost total exclusion of the title character, Wieland is the central figure, and his "transformation" is the central *motif*. The work is a tragedy, Grecian in its unities and in its intensities of horror. The dominating note is struck at the very beginning: the ghastly death of the elder Wieland because he believed he had deliberately disobeyed a divine command—by inference the sacrifice of his family. "I was led to ponder on the mysterious end of my father": over and over this occurs like a recurring chord in music, until at last it is seen to be the device that binds the whole into a unity. The Wieland family is abnormal, but the reader holds the key to this abnormality. The novelist has skillfully furnished all the materials for a clinic. The book is a study in dementia: all four of the main characters are touched with it.

The romance of Wieland has been grotesquely misunderstood. The ventriloquism is only an incident in the book. Wieland did not kill his family because he mistook Carwin's counterfeit for the voice of God. The device of ventriloquism belongs to the strand of seduction. Carwin used his strange power only seven times in all, and in every case but two he used it either to extract himself or Clara from awkward predicaments. Once he tested the courage of Clara with the device and once he used it to confound his rival, Pleyel. The voices which Wieland heard commanding him to kill came not from Carwin but from his own imagination deluded by years of brooding on the ancestral tragedy. The mystery of the voices of Carwin undoubtedly precipitated the final action, but they did not cause it. The careful reader awakes at last to the fact that the deed was caused by dementia and that he has been watching the cumulative growth of the insidious obsession from the earliest chapters. And it has been presented as an old Greek would have presented it, as Nemesis: a man of happiness transformed into a man of sorrows unutterable and through no fault of his own, innocent yet crucified for the sins of others. Clara cries out in agony of soul: "What can I wish for thee? Thou who hast vied with the great preacher of thy faith in sanctity of motives, and in elevation above sensual and selfish! Thou whom thy fate has changed into parricide and savage! Can I wish for the continuance of thy being? No." Clara and Carwin too have been in the grip of diabolic forces and, innocent of intended crime, have been punished like felons. The book is pure tragedy. Into the opening chapter the reader plunges as into an infernal gloom and not once does he emerge into the sunlight until the victim of divine wrath has been destroyed.

There is much to criticise in the romance. The style is overornate and inflated, grotesque with circumlocutions. Instead of *the wind blew* we have "the elemental music was remarkably sonorous"; *he fell in love* becomes "he had not escaped the amorous contagion." Everywhere may be heard the Johnsonian ring and Latinized diction: "His elocution was less sweet than sonorous, and, therefore, better adapted than the mellifluences of his friend to the outrageous vehemence of this drama." But we must not forget that the book was written at the time when all American prose was rhetorical, nor must we forget when laughing at its other absurdities that the book was created in the eighteenth century.

Other flaws in Brown's style are far more serious: his gaspingly short sentence unit—whole paragraphs with sentences like firecrackers; his wordiness; his faulty diction and even faulty grammar. Headlong rapidity of composition accounts partly for these defects. Brown never revised; he never reread his works; slovenliness was inevitable. The most serious structural defect in *Wieland* came from this very source. The Conway element in the plot was not worked out as originally planned. There is no reason for Louisa Conway's presence in Wieland's family. The attempt at the close of the book to explain the Conway incident by means of the new character Maxwell and a new subplot is ludicrous. The tragedy ends in a sprawl.

The reason for this is clear. The mother of Louisa Conway was to have been presented as a victim of Carwin. Halfway through the book Carwin is wanted in Ireland as a felon, for robbery and for the murder of Lady Jane Conway. Brown has even forgotten the name he first gave his victim. As in *The Ring and the Book* each actor in the tragedy tells the story from his own point of view, Clara, Pleyel, and Wieland at length. Carwin also defends himself and explains, but the tale of Carwin, following the *Caleb Williams* formula, took possession of Brown and hurried him to such lengths that it became too unwieldy for inclusion in the novel. Accordingly he cast it aside and improvised an entirely new ending that seemed to give his final moral a double emphasis. (pp. xxxv-xliii)

Brown has been underestimated: he had powers that approached genius. It has been the commonplace to rate him as the strongest man in a feeble age, one who seemed brilliant because of the utter crudeness of the American wilderness into which his life had been cast. But Brown would have been a notable figure in any country and in any age. Had he been born in England and had the encouragement and the advice and the literary atmosphere that he needed he could not have failed even there to be a leading figure in his age. He had a creative imagination. He possessed the power, rare in any epoch, to originate new literary effects. In his own estimation he had but "one merit,— that of calling forth the passion and engaging the sympathy of the reader by means hitherto unemployed by preceding authors." He had, more than this, the power to project his reader into the inner life of his characters; he was able to analyze and to dissect the springs of action; he had poetic vision that cast life into images of beauty; and he had that narrative enthusiasm, rare indeed, that seizes the reader at the start and hurries him despite himself breathless to the end of the tale. John Neal in 1824, in *Blackwood's*, rated him as one of the three original writers that America had produced, Neal including himself among the three [see excerpt above]. He had, Neal wrote, "a sort of absolute sincerity, like that of a man, who is altogether in earnest, and believes every word of his own story. . . . You feel, after he has described a thing—and you have just been poring over the description, not as if you had been reading about it; but, as if you, yourself, had seen it; or at least,—as if you had just parted with a man who *had* seen it—a man, whose word had never been doubted; and who had been telling you of it—with his face flushed." High praise indeed from a man who almost never praised anything American.

Brown's chief defects arose from the speed of his pen. He lacked repose, he lacked finish, he lacked the patience that could recast and replan. These defects proper literary environment would have remedied. The crudeness of his product is partly attributable, as was that of Philip Freneau, his contemporary, to the crude environment in which he was forced to work. His total lack of humor, however, no environment could have supplied, and without this endowment he could never have become a creator of pre-eminent rank. He must be included among that group of talented writers who appeared so suddenly and so dramatically in Europe and America at the close of the eighteenth century and at the opening of the nineteenth, but he must also be rated as one who was not equipped by nature for the highest flights of genius. (pp. xlv-xlvi)

Fred Lewis Pattee, in an introduction to Wieland; or, The Transformation *by Charles Brockden Brown, edited by Fred Lewis Pattee, Harcourt Brace Jovanovich, 1926, pp. ix-xlvi.*

DAVID LEE CLARK   (essay date 1928)

[*In an excerpt from his introduction to* Edgar Huntly, *Clark focuses on Brown's relationship to his literary forebears, his method and purpose in writing fiction, and the scope of his literary influence.*]

From his contemporaries [Brown] drew but little in either matter or manner. They had, however, broken down the Puritan opposition to novel-reading and prepared the soil for sturdier growth. Brown saw here an opportunity and visioned the future of the American novel. He looked about him for distinctly native materials; he saw romance in Indian warfare and in the struggles to conquer a virgin soil; he studied various types of American life; he ransacked our country's history for all that was curious and unique; becoming interested in mental pathology he read avidly in medical journals cases of insomnia, insanity, and other abnormal states. Such aberrations are the warp and woof of Brown's narratives. When to these are added Indian massacres, yellow fever epidemics, and religious fanaticism we have the ingredients of a typical Brown novel.

From the standpoint of subject-matter, then, Brown's novels represent a departure from the prevailing Richardsonian fiction in England and in America. But there was also the Gothic romance, in which species students of Brown have been wont to classify his works. Obviously to do so is to use the term loosely, for the terror element in Brown's narratives is not supernatural, but natural. That there are elements of terror no one will deny, but of hooting owls, swooning maidens, ghosts in armor, premature burials, and all that false brood of terrors which are the very life of a Gothic romance Brown had none. To shock, to thrill, to stimulate swoons—that was its sole purpose. The Gothic school began in a joke and ended in an apology; Jane Austen ridiculed it, and Brockden Brown scorned its puerile machinery. The fact is that Brown was a realist and sought his materials in facts, though often, it will be admitted, on the dim borderland between fact and fancy. He was interested in the human element and all the ills that flesh is heir to. Disorders of mind and diseases of body were to him far more powerful agents of terror than haunted castles; Indian massacres were calculated to excite more fear than fake Alpine robbers; and the fangs of a panther were more horrible than ghosts in armor. Insanity, fanaticism, ventriloquism, somnambulism, the plague, savages,—these were the realities behind his fiction. This difference between Brown's novels and the Gothic romances is significant—significant because it separates him from the School of Terror and puts him squarely in the ranks of the Revolutionaries, with Bage, Holcroft, and Godwin. It is more accurate by far to classify their works as novels of purpose, their aim being the dissemination of the radicalism then stirring the peoples of two continents. It was Bage and Holcroft who taught Godwin to translate the radicalism of *Political Justice* into powerful novels; and indubitably all three, Godwin in particular, gave Brockden Brown the impulse to express in fiction his revolutionary doctrines.

To be specific, of Brown's novels **Wieland** deals with insanity, ventriloquism, spontaneous combustion, and religious fanaticism; **Arthur Mervyn** with the ravages of yellow fever and the vicious lust for wealth; **Ormond** with poverty, plagues, and virtue in distress; **Edgar Huntly** with insanity, Indian outrages, somnambulism, and family feuds; and **Clara Howard** and **Jane Talbot** with the new and vital question of the intellectual and moral emanicpation of women. In fact, both in subject-matter and in general treatment, Brown's novels resemble more the great Greek tragedies than the superficial Gothic romances.

Brown's method of approach was the method of the analyst. He piled up detail on detail, scene on scene; he explained motive, laid bare the soul, analyzed every action with a Defoe-like verisimilitude that holds the reader spellbound. In sheer power of gripping plots and masterful climaxes Brown has few superiors. His weakness, on the other hand, lies in his inability to resolve his plots and scenes into their realizable effects. His narratives are never straightforward: irrelevant details of all kinds are allowed to obtrude upon the reader's main interest. These defects, in the main, are due to haste, for it was his habit to have more than one novel under way at once, and to send parts of these to the printer before he had clearly thought out the sequence. His work is characterized by an unfortunate mingling of crudeness and strength.

However various the subject-matter of Brown's novels, virtue in distress, virtue in the hands of a cruel and inexorable fate, is the central theme of each. Calvinism had spread its gloom, had its deadly hand upon all human activity, and it became the guiding impulse with Brown's characters. This theme he found ready-made in Godwin, Bage, and Holcroft; and from them too he had a pair of characters, common to the Novel of Purpose—a patron and a servant. In the Advertisement to *Sky-Walk* Brown had declared that "the world is governed, not by the simpleton, but by the man of soaring passions and intellectual energy. By the display of such only can we hope to enchain the attention and ravish the souls of those who study and reflect" [see excerpt dated 1798]. This idea Brown shared with the leaders of the Society of the Illuminati, whose principles left their influence upon all his major characters. In their contact with the weak, the inane, the unco guid, Brown's heroes and heroines give to his novels that "contexture of facts capable of suspending the faculties of every soul in curiosity." Here is the prototype of Nietzsche's superman, whose actions are beyond good and evil. In *Wieland* it was Carwin—whose intellectual energy consisted in a mastery of the art of the ventriloquist—who brought calamity upon the Wieland family, for long debased by religious mania. Ormond, in the novel that bears his name, was possessed of a powerful but vicious mind; he was an Illuminatus and thus a stout opponent to all man-made creeds, morals, and institutions. In *Arthur Mervyn* Welbeck's "soaring passion" was the greed of gold and, to obtain it, nothing stood in his way. And so on through the whole list of Brown's novels. Virtue and all the moral maxims dear to the common man are crushed by the driving power of "soaring passions and intellectual energy." This type of character Brown calls the high-minded villain.

Though this conception Brown undoubtedly got from the English revolutionary group of novelists, he makes a significant change. This change lies in the motive behind the villainy. Brown's are systematic and large-minded villains, clothed with mysterious powers, governed by an invisible Empire whose object is the salvation of the world. They are villains by premeditation and for a lofty purpose; Godwin's heroes become criminals in a sudden burst of passion and degenerate into hardened sinners.

The oft-repeated charge by critics that Brown lacked skill in character-drawing is hardly just. Wieland, helplessly driven to crimes of the blackest nature, despite the humanity that rises up in him, and Carwin, impelled to wickedness not because of innate maliciousness, but because of the fascination of evil itself, are powerful and clean-cut studies in speculative pathology. Carwin is without doubt one of the most striking characters in fiction. Again, Ormond, Brown's most fascinat-ing character, is a typical high-minded villain, endowed with noble and generous impulses, who begins life in benevolent service but, on being caught in the web of social errors, turns fiend and cuts his way out regardless of the cost. He is an adept not only in the major sphere of villainy, but a transgressor of all the ordinary conventions and safeguards of society. And Constantia Dudley, upon whom Ormond wreaks all his villainy, is drawn with a vigorous pen. The poet Shelley was passionately fond of her, seeing in her the affecting picture of virtue in distress. Arthur Mervyn, hounding the villain Welbeck, is as striking a character as Caleb Williams.

In his preface to *Edgar Huntly* Brown wrote:

> One merit the writer may at least claim; that of calling forth the passions and engaging the sympathies of the reader by means hitherto unemployed by preceding authors. Puerile superstitions and exploded manners, Gothic castles and chimeras are the materials usually employed for this end. . . . The incidents of Indian hostility and the perils of the western wilderness are far more suitable; and for a native of America to overlook these would admit of no apology. These therefore are, in part, the ingredients of this tale, and these he has been ambitious of depicting in vivid and faithful colours [see excerpt dated 1799].

Here is positive statement that Brown, as has been said, spurned Gothic machinery in favor of a new method and a native material for his novels. The perilous frontier life was to be the setting, and the reader's attention was to center on the Redskins.

Though Mrs. Anna Eliza Bleecker in her "History of Maria Kittle" (1793) had preceded Brown by a number of years in using the Indian as fictional material, it was Brown who demonstrated the real worth of such material and paved the way for Fenimore Cooper. He was moved partly by the novelty of the subject and partly by a spirit of patriotism. His Indians are cruel, crafty Indians, not the idealizations of Cooper. Rousseau's exaltation of the virtues of primitive society had one interesting application in that Europe came to look upon the American Indian as the type of the "noble savage." But such exaltation found no lodgment in the works of Brockden Brown. He knew the Indian not from enchanting distance, but from actual and often bloody contact. Cunning, crafty, nimble, bloodthirsty, the Indian appealed to him as the one genuine basis for a native fiction.

The nearest approximation to Brown's three-fold purpose in writing fiction is seen in *Edgar Huntly*. It "enchains the attention" more completely than any other of his novels; it "instructs the mind" by pointing a moral; and it portrays distinctively American scenes. The work unites Old World intrigues with the hazards of a New World civilization. The story of Huntly and the Indian massacres is in striking contrast with the moral decadence of Europe as seen in the Clithero narrative. But these two elements are so interwoven as to give to the novel a unity rarely achieved by Brown. Even the Weymouth episode has a closer relation to the main threads of the story than is commonly suspected. But Brown certainly intended the main interest of the novel to be the analysis of unusual mental states, a study of somnambulism and insanity. A careful reading reveals that Clithero had inherited a weak mind, that more than once he had been temporarily insane. And Huntly, brooding over the mysterious death of his friend Waldegrave and deeply moved by the plight of Clithero, turns somnambulist and sojourns in the dim borderland between the sane and the insane. That keen insight into the springs of human actions, that subtle analysis of morbid conditions of mind, that almost

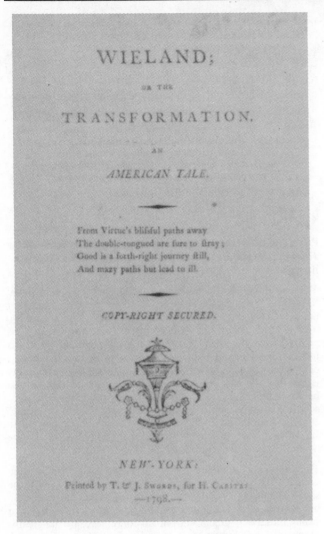

Title page to the first edition of Wieland.

ghoulish force in calling forth terror from the common facts of life are nowhere in Brown so well displayed as in [*Edgar Huntly*].

Brown's place in American literature is a minor one, but it is secure. He was not a lonely figure in a barren land; his contemporaries were many and tuneful. Brown, however, was a star of greater magnitude whose light, though dim, still shines. In passion, in the ugly realism of powerful scenes, in speculative pathology, in pictures of Indian life, and in analysis of motives that stir men's souls, Brown made a distinctive contribution to American literature. Furthermore, he all but created the short-story; to Poe and Hawthorne he may have suggested the scope and the method of that genre. From him Poe perhaps learned something of the secrets of the detective story. His minute analysis of the motives and feelings of souls under great stress must have appealed strongly to Poe. Indeed, Poe's indebtedness to Brown seems to have been not merely general. While one cannot, for instance, positively assert that Poe had before him the story of Huntly's experiences in the cave when he composed "The Pit and the Pendulum," many of the situations and phrases in the latter so distinctly recall Brown's work as to suggest more than mere coincidence. Inferior to Poe in brilliant workmanship, and to Hawthorne in calm and

consistent philosophy of life, Brown was superior to either in the Defoe-like verisimilitude of the scenes he depicted. To Cooper he suggested the lure of the Redskin and the frontier. His kinship with Melville has often been remarked. And Richard H. Dana sang his praises in the *North American Review,* and in his "Paul Felton" too patently imitated Brown. (pp. xiv-xxi)

Though Brown created no school, his influence was pervasive, both at home and abroad. His struggle for American literary independence was notably successful. And the essential quality of his genius will endure. (p. xxii)

> *David Lee Clark, in an introduction to* Edgar Huntly; or, Memoirs of a Sleep-Walker *by Charles Brockden Brown, edited by David Lee Clark, The Macmillan Company, 1928, pp. v-xxii.*

GEORGE SNELL   (essay date 1947)

[*Snell explores Brown's relationship to the apocalyptic tradition in American literature.*]

The history of the novel in America dates from 1798, the year in which Charles Brockden Brown published **Wieland.** In the century and a half that has elapsed, the novel has undergone Protean transformations; it has found new shapes and explored ever-wider ranges of human experience; it has taken various directions and appeared often to have reached limits in depth and breadth; but it continues to flourish and to find variations hitherto unexpected. It has long since severed the umbilical tie that held it to England, yet it has absorbed continuously from Europe without losing its own special qualities. The perfectly indigenous American novel has not, of course, been written and never can be. But there is a sense in which the "American novel" is as distinct and separable an entity as the "Russian novel" or the "French novel."

This could not have been said in Brockden Brown's time. Even after his work was done, and after Irving and Cooper had done theirs, the American novel had not come entirely into existence, although it was showing unmistakable signs of life. But the history of the novel in America is something different from the "American novel," and Brown's is the first name to be encountered in that history. There had been other romancers before him, but no one who was, first and last, a writer; and no novelist whose work is still read today. **Wieland** may not be a great reading experience, but it is a novel that continues to be read, and it is the first novel published by an American, possessing qualities which recommend it to a serious critical consideration.

Brown has this further distinction: he was the shaper of a tradition which affected writers greater than he and which continues today to fructify some of our most serious fiction. It is no accident that we are able to trace back to him an apocalyptical vision, culminating in the novels of William Faulkner, which has been a preoccupation of the American imagination from **Wieland** to *Absalom, Absalom!* It is worthwhile to search for the causes of this preoccupation, an apparent "sport" in the development of American fiction yet in reality an integral part of the American creative imagination equally nourished by a dark strain in our life and by the private tendencies of men of genius able to express it. In Brown we discover foreshadowed all the demonic, macabre or apocalyptic idiosyncrasies of what, to employ an inexact but useful term, amounts to a school in the American novel. (pp. 32-3)

Two immediate circumstances conspired to bring about the creation of the Brown novels. The first was Brown's peculiar sort of morbidity in temperament. A depression of spirits suffered all his life probably had its origin in his lifelong consumption. There are numerous references to it throughout his letters and journals. In one place he asks, "When have I known that lightness and vivacity of mind which the divine flow of health, even in calamity, produces in some men, and would produce in me, no doubt; at least, when not soured by misfortune? Never; scarcely ever; not longer than an half-hour at a time, since I have called myself a man." Also he was extraordinarily sensitive to personal rebuffs, imagining them where they were not intended, and prone to self-reviling upon very little provocation. (p. 35)

Brown, according to all testimony, was a perfectly normal person in all outward respects—a model of moral rectitude, an affectionate husband and father, and an indefatigable worker. Nevertheless he was constantly preoccupied with morbid fancies, saw death not far off, and perhaps consciously, during his youth, paraded the "melancholia" then fashionable in some circles.

This habit of mind served to make Brown especially susceptible to the spell of the "Gothic" romance which at about this time suddenly found favor in Europe. This is the second contingency that prompted the creation of *Wieland* and the other novels. *Caleb Williams, The Monk, The Mysteries of Udolpho* and *The Castle of Otranto,* all coming within a few years, made a powerful impression on him. The extravagant melodrama and psuedo mystery with which they abound, their stage properties of dismal corridors, unmentionable crimes, malignant spirits, dank tarns and haunted castles stimulated his imagination to an unusual degree. He set himself to the creation of a Gothic novel that would put America on the literary map with a vengeance, and in *Wieland* very nearly succeeded. In his own opinion, however, he was not successful. After the book had appeared he modestly wrote, "When a mental comparison is made between this and the mass of novels, I am inclined to be pleased with my own production. But when the objects of comparison are changed, and I revolve the transcendant merits of *Caleb Williams,* my pleasure is diminished, and is preserved from a total extinction only by the reflection that this performance is the first." So he went on, in *Ormond,* to cap the climax with a remarkably apt imitation of Godwin's novel. The plot and manner of *Ormond* are sufficiently Godwinian, but it is the worst of Brown's works in this vein and only a little better than his last two novels, written in a different tradition: *Clara Howard* and *Jane Talbot*—oppressively sentimental tales, tedious almost beyond belief.

But coming from an American, *Wieland* was, at least, fresh and powerful; and, for all its laborious prose, highfalutin phraseology, redundant and turgid rhetoric, not lacking in drama or even in power of characterization. It has also a mordant analytical quality in its delineation of fanatic tendencies among the outlandish protagonists, better developed in the third novel, *Arthur Mervyn.* The plot of *Wieland* revolves about ventriloquism, then in vogue, and its horrors result from the immoral use of his ventriloquist powers by the demonic practical joker, Carwin. Wieland is made to murder his wife and family at the bidding of disembodied voices, and through several hundred pages of spiritual anguish and bloody violence, the secret of Carwin's "joke" is withheld. To say the least, the denouement when it comes is something of a let-down. However, for the readers of Brown's time, ventriloquism, second sight, mes-

merism and like fake "sciences" were held in some esteem. No doubt *Wieland* seemed based on sound doctrine.

What interests us here is not the extravagance of Brown's subject matter, but his manner, which, especially in *Wieland* but also in *Arthur Mervyn* and *Edgar Huntly,* possessed germinative qualities for his successors. Compare, for example, the general tone and style of Poe's "The Case of M. Valdemar" with whole passages in *Wieland,* like this:

> Meanwhile, the disease thus wonderfully generated betrayed more terrible symptoms. Fever and delirium terminated in lethargic slumber, which, in the course of two hours, gave place to death; yet not till insupportable exhalations and crawling putrefaction had driven from his chamber and the house everyone whom their duty did not detain. Such was the end of my father.

Poe's dramatic manipulation and subject matter in many of the *Tales of the Grotesque and Arabesque* bear unmistakable similarity to *Wieland.* (pp. 36-8)

The macabre love-in-death themes ("Ligeia," "Morella") that fascinated Poe are also fully foreshadowed. After murdering his wife, Wieland experiences transports very similar to those of Poe's pathological heroes. "I lifted the corpse in my arms and laid it on the bed. I gazed upon it with delight. Such was the elation of my thoughts that I even broke into laughter. I clapped my hands and exclaimed, 'It is done! My sacred duty is fulfilled. To what have I sacrificed, O my God; thy last and best gift, my wife!'. . . I thought upon what I had done as a sacrifice to duty, and *was calm.*" Poe was able to inject into equally diabolic action a quality of cold deliberation and to surround it with an aura of distorted moral earnestness quite beyond Brown's reach; but the germ evidently is here.

The following comment might very well have been written with Poe in mind: "His great object seems to be exhibit the soul in scenes of extraordinary interest. For this purpose striking and perilous situations are devised, or circumstances of strong moral excitement, a troubled conscience, partial gleams of insanity, or bodings of imaginary evil which haunt the soul, and force it into all the agonies of terror. . . . We are constantly struck with the strange contrast of over-passion and over-reasoning;" but actually, it is a discussion of Brown. With some modifications, it is a comment that might equally apply to the whole school of apocalyptical writers from Brown to Thomas Wolfe. (p. 39)

Brown wrote rapidly and apparently never revised, but apart from haste and lack of respect for his medium, his conception of style placed him in the line of all apocalyptical writers from Sir Thomas Browne to Thomas Wolfe. Is it accidental that these writers invariably produce a luxuriant, involuted prose, or is there some indeterminate connection between their cast of mind, subject matter and its medium of expression? Browne, Coleridge, Melville, Poe, and in our day Faulkner and Wolfe, all formed themselves upon a style of sensuous splendor. Brockden Brown's writing is often bad because of it, but again he achieves striking effects by it. His prose is unwieldy when, instead of writing simply, "I was unhappy," he circumlocutes: "The condition of my mind was considerably remote from happiness"; or when for "I could strike a light," he writes, "by a common apparatus (tinderbox) that lay beside my bed I could instantly produce a light." On the other hand, compare such striking phrases as "His brain seemed to swell beyond its continent" and "What have I to do with that dauntless yet guiltless front? With that foolishly-confiding and obsequious, yet erect and unconquerable, spirit? Is there no means of evading your pursuit? Must I dip my hands, a second time, in blood; and dig for you a grave by the side of Watson?'' with similar passages in Melville or Poe. The seed of the matter, and the pattern of the manner, in both Poe and Melville, it is not too fanciful to think, can be found in the first three novels of Brown. (p. 44)

But without the spur of dark deeds and that peculiar sort of morbidity which alone fired his imagination, he could not produce fiction of vitality. [His last two novels] must have convinced him of this for, though he lived six years longer and wrote voluminously in his *Literary Magazine and American Register,* he produced nothing notable. Dying at thirty-nine, he had apparently said all that was in him; and it was considerable. A beginning had been made; the shape of American fiction had been set in at least one of its characteristic channels; and this was achievement of a significant order. (p. 45)

> *George Snell, ''Charles Brockden Brown: Apocalyptic,'' in his* The Shapers of American Fiction: 1798-1947, *E. P. Dutton & Co., Inc., 1947, pp. 32-45.*

WARNER BERTHOFF   (essay date 1957)

[*Berthoff discusses Brown's treatment of the theme of initiation in* Arthur Mervyn.]

[*Arthur Mervyn*] is unique among Brown's major novels: it ends happily. Otherwise the design is not, superficially, very different. There are the same elements that Brown steadily called for: ''trials of fortitude and constancy,'' illustrations of the ''moral constitution of man,'' the display of ''soaring passions and intellectual energy.'' It is, in fact, his fullest treatment of the fable of initiation. Especially in comparison with the near-allegory of *Edgar Huntly,* the external ''world'' into which the hero advances on his quest for experience seems spacious and substantial; and the novel as a whole seems the least claustral of Brown's work, the most natural in incident and motive, as it is his most moderate and plausible treatment of his hero's inward development. Arthur Mervyn discharges his energies, but quite within his original frame of character. As opposed to Brown's other novels, there is here no overwhelming ''transformation'' (the subtitle of *Wieland*). Arthur survives unharmed and little changed. Instead of anguish and ordeal, there is the steady progress of a ''fearless and sedate manner,'' an ''unalterable equanimity,'' through every danger and error. In *Arthur Mervyn* Brown's dark fables of transformation give way to a comedy of success.

That is not to say that this is a comic novel or that Brown has changed the world of his fiction into a place of happiness and good will. *Arthur Mervyn* is comedy only in the most general sense—with regard to a choice of tone that rejects opportunities to judge life as tragic or damned, and to a plot in which not even the most shocking events are given any especially horrific coloring. Among Brown's principal novels it is the one most free of Gothic sensationalism. It is a bitter comedy, set in a cruel and poisonous city world—a setting defined by the inhumanities of commercial society and by an even more dehumanizing visitation of epidemic pestilence, these being the large trials the hero must pass through. But uniquely in Brown's fiction the hero of *Arthur Mervyn* survives them unscathed; they only spur his successful advance. The world has not changed for the better in Brown's imagination, but here he has invented

a hero who instinctively discovers what can be done with it and in it. (pp. 425-26)

The effect in *Arthur Mervyn* of natural realism and a significant clarity and density of scene is a measure of Brown's success in matching theme and narrative detail. By comparison with his other novels, full of laborious and implausible soliloquies, there is a corresponding simplification in the handling of his hero. Like all Brown's protagonists Arthur is acutely self-conscious, scrutinizing all his feelings and motives, but only in the later stages of the second volume does the characterization come to *depend* on lengthy self-analysis. Arthur is represented rather by what he does, what happens to him; he is not so much characterized as brought to life, thrust into action. The lurid setting of the *Memoirs of a Sleep-Walker* is a symbolic projection of Edgar Huntly's consciousness. But the setting of the *Memoirs of the Year 1793* exists independently (though not unrelatedly), and the character of Arthur Mervyn is his manner of moving through it; his ''maturer thoughts'' emerge out of the particular ''confusion and uproar'' of his city experiences. And where Brown's other narrators stretch their experience into absolute, universal propositions about the nature and condition of man, Arthur Mervyn stops short and is content to formulate a prudential rule of conduct. He makes the practical, short-term adjustment; he is not ''transformed''; he gets along as he can.

Thus, what differentiates him from Brown's other heroes is not some defined quality in his character but his way of carrying his adventures through and winding them up. He is an odd young man; there is a peculiar cast to his successfulness. What Dr. Stevens (the introductory narrator to whom Arthur tells his story) first notices about him is a preternatural gravity. Yellow fever has ''decayed'' his features, but Stevens sees in them traces of ''uncommon but manlike beauty,'' ''pathetic seriousness,'' and feels a ''powerful and sudden claim'' laid on his own affections. This magnetic attractiveness is matched by the force of Arthur's curiosity and the imperturbable meddlesomeness of his good will. What Brown calls curiosity we are more likely to call compulsiveness; behind it lie barely admissible fears. In a literal sense Arthur must escape the malign inheritance which so far has formed his character—not simply ignorance and rusticity but a fatal ''defect of constitution'' that has killed off his brothers and sisters and holds before him the prospect of early death. Before he has reversed this negative destiny, it threatens to overtake him in the form of the pestilence; paradoxically, what chiefly enables him to survive the deadly ''effluvia'' of yellow fever is his calmness, his indifference to personal danger, his low-pitched willingness to let the pestilence be the death of him if it must.

That false fulfillment he may not accept. If the alternative is death, he must take hold of life at any cost. This is the crux of his education out of moral inertia. The ''selfishness'' of this necessity requires for compensation just that energy of compassion which he displays in the novel, for the cost of his education, in Brown's narrative, is an underlying strain of cruelty and inhumanity. That is the cost for Edgar Huntly and Stephen Calvert, too, who must give injury to others to protect themselves, but for them it is equated with suffering and remorse. In *Arthur Mervyn* it is equated with happiness. For Arthur does not give way in any part of his determination to wind up, as he does, ''the happiest of men.''

His relationship to Welbeck, the Byronic forger, is central. The very model of energy and experience, a Vautrin to Arthur's Rastignac, Welbeck is Arthur's mentor, who mocks the common morality of commercial society and lives a devious, high-spirited life of crime. Welbeck's wickedness is equivocal, for as one of his rivals remarks, his extraordinary talents are in good part practiced on fools and sharpers who deserve what they get. But he is not Schiller's virtuous bandit; he also preys on the honest and poor. And he is no superman; in the end the gray business veterans who are his antagonists counter-trick him, spinning out a "tissue of extortions and frauds" that perfectly defines the metropolitan world of "1793." Arthur's first exposure to this world makes him privy to the plot against Welbeck; taken into Welbeck's service, he conceives it his overriding duty to protect his benefactor. Once Welbeck has become an object for benevolence, Arthur clings like a leech. Despite the magnitude of Welbeck's crimes he remains loyal and forgiving, defying law and public opinion. He risks his own fortune in order to save the sinner, is willing to stand accused of partnership in Welbeck's schemes in order to express what he calls his gratitude. All this takes courage and strength of will, to persist in exercising a compassion which has no place in the ways of the world.

To Welbeck, however, Arthur's adhesive benevolence suggests something other than virtuous compassion. "Is there no means of evading your pursuit?" Welbeck cries; "are you actuated by some demon to haunt me, like the ghost of my offences, and cover me with shame?" He cannot endure Arthur's righteousness: "What have I to do with that dauntless yet guiltless front? with that foolishly confiding and obsequious, yet erect and unconquerable spirit?" Arthur's concern is unrelenting. He follows Welbeck even to jail and announces that as a first step toward restoring him "to innocence and peace," he has told Dr. Stevens the whole story as he knows it. Welbeck, with everything to hide, is naturally stupefied and accuses Arthur of perfidy—"This outrage upon promises, this violation of faith." Arthur's energy of goodness is too much for Welbeck, who curses him as an "infernal messenger" and blames him for all the misfortunes since their coming together.

Welbeck is a conscienceless criminal. Yet something in his accusation sticks. Arthur pleads innocence and good intentions. But in the very act of trying to help Welbeck he tips his hand:

> Shall I not visit and endeavor to console thee in thy distress? Let me, at least, ascertain thy condition, and be the instrument in repairing the wrongs which thou hast inflicted. *Let me gain, from the contemplation of thy misery, new motives to sincerity and rectitude.* (Emphasis mine)

His benevolence is selfish, acquisitive, in no way disinterested. In that respect, of course, it is only human and equips him for the speckled world he must exercise it in. But the ambiguity of his motives will not bother him; conscience untroubled, he ignores Welbeck's accusation and piously shepherds him to his death. Granting that his own behavior has been "ambiguous and hazardous, and perhaps wanting in discretion," he nevertheless pleads that his motives are "unquestionably pure." And he caps this complacent judgment with a balanced and now tested formula for success in the world:

> Good intentions, unaided by knowledge, will, perhaps, produce more injury than benefit, and, therefore, knowledge must be gained, but the acquisition is not momentary; is not bestowed unasked and untoiled for. Meanwhile we must not be inactive because we are ignorant. Our good purposes must hurry to performance, whether our knowledge be greater or less.

Hurrying to performance, Mervyn's good purposes are as catalytic in their way as Welbeck's concerted malignance. He is without a sense of privacy, is incapable of embarrassment. He must take charge of every one's destiny and oversee every private catastrophe with his own eyes. Another's suffering is so much grist for the mill of his appetite for experience. The woman who is to complete his march to happiness, Mrs. Fielding, her circumspectness bowled over by his abrupt manners, tells him that she has never met with his like, and he confesses: "Ordinary rules were so totally overlooked in my behavior that it seemed impossible for anyone who knew me to adhere to them. No option was left but to admit my claims to friendship and confidence or to reject them altogether." How discomforting his insidious sociability can be, how ruthless his virtue, he seems to have no idea, and he describes the method of his benevolence without understanding what his strong verb implies: "Every one had my sympathy and kindness, without claiming it, but I *claimed* the kindness and sympathy of every one."

He keeps enough rural innocence, however, to profess astonishment that Mrs. Achsa Fielding, whose kindness and sympathy he takes as his due, should also love him and be eager to marry him. This event, which fulfills his initiation into the world, gives off the curious overtones characteristic of all his displays of feeling and energy. According to Peacock, it stirred Shelley's enthusiasm for Brown to a rare reservation: "The transfer of the hero's affections from a simple peasant girl to a rich Jewess, displeased Shelley extremely, and he could only account for it on the ground that it was the only way in which Brown could bring his story to an uncomfortable conclusion." Shelley's displeasure expressed an abstract prejudgment: the pure young countryman *must* form the pure and not the convenient life-attachment. But the rest of his judgment is oddly penetrating: why should Brown be thought to have wanted to bring his story to an "uncomfortable conclusion"? If Arthur's final happiness is uncomfortable, his own calculations will not admit it. But below his calculations, we see, his mind is troubled; the signs are a fit of sleep-walking and a frightful dream in which a voice cries, "Mervyn shall sleep no more!" and he is stabbed by an enraged apparition of the dead *Mr*. Fielding.

All this is only an interlude before the happy ending; Arthur easily brushes the dream from his mind. But there remains something distasteful about his love. Like his curiosity and his compassion it has an unsavory air of bare-faced selfishness. He is attracted to Mrs. Fielding because she possesses "that very knowledge in which I was most deficient, and on which I set the most value—the knowledge of the human heart." Such knowledge is indeed power; the lust for it we traditionally think of as not less than Satanic. But what has caused Arthur Mervyn a passing uneasiness is not likely to be any qualm on this score; it is rather the suspicion that he may himself be susceptible to love and his own heart exposed, so that his perfect control will be threatened. And in the metropolis of 1793 he would have reason to be uneasy; counterpointing the heartless world of commercial banditry in *Arthur Mervyn* is a wretched succession of misalliances and ill-considered, ill-fated commitments to passion, in a series of secondary episodes which are too complicated to describe but which serve for all their disconnectedness to reinforce the main themes of the book. But Arthur has prudently forestalled such dangers by making a marriage in which no really new commitment need be made and no new emotion is required of him, accepting as his wife an older woman whom he can fondly call his "mamma." In fits of embarrassing complacence he psychoanalyzes himself, recalling proudly how he hated his father but adored a doting mother, and how he easily resisted the advances of his father's wanton second wife, being "so formed that a creature like her had no power over my senses"; thus he can explain away his feeling for Mrs. Fielding ("Was she not the substitute of my lost mamma?") and cheerfully confides this thought to her: "Are you not my lost mamma come back again?"

He has made his place in the world, but there has been no real contest; he is, we see now, the world's peculiar match from the start. He has fulfilled his nature, but by letting it stay partial, deficient. And I should say that it is this deficiency in the hero—and Brown's apparent indifference to it—which more than any structural or stylistic weakness circumscribes *Arthur Mervyn* and sets it below the great Romantic novels of a young man's education. Welbeck can be Arthur's teacher but not, as Balzac's Vautrin is to Rastignac, his tempter, for Arthur has an untemptable and in that one critical respect (despite the vitality and charm that come from his being so consistently himself) an uninteresting character. In the unchallenged fulfillment of his native energies he is unique among Brown's heroes. The essential comedy of his success is that the unwholesome world he moves through (the world projected in most of Brown's fiction) has for the first time been overcome—by a corresponding unwholesomeness of character.

Arthur Mervyn, read in this way, is a cynical book. But the emotions, the operation of mind, back of cynicism are more complex than those that go with mere terror and physical shock. In *Arthur Mervyn* Brown broke out of the mode of psychological melodrama and worked toward a broader and more disturbing image of life. He turned the corner, we may say, from Gothic romance to the more varied prospect of the nineteenth-century novel—a considerable achievement. From another viewpoint we might choose to say that through his steady interest in the perverse irregularities of actual human conduct he challenged the eighteenth-century classifications of human nature and psychology. From yet another (not unrelated) we might see his work as creating an image of society and human character as they will be found anywhere, even in America the new found land, that profoundly challenged the new republic's assumptions of progress and civic virtue, its instinct for optimism. But we could not usefully assert any of these things if the novel were as artless as Brown's fiction is usually made out to be. *Arthur Mervyn* is stamped with the seriousness and integrity, and the vitality, of Brown's own intelligence, qualities that make his writing, despite all that divides and discourages us from it, worth our renewed attention. (pp. 429-34)

> Warner Berthoff, "Adventures of the Young Man: An Approach to Charles Brockden Brown," in *American Quarterly, Vol. IX, No. 4, Winter, 1957, pp. 421-34.*

LARZER ZIFF (essay date 1962)

[*Ziff is an American critic who has examined social and literary influences on American culture in the studies* The American 1890s: Life and Times of a Lost Generation *(1966),* Puritanism in America: New Culture in a New World *(1973), and* Literary Democracy: The Declaration of Cultural Independence *(1981). In the following excerpt, Ziff maintains that in* Wieland *Brown questions the sentimental literary tradition and the optimistic psychology of his age, exposing underlying truths about the depraved nature of humanity.*]

Wieland is conventionally and correctly regarded as a novel of purpose which marks a turn from the stories of love and seduction fathered by Richardson to the kind of story made prominent by Holcroft, Bage, and Godwin. The particular purposes of *Wieland,* however, have never been precisely identified, and this reading is offered in the belief that the novel has been subjected by most students to a form of damnation through faint praise. By marveling that an American in 1798 could produce readable fiction, they place undue emphasis on mere chronology and slight the importance of the novel as part of a more meaningful cultural continuity. *Wieland* is an important novel because of the extraordinary manner in which Brown employs sentiment against itself (rather than simply dismissing it, as it is averred he has done), penetrates beneath the principles of the optimistic psychology of his day, and recognizes the claims which Calvinism makes on the American character.

We may note at the outset that *Wieland* has been poorly planned and changes direction about one-third of the way through. Carwin enters the scene as the conventional seducer, his origins obscure, his present character as a strolling gentleman representing at least the third personality he has assumed, for previously in Spain he had become a convert to Roman Catholicism and had made his "garb, aspect, and deportment . . . wholly Spanish." Clara, the narrator, goes on to note that, "On topics of religion and of his own history, previous to his *transformation* into a Spaniard he was invariably silent." He does, indeed, seduce Clara's maid, as we learn in the denouement, and when the novel approaches its climax we are provided with a newspaper account which connects his name with criminal activity in the British Isles. But this Carwin, the hypocritical Lothario designed to develop into the first seducer in the history of fiction to work his wiles through ventriloquism, never achieves existence. So complete is the change in Brown's plan for him that he is not available in the denouement to accept the responsibilities which his initial presence in the novel incurred, and the Louisa Conway subplot, which has a beginning but no middle because of Carwin's departure from his initial role, must be patched up at the end with the invention of another seducer, one Maxwell, who steps in to take the blame for what Carwin was originally intended to have done.

What has happened to change Carwin's role? Certainly the happy little society with which the author presented us in his exposition is preeminently prepared to receive a guileful seducer. Wieland and his wife, Catharine, live in ornamented rusticity together with the narrator, Clara, Wieland's sister, and Catharine's brother, Henry Pleyel, one who can characterize the interests of the group since it was not until his addition to the society that Wieland's "passion for Roman eloquence was countenanced and fostered by a sympathy of tastes." Wieland, the center of this group, could have had an aristocratic rank in Europe by laying claim to it, but like an American Werther he declined, and in so doing, "He expatiated on the perils of wealth and power, on the sacredness of conjugal and parental duties, and the happiness of mediocrity." He prefers the role of a rustic philosopher, basing his idyll on a profound knowledge of Greek and Roman learning. Clara, his sister, is also a prodigy of sensible enlightenment, one who is perilously ripe for seduction. In her strolls on the meadows of Pennsylvania, she engages herself in philosophical dialogue: "I asked why the plough and the hoe might not become the trade of every human being, and how this trade might be made conducive to, or at least consistent with, acquisition of wisdom and eloquence." The mind which so speculates is powerful; Carwin confesses that when he read Clara's notebook "the intellect which it unveiled, was brighter than my limited and feeble organs could bear.'' The knowing reader recognizes that Carwin's organs are far from feeble.

In addition, to lure us further along the primrose path, Clara displays all the palpitations we expect from a maiden in her circumstances. When Pleyel (the one she believes she truly loves) rallies her on her interest in Carwin, rather than protesting that interest, she says, ''That the belief of my having bestowed my heart upon another, produced in my friend none but ludicrous sensations, was the true cause of my distress.'' But she remains well within the confines of her convention and is too refined either to correct Pleyel's misinterpretation or encourage his desired affection. When she explains why she remains silent, she provides an epitome of the case for *Wieland* as a novel of sentiment and seduction since she gives wholehearted endorsement to the ideal of the palpitating and defenseless female: ''I must not speak. Neither eyes, nor lips, must impart the information. He must not be assured that my heart is his, previous to the tender of his own; but he must be convinced that it has not been given to another; he must be supplied with space whereon to build a doubt as to the true state of my affections; he must be prompted to avow himself. The line of delicate propriety; how hard it is, not to fall short, and not to overleap it.'' In proportion to the delicacy of that line are Carwin's chances for success once that line has been misestimated.

But precisely at this point in the novel, Brown changes direction, and that for the better. Clara sounds the warning as she speaks from the present, the time after the action when she is actually writing the novel, rather than from the historical present, and the subject of her effusion is just the sort of conduct which she has displayed up to this point in the novel. She castigates herself and all such heroines: ''My scruples were preposterous and criminal. They are bred in all hearts, by a perverse and vicious education, and they would still have maintained their place in my heart, had not my portion been set in misery. My errors have taught me thus much wisdom; that those sentiments which we ought not to disclose, it is criminal to harbour.'' For Clara, and for her author, life has intervened between her earlier opinions and this mature pronouncement, and life, they have learned, is not an imitation of art. Clara feels she has learned the lesson too late, but, of course, the author has learned it just in time. And having learned his lesson, having seen the insipidity of the situation, Brown proceeds to reveal his genius, for Clara returns from her self-analysis to the sentiment of the fictional moment and to the combined problem of the mysterious voices and her frustrating desire for love, but Brown proceeds to combine those two complications, not by having Carwin employ ventriloquism as an aid to seduction, which by now the experienced reader of the Richardsonian novel expects, but by using the sentimental expectation validly to deceive the reader, precisely as the good detective novelist develops an attractive but false clue. Such a false clue is dishonest should the author insist upon its being received, but it is artistically permissible if the author offers it and the reader deludes himself by seizing it, and Brown employs the latter manner.

His success is brilliant. For, finally, Clara detects Carwin in her closet immediately after she has heard the mysterious voices, and we are prepared for him, in the best sentimental tradition, to confess the lesser of his crimes, that of deception, but to attempt an evasion of his baser motives. To our surprise, however, Carwin in his seemingly guilty confusion at having been

detected babbles out a full confession of his heinous character and of his immoral designs on Clara, saying that he would have succeeded *had it not been for the mysterious voice*. In our gratification at this complete confirmation of our suspicions about Carwin, we accept his confession; according to the delusive values we have assumed, seduction is the cardinal sin and no one would admit to this intent unless he were the blackest villain. In confessing, Carwin is much in the position of the criminal who has confessed to murder but not to robbery, claiming, indeed, that it was the robber who scared him away from the scene of the murder. So Brown has taken in his reader masterfully, for the problem of the voice remains, indeed, that voice may now even be regarded as beneficent since it checked the seducer. What the unsuspecting reader is yet to learn, however, is that in this novel, to return to the analogy, robbery is a greater crime than murder, and that by accepting the suspect as the murderer, he has, in fact, let the greater criminal go scot free and must avidly follow the remainder of the work to satisfy his curiosity once the error comes home to him. In the terms of *Wieland*, this means that Brown has turned against the sentimental novel and used its expectations to show the reader that life is far more complicated than his novels tell him that it is, that the virtue of maidenly reserve and the vice of masculine lasciviousness are child's play compared with the real horrors of life.

In this respect alone, Brown's achievement in *Wieland* is great. Fielding, before him, had seen the inanity of the sentimental novel as a fit subject for burlesque, and Twain, after him, after the sentimental novel had reached its zenith, and, indeed, in Twain's opinion, had wreaked its havoc on a large part of American society, satirized it. But in *Wieland*, Charles Brockden Brown used the sentimental convention as a formal element and turned upon it within the same work, revealing its hollowness even as he exploited it. To be sure, Brown was a hasty, careless writer and rather than go back and revise his novel so as to fit his change in direction into the work consistently, he accepted his exposition and wrote a number of *deus ex machina* explanations for it in the denouement: killing off Pleyel's wife, allowing Carwin to slink away, and producing one Maxwell to take the blame for what the original Carwin appears to have been created for. But there is a *Wieland* which exists for a large space between the contrived opening and closing, and this *Wieland* is a monument to the often mentioned and little appreciated historical importance of Charles Brockden Brown, an author who saw the vicious effects of a *genre* he had set out to work in, and who artistically converted that *genre* into a telling criticism of itself.

The perception of life which led Brown to this change in direction also has to be understood if we are to appreciate his genius, and to do so we must look at poor Clara Wieland after her discovery of Carwin in the closet. Now suspected of promiscuity by Pleyel, the self-righteous agent of the sentimental values in the novel, and at last convinced that silence about one's true feelings is not a maidenly virtue, she goes to Pleyel to try, unsuccessfully, to reveal the actual state of affairs. Distressed by her inability to persuade him of her innocence, she faints away. When she recovers, she notices that Pleyel is no longer wrathful, but that his features reveal different feelings than he had hitherto evinced towards her in her allegedly fallen state, for he takes her distress to be a sign of her remorse and patronizingly awaits her confession. This insight of Clara's into her situation is the capstone of Brown's triumph. For Clara having seen the artificiality of maidenly reserve does overcome her scruples and goes to Pleyel's house to set matters right only to have his wrathful misunderstanding converted into an equally conventional pity. There is nothing she can do to convince Pleyel, for he matches each of her shows of protestation with the corresponding conventional response of the wronged sentimental lover. Should she protest her innocence, she is brazen; and should she weep, then, worse yet, he is a pitying god looking on Mary Magdalene. The facts of life, Clara realizes, cannot break through the circle of conventional responses with which Pleyel is surrounded. In this scene of an ex-sentimentalist's failure to communicate with the lover still bound by that tradition, Brown achieves one of the greatest condemnations of that tradition in the history of the American novel.

In the heart of *Wieland,* Clara cannot break the vicious circle of sentiment surrounding the others and she relinquishes Pleyel without rancor although in the *deus ex machina* denouement matters are patched up.

A realization of the achievement which results from Brown's change of direction in *Wieland* opens the question of his reasons for so doing. That he did not initially set out to destroy the sentimental tradition is suggested by both the beginning and the end of the novel just as his having turned against the tradition is demonstrated in the heart of the novel. Brown, then, most probably decided on his new approach during the course of the work, and that aspect of the work which seems most obviously to have turned him about is the viewpoint. The tale is told by Clara Wieland, a narrator who not only plays an intimate part in the action but one who is deeply concerned with the motives of all action. So absorbed is she by psychology that finally she and her author discover that human behavior is not what they take, and, in a sense, want it to be, but springs from far dimmer and more turbulent sources.

The psychology on which the work, as a whole, is based is summed up by Clara when she says: "The will is the tool of the understanding, which must fashion its conclusions on the notice of sense. If the senses be depraved it is impossible to calculate the evils that may flow from the consequent deductions of the understanding." The crucial term in this theory, as we come to see, is "depraved." Otherwise the psychology is certainly the stylish one for the late eighteenth century. Man, the *tabula rasa*, is passive to the impressions of sensory experience, impressions which he formulates through his understanding into the basis for his actions. Such a psychology, in spite of Jonathan Edwards' heroic incorporation of it into the body of orthodox Calvinism, sounded the death knell for the doctrine of original sin. Wrong actions will proceed from wrong judgments which, in turn, are to be traced to delusive sensory experience. How novel, then, to have the complication turn on ventriloquism, a phenomenon by which the appearance can be made to contradict the reality so that the senses can be deluded and the rustic philosophers who take part in the plot can be plunged into mysterious episodes. But the finale will demonstrate that the psychology is not wrong, after all, that the senses are the initial guides to conduct and that the mysterious has a natural explanation.

"Depraved" is the key word because Brown, in *Wieland,* discovers that human nature is not so simple as this, and that beside the delusion of senses, which would fit well with the fashionable theory, there is, ultimately, a depravity of senses. This latter contention works against the psychology of his day, but Brown remains true to it once he has discovered it, and Wieland's mania, finally, is not to be explained through ventriloquism, through delusion, but rather through an inherited

depravity which preceded it. Beginning consciously in the camp of the benevolent Philadelphians of the American Philosophical Society (just as he began with the sentimental tradition), Brown ends his journey through the mind by approaching the outskirts of Edwards' camp.

The long hard look Brown took at the murky sources of human behavior achieves an epitome in the very same scene in which he traps the sentimental reader, the scene in which Clara discovers Carwin in the closet. Frustrated at Pleyel's failure to attend the soiree at which she hoped, in the best sentimental manner, to draw him into a confession of his love for her, Clara returns to her lonely home. Brooding upon Pleyel's absence, she fears that he has met with a violent death, and this chain of association from lover to death leads her to think of her father who had met with a mysterious and violent end. From lover and dead father she is now led to a significant association which combines the two notions, that of her brother and the fantasy she has had about him. In this fantasy, Wieland had appeared to her on the far side of an abyss but beckoning and calling her to make haste in joining him even though in so doing she would have been plunged into the pit. "What monstrous conception is this?" she exclaims when she arrives at this point in her thoughts, "My brother!" So jarring is this link in her chain of associations that it forces her into thinking about her thinking, how in that beautiful world of the eighteenth century such a horrible idea could present itself to her, and she is forced to conclude, "Ideas exist in our minds that can be accounted for by no established laws."

This brilliant reproduction of the process of association occurs, as was said, just before Carwin is discovered and the novel turns fully against sentimentalism. Thus, the abandonment of the enlightened psychology and the confused acceptance of supernatural causation lead Brown also to abandon a sentimental reproduction of life. The horrors of incest and inherited depravity which Clara forces back from the threshold of her consciousness by turning to think about thinking are not to be explained away by the *tabula rasa*. While he did not have a theory or even a vocabulary to match his perception of the way the deeper mind works, Brown did not on that account abandon his perception. He adhered to it although the results of this adherence were a mixture of the supernatural with the natural in a novel which he set out to write with every promise of giving up-to-date scientific explanations for all that occurred. Wieland's homicidal actions result, finally, from causes which are inexplicable scientifically. To account for this by pointing out that Brown is here stigmatizing religious fanaticism is inadequate because Wieland's training is singularly free from any sectarianism. The ease with which he is deluded is far more explicable in terms of his lack of preparation than in terms of his prejudiced expectations.

The link between sentimentalism and eighteenth-century optimistic psychology in *Wieland* is, then, profound and meaningful, because, for Charles Brockden Brown at least, the one did not exist apart from the other. His early assault on the sentimental tradition in the novel stemmed from his powers of psychological analysis, and while he did not develop a fully satisfactory esthetic response to the perception, he did turn to a suspicion of scientific enthusiasm and a latent sympathy with some sort of doctrine of inherited depravity. In doing so, he defined the problem of the American artist, setting a pattern for the Hawthorne who was to consider daguerreotypists and inherited curses, and the Melville who was to attempt to trim a craft which eventually sank by hanging the head of Kant on one side and that of Locke on another. To say this is to give far more significance to the conventional remarks about Charles Brockden Brown as a literary precursor than is commonly conveyed. He did not in certain faint ways foreshadow the American novel; rather, he was the first to face the confusion of sentiment and an optimistic psychology, both of which flowed through the chink in the Puritan dike, and to represent American progress away from a doctrine of depravity as a very mixed blessing indeed.

Added to, or resulting from Brown's reversal on the related subjects of sentimentalism and an optimistic psychology is a third prominent aspect of the achievement of *Wieland*, for not only do these turnabouts reveal tensions in the American mind, they govern the way the American setting is handled in the novel. (pp. 51-5)

The America of *Wieland* . . . is a land in which the dreams of prosperity, conjured up by a free society occupying cheap and fertile lands, are realized. But the promises of modern enlightenment, phrased so as to encourage the American in his belief that the past is dead and that the old age of his land, the colonial period with its rigorous Protestant doctrines and aristocratic social formulas, has given way to a new world, these are siren songs. Science and culture, Brown reports, have driven the supernatural and the depraved from the temple, but the rout is a temporary one, for science and culture have not come to grips with the same questions as the dead beliefs attempted to account for. Evil will not go away merely because you refuse to recognize it. Wieland learns this from the voices as Clara learns it in her psychological explorations. The battle which enlightenment seemed to have been carying with such success in the market place of Boston and the assembly halls of Philadelphia was not over. Jonathan Edwards' voice may have been shouted down but America still had to reckon with the realities the old beliefs attempted to explain. This was to be the almost constant theme of Hawthorne and the agony of Melville. They came to it after growing up in an expanding America in which the exploitation of resources was a patriotic duty and the religion of free will held sway in the intellectual centers. But without their experience, writing at the start rather than the height of this expansion, Charles Brockden Brown, too, discovered and then followed this theme. It is fitting that when he did deny the heart of his novel in the optimistic *deus ex machina* ending, he at least sent his characters off to France before permitting them to enjoy their felicity. America was blighted for them.

The subtitle of *Wieland* is *The Transformation,* and the process explicitly referred to is undoubtedly that of the conversion of the enlightened Theodore Wieland into a homicidal maniac, with obvious parallels in the careers of Clara and Carwin. The transformation of the title, interestingly enough, is not followed in detail by Brown. We see the potential for mania in the early Wieland but it is not developed by the author. His insanity is a leap rather than a development.

But there are transformations in the novel which are of greater importance and which are developed in full detail before our eyes, and these constitute the greatness of the work. The novel itself is transformed from a sentimental romance into an anti-sentimental record of life. The viewpoint of the work is transformed from a conventionally superficial and optimistic psychology into one of depth and despair. And the America which forms the milieu in which the novel was written and the subject matter of the action is transformed from the old belief to the new psychology, only to be transformed at last into a doubtful state, hesitant to accept what cannot be explained naturally but

incapable of accounting for the most important aspects of life in a scientific manner.

Charles Brockden Brown's achievement in *Wieland* is considerable, for a half-century before the great literary movement in New England he had perceived the theme and the manner of the American novel, which is to say that like all great literary artists he knew his culture better than it knew itself. His characterization of it is immensely rewarding even though in achieving it he had, at times, to abandon his attitudes the better to pursue his art, and, at other times, to abandon his art the better to pursue life. (pp. 56-7)

Larzer Ziff, "A Reading of 'Wieland'," in PMLA, *Vol. LXXVII, No. 1, March, 1962, pp. 51-7.*

WILLIAM M. MANLY   (essay date 1963)

[*Manly proposes that the use of a first person point of view in* Wieland *unifies the rationalistic, Gothic, and sentimental strains of thought apparent in Brown's novel.*]

Students of Charles Brockden Brown's *Wieland* have often noted its relationship to the Richardsonian sentimental novel. Fred Lewis Pattee was the first to suggest similarities when he wrote in his early Introduction: "The book is to be classed with the seduction novels so popular at the close of the 18th Century—a book of the *Clarissa Harlowe* type" [see excerpt dated 1926]. Leslie Fiedler later elaborated the sentimental seduction theme into the major experience of the novel, and a more recent reading has found *Wieland* to be a sentimental novel with a reactionary middle [see excerpt by Larzer Ziff dated 1962].

Surely there are sentimental-seduction materials in *Wieland:* Clara, the narrator, swoons at several critical moments; she is occasionally dithyrambic with emotion over her would-be lover Pleyel; Carwin, the villain of the piece, at one point confesses to a desire to ravish Clara; and in the denouement he confesses that he has seduced Clara's maid. Yet I would suggest that for all these incidental trappings, the emotional power of *Wieland* does not rely in any essential way on the traditional appeals of the sentimental novel. The felt literary experience which Brown's early novel provides is far closer to the dark ambiguities of reason and emotion in Poe, Hawthorne, and Henry James than to the palpitating excesses of Richardson. Sentiment is only one aspect of the narrator's sensibility, and not the dominant aspect; seduction is only one of a cluster of threats that assail her, and not the dominant threat. The astonishing intensity which Brown generates in such an unevenly written novel reflcts his ability to convey through a first-person narrator the shifting instability of a mind swayed between objective logic and subjective terror, creating thereby a tension which is not resolved until the final pages. The controlling drama of this novel is suggested by another of Pattee's early insights: "The Wieland family is abnormal, but the reader holds the key to this abnormality. The novelist has skillfully furnished all the materials for a clinic. The book is a study in dementia: all four of the main characters are touched with it."

The sensibility of Clara Wieland filters two preoccupations which occur throughout Brown's writing: his avowed interest in rationalism, truth, and purpose; and his equal fascination with the disruption of these qualities in the bizarre, the Gothic, and the sentimental. Though critics have claimed *Wieland* for one or the other of these preoccupations, it seems clear that Brown constructed his tale not around one, but around both—

the one lending dramatic force to the other—and that the dramatic tension so generated is the key to *Wieland*'s central fascination despite its surface flaws. To be fully logical and guided by common sense is, in the mental world of this narrator, to be fully sane; to give reign to one's susceptibilities to supernatural and mystical speculation on mysterious events is to move toward madness. This unresolved dramatic tension begun in the early pages and continued until the final ones not only gives a heretofore slightly regarded unity to this early tale but is clearly its guiding genius.

Clara displays from the beginning a far more rational and controlled intelligence than that of the typical sentimental heroine. Even random samplings of her conversation have a philosophic rigor unknown to Clarissa: "We recalled and reviewed every particular that had fallen under our observation," "he merely deduced from his own reasonings," "I labored to discover the true inferences deducible from his deportment and words." Her analysis of her brother's possible delusion seems to be taken from Locke or Hume entire: "The will is the tool of the understanding, which must fashion its conclusions on the notices of sense. If the senses be depraved it is impossible to calculate the evils that may flow from the consequent deductions of the understanding." The highly rational Pleyel says of her: "I have contemplated your principles, and been astonished at the solidity of their foundation, and the perfection of their structure." This common sense side of Clara reveals the impact of Brown's reading in Locke and Hume, his early interest in Voltaire and the French Deists, and his association with Deistic thinkers in America like Benjamin Franklin. But beyond this, we see in Clara's rationalism Brown's own innate philosophic habit of mind which causes comment among friends and critics alike.

Yet Clara has a more dangerous aspect to her sensibility, a tendency to veer from objective common sense into a melodramatic world of haunting speculation. Working against her tendency to set forth her narrative logically and clearly are sudden shifts as her imagination becomes overwhelmed with horror. Before describing Carwin she writes "My blood is congealed: and my fingers are palsied when I call up this image. Shame on my cowardly and infirm heart!" Three times she pauses to recover herself from soaring sensations which threaten to overwhelm her senses, and toward the end of the tale she morbidly looks toward her own death: "Let my last energies support me in the finishing of this task. Then will I lay down my head in the lap of death. Hushed will be all my murmurs in the sleep of the grave." The indulgence of Clara's imagination sets up an emotional rhythm in the novel which is constantly tugging at the factual foundations on which the tale seems to be based, and injects a hint of instability into the whole.

This tension which Brown is at pains to create through Clara's conflicting predisposition is initiated in her early description of her father's strange death. On the one hand the event is informed with scientific objectivity. The description of her father's day and of the symptoms with which the fatal evening begins are almost clinical; significantly, a man of science, a doctor (Clara's uncle), related the facts to her because she was too young to have understood them at the time. This same rational and scientific uncle will enter the tale in the final scenes to start Clara back on the road to mental health. Clara says of him: "My uncle's testimony is peculiarly worthy of credit, because no man's temper is more skeptical, and his belief is unalterably attached to natural causes." Even the description

of her father's body after the mysterious accident is unemotionally realistic: "My father, when he left the house, besides a loose upper vest and slippers, wore a shirt and drawers. Now he was naked, his skin throughout the greater part of his body was scorched and bruised. His right arm exhibited marks as of having been struck by some heavy body. His clothes had been removed, and it was not immediately perceived that they were reduced to ashes. His slippers and his hair were untouched." It is not surprising that the precisely observed details of this description came from an actual journal report of a similar accident: Clara's tone of factual authenticity is unmistakable.

Yet though she is disposed to view her father's death with a certain objective reserve, another more "Gothic" appeal manifests itself. Throughout the episode Clara dwells intermittently on her father's feeling that he might be doomed by some supernatural agency, and on her mother's thoughts that fatal night. The episode when seen from the eyes of her mother is bathed in emotionalism: "What was it she feared? Some disaster impended over her husband or herself. He had predicted evils but professed himself ignorant of what nature they were. When were they to come? Was this night, or this hour to witness the accomplishment?" This impressionistic speculation on her mother's thoughts long after the event is evidence at the outset of a tendency to color events subjectively, a tendency with which the reader sympathizes—the death is, after all, a mystery—but on which he can only reserve judgment. The peculiar irresolution of the elder Wieland's death is in part the irresolution of Clara'a attitude toward it, an irresolution which the tale will demonstrate to have dangerous consequences.

Brown's dramatization of opposed tendencies in Clara's consciousness is structurally reinforced by the externally opposed personalities of the ultra-rational Pleyel and the ultra-religious Wieland. Their conflicting, and ultimately irreconcilable, attitudes toward experience are defined early: "Pleyel was not behind his friend in knowledge of the history and metaphysics of religion. Their creeds, however, were in many respects opposite. Where one discovered only confirmations of his faith, the other could find nothing but reasons for doubt. Moral necessity, and calvinistic inspiration, were the props on which my brother thought proper to repose. Pleyel was the champion of intellectual liberty, and rejected all guidance but that of his reason." Pleyel, being an outsider, is untouched by the morbid inheritance of a mysterious death which appears to haunt the Wielands; his perspective is like that of Clara's uncle whose nature was "unalterably attached to natural causes." Pleyel is inclined to regard the mysterious voice which Wieland first hears with sociable good humor and skeptical reservation. Wieland, on the other hand, consistently exhibits a mind prone to supernatural brooding and tends to color events with his own interpretation of them. The mysterious voices cause Wieland to fall into a prolonged, introspective meditation which partially isolates him from his friends. Clara remarks of her brother that he always regarded his father's death as "flowing from a direct and supernatural decree," and that he was in some respects an "enthusiast" in religious matters.

Clara is clearly the inheritor of her brother's introspective disposition, which she gradually comes to realize is leading to dangerous alienation from reality, but which she is powerless to control by the application of objective logic. Her emotional commitment to supernatural interference is deepened by her second encounter with the mysterious voice, this time heard not only by Wieland but by Pleyel. She cannot contain an upwelling of enthusiasm: "The tales of apparitions and enchantments did not possess that power over my belief which could even render them interesting. I saw nothing in them but ignorance and folly, and was a stranger even to that terror which is pleasing. But this incident was different from any that I had ever before known. Here were proofs of a sensible and intelligent existence, which could not be denied. Here was information obtained and imparted by means unquestionably super-human." Her use of "proofs" and "unquestionably" at this juncture, while Pleyel is bemused but uncommitted, is an ominous shifting of Clara's mental balance in the direction of Wieland's "enthusiasm"; her assured invocation of the supernatural to explain appearances runs against an underlying tenor of skeptical "scientism" and rationality which has vied for the reader's attention from the beginning. Through Clara's brooding and extravagance Brown begins subtly to establish that the mind which filters the experience of the tale is itself a biased glass which warps the proportions of the events seen; in this respect, the complex tension of the tale becomes focused not on typical sentimental or Gothic situations, but on the problem of separating appearances from realities, truths from fictions, in a manner which suggests Henry James's later technique in "The Turn of the Screw." Clara's vacillation at this point is merely an early tremor in her mental stability but it is a tremor which subtly prepares the reader for those later oscillations between madness and sanity which dominate the tale's central scenes.

Clara grows more and more frenzied as frustration and isolation continue to exacerbate an already divided sensibility. Her tone takes on a desperate quality: "You will believe that calamity has subverted my reason, and that I am amusing you with the chimeras of my brain, instead of facts that really happened. I shall not be surprized or offended, if these be your suspicions." As her instability mounts, her naturally rationalistic, philosophic temper becomes steadily weakened: "I now speak as if no remnant of doubt existed in my mind as to the supernal origin of these sounds; but this is owing to the imperfection of my language, for I only mean that the belief was more permanent, and visited more frequently my sober meditations than its opposite. The immediate effects served only to undermine the foundations of my judgment and precipitate my resolutions."

The subtle dislocation of Clara's narrative is further emphasized by her inexplicable first-sight reaction to Carwin, the ventriloquist villain, a reaction which the reader can neither share nor understand. Having had only a glimpse of Carwin's face (he appears as a rustic stranger), and hearing only a snatch of his conversation to her maid, she is not only moved to tears, but his image continues to preoccupy her for days. The instability which she displays at this juncture is confusing even to herself: "The manner in which I was affected on this occasion, was, to my own apprehension, a subject of astonishment. The tones were indeed such as I never heard before; but that they should, in an instant, as it were, dissolve me in tears, will not easily be believed by others, and can be scarcely comprehended by myself." Clara's involuntary fantasies soon veer to a morbid preoccupation with her father's mysterious death and her own legacy of possible madness; Carwin the stranger is thus only the occasion for a fresh release of melancholy as his image provokes foreshadowings of doom.

This curious reaction, taken together with her response to the voices in the closet plotting her murder, and the warning in the recess—all the startling and inexplicable situations that make up the fabric of this tale—gradually isolate Clara from the free and healthy social intercourse of the novel's beginning, to press her toward the private hell of doubt and uncertainty which characterizes its climax. The progression appears as preordained as a Greek tragedy. We follow those early premonitions and warnings which have intruded into her consciousness and watch them become inexorably realized in the real and threatened mental disintegration of Wieland and Clara herself. One of Brown's major foreshadowing devices, which has heretofore received insufficient, if not irrelevant, treatment, is the dramatic impact and subsequent effect of Clara's dream of Wieland, a dream which not only subtly prepares the reader for Wieland's disastrous transformation in the climactic scenes of violence but gives Clara a dim insight into her own possible mental disintegration if she follows her brother's course. After falling asleep in an isolated summer bower, she dreams she is walking in the evening twilight to her brother's habitation: "A pit, methought, had been dug in the path I had taken, of which I was not aware. As I carelessly pursued my walk, I thought I saw my brother, standing at some distance before me, beckoning and calling me to make haste. He stood on the opposite edge of the gulph. I mended my pace, and one step more would have plunged me into this abyss, had not some one from behind caught suddenly my arm, and exlaimed, in a voice of eagerness and terror, 'Hold! hold!' "

In a curious way, Clara both sees and does not see the pit toward which she is headed in her carelessness; it is a course which her conscious mind neglects but which her subconscious intuits as destructive. The dream is appropriately mysterious; it is an "abyss" toward which her brother beckons her, but with what intention? Recent criticism of *Wieland* has been inclined to interpret the abyss and Clara's fears of her brother as a latent horror of incest, despite the complete lack of objective evidence for such a view within the novel. Clara at no point fears seduction or rape by Wieland but at several points fears the homicidal possibilities of a latent, and perhaps inherited, insanity in her brother. The image of an "abyss" is present at two other crucial points in the narrative, where it is clearly used to mean the gulf of insanity. Furthermore, Clara herself interprets her own dream toward the end of the tale as a prophetic intuition of her brother's incipient transformation into a maniac, an intuition which is repeated in the following waking episode that takes place shortly after her dream.

Alone and in a disturbed state, Clara enters her bedroom prepared to peruse a manuscript, but at her closet door she hesitates, inexplicably overcome with terror: "A sort of belief darted into my mind, that some being was concealed within, whose purposes were evil." She is suddenly haunted by the vision of "An hand invisible and of preternatural strength, lifted by human passions, and selecting my life for its aim," and in the instant the dream of Wieland's temptation to destruction is recalled. She is led to the irresistible conclusion that Wieland is within the closet—"What monstrous conception is this? my brother!" Once again the dream warns her subconscious of danger, but it is quite obviously not sexual assault which she fears but homicidal violence. The very ambiguity of her thoughts and actions in this scene indicates that it is not only Wieland's madness which is dimly presaged, but the scene itself dramatizes a threat to her own sanity that the reader cannot fail to remark. Her irrational compulsiveness here is a subtle prelude to that terrifying compulsive and fanatic behavior of the later Wieland. The disturbed mind faltering in darkness which so fascinates Brockden Brown in this and other novels could well stand as a metaphor for the entire action of this strange tale.

It is not Wieland who emerges from the closet, but Carwin, and this brief direct encounter of Carwin and Clara has been a key scene for those critics who desire to view the tale as Richardsonian. Here, if nowhere else in the novel, sexual assault is presented as a momentary threat. But in the same breath that Carwin alludes to his opportunity to ravish Clara, he professes his inability to do so because she is protected by a "higher power." The scene is short and fraught with mysterious, apologetic behavior on the part of Carwin, who does not appear either here, or anywhere else, as a lusty Lovelace. Even this scene of avowed momentary passion for Clara is later confessed to be a sham expedient, designed to make him seem more flamboyant. Carwin, in fact, is for the most part a shadowy background figure whose final confessions reveal him to be more of a pathetic bumbler than a figure of soaring sexual passion. Though he is the mechanism behind mysterious events, the dramatic heart of the novel is not in the events themselves but in the reaction of Clara and Wieland to them. When the mysteries are brought to light they appear trivial and uninteresting; they have their meaning in the agonies they have produced. Which is only to say again that the central drama of the novel lies not in sex or sensationalism per se, but in Clara's consciousness as she copes with a growing isolation from the sane and normal preoccupations of daily life.

The mysterious alienation of Pleyel (later found to be the work of Carwin) is one more instance of this isolation. The sentimental attraction of Pleyel for Clara is precisely why her isolation from him is so dismaying, for once again the strange has intruded itself into the intimate and familiar to disturb the very foundations of Clara's sanity. To be sure, part of this alienation results from a too scrupulous conventionality which Clara regrets, but this is hardly the most important reason for the alienation, nor is it the point of the whole episode. The incident is organically integrated into Brown's carefully constructed chain of isolation and frustration which with fateful relentlessness is pressing Clara closer and closer to possible disaster, as her emotions and imagination gain control over her reason.

At the climax of the tale those intimations and omens which have plagued Clara from the beginning come to fruition. Wieland's murdered wife and children are discovered, and Wieland himself takes over the narrative for a time (by means of a trial transcript) to portray the consequences of a morbidly hypersensitive sensibility when it is cut loose from any balancing skepticism. Wieland's transcript, which begins so rationally and ends in such horror, is a logical extension of the path on which Clara has been walking, and from which she is only fortuitously saved. In the culminating scenes of the tale, Clara is brought to the brink of complete disorientation: she falls into frenzies, she becomes delirious, and just before Carwin enters for the last time, she is on the point of suicide.

But with Carwin's confession comes catharsis: rationalism begins to be restored and the healthy perspective of fact begins to replace the instability of fancy. This resolution in explanation is actually begun slightly before the confession with the appearance of her uncle, whose rationality and scientific interests take the place of the missing Pleyel. Facts of family history are given, and a medical explanation of Wieland's condition is provided. Yet, as her uncle shows Wieland's madness to be inherited, Clara's dread of her own mental transformation is increased. Shortly after the climactic events she takes to her

bed delirious; once again the ominous image of an abyss, the symbolic inheritance which has haunted her from the beginning, is recalled in a phantasmagoric dream: "Sometimes gleams of light were shot into a dark abyss, on the verge of which I was standing, and enabled me to discover for a moment, its enormous depth and hideous precipices." The ultimate purgation breaking the concatenation of terrors that has dominated her fancy is achieved through a fire from which she is physically and symbolically rescued, a fire which sweeps away the scenes of her past and jars her into a fresh start for the future. As it was fire which destroyed her father to begin the inexorable tragic chain of frustrations and fears that make up *Wieland,* so it is fire that at last breaks that chain to allow Clara to return to a normal life.

This fresh start is the true ending of the novel; from this point on Clara's few pages of "tying up loose ends" act simply to draw out the purgation that Carwin's confession inaugurated and bring the reader back into a world of cause-and-effect sanity. That Brown was careless with some of his details is undeniable, but such carelessness leaves the central experience of the novel untouched. This reading has tried to show that Brown's over-all achievement in *Wieland* is far more of a piece than most critics will acknowledge who approach this early work more as a mine of literary-cultural materials than as a powerful psychological experience. If one must find a tradition for *Wieland,* it must surely lie with those peculiarly American explorations of the tormented psyche which seem ambiguously and resonantly to hover between appearance and reality, fact and imagination, daylight and dream. Brockden Brown is clearly the first of those many in American letters who have grasped the dramatic importance of "point of view" in fiction. (pp. 311-21)

William M. Manly, "The Importance of Point of View in Brockden Brown's 'Wieland'," in *American Literature, Vol. XXXV, No. 3, November, 1963, pp. 311-21.*

LESLIE A. FIEDLER   (essay date 1966)

[*An American critic, novelist, short story writer, essayist, poet, and editor, Fiedler is a commentator on American literature who has generated a great deal of controversy. Using primarily Marxist and Freudian perspectives, he attempts to uncover the origins of modern literature and show how myth is used in it. His critical works, which are often biographical and psychosexual in orientation, have been criticized for their sweeping generalizations. Though some have termed him "the wild man of American literary criticism," Fiedler has been praised for his* Love and Death in the American Novel, *an insightful, provocative, highly individual landmark in literary criticism. In the following excerpt from that work, Fiedler affirms the importance of Brown's contribution to the mythopoeic novel in America and examines* Edgar Huntly *as an example of that tradition.*]

Brown's achievement as a novelist is hard to assess. On only one thing do recent writers who discuss him agree, that his reputation is still moot and that it is somehow important for us now to come to terms with him. Brown remains in an odd way a living writer, because of the polemical tone which a discussion of his work necessarily still assumes. To define his rank and status involves an attempt at redefining the whole tradition of the American novel. Where he is placed depends upon, and in turn determines, the total shape of the literary hierarchy in which he is situated. A conventional "enlightened" attitude toward his work is expressed by Parrington, who believed that though Brockden Brown was possessed of considerable technical skill, his example was "unfortunate" in so far as it represented an adaptation to American uses of the "blood-pudding school" of England. For Parrington, Brown's most admirable feature was his Godwinian politics, which led him to challenge the belief (held by "gentlemen who profited by social wrong") that injustice was "inherent in human nature"; and to insist that the source of that wrong "be sought in institutions rather than in the nature of man." The early American public, however—or at least so Parrington believed—ignored Brown's social theories in favor of his "gross Romanticism," so that his final influence was chiefly harmful.

More recently, George Snell [see excerpt dated 1947] has argued quite oppositely that although Brown is technically inept (Snell finds *Edgar Huntly,* for instance, "utterly incredible"), he was the founder of the "demonic, macabre, apocalyptic" school, which flourishes throughout the history of our literature and reaches a climax in Faulkner's *Absalom, Absalom!* It is certainly true, at any rate, that Cooper borrowed shamelessly from Brown; that Poe, who profited by his example, apparently esteemed him highly; and that Hawthorne not only placed him in his Hall of Fantasy (along with Homer, Shakespeare, Fielding, and Scott) but more generally observed that "no American writer enjoys a more classic reputation on this side of the water." Among his more eminent admirers who had gone on record by that time were Shelley (who ranked his gothic romances with Schiller's *Robbers* and Goethe's *Faust*), Keats, Hazlitt, and Godwin himself, who had returned Brown's admiration with enthusiasm on his own part. Certainly, it is utterly false to say, with a recent Parringtonian critic, that Brown is "liked only by the Professors who are taken in easily by the 'hollow men' of literature."

The problem is somewhat more complex than that. Those who find it difficult to take Brown seriously are, on the one hand, "realists" and, on the other, "formalists." Brown inevitably seems an incompetent and irrelevant writer to anyone who reads the history of our novel as a melodrama with a happy dénouement in which a virtuous but harried realistic tradition, after resisting the blandishments of fantasy, romance, and allegory, was recognized as the true heir to the patrimony. Brown, however, is an anti-realist in almost all respects, moving his irresolute and inconsistent protagonists through a time and space carelessly defined and bearing only a fitful, largely accidental resemblance to the facts of history or geography.

No more is Brown a formalist. He proves, indeed, especially disappointing to the critic who believes, or pretends to, that the novel is at best a skillful and sophisticated arrangement of words, a pleasantly intricate web of sensibility, which is judged good or bad in terms of how complex and various, though finally unified, is its abstract pattern. Brown is a writer careless to the point of shamelessness. He is likely to introduce a character into the action and let him wander about for pages before telling the reader where he comes from, what he is after, or even what his name is. Brown's resolutions are willful, hasty, often a little absurd, depending on broad coincidences hard to credit. Since he wrote four of his novels (plus the fragments of others) at the same time, he sometimes switches incidents or characters or simply names back and forth among them in a bewildering way. Often he will detach an episode for independent expansion or use elsewhere, leaving quite inexplicable vestiges in the original book. He is especially fond of attaching almost identical incidents to different characters in the same book, or of suggesting confusing resemblances between un-related people without ever troubling to justify or exploit those deliberately planted resemblances.

The world through which his characters move is given local names (Philadelphia, for instance, or New York or Perth Amboy), but his scenes have little in common with the places they presumably represent. Only when he describes something monstrous and extraordinary like a city under a pestilence, do his descriptions approach the "reality" of the realists. Only when the real world itself, that is to say, comes to seem a symbolic nightmare does it accommodate itself to the sensibility and dreamlike style of Brown. That is why the set-piece of the anthologies, exempted from blame by his severest critics, is the description of the yellow fever epidemic in *Arthur Mervyn.*

For better or worse, then, Brown established in the American novel a tradition of dealing with the exaggerated and the grotesque, not as they are verifiable in any external landscape or sociological observation of manners and men, but as they correspond in quality to our deepest fears and guilts as projected in our dreams or lived through in "extreme situations." Realistic milieu and consistent character alike are dissolved in such projective fictions, giving way to the symbolic landscape and the symbolic action, which are the hallmarks of the mythopoeic novel. Simply to acknowledge the existence and importance of such a tradition is embarrassing to some readers; for it means, on the one hand, a questioning of the sufficiency of realism, which justifies art by correlating it with science; and on the other, it suggests a disturbing relationship between our highest art and such lowbrow forms of horror pornography as the detective story, the pulp thriller, and the Superman comic book, all of which are also heirs of the gothic.

To understand more specifically, however, the role of Brown in the definition of the American novel, it is necessary to look closely at *Edgar Huntly,* the most successful and characteristic of his gothic romances. *Wieland,* usually preferred to it, is convincing only here and there, being the victim of confusions that Brown could not assimilate (as he did those of *Edgar Huntly*) to the meanings of his story. The plot of the latter book can be summarized with relative simplicity, for a book of Brown. Searching for the murderer of Waldegrave, brother of his fiancée, Huntly discovers Clithero Edny who, beneath the elm under which Waldegrave had been murdered, comes at midnight to dig a pit in which he sits and sobs. Clithero is, it turns out, sleepwalking, tormented by various guilts which do *not* include that for the murder of which Huntly has suspected him. Rather he has (back in Ireland) killed the brother of his protector, Mrs. Lorimer, in a misguided effort at preserving her from that brother's irrational malice. Mrs. Lorimer, however, feels that she is doomed by her protégé's act, since she believes her own life tied by mystic bonds to that of her brother, who was her twin. In anguish over her delusion and the guilt which it imputes to him, Clithero goes mad and attempts to kill his mistress, thus helping to spare her the painful anticipation of her end.

Having told this improbable story to Huntly, Clithero disappears into the Pennsylvania wilderness, through which Huntly (prey of curiosity still) attempts to track him down, only to fall prey to somnambulism himself and to wake one day at the bottom of a pit. As Huntly at this stage of the novel has almost blurred into his alter ego Clithero, so the hole dug by the obsessed Irishman has mysteriously become the vast trap in which Huntly finds himself, confronted with a panther, a tomahawk mysteriously close to hand. The panther killed, then eaten raw and his flesh vomited up again (the whole episode comes to seem a rite of initiation which will prepare Huntly for later demands on his manhood), Huntly succeeds in finding a way out. He is led, however, through subterranean passages to a cave in which Indians hold captive a girl—strange to the main action of the story and quite unintegrated into what follows.

Huntly delivers her from the Indians, but is wounded in the struggle and left for dead; he is reborn again, however (surely he is the most often reborn of heroes), and begins a wilderness trek in which he shoots at and is shot at by unrecognized friends. Absolutely alone at last, with even those who love him turned unwitting foes, he nevertheless manages to return to civilization, where he learns that Waldegrave has been murdered by Indians, perhaps the very ones involved in his own adventure. This information when it comes seems utterly anticlimactic, irrelevant to what has become the real theme of the book. More important for the resolution is the further information that Sarsefield, Huntly's own benefactor, had been the first lover of Mrs. Lorimer. They are married, her husband having meanwhile died as well as her brother, who had hated Sarsefield; but Clithero reappears once more, frightening Mrs. Sarsefield into a miscarriage. He flees again and finally drowns himself to avoid being committed as insane, leaving Huntly free to complete their identification by wooing the daughter of Mrs. Lorimer, with whom Clithero had been in love.

It is a charmingly, a maddeningly disorganized book, not so much written as dreamed, but it convinces the reader, once he has been caught up in the fable, of its most utter improbabilities; for its magic is not the hocus-pocus of make-believe, but the irrational reality of the id. "The miracles of poetry, the transitions of enchantment," Edgar Huntly boasts, "are beggarly and mean compared with those I had experienced. Passage into new forms, overleaping the bars of time and space, reversal of the laws of inanimate and intelligent existence had been mine to perform and witness." Yet all these "perils and wonders" Brown has managed to present without invoking specifically supernatural agencies; not a breach of natural law, justifiable in terms of necromancy or sorcery, but only human madness and especially somnambulism, diseases explicable by medical science, lie at the root of the "marvelous" in *Edgar Huntly.*

Brown's novel is an initiation story, the account of a young man who begins by looking for guilt in others and ends finding it in himself; who starts out in search of answers but is finally satisfied with having defined a deeper riddle than those he attempted to solve. "What light has burst upon my knowledge of myself and mankind . . . ," Edgar Huntly cries. "How . . . enormous the transition from uncertainty to knowledge. . . ." But what has he learned really at the close of this odd murder mystery? That the Indians killed his friend is a piece of information which does not thrill the reader and could not have stirred him to so ecstatic a response. It is more general wisdom that Huntly acquires, discovering that "the crime originated in those limitations which nature has imposed on human faculties." This applies not only to the crime of Clithero of which it is specifically said; it is applicable to all human evil. "How little cognizance have men over the actions and motives of each other. How total is our blindness in regard to our own performances." Any man may wake to find himself at the bottom of a pit. *We are all sleepwalkers!*

But if we walk in our sleep, we also run in our dreams. Life is a nightmare through which we pursue or are pursued in a wilderness where the unexpected and the absurd, the irrelevance of what comes before to what comes after are the basic facts of existence. In *Edgar Huntly,* for instance, the boundaries between person and person are abrogated; people are always turning into each other. Clithero raises his hand to kill Mrs. Lorimer and discovers he is really assaulting his beloved, Clarice. Huntly comes upon a total stranger, a sleepwalker, only to find that he is a sleepwalker, too, and to end under the protection of the same foster-mother, engaged to the same sister-bride.

In this world of transformation, not only do unlikes turn into likes, but things themselves become their own opposites. The best motives lead to the worst ends: attempting to protect Mrs. Lorimer, Clithero kills her brother, almost kills her. The dead prove to be alive; Sarsefield, protector of Huntly, and Wiatte, brother of Mrs. Lorimer, "start to life at the same moment"; while Huntly, as we have seen, is himself apparently dead twice, rises twice to life. Friends become enemies, the protector the destroyer; Sarsefield almost kills Edgar even as Edgar tries to kill him. Through such an unstable world one must flee continually from foes known and unknown: from the lunatic and the brother inexplicably dedicated to evil, from the panther and the Indian and the unwittingly hostile friend—finally, from the principle of destruction in the very self. The image of flight with which the gothic began is in *Edgar Huntly* raised to its highest power, revealed as the image of life itself.

Brown, however, seems to have thought of *Edgar Huntly* as performing in the first instance a specifically American task. In a prefatory note [see excerpt dated 1799], he speaks not only of his resolve to employ for the ends of wonder pathology rather than black magic, "to exhibit a series of adventures . . . connected with one of the most common and wonderful diseases of the human frame," but also of his desire to naturalize gothic terror by presenting it in terms of an action "growing out of the condition of our country." "New springs of action," he insists, "and new motives to curiosity should operate . . . ," since the institutions of our society "differ essentially from Europe." There is a little chauvinism in his plea, a little of the provincial's eagerness to strike a bold cultural pose; but there is also a sense of how unviable (as we have already observed) are the myths and meanings of the European gothic romance in a classless, historyless country. Had some early writer as self-consciously considered the problem of seduction in our literature, the role of love in American fiction might have been far different.

"One merit the writer may at least claim," Brown continues in the preface to *Edgar Huntly,* "that of calling forth the passions and engaging the sympathy of the reader, by means hitherto unemployed by preceding authors. Puerile superstition, and exploded manners; Gothic castles and chimeras, are the materials usually employed for this end. The incidents of Indian hostility, and the perils of the western wilderness are far more suitable; and, for a native of America to overlook these, would admit of no apology." There is something so natural, so inevitable about Brown's proposed substitutions of American for European symbols that it is hard to appreciate, after the fact, how revolutionary a leap of the imagination his project demanded. The very success of his adaptive devices makes it hard to appreciate them yet testifies to how deeply they responded to our imaginative and mythic needs.

For the corrupt Inquisitor and the lustful nobleman, he has substituted the Indian, who broods over the perils of Brown's fictional world in an absolute dumbness that intensifies his terror. Brown's aboriginal shadows do not even speak. They merely threaten by their very presence, their "gigantic forms," "huge limbs," and "fantastic ornaments" representing visually the threat they embody. "I never looked upon or called up the image of a savage," Edgar Huntly says, "without shuddering." There is some sense in Brown of the historic "Indian problem," of the appropriation of their lands by white colonists and their futile dreams of revenge; but "Queen Mab," the spokesman for their cause, though prepared for at some length, does not finally appear in the book. It is not the Indian as social victim that appeals to Brown's imagination, but the Indian as projection of natural evil and the id; his red men are therefore treated essentially as animals, living extensions of the threat of the wilderness, like the panthers with whom they are associated.

For the haunted castle and the dungeon, Brown substitutes the haunted forest (in which nothing is what it seems) and the cave, the natural pit or abyss from which man struggles against great odds to emerge. These are ancient, almost instinctive symbols, the *selva oscura* going back to Dante and beyond, while the cave as a metaphor for the mysteries of the human heart is perhaps as old as literature itself. Brown tries quite consciously to identify the pit in which Edgar Huntly awakes with the terrible womb-tomb dungeons of Mrs. Radcliffe and Monk Lewis. "Methought I was the victim," Huntly says at the moment he becomes aware of where he is, "of some tyrant who had thrust me into a dungeon."

It should be noticed that the shift from the ruined castle of the European prototypes to the forest and cave of Brown involves a shift not just in the manner of saying what the author is after. *The change of myth involves a profound change of meaning.* In the American gothic, that is to say, the heathen, unredeemed wilderness and not the decaying monuments of a dying class, nature and not society becomes the symbol of evil. Similarly not the aristocrat but the Indian, not the dandified courtier but the savage colored man is postulated as the embodiment of villainy. Our novel of terror, that is to say (even before its founder has consciously shifted his political allegiances), is well on the way to becoming a Calvinist exposé of natural human corruption rather than an enlightened attack on a debased ruling class or entrenched superstition. The European gothic identified blackness with the super-ego and was therefore revolutionary in its implications; the American gothic (at least as it followed the example of Brown) identified evil with the id and was therefore conservative at its deepest level of implication, whatever the intent of its authors. (pp. 153-61)

> *Leslie A. Fiedler, "Charles Brockden Brown and the Invention of the American Gothic," in his* Love and Death in the American Novel, *revised edition, Stein and Day Publishers, 1966, pp. 126-61.*

PATRICK BRANCACCIO (essay date 1970)

[*Brancaccio demonstrates how Brown's control of narrative voice in* Arthur Mervyn *reveals the contradictions between unconscious motivation and conscious rationalization of action in Mervyn's character.*]

So much has been written about the debt of American fiction to the tradition of the romance that critics have either overlooked or been hesitant about claiming too much for the realistic strain. Charles Brockden Brown, for example, is generally treated as the ancestor of later romance writers like Hawthorne, Poe, Melville, James, and Faulkner. Following Richard Chase [see Additional Bibliography], Leslie Fiedler has observed that Brown's work belongs to "the mythopoeic novel" in which

"realistic milieu and consistent character alike are dissolved . . . giving way to the symbolic landscape and the symbolic action." But this generalization does not hold true for Brown's *Arthur Mervyn,* a novel in which social milieu is very much a real environment conditioning its characters in a very immediate way. Arthur Mervyn is not only a pre-Freudian portrait of a character whose experiences reveal clear Oedipal feelings, but he is a young man who is moved by the ambitions and anxieties fostered by the American myth of success.

The novel exists in two parts. The first part appeared in 1799, and the second part in 1800. In between Brown brought to completion and published *Edgar Huntley.* The full possibilities of the narrative's social and psychological realism seem to have occurred to Brown in the midst of composition. From a simple demonstration of the ways in which a virtuous young man resists temptation, Brown shifted to an attempt to convey the ironic interplay between Arthur's conscious and unconscious motivation and the sense of bewilderment that results from the ambiguity of appearances. Moreover, Brown responded to the technical demands of his content. His new vision led him to experiment with the techniques of multiple perspective and the device of the unreliable narrator.

Arthur Mervyn is the story of a country boy who comes to seek his fortune in the city. As an ancestor of Robin in Hawthorne's "My Kinsman, Major Molineux," he is an early portrait of a native American type. Soon after entering the city, Arthur becomes involved with a scoundrel who offers to become his patron. Though Arthur becomes embroiled in Welbeck's schemes, he apparently retains the purity of his intentions.

Welbeck is a typical American villain; an earlier version of the confidence man, a forger, an embezzler, and a thief. When charged with complicity in Welbeck's evil schemes, Arthur attempts to clear his name by revealing his history in all its circumstantial detail. In the second half of the novel, he describes his reforming crusade in which he hopes to prove through deeds what he has asserted in words about his noble intentions. He is apparently rewarded with marriage to a wealthy divorcée. But Arthur's tale is called into question through a complex set of narratives within narratives which provide the reader with conflicting views of the same events.

Though the novel is Arthur Mervyn's story, the initial narrator is Dr. Stevens, who serves as the framing consciousness of the first part. Dr. Stevens has taken Mervyn in and nursed him back to health from his attack of yellow fever, the plague that permeates the atmosphere of the entire novel. When Arthur recovers, and some questions arise about his character, he volunteers to explain his past. Arthur has prepared his friend to listen indulgently since he has struck Dr. Stevens from the first as a "simple and ingenuous" youth, whose "uncommon but manlike beauty" the doctor finds difficult to resist. Moreover, Dr. Stevens is a self-consciously benevolent man who is prepared to believe Arthur because of the lip service the young adventurer pays to the virtues of industry, sincerity, purity of mind, and faithfulness. Arthur seems to pursue the ideal of self-improvement through intellectual cultivation and practical "experience."

It is no surprise, then, that Arthur is completely successfuul with Dr. Stevens. The benevolent doctor is not simple-mindedly gullible, but he casts aside his doubts and concludes illogically: "Wickedness may sometimes be ambiguous, . . . but the face of Mervyn is the index of an honest mind." Mr. Wortley, whom Stevens has earlier characterized as a man

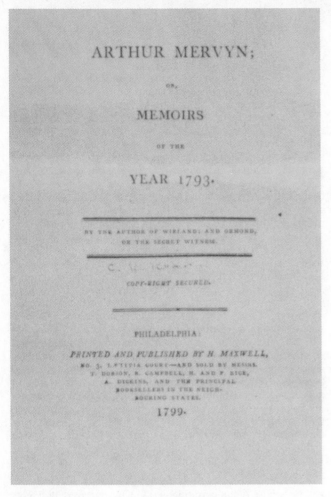

Title page to the first edition of Arthur Mervyn.

"venerable for his discernment and integrity," has not been taken in by Arthur's good looks nor has he succumbed to the charms of his glib tongue. But Stevens is not swayed by Wortley's revelations of Arthur's ties with Welbeck because Arthur has already given him all the details from his own point of view. Wortley and Stevens, then, define the two extreme views of Arthur's narrative. To Wortley, Mervyn's story is a "tissue of ingenious and implausible lies." Stevens believes all. To complicate the dilemma, Arthur never lies about the facts and is never caught in a flat contradiction.

Thus the problem lies not in the literal truth of Arthur's report of the outward events, but in Arthur's interpretation of them. Through his use of multiple perspective, Brown has his various narrators consistently remind us that appearances are ambiguous. Arthur asserts throughout that his intentions are pure. He reinforces this claim with his apparent candor and his complex examination of his motives. But his reliability is called into question because his strategy, as Donald A. Ringe has observed [see Additional Bibliography entry dated 1966], does not remove the possibility that he is self-deluded. Though appearances are deceiving, Brown suggests, they are not always as deceiving as Arthur would have his auditors believe.

The one character who understands Arthur more fully than anyone else is Welbeck. He comprehends Arthur's basic selfishness and his need to rationalize it with pretenses to virtue,

but because he himself is not deluded, he does not appreciate the intensity of Arthur's need or the complex ways in which it expresses itself. (pp. 18-21)

The wide disparity between Arthur's selfish impulses and his rationalizations becomes a source of comedy. In the second half of the novel Arthur abandons his passive role and presents himself as an aggressive do-gooder who wishes to dispel the suspicions about his character in a public and sententious way. In the course of these exploits he reveals himself as a meddlesome, self-righteous bungler who comes close to destroying himself and everyone in his path.

More importantly, Arthur is haunted in this process of image-building by a clearly outlined pattern of Oedipal feelings which deepens the irony of his character and lends coherence to the entire novel. This pattern emerges openly but slowly through Brown's treatment of Mrs. Althorpe, who contradicts Arthur's account of his early life in the country. When Dr. Stevens asks about the source of her charges that Arthur has been guilty of "immoral conduct" with his father's second wife, and that he is a lazy ne'er-do-well who eloped with his father's horse, Mrs. Althorpe can only answer "the unanimous report of the neighbors." Mrs. Althorpe also describes an interview with Arthur in the country which is meant to discredit him but only reveals her own low-minded suspicions. She found Arthur at home knitting socks for his journey and charged him with effeminacy. Moreover, Mrs. Althorpe confuses Arthur's distaste for formal schooling with physical and intellectual idleness. Mrs. Althorpe's narrowmindedness only wins more sympathy for Arthur as a nonconformist in a group of dim-witted and vicious country bumpkins.

The comical display of Arthur's ingenuity in answering her charges, however, is a means of revealing his Oedipal feelings. First, he answers the charge of idleness. He admits that he avoided physical labor but claims it was because of ill health and because he knew his father could afford to pay someone to do his work. Most of all he was concerned for his mother:

> I thought her peace of mind was of some value, and that, if the inclination of either of my parents must be gratified at the expense of the other, the preference was due to the woman who bore me; who nursed me in disease, who watched over my safety with incessant tenderness; whose life and whose peace were involved in mine.

These excessive feelings for his mother lead Arthur into fantasies which transform his tyrannical, sexually competitive father into a meek slave to Arthur's own moral authority: "my mother's person was rescued from brutal violence; he was checked, in the midst of his ferocious career, by a single look or exclamation from me." Even more comically revealing is his answer to the charge that he had illicit relations with the servant girl, Betty Laurence, who later married his father. He would have us believe that she was a creature who "had no power over his senses" and was an object of study for him. Arthur is continually attempting to counteract suggestions that his behavior has been "perverse" with exaggerated expressions of the strength of his moral feeling. In describing his great powers of resistance to temptation, he reveals that voyeuristic, exploitive behavior which becomes the true type of Arthur's "perversion." With seemingly unconscious irony he mentions that his coldness drove Betty "to extremes, which it would serve no good purpose to describe in this audience." The chief irony here is that we can believe the literal truth of Arthur's account. His repressed sexuality is such that from the first pages of the novel he can be found hiding in a bedroom and peering into windows. His zeal for reform never blinds him to enticing sights.

Though, like Warner Berthoff, we may be hesitant to claim "too much for Brown . . . as an ironist," a Freudian reading of character is inevitably ironic for the logic of its analysis depends upon the perception of contradiction between conscious and unconscious levels of motivation. In *The Rhetoric of Fiction* Wayne Booth has warned against such ironic readings especially when they involve a so-called unreliable narrator. Booth is willing to accept the idea of the unreliable narrator only when there is explicit commentary to question him. According to this view there must be some rational norm by which to judge the author's intention—either through the author's voice, a *raisonneur,* or some version of that technique such as a Jamesian *ficelle.* In the absence of such a clearly marked fixed standard Booth rejects such ironic readings as the Freudian view of *The Turn of the Screw.*

But Brown so carefully demonstrates the contradiction between Arthur's unconscious "inclination" and his moralizing that we come to understand repression as the "norm" of his character. It is the fact of this repression which undercuts the worldly success which Arthur achieves at the end through his marriage to Mrs. Fielding. In chapter 39 Arthur assumes the pen for the first time so that we get his story directly rather than having it reported to us by Dr. Stevens. Though this change has been criticized as clumsy, there are important technical and psychological reasons for it. The novel is Arthur's story, and there is some justice in having him tell the most intimate and rewarding episode of his career. He not only looks back with satisfaction and fills in the remaining details of his adventures, but he looks forward with excited expectation toward his forthcoming marriage. There is a sense of ambiguous fulfillment in this act which helps to cap the irony so intricately entangled throughout the novel. We recall that Arthur first hoped to win his fortune in the city through the pen. It was as a copyist that Arthur was first employed by Welbeck, who displayed his maimed hand with the missing finger at their first meeting. Thus through the pen Arthur becomes identified with the financial intrigues and sexual exploitations which make up Welbeck's career. At two critical points in the novel, Arthur finds himself without a pen and searches for one as a pretext to invade Welbeck's private rooms. His involvement with the pen helps to focus all his divided attitudes about his own abilities and dreams. The pen becomes the symbol of the need to realize his financial and sexual ambitions and the need to justify them to the world.

These two compulsions converge in Arthur's first-person narrative of his relationship with Mrs. Fielding. The ostensible reason for his attraction is the quality of her mind, but there are more palpable allures, though beauty is pointedly not one of them. Mrs. Fielding is rich according to Arthur's standards, and she represents worldly sophistication. She is a dark Jewess, a stereotype of the *femme fatale* with a questionable past. She appears at first in bad company, with Mrs. Villars, the madam. She explains the relationship away as an indiscretion in her acceptance of an invitation from a woman she knew nothing about. Yet all Arthur really knows about her comes from the assertions she makes in the romantic tale of desertion and persecution by her husband.

Arthur believes her. She is six years older than he is, and he refers to her repeatedly as his "good mama," thus satisfying the Oedipal tendencies we noted earlier. The approaching con-

summation of these Oedipal feelings raises new anxieties in Arthur. The danger of the father figure is still there, for, according to Achsa Fielding's account, she never obtained a legal divorce.

At the end, when she agrees to marry him in fulfillment of his wildest, though allegedly unconscious desires, Arthur's rapture focuses on his pen: "Move on, My quill! wait not for my guidance. Reanimated with thy master's spirit, all airy light. An hey day rapture. A mounting impulse sways him: lifts him from the earth." But as the day of consummation approaches, an event that never occurs during the time span of the novel, Arthur is troubled by doubts: "I was roused as by a divine voice: 'Sleep no more; Mervyn shall sleep no more.' " In trying to describe the "nameless terror" that seizes him, Arthur clearly reveals his sense of guilt and insecurity in entering this marriage. This feeling culminates in a nightmare of retribution in which the wronged husband appears. He condemns Arthur as a villain: "and drew a steel from his bosom, with which he stabbed him in the heart." When he describes this dream to Mrs. Fielding, her response, unlike Jocasta's, is far from reassuring: "I hate your dream. It is a horrid thought. Would to God it had never occurred to you." Arthur replies innocently: "Why you surely place no confidence in dreams." With a strong sense of forboding, his betrothed answers: "I know not where to place confidence." There is bravado in Arthur's statement at the end when he tells us that the tales of his troubles are over, and in his new happy life he will have no need either to write or to relieve his troubled psyche. In an apostrophe to his pen, he says with ironic insistence, "I believe I will abjure thy company till all is settled with my love. Yes: I *will* abjure thee, so let *this* be thy last office, till Mervyn has been made the happiest of men." Brown has Arthur release his pen, that ambiguous symbol of his male power, with the Oedipus-like self-confidence of attained happiness which caps the irony of this final section.

Arthur, whose direct narration was to have removed all doubts about his character and his future, leaves the reader with a host of new questions. His state of mind at the end completes the impression that his tale is no more a success story than his motives are purely selfless. Far from being a weakness, the device of Arthur's concluding first-person narrative lends a coherence of structure and tone which reveals Brown as far more interested and successful with the techniques of fiction than has been generally recognized. He presents Arthur not as a young man haunted by Gothic terror but as a young American on the make in a competitive, moralistic business culture. Though we do not need to claim for Brown the elaborate self-consciousness or control of a modern psychological novelist, we can recognize that he did explore the possibilities of multiple perspective to suggest the complexities of a character who is neither a simple innocent nor a conscious hypocrite. (pp. 22-7)

Patrick Brancaccio, "Studied Ambiguities: 'Arthur Mervyn' and the Problem of the Unreliable Narrator," in American Literature, *Vol. XLII, No. 1, March, 1970, pp. 18-27.*

SYDNEY J. KRAUSE   (essay date 1973)

[*Krause argues that Brown's complex use of the seduction theme in* Ormond *makes the novel more artistically successful than is usually acknowledged.*]

Of Brockden Brown's four major novels, completed within a two-year outburst, and often rather facilely lumped together as exploitive of gothic sensation, *Ormond* would seem the least gothicized, and, being somewhat heavy on rhetoric, the least dazzling as well. For the effects of terror, critics have mainly contented themselves with allusions to the realistic depiction of the plague, and Ormond's clairvoyance as "secret witness." While Ormond himself is frequently enough cited as Brown's "most complex," and most fully developed Godwinian villain, one does not find the ending—which brings his villainy to its orbital climax—investigated either as a basis of the potency of his character, or as related to literary phenomena of the time. Rather, the ending has been criticized as melodramatic, and as eliciting contradictions in Ormond's character and an unsatisfactory physical (in lieu of a moral and intellectual) resolution to his conflict with Constantia. Donald Ringe, who makes this point, has indeed specifically attributed what he construes to be the "artistic failure" of the book to its "denouement" [see Additional Bibliography entry dated 1966]. I would submit that a consideration of the kind of thematic interest Ormond brings into the novel, along with the enrichment Brown gave to the seduction motif, demonstrate there is validity in one's taking an exactly opposite position.

Though Harry Warfel also disapproved of the ending of *Ormond* on grounds of melodrama, he none the less called it a "hair-raising climax" and went to the heart of the matter of theme in pointing out that "the emphasis on sex occurs not merely through the several scenes of seduction, but it is pervasive throughout the analysis of the fundamental psychology of the characters" [see Additional Bibliography entry dated 1949]. Actually, there can be little doubt from the moment at the end of chapter xi, when Ormond ponders the conflicting accounts of Constantia's character offered by Melbourne and Craig, that a major plot line will ensue from Ormond's decadently savored appraisal of this "exquisite wretch." ("Might not this girl mix a little imposture with her truth? Who knows her temptations to hypocrisy?") Equally important is the fact that the sexual motivation is a readily identifiable blending of the established Richardsonian and gothic seduction motifs of the desperate pursuit of the virtuous maiden. But scant credit has been given to Brown's exceptional treatment of this convention—exceptional to the extent that Ormond's magnificently elaborated assault on Constantia's towering virginity has to be regarded as an unparalleled classic of its kind, exceeding in complexity anything produced by Richardson, Walpole, or any of their followers. With its strongly ironic variation on the stock situation of a master seducer being mastered, it is seduction in a new key.

The action itself is very lucidly ordered in a three-part sequence: the fateful interview in chapter xxvi where Ormond enigmatically warns Constantia of what lies ahead and sees her monumental incredulity as his greatest obstacle, followed by the retrospective account of his earlier rape and murder of the Tartar girl during his soldier-of-fortune stint with the Cossacks, and then the physical assault scene itself in the lonely country mansion. Unmistakable, and useful as they are, the atmospheric gothic trappings—the troubled maiden closeted alone in the desolate house, the mysterious horseman discerned in the gathering dusk, the discovery of Craig's corpse outside her door, the unworkable latch that bars her escape, etc.—are quite the least of it. From the time that Ormond becomes convinced that he can never legitimately possess this girl, who "gratified him in nothing, but left him every thing to hope," to the forewarning of his aim and sour-grapes imputation of lesbianism, on through the final scene wherein, confident of conquest, he bids her to abide the inevitable, Brown orchestrates one of the

most protracted, certainly the subtlest, of seductions in all of gothic and sentimental literature to his time, climaxing it with Ormond's necrophiliac dismissal of Constantia's last-resort defiance: "Choose which thou wilt. . . . Living or dead, the prize that I have in view shall be mine."

No small part of Brown's ingenuity rests on his working within the known moral prohibitions, to which he himself at times editorially subscribed, and transcending them. Meanwhile, the sensual gets *its* due, for in the prior verbal fencing, as the resistance of Constantia's disbelief increases the boldness of Ormond's suggestiveness, Brown gives his reader proportionately more vicarious excitation than is derivable from an achieved rape. The action in *Ormond* is in this regard superior even to the most candidly described rape in the genre—i.e., that given by Matthew Lewis in *The Monk*. Brown's satisfaction of poetic justice is equally complete, fulfilling at the same time the superficial demands of public morality and the deeper concerns of human feeling. The ultra-rational Ormond, advanced thinker that he is and scorner of "sexual sensations" as "a disease" which causes "more entire subversion and confusion of mind than any other," must finally be seen as more the object of ravishment than the victim to whom he threatens it. The situation has its own inner dynamic. Ormond, for example, tells Constantia he pities her, and, from his position of intellectual mastery, he scorns the flimsy claims of honor as below the dignity of enlightened minds; and yet his very mastery is in itself pathetic, for Constantia—unlike almost all other victimized heroines—does find herself drawn to the man, and would consider marriage were he less prone to the sort of callously rationalistic argument he puts forth to overcome her fear of his passion.

An important distinction here is that whereas other authors may have depicted passion in such a way as to stimulate the senses under the guise of exposing it to self-condemnation, Brown allows Ormond to throw an appealingly sensible light on the assumption of a new, "liberated" relationship between the sexes (stemming from nature and approved by reason, it carries neither guilt nor stigma), so that what others might do for the emotions alone Brown would do for the mind as well. Constantia's refusal to come to terms with Ormond's argument and the very fact of her physical, rather than intellectual, conquest of him seem to underscore the vulnerability of conventional morals. The winds of republicanism were blowing rather strongly in the 1790's, and it was thoroughly in character for Ormond, the "disciple," as a contemporary reviewer saw him, "of a new system of belief and conduct, subversive of all established principles" to advocate a wholly rational sex morality. However, while the new attitudes toward sex and marriage were being experimentally entertained—as in Brown's *Alcuin* and a novel like Isaac D'Israeli's *Vaurien* (published a year earlier, in 1797)—such ideas were not normally floated on a take-it-or-leave-it basis when they were made so attractive. (pp. 570-73)

If he seemed uncertain of how to manage sex in his first novel— Clara's dream vision of Wieland beckoning beyond the pit conveys only the vaguest hint of an incest phobia and Carwin's supposed sublimation of an intent to rape her is actually a subterfuge—we find Brown achieving a full realization of its possibilities in *Ormond*. The main thing he did to raise seduction above the run of the mill—and indeed melodramatic— treatment given it in popular fiction was to raise the character endowment of his participants. Quite simply, he gave them some depth as persons. Brown's seducer is the epitome of cultivation. Eminently self-possessed, and deeming himself "superior to the allurements of what is called love," he rated physical gratification at the "bottom" of "his scale of enjoyments." Yet, as with the typical classical figure who places himself above love, he is the first whom Cupid avenges himself on. Constantia also differs from the stereotyped pursued maiden in that she is keenly attracted to her seducer and refuses to see his motive even when he suggests it to her. Interestingly, it is her moral strength that commends Constantia to Ormond. As he observes her from his chimney sweep's disguise, the dignity, steadiness, and even cheerfulness with which she bore her "reverse of fortune," suggested "proofs of a moral constitution from which he supposed the female sex to be debarred." Given all this, it is doubly interesting to see Ormond, frustrated in love, having to stoop to seduction, and to see him bring his dominating intelligence to bear upon the preoccupation of his fallen state. Though he is unexpectedly mastered at the end, that does not detract from the masterful artistry of his attempted assault, for which he deploys as complete an assortment of weaponry as any Renaissance sonneteer might have used: reason, common sense, double entendre, shock, irony, wit, hyperbole, and metaphor. His plea is so thoroughly civilized that on grounds of ingenuity alone Ormond should have won. Perhaps that is one explanation for the mysterious "smile of disdain" which rested upon his face in death—a final gesture, as it were, of ironic superiority over his own physical defeat. Clearly, Ormond is a man who even as seducer retains our interest to the very end.—And much of the success of the final action depends on Brown's maintaining his viability.

Although there appear to have been some inconsistencies in Ormond's conduct, particularly in the self-accommodating relationship he has with Helena Cleves, one may sympathize with her without necessarily feeling that the girl has been badly used. Rather, if one takes note of Ormond's justification and candor (it is Helena's limitedness of mind, her lack of education which precluded his falling in love with her) the man appears to have been more lacking in tact than ethics in his treatment of her. Surprisingly enough, Constantia, whom Helena asks to be her advocate, not only approves of Ormond's handling of the situation, she actually finds herself capable of falling in love with him in spite of it, as Helena's unsuitability points up her own suitability to be his mate. We learn that Constantia's heart "was open at a thousand pores to the love of excellence," and that "the image of Ormond occupied the chief place in her fancy."

As their relationship grows, Constantia delights Ormond by "the facility with which she entered into his meaning." The upshot is: "Her discourse tended to rouse him from his lethargy, to furnish him with powerful excitements, and the time spent in her company seemed like a doubling of existence." He tells Helena he must be Constantia's "husband, or perish." But some difficulties follow. Constantia feels she could love him, but can not allow herself to. She must "guard the avenues to her heart" until he has rectified his erroneous opinions. Meanwhile, Ormond's objections to marriage return.

This, then, is the gist of Ormond's relationship with Constantia prior to the attempted rape. Brown not only created complex characters, he created a complex relationship between them. Ormond is visibly quite different from the single-minded gothic villains. To this point, he is no villain at all. Rather, with his brilliancy of mind, correct taste, and liberalism of outlook, he is a tribute to the Enlightenment, of which he is a model specimen. Moreover, he has fallen deeply in love, and, though he would rather not modify his convictions to win Constantia,

he would rather do that than lose her. Constantia, by the same token finds herself capable of loving him, but is restrained by moral convictions which she cannot modify. What ensues is to some extent a tragedy of the triumph of her will.

It is Constantia's decision to leave for England with Sophia that precipitates the seduction. In the first scene of the concluding sequence, she has just sat down to write Ormond, when he bursts in on her. The man is anguished—and desperate. Whatever concessions he may have been prepared to make have been obviated before he can make them. He looks at the moon and speaks of new impediments appearing (Sophia) after old ones (Dudley) have been removed. Grasping her hand, he asks whether she cannot read his thoughts: "Catch you not a view of the monsters that are starting into birth *here*?" The mounting irony reaches a crescendo when she reminds him that he never scruples to say what he thinks, and he declares there is one excruciating obstacle even to this: "Incredulity in him that hears."

If his looks and allusions will not disclose the monstrosity, and incredulity bars plain talk, then he must try metaphor.

> Tomorrow I mean to ascertain the height of the lunar mountains by travelling to the top of them. Then I will station myself in the track of the last comet, and wait till its circumvolution suffers me to leap upon it; then, by walking on its surface, I will ascertain whether it be hot enough to burn my soles.

Since Constantia will not pursue the ironic tenor of these deductions—that he *will* indeed be forced to attempt the incontemplably monstrous, and hence impossible, and hence lunatic—he must accept her word that in such a predicament "silence is best." "Why speak when the hearer will infer nothing from my speech . . .?" And yet his speech has already conveyed everything by conveying nothing.

Ormond next tries to intimidate her with his powers of clairvoyance, and he does get her to believe this form of the incredible, which it is safer for her to acknowledge. He claims to know what she was about to write him, even her inner motives, and the horror of his seeming to take her very thoughts from her before she can utter them suggests a rape of the mind. He then, in a major speech, proceeds to work in her emotions by launching a prognostication of an unthinkable evil that awaits her—in effect telling her he intends physical rape, without futilely denoting the act. She ought to be able to put two and two together, particularly from his counselling her on how wisely to bear her fate. But, even if she does not, the very ambiguity of the situation should make it ominous enough to render her helpless before the inevitable. Speaking as a rejected lover, his reference is as obvious as the irony of Constantia's apparent failure to grasp it. . . . Having made a considerable play on the implications of their differing value systems, Ormond ends by wishing her well; while Constantia, in her stubborn blindness, and what one begins to suspect is repression, wonders, "What reliance should she place upon prophetic incoherencies thus wild?"

In the lull between the warning and the event, Sophia recounts how the young Ormond had won his commission in the Cossack army. On killing a friend whom he had fought for a Tartar girl after a battle, he proceeded to rape and then stab her as an offering to the ghost of his dead friend. The next day he rushed alone upon a troop of Turkish foragers and brought away no less than "five heads, suspended, by their gory locks," from his horse's mane. These he cast upon his friend's grave to expiate his "offence." Savage as he was then, in his maturity he is the obverse of savage, even when dealing in savagery. One may not like Ormond, but one cannot quite hate him either. There is much one can forgive in a clever man; and among literary seducers there is no one who is even faintly his peer in cleverness.

Constantia's apprehensions notwithstanding, she is not averse to meeting Ormond again. On seeing him come to her of an autumn evening at her South Amboy retreat, she experiences ''some degree of palpitation,'' ''whether from fear or from joy, or from intermixed emotions, it would not be easy to ascertain.'' She is taken aback by the corpse outside her door, and even though she finds Ormond in the downstairs hall, and hears his solemn reminder that the evil he predicted is at hand (''To rescue you I have not come''), she quickly recovers her composure and starts lecturing him about the discrepancy between his ''deportment'' and ''professions . . . of plain dealing.'' The ironic drama of Ormond's presumption of controlling knowledge played against Constantia's unknowing is further intensified. So acutely does he feel his omniscience that Ormond is compelled to empathize with his victim, whereas she, in her iron-clad unawareness, naively concerns herself with propriety. ''Poor Constantia,'' he declares, ''look upon thyself as lost. . . . Summon up thy patience to endure the evil. . . . I would weap for thee, if my manly nature would permit.'' She, in response, cannot decide whether he most deserves ''censure or ridicule,'' and, uncertain of what else to do, concludes it would be ''indiscreet and absurd'' for them to remain alone any longer at the mansion. It is hard to tell which of the two is more amazing.

Ormond presses on, and when she finally demands to know the meaning of his ''prelude'' and the ''full extent of [her] danger,'' he sees it is time to explain his object in terms and with looks, that, this side of lunacy, she hopefully cannot mistake: ''Art thou not a woman? And have I not entreated for thy love and been rejected? . . . My avowals of love were sincere; my passion was vehement and undisguised. It gave dignity and value to a gift in thy power, as a woman, to bestow. . . . What thou refusedst to bestow it is in my power to extort. I came for that end. When this end is accomplished, I will restore thee to liberty.''

Constantia, seeing that all appeals are vain, and escape is impossible, thinks first she can find safety only in the blood of her assailant, but dismisses this idea, since failure means she loses that which is more precious than life. The only way she can assure the preservation of her honor is to turn the penknife upon herself. Heretofore, it had been Ormond who seemed to have all-vanquishing resourcefulness; now it was her turn to claim invincibility. As he advances toward her, she shows the knife and bids him, ''Beware! Know that my unalterable resolution is to die uninjured. . . . one step more, and I plunge this knife into my heart. . . . To save a greater good by the sacrifice of life is in my power. . . .''

Rational to the end, Ormond voices his contempt for her folly: ''so! thou preferrest thy imaginary honor to life! To escape this injury without a name or substance, without connection with the past or future, without contamination of thy purity or thralldom of thy will, thou wilt kill thyself. . . .'' He gives her an out; there is still time for her to come to her senses; still hope, if she will replace her ''cowardice'' with ''wisdom and courage.'' He tells her she may die if she wishes with ''the guilt of a suicide,'' or live with her ''claims to felicity and approbation undiminished.'' And then he brings down his clincher: ''Choose which thou wilt. Thy decision is of moment to thyself, but of none to me. Living or dead, the prize that I have in view shall be mine.'' Escape *is* impossible; but in saying this Ormond seals his own fate.

There has been criticism of Brown's cutting off the action at this point and bringing Sophia in to report its aftermath. However, in the light of all that has gone before, it is doubtful that the mere act of Constantia's stabbing Ormond could have capped this dramatic verbal interchange any better than Ormond's last pronouncement had. Those words are a scene closer. The action almost has to stop here, or it falls.

We also need some sort of pause before we can take in the final blow and the importance of how it came about. Repugnant as killing was to Constantia, even more repugnant, apparently, was the need to kill Ormond, for, when it came right down to it, she in spite of everything ''forbore,'' she said, till her strength was ''almost subdued'' and struck only when ''the lapse of another moment would have placed [her] beyond hope.'' At that, she says her stroke was ''desperate and at random'' and ''answered [her] purpose too well.'' What she recalls is his casting ''a look of terrible upbraiding'' at her.

To its fatal conclusion, this has been no ordinary case of seduction. Constantia goes out of her way to be sympathetic toward her seducer (''O much-erring and unhappy Ormond! That thou shouldst thus untimely perish!''); and it would seem that Brown himself wishes to leave us with as good an impression of him as the situation will allow. That clearly is a significant effect of Brown's not permitting us to see Ormond physically struggling with Constantia. He stands personally condemned for what he does, but in our last glimpse of him alive his proposition of a sanely liberated attitude toward sex makes a good deal of sense in itself, even if it can offer no justification for force. Brown's final irony is that it was Constantia who had won physical mastery, and Ormond, advancing the new doctrine of sex without guilt which exposed the weakness of her morality, who had won intellectual mastery. However far they might have gone in treating rape, no writer of Brown's day went so far as (*a*) to give a character whose mind we respect so plausibly enlightened an argument for freeing sex from moral disgrace, and then (*b*) to allow his argument to stand unrefuted. Though Constantia is its heroine, the book does carry Ormond's name; and, in a passage from ''The Man at Home'' often cited as illustrative of Ormond's character as a man whose ''great energy is employed in the promotion of vicious purposes,'' Brown has his narrator advise:

> In the selection of the subjects of useful history, the chief point is *not the virtue of a character*. The prime regard is to be paid to the *genius and force of mind that is displayed*.

This matter is but part of the total richness of Brockden Brown's treatment of the seduction motif. It has a kind of authority and literary complexity that have not customarily been conceded to Brown and that have never been conceded to ***Ormond***. (pp. 576-84)

Sydney J. Krause, '' 'Ormond': Seduction in a New Key,'' in American Literature, *Vol. XLIV, No. 4, January, 1973, pp. 570-84.*

PAUL WITHERINGTON (essay date 1974)

[*Witherington analyzes the characterization, narrative technique, structure, and themes of* Clara Howard *and* Jane Talbot, *sug-*

gesting that a study of these novels contributes to an understanding of Brown's works as a whole.]

Charles Brockden Brown's most mature novels, and the ones least well known, are *Clara Howard* and *Jane Talbot*. Brown is at last receiving from critics the credit he earned as an innovator in point of view (*Wieland*), a commentator on the American character (*Arthur Mervyn*), and a seer, long before Poe, into the catacombs of consciousness (*Edgar Huntly*). But it was the premature, experimental works that made Brown's reputation and left his last two works to gather dust. For *Clara Howard* and *Jane Talbot* seem such departures from the early experimentation, such capitulations to sentimental "woman's" literature and the epistolary novel, that their maturity—their very slickness, in fact—seems rather a sellout, the indication of, if not the reason for, Brown's early abandonment of creative writing. If they had been written first instead of last, they would be called minor triumphs.

It is my purpose here to argue for proper consideration of *Clara Howard* and *Jane Talbot* among Brown's novels. First, these novels add to our knowledge of the earlier novels by revealing the continuity of Brown's narrative forms, ideas, and tone. To separate any of the novels from the others is somewhat unnatural since all six were published within a three-year period and since at one explosive time in 1799 Brown was working on five of them at once. Second, *Clara Howard* and *Jane Talbot*, especially the latter, model Brown's view of the artist and of his own artistry. Finally, these novels deserve recognition on their own terms for the excellence of structure, point of view, and characterization by which Brown arrives at the paradoxically unhappy culmination of his search for narrative technique. (pp. 257-58)

Whereas the earlier novels seem to show the individual leaving or transcending society, *Clara Howard* and *Jane Talbot* show the victories of social normalcy over individuality and of order over eccentricity and indecisiveness. Brown's drive toward radical ideas cast in radically American forms seems to have stalled, and worse. In the opinion of some critics, Gothic singularity becomes sentimental gush, American scenes and characters are seduced by European forms, and revolutionary themes are turned inside out. About the time of his first novel, *Wieland*, Brown said, "Give me a tale of lofty crimes, rather than of honest folly." But this is prescription, not execution, and "folly" may be the more "honest" subject after all.

Despite Brown's claims in early works to "the exhibition of powerful motives, and a sort of audaciousness of character" [see excerpt dated 1798], all his novels show a similar pattern: the rebellious individual chastened and reunited with society. The difference between the early works and later works is only in degree. In *Wieland*, the arch-villain Carwin confesses like a mischievous child who has misused one of his toys and becomes, in the end, a farmer, while Clara and Pleyel, having suffered for their detachment from the center of society, marry and move to Europe. In *Ormond*, the villain is reduced from noble crimes of the intellect to a passionate attempt at Constantia's virtue, and Constantia, after dispatching him, moves to Europe. Arthur Mervyn chooses an older city woman over a younger country girl and gives up his quixotic adventures for settled married life and an eventual move to Europe. At the end of *Edgar Huntly*, the hero is thoroughly chastised for his desultory and destructive curiosity and returned to the bosom of his oldest friend who has just returned from living in Europe. I emphasize the European "direction" of these endings to show that Americanization of characters and settings was by no means

Brown's habitual concern and to suggest that implicit in the abrupt and often artistically false endings of the early novels may be a quest for another kind of plot and character that would be more compatible with Brown's conservative views of society and art. These "false" endings have been condemned or explained as Brown's concessions to an unsophisticated reading public, with the assumption that the momentary defects of the earlier novels then become expanded into the central concerns of the last two novels. But unleashed from critical assumptions and anthology assessments of Brown as the father of the American novel, one might also say that *Clara Howard* and *Jane Talbot* are the logical end of Brown's quest for form and that however tame they may seem in spirit, however un-American, they are technically superior in that their endings are implicit in their beginnings.

Nor does this bias toward social moderation occur only in the endings. The themes of the last two novels are the themes of the first four novels, phrased in somewhat different terms. All of the novels emphasize the theme of appearance and reality, for example, to dramatize Brown's major issue: what standards can we reasonably adopt to meet the challenges of a world with shifting forms and faithless humanity? In *Wieland*, overemphasis on both reason and religious revelation is tested by Carwin's ventriloquism and mimicry, and a middle ground is established. In the second novel, Ormond, a master of disguise, tests Constantia, who survives only because her narrow base of reason is broadened allegorically by her friends: Sophia provides worldly wisdom; Martinette, courage; and Helena, sensibility. Arthur Mervyn's theory about the sufficiency of a good will is thwarted again and again to show the disastrous results of action without deliberation. Edgar Huntly tramps the deceptive caves and forests of Norwalk to learn that reality is not solid and that the senses, as in *Wieland*, must be bolstered with innate ideas.

In *Clara Howard*, this theme is put almost entirely in social terms. The pitfalls are the ugly pores of gossip, but the message is the same. Love, like any other concern, must submit to reason, to decorum, and often to plain good manners. Moreover, the idea in this novel that an excess of virtue may itself be an evil is a recurring, though spottily developed, motif in the earlier novels. Arthur's bumbling benevolence is the best example, but Edgar Huntly also plays the well-intentioned fool who endangers an entire frontier community with his "phantom in the mask of virtue and duty," and Wieland's voice from God leads to acts of Satanic violence. That this motif is often camouflaged by lofty psychological and archetypal constructions or buried in what appear to be digressions does not affect its importance. Whatever his editorial statements, Brown is consistent throughout his novels in condemning all excesses, whether of vice or enthusiastic virtue.

The theme of moderation takes its final form in *Jane Talbot* with Colden's attempt to find a stabilizing influence, a balance of faith and reason. Like Clara Wieland and Constantia before him, he is criticized for his lack of religious training. He explains his "propensity to reason" in one letter as an excess of deliberation: "Not satisfied with looking at that side of the post that chances to be near me, I move round and round it." But he adds, "The only post, indeed, which I closely examine, is myself, because my station is most convenient for inspecting *that*." His self-conscious point of view renders his knowledge of the world defective and religious faith impossible. It is the trap of self that identifies Brown's earlier villains like Carwin, Ormond, and Welbeck, those unable to "unbosom" themselves to others and share their sensibility. In *Jane Talbot*, the "villain" is simply made more human.

Warner Berthoff has argued convincingly that all Brown's fiction is a dialectic of ideas, "a *formal* alternative to the unreliable simplifications of schematic thought" [see Additional Bibliography]. If Brown's technique is indeed a means of "*discovering* ideas, for exploring and testing them out," we might conclude that the eventual marriages of Clara and Philip, of Jane and Colden, are as effective a means of dramatizing the interaction of ideas as the relationships between static heroes and villains in the early novels. More effective, to the extent that a greater complexity of ideas is made possible in a more human and believable form.

Whether Brown's concerns are metaphysical or social, then, his initial and prevailing tone is moral, as indicated in the prefaces and numerous authorial intrusions. As Lulu Rumsey Wiley puts it, "The author always had a purpose, if not always a plan" [see Additional Bibliography]. Despite his attempts to Americanize Gothic forms, his narratives are continually introducing and then dismantling Gothic paraphernalia, the castle keep or the secret that must be pried from its villainous source. Against these closed circuits of the self, he sets the open flow of benevolence, the sentimental exchange, the conversation that relieves hearts sore for confession. The standard for such exchanges is that of Constantia and Sophia when reunited after a long separation: "Every incident and passion in the course of four years was revived and exhibited." Or that of the reunion of Edgar with Sarsefield: "I wept upon his bosom: I sobbed with emotion which, had it not found passage at my eyes, would have burst my heart-strings." Brown's early unconscious and later conscious reaction against European Gothic forms may not have been so much his desire to replace "Gothic castles and chimeras" with "the perils of the Western wilderness," his statement prefacing *Edgar Huntly,* as his desire to replace the aristocratic class consciousness of European fiction, which Philip describes as pernicious and infectious, with true democratic dignity. Certainly he could not agree with the revolutionary implications of Gothic form, what Devendra P. Varma [in *The Gothic Flame*] calls that "barometer of reaction against the preceding age of literature." For Brown, even in the early novels, the sentimental formula of equal, reciprocal benevolence is the norm, and Gothic is the variation. (pp. 258-62)

While admitting the inconsistencies of Brown's first novels, critics have seen the last two novels only as his refuge from metaphysical pain. But the Romanticism of Brown's early novels may be compared with an experiment that is designed to fail. Consistently and purposefully, eighteenth-century restraint wins over a nineteenth-century impulse toward soaring emotion and strangeness. In this way, the early novels develop toward *Clara Howard* and *Jane Talbot,* theme finally coming to rest in its most appropriate form. Unfortunately, the last two novels have not been reprinted in editions other than Brown's collected works; yet, in a sense, that is how they should be read, as vital conclusions to the conflicts of Brown's life and art.

Clara Howard and *Jane Talbot* indicate more clearly than the other novels, but no more positively, the dilemmas of Brown's artistic career. Two related matters, the moral issue of benevolence in art and the practical issue of the artist and his relation to his benefactor, have not been adequately examined by critics.

Brown's belief in eighteenth-century values of benevolence had a profound effect on his art, as I have shown in an earlier essay [see Additional Bibliography entry dated 1972]. Because art always works by indirection, by suspense rather than by immediate disclosure, thus by the very opposites of benevolence, Brown came to mistrust its premises as he came to understand its ways. In all the novels he shows the folly of a vaulting, voracious ego like that of Arthur Mervyn and Edgar Huntly, and when this ego incorporates also manipulation by deceit or disguise, there are definite overtones of the artist. Carwin tells stories "constructed with so much skill, and rehearsed with so much energy, that all the effects of a dramatic exhibition [are] frequently produced by them." But the underside of this art, his ventriloquism and mimicry, turns him into a "double-tongued deceiver." Ormond, we are told, "blended in his own person the functions of poet and actor, and his dramas were not fictitious but real."

It is likely that Brown associated these criminal egos with the ego of the artist himself and with his own ego. William Dunlap, Brown's biographer, quotes from a contemporary writer's comment on Brown's technique: "He seemed to consider the curiosity of his readers as an engine in his hands, which he might play upon for his amusement merely, and relinquish when he was tired of such sport." The reference to "engine" recalls the words used by Carwin to confess his crime: "I made this powerful engine [his voice] subservient to the supply of my wants and the gratification of my vanity." We know that Brown was extremely sensitive to criticism of his works and that, when his brother wrote to complain about the "excesses" of *Edgar Huntly*, Brown promised thereafter to substitute "moral causes and daily incidents in place of the prodigious or the singular."

This resolution, which led to *Clara Howard* and *Jane Talbot,* must have been born much earlier than *Edgar Huntly.* Brown consistently comments that conversation and social interaction are superior to writing. Long before the composition of the novels, his tone in this regard was set; in a piece written for the *Columbian Magazine,* he defines himself as a "rhapsodist" who "delivers the sentiments suggested by the moment in artless and unpremeditated language. . . . In short he will write as he speaks, and converse with his reader not as an author, but as a man." His characters echo these feelings, from the Wielands to Philip, who writes to Clara Howard: "This is a mode of conversing I would willingly exchange for the more lively and congenial intercourse of eyes and lips; but 'tis better than total silence." At one time a pose, perhaps, this attitude hardened quickly into a position. The letter form demonstrates clearly that letters, like all narrative techniques, are temporary substitutes for benevolent social exchange. In Brown's terms, even the use of point of view can lack benevolence. The experiment with multiple-focus narration in *Wieland* is replaced by a looser point of view in *Ormond,* supposedly a single letter from Constantia to a friend; this focus collapses midway through when Sophia arrives, however, as if Brown is suggesting in spite of himself that wisdom destroys the artifices of art. Colden's many points of view of the pole in *Jane Talbot* are removed when Jane brings him to his senses, or rather, one might say, takes him away from his senses, away from the shifting perspectives of art.

The victory of benevolence over the constricted Gothic ego, whether that ego is criminal or merely lacking in social consciousness, almost always includes a surrender or collapse of some aspect of artistic form that has caused some sort of social paralysis. Brown's antipathy to poses and falsehoods, even in the name of art, made his abandonment of fiction for the anonymity of magazine editorship inevitable. Shortly after the publication of his last novel, Brown became the editor of *The Literary Magazine and American Register*. In his preface to the first issue, he argues for remaining nameless and says, presumably with reference to his novels, "I should enjoy a larger share of my own respect, at the present moment, if nothing had ever flowed from my pen, the production of which could be traced to me." But Brown's turn to editorship brings up a more important issue in Brown's art and life, that of the relationship of the artist to his benefactor. The haven of anonymity may be closely related to a haven of financial security.

All of Brown's novels after *Wieland* deal with problems of money either in the major plot or in subplots. And most of Brown's major characters after *Wieland* are either real or symbolic orphans searching for a home and permanent security. In *Clara Howard* the issue becomes crucial. Clara's father, who had a benefactor in England, becomes the benefactor of Philip in America. Later, Mary Wilmot wants to endow Philip. And after the marriage with Clara, we are told, Clara will continue her father's support of Philip just as she will give Philip, she says, the "treasures" of her heart.

Brown's characters engage in quests for a home, for their lost parentage, for the treasures of love and security. But the price for the individual is high. In the early novels, benefactors tend to be males, ambiguous and morally deficient, like Ormond and Welbeck. In later novels the benefactors are more often females close to the heart of society, morally impeccable, but emotional stranglers. Arthur submits finally to the dark ugly mamma of middle-class conformity, as Fiedler notes; Philip submits to the greater "moral discernment" of Clara; Colden accepts Jane's fortune after his conversion to "simple and true piety." Since only Colden is named directly as a poet, he must serve as the primary example of Brown's view of the artist. Yet his experience has been rehearsed in all the previous novels, and by the time he is named, significantly in Brown's last novel, his fate is a matter of habit.

Colden is first described contemptuously by Mrs. Fielder, Jane's adopted mother, as "a poet, not in theory only, but in practice." But Colden is a very silly artist. He early advocates suicide and talks of art in suicidal terms: "Writing always plants a thorn in my breast." He cannot live, he says, except by the charity of others. A brief example of his poetic reverie included in a letter to Jane is sappy enough to suggest satire, and indeed at the end of it he overturns his ink. Given such foolishness, we almost sympathize with Mrs. Fielder, who is set against his marrying Jane because he is a follower of William Godwin and the "art of the grand deceiver; the fatal art of carrying the worst poison under the name and appearance of wholesome food." Finally, his habitual detachment and artistic schizophrenia—"let me sever myself *from* myself, and judge impartially"—is healed by Jane, who functions in these sections as a helpful anima, "this feminine excellence; this secondary and more valuable self." Thus, he says, "Let me unfold myself *to* myself" as he begins the voyage that brings final unity.

But Colden's anima is not the spirit of creation, Robert Graves's "White Goddess." Jane is the spirit of the social ego, of conservatism and almost virginal normalcy. Her fortune is a "sacred deposit,—an asylum in distress which nothing but the most egregious folly would rob or dissipate." Like the "temple" of her heart, it is open to Colden, but only if he comes on acceptable terms. The stuff of his voyage, he says, "will afford an inexhaustible theme for future conversations," but not, presumably, for his poems or Brown's novels.

From the earliest reviews of his works to the present, Brown has been accused of writing episodic and unplanned stories. Yet Brown was intensely interested in architecture and in drawing and designing, and it would be strange if he had not also been concerned with the architectonics of his novels. In an early literary history, Barrett Wendell suggests that there is a struggle for form in Brown's works: "Paradoxical as it seems, then, these inextricable tangles of autobiography, which made Brockden Brown's construction appear so formless, probably arose from an impotent sense that form ought to be striven for" [see excerpt dated 1900]. With regard to the last two novels, one can go even further, for the form of *Clara Howard* and *Jane Talbot* is remarkably tight, the subplots well integrated, and the point of view consistent. In all the novels, but notably the last ones, Brown wrote far better than he knew.

Letter form offered Brown the compromise of a dependable structure that was at the same time, he felt, more natural, more conversational. Yet the letters of the last novels surely alienate most readers today as they must have alienated some readers in the early 1800's, for Brown came to the epistolary novel when it was being abandoned by other writers. We can hardly imagine Jane writing letters ten hours at a stretch and Colden rereading one of her letters twelve times in two days. Even early critics thought it a flaw that Brown's lovers send their letters about so freely. Richard Henry Dana, Sr., comments sarcastically that "the loveletters go the rounds of the family as regularly as the daily paper." But all Brown's novels except *Arthur Mervyn* employ the letter form, and although it virtually dissolves during the events of the early novels, it has a way of reappearing suddenly and embarrassingly, like a poor relative, to claim its due. In the last novels, at least, that form is functional.

Brown evidently was experimenting in all his fiction with point of view. The stories within stories in *Wieland,* for example, give several versions of the central murder, as William M. Manly has shown [see excerpt dated 1963]. But the briefer letters of the last two novels have immediate possibilities for showing contrasting points of view. The difference between *Wieland* and *Jane Talbot* in this respect resembles the difference in effect between Faulkner's *The Sound and the Fury* and *As I Lay Dying,* the one gaining depth and sustained tone, the other gaining immediacy and flexibility. Longer letters in the last two novels permit ironies such as emerge from the "frame" technique of *Arthur Mervyn* or *Ormond,* what Ernest Marchand has called "nested narratives" [see Additional Bibliography]. At one point in *Clara Howard* there is a letter within a letter within a packet of letters. And in *Jane Talbot,* Brown attains significant differences in style. Colden's reserved, heavily qualified letters are quite different from Jane's direct, passionate ones, and there is considerably more difference in vocabulary than exists in *Wieland,* in which all the characters tend to speak in the same manner.

The plot of *Clara Howard* owes its existence to an unopened letter from Mary to Philip which is misplaced, thereby initiating both the confusion over Mary's disappearance and Philip's quest to find her. On this level, confusion over the mails is highly artificial. But sometimes there is genuine suspense. An "overlap" of letters in *Clara Howard* functions as a flashback. Philip's 15 May letter to Clara, full of despair, comes before Mary's 13 May letter to Clara which reveals the cause of that despair—Philip's hopeless attempts to get Mary to change her mind. Irony and balance are created by simultaneous letters. On 11 May, Philip in a happy mood writes Clara to say he will soon be home, but on the same day Clara in a fit of depression writes Philip saying she is giving him up to Mary. The girls' mutual solution to the affair is dramatized later in Philip's simultaneous reception of their letters urging him to return, one rejecting him as the other—because of that rejection—accepts him. A delicate situation handled delicately, assuming that the reader faithfully attends to each letter's date.

Setting also is used in a thematic way. In *Clara Howard*, Clara is the constant, and all her letters come from New York. Philip travels to Philadelphia and returns to Clara and New York, the moral center of his quest. In *Jane Talbot*, fittingly, geography is more complex. Jane's center is Philadelphia at first, and Colden's is Wilmington and Baltimore, his greater mobility symbolizing his moral transience. But they meet, finally, on neutral ground, New York, suggesting that Jane too has had to bend her original ideas.

The technique of letter juxtaposition is better in *Clara Howard* than in *Jane Talbot*, but the last novel presents the letters as a whole more realistically. The letters making up *Clara Howard* are being sent, an introduction written by Philip tells us, "to—— ——" in order to explain the hardships he has undergone on the way to his present happiness. That Philip should have in his possession all the letters involved is not completely unnatural, for it was the habit in Brown's time to keep records of letters sent as well as those received and also to pass letters about, but it is an unnecessary barrier between author and reader. In *Jane Talbot*, confusion is modified by omission of prefatory material, Brown's only novel to do so. No effort is made to explain who got what packet of letters when, or why, and there is no effort to justify the novel itself as morally useful. One simply accepts the separate letters, as he accepts the omniscient point of view in other novels. The greater freedom here creates a more complex atmosphere with less obviously mechanical sleight of hand. *Jane Talbot* threatens to break out of the letter form and back to the more flexible points of view of earlier novels. Brown's method of rendering personal history, in fact, is finer in this novel than in any of the earlier ones. In her first letter, for example, Jane tells an event of her childhood in very impressionistic fashion, rendering the awareness and unawareness of the five year old who does not yet understand death in a moment that shows character as well as the psychological basis for future behavior.

Characterizations in *Clara Howard* are somewhat stereotyped. Philip, like Arthur in Part II of *Arthur Mervyn*, plays the part of a sentimental clown, but unlike the earlier character, Philip is more pathetic than comic. Proposing a voyage away from the two women, he says, "I shall make myself akin to savages and tigers, and forget that I once was a man." As often in this novel, effects are larger than causes, and Philip does not come off clearly as either a straight or satiric character, whether he is "Philip Sobersides," as he is called by old friends, or the "clown" he imagines himself to be, a judgment reinforced by Mary. Colden, in a similar situation in *Jane Talbot*, is more richly drawn. Though a poet, he is often as cold and wittily distant in his behavior as an overly refined Jamesian lover. Jane complains of his "exaggerations of humility" and of his detachment and lack of passion. He defends himself on the grounds of rational deliberation. When he plans his voyage away from Jane and her stubborn mother, it is with cool intentions, and, unlike Philip, he actually goes, with near fatal results. Philip's "depth of humiliation and horror" is told, not shown, but Colden's adventure, the one thing he must have feared most, jolts him into a very real climate for conversion.

The most remarkable characters in *Jane Talbot*, however, are Jane herself and Frank, her brother, who is perhaps Brown's most believable villain. Like Carwin and Ormond and Welbeck before him, Frank has exotic and probably illegal concerns. Like them, his evil is compounded by secrecy. But Frank's business, speculation and women, is true to life, and his posturing, his alternation of bombastic pride and seductive humility, seems real. His language has a refreshing directness usually reserved for Brown's lower-class characters. He calls Jane an "oddity," "a damned oaf!" and "an idiot—a child—an ape!" as well as a fool and simpleton. He is, as Jane says, "selfish and irascible," but she adds, qualifyingly, "beyond most other men." Brown does not try to make Frank any more singular than his name. Like Brown's earlier villains, Frank is "able to outwit the devil," but unlike the others, he is not outwitted in turn by Brown's audacious innocents. In the manner of sentimental literature, Brown's early stories converted or killed villains, but Frank simply goes away and lives in prosperity. He repays the money he "borrowed" from Jane, but otherwise he makes no concessions. After the early sections of the book, he disappears, and when the novel lags, Brown brings him back for a brief curtain call midway through, still in character.

Brown's women in the early novels tend to be highly rational heroines (Clara in *Wieland* and Constantia in *Ormond*), or cardboard props, or stereotyped innocents like Eliza in *Arthur Mervyn*, or unnamed whores. Much has been made of Brown's attempt to present in Clara Wieland and Constantia a "new," liberated woman, but the price of liberation would seem to be enslavement to all the traditionally masculine foibles of excessive reason. In modern terms, the women of the last two novels are liberated to be themselves. Mary Wilmot is a redoing of Achsa in *Arthur Mervyn* II, an older, full-blooded woman with worldly experience and a yet intact sense of values. Clara Howard comes close to the stiffness of her namesake in *Wieland* and escapes only by being a more shadowy character. Jane, though, is a triumph of Brown's art.

Jane is basically romantic, "the slave of every impulse; blown about by the predominant gale; a scene of eternal fluctuation." She acts spontaneously on numerous occasions, writing Colden to come take her away so they can be married, calling the union she proposes a "pleasing, dreadful thought." To Colden she is "the least suspicious or inquisitive of mortals" and "inattentive" to everyday details. But she is a thinking romantic, not a giddy emotionalist like Philip. Frank says she is accustomed to "*feed on thoughts.*" Like sentimental heroines before her, she is fond of self-analysis: "I have always found an unaccountable pleasure in dissecting, as it were, my heart; uncovering, one by one, its many folds, and laying it before you, as a country is shown in a map." She has strong religious convictions, hard won from her earlier days of easy belief, but she is quite capable of forging an envelope to Mrs. Fielder so her letter will be opened. Since she has been briefly married previously, both her forwardness and her innocence are believable. In short, she is sometimes splendidly unpredictable, "an April girl." When in response to rumors about Colden she says, "I believe and do *not* believe, what I have heard," she shows a complexity impossible to the characters in *Wieland*, for example, whose tragedy is a direct result of their failure to interpret Carwin's ventriloquism ambiguously, to separate what is seen from what is heard.

Jane changes realistically during the novel to parallel Colden's change. At first she has considerable pride and insecurity, but she moves toward greater humility and self-assurance. This progress appears in the architectural referents of her "heart," at first a secluded "temple," than a "mansion," and finally a "frail tenement" which cannot hold her joy. Like Colden, she is mellowed and strengthened by experience, prepared for the marriage which is a merging of selves, a truly human and archetypal union that is more mature than the strongly allegorical endings of earlier novels which stress the ringing out of evil by innocence.

Brown's fiction progressed to a form that adequately expresses his dominant ideas of benevolence and balance, but there is much evidence that Brown did not know he had found that vehicle and that he was unable to make necessary compromises either with form or with idea. What he did well in *Clara Howard* and *Jane Talbot* must have seemed disappointingly shallow by the standards of his early Romantic novels, and yet not shallow enough for his conservative moral views. As a final irony, the culmination of Brown's art was poorly timed with history. The climate favored looser fictional forms and an aesthetic that precluded direct moral preachment. As he grew into the fullness of society and marriage, his own and that of his fictional characters, the mainstream of American literature flowed out of society, and Brown was left in the awkward position of a father with no clear issue. (pp. 263-72)

> Paul Witherington, "Brockden Brown's Other Novels: 'Clara Howard' and 'Jane Talbot'," in Nineteenth-Century Fiction, Vol. 29, No. 3, December, 1974, pp. 257-72.

ALAN AXELROD   (essay date 1983)

[*Axelrod interprets* Edgar Huntly *in terms of the Oedipus myth and argues that all of Brown's major novels illustrate the Oedipal theme.*]

Between Part 1 of *Arthur Mervyn*, which appeared in 1799, and Part 2, 1800, Brown published *Edgar Huntly*. Into Brown's "respectable" novel of Philadelphia, motifs and images of the dangerous wilderness crept with the stealth of infection. In *Edgar Huntly*, however, Brown made these his explicit subjects, as if to thrust the wilderness into the gap between the first and second parts of what, on the surface, seems his most civil novel. The source of unconscious motifs and images in *Wieland*, *Ormond*, and *Arthur Mervyn*, the wilderness emerged in *Edgar Huntly* as a fully acknowledged subject and setting. Even more, in prefatory remarks to the novel, Brown announced it as a duty of the American novelist to depict "incidents of Indian hostility, and the perils of the Western wilderness," declaring that "for a native of America to overlook these would admit of no apology." He even seemed to acknowledge in these remarks the crucial link between the wilderness and the unconscious mind; for he proposed to "exhibit a series of adventures, growing out of the condition of our country, and connected with [somnambulism,] one of the most common and most wonderful diseases or affections of the human frame" [see excerpt dated 1799].

The prefatory remarks to *Edgar Huntly* comprise the most explicit statements the novelist ever made about his work. But even in this novel there is a final and telling evasiveness, perhaps a genuine failure of self-understanding. The ambiguities of *Edgar Huntly* begin with the title character's motives for leaving the safety and comfort of his peaceful manor house for the pain and peril of the wilderness. Waldegrave, Huntly's dear friend and the brother of his fiancée, has been mysteriously

murdered. Huntly conceives it his "duty to . . . God and to mankind" to detect the criminal and see that he is justly "punished." To this end he ventures into the countryside, to the elm beneath which Waldegrave's corpse had been found. Thus, ostensibly, his initial motive for probing the "groves and precipices," the "brooks . . . pits and hollows" of the Pennsylvania frontier is an eminently civilized one: he seeks to introduce justice into the wilderness. (p. 160)

["Duty"] in Brown's fiction often masks some private, self-indulgent, even perverse motive. This is not precisely the case with Huntly. For him, duty is not so much a false motive as it is a very short-lived one. At the fatal elm, in the moonlight, he beholds a human "apparition," which he instantly connects "with the fate of Waldegrave." Half naked, the "robust and strange" figure is busy digging—a grave?—by the elm. Before Huntly can decide what to do, the man drops his spade, sits down by the pit he has dug, and weeps with "heart-bursting grief." Huntly's stern sense of justice immediately yields to sympathy, even as tears—just like those of the wretched figure before him—"find their way spontaneously to" his eyes. "My caution had forsaken me," Huntly reports, "and, instead of one whom it was duty to persecute, I beheld, in this man, nothing but an object of compassion."

So Huntly advances toward him, who, in the meantime, stops weeping and again takes up his spade. He begins to "cover up the pit with the utmost diligence," as if aware of Huntly's presence and wishing to hide something from him. When Huntly calls out, the man merely looks up, gazes at him, but somehow seems not to see the caller, falling once more to oblivious tears. Huntly determines to seek an "interview," but the mysterious figure rises, seizes the spade, and, walking impassively in a profound slumber, brushes past Huntly, as the latter reports, without "appearing to notice my existence." From this point Edgar Huntly's fascination with Clithero Edny mounts to an obsession. He resolves to search the wilderness for Clithero, though he cannot explain why. "For what purpose shall I prosecute this search? What benefit am I to reap from this discovery?" At last Huntly concludes that his most urgent motive is mere curiosity, which, he realizes, "is vicious, if undisciplined by reason, and inconducive to benefit"; but then he glibly concludes that "curiosity, like virtue, is its own reward."

Here, as in the prefatory remarks, Brown seems to acknowledge a character motive only implicit in his earlier novels. Here is an admission of the ascendancy of an essentially irrational impulse over the reasonable motives of civilized duty. Yet, precisely in this admission, Brown causes Edgar Huntly to be most evasive. If his motive for pursuing Clithero is irrational, it is not without reason. Keeping pace with his obsessive attraction to Clithero is the grown conviction that he, Edgar Huntly, has the power to grant the mysterious man absolution for the sin of killing Waldegrave. After twice more pursuing Clithero through a mazelike wilderness landscape, Brown's obsessed hero at last confronts his quarry on the farm of Clithero's employer, Inglefield. Face to face with his pursuer there, Clithero blandly asks Huntly if he wishes to discuss "anything in particular." Three times so far Clithero has led him into the wilderness, and now, reversing roles with his prey, it is Edgar Huntly who insists that Clithero follow *him* down the path back to the portentous elm tree. There he tries to extract a confession, not by threats, but through increasingly sympathetic cajolery. "I can feel for you," Huntly insists. "I act not thus in compliance with a temper that delights in the misery of others.'' This sympathy rapidly intensifies into empathy, as Huntly pleads that ''the explanation I have solicited is no less necessary for your sake than for mine.''

Richard Slotkin, in *Regeneration through Violence,* suggests one reason why the actions of Clithero are so important to Huntly. ''You expect,'' Huntly tells Clithero, ''that, having detected the offender, I will hunt him to infamy and death. You are mistaken.'' But *hunt* Clithero is precisely what Huntly does, going so far, later in the story, as to set out a bait of food for him during a sixth foray into the wilderness. Slotkin, pointing out the ''kinship with the frontier hunters'' suggested by Huntly's very name, associates him with Indian hunters, who ritualistically identify themselves with their prey. Already ''strangely drawn to Clithero,'' Huntly embarks upon a ''hunt [that] carries his sense of kinship to its ultimate point: the hunter identifies himself with the beast he is hunting, becomes one with the thing he wishes to kill.'' In Clithero, then, Huntly recognizes a ''double,'' who ''represents that dark quality of Huntly's own nature which is moved by irresistible passions and impulses and which prefers nighttime and solitude to the genial day and healthy companionship.'' By getting Clithero to confess in order that he can absolve him, Edgar Huntly is really justifying a dark part of his own being and exonerating himself.

While Slotkin's observation accounts for the mythological resonance of Huntly's identification with Clithero, the novel in and of itself sufficiently delineates psychological motives. ''I am no stranger to your cares,'' Huntly attempts to convince Clithero, ''to the deep and incurable despair that haunts you, to which your waking thoughts are a prey and from which sleep cannot secure you.'' When he utters these words, Huntly is as yet unaware that, in diagnosing Clithero's guilt-ridden somnambulism, he is also describing his own. There are many more points at which the identities of hunter and hunted converge. Huntly first sees Clithero digging by moonlight under the elm; in the middle of the novel, we see an identical picture of Huntly, who busies himself beneath the moon digging for what Clithero had buried. It turns out to be a box, identical to one Huntly had discovered earlier in Clithero's room. That first one had been exquisitely crafted, like a puzzle, its seamless lid apparently impossible to open. ''Some spring . . . secretly existed, which might forever elude the senses,'' a piece of handiwork perfectly suited to the enigmatic Clithero. As soon as Huntly runs his hand over the surface of the box, however, it opens. ''A hundred hands might have sought in vain for this spring,'' but it seems as if it had been made expressly for his own hand to open. Disappointingly, there is nothing of interest to Huntly inside, so he decides to exhume whatever he had seen Clithero bury. The second box unearthed, Huntly does not bother with the niceties of secret springs. Impatiently smashing the box under his heel, he finds a manuscript inside written by one Euphemia Lorimer, who had been Clithero's adoptive mother in Ireland, and who (through a complicated but crucial chain of events we shall presently examine) had almost been murdered by Clithero.

Like Clithero, Edgar Huntly is a bit of a carpenter. In a cabinet of his ''own contrivance and workmanship . . . of singular structure,'' containing a secret drawer opened only ''by the motion of a spring, of whose existence none but the maker was conscious,'' Edgar Huntly has hidden his own precious manuscript, the letters of his friend and would-be brother-in-law Waldegrave. Opening the secret drawer one day to fetch the letters, he is shocked to discover them missing. Who could

have taken them—for who but himself knew of the drawer, let alone how to open it? The answer, Huntly finds to his dismay, is that no one but himself had taken the letters. He had opened the drawer in his sleep, sleepwalked into the attic of his uncle's house, and secreted the documents in the angle of the two roof beams. Clithero Edny is shocked in exactly the same manner when he opens his own box to discover that Euphemia Lorimer's papers are missing. Recall that Huntly had smashed the box containing Euphemia Lorimer's manuscript. The empty box Clithero opens is the one Huntly had found in Clithero's room, had opened as if by magic, and had himself found empty. It is empty because Clithero, sleepwalking, had removed the letters and buried them in the other box beneath the elm. Edgar Huntly is forced to acknowledge the somnambulism he shares with Clithero Edny, who ''had buried his treasure with his own hands, as mine had been secreted by myself; but both acts had been performed during sleep.'' As in *Arthur Mervyn,* where secret—antisocial—knowledge is associated with the dark seclusion of a closet, so in *Edgar Huntly* the revelation of an unconscious self is associated with the secret boxes of Clithero and Edgar. These in turn are symbolically parallel with the remote cave in the wilderness and the profound transformation that takes place in it. Huntly's first glimpse of Clithero was as an apparition, ''half naked,'' like a savage. After the initiation ordeal of the cave scene, an adventure into which Clithero Edny had, emotionally, led him, Edgar Huntly emerges from the cavern ''half naked,'' like a savage.

Huntly is anxious to purge Clithero of guilt and grief because he represents the nocturnal, solitary passions of his own nature. These are the very values Brown saw in himself when he explained his identity as a writer to John Bernard. And, as Clithero leads his double, Edgar Huntly, into the wilderness, so Huntly leads Brown, *his* double, after him. Brown follows Huntly not only into a fictional evocation of the Pennsylvania wilds but into that ''metaphysic wilderness'' defined in ''Devotion: An Epistle,'' a territory of dark and uncontrolled intellectual speculation that leads to ''nothing.'' . . . [''Nothing''] comes to be identified with a nihilistic vision of the absurd limits of perception and truth; it is to this vision, after a harrowing physical and emotional chase, that Huntly's human prey finally takes him.

Richard Slotkin argues that Huntly unconsciously identifies with Clithero as the murderer of Waldegrave. Calling Waldegrave ''saintly and paternal,'' Slotkin associates him with the authority of a father, so that Clithero comes to represent for Huntly the fulfillment of a wish to overcome parental control, to exchange civilized restraint for the freedom of savage life. Huntly's natural parents had been killed in an Indian raid when Edgar was a boy. Therefore, in merging his identity with the half-savage Clithero's, becoming something of an Indian himself, Edgar Huntly also identifies quite directly with the murderers of his *natural* parents. Worse, he comes to blame himself for what he thinks has been the Indian slaughter of his *adoptive* parents—an aunt and uncle—and his two sisters, during a raid that took place while Huntly, as a result of his sleepwalking, wandered lost in the forest. (Actually—and significantly—only the uncle, the father-figure, has been slain; Brown spares the aunt/mother and Huntly's sisters.) Huntly is nearly overcome with guilt at the realization that his single-minded pursuit of Clithero has kept him away from the family and home he should have defended. Although we shall see that the ''saintly and paternal'' view of Waldegrave is a serious oversimplification, Slotkin is right to open Brown's text to yet another oedipal reading; but he does not tell the whole complicated story.

Clithero Edny's real crime is not the murder of Waldegrave (slain, it turns out, by those ubiquitous Indians), but the attempted murder of Euphemia Lorimer. Clithero tells the sad tale in a long wilderness "interview" with Edgar. He was born and raised in Ireland (the wild country that gave us Carwin's mentor, Ludloe), the son of a poor tenant farmer. The landlord, living with his wife in Dublin, was a profligate who met a well-deserved end when he challenged a rival for his mistress's favors to a duel. Shortly after the death of her philandering husband, the landlady—Euphemia Lorimer—visited Edny's cottage and was so impressed with young Clithero that she took the boy back to Dublin with her. Ostensibly, he was a servant in the great household, but he soon became more a companion for the lady's son and, finally, was adopted by Mrs. Lorimer as her own boy. Like Huntly, then, Clithero lived with adoptive parents. Idolizing his foster mother as Arthur Mervyn had adored his natural mother and her surrogate in Achsa Fielding, Clithero could not imagine a happier situation than his.

Then he fell in love with Clarice, the illegitimate daughter of Mrs. Lorimer's wicked twin brother, Arthur Wiatte. Like Clithero, Clarice had been adopted by Euphemia, whom she resembles virtually as a twin—a double. As Arthur Mervyn found in Achsa a "mamma" who could gratify his oedipal desires, so Clithero discovered Clarice. Like Arthur, too, Clithero at first believed that his situation was too good to be true. Judging himself socially far below Clarice, he thought that marriage to her was an impossibility. Heartbroken at this realization, he was on the verge of leaving Mrs. Lorimer's household when, as if to put the finishing touch on this oedipal fantasy, the lady herself gave a prospective marriage between her adopted children an enthusiastic blessing.

But Clithero Edny was hardly destined for the bright fantasy future of an Arthur Mervyn. Clarice had to postpone the wedding to journey to the bedside of a dying friend. In the meantime, Arthur Wiatte, Euphemia's twin brother and perhaps the only one-dimensionally evil character Brockden Brown ever created, arrived in Dublin. His appearance there was the more incredible since everyone had supposed him killed some nine years earlier in a mutiny on board the prison ship transporting him to a place of banishment for his crimes. Despite the abuses he had heaped upon her, including coercion into the unhappy marriage with the faithless Lorimer, Euphemia was passionately, pathologically devoted to her evil double. Believing her fate inextricably bound with Wiatte's, she was convinced that her life must end with his. (Neither Clithero nor Brown explains, however, why Euphemia did not die nine years earlier when she supposed her brother had been killed in the mutiny.) Although she had made many sacrifices for Wiatte, attempting desperately to repair the ruin he habitually left in his wake, she did nothing to prevent his transportation, reasoning that, given his depravity, "banishment was the mildest destiny that would befall him." With Wiatte's unexpected return, Clithero and Euphemia's new suitor, Sarsefield (who bears no relation to the Sarsefield mentioned in *Ormond*) feared that he contemplated some horrible revenge upon the sister who, he felt, had conspired to banish him.

Clithero was turning the corner of a Dublin alley when he heard a "hoarse voice" shout, "Damn ye, villain, ye're a dead man!" A pistol shot grazed his cheek, stunning and staggering him, but failing even to knock him down. Seeing that his shot had missed, Clithero's assailant muttered, "This shall do your busi-

ness!" and drew a knife. Like Huntly confronted by the panther, Clithero responded spontaneously, drawing and firing a pistol he had hidden in his pocket. The dead man was Arthur Wiatte.

It mattered little to Clithero that he had acted in self-defense, and, for that matter, without knowing his assailant's identity. All he could think of was how he had signed his "mother's" death warrant by his deed, ending as well any hope of marrying Clarice. Unbalanced by the act that cut short his oedipal romance, Clithero determined to shorten Euphemia's suffering by hastening what he believed to be her inevitable end. In the darkened house, he entered the bedroom he thought was Euphemia's, gazed at a peacefully slumbering figure, raised a dagger, and was about to thrust it home—when his arm was caught by Euphemia Lorimer herself. Having mistaken Clarice's room for Euphemia's, he was about to kill his betrothed. Euphemia, overcome by shock, collapsed into a swoon Clithero mistook for death (a misapprehension under which he labors even as he tells his story to Huntly). He ran, and kept running, onto a ship, across the ocean, and into the woods of Pennsylvania.

Then, his story ended, Clithero runs away from Huntly, too, disappearing "amidst the thickets of the wood." Reasoning that a person capable of attempting to murder his benefactress is also capable of killing Waldegrave, Huntly redoubles his pursuit. But now that Clithero has revealed a specifically oedipal "crime," Huntly is also the more eager to convince him of his innocence. Clithero has led Huntly, and Huntly, Brown, through a wilderness to an oedipal revelation. But if Clithero's dark narrative is properly told in the American wilds, its action had originated in Europe. A more complete incest story than that in *Arthur Mervyn,* involving punishment as well as gratification, it is also a much more cryptic one. Whereas the "Oedipus complex"is blatant in *Arthur Mervyn,* it takes some work to uncover it in *Edgar Huntly,* to recognize that Clithero's betrothed is his adoptive mother's double, and to untangle the role Wiatte plays both in completing the fulfillment of the fantasy and in punishing it. Strictly speaking, Wiatte is Euphemia's brother and Clarice's father, and by virtue of adoption, Clithero and Clarice are brother and sister. However, in the system of symbolic equivalents of Clithero's tale, Wiatte figures as Euphemia's husband (such is her fanatical devotion to him) and Clarice figures for Clithero as the equivalent of Euphemia. Euphemia's quasi-incestuous attachment to Wiatte makes him her "husband," and therefore Clithero's "father," and Clithero's adoptive sibling relationship to Clarice compounds his identification as Wiatte's "son." In killing Arthur Wiatte, then, Clithero consummates an oedipal fantasy with the death of the wicked and oppressive father.

But there is a crucial string attached to this: the very act that consummates the fantasy ends and punishes it. Euphemia had told Clithero that she cannot live without Wiatte, so he proposes to oblige his "mother" by murdering her, thereby adding matricide to patricide. Worse, Clithero had mistaken Clarice's sleeping body for Euphemia's, and is stopped just before he dispatches his sister-mother-bride. Not only, then, does the killing of Wiatte touch off a chain of events that terminates the oedipal fantasy, but, as punishment, Clithero must carry the guilty burden of matricide and sororicide heaped upon patricide. Brown had flirted with brother-sister incest in *Wieland,* and even suggested a combination of brother-sister-mother-son incest in *Arthur Mervyn.* But not even Oedipus the King suffered through the baroque family romance of Clithero Edny, who laments, Oedipus-like, that his "misery has been greater than has fallen to the lot of mortals."

As with the more straightforward oedipal fantasy of *Arthur Mervyn,* the yarn Brown has Clithero spin for Huntly likely betrays an unresolved conflict within the mind of the novelist himself. But speculations about Brown's role in his personal family romance bring us, for the purposes of literary criticism, to a dead end if we do not carry the analysis beyond the merely personal. Like Ormond's seduction and threatened rape of Constantia, and Mervyn's oedipal romances, the story of Clithero is an objectification of a secret knowledge proscribed by the laws and mores of conventional society. Brown thought the revelation so offensive that he could only hint at it in intimations of primal sin and depravity. As bodied forth in Clithero's oedipal patri-matri-sororicide, Brockden Brown banishes these intimations to a wild domain in Pennsylvania. Yet, though one half of the novelist's "double mental existence" casts out this knowledge, it is not forgotten, and the other half is sent across the frontier to hunt it down. We must not overlook in this formulation the crucial fact that Europe, not wilderness America, is the scene of Clithero's drama. This presents a problem of interpretation like the one we encountered in *Ormond,* where the impulses of irrationality are embodied in a European seducer. However, as Ormond approached from the west before he attempted to rape Constantia, so Clithero absconds to the Pennsylvania wilds after his crime. Here he suffers the consequence of European guilt, becoming half savage, thereby enacting the symbolic equivalent of the passions that had driven him from the household of Mrs. Lorimer. Clithero tells his story beneath the elm where he had buried Euphemia's manuscript: the wilderness is a place in which passions are both buried and exhumed, both hidden and revealed.

In *Wieland,* [Brown] reversed Joel Barlow's commonplace utopian image of America as a land of bright revelation. Edgar Huntly, too, sleepwalking out of his lightsome chamber and into a pit hidden within a wilderness cavern, wakes to a New World of utter darkness. At first he believes himself blind.

Writing about the massacre of Theodore Wieland's family, John Greenleaf Whittier judged that the "masters of the old Greek tragedy have scarcely exceeded the sublime horror of this scene from the American novelist" [see excerpt dated 1866]. Whittier may actually have identified in this remark one source of influence upon Brown, who once remarked that the "tragic spectacle has charms congenial to my soul, and I dwell with mingled sadness and delight on the scenes of Sophocles, Racine, and Rome." Had Whittier gone beyond the emotional impact of the ritual atrocity in *Wieland* to discuss the novel's leading intellectual motifs, his observation would have been even more acute. For, in the *Oedipus* of Sophocles, we find the epistemological theme that also obsessed Brown through his four major novels. Like Oedipus, Brown's heroes confront the limit of human capacity to discover and act upon truth. Edgar Huntly, like Oedipus, prides himself on his ability to unravel riddles. He pursues Clithero, confident not only that he is tracking the murderer of Waldegrave but also that he, Huntly, has the power to absolve Clithero of guilt. "You are unacquainted with the man before you," Clithero warns him. "You, like others, are blind to the most momentous consequences of your own actions." And so Huntly is blind. Pursuing Clithero, he really hunts himself. Pitying Clithero for the unconscious, fate-driven nature of his "crime," Huntly discovers that, like him, he is also a sleepwalker, unable to give full account of his actions. (pp. 160-67)

[Brown] shared with Sophocles an insight into the limits of knowledge and judgment. This is demonstrated most succinctly

in Huntly's final, humiliating gesture. Clithero, recovering from serious wounds received at the hands of Indians, retires to the solitude of a wilderness hut. Although Clithero's "fatal and gloomy thoughts seemed to have somewhat yielded to tranquility," Huntly is not content to let him "mope away his life in this unsocial and savage state." He reasons that Clithero is burdened by a mistaken belief that he had caused the death of Euphemia Lorimer. Huntly resolves, therefore, to tell him the truth: that Sarsefield, Edgar's friend and former teacher, recently married Euphemia and has brought her, very much alive, back with him to America. When Clithero refuses to believe that this can be so, Huntly gives him as proof the couple's street address in New York. "'Tis well!" Clithero shouts:

> Rash and infatuated youth, thou hast ratified, beyond appeal or forgiveness, thy own doom. Thou hast once more let loose my steps, and sent me on a fearful journey. Thou has furnished the means of detecting thy imposture. I will fly to the spot which thou describest. I will ascertain thy falsehood with my own eyes. If she be alive, then am I reserved for the performance of a new crime. My evil destiny will have it so. If she be dead, I shall make *thee* expiate.

As he had repeatedly eluded Edgar Huntly in the woods, so Clithero disappears through the door, bound for New York.

But Edgar thinks fast. He dispatches a brief message to Sarsefield, warning him that Clithero is on the loose, and follows this note with a longer letter explaining the matter in detail. Sarsefield, in return, writes to Huntly about the consequences of his having set Clithero on Euphemia's trail, and about the additional consequence of his note and letter. Edgar's first brief note Sarsefield had narrowly prevented Euphemia from reading. She was on the verge of opening it when he entered the

A portrait of Brown around 1809.

room and stopped her. "See how imminent a chance it was that saved my wife from a knowledge of its contents!" Sarsefield writes. For Euphemia was pregnant, and there could be no telling what terrible effect news about Clithero would have had on her in that delicate condition. This notwithstanding, Edgar's first note was at least timely. Sarsefield alerted the authorities, who apprehended Clithero Edny in New York. Sailing back to Pennsylvania for confinement in the lunatic asylum, Clithero jumped overboard—an escape attempt or suicide?—and drowned.

But it was Euphemia Lorimer-Sarsefield who received the second letter when her husband was out of the house. After nearly dying from the shock of the news about Clithero, Euphemia suffered a miscarriage. Not only is this event the novel's epistemological coup de grâce, reiterating once and for all the myopic range of human foresight, it also sets the seal on Huntly's identification with Clithero and his oedipal romance. Richard Slotkin rightly observes that it is Huntly who fulfills Clithero's destiny, striking "down the woman and the child in her womb by a rash, unthinking deed." Actually, Huntly is implicated in Clithero's oedipal romance even more deeply than Slotkin acknowledges. Sarsefield, husband of the novel's central mother-wife, serves Huntly as a surrogate father. Huntly identifies himself as Sarsefield's "pupil" and "child," while the mentor in turn confesses "parental affection" for Edgar. Moreover, apparently unaware of Edgar's attachment to Mary Waldegrave, Sarsefield hints at a prospective marriage between his "son" Edgar and his adopted daughter—Clarice. Sarsefield declares to Huntly that Euphemia "longs to embrace you as a son. To become truly her son will depend upon your own choice, and that of one [Clarice] who was the companion of our voyage [from Europe to America]." Searching out the incestuous murderer, Edgar Huntly, like Oedipus, reveals the guilt in himself.

When he formulated the theory of the Oedipus complex, Sigmund Freud recognized the epistemological "moral" implicit in the legend of the Theban king. Freud quotes the chorus that closes Sophocles' play: "Fix on Oedipus your eyes, / Who resolved the dark enigma, noblest champion and most wise," but who, Freud cautions, lives like the rest of us, in ignorance of our deepest desires. Edgar Huntly concludes, after he has discovered himself a sleepwalker: "Disastrous and humiliating is the state of man! By his own hands is constructed the mass of misery and error in which his steps are forever involved." It is the blinding revelation for which he has hunted through the wilderness, and having caught it, it is destined to hunt and haunt him, just as it had Clithero Edny.

Renaissance Europeans were capable of asking: "Has the discovery of America been useful or harmful to mankind?" . . . Like the early European explorers, Huntly enters the New World on what he believes to be a civilized mission. He ventures into the wilderness expecting to emerge unchanged, indeed expecting to change a half-naked and half-savage apparition he finds there. But like the Europeans of the Renaissance, both Edgar Huntly and Brockden Brown return from contact with the New World profoundly changed, transformed.

There is an intriguing excursus in the novel which makes the "saintly" Waldegrave resemble the devious Ormond. Among the letters of Waldegrave, which Huntly treasures in his secret box, are youthful pronouncements upon the nature of reality. Virtually identical with Ormond's dangerous creed, Waldegrave's early belief was in a godless and wholly material universe in which necessity replaces providence, and physical matter the soul. Waldegrave suffered a conversion by and by,

becoming a kind of wilderness missionary. Unlike the senior Wieland, however, he sets up as a rational teacher of poor blacks rather than as a fanatical preacher to the Indians. Despite this overwhelming testimony of mature piety, Huntly considers his friend's early doctrines harmful enough to withhold them from his fiancée, Mary, Waldegrave's sister. When she does request the letters, Huntly feels duty-bound to sort through and censor them before sending them on. But when he goes to get them in the secret drawer of his specially constructed box, he discovers that they are missing. Knowing that only he could have opened the drawer, Huntly is forced to recognize that he is a somnambulist when he finds the letters hidden in the attic.

None of this is essential to Brown's plot. Edgar Huntly could have discovered his sleepwalking affliction more dramatically as a direct result of his experience in the cave scene. Nor does the plot demand our knowing about Waldegrave's early beliefs. If the novel itself, then, does not call for the Waldegrave detour, something in Brown must have. We know from the novelist's identification with Ormond, and from his description of writing as an unconscious and unwilled act, that he was himself drawn to the atheistic, even nihilistic, ideas of the young Waldegrave. This warrants further speculation about Huntly's treatment of his friend's letters, and also about the fate for which Brockden Brown reserves Waldegrave. Edgar's somnambulistic removal of the "dangerous" letters invites two contrary interpretations. Either the unconscious act suggests Brown's own desire to rid himself of seductive Ormondesque ideas, or it hints at a desire to preserve them, to hide them from the world and even from the censorship of his own conscious self. As to the significance of Waldegrave's having met his death in the woods at the hands of "savages," if Brown associated Waldegrave's early radicalism with the anarchistic values of the wilderness, perhaps Waldegrave's murder is the execution of poetic justice, the wild consequence of wild ideas. Or perhaps the poetic justice is the revenge the wilderness exacts upon one who has abandoned its values; Waldegrave suffers for having turned from radicalism to the bright Christianity of conventional society.

The name "Waldegrave," as a combination of the German *Wald* ("woods") and the English word *grave*, serves to link Waldegrave's letters, which Huntly hides in the attic, with Euphemia Lorimer's journal, which Clithero buries in a woodland "grave." The name also underscores the ambiguity of both Huntly's and Clithero's acts of concealment, since we are uncertain whether committing the documents to a wilderness grave signifies a desire to destroy or to preserve them. We may risk conjuring with the curious name even further. A *waldgrave*—from the German *waldgraf*—was, in "mediaeval Germany, an officer having jurisdiction over a royal forest" (*OED*). So, in perpetrating the fictional murder of a character named Waldegrave (a man whose youthful ideas savored of the "wild"), Brown possibly destroys a guardian of the forest, a kind of wilderness genius loci. Or perhaps it is Waldegrave in his saintly aspect who is destroyed—not the writer of atheist doctrine, but the pious master of a school for indigent blacks. The first interpretation would suggest Brown's repudiation of the antisocial territory of the wilderness; the second suggests that he wished to overcome the "waldgrave" who guards the forest *against* him, who prevents his entry into that unconscious territory. Waldegrave, then, emerges as an emblem of Brown's enduring ambivalence. A "sinner" turned "saint," he is associated both with the anarchistic spirit of the forest and with the repressive force that prevents access to it.

Suggestive as the ambiguities of Waldegrave are, it is important to realize that he is but a ghost in *Edgar Huntly,* dead before the narrative begins. Richard Slotkin's insights notwithstanding, Waldegrave is not a surrogate father for Huntly. Brotherly, not fatherly, and a prospective brother-in-law at that, Waldegrave yields to Sarsefield as the principal father-figure. In the letter to Edgar Huntly that ends the novel, Sarsefield reproves his "son" for having so rashly sent Clithero Edny and the two fatal messages to him and his wife: "I assure you, Edgar, my philosophy has not found itself lightsome and active under this burden. I find it hard to forbear commenting on your rashness in no very mild terms. You acted in direct opposition to my counsel and to the plainest dictates of propriety." Considering that he refers to something which cost him an unborn child and very nearly its mother as well, this is a laughably mild reproof. In fact, it is downright fatherly: "Be more circumspect and more obsequious for the future," he cautions. For its tone of paternal counsel, the reproof is the more humiliating. In *Edgar Huntly* the oedipal drama is played out to the end, through gratification as well as punishment, with the father triumphant at the last. We are left only to imagine the burden of Clithero-like guilt Huntly will have to bear for the grief he has brought upon Euphemia and her new husband. Insofar as the oedipal adventure is associated with the seductive and dangerous freedom of the wilderness, the conclusion to *Edgar Huntly* signals Brown's retreat from the frontier his hero had crossed.

In the respectable guise of an urban American success story, Brown consummated, quite without attendant punishment and guilt, a simpler oedipal fantasy. The second part of *Arthur Mervyn,* in which the young hero meets and is about to marry his "new mamma," appeared a year after *Edgar Huntly.* The novelist has Arthur close his story this way:

> What more can be added?
>
> What more? Can Achsa ask what more? She who has not been *only* a wife—
>
> But why am I indulging this pen-prattle? The hour she fixed for my return to her is come, and now take thyself away, quill. Lie there, snug in thy leathern case, till I call for thee, and that will not be very soon. I believe I will abjure thy company till all is settled with my love. Yes: I *will* abjure thee, so let *this* be thy last office, till Mervyn has been made the happiest of men.

Unlike Arthur, Brockden Brown did not literally put away his pen when he finished the second part of *Mervyn:* he continued to ply it for another decade, until his death in 1810. But he did emerge from the completion of *Arthur Mervyn* a remarkably transformed writer.

What more could be added, what more—after the novelist had pursued himself across the frontier of consciousness, and into a wilderness of both dream and nightmare? Having glimpsed perhaps too much already, the respectable citizen of Philadelphia did not put out his eyes for shame, but shut them for the remainder of his life and career to the world of Wieland, Ormond, Edgar Huntly, and even Arthur Mervyn. (pp. 168-72)

> *Alan Axelrod, in his* Charles Brockden Brown: An American Tale, *University of Texas Press, 1983, 203 p.*

ADDITIONAL BIBLIOGRAPHY

Bell, Michael Davitt. " 'The Double-Tongued Deceiver': Sincerity and Duplicity in the Novels of Charles Brockden Brown." *Early American Literature* IX, No. 2 (Fall 1974): 143-63.

Focuses on the clash between innocence and experience in *Wieland, Ormond, Edgar Huntly,* and *Arthur Mervyn.*

————. "Sentiments and Words: Charles Brockden Brown." In his *The Development of American Romance: The Sacrifice of Relation,* pp. 40-61. Chicago: University of Chicago Press, 1980.

Examines the major themes of Brown's fiction within the context of his philosophical development from idealism to skepticism.

Bellis, Peter J. "Narrative Compulsion and Control in Charles Brockden Brown's *Edgar Huntly.*" *South Atlantic Review* 52, No. 1 (January 1987): 43-57.

Describes the tension created by the narrator's desire to both relive and forget traumatic history in *Edgar Huntly.*

Bernard, Kenneth. "Charles Brockden Brown." In *Minor American Novelists,* edited by Charles Alva Hoyt, pp. 1-9. Crosscurrents/Modern Critiques, edited by Harry T. Moore. Carbondale: Southern Illinois University Press, 1970.

Identifies utopian idealism and Puritan pessimism as tension-producing opposites in Brown's fiction.

Berthoff, W. B. " 'A Lesson on Concealment': Brockden Brown's Method in Fiction." *Philological Quarterly* XXXVIII, No. 1 (January 1958): 45-57.

Argues that Brown used narrative to discover, explore, and test ideas. Berthoff illustrates this contention by an analysis of Brown's short story "A Lesson on Concealment; or, Memoir of Mary Selwyn."

Bredahl, A. Carl, Jr. "Transformation in *Wieland.*" *Early American Literature* XII, No. 2 (Fall 1977): 177-92.

Interprets *Wieland* as an exploration of the transformational powers of the literary imagination and asserts that this is a particularly American theme.

Butler, David L. *Dissecting a Human Heart: A Study of Style in the Novels of Charles Brockden Brown.* Washington, D.C.: University Press of America, 1978, 130 p.

An examination of Brown's style that treats such subjects as the rhetorical tradition, the literary climate of America in Brown's age, Brown's literary opinions and theory, and his intellectual interests.

Chase, Richard. "Brockden Brown's Melodramas." In his *The American Novel and Its Tradition,* pp. 29-41. Garden City, N.Y.: Doubleday & Co., Anchor Books, 1957.

Analyzes Brown's use of melodrama in his novels and notes the influence of his innovations on later American novelists.

Clark, David Lee. *Charles Brockden Brown: Pioneer Voice of America.* Durham, N.C.: Duke University Press, 1952, 363 p.

An important biography that emphasizes Brown's radical political and social thought and investigates various aspects of his work. The study is enhanced by the use of materials from unpublished Brown manuscripts made available to the critic by Brown's family.

Cleman, John. "Ambiguous Evil: A study of Villains and Heroes in Charles Brockden Brown's Major Novels." *Early American Literature* X, No. 2 (Fall 1975): 190-219.

A comparative study of Brown's major characters.

Coad, Oral Sumner. "The Gothic Element in American Literature before 1835." *Journal of English and Germanic Philology* XXIV (1925): 72-93.

Asserts Brown's importance as America's first Gothic novelist in a discussion of the Gothic strain in American literature.

Cowie, Alexander. "Vaulting Ambition: Brockden Brown and Others." In his *The Rise of the American Novel,* pp. 69-114. New York: American Book Co., 1948.

Includes a biographical introduction, a survey of Brown's novels, and considerations of his social views, literary theory, and critical reputation.

Dunlap, William. *Memoirs of Charles Brockden Brown, the American Novelist.* London: Henry Colburn and Co., 1822, 337 p.

An abridged version of Dunlap's biography of 1815. Begun by Paul Allen and continued by Dunlap at the request of Brown's family, the biography contains fragments of Brown's work unavailable elsewhere and remains the most important source of information about Brown's life, although scholars agree that it is difficult to read and marred by Dunlap's biases.

Fleischmann, Fritz. "Charles Brockden Brown: Feminism in Fiction." In *American Novelists Revisited: Essays in Feminist Criticism,* edited by Fritz Fleischmann, pp. 6-41. A Publication in Women's Studies, edited by Barbara Haber. Boston: G. K. Hall & Co., 1982.
Traces Brown's attitude toward women's rights throughout his fiction.

Franklin, Wayne. "Tragedy and Comedy in Brown's *Wieland.*" *Novel* 8, No. 2 (Winter 1975): 147-63.
Notes parallels between *Wieland* and Shakespeare's comedies and tragedies in character, plot, theme, and intent.

Grabo, Norman S. *The Coincidental Art of Charles Brockden Brown.* Chapel Hill: University of North Carolina Press, 1981, 209 p.
Maintains that coincidental occurrences in Brown's fiction are part of a conscious, discernible, artistic pattern and analyzes each of the novels to support this thesis.

Hedges, William. "Charles Brockden Brown and the Culture of Contradictions." *Early American Literature* IX, No. 2 (Fall 1974): 107-42.
Treats Brown's fiction in terms of its relationship to such ideological opposites as progress and tradition present in the American culture of his age.

Hirsch, David H. "Charles Brockden Brown as a Novelist of Ideas." *Books at Brown* XX (1965): 165-84.
Proposes that the shortcomings associated with Brown's fiction are the result of the failure of his Gothic and sentimental rhetoric to accommodate the French and Godwinian philosophical ideas he wished to disseminate.

Hume, Robert D. "Charles Brockden Brown and the Uses of Gothicism: A Reassessment." *ESQ* 18, No. 1 (1972): 10-18.
Considers Brown's use of Gothic elements in his novels and compares his works with those of other writers in the Gothic tradition.

Jordan, Cynthia S. "On Rereading *Wieland:* 'The Folly of Precipitate Conclusions'." *Early American Literature* XVI, No. 2 (Fall 1981): 154-74.
Argues that the ending of *Wieland* expresses the dangers of believing that permanent stability and structure can be achieved in life.

Kimball, Arthur. *Rational Fictions: A Study of Charles Brockden Brown.* Linfield Studies. McMinnville, Oreg.: Linfield Research Institute, 1968, 238 p.
Examines Brown's novels within the context of late eighteenth-century ideas and events.

Krause, Sydney J. "*Ormond:* How Rapidly and How Well 'Composed, Arranged and Delivered'." *Early American Literature* XIII, No. 3 (Winter 1978-79): 238-49.
Explores Brown's writing habits as reflected in the strengths and weaknesses of *Ormond.*

———. "*Edgar Huntly* and the American Nightmare." *Studies in the Novel* XIII, No. 3 (Fall 1981): 294-302.
Views *Edgar Huntly* as an early example of the theme of obsessive pursuit of an unobtainable American dream.

Levine, Paul. "The American Novel Begins." *American Scholar* 35, No. 1 (Winter 1965-66): 134-48.
Postulates that Brown's works anticipate rather than begin the tradition of the American novel.

Levine, Robert S. "*Arthur Mervyn's* Revolutions." *Studies in American Fiction* 12, No. 2 (Autumn 1984): 145-60.
Concludes that the many upheavals and twists of fate in *Arthur Mervyn* reflect the influence of the post-French Revolutionary era on Brown's art.

Lewis, R.W.B. "The Hero in Space: Brown, Cooper, Bird." In his *The American Adam: Innocence, Tragedy and Tradition in the Nineteenth Century,* pp. 90-109. Chicago: University of Chicago Press, 1955.
Identifies *Arthur Mervyn* as a prototypical American expression of the themes of evil and innocence.

Loshe, Lillie Deming. "The Gothic and the Revolutionary" and "Early Historical Novels and Indian Tales." In her *The Early American Novel,* pp. 29-58, 59-81. 1907. Reprint. New York: Columbia University Press, 1930.
Examines various aspects of Brown's novels, including their characters, realistic detail, similarities to Godwin's fiction, and portrayal of native Americans.

Lyttle, David. "The Case against Carwin." *Nineteenth-Century Fiction* 26, No. 3 (December 1971): 257-69.
Analyzes the character of Carwin in *Wieland* and *Carwin, the Biloquist.*

Marchand, Ernest. Introduction to *Ormond,* by Charles Brockden Brown, edited by Ernest Marchand, pp. ix-xliv. New York: American Book Co., 1937.
A general overview of ideas that influenced Brown's novels, with specific consideration of *Ormond.*

Nelson, Carl. "A Just Reading of Charles Brockden Brown's *Ormond.*" *Early American Literature* VIII, No. 2 (Fall 1973): 163-78.
Claims that the role of the narrator in *Ormond* is central to an interpretation of the novel.

———. "A Method for Madness: The Symbolic Patterns in *Arthur Mervyn.*" *West Virginia University Philological Papers* 22 (1975): 29-50.
A psychological interpretation of *Arthur Mervyn* that explores symbolic setting, thematic structure, and language.

Parker, Patricia L. *Charles Brockden Brown: A Reference Guide.* A Reference Publication in Literature, edited by Everett Emerson. Boston: G. K. Hall & Co., 1980, 132 p.
An annotated list of works about Brown.

Patrick, Marietta Stafford. "Romantic Iconography in *Wieland.*" *South Atlantic Review* 49, No. 4 (November 1984): 65-74.
Argues that Jungian archetypes of transformation provide structure in *Wieland.*

Petter, Henri. *The Early American Novel.* Columbus: Ohio State University Press, 1971, 500 p.
A descriptive and critical survey of the early American novel containing a discussion of Brown's heroines in *Clara Howard* and *Jane Talbot* and an examination of character development in each of the other major novels.

Quinn, Arthur Hobson. "Charles Brockden Brown and the Establishment of Romance." In his *American Fiction: An Historical and Critical Survey,* pp. 25-39. New York: D. Appleton Century Co., 1936.
Regards Brown's novels as romances that deal with selected extraordinary events of everyday life.

Ringe, Donald A. *Charles Brockden Brown.* Twayne's United States Authors Series, vol. 98. New York: Twayne Publishers, 1966, 158 p.
A detailed analysis and evaluation of Brown's novels.

———. "Charles Brockden Brown." In *Major Writers of Early American Literature,* edited by Everett Emerson, pp. 273-94. Madison: University of Wisconsin Press, 1972.
Discusses Brown in terms of his literary influences and provides a general analysis of his novels.

Rosenthal, Bernard, ed. *Critical Essays on Charles Brockden Brown.* Critical Essays on American Literature, edited by James Nagel. Boston: G. K. Hall & Co., 1981, 246 p.
A collection of criticism of Brown's works covering early reviews and modern essays.

Schulz, Dieter. *"Edgar Huntly* as Quest Romance." *American Literature* XLIII, No. 3 (November 1971): 323-35.

Finds that *Edgar Huntly* deviates from the traditional pattern of quest romance, foreshadowing the development of later American fiction.

Seltzer, Mark. "Saying Makes It So: Language and Event in Brown's *Wieland."* *Early American Literature* XIII, No. 1 (Spring 1978): 81-91.

Relates repetitive patterns of speech and action in *Wieland* to Brown's narrative structure and theme.

Vilas, Martin S. *Charles Brockden Brown: A Study of Early American Fiction.* Burlington, Vt.: Free Press Association, 1904, 66 p.

Examines Brown's life and works and evaluates his lasting influence on American literature.

Warfel, Harry R. Introduction to *The Rhapsodist, and Other Uncollected Writings,* by Charles Brockden Brown, edited by Harry R. Warfel, pp. v-xii. New York: Scholars' Facsimiles & Reprints, 1943.

Contends that an examination of Brown's early nonfiction aids in understanding the form of his later work.

———. *Charles Brockden Brown: American Gothic Novelist.* Gainesville: University of Florida Press, 1949, 255 p.

A biographical study that links Brown's works to the intellectual atmosphere of his time.

Wiley, Lulu Rumsey. *The Sources and Influence of the Novels of Charles Brockden Brown.* New York: Vantage Press, 1950, 381 p.

An inquiry into the literary and cultural background of Brown's novels and an examination of their influence on later writers.

Witherington, Paul. "Image and Idea in *Wieland* and *Edgar Huntly."* *The Serif* III, No. 4 (December 1966): 19-26.

Suggests a connection between Brown's search for imagery to convey moral and psychological ideas and his ultimate rejection of fictional forms.

———. "Benevolence and the 'Utmost Stretch': Charles Brockden Brown's Narrative Dilemma." *Criticism* XIV, No. 2 (Spring 1972): 175-91.

Discusses the tension between Brown's philosophy of benevolence and his perception of the power of the artistic imagination.

———. "Charles Brockden Brown: A Bibliographical Essay." *Early American Literature* IX, No. 2 (Fall 1974): 164-87.

Provides an annotated history of Brown criticism along with information on editions, manuscripts and letters, and biographies.

Thomas Carlyle

1795-1881

Scottish philosopher, social critic, essayist, historian, biographer, translator, and editor.

Known as the "sage of Chelsea," Carlyle was a satirical, dogmatic social critic of the Victorian era. He fiercely condemned the failings of his society in a revolutionary prose style noted for its striking imagery and bludgeoning force. Judging that Victorian civilization—increasingly preoccupied with mechanization, materialism, science, and moral and social utilitarianism—suffered from spiritual bankruptcy, Carlyle called for a social, moral, and spiritual renaissance in such controversial, idiosyncratic works as *Sartor Resartus, The French Revolution,* and *Past and Present.* Carlyle's writings prompted extreme reactions, both of enthusiastic admiration and violent condemnation, during his lifetime. While this partisan fervor has abated in the present century, Carlyle is remembered as a prophet of his age, and he remains a relevant voice in our own.

The son of a hardworking stonemason turned farmer, Carlyle was born in Ecclefechan, Scotland. He was educated at local schools before attending Edinburgh University, where he showed a talent for mathematics. Although his Calvinist parents wished him to become a minister, Carlyle found that he had no vocation. However, while he ultimately rejected the Calvinist faith, its emphasis on the moral value of duty and its concept of the elite deeply influenced his writing. After leaving the university, Carlyle taught at Annan and Kirkealdy for a few years, returning to Edinburgh in 1818. Here he satisfied his growing desire to write with occasional book reviews and other hackwork, but nonetheless became increasingly despondent, plagued as he was by chronic digestive problems, uncertainty over the choice of a profession, and tormenting religious doubts. Since his rejection of Calvinism he had come to the conclusion that existence was meaningless, fearing that such a world as he knew could only be the province of the devil. It was probably in the summer of 1822 that Carlyle experienced the spiritual conversion he later described in *Sartor Resartus.* In essence, Carlyle believed in the ineffable mystery of the world and the power of his own self-will: "[There] rushed . . . a stream of fire over my whole soul; and I shook base Fear away from me forever. I was strong, of unknown strength; a spirit, almost a god."

Another decisive influence on Carlyle during these years in Edinburgh was his discovery of German creative and philosophical writers, particularly Johann Wolfgang von Goethe, who always remained his literary hero. In the early 1820s Carlyle published a number of essays and works on German subjects, including a translation of Goethe's novel *Wilhelm Meisters Lehrjahre* and a biography of Friedrich Schiller. Carlyle married Jane Baillie Welsh in 1826 after a five-year courtship; the marital relationship between these two headstrong and creative people has occasioned much interest and controversy. For several months the couple lived mostly in remote Craigenputtock, where Carlyle began his writing career in earnest, contributing to the *Edinburgh Review* and the *Foreign Review.* With the appearance of his essays "Signs of the Times" and "Characteristics" in the *Edinburgh Review* in 1829 and 1831, Carlyle launched his career as a social critic, sounding many

of the themes he was to expand upon in his later work, particularly his vision of Victorian England as a society deadened by technological and spiritual mechanization.

Carlyle's first important work, *Sartor Resartus,* was published serially in *Fraser's Magazine* in 1833-34 and was received with consternation ad confusion by most reviewers. Soon afterwards, the Carlyles moved to the Chelsea district of London, where Carlyle firmly established himself as a major literary figure with the publication of *The French Revolution* in 1837. Thereafter he was lionized by some and derided by others, but remained throughout his life a critical influence on English society. He counted among English friends and acquaintances John Stuart Mill, Charles Dickens, John Forster, Alfred, Lord Tennyson, and Robert Browning; in America, his admirers included Ralph Waldo Emerson, who enthusiastically promoted Carlyle's work. A coterie of "disciples" formed around Carlyle during the following years as he produced his other major works, including *On Heroes, Hero-Worship, and the Heroic in History* (originally a series of lectures), *Past and Present, Oliver Cromwell's Letters and Speeches, Latter-Day Pamphlets,* and *History of Friedrich II. of Prussia, Called Frederick the Great.* Carlyle's detractors were as fervent as his disciples, however, and controversy followed the publication of each of his books. In 1866 Carlyle was devastated

60

by his wife's death. He prepared but did not publish two tributes to her: *Reminiscences,* a searingly honest account of Jane's life and his own, and a collection of her letters. Carlyle spent his remaining years in Chelsea in partial retirement, attended by his disciples, particularly his niece Mary Aitken and James Anthony Froude, a prominent man of letters and Carlyle's first biographer. Still highly esteemed by his contemporaries, Carlyle declined the government's offer of a knighthood. When he died at the age of eighty-five, he was buried, as he desired, at Ecclefechan rather than Westminster Abbey.

The Victorian era was a dynamic period in English history, when the rapid rise of industry altered social conditions, accelerating change and the need for change. Most of Carlyle's writings are a reaction to this volatile period of upheaval, as he sought to arrest and correct the problems he perceived. Above all, Carlyle believed that Victorian society had replaced the moral, social, and political values that had traditionally upheld the nation with the unworthy motives of economic profit, technological and scientific "progress," and liberal social reform. Democratization had resulted in political leaders who lacked the ability to lead or to inspire reverence in their followers; industrialization had given rise to the debasement of social economics from the old hierarchical relationship between landlord and tenant (with all its attendant reciprocal social ties) to a soulless business arrangement founded merely on the "cash nexus" between employer and worker. Further, religious institutions had lost their wonted force and effectiveness, contributing to a general weakening of faith and a consequent spiritual crisis. Victorian society, according to Carlyle, was plagued by "mechanization": mechanization not only in the rise of industry but in every aspect of human civilization. In response, Carlyle set out to be the catalyst of an essentially spiritual renewal of society based on the transcendent mystery and divinity that exists in every facet of the universe, especially in humanity.

Carlyle treated these themes in his many and varied works, the two most important of which are generally thought to be *Sartor Resartus* and *The French Revolution. Sartor Resartus*—part philosophical treatise, part autobiography, part novel—is a curious blend of probing, satirical social criticism and spiritual thought. Carlyle adopted the persona of biographer and editor of the life and work of the German Diogenes Teufelsdröckh (God-Begotten Devil's Dung), Professor of Things in General at the University of I Know Not Where and author of the "philosophy of clothes" elucidated in *Sartor Resartus* (which means "the tailor re-tailored"). "Teufelsdröckh's" writings elaborate the book's central metaphor: social customs and mores and political and religious institutions are but the "clothing" of essential realities, even as the body is the clothing of the soul. Teufelsdröckh's biography—based largely on Carlyle's own—traces his development from the "Everlasting No" of spiritual desolation through the "Centre of Indifference" to the "Everlasting Yea," a spiritual renewal in which Teufelsdröckh recognizes the omnipresence of divinity and humankind's share in it. *Sartor Resartus* articulates many other themes that recur in Carlyle's works: the imperatives of action and work in the individual's life and the corresponding concept of duty, the necessity for hero worship both to regulate politics and to fulfill humanity's need to obey and reverence the superior, and the dangers of utilitarianism to morals and politics.

Vying with *Sartor Resartus* as Carlyle's most famous book, and among his most controversial, *The French Revolution* is, in the words of John Stuart Mill, "not so much a history, as

an epic poem." Indeed, Mill's words are still echoed, for Carlyle's first history was a deliberate break with established historiography. Carlyle contemptuously rejected what he termed the "dryasdust" method of presenting history as an unadorned series of facts, and *The French Revolution* has been hailed as a vibrant, imaginative, and dramatic recreation of its subject. "Never, indeed, was history written in so mad a vein," marvelled William Henry Smith in 1843. *The French Revolution* betrays its author's bias. While clearly sympathetic to the plight of the revolutionaries, and mindful of the necessity to change corrupt or outdated social institutions, Carlyle abhorred anarchy and feared the rule of the people.

Carlyle's distrust of the multitude increased with time, and he became an adamant opponent of democracy: his later political works and biographies demonstrate his conviction that the successful state is governed by strong individuals, not the people. *On Heroes, Hero-Worship, and the Heroic in History* outlines his thesis that the vast majority of people, unsuited to rule, are in need of heroes to provide strong leadership. *Oliver Cromwell* and *Frederick the Great,* treatments of two of Carlyle's personal heroes, are illustrations of this same theme. In *Past and Present,* Carlyle favorably contrasted medieval society, exemplified by the abbey of Bury St. Edmunds, with the parliamentary democracy of his own day. The substitution of democracy for the medieval concept of a fixed social hierarchy, Carlyle believed, had resulted in political incompetence—in that those fittest to rule were hindered by the power of the majority—and social fragmentation, as a society of supposed equals had no defined reciprocal relationships based on the responsibilities of the different social classes toward one another. *Latter-Day Pamphlets,* a series of essays on topical issues, is considered Carlyle's most combative, dogmatic, and offensive work. "Model Prisons" blasts the new enlightened, humanitarian approach to penal reform as a travesty of the ideal of justice. *Occasional Discourse on the Nigger Question* (published as a separate work but usually linked with this series) opposes the emancipation of American and West Indian slaves. "The Present Time" treats the same theme, arguing that democracy is in effect anarchy and that "freedom" for the poor and underprivileged is a worthless concept if it means, as Carlyle believed it generally does, the freedom to starve to death rather than live under the care (and constraint) of a benevolent leader.

Carlyle's literary style, considered one of the most distinctive and explosive in English, marked a revolutionary departure from the measured, decorous prose of the Victorian era. Inverted syntax, German idiom, coinages of compound words, unusual metaphors, ubiquitous allusions, and typographical oddities combine to create a prose style noted for both its obscurity and its forceful intensity.

Few authors have received the extraordinary amount of critical attention devoted to Carlyle in the nineteenth century. Early reviewers were generally split along partisan lines with regard to Carlyle's social and political commentary. His vigorous denunciation of sham and pretense touched a chord with many, to whom Carlyle was a sort of social savior, a fearless speaker of truth whose mockery and irony could not disguise his essential philanthropy. Others objected to Carlyle's radicalism and complained that his social criticism was purely destructive, offering no positive alternatives to the conditions he decried. Similarly, Carlyle's vaguely defined mysticism, which he called "natural supernaturalism," called forth opposing reactions. There were those who viewed Carlyle's celebration of reverent awe and wonder as an expression of the deepest faith and morality, and there were others for whom Carlyle's lack of specific doctrine rendered him theologically suspect. Critics were equally divided with regard to Carlyle's style. Henry David Thoreau praised it as "the richest prose style we know of"; William Edmonstoune Aytoun dismissed it as "intolerable twaddle"; William Henry Smith shrugged: "Such is *Carlylism;* and that is all that can be said upon the matter." Yet, notwithstanding the diversity of their judgments, critics were united in their acknowledgment of Carlyle's pivotal influence on his society and his role as a catalyst to thought.

After Carlyle's death, an extra-literary but persistent controversy caused his reputation to plummet. Froude published Carlyle's *Reminiscences* in 1881, and many found the man presented therein unattractive in his indulgent self-recriminations regarding Jane's death and captious and mean-spirited in his sarcastic appraisals of his contemporaries. Following closely upon this, Froude's biography of his mentor portrayed Carlyle as an egocentric, irascible, and sometimes cruel man. Most shocking of all to late nineteenth-century readers were Froude's veiled but obvious allusions to Carlyle's impotence and his subtle hints that the Carlyles' marriage was never consummated. Such charges engendered outraged defences from Carlyle's relations and friends, fueling interest in his life and personality.

With the passage of time, the controversy surrounding Carlyle's personal life diminished—but so did the force of his writings. To a civilization in which democracy and industrialization—anathema to Carlyle—had gained the ascendancy, his relevance was greatly lessened. Indeed, the reign of his influence was declared ended in 1921 by Edmund Gosse, who wrote: "Carlyle has lost his potency and his magic." But Gosse's words are denied by the considerable attention Carlyle has received during the twentieth century. At times he has been reviled: the virulent, acidic essays of *Latter-Day Pamphlets* have contributed to a perception of Carlyle as a rabid reactionary while *On Heroes and Hero-Worship* has caused some to brand him as a proponent of totalitarian government and an advocate of repression comparable to Adolph Hitler. In general, however, modern criticism of Carlyle has become less factional and more scholarly, focusing on the philosophical bases of his thought and the literary qualities of his work. While many of Carlyle's sociopolitical ideals are considered as superannuated as the times that gave them birth, critics assert that Carlyle's importance remains palpable. The pugnacious, dogmatic, and defiantly unique sage of Chelsea, in his unrelenting battle against social mechanization and earnest emphasis on the transcendent over the prosaic, exerted a powerful influence on the Victorian era and thus helped to shape the evolution of the modern world.

(See also *Dictionary of Literary Biography*, Vol. 55: *Victorian Prose Writers before 1867*.)

PRINCIPAL WORKS

Wilhelm Meister's Apprenticeship [translator; from *Wilhelm Meisters Lehrjahre* by Johann Wolfgang von Goethe] (novel) 1824
The Life of Friedrich Schiller (biography) 1825
*Sartor Resartus (prose) 1836
The French Revolution (history) 1837
**Critical and Miscellaneous Essays. 4 vols. (essays) 1838-39

On Heroes, Hero-Worship, and the Heroic in History (lectures) 1841
Past and Present (prose) 1843
Oliver Cromwell's Letters and Speeches. 2 vols. [editor] (letters and speeches) 1845
Latter-Day Pamphlets (essays) 1850
The Life of John Sterling (biography) 1851
Occasional Discourse on the Nigger Question (essay) 1853
The Collected Works of Thomas Carlyle. 16 vols. (prose, history, essays, biography, and translations) 1857-58
History of Friedrich II. of Prussia, Called Frederick the Great. 6 vols. (biography) 1858-65
Shooting Niagara: And After? (essay) 1867
Reminiscences (memoir) 1881
The Correspondence of Thomas Carlyle and Ralph Waldo Emerson, 1834-1872. 2 vols. (letters) 1883
Letters and Memorials of Jane Welsh Carlyle. 3 vols. [editor, with James Anthony Froude] (letters and memoir) 1883
Early Letters of Thomas Carlyle. 2 vols. (letters) 1886
Correspondence between Goethe and Carlyle (letters) 1887
The Works of Thomas Carlyle. 30 vols. (prose, history, essays, biographies, and translations) 1896-99
The Love Letters of Thomas Carlyle and Jane Welsh. 2 vols. (letters) 1909
Letters of Thomas Carlyle to John Stuart Mill, John Sterling, and Robert Browning (letters) 1923

*This work was originally published in the periodical *Fraser's Magazine* in 1833-34.

**The essays in this collection were first published in periodicals.

[ALEXANDER HILL EVERETT] (essay date 1835)

[*Everett, an American diplomat, essayist, poet, and translator, served as editor of the influential* North American Review *from 1830 to 1835. He was also interested in European Romanticism, and his translations of Goethe are considered among the best in American letters. In this excerpt from his review of* Sartor Resartus, *he comments on the unusual, tongue-in-cheek form of the work and prophesies a bright literary future for the author.*]

This little work [*Sartor Resartus*], which, as the title-page informs us, was first published in successive portions in *Fraser's Magazine*, comes before us under rather suspicious circumstances. It purports to be a sort of commentary, by an anonymous writer, on a late work upon the Philosophy of Dress, or Clothes, by Dr. Diogenes Teufelsdroeckh, Professor of the Science of Things in General at the University of Weissnichtwo in Germany. The commentator represents himself as having made the acquaintance of this writer, some years ago, on a visit to the place of his residence; and gives a pretty full description of his personal habits and character, to which we may advert hereafter. Some time after his return, the commentator, or, as he calls himself, the editor, received from his German friend a copy of the work just alluded to, the title of which, at full, is as follows: *Die Kleider, ihr Werden und Wirken,* (Clothes, their origin and influence,) *von Diogenes Teufelsdroeckh, J. U. D. &c. Stillschweigen and Co. Weissnichtwo.* (p. 454)

Our commentator, or, editor, as he prefers to call himself, on the first perusal of this "remarkable volume," perceived that it exhibited what he affects to consider as an entirely new system of philosophy, and in the author an almost unexampled personal character. Having mastered the contents of the work, he was deliberating rather anxiously upon the best method of imparting to the public the treasure which he supposed himself to have acquired, when his zeal was still farther excited by a letter which he unexpectedly received from Counsellor *Heuschrecke,* the most intimate friend of Teufelsdroeckh, with whom our editor had not been in previous correspondence. The counsellor, it seems, after much extraneous matter, entered at large upon the subject of the work in question, described it as creating an extraordinary sensation throughout all Germany, and at length hinted, with much circumlocution, at the practicability of conveying some knowledge of it and of its author to England, and through England to the Far West. The counsellor added, that if our commentator were disposed to undertake a biography of Professor Teufelsdroeckh, he (Counsellor Heuschrecke) had it in his power to furnish the requisite documents. This letter decided the previously irresolute purpose of our editor, and he immediately made an arrangement with the publisher of *Fraser's Magazine,* to furnish him with a series of articles upon the Philosophy of Clothes, and its author.

After commencing and making some progress in his work, the editor represents himself as receiving from his correspondent Heuschrecke another voluminous and discursive letter, accompanying the promised documents, which proved to be a sort of irregular autobiography, consisting of a mass of papers, written by the professor himself upon all sorts of subjects, including his own life and adventures;—the whole deposited in "six considerable paper bags, carefully sealed, and marked successively in gilt China-ink, with the symbols of the six southern zodiacal signs, beginning at Libra." The editor complains very much of the confusion in which he found these materials, and of the great trouble that he had in collecting from them the facts which he wanted. By dint of hard labor and great perseverance, he finally succeeded in putting together a sort of biography, which occupies the second book of the commentary before us. In the third and last, the editor returns to his task, and concludes his summary of the contents of the work.

Such is the account, given by the "present editor," of the origin of this little work. Though professing in general a good deal of respect for his author, he at times deals pretty freely with him:—"Thou foolish Teufelsdroeckh!" and "Thou rogue!" are among the titles which are occasionally bestowed on him. For ourselves, we incline to the opinion, that the only rogue in the company is the "present editor." We have said that the volume came before the public under rather suspicious circumstances, and, after a careful survey of the whole ground, our belief is, that no such persons as Professor Teufelsdroeckh or Counsellor Heuschrecke ever existed; that the six paper bags, with their China-ink inscriptions and multifarious contents, are a mere figment of the brain; that the "present editor" is the only person who has ever written upon the Philosophy of Clothes; and that the **Sartor Resartus** is the only treatise that has yet appeared upon that subject;—in short, that the whole account of the origin of the work before us, which the supposed editor relates with so much gravity, and of which we have given a brief abstract, is in plain English, a *hum.* (pp. 455-56)

In short, our private opinion is . . . that the whole story of a correspondence with Germany, a university of Nobody-knows-

where, a Professor of Things in General, a Counsellor Grasshopper, a Flower-Goddess Blumine, and so-forth, has about as much foundation in truth, as the late entertaining account of Sir Harry Herschel's discoveries in the moon. Fictions of this kind are, however, not uncommon, and ought not, perhaps, to be condemned with too much severity; but we are not sure that we can exercise the same indulgence in regard to the attempt, which seems to be made to mislead the public as to the substance of the work before us, and its pretended German original. Both purport, as we have seen, to be upon the subject of Clothes, or dress. *Clothes, their Origin and Influence,* is the title of the supposed German treatise of Professor Teufelsdroeckh, and the rather odd name of **Sartor Resartus**,—the Tailor Patched,—which the present editor has affixed to his pretended commentary, seems to look the same way. But though there is a good deal of remark throughout the work in a half-serious, half-comic style upon dress, it seems to be in reality a treatise upon the great science of Things in General, which Teufelsdroeckh is supposed to have professed at the university of Nobody-knows-where. Now, without intending to adopt a too rigid standard of morals, we own that we doubt a little the propriety of offering to the public a treatise on Things in General, under the name and in the form of an Essay on Dress. For ourselves, advanced as we unfortunately are in the journey of life, far beyond the period when dress is practically a matter of interest, we have no hesitation in saying, that the real subject of the work is to us more attractive than the ostensible one. But this is probably not the case with the mass of readers. To the younger portion of the community, which constitutes every where the very great majority, the subject of dress is one of intense and paramount importance. An author who treats it appeals, like the poet, to the young men and maidens,—*virginibus puerisque,*—and calls upon them by all the motives which habitually operate most strongly upon their feelings, to buy his book. When, after opening their purses for this purpose, they have carried home the work in triumph, expecting to find in it some particular instruction in regard to the tying of their neckcloths, or the cut of their corsets, and meet with nothing better than a dissertation on Things in General, they will,—to use the mildest terms,—not be in very good humor. If the last improvements in legislation, which we have made in this country, should have found their way to England, the author, we think, would stand some chance of being *Lynched.* Whether his object in this piece of *supercherie* be merely pecuniary profit, or whether he takes a malicious pleasure in quizzing the dandies, we shall not undertake to say. In the latter part of the work, he devotes a separate chapter to this class of persons, from the tenor of which we should be disposed to conclude, that he would consider any mode of divesting them of their property very much in the nature of a spoiling of the Egyptians.

The only thing about the work, tending to prove that it is what it purports to be, a commentary on a real German treatise, is the style, which is a sort of Babylonish dialect, not destitute, it is true, of richness, vigor, and at times a sort of singular felicity of expression, but very strongly tinged throughout with the peculiar idiom of the German language. This quality in the style, however, may be a mere result of a great familiarity with German literature, and we cannot, therefore, look upon it as in itself decisive, still less as outweighing so much evidence of an opposite character.

From what has been said, our readers will gather, with sufficient assurance, that the work before us is a sort of philosophical romance in which the author undertakes to give, in the form of a review of a German treatise on dress, and a notice of the life of the writer, his own opinions upon Matters and Things in General. The hero, Professor Teufelsdroeckh, seems to be intended for a portrait of human nature as affected by the moral influences to which, in the present state of society, a cultivated mind is naturally exposed. Teufelsdroeckh is a foundling, brought up by poor but respectable parents, and educated for the legal profession. He is called to the bar, or as the phrase is in Germany, admitted as a listener (*auscultator*), and having little business and no property, finds himself rather at a loss for the means of subsistence. While lingering in this uncertain state, he forms an acquaintance with an English traveller, named Towgood, and is patronized to a certain extent by Count Zahdarm, a nobleman whose lady occasionally invites him to a sort of entertainment, which would be called here a blue-stocking party, or *Blue Congress,* but which is dignified in Germany by the more classical title of an *æsthetic tea.* At one of these ''æsthetic teas,'' he falls in love with the Flower-Goddess Blumine, alluded to above, who seems to be a sort of *demoiselle de compagnie* to the Countess, and who, after lending for a time an apparently favorable ear to his suit, all at once changes her mind, and marries his English friend Towgood. The result increases the uneasiness under which Teufelsdroeckh was previously laboring, and he finally quits his profession and place of residence, and sets forth upon his travels, which appear to have been extensive, and are described with sufficient exactness, though in general terms. The worst thing about his case is, that in addition to want, idleness, and disappointment in love and friendship, he fell into a kind of scepticism, or rather absolute unbelief. From this, however, he is gradually restored by a series of changes in his intellectual and moral character, amounting altogether to a sort of philosophical conversion. These changes are described in successive chapters under the titles of the *Everlasting No,* the *Centre of Indifference,* and the *Everlasting Yes,* which may be said to constitute the kernel of the work. Being now in a comfortable frame of mind, the wanderer appeals to his pen as a means of obtaining subsistence, and by a diligent use of it obtains pretty soon the professorship of Things in General at the University of Nobody-knows-where. Here he flourishes in tranquil contentment, and publishes the remarkable, close-printed, close-meditated volume, which forms the subject of the present editor's learned commentary. (pp. 458-60)

[*Sartor Resartus*] contains, under a quaint and singular form, a great deal of deep thought, sound principle, and fine writing. It is, we believe, no secret in England or here, that it is a work of a person to whom the public is indebted for a number of articles in the late British Reviews, which have attracted great attention by the singularity of their style, and the richness and depth of their matter. Among these may be mentioned particularly those on **"Characteristics"** and the **"Life of Burns"** in the *Edinburgh Review,* and on **"Goethe"** in the *Foreign Quarterly.* We have been partly led to take this notice of the work before us by the wish, which the author expresses, that a knowledge of his labors might penetrate into the Far West. We take pleasure in introducing to the American public a writer, whose name is yet in a great measure unknown among us, but who is destined, we think, to occupy a large space in the literary world. (pp. 481-82)

[Alexander Hill Everett], ''Thomas Carlyle,'' in The North American Review, Vol. XLI, No. 89, October, 1835, pp. 454-82.

RALPH WALDO EMERSON   (essay date 1836)

[*Emerson was one of the most influential figures of the nineteenth century. An American essayist and poet, he founded the Transcendental movement and shaped a distinctly American philosophy that embraces optimism, individuality, and mysticism. His philosophy stresses the presence of ongoing creation and revelation by a god apparent in everything and everyone, as well as the essential unity of all thoughts, persons, and things in the divine whole. He and Carlyle began to correspond after Emerson read and admired* Sartor Resartus *in 1834. Emerson then vigorously promoted Carlyle's books in America, writing a preface for the 1836 American edition of* Sartor, *excerpted below, and supervising the American publication of* The French Revolution *and* Past and Present. *Emerson here introduces* Sartor *to readers, commenting on its peculiar style and profound theme. For additional criticism by Emerson, see excerpt dated 1843.*]

The Editors have no expectation that this little work [*Sartor Resartus*] will have a sudden and general popularity. They will not undertake, as there is no need, to justify the gay costume in which the Author delights to dress his thoughts, or the German idioms with which he has sportively sprinkled his pages. It is his humor to advance the gravest speculations upon the gravest topics in a quaint and burlesque style. If his masquerade offend any of his audience, to that degree that they will not hear what he has to say, it may chance to draw others to listen to his wisdom; and what work of imagination can hope to please all? But we will venture to remark that the distaste excited by these peculiarities, in some readers, is greatest at first, and is soon forgotten; and that the foreign dress and aspect of the work are quite superficial, and cover a genuine Saxon heart. We believe, no book has been published for many years, written in a more sincere style of idiomatic English, or which discovers an equal mastery over all the riches of the language. The author makes ample amends for the occasional eccentricity of his genius, not only by frequent bursts of pure splendor, but by the wit and sense which never fail him.

But what will chiefly commend the book to the discerning reader is the manifest design of the work, which is, a Criticism upon the Spirit of the Age,—we had almost said, of the hour, in which we live; exhibiting, in the most just and novel light, the present aspects of Religion, Politics, Literature, Arts, and Social Life. Under all his gaiety, the writer has an earnest meaning, and discovers an insight into the manifold wants and tendencies of human nature, which is very rare among our popular authors. The philanthropy and the purity of moral sentiment, which inspire the work, will find their way to the heart of every lover of virtue. (pp. iii-v)

Ralph Waldo Emerson, in a preface to Sartor Resartus *by Thomas Carlyle, James Munroe and Company, 1836, pp. iii-v.*

[JOHN STUART MILL]   (essay date 1837)

[*The author of* On Liberty *(1859),* Utilitarianism *(1863), and* The Subjection of Women *(1869), Mill is regarded as one of England's greatest philosophers and political economists. Educated at home under an exacting regimen designed by his father James Mill, an ardent disciple of utilitarian philosopher Jeremy Bentham, Mill became, while still in his teens, a prominent exponent of utilitarianism and a prolific essayist for the* Westminster Review *(later the* London and Westminster Review*). In his early twenties, Mill suffered a ''mental crisis,'' which he attributed to the lack of emotional and imaginative outlets in his strictly intellectual upbringing. He turned to the works of William Wordsworth and Samuel Taylor Coleridge, among others, as a means of supplying* *this lack, and was later instrumental in modifying the radical utilitarianism of Bentham to include the consideration of such human intangibles as idealism, emotion, and imagination. Mill and Carlyle became friends in the early 1830s. Mill enthusiastically supported Carlyle's plan to write a history of the French Revolution, and in February of 1835 Carlyle gave his friend the first volume of his manuscript to critique. Mill's house-keeper, mistaking the manuscript for wastepaper, threw it in the fire, destroying a work it had taken Carlyle five months to complete. As he had no other copy, he was forced to completely reconstruct the book. In this excerpt from a review of* The French Revolution, *Mill pronounces the work unique in the realism and immediacy of its portrayal of character and scene and evaluates the socio-political opinions expressed in the history. He also predicts that the book will be controversial due to its startling originality of both style and content. Mill later wrote in his autobiography: "I believe that the early success and reputation of Carlyle's* French Revolution, *were considerably accelerated by what I wrote about it in the* [London and Westminster Review]. *Immediately on its publication, and before the commonplace critics, all whose rules and modes of judgment it set at defiance, had time to pre-occupy the public with their disapproval of it, I wrote and published a review of the book, hailing it as one of those productions of genius which are above all rules, and are a law to themselves." In later years, Mill and Carlyle drifted apart, as the fundamental differences between their social and ethical philosophies became a barrier to friendship.*]

[*The French Revolution*] is not so much a history, as an epic poem; and notwithstanding, or even in consequence of this, the truest of histories. It is the history of the French Revolution, and the poetry of it, both in one; and on the whole no work of greater genius, either historical or poetical, has been produced in this country for many years.

It is a book on which opinion will be for some time divided; nay, what talk there is about it, while it is still fresh, will probably be oftenest of a disparaging sort; as indeed is usually the case, both with men's works and with men themselves, of distinguished originality. For a thing which is unaccustomed, must be a very small thing indeed, if mankind can at once see into it and be sure that it is good: when, therefore, a considerable thing, which is also an unaccustomed one, appears, those who will hereafter approve, sit silent for a time, making up their minds; and those only to whom the mere novelty is a sufficient reason for disapproval, speak out. We need not fear to prophesy that the suffrages of a large class of the very best qualified judges will be given, even enthusiastically, in favour of the volumes before us; but we will not affect to deny that the sentiment of another large class of readers (among whom are many entitled to the most respectful attention on other subjects) will be far different; a class comprehending all who are repelled by quaintness of manner. For a style more peculiar than that of Mr Carlyle, more unlike the jog-trot characterless uniformity which distinguishes the English style of this age of Periodicals, does not exist. Nor indeed can this style be wholly defended even by its admirers. Some of its peculiarities are mere mannerisms, arising from some casual association of ideas, or some habit accidentally picked up; and what is worse, many sterling thoughts are so disguised in phraseology borrowed from the spiritualist school of German poets and metaphysicians, as not only to obscure the meaning, but to raise, in the minds of most English readers, a not unnatural nor inexcusable presumption of there being no meaning at all. Nevertheless, the presumption fails in this instance (as in many other instances); there is not only a meaning, but generally a true, and even a profound meaning; and, although a few dicta about the "mystery" and the "infinitude" which are in the universe and in man, and such like topics, are repeated in varied phrases greatly too often for our taste, this must be borne with, proceeding, as one cannot but see, from feelings the most solemn, and the most deeply rooted which can lie in the heart of a human being. These transcendentalisms, and the accidental mannerisms excepted, we pronounce the style of this book to be not only good, but of surpassing excellence; excelled, in its kind, only by the great masters of epic poetry; and a most suitable and glorious vesture for a work which is itself, as we have said, an epic poem.

To any one who is perfectly satisfied with the best of the existing histories, it will be difficult to explain wherein the merit of Mr Carlyle's book consists. If there be a person who, in reading the histories of Hume, Robertson, and Gibbon (works of extraordinary talent, and the works of great writers) has never felt that this, after all, is not history—and that the lives and deeds of his fellow-creatures must be placed before him in quite another manner, if he is to know them, or feel them to be real beings, who once were alive, beings of his own flesh and blood, not mere shadows and dim abstractions; such a person, for whom plausible talk *about* a thing does as well as an image of the thing itself, feels no need of a book like Mr Carlyle's; the want, which it is peculiarly fitted to supply, does not yet consciously exist in his mind. That such a want, however, is generally felt, may be inferred from the vast number of historical plays and historical romances, which have been written for no other purpose than to satisfy it. Mr Carlyle has been the first to shew that all which is done for history by the best historical play, by Schiller's *Wallenstein,* for example, or Vitet's admirable trilogy, may be done in a strictly true narrative, in which every incident rests on irrefragable authority; may be done, by means merely of an apt selection and a judicious grouping of authentic facts.

It has been noted as a point which distinguishes Shakespeare from ordinary dramatists, that *their* characters are logical abstractions, his are human beings: that their kings are nothing but kings, their lovers nothing but lovers, their patriots, courtiers, villains, cowards, bullies, are each of them that, and that alone; while his are real men and women, who have these qualities, but have them in addition to their full share of all other qualities (not incompatible), which are incident to human nature. In Shakespeare, consequently, we feel we are in a world of realities; we are among such beings as really could exist, as do exist, or have existed, and as we can sympathise with; the faces we see around us are human faces, and not mere rudiments of such, or exaggerations of single features. This quality, so often pointed out as distinctive of Shakespeare's plays, distinguishes Mr Carlyle's history. Never before did we take up a book calling itself by that name, a book treating of past times, and professing to be true, and find ourselves actually among human beings. We at once felt, that what had hitherto been to us mere abstractions, had become realities; the "forms of things unknown," which we fancied we knew, but knew their names merely, were, for the first time, with most startling effect, 'bodied forth' and "turned into shape." Other historians talk to us indeed of human beings; but what do they place before us? Not even stuffed figures of such, but rather their algebraical symbols; a few phrases, which present no image to the fancy, but by adding up the dictionary meanings of which, we may hunt out a few qualities, not enough to form even the merest outline of what the men *were,* or possibly *could* have been; furnishing little but a canvas, which, if we ourselves can paint, we may fill with almost any picture, and if we cannot, it will remain for ever blank.

Take, for example, Hume's history; certainly, in its own way, one of the most skilful specimens of narrative in modern literature, and with some pretensions also to philosophy. Does Hume throw his own mind into the mind of an Anglo-Saxon, or an Anglo-Norman? Does any reader feel, after having read Hume's history, that he can now picture to himself what human life was, among the Anglo-Saxons? how an Anglo-Saxon would have acted in any supposable case? what were his joys, his sorrows, his hopes and fears, his ideas and opinions on any of the great and small matters of human interest? Would not the sight, if it could be had, of a single table or pair of shoes made by an Anglo-Saxon, tell us, directly and by inference, more of his whole way of life, more of how men thought and acted among the Anglo-Saxons, than Hume, with all his narrative skill, has contrived to tell us from all his materials?

Or descending from the history of civilization, which in Hume's case may have been a subordinate object, to the history of political events: did any one ever gain from Hume's history anything like a picture of what may actually have been passing, in the minds, say, of Cavaliers or of Roundheads during the civil wars? Does any one feel that Hume has made him figure to himself with any precision what manner of men these were; how far they were like ourselves, how far different; what things they loved and hated, and what sort of conception they had formed of the things they loved and hated? And what kind of a notion can be framed of a period of history, unless we begin with that as a preliminary? Hampden, and Strafford, and Vane, and Cromwell, do these, in Hume's pages, appear to us like beings who actually trod this earth, and spoke with a human voice, and stretched out human hands in fellowship with other human beings; or like the figures in a phantasmagoria, colourless, impalpable, gigantic, and in all varieties of attitude, but all resembling one another in being shadows? And suppose he had done his best to assist us in forming a conception of these leading characters; what would it have availed, unless he had placed us also in the atmosphere which they breathed? What wiser are we for looking out upon the world though Hampden's eyes, unless it be the same world which Hampden looked upon? and what help has Hume afforded us for this? Has he depicted to us, or to himself, what all the multitude of people were about, who surrounded Hampden; what the whole English nation were feeling, thinking, or doing? Does he shew us what impressions from without were coming to Hampden—what materials and what instruments were given to him to work with? If not, we are well qualified, truly, from Hume's information, to erect ourselves into judges of any part of Hampden's conduct!

Another very celebrated historian, we mean Gibbon—not a man of mere science and analysis, like Hume, but with some (though not the truest or profoundest) artistic feeling of the picturesque, and from whom, therefore, rather more might have been expected—has with much pains succeeded in producing a tolerably graphic picture of here and there a battle, a tumult, or an insurrection; his book is full of movement and costume, and would make a series of very pretty ballets at the Opera-house, and the ballets would give us fully as distinct an idea of the Roman empire, and how it declined and fell, as the book does. If we want that, we must look for it anywhere but in Gibbon. One touch of M. Guizot removes a portion of the veil which hid from us the recesses of private life under the Roman empire, lets in a ray of light which penetrates as far even as the domestic hearth of a subject of Rome, and shews us the government at work making that desolate; but no similar gleam of light from Gibbon's mind ever reaches the subject; *human*

life, in the times he wrote about, is not what he concerned himself with.

On the other hand, there are probably many among our readers who are acquainted (though it is not included in Coleridge's admirable translation) with that extraordinary piece of dramatic writing, termed *Wallenstein's Camp*. One of the greatest of dramatists, the historian of the Thirty Years' War, aspired to do, in a dramatic fiction, what even *his* genius had not enabled him to do in his history—to delineate the great characters, and, above all, to embody the general spirit of that period. This is done with such life and reality through ten acts, that the reader feels when it is over as if all the prominent personages in the play were people whom he had known from his childhood; but the author did not trust to this alone: he prefixed to the ten acts, one introductory act, intended to exhibit, not the characters, but the element they moved in. It is there, in this preliminary piece, that Schiller really depicts the Thirty Year's War; without that, even the other ten acts, splendid as they are, would not have sufficiently realized it to our conception, nor would the Wallensteins and Piccolominis and Terzskys of that glorious tragedy have been themselves, comparatively speaking, intelligible.

What Schiller must have done, in his own mind, with respect to the age of Wallenstein, to enable him to frame that fictitious delineation of it, Mr Carlyle, with a mind which looks still more penetratingly into the deeper meanings of things than Schiller's, has done with respect to the French Revolution. And he has communicated his picture of it with equal vividness; but he has done it by means of real, not fictitious incidents. And therefore is his book, as we said, at once the authentic History and the Poetry of the French Revolution.

It is indeed a favourite doctrine of Mr Carlyle, and one which he has enforced with great strength of reason and eloquence in other places, that all poetry suitable to the present age must be of this kind: that poetry has not naturally any thing to do with fiction, nor is fiction in these days even the most appropriate vehicle and vesture of it; that it should, and will, employ itself more and more, not in inventing unrealities, but in bringing out into ever greater distinctness and impressiveness the poetic aspect of realities. For what is it, in the fictitious subjects which poets usually treat, that makes those subject poetical? Surely not the dry, mechanical *facts* which compose the story; but the *feelings*—the high and solemn, the tender or mournful, even the gay and mirthful contemplations, which the story, or the manner of relating it, awaken in our minds. But would not all these thoughts and feelings be far more vividly aroused if the facts were *believed*; if the men, and all that is ascribed to them, had actually *been*; if the whole were no play of imagination, but a truth? In every real fact, in which any of the great interests of human beings are implicated, there lie the materials of all poetry; there is, as Mr Carlyle has said, the fifth act of a tragedy in every peasant's deathbed; the life of every heroic character is a heroic poem, were but the man of genius found, who could *so* write it! Not falsification of the reality is wanted, not the representation of it as being any thing which it is not; only a deeper understanding of what it is; the power to conceive, and to represent, not the mere outside surface and costume of the thing, nor yet the mere logical definition, and *caput mortuum* of it—but an image of the thing itself in the concrete, with all that is loveable or hateable or admirable or pitiable or sad or solemn or pathetic, in it, and in the things which are implied in it. That is, the thing must be presented as it can exist only in the mind of a great poet: of one gifted with the two essential elements of the poetic character—creative imagination, which, from a chaos of scattered hints and confused testimonies, can summon up the Thing to appear before it as a completed whole: and that depth and breadth of feeling which makes all the images that are called up appear arrayed in whatever, of all that belongs to them, is naturally most affecting and impressive to the human soul.

We do not envy the person who can read Mr Carlyle's three volumes, and not recognize in him both these endowments in a most rare and remarkable degree. What is equally important to be said—he possesses in no less perfection that among the qualities necessary for his task, seemingly the most opposite to these, and in which the man of poetic imagination might be thought likeliest to be deficient; the quality of the historical day-drudge. A more pains-taking or accurate investigator of facts, and sifter of testimonies, never wielded the historical pen. We do not say this at random, but from a most extensive acquaintance with his materials, with his subject, and with the mode in which it has been treated by others.

Thus endowed, and having a theme the most replete with every kind of human interest, epic, tragic, elegiac, even comic and farcical, which history affords, and so near to us withal, that the authentic details of it are still attainable; need it be said, that he has produced a work which deserves to be memorable? a work which, whatever may be its immediate reception, ''will not willingly be let die;'' whose reputation will be a growing reputation, its influence rapidly felt, for it will be read by the writers; and perhaps every historical work of any note, which shall hereafter be written in this country, will be different from what it would have been if this work were not. (pp. 17-22)

[What] (it may be asked) are Mr Carlyle's *opinions*?

If this means, whether he is Tory, Whig, or Democrat; is he for things as they are, or for things *nearly* as they are; or is he one who thinks that subverting things as they are, and setting up Democracy is the main thing needful? we answer, he is none of all these. We should say that he has appropriated and made part of his own frame of thought, nearly all that is good in all these several modes of thinking. But it may be asked, what opinion has Mr Carlyle formed of the French Revolution, as an event in universal history; and this question is entitled to an answer. It should be, however, premised, that in a history upon the plan of Mr Carlyle's, the opinions of the writer are a matter of secondary importance. In reading an ordinary historian, we want to know his opinions, because it is mainly his *opinions* of things, and not the things themselves, that he sets before us; or if any features of the things themselves, those chiefly, which his *opinions* lead him to consider as of importance. . . . [This] is not Mr Carlyle's method. Mr Carlyle brings the thing before us in the *concrete*—clothed, not indeed in *all* its properties and circumstances, since these are infinite, but in as many of them as can be authentically ascertained and imaginatively realized; not prejudging that some of those properties and circumstances will prove instructive and others not, a prejudgment which is the fertile source of misrepresentation and one-sided historical delineation without end. Every one knows, who has attended (for instance) to the sifting of a complicated case by a court of justice, that as long as our image of the fact remains in the slightest degree vague and hazy and undefined, we cannot tell but that what we do *not* yet distinctly see may be precisely that on which all turns. Mr Carlyle, therefore, brings us *acquainted* with persons, things, and events, before he suggests to us what to think of them: nay, we see that this is the very process by which he arrives at his own

thoughts; he paints the thing to himself—he constructs a picture of it in his own mind, and does not, till afterwards, make any logical propositions about it at all. This done, his logical propositions concerning the thing may be true, or may be false; the thing is there, and any reader may find a totally different set of propositions in it if he can; as he might in the reality, if *that* had been before him.

We, for our part, do not always agree in Mr Carlyle's opinions either on things or on men. But we hold it to be impossible that any person should set before himself a perfectly true picture of a great historical event, as it actually happened, and yet that his judgment of it should be radically wrong. Differing partially from some of Mr Carlyle's detached views, we hold his theory, or theorem, of the Revolution, to be the true theory; true as far as it goes, and wanting little of being as complete as any theory of so vast and complicated a phenomena can be. Nay, we do not think that any rational creature, now that the thing can be looked at calmly, now that we have nothing to hope or to fear from it, can form any second theory on the matter.

Mr Carlyle's view of the Revolution is briefly this: That it was the breaking down of a great Imposture: which had not always been an Imposture, but had been becoming such for several centuries.

Two bodies—the King and Feudal Nobility, and the Clergy—held their exalted stations, and received the obedience and allegiance which were paid to them, by virtue solely of their affording *guidance* to the people: the one, directing and keeping order among them in their conjunct operations towards the pursuit of their most important temporal interests; the other, ministering to their spiritual teaching and culture. These are the grounds on which alone any government either claims obedience or finds it: for the obedience of twenty-five millions to a few hundred thousand never yet was yielded to avowed tyranny.

Now, this guidance, the original ground of all obedience, the privileged classes *did* for centuries give. The King and the Nobles led the people in war, and protected and judged them in peace, being the fittest persons to do so who then existed; and the Clergy did teach the best doctrine, did inculcate and impress upon the people the best rule of life then known, and did believe in the doctrine and in the rule of life which they taught, and manifested their belief by their actions, and believed that, in teaching it, they were doing the highest thing appointed to mortals. So far as they did this, both spiritual and temporal rulers deserved and obtained reverence, and willing loyal obedience. But for centuries before the French Revolution, the sincerity which once was in this scheme of society was gradually dying out. The King and Nobles afforded less and less of any real guidance, of any real protection to the people; and even ceased more and more to fancy that they afforded any. All the important business of society went on without them, nay, mostly in spite of their hindrance. The appointed spiritual teachers ceased to do their duty as teachers, ceased to practise what they taught, ceased to believe it, but alas, not to cant about it, or to receive wages as teachers of it. Thus the whole scheme of society and government in France become one great Lie: the places of honour and power being all occupied by persons whose sole claim to occupy them was the pretence of being what they were not, of doing what they did not, nor even for a single moment attemped to do. All other vileness and profligacy in the rulers of a country were but the inevitable consequences of this inherent vice in the condition of their existence. And, this continuing for centuries, the government growing ever more and more consciously a

Lie, the people ever more and more perceiving it to be such, the day of reckoning, which comes for all impostures, came for this: the Good would no longer obey such rulers, the Bad ceased to be in awe of them, and both together rose up and hurled them into chaos.

Such is Mr Carlyle's idea of what the Revolution was. And now, as to the melancholy turn it took, the horrors which accompanied it, the iron despotism by which it was forced to wind itself up, and the smallness of its positive results, compared with those which were hoped for by the sanguine in its commencement.

Mr Carlyle's theory of these things is also a simple one: That the men, most of them good, and many of them among the most instructed of their generation, who attempted at that period to regenerate France, failed in what it was impossible that any one should succeed in: namely, in attempting to found a government, to create a new order of society, a new set of institutions and habits, among a people having no convictions to base such order of things upon. That the existing government, habits, state of society, were bad, this the people were thoroughly convinced of, and rose up as one man, to declare, in every language of deed and word, that they would no more endure it. What was, was bad; but what was good, nobody had determined; no *opinion* on that subject had rooted itself in the people's minds; nor was there even any person, or any body of persons, deference for whom was rooted in their minds and whose word they were willing to take for all the rest. Suppose, then, that the twelve hundred members of the Constituent Assembly had even been gifted with perfect knowledge what arrangement of society was best;—how were they to get time to establish it? Or how were they to hold the people in obedience to it when established? A people with no preconceived reverence, either for it or for them; a people like slaves broke from their fetters—with all man's boundless desires let loose in indefinite expectation, and all the influences of habit and imagination which keep mankind patient under the denial of what they crave for, annihilated for the time, never to be restored but in some quite different shape?

Faith, doubtless, in representative institutions, there was, and of the firmest kind; but unhappily this was not enough: for all that representative institutions themselves can do, is to give practical effect to the faith of the people in something else. What is a representative constitution? Simply a set of contrivances for ascertaining the convictions of the people; for enabling them to declare what men they have faith in; or, failing such, what things the majority of them will insist upon having done to them—by what *rule* they are willing to be governed. But what if the majority have not faith in any men, nor know even in the smallest degree what things they wish to have done, in what manner they would be governed? This was the condition of the French people. To have made it otherwise was possible, but required time; and time, unhappily, in a Revolution, is not given. A great man, indeed, may do it, by inspiring at least faith in himself, which may last till the tree he has planted has taken root, and can stand alone; such apparently was Solon, and such perhaps, had he lived, might have been Mirabeau: nay, in the absence of other greatness, even a great quack may temporarily do it; as Napoleon, himself a mixture of great man and great quack, did in some measure exemplify. Revolutions sweep much away, but if any Revolution since the beginning of the world ever founded anything, towards which the minds of the people had not been growing for generations previous, it has been founded by some individual man.

Much more must be added to what has now been said, to make the statement of Mr Carlyle's opinions on the French Revolution anything like complete; nor shall we any further set forth, either such of those opinions as we agree in, or those, far less numerous, from which we disagree. Nevertheless, we will not leave the subject without pointing out what appears to us to be the most prominent defect in our author's general mode of thinking. His own method being that of the artist, not of the man of science—working as he does by figuring things to himself as wholes, not dissecting them into their parts—he appears, though perhaps it is but appearance, to entertain something like a contempt for the opposite method; and to go as much too far in his distrust of analysis and generalization, as others (the Constitutional party, for instance, in the French Revolution) went too far in their reliance upon it.

Doubtless, in the infinite complexities of human affairs, any general theorem which a wise man will form concerning them, must be regarded as a mere approximation to truth; an approximation obtained by striking an average of many cases, and consequently not exactly fitting any one case. No wise man, therefore, will stand upon his theorem only—neglecting to look into the specialties of the case in hand, and see what features *that* may present which may take it out of any theorem, or bring it within the compass of more theorems than one. But the far greater number of people—when they have got a formula by rote, when they can bring the matter in hand within some maxim "in that case made and provided" by the traditions of the vulgar, by the doctrines of their sect or school, or by some generalization of their own—do not think it necessary to let their mind's eye rest upon the thing itself at all; but deliberate and act, not upon knowledge of the thing, but upon a hearsay of it; being (to use a frequent illustration of our author) provided with spectacles, they fancy it not needful to use their eyes. It should be understood that general principles are not intended to dispense with thinking and examining, but to help us to think and examine. When the object itself is out of our reach, and we cannot examine into it, we must follow general principles, because, by doing so, we are not so likely to go wrong, and almost certain not to go so far wrong, as if we floated on the boundless ocean of mere conjecture; but when we are not driven to guess, when we have means and appliances for observing, general principles are nothing more or other than helps towards a better use of those means and appliances.

Thus far we and Mr Carlyle travel harmoniously together; but here we apparently diverge. For, having admitted that general principles (or *formulæ*, as our author calls them, after old Mirabeau, the crabbed *ami des hommes*) are helps to observation, not substitutes for it, we must add, that they are *necessary* helps, and that without general principles no one ever observed a particular case to any purpose. For, except by general principles, how do we bring the light of past experience to bear upon the new case? The essence of past experience lies embodied in those logical, abstract propositions, which our author makes so light of:—there, and no where else. From them we learn what has ordinarily been found true, or even recall what we ourselves have found true, in innumerable unnamed and unremembered cases, more or less resembling the present. We are hence taught, at the least, what we shall *probably* find true in the present case; and although this, which is only a probability, may be lazily acquiesced in and acted upon without further inquiry as a certainty, the risk even so is infinitely less than if we began without a theory, or even a probable hypothesis. Granting that all the facts of the particular instance are within the reach of observation, how difficult is the work of observing, how almost impossible that of disentangling a complicated case, if, when we begin, no one view of it appears to us more probable than another. Without a hypothesis to commence with, we do not even know what end to begin at, what points to enquire into. Nearly every thing that has ever been ascertained by scientific observers, was brought to light in the attempt to test and verify some theory. To start from a theory, but not to see the object through the theory; to bring light with us, but also to receive other light from whencesoever it comes; such is the part of the philosopher, of the true practical *seer* or person of insight.

Connected with the tendency which we fancy we perceive in our author, to undervalue general principles is another tendency which we think is perceptible in him, to set too low a value on what constitutions and forms of government can do. Be it admitted once for all, that no form of government will enable you, as our author has elsewhere said, "given a world of rogues, to produce an honesty by their united action;" nor when a people are wholly without faith either in man or creed, has any representative constitution a charm to render them governable well, or even governable at all. On the other hand, Mr Carlyle must no less admit, that when a nation *has* faith in any men, or any set of principles, representative institutions furnish the only regular and peaceable mode in which that faith can quietly declare itself, and those men, or those principles, obtain the predominance. It is surely no trifling matter to have a legalized means whereby the guidance will always be in the hands of the Acknowledged Wisest, who, if not always the really wisest, are at least those whose wisdom, such as it may be, is the most available for the purpose. Doubtless it is the natural law of representative governments that the power is shared, in varying proportions, between the really skilfullest and the skilfullest quacks; with a tendency, in easy times, towards the preponderance of the quacks, in the "times which try men's souls," towards that of the true men. Improvements enough may be expected as mankind improve, but that the best and wisest shall always be accounted such, *that* we need not expect; because the quack can always steal, and vend for his own profit, as much of the good ware as is marketable. But is not all this to the full as likely to happen in every other kind of government as in a representative one? with these differences in favour of representative government, which will be found perhaps to be its only real and universal pre-eminence: That it alone is government by consent—government by mutual compromise and compact; while all others are, in one form or another, governments by constraint: That it alone proceeds by quiet muster of opposing strengths, when that which is really weakest sees itself to be such, and peaceably gives way; a benefit never yet realized but in countries inured to a representative government; elsewhere nothing but actual blows can show who is strongest, and every great dissension of opinion must break out into a civil war.

We have thus briefly touched upon the two principal points on which we take exception, not so much to any opinion of the author, as to the tone of sentiment which runs through the book; a tone of sentiment which otherwise, for justness and nobleness, stands almost unrivalled in the writings of our time. A deep catholic sympathy with human nature, with all natural human feelings, looks out from every page of these volumes; justice administered in love, to all kind of human beings, bad and good; the most earnest exalted feeling of moral distinctions, with the most generous allowances for whatever partial confounding of these distinctions, either natural weakness or perverse circumstances can excuse. No greatness, no strength, no

goodness or lovingness, passes unrecognized or unhonoured by him. All the sublimity of "the simultaneous death-defiance of twenty-five millions" speaks itself forth in his pages—not the less impressively, because the unspeakable folly and incoherency, which always in real life are not one step from, but actually pervade, the sublimities of so large a body (and did so most notably in this instance) are no less perceptible to his keen sense of the ludicrous. We presume it is this which has caused the book to be accused, even in print, of "flippancy," a term which appears to us singularly misapplied. For is not this mixture and confused entanglement of the great and the contemptible, precisely what we meet with in nature? and would not a history, which did not make us not only see this, but feel it, be deceptive; and give an impression which would be the more false, the greater the general vivacity and vigour of the delineation? And indeed the capacity to see and feel what is loveable, admirable, in a thing, and what is laughable in it, at the same time, constitutes humour; the quality to which we owe a Falstaff, a Parson Adams, an Uncle Toby, and Mause Headriggs and Barons of Bradwardine without end. You meet in this book with passages of grave drollery (drollery unsought for, arising from the simple statement of facts, and a true natural feeling of them) not inferior to the best in Mr Peacock's novels; and immediately or soon after comes a soft note as of dirge music, or solemn choral song of old Greek tragedy, which makes the heart too full for endurance, and forces you to close the book and rest for a while.

Again, there are aphorisms which deserve to live for ever; characters drawn with a few touches, and indicating a very remarkable insight into many of the obscurest regions of human nature; much genuine philosophy, disguised though it often be in a poetico-metaphysical vesture of a most questionable kind; and, in short, new and singular but not therefore absurd or unpractical views taken of many important things. A most original book; original not least in its complete sincerity, its disregard of the merely conventional: every idea and sentiment is given out exactly as it is thought and felt, fresh from the soul of the writer, and in such language (conformable to precedent or not) as is most capable of representing it in the form in which it exists there. And hence the critics have begun to call the style "affected;" a term which conventional people, whether in literature or society, invariably bestow upon the unreservedly natural.

In truth, every book which is eminently original, either in matter or style, has a hard battle to fight before it can obtain even pardon for its originality, much less applause. Well, therefore, may this be the case when a book is original, not in matter only or in style only, but in both; and, moreover, written in prose, with a fervour and exaltation of feeling which is only tolerated in verse, if even there. And when we consider that Wordsworth, Coleridge, and others of their time, whose deviation from the beaten track was but a stone's throw compared with Mr Carlyle, were ignominiously hooted out of court by the wise tribunals which in those days dispensed justice in such matters, and had to wait for a second generation before the sentence could be reversed, and their names placed among the great names of our literature, we might well imagine that the same or a worse fate awaits Mr Carlyle; did we not believe that those very writers, aided by circumstances, have made straight the way for Mr Carlyle and for much else. This very phenomenon, of the different estimation of Wordsworth and Coleridge, now, and thirty years ago, is among the indications of one of the most conspicuous new elements which have sprung up in the European mind during those years: an insatiable demand for realities, come of conventionalities and formalities what may; of which desire the literary phasis is, a large tolerance for every feeling which is natural and not got-up, for every picture taken from the life and not from other pictures, however it may clash with traditionary notions of elegance or congruity. The book before us needs to be read with this catholic spirit; if we read it captiously, we shall never have done finding fault. But no true poet, writing sincerely and following the promptings of his own genius, can fail to be contemptible to any who desire to find him so; and if even Milton's *Areopagitica,* of which now, it would seem, no one dares speak with only moderate praise, were now first to issue from the press, it would be turned from with contempt by every one who will think or speak disparagingly of this work of Mr Carlyle. (pp. 43-52)

[*John Stuart Mill*], *in a review of "The French Revolution: A History," in* The London and Westminster Review, *Vol. XXVII, No. 11, July, 1837, pp. 17-53.*

[WILLIAM MAKEPEACE THACKERAY] (essay date 1837)

[*Thackeray is best known for his satiric sketches and novels of upper- and middle-class English life, including* Vanity Fair: A Novel without a Hero (1848). *He is credited with bringing a simpler style and greater realism to English fiction. In this excerpt from a review that pleased Carlyle, Thackeray heartily recommends* The French Revolution.]

Since the appearance of [*The French Revolution*], within the last two months, it has raised among the critics and the reading public a strange storm of applause and discontent. To hear one party you would fancy that the author was but a dull madman, indulging in wild vagaries of language and dispensing with common sense and reason, while, according to another, his opinions are little short of inspiration, and his eloquence unbounded as his genius. We confess, that in reading the first few pages we were not a little inclined to adopt the former opinion, and yet, after perusing the whole of this extraordinary work, we can allow, almost to their fullest extent, the high qualities with which Mr. Carlyle's idolators endow him.

But never did a book sin so grievously from outward appearance, or a man's style so mar his subject and dim his genius. It is stiff, short, and rugged, it abounds with Germanisms and Latinisms, strange epithets, and choking double words, astonishing to the admirers of simple Addisonian English, to those who love history as it gracefully runs in Hume, or struts pompously in Gibbon—no such style is Mr. Carlyle's. A man, at the first onset, must take breath at the end of a sentence, or, worse still, go to sleep in the midst of it. But these hardships become lighter as the traveller grows accustomed to the road, and he speedily learns to admire and sympathize; just as he would admire a Gothic cathedral in spite of the quaint carvings and hideous images on door and buttress.

There are, however, a happy few of Mr. Carlyle's critics and readers to whom these very obscurities and mysticisms of style are welcome and almost intelligible; the initiated in metaphysics, the sages who have passed the veil of Kantian philosophy, and discovered that the "critique of pure reason" is really that which it purports to be, and not the critique of pure nonsense, as it seems to worldly men: to these the present book has charms unknown to us, who can merely receive it as a history of a stirring time, and a skilful record of men's worldly thoughts and doings. Even through these dim spectacles a man may read and profit much from Mr. Carlyle's volumes.

He is not a party historian like Scott, who could not, in his benevolent respect for rank and royalty, see duly the faults of either: he is as impartial as Thiers, but with a far loftier and nobler impartiality.

No man can have read the admirable history of the French ex-Minister who has not been struck with this equal justice which he bestows on all the parties or heroes of his book. He has completely mastered the active part of the history: he has no more partiality for court than for regicide—scarcely a movement of intriguing king or republican which is unknown to him or undescribed. He sees with equal eyes Madame Roland or Marie Antoinette—bullying Brunswick on the frontier, or Marat at his butcher's work or in his cellar—he metes to each of them justice, and no more, finding good even in butcher Marat or bullying Brunswick, and recording what he finds. What a pity that one gains such a contempt for the author of all this cleverness! Only a rogue could be so impartial, for Thiers but views this awful series of circumstances in their very meanest and basest light, like a petty, clever statesman as he is, watching with wonderful accuracy all the moves of the great game, but looking for no more, never drawing a single moral from it, or seeking to tell aught beyond it.

Mr. Carlyle, as we have said, is as impartial as the illustrious Academician and Minister; but with what different eyes he looks upon the men and the doings of this strange time! To the one the whole story is but a bustling for places—a list of battles and intrigues—of kings and governments rising and falling; to the other, the little actors of this great drama are striving but towards a great end and moral. It is better to view it loftily from afar, like our mystic poetic Mr. Carlyle, than too nearly with sharp-sighted and prosaic Thiers. Thiers is the *valet de chambre* of this history, he is too familiar with its dishabille and off-scourings: it can never be a hero to him.

It is difficult to convey to the reader a fair notion of Mr. Carlyle's powers or his philosophy, for the reader has not grown familiar with the strange style of this book, and may laugh perhaps at the grotesqueness of his teacher: in this some honest critics of the present day have preceded him, who have formed their awful judgments after scanning half a dozen lines, and damned poor Mr. Carlyle's because they chanced to be lazy. . . .

The reader, we think, will not fail to observe the real beauty which lurks among all these odd words and twisted sentences, living, as it were, in spite of the weeds; but [the book] . . . requires time and study. A first acquaintance with it is very unprepossessing, only familiarity knows its great merits, and values it accordingly. . . .

[The book] is written in an eccentric prose, here and there disfigured by grotesque conceits and images; but, for all this, it betrays most extraordinary powers—learning, observation, and humour. Above all, it has no CANT. It teems with sound, hearty, philosophy (besides certain transcendentalisms which we do not pretend to understand), it possesses genius, if any book ever did. It wanted no more for keen critics to crie fie upon it! Clever critics who have such an eye for genius, that when Mr. Bulwer published his forgotten book concerning Athens, they discovered that no historian was like to him; that he, on his Athenian hobby, had quite out-trotted stately Mr. Gibbon; and with the same creditable unanimity they cried down Mr. Carlyle's history, opening upon it a hundred little piddling sluices of small wit, destined to wash the book sheer away; and lo! the book remains, it is only the poor wit which has run dry.

[*William Makepeace Thackeray*], *in a review of "The French Revolution," in* The Times, *London, August 3, 1837, p. 6.*

[JOHN STERLING]   (essay date 1839)

[*Sterling was an English man of letters and a friend of Carlyle. Carlyle's* Life of Sterling, *considered his gentlest and most lyrical work, is a moving biography written after Sterling's death in 1844. The following excerpt presents salient points from Sterling's long, comprehensive review of the philosophy and merit of* Critical and Miscellaneous Essays *and* Sartor Resartus. *For Sterling's more personal reaction to* Sartor, *see Additional Bibliography.*]

All countries at all times require, and England perhaps at present not less than others, men having a faith at once distinct and large, the expression of what is best in their time, and having also the courage to proclaim it, and take their stand upon it. Many a one there is among us, prompted by the blind fire of feeling and the blast of conscience, who adopts fervently, even fiercely, some mode or fragment of an old creed, pushes it to all extremes, presses it on all hearers, and exhibits all the self-reliance and vehemence of a prophet, but one to whom clear vision is wanting. For where the general insight and elevation necessary in our day for an adequate view of man, exist, there must the difficulties be most keenly felt which lie in the way of any recognised tradition, or render it at least insufficient. Knowledge without belief, and belief without knowledge, divide in the main the English world between them. The apparent exceptions are generally cases of compromise, when men are content to half-believe one thing, and half-say another; for a whole belief would demand its own complete expression. And in the repeating by rote, for the sake of quiet, of popular creeds and formulas, the sense of discontent and doubt which lurks in the heart asserts itself by stammering and reluctant sighs or sneers. Semi-sincere persuasions, semi-candid declarations, make up our limbo of public opinion. There is often, perhaps most often, heart in the words; but often too— how often who dare ask? within the heart a lie.

It is not to be denied that we have also in literature and society many a man who proposes his scheme of human life and of the universe. But they almost all labour under the evil that these schemes are fatally partial or superficial. Some one breaks off a corner of our nature—calls it suggestion, or association, or self-interest, or sympathy, or pleasure and pain, or profit and loss, or the nervous system; and lifting up the fragment, says, "Behold! this is the essence of man." He builds a hut with a few stones of Thebes or Babylon in the corner of some immeasureable ruin, and exclaims, "Lo! the hundred-gated town restored—See here rebuilt the city of the great King."

As these theories, which all have their plausibility, their use, and their vestige of truth in them, take in but some small grains, but some faint shadows of what man is, therefore the living soul of man, with its longings and capacities of faith, refuses to acknowledge them. They sprung from no unfathomable depth of craving for reality, glow with no full stream of life; and accordingly they have no hold on any but the cold and recluse spinner of inferences; or the empty self-seeker of this world, who considers knowledge as ornamental, and looks at himself in the mirror, whether of glass or of human eyes, with more complacency when he can say, "I, too, am a philosopher."

Of all such pale and shrivelled theories it is the common characteristic that they belong to minds skilled more or less in dialectics and the management of terms, but poorly furnished with the large and solid stuff of human nature which should furnish the premises of their schemes. The senses indeed may be acute, and the appetites voracious, as well as the understanding quick and patient; but the breast is comparatively empty of love, of hope, of awe; the will disdains to bow under aught higher than itself; and the dead artificial parasol of self-conceit, which can be raised or lowered, opened or folded, painted and tricked out at pleasure, is substituted for the infinite concave of Heaven, beneath whose vault man walks at once humbled and inspired.

Of such speculators it is the inevitable and deadly lot that the overpowering consciousness of what is lowest and most chaotic in us, rather than of the higher and brighter—the spirit-man— supplies the materials which the intellect works on, from which it draws its thin unbroken clue of speculation. And having only this to start from and to shape with, the finer and truer the power of syllogizing, the more coherently worthless is the whole result. Of far nobler and more fruitful promise than such a man is the poor bewildered visionary, perhaps fanatic, who feels a surge of dim forces in his soul, which he cannot explain, or can only explain into something as unsubstantial as a dream. On his great world of life, now confused and dark, peace will assuredly one day descend and morning open. He will find that Paradise was preparing for him while it seemed to him that all was hell.

But in our day such visionaries are less and less possible. The spread of shallow but clear knowledge, like the cold snow-water issuing from the glaciers, daily chills and disenchants the hearts of millions once credulous. Daily, therefore, does it become more probable that millions will follow in the tract of those who are called their betters. Thus will they find in the world nothing but an epicurean stye, to be managed, with less dirt and better food, by patent steam-machinery; but still a place for swine, though now the swine may be washed, and their victuals more equally divided.

Is it not then strange that in such a world, in such a country, and among those light-hearted Edinburgh Reviewers, a man should rise and proclaim a creed; not a new and more ingenious form of words, but a truth to be embraced with the whole heart, and in which the heart shall find as his has found, strength for all combats, and consolation, though stern not festal, under all sorrows? Amid the masses of English printing sent forth every day, part designed for the most trivial entertainment, part black with the narrowest and most lifeless sectarian dogmatism, part, and perhaps the best, exhibiting only facts and theories in physical science, and part filled with the vulgarest economical projects and details, which would turn all life into a process of cookery, culinary, political, or sentimental—how few writings are there that contain like [*Critical and Miscellaneous Essays*] a distinct doctrine as to the position and calling of man, capable of affording nourishment to the heart and support to the will, and in harmony at the same time with the social state of the world, and with the most enlarged and brightened insight which human wisdom has yet attained to?

We have been so little prepared to look for such an appearance that it is difficult for us to realize the conception of a genuine coherent view of life thus presented to us in a book of our day, which shall be neither a slight compendium of a few moral truisms, flavoured with a few immoral refinements and paradoxes, such as constitute the floating ethics and religion of the time; nor a fierce and gloomy distortion of some eternal idea torn from its pure sphere of celestial light to be raved about by the ignorant whom it has half-enlightened, and half made frantic. But here, in our judgment—that is, in the judgment of one man who speaks considerately what he fixedly believes— we have the thought of a wide, and above all, of a deep soul, which has expressed, in fitting words, the fruits of patient reflection, of piercing observation, of knowledge many-sided and conscientious, of devoutest awe, and faithfullest love. (pp. 1-3)

For professed philosophers, knowledge is the end of existence. They live in order to think. The universe presents itself to them as a conflux of forces, subter-human, human, and superhuman, working to the perpetual production and sustenance of a bound-less living whole, which it is their special vocation to apprehend and contemplate, and so to rise to the view of the primordial truth, which originates and lights up all. Now with Mr Carlyle this is not the case. He casts aside all slighter and more partial theories than those matured by these great thinkers, as insuf-ficient for the spirit of a wise man in our day. But by him the best wisdom is valued as a means of the best work. To know is not his end, but to be. He seeks to be wise in order to be worthy; and by the same measure strives to judge whatever representation or fact of human life is brought before him. To struggle manfully in doing the highest work within our power, at all costs of outward contradiction; to be consistent and com-plete in a true purpose, down to the most trifling detail of every day, word, and thought; and to live thus, not by calculation, with pedantic self-conscious accuracy, but by dint of an im-pulse of heroism and conviction energizing in the whole char-acter, and moulding it altogether;—this is the task which in his view is given to man.

Therefore to the noblest of mere philosophers he stands related somewhat in this way:—The speculative seer, if of a high and genuine order, must needs, by spiritual instinct, regard the universe as a divine vision, and the reason as an inspired organ for beholding this; which is equally the implicit faith of phi-losopher, poet, and hero. But the sage is by nature and purpose also a dialectician, and labours to define the primal truth he sees; to pursue it into all its ramifications; and show that these afford, or indeed are, the true solution of all the facts and classes of facts, which direct observation discloses to all men, but which it cannot interpret. Now the systematic process of ratiocination is one from which Mr Carlyle turns with com-parative indifference. He values the master truth of the phi-losopher, not as an idea to be worked upon, and minutely evolved by the understanding, but to be taken into the character and affections, to rule the will, and to shape and glorify the whole structure of the man and of his life.

Neither does he exactly resemble the poets, in whom he so much delights, and whose worth he has so keenly insisted on. These men, especially Goethe, Schiller, and Jean Paul, but also all great creative singers, having a true insight into the wondrousness and depth of things, and the harmony in which they grow together in the midst of conflicts and jarrings which are themselves essential to this harmony—do not make it their business to unfold the idea of it as an object of speculation. Neither do they directly labour to realize it more evidently in practice and fact. But stirred and enlightened by it, and filled from it with a breath of its melodious joy, they shape its images as given them from without, and new-born within their souls, into fresh and fair semblances that reproduce in partial shows of the whole, a more vocal and facile display of its true being.

Jane Carlyle in 1854.

Their own delight in the beauty and worth of real existence pours itself into their reproduction of it. Aiming neither at teaching men as the philosopher, nor at exciting and organizing them anew on a nobler model, as the practical hero,—they do indirectly impart their own living consciousness of truth, and draw men, without exhorting them, towards the higher regions where the poet dwells rejoicing.

Such is not the case with Mr Carlyle; he does not rest at ease in the contemplation of fair pictures of life, leaving them to find their own reception, and work silently their own vague effect upon mankind. The practical problem and struggle of Man entirely possesses him. With its force he speaks, towards its aim he works. He seldom relaxes to enjoy the aspect of images, however beautiful, however familiar to his heart, un-less they have a direct significance and efficiency for this end. And finding no sufficient peace in the music of sweet song, he loves the resounding lyre which builds up the walls of cities, or the blast of the trumpet which throws them down.

Not that he wants poetry any more than philosophy. But they are his wings and not his heaven. His heart and mouth are full of them, but they are not the springs of his existence. The man among the Germans, whose works at first sight his undoubtedly the most resemble, is that strange, huge mass of lambent, innocuous fire, full of gas-jets and grotesque tongues, and salamanders and flaming eyes—Jean Paul Richter. They are like, in the apparent rudeness, harshness, lawless capricious-ness of style; full of meanings and images, but these looking incoherent, or at least as yet unreconciled. Both constantly use words sanctioned by no custom or even precedent, and, of course, though often expressive, sometimes not compensating for their oddness by any special felicity. In both it looks as if there were strong, nay overpowering, self-will and self-consciousness. The thought, as well as speech, often finds its sufficient explanation in the peculiarities of individual character, rather than in the demands and laws of the matter handled. In neither is there much exercise of skill in logical abstractions, and their discipline; or much clear delineation of objects, uncoloured by the particular and casual feelings of the artist. As to their views of human life they have also much in common. The ground in both appears to be furnished by a deep and fervid sense of whatever is noblest and fairest in man's active powers,—and this realized not only in the imaginative consciousness, but in the personal character of each. Alike they shrink with even fastidious and self-complacent vivacity from all the forms, blazonries, and authorities of social existence, when these happen to be insufficiently supported by the worth of the men whom Nature's habitual irony has thus dignified. A fine and genuine, nay stern and sublime, enthusiasm, a puritanic Quixotism, for the lovely, the true, the right, the everlasting,—is heightened and softened in both by the perpetual presence of a graver than Cervantean humour, which blends with and repeats the lofty feeling in a mode of kindred contrast. Both the German and the Englishman use whatever portions and aspects of the phenomenal world they advert to, neither for their simple and direct beauty, nor as facts having their meaning and purport in themselves; but as hints and whispers of a higher and unseen world, the proper abode of man. In each there is a fulness and warmth of nature, which would suffice to place them among the sacred band, the immortals of history. And in each also there is something unfashioned, excessive, tumultuous, far indeed from the vulgar chaotic fury and darkness of passions and prejudices, but still at war with the brightness and heavenly peace which are rather suggested and promised to the heart than made apparent to the eye. (pp. 8-10)

The clearness of the eye to see whatever is permanent and substantial, and the fervour and strength of heart to love it as the sole good of life, are . . . , in our view, Mr Carlyle's pre-eminent characteristics, as those of every man entitled to the fame of the most generous order of greatness. Not to paint the good which he sees and loves, or see it painted, and enjoy the sight; not to understand it, and exult in the knowledge of it; but to take his position upon it, and for it alone to breathe, to move, to fight, to mourn, and die—this is the destination which he has chosen for himself. His avowal of it and exhortation to do the like is the object of all his writings. (p. 11)

[Neither] is for him the solid, abiding, inexhaustible, that merely which is received as such by popular acquiescence. It must needs be a truth which the spirit, cleared and strengthened by manifold knowledge and experience, and above all, by strong and steadfast endeavour, can rest in, and say: This I mean, not because it is told me, were my informants all the schools of Rabbins or a hierarchy of angels; but because I have looked into it, tried it, found it healthful and sufficient, and thus know that it will stand the stress of life. We may be right or wrong in our estimate of Mr Carlyle, but we cannot be mistaken in supposing that on this kind of anvil have all truly great men been fashioned, and of metal thus honest and enduring.

Further, it must be said, that true as is his devotion to the truth, so flaming and cordial is his hatred of the false, in whatever shapes and names delusions may show themselves. Affectations, quackeries, tricks, frauds, swindlings commercial or literary, baseless speculations, loud ear-catching rhetoric, melo-

dramatic sentiment, moral drawlings and hyperboles, religious cant, clever political shifts, and conscious or half-conscious fallacies, all in his view, come under the same hangman's rubric,—proceed from the same offal heart. However plausible, popular and successful, however dignified by golden and purple names, they are lies against ourselves,—against whatever in us is not altogether reprobate and infernal. His great argument, theme of his song, spirit of his language, lies in this, that there is a work for man worth doing, which is to be done with the whole of his heart, not the half or any other fraction. Therefore, if any reserve be made, any corner kept for something unconnected with this true work and sincere purpose, the whole is thereby vitiated and accurst. So far as his arm reaches he is undoing whatever in nature is holy; ruining whatever is the real creation of the great worker of all. This truth of purpose is to the soul what life is to the body of man; that which unites and organizes the mass, keeping all the parts in due proportion and concord, and restraining them from sudden corruption into worthless dust.

From this turn of mind and ground-plan of conviction it follows, that to Mr Carlyle the objects of chief interest are memorable persons—men who have fought strongly the good fight. And more especially, though not exclusively, does he revere and study those living nearest to our own time and circumstances, in whom we may find monumental examples of the mode in which our difficulties are to be conquered. These men he rejoices, and eminently succeeds, in delineating; in enabling us to see what is essential and physiognomical in each, and how the facts of nature and society favoured and opposed the formation of his life into a large completeness. The hindrances such a man had to overcome, the energies by which he vanquished them, and the work, whatever it may have been, which he thus accomplished for mankind, appear in these pictures with lucid clearness, marked with a force and decision of hand and style worthy of the greatest masters.

Thus having taken anxious measure of the perplexities and dangers of human life in its higher progresses, he has learnt also to pity, with a mother's tenderness, the failings and confusions of those against whom these hostile forces have prevailed. His proudest and most heroic odes in honour of the conquerors are mingled with or followed by some strain of pity for those who have fallen and been swallowed up in the conflict. The dusky millions of human shapes that flit around us, and in history stream away, fill him with an almost passionate sorrow. Their hunger and nakedness, their mistakes, terrors, pangs, and ignorances, press upon his soul like personal calamities. Of him, more than of all other English writers, perhaps writers of any country, it is true, that not in words and fits of rhetorical sentiment, but in the foundation of his being, man, however distant and rude a shadow, is to him affecting, venerable, full of a divine strength, which, for the most part, is rather cramped and tortured than ripened to freedom in this fleshly life and world. This kind of feeling must be felt as truly distinguishing him by all who read his works. For though similar expressions to some of his have been used by many, from no one, at least in our language, have they proceeded with so resolute and grand a force of radiant clearness and adamantine conviction. (pp. 12-13)

[Anyone] who should take up [Carlyle's writings] . . . would doubtless be startled at the strangeness of the style which prevails more or less throughout them. They are not careless, headlong, passionate, confused; but they bear a constant look of oddity which seems at first mere wilful wantonness, and which we only afterwards find to be the discriminating stamp of original and strong feeling. . . . [His] sensibilities are burning with a slow, immense fire, kindled by the very theme on which he writes, and compelling him to write. The greatness and weakness, the infinite hopes and unquenchable reality of human life; the aching pressure of the body and its wants on the myriads of millions in whom celestial force sleeps and dreams of hell; the sight of follies, frauds, cruelties, and lascivious luxury in the midst of a race thus endowed and thus suffering; and the unconquerable will and thought with which the few work out the highest calling of all men; these it is, and not self-indulging distresses and theatrical aspirations of his own, which boil and storm within. Therefore does he speak with the solid strength and energy which gives so serious, and rugged an aspect to his sentences; while, perpetually checking himself, from a wise man's shame at excessive emotion, and from the knowledge that others will but half sympathize with him, he adds to his most weighty utterances a turn of irony which relieves the excessive strain.

It must also be considered that, having looked piercingly and bravely into the doings of the world, and found much thereof false, and much more only half true, he is constantly led to speak of things either held in esteem or blandly tolerated, and to convey his knowledge of their worthlessness in a tone of quiet, deliberate scorn, which couples itself in friendly dissonance with his fervid worship of many a ragged, outcast heroism;—as the answer of an Arab Sheik to the messenger of a Pasha requiring the free son of the desert to pay tribute, compared with his welcome to his tents of the naked, wandering stranger.

Add to this, that Mr Carlyle's resolution to convey his meaning at all hazards, makes him seize the most effectual and sudden words in spite of usage and fashionable taste: and that, therefore, when he can get a brighter tint, a more expressive form, by means of some strange—we must call it—Carlylism; English, Scotch, German, Greek, Latin, French, Technical, Slang, American, or Lunar, or altogether superlunar, transcendental, and drawn from the eternal Nowhere,—he uses it with a courage which might blast an academy of lexicographers into a Hades, void even of vocables. (pp. 21-2)

Furthermore, it may be observed, on the choice of words shown in this author's writings, that his clear and irresistible eye for the substantial and significant in all objects, and his carelessness of the merely abstract, show themselves in an immediateness and prominence of expression, to which we see nothing in its kind equal in modern English books. His style is not so much a figured as an embossed one. The shapes which it exhibits have not only neatness and strength, which those of a clever rhetorician often have; but a truth and life, which show them to be prompted by the writer's feeling and experience of things, and not arranged from a calculation of what will be the effect on others. (p. 23)

Among the works of Mr Carlyle, there is one fiction—*Sartor Resartus—The Life and Opinions of Herr Teufelsdröckh*. This consists of two intertwisted threads, though both spun off the same distaff, and of the same crimson wool. There is a fragmentary, though, when closely examined, a complete biography of a supposed German professor, and, along with it, portions of a supposed treatise of his on the philosophy of clothes. Of the three books, the first is preparatory, and gives a portrait of the hero and his circumstances. The second is the biographical account of him. The third, under the rubric of

extracts from his work, presents us with his picture of human life in the nineteenth century.

How so unexampled a topic as the philosophy of clothes can be made the vehicle for a philosophy of man, those will see who read the book. But they must read with the faith that, in spite of all appearances to the contrary, it is the jest which is a pretence, and that the real purport of the whole is serious, yea, serious as any religion that ever was preached, far more serious than most battles that have ever been fought since Agamemnon declared war against Priam. (pp. 52-3)

In this book that strange style appears again before us in its highest oddity. Thunder peals, flute-music, the laugh of Pan and the nymphs, the clear disdainful whisper of cold stoicism, and the hurly-burly of a country fair, succeed and melt into each other. Again the clamour sinks into quiet, and we hear at last the grave, mild hymn of devotion, sounding from a far sanctuary, though only in faint and dying vibrations. So from high to low, from the sublime to the most merely trivial, fluctuates the feeling of the poet. Now in a Vulcan's cave of rock, with its smoke and iron tools, and gold and rubies; now in dismal mines and dens, and now in fairy bowers, shifting to the vulgarest alleys of stifling cities; yet do we always feel that there is a mystic influence around us, bringing out into sharp homely clearness what is noblest in the remote and infinite, exalting into wonder what is commonest in the dust and toil of every day. In this enchanted island, Prospero, the man of serene art, rules indeed supreme, and has his bidding lightly done, but oftener by a band of shaggy Calibans than by a choir of melodious Ariels. And it is most bewildering of all—for is not the common that which, by disclosing its strangeness, has ever the greatest power to amaze us?—that the Prospero is a man of our age, in our familiar garb, with no magic instruments but the words we all use. Even the Calibans and Ariels of the vision are the dull, customary tribe—peasant, artisan, gentleman, and lady, whom we know by rote as the obvious alphabet of our lives.

'Tis weird work all. If Jean Paul presents to us milk and wine, here, instead of wine, is alcohol and something more, and the milk what one might fancy not of a cow, but a she-mammoth.

Hopeless is the contrast, the contradiction which the book at first presents to all our common world, its laws, and usages, and familiar insignificance. Nothing beautiful is here; nothing calmly, manifestly wise. We look at it not for its worth, but its oddity. Gradually the eye learns to find some dawning coherence and stability, as if it were not merely mist. Then one entanglement untwists itself after another; joint and lineament, plan and structure, appear, intricate indeed, but palpable. At last we cross ourselves, and know not whether to laugh or weep when we find that we were puzzled, not by the want of aught real and substantial in the object, but by the presence of so many more forms of truth and nature than we commonly discern in life; and which yet, although we knew them not, were ever there. These shadows, too, now no longer illusive, are all compacted by their own vital unity, which excludes the unmeaning and alien, and brings the expressive and lasting elements of our time and being, however seemingly discordant, into smooth, indissoluble conjunction. In what seemed a fair-booth, half smoke, half canvass, full of puppets, toys, dolls, refuse trinkets, peering vaguely through thick confusion, there is discovered to be implied nothing less than a model, and that a living one, of the world itself, such as God in his eternity, and man in his six thousand years, have made it. The image is not indeed complete, but broad, full, bright, and most genuine, created and imparted by an earnest soul, to which nothing that lives and grows, and is not a mere idle falsehood, comes as worthless. It is, in fine, a system of highest philosophy in figures of liveliest truth, and wanting only—though this is not a small want—the soft musical roundness and honeyed flow of song, to be a poem such as these latter days of English song have not produced.

Much there is that at the tenth, no less than at the first perusal, must seem affected, arbitrary, and little more than mere burlesque. But the law which unites the capacity for all that is highest and most beautiful with the tendency to see meaning in the commonest, even sordid things—and the experience of all strongest hearts that they must often needs escape, if they would not break upon the spot, from the fierce immensity of feeling into the homely fire-side circle of the ludicrously vulgar,—these (which to no one knowing what is in man, and not merely what comes out of him, can be unknown truths) explain so many seeming anomalies and discords, that all the rest may well be believed equally fitting, or if not, yet but pardonably wrong.

There are, indeed, persons of high faculties and excellent cultivation, to whom a limited, conventional rather than convictional, standard, will make the whole distasteful. But, blessed be that endless dawning which for ever discloses more and more of the eternal within the narrow bounds of time, this temper is ceasing to be that of our age. Those who read the book for the worth that is in it, will assuredly not miss their reward. (pp. 53-5)

The book is the most extraordinary mixture we know of the purest and rarest truth with much truth in itself of equal depth, but here exaggerated into not merely hyperbolical phrases—of which, indeed, there is little if anything—but hyperbolical opinions; opinions, that is, which have fallen over the battlements they were placed to defend, and been dashed into separate pieces or confused lumps. Any man who, although thus erring, at the same time utters much and original wisdom and poetry, is of course a person of strong abilities, and, if all is done with unaffected earnestness, must be of strong character also. Here purpose and faculty, will and talents, are combined and exist in friendly union, and all in the highest vigour; and it is not the least charm of the book that it supplies some seminal hints on the mode in which a mind so marked and so capacious has been formed and ripened. Nay, a zealous student will often be inclined to suspect that, in Teufelsdröckh, a British biography looks through the widely different and much exaggerated mask of a German one. (pp. 57-8)

Here must end our remarks on the admirable writings of a great man. Could it be hoped, that by what has been said, any readers, and especially any thinkers, will be led to give them the attention they require, but also deserve, in this there would be ample repayment, even were there not at all events a higher reward, for the labour, which is not a slight one, of forming and asserting distinct opinions on a matter so singular and so complex. For few bonds that unite human beings are purer or happier than a common understanding and reverence of what is truly wise and beautiful. This also is religion. Standing at the threshold of these works, we may imitate the saying of the old philosopher to the friends who visited him on their return from the temples—Let us enter, for here too are gods. (p. 68)

[*John Sterling*], in a review of "*Critical and Miscellaneous Essays*," in The London and Westminster Review, *Vol. XXXIII, No. 1, October, 1839, pp. 1-68.*

[WILLIAM HENRY SMITH]   (essay date 1843)

[*Smith surveys Carlyle's writings to date, noting destructive critical technique, partiality, and stylistic eccentricity as the author's primary weaknesses, moral intent and integrity as his prevailing strengths.*]

Mr Carlyle—an astute and trenchant critic might, with show of justice, remark—assumes to be the reformer and castigator of his age—a reformer in philosophy, in politics, in religion—denouncing its *mechanical* method of thinking, deploring its utter want of *faith*, and threatening political society, obstinately deaf to the voice of wisdom, with the retributive horrors of repeated revolutions; and yet neither in philosophy, in religion, nor in politics, has Mr Carlyle any distinct dogma, creed, or constitution to promulgate. The age is irreligious, he exclaims, and the vague feeling of the impenetrable mystery which encompasses us, is all the theology we can gather from him; civil society, with its laws and government, is in a false and perilous position, and for all relief and reformation, he launches forth an indisputable morality—precepts of charity, and self-denial, and strenuous effort—precepts most excellent, and only *too* applicable; applicable, unfortunately, after an *à priori* fashion—for if men would but obey them, there had been need of few laws, and of no remedial measures.

This man of faith—our critic might continue—has but one everlasting note; and it is really the most sceptical and melancholy that has ever been heard, or heard with toleration, in our literature. He repeats it from his favourite apostle Goethe; "all doubt is to be cured only—by action." Certainly, if *forgetting* the doubt, and the subject of doubt, be the sole cure for it. But that other advice which Mr Carlyle tells us was given, and in vain, to George Fox, the Quaker, at a time when he was agitated by doubts and perplexities, namely, "to drink beer and dance with the girls," was of the very same stamp, and would have operated in the very same manner, to the removing of the pious Quaker's doubts. Faith! ye lack faith! cries this prophet in our streets; and when reproved and distressed scepticism enquires where truth is to be found, he bids it back to the loom or the forge, to its tools and its workshop, of whatever kind these may be—there to forget the enquiry.

The religion, or, if he pleases, the formula of religion, which helps to keep men sober and orderly, Mr Carlyle despises, ridicules; "old clothes!" he cries, empty and ragged. It is not till a man has risen into frenzy, or some hot fanaticism, that he deserves his respect. An Irving, when his noble spirit, kindled to fever heat, is seized with delirium, becomes worthy of some admiration. A Cromwell is pronounced emphatically to have believed in a God, and *therefore* to have been "by far the remarkablest governor we have had here for the last five centuries or so." Meanwhile, is it the faith of an Irving, or the God of a Cromwell, that our subtle-minded author would have us adopt, or would adopt himself? If he scorn the easy, methodical citizen, who plods along the beaten tracks of life, looking occasionally, in his demure, self-satisfied manner, upwards to the heavens, but with no other result than to plod more perseveringly along his very earthy track, it follows not that there is any one order of fanatic spirits with whom he would associate, to whose theology he would yield assent. Verily, no. He demands faith—he gives no creed. What is it *you* teach? a plain-speaking man would exclaim; where is your church? have you also your thirty-nine articles? have you nine? have you *one* stout article of creed that will bear the rubs of fortune—bear the temptations of prosperity or a dietary system—stand both sunshine and the wind—which will keep virtue steady when disposed to reel, and drive back crime to her penal caverns of remorse? What would you answer, O philosopher! if a simple body should ask you, quite in confidence, where wicked people go to?

Were it not better for those to whom philosophy has brought the sad necessity of doubt, to endure this also patiently and silently, as one of the inevitable conditions of human existence? Were not this better than to rail incessantly against the world, for a want of that sentiment which *they* have no means to excite or to authorize?

The same inconsequence in politics. We have *Chartism* preached by one not a Chartist—by one who has no more his *five points* of Radicalism than his five points of Calvinistic divinity—who has no trust in democracy, who swears by no theory of representative government—who will never believe that a multitude of men, foolish and selfish, will elect the disinterested and the wise. Your constitution, your laws, your "horse-haired justice" that sits in Westminster Hall, he likes them not; but he propounds himself no scheme of polity. Reform yourselves, one and all, ye individual men! and the nation will be reformed; practise justice, charity, self-denial, and then all mortals may work and eat. This is the most distinct advice he bestows. Alas! it is advice such as this that the Christian preacher, century after century, utters from his pulpit, which he makes the staple of his eloquence, and which he and his listeners are contented to applaud; and the more contented probably to applaud, as, on all hands, it is tacitly understood to be far *too good* to be practised.

In fine, turn which way you will, to philosophy, to politics, to religion, you find Mr Carlyle objecting, denouncing, scoffing, rending all to pieces in his bold, reckless, ironical, manner—but *teaching* nothing. The most docile pupil, when he opens his tablets to put down the precious sum of wisdom he has learned, pauses—finds his pencil motionless, and leaves his tablet still a blank.

Now all this, and more of the same kind, which our astute and trenchant critic might urge, may be true, or very like the truth, but it is not the whole truth.

"To speak a little pedantically," says our author himself, in a paper called **"Signs of the Times,"**

> there is a science of *Dynamics* in man's fortune and nature, as well as of *Mechanics*. There is a science which treats of, and practically addresses, the primary, unmodified, forces and energies of man, the mysterious springs of love, and fear, and wonder, of enthusiasm, poetry—religion, all which have a truly vital and *infinite* character; as well as a science which practically addresses the finite, modified developments of these, when they take the shape of immediate 'motives,' as hope of reward, or as fear of punishment. Now it is certain, that in former times the wise men, the enlightened lovers of their kind, who appeared generally as moralists, poets, or priests, did, without neglecting the mechanical province, deal chiefly with the dynamical; applying themselves chiefly to regulate, increase, and purify, the inward primary powers of man; and fancying that herein lay the main difficulty, and the best service they could undertake.

In such *Dynamics* it is that Mr Carlyle deals. To speak in our own plain common-place diction, it is to the elements of all religious feeling, to the broad unalterable principles of morality, that he addresses himself; stirring up in the minds of his readers those sentiments of reverence to the Highest, and of

justice to all, even to the lowest, which can never utterly die out in any man, but which slumber in the greater number of us. It is by no means necessary to teach any peculiar or positive doctrine in order to exert an influence on society. After all, there is a moral heart beating at the very centre of this world. Touch *it*, and there is a responsive movement through the whole system of the world. Undoubtedly external circumstances rule in their turn over this same central pulsation: alter, arrange, and modify, these external circumstances as best you can, but he who, by the *word* he speaks or writes, can reach this central pulse immediately—is he idle, is he profitless? (pp. 121-22)

It is not by teaching this or that dogma, political, philosophical, or religious, that Mr Carlyle is doing his *work,* and exerting an influence, by no means despicable, on his generation. It is by producing a certain moral tone of thought, of a stern, manly, energetic, self-denying character, that his best influence consists. Accordingly we are accustomed to view his works, even when they especially regard communities of men, and take the name of histories, as, in effect, appeals to the individual heart, and to the moral will of the reader. His mind is not legislative; his mode of thinking is not systematic; a state economy he has not the skill, perhaps not the pretension, to devise. When he treats of nations, and governments, and revolutions of states, he views them all as a wondrous picture, which he, the observer, standing apart, watches and apostrophizes; still revealing *himself* in his reflections upon them. The picture *to the eye,* he gives with marvellous vividness; and he puts forth, with equal power, that sort of world-wide reflection which a thinking being might be supposed to make on his first visit to our planet; but the space between—those intermediate generalizations which make the pride of the philosophical historian—he neglects, has no taste for. Such a writer as Montesquieu he holds in manifest antipathy. His *History of the French Revolution,* like his *Chartism,* like the work now before us, his *Past and Present,* is still an appeal to the consciousness of each man, and to the high and eternal laws of justice and of charity—lo, ye are brethren! . . .

It accords with the view we have here taken of the writings of Mr Carlyle, that of all his works that which pleased us most was the one most completely *personal* in its character, which most constantly kept the reader in a state of self-reflection. In spite of all its oddities and vagaries, and the chaotic shape into which its materials have been thrown, the *Sartor Resartus* is a prime favourite of ours—a sort of volcanic work; and the reader stands by, with folded arms, resolved at all events to secure peace within his own bosom. But no sluggard's peace; his arms are folded, not for idleness, only to repress certain vain tremors and vainer sighs. He feels the calm of self-renunciation, but united with no monkish indolence. (p. 123)

Many a man in his hour of depression, when resolution is sicklied over by the pale cast of thought, will find, in the writings of Carlyle, a freshening stimulant, better than the wine-cup, or even the laughter of a friend, can give. In some of his biographical sketches, with what force has he brought out the moral resolution which animated, or ought to have animated, the man of whom he is writing! (p. 124)

The *History of the French Revolution* deserves, no doubt, notwithstanding the sort of partiality we have intimated for its wild predecessor, to be considered as the greatest work of Mr Carlyle; but it is the work of which criticism, if she ventures to speak at all, must speak with the loudest and most frequent protests. There are certain grave objections which cannot be got over. As to the *style,* indeed, Mr Carlyle is, on this head, (except, occasionally, when writing for some *Review* in which a very violent departure from the English language would not be advisable,) far above all criticism. The attempt to censure the oddities with which it abounds—the frequent repetition—the metaphor and allusion used again and again till the page is covered with a sort of slang—would only subject the critic himself to the same kind of ridicule that would fall upon the hapless wight who should bethink him of taking some Shandean work gravely to task for its scandalous irregularities, and utter want of methodical arrangement. Such is *Carlylism;* and this is all that can be said upon the matter. But the style which seemed not altogether unnatural, and far from intolerable, in Herr Teufelsdrockh, becomes a strangely inconvenient medium of communication where a whole history is to be told in it. The mischief is, that it admits of no safe middle path: it must arrest attention for its novelty, its graphic power, its bold originality; or it must offend by its newfangled phrase, its jerking movement, and its metaphor and allusion reduced into a slang. Meanwhile, there is so much in a history which needs only to be told—so much, which even this author, *skip* how he may, must relate, for the sake merely of preserving a continuous narrative—and where the perfection of style would be, as all the world knows, that it should draw no attention whatever to itself. A style like this of our author's, once assumed, cannot be laid down for a moment; and the least important incident is related with the same curiosity of diction, and the same startling manner, that delighted us in the *Siege of the Bastile.* To convey mere *information,* it seems quite unserviceable. (p. 125)

The basis of a history is surely, after all, the narrative, and whatever may be the estimate of others, the *historian* proceeds on the supposition that the facts he has to relate are, for their own sake, deserving to be had in remembrance. If not, why is he there recording and verifying them? But Mr Carlyle proceeds throughout on quite the contrary supposition, that the fact for itself is worth nothing—that it is valuable only as it presents some peculiar picture to the imagination, or kindles some noteworthy reflection. He maintains throughout the attitude of one who stands apart, looking *at* the history; rarely does he assume the patient office of that scribe whom we remember to have seen in the frontispiece of our school histories, recording faithfully what the bald headed Time, sitting between his scythe and his hour-glass, was dictating.

Never, indeed, was history written in so mad a vein—and that not only as regards style, but the prevailing mood of mind in which the facts and characters are scanned. That mood is for the most part ironical. There is philanthropy, doubtless, at the bottom of it all; but a mocking spirit, a profound and pungent irony, are the manifest and prevailing characteristics. It is a philanthropy which has borrowed the manner of Mephistopheles. It is a modern Diogenes—in fact it is Diogenes Teufelsdrockh himself, surveying the Revolution from his solitary watch-tower, where he sits so near the eternal skies, that a whole generation of men, *whirling off in wild Sahara waltz into infinite space,* is but a spectacle, and a very brief and confused one. This lofty irony, pungent as it is, grows wearisome. By throwing a littleness on all things, it even destroys the very aliment it feeds on; nothing, at last, is worth the mocking. But the weariness it occasions is not its greatest fault. It leads to a most unjust and capricious estimate of the characters and actions of men. Capricious it must, of necessity, become. To be ironical always was insufferable; even for the sake of artistical effect, some personages, and some events, must be treated with a natural feeling of respect or abhorrence;

yet if one murder is to be recorded with levity, why not another?—if one criminal is to be dismissed with a jest, levelled perhaps at some personal oddity, why is an earnest indignation to be bestowed on the next criminal that comes under notice? The distinctions that will be made will be not fair judgments, but mere favouritism. Situated thus—plain moral distinctions having been disparaged—Mr Carlyle has given way to his admiration of a certain *energy* of character, and makes the possession of this sole excellence the condition of his favour, the title to his respect, or perhaps, we should say, to an immunity from his contempt. The man who has an *eye*—that is, who glares on you like a tiger—he who, in an age of revolution, is most thoroughly revolutionary, and *swallows all formulas*—he is made a hero, and honourable mention is decreed to him; whilst all who acted with an ill-starred moderation, who strove, with ineffectual but conscientious effort, to stay the wild movement of the revolution, are treated with derision, are dismissed with contempt, or at best with pity for their *weakness.* (pp. 125-26)

Well may *energy* or *will* stand in the place of goodness with Mr Carlyle, since we find him making . . . this strange paradoxical statement: "*Bad* is by its nature negative, and can do *nothing;* whatsoever enables us to *do* any thing is by its very nature *good.*" So that such a thing as a *bad deed* cannot exist, and such an expression is without meaning. Accordingly, not only is energy applauded, but that energy applauded most that *does most.* Those who exercised their power, and the utmost resolution of mind, in the attempt to restrain the Revolution, are not to be put in comparison with those who *did something*—who carried forward the revolutionary movement. . . .

But what criticism has to say in *praise* of this extraordinary work, let it not be said with stint or timidity. The bold glance *at* the Revolution, taken from his Diogenes' station, and the vivid descriptions of its chief scenes, are unrivalled.

That many a page sorely tries the reader's patience is acknowledged, and we might easily fill column after column with extracts, to show that the style of Mr Carlyle, especially when it is necessary for him to descend to the common track of history, can degenerate into a mannerism scarce tolerable, for which no term of literary censure would be too severe. We have, however, no disposition to make any such extracts; and our readers, we are sure, would have little delight in perusing them. On the other hand, when he does succeed, great is the glory thereof. . . . (p. 127)

[It is time that we turned to *Past and Present*], the perusal of which has led us to these remarks upon Mr Carlyle. We were desirous, however, of forming something like a general estimate of his merits and demerits before we entered upon any account of his last production. (p. 129)

Past and Present, if it does not enhance, ought not, we think, to diminish from the reputation of its author; but as a *mannerism* becomes increasingly disagreeable by repetition, we suspect that, without having less merit, this work will have less popularity than its predecessors. The style is the same "motley wear," and has the same jerking movement—seems at times a thing of shreds and patches hung on wires—and is so full of brief allusions to his own previous writings, that to a reader unacquainted with these it would be scarce intelligible. With all this it has the same vigour, and produces the same vivid impression that always attends upon his writings. Here, as elsewhere, he pursues his author-craft with a right noble and independent spirit, striking manifestly for truth, and for no other cause; and here also, as elsewhere, he leaves his side unguarded, open to unavoidable attack, so that the most blundering critic cannot fail to hit right, and the most friendly cannot spare.

The *past* is represented by a certain Abbot Samson, and his abbey of St Edmunds. . . . Our author will look, he tells us, face to face on this remote period, "in hope of perhaps illustrating our own poor century thereby." Very good. To get a station in the past, and therefrom view the present, is no ill-devised scheme. But Abbot Samson and his monks form a very limited, almost a domestic picture, which supplies but few points of contrast or similitude with our "own poor century," which, at all events, is very rich in point of view. When, therefore, he proceeds to discuss the worldwide topics of our own times, we soon lose all memory of the Abbot and his monastery, who seems indeed to have as little connexion with the difficulties of our position, as the statues of Gog and Magog in Guildhall with the decision of some election contest which is made to take place in their venerable presence. On one point only can any palpable contrast be exhibited, namely, between the religious spirit of his times and our own.

Now, here, as on every topic where a comparison is attempted, what must strike every one is, the manifest partiality Mr Carlyle shows to the past, and the unfair preference he gives it over the present. Nothing but respect and indulgence when he revisits the monastery of St Edmunds; nothing but censure and suspicion when he enters, say, for instance, the precincts of Exeter Hall. Well do we know, that if Mr Carlyle could meet such a monk alive, as he here treats with so much deference, encounter him face to face, talk to him, and hear him talk; he and the monk would be intolerable to each other. (pp. 129-30)

Mr Carlyle censures our poor century for its lack of faith; yet the kind of faith it possesses, which has grown up in it, which is *here* at this present, he has no respect for, treats with no manner of tenderness. What *other* would he have? He deals out to it no measure of philosophical justice. He accepts the faith of every age but his own. He will accept, as the best thing possible, the trustful and hopeful spirit of dark and superstitious periods; but if the more enlightened piety of his own age be at variance even with the most subtle and difficult tenets of his own philosophy, he will make no compromise with it, he casts it away for contemptuous infidelity to trample on as it pleases. When visiting the past, how indulgent, kind, and considerate he is! . . . But when he turns from the past to the present, all this charity and indulgence are at an end. He finds in his own mechanico-philosophical age a faith in accordance with its prevailing modes of thought—a faith lying at the foundation of whatever else of doctrinal theology it possesses—a faith diffused over all society, and taught not only in churches and chapels to pious auditories, but in every lecture-room, and by scientific as well as theological instructors—a faith in God, as creator of the universe, as the demonstrated author, architect, originator, of this wondrous world; and lo! this same philosopher who looked with encouraging complacency on Abbot Samson bending in adoration over the exhumed remains of a fellow mortal, and who listens without a protest to the cries of sanguinary enthusiasm, rising from a throng of embattled Christians, steps disdainfully aside from this faith of a peaceful and scientific age; he has some subtle, metaphysical speculations that will not countenance it; he demands that a faith in God should be put on some other foundation, which foundation, unhappily, his countrymen, as yet unskilled in transcendental metaphisics, cannot apprehend; he withdraws his sympathy

from the so trite and sober-minded belief of an industrious, experimental, ratiocinating generation, and cares not if they have a God at all, if they can only make his existence evident to themselves from some commonplace notion of design and prearrangement visible in the world. (pp. 130-31)

Do we ask Mr Carlyle to falsify his own transcendental philosophy for the sake of his weaker brethren? By no means. Let him proceed on the "high *à priori* road," if he finds it—as not many do—practicable. Let men, at all times, when they write as philosophers, speak out simply what they hold to be truth. It is his *partiality* only that we here take notice of, and the different measure that he deals out to the past and the present. Out of compliment to a bygone century he can sink philosophy, and common sense too; when it might be something more than a compliment to the existing age to appear in harmony with its creed, he will not bate a jot from the subtlest of his metaphysical convictions.

Mr Carlyle not being *en rapport* with the religious spirit of his age, finds therein no religious spirit whatever; on the other hand, he has a great deal of religion of his own, not very clear to any but himself. . . . (p. 131)

The whole parallel which he runs between past and present is false—whimsically false. At one time we hear it uttered as an impeachment against our age, that every thing is done by committees and companies, shares and joint effort, and that no one man, or hero, can any longer move the world as in the blessed days of Peter the Hermit. Were we disposed to treat Mr Carlyle as members of Parliament, by the help of their *Hansard*, controvert each other, we should have no difficulty in finding amongst his works some passage—whether eloquent or not, or how far intelligible, would be just a mere chance—in which he would tell us that this capacity for joint effort, this habit of co-operation, was the greatest boast our times could make, and gave the fairest promise for the future. (pp. 132-33)

But we are not about to proceed through a volume such as this in a carping spirit, though food enough for such a spirit may be found; there is too much genuine merit, too much genuine humour, in the work. What, indeed, is the use of selecting from an author who *will* indulge in all manner of vagaries, whether of thought or expression, passages to prove that he can be whimsical and absurd, can deal abundantly in obscurities and contradictions, and can withal write the most motley, confused English of any man living? Better take, with thanks, from so irregular a genius, what seems to us good, or affords us gratification, and leave the rest alone. (p. 133)

[We] regard the chief *value* of Mr Carlyle's writings to consist in the *tone of mind* which the individual reader acquires from their perusal;—manly, energetic, enduring, with high resolves and self-forgetting effort; and we here again, at the close of our paper, revert to this remark: *Past and Present*, has not, and could not have, the same wild power which *Sartor Resartus* possessed, in our opinion, over the feelings of the reader; but it contains passages which look the same way, and breathe the same spirit. (pp. 137-38)

[*William Henry Smith*], in a review of "*Past and Present*," in Blackwood's Edinburgh Magazine, *Vol. LIV, No. CCCXXXIII, July, 1843, pp. 121-38.*

[RALPH WALDO EMERSON] (essay date 1843)

[*In the following excerpt from a review of* Past and Present *that gave much satisfaction to Carlyle, Emerson extols the perspicuity and style of the work, faulting only Carlyle's exaggeration. For further commentary by Emerson, see excerpt dated 1836.*]

[*Past and Present*] is Carlyle's new poem, his *Iliad* of English woes, to follow his poem on France, entitled the *History of the French Revolution*. In its first aspect, it is a political tract, and since Burke, since Milton, we have had nothing to compare with it. It grapples honestly with the facts lying before all men, groups and disposes them with a master's mind,—and with a heart full of manly tenderness, offers his best counsel to his brothers. Obviously it is the book of a powerful and accomplished thinker, who has looked with naked eyes at the dreadful political signs in England for the last few years, has conversed much on these topics with such wise men of all ranks and parties as are drawn to a scholar's house, until such daily and nightly meditation has grown into a great connexion, if not a system of thoughts, and the topic of English politics becomes the best vehicle for the expression of his recent thinking, recommended to him by the desire to give some timely counsels, and to strip the worst mischiefs of their plausibility. It is a brave and just book, and not a semblance. "No new truth," say the critics on all sides. Is it so? truth is very old; but the merit of seers is not to invent, but to dispose objects in their right places, and he is the commander who is always in the mount, whose eye not only sees details, but throws crowds of details into their right arrangement and a larger and juster totality than any other. The book makes great approaches to true contemporary history, a very rare success, and firmly holds up to daylight the absurdities still tolerated in the English and European system. It is such an appeal to the conscience and honor of England as cannot be forgotten, or be feigned to be forgotten. It has the merit which belongs to every honest book, that it was self-examining before it was eloquent, and so hits all other men, and, as the country people say of good preaching, "comes bounce down into every pew." Every reader shall carry away something. The scholar shall read and write, the farmer and mechanic shall toil with new resolution, nor forget the book when they resume their labor.

Though no theocrat, and more than most philosophers a believer in political systems, Mr. Carlyle very fairly finds the calamity of the times not in bad bills of Parliament, nor the remedy in good bills, but the vice in false and superficial aims of the people, and the remedy in honesty and insight. Like every work of genius, its great value is in telling such simple truths. (pp. 96-7)

It requires great courage in a man of letters to handle the contemporary practical questions; not because he then has all men for his rivals, but because of the infinite entanglements of the problem, and the waste of strength in gathering unripe fruits. The task is superhuman; and the poet knows well, that a little time will do more than the most puissant genius. Time stills the loud noise of opinions, sinks the small, raises the great, so that the true emerges without effort and in perfect harmony to all eyes; but the truth of the present hour, except in particulars and single relations, is unattainable. Each man can very well know his own part of duty, if he will; but to bring out the truth for beauty and as literature, surmounts the powers of art. The most elaborate history of to-day will have the oddest dislocated look in the next generation. The historian of to-day is yet three ages off. The poet cannot descend into the turbid present without injury to his rarest gifts. Hence that necessity of isolation which genius has always felt. He must stand on his glass tripod, if he would keep his electricity.

But when the political aspects are so calamitous, that the sympathies of the man overpower the habits of the poet, a higher than literary inspiration may succor him. It is a costly proof of character, that the most renowned scholar of England should take his reputation in his hand, and should descend into the ring, and he has added to his love whatever honor his opinions may forfeit. To atone for this departure from the vows of the scholar and his eternal duties, to this secular charity, we have at least this gain, that here is a message which those to whom it was addressed cannot choose but hear. Though they die, they must listen. It is plain that whether by hope or by fear, or were it only by delight in this panorama of brilliant images, all the great classes of English society must read, even those whose existence it proscribes. Poor Queen Victoria,—poor Sir Robert Peel,—poor Primate and Bishops,—poor Dukes and Lords! there is no help in place or pride or in looking another way; a grain of wit is more penetrating than the lightning of the night-storm, which no curtains or shutters will keep out. Here is a book which will be read, no thanks to anybody but itself. What pains, what hopes, what vows, shall come of the reading! Here is a book as full of treason as an egg is full of meat, and every lordship and worship and high form and ceremony of English conservatism tossed like a football into the air, and kept in the air with merciless kicks and rebounds, and yet not a word is punishable by statute. The wit has eluded all official zeal; and yet these dire jokes, these cunning thrusts, this flaming sword of Cherubim waved high in air illuminates the whole horizon, and shows to the eyes of the universe every wound it inflicts. Worst of all for the party attacked, it bereaves them beforehand of all sympathy, by anticipating the plea of poetic and humane conservatism, and impressing the reader with the conviction, that the satirist himself has the truest love for everything old and excellent in English land and institutions, and a genuine respect for the basis of truth in those whom he exposes.

We are at some loss how to state what strikes us as the fault of this remarkable book, for the variety and excellence of the talent displayed in it is pretty sure to leave all special criticism in the wrong. And we may easily fail in expressing the general objection which we feel. It appears to us as a certain disproportion in the picture, caused by the obtrusion of the whims of the painter. In this work, as in his former labors, Mr. Carlyle reminds us of a sick giant. His humors, are expressed with so much force of constitution, that his fancies are more attractive and more credible than the sanity of duller men. But the habitual exaggeration of the tone wearies whilst it stimulates. It is felt to be so much deduction from the universality of the picture. It is not serene sunshine, but everything is seen in lurid storm-lights. Every object attitudinizes, to the very mountains and stars almost, under the refractions of this wonderful humorist, and instead of the common earth and sky, we have a Martin's Creation or Judgment Day. A crisis has always arrived which requires a *deus ex machinâ*. One can hardly credit, whilst under the spell of this magician, that the world always had the same bankrupt look, to foregoing ages as to us,—as of a failed world just recollecting its old withered forces to begin again and try to do a little business. It was perhaps inseparable from the attempt to write a book of wit and imagination on English politics, that a certain local emphasis and of effect, such as is the vice of preaching, should appear, producing on the reader a feeling of forlornness by the excess of value attributed to circumstances. (pp. 98-100)

And yet the gravity of the times, the manifold and increasing dangers of the English state, may easily excuse some over-coloring of the picture, and we at this distance are not so far removed from any of the specific evils, and are deeply participant in too many, not to share the gloom, and thank the love and the courage of the counsellor. This book is full of humanity, and nothing is more excellent in this, as in all Mr. Carlyle's works, than the attitude of the writer. He has the dignity of a man of letters who knows what belongs to him, and never deviates from his sphere; a continuer of the great line of scholars, and sustains their office in the highet credit and honor. If the good heaven have any word to impart to this unworthy generation, here is one scribe qualified and clothed for its occasion. One excellence he has in an age of Mammon and of criticism, that he never suffers the eye of his wonder to close. Let who will be the dupe of trifles, he cannot keep his eye off from that gracious Infinite which embosoms us. As a literary artist, he has great merits, beginning with the main one, that he never wrote one dull line. How well read, how adroit, what thousand arts in his one art of writing; with his expedient for expressing those unproven opinions which he entertains but will not endorse, by summoning one of his men of straw from the cell, and the respectable Sauerteig, or Teufelsdrock, or Dryasdust, or Picturesque Traveller says what is put into his mouth and disappears. That morbid temperament has given his rhetoric a somewhat bloated character, a luxury to many imaginative and learned persons, like a showery south wind with its sunbursts and rapid chasing of lights and glooms over the landscape, and yet its offensiveness to multitudes of reluctant lovers makes us often wish some concession were possible on the part of the humorist. Yet it must not be forgotten that in all his fun of castanets, or playing of tunes with a whiplash like some renowned charioteers,—in all this glad and needful venting of his redundant spirits,—he does yet ever and anon, as if catching the glance of one wise man in the crowd, quit his tempestuous key, and lance at him in clear level tone the very word, and then with new glee returns to his game. He is like a lover or an outlaw who wraps up his message in a serenade, which is nonsense to the sentinel, but salvation to the ear for which it is meant. He does not dodge the question, but gives sincerity where it is due.

One word more respecting this remarkable style. We have in literature few specimens of magnificence. Plato is the purple ancient, and Bacon and Milton the moderns of the richest strains. Burke sometimes reaches to that exuberant fulness, though deficient in depth. Carlyle in his strange half mad way, has entered the Field of the Cloth of Gold, and shown a vigor and wealth of resource, which has no rival in the tourney play of these times;—the indubitable champion of England. Carlyle is the first domestication of the modern system with its infinity of details into style. We have been civilizing very fast, building London and Paris, and now planting New England and India, New Holland and Oregon,—and it has not appeared in literature,—there has been no analogous expansion and recomposition in books. Carlyle's style is the first emergence of all this wealth and labor, with which the world has gone with child so long. London and Europe tunnelled, graded, cornlawed, with trade-nobility, and east and west Indies for dependencies, and America, with the Rocky Hills in the horizon, have never before been conquered in literature. This is the first invasion and conquest. How like an air-balloon or bird of Jove does he seem to float over the continent and stooping here and there pounce on a fact as a symbol which was never a symbol before. This is the first experiment; and something of rudeness and haste must be pardoned to so great an achievment. It will be done again and again, sharper, simpler, but fortunate is he who did it first, though never so giant-like and fabulous. This grandiose character pervades his wit and his imagination.

We have never had anything in literature so like earthquakes, as the laughter of Carlyle. He "shakes with his mountain mirth." It is like the laughter of the Genii in the horizon. These jokes shake down Parliament-house and Windsor Castle, Temple, and Tower, and the future shall echo the dangerous peals. The other particular of magnificence is in his rhymes. Carlyle is a poet who is altogether too burly in his frame and habit to submit to the limits of metre. Yet he is full of rhythm not only in the perpetual melody of his periods, but in the burdens, refrains, and grand returns of his sense and music. Whatever thought or motto has once appeared to him fraught with meaning, becomes an omen to him henceforward, and is sure to return with deeper tones and weightier import, now as promise, now as threat, now as confirmation, in gigantic reverberation, as if the hills, the horizon, and the next ages returned the sound. (pp. 100-02)

> [*Ralph Waldo Emerson*], *in a review of "Past and Present," in* The Dial: Magazine for Literature, Philosophy, and Religion, *Vol. IV, No. I, July, 1843, pp. 96-102.*

EDGAR ALLAN POE   (essay date 1843)

[*Considered one of America's outstanding men of letters, Poe is best known for his bizarre and macabre short stories. Among his theories as a literary critic was his belief that through the calculated use of language an author may express, though always imperfectly, a vision of truth and the absolute condition of all existence. In this excerpt from comments made in 1843, Poe ridicules Carlyle's obscurity.*]

Mr. Tennyson is quaint only; he is never, as some have supposed him, obscure—except, indeed, to the uneducated, whom he does not address. Mr. Carlyle, on the other hand, is obscure only; he is seldom, as some have imagined him, quaint. So far he is right; for although quaintness, employed by a man of judgment and genius, may be made auxiliary to a *poem,* whose true thesis is beauty, and beauty alone, it is grossly, and even ridiculously, out of place in a work of prose. But in his obscurity it is scarcely necessary to say that he is wrong. Either a man intends to be understood, or he does not. If he write a book which he intends *not* to be understood, we shall be very happy indeed not to understand it; but if he write a book which he means to be understood, and, in this book, be at all possible pains to prevent us from understanding it, we can only say he is an ass—and this, to be brief, is our private opinion of Mr. Carlyle, which we now take the liberty of making public.

> *Edgar Allan Poe, in an extract in* Thomas Carlyle: The Critical Heritage, *edited by Jules Paul Seigel, Routledge & Kegan Paul, 1971, p. 302.*

HENRY D. THOREAU   (essay date 1847)

[*Thoreau was one of the key figures of the American Transcendental movement. His* Walden; or, Life in the Woods (1854), *a record of two years that he spent living alone in the woods near Concord, Massachusetts, is considered one of the finest prose works in American literature. Part autobiography, part fiction, part social criticism, Walden is a highly individual work in which Thoreau advocated a simple, self-sufficient way of life in order to free the individual from self-imposed social and financial obligations. Thoreau also pleaded for a more intimate relationship between human beings and nature as an antidote to the deadening influence of an increasingly industrialized society. The following excerpt is taken from a retrospective of Carlyle's career in which*

When we remember how [Carlyle's works] came over to us,
with their encouragement and provocation from mouth to mouth,
and what commotion they created in many private breasts, we
wonder that the country did not ring, from shore to shore, from
the Atlantic to the Pacific, with its greeting; and the Boons
and Crockets of the West make haste to hail him, whose wide
humanity embraces them too. Of all that the packets have
brought over to us, has there been any richer cargo than this?
What else has been English news for so long a season? What
else, of late years, has been England to us—to us who read
books, we mean? Unless we remembered it as the scene where
the age of Wordsworth was spending itself, and a few younger
muses were trying their wings, and from time to time, as the
residence of Landon; Carlyle alone, since the death of Coleridge, has kept the promise of England. It is the best apology
for all the bustle and the sin of commerce, that it has made us
acquainted with the thoughts of this man. Commerce would
not concern us much if it were not for such results as this.
New England owes him a debt which she will be slow to
recognize. His earlier essays reached us at a time when Coleridge's were the only recent words which had made any notable
impression so far, and they found a field unoccupied by him,
before yet any words of moment had been uttered in our midst.
He had this advantage, too, in a teacher, that he stood near to
his pupils; and he has no doubt afforded reasonable encouragement and sympathy to many an independent but solitary
thinker. Through him, as usher, we have been latterly, in a
great measure, made acquainted with what philosophy and
criticism the nineteenth century had to offer—admitted, so to
speak, to the privileges of the century; and what he may yet
have to say, is still expected here with more interest than any
thing else from that quarter.

It is remarkable, but on the whole, perhaps, not to be lamented,
that the world is so unkind to a new book. Any distinguished
traveler who comes to our shores, is likely to get more dinners
and speeches of welcome than he can well dispose of, but the
best books, if noticed at all, meet with coldness and suspicion,
or, what is worse, gratuitous, off-hand criticism. It is plain
that the reviewers, both here and abroad, do not know how to
dispose of this man. They approach him too easily, as if he
were one of the men of letters about town, who grace Mr.
Somebody's administration, merely; but he already belongs to
literature, and depends neither on the favor of reviewers, nor
the honesty of booksellers, nor the pleasure of readers for his
success. He has more to impart than to receive from his generation. He is another such a strong and finished workman in
his craft as Samuel Johnson was, and like him, makes the
literary class respectable. As few are yet out of their apprenticeship, or even if they learn to be able writers, are at the
same time able and valuable thinkers. The aged and critical
eyes, especially, [are] incapacitated to appreciate the works of
this author. To such their meaning is impalpable and evanescent, and they seem to abound only in obstinate mannerisms,
Germanisms, and whimsical ravings of all kinds, with now
and then an unaccountably true and sensible remark. On the
strength of this last, Carlyle is admitted to have what is called
genius. We hardly know an old man to whom these volumes
are not hopelessly sealed. The language, they say, is foolishness and a stumbling-block to them; but to many a clear-headed
boy, they are plainest English, and despatched with such hasty
relish as his bread and milk. The fathers wonder how it is that
the children take to this diet so readily, and digest it with so

little difficulty. They shake their heads with mistrust at their
free and easy delight, and remark that "Mr. Carlyle is a very
learned man;" for they, too, not to be out of fashion, have got
grammar and dictionary, if the truth were known, and with the
best faith cudgelled their brains to get a little way into the
jungle, and they could not but confess, as often as they found
the clue, that it was as intricate as Blackstone to follow, if you
read it honestly. But merely reading, even with the best intentions, is not enough, you must almost have written these
books yourself. Only he who has had the good fortune to read
them in the nick of time, in the most perceptive and recipient
season of life, can give any adequate account of them.
(pp. 146-47)

[Carlyle's] style is eminently colloquial—and no wonder it is
strange to meet with in a book. It is not literary or classical;
it has not the music of poetry, nor the pomp of philosophy,
but the rhythms and cadences of conversation endlessly repeated. It resounds with emphatic, natural, lively, stirring tones,
muttering, rattling, exploding, like shells and shot, and with
like execution. So far as it is a merit in composition, that the
written answer to the spoken word, and the spoken word to a
fresh and pertinent thought in the mind, as well as to the half
thoughts, the tumultuary misgivings and expectancies, this author is, perhaps, not to be matched in literature. In the streets
men laugh and cry, but in books, never; they "whine, put
finger i' the eye, and sob" only. One would think that all
books of late, had adopted the falling inflexion. "A mother,
if she wishes to sing her child to sleep," say the musical men,
"will always adopt the falling inflexion." Would they but
choose the rising inflexion, and wake the child up for once.

He is no mystic either, more than Newton or Arkwright, or
Davy—and tolerates none. Not one obscure line, or half line,
did he ever write. His meaning lies plain as the daylight, and
he who runs may read; indeed, only he who runs *can* read,
and keep up with the meaning. It has the distinctness of picture
to his mind and he tells us only what he sees printed in largest
English type upon the face of things. He utters substantial
English thoughts in plainest English dialects; for it must be
confessed, he speaks more than one of these. All the shires of
England, and all the shires of Europe, are laid under contribution to his genius; for to be English does not mean to be
exclusive and narrow, and adapt one's self to the apprehension
of his nearest neighbor only. And yet no writer is more thoroughly Saxon. In the translation of those fragments of Saxon
poetry, we have met with the same rhythm that occurs so often
in his poem on the French Revolution. And if you would know
where many of those obnoxious Carlyleisms and Germanisms
came from, read the best of Milton's prose, read those speeches
of Cromwell which he has brought to light, or go and listen
once more to your mother's tongue. So much for his German
extraction.

Indeed, for fluency and skill in the use of the English tongue,
he is a master unrivaled. His felicity and power of expression
surpass even any of his special merits as a historian and critic.
Therein his experience has not failed him, but furnished him
with such a store of winged, aye, and legged words, as only
a London life, perchance, could give account of; we had not
understood the wealth of the language before. Nature is ransacked, and all the resorts and purlieus of humanity are taxed,
to furnish the fittest symbol for his thought. He does not go
to the dictionary, the word-book, but to the word-manufactory
itself, and has made endless work for the lexicographers—yes,
he has that same English for his mother-tongue, that you have,

Carlyle's birthplace in Ecclefechan.

but with him it is no dumb, muttering, mumbling faculty, concealing the thoughts, but a keen, unwearied, resistless weapon. He has such command of it as neither you nor I have; and it would be well for any who have a lost horse to advertise, or a town-meeting warrant, or a sermon, or a letter to write, to study this universal letter-writer, for he knows more than the grammar or the dictionary.

The style is worth attending to, as one of the most important features of the man which we at this distance can discern. It is for once quite equal to the matter. It can carry all its load, and never breaks down nor staggers. (pp. 147-48)

One wonders how so much, after all, was expressed in the old way, so much here depends upon the emphasis, tone, pronunciation, style, and spirit of the reading. No writer uses so profusely all the aids to intelligibility which the printer's art affords. You wonder how others had contrived to write so many pages without emphatic or italicised words, they are so expressive, so natural, so indispensable here, as if none had ever used the demonstrative pronouns demonstratively before. In another's sentences the thought, though it may be immortal, is, as it were, embalmed, and does not *strike* you, but here it is so freshly living, even the body of it, not having passed through the ordeal of death, that it stirs in the very extremities, and the smallest particles and pronouns are all alive with it. It is not simple dictionary *it,* yours or mine, but IT. The words did not come at the command of grammar, but of a tyrannous,

inexorable meaning; not like standing soldiers, by vote of parliament, but any able-bodied countryman pressed into the service, for "sire, it is not a revolt, it is a revolution."

We have never heard him speak, but we should say that Carlyle was a rare talker. He has broken the ice, and streams freely forth like a spring torrent. He does not trace back the stream of his thought, silently adventurous, up to its fountain-head, but is borne away with it, as it rushes through his brain like a torrent to overwhelm and fertilize. He holds a talk with you. His audience is such a tumultuous mob of thirty thousand, as assembled at the University of Paris, before printing was invented. Philosophy, on the other hand, does not talk, but write, or, when it comes personally before an audience, lecture or read; and therefore it must be read to-morrow, or a thousand years hence. But the talker must naturally be attended to at once; he does not talk on without an audience; the winds do not long bear the sound of his voice. Think of Carlyle reading his **French Revolution** to any audience. One might say it was never written, but spoken; and thereafter reported and printed, that those not within sound of his voice might know something about it. (p. 148)

Such a style—so diversified and variegated! It is like the face of a country; it is like a New England landscape, with farmhouses and villages, and cultivated spots, and belts of forests and blueberry-swamps round about it, with the fragrance of shad-blossoms and violets on certain winds. And as for the reading of it, it is novel enough to the reader who has used only the diligence, and old-line mail-coach. It is like traveling, sometimes on foot, sometimes in a gig tandem; sometimes in a full coach, over highways, mended and unmended, for which you will prosecute the town; on level roads, through French departments, by Simplon roads over the Alps, and now and then he hauls up for a relay, and yokes in an unbroken colt of a Pegasus for a leader, driving off by cart-paths, and across lots, by corduroy roads and gridiron bridges; and where the bridges are gone, not even a string-piece left, and the reader has to set his breast and swim. You have got an expert driver this time, who has driven ten thousand miles, and was never known to upset; can drive six in hand on the edge of a precipice, and touch the leaders anywhere with his snapper.

With wonderful art he grinds into paint for his picture all his moods and experiences, so that all his forces may be brought to the encounter. Apparently writing without a particular design or responsibility, setting down his soliloquies from time to time, taking advantage of all his humors, when at length the hour comes to declare himself, he puts down in plain English, without quotation marks, what he, Thomas Carlyle, is ready to defend in the face of the world, and fathers the rest, often quite as defensible, only more modest, or plain spoken, or insinuating, upon ''Sauerteig,'' or some other gentleman long employed on the subject. Rolling his subject how many ways in his mind, he meets it now face to face, wrestling with it at arm's length, and striving to get it down, or throws it over his head; and if that will not do, or whether it will do or not, tries the back-stitch and side-hug with it, and downs it again—scalps it, draws and quarters it, hangs it in chains, and leaves it to the winds and dogs. With his brows knit, his mind made up, his will resolved and resistless, he advances, crashing his way through the host of weak, half-formed, *dilettante* opinions, honest and dishonest ways of thinking, with their standards raised, sentimentalities and conjectures, and tramples them all into dust. See how he prevails; you don't even hear the groans of the wounded and dying. Certainly it is not so well worth the while to look through any man's eyes at history, for the time, as through his; and his way of looking at things is fastest getting adopted by his generation.

It is not in man to determine what his style shall be. He might as well determine what his thoughts shall be. We would not have had him write always as in the chapter on Burns, and the **Life of Schiller,** and elsewhere. No; his thoughts were ever irregular and impetuous. Perhaps as he grows older and writes more he acquires a truer expression; it is in some respects manlier, freer, struggling up to a level with its fountain-head. We think it is the richest prose style we know of. (pp. 148-49)

We believe that Carlyle has, after all, more readers, and is better known to-day for . . . [his] originality of style, and that posterity will have reason to thank him for emancipating the language, in some measure, from the fetters which a merely conservative, aimless, and pedantic literary class had imposed upon it, and setting an example of greater freedom and naturalness. No man's thoughts arre new, but the style of their expression is the never failing novelty which cheers and refreshes men. If we were to answer the question, whether the mass of men, as we know them, talk as the standard authors and reviewers write, or rather as this man writes, we should say that he alone begins to write their language at all, and that the former is, for the most part, the mere effigies of a language, not the best method of concealing one's thoughts even, but frequently a method of doing without thoughts at all. (p. 149)

But for style, and fine writing, and Augustan ages—that is but a poor style, and vulgar writing, and a degenerate age, which allows us to remember these things. This man has something to communicate. Carlyle's are not, in the common sense, works of art in their origin and aim; and yet, perhaps, no living English writer evinces an equal literary talent. They are such works of art only as the plough, and corn-mill, and steam-engine—not as pictures and statues. Others speak with greater emphasis to scholars, as such, but none so earnestly and effectually to all who can read. Others give their advice, he gives his sympathy also. It is no small praise that he does not take upon himself the airs, has none of the whims, none of the pride, the nice vulgarities, the starched, impoverished isolation, and cold glitter of the spoiled children of genius. He does not need to husband his pearl, but excels by a greater humanity and sincerity.

He is singularly serious and untrivial. We are every where impressed by the rugged, unwearied, and rich sincerity of the man. We are sure that he never sacrificed one jot of his honest thought to art or whim, but to utter himself in the most direct and effectual way, that is the endeavor. These are merits which will wear well. When time has worn deeper into the substance of these books, this grain will appear. No such sermons have come to us here out of England, in late years, as those of this preacher; sermons to kings, and sermons to peasants, and sermons to all intermediate classes. It is in vain that John Bull, or any of his cousins, turns a deaf ear, and pretends not to hear them, nature will not soon be weary of repeating them. There are words less obviously true, more for the ages to hear, perhaps, but none so impossible for this age not to hear. What a cutting cimiter was that [*Past and Present*], going through heaps of silken stuffs, and glibly through the necks of men, too, without their knowing it, leaving no trace. He has the earnestness of a prophet. In an age of pedantry and dilettantism, he has no grain of these in his composition. There is no where else, surely, in recent readable English, or other books, such direct and effectual teaching, reproving, encouraging, stimulating, earnestly, vehemently, almost like Mahomet, like Luther; not looking behind him to see how his *Opera Omnia* will look, but forward to other work to be done. His writings are a gospel to the young of this generation; they will hear his manly, brotherly speech with responsive joy, and press forward to older or newer gospels.

We should omit a main attraction in these books, if we said nothing of their humor. Of this indispensable pledge of sanity, without some leaven, of which the abstruse thinker may justly be suspected of mysticism, fanaticism, or insanity, there is a superabundance in Carlyle. Especially the transcendental philosophy needs the leaven of humor to render it light and digestible. In his later and longer works it is an unfailing accompaniment, reverberating through pages and chapters, long sustained without effort. The very punctuation, the italics, the quotation marks, the blank spaces and dashes, and the capitals, each and all are pressed into its service. (pp. 149-50)

Carlyle's humor is vigorous and Titanic, and has more sense in it than the sober philosophy of many another. It is not to be disposed of by laughter and smiles merely; it gets to be too serious for that—only they may laugh who are not hit by it. For those who love a merry jest, this is a strange kind of fun— rather too practical joking, if they understand it. The pleasant humor which the public loves, is but the innocent pranks of the ballroom, harmless flow of animal spirits, the light plushy pressure of dandy pumps, in comparison. But when an elephant takes to treading on your corns, why then you are lucky if you sit high, or wear cowhide. His humor is always subordinate to a serious purpose, though often the real charm for the reader, is not so much in the essential progress and final upshot of the chapter, as in this indirect sidelight illustration of every hue. He sketches first with strong, practical English pencil, the essential features in outline, black on white, more faithfully than Dryasdust would have done, telling us wisely whom and what to mark, to save time, and then with brush of camel's hair, or sometimes with more expeditious swab, he lays on the bright and fast colors of his humor everywhere. One piece of solid work, be it known, we have determined to do, about which let there be no jesting, but all things else under the heavens, to the right and left of that, are for the time fair game. To us this humor is not wearisome, as almost every other is. Rabelais, for instance, is intolerable; one chapter is better than a volume—it may be sport to him, but it is death to us. A mere humorist, indeed, is a most unhappy man; and his readers are most unhappy also. . . .

But, after all, we could sometimes dispense with the humor, though unquestionably incorporated in the blood, if it were replaced by this author's gravity. (p. 150)

We confess that Carlyle's humor is rich, deep, and variegated, in direct communication with the back bone and risible muscles of the globe—and there is nothing like it; but much as we relish this jovial, this rapid and detergeous way of conveying one's views and impressions, when we would not converse but meditate, we pray for a man's diamond edition of his thought, without the colored illuminations in the margin—the fishes and dragons, and unicorns, the red or the blue ink, but its initial letter in distinct skeleton type, and the whole so clipped and condensed down to the very essence of it, that time will have little to do. We know not but we shall immigrate soon, and would fain take with us all the treasures of the east, and all kinds of *dry,* portable soups, in small tin canisters, which contain whole herds of English beeves, boiled down, will be acceptable.

The difference between this flashing, fitful writing and pure philosophy, is the difference between flame and light. The flame, indeed, yields light, but when we are so near as to observe the flame, we are apt to be incommoded by the heat and smoke. But the sun, that old Platonist, is set so far off in the heavens, that only a genial summer-heat and ineffable daylight can reach us. But many a time, we confess, in wintery weather, we have been glad to forsake the sun-light, and warm us by these Promethean flames.

Carlyle must undoubtedly plead guilty to the charge of mannerism. He not only has his vein but his peculiar manner of working it. He has a style which can be imitated, and sometimes is an imitator of himself. (p. 151)

Carylye's works, it is true, have not the stereotyped success which we call classic.They are a rich but inexpensive entertainment, at which we are not concerned lest the host has strained or impoverished himself to feed his guests. It is not the most lasting word, nor the loftiest wisdom, but rather the word which comes last. For his genius it was reserved to give expression to the thoughts which were throbbing in a million breasts. He has plucked the ripest fruit in the public garden; but this fruit already least concerned the tree that bore it, which was rather perfecting the bud at the foot of the leaf stalk. His works are not to be studied, but read with a swift satisfaction. Their flavor and gust is like what poets tell of the froth of wine, which can only be tasted once and hastily. (p. 152)

* * * * *

[Carlyle is] the best tempered, and not the least impartial of reviewers. He goes out of his way to do justice to profligates and quacks. There is somewhat even Christian, in the rarest and most peculiar sense, in his universal brotherliness, his simple, child-like endurance, and earnest, honest endeavor, with sympathy for the like. And this fact is not insignificant, that he is almost the only writer of biography, of the lives of men, in modern times. So kind and generous a tribute to the genius of Burns cannot be expected again, and is not needed. We honor him for his noble reverence for Luther, and his patient, almost reverent study of Goethe's genius, anxious that no shadow of his author's meaning escape him for want of trustful attention. There is nowhere else, surely, such determined and generous love of whatever is manly in history. His just appreciation of any, even inferior talent, especially of all sincerity, under whatever guise, and all true men of endeavor, must have impressed every reader. Witness the chapters on Werner, Heyne, even Cagliostro, and others. He is not likely to underrate his man. We are surprised to meet with such a discriminator of kingly qualities in these republican and democratic days, such genuine loyalty all thrown away upon the world. (p. 238)

Notwithstanding the very genuine, admirable, and loyal tributes to Burns, Schiller, Goethe, and others, Carlyle is not a critic of poetry. In the book of heroes, Shakspeare, the hero, as poet, comes off rather slimly. His sympathy . . . is with the men of endeavor; not using the life got, but still bravely getting their life. "In fact," as he says of Cromwell, "every where we have to notice the decisive, practical *eye* of this man; how he drives toward the practical and practicable; has a genuine insight into what *is* fact." You must have very stout legs to get noticed at all by him. He is thoroughly English in his love of practical men, and dislike for cant, and ardent enthusiastic heads that are not supported by any legs. He would kindly knock them down that they may regain some vigor by touching their mother earth. We have often wondered how he ever found out Burns, and must still refer a good share of his delight in him to neighborhood and early association. The *Lycidas* and *Comus* appearing in *Blackwood's Magazine,* would probably go unread by him, nor lead him to expect a *Paradise Lost.* The condition of England question is a practical one. The condition of England demands a hero, not a poet. Other things demand a poet; the poet answers other demands. Carlyle in London, with this question pressing on him so urgently, sees no occasion for minstrels and rhapsodists there. Kings may have their bards when there are any kings. Homer would *certainly* go a begging there. He lives in Chelsea, not on the plains of Hindostan, nor on the prairies of the West, where settlers are scarce, and a man must at least go *whistling* to himself.

What he says of poetry is rapidly uttered, and suggestive of a thought, rather than the deliberate development of any. He answers your question, What is poetry? by writing a special poem, as that Norse one, for instance, in the **Book of Heroes,** altogether wild and original;—answers your question, What is light? by kindling a blaze which dazzles you, and pales sun and moon, and not as a peasant night, by opening a shutter. And, certainly, you would say that this question never could be answered but by the grandest of poems; yet he has not dull breath and stupidity enough, perhaps, to give the most deliberate and universal answer, such as the fates wring from illiterate and unthinking men. He answers like Thor, with a stroke of his hammer, whose dint makes a valley in the earth's surface. . . .

There is indeed more poetry in this author than criticism on poetry. He often reminds us of the ancient Scald, inspired by the grimmer features of life, dwelling longer on Dante than on Shakspeare. We have not recently met with a more solid and unquestionable piece of poetic work than that episode of "The Ancient Monk," in *Past and Present,* at once idyllic, narrative, heroic; a beautiful restoration of a past age. There is nothing like it elsewhere that we know of. *The History of the French Revolution* is a poem, at length got translated into prose; an *Iliad,* indeed, as he himself has it—"The destructive wrath of Sansculotism: this is what we speak, having unhappily no voice for singing." (p. 239)

One more merit in Carlyle, let the subject be what it may, is the freedom of prospect he allows, the entire absence of cant and dogma. He removes many cart-loads of rubbish, and leaves open a broad highway. His writings are all enfenced on the side of the future and the possible. He does not place himself across the passage out of his books, so that none may go freely out, but rather by the entrance, inviting all to come in and go through. No gins, no net-work, no pickets here, to restrain the free thinking reader. In many books called philosophical, we find ourselves running hither and thither, under and through, and sometimes quite unconsciously straddling some imaginary fence-work, which in our clairvoyance we had not noticed, but fortunately, not with such fatal consequences as happen to those birds which fly against a white-washed wall, mistaking it for fluid air. As we proceed the wreck of this dogmatic tissue collects about the organs of our perception, like cobwebs about the muzzles of hunting dogs in dewy mornings. If we look up with such eyes as these authors furnish, we see no heavens, but a low pent-roof of straw or tiles, as if we stood under a shed, with no sky-light through which to glimpse the blue.

Carlyle, though he does but inadvertently direct our eyes to the open heavens, nevertheless, lets us wander broadly underneath, and shows them to us reflected in innumerable pools and lakes. We have from him, occasionally, some hints of a possible science of astronomy even, and revelation of heavenly arcana, but nothing definite hitherto. . . .

[Carlyle's works] contain not the highest, but a very practicable wisdom, which startles and provokes, rather than informs us. Carlyle does not oblige us to think; we have thought enough for him already, but he compels us to act. We accompany him rapidly through an endless gallery of pictures, and glorious reminiscences of experiences unimproved. "Have you not had Moses and the prophets? Neither will ye be persuaded if one should rise from the dead." There is no calm philosophy of life here, such as you might put at the end of the Almanac, to hang over the farmer's hearth, how men shall live in these winter, in these summer days. No philosophy, properly speaking, of love, or friendship, or religion, or politics, or education, or nature, or spirit; perhaps a nearer approach to a philosophy of kingship, and of the place of the literary man, than of any thing else. A rare preacher, with prayer, and psalm, and sermon, and benediction, but no contemplation of man's life from serene oriental ground, nor yet from the stirring occidental. (p. 241)

There is no philosophy here for philosophers, only as every man is said to have his philosophy. No system but such as is the man himself; and, indeed, he stands compactly enough. No progress beyond the first assertion and challenge, as it were, with trumpet blast. One thing is certain, that we had best be doing something in good earnest, henceforth forever; that's an indispensable philosophy. The before impossible precept, "*know*

thyself," he translates into the partially possible one, "*know what thou canst work at.*" *Sartor Resartus* is, perhaps, the sunniest and most philosophical, as it is the most autobiographical of his works, in which he drew most largely on the experience of his youth. But we miss everywhere a calm depth, like a lake, even stagnant, and must submit to rapidity and whirl, as on skates, with all kinds of skillful and antic motions, sculling, sliding, cutting punch-bowls and rings, forward and backward. The talent is very nearly equal to the genius. Sometimes it would be preferable to wade slowly through a Serbonian bog, and feel the juices of the meadow. We should say that he had not speculated far, but faithfully, living up to it. He lays all the stress still on the most elementary and initiatory maxims, introductory to philosophy. It is the experience of the religionist. (pp. 241-42)

Beside some philosophers of larger vision, Carlyle stands like an honest, half-despairing boy, grasping at some details only of their world systems. (p. 242)

To sum up our most serious objections, in a few words, we should say that Carlyle indicates a depth,—and we mean not impliedly, but distinctly,—which he neglects to fathom. We want to know more about that which he wants to know as well. If any luminous star, or undissolvable nebula, is visible from his station, which is not visible from ours, the interests of science require that the fact be communicated to us. The universe expects every man to do his duty in his parallel of latitude. We want to hear more of his inmost life; his hymn and prayer, more; his elegy and eulogy, less; that he should speak more from his character, and less from his talent; communicate centrally with his readers, and not by a side; that he should say what he believes, without suspecting that men disbelieve it, out of his never-misunderstood nature. Homer and Shakspeare speak directly and confidently to us. The confidence implied in the unsuspicious tone of the world's worthies, is a great and encouraging fact. Dig up some of the earth you stand on, and show that. If he gave us religiously the meagre results of his experience, his style would be less picturesque and diversified, but more attractive and impressive. His genius can cover all the land with gorgeous palaces, but the reader does not abide in them, but pitches his tent rather in the desert and on the mountain peak.

When we look about for something to quote, as the fairest specimen of the man, we confess that we labor under an unusual difficulty; for his philosophy is so little of the proverbial or sentential kind, and opens so gradually, rising insensibly from the reviewer's level, and developing its thought completely and in detail, that we look in vain for the brilliant passages, for point and antithesis, and must end by quoting his works entire. What in a writer of less breadth would have been the proposition which would have bounded his discourse, his column of victory, his Pillar of Hercules, and *ne plus ultra,* is in Carlyle frequently the same thought unfolded; no Pillar of Hercules, but a considerable prospect, north and south, along the Atlantic coast. There are other pillars of Hercules, like beacons and light-houses, still further in the horizon, toward Atlantis, set up by a few ancient and modern travelers; but, so far as this traveler goes, he clears and colonizes, and all the surplus population of London is bound thither at once. What we would quote is, in fact, his vivacity, and not any particular wisdom or sense, which last is ever synonymous with sentence, [*sententia,*] as in his cotemporaries, Coleridge, Landor and Wordsworth. (pp. 242-43)

Who lives in London to tell this generation who have been the great men of our race? We have read that on some exposed place in the city of Geneva, they have fixed a brazen indicator for the use of travelers, with the names of the mountain summits in the horizon marked upon it, "so that by taking sight across the index you can distinguish them at once. You will not mistake Mont Blanc, if you see him, but until you get accustomed to the panorama, you may easily mistake one of his court for the king." It stands there a piece of mute brass, that seems nevertheless to know in what vicinity it is: and there perchance it will stand, when the nation that placed it there has passed away, still in sympathy with the mountains, forever discriminating in the desert.

So, we may say, stands this man, pointing as long as he lives, in obedience to some spiritual magnetism, to the summits in the historical horizon, for the guidance of his fellows.

Truly, our greatest blessings are very cheap. To have our sunlight without paying for it, without any duty levied,—to have our poet there in England, to furnish us entertainment, and what is better provocation, from year to year, all our lives long, to make the world seem richer for us, the age more respectable, and life better worth the living,—all without expense of acknowledgment even, but silently accepted out of the east, like morning light as a matter of course. (p. 245)

*Henry D. Thoreau, "Thomas Carlyle and His Works,"
in* Graham's Magazine, *Vol. XXX, Nos. 3 and 4,
March and April, 1847, pp. 145-52; 238-45.*

[WILLIAM EDMONSTOUNE AYTOUN]   (essay date 1850)

[*In the following excerpt from a review of* Latter-Day Pamphlets, *Aytoun censures Carlyle's misguided political views and objectionable prose.*]

It is nothing unusual, in this wayward world of ours, to find men denouncing, with apparent sincerity, that very fault which is most conspicuous in themselves. How often do we detect the most quarrelsome fellow of our acquaintance, the Hotspur of his immediate circle, uttering a grave homily against intemperance of speech, and rebuking for some casual testiness a friend, whose general demeanour and bearing give token of a lily-liver? What more common than to hear the habitual drunkard railing at the sin of inebriety, and delivering affecting testimony against the crying iniquity of the ginshop? . . .

Mr Thomas Carlyle has, of late years, devoted a good deal of his leisure time to the denunciation of shams. The term, in his mouth, has a most extended significance indeed—he uses it with Catholic application. Loyalty, sovereignty, nobility, the church, the constitution, kings, nobles, priests, the House of Commons, ministers, Courts of Justice, laws, and lawgivers, are all alike, in the eyes of Mr Carlyle, shams. Nor does he consider the system as of purely modern growth. England, he thinks, has been shamming Isaac for several hundred years. Before the Commonwealth it was overridden by the frightful Incubus of Flunkeyism: since then, it has been suffering under Horsehair and Redtapism, two awful monsters that present themselves to Mr Carlyle's diseased imagination, chained at the entrances of Westminster Hall and Downing Street. Cromwell, perhaps, was not a sham, for in the burly regicide brewer Mr Carlyle discerns certain grand inarticulate strivings, which elevate him to the heroic rank. The gentlemen of the present age, however, are all either shams or shamming. (p. 641)

It is natural to suppose that an individual who habitually deals in such wholesale denunciation, and whose avowed wish is to regenerate and reform society upon some entirely novel principle, must be a man of immense practical ability. The exposer of shams and quackeries should be, in his own person, very far indeed above suspicion of resembling those whom he describes, or tries to describe, in language more or less intelligible. If otherwise, he stands in imminent danger of being treated by the rest of the world as an impertinent and egregious impostor. Now, Mr Thomas Carlyle is anything but a man of practical ability. Setting aside his style for the present, let us see whether he has ever, in the course of his life, thrown out a single hint which could be useful to his own generation, or profitable to those who may come after. If he could originate any such hint, he does not possess the power of embodying it in distinct language. He has written a history of the French Revolution, a pamphlet on Chartism, a work on Heroes and Hero-worship, and a sort of political treatise entitled *Past and Present*. Can any living man point to a single practical passage in any of these volumes? If not, what is the real value of Mr Carlyle's writings? What is Mr Carlyle himself but a Phantasm of the species which he is pleased to denounce?

We have known, ere now, in England, political writers who, single-handed, have waged war with Ministers, and denounced the methods of government. But they were men of strong masculine understanding, capable of comprehending principles, and of exhibiting them in detail. They never attempted to write upon subjects which they did not understand: consequently, what they did write was well worthy of perusal, more especially as their sentiments were conveyed in clear idiomatic English. . . . Mr Carlyle, on the other hand, can never stir one inch beyond the merest vague generality. If he were a doctor, and you came to him with a cut finger, he would regale you with a lecture on the heroical qualities of Avicenna, or commence proving that Dr Abernethy was simply a Phantasm-Leech, instead of whipping out his pocketbook, and applying a plaster to the wound. Put him into the House of Commons, and ask him to make a speech on the budget. No baby ever possessed a more indefinite idea of the difference between pounds, shillings, and pence. He would go on maundering about Teufelsdrökh, Sauerteig, and Dryasdust, Sir Jabez Windbag, Fire-horses, Marsh-jötuns, and vulturous Choctaws, until he was coughed down as remorselessly as ever was Sir Joshua Walmsley. And yet this is the gentleman who has the temerity to volunteer his services as a public instructor, and who is now issuing a series of monthly tracts, for the purpose of shedding a new light upon the most intricate and knotty points of the general policy of Great Britain! (p. 642)

[Mr Carlyle] does not favour us with propositions at all; he contents himself with abusing men and matters in a barbarous, conceited, uncouth, and mystical dialect.

One peculiarity there is about the *Latterday Pamphlets,* as contradistinguished from their author's previous lucubrations, which has amused us not a little. Mr Carlyle has hitherto been understood to favour the cause of self-styled Liberalism. His mania, or rather his maunderings, on the subject of the Protector gained him the applause of many who are little less than theoretical republicans, and who regard as a glorious deed the regicide of the unfortunate Charles. Moreover, certain passages in his *History of the French Revolution* tended to strengthen this idea; he had a kindly side for Danton, and saw evident marks of heroism in the loathsome miscreant whom, in his usual absurd jargon, he styles "the pale seagreen Incorruptible," Robespierre. On this ground, his works were received with approbation by a section of the public press; and we used to hear him lauded and commended as a writer of the profoundest stamp, as a deep original thinker, a thorough-paced philanthropist, the champion of genuine greatness, and the unflinching enemy of delusions. Now, however, things are altered. Mr Carlyle has got a new crochet into his head, and to the utter discomfiture of his former admirers, he manifests a truculent and ultra-tyrannical spirit, abuses the political economists, wants to have a strong coercive government, indicates a decided leaning to the whip and the musket as effectual modes of reasoning, and, in short, abjures democracy! The sensation caused by this extraordinary change of sentiment has been as great as if Joe Hume had declared himself a spendthrift. (p. 643)

Flat burglary as ever was committed! O villain! thou wilt be condemned into everlasting redemption for this—so say the political Dogberrys to the gentleman whom they used to applaud. We are not surprised at their wrath. It *is* rather hard to be told at this time of day that ballot-boxes and extension of the suffrage are included in Mr Carlyle's catalogue of Shams, and that Messrs Thompson, Fox, and Co., must even submit to the charge of talking unveracities and owlism. Surely there is some mistake here. Not a whit of it. Mr Carlyle is in grim earnest, and lays about him like a man. . . .

Sham-kings may and do exist, thinks Mr Carlyle, but the greatest unveracity of all is this same Democracy, which people were lately so very willing to applaud. It must be admitted that our author is perfectly impartial in the distribution of his strokes. He has no love for Kings, or Metternichs, or Redtape, or any other fiction or figure of speech whereby he typifies existing governments: he disposes of them in a wholesale manner of Impostors and Impostures. But no more does he regard with affection Chartist Parliament, Force of Public Opinion, or "M'Crowdy the Seraphic Doctor with his last evangel of Political Economy." M'Culloch is, in his eyes, as odious as the First Lord in Waiting, whoever that functionary may be. Clenching both his fists, he delivers a facer to the Trojan on the right, and to the Tyrian on the left. Big with the conviction that all Governments are wrong, as presently or lately constituted, he can see no merit, but the reverse, in any of the schemes of progress, or reform, or financial change, which have yet been devised. (p. 644)

Now, reader, what do you think of all this? We doubt not you are a good deal puzzled: and an admission to that effect would be no impeachment of your intellect. Well then, let us try to extract from these pamphlets of Mr Carlyle some tendency, if not distinct meaning, which may at least indicate the current of his hopes and aspirations. Putting foreign governments altogether out of the question, we gather that Mr Carlyle considers this realm of Britain as most scandalously misgoverned; that he looks upon Downing Street as an absolute sewer; that he decidedly yields to Mr Hawes in reverence for Lord John Russell; that he regards the Protectionists as humbugs; that he laughs at ballot-boxes, despises extension of the suffrage, and repudiates, as a rule of conduct, the maxim about the markets, which indeed, by this time, stinks in every British nostril as yet unplugged with calico; that he detests the modern brood of political economists with a cordiality which does him credit; and that he is firmly convinced that democracy is a thing forever impossible. This is a tolerably extensive creed, though as yet entirely a negative one—is there no one point upon which Mr Carlyle will condescend to be positive?

Yes, one there is; not apparent perhaps to the casual reader, but detectible by him who studies closely those pages of oracular thought—a point very important at the present moment, for this it is—that there is ONE MAN existing in her Majesty's dominions who could put everything to rights, if he were only allowed to do so. Who that man is we may possibly discover hereafter. At present we are hardly entitled to venture beyond the boundaries of dim conjecture. Nor is it very clear in what way the Unknown, or rather the Undeveloped, is to set about his exalted mission. Is he to be minister—or something more? Perhaps Mr Carlyle did not like to be altogether explicit on such a topic as this; but we may possibly gain a little light from indirect and suggestive passages. Take this for example:

> Alas, it is sad enough that anarchy is here; that we are not permitted to regret its being here,—for who that had, for this divine Universe, an eye which was human at all, could wish that shams of any kind, especially that Sham Kings should continue? No: at all costs, it is to be prayed by all men that Shams may *cease*. Good Heavens, to what depths have we got, when this to many a man seems strange! Yet strange to many a man it does seem; and to many a solid Englishman, wholesomely digesting his pudding among what are called the cultivated classes, it seems strange exceedingly, a mad ignorant notion, quite heterodox, and big with mere ruin. He has been used to decent forms long since empty of meaning, to plausible modes, solemnities grown ceremonial,— what you in your iconoclast humour call shams,— all his life long; never heard that there was any harm in them, that there was any getting on without them. Did not cotton spin itself, beef grow, and groceries and spiceries come in from the East and the West, quite comfortably by the side of shams? Kings reigned, what they were pleased to call reigning; lawyers pleaded, bishops preached, and honourable members perorated; and to crown the whole, as if it were all real and no sham there, did not scrip continue saleable, and the banker pay in bullion, or paper with a metallic basis? "The greatest sham, I have always thought, is he that would destroy shams."

> Even so. To such depths have *I*, the poor knowing person of this epoch, got;—almost below the level of lowest humanity, and down towards the state of apehood and oxhood! For never till in quite recent generations was such a scandalous blasphemy quietly set forth among the sons of Adam; never before did the creature called man believe generally in his heart that this was the rule in this Earth; that in deliberate long-established lying could there be help or salvation for him, could there be at length other than hindrance and destruction for him.

We have been sorely tempted to mark with italics certain portions of the above extract, but on second thoughts we shall leave it intact. After applying ourselves most diligently to the text, with the view of eliciting its meaning, we have arrived at the conclusion, that it is either downright nonsense, or something a great deal worse. Observe what he says. It is to be prayed for by all men that Shams may cease—more especially Sham Kings. But certain solid Englishmen are not prepared for this. They have been "used to decent forms long since fallen empty of meaning, to plausible modes, solemnities grown ceremonial,—what you in your iconoclast humour call shams." They thought no harm of them. "Kings reigned, what they were pleased to call reigning; lawyers pleaded, bishops preached, and honourable members perorated," &c. And those who differ in their estimate of these things from Mr Carlyle are "almost below the level of lowest humanity, and down towards the state of apehood and oxhood:''—and their belief is a ''scandalous blasphemy.'' So then, the Monarchy is a sham, and so are the laws, the Church, and the Constitution! They are all lies, and in deliberate long-established lying there can be no help or salvation for the subject! This may not be Mr Carlyle's meaning, and we are very willing to suppose so; but he has no title to be angry, were we to accept his words according to their evident sense. If men, through conceit or affectation, will write in this absurd and reckless fashion, they must be prepared to stand the consequences. The first impression on the mind of every one who peruses the above passage must be, that the author is opposed to the form of government which is unalterably established in these kingdoms. If this be so, we should like to know in what respect such doctrines differ from the pestilential revolutionary trash which has inundated France and Germany? What kind of overturn does Mr Carlyle contemplate, for overturn there must be, and that of the most extensive kind, if his views are ever destined to be realised? Is it not, perhaps, as melancholy a spectacle as may be, to find a man of some genius, and considerable learning, attempting to unsettle the minds of the young and enthusiastic, upon points distinctly identified with all that is great and glorious in our past history; and insinuating doctrines which are all the more dangerous on account of the oblique and uncertain language in which they are conveyed? Fear God and honour the King, are precepts not acknowledged by Mr Carlyle as the rudiment and foundation of his faith. He does not recognise them as inseparably linked together. He would set up instead some wretched phantom of his own imagination, framed out of the materials which he fondly supposes to be the attributes of the heroic character, and he would exalt that above all other authority, human and divine. He is, if we do not entirely misconstrue the tenor of these pamphlets, possessed at this moment with the notion of the advent of another Cromwell, the sole event which, as he thinks, can save England from being swallowed up by the evils which now beset her. (pp. 645-46)

Cromwellism, then, if we may use the term, is Mr Carlyle's secret and theory. Cromwellism, is, we know, but another phrase for despotism; and we shall not put so harsh a construction on the term as to suppose that it necessarily involves extinguishment of the royal function. The example of Richelieu is sufficient to save us from such a violent interpretation, and therefore we may fairly assume that our author contemplates nothing more than the lodgment of the executive power in the hands of some stern and inexorable minister. To this the whole of his multitudinous political ravings, when melted into intelligible speech, would seem to tend. He has little regard for Kings, despises Lords, contemns Bishops, scouts the House of Commons, sneers at Chartists, repudiates the political economists, spurns the mob, and laughs at the Ten-pounders. There is here a tolerably extensive range of scorn—we doubt whether it could have been equalled by the reflective philosospher of the tub. (pp. 646-47)

Was there ever so tantalising a fellow? We only know of one parallel instance. Sancho, after a judicial hearing at Barrataria, sits down to dinner, but every dish upon which he sets his fancy is whisked away at the command of a gaunt personage stationed on one side of his chair, having a wholesome rod in his hand. Fruit, meat, partridges, stewed rabbits, veal, and olla-podrida, vanish in succession, and for the removal of each some learned reason is assigned by the representative of Esculapius. We give the remainder of the anecdote in the words of Cervantes.

Sancho, hearing this, threw himself backward in his chair, and, looking at the doctor from head to foot, very seriously, asked him his name, and where he had studied. To which he answered: ''My Lord Governor, my name is Doctor Pedro Rezio de Aguero; I am a native of a place called Tirteafuera, lying between Caraquel and Almoddobar del Campo on the right hand, and I have taken my doctor's degree in the University of Ossuna.'' ''Then hark you,'' said Sancho in a rage, ''Signor Doctor Pedro Rezio de Aguero, native of Tirteafuera, lying on the right hand as we go from Caraquel to Almoddobar del Campo, graduate in Ossuna, get out of my sight this instant— or, by the light of heaven! I will take a cudgel, and, beginning with your carcase, will so belabour all the physic-mongers in the island, that not one of the tribe shall be left!—I mean of those like yourself, who are ignorant quacks; for those who are learned and wise I shall make much of, and honour, as so many angels. I say again, Signor Pedro Rezio, begone! or I shall take the chair I sat on, and comb your head with it, to some tune, and, if I am called to an account for it, when I give up my office, I will prove that I have done a good service, in ridding the world of a bad physician, who is a public executioner.''

Mr Carlyle, though he may not be aware of it, is even such a political doctor. He despises De Lolme on the British Constitution, and peremptorily forbids his patient to have anything to do with that exploded system. ''I should like to have,'' says the pupil placed under his charge, ''in the first place, a well-regulated constituted monarchy.'' '''Tis a sham!'' cries Signor Doctor Thomas Carlyle—''Are solemnly constituted Impostors the proper kings of men? Do you think the life of man is a grimacing dance of apes? To be led always by the squeak of a paltry fiddle? Away with it!'' The wand is waved, and constitutional monarchy disappears. ''Well then,'' quoth the tyro, ''suppose we have an established Church and a House of Peers?'' ''Avaunt, ye Unveracities—ye Unwisdoms,'' shrieks the infuriated graduate. ''What are ye but iniquities of Horsehair? O my brother! above all, when thou findest Ignorance, Stupidity, Brute-mindedness,—yes, there, with or without Church-tithes and Shovelhat, or were it with mere dungeons, and gibbets, and crosses, attack it, I say; smite it wisely, unweariedly, and rest not while thou livest and it lives! Instead of heavenly or earthly Guidance for the souls of men, you have Black or White Surplice Controversies, stuffed Hair-and-leather Popes;— terrestrial Law-words, Lords, and Lawbringers organising Labour in these years, by passing Corn Laws. Take them away!'' ''What say you to the House of Commons, doctor?'' ''Owldom! off with it.'' ''A Democracy?'' ''On this side of the Atlantic and on that, Democracy, we apprehend, is for ever impossible.'' ''And why will none of these things do?'' ''Because,'' quoth the graduate with a solemn aspect, ''you perceive we have actually got into the New Era there has been such prophesying of: here we all are, arrived at last;—and it is by no means the land flowing with milk and honey we were led to expect! very much the reverse. A terrible new country this: no neighbours in it yet, that I can see, but irrational flabby monsters (philanthropic and other) of the giant species; hyaenas, laughing hyaenas, predatory wolves; probably *devils*, blue (or perhaps blue-and-yellow) devils, as St Guthlac found in Croyland long ago. A huge untrodden haggard country, the chaotic battlefield of Frost and Fire, a country of savage glaciers, granite-mountains, of foul jungles, unhewed forests, quaking bogs;—which we shall have our own ados to make arable and habitable, I think!'' What wonder if the pupil, hearing this pitiable tirade, should bethink him of certain modes of treatment prescribed by the faculty, in cases of evident delirium, as extremely suitable to the symptoms exhibited by his beloved preceptor?

Let us now see what sort of government Mr Carlyle would propose for our adoption, guidance, and regeneration. Some kind of shapes are traceable even in fog-banks, and the analogy encourages us to persevere in our Latter-day researches.

Mr Carlyle is decidedly of opinion that it is our business to find out the very Noblest possible man to undertake the whole job. What he means by Noblest is explicitly stated. "It is the Noblest, not the Sham-Noblest; it is God Almighty's Noble, not the Court-Tailor's Noble, nor the Able-Editor's Noble, that must in some approximate degree be raised to the supreme place; he and not a counterfeit—under penalties." This *Noblest*, it seems, is to have a select series or staff of *Noblers,* to whom shall be confided the divine everlasting duty of directing and controlling the Ignoble. The mysterious process by means of which "the Noblest" is to be elevated—when he is discovered—is not indicated, but the intervention of ballot-boxes is indignantly disclaimed. "The Real Captain, unless it be some Captain of mechanical Industry hired by Mammon, where is he in these days? Most likely, in silence, in sad isolation somewhere, in remote obscurity; trying if, in an evil ungoverned time, he cannot at least govern himself." There are limits to human endurance, and we maintain that we have a right to call upon Mr Carlyle either to produce this remarkable Captain, or to indicate his whereabouts. He tells us that time is pressing—that we are moving in the midst of goblins, and that everything is going to the mischief for want of this Noblest of his. Well, then, we say, where is this Captain of yours? Let us have a look at him—give us at least a guess as to his outward marks and locality—does he live in Chelsea or Whitehall Gardens; or has he been, since the general emigration of the Stags, trying to govern himself in sad isolation and remote obscurity at Boulogne? If you know anything about him, out with it—if not, why pester the public with these sheets of intolerable twaddle? (pp. 647-49)

Let us now suppose that Mr Carlyle has succeeded in his quest after capable men—that he has fairly bolted his Noblest, like an overgrown badger, from the hole in which he lies presently concealed, and has surrounded him with a staff of the Nobler, including, we presume, the author of the *Latter-day Pamphlets.* Noblest and Nobler must now go to work in serious earnest, taking some order with the flabby monsters, laughing hyaenas, predatory wolves, and blue, or blue and yellow devils, which abound in this New Era. What is the first step to be adopted? (p. 651)

[Let us hear a few sentences] of the speech to be made by the new British Minister to the assembled paupers . . .—

> But as for you, my indigent incompetent friends, I have to repeat, with sorrow but with perfect clearness, what is plainly undeniable, and is even clamorous to get itself admitted, that you are of the class of *slaves,*—or if you prefer the word of *nomadic, and now even vagrant and vagabond servants that can find no master on those terms;* which seems to me a much uglier word. Emancipation? You have been emancipated with a vengeance! Foolish souls! I say the whole world cannot emancipate you. Fealty to ignorant unruliness, to gluttonous sluggish Improvidence, to the Beerpot and the Devil, who is there that can emancipate a man in that predicament? Not a whole Reform Bill, a whole French Revolution executed for his behoof alone.

In this style, Noblest proceeds for a page or two, haranguing the unlucky paupers upon the principle that poverty is crime; taunting them with previous doles of Indian meal and money, and informing them that the Workhouses are thenceforward inexorably shut. Finally, he announces that they are to be embodied into industrial regiments, with proper officers; and marched off

> to the Irish Bogs, to the vacant desolations of Connaught now falling into Cannibalism, to mis-tilled Connaught, to ditto Munster, Leinster, Ulster, I will lead you; to the English fox covers, furze-grown Commons, New Forests, Salisbury Plains; likewise to the Scotch Hillsides, and bare rushy slopes which as yet feed only sheep.

All these are to be tilled by the slave regiments under the following penalties for recusancy.

> Refuse to strike into it; shirk the heavy labour, disobey the rules—I will admonish and endeavour to incite you; if in vain, I will flog you; if still in vain, I will at last shoot you,—and make God's Earth, and the forlorn-hope in God's Battle, free of you. Understand it, I advise you.

O rare Thomas Carlyle!

The language in which this significant and notable plan is conveyed, is more original than the plan itself. Other Liberals than Mr Carlyle have propounded the doctrine that the pauper is a slave of the state. A century and a half ago, Fletcher of Saltoun wrote a treatise to that effect, and probably a more determined republican than Fletcher never stepped in upper leathers. But somehow or other, although Scotland was then less scrupulous in matters of personal freedom than the sister kingdom, the scheme was by no means received with acclamation. Heritable jurisdictions were all very well in their way, but the idea of reducing the peasantry to the state of Russian serfdom, was rather more than the free parliament of the Scots Estates could contrive to stomach. It has been very shrewdly remarked that there is a wide circle in politics, whereof the connecting link lies between ultra-liberalism and absolute tyranny. Mr Carlyle, without meaning it, gives us a fair exemplification of this in the present pamphlets. (pp. 651-52)

We must now take our leave of Mr Carlyle, sincerely regretting that we cannot, with any degree of truth, congratulate him either on the tone or the character of his late lucubrations. These pamphlets, take them altogether, are about the silliest productions of the day; and we could well wish, for his sake, that they had never been compiled. (p. 657)

If Mr Carlyle feels that his vocation is political—if the true spirit of the prophet is stirring within him—he ought to endeavour in the first place to think clearly, and, in the second, to amend his style. At present his thoughts are anything but clear. The primary duty of an author is to have a distinct understanding of the matter which he proposes to enunciate, for unless he can arrive at that, his words must necessarily be mystical and undefined. If men are to be taught at all, let the teaching be simple, and level to the common capacity; and let the teacher be thoroughly conversant with the whole particulars of the lesson. We have a strong suspicion that Cassandra must have been a prophetess reared in the same school as Mr Carlyle. Her predictions seem to have been shrouded in such thorough mysticism, that no one gave her credit for inspiration; and in consequence the warnings which might have saved Troy, were spoken to the empty winds. Here, perhaps, we ought to guard ourselves against a similar charge of indistinctness. We by no means intend to certify that Mr Carlyle is a prophet, or that there is any peculiar Revelation in these *Latter-day Pamphlets* which can avert the fall of Britain, should that sad catastrophe be foredoomed. We simply wish to express our regret that Mr Carlyle, who may lay claim to the possession of some natural genius and ability, will not allow us the privilege of understanding the true nature of his thoughts, and therefore exposes himself to a suspicion that the indistinctness lies quite as much in the original conception of the ideas, as in the language by means of which they are conveyed.

As to his style, it can be defended on no principle whatever. . . . [In] Mr Carlyle's sentences and periods, there is no touch or sound of harmony. They are harsh, cramped, and often ungrammatical; totally devoid of all pretension to ease, delicacy, or grace. In short, we pass from the *Latter-day Pamphlets* with the sincere conviction that the author as a politician is shallow and unsound, obscure and fantastic in his philosophy, and very much to be reprehended for his obstinate attempt to inculcate a bad style, and to deteriorate the simple beauty and pure significancy of our language. (pp. 657-58)

[William Edmonstoune Aytoun], "Latter-Day Pamphlets," in Blackwood's Edinburgh Magazine, Vol. LXVII, No. CCCCXVI, June, 1850, pp. 641-58.

[GEORGE ELIOT] (essay date 1852)

[*Eliot is considered one of the foremost English novelists of the nineteenth century. Her novels, including* The Mill on the Floss *(1860) and* Middlemarch *(1871-72), explore psychological and moral issues while providing intimate pictures of everyday life informed by a profound insight into human character. In the following excerpt, she admires* The Life of John Sterling *as Carlyle's most touching and affecting work.*]

[*The Life of John Sterling* is] a labour of love, and to this is owing its strong charm. Carlyle here shows us his "sunny side." We no longer see him breathing out threatenings and slaughter as in the *Latter-Day Pamphlets*, but moving among the charities and amenities of life, loving and beloved—a Teufelsdröckh still, but humanized by a Blumine worthy of him. We have often wished that genius would incline itself more frequently to the task of the biographer,—that when some great or good personage dies, instead of the dreary three or five volumned compilations of letter, and diary, and detail, little to the purpose, which two-thirds of the reading public have not the chance, nor the other third the inclination, to read, we could have a real *Life*, setting forth briefly and vividly the man's inward and outward struggles, aims, and achievements, so as to make clear the meaning which his experience has for his fellows. A few such lives (chiefly, indeed, autobiographies) the world possesses, and they have, perhaps, been more influential on the formation of character than any other kind of reading. But the conditions required for the perfection of life writing,—personal intimacy, a loving and poetic nature which sees the beauty and the depth of familiar things, and the artistic power which seizes characteristic points and renders them with life-like effect,—are seldom found in combination. *The Life of Sterling* is an instance of this rare conjunction. Its comparatively tame scenes and incidents gather picturesqueness and interest under the rich lights of Carlyle's mind. We are told neither too little nor too much; the facts noted, the letters selected, are all such as serve to give the liveliest conception of what Sterling was and what he did; and though the book speaks much of other persons, this collateral matter is all a

kind of scene-painting, and is accessory to the main purpose. (p. 249)

From the period when Carlyle's own acquaintance with Sterling commenced, the *Life* has a double interest, from the glimpses it gives us of the writer, as well as of his hero. We are made present at their first introduction to each other; we get a lively idea of their colloquies and walks together, and in this easy way, without any heavy disquisition or narrative, we obtain a clear insight into Sterling's character and mental progress. Above all, we are gladdened with a perception of the affinity that exists between noble souls, in spite of diversity in ideas—in what Carlyle calls "the logical outcome" of the faculties. This *Life of Sterling* is a touching monument of the capability human nature possesses of the highest love, the love of the good and beautiful in character, which is, after all, the essence of piety. The style of the work, too, is for the most part at once pure and rich; there are passages of deep pathos which come upon the reader like a strain of solemn music, and others which show that aptness of epithet, that masterly power of close delineation, in which, perhaps, no writer has excelled Carlyle. (pp. 250-51)

[George Eliot], "Contemporary Literature of England," in The Westminster Review, Vol. LVII, No. CXI, January 1, 1852, pp. 247-51.

JOHN G. WHITTIER (essay date 1854)

[*A noted American poet, abolitionist, journalist, and critic, Whittier encouraged the idea of American literary nationalism. His works are noted for their moral content, simple sentiment, and humanitarianism. In the following excerpt, he decries the immorality of Carlyle's proslavery stance in* Occasional Discourse on the Nigger Question.]

A late number of *Fraser's Magazine* contains an article bearing the unmistakable impress of the Anglo-German peculiarities of Thomas Carlyle, entitled *An Occasional Discourse on the Negro Question,* which would be interesting as a literary curiosity were it not in spirit and tendency so unspeakably wicked as to excite in every rightminded reader a feeling of amazement and disgust. With a hard, brutal audacity, a blasphemous irreverence, and a sneering mockery which would do honor to the devil of Faust, it takes issue with the moral sense of mankind and the precepts of Christianity. Having ascertained that the exports of sugar and spices from the West Indies have diminished since emancipation,—and that the negroes, having worked, as they believed, quite long enough without wages, now refuse to work for the planters without higher pay than the latter, with the thriftless and evil habits of slavery still clinging to them, can afford to give,—the author considers himself justified in denouncing negro emancipation as one of the "shams" which he was specially sent into this world to belabor. Had he confined himself to simple abuse and caricature of the self-denying and Christian abolitionists of England—"the broad-brimmed philanthropists of Exeter Hall"—there would have been small occasion for noticing his splenetic and discreditable production. Doubtless there is a cant of philanthropy—the alloy of human frailty and folly—in the most righteous reforms, which is a fair subject for the indignant sarcasm of a professed hater of shows and falsities. Whatever is hollow and hypocritical in politics, morals, or religion comes very properly within the scope of his mockery, and we bid him God speed in applying his satirical lash upon it. Impostures and frauds of all kinds deserve nothing better than detection and exposure. Let him blow them up to his heart's content, as Daniel did the image of Bell and the Dragon.

But our author, in this matter of negro slavery, has undertaken to apply his explosive pitch and rosin, not to the affectation of humanity, but to humanity itself. He mocks at pity, scoffs at all who seek to lessen the amount of pain and suffering, sneers at and denies the most sacred rights, and mercilessly consigns an entire class of the children of his heavenly Father to the doom of compulsory servitude. He vituperates the poor black man with a coarse brutality which would do credit to a Mississippi slave driver, or a renegade Yankee dealer in human cattle on the banks of the Potomac. His rhetoric has a flavor of the slave pen and auction block—vulgar, unmanly, indecent—a scandalous outrage upon good taste and refined feeling—which at once degrades the author and insults his readers.

He assumes (for he is one of those sublimated philosophers who reject the Baconian system of induction and depend upon intuition without recourse to facts and figures) that the emancipated class in the West India islands are universally idle, improvident, and unfit for freedom; that God created them to be the servants and slaves of their ''born lords,'' the white men, and designed them to grow sugar, coffee, and spices for their masters, instead of raising pumpkins and yams for themselves; and that, if they will not do this, ''the beneficent whip'' should be again employed to compel them. He adopts, in speaking of the black class, the lowest slang of vulgar prejudice. ''Black Quashee,'' sneers the gentlemanly philosopher,—''black Quashee, if he will not help in bringing out the spices, will get himself made a slave again, (which state will be a little less ugly than his present one,) and with beneficent whip, since other methods avail not, will be compelled to work.''

It is difficult to treat sentiments so atrocious and couched in such offensive language with any thing like respect. Common sense and unperverted conscience revolt instinctively against them. The doctrine they inculcate is that which underlies all tyranny and wrong of man towards man. It is that under which ''the creation groaneth and travaileth unto this day.'' It is as old as sin; the perpetual argument of strength against weakness, of power against right; that of the Greek philosopher, that the barbarians, being of an inferior race, were born to be slaves to the Greeks; and of the infidel Hobbes, that every man, being by nature at war with every other man, has a perpetual right to reduce him to servitude if he has the power. It is the cardinal doctrine of what John Quincy Adams has very properly styled ''the Satanic school of philosophy''—the ethics of an old Norse sea robber or an Arab plunderer of caravans. It is as widely removed from the ''sweet humanities'' and unselfish benevolence of Christianity as the faith and practice of the East India Thug or the New Zealand cannibal.

Our author does not, however, take us altogether by surprise. He has before given no uncertain intimations of the point towards which his philososphy was tending. In his brilliant essay upon Francia of Paraguay, for instance, we find him entering with manifest satisfaction and admiration into the details of his hero's tyranny. In his [*Oliver Cromwell's Letters and Speeches*]— in half a dozen pages of savage and almost diabolical sarcasm directed against the growing humanity of the age, the ''rose-pink sentimentalisms,'' and squeamishness which shudders at the sight of blood and infliction of pain—he prepares the way for a justification of the massacre of Drogheda. More recently he has intimated that the extermination of the Celtic race is the best way of settling the Irish question; and that the enslavement and forcible transportation of her poor, to labor under armed taskmasters in the colonies, is the only rightful and proper remedy for the political and social evils of England. In the

A manuscript page from Latter-Day Pamphlets.

[*Occasional Discourse on the Negro Question*] we see this devilish philosophy in full bloom. The gods, he tells us, are with the strong. Might has a divine right to rule—blessed are the crafty of brain and strong of hand! Weakness is crime. *''Vae victis!''* as Brennus said when he threw his sword into the scale—Woe to the conquered! The negro is weaker in intellect than his ''born lord,'' the white man, and has no right to choose his own vocation. Let the latter do it for him, and, if need be, return to the ''beneficent whip.'' ''On the side of the oppressor there is power;'' let him use it without mercy, and hold flesh and blood to the grindstone with unrelenting rigor. Humanity is squeamishness; pity for the suffering, mere ''rose-pink sentimentalism,'' maudlin and unmanly. The gods (the old Norse gods doubtless) laugh to scorn alike the complaints of the miserable, and the weak compassions and ''philanthropisms'' of those who would relieve them. This is the substance of Thomas Carlyle's advice; this is the matured fruit of his philosophic husbandry—the grand result for which he has been all his life sounding ''unfathomable abysses'' or beating about in the thin air of Transcendentalism. Such is the substitute which he offers us for the Sermon on the Mount. (pp. 34-9)

A more recent production, *Latter Day Pamphlets,* in which man's capability of self-government is more than doubted, democracy somewhat contemptuously sneered at, and the ''model republic'' itself stigmatized as a ''nation of bores,'' may have a salutary effect in restraining our admiration and in lessening our respect for the defender and eulogist of slavery. The sweeping impartiality with which in this latter production he applies the principle of our ''peculiar institution'' to the laboring poor man, irrespective of color, recognizing as his only inalienable right "the right of being set to labor" for his "born lords," will, we imagine, go far to neutralize the mischief of his [*Occasional Discourse on the Negro Question*].

It is a sad thing to find so much intellectual power as Carlyle really possesses so little under the control of the moral sentiments. In some of his earlier writings—as, for instance, his beautiful tribute to the Corn Law rhymer—we thought we saw evidence of a warm and generous sympathy with the poor and the wronged, a desire to ameliorate human suffering, which would have done credit to the "philanthropisms of Exeter Hall" and the "Abolition of Pain Society." Latterly, however, like Molière's quack, he has "changed all that;" his heart has got upon the wrong side; or rather, he seems to us very much in the condition of the coal burner in the German tale who had swapped his heart of flesh for a cobble stone. (pp. 45-6)

> *John G. Whittier, "Thomas Carlyle on the Slave Question," in his* Literary Recreations and Miscellanies, *Ticknor and Fields, 1854, pp. 34-46.*

HARRIET MARTINEAU   (essay date 1855)

[*An English author, Martineau wrote* Illustrations of Political Economy *(1832-34), a series of stories calling for social reform. She was acquainted with Carlyle, who liked her despite her liberal, utilitarian views. In her autobiography, which she wrote in 1855, Martineau attributed Carlyle's ferocity of manner and writing to his love and sympathy for humanity: "He does not know what to do with his [excess of sympathy], and with its bitterness, seeing that human life is full of pain to those who look out for it: and the savageness which has come to be a main characteristic of this singular man is, in my opinion, a mere expression of his intolerable sympathy with the suffering." In the following excerpt, also from her autobiography, Martineau explains her preferences among Carlyle's works and hails his potency as a force for moral regeneration.*]

[Carlyle's] mind has always seemed to me as inaccessible as Wordsworth's, or any other constitutionally isolated like theirs: and therefore it is that I prefer to an outpouring of his own notions, which we have heard as often as he has written didactically, and which were best conveyed in his *Sartor Resartus,* a commentary on a character, as in biography, or on events, as in a history. For many reasons, I prefer his biographies. I do not think that he can do any more effectual work in the field of philosophy or morals: but I enjoy an occasional addition to the fine gallery of portraits which he has given us. I am now too much out of the world to know what is the real condition of his fame and influence: but, for my own part, I could not read his *Latter Day Pamphlets,* while heartily enjoying his *Life* of his friend Sterling, and, in the main, his *Cromwell.* No one can read his *Cromwell* without longing for his *Frederick the Great:* and I hope he will achieve that portrait, and others after it. However much or little he may yet do, he certainly ought to be recognised as one of the chief influences of his time. Bad as is our political morality, and grievous as are our social short-comings, we are at least awakened to a sense of our sins: and I cannot but ascribe this awakening mainly to Carlyle. What Wordsworth did for poetry, in bringing us out of a conventional idea and method to a true and simple one, Carlyle has done for morality. He may be himself the most curious opposition to himself,—he may be the greatest mannerist of his age while denouncing conventionalism,—the greatest talker while eulogising silence,—the most woeful complainer while glorifying fortitude,—the most uncertain and stormy in

mood, while holding forth serenity as the greatest good within the reach of Man: but he has nevertheless infused into the mind of the English nation a sincerity, earnestness, healthfulness and courage which can be appreciated only by those who are old enough to tell what was our morbid state when Byron was the representative of our temper, the Clapham Church of our religion, and the rotten-borough system of our political morality. If I am warranted in believing that the society I am bidding farewell to is a vast improvement upon that which I was born into, I am confident that the blessed change is attributable to Carlyle more than to any single influence besides. (pp. 386-87)

> *Harriet Martineau, in an excerpt in her* Harriet Martineau's Autobiography, Vol. I, *Smith, Elder, & Co., 1877, pp. 386-87.*

JAMES RUSSELL LOWELL   (essay date 1871)

[*Lowell was a celebrated American poet and essayist and the editor of two leading journals, the* Atlantic Monthly *and the* North American Review. *He is noted for his satirical and critical writings, including* A Fable for Critics *(1848), a book-length poem featuring witty critical portraits of his contemporaries. Commentators generally agree that Lowell displayed a judicious critical sense, and despite the fact that he sometimes relied upon impressions rather than critical precepts, most literary historians rank him with the major nineteenth-century American critics. In the following excerpt from a retrospective of Carlyle's career, Lowell contends that the author's work has progressively degenerated from conviction to dogma, indignation to railing, sincerity to formula. Still, Lowell believes Carlyle is due "reverential gratitude" for the achievements of his prime.*]

Mr. Carlyle is an author who has now been so long before the world, that we may feel toward him something of the unprejudice of posterity. It has long been evident that he had no more ideas to bestow upon us, and that no new turn of his kaleidoscope would give us anything but some variation of arrangement in the brilliant colors of his style. It is perhaps possible, then, to arrive at some not wholly inadequate estimate of his place as a writer, and especially of the value of the ideas whose advocate he makes himself, with a bitterness and violence that increase, as it seems to us, in proportion as his inward conviction of their truth diminishes. (p. 121)

In the earliest authorship of Mr. Carlyle we find some not obscure hints of the future man. Nearly fifty years ago he contributed a few literary and critical articles to the *Edinburgh Encyclopaedia.* The outward fashion of them is that of the period; but they are distinguished by a certain security of judgment remarkable at any time, remarkable especially in one so young. British criticism has been always more or less parochial; has never, indeed, quite freed itself from sectarian cant, and planted itself honestly on the aesthetic point of view. It cannot quite persuade itself that truth is of immortal essence, totally independent of all assistance from quarterly journals or the British army and navy. Carlyle, in these first essays, already shows the influence of his master, Goethe, the most widely receptive of critics. In a compact notice of Montaigne, there is not a word as to his religious scepticism. The character is looked at purely from its human and literary sides. . . . We find here no uncertain indication of that eye for the moral picturesque, and that sympathetic appreciation of character, which within the next few years were to make Carlyle the first in insight of English critics and the most vivid of English historians. In all his earlier writing he never loses sight of his master's great rule, *Den Gegenstand fest zu halten.* He accordingly gave to Englishmen the first humanly possible likeness of Voltaire, Diderot, Mirabeau, and others, who had hitherto been measured by the usual British standard of their respect for the geognosy of Moses and the historic credibility of the Books of Chronicles. What was the real meaning of this phenomenon? what the amount of this man's honest performance in the world? and in what does he show that family-likeness, common to all the sons of Adam, which gives us a fair hope of being able to comprehend him? These were the questions which Carlyle seems to have set himself honestly to answer in the critical writings which fill the first period of his life as a man of letters. In this mood he rescued poor Boswell from the unmerited obloquy of an ungrateful generation, and taught us to see something half-comically beautiful in the poor, weak creature, with his pathetic instinct of reverence for what was nobler, wiser, and stronger than himself. Everything that Mr. Carlyle wrote during this first period thrills with the purest appreciation of whatever is brave and beautiful in human nature, with the most vehement scorn of cowardly compromise with things base; and yet, immitigable as his demand for the highest in us seems to be, there is always something reassuring in the humorous sympathy with mortal frailty which softens condemnation and consoles for shortcoming. The remarkable feature of Mr. Carlyle's criticism (see, for example, his analysis and exposition of Goethe's *Helena*) is the sleuth-hound instinct with which he presses on to the *matter* of his theme,—never turned aside by a false scent, regardless of the outward beauty of form, sometimes almost contemptuous of it, in his hunger after the intellectual nourishment which it may hide. The delicate skeleton of admirably articulated and related parts which underlies and sustains every true work of art, and keeps it from sinking on itself a shapeless heap, he would crush remorselessly to come at the marrow of meaning. With him the ideal sense is secondary to the ethical and metaphysical, and he has but a faint conception of their possible unity.

By degrees the humorous element in his nature gains ground, till it overmasters all the rest. Becoming always more boisterous and obtrusive, it ends at last, as such humor must, in cynicism. In *Sartor Resartus* it is still kindly, still infused with sentiment; and the book, with its mixture of indignation and farce, strikes one as might the prophecies of Jeremiah, if the marginal comments of the Rev. Mr. Sterne in his wildest mood had by some accident been incorporated with the text. In *Sartor* the marked influence of Jean Paul is undeniable, both in matter and manner. It is curious for one who studies the action and reaction of national literatures on each other, to see the humor of Swift and Sterne and Fielding, after filtering through Richter, reappear in Carlyle with a tinge of Germanism that makes it novel, alien, or even displeasing, as the case may be, to the English mind. Unhappily the bit of *mother* from Swift's vinegar-barrel has had strength enough to sour all the rest. The whimsicality of *Tristram Shandy,* which, even in the original, has too often the effect of forethought, becomes a deliberate artifice in Richter, and at last a mere mannerism in Carlyle.

Mr. Carlyle in his critical essays had the advantage of a well-defined theme, and of limits both in the subject and in the space allowed for its treatment, which kept his natural extravagance within bounds, and compelled some sort of discretion and compactness. The great merit of these essays lay in a criticism based on wide and various study, which, careless of tradition, applied its standard to the real and not the contemporary worth of the literary or other performance to be judged, and in an unerring eye for that fleeting expression of the moral features of character, a perception of which alone makes the

drawing of a coherent likeness possible. Their defect was a tendency, gaining strength with years, to confound the moral with the aesthetic standard, and to make the value of an author's work dependent on the general force of his nature rather than on its special fitness for a given task. In proportion as his humor gradually overbalanced the other qualities of his mind, his taste for the eccentric, amorphous, and violent in men became excessive, disturbing more and more his perception of the more commonplace attributes which give consistency to portraiture. His *French Revolution* is a series of lurid pictures, unmatched for vehement power, in which the figures of such sons of earth as Mirabeau and Danton loom gigantic and terrible as in the glare of an eruption, their shadows swaying far and wide grotesquely awful. But all is painted by eruption flashes in violent light and shade. There are no half-tints, no gradations, and we find it impossible to account for the continuance in power of less Titanic actors in the tragedy like Robespierre, on any theory whether of human nature or of individual character supplied by Mr. Carlyle. Of his success, however, in accomplishing what he aimed at, which was to haunt the mind with memories of a horrible political nightmare, there can be no doubt.

Goethe says, apparently thinking of Richter, ''The worthy Germans have persuaded themselves that the essence of true humor is formlessness.'' Heine had not yet shown that a German might combine the most airy humor with a sense of form as delicate as Goethe's own, and that there was no need to borrow the bow of Philoctetes for all kinds of game. Mr. Carlyle's own tendency was toward the lawless, and the attraction of Jean Paul made it an overmastering one. Goethe, we think, might have gone farther, and affirmed that nothing but the highest artistic sense can prevent humor from degenerating into the grotesque, and thence downwards to utter anarchy. Rabelais is a striking example of it. The moral purpose of his book cannot give that unity which the instinct and forethought of art only can bring forth. Perhaps we owe the masterpiece of humorous literature to the fact that Cervantes had been trained to authorship in a school where form predominated over substance, and the most convincing proof of the supremacy of art at the highest period of Greek literature is to be found in Aristophanes. Mr. Carlyle has no artistic sense of form or rhythm, scarcely of proportion. Accordingly he looks on verse with contempt as something barbarous,—a savage ornament which a higher refinement will abolish, as it has tattooing and nose-rings. With a conceptive imagination vigorous beyond any in his generation, with a mastery of language equalled only by the greatest poets, he wants altogether the plastic imagination, the shaping faculty, which would have made him a poet in the highest sense. He is a preacher and a prophet,—anything you will,—but an artist he is not, and never can be. It is always the knots and gnarls of the oak that he admires, never the perfect and balanced tree.

It is certainly more agreeable to be grateful for what we owe an author, than to blame him for what he cannot give us. But it is sometimes the business of a critic to trace faults of style and of thought to their root in character and temperament,—to show their necessary relation to, and dependence on, each other,—and to find some more trustworthy explanation than mere wantonness of will for the moral obliquities of a man so largely moulded and gifted as Mr. Carlyle. So long as he was merely an exhorter or dehorter, we were thankful for such eloquence, such humor, such vivid or grotesque images, and such splendor of illustration as only he could give; but when he assumes to be a teacher of moral and political philosophy, when he himself takes to compounding the social panaceas he has made us laugh at so often, and advertises none as genuine but his own, we begin to inquire into his qualifications and his defects, and to ask ourselves whether his patent pill differs from others except in the larger amount of aloes, or has any better recommendation than the superior advertising powers of a mountebank of genius. Comparative criticism teaches us that moral and aesthetic defects are more nearly related than is commonly supposed. Had Mr. Carlyle been fitted out completely by nature as an artist, he would have had an ideal in his work which would have lifted his mind away from the muddier part of him, and trained him to the habit of seeking and seeing the harmony rather than the discord and contradiction of things. His innate love of the picturesque, (which is only another form of the sentimentalism he so scoffs at, perhaps as feeling it a weakness in himself,) once turned in the direction of character, and finding its chief satisfaction there, led him to look for that ideal of human nature in individual men which is but fragmentarily represented in the entire race, and is rather divined from the aspiration, forever disenchanted to be forever renewed, of the immortal part in us, than found in any example of actual achievement. A wiser temper would have found something more consoling than disheartening in the continual failure of men eminently endowed to reach the standard of this spiritual requirement, would perhaps have found in it an inspiring hint that it is mankind, and not special men, that are to be shaped at last into the image of God, and that the endless life of the generations may hope to come nearer that goal of which the short-breathed threescore years and ten fall too unhappily short.

But Mr. Carlyle has invented the Hero-cure, and all who recommend any other method, or see any hope of healing elsewhere, are either quacks and charlatans or their victims. His lively imagination conjures up the image of an impossible he, as contradictorily endowed as the chief personage in a modern sentimental novel, and who, at all hazards, must not lead mankind like a shepherd, but bark, bite, and otherwise worry them toward the fold like a truculent sheep-dog. If Mr. Carlyle would only now and then recollect that men are men, and not sheep,—nay, that the farther they are from being such, the more well grounded our hope of one day making something better of them! It is indeed strange that one who values Will so highly in the greatest, should be blind to its infinite worth in the least of men; nay, that he should so often seem to confound it with its irritable and purposeless counterfeit, Wilfulness. The natural impatience of an imaginative temperament, which conceives so vividly the beauty and desirableness of a nobler manhood and a diviner political order, makes him fret at the slow moral processes by which the All-Wise brings about his ends, and turns the very foolishness of men to his praise and glory. Mr. Carlyle is for calling down fire from Heaven whenever he cannot readily lay his hand on the match-box. No doubt it is somewhat provoking that it should be so easy to build castles in the air, and so hard to find tenants for them. It is a singular intellectual phenomenon to see a man, who earlier in life so thoroughly appreciated the innate weakness and futile tendency of the "storm and thrust" period of German literature, constantly assimilating, as he grows older, more and more nearly to its principles and practice. It is no longer the sagacious and moderate Goethe who is his type of what is highest in human nature, but far rather some Götz of the Iron Hand, some assertor of the divine legitimacy of *Faustrecht*. It is odd to conceive the fate of Mr. Carlyle under the sway of any of his heroes,—how Cromwell would have scorned him as a babbler more long-winded than Prynne, but less clear and practical,—how Friedrich would have scoffed at his tirades as *dummes Zeug*

not to be compared with the romances of Crébillon *fils*, or possibly have clapped him in a marching regiment as a fit subject for the cane of the sergeant. Perhaps something of Mr. Carlyle's irritability is to be laid to the account of his early schoolmastership at Ecclefechan. This great booby World is such a dull boy, and will not learn the lesson we have taken such pains in expounding for the fiftieth time. Well, then, if eloquence, if example, if the awful warning of other little boys who neglected their accidence and came to the gallows, if none of these avail, the birch at least is left, and we will try that. The dominie spirit has become every year more obtrusive and intolerant in Mr. Carlyle's writing, and the rod, instead of being kept in its place as a resource for desperate cases, has become the alpha and omega of all successful training, the one divinely-appointed means of human enlightenment and progress,—in short, the final hope of that absurd animal who fancies himself a little lower than the angels. Have we feebly taken it for granted that the distinction of man was reason? Never was there a more fatal misconception. It is in the gift of unreason that we are unenviably distinguished from the brutes, whose nobler privilege of instinct saves them from our blunders and our crimes.

But since Mr. Carlyle has become possessed with the hallucination that he is head-master of this huge boys' school which we call the world, his pedagogic birch has grown to the taller proportions and more ominous aspect of a gallows. His article on Dr. Francia was a panegyric of the halter, in which the gratitude of mankind is invoked for the self-appointed dictator who had discovered in Paraguay a tree more beneficent than that which produced the Jesuits' bark. Mr. Carlyle seems to be in the condition of a man who uses stimulants, and must increase his dose from day to day as the senses become dulled under the spur. He began by admiring strength of character and purpose, and the manly self-denial which makes a humble fortune great by steadfast loyalty to duty. He has gone on till mere strength has become such washy weakness that there is no longer any titillation in it; and nothing short of downright violence will rouse his nerves now to the needed excitement. At first he made out very well with remarkable men; then, lessening the water and increasing the spirit, he took to Heroes: and now he must have downright *in*humanity, or the draught has no savor;—so he gets on at last to Kings, types of remorseless Force, who maintain the political views of Berserkers by the legal principles of Lynch. Constitutional monarchy is a failure, representative government is a gabble, democracy a birth of the bottomless pit; there is no hope for mankind except in getting themselves under a good driver who shall not spare the lash. And yet, unhappily for us, these drivers are providential births not to be contrived by any cunning of ours, and Friedrich II. is hitherto the last of them. Meanwhile the world's wheels have got fairly stalled in mire and other matter of every vilest consistency and most disgustful smell. What are we to do? Mr. Carlyle will not let us make a lever with a rail from the next fence, or call in the neighbors. That would be too commonplace and cowardly, too anarchical. No; he would have us sit down beside him in the slough, and shout lustily for Hercules. If that indispensable demigod will not or cannot come, we can find a useful and instructive solace, during the intervals of shouting, in a hearty abuse of human nature, which, at the long last, is always to blame.

Since *Sartor Resartus* Mr. Carlyle has done little but repeat himself with increasing emphasis and heightened shrillness. Warning has steadily heated toward denunciation, and remonstrance soured toward scolding. The image of the Tartar prayer-mill, which he borrowed from Richter and turned to such humorous purpose, might be applied to himself. The same phrase comes round and round, only the machine, being a little crankier, rattles more, and the performer is called on for a more visible exertion. If there be not something very like cant in Mr. Carlyle's later writings, then cant is not the repetition of a creed after it has become a phrase by the cooling of that white-hot conviction which once made it both the light and warmth of the soul. We do not mean intentional and deliberate cant, but neither is that which Mr. Carlyle denounces so energetically in his fellow-men of that conscious kind. We do not mean to blame him for it, but mention it rather as an interesting phenomenon of human nature. The stock of ideas which mankind has to work with is very limited, like the alphabet, and can at best have an air of freshness given it by new arrangements and combinations, or by application to new times and circumstances. Montaigne is but Ecclesiastes writing in the sixteenth century, Voltaire but Lucian in the eighteenth. Yet both are original, and so certainly is Mr. Carlyle, whose borrowing is mainly from his own former works. But he does this so often and so openly, that we may at least be sure that he ceased growing a number of years ago, and is a remarkable example of arrested development.

The cynicism, however, which has now become the prevailing temper of his mind, has gone on expanding with unhappy vigor. In Mr. Carlyle it is not, certainly, as in Swift, the result of personal disappointment, and of the fatal eye of an accomplice for the mean qualities by which power could be attained that it might be used for purposes as mean. It seems rather the natural corruption of his exuberant humor. Humor in its first analysis is a perception of the incongruous, and in its highest development, of the incongruity between the actual and the ideal in men and life. With so keen a sense of the ludicrous contrast between what men might be, nay, wish to be, and what they are, and with a vehement nature that demands the instant realization of his vision of a world altogether heroic, it is no wonder that Mr. Carlyle, always hoping for a thing and always disappointed, should become bitter. Perhaps if he expected less he would find more. Saul seeking his father's asses found himself turned suddenly into a king; but Mr. Carlyle, on the lookout for a king, always seems to find the other sort of animal. He sees nothing on any side of him but a procession of the Lord of Misrule, in gloomier moments, a Dance of Death, where everything is either a parody of whatever is noble, or an aimless jig that stumbles at last into the annihilation of the grave, and so passes from one nothing to another. Is a world, then, which buys and reads Mr. Carlyle's works distinguished only for its "fair, large ears"? If he who has read and remembered so much would only now and then call to mind the old proverb, *Nec deus, nec lupus, sed homo!* If he would only recollect that, from the days of the first grandfather, everybody has remembered a golden age behind him!

The very qualities, it seems to us, which came so near making a great poet of Mr. Carlyle, disqualify him for the office of historian. The poet's concern is with the appearances of things, with their harmony in that whole which the imagination demands for its satisfaction, and their truth to that ideal nature which is the proper object of poetry. History, unfortunately, is very far from being ideal, still farther from an exclusive interest in those heroic or typical figures which answer all the wants of the epic and the drama and fill their utmost artistic limits. Mr. Carlyle has an unequalled power and vividness in painting detached scenes, in bringing out in their full relief the oddities or peculiarities of character; but he has a far feebler sense of those gradual changes of opinion, that strange communication of sympathy from mind to mind, that subtile influence of very subordinate actors in giving a direction to policy or action, which we are wont somewhat vaguely to call the progress of events. His scheme of history is purely an epical one, where only leading figures appear by name and are in any strict sense operative. He has no conception of the people as anything else than an element of mere brute force in political problems, and would sniff scornfully at that unpicturesque common-sense of the many, which comes slowly to its conclusions, no doubt, but compels obedience even from rulers the most despotic when once its mind is made up. . . . Were it not for the purely picturesque bias of Mr. Carlyle's genius, for the necessity which his epical treatment lays upon him of always having a protagonist, we should be astonished that an idealist like him should have so little faith in ideas and so much in matter.

Mr. Carlyle's manner is not so well suited to the historian as to the essayist. He is always great in single figures and striking episodes, but there is neither gradation nor continuity. He has extraordinary patience and conscientiousness in the gathering and sifting of his material, but is scornful of commonplace facts and characters, impatient of whatever will not serve for one of his clever sketches, or group well in a more elaborate figure-piece. He sees history, as it were, by flashes of lightning. A single scene, whether a landscape or an interior, a single figure or a wild mob of men, whatever may be snatched by the eye in that instant of intense illumination, is minutely photographed upon the memory. Every tree and stone, almost every blade of grass; every article of furniture in a room; the attitude or expression, nay, the very buttons and shoe-ties of a principal figure; the gestures of momentary passion in a wild throng,—everything leaps into vision under that sudden glare with a painful distinctness that leaves the retina quivering. The intervals are absolute darkness. Mr. Carlyle makes us acquainted with the isolated spot where we happen to be when the flash comes, as if by actual eyesight, but there is no possibility of a comprehensive view. No other writer compares with him for vividness. He is himself a witness, and makes us witnesses of whatever he describes. This is genius beyond a question, and of a very rare quality, but it is not history. He has not the cold-blooded impartiality of the historian; and while he entertains us, moves us to tears or laughter, makes us the unconscious captives of his ever-changeful mood, we find that he has taught us comparatively little. His imagination is so powerful that it makes him the contemporary of his characters, and thus his history seems to be the memoirs of a cynical humorist, with hearty likes and dislikes, with something of acridity in his partialities whether for or against, more keenly sensitive to the grotesque than the simply natural, and who enters in his diary, even of what comes within the range of his own observation, only so much as amuses his fancy, is congenial with his humor, or feeds his prejudice. Mr. Carlyle's method is accordingly altogether pictorial, his hasty temper making narrative wearisome to him. In his *Friedrich,* for example, we get very little notion of the civil administration of Prussia; and when he comes, in the last volume, to his hero's dealings with civil reforms, he confesses candidly that it would tire him too much to tell us about it, even if he knew anything at all satisfactory himself.

Mr. Carlyle's historical compositions are wonderful prose poems, full of picture, incident, humor, and character, where we grow familiar with his conception of certain leading personages, and even of subordinate ones, if they are necessary to the scene, so that they come out living upon the stage from the dreary limbo of names; but this is no more history than the historical plays of Shakespeare. There is nothing in imaginative literature superior in its own way to the episode of Voltaire in the *Fritziad*. It is delicious in humor, masterly in minute characterization. We feel as if the principal victim (for we cannot help feeling all the while that he is so) of this mischievous genius had been put upon the theatre before us by some perfect mimic like Foote, who had studied his habitual gait, gestures, tones, turn of thought, costume, trick of feature, and rendered them with the slight dash of caricature needful to make the whole composition tell. It is in such things that Mr. Carlyle is beyond all rivalry, and that we must go back to Shakespeare for a comparison. But the mastery of Shakespeare is shown perhaps more strikingly in his treatment of the ordinary than of the exceptional. His is the gracious equality of Nature herself. Mr. Carlyle's gift is rather in the representation than in the evolution of character; and it is a necessity of his art, therefore, to exaggerate slightly his heroic, and to caricature in like manner his comic parts. His appreciation is less psychological than physical and external. . . . If his sympathies bore any proportion to his instinct for catching those traits which are the expression of character, but not character itself, we might have had a great historian in him instead of a history-painter. But that which is a main element in Mr. Carlyle's talent, and does perhaps more than anything else to make it effective, is a defect of his nature. The cynicism which renders him so entertaining precludes him from any just conception of men and their motives, and from any sane estimate of the relative importance of the events which concern them. . . . The cynical view is congenial to certain moods, and is so little inconsistent with original nobleness of mind, that it is not seldom the acetous fermentation of it; but it is the view of the satirist, not of the historian, and takes in but a narrow arc in the circumference of truth. Cynicism in itself is essentially disagreeable. It is the intellectual analogue of the truffle; and though it may be very well in giving a relish to thought for certain palates, it cannot supply the substance of it. Mr. Carlyle's cynicism is not that polished weariness of the outsides of life which we find in Ecclesiastes. It goes much deeper than that to the satisfactions, not of the body or the intellect, but of the very soul itself. It vaunts itself; it is noisy and aggressive. What the wise master puts into the mouth of desperate ambition, thwarted of the fruit of its crime, as the fitting expression of passionate sophistry, seems to have become an article of his creed. With him

> Life *is* a tale
> Told by an idiot, full of sound and fury,
> Signifying nothing.

He goes about with his Diogenes dark-lantern, professing to seek a man, but inwardly resolved to find a monkey. He loves to flash it suddenly on poor human nature in some ridiculous or degrading posture. He admires still, or keeps affirming that he admires, the doughty, silent, hard-working men who, like Cromwell, go honestly about their business; but when we come to his later examples, we find that it is not loyalty to duty or to an inward ideal of high-mindedness that he finds admirable in them, but a blind unquestioning vassalage to whomsoever it has pleased him to set up for a hero. (pp. 122-38)

In the earlier part of his literary career, Mr. Carlyle was the denouncer of shams, the preacher up of sincerity, manliness, and of a living faith, instead of a droning ritual. He had intense convictions, and he made disciples. With a compass of diction unequalled by any other public performer of the time, ranging as it did from the unbooked freshness of the Scottish peasant to the most far-sought phrase of literary curiosity, with humor, pathos, and eloquence at will, it was no wonder that he found eager listeners in a world longing for a sensation, and forced to put up with the West-End gospel of *Pelham*. If not a profound thinker, he had what was next best,—he felt profoundly, and his cry came out of the depths. . . . Mr. Carlyle won his first successes as a kind of preacher in print. His fervor, his oddity of manner, his spugnacious paradox, drew the crowd; the truth, or, at any rate, the faith that underlay them all, brought also the fitter audience, though fewer. But the curse was upon him; he must attract, he must astonish. Thenceforth he has done nothing but revamp his telling things; but the oddity has become always odder, the paradoxes more paradoxical. No very large share of truth falls to the apprehension of any one man; let him keep it sacred, and beware of repeating it till it turn to falsehood on his lips by becoming ritual. Truth always has a bewitching savor of newness in it, and novelty at the first taste recalls that original sweetness to the tongue; but alas for him who would make the one a substitute for the other! We seem to miss of late in Mr. Carlyle the old sincerity. He has become the purely literary man, less concerned about what he says than about how he shall say it to best advantage. The Muse should be the companion, not the guide, says he whom Mr. Carlyle has pronounced ''the wisest of this generation.'' What would be a virtue in the poet is a vice of the most fatal kind in the teacher, and, alas that we should say it! the very Draco of shams, whose code contained no penalty milder than capital for the most harmless of them, has become at last something very like a sham himself. Mr. Carlyle continues to be a voice crying in the wilderness, but no longer a voice with any earnest conviction behind it. (pp. 139-40)

With the gift of song, Carlyle would have been the greatest of epic poets since Homer. Without it, to modulate and harmonize and bring parts into their proper relation, he is the most amorphous of humorists, the most shining avatar of whim the world has ever seen. Beginning with a hearty contempt for shams, he has come at length to believe in brute force as the only reality, and has as little sense of justice as Thackeray allowed to women. We say *brute force* because, though the theory is that this force should be directed by the supreme intellect for the time being, yet all inferior wits are treated rather as obstacles to be contemptuously shoved aside than as ancillary forces to be conciliated through their reason. But, with all deductions, he remains the profoundest critic and the most dramatic imagination of modern times. Never was there a more striking example of that *ingenium perfervidum* long ago said to be characteristic of his countrymen. His is one of the natures, rare in these latter centuries, capable of rising to a white heat; but once fairly kindled, he is like a three-decker on fire, and his shotted guns go off, as the glow reaches them, alike dangerous to friend or foe. Though he seems more and more to confound material with moral success, yet there is always something wholesome in his unswerving loyalty to reality, as he understands it. History, in the true sense, he does not and cannot write, for he looks on mankind as a herd without volition, and without moral force; but such vivid pictures of events, such living conceptions of character, we find nowhere else in prose. The figures of most historians seem like dolls stuffed with bran, whose whole substance runs out through any hole that criticism may tear in them, but Carlyle's are so real in comparison, that, if you prick them, they bleed. He seems a little wearied, here and there, in his *Friedrich*, with the multiplicity of detail, and does his filling-in rather shabbily; but he still remains in his own way, like his hero, the Only, and such episodes as that of Voltaire would make the fortune of any other writer. Though not the safest of guides in politics or practical philosophy, his value as an inspirer and awakener cannot be over-estimated. It is a power which belongs only to the highest order of minds, for it is none but a divine fire that can so kindle and irradiate. The debt due him from those who listened to the teachings of his prime for revealing to them what sublime reserves of power even the humblest may find in manliness, sincerity, and self-reliance, can be paid with nothing short of reverential gratitude. As a purifier of the sources whence our intellectual inspiration is drawn, his influence has been second only to that of Wordsworth, if even to his. (pp. 148-49)

> James Russell Lowell, "Carlyle," in his My Study Windows, *James R. Osgood and Company, 1871, pp. 115-49.*

[LESLIE STEPHEN] (essay date 1881)

[*Stephen is considered one of the most important English literary critics of the late Victorian and early Edwardian eras. In his criticism, which was often moralistic, Stephen argued that all literature is nothing more than an imaginative rendering, in concrete terms, of a writer's philosophy or beliefs. It is the role of criticism, he contended, to translate into intellectual terms what the writer has told the reader through character, symbol, and plot. Stephen's analyses often include biographical judgments. As Stephen once observed, "The whole art of criticism consists in learning to know the human being who is partially revealed to us in his spoken or his written words." In the following excerpt, Stephen eulogizes Carlyle, emphasizing his friend's moral integrity and intensity.*]

I do not propose at the present time to attempt anything like a critical estimate of the great man who has just passed from our midst. Better occasions may offer themselves for saying what has to be said in that direction. For the present it would seem that there is little need of speech. Much has been written, and not a little admirably written, in commemoration of the teacher and the message which he delivered to mankind; as also there has not been wanting the usual snarl of the cynic irritated by a chorus of eulogy. Even the feeblest of critics could scarcely fail to catch some of the characteristic features of one of the most vigorous and strongly-marked types that ever appeared in our literature. The strongest amongst them would find it hard to exhaust the full significance of so remarkable a phenomenon. Despair of saying anything not palpably inadequate or anything not already said by many writers might suggest the propriety of silence, were it not that in any review which claims a literary character it might seem unbecoming not to make some passing act of homage to one who was yesterday our foremost man of letters. To do justice to such a theme we ought to have been touched by the mantle of the prophet himself. We should have been masters of the spell wrought by his unique faculty of humorous imagination. When Mr. Carlyle spoke, as he has spoken in so many familiar passages, of the death of a personal friend, or of one of those heroes whom he loved with personal affection, he could thrill us with a pathos peculiar to himself; for no one could adopt more naturally or interpret more forcibly the mood of lofty Stoicism, dominating without deadening the most tender yearning; or enable us at once to recognise the surpassing value of a genuine hero and to feel how dreamlike and transitory all human life appears in presence of the eternal and infinite, and how paltry a thing, in the moments when such glimpses are vouchsafed to us, is the most towering of human ambitions. To express adequately these solemn emotions is the prerogative

of men endowed with the true poetic gift. It will be enough for a prosaic critic to recall briefly some of the plain and tangible grounds which justify the pride of his fellow-countrymen—especially of those who follow his calling—in Mr. Carlyle's reputation. (p. 349)

Carlyle, as we all know, indulged in much eloquent declamation upon the merits of silence as compared with speech. Like many other men of literary eminence, he seemed rather to enjoy the depreciation of his own peculiar function.... Heartily as Carlyle loved certain great literary teachers, more or less congenial to his own temperament, he always places them on a level distinctly beneath that of statesman or soldier.... (p. 350)

Carlyle at another period might have been a Knox heading a great spiritual movement, or at least a Cameronian preacher stimulating the faith of his brethren under the fire of persecution. Under actual circumstances, no precise post in the army of active workers was open to him; and he was forced to throw in his lot with the loose bands of literary skirmishers each of whom has to fight for his own hand, and to strike in here and there without concert or combination.... The qualities which he admired with his whole soul were force of will, intensity of purpose, exclusive devotion to some worthy end. What he hated from the bottom of his heart were any practices tending to dissipate the energy which might have accomplished great things or to allow it to expend itself upon unreal objects. We may remember, to quote one amongst a thousand instances, his references to that remarkable religious reformer, Ram Dass, who declared himself to have fire enough in his belly to burn up the sins of the whole world. A man, according to his view, is valuable in proportion as he has a share of that sacred fire. We are tempted unfortunately to use it up merely for cooking purposes, or to turn it to account for idle pyrotechnical displays. He is the greatest who uses the fire for its legitimate purposes and in whom it burns with the whitest and most concentrated heat. Perhaps in enforcing this doctrine from every possible point of view, Carlyle may have shown some want of appreciation for certain harmless and agreeable modes of dissipating energy. The Puritan in grain—and certainly the name applies to no one if not to Carlyle—finds a difficulty in coming to an understanding with the lover of a wider culture. But, in any case, it is not really a question between the means of speech and of action, but between those who have and those who have not an overpowering sense of the paramount importance of the ends to be obtained.

Now it may be fairly said that Carlyle's words have in this sense the quality of deeds. Intensity is the cardinal virtue of his style. The one essential thing with him is to make a deep impression; he must strike at the heart of the hearers and grasp at once the central truth to be inculcated; he cares less than nothing for the rules of art so long as he can gain his end; and will snatch at any weapons in his power, whether he is to be grotesque or sublime, tender or cynical in expression, or to produce an effect not capable of being tabulated under any critical category. The blemishes as well as the surpassing merits of his writings spring equally from a characteristic which naturally makes him unintelligible and at times offensive to men of different temperaments. Now whatever the literary consequences, the man's own personality derived from it a singular impressiveness. Great men are sometimes disappointing; but no one could possibly be disappointed who made a pilgrimage to the little house in Chelsea. It is a feeble expression of the truth to say that the talk resembled the writing; it seemed more frequently to be the quintessence of this writing. Ever after-wards, if you took up *Sartor Resartus* or the **French Revolution,** you seemed to have learnt the inevitable cadence of the sentences; you heard the solemn passages rolled out in the strong current of broad Scotch, and the grotesque phrases recalled the sudden flash of the deep-set eyes and the huge explosions of tremendous laughter full of intense enjoyment, and yet dashed with an undertone of melancholy; or you saw the bent frame in its queer old dressing-gown, taking the pipe from its lips and rapping out some thundering denunciation of modern idols with more than Johnsonian vigour. You came to understand how the oddities which strike some hasty readers as savouring of affectation really expressed the inmost nature of the man; and that the strange light cast upon the world represented the way in which objects spontaneously presented themselves to his singularly constituted imagination. Instead of fancying that he had gradually learnt a queer dialect in order to impress his readers, you came to perceive that the true process was one of gradually learning to trust his natural voice where he had at first thought it necessary to array himself more or less in the conventional costume of ordinary mortals. Briefly it became manifest that the contortions of the Sibyl (to quote Burke's phrase about Johnson) was the effect of a genuine inspiration, and the very reverse of external oddities adopted of *malice prepense.* (pp. 350-52)

Some writers complain that Carlyle did not advance any new doctrine, or succeed in persuading the world of its truth. His life failed, it is suggested, in so far as he did not make any large body of converts with an accepted code of belief. But here, as it seems to me, the criticism becomes irrelevant. No one will dispute that Carlyle taught a strongly marked and highly characteristic creed, though one not easily packed into a definite set of logical formulae. If there was no particular novelty in his theories, that was his very contention. His aim was to utter the truths which had been the strength and the animating principles of great and good men in all ages. He was not to move us, like a scientific discoverer, by proclaiming novelties, but to utter his protest in behalf of the permanent truths, obscured in the struggle between conflicting dogmas and drowned in the anarchical shrieks of contending parties. He succeeded in so far as he impressed the emotions and the imagination of his fellows, not in so far as he made known to them any new doctrine. Nor was his life to be called a failure, judged by his own standard, because he failed to produce any tangible result. Rightly or wrongly, Carlyle was no worshipper of progress, nor, indeed, a believer in its existence. The fact that an opinion did not make its way in the world was not even a presumption against its truth and importance in a world daily growing more and more chaotic, plunging wildly over Niagaras, falling more hopelessly under the dominion of shams and pursuing wilder phantasms into more boundless regions of distracted bewilderment. His duty was accomplished when he had liberated his own soul; when he had spoken so much truth as it was given to him to perceive, and left it to work as it might in the general play of incalculable forces. Here is truth: make what you can of it; if you can translate it into action, so much the better; if it only serves to animate a few faithful Abdiels, struggling with little hope and even less success against the manifold perplexities of a collapsing order, it has at least been so far useful. The sower must be content when he has cast the seed; he must leave it to the Power which rules the universe to decide whether it shall bear fruit a thousandfold, or be choked amongst the tares which are sprouting up in every direction with a growth of unparalleled luxuriance. He has

played his part; and the only pay which he desires or deserves is the consciousness of having played it manfully. (pp. 355-56)

Some people would have been more attracted to [Carlyle] had he not been armed with [a] grand stoical independence. They feel that there is something harsh about him. They utterly fail to perceive his intense tenderness of feeling, because they cannot understand the self-restraint which forbade him to wear his heart upon his sleeve. They see indifference to suffering in his profound conviction of the impotence of spasmodic attempts at its relief; and fancy that he was cynical when, in fact, he was only condemning that incontinence of sentiment which cannot bear to recognise the inexorable barriers of human fate. They cannot understand that a man can really be content to give the most concentrated expression to a melancholy view of human life without fidgeting over the schemes of practical reform. There seems to be a kind of antithesis between the apparent pride of a self-contained independence and the ardent sympathies of genuine benevolence. I do not think, indeed, that any one can really love Carlyle's books without becoming sensible of the emotional depth which underlies his reserve and his superficial harshness; nor is it possible to read the **Life of Sterling**—the most purely charming of his writings—without understanding the invincible charm of the man to a fine and affectionate nature. . . . Carlyle remains the noblest man of letters of his generation; the man who devoted himself with the greatest persistency to bringing out the very best that was in him; who least allowed himself to be diverted from the highest aims; and who knew how to confer a new dignity upon a character not always—if the truth must be spoken—very remarkable for dignity. He showed his eccentricity—as a critic naïvely tells us—by declining the mystic letters G.C.B. But he missed none of the dignity which comes from the unfeigned respect borne by all honest men to a character of absolute independence, the most unspotted honour in every relation of life, and the exclusive devotion of a long life to the high calling imposed by his genius. (pp. 356-57)

For near fifty years [Carlyle's little house in Chelsea] was the scene of the laborious industry of the greatest imaginative writer of the day, and the goal of pilgrimages from which no one ever returned without one great reward—the sense, that is, of having been in contact with man who, whatever his weaknesses or his oddities, was utterly incapable of condescending to unworthy acts or words, or of touching upon any subject without instinctively dwelling upon its deepest moral significance. If his views of facts might be wrong or distorted and his teaching grotesque in form, it could never be flippant or commonplace, or imply any cynical indifference to the deepest interests of humanity. The hero in literature is the man who is invariably and unflinchingly true to himself; who works to his end undistracted by abuse or flattery, or the temptations of cheap success; whose struggles are not marked by any conspicuous catastrophes or demands for splendid self-sacrifices; who has to plod on a steady dull round of monotonous labour, under continual temptation to diverge into easier roads, and with the consciousness that his work may meet with little acceptance, or with a kind of acceptance which is even more irritating than neglect; and who must therefore place his reward chiefly in the work itself. Such heroism requires no small endowment of high moral qualities; and they have seldom or never been embodied more fully than in this sturdy, indomitable Scotchman, whose genius seemed to be the natural outcome of the concentrated essence of the strong virtues of his race. (p. 358)

[*Leslie Stephen*], *''Thomas Carlyle,'' in* The Cornhill Magazine, *Vol. XLIII, March, 1881, pp. 349-58.*

GERARD HOPKINS, S. J.   (letter date 1881)

[*Hopkins, whose poetry is distinguished by his striking diction and pioneering use of meter, is considered a major English poet. Although his work was almost completely unknown in the nineteenth century, he is now firmly established as an outstanding innovator and a major force in the development of modern poetry. In the following excerpt from a letter to Richard Watson Dixon, Hopkins grudgingly admits Carlyle's genius.*]

[There] was something in some letter of yours some while ago I wanted to return to, but now it has escaped me. It was, I think, about Carlyle. Your words surprised me '—of some genius': they would commonly be thought, and so they appear to me, too weak. I do not like his pampered and affected style, I hate his principles, I burn most that he worships and worship most that he burns, I cannot respect (no one now can) his character, but the force of his genius seems to me gigantic. He seems to me to have more humour than any writer of ours except Shakspere. I should have called him the greatest genius of Scotland. And yet after all I could fancy your making a good case against him, especially bearing the rule in mind *nemo coronabitur nisi qui legitime certaverit:* always to be affected, always to be fooling, never to be in earnest (for as somebody said, he is terribly earnest but never serious—that is never *in* earnest) is not to fight fair in the field of fame. (p. 59)

> *Gerard Hopkins, S. J., in a letter to Richard Watson Dixon on September 24, 1881, in* The Correspondence of Gerard Manley Hopkins and Richard Watson Dixon, *edited by Claude Colleer Abbott, Oxford University Press, London, 1935, pp. 58-9.*

JAMES ANTHONY FROUDE   (essay date 1884)

[*Froude was an English historian and a younger contemporary of Carlyle. He met the Carlyles in 1849, becoming their friend as well as Carlyle's most ardent disciple. After Carlyle's death, Froude published* Reminiscences, Jane Carlyle's letters, *and a four-volume biography of his mentor. The latter work sparked a fierce controversy by alluding to Carlyle's alleged mistreatment of his wife and sexual impotence. Carlyle's outraged defenders included his niece Mary Aitken and her husband, Carlyle's nephew Alexander Carlyle, who accused Froude not only of untruthfulness but of acting improperly in issuing any biography at all. Froude protested that Carlyle had designated him as official biographer, releasing personal documents to him for that reason; Froude added that his sincere regard for Carlyle could not be allowed to interfere with his responsibility to report biographical truth. For commentary by several of the principals in the controversy—Froude, Alexander Carlyle, and Frank Harris—as well as for Waldo H. Dunn's overview of the affair, see the Additional Bibliography. In the following excerpt from his biography of Carlyle, Froude relates* The French Revolution *to its author's moral convictions.*]

[*The History of the French Revolution*] gave Carlyle at a single step his unique position as an English man of letters, and . . . it is in many respects the most perfect of all his writings. In his other works the sense of form is defective. He throws out brilliant detached pictures, and large masses of thought, each in itself inimitably clear. There is everywhere a unity of purpose, with powerful final effects. But events are not left to tell their own story. He appears continually in his own person, instructing, commenting, informing the reader at every step of his own opinion. His method of composition is so original that it cannot be tried by common rules. The want of art is even useful for the purposes which he has generally in view; but it

interferes with the simplicity of a genuine historical narrative. The *French Revolution* is not open to this objection. It stands alone in artistic regularity and completeness. It is a prose poem with a distinct beginning, a middle, an end. It opens with the crash of a corrupt system, and a dream of liberty which was to bring with it a reign of peace and happiness and universal love. It pursues its way through the failure of visionary hopes into regicide and terror, and the regeneration of mankind by the guillotine. It has been called an *epic*. It is rather an Æschylean drama composed of facts literally true, in which the Furies are seen once more walking on this prosaic earth and shaking their serpent hair.

The form is quite peculiar, unlike that of any history ever written before, or probably to be written again. No one can imitate Carlyle who does not sincerely feel as Carlyle felt. But it is complete in itself. The story takes shape as it grows, a definite organic creation, with no dead or needless matter anywhere disfiguring or adhering to it, as if the metal had been smelted in a furnace seven times heated, till every particle of dross had been burnt away. As in all living things, there is the central idea, the animating principle round which the matter gathers and developes into shape. Carlyle was writing what he believed would be his last word to his countrymen. He was not looking forward to fame or fortune, or to making a position for himself in the world. He belonged to no political party, and was engaged in the defence of no theory or interest. For many years he had been studying painfully the mystery of human life, wholly and solely that he might arrive at some kind of truth about it and understand his own duty. He had no belief in the virtue of special 'Constitutions.' He was neither Tory, nor Whig, nor Radical, nor Socialist, nor any other 'ist.' He had stripped himself of 'Formulas' 'as a Nessus shirt,' and flung them fiercely away from him, finding 'Formulas' in these days to be mostly 'lies agreed to be believed.' In the record of God's law, as he had been able to read it, he had found no commendation of 'symbols of faith,' of church organisation, or methods of government. He wrote, as he said to Sterling, 'in the character of a man' only; and of a man without earthly objects, without earthly prospects, who had been sternly handled by fate and circumstances, and was left alone with the elements, as Prometheus on the rock of Caucasus. Struggling thus in pain and sorrow, he desired to tell the modern world that, destitute as it and its affairs appeared to be of Divine guidance, God or justice was still in the middle of it, sternly inexorable as ever; that modern nations were as entirely governed by God's law as the Israelites had been in Palestine— laws self-acting and inflicting their own penalties, if man neglected or defied them. And these laws were substantially the same as those on the Tables delivered in thunder on Mount Sinai. You shall reverence your Almighty Maker. You shall speak truth. You shall do justice to your fellow-man. If you set truth aside for conventional and convenient lies; if you prefer your own pleasure, your own will, your own ambition, to purity and manliness and justice, and submission to your Maker's commands, then are whirlwinds still provided in the constitution of things which will blow you to atoms. Philistines, Assyrians, Babylonians, were the whips which were provided for the Israelites. Germans and Huns swept away the Roman sensualists. Modern society, though out of fear of barbarian conquerors, breeds in its own heart the instruments of its punishment. The hungry and injured millions will rise up and bring to justice their guilty rulers, themselves little better than those whom they throw down, themselves powerless to rebuild out of the ruins any abiding city; but powerful to destroy, powerful to dash in pieces the corrupt institutions which have been the shelter and the instrument of oppression.

And Carlyle *believed* this—believed it singly and simply as Isaiah believed it, not as a mode of speech to be used in pulpits by eloquent preachers, but as actual literal fact, as a real account of the true living relations between man and his Maker. The established forms, creeds, liturgies, articles of faith, were but as the shell round the kernel. The shell in these days of ours had rotted away, and men supposed that, because the shell was gone, the entire conception had been but a dream. It was no dream. The kernel could not rot. It was the vital force by which human existence in this planet was controlled, and would be controlled to the end.

In this conviction he wrote his spectral *History of the French Revolution.* Spectral, for the actors in it appear without their earthly clothes: men and women in their natural characters, but as in some vast phantasmagoria, with the supernatural shining through them, working in fancy their own wills or their own imagination; in reality, the mere instruments of a superior power, infernal or divine, whose awful presence is felt while it is unseen.

To give form to his conception, Carlyle possessed all the qualities of a supreme dramatic poet, except command of metre. He has indeed a metre, or rather a melody, of his own. The style which troubled others, and troubled himself when he thought about it, was perhaps the best possible to convey thoughts which were often like the spurting of volcanic fire; but it was inharmonious, rough-hewn, and savage. It may be said, too, that he had no 'invention.' But he refused to allow that any real poet had ever 'invented.' The poet had to represent truths, not *lies,* or the polite form of lies called fiction. Homer, Dante, believed themselves to be describing real persons and real things. Carlyle 'created' nothing; but with a real subject before him he was the greatest of historical painters. He took all pains first to obtain an authentic account of the facts. Then, with a few sharp lines, he could describe face, figure, character, action, with a complete insight never rivalled except by Tacitus, and with a certain sympathy, a perennial flashing of humour, of which Tacitus has none. He produces a gallery of human portraits each so distinctly drawn, that whenever studied it can never be forgotten. He possessed besides another quality, the rarest of all, and the most precious, an inflexible love of truth. It was first a moral principle with him; but he had also an intellectual curiosity to know everything exactly as it was. Independently of moral objections to lies, Carlyle always held that the fact, if you knew it, was more interesting than the most picturesque of fictions, and thus his historical workmanship is sound to the core. He spared himself no trouble in investigating; and all his effort was to delineate accurately what he had found. Dig where you will in Carlyle's writings, you never come to water. Politicians have complained that Carlyle shows no insight into constitutional principles, that he writes as if he were contemptuous of them or indifferent to them. Revolutionists have complained of his scorn of Robespierre, and of his tenderness to Marie Antoinette. Catholics find Holy Church spoken of without sufficient respect, and Tories find kings and nobles stripped of their fine clothes and treated as vulgar clay. But Constitutions had no place in Carlyle's Decalogue. He did not find it written there that one form of government is in itself better than another. He held with Pope:—

> For forms of government let fools contest;
> Whate'er is best administered is best.

His sympathies were with purity, justice, truthfulness, manly courage, on whichever side he found them. His scorn was for personal cowardice, or cant, or hollow places of any kind in the character of men; and when nations are split into parties, wisdom or folly, virtue or vice, is not the exclusive property of one or the other.

A book written from such a point of view had no 'public' prepared for it. When it appeared, partisans on both sides were offended; and to the reading multitude who wish merely to be amused without the trouble of thinking, it had no attraction till they learned its merits from others. But to the chosen few, to those who had eyes of their own to see with, and manliness enough to recognise when a living man was speaking to them, to those who had real intellect, and could therefore acknowledge intellect and welcome it whether they agreed or not with the writer's opinions, the high quality of the *French Revolution* became apparent instantly, and Carlyle was at once looked up to, by some who themselves were looked up to by the world, as a man of extraordinary gifts; perhaps as the highest among them all. (pp. 75-80)

James Anthony Froude, in his Thomas Carlyle: A History of His Life in London, 1834-1881, *Vol. I, Longmans, Green, and Co., 1884, 392 p.*

VIDA D. SCUDDER   (essay date 1898)

[*Seeing* Sartor Resartus *as at once a work of romanticism and realism that advocates both spiritual renewal and social reform, Scudder stresses the book's continuing relevance.*]

To the generation of 1840, *Sartor* must have been completely baffling. It scouted modern civilization *in toto.* It violated every literary tradition. It jeered at the most cherished conventions, religious and social. Instead of well-marshaled paragraphs, it presented a chaos of seemingly incoherent quotations; instead of lucid dogmatism, bewildered inquiry; instead of tangible theme, definitely treated, a phantasmagoria of ironical observation and mystical dream. What reception could be expected? (p. 145)

For us looking back, however, *Sartor* is not hard to place. It is the last, perhaps the noblest utterance of the early romantic movement in England; and it is also the first notable and sincere expression of the attitude which seeks to see modern life with no glamour of delusion. Thus it belongs both to the future and to the past, to romanticism and to realism: a germinal book indeed. (pp. 145-46)

[The] work of romanticism could not be accomplished till it turned not only philosopher, but realist. It had to leave coquetry with turrets and armor, and to seek satisfaction for its audacious instinct in wooing the wonder of the actual world. It had to bring the idealism won from speculation to bear on the social facts about it. The moment when it made the change is profoundly significant. This moment *Sartor Resartus* preserves. The romantic temper, deepened, Germanized, and brought with grim resolution to face, not the dreams of the past, but the facts of the present,—such is the mood of this strange book.

It made its way in time, as new life will. It found those for whom it was written: the children of the future. To the young men of England, it remained for more than one generation a sort of gospel. What they first discovered and chiefly valued was doubtless its noble religious message. Teufelsdröckh, the hero, was the earliest in England of those spiritual sons of romance—a John Inglesant, a Marius the Epicurean—whose

Carlyle's home in Craigenputtock, where he wrote Sartor Resartus.

inner fortunes the reading public has shared with so keen a sympathy. In his experience the age found what many of its earnest children desired: the rejection of creeds with the renewal of faith.

However, the real import of *Sartor Resartus* is only in part spiritual and personal. The vibrations of the French Revolution were still in the air, and the social animus of the book is throughout as strong as the religious. When we first see the little Professor Teufelsdröckh, he is toasting "The Cause of the Poor, in God's name, and the Devil's," amid the plaudits of Weissnichtwo. Carlyle takes all pains to emphasize the twofold sweep of his radicalism. At the very outset, he couples with the "clear, logically founded transcendentalism" of his hero, a "meek, silent, deep-seated sans-culottism," and the "sans-culottism" remains at least as prominent as the "transcendentalism" in the Professor's mystifying personality. The mock horror with which Carlyle cites his utterances is never so charged with hidden zest and even mischief, as when Teufelsdröckh breaks into some sweeping attack on social creeds. At the queer end of the story, the bewildering hero vanishes from the scene; apparently, though the hint is given with bated breath, he has betaken himself to the society of the Saint Simonians, those early French socialists whose vagaries, as we know from other sources, had always a certain attraction for Carlyle. The word Socialism is never mentioned in the book: half a century was to pass before the sound of that word was to strike habitual terror to English ears; but into socialistic fellowship, nevertheless, disappears from view the first hero of the modern social movement in English literature.

The spiritual and social elements of the book are indeed so united that separation is impossible. A "speculative radical,

and that of the very darkest tinge," like the Professor, convinced that "custom doth make dotards of us all" "and weaves airraiment for all the Spirits of the Universe," no sooner discovers the central truth that "man is a spirit" than he proceeds to a supreme disregard of man's "clothes," "acknowledging for the most part in the solemnities and paraphernalia of civilized life, which we make so much of, nothing but so many cloth-rags, turkey-poles, and 'bladders with dried peas.'" The whimsical "clothes-philosophy" was probably the most felicitous form in which Carlyle's universal challenge could have been uttered. Who can forget the startling chapter in which Teufelsdröckh forces us to look at the World out of Clothes: society in its "birthday-suit," mother-naked, engaged in its accustomed pursuits? The whole book produces much the rueful effect of such a scene, and conventions of society and religion still disappear with equal celerity as we turn its pages.

To a modern reader, indeed, the social teachings of *Sartor Resartus* strike home with more freshness than the religious. It was in every sense a work of transition, but the spiritual transition which it signaled has been accomplished long ago, and its message comes to us with force truly, but not with novelty. The social challenge of the book, on the other hand, rings audacious as ever, for the social transition of which it gives perhaps the first hint in imaginative prose has lasted seventy years, and is still in progress.

The starting-point of the entire book is that sense of the social organism which we sometimes vaunt for a recent discovery. To Carlyle, society is no result of a "social contract," no fortuitous collection of individuals; it is a living unity of fellowship. As a direct consequence of this abstract conception his thought thrills with the intense consciousness, so alien to our forefathers, of the silent multitudes by whose toil we live. *Sartor Resartus* is one of the first books in which the modern working-class is recognized and its condition noted. The thought of Langland, unheeded through the centuries, finds here at last an echo, and the reverence for labor, revived by Wordsworth, is reiterated with new earnestness. . . . From this deep feeling for our organic unity with the workers, it naturally follows that Carlyle makes the connection that Swift failed to make, because he lacked the feeling. Luxury and poverty, in *Sartor Resartus,* appear no longer as puzzling, independent phenomena. They are sternly related. Carlyle's contrasting pictures of Poor Slaves and Dandies, striking studies of social extremes as were ever drawn, are placed side by side with highest art. They might be printed in the Labor Press to-day, unchanged except for a few details in the costume of the dandy.

Three generations have passed, and we see the instinct which animates Carlyle's thought so far, almost universal. Yet there are ways in which he is distinctly in advance of us still. For his accent, unlike our own, falls constantly on the non-material aspects of social need. He is alive to the physical distress of the poor; but the son of a Scotch mason, inured to poverty from childhood, was no sentimentalist, nor do hardship and privation seem in themselves great evils to him. What tortures him with agony fierce and broken in expression is the thought of the multitudes spiritually disinherited; by the very conditions of modern industry, consigned to mental apathy worse than physical death. (pp. 147-51)

Carlyle's attitude is still very rare. The right of every man to material subsistence has become a familiar thought since the days of the old economists, and the public now at least laments, if it does not remedy, the stunted physique and bad physical conditions of the wage-earner. But the right of the spirit to life is a claim strange to the majority. Most people take it comfortably for granted that society has done its full duty to a man when it enables him, by the devotion of all his waking hours, to provide comfortably for his keep. In the miners' strike of 1897 in Pennsylvania, it was said that the death of a mule was regarded by the operators of the mines as a greater pecuniary loss than the death of a man. Why? It took money to replace the mule: none to replace the miner. "And yet there must be something wrong," wrote Carlyle in 1833:

> A full-formed Horse will, in any market, bring from twenty to as high as two-hundred Friedrichs d'or: such is his worth to the world. A full-formed Man is not only worth nothing to the world, but the world could afford him a round sum would he simply engage to go and hang himself. Nevertheless which of the two was the more cunningly-devised article, even as an Engine? Good Heavens! A white European Man, standing on his two Legs, with his two five-fingered Hands at his shackle-bones, and miraculous Head on his shoulders, is worth, I should say, from fifty to a hundred Horses!

Truly, our problems have not changed. We should be wrong, however, did we say that no advance had been made since the emotional utterances of Carlyle. He recognized the evils of unemployment and industrial waste. We have gone one step further: we have analyzed them by statistics.

While Carlyle brooded in Craigenputtock, certain Tories of the old school were thinking in lines not wholly dissimilar from his own. Wordsworth and Southey, too, felt the dangers springing unperceived from the new industrial methods. But they faced the past, he the future; for they could see the evils, but

could not construe the needs of their times. Teufelsdröckh is no "Adamite," rejecting with revolutionary ardor all social forms on principle, and pleading with Rousseau for a return to nature; neither is he a conservative. His quest is positive, and it makes, however vaguely, for reconstruction. It is this quest which imparts the impressiveness of suspense to the mournful pages of *Sartor*. Metaphor after metaphor shows in concrete glowing symbol Carlyle's one conviction: that the old order was changing, and that on the moral purpose of the people depended the nature of the new order which should be born. Let society throw aside its outworn garment, and give over cobbling this tear, that rent. Let it prepare for itself a new garment, clean and fresh. Such thought was not unknown; but in Carlyle's day it had been silenced, seemingly forever, by the resurgence of the tide of custom. . . . Carlyle sounded anew . . . the hope, the threat, of change. He first, in sober prose, promoted what Arnold so keenly desired: the free play of consciousness round things as they are, which can loosen them from their conventional moorings. By searching hint, by mysterious allusion, by words veiled yet electric, he quickened again the dying consciousness of social renewal.

This consciousness is the starting-point of all our social thought. Even in moods most near to despair, its life-communicating power animates modern literature with a force that impels toward the unknown. We know how from the most earnest speculation of earlier centuries such instinct for renewal is absent; absent even from those whom we can see most clearly to have had the spirit of the future. Langland, in the fourteenth century, marvelously like Carlyle in many ways, with the same burning sense of social injustice, the same reverence for poverty and labor, yet rested content with a purely ethical plea for reform of spirit, and regarded king, priest, knight, and workman as parts of an immutable social order. More, with the young daring of the Renascence, dreamed an ideal state after Plato, but did not hope to see in his own day the customs of the Utopians established in England. Swift, in the century of acquiescence, criticised unsparingly, condemned unreservedly, cried out in horror, and paused. Then came the Revolution. Poets and statesmen beheld for one brief instant the vision of a new earth below a new heaven, sought wildly to realize it, failed, uttered it in one burst of song, and fell on silence. With *Sartor Resartus* sounds again the new note: indomitable, though not triumphant. Tentative it is now; charged with apprehension and solemnity; yet none the less assured. (pp. 152-56)

Full of passion, expressing solitude and the stress of solitude, the strange little book speaks in hints elusive and abrupt. It is tentative, emotional, vague. But in it the iconoclastic work of the romantic movement at its acme finds a climax, and the new method of facing actual civilization with open soul, pitiful heart, and observant mind finds a prophecy. The book seems written by one breathless with the eager strain of his own thought. It is a torch borne by a runner in the torch-race of freedom; its flame is mingled with smoke, torn, tossed, even blown backward by conflicting winds; but it is living still, and though it may now no longer warm nor illumine, it still serves as a signal-fire. (p. 156)

> *Vida D. Scudder, "The Awakening: 'Sartor Resartus',' in her* Social Ideals in English Letters, *Houghton, Mifflin and Company, 1898, pp. 143-56.*

EDMUND GOSSE   (essay date 1921)

[*An English literary historian, critic, and biographer, Gosse wrote extensively on seventeenth- and eighteenth-century English lit-*

erature. In the following excerpt, he argues that Carlyle has justly lost his audience and influence.]

Where does Carlyle stand to-day in public esteem? When great wealth has been accumulated, even financial ruin does not prevent money from lurking here and there in corners of an estate, and doubtless a numbering of the people would reveal the survival of a considerable clan of Carlyle's worshippers. But, in the main, and comparing their loyalty to-day with what it was sixty years ago, it can hardly be questioned that no one of the great Victorians has declined in influence so steadily, and shows so little evidence of being restored to favour as the once almost omnipotent author of *Heroes and Hero-Worship.* He, at all events, is a hero whose shrine is abundantly neglected to-day. . . .

Whether we regret it or not, the fact has to be faced that there was something in the texture of Carlyle's mind, in the character of his expressed thought, which soon destroyed its attraction and its stimulus. A large portion of his writing has ceased to be interesting; his pages create fatigue and impatience in youthful readers, who read only because there persists a tradition that they must be read. Philosophers declare that this is unjust, and they point to scattered beauties of a very high order. They are right in doing so, but at present their appeal is all in vain. Carlyle has lost his potency and his magic. (p. 301)

[Carlyle] was futile as a prophet. He failed altogether to read the signs of the future aright; he underrated mechanism, and had no conception of its value in the reduction of human distress; he professed to hope for the race, but he started in a determination to be disappointed. What is to be thought of a political watchman of the night who could see nothing in Lord Beaconsfield in 1875 except "a cursed old Jew, not worth his weight in cold bacon"? What is to be thought of a military observer who declared the Prussian army to be the ultimate expression of good government in its "victory over chaos"? These outbursts might amuse for a moment, or even for a generation, but long ago they became merely tiresome.

Incessant yelping is one of the most wearisome things in the world, and Carlyle, with all his monstrous talent, has ruined his own reputation by his impetuous irritability. Nothing endears the handsomest dog to those whom he disturbs all through the night by his perpetual bayings at the moon. What George Meredith called Carlyle's "hideous blustering impatience in the presence of progressive facts" expressed itself in a series of more or less melodious howls which roused attention at first, and then grew taken for granted, and then became an insupportable bore. Let any one to-day judge for himself, not taking the Victorian eulogists nor such a perfectly honest but prejudiced guide as Mr. Augustus Ralli, but planting himself down in an easy-chair with the actual text of *Past and Present* in his hands and the *Latter-Day Pamphlets* on the table at his side. Will he pass an agreeable, or a useful, or even a tolerable hour in the company of these famous treatises? I think not.

He will read about "infinite sorrowful jangle" and the identity of "might and right." He will learn that the Practical aristocrat in combination with the Titular will make Chaos Cosmos, and that those who do not realise this fact had better stay at home and hunt rats. He will find himself suffocating in a sort of cloud of poisonous anger; wherever the author takes him, his fellow-creatures are described, even the gentlest and most unselfish, as "apes" with "angry dog-faces." If we wish to know why Carlyle has ceased to be an influence, let us listen—briefly, for the sound is not a pleasant one—to the roarings of

Latter-Day Pamphlets and the denunciations of our Scavenger Age.

Hitherto, I have spoken—very briefly and imperfectly, for want of space—as the Devil's Advocate. But so great an artificer of British speech must not be relinquished in so summary a fashion. If I plead for a dismissal from our text-books of the public scold, who tormented his contemporaries by his tempest and agony of thought, who blew hot and cold with a pertinacity enough to drive the Satyr of criticism crazy, who preached the doctrine of Silence with vociferous and laughable volubility, who looked upon Germany as the only perfect and imitable State—if I dare to express the belief that several of Carlyle's most famous books are only just redeemed from failure by the amazing felicity of particular passages, I am not, therefore, blind to his splendour or deaf to his music. He was not, I contend, a prophet of any permanent importance, but he was an artist of the highest originality. He knew nothing of human character, but he could paint the exterior of life with a vividness which has not been surpassed, which has very rarely been equalled. He could not fathom the tenderness of the author of *The Vicar of Wakefield,* but he could bring before us, once and for ever, "an Irish blackguard, with a fine brain, and sun-like eyes, and a great fund of goosery."

He had little insight into the meditations of Wordsworth, but he could imprint for ever upon our memories the solemn poet, isolated at a London dinner-table, and "munching what appeared to be raisins." This pictorial quality animates *The French Revolution,* which is, doubtless, the masterpiece among Carlyle's set productions. But it positively inspires the *Reminiscences* and the *Correspondence,* the best of his thirty volumes. It fluctuates through the huge *Frederick,* and it is not absent from the *Cromwell.* It constantly flashes out in the early critical essays, any one of which is worth all the political and controversial treatises put together. It is these latter, with their lugubrious contempt for everything and everybody, which have disgusted modern readers, and have led to a disaffection which unjustly includes Carlyle's best performances. (pp. 305-07)

Edmund Gosse, "Carlyle," in his Books on the Table, *Charles Scribner's Sons, 1921, pp. 299-307.*

JOSEPH ELLIS BAKER (essay date 1933)

[*Baker discusses parallels between Carlyle's sociopolitical views and those of Adolph Hitler.*]

It is too often assumed that Hitler's philosophy is so strange that it can never be comprehended by the Anglo-Saxon mind. Now whatever may be true of Hitler's practice, his ultimate intentions, and his underlying motives, it should be noticed that his philosophy itself, as it is set forth in his book, *My Battle* might be treated in a footnote to our reading of one of the best-known writers of English prose. For people of English culture, the best approach to the ideology of the latest revolution on the Continent lies through Thomas Carlyle. Before we condemn the German people as the victims of mass insanity we should realize that the Nazi program as it has been presented to them—we are not speaking of the actual working-out of the movement, which can be judged only by expert observers on the spot day after day—bears a very close resemblance to a solution of the problems of our industrial civilization that we have long accepted as a part of our traditional intellectual heritage. . . .

We need an international interpreter to introduce us to Hitler and the movement Hitler represents. Carlyle is the man. He has become one of the major prophets of the twentieth century becuase he was hopelessly out of harmony with the nineteenth. He was a sour, dour, canny Scotchman who refused to be swept off his feet by the spirit of the age. He had his doubts about all the "modern" movements: democracy, science, business—or at least those movements as they understood themselves, officially, in his own time. And now that these movements have reached a certain stature, are ready for new blueprints, here is Carlyle, as alive as ever, saying:

> In the midst of plethoric plenty, the people perish; with gold walls and full barns, no man feels himself safe or satisfied. Workers, Master Workers, Unworkers, all men, come to a pause; stand fixed, and cannot farther. Fatal paralysis spreading inwards, from the extremities. . . .

Many men have said that, are saying that. Carlyle's significance, like Hitler's or Mussolini's, is that while he seems ultraradical, he also seems ultra-reactionary. He lays claim to the future, but he does not throw away the national past. As Hitler would have Germany substitute her own heroes and northern myths for the Old Testament; and as Mussolini wishes to revive the Mediterranean glories of ancient Rome, Carlyle finds in Oliver Cromwell and in a medieval English monk the models for the modern British statesman or industrialist. Let us get down to the basis of the paradox. We have been taught to see the world as a conflict between capitalism and communism. But Carlyle and the fascists refuse to accept the postulate that there is inevitable conflict between labor and the ruling class, or that their only relation to each other is economic.

In contrast to capitalism and commmunism, fascism is nationalistic, aristocratic, and idealistic—idealistic in the philosophic sense, most thoroughly explored by the great German philosophers and brought over into English literature by Carlyle in his conception that the world we grasp through the senses and the intellect is merely the clothes of a deeper, true reality. To a man with "clear vision in his heart" certain ideals—such as duty to the community—are more real than anything that can be seen, or measured, or bought, or subjected to "equal distribution." To have a sound art, a sound state, a sound social life, we must recognize these values, devote ourselves to them enthusiastically, and not allow them to be overthrown by mere majority vote. Liberalism is poisonous. Uncontrolled freedom to expoit other men's pocket-books is no worse than uncontrolled freedom to exploit other men's minds through an antisocial press. Nature throws us into the midst of battle, and if the best people become tolerant, ceasing to fight for human culture, civilization will be swamped by the very numerical superiority of lower-type men and their political demagogues and journalistic, artistic, and cinematic panders. The best men must not be pacifists. Hitler speaks of the right of victory for the best and the strongest *(Stärkeren).* "In all battles," says Carlyle,

> if you await the issue, each fighter has prospered according to his right. His right and his might, at the close of the account, were one and the same . . . (the Truth) is part of Nature's own Laws, coöperates with the World's eternal Tendencies, and cannot be conquered. . . .

Against the liberal's demand for freedom fascism sets up the military ideal of discipline: disciplined men working under disciplined leaders. It is in this sense, rather than for specific threats, that Hitler can be called thoroughly military. His book,

beginning with its very title, *My Battle,* is full of war-consciousness, even when he is not writing of soldiers or armies—it is the spirit of a militant Church, a faith more than a campaign. An officer, and a gentleman—or a Christian—will consider first the welfare of the state, not his own personal profit. He differs from the financier, the communist, and "historical materialism" in that he does not place the economic motive first either in his own conduct or in his interpretation of the human beings with whom he has to deal. Service to the state, even going as far as self-sacrifice, is the mark of the hero. The higher the form of life, Hitler tells us, the less the egoism. Animals care only for themselves. The first extension beyond the self was the family. Evolution has carried this so far that in some races the best men are glad to give up their own lives in battle for the country; it was such volunteer willingness to stand foremost in the face of danger that wiped out so many of the best men in the World War, leaving the way open for inferior men to destroy the German Empire from within. A wonderful illustration of this idealistic disposition is offered by the word "Work" *(Arbeit)* which to such a man does not mean selfish activity but creative work in harmony with the general welfare. For selfish activity we have other words, such as *Wucher* (usury, interest), and *Diebstahl* (theft). The very word "Worker" is part of the official name of Hitler's party, the Nationalsozialistischen Deutschen Arbeiterpartei, the National Socialistic German Worker's Party. Every genuine human *Kultur* (the meaning of the word is as broad as the English word "civilization" and as high as "culture") presupposes first the mind that places the welfare of the community before self-interest. This makes possible the development of all those great works of mankind which bring to the creator little recompense but to posterity the richest blessings. German has another great word, *Pflichterfüllung* (fulfilment of duty) which means not to satisfy oneself but to serve the whole. At the basis of this lies *Idealismus,* in opposition to *Egoismus.*

Almost all of these ideas from Hitler could be expressed in familiar old phrases from Carlyle: "Man is created to fight; he is perhaps best of all definable as a born soldier." "Obedience is our universal duty and destiny." "Liberty when it becomes the 'Liberty to die by starvation' is not so divine." Carlyle thinks that " 'enlightenment Egoism,' never so luminous, is not the rule by which man's life can be led. That 'Supply-and-demand' . . . are not, and will never be, a practical Law of Union for a Society of Men. That Poor and Rich, the Governed and Governing, cannot long live together on any such Law of Union." He objects to an age when

> all human dues and reciprocities have been fully changed into one great due of *cash payment;* and man's duty to man reduces itself to handing him certain metal coins. . . . How human affairs shall now circulate everywhere not healthy lifeblood in them, but, as it were, a detestable copperas banker's ink; and all is grown acrid, diverse, threatening dissolution.

He constantly preached the Gospel of Work: "Labor is Life." "Work is Worship." "There is a perennial nobleness and even sacredness, in Work." "This same 'sense of the Infinite nature of Duty' is the central part of all with us."

These are not superificial parallels, since they lay the very foundation for the doctrines of both Carlyle and Hitler. Of course the two men, a century apart, are not in all respects identical, and it is impossible to say how far away from his theory even the English writer would be carried if he found himself filling the shoes of Frederick the Great instead of using him as subject for a biography.

As he was opposed to democratic freedom, which is the condition that makes possible capitalistic individualism, so Carlyle was also opposed to the democratic theory of human equality, which is the basis of communism. No nation, Carlyle believes, has ever subsisted on democracy. In the ancient republics the mass of the people were slaves, and the citizens were really aristocrats. Whether we call a monarch a dictator or a king makes little difference; "there is in every Nation and Community a *fittest,* a wisest, bravest, best; whom could we find and make King over us, all were in truth very well." Thus besides the dictator there are local monarchs, the new aristocracy; "we must have an Aristocracy of Talent!" But it is not to be the existing "Phantasm-Aristocracy, no longer able to *do* its work, not in the least conscious that it has any work longer to do . . . careful only to clamor for the *wages. . . .*" Thus Carlyle is poles apart from the ordinary conservative. But he is interstellar distances remote from the humanitarians, the social democrats, and the communists, for he is willing to use the test of the strongest (in the broadest sense) to determine the best; and because he would have us approach our great men not as subjects for "debunking" biographies but as objects of reverence. "No sadder proof can be given by a man of his own littleness than disbelief in great men." This hero worship is in the greatest contrast to any form of rule by majorities—"the wise and noblest minded . . . was not the majority in my time," and Parliament he calls a "National Palaver." Carlyle was a humanist rather than a humanitarian, interested not in making society serve (through applied science and democratic government) the greatest good of the greatest number, but rather in keeping the way open for the rise of the best men, with the people ready to follow loyally such aristocrats. "Dim all souls of men to the divine, the high and awful meaning of Human Worth and Truth, we shall never, by all the machinery in Birmingham, discover the True and Worthy."

Hitler agrees with Carlyle: The state must be organized on the *"aristokratischen Prinzip,"* based not upon any thought of the *"Majorität"* but upon personality. Not the mass, not the majority, but single persons have given to mankind inventions, organization, and thought. The state then must not hinder gifted individuals from rising out of the mass, but must encourage this process. "The Jewish doctrine of Marxism turns aside from Nature's aristocratic principle and in the place of the eternal prerogatives of Power and Strength sets the dead weight of number."

Before all, the hard struggle for life itself provides for the selection of brains. . . . This process of selection still takes place today in the realm of thought, of artistic creation, indeed even of economic life. . . . The administration of the state and even the forces embodied in the organized defense of the nation are likewise ruled by this idea. Everywhere here, still, is dominant the idea of personality, its authority over the inferior and responsibility towards the higher person. Only political life has today already turned away from this natural principle.

In politics only (since the world has been made safe for democracy) is a man responsible to his inferiors. Obedient to the leaders must be a people properly educated—not pedantically, but humanistically, with first attention to the development of character, including especially the capacity for Silence. (Yes, it is Hitler speaking, not Carlyle!) In this materialistic age, when our economic life gives such importance to special departments of knowledge, such as mathematics, or physics, or chemistry, there is great danger that the general education of a nation will be more and more narrowed to the sciences, which

always threaten to sink into the service of Mammon. (Hitler, still, speaking Carlylese!) Rather our general education must correspond to the humanistic branches. Otherwise we renounce a kind of strength (or rather, plural, *Kräfte*) *always* of more importance for the maintenance of the nation than all technical knowledge. Especially we must not allow ourselves to be dissuaded from the study of antiquity. Roman history remains the best of teachers, not only for today, but for all time. The Hellenic ideal of culture ought to be preserved for us in its typical beauty. We must not, merely because of the difference between single nations, allow the great common possessions of the race to be broken up. "The battle that rages today has great scope: a culture—a civilization—that holds in itself thousands of years, that embraces the Greek and the German, is fighting for its existence."

Beyond the parallel between Carlyle and Hitler as to situation, philosophy, and emotional tone, it is impossible for us to go. What would Carlyle say about Hitler's rule in Germany as it has shown itself in actuality? That would be the book of the year.

Joseph Ellis Baker, "Carlyle Rules the Reich," in
The Saturday Review of Literature, *Vol. X, No. 19,*
November 25, 1933, p. 291.

EDITH BATHO AND BONAMY DOBRÉE (essay date 1938)

[*Batho and Dobrée maintain that Carlyle's prose, while frequently "intolerable," reveals an unmistakable artistry.*]

[Carlyle] never ceased to be the obstinate peasant of Ecclefechan. His nature was as tortured and "impossible" as his grotesque prose. With his violently puritan, pleasure-hating nature, akin to that of John Knox, he tried to absorb German romanticism, and even the monstrous transcendentalism of Novalis. He longed to be what he was utterly incapable of being, a man of action. "Brave young friend . . . you are, what I am not, in the happy case to learn to *be* something and to *do* something, instead of eloquently talking about what has been and was done and may be!" The sort of man of action he would have liked to be was a mixture of Frederick the Great and Jeremiah. He loved denunciation, one is bound to think, for its own sake; he would have wished to-day, perhaps, to be Hitler (their utterances are not unlike), a dictator with a torrent of words at his command. A dictator was what he called aloud for, in an anguished rush of rhetoric. His hatreds were many and manifest, it is hard to discover his loves. He believed that nothing could prosper which was not founded upon what he called veracity, the will of nature, or the commands of God: but everything that he personally disliked was what he meant by unveracious, or contrary to the will of God—Parliaments, Popery, Progress—and if he maintained that men were Godlike individuals, he also asserted that they were mostly fools. His ideas usually came out in a fury of sound which makes him nearly unreadable; his strange concatenations of words and phrases, his jibes and jeers and capital letters, his Germanic constructions, his smokiness, his thunderousness (with its occasional lightning flashes), make it intolerable to read him. . . . At first the tremendous nervous vigour appeals; for a few paragraphs one feels an accession of strength: but soon the effect is numbing; it is like the mad rantings of Nathaniel Lee. The storm goes on raging, but one ceases to take any notice.

Yet with all his vociferations Carlyle was an artist. It is not only that he occasionally struck out a memorable phrase, but that he could create a vision of the past. He is not, we are told, to be trusted as a historian, for though he went through enormous travail in seeking out original documents, he distorted history to suit his own arguments. No doubt every historian necessarily does this to some extent; but Carlyle seems to have made no attempt to guard against it; the lower veracity must make way for the higher. For him history was a moral weapon with which to bludgeon his opponents, and in the process of using history to this end he painted the most magnificent series of wildly Turnerian landscapes, filled with figures as active and diverse, as multitudinous and immediate as those of Peter Breughel, and as strange as those of Hieronymus Bosch. *The French Revolution* is a superb phantasmagoria: the Abbot in *Past and Present* an eternally great imaginary portrait. What they are meant to convey need no longer matter. And there are, it is true, certain qualities in the prose which make for the effects; the vigour in the soil which made the brambles into such scratchy hedges also made the corn sprout luxuriantly.

And if he was wrong-headed and perverse in a dozen ways, in one respect, in his greatest hatred and contempt, he was right. He loathed Mammon and his works with all his heart. He hated orthodox economics, "the dismal science" with its "inexorable laws", its *laisser faire,* its reduction of men to hopeless slavery. He could not analyse what the horror and the blasphemy were due to, and laid the charge to the door of democracy ("physical-force Chartism" seems to have inspired him with a terror which never left him), but he knew in his deepest part that the whole thing was fundamentally wrong. (pp. 106-08)

Edith Batho and Bonamy Dobrée, "General Prose Writers," in their The Victorians and After: 1830-1914, *The Cresset Press, 1938, pp. 103-21.*

LOUISE MERWIN YOUNG (essay date 1939)

[*Young discusses Carlyle's conception and practice of historiography and assesses his rank as a historian.*]

In Carlyle's interpretation of the historic process and in his theory and practice of historical writing, several older streams of thought converged. He perpetuated the tradition of literary history bequeathed by the great historians of the eighteenth century. But he revitalized the tradition by introducing the leavening influences of romanticism in the several aspects represented by Herder, Schiller, Scott and Burke. To the romantic impulse he added the stimulating influence of the sociological and psychological discoveries with regard to the nature of the social organism, and the dual qualities of continuity and impermanence characterizing the historic process. Carlyle's thought remained a thing apart from other streams of thought undergoing a parallel development, such as the environmental philosophy of history of Thomas Buckle and his followers, the application of the Hegelian dialectic in the economic materialism of Karl Marx, and the new school of scientific historiography which recognized Ranke as its master. Although Carlyle's claim to distinction both as a thinker and a historian rests on a broader basis than do the claims of any of the representatives of these more specialized trends, the nature of the times obscured his significance. This fact alone would lend historical interest to any study of Carlyle's performance as a historian.

The larger issues relating to a definition of history and the true function of the historian have a contingent relationship to our problem. How far, for example, may a historian go in defining his medium and setting the limits of his task? Dryasdust cur-

rently assumes full jurisdictional rights in this province, although in Carlyle's day the license was freer. Again, what is history? An art or a science? Carlyle believed firmly that history was related to poetry, even though its method was scientific. His career may be said to bring to a close the age of the gifted amateurs, the product of whose efforts belongs as much to literature as to history.

Historiography, or the art of writing history, is a term whose content has always depended on the general intellectual environment to which it stands related, and of which it is the product. Thomas Buckle remarked that there would "always be a connection between the way in which men contemplate the past and the way they contemplate the present." This fact, indeed, gives to history one of its most compelling qualities. Every age, whatever its technical equipment or philosophic shortcomings, has something authentic to give us even if it only interprets the record of the past in the light of its own ideas, and in ways acceptable to itself. The question of a general definition of history, and of those who may properly be called historians, has been debated vigorously, even acrimoniously, since the day of Aristotle and possibly even before, successive ages contributing their own specially conditioned views. The best we can do, it appears, is to admit that no wholly satisfactory definition is conceivable of so Protean a literary form; and to grant that great history, like great art, may be recognized more easily by its effect than by its form and content. One who has read Herodotus and Plutarch, Thucydides and Tacitus, Clarendon and the venerable Bede, Gibbon and Mommsen, Ranke and Carlyle, will have little difficulty in recognizing fine historical writing when he sees it, even though he may be unable to define the qualities which make the works histories and which make them great. The distance between Bede's plain chronicle and Tacitus' passionate indictment of the Empire is unbridgeable by definition. Yet that both are histories and have certain elements in common none will deny. Nor will many deny the further fact that they are read today with enduring pleasure, not merely because they are histories but because they are works of art at the same time.

Lytton Strachey defined the three essential attributes of the historian as "a capacity for absorbing facts, a capacity for stating them, and a point of view." Charles A. Beard improved upon this definition by a further qualification. In his view the title of historian should be granted only to those who pursue the subject to its fullness and "try to comprehend the intellectual operations which they themselves are performing." These four qualifications summarize admirably the main aspects of Carlyle's technical equipment as a historian. They are based on the assumption that the historian must have a clear conception of his task, a definite theory of his function, a specific approach to his material and a general philosophy acting as a controlling force in guiding the operation of selecting and organizing his material. . . . Carlyle possessed all of these; and had, in addition, a thorough understanding of the intellectual operations he was performing.

In addition to these qualifications, however, Carlyle possessed one more, possibly the greatest of all—a qualification which Professor Saintsbury defined as the "historic sense." This quality, according to Professor Saintsbury, consists of the "power of seizing, and so of portraying a historic character, incident or period as if it were alive, not dead." The imagination of the reader is excited to a degree that, even if he is convinced the thing did not happen, he sees that it might have happened. It is apparent that the historic sense is really just a special case of the poetic sense which makes of poetry an "image of man and nature . . . not standing upon external testimony, but carried alive into the heart by passion." Unlike the poet, whose invention works upon the materials of his observation, the historian is constrained to remain within the limits of historical facts; but the function of the imagination is much the same in either case. The kinship of history with poetry is thus established.

It will be acknowledged at once that many excellent historians have been entirely lacking in the "historic sense." A sense for the past they almost always have and a scholar's pleasure in adding to the sum total of useful knowledge. But the quickening perception of past events and peoples, in terms not only of space and time but of subtler moral qualities lending themselves to individuation is a power of imagination granted to few. Tacitus and Herodotus possessed such power; so did Homer and Shakespeare. Among English historians before Carlyle, only Clarendon possessed it to any significant degree; while Gibbon and Scott had it to a lesser degree. Carlyle possessed it, however, to a degree equaled by "none ever before or since." Saintsbury called him "one of the Deucalions of literature," who "cannot cast a stone but it becomes alive." Lowell likened the figures of most historians to "dolls stuffed with bran, whose whole substance runs out through any hole criticism may tear in them," while Carlyle's are so real that "if you prick them they bleed." William Roscoe Thayer remarked that turning to Carlyle after reading most historians was like coming out of a museum of mummies into a crowd of living, breathing people.

The roots of the "historic sense" lie buried deep in two primary qualities—qualities by no means peculiar to those called geniuses—a sense of the past and acute powers of observation and investigation. These qualities may be traced in an unbroken development from the earliest period of Carlyle's career. Taken together, they constitute the "historico-biographical faculty," which determined the character of all of Carlyle's writings, whether on professedly historical topics or not. His interest in the past is oddly reminiscent of the feeling of the hero in Henry James' novel that it was only when "life was framed in death that the picture was really hung up." Carlyle recorded, in *Sartor Resartus,* the stirring of his infant imagination by the discovery that "Entepfuhl stood in the middle of a Country, of a World; that there was such a thing as history, as Biography; to which I also, one day, by hand and tongue, might contribute." His imagination opened wide to the "grandeur and mystery of time" on the day when, as a small child, he realized that Ecclefechan burn "had flowed and gurgled, through all changes of time and fortune from beyond the earliest date of History." It was a visible link between him and the legions of Caesar who had encamped on nearby Burnswark. By means of it, all the past events which the simple brook had witnessed became part of what Croce calls the "contemporaneous present" and partook of its reality. Time was reduced to its proper significance as a mere convenience or mode of thought. The child only sensed the truth to which Kant gave him the key and a philosophic construction many years later, but the recollected experience gives us an intimation of one of the most extraordinary qualities of Carlyle's mind. (pp. 4-8)

Posterity will be the ultimate judge of Carlyle as a historian. If men continue to read him, and his undoubted literary genius will assure that, his histories will continue to exercise an influence on the world. . . . Our belief in Carlyle's claim to be ranked among the great historians is based fundamentally, not on his transcendentalism, nor his poetic style, but on his re-

markable capacity to present a "plain record" of "actual and palpable circumstances" rescued from the past. His literary excellence will contribute in large measure to his permanent fame, but great as his service was to literature, his service to history was still greater. His insight into the motives of men, his extraordinary power of revivifying the past in terms of human experience, his sociological analysis of the nature of the historic process and his philosophic interpretations of the ultimate meaning of history offer a broad basis for the assumption that his historical writings will be among those works of art which will endure. (pp. 185-86)

> *Louise Merwin Young, in her* Thomas Carlyle and the Art of History, *University of Pennsylvania Press, 1939, 219 p.*

BASIL WILLEY   (essay date 1949)

[*Willey investigates Carlyle's spiritual and political ideas.*]

Carlyle was a man with a message, if ever there was one, and the message was essentially that of the great Romantic poets and thinkers, applied to the condition of England in the days of Chartism and the dismal science. (p. 102)

A full examination of Carlyle's teaching has to include an analysis of his style, for of him it is abundantly true that the style *is* the man. Carlylese is as distinct a dialect as Miltonics, though a style as Gothic in its chiaroscuro as Milton's is classical in its inversions and intonations. It is certainly (as Keats said of *Paradise Lost*) 'unique', a 'curiosity', and not to be taken as a model. But it has a strange vitality, and indeed it is only great energy of intellect and imagination which can thus make for itself a new language out of an old one. Like others who have forged a highly individual style, Carlyle began by writing the ordinary English of his time, and those who find his mature work unreadable may prefer his early manner. But there can be no doubt that Carlylese, with all its faults, was intensely expressive both of Carlyle's personality and of his relationship to his age: that, namely, of a prophet-sage who, in virtue of a few simple and profound intuitions, hurls lifelong defiance at all the main tendencies of the modern world. Carlyle can never write urbanely; he is always on the stretch. He will not consent to use the current verbal coin; every phrase (and many actual words) must come molten from the forge. For Carlyle writes almost exclusively from the heart or the solar-plexus, not from the head. He sees by flashes and does not think connectedly; summer-lightning, not sunshine, is the light that guides him. So anxious is he not to occupy common ground with his reader, so anxious to keep clear of accepted assumptions and catchwords, that the use of standard English, which implies a certain solidarity between writer and reader, a sharing of presuppositions as between man and man (not to say 'gentleman and gentleman'), becomes impossible for him. Everything he says must be said uniquely, as if for the first time; the constant implication being: 'when I say anything, I mean unspoken volumes, and not the cliché anyone else would mean'. All this makes him fatiguing to read, but it is also the secret of his extraordinary power of transmuting any person, scene or object, at a touch, into an emanation of the Carlylean vision. (pp. 103-04)

'A man's religion' (he said in *Heroes*) 'is the chief fact with regard to him'; let us follow his lead and take his own religion first. It is not easy to divide his thought into 'aspects', for to him, as to Coleridge, 'the unity of all had been revealed', and one of the main sources of his influence was his power of suggesting that all topics were aspects of one topic, and that the most important of all. God and man, supernatural and natural, spirit and matter, sacred and profane:—it was precisely by fusing and obliterating all these time-honoured distinctions in his visionary furnace that he cast a spell over his listeners, and gave them a sense of deepened insight. It is thus impossible to consider his religion without considering the whole of his thought, even if for the sake of presentation we must make some subdivisions.

Carlyle is remembered, and his influence was felt, as an up-holder of the spiritual view of the world in an age of increasing materialism and unbelief. Yet he is the most remarkable ex-ample of a phenomenon which I take to be typical of the nineteenth century, that of the religious temperament severed from 'religion'. Few 'secular' writers of his time can have used the name of God more constantly, yet he meant by this word, as Sterling pointed out, something other than the God of Christianity. (p. 105)

Carlyle belonged to the company of the escaped Puritans. Re-jecting Church, creed and sacrament—all that he described as 'Hebrew Old-Clothes'—he yet retained the deep intuitions of his Calvinistic peasant-childhood, and it was from the un-questioned moral certainties of Puritanism that he derived both his satiric animus and his prophetic energy. . . . In a real sense Carlyle *did* make religion his great lifelong study; all the pos-itives in his teaching are on the side of faith and against unbe-lief. The evils which he denounced were all due, he taught, to spiritual paralysis, lack of reverence, lack of wonder—in a word, to lack of religious belief. Like a Hebrew prophet, he recalls his age from following the idols of materialism, utili-tarianism, democracy and the like, to the worship of the true God. Men's hearts and minds were stricken with the blight of eighteenth century rationalism; the universe had gone dead and mechanical; the nations would perish unless they could recap-ture the vision of God working in Nature and history, and learn that the meaning of life lay in dutiful service, and not in motive-grinding or the felicific calculus. In all this Carlyle's affinity with the religious side of Romanticism is manifest enough. In so far as the Romantic Movement meant a rejection of the flimsy superficialities of the age of reason, an awakening to fuller and richer insights into reality and into the relation of past and present, and an acknowledgement of the authenticity of Imagination and of Faith—then Carlyle's work can be seen as a vigorous continuation of that movement. The same forces led Coleridge from Unitarianism to Anglicanism, and Newman from the Church of England to Rome. The path of Carlyle's pilgrimage diverged widely from theirs, but his starting-point was the same: the demand for a deeper and more spiritual interpretation of experience than had been available in the pre-vious century. (pp. 106-08)

Carlyle's 'conversion' or spiritual rebirth has become familiar from the account given in *Sartor Resartus* of Teufelsdröckh's victory over the 'Everlasting No'—an account which, he has told us, is true to his own experience. As in the story of many mystics, his illumination was preceded by a dark night of the soul—the 'fixed starless Tartarean black', in which doubt has darkened into unbelief. (pp. 113-14)

The Christian reader will notice . . . a lack of conformity with the established pattern of conversion: there is no contrition, no reliance upon grace or redeeming love, but on the contrary, much proud and passionate self-assertion. The emotion that follows release is hatred and defiance of the Devil, rather than love and gratitude towards God. Nevertheless, he had found a

faith, and never afterwards lost it. . . . What he has attained is not humility and love, but a spiritual elevation from whence he can look down, with mingled compassion and scorn, on 'the welterings of my poor fellow-creatures, still stuck in that fatal element'—a point of vantage which removes him far above 'Puseyisms, Ritualisms, Metaphysical controversies and cob-webberies' and leaves him with no feeling 'except honest silent pity for the serious or religious part of them, and occasional indignation . . . at the frivolous, *secular* and impious part, with their Universal Suffrages, their Nigger Emancipations, Slug-gard-and-Scoundrel Protection Societies, and "Unexampled Prosperities", for the time being!'

From this time onwards Carlyle increasingly assumes the tone of a religious seer, proclaiming that God lives and reigns, and executes judgment amongst the nations. His *French Revolu-tion,* which more than any other single work won him fame, is unlike any book of history since the Pentateuch; it is a Vision of Judgment, in which the wrath of God is seen, as of old, descending upon a sinful and corrupt generation. Indeed the Revolution, the palmary modern instance of the workings of eternal divine justice, was ever in Carlyle's mind the main evidence for the reality of a moral order in the world. Believe in God, seek the Truth, and do the Duty nearest to hand! is the burden of his message. (pp. 115-16)

The strength of Carlyle lay in the passionate sincerity with which he believed in his own 'God'. This 'God' may have been, as Sterling and others complained, a mere 'formless Infinite' or an 'inscrutable Necessity', but it was real to him, it may be conjectured, as the God of Christianity was to few 'Christians' of that age. But Carlyle's appeal to the many who were religiously inclined yet dissatisfied with orthodoxy, the exhilarating sense of release and renewal he brought them, were due not merely to the fiery energy of his own conviction. They were due also to this; that Carlyle's teaching powerfully reinforced two tendencies which had for long been gathering momentum in the mind of Europe—the tendency to find God in Nature, and the tendency (produced, like the former, by the scientific movement) to regard all translations of picture-think-ing into concept and law as closer approximations to Truth. Substitute 'the Immensities and Eternities' for God, substitute 'the Temple of the Universe' for the Church, 'Literature' for the Bible, 'Heroes' for saints, 'Work' for prayer, and the like: do all this, and you have at one stroke destroyed 'superstition' and provided a true religion for honest men in these latter days. Here at last was a creed which *did* 'correspond to fact'; which could be believed without putting out the eyes of the mind. . . .

> Often also could I see the black Tempest marching in anger through the distance: round some Schreck-horn, as yet grim-blue, would the eddying vapour gather, and there tumultuously eddy, and flow down like a mad witch's hair; till, after a space, it vanished, and, in the clear sunbeam, your Schreckhorn stood smiling grim-white, for the vapour had held snow. How thou fermentest and elaboratest in thy great fermenting vat and laboratory of an Atmosphere, of a World, O Nature!—Or what is Nature? Ha! why do I not name thee GOD? Art not thou the 'Living Garment of God'? O Heavens, is it, in very deed, HE, then, that ever speaks through thee; that lives and loves in thee, that lives and loves in me?

Thus does Carlyle translate the old conversion-story into the language of Nature-worship. Many of the characteristics of his style, too, are here illustrated: the tone of rapt soliloquy; the touch of Gothic terror; the poetic fury, checked however by the abrupt changes of rhythm and by such a phrase as 'your Schreckhorn'; the volte-face at 'Ha!'; the catch in the throat, and the freely flowing unction of the final rhetorical question. Having thus woven his spell, and won your emotional assent, he can then complete the incantation in a strain of exalted tenderness, leading up to a clinching affirmative:

> Fore-shadows, call them rather fore-splendours, of that Truth, and Beginning of Truths, fell mysteriously over my soul. Sweeter than Dayspring to the Ship-wrecked in Nova Zembla; ah, like the mother's voice to her little child that strays bewildered, weeping, in unknown tumults; like soft streamings of celestial music to my too-exasperated heart, came that Evangel. The Universe is not dead and demoniacal, a channel house with spectres; but godlike, and my Father's!

It was in this way that Carlyle offered to his readers 'God's Universe' as a 'Symbol of the Godlike', and 'Immensity' for a Temple; it was an appeal which (as Pascal had long ago declared) could influence only those who already believed in God on other grounds. But there were plenty of these, and the appeal met with eager response. (pp. 117-19)

The man to whom the Universe has become a Temple will pass through life in a marvelling temper; he will know that 'in every object there is inexhaustible meaning', and that 'the eye sees in it what the eye brings means of seeing'. Wonder is the basis of all true worship, and Carlyle, anticipating D. H. Lawrence here (as often), attacks Science for having killed the emotion of wonder:

> The man who cannot wonder . . . were he President of innumerable Royal Societies . . . is but a Pair of Spectacles behind which is no Eye. . . . Doth not thy cow calve, doth not thy bull gender? Thou thyself, wert thou not born, wilt thou not die? ''Explain'' me all this . . . or, what were better, give it up, and weep not that the reign of wonder is done, and God's world all disembellished and prosaic, but that thou hitherto art a Dilettante and sandblind Pedant!

If Carlyle here looks forward to Lawrence, he looks back also to Wordsworth and Coleridge: 'to excite a feeling analogous to the supernatural by awakening the mind's attention from the lethargy of custom'—this was continually his aim. He developed, indeed, an explicit doctrine of the identity of natural and supernatural, not by denying the supernatural, but by raising the natural to the higher level. . . . It was indeed the 'gist' of his whole message, for by means of it he was able to reconcile the contraries that met in him: the impulse to deny, and the impulse to affirm. The Church is dead?—then worship in the temple of the universe; Heaven is a fable? but Infinitude remains; miracles are discredited? but Nature is a miracle; the Bible is incredible? but History is a Bible; Revelation is a fairy-tale? but the true Shekinah is Man, and in worshipping Heroes we are acknowledging the godlike in human form.

Carlyle possessed a power of double-vision or second-sight which, in another age, might have made him a great satirist. He had the satirist's awareness of the disparities between the ideal and the actual, the real and the illusory, the genuine and the spurious; but, though satire abounds in his work, he was too much a Romantic to maintain the satiric poise. Tenderness and *Schwärmerei* were continually breaking in, so that he remains on the whole a humorist. But this second-sight gave him the power to see persons, things and events in a spectral and visionary light; when this clairvoyance was upon him he beheld objects not as objects, but as symbols of invisible forces, or

as patterns in a divine drama. From this kind of insight springs much of the power and pathos of his historical work, and his portraits of men and women; people in action, while remaining human, are simultaneously seen as impelled to glory or disaster by unalterable invisible law, as the human units in Hardy's *Dynasts* are unwitting agents of the Immanent Will. To Carlyle this visionary power often brought great suffering: he speaks of it as a 'detestable state of enchantment'. Yet, now that the force of his 'message' is spent, this power may well seem to be the most unequivocal sign of his greatness. I mention it while speaking of his 'religion', because it was closely connected with his grasp of unseen realities. (pp. 121-23)

In the light of the foregoing we may now briefly consider some of Carlyle's moral and political ideas. His idealism was a part of his religiosity: The World is the vesture of God, matter of thought, the transient of the eternal; every object is 'a window through which we may look into Infinitude itself'. The clue to History is the account of men's inmost thoughts—hence, of their religion: 'the thoughts they had were the parents of the actions they did . . . it was the unseen and spiritual in them that determined the outward and actual'. Indeed, History is essentially Biography, and above all the Biography of Great Men. Thus unequivocally does Carlyle deny the doctrine of 'historical materialism', which asserts that thoughts, ideals, religions, arts and the like are epiphenomena: mirages floating upon the economic sands. But I have found no hint that Carlyle knew the writings of Marx; the enemy, for him as for Coleridge, was 'The Unbelieving Century' (the eighteenth), and its legacy in his own time. The eighteenth century suffered from 'spiritual paralysis'; it was sceptical, utilitarian, mechanical. . . . The battle of Belief against Unbelief is never-ending; in the eighteenth century Unbelief was in the ascendant, for the old ways of believing were in decay. Carlyle can find a word of negative praise for Benthamism, as an honest attempt to make whatever could be made of a 'dead iron machine' worked by 'Gravitation and selfish Hunger'. But the 'doctrine of motives', the view that the ultimate springs of action are love of pleasure and fear of pain, was the object of his special abhorrence. 'Foolish Wordmonger and Motive-grinder, who in thy Logic-mill hast an earthly mechanism for the Godlike itself, and wouldst fain grind me out Virtue from the husks of Pleasure,—I tell thee, Nay!'. . . Enlightened egoism 'is not the rule by which man's life can be led'; *'Laissez-faire'*, 'Supply-and-demand', and 'Cash-payment for the sole nexus' are not valid laws of union for a society of human beings. The true laws were understood in the age of Abbot Samson, when wild-fowl screamed over Lancashire, the coal and iron seams slept undisturbed side by side, and the Ribble and the Aire were 'as yet unpolluted by dyer's chemistry'; when Religion was 'not yet a horrible restless Doubt, still less a far horribler composed Cant; but a great heaven-high Unquestionability, encompassing, interpenetrating the whole of Life'.

Carlyle's analysis of modern society resembles Arnold's, but with a change of nomenclature; the 'Barbarians' become the exponents of Dilettantism or Donothingism, and the 'Philistines' of Mammonism. The latter have this superiority over an idle, game-preserving aristocracy, that their Mammonism at least makes them *work;* for Plugson of Undershot, therefore, Carlyle has a measure of respect—he, at any rate, is 'real'. 'Not that we want *no* aristocracy', he wrote in his Journal, Oct. 1830, 'but that we want a *true* one.' (pp. 126-27)

Carlyle's attitude towards the Masses is like that of Langland: a blend of compassion for human misery with scorn for the

The Carlyle residence in Chelsea.

nostrums of 'democracy'. It is in the name of the toiling millions that he denounces *laissez-faire* and the cash nexus, but the remedy is not to be found in mere political enfranchisement. The Reform Bill has proved a Barmecide Feast; the franchise has been extended, but there remain as before hunger, unemployment, lack of security, lack of hope, sense of injustice. . . . What is needed is a true Aristocracy, an Aristocracy of the Wise, and a true Priesthood; the only 'right' of man is the right to be wisely governed. God made the world for 'degree' (hierarchy), and in feudal times, before cash became the sole nexus, an Idea was really at work in the actual, that, namely, of the organic Christian society. Rebellion is an ugly thing, but if our present nobility and clergy can do nothing, others will. The 'Toiling Millions' are in 'most vital need and passionate instinctive desire'—not of Votes, but of 'Guidance'; guidance by 'Real Superiors'. England will either learn how to find its Heroes, or it will cease to exist among Nations. Hero-worship is the essence and practical perfection of all manner of worship; it has a mystical foundation, for in the Great Man Heaven reveals itself.

This of course is the part of Carlyle's teaching which is least endurable to us today. He correctly diagnosed the weaknesses and exposed the cant of Victorian 'democracy': its reliance upon *laissez-faire* economics, its superficial conception of freedom, its belief in the virtues of political enfranchisement, its deficiency in purpose, idea or soul. Given such defects (and

most agree that it had these defects), 'democracy' was likely enough to relapse into dictatorship. But Carlyle's heroes, it must be remembered, are not all Führers: they are also the Prophets—Buddha, Mahomet, Christ; the poets—Dante, Shakespeare, Goethe, Burns; the men of letters—Johnson or Rousseau. True, they are above all the kings, soldiers and governors: Caesar, Cromwell, Frederick, Napoleon; but Cromwell was the chief of Heroes, because he was the soldier of God. I do not think that Carlyle would have mistaken Hitler for a Cromwell, any more than Plato would have mistaken him for a Philosopher-king. He is commonly supposed, indeed, to have believed and taught that 'Might is Right', and even some of his devoted admirers were shocked at his apparent 'abdication of all moral judgment on atrocious actions and abandoned men,—a Mirabeau and a September massacre'. Carlyle had an imagination too dramatic and superheated ('my work', he said, 'needs all to be done with my nerves in a kind of blaze'); he often delights in exhibitions of mere energy, or in historical convulsions wherein judgment is executed by fire and whirlwind. But, as he was careful to explain, what he really meant was that in a world governed by a righteous Providence, might is right *in the long run;* Injustice and Untruth cannot long flourish in such a world (witness the French Revolution, the supreme object-lesson). The strong class, nation or man, will in the long view be the just and the righteous, because to be strong *means* to be righteous. He admits that 'Might and Right do differ frightfully from hour to hour; but give them centuries to try it in, they are found to be identical'— which is small comfort, perhaps, to dwellers in one of the intermediate centuries. To Lecky, who had accused him of supposing all might as such to be right, he replied: 'I shall have to tell Lecky one day that quite the converse or *re*verse is the great and venerable author's real opinion—namely, that right is the eternal symbol of might . . . and that, in fact, he probably never met with a son of Adam more contemptuous of might except where it rests on the above origin.'

Carlyle could not be expected to see (what we see so clearly as to make discussion tiresome) that hero-worship, as a cure for democracy, might be far worse than the disease, or that the 'passionate instinctive desire' for a Leader might be satisfied quite as easily by a Hitler as by a Cromwell. What we can learn from Carlyle is that 'democracy', in order to survive, must be born again; it must unlearn its economic idolatries, cease to be self-seeking and mechanical, and recapture its soul by returning to its own inmost ideas, which will turn out, on reflexion, to be those of Christianity. We seem to discern now that the old 'liberal' values—Liberty, Equality, Fraternity, the Rights of Man, tolerance, reverence for each individual as an end and not a means—can only flourish if they are rooted in the religion from which they originally sprang, and that the instinctive need for an object of worship, if not properly satisfied, will send us seeking after strange gods. (pp. 129-31)

Basil Willey, "Thomas Carlyle," in his Nineteenth Century Studies: Coleridge to Matthew Arnold, *Chatto & Windus, 1949, pp. 102-31.*

JOHN HOLLOWAY   (essay date 1953)

[*In the following excerpt from his highly respected study* The Victorian Sage, *which contains a chapter on Carlyle as a historian, Holloway discusses how Carlyle's distinctive use of language reflects and supports four basic premises of his "antimechanism" philosophy.*]

'Life-Philosophy' Knowledge

[Carlyle] wants to state, and to clinch, the basic tenets of a 'Life-Philosophy', of something that will veritably transform men's outlook. 'We shall awaken; and find ourselves in a world greatly widened.' 'Pray that your eyes be opened that you may see what is before them! The whole world is built, as it were, on Light and Glory.' He is writing for 'these mean days that have no sacred word'; he envies the preacher his pulpit, and he does so because he feels that his own message has an almost sacred quality. 'What am I? What *is* this unfathomable Thing I live in, which men name Universe? What is Life; what is Death? What am I to believe? What am I to do?' Carlyle puts these questions into the mouth of the Young Mahomet; he means to answer them himself.

Insight into 'the sacred mystery of the Universe' is not, in Carlyle's view, hard to get. It is the '*"open* secret"',—open to all'; and it is open to all because everyone has the conclusive evidence for it of introspection. 'Men at one time read it in their Bible. . . . And if no man could now see it by any Bible, there is written in the heart of every man an authentic copy of it direct from Heaven itself: there, if he have learnt to decipher Heaven's writing . . . every born man may still find some copy of it.' In his later books Carlyle tends to call this power of knowledge 'conscience'; in the earlier ones Goethe's influence is more prominent, and he discredits clear utterance, rigid argument, and 'mere logic' instead. It is at this time that he writes 'not our Logical, Mensurative faculty, but our Imaginative one is King over us. . .'. But to call this power of knowledge Imagination or Conscience is hardly important, so long as it is steadily contrasted with the knowledge that comes from strict logic and abstract argument.

But this account is an exaggeration. Insight did not come, in Carlyle's opinion, quite so easily. The secret, though 'open to all' was 'seen by almost none'. A man must be of 'loyal heart', as he says; and even if he is, 'to *know;* to get into the truth of anything, is ever a mystic act', bringing not any facile through-and-through comprehension, but an imperfect glimpse of some basic puzzling truth. 'Believe it thou must; understand it thou canst not.' Moreover, there must be an initial leap. The effort precedes the insight. Knowledge of God comes from confident belief in him; and if we want to discover what our duties are, we must first actually set our hand to the duty which seems to be the nearest. Whether we are willing to pay this price is no trivial matter. In the search for ultimate truth, the Imagination is one of only two things: 'Priest and Prophet to lead us heavenward; or Magician and Wizard to lead us hellward'. But if it is allowed to operate correctly it will transform our lives, for the state of illumination, of truly understanding the fundamentals about man and the world, is to ordinary life as waking is to sleeping, or open to closed eyes; and indeed, these contrasts are among Carlyle's favourites.

The Live Cosmos

The philosophy of Carlyle is simple, and it hardly changes all through his life. It is a revolt; or rather, a counter-revolution. In a word, it is *anti-mechanism*. Its main tenets are:

(1) the universe is fundamentally not an inert automatism, but the expression or indeed incarnation of a cosmic spiritual life;

(2) every single thing in the universe manifests this life, or at least could do so;

(3) between the things that do and those that do not there is no intermediate position, but a gap that is infinite;

(4) the principle of cosmic life is progressively eliminating from the universe everything alien to it; and man's duty is to further this process, even at the cost of his own happiness.

Such is Carlyle's outlook in brief—regardless of the apparent inconsistencies latent in it at certain points. Its sources do not matter, except that one of them provided him with an invaluable means of expressing this outlook in a really vivid and telling way, expounding what he had to say and simultaneously making it convincing. The doctrine of self-renunciation may recall Carlyle's admiration for Goethe, and the belief that what the senses show of the world is not reality but only appearance recalls Fichte and the German Idealists; but judged as a whole, Carlyle's view of life is enormously indebted to Scottish Calvinism. The omnipotence and omnipresence of God, a universe governed everywhere by relentless necessity, a final division between elect and damned, renunciation of temporal pleasures, and the delusiveness (in a non-philosophical sense) of the shows of the world are Calvin's tenets; and of course they were largely accepted in the England of Carlyle's time, so far as this was nonconformist or evangelical, and have indeed some measure of affinity with Christianity of any and every kind. It was therefore a powerful weapon for Carlyle, to write in a language which is influenced through and through by that of the Authorized Version. This revived a whole world of associations that were deeply rooted in his readers' minds. Even if they had become dissatisfied (as Carlyle was himself) with orthodox Church Christianity, Biblical language might still mean a great deal to them, and its use by Carlyle could attach his outlook to an elaborately developed world view with which his readers would be deeply familiar, and for which they would probably have a deep though perhaps a qualified sympathy. Actually, by using this Biblical language and at the same time often sharply criticizing conventional religion, Carlyle gets the best of both worlds. (pp. 21-4)

[The] texture of Carlyle's writing very often draws unconsciously on the associations and on the whole cosmic outlook of the Bible; and in doing so, of course, it encourages belief in the first of the guiding principles mentioned above, that the universe is not a mechanism but expresses a principle of cosmic life.

But it is important to remember what this principle meant, and upon what part of that meaning Carlyle wanted to insist. The universe was not a mechanism, but it was still governed by law. 'I, too, must believe . . . that God . . . does indeed never change; that Nature . . . does move by the most unalterable rules.' But they were rules of a distinctive kind, and Carlyle goes on, 'What are the Laws of Nature? To me perhaps the rising of one from the dead were no violation of these Laws, but a confirmation; were some far deeper Law, now first penetrated into, and by Spiritual Force, even as the rest have all been, brought to bear on us with its Material Force.' 'Even as the rest have all been'; this is the crucial phrase. Carlyle wrote for those all too ready, perhaps, to believe that the rules of Nature were unalterable; for him it was of more significance to show that these laws expressed a 'Spiritual Force'.

At the expense, it must be admitted, of leaving little or no impression of system, there is much in Carlyle's language to suggest this life in the universe. It is possible to distinguish three devices whereby he seeks this effect, and two of these can be discussed quite briefly. First, at the simplest level, is his style: a wild, passionate energy runs through it, disorderly and even chaotic, but leaving an indelible impression of life, force, vitality. The main units of sense and still more of the phrases are brief; punctuation is heavy, expression marks are used in lavish profusion. On the other hand there is little of sustained or close-knit argument demanding concentrated, dispassionate study; the reader is hurried, as if by an all-pervading and irresistible violence, from one problem to another.

Second comes another device, which might be called the dramatization of discussions. Carlyle does not always speak in his own person; his discussion is enlivened by a variety of characters, most fictitious and some not, who interrupt the author, confirm his outlook, defend their own, contradict him, and illustrate the points of view that he wishes to commend or condemn. *Sartor Resartus* is entirely based on this technique: Carlyle merely introduces and comments on the manuscripts of a mythical German Professor Teufelsdröckh, who appears as the real author of the Clothes-Philosophy. Teufelsdröckh comes again in *Past and Present*, this time with 'Sauerteig' (of the Pig-Philosophy), and the 'Houndsditch Indicator'. The same device is employed in the Introduction to *Cromwell's Letters and Speeches,* where the second speaker, 'my impatient friend', is anonymous although clearly he is a mouthpiece for Carlyle; and a variety of unidentified speakers, together with 'Sauerteig', 'Crabbe' of the 'Intermittent Reflector', the 'Department of Woods and Forests', 'John Bull', 'Ben Brace', 'Gathercoal' and the egregious M'Crowdy, all do something to diversify the pages of *Latter-Day Pamphlets*. This method tends to be naïve and crude, though not without effect. It seems to have grown on Carlyle until he used it for its own sake, but its intrinsic tendency to make the style more varied, violent, surprising, and forceful is indisputable, especially since Carlyle often employed his mythical personages to deliver the wildest passages of rhetoric.

The third feature is Carlyle's use of figurative language. It is probably the most influential of all. In different ways, figurative language operates through both its content and its organization. The importance of its content is easily seen. Time and again Carlyle's images are of some power or force or energy, disorderly perhaps, but passionate, violent, irrepressible. First, the image of fire runs like a bright thread through everything he wrote. . . . Fire—and light too—becomes almost the permanent context of Carlyle's argument, appearing in the least expected and most trivial places. In *Cromwell*, for example, he even speaks of 'editing' documents 'by fire', when he simply means destroying those that are useless.

Two other kinds of image acquire this contextual function in varying degrees: those of moving water and of animal life. Sometimes these are fused with images of fire or light; 'the inner fountains of life may again begin, like eternal Light-fountains'; 'this Planet, I find, is but an inconsiderable sand-grain in the continents of Being . . . that eternal Light-Sea and Flame-Sea'. But images of water are frequent alone: 'the roaring Billows of Time'; 'a life-purpose . . . like an ever-deepening river . . . it runs and flows'; 'the undiscovered Sea of Time'; 'the Scotch people . . . look into a sea of troubles, shoreless, starless, on which there seems no navigation possible'. The different uses to which Carlyle puts the images of *stream* and *ocean* are not relevant at present; both suggest a world that is all power and life, whether clear and purposeful like a stream, or turbulent and confused like a stormy sea.

Perhaps Carlyle's animal imagery also contributes something, by its astonishing frequency and variety. His work is a veritable verbal menagerie: within a mere sixty pages of *Latter-Day Pamphlets,* for example, the ape, wolf, ox, dog, pig, ass, hyena, dragon, serpent, sparrow, python, buzzard, eagle, owl, mouse, horse, mole, rat, beaver, spider, wren and canary all make their appearance in metaphorical uses, many of them several times over. Elsewhere, there are Kilkenny cats, beetles, lions, crows, bees, beagles, boa-constrictors, ostriches, cormorants, camels, lynxes, krakens, hydras, centaurs, chimeras, megatherions, and a multitude of anonymous monsters. The ass chews a thistle, the boa-constrictor wrestles with the lion, the Kilkenny cats are at their legendary occupation, the owl screeches, the apes gibber and chatter. Whether his images enlighten us about the good things in the world or the bad, this effect is equally present: everything seems busy with a restless, overwhelming life.

The impression is accentuated: images that do not suggest life and energy by themselves can do so through their sequence. This is conspicuous in the chapter on 'Natural Supernaturalism' of *Sartor Resartus*. Here Carlyle's purpose is exactly that now under discussion—to convince his readers that the universe pulsates with life. We are dealing here with a mixture, in fact, of metaphors or comparisons, and simple vivid images: but what they contribute to the book lies partly in what supervenes upon them because they all come so close together. It is their extraordinary sequence which hurries the reader first to the day on which the world was created, then to 'Sirius and the Pleiades', then under the sea, then to the planets in their courses, then from the laws of Nature as 'celestial hieroglyphics' to the laws of Nature as an 'inexhaustible Domestic-Cookery Book', then to the inside of the human body, then to the surface of the earth, the 'habitable flowery Earth-rind', then back to the Creation and forward to the Cataclysm, then to 'stretch forth my hand and clutch the Sun', then down into Hell, at least by implication ('Orpheus' and 'a huge Troglodyte Chasm') and up to Heaven, and at last (should we have retained breath enough to follow so far)

> like some wild-flaming, wild-thundering train of Heaven's Artillery, does this mysterious MANKIND thunder and flame, in long-drawn, quick-succeeding grandeur, through the unknown Deep . . . like a God-created, fire-breathing Spirit-host, we emerge from the Inane; haste stormfully across the astonished Earth; then plunge again into the Inane. Earth's mountains are levelled, and her seas filled up, in our passage.

That seems almost to happen in this passage too. It is the astonished reader who is made to hasten stormfully throughout the Cosmos, and by a well-known process of association to transfer the violence of his journey to the Cosmos through which in imagination he journeys.

The Ocean rolling round the Islet

So much for how Carlyle gives expression to the first principle, that the world is filled with cosmic life. The second was that this spiritual life might be manifested by everything in the universe, however apparently humble it may be. Vivifying this doctrine was a very important part of Carlyle's purpose. Ultimately, like every other writer of his kind, he wants to make the reader see familiar things in a new way, to dwell on and emphasize aspects of them that were overlooked or neglected before. Things are more than the casual eye takes in: the lowest resembles and indeed is in continuity with the highest. Explicit statements of the view are frequent enough in Carlyle. But hints and reminders and particular illustrations pervade his work like an atmosphere, and Carlyle thereby achieves a twin purpose: he spreads the character of those things agreed to be noble or exalted to everything in the universe, and thus he emphatically reinforces our impression that this universe is a giant system moving according to a single pattern.

It is fanciful, perhaps, but not unilluminating, to compare this technique with the form of a *passacaglia* in music. Sooner or later one hears the theme unadorned; but in various modified forms it runs without interruption, the unadorned version audible below. Carlyle approximates to the plain statement in, for example, the words he gives King William Rufus in an attack upon the rigidities of medieval Catholicism: 'Behold . . . the world is *wider* than any of us think . . . there are . . . immeasurable Sacrednesses in this that you call . . . Secularity'. The variations are numerous: 'Sooty Manchester,—it too is built on the infinite Abysses; overspanned by the skyey Firmaments . . . every whit as wonderful . . . as the oldest Salem or Prophetic City'. 'The Present Time, youngest-born of Eternity, child and heir of all the Past Times with their good and evil.' In these the intention and the effect are clear. Greater interest attaches to passages which at first sight seem like nothing more than idyllic descriptive interludes. For example, from **Cromwell's Letters and Speeches**, 'Oliver farmed part or whole of these . . . lands . . . past which the river Ouse slumberously rolls . . . his cattle grazed here, his ploughs tilled here'—so far the passage is plain description; but Carlyle continues 'the heavenly skies and infernal abysses overarched and underarched him here'. . . . (pp. 26-32)

Often, in Carlyle, the lightest touches remind the reader that the world is wider than it seems. For example, he is fond of imagery of green landscapes; and it does not come without its influence. 'The green foliage and blossoming fruit-trees of Today . . . the leafy blossoming Present Time'; 'Man's life . . . no idle promenade through fragrant orange-groves and green flowery spaces'; 'Work is Worship . . . *its* Cathedral . . . coped with the star-galaxies; paved with the green mosaic of land and ocean'; 'Chaos is dark . . . let light be, and there is instead a green and flowery world'; 'Wisdom . . . rests there, as on its dark foundations does a habitable flowery Earth-rind.' Thus a thought of the whole earth and of all the living things that spread over it is worked more intimately still into the texture of the argument. Ultimately, these passages set every immediate and restricted topic in a wider context, in the context of the whole earth, or indeed the whole universe; and they modify the reader's attitude until he tends to think of any small things as like the grandest and most beautiful and most alive things he knows, and as influenced by them through a direct and genuine continuity. Carlyle's argument is a foreground that is developed against a background; and by sustaining an ever-present sense that this background is grand and awe-inspiring, he is able, without explicit reference, to diffuse our attitude towards it until we have the same attitude towards his immediate subject.

Carlyle's intention in this respect is most clearly seen in his use of the word 'miracle'. He wishes to say that every existing thing is miraculous; this indeed is almost his central tenet. 'Daily life is girt with Wonder, and based on Wonder, and thy very blankets and breeches are Miracles.' What we have been exploring is a device which makes us see things under the influence of those other more portentous things that they are girt with.

Shams and Diabolisms

Between the second and the third of Carlyle's central tenets there is perhaps a latent contradiction, for the second explains how everything reflects the cosmic life, and the third how some things in the universe most emphatically lack it. Our problem, however, is not whether he solves this contradiction in logical terms, but how the two parts of it are developed and amplified and made emotionally convincing. And certainly, in pursuing this problem, we discover two contrasting techniques: for the second tenet was conveyed to the reader by devices that hinted at unsuspected affinities, while the third is constantly reinforced through expressions which crystallize a single, pervasive, fundamental dichotomy in the world.

Consider first the plain statement of this dichotomy, and then the indirect devices that keep the reader attuned to it. Carlyle praises Dante, for example, because he 'felt Good and Evil to be the two polar elements of this Creation, on which it all turns; that these two differ not by *preferability* of one to the other, but by incompatibility absolute and infinite; that the one is excellent and high as light and Heaven, the other hideous, black as Gehenna and the Pit of Hell'. Absolute contrasts of this kind attract Carlyle: Revenge is a divine feeling, *but its excess is diabolic;* historical periods differ not merely greatly, *but infinitely.* All good, and all bad things are assimilated: 'at bottom the Great Man, as he comes from the hand of Nature, is ever the same kind of thing', while 'independence, in all kinds, is rebellion', and untruths are all the Devil's.

This contrast runs sharply through Carlyle's work, because the vocabulary he uses for comment and evaluation tends always to draw upon it. The first quotation from **Heroes and Hero-Worship** above did so by comparing the good to Heaven and Light, the bad to Hell and darkness. The other quotations illustrate Carlyle's use of the contrast between what is divine and what is diabolic, but the contrast between light and dark is perhaps more prominent still. Cromwell's work was for 'the Protestant world of struggling light against the Papist world of potent darkness'. Elsewhere, Cromwell is as a 'luminous body . . . crossing a dark Country, a dark Century'; and—a hint of the same—the intellect of the Younger Vane is 'atrabiliar'. Carlyle rings many changes, but the guiding principle is simply that there are contrasting extremes and nothing whatever between them. Occasionally he cannot avoid speaking of something good but imperfect; even so he retains the contrast as sharply as he can by employing the usual metaphor in a modified way: perfect religion is like light, imperfect religion (at least in some cases) like 'red smoky scorching fire'. It can be purified into light, and 'Is not Light grander than Fire? It is *the same element* in a state of purity.' Thus it is that Carlyle manages to say something of intermediates within a vocabulary that draws the advantages of precluding them.

But the contrast is equally fundamental if made between *true* light and *false* or factitious light. The contrast between the 'true' and the 'sham' in Carlyle is worked out for light in expressions like 'a poor paper-lantern with a candle-end in it', and in the attack on those who believe that 'Heroism means gas-lighted Histrionism; that seen with ''clear eyes'' (as they call Valet-eyes), no man is a Hero'. This quotation introduces two new methods employed by Carlyle to emphasize his basic contrast. The 'seeing eye' is a frequent alternative for light: 'Thor red-bearded, with his blue sun-eyes', and then the contrast is made, for example, in passages like this about Mirabeau: 'he has an *eye*, he is a reality; while others are formulas and eye-*glasses*' (alternatives elsewhere to the eye-glass are glass-eyes and spectacles). In view of this, the expressions above, 'gas-lighted Histrionism' and 'Valet-eyes', are exactly comparable in Carlyle's vocabulary, and they introduce, as two further illustrations of the ultimate contrast, the contrast of real life with acting, and that of master with servant. The first takes many different forms: 'Well may the buckram masks start together, terror-struck . . . let whosoever is but buckram and a phantasm look to it'; 'considering the Treaty mainly as a piece of Dramaturgy, which must . . . leave a good impression on the Public'. The contrast between master and servant is conspicuous in Carlyle's frequent tirades against flunkies and valets and 'Valetism, the *reverse* of Heroism'; 'England will . . . learn to reverence its Heroes and distinguish them from its Sham-heroes and Valets and gas-lighted Histrios'.

Another slash at actors introduces a fresh contrast. Government, says Carlyle, in *Latter-Day Pamphlets,* is 'really a heroic work, and cannot be done by histrios, and dexterous talkers having the honour to be'; and many times the contrast of good with bad is likened to that of deed with mere word. 'Not a better Talking-Apparatus . . . but an infinitely better Acting-Apparatus' (that is, Doing-Apparatus) is wanted. This explains the innumerable attacks on 'cant' and 'jargon'; and the tirades against quacks too, for a quack is one who talks of his healing powers but cannot do anything—this is brought out in the words 'Sir Jabesh Windbag . . . or what other Cagliostro'. The attacks on 'dilettantes' serve the same purpose—'unserious Dilettantism . . . grinning with inarticulate incredulous incredible jargon about all things'.

The next comparison represents good by the human, and bad by the animal. The type appears in the 'dusky potent insatiable animalism' of a 'Chartist Notability' (the word 'dusky' hints, of course, at the analogy with darkness). It is best illustrated in the analogy between cynics and 'Apes . . . *gibbering and chattering* very genuine nonsense . . . they sit . . . with their wizened *smoke*-dried visages . . . looking out through those *blinking smoke-bleared eyes* of theirs, into the wonderfulest universal *smoky Twilight* and undecipherable disordered Dusk of Things'. In this passage of intricate rhetoric, the cynic is belittled first by the analogy with the sub-human, and then through the hints of idle chatter, smoke, defective eyes, and darkness. All these metaphors have their established and characteristic function in Carlyle, and here their fusion and interaction is plain.

The Growth of Metaphor

Figurative language in Carlyle is so elaborate that a question arises which is really prior to that of its use; for his work displays not merely its use, but its creation. The valet, the eyeglass, the smoke, the buckram mask—these metaphors are scarcely intelligible unless sooner or later they are 'cashed', and their significance explained. They are 'technical-term' metaphors, effective through other metaphors used prior to them and effective of themselves. But once a connection is made between metaphors that need an introduction and those that need none, the former can vary and amplify the latter. Carlyle uses this method elaborately. He develops a figurative language that becomes more and more esoteric; and the developments do not occur in isolation, but interconnect and sometimes fuse.

Since, of necessity, this has already been a good deal illustrated, it will be enough here to give two examples which display the whole process of image-creation. Consider first how the metaphor of darkness is elaborated. Carlyle asserts that the surviving materials for a life of Cromwell are the 'dreariest

continent of shot-rubbish the eye ever saw . . . in *lurid twilight* . . . peopled only by *somnabulant* Pedants . . . and doleful creatures . . . by *Nightmares,* pasteboard Norroys, griffins, wiverns and chimeras dire'. The sleep-metaphor, as an adjunct to darkness, reappears: 'Such darkness, thick sluggish clouds of cowardice . . . thickening as if towards the eternal sleep'. What of the griffins and wiverns? They echo another extension of the darkness-metaphor, to be seen in the 'thousand-fold wrestle with pythons and mud-demons . . . enormous Megatherions, as were ever born of mud, loom huge and hideous out of the twilight Future' of *Latter-Day Pamphlets.* In this work the same figure is plentiful: 'British industrial existence . . . one huge poison-swamp of reeking pestilence . . . communicating with the Nether Deeps . . . that putrefying well of abominations . . . the universal Stygian quagmire of British industrial life'. These passages, besides utilizing the idea that darkness gives rise to monsters, also fuse the metaphor of darkness with that of the swamp, contrast to the fresh flowing stream of healthy life. Later in the same work comes 'a dim horn-eyed owl-population'. The owl, with these same associations, appears often enough: 'a too miserable screech-owl phantasm of talk and struggle' (here 'screech-owl' is reminiscent of 'darkness' and also 'jargon'); 'the human Owl, living in his perennial London fog, in his Twilight of all imaginable corrupt exhalations'. Already, in an earlier passage, we have been given a hint as to what these exhalations may include: 'accumulated owl-droppings and foul guano-mountains', which once more fuses the darkness and the swamp. Sleep, the owl and the swamp, reappear in *Latter-Day Pamphlets:* 'twenty-seven millions of my fellow-countrymen, sunk deep in Lethean sleep, with mere owl-dreams of Political Economy . . . in this pacific thrice-infernal slush-element'. Thus it becomes clear that the metaphor of darkness is used to *coin* metaphors of sleep, monsters, the owl and the muddy swamp; and through the guano and the mud, owl and swamp share more of each other's qualities than a joint affinity with darkness, and jointly contrast with Carlyle's image of flowing water with its characteristic meaning.

The concept of 'silence' also illustrates how Carlyle develops and utilizes a whole interconnected vocabulary of figurative expressions. In one way or another, it serves to amplify each of the three basic tenets discussed so far. It expresses, first, the belief that the universe possesses a mysterious life: 'It is fit that we *say* nothing, that we think only in silence; for what words are there! The Age of Miracles past? The Age of Miracles is forever here!—'. Second, it reminds us that the universe is vast in space; and by doing so is a symbol that everything, however trivial apparently, has really something of the greatness of those spaces: 'The SILENCE of deep Eternities, of Worlds from beyond the morning-stars, does it not speak to thee? . . . the Stars in their never-resting courses, all Space and all Time, proclaim it to thee in continual silent admonition'. Sometimes these two ideas are fused: 'The divine Skies all silent'. Third, silence is an antithesis of speech, and serves in the rich vocabulary that contrasts the sham and the true: 'Silence . . . here and there . . . how eloquent in answer to . . . jargon'. (pp. 32-9)

But the most interesting extension from the concept of silence is Carlyle's occasional use of the word 'open'. Sometimes he links this with silence directly—'while the world lay yet silent, and the heart true and open'; and sometimes there is an indirect link, through the word 'secret': 'SILENCE and SECRECY! Altars might still be raised to them'; and 'the open secret'. Then the concept 'open' is used for all the three tasks which 'silence' proved to carry out: reminding us, that is, of the world's mysterious life, of its vast extent in space, and of the contrast between real and sham. It recalls (1) the mysterious life of the world in such a phrase as 'the sacred mystery of the universe; what Goethe calls "the open secret"'. But (2) the secret is open because the mystic force shows itself everywhere throughout the world. 'That divine mystery', Carlyle continues, 'which lies everywhere in all Beings . . . of which all Appearance, from the starry sky to the grass of the field, but especially the Appearance of Man and his work, is but the *vesture*, the embodiment that renders it visible.' Finally (3), the *opened* heart is something true and real, not a sham: 'Wholly a blessed time: when jargon might abate, and here and there some genuine speech begin. When to the noble opened heart . . . the difference between . . . true and false, between work and sham-work, between speech and jargon, was once more . . . infinite.'

These then, are some of the methods whereby Carlyle preserves, throughout the whole texture of his work, an ultimate and absolute contrast between what in his view is good and what bad. They are methods embedded so deeply and intimately in his language that, so far at least as they are successful, they permanently sustain the attitude that Carlyle desires in the reader. The general effect of this basic contrast is plain enough: it makes Carlyle's philosophy simple, and makes it emphatic. Palliation disappears. The normal judgement to pass on anything is one of outright commendation or censure; qualified judgements, if any, preserve abstract accuracy, but tend to evoke the same attitudes as they would if unqualified.

This irreducible distinction is worked into the texture of Carlyle's argument in another way. Like Newman, Carlyle believes the universe to be a system; but what makes it a system for him must largely be explained through this contrast, since he sees the system of the world as two great movements that spread the good in the world everywhere and annihilate the bad. Thus the third tenet is what gives content to the fourth. Destiny is 'Didactic Destiny' and the universe is 'a Temple and Hall of Doom'; what destiny teaches being that

> a divine message, or eternal regulation of the Universe there verily is, in regard to every conceivable procedure and affair of man: faithfully following this, said procedure or affair will prosper, and have the whole Universe to second it, and carry it, across the fluctuating contradictions, towards a victorious goal; not following this; mistaking this, disregarding this, destruction and wreck are certain for every affair.

Certainly, this has its optimistic side. There is an 'inevitable necessity . . . in the nature of things' for human progress; 'a man is right and invincible . . . while he joins himself to the great deep Law of the World'. But there is a pessimistic side too: 'no world, or thing here below, ever fell into misery, without having first fallen into folly, into sin against the Supreme Ruler of it, by adopting as a law of conduct what was not a law, but the reverse of one'. In one direction or the other, however, the event must turn: 'the Highest did of a surety dwell in this Nation . . . leading . . . this Nation heavenward . . . or else the terrible *inverse*'. Vice and Virtue have, one as much as the other, their ultimate, uncompromising rewards.

The Control of Meaning

So far we have been concerned with how Carlyle's distinctive tenets are lent support by his style, his imagery, and his diction. The next problem—and it is a particularly important one in his case—is to see how some of his arguments and assertions are less factual than verbal.

Arguments and assertions cannot ever, perhaps, become verbal, unless they contain vague expressions. Newman's verbal discussions . . . consist largely of refusing to employ words in loose or unusual senses, and insisting upon their normal, or some other rather strict sense. His discussions claim to revert to exact standard usage. This meticulous, perhaps rather pedestrian approach made little appeal to Carlyle; and his verbal arguments justify the use of words in new, surprising, paradoxical or unexpectedly pregnant senses. The number, the variety of these arguments is amazing. In order to say what he wished to say, Carlyle had to remould and modify a quite appreciable part of the language. On a scale not fully recognized, he created language.

Therefore, before we see how he used language, we must see how he made it. But the two processes, though distinguishable in theory, can scarcely be isolated in practice. Carlyle's figurative language has already raised a problem: just as esoteric metaphors are used in a context which clarifies their meaning, and yet at the same time are really describing something, so individual words often acquire their new senses exactly through their appearance in new metaphors. If we attempt to trace the stages by which Carlyle transformed language, we often find a range of sentences from those whose sole purpose is to modify the sense of an expression, to those that take a modified sense for granted and merely employ it. The task of analysis is easier, though, if we consider these two extremes. Creating and exploiting new senses may not be rigidly separable, but the two processes can be observed in their turn.

The earliest stage in coining a sense is apparently to suggest that the real meaning of a word is not properly known. Thus 'Hast thou ever meditated on that word, Tradition?' or '"Cheap and nasty"; there is a pregnancy in that poor vulgar proverb, which I wish we better saw and valued'; or 'the Poet . . . communicates . . . a certain character of "infinitude", to whatsoever he delineates. This, though not very precise, yet on so vague a matter is worth remembering: if well meditated some meaning will gradually be found in it.' Next, a hint is given of the kinds of sense that may have escaped us: 'Is not the poorest nature *a mystery* . . . is he not an individual? And who shall explain all the significance of that one word?' 'This *momentous* and now almost forgotten truth, *Man is still Man*'— the enquiry, that is, has for goal the momentous and mysterious. Next a sense is more or less explicitly given, but some qualifying phrase is employed to make it acceptable in spite of its strangeness. 'To know a thing, what we can call knowing, a man must first *love* the thing, sympathize with it: that is, be *virtuously* related to it.' 'Let Oliver take comfort in his . . . melancholies. The quantity of sorrow he has, does it not mean withal the quantity of *sympathy* he has, the quantity of faculty and victory he shall yet have?'; 'the very editor . . . had, if reading mean understanding, never *read* them'; '"Reign of God" . . . giving place to modern Reign of the No-God, whom men name Devil'; 'all real "Art" is definable as Fact, or say as the disimprisoned "Soul of Fact"'; '*virtue to produce belief*, which is the highest and in reality the only literary success'; 'You are of the nature of *slaves*—or if you prefer the word, of *nomadic, and now even vagrant and vagabond, servants that can find no master on those terms;* which seems to me a much uglier word.'

Some phrase or another, or perhaps only a word in italics, has occurred in all these cases to indicate a novel sense; and often the novel sense is introduced not at once, but in two stages, of which the first is nearer to normal usage than the second.

The examples above deserve careful attention, because they also show how giving novel senses to words can make them terms of more emphatic praise or blame. This is explicit in the last two examples, but easily seen in the others and extremely important. Two further points are significant. First, a word may only be given a novel sense ('know', 'sorrow', 'read' and the rest) if its own sense is vague in part, and the senses of some other words are precise in part. Thus in their contexts, 'love', 'sympathize', 'virtuously', 'victory', 'understand' and the others do what is required of them because their meaning is definite and is not in question. Second, this process is entirely different from 'defining one's terms'. Carlyle does not wish to be thought of as explicitly allotting his own senses to these words, but as discovering what really they mean already, what their existing present use both depends upon, and perhaps conceals. But that the senses of the words are not being simply discovered, but really being changed, is clear from such phrases as 'does it not mean withal', or 'whom men name'; yet these occur indifferently with 'of the nature of' and 'in reality', which proves that Carlyle is claiming to discover the true meaning, not to prescribe his own.

Sometimes Carlyle unfolds the full meaning of a term as he sees it in a long and elaborate discussion. Thus in two chapters of *Past and Present* he expands the concept of *work*. Elaborating the meaning and applying it go on together, but the varieties of amplification are easy to trace. Near the beginning comes the simple call to reflection: 'It has been written, "an endless significance lies in Work"'. Then he begins to add new ideas to the meaning: 'there is a perennial nobleness, and even sacredness, in Work'. 'Work is of a religious nature:—work is of a *brave* nature; which it is the aim of all religion to be.' 'Religion' is already a powerful and definite term of praise; and next, religious authority is invoked to the same end—'we do entirely agree with those old monks, *Laborare est Orare*. In a thousand senses, from one end of it to the other, true Work *is* Worship.'

Another important stage in the expansion is: 'Work . . . is in communication with Nature'. At first, illustrations of this point are literal: 'foul jungles are cleared away, fair seed-fields rise instead'; 'true hand-labour . . . wide as the Earth . . . sweat of the brow'. Then metaphors follow: as some raise fair seedfields from jungles, so Christopher Wren raised a cathedral from London's ashes; the sweat of hand-labour leads us to sweat of the brain and heart, to Kepler, Newton, poets, martyrs, finally to 'that "Agony of bloody sweat"' which all men have called divine'. And now the two parts of the elaboration can be seen working together, for this last point seems naturally to confirm that 'properly speaking, all true Work is Religion'. There are other metaphors. To have 'found' one's work is to have a life purpose, to follow it as it runs like a clear stream 'through the sour mud-swamp of one's existence'; and this leads naturally through 'all work of man is as the swimmer's: a waste ocean threatens to drown him; if he front it not bravely', to literal examples again, Columbus and the Vikings. Finally there is amplification by contrast. The religion of the 'idle man' is that 'beggary or thievery' may suffice; work without religion is 'eye-service, greedy grasping of wages . . . manufacture of semblances . . . lath-and-plaster . . . stuffed hair-and-leather . . . Galvanism'—and throughout the whole passage, of course, in both expansion and contrast, the metaphors are Carlyle's own distinctive metaphors, and mean what he has made them mean.

One can distinguish here five activities: 'scene-setting', or the suggestion that a hidden meaning awaits discovery, if only we will meditate; verbal paradox (qualified conspicuously or inconspicuously so as to make it plausible); illustration; elaboration by metaphor; and expansion through contrast. Now, having seen the new sense of 'work' perfected, we can trace the uses to which it is put. First, Carlyle discredits abstract theoretical enquiry: since work communicates with Nature, the knowledge that 'will hold good in working' is to be valued, other knowledge on the whole not. Second, because work is divine, our well-being must be in it alone; and since 'all works . . . are a making of Madness sane;—truly enough a religious operation', we must struggle unremittingly against disorder, chaos and abuse. Third, we must not complain of a life of toil in the plain sense of physical labour, for if we call it labour at all, we must do so on Carlyle's terms, and then it is noble and divinely ordained. Even industrial manufacture is divine—'Labour is not a devil, even while encased in Mammonism; Labour is ever an imprisoned God, writhing unconsciously or consciously to escape out of Mammonism'—and the industrialist, or 'Master-Worker' is thus intrinsically a power for good. Next, the word 'wages' is given an expanded sense through the expanded sense of 'work'. If work is really sacred, religious, divine, 'the "wages" of every noble Work do . . . lie in Heaven'. Undeniably, the worker must be paid what enables him to go on working; but there cannot be, in money, wages exactly proportionate to work done—indeed, 'money-wage' is a contradiction. Work, life-purpose, Life cannot be sold, because its worth is infinite. At bottom it must be given away. Earthly happiness, money and the means to it, are incommensurate with what is divine.

That all valuable knowledge is practical, that we should work hard without complaining, should create order out of disorder, respect industry and industrialists, insist only on a subsistence rate of payment—all these propositions may be true or false. For the moment what matters is how Carlyle leads his readers to accept them through claiming to elaborate in full the *accepted* meaning of a single crucial term. This device is essential to how he expresses the 'life-philosophy'. (pp. 39-46)

Paradox and Truism

Paradoxes in Carlyle are too frequent to need full illustration; but what might be called the positive paradoxes must be distinguished from the negative, because their functions are quite different. 'Nature is *preter*natural' is an example of the first, while that the Poem written only for sucess has 'not yet become a Thing' or that 'We have sumptuous garnitures for our Life, but have forgotten how to *live*' is of the second. Of these two kinds of paradox, the first exalts our notion of the subject by employing a word that would normally be used only of something superior to it, the second belittles the subject by withholding a word that would normally be employed of it; and in both, the word in question serves as a term of praise. Sometimes one can find Carlyle writing two contrasting assertions, where the term of praise used in one is withheld in the other. Thus by contrast with the bad poem which is not yet a Thing, 'all real "Art" is definable as Fact'.

The paradox that the commercial poem is not yet a 'Thing' has a special interest; it suggests the general value of such writing. Carlyle is at pains to make his statement acceptable to the reader and he begins by speaking only of a Poem which is being planned. 'Thy No-Thing of an Intended Poem, O Poet who hast looked only to reviewers . . . behold it has not yet become a Thing.' Since this poem is still only 'intended', the statement is true literally. But it is soon transformed into paradox, for Carlyle goes on: '. . . The Truth is not in it!'; and then comes the crucial transition, and the by now familiar claim that a special sense is the only sense: 'Though printed, hot-pressed . . . to the twentieth edition: what is all that? The Thing, *in philosophical uncommercial language,* is still a No-Thing.' 'Still' hides the shift from one sense of 'thing' used in an unequivocal and clearly true statement, to another sense, used of something not intended but by now produced, in a paradox. Carlyle has prefaced his paradox by a non-paradoxical verbal equivalent. . . . (pp. 50-1)

It is natural to ask whether in these passages at least, Carlyle is not a fraud; and one is tempted to say that he is. Yet this hardly follows. Certainly, these passages comprise trains of association that could induce an unreflecting reader to accept Carlyle's conclusion, and yet have no ground for it whatever; and sometimes perhaps, when the reader discovers himself fallen into this trap, he may reasonably claim to have been preceded there by the author. But this is interpretation at a fairly crude level, and assumes that if Carlyle's prose has any value at all, it has the value of a sequence of logically developing propositions whose sense is plain at once. What warrant is there for this assumption?

But, it may be asked, what alternative is there to it? An alternative does exist. It is that a discussion may consist of what might be called 'nodal' propositions, with a far from immediately plain sense, but introduced, familiarized, made easier for the reader to grasp, by a variety of techniques that would indeed be sophistical, if their interpretation could be nothing but logical; but not otherwise. The intervening passages do not prove the nodal propositions, but they work upon the reader, they quicken his insight until he can grasp their point directly for himself. This by itself, though, is insufficient. Of what value to him can these nodal propositions be, if they are not logically proved, but simply asserted, dogmatically though perhaps alluringly? That they are important (as is seen whenever they are examined in Carlyle) in praising one object or disparaging another, in evoking the emotions of respect or disrespect, is not enough; for these emotions can be evoked by trickery.

But the solution lies along these lines: emotions are not always and necessarily evoked by trickery, and a criterion can be found to distinguish genuine from sophistical evocation. For though language can evoke emotions, so can things themselves; and language, even when it fails to state or describe, has a legitimate emotive power if it operates not independently, in a beautiful though empty mist, but by re-directing our attention to objects, concentrating it upon them, and thereby making us notice aspects of them that previously we had overlooked. A vital distinction exists between one emotive use of words, as it is called, and another. With the first, when we turn from the language to the things of which it is alleged to speak, experience cancels our incipient emotions, and prompts us to discard a tissue of sophistical nonsense. With the second, experience reinforces and completes what language began. This distinction between usefully and fraudulently evocative language remains, even should we all disagree about which attempts are of which kind; but many people are likely to find themselves in agreement that certain attempts are of one kind, and others of the other. As for Carlyle, most readers would agree that some of his nodal propositions were aids to insight, and some of them emphatically were not.

So much for the paradoxical element in Carlyle's work; its apparent contrary is the element of truism. 'Truism' means here a statement that is true solely from how the words in it

are defined; and seems the opposite of paradox, because just as a paradox cannot really (we are inclined to say in our down-to-earth moments) be true, so a truism cannot really be false. But Carlyle controls the senses of his words so thoroughly that the contrast is illusory. What is a paradox at one extreme, interpreted in a perfectly straightforward sense, is a truism at the other, when the special sense given to some crucial word is made fully explicit. This is often why Carlyle says that some apparent extravagance will become obvious when meditated upon, especially if the meditation is carried out in just the required spirit.

With patience, every intermediate variety between paradox and truism can be traced. 'Independence, in all kinds, is rebellion', is at one extreme; then, perhaps a shade less belligerently paradoxical, come those sentences quoted previously, where there is a hint that the meanings must be considered as well as the things themselves; then statements which hint that a word may have two quite unrelated senses, or a true sense and a false sense, like 'properly speaking, the land belongs to . . . God'. There are two interesting specimens of the next position on the scale. One runs: 'were your Superiors worthy to govern, and you worthy to obey, reverence for them were even your only possible freedom'; and the other:

> Despotism is essential in most enterprises . . . they do not tolerate "freedom of debate" on board a Seventy-four! . . . yet observe . . . Freedom, not no-mad's or ape's Freedom, but man's Freedom; this is indispensable. . . . To reconcile Despotism with Freedom . . . do you not already know the way? It is to make your Despotism *just.* Rigorous as Destiny; but just too, as Destiny and its Laws.

These two passages are almost the same in meaning. Their interest is that they make paradoxical assertions only upon some condition which goes far to turn the paradox into a truism. To be sure, this condition is put indirectly, and is by no means conspicuous. But they could be paraphrased, at loss only of subtlety in presentation, as 'obedience is freedom if of worthy subjects to worthy superiors', and 'despotism brings freedom, if it is just despotism'. In this form the tendency towards truism is plain, either because despotism failing to bring freedom would quite likely be regarded as *ipso facto* not 'just' despotism, or because anything that just despotism failed to bring would not be freedom 'properly speaking', or of the human and not merely nomadic or simian kind.

Assertions like this are common in Carlyle; and either by a word like 'true' or 'real' or by some device of typography, they indicate that a word used has a special sense and leave the question open whether or not this sense will suffice to render the whole assertion a truism. For example, 'the grand problem yet remains . . . finding government by your Real-Superiors'; 'a revolt against *false* sovereigns . . . the painful but indispensable first preparative for true sovereigns'; 'Europe requires a real Aristocracy, a real Priesthood. . . . False Aristocracies are insupportable . . . true aristocracies are . . . indispensable'; 'A Time of Miracle; as indeed all "Times" are . . . when there are MEN alive . . .'; 'the god-made king is needed'.

These distinctive words like 'true' and 'real'—and italics too—insist that the reader give to an assertion just that sense which makes it true. But the insistence is unnecessary if it is difficult for him to do otherwise, and some words naturally carry the implication required by the author. Carlyle speaks of struggling 'as for life in reforming our foul ways . . . alleviating . . . our people; seeking . . . that something like spiritual food be imparted them, some real governance . . . be provided them!' Here 'governance' requires the word 'real' to give it a sense in which it is a truism to call it desirable, but the idiom of the language makes us take for granted that 'spiritual' food is desirable. Here Carlyle combines two techniques: he precedes an assertion that is explicitly qualified so as to be a truism, by an assertion that is a truism through the most natural sense of the words it contains.

Ungarnished truisms are common in Carlyle's work: 'Many things can be done . . . had we once got a soul': inability to do the things would show that *ipso facto* we still lacked a soul. 'The . . . Wise will have . . . to take command of the . . . Foolish' if ever it proved that this relation ought not to hold, *ipso facto* either 'wise' or 'foolish' would have been misused. 'The one enemy we have in this Universe is Stupidity' any apparently stupid thing that proved useful is *ipso facto* not stupid really, any inimical thing is *ipso facto* stupid at bottom, even if not apparently. 'All the millenniums that I ever heard of heretofore were to be preceded by a "chaining of the Devil"'—if the Devil proves not to have been chained, *ipso facto* what has come is not a millennium.

Perhaps the reader will at this point lose patience once for all with Carlyle and I fear with the analysis of him too. Yet in spite of appearances these truisms are not worthless, because they are not empty. There is an ambiguity in their crucial terms that gives some point to them after all. When these terms are given one interpretation, the sentences follow by definition, and when another, they are controversial but substantial generalizations. Their air of incontrovertibility is a persuasive or rhetorical device, making the controversial seem non-controversial; but, though Carlyle may unconsciously trick the reader, it is not into nothing. This can easily be seen.

'Abler men in Downing Street, abler men to govern us'—that these would help may be a truism, but after it has been enunciated at the head of a paragraph, Carlyle goes on to make it controversial: 'the Able Man . . . is definable as the born enemy of Falsity and Anarchy, the born soldier of Truth and Order'. This is vague enough, certainly; but it by no means follows by definition that this ability is desirable in Downing Street or elsewhere; and the definition is much further elaborated. Later, Carlyle reverts to this topic. What is required is 'an increased supply of Human Intellect to Downing Street', and Intellect is 'otherwise definable as Human Worth'. Further, it can be pursued only by 'devout prayer to Heaven'; in this Christian context 'Worth', and 'Intellect' too perhaps, have relatively precise meanings, and once again we see how Carlyle is drawing upon an established religious tradition. Compare '"Organization of Labour";—which must be taken out of the hands of absurd windy persons, and put into the hands of wise, laborious, modest and valiant men'; here there is an elaborate fusion of what is controversial with what is not. 'Absurd', 'windy', and on the other hand 'wise' can scarcely be given senses that do not leave the whole assertion a truism; 'laborious', 'modest' and 'valiant' all introduce something of a more or less controversial nature, though Carlyle has so broken down the normal resistance of language that in reading the sentence one begins to feel how their meaning could be adjusted to make them apt by definition alone. A good deal later, Carlyle further elaborates his concept of a wise man: 'other men . . . a totally other sort of men, different as light is from dark, as star-fire is from street-mud'; and this illustrates again how each more restricted assertion, in a work of this kind, tends to rely upon the whole cumulative strength of the 'Life-Philosophy', and how our un-

derstanding of the life-philosophy cannot be put into any formula or rubric, but is a sense of something, an understanding built up in us gradually by all the techniques which this chapter has been examining, and, strangely enough, revived in our minds even by what seems to draw on it.

Carlyle's truisms then, are not simply empty, just as his paradoxes are not simply false. Rather, we discover two different methods of making controversial statements leave their impress on the reader: paradox is impressive and memorable because surprising and striking, truism because incontrovertible. These assertions derive their persuasive and rhetorical power from their form. But they make a contribution of substance too, because the senses of words are manipulated until the paradox is no longer paradoxical, the truism no longer trite. The paradox is mollified, as it were, until it just relapses into a proper sense, and the truism is progressively charged with meaning until it just manages to acquire one. In both cases, the ultimate result is not very different. Once the reader is alive to this kind of ambiguity, he can see Carlyle combining and alternating between these methods with presumably unconscious skill traceable on every page.

Early in this [essay] four principles were advanced as a summary of Carlyle's philosophy. It is now possible to see more clearly how the whole texture and detail of his work is what really interprets them. A sense of the life and energy that pervades the world is amassed gradually for his reader by the febrile style, by the constant dramatization of apparently abstract argument, by a wide variety of metaphors, and sometimes by the bewilderingly erratic sequence of ideas and images. The integration of the universe, as Carlyle sees it, and its permeation by this cosmic life, is suggested by innumerable passing deviations from small things to great. What is almost a new linguistic continent of distinctive or even esoteric metaphor makes Carlyle's sense of a cosmic fissure between good and bad, real and sham, enter every fragment of what he wrote; and it is the living quality of the cosmos, and this great split through it, which generate Carlyle's sense of the course of history. These devices would give a vivid sense of his world view, even if he never generalized at all. But his broader assertions draw upon a remoulding of the senses of words so extensive and elaborate that it might almost be called a new linguistic continent too. As a result, the more discursive parts of his work must be seen not as logical argument, but as sequences of verbal marches and countermarches—as formulae which prepare the reader's mind for, and converge upon, some nodal or crucial assertion. And this nodal assertion will prove acceptable (if at all) not on logical grounds, but because, prepared and sensitized as he is, the reader may glimpse how, in a strained and cryptic way, it is a revelation of some important and elusive truth, an assertion which, if it is put to the test, illuminates the whole bias of experience. Finally, by the frequent use of Biblical diction, Carlyle attaches his whole exposition to a philosophy or world view which is deeply familiar and widely sympathetic. No part of Carlyle's prose seems quite unrelated to his overriding purpose. (pp. 51-7)

> *John Holloway, "Carlyle," in his* The Victorian Sage: Studies in Argument, *Macmillan & Co., Ltd., 1953, pp. 21-57.*

JOHN LINDBERG   (essay date 1960)

[*Lindberg sees a ruling artistic unity in* Sartor Resartus, *designating the work a novel.*]

It would be absurd to claim to find the unity of a novel by James in the wonderful *olla podrida* that makes up *Sartor Resartus,* and yet I do believe the book displays artistic form, not only of theme and style but also, and even basically, of that sort of structure involving relationships between distinct characters participating in a series of actions demanded by a plot moving to a preconcerted judgment about life. In short, *Sartor Resartus* deserves to be recognized as a true novel, and not just the sort of book we call a novel because no other term fits. But it is true that Carlyle discharged all of his gifts indiscriminately into the book in an access of bitterness at his failure to win literary recognition, as though he would create in spite of his inexperience and the indifference of the world, so that the structural merit of the book may easily fail to strike the reader who first notices the bewildering mixture of philology, topical and universal satire, literary and historical allusion, philosophy, irony, humor, anger, and buffoonery. (p. 20)

Sartor Resartus is the story of an orphan reared in an idyllic natural setting by doting foster-parents, bred in the deadening traditions of a formalistic educational system, disappointed in love, disgusted with the demands of a materialistic society, undergoing a religious conversion and winning through all adversity to a renewed sense of purpose and service. Put so flatly, the story is much like many popular novels of the time for which *Sartor Resartus* may have helped prepare the British public—*Great Expectations* and *Henry Esmond,* perhaps—and of course its immediate literary ancestors were *Werther* and *Meister,* which last Carlyle had already translated. *Sartor Resartus* may be a transitional medium for the *Bildungsroman* from German to English Romanticism, although it does clearly reflect Carlyle's love for Fielding and Smollett. Of course I am not the first to make these points, but they seem especially relevant in establishing the artistic unity, not to say conventionality, of *Sartor Resartus.*

But Carlyle's development of this traditional basis is not conventional and we must firmly relate the unusual development to the traditional basis if we are to see an artistic structure uniting the disparate elements of the book.

First, Carlyle adopts a disguise for his novel and pretends to be writing a straightforward biography, in this way winning room for inventive episodes, using the conventions of both forms to create a unique form, a "special world" with "a most complex structure, having a logic of its own which governs feeling and speech. It is at once a way of looking at things, a way of feeling, and a way of speaking." I have said that Carlyle used the conventions of biography to disguise the fact that he was actually inventing a fictitious story; this conception of a disguise or a mask is absolutely essential to a full appreciation of the artistic integrity of the book. Carlyle himself confesses to it, putting into the mouth of his hero these words: "Alas, the panoply of Sarcasm was but as a buckram case, wherein I had striven to envelope myself; that so my own poor Person might live safe there, and in all friendliness, being no longer exasperated by wounds."

The position in *Sartor Resartus* where these words occur is most important, and they would not mean so much if they appeared at any other place in the structure of the book. The words are spoken in retrospect by the mature Teufelsdröckh, and he is contemplating himself as a young man forced to make his own way before the indifference of the world, just out of the university and casting desperately about for some means of subsisting without compromising his ideals. The envelope of sarcasm around young Teufelsdröckh corresponds precisely to the unique form of *Sartor Resartus,* Carlyle deciding to invent it at the same stage in his careeer as the one at which Teufelsdröckh perfects his idiosyncratic personality in his own development.

In the structure of *Sartor Resartus,* those elements of the book based primarily on Carlyle's own life end with these words, almost exactly half-way through the story, and the rest of Teufelsdröckh's history becomes an explanation of his opinions, a record of religious and philosophical beliefs capable of comforting people in general as well as the individual who formed them. The chapters on religious conversion immediately succeeding these words about the envelope of sarcasm have given comfort to many generations of men, and represent also a climax in Carlyle's inner experience; his "way out of the Everlasting No was . . . by three paths: . . . the way of religion, the way of Weltanschauung and the way of prophecy."

"Weltanschauung" came to be a basic conception in the function of the masking device Carlyle created in *Sartor Resartus.* As his chapter on "Symbols" makes clear, he regarded literature as "concealment and yet revelation . . . by Silence and Speech acting together, comes a double significance." Just as literature represents the world, so the world represents the transcendent reality of the divine creative spirit, and Carlyle conceived of art as the sacred communication of divine intuitions about the dualism between creation and the substance created in the universe. Literature was a pulpit, and traditional forms might be modified at need to express the baffling ambivalence to be seen at work in the world, both revealing and concealing Truth.

Thus the disguising or masking function of the unique form of *Sartor Resartus* both answered a deep personal need for protection from the indifference of Carlyle's audience and also gave Carlyle the necessary freedom to exploit all the latent possibilities of "a truly useful and philosophic . . . *Essay on Metaphors.*"

To discuss Carlyle's unusual treatment of the material of fiction, we may note his use of the three salient features of a novel—character, plot, and scene. We may say of these what we have said of the autobiographical parts of the book—that they develop from fairly specific to general relevance. This general relevance is always to the transcendental theme of the work.

The main characters are Teufelsdröckh's editor—to be referred to as the Editor in order to distinguish him from Carlyle—and the Philosopher himself, Diogenes Teufelsdröckh, whose name symbolizes the ambivalence of the world as he presents it in his Clothes-Philosophy. The Clothes-Philosophy further develops the dualistic symbolism in the book by representing the created universe both masking and adumbrating its creator.

We never do actually meet the Philosopher, who always appears to us in the guise of his work, the Clothes-Philosophy, and then only as well as the Editor's imperfect sympathy allows. For this is the conflict of the novel, the imperfect sympathy of the Editor for his Philosopher, and the radical inability of the Philosopher to express himself in terms acceptable to his Editor.

Between these opposite poles the Clothes-Philosophy springs into being, drawing its force from the struggle of Editor and Philosopher to understand their opposed world-views. Consequently, the relationship between the characters must deteriorate as their main ideas take over the book, and so it is;

A photograph of Carlyle in 1867.

from a cozy *Bierstube*-atmosphere of a student revering a professor, the characters develop away from each other until at the end of the book only the Clothes-Philosophy is left on the stage.

Quite without paradox, then, I maintain that the Clothes-Philosophy, growing out of a conflict between characters, is fully fictive and dynamic, no mere construction of logic but a living symbol of Carlyle's attitude toward the world. I say "living symbol" because of course both Editor and Philosopher represent aspects of Carlyle, who is dramatizing an inner conflict of his own as well as staging a transcendental philosophy.

Sartor Resartus may have no plot in the conventional sense. The adventures of Teufelsdröckh constitute a story of some scope but they occupy only the second "book," the one allegedly composed of the Philosopher's memoirs, and a plot must implicate all of the main characters if a novel is to have unity. If we discard the usual idea of a plot, which limits it to a series of events in time and place, and attempt to conceive of a plot as the interrelationships entered into between characters because of their dispositions toward each other, then it may be that *Sartor Resartus* has a very strong plot indeed, one which like the characterization undergoes a complication from topical to general relevance.

The plot of *Sartor Resartus* has a pronounced rhythm caused by the alternation between the free speaking of each character and the contradiction determined by that free speech. This rhythm appears in full swing even in the smallest divisions of the book and rises to a series of climaxes as Editor and Philosopher clash.

First, the Editor is the main speaker in Book I, followed by Teufelsdröckh speaking through his memoirs in Book II; after

full characterization, Book III is concerned with the central conflict, the meaning and exposition of the Clothes-Philosophy. Second, each "book" is a running argument between Editor and Philosopher, each character speaking in alternating chapters and the argument culminating in a striking affirmation from the Philosopher and a more or less qualified denial from the Editor; this arrangement is apparent even from a glance at the chapter-headings.

My final point about the plot should be stressed to counteract the idea of Carlyle that must arise of sad necessity from reading him in anthologies. The rhythmic development of the relationship between Editor and Philosopher assigns a subordinate and contributory rather than a central importance to the climax of Book II; after the religious conversion recounted in the middle of *Sartor Resartus*, there yet remains the climax of the work as a whole in Book III—those eloquent chapters entitled "The Phoenix," "Organic Filaments," and especially "Natural Supernaturalism," where for himself and the world Teufelsdröckh achieves his ultimate victory in vision and idea.

As for scene, the setting of *Sartor Resartus* is the world of the book itself. I think Carlyle has permitted us no doubt of his intentions here. The Clothes-Philosophy is the theme of the work and from the first it occupies all concerned. Not only do we never meet the Philosopher except through his work, but the Editor claims himself to be "insignificant . . . a voice publishing tidings of the Philosophy of Clothes; undoubtedly a Spirit addressing Spirits: whoso hath ears, let him hear."

The setting of the book is an aural fantasy, a serendipitous internal consistency of the symbolic power of words. The autobiographical memoirs on which the Editor hopes to rely are fragmentary, visionary, disorganized, and as he comes to suspect at the end of Book II, "partly a mystification" meant to "deceptively inlock both Editor and Hofrath [the general reader, as I interpret the role of the good counselor] in the labyrinthic tortuosities and covered-ways'" of the Clothes-Philosophy.

Teufelsdröckh's "outward Biography, therefore, which . . . we saw churned utterly into spray-vapour, may hover in that condition," while the Editor and reader now devote themselves to the Clothes-Philosophy entirely in Book III. And in Book III the whole volume is made to depend on the validity of the Clothes-Philosophy alone when the Philosopher simply disappears from the knowledge of man—"Professor Teufelsdröckh, be it known, is no longer visibly present at Weissnichtwo, but again to all appearance lost in space!"

The Philosopher is "again . . . lost in space" as he was once before when like Christ he wandered in the wilderness to seek within himself his purpose and work in the world (climax of Book II). Having brought his prophetic vision to completion in the Clothes-Philosophy, he may disappear, leaving as his memorial the work he had before disappeared to find.

The Philosopher, the Editor, the Hofrath or the reader inasmuch as he has become implicated in the meaning of the Clothes-Philosophy, all are marked by the common fate of man, a fate symbolized by the unexpected, sudden disappearance of Teufelsdröckh—an end Carlyle constantly stressed by his favorite quotation, with which he concluded the climax of *Sartor Resartus:*

> We *are such stuff*
> As dreams are made of, and our little Life
> Is rounded with a sleep!

In the face of his world, which was much like ours in its quest for secure values, Carlyle was determined not to fade and leave not a wrack behind. *Sartor Resartus,* firm in its artistic unity, remains as the inspired vision of a magician whose labors now are ended. (pp. 20-3)

John Lindberg, "The Artistic Unity of 'Sartor Resartus'," in The Victorian Newsletter, No. 17, Spring, 1960, pp. 20-3.

G. B. TENNYSON   (essay date 1965)

[*In this excerpt, drawn from his full-length study of* Sartor Resartus, *Tennyson analyzes in turn the three books of the work, investigating their functions and themes.*]

[Nowhere did Carlyle] find a more perfect embodiment for the turbulences of the age and the insights of his own mind than in the interchange and struggle of the commonsense Editor with the life and mind of the mystical Teufelsdröckh [in *Sartor Resartus*]. For here Carlyle was able to embody his own double awareness that everything has two aspects, the spiritual and the material, or as he put it, "two authentic Revelations, of a God and of a Devil; the Pulpit, namely, and the Gallows." If in *Sartor* the material side is condemned, abused, and frequently violated, it is because the need to show that there is a genuine spiritual life in the universe was far greater than the need to call the attention of society to the material world, which is in any case too much with us. Thus the style often operates to annihilate the finite world entirely, and structurally Teufelsdröckh always threatens to swallow up the Editor; but this serves the moral purpose of leaving no doubt as to which is superior, finite or infinite, material or spiritual. The structure and style of *Sartor* join in leading us to use the material world as a window onto the divine. But both ineluctably are, and our task is to see them in proper perspective.

If there is a single aim toward which the double vision of structure and style is directed, that aim is to make one *see.* Indeed, the metaphor of vision and blindness stands behind even the pervasive imagery of light and dark, investing it all with a moral dimension. *Insight* may be the key word to *Sartor* after all: Carlyle has had an insight into the nature of man and society; *Sartor* leads the reader to the same insight. The assertion properly is, not either finite or infinite, but both. Man and society are still man and society. Furthermore, both are organisms; both live. The feeling of pulsating, onrushing life conveyed by Carlyle's prose enlists the reader's support for Carlyle's beliefs in a way that no amount of discursive reasoning can do.

By now everyone knows what the clothes metaphor stands for, that clothes are figuratively the institutions, beliefs, customs, and conventions of man and society. Yet a further purpose of the painstaking identification of clothing with the practices of society is to strip the clothes off. Carlyle fashions the clothes metaphor less to apparel society than to denude it. Swift creates his clothes metaphor in *A Tale of a Tub* to comment on a particular set of beliefs, Christianity, and to show that one set of beliefs is superior to its rivals, that one suit of clothes fits man better than any other. Carlyle's metaphor is both more intensive and more extensive. All of society's old clothes are ill fitting and must be removed. *Sartor* abounds in allusions to nakedness, stripping away, disrobing—all designed to make us look at the fundamental object, man, so that we too see that he and his society are wearing tatters in this "Ragfair of a World." The time has come, Carlyle argues, to divest society of its clouts and deposit them where they belong—in the Monmouth Street Old Clothes market. There is no specific record

that Carlyle was familiar with the fact that tearing off one's clothes is [according to Eric Voegelin] a "ritual gesture of revulsion against blasphemy," but the correspondence between the ancient Hebrew gesture and what Teufelsdröckh does for society is astonishingly close. The blasphemy, of course, resides in the decay into which divine institutions have been let fall and the hypocritical lip service those institutions continue to receive while the meaning they once symbolized is no longer operative. Let us, cries Teufelsdröckh, have new finite embodiments of the eternal truths that are ever there underneath the "adventitious wrappages," in the very nature of the organism that is the human being.

The insight that man is an organism applies with equal force to society. If we can but peer beneath the outer coverings, the "hulls," "husks," and "garnitures," and other pejorative terms Carlyle employs to make these externals appear contemptible, we will see that a living unity lies revealed. The perception of organic life in man and society is one of the most important, although not the most original, of Carlyle's insights. The clothes metaphor dovetails with this insight at the most crucial point because clothes, in themselves lifeless, nevertheless presuppose a body. Machines are not clothed; society is, and man is. Even nature becomes the "living garment of God." Once the clothes metaphor in its widest extension is firmly planted in the reader's mind, Carlyle is able to play on the contrast between outer and inner, material and spiritual, real and ideal, dead and living, as on an instrument of which he is the designer and sole performer.

All of this is there in germ in Book One of *Sartor Resartus:* the double vision of material and spiritual, the stripping away of old clothes, the irreducible mystery and divinity of man. In "Pure Reason" the message is explicitly stated several times:

> "To the eye of vulgar Logic," says he, "what is man? An omnivorous Biped that wears Breeches. To the eye of Pure Reason what is he? A Soul, a Spirit, and divine Apparition. Round his mysterious ME, there lies, under all those wool-rags, a Garment of Flesh (or of Senses), contextured in the Loom of Heaven; whereby he is revealed to his like, and dwells with them in UNION and DIVISION; and sees and fashions for himself a Universe, with azure Starry Spaces, and long Thousands of Years. Deep-hidden is he under that strange Garment; amid Sounds and Colours and Forms, as it were, swathed-in, and inextricably over-shrouded: yet it is sky-woven, and worthy of a God. Stands he not thereby in the centre of Immensities, in the conflux of Eternities?"

And again in "Prospective," where the Editor looks ahead to the task he has undertaken: "'Nay, if you consider it, what is Man himself, and his whole terrestrial Life, but an Emblem; a Clothing or visible Garment for that divine ME of his, cast hither, like a light-particle, down from Heaven?'" Finally, in Book One, the extension of the insight to cover all things: "'Thus in this one pregnant subject of CLOTHES, rightly understood, is included all that men have thought, dreamed, done, and been: the whole External Universe and what it holds is but Clothing, and the essence of all Science lies in the PHILOSOPHY OF CLOTHES'."

Carlyle recognized that the essence of his insight lay already in Book One, and he originally proposed to stop there and publish it as a long article. Then he realized that the development of the ideas in Book One was not extensive enough. The demands made on the reader are too radical for the full impact to be felt by a reading of Book One alone. In the context of the three books, Book One succeeds chiefly in introducing the reader to the terms necessary for an investigation of man and society, and above all in posing again and again the fundamental and ancient question to which *Sartor* as a whole is addressed: what is man that God is mindful of him? (pp. 285-88)

[Carlyle] has a strong sense of the dramatic and is quite capable of constructing miniature dramas throughout. He continually personifies, investing abstracts with qualities one likes or dislikes. But the overall rhythm of *Sartor* is not dramatic, even while that of Book Two may well be. . . . *Sartor* is closer to being a sermon: the text is enunciated in Book One, and Book Two is the *exemplum*. As if to confirm the homiletic nature of *Sartor*—though confirmation is hardly necessary when we consider the whole drift of Carlyle's efforts from 1814 on—Carlyle wrote in his journal in October 1831:

> What an advantage has the Pulpit, when you address men arranged to hear you, and in a vehicle which long use has rendered easy: how infinitely harder when you have all to create, not the ideas only and the sentiments, but the symbols and the mood of mind! Nevertheless in all cases, where man addresses man, on his spiritual interests especially, there is a *sacredness,* could we but evolve it, and think and speak in it. . . .
>
> —Is *Art* in the old Greek sense possible for man at this late era? Or were not (perhaps) the Founder of a Religion our true Homer at present?—The *whole Soul* must be illuminated, made harmonious: Shakespeare seems to have had no religion, but his Poetry.—

At this time Carlyle was in London trying to market his manuscript. Back in Scotland the following spring, *Sartor* still with him and unpublished, he wrote in his journal: "Every man that writes is writing a new Bible; or a new Apocrypha; to last for a week, or for a thousand years: he that convinces a man and sets him working is the doer of a *miracle*."

Carlyle's intention at any rate is clear: *Sartor,* like a sermon, addresses man's spiritual interests and as such is possessed of a *sacredness.* The question is merely how accurately the undertaking has been received by its audience, whether the author and reader have evolved the sacredness. We generally consider it one of the more eccentric characteristics of the Victorian age that any reader ever saw in *Sartor* a pattern for faith. Yet, from the nature of the work itself and Carlyle's explicit statements, that is obviously what *Sartor* was designed to offer. Book Two, as the *exemplum* of the sermon, provides the pattern for the individual. The application of Book Two is primarily tropological; it offers us the spiritual development of a man coming to right understanding in times as turbulent as the present. . . . Let us concentrate on the spiritual dimension of the allegory as a means of seeing the kind of pattern that Carlyle devises for Teufelsdröckh and that became in turn the classic pattern of Victorian doubt, denial, and affirmation.

In keeping with the suggestion of denuding society, Carlyle also posits a denuding of the individual. Teufelsdröckh is another Adam; yet he is set down not in Eden but in the barren desert of modern life. Beyond that, he is fatherless, an important Christian allusion that is not forgotten when affirmation is reached. In the early part of Book Two Teufelsdröckh is fitted out with the current clothes of society, but they are simply inadequate. The Editor, as always, glosses Teufelsdröckh's spiritual development at crucial points. Up to his university years the situation is as follows: "So much we can see; darkly, as through the foliage of some wavering thicket: a youth of no

common endowment, who has passed happily through Childhood, less happily yet still vigorously through Boyhood, now at length perfect in 'dead vocables,' and set down, as he hopes, by the living Fountain, there to superadd Ideas and Capabilities."

Ideas and capabilities are not forthcoming from a "Rational University," and Teufelsdröckh begins to fall into doubt. Even friendship is denied him, although he experiences a pale shadow of it in his association with Herr Towgood. In "Getting Under Way" the Editor's gloss makes clear that the situation is extremely grave. . . . (pp. 290-92)

The turn to the lady known as Blumine is the last hope of a desperate man. His motivation is, as ever, spiritual: "A visible divinity dwelt in [women]; to our young friend all women were holy, were heavenly." Repeatedly in the autobiographical notes dealing with the love affair the Editor seeks in vain for items of "psychological" (i.e. novelistic) interest, but concludes: "To all which questions, not unessential in a Biographic work, mere Conjecture must for the most part return answer." The reason is that psychology is not at issue; spirituality is. Blumine is the agency through which Teufelsdröckh reaches despair. Accordingly, when Blumine parts with him, "'thick curtains of Night rushed over his soul, as rose the immeasurable Crash of Doom; and through the ruins as of a shivered Universe was he falling, falling, towards the Abyss'." . . . (p. 293)

[Let] us stress that the experience strips Teufelsdröckh of every external covering with which education and society have provided him. He becomes the prototype of the "poor forked animal." Just as his low point is a denial of God, so the way back begins with a denial of the devil. At the central moment in Teufelsdröckh's drama he too sees himself alone in the universe, and he defies hell. But as he does so, he gains strength from outside: "'And as I so thought, there rushed like a stream of fire over my whole soul.'" The experience is characteristic of mystics at the moment of conversion. What gives Carlyle's its particular depth and relevance is that he proceeds from that point to carry his protagonist all the way back.

Carlisle Moore has pointed out [in a 1963 article in *Victorian Studies*] that a subsequent "prolonged period of doubt . . . delays and modifies" the original mystic experience. In Teufelsdröckh's case it is the Centre of Indifference. During this period Teufelsdröckh is far from spiritually secure; there are still times of misery and doubt; but there are signs of regeneration: "In a word, he is now, if not ceasing, yet intermitting to 'eat his own heart'; and clutches round him outward on the Not-me for wholesomer food." Teufelsdröckh himself glosses the whole meaning of his experience in spiritual terms:

> "Has not thy Life been that of most sufficient men (*tüchtigen Männer*) thou hast known in this generation? An outflush of foolish young Enthusiasm, like the first fallow-crop, wherein are as many weeds as valuable herbs: this all parched away, under the Droughts of practical and spiritual Unbelief, as Disappointment, in thought and act, often-repeated gave rise to Doubt, and Doubt gradually settled into Denial! If I have had a second-crop, and now see the perennial greensward, and sit under umbrageous cedars, which defy all Drought (and Doubt); herein too, be the Heavens praised, I am not without examples, and even exemplars."

The feeling of understanding the world, the perception of truths previously hidden, and the positive out-going grip of life are the final result of the conversion experience. Unlike some subsequent Victorian mystics, notably Tennyson, Teufelsdröckh experiences something like a second trance-like state, less intense than that moment on the Rue de l'Enfer, but nevertheless of considerable consequence in ascertaining the extent of the mysticism involved. It follows immediately upon Teufelsdröckh's exclamation: "'Or what is Nature? Ha! why do I not name thee God? Art not thou the "Living Garment of God"? O Heavens, is it, in very deed, HE, then, that ever speaks through thee; that lives and loves in thee, that lives and loves in me?'" Immediately that Teufelsdröckh brings himself to name God as the real meaning of nature, he experiences his second moment of mystic oneness with the divine, and at last Teufelsdröckh recognizes that he has a Father. . . . (pp. 293-95)

The "Everlasting No" was the turning-point in the spiritual development of Teufelsdröckh's soul; the "Everlasting Yea," however, is the climax. . . . [It] really involves a descent into the depths of the soul; and the turning point is what starts the soul on the way back up. . . . "Descend, so that ye may ascend" is an Augustinian injunction figuratively followed by Teufelsdröckh, for his chthonic descent stops only in Hell (Rue de l'Enfer), and then he begins the ascent which takes him to an alpine peak ("'Beautiful it was to sit there, as in my skyey Tent, musing and meditating; on the high table-land, in front of the mountains; over me, as roof, the azure Dome, and around me for walls, four azure-flowing curtains,—namely, of the Four azure Winds, on whose bottom-fringes also I have seen gliding.'"), where he experiences the softer, gentler "foresplendours of Truth." The language of the experience itself is calculated to win the reader's emotional assent to what Teufelsdröckh has undergone. And it recalls, even to the imagery, the assertions in "Pure Reason" in which man is called "himself a Universe, with azure Starry Spaces, and long Thousands of Years."

The soul has found such assurance as there is to find in the world. For all Carlyle's dogmatism this assurance is not presented as all-sufficient; mystery remains and will ever remain. But the degree of conviction attained transforms Teufelsdröckh, producing in him at once a feeling of sympathy and love for his fellow-man ("'O my Brother, my Brother, why cannot I shelter thee in my bosom, and wipe away all tears from thy eyes!'") and an acceptance of the world as it is ("'Truly, the din of many-voiced Life, which, in this solitude, with the mind's organ, I could hear, was no longer a maddening discord, but a melting one; like inarticulate cries, and sobbings of a dumb creature, which in the ear of Heaven are prayers'"). The experience is then generalized into a principle: *'The Fraction of Life can be increased in value not so much by increasing your Numerator as by lessening your Denominator'*—that is, *Entsagen*. And the principle becomes an exhortation: "'Love not pleasure; love God. This is the EVERLASTING YEA, wherein all contradiction is solved: wherein whoso walks and works, it is well with him.'" Following that, there are practical, social, and ethical inferences to be drawn, which indeed are immediately embarked on, with the exhortation to *'Do the Duty which lies nearest thee.'* All of this is part of the grand climax of Book Two, with its paean to light and order and its exhortation to produce:

> I too could now say to myself: Be no longer a Chaos, but a World, or even Worldkin. Produce! Produce! Were it but the pitifullest infinitesimal fraction of a Product, produce it, in God's name! 'Tis the utmost thou hast in thee: out with it, then. Up, up! Whatsoever thy hand findeth to do, do it with thy whole might. Work while it is called Today; for the Night cometh, wherein no man can work.

Carlyle is not content to exemplify the problem of society through one man; he does the same thing for society itself. Book Three tells the tale. All that has been shadowed forth in Book One about the symbolic nature of clothes and all that the soul undergoes in Book Two is hammered home in Book Three in respect to Society. The analysis of society's maladies is inherent and foreshadowed in Book One. The moment we begin to look at institutions as clothing, and the moment we begin to look at society without its clothing, we begin to see things in a new light. The first part of Book Three is devoted to establishing the fact that society is dead: its church clothes are out at elbow, its symbols superannuated, its respect for the dignity of the individual vanished utterly away, and its aristocracy busy "Preserving their Game!" "Teufelsdröckh," says the Editor, "is one of those who consider Society, properly so called, to be as good as extinct." The powerful group of chapters that follows the depiction of society's dead or at least moribund state forms Teufelsdröckh's prescription for the improvement of society promised in Book One. The section also parallels on the social scale the personal experience of Teufelsdröckh from the biography of Book Two. The fire and phoenix imagery of this climactic section of *Sartor* echoes the fire imagery of Teufelsdröckh's death and forms further a subdivision of the light imagery of the whole book:

> "The Soul Politic having departed," says Teufelsdröckh, "what can follow but that the Body Politic be decently interred, to avoid putrescence? Liberals, Economists, Utilitarians enough I see marching with its bier, and chanting loud paeans, towards the funeral-pile, where, amid wailings from some, and saturnalian revelries from the most, the venerable Corpse is to be burnt."

Combustion and clothing imagery meet in "The Phoenix" and "Old Clothes" to depict a society in its final tottering moments:

> "The World," says he, "as it needs must, is under a process of devastation and waste, which, whether by silent assiduous corrosion, or open quicker combustion, as the case chances, will effectually enough annihilate the past Forms of Society; replace them with what it may. For the present, it is contemplated that when man's whole Spiritual interests are once *divested*, these innumerable stript-off Garments shall mostly be burnt; but the sounder Rags among them be quilted together into one huge Irish watch-coat for the defence of the Body only!"

As Teufelsdröckh's old man was destroyed in the fire-consummation in Hell, so society will burn away: "'When the Phoenix is fanning her funeral pyre, will there not be sparks flying! Alas, some millions of men, and among them such as a Napoleon, have already been licked into that high-eddying Flame, and like moths consumed there'." As we survey the history of the time since Carlyle wrote, we should be more inclined to acknowledge his prophetic gifts than we have been.

As society smolders and as old clothes are cast away, we have an accumulation of ideas and beliefs that Teufelsdröckh delights to study, for his sojourn in the Old Clothes Market is a declaration of the beauty of the study of history. Society's old clothes are objects of reverence when once they have been removed, for in them one sees "'the whole Pageant of Existence [passing] awfully before us; with its wail and jubilee, mad loves and mad hatreds, church-bells and gallows-ropes, farce-tragedy, beast-godhood,—the Bedlam of Creation!'"

But the parallels with the experience of the individual soul are clear: society lies dying—not in quite the same blaze of glory the Old Teufelsdröckh died in, for there are thousands of contingencies that mitigate against a rapid destruction of even worn-out symbols. But society is dying all the same, and it too must pass through a center of indifference, or more properly is even now passing through such a period, an age of transition, if Carlyle's reading of the *Zeitgeist* is right. "Organic Filaments" is to society what the Centre of Indifference was to Teufelsdröckh:

> For us, who happen to live while the World-Phoenix is burning herself, and burning so slowly that, as Teufelsdröckh calculates, it were a handsome bargain would she engage to have done "within two centuries," there seems to lie but an ashy prospect. Not altogether so, however, does the Professor figure it. "In the living subject," says he, "change is wont to be gradual: thus, while the serpent sheds its old skin, the new is already formed beneath. Little knowest thou of the burning of a World-Phoenix, who fanciest that she must first burn-out, and lie as a dead cincereous heap; and therefrom the young one startup by miracle, and fly heavenward. Far otherwise! In that Fire-whirlwind, Creation and Destruction proceed together; ever as the ashes of the Old are blown about, do organic filaments of the New mysteriously spin themselves: and amid the rushing and the waving of the Whirlwind-element come tones of a melodious Deathsong, which end not but in tones of a more melodious Birthsong. Nay, look into the Fire-whirlwind with thy own eyes, and thou wilt see."

The fire-death of society is like the continued but diminished ravings of Teufelsdröckh's "old inward Satanic School" in the Centre of Indifference. During this period the organic filaments are mysteriously fashioning new clothes for Teufelsdröckh's soul. At the end of the Centre of Indifference, Teufelsdröckh's soul is described as follows: "We should rather say that Legion, or the Satanic School, was now pretty well extirpated and cast out, but next to nothing introduced in its room; whereby the heart remains, for the while, in a quiet but no comfortable state." So in "Organic Filaments" the modern age is described: "'Or what if the character of our so troublous Era lay even in this: that man had forever cast away Fear, which is the lower; but not yet risen into perennial Reverence, which is the higher and the highest?'" But hope is at hand: "'If, in the most parched season of Man's History, in the most parched spot of Europe [i.e. eighteenth-century Paris], when Parisian life was at best but a scientific *Hortus Siccus,* bedizened with some Italian Gumflowers, such virtue could come out of it; what is to be looked for when Life again waves leafy and bloomy, and your Hero-Divinity shall have nothing apelike, but be wholly human?'"

Society, having passed through its Everlasting No in the atheistic eighteenth century, and passing now in the nineteenth through its Centre of Indifference, is slowly approaching its own Everlasting Yea. This will be "Natural Supernaturalism," the affirmation of a positive force in society just as the Everlasting Yea is Teufelsdröckh's personal affirmation. Only after the procedure of denial and destruction has been completed, only after the thousands of unseen forces in society gather new forms about them, can the soul of society, like the soul of man, attain a positive grasp on the divine. In all which speculation Teufelsdröckh is engaging in prophecy, the poet's highest calling; for at the moment society is yet in its death throes. By way of pointing the path for society, Teufelsdröckh urges the reader to pierce through both space and time, which are merely "Forms of Thought" that "hide from us the brightest God-effulgences." With the aid of Teufelsdröckh's mantic space

and time-annihilating hats, the reader can pierce through to the future, to the "Fire-Consummation" of society, and see what Teufelsdröckh already saw in his skyey tent, the "fore-splendours" of Truth.

That Carlyle's formulation of the society of the future is blessedly free from the programmatic earthly paradise of many nineteenth-century planners is attested to by the mystery-haunted conclusion of "Natural Supernaturalism":

> "Thus, like some wild-flaming, wild-thundering train of Heaven's Artillery, does this mysterious MANKIND thunder and flame, in long-drawn, quick-succeeding grandeur, through the unknown Deep. Thus, like a God-created, fire-breathing Spirit-host, we emerge from the Inane; haste stormfully across the astonished Earth; then plunge again into the Inane. Earth's mountains are levelled, and her seas filled up, in our passage: can the Earth, which is but dead and a vision, resist Spirits which have reality and are alive? On the hardest adamant some footprint of us is stamped-in; the last Reader of the host will read traces of the earliest Van. But whence?—O Heaven, whither? Sense knows not; Faith knows not; only that it is through Mystery to Mystery, from God and to God."

The final chapters of **Sartor** stand as a coda to the biography and the clothes philosophy, perhaps even marring the symmetry. The Editor, professing himself exhausted by the demands of Natural Supernaturalism, but thoroughly persuaded of its profundity, turns to its practical applications. If we can see Book Two as an *exemplum* of the clothes philosophy introduced in Book One, the chapters dealing with the Dandiacal Body and tailors are *exempla* of the further text enunciated in Book Three. From an architectonic point of view, Book Three might well have been concluded with a chapter from the Editor following "Natural Supernaturalism," but the excursion into the practical realm was made to satisfy Carlyle's immense concern with practical social problems.

"The Dandiacal Body" attacks the do-nothing aristocracy that has failed to provide leadership and warns that the two nations, the rich and the poor, are headed for irreversible conflict. "Tailors" utters a paean to poets and artists and an admonition to the world to heed its prophets. Then, his work done, the Editor lays down his pen, and Teufelsdröckh emerges into the present, perhaps to the Paris Revolution of July 1830, or, as the Editor surmises, "actually in London."

Carlyle's measure of the needs of the age was essentially accurate; but he may have miscalculated the extent to which his prescription for solution would or could be acted upon. For it was the way of a soul in Book Two that most completely fastened itself on the Victorian imagination. The social applications in Book Three were, in Carlyle's view, never really grasped. The tailor has certainly been retailored, but has he also given society a new suit of clothes that it will happily wear? (pp. 295-303)

G. B. Tennyson, in his "Sartor" *Called* "Resartus": The Genesis, Structure, and Style of Thomas Carlyle's First Major Work, *Princeton University Press, 1965, 354 p.*

GEORGE LEVINE (essay date 1968)

[*Levine analyzes selected passages of Carlyle's prose to investigate the link between substance and literary style.*]

The first step in any attempt to come to terms with Carlyle's style is, necessarily, to show that the mannerism is a reflex of the substance, that the style is the best possible means for the expression of the ideas, attitudes, and sensed relation to audience with which Carlyle worked. A defense of Carlyle in this way can be found in an altogether unexpected quarter. Henry James, the stylist of nuance, and artificer of elaborate and—from what would certainly have been Carlyle's point of view—trivial fictions, once said, "Carlyle's extemporized, empirical style seems to us the very substance of his thought. If the merit of style lies in complete correspondence with the feeling of the writer, Carlyle's is one of the best" [see Additional Bibliography]. To be sure, James concludes with an inevitable Jamesian paradox and qualification: "It is not defensible, but it is victorious." But if Carlyle's style is the substance of his thought and feeling, it is more than merely "defensible." James's implicit assumption that Carlyle's style triumphs over the lack of craftsmanship is misguided. Carlyle was a very careful workman. The extemporized appearance of it (except, one assumes, in the letters) is the product of careful deliberation rather than an unconsidered dash at paper by a man overheated with passion. The passion one recognizes in the prose is, undoubtedly, genuine, but it is usually also—and obviously—controlled and directed, at least in his more serious and ambitious works.

The problem, in any case, is not to examine Carlyle's intention and preformulated strategies, but to see how the prose works, to see if in fact James is right and that the style is the appropriate vehicle of the ideas and feelings that inform it. To do this I want to turn here briefly to a passage from one of the essays in which Carlylese, though shaping itself into the form that in the later works became almost a parody of itself, was not fully formed; by so doing I hope to be able to work out fairly precisely how important the fully formed style was for the expression of Carlyle's characteristic attitudes. In **"Signs of the Times,"** stylistically restricted both because it is fairly early and because it was written for the same *Edinburgh Review* in which Macaulay was making his name and for which the spokesman of the Whig aristocracy regularly wrote, we can see early and mature Carlyle at work together. The ideas are those that he was to develop for the rest of his career. The manner is, however, less radical and violent. The essay begins in this way:

> It is no very good symptom either of nations or individuals, that they deal much in vaticination. Happy men are full of the present, for its bounty suffices them; and wise men also, for its duties engage them. Our grand business undoubtedly is, not to *see* what lies dimly at a distance, but to *do* what lies clearly at hand.

The pervasive revulsion from theorizing and speculation accompanied by an alternative insistence on work is immediately recognizable as Carlylean. The form, however, in its extraordinarily neat and rhythmic antitheses, is not what one expects from Carlyle and obviously represents a continuation of an eighteenth-century mode, a mode spectacularly exploited by Macaulay. Moreover, in its very neatness it implies a rationalism that Carlyle spent the best part of his career attacking and that is implicitly attacked in the passage itself. In one respect, the style here is a just expression of the vision implied; but in another, the style is in fact struggling against the ideas and attitudes it is meant to convey.

The central and obvious point of the passage is to set up a dichotomy between two ways of settling contemporary difficulties. In this respect, it is all of a piece with the constant tendency of Carlyle's vision—to see the world as divided between good and evil, right and wrong. Carlyle's essentially dualist position does not change throughout his career. Teufelsdröckh will later exclaim, "Close thy Byron; open thy Goethe"; "Love not pleasure, Love God." There are, as Carlyle sees it, only two possibilities for every man and every nation. If you do the one, you must reject the other. And yet, at his best, Carlyle manages to avoid the impression that his vision is thus simplistic; the particular passage under discussion does not in fact equal Carlyle's fully worked out sense of the world and this because its style is artificially limiting, imposing formal bounds beyond which Carlyle needed to grow to become the enormously influential writer he eventually was.

In Carlyle's canon there are certainly hundreds of passages which express, in one way or another, the dualism implicit in this passage. It will be useful to examine at least one such fully Carlylean passage to see what Carlylese does that the inherited eighteenth-century form could not do. Here is a characteristic passage from *Past and Present:*

> Yes, friends: Hero-kings and a whole world not unheroic,—there lies the port and happy haven, towards which, through all these stormtost seas, French Revolutions, Chartisms, Manchester Insurrections, that make the heart sick in these bad days, the Supreme Powers are driving us. On the whole, blessed be the Supreme Powers, stern as they are! Towards that haven will we, O friends; let all true men, with what of faculty is in them, bend valiantly, incessantly, with thousandfold endeavour, thither, thither! There, or else in the Ocean-abysses, it is very clear to me, we shall arrive.

The alternatives are once more clearly expressed—the heroic world or the Ocean-abysses. But the differences in tone, structure, and diction are immediately apparent. Here we have pure Carlylese.

The qualities of this passage that draw attention to themselves are very different from those that make the earlier passage striking. In opposition to intellectual neatness one finds here a passionate and energetic movement that makes the final antithesis ("There"—"Ocean-abysses") dramatic rather than witty. Moreover, the antithesis (though Carlyle is not averse, even in his later career, to using sparingly the balance one finds in the **"Signs of the Times"** passage) is clearly not of the balanced kind we expect from eighteenth-century prose. For the sake of the drama of the passage, "Ocean-abysses" carries far more weight in the final sentence than "There." But within the structure of the complete paragraph, the "Ocean-abysses" are outweighed. The paragraph moves with great energy away from the Ocean to the "port and happy haven." It moves, through the central "stormtost" activity of the Ocean, "Towards that haven . . . thither, thither!" This dramatic pattern is repeated, as I shall try to show, in each important sentence. And then, as the strenuous labor of "all true men" seems to have borne us to the haven, the "Ocean-abysses" dramatically remind us of the consequence of not undertaking the struggle.

The dualism, then, is dramatically rather than intellectually presented. The finality of the strangely ordered final sentence pronounces a kind of doom as it makes its threat. Notice what non-Carlylean structure would likely have made of the same words: "It is very clear to me that we shall arrive there or else in the Ocean-abyssess." The consecutiveness of the normal English structure deprives the sentence both of the sense of struggle implicit in the original's fragmentation and then of the finality of the last phrase—"we shall arrive." Typically, in this passage the Carlylean inversions of normal word order serve to create a surface tension that reflects the very substance of the passage's meaning. The insistence on *doing,* and on the difficulty of doing, explicit in the penultimate sentence, emerges strenuously in the laboring of the syntax; and the utter disregard of logical antithesis and balance is justified because Carlyle is not so much thinking as acting. The drama and the passion of Carlyle's style are, then, part of its meaning.

But the drama is only possible because Carlyle sees what he is discussing not in logical but in metaphorical terms. The alternative is not conceived as dictatorship or disorder but as hero-populated harbor or chaotic ocean. Thus, the passage in fact describes a voyage to a harbor, and it envisages what the voyage will be like and what it will require of the crew. The great eruptions of disorder that Carlyle knew actually become the "stormtost seas"; all these eruptions are turned into plural forms to suggest that they are not merely isolated instances. The effort to come through these seas will necessarily be strenuous, and the strenuousness is reflected in the interesting assonating and alliterative line, broken into very small fragments: "let all true men, with what of faculty is in them, bend valiantly, incessantly, with thousandfold endeavour, thither, thither!"

Although I greatly distrust analysis of sound patterns as a guide to meaning (how easy, for instance, it would be to say that the difficulty of pronouncing all those "th's" reflects the strenuousness of the endeavour), it is hard to resist the implication that lines such as this suggest a very conscious artist. And the accumulation of the "e" vowel, the echoing of the "n" sound, and the finally culminating "thi" pattern in "thither" do seem to enforce the sense of direction impelling the voyager forward. The anti-artist Carlyle has needed to resort to the techniques of the artist.

The central components of a poetic mode are here, however gross and lacking in subtlety one may feel that mode to be. The meaning is in the style and the style is fundamentally dramatic, metaphorical, rhythmic, rather than witty and abstract. It should be agreed, moreover, that the rhythms, at least, are much subtler and more functional here than are those of the first passage cited. The eighteenth-century pattern suggests a witty enforcement of a dualist pattern; the subtler pattern complicates while reasserting the dualism dramatically rather than intellectually.

It is worth proceeding further in examining the newly complicated dualism. Carlyle's style characteristically expresses dualism, in a way I have described elsewhere, by elaborating extensively on the aspects of the negative pole and then dramatically and emphatically destroying the elaboration by the assertion of a single, all-potent positive. That basic pattern is present here, although because the passage is engaged in describing a struggle, the annihilation of the negative is not complete. The argument that it should be annihilated is, however, forcefully present in the style itself. The positive pole is presented first—"Hero-kings and a whole world not unheroic"— but the center of the paragraph immediately shifts to the "stormtost seas" which later become "Ocean-abysses." The most characteristic formulation is in the pluralizing, already referred to, of the various manifestations of the age's sickness—the "French Revolutions, Chartisms, Manchester Insurrections." The direction away from this multi-faceted evil is, however, single and insistent: "thither, thither!" Notice how the very sentence that introduces the evils is constructed

to conquer them: "there lies the port and happy haven." The sentence moves, then, through the evil and brings us out the other side, assured that there "the Supreme Powers are driving us." The penultimate sentence of the paragraph, already discussed, has a similar shape and ends with the same affirmation of driving toward the haven—"thither." Although the paragraph does not settle for asserting the positive pole once and in one way, the impression of unity holds strongly against the chaos of the negative.

Carlyle's dualism, in fact, tends to be based on a vision of the world which sees evil manifested in endless variety, since evil is merely appearance and always finite, while the good is the single, indivisible, infinite fact of God—the reality that underlies all appearance. Goodness tends to be single, unchanging, and all-pervasive (it is always the port of the Hero-king towards which the passage moves); and Carlyle's favorite symbol for the unchanging single reality is the polar- or lode-star. (pp. 104-09)

I would suggest, finally, that the *Past and Present* passage is informed by at least one more aspect of Carlyle's mature vision not present in the earlier one—the vision of the world as interconnected energy and movement. One of the clearest and most representatively Carlylean statements of this view comes in the *French Revolution:*

> How true that there is nothing dead in this Universe; that what we call dead is only changed, its forces working in inverse order! "The leaf that lies rotting in moist winds," says one, "has still force; else how could it *rot*?" Our whole Universe is but an Infinite Complex of Forces; thousandfold, from Gravitation up to Thought and Will; man's Freedom environed with Necessity of Nature: in all which nothing at any moment slumbers, but all is forever awake and busy. The thing that lies isolated inactive thou shalt nowhere discover; seek everywhere, from the granite mountain, slow-mouldering since Creation, to the passing cloud-vapour, to the living man; to the action, to the spoken word of man.

Carlylese regularly "evinces," as John Holloway has remarked [see excerpt dated 1953], "a wild, passionate energy . . . disorderly and even chaotic, but leaving an indelible impression of life." It is this "wild, passionate energy" that is usually taken to be the most characteristic general quality of Carlylese. But I would suggest that the disorderliness is more apparent than real (at least when Carlyle is working at his best) and that the wild, passionate energy is regularly directed to turn back in on itself and to rest upon the single immutable fact of God. This is so whether, in any given passage, that Fact be the port of Hero-kings, the Polar Star, or Life itself as the ultimate unchanging source of all energy. It is true that since Carlyle's whole way of seeing things rejects logical continuity, his greatest works give the impression of disorder. But if one examines the neatly organized *Edinburgh Review* essays, **"Signs of the Times"** and **"Characteristics,"** both expounding in more and more characteristic ways the Carlylean vision, one finds that the organization is less effective in expressing this vision than the apparent disorder of *Sartor* or *Past and Present*.

Carlyle creates the impression of wild and passionate energy in several ways. We have already seen something of the effect of inversion of normal word order, of pluralizing of particular facts and events, of manipulation of patterns of sound. Another obvious device is coinage of compound words, suggesting the need to break through conventional means of expression; we have seen some of the less violent ones: Hero-kings, Ocean-abysses, Dream-Grottoes, cloud-vapour. Such words are usually linked to Carlyle's compulsion to work metaphorically and they seem to imply a kind of compression of large meanings into short compass. Moreover, Carlyle's prose tends to be clogged with allusions to facts, events, things. The passages I have chosen to discuss have many fewer such allusions than are typical, but the kind of thing I mean can be seen in the sequence "French Revolutions, Chartisms, Manchester Insurrections," or "The granite mountain, . . . passing cloud-vapour, . . . living man; . . . action, . . . spoken word."

Within the small compass of paragraphs or chapters it can, I think, be shown that the violence is part of a larger and coherent pattern, frequently a dramatic one. The violence and energy of the passage from the *French Revolution* can be seen to work in much the way the device of Teufelsdröckh's six paper bags works in *Sartor Resartus*. Those six bags, full of the chaos and leavings of Teufelsdröckh's life—notes, laundry-bills, records of dreams, Metaphysico-theological Disquisitions, street-advertisements—are somehow capable of giving in a symbolic or metaphorical way the essence of Teufelsdröckh's character. The bags are a chaos more complete than the chaos of the Clothes volume itself. Yet, "Over such a universal medley of high and low, of hot, cold, moist and dry, is [the Editor] here struggling (by union of like with like, which is Method) to build a firm Bridge for British-travellers." The assumption underlying this bridge-building is that all things are organically connected and that it doesn't ultimately make much difference what aspect of life one focuses on since every fact can be taken as another expression in the world of Space and Time of the great Fact that lies outside that world. In the *French Revolution* passage a similar assumption is at work and can be spotted in the key injunction, "seek everywhere." Wherever we seek—in the rotting leaf, the granite mountain, the cloud-vapour, man, and each of man's actions and words—we find the principle of life and energy. The whole great history makes clear that the source of this life and energy, whatever its violent expression in time, is in the unchanging truth of Carlyle's God. This vision tends to give to Carlyle's larger works a chaotic appearance; but his characteristic structure is that of theme-and-variations because whatever the particular subject he discusses he is always brought back to the single fact which gives life to his subject. The ultimate Carlylean dualism is between appearances and reality. He discusses the appearance, which takes on the qualities of life because of its relation to the reality, in order to get back to the reality. And all the energy of his prose is to bring him back to the still center, where the polar star, apparently only twinkling in the distance, is steadfast and glowing. Over the surging of the waves of the Ocean-abysses can be made out the happy haven of the port of the Hero-kings. (pp. 109-11)

> *George Levine, "The Use and Abuse of Carlylese,"*
> in The Art of Victorian Prose, *edited by George Levine and William Madden, Oxford University Press, 1968, pp. 101-26.*

HEDVA BEN-ISRAEL (essay date 1968)

[*Ben-Israel discusses the antecedents, political interpretations, and form of* The French Revolution.]

Carlyle's [*History of the French Revolution*], when it came out in 1837, established his fame. It is the best known of the English histories of the event, and belongs with Michelet and Lamartine to the class of books which are not brought up to date in new editions. It is often considered as a piece of literature rather than a history, and this raises a central question in Carlylean studies, that of the standards which should be used in estimating Carlyle as a historian. This question has been raised by a group of students of English and history who have attempted a revaluation of Carlyle on the ground that previous estimates had used irrelevant and anachronistic standards. They say that Carlyle was most underrated at the end of the last century when dry, scientific and purely factual writing was the fashion in English historiography. They want to judge Carlyle 'in the light of what he endeavoured to do' as a literary and not as a scientific historian, as an heir of Gibbon and not as a contemporary of Ranke. This criticism is directed against narrow professional historians who apply to Carlyle standards which did not exist in his time. It is not, however, clear that such a narrowly professional school exists. Gooch who is mentioned in this connection does criticize Carlyle's errors as well as his interpretations. But Gooch belongs to a different tradition of Carlylean criticism, deriving from Mill and Morley and discoverable in Trevelyan [see Additional Bibliography] and Aulard. At the same time the conclusions of both Mill and Aulard are favourable to Carlyle's scholarship and historical merit.

Those who seek to save Carlyle from the narrow clutch of the professional critics, defend him by applying standards which he himself would not have acknowledged because they are not the standards of history which he knew and pursued. They argue, roughly, that Carlyle regarded history writing as an art. He must therefore be judged, like a creative artist, by the standards that he set himself. The faults which he knew that he had failed to overcome, they glorify into achieved aims. The 'literary' aims which he indeed professed, he tried to achieve not at the expense of historical accurate and factual truth, but emphatically through it.

What Carlyle's own historical aims and methods were must be shown with reference to his own discussions of them, to the process by which he studied and wrote history, and to the *French Revolution* as it stands. His works abound in theoretical discussions of history writing, because, of all the English historians of his time, he was the most conscious of the problems involved and of the transformations which existing historical conventions were undergoing, especially abroad. In his essays on history, mostly written before the Histories themselves, he discussed the theoretical problems of research and scientific history and foresaw the division of labour that must come in historical work. He discussed the difference between narratives which recreate history and those which discuss aspects of history; and he saw the danger and the limitations of drudgery as well as its necessity and its possible elevation.

Carlyle was strongly influenced by German thought and enthusiastic over the translation of Niebuhr into English. He announced it to Goethe in 1829, adding that German influence had reached the universities. The German influences which were strongest on him were those of the period preceding the beginning of the historical movement proper. But though his teachers were Herder and Schiller, he knew the work of Niebuhr and Ranke well; and it is not the plea of ignorance that can shield him against the charge that his methods were insufficiently critical.

Carlyle was even more influenced by the Romantic movement in literature and by its element of rebellion. But in him individual and intellectual rebellion were stronger than social. There is little in common between Shelley expressing in poetry

Godwin's rationalistic ideas and Carlyle developing in tortuous prose his own subjective way of thought, under the influence of Burke amongst others.

Romanticism influenced Carlyle's historical writing in several ways. An unlearned, intuitive enthusiasm appears in his earliest references to historical subjects. His early letters contain a conventional pattern of sympathies such as are familiar in the young and romantic liberals who were taught by Madame de Staël. He frowns at the cold and cruel Revolution and responds warmly to Napoleon, moved especially by the tragic quality of his fall. 'Since the days of Prometheus Vinctus', he knows of nothing more sublime than this great man's torment. 'Captive, sick, despised, forsaken;—yet arising above it all, by the stern force of his unconquerable spirit, and hurling back on his mean oppressors the ignominy they strove to load him with.' This early romanticism survived many developments and formed the emotional basis for his theory of heroes in history.

Carlyle's starting-points in history were a passionate interest in human facts and an endless quest for the answers to the questions which troubled his soul. The human curiosity may have been shallow at first, but it was a stimulus to investigation and it led to a search for true reality. Only that which 'really happened' was really exciting to Carlyle. At the root of his philosophic restlessness and his devotion to history was the belief that history was a bible written by God and that it was the historian's function to interpret Providence and expound the essentially moral nature of the world. As a result of all this he was driven to much hard thinking about the meaning of the Revolution. The inquisitive and the philosophic nature of his interest in history explain the two qualities on which he prides himself in this book—the ability to portray stark reality, and at the same time to reveal profound truth behind it. This also explains the contradictory appreciations of the work, which some have called a mere painting and others a sermon on the text of the Revolution.

The passion for human detail was a romantic interest by which even Alison was touched. The subject of Carlyle's investigations for the *History* was human behaviour. This is why his book appears to some a psychological study or a sociological case book. Human interest was in the air and was, in time, to produce social histories, but Carlyle was the first to write a human history of the French Revolution.

Another important romantic influence on Carlyle was the romantic poets' theory of artistic creation. It shaped his own work, for he actually put into practice a subconscious method of writing history. It is the source of much that is extraordinary in his work and for which explanations are often sought elsewhere. Applied to the history of the Revolution, this notion meant a rejection of thought about the event and also of historical perspective. Distance produced the generalizations which Carlyle did not want. To grasp the Revolution historically he lost himself inside the intricate period, wandered about it aimlessly and unsystematically in the hope that close contact would somehow create the right reaction. The process of creating true history for Carlyle was as subconscious as the process of creating poetry was in Wordsworth's theory. To promote a genuine reaction, a historian makes sure that the picture which gives the stimulus is authentic. Once the right reaction has been brought about, it is this which directs the recreation of reality. Writing history was so painful for Carlyle because, while playing a highly active role, he considered himself a passive factor. All he could do was feverishly to pile on the fuel and wait for the flame to burst out and illuminate a picture in his mind.

This notion did much to produce both the best and the worst in Carlyle's book. It led to its greatest fault, the lack of proportion. Many of the individual faults, the neglect of Europe and the provinces, of the past and of the future, of events and of phases, of whole spheres of economic and constitutional development, are connected with this defect. Because Carlyle trusted his reactions, he wrote only of what evoked the strongest reactions. He imagined that as long as he was telling the truth he could not go wrong, and in this he laid himself open to attack from historians who demand the whole truth.

The romantic method of creation also let him down in his use of sources, the second great point of criticism against him. He seems to have believed that the reconstruction of any historical object is the result of a multitude of both objective and subjective processes, some of them unconscious, which create a different picture of the object in the mind of every reader. The extraordinary thing is that his own characterizations are generally accepted as remarkably true. But this method, so successful in the treatment of personalities, often proved inadequate when applied to ordinary historical facts.

An attitude to history was also at the root of the unique impartiality which Carlyle claimed and which was claimed for him by historians like Trevelyan and Aulard. The claim seems strange when it is applied to a man who despised even toleration as 'indifferentism'. And detachment would have been a negation of his basic condition for the writing of history, which required a vision seen as if from inside historical objects. His impartiality could not exclude identification and sympathy. What it meant to him was a resolution to avoid a superstructure of systematic ideas. It meant also a sense of the irrelevance of political judgments in histories of the Revolution. He had passed through the stage of seeing all sides and avoiding extremes, and he must have rejected the contention that the aims of the Revolutionaries can only be seen clearly from a distance. Despair of getting at truth through 'mazes of speculation' drove him to extreme persistence in the attempt to paint reality only. His impartiality was therefore a result, not of a political attitude (though it is true that he stood outside all parties) but of a search for a historical truth which is achieved by an historian who abandons himself to the impact of as much reality as he can find, bringing to it nothing from outside, least of all a pattern of politics.

Carlyle's earliest publication, a series of articles written in 1819-22 for Brewster's *Encyclopaedia,* is often ignored or dismissed as hackwork. Some of the articles are connected with the French Revolution and constitute straight historical writing. He used German works and made historical guesses. The best reading is the article on Chatham, full of hero-worship not yet vitiated by any extremes of opinion or political bitterness. The article on Nelson, based on Southey's *Life,* gives good accounts of the battles, and dramatizes the death scene. Nelson's 'sense of rectitude', writes Carlyle, 'embodied itself in a feeling of loyalty to the King and of hatred to all Frenchmen'. In his article on Moore, Carlyle dismisses this man's Revolutionary writings as no longer interesting. The articles on Pitt and Necker contain the narrative of the Revolutionary period on which Carlyle's subsequent picture rested.

The most conspicuous quality of the historical articles is the conventionality and the caution with which politics are treated. There is no hint of the forthrightness which we expect to find in Carlyle. The writer here balances his judgments so carefully that they sometimes cease to make sense. The question arises whether Carlyle then had any political views which he toned down for the sake of the detachment required in an encyclo-paedia, or out of his anxiety to make his first appearance in print, or whether he was as impartial as he was non-committal. The artificiality of his elaborate ambiguities in dealing for instance with the question of war and peace in 1793 or with Pitt's abandonment of reform, when compared with the gen-uineness of passages in the article on Chatham, indicates that he was keeping himself in check on controversial questions. This need might have fostered his strange bitterness of later years towards hackwork or writing for periodicals.

If the articles contain some 'cant' which later made Carlyle blush, they also hinted at better things to come. The statement, for instance, that 'the Revolution might be accelerated or re-tarded, it could not be prevented or produced', was not in itself unusual, but it stands out among the historical judgments pre-sented here. It marks Carlyle as an independent thinker, who could already accept the royalist theories on incitement without believing that incitement caused the Revolution, and who, while hating misrule and violence, blamed no one for either. There is, apart from the forced detachment, the ability to see and express the contradictory points of view and to make the most of each case, the anti-revolutionary and even the anti-reformist. In all this one discerns a faint foreshadowing of the peculiar kind of impartiality which Carlyle later exercised from the omniscient level of the *History*. The compact, ambiguous and problematical rendering of various points of view hints at a characteristic peculiar to Carlyle, that of presenting both sit-uations and questions of judgment in the confused, uncertain way in which they appear to the people concerned. They may be distorted historically, but they are true to the working of human nature and they create, out of a multitude of false and subjective reactions, the atmosphere and psychological back-ground which make history credible. (pp. 127-33)

Carlyle was right when he complained that the public expected writers to range themselves behind some party. He himself refused to do this, but when his *History* came out, readers never tired of guessing his political views, bringing out through their contradictions the book's political independence. (p. 144)

The main views ascribed to Carlyle are, on the one hand, that he wrote the Radical antidote to Burke, and, on the other, that he stood directly behind Burke, expounding the latter's views to a later generation. It is true that Carlyle shared Burke's condemnation of the 'philosophes' as irreverent and irreligious, and that he saw the springs of human action in deep irrational passions. But he differed radically from Burke's assumptions concerning the old régime, which he saw as fit only for de-struction. Unlike Burke, he saw everything in history as mortal and mutable. Of all the English historians of the Revolution, not excepting Morse Stephens, Carlyle alone wrote, not as 'affected' by the Revolution but as related to it. His use of the pronoun 'us' when lost among the *sansculottes,* particularly endeared him to Aulard.

Carlyle's hatred for the Radicals grew in the course of his study. Radicals and Girondins discredited each other for him. At the appropriate place in his *History* he stops to write, in a letter to Mill, that he was sick of the Girondins, who like respectable radical Members were patronizing about the masses, formalistic, narrow and barren. 'The Mountain was perfectly under the necessity of flinging such men to the Devil.' At the same moment Croker and Carlyle were attacking the myth of the virtuous Girondins from different angles, equally deter-mined to reject a formulated set of Revolutionary sympathies adapted to liberal politics.

It is often said against Carlyle that he saw the Revolution as purely destructive and ignored its constructive efforts and re-sults. Carlyle did not intend to give his views on the whole of the period or on the results. Because this is usually assumed, he is also criticized for having presented the Revolution as beginning and ending suddenly and for ignoring its European, constitutional and economic aspects. Carlyle often insisted in letters and in the *History* that he was writing a history of sansculottism. It is possible to hold that sansculottism was a phenomenon which grew independently of the reforming ten-dencies which preceded and followed the Revolution. Carlyle connected the Revolution with its past and future, in the **"Signs"** and in **"Voltaire"** of 1829, but he saw the connection through ideas and not through institutions. In **Heroes** he said that the Revolution of 1830 destroyed the meteoric quality of the Great Revolution and showed that it was not 'a transitory ebullition of Bedlam, but a genuine product of this earth'. Ever since Mackintosh there had been a tendency in English historiog-raphy to separate the constructive from the destructive Revo-lution. When Macaulay in 1832 glorified the Revolution for its very destructive work he was making a theoretic case for destructive legislation. But Carlyle's eyes were fixed on the destruction which originated from the masses. Though he had infinitely more pity for the passions which move men to vio-lence, and though he allowed the *sanculotte* an inarticulate striving after a lofty idea, he did not give violence either moral or political sanction. The idealist view that moral and not ma-terial forces shape history was basic in his interpretation. He said that ideas and not actions leave a mark on history, and that no calculations of profit brought about revolutions. The English Revolution was fought for conscience, and in the French Revolution too there was an idea. Carlyle never lost the balance between material and ideal forces in the Revolution. Such bal-ance generally characterizes the English historians of the Rev-olution. Bread and a vision both play a part in their versions. There are in Carlyle's *History* general reflections which give rise to theories of social changes. Society is a self-generating organism and revolutions are legitimate forces released to crush decaying institutions. On the other hand there are reflections which see the Revolution as a violent punishment. The Rev-olution can also be seen in the context of a theory of historical cycles, or it can be said that it provided scope for the action of Carlyle's heroes. The abundant contradictions baffle any attempt to reduce Carlyle's views to a system. The mob is the beast and the mob is the hero, the mob is incited, and the mob is nature itself, genuine and morally authoritative. The Rev-olution is sansculottism, born with anarchy and dead with Ther-midor, but it is also history incarnate, a microcosm of world change, the authentic process designed by God. It is difficult to impose a system, even within a single one, of the sources for Carlyle's view of the Revolution; it is impossible to bring them all into harmony.

It is true that Carlyle went to the Revolution eager to understand it, and, through it, the whole of history. When he had done with it he was no wiser as to a system than before. The authentic feeling of chaos was the reality he achieved and because it covered a conglomeration of phenomena it gave him the sat-isfaction of truth. He sensed perhaps that the Revolution was producing its own causes and motive forces, when he made sheer mad and destructive forces develop a will and an idea of their own.

The distinctive novelty of Carlyle's book is not in interpretation but in historical form. The ring of truth that brought it success was partly due to the choice of the narrative form. A story will be listened to. Carlyle knew only the dramatic narrative form for history writing. Theory and practice influenced each other with him. He both rationalized his preferences and consciously put theory into practice. The form he chose was best suited to perform the tasks he allotted to history and it best suited the age which was awakening to romance, to the live and human interest in the past which Scott had done so much to foster. In the English historiography of the Revolution, nothing was more wanted. Tired of being told what to think about the Revolution, people were glad to glimpse a painting of it. The pamphleteers, lectures, critics, reviewers and early historians, all sought to say something true about it. Alison, before Carlyle attempted a proper narrative, was moved by the human interest, and he had great success. But his volumes were bulky and dull and his tone was political and conventional, so that his book had the popularity of a duty more than of a delight. Carlyle reclaimed the history of the Revolution from the politicians, the teachers, the critics, and the reviewers by following a different course with a different aim. The English approach to the Revolution had by then developed distinctive lines. The preoccupation with other historians, even in scholars like Croker, went far to limit the serious English interest to an academic discipline, to an analysis of books and writers. Contributions were largely made by correction and criticism rather than by independent reconstruction. Carlyle alone noticed that something was wrong. He said that the history itself lay shrouded while writers worried about what the Whigs said, what the Tories, what the Priests or the Freethinkers, and, above all, what they would 'say of *me* (the historian) for what I say of it'. The historical faculty was directed at the 'Writings and the Writers both of which are quite extraneous'. He therefore wrote a pure narrative, a story told by the traditional omniscient observer. He used books for information but rarely commented on them, unless they were by the actors. The Revolution is his only theme. Carlyle, in premature boldness, did what Croker in learned timidity dared not attempt. The scholar retreated before the vastness of his own knowledge into a study of episodes. The artist, mentally excited, was eager to shape his materials almost before they were gathered. Carlyle set out with little more than a deeply aroused interest and a multitude of conflicting opinions, studying and writing about the event simultaneously. (pp. 144-47)

> Hedva Ben-Israel, ''Carlyle and the French Revolution,'' in her *English Historians on the French Revolution, Cambridge at the University Press, 1968, pp. 127-47.*

ALICE CHANDLER (essay date 1970)

[*Chandler explicates* Past and Present *in the context of Carlyle's sociopolitical medievalism.*]

The inspiration [for *Past and Present*] came in September 1842 when Carlyle visited in rapid succession the workhouse of St. Ives and the ruins of St. Edmund's Abbey. The differences between the two places epitomized for him the decline of England since the Middle Ages. In the workhouse healthy inmates sat enchanted in their ''Bastille,'' victims of a do-nothing government and a laissez faire economy; in the abbey they had once received wise government in their prosperity and ample charity in their need. Carlyle seized on this contrast both as artist and social critic and expanded it into a comparison between a vital and ordered past and a chaotic and impotent present. From it was born *Past and Present*. . . . (p. 138)

Carlyle begins his book with a description of the condition of England which is meant to shock the reader so that he remembers it throughout the subsequent discussions of past, present, and future. In three stages he builds up a memorable image of horror. First, a paradox: ''England is full of wealth and multifarious produce, supply for human want in every kind; yet England is dying of inanition.'' Then, an ironic report by the Picturesque Tourist on the workhouses (''pleasantly so named because work cannot be done in them''), which reproduces Carlyle's experience in September at the workhouse of St. Ives. And finally, a Dantesque scene from the inmost circle of Hell, the trial at the Stockport Assizes where a mother and father were found ''guilty of poisoning three of their children to defraud a burial society of some £3 8s due on the death of each child.'' In prosperous Britain, he writes,

> A human Mother and Father had said to themselves, What shall we do to escape starvation? We are deep sunk here in our dark cellar; and help is far.—Yes, in the Ugolino Hunger-tower stern things happen; best-loved little Gaddo fallen dead on his Father's knees! The Stockport Mother and Father think and hint: Our poor little starveling Tom, who cries all day for victuals, who will see only evil and not good in this world: if he were out of misery at once; he well dead, and the rest of us perhaps kept alive? It is thought, and hinted; at last it is done. And now Tom being killed, and all spent and eaten, Is it poor little starveling Jack that must go, or poor little starveling Will?—What a committee of ways and means.

With this dreadful text for his lay sermon, Carlyle can go on to explain that England's basic weakness is that her leaders . . . have ceased to lead. The artistocracy is interested only in preservation of game and corn laws; the millocracy, only in making money. Neither remembers its duty to assure its tenants and workers of the simple social justice of '''a fair day's-wages for a fair day's-work'.'' The result of their callousness is that the English horse is a good deal better off than the English man, for he at least is assured food and a stable, while millions of Englishmen go naked, hungry, unroofed, and what is worse, unbound by social ties. No wonder, Carlyle insists, that revolution is upon us.

In these opening chapters of *Past and Present*, Carlyle is more concerned with pointing his finger at England and saying ''thou ailest here and here'' than with finding any remedy for these ailments. One thing he does make clear, however, is that the reform must be spiritual. If the proximate cause of all this suffering is that man has forgotten social justice, the final cause is that he has forgotten God, that he is possessed of the inane idea that nature is dead, an ancient eight-day clock, ''still ticking, but dead as brass.'' Going back to his Goethe and his Fichte, Carlyle places his hope in leaders whose spiritual wisdom teaches them the practical thing to do. His final wish, therefore, in this section is for ''Hero Kings, and a whole world not unheroic.''

To show what heroes can do Carlyle goes back in the second book of *Past and Present* to the ''world not unheroic'' of the Middle Ages. As he had done in so early a work as the *History of German Literature,* he compares the spiritual chaos of the present with the heart-whole faith of the past. But he now fills out the general theme with details, significant in themselves and useful for their contrast with modern times. Drawing heavily on Jocelin's chronicle [the *Chronica Jocelini de Brakelonda,* Carlyle's sourcebook for the medieval section of *Past and Present*], he transforms his record of St. Edmund's Abbey into what might be called a morality play for moderns, except that "morality play" is too abstract a term for the fullness of life and scene that he presents, and "Everyman," too weak a name for his heroic protagonists.

The first hero on whom the time-curtain rises is the good Landlord Edmund, who ruled a large tract of land in the eastern counties. A real man, Carlyle insists, he lived the ordinary life of his time: wore leather shoes and a sturdy body-coat, procured his breakfast, and somehow managed to reconcile the contradictions of life. But his reality is asserted only to make more effective the contrast between him and his nineteenth-century successors. Carlyle remarks with his customary irony that many things are not known about him: "With what degree of wholesome rigour his rents were collected we hear not. Still less by what methods he preserved his game . . . and if the partridge-seasons were 'excellent,' or were indifferent. Neither do we ascertain what kind of Corn-Bill he passed, or wisely-adjusted Sliding-scale." What is known is that far from busying himself merely with tailors and wine merchants, he stood bravely in defense of his own. When certain "Heathen Physical-Force Ultra-Chartists, 'Danes' as they were then called, [came] into his territory with their 'five points,' or rather with their five-and-twenty thousands points . . . of pikes," he resisted the incoming anarchy to the utmost. "Cannot I die," said he, and did so, barbarously tortured, but in his martyrdom eventually triumphant over them.

No wonder then that in an age of hero worship Edmund needed no yeomanry-cavalry to keep his tenants in order:

> For his tenants, it would appear, did not in the least complain of him; his labourers did not think of burning his wheat stacks, breaking into his game-preserves; very far the reverse of all that. Clear evidence, satisfactory even to my friend Dryasdust, exists that, on the contrary, they honoured, loved, admired this ancient Landlord to a quite astonishing degree,—and indeed at last to an immeasurable and inexpressible degree; for finding no limits or utterable words for their sense of his worth, they took to beatifying and adoring him! "Infinite admiration," we are taught, "means worship."

Landlord Edmund is for Carlyle a typically heroic character of the early Middle Ages. After telling his story, which culminates with the founding of St. Edmund's Abbey, Carlyle skips several hundred years to describe the slipshod state of the abbey in the twelfth century, a state suggestive of England in the nineteenth. The ideal, Carlyle asserts in one of the bursts of hard-headed pragmatism that are as typical as his mysticism, "had always to grow in the Real, and to seek out its bed and board there, often in a very sorry way." Three centuries after its founding, St. Edmund's Abbey's way was of the sorrow-fulest. The abbot was one Hugo—old, as Jocelin informs us, somewhat blind, and the victim of his flatterers' zeal and his own idleness. "Wrapt in his warm flannels and delusions," he had let the monastery's account books fall into a dreadful state. As with the complacent Whig leaders of the 1830s, his expenditures each year exceeded his income, until at his death there was no money left in his exchequer and a national debt, so to speak, of £1,400.

Abbot Hugo dead, who was to replace him? Who was to lead the abbey—or England—out of chaos? This is an important question for Jocelin, who devotes many pages of his chronicle to narrating the conversations and transactions involved in electing his successor. It is important to Carlyle, too, who retells his

story with great care. As an artist he could not help but be delighted by the life breathing from Jocelin's gossipy pages— the *dixit quidam de quodam* ("said one monk of another") that enliven his record. But as a sermon-writer he was even more impressed by the meaning behind these discussions. For elections are but another form of hero worship, and hero worship is the only significant social act. "Given the men a People choose," Carlyle asserts, "the People itself, in its exact worth and worthlessness is given."

Besides, Carlyle's generation was particularly interested in the mechanics of election. The Reform Bill had been the chief political accomplishment of the 1830s, and the question of extending this reform agitated the English political scene until late in the sixties. Carlyle, therefore, makes a point of showing that the devices of "midwifery," as he terms the mode of election, are relatively unimportant, not to be compared in importance to the spirit in which the choice is carried out.

Judged by this test, the medieval monastery is far superior to modern society, for it can choose a true hero for its leader. The new Abbot Samson possesses all the Carlylean virtues: faith, energy, discipline, and compassion. His first words on ascending to the difficult task of restoring order to the abbey are "miserere mei Deus," since he knows that if spiritual strength is granted him, adequate deeds will follow. However, he also knows that it is the duty of every leader to watch the account books. Faced with Abbot Hugo's accumulated debts, "boundless seemingly as the National Debt of England," Samson immediately institutes radical economic reforms—just as Carlyle hoped Prime Minister Robert Peel would do. There are only two ways, Carlyle points out, to reduce debt: "increase in industry in raising income, increase in thrift in laying out." Samson applies both with an intelligence and vigor that might well serve as a model to the current English government.

As his nineteenth-century descendants should also be, Samson is interested in justice as well as economics. The reaping tax had once driven women to rush out after the tax collectors like "Female Chartists," shrieking and waving their distaffs. Under Samson that tax ceases to be a burden on the poor, as does the Lakenheath eel toll and other exactions. Everywhere, in short, that "Disorder may stand or lie," Carlyle says, Abbot Samson "is the man that has declared war on it." If his monks are remiss in carrying out their duties toward his people, he chastises or even replaces them. If the courts are venal, he brings justice to them. If Parliament has fallen into decay—"some Reform Bill, then as now, being greatly needed"—he fights for reform, although in opposition to King John himself.

At times, indeed, the very efficiency of Samson's justice shows a ruthlessness frightening to modern readers who have grown more skeptical than Carlyle about the value of substituting abstract authority for human values. . . . For Carlyle, however, all that is dictatorial in Samson's actions is redeemed by his ability to see, speak, and do the truth. In all his actions, a deep piety and reverence is apparent—most obviously so in his capacity for hero worship, for reverencing the divine in human shape. (pp. 138-44)

It is with these seven centuries, or rather the difference between them—between, that is, the twelfth and nineteenth centuries— that Carlyle is mainly concerned. However brilliantly his narrative of St. Edmund's Abbey goes and however alive his characters based on Boswell-Jocelin become, sheer history is not his aim. His underlying theme is always past and present, the contrast between a medieval society that deifies St. Edmund and a modern one that lets Robert Burns gauge ale barrels in Dumfries. (p. 144)

Faith is the key to Carlyle's medievalism. Like many of the English and Continental medievalists he had read, he sees the Middle Ages as a period of belief—belief as distinguished from mere religious observance. Abbot Samson's faith is evidenced not in his creed or his rituals, but in the thousand daily acts that show his belief in a meaningful universe. "Practical-devotional," Carlyle calls it, and with his usual use of the medieval-modern contrast goes on to differentiate it from the sickly "isms" of the present day as neither a ghastly Methodism with its eye turned ever on its navel, nor a mere Dilettantism, a galvanized spasmodic Puseyism, but a faith whose contrast with such foolishness can strike one dumb.

Faith is not the only lesson the modern state can learn from the Middle Ages. It can also learn the lesson of leadership, which is faith's corollary. Without religion, Carlyle concluded, inaction and sham stifle every hope of government. With it, men can find the leaders or heroes for whom all things are possible. In contrast to the modern do-nothing state, the feudal one seemed to him rugged and stalwart, "full earnestness, of a rude God's truth," and led by a never-idle aristocracy. (pp. 144-45)

The aristocracy had the reaping of the land in return for ruling it; and the peasant, though he no doubt "got cuffs as often as pork partings" was at least far better off than the modern workman rotting in the workhouse or slaughtering his children for the burial fee. Surely, Carlyle claims, this was a far juster society than that of today, in which a corn-lawing, game-preserving aristocracy had the reaping without the ruling and the peasantry had only the name of freedom in place of the far more valuable reality of security and leadership. Referring to characters from Scott's *Ivanhoe,* as he does several other times in the book to form a common reference point for his reader, Carlyle sums up this view in a memorable passage:

> Gurth, born thrall of Cedric the Saxon, has been greatly pitied by Dryasdust and others. Gurth, with the brass collar round his neck, tending Cedric's pigs in the glades of the wood, is not what I call an exemplar of human felicity: but Gurth, with the sky above him, with the free air and tinted boscage and umbrage round him, and in him at least the certainty of supper and social lodging when he came home; Gurth to me seems happy, in comparison with many a Lancashire and Buckinghamshire man of these days, not born thrall of anybody! Gurth's brass collar did not gall him: Cedric *deserved* to be his master. The pigs were Cedric's, but Gurth too would get his parings of them. Gurth had the inexpressible satisfaction of feeling himself related indissolubly, though in a rude brass-collar way, to his fellow mortals in this Earth. He had superiors, inferiors, equals.—Gurth is now "emancipated" long since; has what we call "Liberty." Liberty, I am told, is a divine thing. Liberty when it becomes the "Liberty to die by starvation" is not so divine!
>
> Liberty? the true liberty of a man, you would say, consisted in his finding out, or being forced to find out the right path, and to walk thereon. To learn, or be taught, what work he actually was able for; and then by permission, persuasion, and even compulsion, to set about doing of the same.

By denying the importance of liberty, Carlyle also denies the responsibility of the common man. Indeed, his whole conception of the hero, which was to grow more important in his

thinking in the years after he wrote *Past and Present,* implies the inadequacy of most men to cope with the conditions of existence. (pp. 145-46)

After showing, primarily in Books II and III of *Past and Present,* the ways in which the Middle Ages were superior to the modern, Carlyle goes on in Book IV to apply the lessons of the past to the present and future. Artistically this section is much less successful. His satiric figures—Pandarus Dog-draught, Sir Jabesh Windbag, the Duke of Windlestraw—are far less convincing than the historical heroes he took from Jocelin. Lacking a clear narrative thread, he lapses, as he does so often, into repetition and dogmatism. In spite of its faults, however, the last half of the book is extremely interesting to the modern reader. It not only applies medieval concepts to nineteenth-century problems but makes suggestions still valid in the twentieth.

Essentially, Carlyle is looking here, as always, for a hero to lead society out of its wasteland, and he finds leadership possible in two groups, the aristocrats and the industrialists. His treatment of the aristocrat is perhaps the less original of the two. It is one of the last expressions in English literature of a new feudalism based on the return of large landholders to their historical role of ruling the nation. Nevertheless, Carlyle's program for landholders is not as purely manorial as Scott's or Cobbett's. Living in the age of reform, he thinks, instead, of parliamentary action. The first step, he suggests, is that the landowners give up their corn laws, thus giving England a ten-year breathing space of new prosperity in which to solve her other problems. After that they can participate, again through Parliament be it noted, in a series of projects and reforms that will restore the English government, though in a new form, to her medieval function of serving the people's welfare.

The landed classes, however, were not to carry out these reforms alone. Carlyle's most original contribution to the development of English medievalism is in adapting the idea of the paternal leadership of society to an industrial age. He makes the manufacturers and businessmen take on responsibilities previously reserved for the landed aristocracy. All the previous medievalists, most of them born a generation before Carlyle, had had an emotional belief in England as an agricultural country; their medievalism was essentially a mode of advocating a return to the land. Carlyle alone fully appreciated the inevitability of industrialism. Unlike his predecessors, he did not think it possible to diminish the importance of commerce and industry and make a neofeudal agriculture serve as the basis of a national economy. As Carlyle put it, "the Gospel of Richard Arkwright once promulgated, no monk of the old sort is any longer possible in this world"—nor any Landlord Edmund either. The future lay not in an impossible revival of St. Edmund's Abbey, but, however dreadful now, with the flame-mountains, "flaming with steam fires and useful labor" of Lancashire, Yorkshire, and counties and nations to come.

With obvious indebtedness to Saint-Simon, though offering far greater detail, Carlyle tries to promulgate a new gospel for the guidance of the industrialists, who will be responsible for the laboring millions of England. "This that they call 'Organizing of Labour,'" Carlyle writes, "is, if well understood, the Problem of the whole Future." With his usual flair for names, Carlyle invents a typical industrialist, Plugson of Undershot, and lectures for his benefit. Much is wrong with Plugson, Carlyle insists. He is possessed by mammonism, thinks money-making the great aim of life, and fears financial failure like the terrors of hell. So intent is he upon wealth-getting that he has forgotten all other ties to mankind except that of cash payment, and in order to extract the last cent of profit from his mills keeps that cash payment to a minimum, letting his workers choke in thick cotton-fuzz and copperas fumes. Buccaneer like, he addresses his workers: "Noble-spinners, this is the Hundred Thousand we have gained, wherein I mean to dwell and plant vineyards; the hundred thousand is mine; the three and sixpence daily [is] yours."

For all that, Carlyle finds hope in Plugson. At least he is a worker and work, however mammonish, helps man communicate with nature, each completed job showing more clearly the next thing to do. Just as the buccaneer and pirate gave way to the medieval lord (a rude fellow perhaps, but one willing to defend his land and stand by his retainers in plenty or want), so the modern Captain of Industry must also give way to a better leader who will be attached to his workers by kindly feelings as well as the cash-nexus. Echoing the ideal of knighthood defined in such medieval works as *Piers Plowman* or the *Prose Lancelot,* Carlyle proposes a "chivalry of labor" in which the industrialists shall govern their men with wisdom and kindness. The suggestions, however, in spite of their feudal inspiration, are completely forward looking, similar to some of the more liberal developments in present-day capitalism.

One of his ideas is permanence of contract, an acknowledgment of the fact that while "men cannot now be bound to men by brass collars," they also cannot be constantly in danger of unemployment and need whenever the market drops or cheaper labor becomes available. If they were bound together for a sizable length of time, the workman would wish to see his master's interests prosper and the master his workmen's. The one would put his best efforts into his job, while the other would make sure by adequate wages and conditions of work that the men he was bound to retain would be healthy and willing. Carlyle even suggests, though very tentatively, that the two classes might be merged to a degree by some form of what we would call profit-sharing or stock bonuses so that industry might "become in practical result what in essential fact and justice it ever is, a joint enterprise."

But for all this modernism Carlyle's underlying motif is always feudalism. How "reconcile Despotism with Freedom?" he asks. "Is that such a mystery? Do you not already know the way? It is to make your Despotism *just.*" The Middle Ages were essentially a military organization and their symbol might be "arms and the man." Carlyle thinks that the industrial ages might be similarly militarized under the banner of "tools and the man." Working together, the industrialists, the landed aristocrats, and the "natural aristocrats" (men of genius) might through parliamentary action create "an army ninety-thousand strong, maintained and fully equipt in continual real action and battle against Human Starvation, against Chaos, Necessity [and] Stupidity." There is no question in his mind that to accomplish this end, unbridled laissez faire must be replaced by state control: "Legislative interference, and interferences not a few, are indispensable." His age already had factory inspectors, why could it not also have mine inspectors, furrowfield inspectors, sanitary regulations, an education bill, a teaching service, and an effective emigration service? Hierarchical and paternalistic, these schemes show the influence of Carlyle's idealized Middle Ages upon his conception of an industrialized Utopia.

All this seems very far from the earlier agrarian medievalism and yet Carlyle's feudalization of industry is simply the next step in the tradition. All humanitarians realized that the condition of England demanded change. Those who were conser-

vatives, as all medievalists tended to be, saw in the medieval ideal of the guided society a rough sketch of the changes to be made. Religion, a deep spiritual faith, was one of the values it offered both the English and Continental medievalists—the same faith that was being sought in Romantic poetry. Paternalism was another advantage. Man was a "poor, bare, forked, animal" according to the conservatives' fearful yet pitying view. The Middle Ages provided him with adequate food and shelter and, more important, with the ties and traditions that by making him content would eliminate the danger of revolt.

Carlyle's contribution to English medievalism was first to make the contrast between modern and medieval England sharper and more horrifying than it had ever been. He could do this partly because the current condition of England had grown worse over the years and partly because he knew how to etch forever on our memories the image of the St. Ives workers and the Stockport mother. His Middle Ages shared a vividness equalled only by Scott's. Carlyle gave new direction to the practical application of medievalism, transferring its field of action from agriculture, which was no longer the center of English life, to manufacturing, in which its lessons could be extremely valuable. Plugson of Undershot's most direct descendants, perhaps, are the Tory Disraeli's Millbank and the Socialist Shaw's Undershaft—a combination that is a good symbol of Carlyle's paradoxical Tory-radicalism. Plugson's influence and that of other aspects of Carlyle's medievalism are to be found throughout the literature of the Victorian age and, indirectly at least, in much of the social legislation of the past hundred and more years. (pp. 147-51)

Alice Chandler, "Faith and Order: Carlyle," in her A Dream of Order: The Medieval Ideal in Nineteenth-Century English Literature, 1970. *Reprint by Routledge & Kegan Paul, 1971, pp. 122-51.*

PHILIP ROSENBERG   (essay date 1974)

[*In this excerpt from his book* The Seventh Hero: Thomas Carlyle and the Theory of Radical Activism, *Rosenberg analyzes Carlyle's conception of hero worship, or "charismatic followership," arguing that Carlyle's ideal entails perpetual resistance rather than passive submission.*]

Behind Carlyle's critique of democracy as an inadequate way of meeting the needs of the people—that is, as an inadequate method of organizing England for political and social regeneration—lay a positive sense of the direction English political life must take. The so-called hero theory served Carlyle as a focal point around which he could arrange all that he wanted to affirm about contemporary political reality. For him the hero theory was both a historical and a moral principle, and his claim that it "lay most legible" in all that he had written is not far from the truth.

There is nothing in the least complex or intricate about Carlyle's conception of heroes, their role in history, and the role he would have them play in society as he wants it to be, although the amount of polemical ink spilled on the subject can lead one to imagine that Carlyle's thinking about heroes and the heroic is a mass of subtleties which requires considerable critical unraveling. The hero theory is neither more nor less than the claim that, in the final analysis, the process we call history is a web of individual actions.

Carlyle begins his one book devoted specifically to the subject of heroes [*On Heroes and Hero-Worship and the Heroic in History*] with the statement that "Universal History, the history of what man has accomplished in this world, is at bottom the History of the Great Men who have worked here.'' It is an unfortunate opening, in that it has provided so convenient— though inaccurate—an encapsulation of his hero theory that practically all of the critical literature on the subject has amounted to little more than an extended gloss on this single text. For example, in Sidney Hook's *The Hero in History* we find that scornful attention is directed at ''the Carlylean fantasy that the great man was responsible for the very conditions of his emergence and effectiveness,'' a conclusion which Hook apparently derives from Carlyle's statement that great men are at the ''bottom'' of the historical process. Hook then goes on to contrast Carlyle's excesses in this department with the more reasonable ideas of other thinkers who limited the latitude of history's great men to the area marked out by routinely present possibilities. . . . (pp. 188-89)

Surely Hook is right to call the idea of an omnipotent hero capable of turning the course of history an excess, but the fantasy is Hook's rather than Carlyle's. Indeed, one does not even know where to begin refuting such an interpretation— and it has been so influential, so commonly received as true, that its pernicious effects on Carlyle's reputation are beyond computation—for it is so totally unrelated to anything Carlyle wrote as to be beyond contradiction. Were it not for the fact that this sort of mangling of Carlyle by Hook and others has been so influential, one would of course ignore these parodies

of Carlyle's thought. As it is, one must deal with them, and perhaps one may even be thankful to these distortions for providing an occasion for clarifying just how much Carlyle's hero theory means to imply about the role of the hero in history.

If one begins by applying a little common sense to the matter, one recognizes at once that the statement that history is fundamentally the history of great men makes no outlandish claims at all. It is, on the contrary, almost a truism. By opening any history book at random one can see immediately that there are far more capital letters than the number of sentences in the book might lead one to expect. Indexes are compiled for history books on the basis of the perception that the most salient moving forces of history are entities with proper names. Great men are, obviously, what most historical writing is concerned with, and it is therefore reasonable to assume that they are crucial to history itself.

Nowhere does Carlyle imply that these great men have an absolute power over the historical milieu in which they work. On the contrary, he was acutely aware of the importance of the character of an age in determining the range of achievement possible in that age; before one could determine what actions were possible at a given moment it was necessary to read the ''signs of the times,'' as Carlyle indicated by inaugurating his career as a social commentator with an essay under that title. Thus Carlyle would not have written, as Albert Mathiez did

Carlyle's study, where he wrote Frederick the Great.

in describing the political situation on the eve of the French Revolution, that "What was wanted at the head of the monarchy, to dominate the crisis which threatened, was a king. But there was nobody but Louis XVI." Carlyle never permitted himself to forget that forces far larger than those which any man could have at his disposal already had dictated that "the French Kingship had not, by course of Nature, long to live." In such a context, Louis' incompetence could only "accelerate Nature," and, conversely, a heroic king could have done no more than retard it. Although Carlyle does, indeed, exhort the king to take bold and forthright action, he generally does so with an ironic awareness that such action could be no more than a dignified, lovely, but nonetheless vain gesture. (pp. 189-90)

The frequent apostrophes in his *History of the French Revolution* should not be taken to mean that Carlyle imagined that bold and heroic action could deflect the larger forces of history; it was, rather, a question of meeting those forces with dignity. Thus Carlyle often calls upon a hero or would-be hero to act, to give some existential gesture asserting defiance of an unacceptable and unalterable state of affairs. Even after Louis is sentenced to death, Carlyle continues to urge him to action, not because he believes any possible action could stay his execution, but precisely because it cannot. "The silliest hunted deer dies not so," Carlyle reminds the king.

So far is Carlyle from holding the doctrines of historical indeterminacy that Hook attributes to him that he is at great pains to point out, in connection with each of the heroes he discusses, the extent to which the hero's actions were shaped and conditioned by the world around him. The hero must be, he insists time and time again, in touch with "reality": "A man is right and invincible, virtuous and on the road towards sure conquest," Carlyle announces, "precisely while he joins himself to the great deep Law of the World, in spite of all superficial laws, temporary appearances, profit-and-loss calculations; he is victorious while he coöperates with that great central Law, not victorious otherwise. . . ." (p. 191)

[The] greatness of the hero derives from his ability to recognize an as yet unrealized truth and to assist as midwife at its birth. Luther, Carlyle points out, did not bring the Reformation, for "the Reformation simply could not help coming." The Carlylean hero is never a man who fashions history out of his own will, but is at all points a man willing, Carlyle says, to submit to the "great deep Law of the World," just as Hegel says that his world-historical man is one "whose own particular aims involve those large issues which are the will of the World-Spirit." Thus a hero like Cromwell is impotent to act until historical developments have prepared the way for his mission:

> Long years he had looked upon it [the godlessness of the king's government], in silence, in prayer; seeing no remedy on Earth; trusting well that a remedy in Heaven's goodness would come,—that such a course was false, unjust, and could not last for ever. And now behold the dawn of it; after twelve years silent waiting, all England stirs itself; there is to be once more a Parliament, the Right will get a voice for itself: inexpressible well-grounded hope has come again into the Earth. Was not such a Parliament worth being a member of? Cromwell threw down his ploughs, and hastened thither.

Just as Cromwell is, Carlyle makes clear, in an important sense a product of the movement he led, so it is true of all of Carlyle's heroes that they act in response to the social needs of the cultures which produced them. "Before the Prophet can arise

who, seeing through it [the false idol worshipped by the people], knows it to be mere wood, many men must have begun dimly to doubt that it was little more." In this fact lies the open secret of Carlyle's theory of heroes and hero-worship, for on page after page Carlyle tirelessly reiterates that the hero is the virtual delegate of his followers, led on and incited by them, reflecting their desires back to them in the form of leadership. (pp. 192-93)

In thus acknowledging that the hero's career is shaped by the society in which he finds himself, Carlyle made sure that his hero theory was at all points compatible with his awareness of the role the masses of anonymous men play in history. "Social Life is the aggregate of all the individual men's Lives who constitute society; History is the essence of innumerable Biographies," he had written years earlier, and there is no contradiction between this statement and the one with which he opens *On Heroes and Hero-Worship*. For Carlyle the idea that history should be the biography of great men and the idea that it should be the essence of the biographies "of all the individual men . . . who constitute society" were alternative forms of the same truth. A hero was a great man precisely because he was able to speak articulately "what all men were longing to say."

Carlyle's hero theory is Hegelian and Weberian rather than Nietzschean. For Nietzsche the context in which the hero can realize himself is a society of mass men, of "herd animals." . . . The willfulness of the hero and the will-lessness— that is, the willing submission—of his followers are the key variables in the etiology of power as Nietzsche traces it.

Carlyle, however, speaks of submission in connection with the hero theory only rarely, and when he does it is significantly the hero rather than the hero-worshipper who must submit. The hero's role in "this great God's-World," Carlyle writes, is "to conform to the Law of the Whole, and in devout silence follow that; not questioning it, obeying it as unquestionable." In stark contrast to the Nietzschean idealization of will, Carlyle asserts that "Great souls are always loyally submissive, reverent to what is over them; only small mean souls are otherwise." Nowhere is the hero-worshipper called upon for anything like the total surrender of self that characterizes the hero. On the contrary, the role of hero-worshipper is entered into by exercising discretionary choice in "electing" the hero as one's leader and oneself as his follower. In both *Past and Present* and *On Heroes and Hero-Worship* Carlyle lays great emphasis on the importance to a society of selecting the leaders it will follow. Thus Carlyle, who . . . satirized political elections, nevertheless maintained that an election "is a most important social act; nay, at bottom, the one important social act." The contradiction between these starkly opposite evaluations of the worth of elections is, I think, on the surface merely. The elections which Carlyle speaks of as among the most important social acts are not at all like the routinely administered ballotings by which one chooses between candidates for institutional office; indeed, as we shall see shortly, the decision to follow a hero is invariably a repudiation of the routinely offered choices. Electing a leader in Carlyle's sense is a matter of great moment and takes on some of the characteristics associated with a religious conversion, for it constitutes no less than a decision as to what one's own calling is to be; to be truly meaningful, an election must be not so much a choice *between* potential leaders as a choice *of* a leader. What is more, insofar as it is a true election it is in a very real sense an election of oneself into the role of charismatic followership as much as it is an election of the hero. Such an "election" is the beginning of action for the individual making the decision, for in casting one's lot with a hero one commits oneself to an active role in the cause the hero leads; in contrast, the political election is an end of action, for in casting a ballot one votes for a candidate to whom, if he is successful, one will delegate one's potential for action.

Carlyle's belief that the hero is called upon to submit to superior powers whereas his followers are permitted to exercise discretion in choosing or not choosing to follow him is a logical corollary of his understanding of herohood as primarily a matter of insight into the true state of social or even cosmic affairs. In this respect the distinction between the hero and the hero-worshipper exclusively depends upon the fact that the former has his insight directly, via an intuitive apprehension of reality or an explicit communication from god, whereas the follower gains insight only indirectly, from the mouth of the hero himself. Followership, therefore, is essentially a voluntaristic, non-coercive relationship to the hero, for the follower "obeys those whom he esteems better than himself, wiser, braver; and will forever obey such; and even be ready and delighted to do it."

In recognizing that submission is relevant to hero-worship primarily with regard to the hero's relationship to *his* source of authority rather than with regard to the follower's relationship to the hero, Carlyle anticipated what was to become, in the writings of Max Weber, one of the most important and paradoxical aspects of the theory of charismatic power. Thus Weber notes on the one hand that the charismatic leader "does not derive his 'right' from their [his followers'] will, in the manner of an election. Rather, the reverse holds: it is the *duty* of those to whom he addresses his mission to recognize him as their charismatically qualified leader." But on the other hand it is also the case that "The genuinely charismatic ruler is responsible precisely to those whom he rules," for although he invariably does not "regard . . . his quality [of charisma] as dependent on the attitudes of the masses toward him," the fact remains that "It is recognition on the part of those subject to authority which is decisive for the validity of charisma." In other words, although the hero is self-appointed—that is, he sees himself as appointed by god or by necessary forces in world history—and tends to see his followers as duty-bound to acquiesce in his charismatic authority (just as he himself is duty-bound to acquiesce in the dictates of his authority source), it is nevertheless the case that the followers have no duty to the hero except insofar as they accept the validity of his charisma and acknowledge that his path is the true one for them.

Carlyle drew two conclusions from this understanding of the nature of duty in a charismatic relationship. In the first place, he maintained that hero-worship is in no way incompatible with the traditional Protestant emphasis on "private judgment." The notion that Protestantism stands for freedom of private judgment as against the institutionally coerced judgments of Roman Catholicism is, Carlyle argues, deeply mistaken. The Catholic Church may indeed define for its votaries various forms of belief, but it can do so only because its votaries are convinced that Roman Catholicism is on the whole valid. "The sorriest sophistical Bellarmine, preaching sightless faith and passive obedience, must first, by some kind of *conviction,* have abdicated his right to be convinced. His 'private judgment' indicated that, as the advisablest step *he* could take."

At first glance this argument itself seems somewhat sophistical, and we may well wonder at the validity of contending that the abdication of the right to judgment constitutes a legitimate exercise of judgment. In this connection, however, we should note that the case here is not really comparable to the seemingly analogous case, discussed by John Stuart Mill, involving the question of whether the concept of freedom entails the right to sell oneself into slavery. The difference between the two—and it is enough of a difference to render them incommensurable—is that the situation Carlyle is dealing with involves an ongoing process whereas Mill is concerned with what obviously must be a single irreversible event. The person who accepts the role of followership and thereby exercises his option to renounce his private judgment does so for as long as and insofar as he continues to be convinced of the validity of the charismatic claims of the leader.

The second conclusion Carlyle derived from his understanding of the role of submission with respect to charismatic authority led him to minimize the distinction between hero and hero-worshipper. As he saw it, both parties in the relationship submit to what they take to be the true and just mandate of god and/or history and are, through this submission, acting out of their own convictions. Unlike Nietzsche, for whom hero and hero-worshipper are diametrically opposed concepts, Carlyle argues that the difference between them is merely one of degree, for the hero is a man with enough power of vision to see the truth of the world as it stands before him, whereas the follower has power of vision sufficient only for seeing the truth when it is shown to him. It is for this reason that Carlyle was able to say that hero-worship itself is a form of heroism. (pp. 193-96)

There is nothing fanciful in Carlyle's notion that only a heroic mind can choose to follow a hero, for the hero and his followers are always a band of rebels, compacted together in a daring and invariably dangerous mission. The charismatic leader and his followers are inevitably a revolutionary force inasmuch as their mission is based on a sense of duty unconnected to the institutional sources which legitimate authority in the socio-political world. From the point of view of legitimate institutions, therefore, charismatic authority at best can stand as merely an alternative to them, but in most cases it will directly threaten them. (p. 197)

Because charisma is by definition a counterlegitimate force, the charismatic leader requires of his followers the courage to renounce all normal ties to society and to turn their backs on what they have been taught to see as a legitimate order. The type of "passive obedience" Ernst Cassirer accuses Carlyle of preaching [see Additional Bibliography] can have no place in the camp of the hero. It was not docility of temperament that induced "thirteen followers" to take up Muhammad's mission and go with him into the desert; if those who followed Cromwell can be accused of passive obedience, then legitimate authority is in more trouble than it realizes. "I am come to set a man at variance against his father," Jesus warned his disciples as a way of reminding them that charismatic followerhood demands the courage to say no to all normal bonds of loyalty. "He that loveth father or mother more than me is not worthy of me," he declared, making clear that it is precisely passive obedience that must be renounced if one is to join in the active obedience of charismatic followership.

Although critics of theories such as Carlyle's often contend that submission to a charismatic leader readily degenerates into a permanent system of subordination, in fact this danger is effectively minimized by the principled nature of Carlyle's support of charismatic leadership. Charisma is, as Weber explains, an extremely unstable political base. It tends either to collapse when faced with temporary defeats or to routinize itself into an institutional structure which is by its nature no longer charismatic. Although this latter possibility has led to the charge that Carlyle's hero theory is inherently totalitarian, such a criticism could be valid only if Carlyle's ideas about heroes were considerably less self-conscious than they are, if they had been developed as political propaganda rather than as political theory. As propaganda, a defense of the prerogatives of any particular leader on the grounds of his charismatic election indeed could be transformed readily into support of the leader even after he had used his charismatic mandate to build a system of dictatorial institutions.

As theory, however, the defense of the charismatic hero retains its integrity despite practical disappointments. It is in the nature of political theory to be self-conscious and critical, to stand aside from the pragmatic vicissitudes of politics and to measure them by its own unchanging yardstick. The hero, being human and fallible, may attempt to cash in his charisma, to erect a dictatorial apparatus, but it is precisely at this point that those who, like Carlyle, are committed on principle to nonbureaucratic and nonstatist types of leadership will turn from him as from a traitor. Moreover, it is not inconceivable that a charismatic leader himself, if he is in principle committed to maintaining the charismatic and revolutionary nature of his own rule, would resist attempts to institutionalize his leadership. (pp. 197-98)

Perhaps Carlyle was being naive in his belief that charismatic leaders and their followers could remain true to their principles, but I can find nothing inherently unreasonable in his faith that there is no better training for resistance to the imposition of power than the combination of self-assertion and self-discipline required for membership in a band of rebel followers. And when these traits are combined with a conscious, theoretical commitment to charismatic rebellion itself, the dangers of a lapse into totalitarianism are, at the very most, no greater than they inevitably must be so long as the means of massive coercion exist.

Carlyle's call for a rebirth of the spirit of hero-worship is, we should now be able to see, a call for resistance rather than for submission. When Carlyle criticized contemporary culture on the grounds that the mass of men no longer seemed able or willing to find and follow heroes, he distinguished between two contrasting types of non-hero-worshippers. On the one hand there are the "Valets," a term taken, via Hegel or, more likely, Goethe, from the aphorism that no man is a hero to his valet and applied to all those who are constitutionally or on principle opposed to acknowledging the existence of men superior to themselves. The second type of non-hero-worshipper is the "Flunkey," the very antithesis of the Valet. Just as the Valet is the man temperamentally indisposed to perceiving heroism where it exists, so the Flunkey is a man temperamentally disposed to perceiving it where it does not exist. It is Flunkeyism, Carlyle warns, that will be the undoing of democracy in England, for the very deference which Bagehot was to celebrate a few decades later as the magical mortar that held the British socio-political system together meant to Carlyle that, for the most part, the *demos* of England was fatally disposed to defer to its social superiors rather than to its true betters. Never much worried that the masses, under democracy, would become self-willed and disinclined to accept the leadership of wiser men, Carlyle greatly feared that, through an excess of deference, they would submit themselves to the leadership of respectable quacks. "Seek only deceitful Speciosity, money with gilt-carriages, 'fame' with newspaper-paragraphs, whatever name it bear, you will find only deceitful Speciosity; godlike Reality will be forever far from you," he warned.

Time and again, therefore, Carlyle uses the hero theory to remind his readers of the dangers of excessive willingness to defer to self-proclaimed or socially acknowledged superiors. In this sense, the first task of the man who would worship heroes is a revolutionary task—the withholding of deference from all those not worthy of it and the ejection of them from government. (pp. 198-99)

Most commentators on Carlyle's hero theory have emphasized the hero-worshipper's loyalty to his leader, and in doing so they have forgotten that loyalty in this context must be preceded by a courageous act of disloyalty to the established order, which is the habitat of the "knaves and dastards" whose arrestment is the first order of business in a heroic world. In general, the literary critics who have had their innings with Carlyle have followed Freud in assuming that the relationship between a follower and a charismatic leader is modeled on and therefore stands as a continuation of normal patrilineal authority. The family, according to Freud, is the prototype of all authority relationships: "What began in relation to the father," Freud wrote, "is completed in relation to the group," for "The leader of the group is still the dreaded primal father. . . ." Such an analysis of group leadership is valid only if one is aware—as Freud himself was but as literary Freudians tend not to be— that an identification of this nature is a two-edged weapon, for to whatever extent the leader of the group "is still" the primal father, he is also precisely *not* the father. To say that the charismatic leader replaces the father is to indicate some of the tensions inherent in the situation of the follower, who can perceive himself as loyal insofar as he sees the hero as the father, and can perceive himself as criminal insofar as he sees the hero as taking the place of the father. Undoubtedly, no relationship of charismatic leader and follower is totally free of this ambivalence, and there is probably no point at all in taking either of the polarized halves of it to be the essential feature of the relationship as a whole. It is simultaneously true that the charismatic figure continues "what began in relation to the father" and that, as Max Weber observed, charisma "is contrary to all patriarchal domination." The charismatic hero takes on the roles of father, priest, and king, but in doing so he is a stranger in the father's place, an iconoclast in the priest's, and a regicide in the king's.

"I am for permanence in all things," Carlyle wrote, knowing full well that there could be no permanence in the historical world. All clothes grow old, he had recognized from the start, and require to be cast off; new clothes must be made to replace them. With each moment that passes, some bold and heroic insight ossifies itself into an institutional form, routinizes itself, and thus becomes no longer capable of generating true political action. It becomes, in Karl Mannheim's terminology, an occasion for administrative and reproductive functioning rather than for political creativity. With each moment, therefore, one hopes that a hero will arise to call upon all those who are willing to become "sansculottes"—to go with him outside of the institutional sphere, and there establish a new order, a new culottism, which is in turn fated to be overthrown by the next sansculottes.

"[I]n this Time-World of ours there is properly nothing else but revolution and mutation," Carlyle had acknowledged in his ***History of the French Revolution,*** and it therefore followed that the only permanence possible to man was the permanence of revolutionary change itself. In his attempt to build a political system on the basis of revolutionary charisma, Carlyle had finally arrived at the only possible completion for the system of his thought. From whichever angle one approaches it, all of Carlyle's thought points to this one overriding conclusion. In terms of his lifelong search for a mode of self-realization, a way out of the enervating solipsism of the world of self-centered egoism, which would at the same time avoid the alienation or annihilation of self that resulted from simple work in the routinely present world of organized social categories, Carlyle had long known that creative action in the time-world of history was the possibility that must be explored. Yet the hero-actor must be a revolutionary because all true action is inherently revolutionary, a repudiation of the world of formula and a commitment to the creation of new modes of social interrelationship. As a political ideology which takes as its highest ideal a continuous openness to historical action, Carlyle's theory of political action is a doctrine of permanent revolution.

Moreover, revolution entails by definition the universalization of herohood, as Carlyle had shown by laying bare the way the French Revolution had abrogated the monopoly of political action formerly enjoyed by kings, courtiers, and legislators, and had moved the historical arena out onto the streets. "The most indubitable feature of a revolution," Leon Trotsky has written, in a statement which accurately reflects Carlyle's sense of the matter,

> is the direct interference of the masses in historic events. In ordinary times the state, be it monarchical or democratic, elevates itself above the nation, and history is made by specialists in that line of business—kings, ministers, bureaucrats, parliamentarians, journalists. . . . The history of a revolution is for us first of all a history of the forcible entrance of the masses into the realm of rulership over their own destiny.

Carlyle's hero is preeminently the man who forces his way into the realm of rulership over his own destiny, and his followers are those who make it possible for him to do so by their readiness to enter the world of creative action with him. This asymmetrical dependency in the relationship of leader and follower is at the heart of the radical meaning of Carlyle's hero theory, for the presence of a heroic disposition among those from whom the hero is to draw his followers is . . . a vital prerequisite for the hero's own career. Conversely, the heroic readiness of the masses makes the existence of the hero, as authoritative leader of others, in an important sense irrelevant. The very process which makes the hero possible, the coming into being of a mass of people prepared and willing to act resolutely on what they believe to be the true nature of things, necessarily creates a revolutionary situation in which the people will refuse to tolerate sham, quackery, and the imposition upon themselves of government by those unfit to govern.

For this reason Carlyle, who preached of the duty to find and follow a hero, never felt the personal necessity of subordinating himself to a leader, never found a contemporary hero to worship. More than a few students of Carlyle have noted this fact as a discrepancy in his teachings on hero-worship, maintaining that secretly Carlyle always had himself in mind when he spoke of heroes. Far from being a discrepancy, however, this is as it should be. *On Heroes and Hero-Worship* deals with six types of heroism, but it points inexorably toward a seventh hero—the hero as oneself. Precisely because true hero-worship is to Carlyle a form of heroism, the coming of the hero is not a matter of crucial moment to the man ready for action. "[W]e will strive and incessantly make ready, each of us, to be worthy to serve and second such a First-Lord!" Carlyle writes of the

hero. "We shall then be as good as sure of his arriving; sure of many things, let him arrive or not."

With his hopes centered on the formation of a world permanently open to political action—a permanently revolutionary world—Carlyle felt, as he reflected on the centuries of revolution that had commenced with the Protestant Reformation, much reason for optimism. "In all this wild revolutionary work, from Protestantism downwards, I see the blessedest result preparing itself. . . . If Hero mean *sincere man*, why may not every one of us be a Hero?" he asked in 1840. Why not, indeed, he answered three years later: "'Hero-worship,' if you will,—yes, friends; but, first of all, by being ourselves of heroic mind. A whole world of Heroes . . . that is what we aim at!" (pp. 200-03)

> *Philip Rosenberg, in his* The Seventh Hero: Thomas Carlyle and the Theory of Radical Activism, *Cambridge, Mass.: Harvard University Press, 1974, 235 p.*

JULES P. SEIGEL   (essay date 1976)

[*Seigel accents the frustrated anger and overriding pessimism of* Latter-Day Pamphlets, *likening the work to an epic in its dark vision of a modern hell.*]

Even serious readers of Victorian literature are apt to pass quickly over Carlyle's *Latter-Day Pamphlets*, briefly noting his attacks against the dogmas of progress, sacred nineteenth century institutions and minority groups, noting the aggressive and abusive tone and the seemingly chaotic structure of the work. Often the *Pamphlets* are dismissed and perhaps, in the minds of many sensitive and otherwise sympathetic readers, for good reasons. Coming to the *Latter-Day Pamphlets* after two world wars, and the unbelievable Nazi holocaust, Carlyle's attacks against Jamaican blacks sitting idle, up to their ears in pumpkins, and Irish paupers too lazy to work, weary us. His strident talk of beneficent whips and leather along the backs of the unemployed in these times when all forms of individual life seem threatened set us on edge. Yet we have no choice but to agree that the bloom held out by the promises of nineteenth century democracy has wilted, that the dogmas of democracy are upheld only by sacrifices, and that bureaucracy, democracy's offspring, has succeeded at producing as many evils as it has benefits. And Carlyle's criticism of the machinery and methodology of nineteenth century democracy in the *Pamphlets* has a bitter, cutting tone matched by no other prophetic voices of his time.

What actually were the reasons for such vitriolic outbursts, for this fierce and unbalanced work which, as David Masson said, brought the general antipathy towards Carlyle to a crisis and made him "unpopular with at least one half of the kingdom"? One explanation was that the Sage of Chelsea had taken to whisky; another, suggested by William B. Aytoun, was that the work was a product of a "diseased imagination" [see excerpt dated 1850]. Yet the *Pamphlets* do not, as Albert J. La Valley has shown [see Additional Bibliography], "represent a complete volte-face from his earlier political and social writings. They may be frightening in both what they say and how they say it, but they are still an outgrowth of Carlyle's earlier social writings". One recognizes not only familiar language but also familiar themes: there is the continuing search for heroes, the call for action and not words (the need for silence), the necessity of work and redemption, attacks against the immorality of the economics of the day, against selfish beaverism and huckstering, against the foolishness of parliamentary reform rather than reform of the self, and against the hypocrisy of organized religion. His cutting satire in the *Pamphlets* lays bare evils still recognizable in the modern world, such as consumerism and the special rhetorics—bureaucratic and private—which exert unbelievable control over the people. Everything is, in Carlyle's words, either "Fit for the market; not fit". In his general exposure of the immorality of rhetoric—simply *lying*, as he puts it—he points to the corrosive effects it has in a modern democracy: "Words will not express what mischiefs the misuse of words has done, and is doing, in these heavy laden generations". These familiar Carlylisms are expressed in his harshest and most direct style.

Yet his vision is intensified and his anxiety heightened. The language is violent as Carlyle agitates, urges and threatens. His voice becomes one of desperation as he strikes out trying to put down simultaneously all his disjointed and painful observations. It is precisely this formlessness, a stylistic neurosis, that characterizes the *Pamphlets*. The familiar themes and images, however unsystematically presented, seem mainly held together by the urgency of the writer's voice, painfully haranguing, relentlessly arguing his readers into accepting his prophetic message. It is obvious that Carlyle's many personae (Jefferson Brick, Crabbe, Prime Minister, Benevolent Man, Future, and others) all have the same voice—authoritative, satirical, and aggressive. His is a sensibility marked by frustration; often grotesque, consistently angry. As George Levine has suggested, Carlyle has "identified himself with his creation, and Carlylese becomes the staple mode of expression at the same time as its sustaining tensions and its implicit faith in the possibilities of this world have broken down".

Levine argues that the earlier works of Carlyle could survive artistic analysis, but he questions whether analysis could do anything for the inartistic *Latter-Day Pamphlets*. For him the *Pamphlets* are triumphs of negativism, unrelieved by the flexibility of the earlier and more obviously coherent works.... What has happened is that the "vision of the world is unrelievedly bleak and disillusioned.... Carlyle ... is responding wildly and incoherently—and ineffectually—to all the aspects of his society which repel him". Fragmentation and splintering replace a sustained artistic and structural tension.

Carlyle's earlier fears of democracy were intensified by the outbreak of the revolutions of 1848, harbingers of inevitable democracy. These fears were then exaggerated by his growing awareness of the misery of Ireland. Together they represented the most fearful elements of an expanding democracy—an uncontrolled population without work, without direction, bereft of leadership, lost in social chaos and anarchy. It was the confusion and complexity of democracy which Carlyle now envisioned as a reality. Its great convulsions would inevitably destroy his essential vision of nature as a hierarchical structure—a simplistic and neatly ordered society and universe. To his Calvinistic sensibility democracy was also noisy and dirty—personally obnoxious.... The *Latter-Day Pamphlets* register a series of traumatic and fearful responses to a modern democratic culture. All the corollaries of democracy—decision by universal ballot, in particular, never a true way of electing the "best"—the greater distribution of "wealth", and the doctrines of progress, all become magnified and grotesquely distorted by an imagination which is able on the one hand to see the disease and corruption inherent in the political and economic systems themselves, but, on the other, is unable to dissociate that which it created itself from its own particular disoriented vision. (pp. 156-58)

His aggressive stance in the face of advancing democracy and growing poverty, disease, and population derives more from his fear of the multiple unknowns inherent in these social phenomena than from any particular plan to stem the movements; though Carlyle does offer such concrete proposals in the *Latter-Day Pamphlets* as organized work forces or agricultural regiments to reclaim waste lands. Yet the *Pamphlets* are mainly his painfully-recorded responses; an answer to the crisis, and a search for some sort of artistic form to his response. In a strange way, Carlyle is both the prophet and the prophecy. (p. 158)

Carlyle had lost his former hope of regeneration of the self in the face of social fragmentation. Throughout the *Pamphlets* there are points where Carlyle reasserts his earlier faith, but they appear sporadically and outside the consistent tone of accusation. The follies of democratic bureaucracy he dwells on continually irritated him. Prompted by a vision of a diseased society, Carlyle's stance becomes largely responsive and captious rather than synthetic and creative. The obnoxious elements he sees in society grate sharply on his senses, as shown by the imagery of excrement and slime. There is also recurring imagery of economics ("spiritual banknotes", "gold bullion of human culture", "nature keeps silently a most exact Savings-Bank") which jostles against imagery of technology (of railroad miracles: "The distances of London to Aberdeen, to Ostend, to Vienna, are still infinitely inadequate to me! Will you teach me the winged flight through Immensity, up to the Throne dark with excess of bright!"). Every image is charged with the sense of a newly-emerging society, and with its overwhelming presence.

Carlyle found himself faced with a problem of epic dimension; its scope was nothing less than the known world; and he felt himself called upon to prophesy about it passionately. It was a subject of the immediate present, a subject yet of cosmic proportion, and a subject beyond the scope of biography or past history—both genres already familiar to Carlyle. In a way he was attempting to write a latter-day epic, but given his anxiety during these months and his anger and confusion, what finally emerges is a series of long pamphlets which participate in several literary styles, prophetic, satiric, and epic. Most obvious in tone is the voice of the Biblical prophet, condemning and exhorting. This voice, however, fuses with that of the satirist, viciously and brutally laying bare to the bone with directness and often times with embarrassing incisiveness. It is a voice which may be compared to that of Eldridge Cleaver's in *Soul on Ice*, a work which, like the *Pamphlets*, engages in angry satire and the most acute name calling.

Yet, still interesting, in certain ways, is the use Carlyle makes of the traditional epic. The *Pamphlets* are clearly a continuation of the epic theme of democracy which was so brilliantly and coherently handled in *The French Revolution*. As most readers notice there seems more coherence in the *Pamphlets* in terms of texture (imagery and theme) and tone than there is in terms of any formal structure, such as that of the epic. Yet there is also an attempt, either consciously or unconsciously, to superimpose, if nothing else, the sense of being epic. It may even be of significance that Carlyle made it clear that he wanted to write twelve pamphlets, one for each month of the year, but also the number of books that one finds in such secondary epics as the *Aeneid* and *Paradise Lost*.

Carlyle's personae have long, set speeches resembling those of the epic, and yet they are all in the same voice—that of Carlyle himself. The *Pamphlets*, in imagery and tone, collectively resemble a descent into hell itself, though it is the hell of a democratically-oriented society. It is both reminiscent of the epic and yet almost a burlesque, for if the times had called for a mythic hero of the calibre of Hercules, his modern counterpart has to be Robert Peel. Carlyle's language, too, is not like the high style of the epic; rather it is usually a satiric, biting, and oracular tone. Yet one might say that Carlyle's audience is at one moment invited to feel awe by the grim rehearsal of what he sees as the universal moral and social decadence of the present, and then to respond to his ridicule. Finally, in the broad political sweep of the *Pamphlets*, he is not unlike a modern epicist. (pp. 162-63)

For Milton the symbolic act of man's disobedience brought death to man and the loss of Eden. It is a personal sin which each man must subdue in order to regain paradise and overcome a hell which in Christian terms is individualized. So, too, Carlyle sees Democracy as demonic, symbolic of potential death, a force which once unleashed, it will "behove us to solve or die". He presents a myth of social degradation and alienation, and not chiefly religious alienation and personal death as in *Sartor*. . . . Societal death is seen throughout in the images of asphyxiation, the absence of lungs; his is a culture, as Carlyle puts it, slowly wheezing to death.

Carlyle's prophesying of a political apocalypse is also somewhat epical. The *Latter-Day Pamphlets* contain a sense of inevitable change; ultimate chaos seems always at hand. The whole world—from England, and the continent, to America— is on the brink of disaster. As Thomas Greene notes [in *The Descent from Heaven: A Study of Epic Continuity* (1963)], the epic poet must attempt to "clear away an area he can apprehend, if not dominate, and commonly this area expands to fill the epic universe, to cover the known world and reach heaven and hell. Epic characteristically refuses to be hemmed in, in time as well as space; it raids the unknown and colonizes it. It is the imagination's manifesto, proclaiming the range of its grasp, or else it is the dream of the will, indulging its fantasies of power".

Although, then, there is no tightly structured development throughout the pages of the *Latter-Day Pamphlets* of the epic theme of Democracy, its presence is everywhere, affecting the actions of all the characters and all the institutions. Democracy has arrived and has been announced to the world in message after message; it is as if "all the populations of the world were rising or had risen into incendiary madness". In another metaphor Democracy is seen as some vital force rising from the bowels of the earth and forcing itself upon the political and social realities of the mid-nineteenth century world. Or, again, it is a bottomless volcano or "universal powder-mine of most inflammable mutinous chaotic elements, separated from us by a thin earth rind" and is fanned into anarchy by "students, young men of letters, advocates, editors, hot inexperienced enthusiasts, or fierce and justly bankrupt desperadoes". Democracy is the "grand, alarming, imminent and indisputable Reality" and its problems must be solved or the world will die. No force seems at all able to drive it back to its elemental depths.

Society, indeed the Victorian world, is the scene of a cosmic night battle. Democracy, on the one hand, is a reality and will not retreat, and the laws of nature, on the other hand, are inflexible and hierarchical, as Carlyle sees them. What we have is a confrontation out of which Carlyle, in the overview of the *Latter-Day Pamphlets*, is unable to imagine a resynthesis along the lines of *Sartor Resartus, Past and Present*, or, for that matter, *The French Revolution*. This, it seems, is another basic reason that the *Pamphlets* appear so incohesive, disconcerting, and uneven. Carlyle, too, feels himself led towards personal disillusionment and self-destruction. Democracy is the devil, so to speak; it represents the present confusion, the complexity of modern life in confrontation with nature; and the staging area is the whole world. . . . (pp. 164-65)

Surely the resolution for Carlyle was not to be found in the ballot boxes which he felt would never be able to replace the natural hierarchy of God's world: the noble will always remain in high places, the ignoble in low. . . .

The theme of the confrontation and the subsequent deadlock between Democracy and nature is reflected in Carlyle's language as well, which, although alluding to primitive animals, to Megatherions and Pythons, and mud-demons, suggests a reversal in the evolutionary process. It is as if civilization is not evolving but devolving into the primeval mud out of which it was bred. Democracy and its anarchical tendencies, its uncontrollability and unruliness, is represented by the "Irish Giant, named of Despair" who is advancing upon London, laying waste the English towns and villages. . . . (p. 166)

In terms of imagery the *Latter-Day Pamphlets* are consistently negative, and one might say that Carlyle is describing a true social hell, one which is viewed as near death, and slowly being asphyxiated. Throughout the *Pamphlets*, society is alluded to in classical terms as Stygian deeps, Phlegethon, and the mud of Lethe; yet the hell which emerges is modern. The *Pamphlets* describe a world of chaos, foul odours, vulgarity, filth, ultimate selfishness, characterized by slime, serpents, dung heaps, and finally the pig philosophy. The consciousness of the *Pamphlets* is one of pervasive contempt and disgust. Yet there is some method in Carlyle's characterization of this living hell. What is suggested is a Dantesque vision, beginning with lesser or social evils and descending deeper into hell, to the source of all evil: spiritual evil, that point from which all social disorder emanates. This is symbolized by Jesuitism, the subject of the final pamphlet and the one which Carlyle felt was his best.

In **"The Present Time"**, the first pamphlet, Carlyle circles the perimeter of hell. His descriptions are general and have an epical sweep to them. This is the *Pamphlet* which announces the theme of democracy, the advent of cosmic change. The following *Pamphlets* particularize the social hell, the sickness and dehumanizing effects of institutions, and the move through the thin earth rind of **"Parliaments"** and **"Downing Street"**, to the ultimate source of social corruption—egotism, selfishness—the stomach and the purse. . . . (pp. 167-68)

The social institutions attacked throughout the *Pamphlets* are familiar—ineffective philanthropy (**"Model Prisons"**); the dehumanizing effect of red tape (**"Downing Street"**); mechanical rather than wise leadership (**"New Downing Street"**); hypocrisy of political rhetoric (**"Stump Orator"**); uselessness of parliamentary government (**"Parliaments"**); worship of money (**"Hudson's Statue"**), and finally **"Jesuitism"**. The inhabitants of this social hell move centripetally from lesser to more serious sins: they range from ineffective bureaucrats such as Felicissimus Zero who gallops his thunder horse in circles and huckstering railroad kings such as George Hudson (**"Copper Vishnu of the Scrip Ages"**) to Ignatius Loyola who inhabits the dead centre.

The centre of Carlyle's hellish vision is dominated by the pig philosophy, a form of metaphorical sensualism. All Carlyle's images of darkness, aggression, and confusion, mud-pythons, dung heaps, beaver intellect, "spiritual Vampires and obscene Nightmares", and the "world-wide jungle of redtape", are attached to this central image of the Pig Philosophy: *Schweinsche Weltansicht*, which, in effect, embraces the universe. The first principle of the Pig Philosophy states: "The Universe, so far as sane conjecture can go, is an immeasurable Swine's trough, consisting of solid and liquid, and of other contrasts and kinds;—especially consisting of attainable and unattainable, the latter in immensely greater quantities for most pigs". Pighood is the physical and mental condition of the world and, objectionable as it may seem, is the dominant image of the *Pamphlets* and the one toward which all others have been moving.

The universe, the "Swine's-trough", is a place where aggressive huckstering, the making of money, the Veritable Age of Gold reigns. In it man's duty is to consume ("to diminish the quantity of the unattainable and increase that of the attainable"); Paradise is the "unlimited attainability of Pig-wash; perfect fulfilment of one's wishes;" and justice is getting one's share of the "Swine's-trough" and "not any portion" of mine. One's share is defined as whatever one can "contrive to get without being hanged or sent to the hulks". People become pigs and greedily engage in "consumerism". The system of consuming is, moreover, defended by a corrupt legal system of lawyers (**"Servants of God"**), and by a hypocritical church which itself is no longer able to distinguish between a heaven and a living hell. Harsh though Carlyle's satire may be, it is successful in magnifying the diseases of a capitalistic economy fostered by a growing democracy.

Seen another way, the world is poisoned, and Ignatius Loyola is the symbol of its having happened; the dead world is seen as a "spiritual mummyhood"; the people are now devoted only to "cookery" and to "scrip", to prurient appetites, and to the acceptance of worn-out traditions as truth. The world has been infected by the "deadly virus of lying" and "prussic-acid and chloroform are poor to it". A fatal poison such as hydrocyanic acid or the fumes of chloroform—though actually able to destroy consciousness—are ineffective against the widespeard disease of lying. In this same context Carlyle switches the image: "Jesuit chloroform stupefied us all". The human race is now "sunk like steeping flax under the wide-spread fetid Hell-waters,—in all spiritual respects dead, dead; voiceless towards Heaven for centuries back; merely sending up, in the form of mute prayer, such an odour as the angels never smelt before". It is a corrupt and foul world, rotten to the core, and a "detestable devil's poison circulates in the life-blood of mankind; taints with abominable deadly malady all that mankind do. Such a curse never fell on man before". Life is being destroyed. . . . It is as if Carlyle has awakened from a dream and now faces the "consciousness of Jesuitism". It lies around him like the "valley of Jehoshaphat, . . . one nightmare wilderness, and wreck of deadmen's bones, this false modern world; and no rapt Ezekiel in prophetic vision imaged to himself things sadder, more horrible and terrible, than the eyes of men, if they *are* awake, may now deliberately see". Jesuitism, then, symbolizes the psychology of the new modern consciousness, now a reality.

There is, moreover, the contemptuous and bitter realization by Carlyle that Christian institutions have failed to embody a true belief for the modern world. They are blind, and their churchmen are pictured by Gathercoal (a "Yankee friend" of his) as apes "'with their wretched blinking eyes, squatting round a fire which they cannot feed with new wood; which they say will last forever without new wood,—or, alas, which they say is going out forever: it is a sad sight!'" (pp. 168-70)

The epic "hero" of the **Latter-Day Pamphlets** is Carlyle himself as he takes on the role of latter-day *Vates* and epicist. His heroic mood must be seen in the familiar Carlylean context that all history was epic, that as long as societies remained "simple and in earnest" they knew unconsciously that their history was "Epic and Bible, the clouded struggling Image of a God's Presence, the action of heroes and god inspired men". Furthermore, the noble intellect who "could disenthral such divine image, and present it to them clear, unclouded, in visible coherency comprehensible to human thought, was felt to be a *Vates* and the chief of intellects". It was not necessary to ask that he write an epic or deliver a prophecy: "Nature herself compelled him".

It may be said that Carlyle himself was compelled to write the **Pamphlets,** and to deliver his prophecy. When he asks rhetorically, "Who are they, gifted from above, that will convert voluminous Dryasdust into an Epic and even a Bible?"—one must feel that Carlyle himself is assuming the role of epic poet and latter-day prophet. His contempt for the fine arts as they are shown in the **Pamphlets** rules out his contemporaries. If these are "Human Arts" at all, Carlyle writes, "where have they been wool-gathering, these centuries long; wandering literally like creatures fallen mad!" As Carlyle has it, the fine arts have been converted into "after-dinner amusements; slave adjunct to the luxurious appetites" of one "big ugly Nawaub"—which all Europe has become.

His tone is strained to hoarseness, for if he has a covert "hero" it is Sir Robert Peel who is seen as the modern Hercules who must clean the bureaucratic Augean stables of layers of filth, corruption, of dead pedantries and accumulations of jungles of red tape and administrative droppings. Government, in fact, is a cesspool. . . . Peel is called upon to lead England through the present morass, up the "long, steep journey" as if out of hell itself, and "snatch the standard"; and thus become a hero of his country.

It would be easy to agree with Northrop Frye [in *Anatomy of Criticism* (1957)] that Carlyle's style in general is "tantrum prose", the prose of denunciation, of propaganda, of rhetoric in which "we feel that the author's pen is running away with him. . . ." As the prose grows more incoherent, writes Frye, the more it seems to express "emotion apart from or without intellect". It lapses into emotional jargon, consisting of "obsessive repetition of verbal formulas". To a great extent this is true, but a close reading of Carlyle's **Pamphlets** shows that the writer, though angered, still has a certain control over the work. It is in essence the response of an outraged sensibility to modern madness. No reader of the **Pamphlets** can deny that Carlyle has anticipated the terrors of modernism, its nightmarish qualities, its insanity. If the **Pamphlets** are an over-reaction, they nevertheless dramatize symbolically the consciousness of one man unable to cope with what he envisioned ultimately as the loneliness, the "restless gnawing ennui" of modern life. His responses were precipitous and spontaneous, angry and brutal, yet almost always conveying the sense of futility, of the loss of hope. Periodically Carlyle reasserted his older, hopeful visions in his direct addresses to the young men of England, but these calls for redemption, for new and dedicated leaders, are lost in the overwhelming rhetorical structure of the work—a work which is unified by a myth of decadence and by a tone of impending crisis of total destruction and with virtually no hope of renovation. The inconclusiveness of Carlyle's vision—since structurally there is no myth of a future regenerated society—reveals the depth of his frustration. The *Pamphlets* are a prophetic warning, an ugly result of what has happened to one psychology when confronted with the new, the transitional, the relatively unknown. . . . To the many Victorians this work was deeply disappointing. It is decidedly negative: there is no tailor retailored. Rather we are left with the feeling that Carlyle's reality, his vision of England of 1850, was truly one of social and psychological chaos:

> we are not properly a society at all; we are a lost gregarious horde, with Kings of Scrip on this hand, and Famishing Connaughts and Distressed Needle-women on that—presided over by the Anarch Old. A lost horde,—who, in bitter feeling of the intolerable injustice that presses upon all men, will not long be able to continue ever gregarious; but will have to split into street-barricades, and internecine battle with one another; and to fight, if wisdom for some new real *Peerage* be not granted us, till we all die, mutually butchered, and *so* rest,—so if not otherwise!

(pp. 171-73)

> *Jules P. Seigel, " 'Latter-Day Pamphlets': The Near Failure of Form and Vision," in* Carlyle Past and Present: A Collection of New Essays, *edited by K. J. Fielding and Rodger L. Tarr, Vision Press, 1976, pp. 155-76.*

A. L. Le Quesne (essay date 1982)

[*In the following excerpt from the conclusion of his study of Carlyle, Le Quesne assesses the author's ultimate importance, finding that it lies not in his continuing relevance but in his profound influence on his own generation.*]

The question whether Carlyle was a great man is both easy and hard to answer. Few men have been more unanimously recognised as great by their contemporaries and by those who knew them. But if one is asked to define the nature of that greatness exactly, the difficulties soon appear. Compared with thinkers like Burke and Marx, Carlyle has added nothing to the permanent stock of the world's ideas. The problem is compounded by the fact that, in the last hundred years, the world has not gone his way. Carlyle's notion of radicalism, which rested on a transformation of human relationships based on a fundamentally religious understanding of man's place in the universe, may be potentially the most fruitful one; but, in twentieth-century terms, it was a radicalism of the right, and that radicalism, disfigured by its own twentieth-century excesses, has lost out in practice to the rival radicalism of the left, based on the pursuit of egalitarianism and the transfer of political power. One is back with the familiar question of whether it is worth arguing with the course of history (especially given Carlyle's own propensity to regard history as the final court of appeal). Maybe the same is true of his historiography: perhaps Carlyle's notion of the function of history, with its emphasis on total imaginative recreation and the interpretation of the past as a record of the relationship of human societies with the transcendent justice (or is it the transcendent reality?) that overrules them, was a similar blind alley, which all later historiography has resolutely and wisely rejected. But this can be granted only with the major reservation that *The French Revolution,* at least, showed that this kind of history *could* be written, and written wonderfully.

If Carlyle was neither philosopher, political thinker, social theorist or historian of the first order, what was he? He was an important transmitter of the ideas of the late eighteenth-century German intellectual revolution to Britain; but others share this distinction, and it could hardly be made the basis of a claim to greatness. He was the author of two great masterpieces of the literary imagination, *Sartor Resartus* and *The French Revolution;* recent academic interest in Carlyle has been largely confined to critics and literary scholars, and it is as a literary figure that Carlyle's contemporary reputation stands highest. It is, though, ironic if this is to be the basis of Carlyle's claim to greatness, for there are few roles for himself that Carlyle would have repudiated more vehemently than that of the artist. He abhorred the notion of art, literary or otherwise, as an end in itself. The one acceptable role for the writer of his own luckless generation, he repeatedly insisted, was as prophet. . . . He was not interested in writing for posterity: he wanted to deliver a message to his own generation. Perhaps the most penetrating nineteenth-century judgement of Carlyle's importance was made by George Eliot as early as 1855 [see excerpt above], and it carries more weight because she could never be classed as one of his disciples but at most as his detached and discriminating admirer:

> It is an idle question to ask whether his books will be read a century hence; if they were all burnt as the grandest of Suttees on his funeral pile, it would be only like cutting down an oak after its acorns have sown a forest. For there is hardly a superior or active mind of this generation that has not been modified by Carlyle's writings; there has hardly been an English book written for the last ten or twelve years that would not have been different if Carlyle had not lived.

The true nature of Carlyle's greatness is missed if one insists on looking for *enduring* memorials of it, even though those memorials may in fact exist (the books *are* still read; Carlyle *is* often recognised as one of the major originators of a tradition of moral criticism of industrial society that persists vigorously to the present day). Carlyle never saw himself as an artist, or an original thinker. He aspired to be a prophet, a man with a message for his age, and for one brief decade he fulfilled that role. It is not every generation that needs, or deserves, a prophet, and those that need one do not always find one; but the generation of the 1840s was lucky. In Carlyle they found the greatest example of the type in modern times, a man who could express memorably the anxieties and the aspirations they felt, but were only half aware of, or could not themselves articulate. Carlyle fulfilled this role for a bare decade, in a lifetime of eighty years, and even for this decade his success was incomplete. He never succeeded in producing a programme of practical action in sufficiently concrete terms (a notion which he himself would have dismissed as a mere formula, and hence an illusion; but is this more than an escape?); and before long, the pursuit of his own private compulsions drove him away tangentially from the best minds of the generation that had revered him. There is pathos in recalling the passage on Mirabeau from *The French Revolution* in which the half-conscious identification with Carlyle himself occurs: 'like a burning mountain he blazes heaven-high; and, for twenty-three resplendent months, pours out, in flame and molten fire-torrents, all that is in him, the Pharos and Wonder-sign of an amazed Europe;—and then lies hollow, cold for ever!' Carlyle's time of greatness was longer than Mirabeau's, but still short enough; for prophets are ephemeral creatures by the nature of their calling. Carlyle's achievement is local in both time and place. He is neither a philosopher, nor a major figure of European, as distinct from British, intellectual history. Nevertheless, in the years between 1837 and 1848 his social criticism was characterised by an immensely fruitful tension, between the moral and the practical, between marvel and horror at the achievements and monstrosities of industrialism, that was equalled by no other critic of the nineteenth century, and by an inconsistent but nevertheless profound humanity that enabled him to function as the voice and the conscience of the most open and socially sensitive generation of the nineteenth century. (pp. 92-4)

A. L. Le Quesne, in his Carlyle, *Oxford University Press, Oxford, 1982, 99 p.*

ADDITIONAL BIBLIOGRAPHY

Annan, Noel. "Historians Reconsidered: Carlyle." *History Today* II, No. 10 (October 1952): 659-65.
    Assesses Carlyle's achievement as a historian.

Bentley, Eric. *The Cult of the Superman: A Study of the Idea of Heroism in Carlyle and Nietzsche, with Notes on Other Hero-Worshippers of Modern Times*. Gloucester, Mass.: Peter Smith, 1969, 277 p.
    A comparative study of the antidemocratic concept of hero worship in the thought of Carlyle, Friedrich Nietzsche, Richard Wagner, and Bernard Shaw, among others.

Birrell, Augustine. "Carlyle." In his *Obiter Dicta, first and second series*, pp. 1-28. London: Duckworth & Co., 1913.
    An 1884 assessment of Carlyle's works in every genre. Birrell labels the author a mystic, philosophical idealist, realist, and humorist.

[Browning, Elizabeth Barrett], and Horne, Richard Hengist. "Thomas Carlyle." In *A New Spirit of the Age*, edited by Richard Hengist Horne, pp. 433-50. London: Oxford University Press, 1907.
    An 1844 discussion of Carlyle's general philosophy and aims, stressing his significance as a prophet and teacher.

Calder, Grace J. *The Writing of "Past and Present": A Study of Carlyle's Manuscripts*. New Haven: Yale University Press, 1949, 214 p.
    An in-depth study of Carlyle's composition of *Past and Present*. Calder compares Carlyle's rough drafts with the printer copies and final version to trace the development of the book's style. She concludes: "Both the highly developed technique of the craftsman and the mysterious inspiration of the creator are written large on the manuscript pages of *Past and Present*."

Carlyle, Alexander. "Frank Harris and His (Imaginary) 'Talks with Carlyle'." *English Review* IX (November 1911): 599-608.
    An indignant rejection, by Carlyle's nephew, of Frank Harris's revelatory conversations with Carlyle (see entry below). Offering evidence to prove that the supposed conversations could never have taken place, Alexander Carlyle accuses Harris of "base ingratitude and cynical brutality." Appended to this essay is an answer from Harris, who insists on his own veracity and brands Alexander Carlyle "an old watch-dog of the Carlyle clan, who has been kept on the chain, so to speak, so long that he's not responsible for his mad temper."

————, and Crichton-Brown, Sir James. *The Nemesis of Froude: A Rejoinder to James Anthony Froude's "My Relations with Carlyle."* London: John Lane, The Bodley Head, 1903, 182 p.
    Rebuts Froude's posthumous *My Relations with Carlyle* (see entry below), labeling it "a kind of literary garbage." The authors write to vindicate Carlyle's character, calling him "morally as well as intellectually great."

Cassirer, Ernst. "The Preparation: Carlyle." In his *The Myth of the State*, pp. 189-223. New Haven: Yale University Press, 1946.
    A close analysis of Carlyle's conception of hero worship and its social and political implications. Cassirer concludes that Carlyle's theories can in no way be equated with those of Nazism.

Cazamian, Louis. *Carlyle*. Translated by E. K. Brown. New York: Macmillan Company, 1932, 289 p.
    A 1913 study aiming toward "an interpretation of Carlyle as a whole, leaving out all minor issues . . . to build, if possible, a coherent picture."

Chesterton, G. K. "Thomas Carlyle." In his *Varied Types*, pp. 109-22. New York: Dodd, Mead and Co., 1909.
    Praises Carlyle for irrationality and censures him for consistency in a wry assessment.

Clubbe, John, ed. *Carlyle and His Contemporaries: Essays in Honor of Charles Richard Sanders*. Durham, N.C.: Duke University Press, 1976, 371 p.
    A collection of biographical and critical essays.

Cobban, Alfred. "Carlyle's *French Revolution*." *History* XLVIII, No. 164 (October 1963): 306-16.
    Assesses *The French Revolution*, citing faults of perspective, interpretation, and reliability, but praising the work's immediacy and skillful portraiture.

Deneau, Daniel P. "Relationship of Style and Device in *Sartor Resartus*." *The Victorian Newsletter*, No. 17 (Spring 1960): 17-20.
    Maintains that Carlyle's failure to adequately differentiate Teufelsdröckh's style from the narrator's weakens *Sartor Resartus*.

Dunn, Waldo H. *Froude & Carlyle: A Study of the Froude-Carlyle Controversy*. 1930. Reprint. Port Washington, N.Y.: Kennikat Press, 1969, 365 p.
    Recapitulates the controversy surrounding Froude's biographical revelations. In his verdict of the affair, Dunn upholds Froude's veracity and honorable conduct.

Emerson, Ralph Waldo. "Carlyle." In his *The Portable Emerson*, rev. ed., edited by Carl Bode and Malcolm Cowley, pp. 621-26. New York: Penguin Books, 1981.
    Observations on Carlyle's character and opinions.

Fletcher, Jefferson B. "Newman and Carlyle: An Unrecognized Affinity." *The Atlantic Monthly* 95, No. 5 (May 1905): 669-79.
    Relates Carlyle's "doctrine of the Unconscious" to John Henry Newman's theory of belief.

Froude, James Anthony. *My Relations with Carlyle*. London: Longmans, Green, and Co., 1903, 80 p.
    A vindication (written in 1887 and published after Froude's death by his family) of his actions and decisions regarding the publication of *Reminiscences* and his biography of Carlyle. Froude claims that his ruling object was to serve the interests of Carlyle and of truth, writing: "The only 'Life' of a man which is not worse than useless is a 'Life' which tells all the truth so far as the biographer knows it." This work was fiercely contested by Alexander Carlyle and Sir James Crichton-Brown (see entry above).

Garnett, Richard. *Life of Thomas Carlyle*. London: Walter Scott, 1887, 214 p.
    An early biography. Garnett includes a critical chapter summing up the philosophy and achievements of Carlyle, who "will be honoured by posterity for his influence on human life, rather than for his supremacy as a literary artist."

Gascoyne, David. *Thomas Carlyle*. London: Longmans, Green & Co., 1952, 44 p.
    A critical survey of Carlyle's writings. Gascoyne attempts to vindicate Carlyle from what he believes are prevalent misconceptions concerning his philosophy, establishing him as a thinker of significant and continuing importance.

Goldberg, Michael. *Carlyle and Dickens*. Athens: University of Georgia Press, 1972, 248 p.
    Examines the developing influence of Carlyle on Charles Dickens's social criticism.

Grierson, H.J.C. *Carlyle & Hitler*. London: Cambridge at the University Press, 1933, 63 p.
    An examination of Carlyle's theory of the hero. Although Grierson makes no explicit parallels between Carlyle and Adolph Hitler,

he notes that recent events in Germany demonstrate that acceptance of Carlyle's theory of the hero fosters an atmosphere favorable to the emergence of such a leader as Hitler.

Guernsey, Alfred. *Thomas Carlyle: His Life, His Books, His Theories.* New York: D. Appleton and Co., 1900, 219 p.
    A biography, written a few years before Carlyle's death, approaching the author through his works and including passages of Carlyle's conversation as recorded by an acquaintance.

Halliday, James L. *Mr. Carlyle, My Patient: A Psychosomatic Biography.* London: William Heinemann, 1949, 227 p.
    A psychosexual biography. In a chapter on Carlyle's writing, Halliday relates his subject's literary qualities to his psychological traits and warns that reading Carlyle's books (particularly *Sartor Resartus*) "may be a factor in preventing the development of more mature attitudes or even in precipitating psychotic breakdown."

Harris, Frank. "Talks with Carlyle." *English Review* VII (February 1911): 419-34.
    A controversial memoir of Carlyle. Claiming intimacy with the author, Harris recounts conversations that purportedly took place beween the two, frequently revealing unattractive aspects of Carlyle's character. Particularly offensive to some is a section in which Harris describes Carlyle's tearful confession of his sexual inadequacies. For Alexander Carlyle's response to this essay and Harris's rebuttal, see the entry above.

Harrold, Charles Frederick. "Carlyle's General Method in *The French Revolution*." *PMLA* XLIII, No. 4 (December 1928): 1150-69.
    Examines Carlyle's methods of historical scholarship in writing *The French Revolution*, asserting that "his treatment of sources is, on all major accounts, entirely faithful to the facts presented in them, and that all departures from the original versions of an event are confined to minor details which, however, enliven and enrich the narrative."

———. "The Mystical Element in Carlyle (1827-34)." *Modern Philology* XXIX, No. 4 (May 1932): 459-75.
    Investigates mystical aspects of Carlyle's thought.

———. *Carlyle and German Thought: 1819-1834.* Yale Studies in English, vol. LXXXII. New Haven: Yale University Press, 1934, 346 p.
    A comprehensive study of how Carlyle's thought was influenced by German literature and philosophy.

———. "The Nature of Carlyle's Calvinism." *Studies in Philology* XXXIII, No. 3 (July 1936): 475-86.
    Explains Carlyle's social theories in terms of his adherence to Calvinist theology.

Hearn, Lafcadio. "On the Philosophy of *Sartor Resartus*." In his *Interpretations of Literature*, Vol. 1, edited by John Erksine, pp. 208-32. New York: Dodd, Mead and Co., 1915.
    Summarizes and explicates what Hearn considers the most salient aspects and compelling theses of *Sartor*.

Hood, Edwin Paxton. *Thomas Carlyle: Philosopher, Thinker, Theologian, Historian, and Poet.* 1875. Reprint. New York: Haskell House Publishers, 1970, 502 p.
    An early critical biography.

Ikeler, A. Abbott. *Puritan Temper and Transcendental Faith: Carlyle's Literary Vision.* Columbus: Ohio State University Press, 1972, 226 p.
    A discussion of how Carlyle's views were shaped by the conflicting currents of transcendental idealism and orthodox Calvinism.

James, Henry, Jr. "The Correspondence of Carlyle and Emerson." *The Century Magazine* XXVI, No. 2 (June 1883): 265-72.
    A laudatory review of *The Correspondence of Thomas Carlyle and Ralph Waldo Emerson*.

John, Brian. "The Fictive World of Thomas Carlyle." In his *Supreme Fictions: Studies in the Work of William Blake, Thomas Carlyle, W. B. Yeats, and D. H. Lawrence*, pp. 75-147. Montreal: McGill-Queen's University Press, 1974.

An analysis of Carlyle's fictional techniques.

Kaplan, Fred. *Thomas Carlyle: A Biography.* Ithaca: Cornell University Press, 1983, 614 p.
    A biography "self-consciously" modeled on Carlyle's own biographical methods. Kaplan discusses Carlyle's works "only insofar as they are important to the narrative and illumine the central biographical and cultural issues."

LaValley, Albert J. *Carlyle and the Idea of the Modern: Studies in Carlyle's Prophetic Literature and Its Relation to Blake, Nietzsche, Marx, and Others.* New Haven: Yale University Press, 1968, 351 p.
    Combines literary analyses of Carlyle's work with comparisons of Carlyle and modern writers in order to "demonstrate [Carlyle's] central role in a dominant modern tradition, that of the artist as problematic prophet, the seer who is himself a quester into self and society."

Lehman, B. H. *Carlyle's Theory of the Hero: Its Sources, Development, History, and Influence on Carlyle's Work.* 1928. Reprint. New York: AMS Press, 1966, 212 p.
    Analyzes Carlyle's work in light of his preoccupation with the idea of the hero.

Leicester, H. M., Jr. "The Dialectic of Romantic Historiography: Prospect and Retrospect in *The French Revolution*." *Victorian Studies* XV, No. 1 (September 1971): 5-17.
    Compares Carlyle's abstract historical theory to his actual practice in *The French Revolution*.

Levine, George. "*Sartor Resartus* and the Balance of Fiction." In his *The Boundaries of Fiction: Carlyle, Macaulay, Newman*, pp. 19-78. Princeton: Princeton University Press, 1968.
    Examines the relationship of *Sartor* to Victorian fiction.

Mazzini, Joseph. "On the Genius and Tendency of the Writings of Thomas Carlyle." In his *Life and Writings of Joseph Mazzini: Critical and Literary*, Vol. IV, pp. 56-109. London: Smith, Elder, & Co., 1891.
    An analysis, originally published in 1843 in the *British and Foreign Review*, of the ideals and convictions expressed in Carlyle's writings.

Metzger, Lore. "*Sartor Resartus*: A Victorian *Faust*." *Comparative Literature* XIII, No. 4 (Fall 1961): 316-31.
    Details the influence of Goethe's *Faust* on *Sartor*.

Moore, Carlisle. "The Persistence of Carlyle's 'Everlasting Yea'." *Modern Philology* LIV, No. 3 (February 1957): 187-96.
    Contends that Carlyle partially lost his positive faith in God, humanity, and society as he grew older and more bitter.

———. "Thomas Carlyle." In *The English Romantic Poets & Essayists: A Review of Research and Criticism*, rev. ed., edited by Carolyn Washborn Houtchens and Lawrence Huston Houtchens, pp. 333-78. London: University of London Press, 1966.
    Describes and evaluates bibliographies, biographies, and literary criticism in Carlyle studies.

Neff, Emery. *Carlyle.* New York: W. W. Norton & Co., 1932, 282 p.
    A standard study of Carlyle's life and work.

[Oliphant, Margaret]. "Thomas Carlyle." *Macmillan's Magazine* XLIII, No. 258 (April 1881): 482-96.
    Combines a review of *Reminiscences* with Oliphant's own sympathetic memories of the author and his circle.

Pankhurst, Richard K. P. *The Saint Simonians, Mill, and Carlyle: A Preface to Modern Thought.* London: Sidgwick & Jackson, Lalibela Books, 1957, 154 p.
    Discusses the relation of Carlyle and John Stuart Mill to nineteenth-century Saint-Simonism.

Ralli, Augustus. *Guide to Carlyle.* 2 vols. London: George Allen & Unwin, 1920.
    Combines biography, literary criticism, and detailed, objective summaries of each of Carlyle's works.

Roe, Frederick William. *Thomas Carlyle as a Critic of Literature*. New York: Columbia University Press, 1910, 152 p.
  Assesses Carlyle's literary criticism and his significance to the development of criticism in England.

Roellinger, Francis X., Jr. "The Early Development of Carlyle's Style." *PMLA* LXXII, No. 5 (December 1957): 936-51.
  Argues that *Sartor Resartus* represented a radical, not a gradual, change in Carlyle's prose style.

Sanders, Charles Richard. "The Victorian Rembrandt: Carlyle's Portraits of His Contemporaries." *Bulletin of the John Rylands Library* 39, No. 2 (March 1957): 521-57.
  Assesses Carlyle's descriptions of his contemporaries.

———. "The Byron Closed in *Sartor Resartus*." *Studies in Romanticism* III, No. 2 (Winter 1964): 77-108.
  A detailed examination, drawing on biographical and textual evidence, of Carlyle's attitude toward Byron and his work.

Seigel, Jules Paul, ed. *Thomas Carlyle*. The Critical Heritage Series, edited by B. C. Southam. London: Routledge & Kegan Paul, 1971, 526 p.
  A collection of excerpted criticism on Carlyle's works covering the years 1834 to 1881.

Shine, Hill. *Carlyle's Fusion of Poetry, History, and Religion by 1834*. Chapel Hill: University of North Carolina Press, 1938, 85 p.
  A study of how Carlyle formed his unique philosophy from a variety of sources.

———. *Carlyle's Early Reading, to 1834, with an Introductory Essay on His Intellectual Development*. Lexington: University of Kentucky Libraries, 1953, 353 p.
  A comprehensive listing of Carlyle's comments on books he read.

Sterling, John. Letter to Thomas Carlyle. In *The Life of John Sterling*, by Thomas Carlyle, pp. 95-103. London: Chapman and Hall, 1871.
  A letter dated 29 May 1835 critiquing *Sartor Resartus*. Although he objects to some of the work's language as "positively barbarous," Sterling is deeply affected by "the genius and moral energy of the book."

Stewart, Herbert L. "Carlyle's Place in Philosophy." *The Monist* XXIX, No. 2 (April 1919): 161-89.
  Assesses Carlyle as a philosophical thinker, noting that he constructed a viable system of ethics and metaphysics even while rejecting metaphysical inquiry as a "disease."

Strachey, George. "Carlyle and the 'Rose-Goddess'." *The Nineteenth Century* XXXII, No. 187 (September 1892): 470-86.
  Draws on *Reminiscences* and Carlyle's letters to illustrate his life, particularly his relations to the Stracheys, the Bullers, and Kitty Kirkpatrick. Strachey, the son of Carlyle's friends Edward and Julia Strachey, expresses his family's belief that the characters of *Sartor Resartus* represent real people and supplies his own personal remembrance of the author.

Strachey, Lytton. "Carlyle." In his *Portraits in Miniature and Other Essays*, pp. 178-90. New York: Harcourt, Brace and Co., 1931.
  Contends that Carlyle's genius and artistry are flawed by his "obsession" with moralizing and his distorted sense of self.

Taylor, A. J. P. "The Art of Writing History." *The Listener* L, No. 1272 (16 July 1953): 108-09.
  Contrasts the historical methods and styles of Carlyle and Thomas Babington Macaulay.

Tennyson, G. B. "Thomas Carlyle." In *Victorian Prose: A Guide to Research*, edited by David J. DeLaura, pp. 33-104. New York: Modern Language Association of America, 1973.
  Provides comprehensive bibliographical information on works by and about Carlyle.

Thompson, Francis. "Carlyle." In his *Literary Criticisms*, edited by Rev. Terence L. Connolly, S. J., pp. 163-66. New York: E. P. Dutton and Co., 1948.
  Praises the dramatic immediacy of *The French Revolution*. Thompson's remarks were first published in the *Academy* in 1903.

Tillotson, Geoffrey. "Carlyle." In his *A View of Victorian Literature*, pp. 55-111. Oxford: Clarendon Press, 1978.
  A general discussion of Carlyle, focusing on the author's essential sympathy for humanity and the extent of his influence on other Victorian writers.

Towne, Jackson E. "Carlyle and Oedipus." *The Psychoanalytic Review* XXII, No. 3 (July 1935): 297-305.
  Posits that Carlyle's neuroses were the result of his Oedipus complex.

Trevelyan, G. M. "Carlyle as an Historian." *The Nineteenth Century* XLVI, No. 271 (September 1899): 493-503.
  Asserts Carlyle's right to be considered a true, if unorthodox, historian, emphasizing the merits of his poetic writing, his humor, and his insight into the human mind.

Trowbridge, Ronald L. "Thomas Carlyle's Masks of Humor." *Michigan Academician* III, No. 2 (Fall 1970): 57-66.
  Attests to the humor in Carlyle's work.

Wellek, René. "Carlyle and German Romanticism" and "Carlyle and the Philosophy of History." In his *Confrontations: Studies in the Intellectual and Literary Relations between Germany, England, and the United States during the Nineteenth Century*, pp. 34-81, 82-113. Princeton: Princeton University Press, 1965.
  Two essays. The first discusses Carlyle's links to Romanticism and German literature; the second assesses him as a historian, denying that he adhered to a set of philosophical historical principles but suggesting that "his insight into some features of the historical process may be deeper than that of the professional historians of the nineteenth century."

Whitman, Walt. "Death of Carlyle." In his *Rivulets of Prose*, edited by Carolyn Wells and Alfred F. Goldsmith, pp. 139-64. New York: Greenberg, 1928.
  An admiring commentary on Carlyle written in 1882 and after. Whitman remarks: "As a representative author, a literary figure, no man else will bequeath to the future more significant hints of our stormy era, its fierce paradoxes, its din, and its struggling parturition periods, than Carlyle."

(Jacobine) Camilla (Wergeland) Collett

1813-1895

Norwegian novelist, essayist, memoirist, and short story writer.

Collett was a pioneering feminist writer and the first realistic novelist of Norway. Her writings include stories, memoirs, and feminist polemics, but her best-known work is the influential novel *Amtmandens døtre* (The Governor's Daughters), known to readers as a passionate appeal for the rights of Norwegian women to improved social status and emotional freedom. Considered controversial and sensational by its initial audience, the novel brought its author first notoriety and eventually lasting fame in Norway. Although few modern English-language scholars study her works, those who do acknowledge Collett's influence on such writers as Henrik Ibsen and Jonas Lie and recognize her dual importance as an early Scandinavian feminist and realistic novelist.

Collett was born Jacobine Camilla Wergeland in Kristiansand and grew up in Eidsvoll, where her father was pastor. At first tutored at home with her brothers, she was later sent abroad to attend finishing school. She returned to Norway at the age of sixteen or seventeen. In Christiania (now Oslo), she met and fell in love with the poet and critic J. S. Welhaven. Collett became unwittingly embroiled in a literary and political feud between Welhaven, who believed that terse, formalistic poetry (as sanctioned by Danish universities and the intelligentsia) represented the artistic ideal, and her brother Henrik, a celebrated lyric poet who advocated Norwegian independence from Danish cultural hegemony. More pertinent to her subsequent writing, however, was her vacillating personal relationship with Welhaven. The years of Collett's association with Welhaven were by all accounts intensely frustrating for her—in love with the young poet, she was prevented by social restrictions from either declaring or acting openly upon her feelings. For his part, Welhaven was noncommittal, hinting in his letters at passion but remaining ultimately undecided. In 1836 the two finally called an end to their equivocal relationship. Five years later she married lawyer and literary critic Peter Jonas Collett.

It was Peter Jonas Collett who encouraged his wife to write her first short stories, many of which appeared in the daily *Den constitutionelle* (the Constitutionalist) and were later collected and published as *Fortællinger* (Stories). Collett continued to write after her husband's death in 1851, publishing her only novel, the feminist masterpiece *Amtmandens døtre,* in 1855. Due to its radical premise—that women merited the same emotional and social freedom as men—the novel was not initially well received, but within Collett's own lifetime changing social conditions in Norway brought the work into favor. Collett spent many of her later years abroad, traveling throughout Europe and publishing stories, memoirs, and fiery feminist polemics. In 1893, on her eightieth birthday, Collett was honored by her compatriots, including Ibsen, for her contributions not only to literature but also to Norwegian society through her position as her country's foremost advocate of the emancipation of women. She died two years later in Christiania.

Collett described *Amtmandens døtre* as "a shriek," "a cry that escaped me, my life's long-withheld despairing cry," and indeed critics agree that the novel is informed by its author's

passionate intensity. In parallel stories of the lives of three sisters, *Amtmandens døtre* explores the helplessness of women to assume active control of their love relationships and thus their lives. The faults in construction and characterization that critics have noted in the novel are overshadowed by Collett's compassion for her subjects and the realism of her portrayal of their predicament. In later feminist works, including the collection of essays *Sidste blade* (Last Leaves), Collett turned her attention to direct social and political reform. Another work, the 1877 essay *Fra de stummes leir* (From the Camp of the Dumb), is an astringent assessment of the negative, unfair portrayal of women in literature. It is said that Collett's criticism of Ibsen in this work caused the noted dramatist to alter the representation of women in his writings. In a different vein, Collett's memoir of her childhood and youth, *I de lange nætter* (During the Long Nights), is considered her most charming and engaging work.

But it is for *Amtmandens døtre,* autobiographical in spirit if not in detail, that Collett is primarily remembered. As the first Norwegian novel written with a social purpose, *Amtmandens døtre* remains an affecting and effective attack on the social conventions that required women to be passive. For this novel, Collett continues to be known in Norway, in the words of Agnes Mathilde Wergeland, as "our greatest authoress and our valkyrie."

PRINCIPAL WORKS

Amtmandens døtre (novel) 1855; revised edition, 1879
Fortællinger (short stories) 1861
I de lange nætter (memoirs) 1863
Sidste blade. 5 vols. (essays) 1868-73
Fra de stummes leir (essay) 1877
Camilla Collets skrifter. 11 vols. (novel, essays, memoirs, and short stories) 1892-94

*Most of the stories in this collection were originally published in the daily newspaper *Den constitutionelle* (the Constitutionalist).

THE ATHENAEUM (essay date 1895)

[*In the following excerpt from an obituary of Collett, the anonymous commentator pays tribute to the Norwegian author.*]

An interesting figure has passed away in the person of Jacobine Camilla Collett, the latest survivor of the Norwegian writers of the beginning of the century. . . .

It was not until 1855 that Mrs. Collett published her first and best book, the very remarkable novel of **The Sheriff's Daughters** (*Amtmandens Döttre*), a work which created a great sensation in Norway, and which has been translated into most of the languages of Europe. In 1863 she produced **In the Long Nights** (*I de Lange Nætter*), and in 1868 **Last Leaves** (*Sidste Blade*). She has taken the leading part in all questions of women's rights in Norway, and has published a great deal of polemical matter on this subject. Preserving her faculties to the last, her old age was both brilliant and attractive. Of late years Mrs. Collett had occupied a unique place in Christiania, and her death closes a chapter in the intellectual life of modern Norway.

> E. G., "Madame Camilla Collett," in The Athenaeum, No. 3516, March 16, 1895, p. 345.

AGNES MATHILDE WERGELAND (essay date 1913)

[*In remarks written to celebrate the centenary of Collett's birth, Wergeland emphasizes her important role in Norwegian culture, extolling the personal virtues and writings of "our greatest authoress and our valkyrie."*]

What wonderful power lies in a name! Especially in a dear and great name such as [Camilla Collett's]; a name made significant by her own unspoiled individuality. It is a nimbus; something indescribable about it forces us to pause and long observe it. Björnson has likened such a name to a constellation shining down upon us in peaceful, ever memorable greatness. But in Camilla Collett's name we are as much fascinated by the secret, the mysterious, as by the transparent and clear. We think of winged flight, of the song of hidden birds, of the gentle falling of white cherry petals. The charm of the mountain nymph rests on this name. It reminds us of the leafy woods, the river bank lying amid alder and hazel, and the silent occult spirit-haunted life of the woods of Norway.

She was perhaps the most characteristic phenomenon in our history—this clergyman's daughter from Eidsvold, who became our greatest authoress and our valkyrie, who for more than a generation in a little corner of the world carried on the struggle for the rights of the woman-heart, of the human soul,

against the power of all conventionalities and customs and fought it with triumph. Yet with all her ideal courage and her ire, she remained the same shy, reserved person as in her youth, the same mimosa in the presence of outsiders, especially of the great public, which repelled her by its obtrusion, its lack of regard for talent other than amusing, its indifference to the mental real values. But many a mother and father, many a young girl and boy, read what she wrote and imbibed strength to defend, to strike a blow for worth, to prevent the flower of existence from being trodden under foot. Thus she lived among us year by year, unknown to the multitude, hidden from the masses, forgotten by many, until she felt her existence too cramped, too pallid and deathlike, and withdrew abroad to surroundings which better suited her nature. There among artists and authors and their works she breathed the free air of eternal ideas and great accomplishments. Self-exiled thus as she was, she nevertheless continued to bring to her native land the fruits of her thoughts, her work, and her struggle.

It is now a hundred years since Camilla Collett was born. The history of her life has been written by her son, a fascinating book which makes him, who wrote it, and her, who inspired it, almost equally great. Unaffected and unostentatious as herself, it tells in a big clear way, mostly in her own words, the story of her development. Her career was in the best sense free from blemish, her speech as pure as her thoughts. She was not ignorant of the shady side of existence, but she abhorred all things questionable, gossip, and foulness. None of these penetrated her life or her books. Her greatest work, **The Daughters of the County Magistrate,** has few parallels in any literature. It was the child of her sorrows, and it is a sorrowful book; yet it is so exceedingly charming, so beautiful in tone, so delicate in feeling, so artistically moulded and balanced, so elevated, so powerful in its pathos, as to be almost alone in its kind. Of all the books I have read I can scarcely recollect any that made such an ineffaceable impression upon me. If any, perhaps those of Turgenieff, with whom indeed Fru Collett has much in common, in viewpoint and manner and incomparable mastery of language. Yet there is a difference. While he in sad resignation seems to say: "Well, the world is not any better," she with wrath dissolved in irony exclaims: "Beyond all criticism, the world is absurd!" (pp. 64-6)

The brilliance, firmness, purity, and beauty of her style—its diamondlike quality—is what decides her high rank as a writer. By virtue of this, her books, though few, withstand the influence of time and her name retains its lustre undimmed by the greatness of later authors. Fru Aubert in a late book says truly that mighty geniuses known by all the world have since enriched our literature; but hardly any creative work has so revolutionized minds as did Fru Collett's **The Daughters of the County Magistrate.** And with the assurance of one who lived through the period she declares, "The book had this power because it was Norwegian, because it began a new form of activity in our social development, and because it was expressed in a style which after fifty years remains unsurpassed in our literature." (p. 70)

The sensation caused by the book is a matter of common knowledge. "How well one knew it all, and yet how fresh and kindling the idea! Who can ever forget it?" says Fru Aubert. The author showed a first hand knowledge of the situation treated, the persons were drawn with an acute sense of their peculiarities, made alive and different; the conversations were dramatic; nature was described as only a true worshipper can describe it; and above all there was true and deep feeling, never prolix, but with fine restraint seeking its contrast and outlet in humor. Such were the qualities by which the unknown writer held her readers. If further analyzed, the book shows experience, an eye for the deeper emotions and for the strange parody that plays havoc with our lives and brings results entirely opposite to those anticipated. It warns us by showing in a hollow mirror a contorted image of what is to be our lot. In this particular Fru Collett is certainly related to George Eliot. Margrethe gives Cold such good advice concerning the young girl who is to be his choice. "Do not ravish her love, let her feeling ripen of itself. Like the must, it needs time to ferment, and if it is pure, it will overflow of its own sweetness." But this restraining of his own emotion in order that hers may freely unfold, brings disaster. The story of the poor old spinster, once "the prettiest most fêted girl in all the parish," who went daft from shame because she had confessed her love to the man she loved, becomes to Sophie such a hollow mirror wherein she shudderingly sees her own fate parodied (for she did not go daft); while Cold's noble delicate remarks seem to her the flower-decked trap into which she falls.

This scene is with a great deal of art made the central point of the book. Here the chief actors show their characters, from here their fate is worked out in logical sequence. People's thoughts were especially occupied with the tendency of the novel. "What is it she wishes?" they said. "Does she want the ladies to propose?" Fru Collett herself says that she wished to reinstate feeling in its rights. She somewhere calls the book "a cry that escaped me, my life's long-withheld despairing cry." The book was indeed herself, what she had lived through, only resuscitated, risen from her soul's depth as another reality. Hence no one can criticize this work for shallowness, lack of inventive power, insufficiency of imaginative transformation. On the contrary, the poetic has become the real and the reality is absorbed in the poetic.

Why did this book come to be, in a sense, Fru Collett's only great creative contribution to our literature? She herself says she was not fond of writing, and found no satisfaction in forced productivity. Besides, a contempt for fiction, which sometimes develops with maturer years, seems to have taken possession of her. She says somewhere, "If those who truly had lived, even though the life had not been remarkable, would with the courage of truth tell their experience, people would have reading more effectual in the progress of mankind than many of the fables with which we are now punished."

In accordance with this view, she published her personal and family memoirs in *The Long Nights*. This book is one of the most interesting memoirs to be found in any literature, and is written not only with intensity of feeling but with evident enjoyment as well. Yet it seems to have brought its author at the time only unpleasant remarks;—"It is, of course, nothing but lamentations," she "speaks all the time herself," and more of that kind. Hence she nearly lost courage and desire to bring forth anything for a public so plainly unappreciative. "Ask the plant which never sees sunshine why it does not have flower after flower," she says in *Last Leaflets*.

But a great talent cannot be so easily crushed. It made a new opening for itself in which the unpleasantness of being exposed to the gaze of the public and the suffering it cost her to write disappeared before the enthusiasm of serving a cause, an idea. And the idea lay beforehand in her soul, as a seed ready for growth. "There are facts in our existence that are not worth thinking too deeply about," says Louise in *The Daughters*, "perhaps it is fortunate that so few do think about them. We,

who are the equals of men in the scale of living beings, who are just as noble, just as gifted as they, and are unsullied by their vices, we, while we are the objects of their choice and refusal are yet valued so singularly low." On the whole, Louise, her fate, her speech, the entire episode relating to her in its bold bitter beauty, its terseness and energy, its harsh reality (it frightened people so that in the next edition Fru Collett had to tone it down a bit)—this entire portion of the book was already a challenge to a fight for the cause of woman.

Life had prepared Fru Collett for such a fight. She had herself experienced how unfortunate it is in youth to have only one's heart to live on because one's hands are tied. She had seen great talents among those of her own age "vegetate within the family and die the natural death so likely to come to gifts in a woman." And she looked further and saw that "our country cannot employ its daughters. A thousand forces are left unused, miserably wasted, as is the champignon, which the peasant not knowing its value or use tramples under foot." She had observed long before the gap between men's and women's morals, for almost every household in the parishes had its Borgia, its Bluebeard in miniature; and she had seen the honorable wives—the pale, mute, griefworn, degraded wives—of these scandalous husbands. And even more deeply impressed upon her was the fact that she had seen good natural abilities in women restrained till they were transformed into evil. She had herself lived through "the greatest sorrow a human being can undergo, and to the grief and bereavement was added the experience of *a widow's lot in this land.*" For again she looked further and saw that for other widows it was no different; that a woman was nothing in herself, did not exist as an individual, as a member of society, but only as a member of a family. To free the individual, to set in motion the forces for good, became thus Fru Collett's aim. "Emancipation, this watchword of your scorn," she exclaims, "means nothing but the deliverance of women's good natural salutary gifts; it is the false womanliness in them that emancipation will do away with and will put the true womanliness in its place." Healthy activity in some practical or intellectual direction she declared would bring an important liberation. And such liberation "will react upon women's emotional life, making it healthier and stronger. The age of unhealthy overwrought sentiment will then be past."

The necessity for the same moral duty, the same responsibility for man as for woman, was to her a matter of chief importance. And she who was herself so chaste that she had to battle with her own sensitiveness in order to touch moral questions, gave Mrs. Butler's *Voice in the Desert* a warm and deeply felt welcome. She took up these needed reforms in legislation as well as in literature. Her polemical *Woman in Literature* tore big rents in the accepted standards. Especially the French legislation and the French novel received the sharp arrows of her wit and her indignation. But also in our own literature she pointed out the painful fact that the type of woman had deteriorated.

Fru Collett now always wrote under her own name. The dual sides of her nature, which she recognized by having "Hardie et Timide" engraved in her seal, were no longer at war. She was timid for herself, but bold for her cause. The blows and adversity resulting from her battle she considered as afflictions undergone for the sake of her cause.

But she had not only adversity. She gained companions in arms as well, warm faithful friends and admirers. With bitter-sweet humor, she called herself a goodwife who tried to stem and turn the tide, and she named one of her books *Against the Tide*.

Yet in time she found that the tide did turn her way, that her cause made progress. (pp. 94-9)

Her long often gloomy day passed away in a beautiful evening glow. A great multitude from all over the land paid homage to her on her eightieth birthday, bringing from each and every one a special expression of gratitude for the way she had awakened, spurred, strengthened, or simply given joy. Her reform work and her poetic work gathered into one great light which shone over the whole land. And a few years after, she died, at home, among her own, as she had desired.

Fru Collett's importance in the recent history of our country is great. Her unusual personality, possessing something of the fairy princess, something of the saga woman; her unique position in the centre of clashing views, with family relations and affections ranged against intellectual sympathies and educational affinities; her style, so elastic, graceful, strong and buoyant; her subjects and her treatment of them so superior that our knowledge of the country and the times would be incomplete without her writings; her battle as path-breaker and pioneer for her sex;—all these secure to her an eminent rank among our remarkable personalities and our greatest authors. (pp. 100-01)

> *Agnes Mathilde Wergeland, "Camilla Collett: A Centenary Tribute," in her* Leaders in Norway and Other Essays, *edited by Katharine Merrill, 1916. Reprint by Books for Libraries Press, 1966, pp. 64-101.*

OLA RAKNES (essay date 1923)

[*Raknes appreciatively surveys Collett's career, noting the author's unique contributions to Norwegian literature and culture.*]

In Norwegian history Camilla Collett represents two important innovations: in our literature she is the first to introduce the *roman à thèse,* and in politics she is our first champion of the emancipation of women. To her, literature was little else than a means to fight for her ideas, such as life had formed them for her. . . . For of Camilla Collett we may say that she spent the first half of her life in gaining experience, which in the latter half she founded her writings upon, for other sufferers of her sex to benefit by it. (p. 113)

The works of Camilla Collett may be roughly divided into three parts, a division corresponding not only to their contents but also to their order of publication. The first part consists of works of fiction, what we in Norway call *skjønliteratur,* the second part of her recollections, and the third of polemical and propagandist writings. The division is, however, only a rough one, for we everywhere find definite moral purpose, personal memories, and striving after artistic effect. (pp. 120-21)

[Her] first publications were the stories and sketches in *Den Constitutionelle.* In the very first of them she argues against the oppression of women by social etiquette. The following articles are sketches from peasant life, partially occasioned by and protesting against the descriptions Asbjørnsen had given as framework of his popular legends and tales. . . . Some of the other articles are still interesting as good descriptions of the life of the country functionaries, and as acute criticisms of society life, both in the country and in the capital.

But all those things are little more than experiments which only imperfectly show us the great qualities of the author. These are to be sought in her chief work, her great novel *Amtmandens Døttre,* published . . . in 1855.

The County Sheriff's Daughters consists of several distinct stories running parallel. The principal one is the love story of the sheriff's youngest daughter, Sophie, and of George Cold, the sheriff's secretary. The other stories are those of the love and marriage of the other sisters, told with the purpose of setting forth Sophie's misfortune as the common lot of women.

George Cold is a young man of the educated class, but without relations, so that only his personal qualities have opened to him the most exclusive society of the Norwegian capital. The men envy him, the women adore him, and he has made more than one conquest among them, has even been engaged once or twice. But intimacy with women has opened his eyes, he thinks: he has never met any woman whose intelligence or character were worthy of him, and now he believes himself immune from any attack from the other sex. So minded he arrives at the sheriff's house. At first there seems to be but small danger of his falling in love with anybody—in spite of the recognized risk of such things happening whenever a young man comes to live in a family where there are unmarried and marriageable daughters. In the sheriff's house there are two unmarried girls. But the elder is too homely, too silly, and too sentimental to make any deep impression on him, and the younger is only a child, taciturn and recalcitrant, and too shy for him to form any opinion of her deeper nature. By chance he discovers that her reticence is not natural, but an attitude she has imposed upon herself from fear of being exploited as her married sisters have been, and also of having her most intimate sentiments violated. From that moment he begins to take an interest in the young girl, although he still regards her as a child. She goes abroad to complete her education (just as the young Camilla Wergeland had done), and when she returns, Cold suddenly discovers that from a child she has grown into a young woman. Without any thought of love, he takes a pleasure in guiding this awakening soul. As might be expected, she falls in love with her tutor, and without knowing it, he falls in love too. When at last he discovers it, he at once resolves to declare his feelings to her. A chance makes him come to her just in time to save her from another suitor who will not accept her refusal. In her joyous excitement at being saved, she gets the start of him by telling him of her love first. He responds wholeheartedly to it, and everything seems to be very well, when an old friend of his turns up just as they are going to make their love known to her parents. Cold is afraid of the cynicism of this friend, afraid that his newborn happiness should be profaned, and so he disowns his love and speaks lightly of the young girl, in terms that are likely to wound her if ever reported to her. By a most unfortunate chance—there are rather many such chances in the book—she overhears their conversation. Judging by what she has seen of other men, Sophie never doubts that George Cold has spoken the truth to his friend, so he must have lied to her and made fun of her confession. Broken-hearted and bewildered, she refuses to speak to him, and he, who has not the slightest idea of the cause of her change towards him, is obliged to leave her without an explanation. A relatively short time after, she accepts the hand and fortune of Dean Rein, who might have been her father. Not till the eve of her wedding day does she learn from George's lips the fatal mistake. But it is already too late, the wheels of the machine called a fashionable wedding have already caught hold of her, and she feels that she would be crushed if she tried to escape.

To her sisters the same or similar things happen, everywhere woman's love is trampled underfoot as an obstacle to the superior interests of the family, or sacrificed to the true vocation of woman, as the sheriff's wife puts it.

It is easy to find fault with this novel: the composition is too loose, many characters are there only to illustrate the thesis of the author without throwing any additional light on the principal characters, the reflections and soliloquies occupy too much space, the characters are not sufficiently individualized, and more such things. But what makes up for all that is the author's penetrating analysis of the feelings, her masterly exposition of the degrading situation of the society woman, the truthful pictures of society life in the country, and above all, the deep compassion for the sufferings of women. There is also the natural, clear, direct, sententious style, visibly influenced by George Sand and other French writers of the time. (pp. 121-23)

The County Sheriff's Daughters was at once hailed as the most important novel of the young Norwegian literature, and its importance was constantly growing for more than thirty years. Of the authors that have been strongly influenced by it we mention Henrik Ibsen and Jonas Lie, who have both acknowledged their indebtedness.

It is *The County Sheriff's Daughters* that places Camilla Collett among the great authors of Norwegian literature. But she has also written at least one other book that is still much read, and which probably will hold its place as long as the first. The book is the volume of recollections called *I de Lange Nætter* (*During the Long Nights*), published in 1863. It is certainly one of the most valuable as well as the most charming volumes of memoirs of our literature—which is rather poor in this respect. Its historical importance is largely due to the fact that it contains so much first-hand information about three remarkable personalities—the author herself, her brother Henrik, and her father Nicolai Wergeland. (p. 124)

However great the historical value of the *Long Nights* may be, its purely literary value is greater still. Camilla Collett's style is nowhere more limpid and full of grace, and never did she attain a fuller expression of her peculiar way of seeing and feeling. What the book lacks in force as compared with *The County Sheriff's Daughters,* it makes up for by its charm, and probably nothing of what its author has written is better loved.

Between those two books, Camilla Collett had published, in 1861, a volume of *Fortællinger* (*Stories*), containing the articles and sketches of which we have already spoken, with the addition of a new sketch, "**Octoberphantasier,**" criticizing the life and manners of Kristiania society. After the *Long Nights* she did not publish any new book for five years, and then, thinking that her literary activity was at an end, she called her book *Sidste Blade* (*Last Leaves,* with the sub-title *Recollections and Confessions*). They were, however, not to be her last leaves, she was still to publish no fewer than five books, some of them quite bulky ones, and a number of articles that she did not think worthy of being incorporated.

In the first of these volumes, called *Last Leaves, Second and Third Series,* she for the first time sets up the emancipation of women as a political programme, and from this time all her forces were consecrated to that cause. She was, therefore, inclined to put this book foremost among her writings as the one that contained the first clear statement of her aims. The other four volumes were *Last Leaves, Fourth and Fifth Series, Fra de Stummes Leir* (*From the Camp of the Dumb*), *Mod Strømmen* (*Against the Tide*), and *Against the Tide, Second Series.* The most interesting of these last volumes, all occupied with the woman question, is the one called *From the Camp of*

J. S. Welhaven.

the Dumb. The author there reviews a great number of modern books, Norwegian and foreign, chiefly with the object of showing how the false, conventional views on woman have vitiated the works of even the best-intentioned authors. In spite of its exaggerations the book contains a great number of remarks that are still of interest, and that not only to the historian of literature.

We have already mentioned the great progress of the cause to which Camilla Collett had devoted her life. But she was of those natures that always have the feeling, not of what has been accomplished, but of what still remains to be done. Her own writings she (in a letter to Theodore Stanton) compares to those Arctic explorers who never return: they may find the northern passage, but one hears no more of them. "I am neither discontented nor glad, only tired. I repent of nothing that I have written, a later generation must judge."

What we meet in the part of Camilla Collett's work that is still living, is above all the soul of a highly gifted and great-hearted woman, with her courage and her shyness, with her hopes and disillusions, with her joys and sufferings, with her entire womanliness. Speaking of her place in the company of our great authors, we may use Welhaven's words of her appearance in society:

> Among the brilliant assembly
> she wore a crown invisible,
> for she alone walked in an aura
> of mild and graceful womanhood.

(pp. 125-26)

Ola Raknes, "Camilla Collett," in Chapters in Norwegian Literature: Being the Substance of Public Lectures, Given at University College, London, during the Sessions 1918-1922 *by Illit Grøndahl and Ola Raknes, 1923. Reprint by Books for Libraries Press, 1969, pp. 113-26.*

JOSEF WIEHR (essay date 1925)

[*Wiehr describes Collett's social, political, and literary beliefs as they are expressed in her works, emphasizing her seminal contribution to feminism.*]

Among the intellectual and social aristocracy of nineteenth century Norway, Camilla Collett, the daughter of Nicolai Wergeland, occupies a position in the front ranks, despite the fact that the status of the Norwegian women was still a very unfavorable one in her days. While she did not attain the name and fame of her brother Henrik Wergeland and possessed very little, if any, of the former's poetic genius, she exercised a most potent and far-reaching influence in the struggle for the emancipation of her sex. (p. 335)

Only about half her writings may be classed as belonging to the category of *belles lettres*; all the rest is largely polemic and frequently tinged by a strong personal note. She states of her literary work:

> Det savner vistnok, dette mit Forfatterskab, et vir-keligt Forstudium, som en ung Pige i min Tid ikke synderlig tænkte paa, heller ikke hadde nogen Ad-gang til at erhverve sig. Det har maaske ikke engang været mit rette Kald. Som en Frugt af Sorgen og Ensomheden blev det mere til en Hjertes end en Aan-dens, Forstandens Sag. Jeg optegnede saa godt jeg kunde et Livs triste Erfaringer og mine Tanker de-rom, fæstnet og lutret med Samlivet med den skarpest og sundest dømmende Aand, jeg nogensinde har kjendt.

> [It lacks, to be sure, this authorship of mine, all real preparation, of which a young girl in my days did not seriously think, and which she had no opportunity to acquire, either. It (authorship) may not even have been my true calling. As a fruit born of sorrow and loneliness, it turned out to be more an affair of the heart than of the intellect and of the reason. I re-corded, as well as I could, life's sad experiences and what I thought of them, strengthened and enobled by the closest contact with the keenest and wisest mind which I have ever known.]

But whatever the esthetic shortcomings of her literary produc-tions may be, she has created at least one work which entitles her to a place of honor in the history of Norwegian literature: *Amtmandens Døtre* (*The Daughters of the Magistrate*), which may well be regarded as the first novel of importance written in the Norse tongue. *Amtmandens Døtre* is distinguished by superiority of style, careful, realistic portrayal of details, splen-did description of natural scenery and interiors, and an abun-dance of new ideas. The theme is a defense of a woman's love as the only decisive factor in marriage. But it is usually flattered vanity, economic, or, rather, mercenary considerations, and an inherited habit of submissiveness which induces most women to marry a certain man. Men, with whom the actual choice seems to rest, are equally short-sighted. They forget that the only essential to marital happiness is a woman's love, and even if they are aware that it is lacking, they console themselves with the thought that somehow it will blossom forth mysteri-ously after marriage. . . . Though times have greatly changed, and women are now enjoying far greater liberty than three generations ago, the problem dealt with in Mrs. Collett's novel has by no means been solved, and many a precept set forth in *Amtmandens Døtre* is as pertinent today as it was in 1854. The novel has seen at least five editions, which is proof in itself that it still makes an appeal and has a message to convey. Aside from several short stories, Camilla Collett has not written any other fiction, but all her productions with the exception of a few that are purely polemic are of high literary merit. Her style is original and brilliant in all her works.

Those of her writings that appeared in the seventies and eighties deal chiefly with the cause of woman. Her theory is that woman is by no means inferior to man, in fact, she is his superior in all essentials, especially in the realm of emotions and morals. If intellectually she falls below the standard of the male, it is simply due to the fact that her mind has been systematically dwarfed through thousands of years of oppression and subju-gation. At the bottom of it all lies the insane egotism of man. Present day society is tottering along on the edge of a precipice and is sure to perish if not saved by the women of the world. But to accomplish this task, these latter must be accorded full equality with the men; not, perchance, merely equality before the law, grudgingly granted, but one based on mutual respect and confidence, which will lead to sincere cooperation, perfect harmony, and peace the world over. In former days, during the middle ages, nay, even during the first part of the nineteenth century, the influence of women was far greater than at the present, and they were then held in higher esteem by the other sex. Nowadays man not even hates woman any longer, but is totally indifferent to her except as an object of exploitation and a means to gratify his sensuality. It is, however, a hopeful sign that he begins to fear her, for this presupposes respect and consequently the possibility that he some future day may love her once more. The most deplorable fact is that woman has become so degraded by perpetual abuse and enslavement that she is really no longer conscious of the perpetual wrong in-flicted upon her. Her own apathy, ignorance, and servility are the worst obstacles to her emancipation. Out of sheer self-interest and for the sake of self-preservation, society should above all endeavor to alleviate the lot of womankind. (pp. 340-42)

To most readers, Camilla Collett's attitude must necessarily seem one-sided, the great mass of her arguments is, however, well chosen and to the point. But it is not a wholly logical and fair procedure when she attributes Monod's views to a poor Stockholm preacher, whose exposition of the duties of women she rejects, and then proceeds to argue on the fictitious as-sumption that he is in full accord with Monod. Nor are certain examples from the animal world, tending to show that the male of certain species sacrifices himself for the female, particularly in the breeding season, felicitously chosen or convincing. The following, holding up the social organization of the bees as a model for mere man, is outright ludicrous.

> Han mindedes med Beundring en liden Stat, hvori det eneste Femininum, der fandtes, var ophøiet til Eneherskerinde, medens alle Maskulinerne var Ar-beidere! . . . . Hun hadde slet intet andet at gjøre end at tage imod Hyldningen, sole sig og lege nogle tus-end Skokke Egg om Maaneden. . . .

> [He recalled with admiration a little state in which the only female individual to be found was made the absolute ruler, while all the males were work-ers. . . . . She had nothing to do but receive homage, bask herself in the sun, and lay a few hundred thou-sand eggs each month.]

(pp. 343-44)

Like Byron she holds that, at present, at least, love, wifehood, and motherhood are the only realms to which a woman is given access, while man has selfishly reserved to himself all the varied activities of life. Under the circumstances, it is all the more important that every woman should determine the choice of her mate herself, and only in accordance with the dictates of her heart. At present, she is denied this right and must passively abide her fate, unless she prefers the lamentable existence of the spinster. It is the woman who by all means should do the choosing, since her judgment in these matters is far more reliable than that of the mere male. Moreover, just the best men are very apt to make a poor choice.

One of the great wrongs inflicted upon the women of modern times is the twofold moral standard, sanctioned by social convention and even upheld by the laws of various countries. Its evil effects have not been confined to the unfortunate women, but have poisoned the whole race. (p. 344)

But while Mrs. Collett pleads for more restraint on the part of man, for more tolerance toward her own sex, she emphatically rejects all doctrines of free love, not because she is opposed to it in principle, but because she clearly recognizes that mankind in general and men in particular utterly lack that high sense of moral responsibility which alone would make such relations compatible with the interest of women and the safety of the race.

Literature is a mirror of life, Camilla Collett correctly contends; hence a certain knowledge about human existence, social conditions, conventions, prejudices, and so forth, may readily be gained from the study of the literature of a given period. With this end in view, she read and appraised many of the novels of her day. In no case is she concerned in the literary or esthetic value of the work in question; it is only the attitude of the particular author toward women which interests her. She finds that modern novelists almost without exception represent a type of women who rebel and resist, but infallibly are defeated and conquered in the end. This independent minded and individualistic type must, however, not be interpreted as an indication that the women are gaining more influence in life; it was created by the various authors merely to add new spice and zest to the game of pursuit and conquest. The worst offenders, it seems to Mrs. Collett, are the French novelists of last century. (pp. 346-47)

A number of literary men of first magnitude, such as Goethe, Byron, Bulwer Lytton, Dumas *fils,* Flaubert, Cherbuliez, and Spielhagen, are shown off in all their unscrupulous male conceit and egotism. Mrs. Collett's comment on the different works is often very interesting, and there is a good deal to be said for her point of view. Most important in this respect are her discussions of some of the works of Ibsen and Jonas Lie. But as has been said before: the one and only feature which she considers is the attitude of the particular author toward women. The basic question of our present day life is for her "the relations between the sexes and the position in our social order which will finally be accorded to women."

And inseparable from this conviction, as a matter of fact, the logical prerequisite of it, is her firm belief in the superiority of women in all but mere physical strength. Here, Mrs. Collett readily admits that woman is the weaker vessel and, accordingly, demands that due recognition should be taken of the fact by special concessions.

In spite of the greater impartiality and dispassionate judgment which she vindicates to women, she is an extreme partisan. Virtually all her evaluations of persons and institutions are based solely on the relations they have to the so-called emancipation of women. Needless to say that she hailed with enthusiasm every comrade in arms. Aurore Dudevant, née Dupin, (George Sand), Mary-Ann Evans, (George Eliot), Rahel Levin, Stuart Mill, Ernest Legouvé, Frederika Bremer, Josephine But-

ler, and the like, are names inscribed on her roll of honor in letters of gold. Somewhat surprising is her estimate of Heinrich Heine. Him she considers an innocent victim of our perverse social order. . . . (pp. 348-49)

Utterances on other topics than the woman's question are numerous and vary from minute discussions of the customary Christiania meal hours to expectorations upon the pessimism of Schopenhauer and Strindberg. Camilla Collett was a humanitarian, anti-militarist, pacifist, and monarchist. Men like Napoleon and Richelieu were for her but monsters. Her sympathy was always with the weak and the suffering, and her compassion extended to the dumb animals as well. In this connection, her attitude toward vivisection deserves mention. She sees in it nothing but perverted sensuality and cruelty, and actually suggests that the people should take the law into their own hands and forcibly put a stop to this pernicious practice. On the question of the education of children, Mrs. Collett's views far from coincide with those of the majority. While she favors co-education, out of door exercise and sport, constant association of the two sexes during the period of childhood and adolescence, and respect for individuality, she deeply laments the growing disrespect for authority of any kind on the part of the young. (pp. 349-50)

Camilla Collett desired that the status of woman should be changed radically, that male authority should cease, but she, by no means, should have liked to see a general recasting of our present day economic and social conditions and institutions. She was an idealist, individualist, aristocrat, monarchist, and conservative. Politics, she abhorred, and she protested against being identified with any political party.

> Har der noget i min Produktion lignet en *politisk* Bekjendelse, saa bunder det dog paa den samme uryggelige Grundsyn, hvorpaa denne Produktion er bygget: mit "Høire" og "Venstre" heder *Mend* og *Kvinde.*
>
> [If anything in my production resembled a political creed, it rests, nonetheless, on the same immutable basic conception whereupon my production has been erected: my "Right" and "Left" (conservative and liberal) is *man* and *woman.*]

This utterance is the key to her philosophy of life, but it also reveals her limitations, her one-sidedness, and partiality. Like Ibsen, she was both pessimist and optimist; pessimist in her appraisal of the existing conditions, optimist in her steadfast hope for a better future, her firm belief in the possibility of great advance, and in the loftiness of her ideals.

All her life long, she was a loyal adherent of the descendants of Bernadotte on the Swedish throne and a staunch monarchist. Democracy spelled for her dissolution of society; the ambition of the French people at the time of the Revolution to eliminate class distinctions is designated as madness (afsindig). It is true that Camilla Collett possessed deep and genuine sympathy for all who had to suffer and were wronged, that she freely used her material means to alleviate want and misery, but the great mass of her inquiries into certain actual conditions and her remedial suggestions concern the interests of women of the upper class. Thus, for instance, she protested repeatedly against the exclusion of women from certain social or semi-public functions, as the funeral of the Schweigaards. That ninety-nine men out of every hundred, together with their wives and daughters, also were excluded since they happened to be teamsters, dock laborers, coal trimmers, cobblers, and the like, seemed to her as it should and must be. (pp. 350-51)

Within each social group, she demanded, indeed, full equality for women, whether it is the right of succession to the Danish throne or the right of admission to Christiania University, but these groups themselves must not be disturbed. The levelling tendencies of the age seem to her sheer evils. (p. 352)

[Camilla Collett] made no secret of her strong likes and dislikes and always took her own superiority for granted. She possessed, however, not only the courage to stand by her convictions, but she was also bold enough to make public profession of them. In dealing with the various problems of the day, she did not shrink from the repulsive, as, for instance, where she deals with legalized prostitution. False modesty and prudishness, she regarded as two of the most serious faults of her sex. . . .

Camilla Collett continued to write as long as she was able to wield a pen, which means, almost to the very day of her death. Toward the close of her life, she received many tokens of respect and gratitude from her fellow countrymen; but better still, she lived to see considerable progress made in the cause of her sex. If the women of Norway today are as free as any, Camilla Collett's share in their liberation has not been a small one. Her life work is appropriately characterized in the following lines:

> Være Forfatter efter Tidens Behøv er ogsaa at udtale Sandheder, som andre tænker, eller dunkelt tænker, eller slet ikke tænker, udtale dem træffende og overbevisende, oprivende og lægende, og med sin Smule Livslykke og Dagsfred indestaa derfor.

> [To be an author, such as the age requires, consists also in giving utterance to thoughts which others think, or vaguely ponder, or not conceive at all, express them in striking and convincing, rousing and, at the same time, healing manner, and to stake one's mite of happiness and the peace of one's days in this cause.]

(p. 353)

Josef Wiehr, ''Camilla Collett,'' in The Journal of English and Germanic Philology, *Vol. XXIV, No. 3, July, 1925, pp. 335-53.*

THEODORE JORGENSON   (essay date 1933)

[*Jorgenson stresses Collett's passionate feminism as well as the significant influence she exerted on both Norwegian literature and society.*]

Realistic by nature and experience rather than by theory was the leading woman writer of the nineteenth century, Camilla Collett. Her novel *The Governor's Daughters,* published in 1855, was the cry of an indignant soul who felt that the natural rights of womanhood were given little attention in the social and economic order of the time. (p. 296)

Madame Collett writes with a passionate intensity, pours her indignation forth as a representative of womanhood desirous above all other things of becoming functioning and self-determining free human beings. She directs her attack first of all at the social inequality existing between young men and young women. The men seek their life companions; the women must wait, be modest, reticent, and obedient. An actively aggressive and creative girl was in her day thought of as rather intolerable, yet such is precisely the free woman of the authoress' own heart.

In like manner she attacks the conventional marriage. Woman cannot choose her own destiny; the home as well as society is male-determined. Though nature makes it abundantly clear that the task of rearing the coming generation is preëminently woman's, and that in consequence a matriarchate cannot fail to be more satisfying than a home based on patriarchal dominion—especially if the sexes attain economic independence—in spite of these self-evident facts, woman remains in the status of the agricultural economy of the Middle Ages. She is the mother of her husband's children, and in society her standing is determined with reference to whether she is the wife of the pastor, the banker, or the professor so and so. Should the trying experience be hers of losing her husband, she loses forthwith all standing and influence in the social circles of her late master. She is then but a widow with small children to take care of. In the eyes of nature she is distinctly fulfilling her life purpose, but in the eyes of the world she is a nonentity because she is but a woman; she is a widow, a remnant.

In our day the reasoning here indicated is by no means unfamiliar to the enlightened public. The arguments for feminine independence and for a creative functional existence of womanhood are everywhere tacitly admitted; women themselves assume a different attitude now from that of the middle of the nineteenth century. To the generation of the fifties, Camilla Collett's book was shocking to say the least. Its influence on modern Norwegian literature can hardly be overestimated. Björnson, Ibsen, Jonas Lie, the naturalists of the eighties, and the entire development of the last seventy-five years need to be considered in relation to her work and her character. When she died in 1895, the social change which she advocated had, at least in theory, largely been accomplished. (pp. 297-98)

Theodore Jorgenson, ''Realism,'' in his History of Norwegian Literature, *The Macmillan Company, 1933, pp. 289-310.*

HARALD BEYER   (essay date 1952)

[*In this excerpt from a survey of Norwegian literature originally published in Oslo in 1952, Beyer discusses Collett's personality and experiences, linking these to her writing.*]

If we examine what kind of literature Norwegians were reading in the first half of the nineteenth century, we find that just as in our day, novels were the most popular form. The farmers were still reading the old ''folk books,'' late versions of the medieval romances. In the cities the ladies especially were reading foreign novels in frequently poor Danish translations, mostly borrowed at lending libraries. In the early years they were mostly German middle-class novels. Around 1850 they were mostly translations from English—Walter Scott, Bulwer-Lytton, Charles Dickens, Frederick Marryat, and Fenimore Cooper. The most popular French novels were those of Alexandre Dumas, Victor Hugo, and Eugène Sue, while among Germans there were Hackländer and Theodor Mügge. Danish authors like Mme Gyllembourg and Carl Bernhard and Swedish ones like Fredrika Bremer and Emilie Flygare-Carlén were eagerly perused.

But there were few Norwegian novels to choose from, and none of them good. The lyric was the only form of literature that had as yet reached a high cultivation in Norway. Mauritz Hansen's stories were ''read in all cultured homes,'' but his novels were too improbable and unrealistic. Critics of the time often deplored the absence of Norwegian novels which could reflect the social life of the country. The answer to their demands came with Camilla Collett's novel *The Governor's Daughters* (*Amtmandens Døttre*).

Camilla Collett, born Wergeland (1813-1895), belonged to the age group of the national romantics, but her authorship fitted rather into that of Ibsen and Bjørnson. She had many traits of the transitional personality. No one felt more keenly than she the contrast between the dreams and reality. It was the source of her inspiration and the undercurrent in her writing. At bottom she was a romanticist who never became wholly reconciled to reality.

She had many traits in common with her father Nicolai Wergeland, and her brother Henrik, including the melancholia and persecution complex of the former and the vivid emotional life of the latter. She had some of Henrik's imaginative capacity and his love of nature, together with his tendency to see his own experiences in a larger perspective. Just as Henrik identified himself with humanity, so she identified herself with womankind. The fact that melancholy predominated in her character, while optimism predominated in his, may be due to the bitter disappointment in love which she experienced in her youth. To Welhaven the affair with Camilla was a mere episode, but to her it became a fate. The fact that she loved Welhaven during the crucial years of controversy, and had to stand midway between St. Sebastian, as she called him, and her own father and brother, determined her development. Therefore we can read her diaries, letters, and notations from her youth as the great social novel of the 1830's. These documents, which were published at her own request after her death, surpass in dramatic intensity and passionate force anything she herself published.

In 1841 she was married to Peter Jonas Collett, one of the best men in the Intelligentsia, who gave her spirit a short respite and encouraged her to write. She wrote down folk tales she had heard and helped Asbjørnsen with some of the "frame stories" in his *Fairy Tales*, and wrote some sketches and short stories. But not until she became a widow did she complete *The Governor's Daughters* which appeared anonymously in 1854-1855.

This extraordinary book was the first novel of social purpose in Norway. It had a great influence on later Norwegian writing, on Ibsen's *Comedy of Love*, and some of Jonas Lie's stories. It was the first omen of the generation of writers who dominated the 1870's and 1880's, above all the writing of Alexander Kielland. When it appeared, it was not well received by the critics, but it gave to many of its woman readers a feeling of release and liberation, and it was later reprinted time and again.

The position of woman in home and society had been discussed in the novels of other countries from the 1830's on, by George Sand in France and Fredrika Bremer in Sweden. But in Norway it had never been discussed in any major work of literature. Henrik Wergeland had anticipated the theme in one of his sketches from 1833 about "Old Maids"; "I thought that Mina would neither have been sour, lazy, thin, faded, wrinkled, prudish, malicious, hysterical, or finally consumptive and laid in an early grave if this confounded class difference, which is less founded in superior spiritual advantages than people think, had not forbidden her from attaining 'a woman's purpose.'"

In Camilla Collett's case, however, her own experiences were more influential than reading in opening her eyes to woman's need for a different education than the one that prepares her only for a socially desirable marriage. Her mission came to be a struggle on behalf of woman's right to love. Neither the man nor the woman shall choose, but the woman's love alone, to which she attributed mystic qualities. In *The Governor's Daughters* she did not primarily ask for practical reforms; her interests turned in this direction later. Instead she demanded a change of attitude, an understanding of the woman's heart. Into this cause she flung all her glowing passion, writing with bitterness and sympathy and an amazing boldness. She spoke of her novel as a "shriek," and many felt it to be just that.

The Governor's Daughters is not a perfect work of art, but still it is her most important contribution to literature. A more charming book is *In the Long Nights* (*I de lange Nætter*) with vivid pictures from her childhood and youth, above all of her father and brother. The rest of her writing was mostly agitation on behalf of the feminist cause, ironic and polemical, often bitter and aggressive. Camilla Collett felt herself to be persecuted and misunderstood, but on her eightieth birthday she was honored by men and women of all political persuasions. Henrik Ibsen was her escort at the great banquet that was held in her honor.

Her example helped to encourage other women to enter the literary arena, most of them minor though interesting figures. Not until Amalie Skram did one arrive who could equal or surpass the writing of Camilla Collett. (pp. 160-62)

Harald Beyer, "Dreams and Reality," in his A History of Norwegian Literature, *edited and translated by Einar Haugen, New York University Press, 1956, pp. 154-66.*

BRIAN W. DOWNS   (essay date 1966)

[*Downs describes and critiques* Amtmandens døtre, *noting the novel's dearth of imagination but praising it as a pioneering exposition of feminist issues.*]

[The] first Norwegian novel of any stature [is] Camilla Collett's *The Sheriff's Daughters* (*Amtmandens Døttre*), published in 1855—176 years after *The Princess of Cleves* and 114 years after *Pamela*.

Sheriff Ramm, after whose three surviving girls *The Sheriff's Daughters* takes its title, is stationed in a thinly populated district far from the capital. There is scarcely any society, and what there is of it is notably deficient in young men who by any standard could be thought 'eligible', since these anticipate their eligibility by seeking their fortunes—and their wives—elsewhere. The brightest of the daughters, having missed her chance when she was sent to live for two years in Copenhagen, is, like her two elder sisters, thrown back on the family tutor-cum-secretary, this time a young man of intelligence, charm, some means and a face strikingly like that of Lord Byron. Sophie and Georg Cold genuinely fall in love with one another. By an unlucky chance, however, Sophie overhears a conversation between Cold and a visiting friend, intended to throw the latter's prying off the scent, and infers from it that she has been deceived in believing her passion to be returned. Before there is time to clear up the misunderstanding she goes off with her mother to stay with an elderly connexion, a rural dean, a widower with children, and, emotionally quite untouched, accepts his lukewarm proposal of marriage: her elder sister, Amalie, poorly and unhappily married though she is, has advised her that she cannot hope for anything better. Sophie and the rural dean go to the altar together with his entirely colourless curate and the youngest of the girls.

The Sheriff's Daughters is built on a grievance; the authoress called it a 'shriek'. Her point is not so much that girls like the Ramms are badly placed for finding husbands (to which the purpose of their lives is directed) as that their scope for falling in love is restricted, passion being the only true basis for marriage (and, one may refine, passion on the woman's part, almost irrespective of her partner's erotic temperature). This insistence on passion may be romantic at bottom, but, in the presentation it is entirely subdued to the realism of the rest. The middle-class rural *milieu* is firmly though not minutely depicted; the characters, but for Cold, are ordinary—the men mostly clods and the women often shrews—and faithfully exhibited as such. The style is level, correct and flat, heightened neither by grace nor by humour, the construction pedestrian, if adequate; the 'fatal misunderstanding' may just pass, and a dissipation of interest between the three girls is averted.

Fru Collett may have had none of the imaginative power of her contemporaries Emily and Charlotte Brontë, whose novels equally centred on passionate young women in bleak surroundings, but her pioneer work provided a worthy exemplar: twenty years were to elapse before it was rivalled. Its preoccupation with 'the woe of women' set a tone which re-echoed through many a more distinguished work of later date and a host of lesser products. (pp. 13-14)

Brian W. Downs, "Preliminary," *in his* Modern Norwegian Literature: 1860-1918, *Cambridge at the University Press, 1966, pp. 1-16.*

ADDITIONAL BIBLIOGRAPHY

Kielland, Eugenia. "New Books on Norwegian Women." *The American-Scandinavian Review* XXVI, No. 4 (December 1938): 346-51.
> Contains a biographical sketch. Kielland praises Collett's books as "one passionate cry for justice and humane conditions for women."

Skard, Sigmund. "Tense Interlude." In *The Voice of Norway*, by Halvdan Koht and Sigmund Skard, pp. 215-23. Morningside Heights, N.Y.: Columbia University Press, 1944.
> Cites the drama of Collett's personal life and the intensity of her feminist writings as the reasons she was "a general symbol of liberty and a constant reminder of the new responsibilities of literature in the struggle for freedom."

Wildhagen, Fredrik Chr. "Norwegian Memoirs." *The American-Scandinavian Review* XXI, Nos. 6-7 (June-July 1933): 353-56.
> Briefly reviews a collection of Collett's letters, calling the edition "a very important contribution to the intellectual history of Norway."

Johann Wolfgang von Goethe

1749-1832

(Also Göthe; Göethe) German poet, novelist, dramatist, short story and novella writer, essayist, critic, biographer, autobiographer, memoirist, and librettist.

The following entry presents criticism of Goethe's novel *Die Leiden des jungen Werthers* (1774; revised edition, 1787; translated as *The Sorrows of Werter*, 1779; also translated as *The Sufferings of Young Werther*, 1957). For additional criticism on Goethe's career and *Werther*, see *NCLC*, Vol. 4.

Werther was, in its era, one of the most popular and influential works in German literature. An epistolary novel depicting the turbulent emotional life of a young man whose involvement in a love triangle eventually leads to his suicide, *Werther* came to be seen as representative of an entire generation of German youth. The novel immediately created a tremendous sensation, fueling speculation regarding its autobiographical elements, inspiring numerous imitations, and catapulting Goethe to fame throughout Germany and all of Europe. While its popularity diminished greatly in subsequent years, *Werther*'s interest to scholars as autobiography and as a representative work of the Sturm und Drang (Storm and Stress) movement has continued unabated.

Published near the beginning of Goethe's long and prolific literary career, *Werther* was his first novel and is generally considered the final work of his youthful period. During this time, Goethe composed poetry, dramas, and criticism while honoring his father's wishes by studying law, first at the University of Leipzig and later at the University of Strasbourg. At Strasbourg he met the German poet and philosopher Johann Gottfried von Herder, who was the leader of a literary revolt that eventually became known as the Sturm und Drang movement. Writing in a time of transition from the Enlightenment to the Romantic era, Herder and his followers rejected the influence of French classicism and the emphasis on reason common to Enlightenment thinkers, arguing instead for the return to nature, the importance of intuition, and the supremacy of personal emotion. Responding to Herder's ideas, Goethe developed a reverence for William Shakespeare, Jean-Jacques Rousseau, and German folk songs. These influences are evident in his work immediately preceding *Werther*: his lyric poetry of the early 1770s and particularly his drama *Götz von Berlichingen mit der eisernen Hand (Goetz of Berlichingen with the Iron Hand)*. Modeled after Shakespeare's history plays and featuring action and intense emotion, this popular drama of 1773 first brought Goethe to the attention of his contemporaries and is generally viewed as the most important literary production of the Sturm und Drang movement; published one year later, *Werther* also demonstrates the influence of the Sturm und Drang movement.

The characters and events of *Werther* are largely drawn from Goethe's life. While commentators cite numerous sources for the novel, they agree that much of it derives from Goethe's experiences in the town of Wetzlar in the spring and summer of 1772, two years prior to publishing *Werther*. As part of his legal training, he spent four months there at the Reichskammergericht, the Supreme Court of the Holy Roman Empire. In

Wetzlar he met Charlotte Buff, a young woman who managed the household for her widowed father and ten siblings. Although she was engaged to his friend Johann Christian Kestner, a secretary to the Hanover legation at the court, Goethe soon fell in love with her. He left Wetzlar in September 1772. Shortly after, on a visit to his friend, the German novelist Sophie von La Roche, whose daughter, Maximiliane, also captured his heart, he received news that an acquaintance in Wetzlar, Karl Wilhelm Jerusalem, had committed suicide. Jerusalem had long been despondent, probably due in part to his unreturned love for the wife of a friend and to his unsatisfactory position at the court, where he had been shunned by aristocratic society. When Goethe learned that Jerusalem had committed suicide, he requested and received from Kestner a detailed description of the actions leading up to it. While these sources for the novel are widely acknowledged, the circumstances of its composition are less clear. Goethe states in his autobiography, *Aus meinem Leben: Dichtung und Wahrheit (The Autobiography of Goethe: Truth and Poetry from My Own Life)*, written forty years later, that he set to work on the novel immediately after he learned of Jerusalem's death and wrote it in the space of four weeks. Yet this contradicts surrounding passages in the autobiography in which he relates its composition to a later visit he made to Maximiliane and her new husband, Peter Brentano, in early 1774. Many critics now conjecture that Goethe may have devised the plan for the novel in 1772 after learning of Jerusalem's death, but that he did not actually write *Werther* until 1774.

The story of *Werther* is quite simple. The novel, which is broken into two parts, consists of letters from Werther to his friend, Wilhelm, detailing his experiences and his reactions to them. Throughout, Werther displays the unrestrained emotionalism for which the character became famous: believing that his own feelings provide the only meaningful standard of truth and experience of reality, Werther luxuriates in his sensations of passion. In the first part of the novel, believed to be primarily drawn from Goethe's relationships with Charlotte and Kestner, Werther describes his arrival at Wahlheim, his first meeting with Lotte and developing feelings for her, his friendship with Albert, her fiancé, and his eventual departure when he becomes overwhelmed with despair because of his unrequited love for Lotte. In the second part of the novel, which critics agree incorporates information from Jerusalem's life, Werther relates his dissatisfaction in his new position under an ambassador at court, his feelings of humiliation when he suffers a social snub at the home of an aristocratic friend, his later stay at the estate of a prince, and his return to Wahlheim to see Lotte. Near the end, after the editor breaks in to explain that the story has been pieced together from several reports, Werther's final days at Wahlheim are recounted, including his borrowing of a set of pistols from Albert and his subsequent suicide.

Upon completing *Werther*, Goethe sent a copy to his friends in Wetzlar. The novel's blend of fact and fiction worried Kestner, who was concerned that readers would confuse the characters in the novel with him and Charlotte. Goethe, too, seems to have alluded to this problem when he described his poetic intent: "The poet transmutes life into an image. The common crowd desires to lower the image again by turning it into the original material." According to many commentators, Kestner's letter to the author anticipating this reaction by the "common crowd" probably contributed to Goethe's decision to revise *Werther*. In the second version, published in 1787, Goethe made several changes: he modified Albert's portrait to make him a more appealing character; he altered Lotte's portrait to eliminate any impression of ambiguity in her feelings for Werther; he toned down some of the exuberant language characteristic of the Sturm und Drang movement and standardized spelling and grammar, so that the result is in keeping with his development toward a neoclassical style; he diminished the effect of the snub that Werther receives, which had prompted questions about his motives for suicide; he introduced the story of the peasant lad who falls in love with the woman he works for and then kills his rival, which contrasts with Werther's experiences; and he expanded and moved some of the editor's passages, thereby strengthening the narrator's role. While both versions of *Werther* have sparked interest in the novel's use of historical events and individuals, critics have consistently stressed Goethe's artistry in transforming reality into imaginative fiction.

When *Werther* was published in 1774, the effect was immediate, widespread, and profound. The novel quickly became controversial, and extreme reactions characterized much of the contemporary response. Many youthful fans hailed it as an accurate portrait of the feelings of an entire generation, agreeing with Thomas Carlyle that it expressed "the nameless unrest and longing discontent that was then agitating every bosom"; in fact, several suicides were attributed to its influence. Other readers condemned the work as an immoral apology for suicide, and authorities in some areas banned it to protect the public. Interest in the novel was fueled by readers' tendencies to treat it as a roman à clef describing the author's own experiences, and many avidly sought out information about the individuals and events on which it was based. Werther and Lotte quickly passed into popular culture, as they were depicted on fans, jewelry, gloves, porcelain, and other household objects. Although Goethe had been known in Germany since the publication of *Goetz of Berlichingen*, his first novel made him famous—throughout the rest of his life he was viewed as "the author of *Werther*"—and initiated his international reputation. Promptly translated into several languages and widely imitated, parodied, and challenged throughout Europe, *Werther* became the first modern German work to achieve recognition outside Germany.

The critical reception of *Werther* in the nineteenth and twentieth centuries parallels that of Goethe's works as a whole. While the novel quickly became a part of Germany's literary heritage, *Werther*'s popularity soon diminished in England and the United States. The little commentary on the novel that appeared in the nineteenth century was dominated by historical studies, often focusing on its sources. One notable piece during this period is the respected study of Goethe by George Henry Lewes. Critical appreciation of Goethe has increased dramatically in the twentieth century. While most agree that *Werther* is not Goethe's greatest work, the novel has enjoyed a resurgence of interest on the part of modern scholars. Some continue to follow a historical approach, investigating the similarities between the work and its original sources, especially the degree to which Werther is patterned after the author, and examining his account of the novel's composition in his autobiography. Several critics see the novel primarily as a portrait of society and an expression of the Weltschmerz that gripped the era. Yet others consider the novel first and foremost a portrait of an individual: these critics focus directly on Werther's character and personality, his outpouring of personal feelings, and his psychological makeup, often delving into the motivations for and significance of his suicide. The influence of other literary works on *Werther* is also explored, including its relation to earlier epistolary novels, to the sentimental traditions in English and German literature, and to the Sturm und Drang movement. In recent years, the novel's literary qualities have received closer analysis, as scholars have evaluated its style, structure, form, and narration, especially examining the role of the editor in the first and second versions. Although the novel may never regain the broad popularity it initially enjoyed, the diversity of interpretations that *Werther* continues to inspire, more than two centuries after it was published, testifies to its enduring appeal.

JOHANN CHRISTIAN KESTNER (letter date 1774)

[*Goethe sent a copy of* Werther *to Kestner and Charlotte shortly after he completed it in 1774; Kestner soon responded with this letter, in which he criticizes the novel's characterization as at once untrue yet too revealing of actual people. Critics agree that Goethe took these remarks to heart, incorporating some of Kestner's suggestions into the revised text of 1787. For Goethe's response to Kestner's concerns and for additional criticism by Kestner, see excerpts below dated 1774.*]

Your **Werther** might have given me great pleasure, since it could have reminded me of many interesting scenes and incidents. But as it is, it has in certain respects given me little edification. You know I like to speak my mind.

It is true, you have woven something new into each person, or have fused several persons into one. So far good. But if in this interweaving and fusing you had taken counsel of your heart, you would not have so prostituted the real persons whose features you borrow. You wished to draw from nature, that your picture might be truthful; and yet you have combined so much that is contradictory, that you have missed the very mark at which you aimed. The distinguished author will revolt against this judgment, but I appeal to reality and truth itself when I pronounce that the artist has failed. The real Lotte would, in many instances, be grieved if she were like the Lotte you have there painted. I know well that it is said to be a character compounded of two, but the Mrs. H. whom you have partly inwoven was also incapable of what you attribute to your heroine. But this expenditure of fiction was not at all necessary to your end, to nature and truth, for it was without any such behaviour on the part of a woman—a behaviour which must ever be dishonourable even to a more than ordinary woman— that Jerusalem shot himself.

The real Lotte, whose friend you nevertheless wish to be, is in your picture, which contains too much of her not to suggest her strongly: is, I say—but no, I will not say it, it pains me already too much only to think it. And Lotte's husband—you called him your friend, and God knows that he was so—is with her.

The miserable creature of an Albert! In spite of its being an alleged fancy picture and not a portrait, it also has such traits of an original (only external traits, it is true, thank God, only external), that it is easy to guess the real person. And if you wanted to have him act so, need you have made him such a blockhead? that forthwith you might step forward and say, See what a fine fellow I am! (pp. 156-57)

> *Johann Christian Kestner, in an extract from a letter to Johann Wolfgang von Goethe in 1774, in* The Life of Goethe *by George Henry Lewes, second edition, 1864. Reprint by Frederick Ungar Publishing Co., 1965, pp. 156-57.*

JOHANN WOLFGANG VON GOETHE   (letter date 1774)

[*Here, Goethe responds to Kestner's remarks on the novel (see excerpt above dated 1774). For additional comments by Goethe, see excerpts dated 1814 and 1824.*]

Here I have thy letter, Kestner! On a strange desk, in a painter's studio, for yesterday I began to paint in oil, I have thy letter, and must give thee my thanks! Thanks, dear friend! Thou art ever the same good soul! O that I could spring on thy neck, throw myself at Lotte's feet, one, one minute, and all, all that should be done away with, explained, which I could not make clear with quires of paper! O ye unbelieving ones! I could exclaim. Ye of little faith! Could you feel the thousandth part of what **Werther** is to a thousand hearts, you would not reckon the sacrifice you have made towards it! Here is a letter, read it, and send me word quickly what thou thinkest of it, what impression it makes on thee. Thou sendest me Hennings' letter; he does not condemn me; he excuses me. Dear brother Kestner! if you will wait, you shall be contented. I would not, to save my own life, call back **Werther,** and believe me, believe in

me, thy anxieties, thy *gravamina* will vanish like phantoms of the night if thou hast patience; and then, between this and a year, I promise you in the most affectionate, peculiar, fervent manner, to disperse, as if it were a mere north-wind fog and mist, whatever may remain of suspicion, misinterpretation, etc., in the gossiping public, though it is a herd of swine. **Werther** must—must be! You do not feel *him,* you only feel *me* and *yourselves;* and that which you call *stuck on,* and in spite of you, and others, is *interwoven.* If I live, it is thee I have to thank for it; thus thou art not Albert. And thus—

Give Lotte a warm greeting for me, and say to her: "To know that your name is uttered by a thousand hallowed lips with reverence, is surely an equivalent for anxieties which would scarcely, apart from anything else, vex a person long in common life, where one is at the mercy of every tattler".

If you are generous and do not worry me, I will send you letters, cries, sighs after **Werther,** and if you have faith, believe that all will be well, and gossip is nothing, and weigh well your philosopher's letter, which I have kissed.

O then!—hast not felt how the man embraces thee, consoles thee, and in thy—in Lotte's worth, finds consolation enough under the wretchedness which has terrified you even in the fiction? Lotte, farewell,—Kestner, love me, and do not worry me. (pp. 158-59)

> *Johann Wolfgang von Goethe, in an extract from a letter to Johann Christian Kestner on November 21, 1774, in* The Life of Goethe *by George Henry Lewes, second edition, 1864. Reprint by Frederick Ungar Publishing Co., 1965, pp. 158-59.*

JOHANN CHRISTIAN KESTNER   (letter date 1774)

[*In this extract from a letter to a friend, Kestner outlines to what extent the characters in the novel were drawn from real life. For additional criticism by Kestner, see excerpt above dated 1774.*]

In the first part of **Werther,** Werther is Goethe himself. In Lotte and Albert he has borrowed traits from us, my wife and myself. Many of the scenes are quite true, and yet partly altered; others are, at least in our history, unreal. For the sake of the second part, and in order to prepare for the death of Werther, he has introduced various things into the first part which do not at all belong to us. For example, Lotte has never either with Goethe or with any one else stood in the intimate relation which is there described; in this we have certainly great reason to be offended with him, for several accessory circumstances are too true and too well known for people not to point to us. He regrets it now, but of what use is that to us? It is true he has a great regard for my wife; but he ought to have depicted her more faithfully in this point, that she was too wise and delicate ever to let him go so far as is represented in the first part. She behaved to him in such a way as to make her far dearer to me than before, if this had been possible. Moreover, our engagement was never made public, though not, it is true, kept a secret: still she was too bashful ever to confess it to any one. And there was no engagement between us but that of hearts. It was not till shortly before my departure (when Goethe had already been a year away from Wetzlar at Frankfurt, and the disguised Werther had been dead half a year) that we were married. After the lapse of a year, since our residence here, we have become father and mother. The dear boy lives still, and gives us, thank God, much joy. For the rest, there is in Werther much of Goethe's character and manner of thinking.

Lotte's portrait is completely that of my wife. Albert might have been made a little more ardent. The second part of **Werther** has nothing whatever to do with us. . . . When Goethe had printed his book, he sent us an early copy, and thought we should fall into raptures with what he had done. But we at once saw what would be the effect and your letter confirms our fears. I wrote very angrily to him [see excerpt above]. He then for the first time saw what he had done; but the book was printed, and he hoped our fears were idle. (pp. 159-60)

> *Johann Christian Kestner, in an extract from a letter to Hennings in 1774, in* The Life of Goethe *by George Henry Lewes, second edition, 1864. Reprint by Frederick Ungar Publishing Co., 1965, pp. 159-60.*

CHARLOTTE SMITH   (poem date 1789)

[*The following poem, written by an extremely popular English sentimental novelist, is only one example of the many creative tributes* Werther *inspired from artists throughout Europe. The sonnet, written from the viewpoint of Werther, conveys the depth of his love for Lotte.*]

> Go! cruel tyrant of the human breast!
>   To other hearts, thy burning arrows bear;
> Go, where fond hope, and fair illusion rest!
>   Ah! why should love inhabit with despair!
> Like the poor maniac I linger here,
>   Still haunt the scene, where all my treasure lies;
> Still seek for flowers, where only thorns appear,
>   'And drink delicious poison from her eyes!'
> Towards the deep gulph that opens on my sight
>   I hurry forward, passion's helpless slave!
> And scorning reason's mild and sober light,
>   Pursue the path that leads me to the grave!
> So round the flame the giddy insect flies,
> And courts the fatal fire, by which it dies!

> *Charlotte Smith, "Sonnet XXI," in her* Elegiac Sonnets, *Vol. 1, fifth edition, T. Cadell, 1789, p. 21.*

THE WEEKLY MAGAZINE   (essay date 1798)

[*This brief anonymous review, which castigates* Werther *as immoral, is representative of much of the contemporary response to the novel.*]

Books enter so immediately into our concerns, present and future, that they can never be too much valued, or too carefully chosen. The recreations and studies of youth greatly influence their morals through life. The prevailing passion for novels particularly merits regard. There are some books of this kind which no parent should suffer to enter the hands of her child; which no bookseller should sell. Among these I shall only mention the **Sorrows of Werter,** a book which has proved the bane of more than one family.

There are, however, numerous novels which tend rather to enlarge the heart and to produce only the most generous emotions. It has been questioned by moralists whether Richardson should ever have drawn his character of Lovelace, because it exhibits a monster of depravity. Much may be urged against the delineation of such characters; but, so long as they exist, it appears to be no more than proper to display their deformity in order to guard youth against them. The character of Lovelace is not dressed up in alluring colours like that of Werter; nature is displayed where it is depraved, in lines so strong as to excite abhorrence; Werter, on the contrary, is drawn with a richness, that, however pitiable the real character might be, the danger

of a mistaken passion or an immoral indulgence of amorous affection, is too great to be safely or prudently entrusted to the consideration of minds not strongly formed. (p. 331)

> *"The Ubiquitarian—No. IX," in* The Weekly Magazine, *Vol. I, No. 11, April 14, 1798, pp. 331-32.*

JOHANN WOLFGANG von GOETHE   (essay date 1814)

[*The following excerpt is taken from Goethe's autobiography, in which he describes the circumstances that inspired* Werther. *In the first section of the excerpt, he chronicles his relations with the real-life models for the principal characters in* Werther. *In the second section, Goethe explains how he arrived at his decision to employ the epistolary form, recalls the world-weariness that affected his contemporaries and prompted his own thoughts of suicide, and describes his relationship with Maximiliane von La Roche, the wife of Peter Brentano. Finally, he relates his response to critical reaction to the novel. Since the publication of this portion of the autobiography in 1814, many critics have questioned Goethe's recollection of the timing of the novel's composition. For additional commentary by Goethe, see excerpts dated 1774 and 1824.*]

[My] resolution to let my inner nature follow its own course and to let outer nature influence me in its own capacity brought me to the strange circumstances under which **Werther** was conceived and written. I was trying to free myself inwardly of everything alien, to observe external things lovingly, and to let all beings, from the human down to those barely perceptible, have their effect on me, each in its own way. Thus there arose a marvelous feeling of kinship with individual objects in nature, and a heartfelt accord or harmony with the whole, so that every alternation affected me deeply, whether it was of places or regions, or of times of day and seasons, or of whatever else might occur. The artist's gaze joined the poet's, while the beautiful rural landscape, brightened by its friendly river, inclined me even more to solitude and fostered my quiet but wide-ranging contemplations.

But ever since I had left that family circle in Sesenheim, and then my circle of friends in Frankfurt and Darmstadt, there had been an emptiness in my bosom that I could not fill. Consequently I found myself in a state where, in order to take us unawares and bring all good resolutions to naught, an affection only needs to approach in a light disguise.

And since the writer has now arrived at this stage of his undertaking, this book will become what it is really supposed to be. It was not declared to be an independent entity, but was meant to fill the gaps in an author's life, to complete many fragments, and to preserve the memory of bold enterprises now lost and forgotten. What is already done, however, cannot, and should not, be repeated. Also, it would now be in vain for the poet to try to summon up his dimmed mental powers, useless for him to ask them to revive the sweet attachment that so greatly enriched his sojourn in the Lahn valley. Fortunately, his guiding genius provided for that earlier by prompting him, in his capable youth, to capture and describe the recent past, and to be bold enough to set it before the public at a favorable moment. It probably needs no further explanation that I am referring here to the little book **Werther.** However, I shall by and by reveal a few things about the persons depicted in it, and about the sentiments portrayed.

Among the young men attached to the legation for advance training in their future careers was one whom we usually called simply "the Fiancé" [Johann Christian Kestner]. He was distinguished by his calm evenness of manner, the clarity of his views, and the precision of his actions and statements. His cheerful willingness, his unremitting diligence recommended him so highly to his superiors that they promised soon to find him a position. On the strength of this he ventured to become engaged to a young woman [Charlotte Buff] who in every respect suited his disposition and desires. After her mother's death she had proved very efficient in managing a large family of younger children, and all alone had sustained her father in his widowerhood. Therefore her future husband could hope that she would do the same for him and his progeny, and could anticipate assured domestic happiness. Everyone, even with no such personal goals in mind, declared her to be a desirable young woman. She was of the type that is created to arouse general approval rather than inspire violent passions. A slightly built, nicely shaped figure; a pure, healthy nature and the happy, busy interest in life which goes with it; unpretentious performance of daily duties—all of these were hers. It always warmed my heart to observe such qualities, and I was happy to associate with those who possessed them. And if I did not always have occasion to render them genuine service, I would share with them, rather than with others, the enjoyment of those innocent pleasures which are always at youth's disposal and can be had without great effort and expense. Furthermore, since it is well known that women dress only for each other and never tire of adding to their finery among themselves, I much preferred girls like her, whose simple cleanliness was a tacit assurance to their male friend, their fiancé, that they really dressed only for him, and that their whole life could continue like this without great ceremony and expense.

Such persons are not overconcerned with themselves. They have time to observe the world around them and enough composure to adapt and conform to it. Without great effort, they become wise and understanding, and need few books for their cultural development. Thus the fiancée. Her betrothed, being of a thoroughly upright and trusting disposition, soon introduced her to everyone he esteemed. Because he spent the greatest part of the day zealously attending to business, he was glad to see his intended, after household duties were done, amuse herself otherwise and enjoy sociable strolls and country picnics with male and female friends. Lotte—for obviously that is her name!—was unassuming in a double sense: first, she was inclined by nature more to general kindliness than to particular affections, and then, after all, she had decided on a man worthy of herself, who evidently had declared himself ready to join his destiny to hers for life. The atmosphere around her was most cheerful. Indeed, pleasant as it is to see parents lavishing constant care on their children, there is something still more beautiful about siblings doing the same for siblings. In the former case we believe we are mainly seeing natural instinct and civil custom, in the latter, free choice of the heart.

The new arrival, quite free of any ties, felt unconcerned in the presence of a girl who, since she was already spoken for, would not interpret his most agreeable services as wooing, and thus could take the more delight in them. He calmly let matters proceed, but was soon so entangled and enchained, yet also treated so trustingly and amicably by the young couple, that he no longer recognized himself. Idle and dreamy because the present did not satisfy him, he found what he was lacking in this female friend who, by living for the whole year, seemed to live just for the present moment. She was glad to have him as a companion, and soon he could not do without being near her, for she was his link to the everyday world, and so they were soon inseparable companions on the fields and meadows,

in the vegetable and flower gardens of this extensive household. The fiancé, for his part, was also present, if his duties permitted. All three had grown accustomed to each other without meaning to, and did not know how it had come about that they were indispensable to each other. So, right through the splendid summer, they lived a genuine German idyll, for which the fertile land provided the prose, and pure affection the poetry. Wandering through fields of ripe grain, they took refreshment from the dewy morning; the song of the lark, the call of the quail were pleasant sounds; hours filled with heat followed; tremendous thunderstorms came up, but we just huddled together, and many a little family irritation was easily soothed with unfailing love. And so one ordinary day followed another, and all seemed to be festival days: the whole calendar should have been printed in red. I will be understood by anyone who remembers what was predicted for the happy-unhappy lover of the new Héloise: "And, sitting at the feet of his beloved, he will card hemp, and he will wish to continue carding hemp, today, tomorrow, and the next day, indeed for his whole life."

Only a little, but perhaps as much as necessary, can now be said about a young man whose name has subsequently been mentioned only too often. It was Jerusalem, the son of the liberal and sensitive theologian. He too was attached to a legation. An agreeable figure of middle height, well built, with a face more round than oval, he had soft, calm features and everything else that goes to make up a handsome blond youth, also blue eyes that could be called interesting rather than expressive. His clothing was of the kind customary among the Low Germans, imitated from the English: a blue tailcoat, buff-colored vest and breeches, and boots with brown tops. The author never visited or received him, although he met him occasionally at friends' places. The young man's statements were unremarkable, but amiable. He took part in the most varied creative endeavors, but especially liked drawings and sketches that caught the quiet character of lonely areas. On these occasions he would pass around etchings by Gessner and encourage us amateurs to take these as our model. He entered seldom or not at all into [our] nonsensical chivalric masquerade, but instead lived to himself and with his own ideas. There was talk about his pronounced passion for the wife of a friend, although they were never seen together in public. In general there was not much to be said about him except that he studied English literature. As the son of a prosperous man he neither had to devote himself anxiously to his work nor urgently seek immediate placement in a position. (pp. 399-402)

．．．．．

[While *Götz von Berlichingen*] was being conceived, written, rewritten, printed, and distributed many other images and ideas were stirring in [the author's] mind. Those meant for dramatic treatment had the advantage of being thought through most often and nearly completed, but simultaneously a transition developed to a different kind of presentation, which is not ordinarily considered dramatic and yet has a great relationship to drama. This transition was brought about mainly by the author's peculiar habit of recasting even soliloquy as dialogue.

Being accustomed to spend his time preferably in company, he transformed even solitary thinking into social conversation, and in the following way: namely, when he found himself alone, he would summon up in spirit some person of his acquaintance. He would ask this person to be seated, pace up and down by him, stand in front of him, and discuss whatever subject he had in mind. The person would occasionally answer him and indicate, with the customary gestures, his agreement or disagreement; and everyone has a particular way of doing this. Then the speaker would continue, and expand on whatever seemed to please his guest; or he would qualify what the latter disapproved of, and define it more clearly, and even finally be willing to abandon his thesis. The most curious aspect of this was that he never chose persons of his closer acquaintanceship, but those he saw only rarely, nay, often some who lived in far-off places and with whom he had merely a passing relationship. But usually they were persons more receptive than communicative in nature, open-minded and prepared to be calmly interested in matters within their ken, although sometimes he would also summon contentious spirits to these dialectical exercises. Persons of both sexes, and of every age and condition, submitted to this and proved agreeable and charming, because the conversation was only about subjects they liked and understood. Yet many of them would have been greatly amazed, had they been able to find out how often they were summoned to these imaginary conversations, since they would hardly have come to a real one.

It is quite clear that such thought-conversations are closely related to correspondence, except that the latter responds to an established familiarity, while the former creates a new, ever-changing familiarity for itself, with no reply. Thus, when the author had to depict that ennui with life felt by some people who are not beset by any real trouble, it immediately occurred to him to portray his sentiments in letters. For every distemper is generated and nurtured by solitude. Whoever yields to it, flees all counteraction, and what counteracts it more than any sort of cheerful company? Other people's enjoyment of life is a painful reproach to him, and so the very thing that ought to draw him out actually turns him back upon his innermost self. If he cares to discuss this at all, it will be through letters, for no one, after all, can immediately oppose a written effusion, be it joyous or ill-humored. An answer composed of counter-arguments, however, gives the recluse an opportunity to become more entrenched in his melancholy thoughts and reason to become still more obdurate. The letters of Werther written in this spirit probably owe their manifold appeal to the fact that their various contents were first rehearsed in imaginary dialogues with several individuals, whereas in the composition itself they seem to be directed to only *one* friend and sympathizer. It is perhaps not altogether advisable to say more about the writing of this much-discussed little work; something about its contents, however, can be added.

The aforementioned disgust with life has both its physical and moral causes. Let investigation of the former be left to physicians, of the latter, to moral philosophers; and we shall pay heed only to the main point in this so frequently treated material, the point where that phenomenon stands out most clearly. All our pleasure in life depends on the regular recurrence of external things. The alternation of day and night, of seasons, of blossoms and fruits, and of everything else each epoch brings—these are the real foundation of life on earth. The more receptive we are to such pleasures, the happier we feel. If, however, these various phenomena surge and fall before us and we take no interest in them, if we are insensitive to these lovely offerings, then the greatest of evils sets in, the gravest illness, which is to view life as a repugnant burden. It is told of an Englishman that he hanged himself so as not to be forced to dress and undress every day. I knew an honest gardener, the overseer of a large park, who once cried out in annoyance: "Must I then constantly watch these rainclouds move from west to east?" It is said of one of our most excellent men that he was vexed with seeing the spring grow verdant again and

wished it might look red for a change. These are truly symptoms of life-weariness, which not infrequently results in suicide and was more prevalent among philosophical, introverted people than one might believe.

But there is no more effective cause of this weariness than the recurrence of love. It is correctly said that the first love is the only one, for the supreme sense of love gets lost in the second and because of the second. The concept of eternity and affinity that really exalts and sustains love is destroyed, so that it seems as transitory as everything else that recurs. The separation of the physical from the moral part of it, which in the complex cultivated world divides the feelings of love from those of desire, also produces an exaggeration here that cannot bring good results.

Furthermore a young man will soon perceive, perhaps not in himself but at least in others, that moral epochs alternate just like seasons. The grace extended by the great, the favor shown by the powerful, the advancement offered by persons in active life, the affection of the crowd, and the love of individuals, all of these fluctuate, and we cannot hold fast to them any more than to the sun, moon, and stars. And yet these things are not mere natural phenomena. It is by our own fault or that of others, or through chance or destiny, that they escape us; but they do alternate, and we are never in secure possession of them.

However, what gives a sensitive youth the greatest concern is the inevitable recurrence of our errors. How late we come to the realization that while we are developing our virtues we are simultaneously cultivating our faults! The former rest upon the latter as though on roots, which branch out in secret as vigorously and diversely as our virtues do in the light of day. Because we usually exercise our virtues with conscious will, whereas our faults take us unawares, the former seldom give us any joy, and the latter always distress and torment us. This is the hardest part about acquiring knowledge of oneself, and what makes it almost impossible. Add the seething blood of youth and an imagination easily paralyzed by individual things; add also the shifting currents of the time, and it will not be found unnatural if someone strives impatiently to be freed of such a dilemma.

Yet these gloomy thoughts, which, if one yields to them, can lead to infinity, could not have found such marked development in the minds of German youth if the latter had not been stimulated and assisted in this sad business by external suggestion. English literature was responsible, especially the poetry, whose great merits are coupled with a grave melancholy that infects everyone who studies it. The talented Briton sees himself surrounded from youth onwards by a world full of significance, which stimulates all his energies. Sooner or later he perceives that he has to muster all his wits to come to terms with it. How many of their poets have not led lusty and dissolute lives in their youth and soon found themselves justified in accusing earthly things of vanity! How many of them have tried their mettle in world affairs, where they have played either major or minor roles in parliament, at court, in the ministry, in ambassadorial posts, taking an active part at times of internal unrest and changes of regime and government, only to undergo more sad experiences than happy ones, if not personally, at any rate with respect to their friends and patrons! How many of them have not been banished, exiled, imprisoned, and deprived of their estates!

But even just to be a spectator at such great events demands gravity of a person, and to what can gravity lead except meditation on the transitoriness and vanity of all earthly things? Since Germans are also grave, English poetry suited them very well and seemed imposing because it issued from superior circumstances. Great, sound, worldly-wise understanding was to be found in it everywhere, a profound, tender heart, the best of intentions, and passionate endeavor, the most splendid qualities for which an intelligent, cultured person can be praised—but all of these together still do not make a poet. True poetry makes itself known by the fact that it, as a secular gospel, can free us from our oppressive earthly burdens with its inner serenity and external delights. Like an air balloon it lifts us, with our ballast attached, into higher regions and lets the tangled maze of earth lie unrolled before us in bird's eye perspective. The sprightliest and the gravest works have an identical purpose, which is to moderate pleasure and pain by means of a felicitous, ingenious presentation. Now let the majority of English, mostly moral-didactic poems be viewed in this light, and as a rule they will show nothing more than a gloomy weariness with life. (pp. 424-27)

I have no doubt that in contrast to this I could be shown sprightly works and cheerful poems; but certainly the majority and the best of these go back to an older period, while the modern ones that might be included tend toward satire, are bitter, and are especially scornful of women.

Suffice it to say that those serious poems . . . , the ones that were debilitating to human nature, were our favorite selections and we preferred them to all others. Depending on our dispositions, some of us turned to the lighter, elegiac kind of grief, others to the heavy burden of total despair. Oddly enough, it was our father and mentor Shakespeare, otherwise the dispenser of such pure cheerfulness, who himself fueled this distemper. Hamlet and his soliloquies were spectres that continued to haunt all youthful minds. Everyone knew the main passages by heart and gladly recited them, and everyone thought he had a right to be as melancholy as the prince of Denmark, though he had seen no ghost and had no royal father to avenge.

In order, as it were, to supply this pervading gloom with a thoroughly suitable locale, Ossian lured us off to Ultima Thule, where we roamed about on the infinite gray heath amidst protruding mossy gravestones, looking around us at the grass blown by a chill wind, and above us at the heavily clouded sky. Only by moonlight did this Caledonian night really become day: perished heroes and vanished maidens hovered about us, and we actually began to believe that we had seen the ghost of Loda in its fearsome form.

It was in this element and environment and while given to this sort of favorite pursuit and study that we, who were tormented by unfulfilled desires and bereft of any external stimulus to significant actions, who had no other prospects than that of being stuck in a tedious, spiritless civil routine, embraced the thought, in something like an exhilaration of depression, that we could abandon life at will, if it no longer pleased us; and thus we had at least a scanty defense against the injustice and boredom of those days. These sentiments were universal enough to give *Werther* its great effectiveness, for the book went to the heart of the matter and gave an open, comprehensible portrayal of the innermost workings of a morbid youthful folly. How very familiar the English were with this misery is proved by the following notable lines written before the appearance of *Werther:*

> To griefs congenial prone,
> More wounds than nature gave he knew,
> While misery's form his fancy drew
> In dark ideal hues and horrors not its own.

Suicide is a phenomenon of human nature that demands everyone's attention and needs reassessment in every epoch, however much it may already have been discussed and treated. Montesquieu grants his heroes and great men the right to take their lives at will, saying that everyone must be at liberty to conclude the fifth act of his tragedy as he pleases. However, my subject here is not those who have led a significant, active life, who have dedicated their days to some great realm or to the cause of freedom. When the idea that inspired such persons has vanished from the earth, we do not begrudge them the wish to pursue it in the other world. Here we are concerned with those who actually become disgusted with life because they have placed exaggerated demands on themselves, whereas, in the most peaceful situation imaginable, there is a dearth of deeds. Since I was in that state myself and know best what pain I suffered, what exertions it cost me to escape that pain, I shall not conceal that I deliberately meditated on the various kinds of death that can be chosen.

It is such an unnatural thing for a person to sever connections with himself, and not only injure but annihilate himself, that he will often seize on a mechanical means of putting his resolve into effect. When Ajax falls on his sword, it is the weight of his body that does him this last service. When a warrior charges his shield bearer not to let him fall into enemy hands, this is again making sure of an external force, although a moral rather than a physical one. Women seek to cool their despair in water, and the least strenuous way of assuring the swiftness of the deed is the gun, which is a very mechanical means. One only reluctantly mentions hanging, because it is an ignoble death. It is most apt to be encountered in England, where, from childhood on, one sees many a person hanged, and the punishment is not exactly a dishonor. Poison and the cutting of veins are for those who plan a slow exit from life, and the very fastidious, quick, and painless death from an adder's bite was fitting for a queen who had spent her life in splendor and pleasure. But all of these are external devices; they are enemies with which a person concludes a pact against himself.

In my consideration of all these methods and my further examination of history, I found no one who had performed the deed with as much grandeur and freedom of spirit as Emperor Otho. He saw himself at a disadvantage, but by no means in extremity, as a general; yet he decided, in the best interests of the empire that in a certain sense was already his, and to spare many thousands of lives, to depart this world. He cheerfully enjoyed a supper with his friends, and the next morning they found he had plunged a sharp dagger into his heart with his own hand. This was the only deed I considered worthy of imitation, and I convinced myself that if anyone could not act like Otho in this regard he should not be permitted to take voluntary leave of this world. This conviction not only saved me from the intention of suicide but from the melancholy thought of it which had taken hold of idle youth in these splendidly peaceful times. Among other items in my considerable collection of weapons was a valuable, well-honed dagger. I always laid this next to my bed, and before extinguishing the light I would try to bring myself to sink its sharp tip a few inches deep into my chest. Since I never could do it, I finally laughed at myself, cast away all hypochondriacal whimsies, and resolved to live. But to do this cheerfully, I had to complete a literary assignment that would express everything I had felt, thought, and fancied about this important point. The elements of it had been wandering around within me for a few years, and now I collected them, concentrating my mind on those instances which had most oppressed and worried me. But nothing would take shape for me: I lacked an event, a plot, in which to incorporate these things.

All at once I heard the news of Jerusalem's death, and on the very heels of the general rumor there followed the most exact and detailed description of the occurrence. At this moment I found the plan for **Werther.** From all sides the whole thing crystallized into a solid mass, just as water in a bucket, when at the freezing point, can be immediately changed to firm ice by the slightest shock. It was particularly opportune for me to have this singular prize within my grasp, to concentrate on a work of such significant and varied content and finish all its parts, since I had again gotten into an embarrassing situation, with even fewer good prospects than the others, and presaging nothing but depression, if not vexation.

It is always disastrous to enter into new circumstances that are foreign to one's tradition. We are often lured into a false interest, and although the incompleteness of such situations is distressing, we see no means either of making them whole or renouncing them.

Mrs. von La Roche had sent her elder daughter off to married life in Frankfurt and often came to visit her, but was unable to adjust to a situation she herself had chosen. Instead of feeling comfortable in it or bringing about some change, she indulged in so many lamentations that one would really have thought her daughter was unhappy. Yet it was unclear what the source of this unhappiness was, since the young woman lacked for nothing and her husband refused her nothing. Meanwhile I was being well received in the house and associated with the whole circle, which consisted of persons who had either promoted the marriage or were wishing it the best success. . . . Suddenly I saw myself at home in a foreign circle and was prompted, indeed urged, to participate in their activities, pleasures, even their religious exercises. My earlier relationship to the young wife, actually a fraternal one, was continued after her marriage. We were compatible because of our age, and I was the only one in the whole circle from whom she heard an echo of those intellectual tones to which she had been accustomed from childhood onwards. We went on living side by side in childlike trust and, while there was no admixture of passion in our association, it was quite tormenting, because she also was uncomfortable in her new situation. Though blessed with material goods, she had been transported from cheerful Thal-Ehrenbreitstein and her happy youth into a gloomily situated commercial house, where she was already expected to act as mother to several stepchildren. I was hemmed in by all these new family circumstances without having any real share in them or any contribution to make. If there was mutual peace, that seemed to be taken for granted; but in instances of annoyance most of the participants turned to me, and my lively sympathy usually made things worse rather than better. Before long, the situation grew quite intolerable for me. All the ennui that such false relationships generally produce seemed to weigh on me doubly and triply, and a mighty new resolve was required if I was to be liberated from this.

Jerusalem's death, which was caused by his unfortunate love for a friend's wife, shook me out of my dream. I did not take a merely objective view of his experiences and mine; on the contrary, their similarity with what was happening to me at this moment put me into a state of emotional excitement. Thus the production just undertaken by me was inevitably filled with an incandescence permitting no distinction between poetry and reality. Outwardly I totally isolated myself, refusing my friends' visits, and inwardly, too, I set aside everything that did not

directly pertain to my work. On the other hand, I assembled everything that had any reference to my plan and reviewed my latest experiences in life, which had not yet been put to any literary use. Under such circumstances, and after such long and often secret preparations, I wrote **Werther** in four weeks, without having written down in advance any scheme for the whole work, or a treatment of any part of it.

The now finished manuscript lay before me in a first draft, with few corrections and emendations. It was bound at once, for binding is to a piece of writing approximately what a frame is to a picture: one can more easily see then if it really amounts to anything. Since I had written this little work rather unconsciously, like a somnambulist, I was amazed myself when I looked through it to make changes and improvements. But in the expectation that many additional improvements would occur to me after a while, when I looked at it from a certain distance, I let my younger friends read it. The effect on them was all the greater because, contrary to habit, I had not talked to anyone about it beforehand or revealed my intention. Of course, here again it was the subject matter that actually produced the effect, and therefore they were in a mood precisely opposite to mine. For through this composition, more than any other, I had saved myself from a stormy element on which I had been tossed back and forth most violently, by my own and others' doing, by chance and chosen mode of life, by resolve and rashness, by obstinacy and pliancy. I felt as glad and free again as after a general confession, and entitled to a new life. The old home remedy had served me supremely well this time. But whereas I felt relieved and serene for having transformed reality into poetry, my friends were misled into thinking that poetry must be transformed into reality, that they must reenact the novel, and possibly shoot themselves. And what began here among a few, afterwards took place in the public at large, and the little book that had been of such great profit to me was decried as hurtful in the extreme. (pp. 428-32)

The impression made by my little book was great, nay, immense, and principally because it appeared at just the right time. For as only a modicum of priming powder is needed to detonate a powerful mine, so the explosion that now occurred among the public was a mighty one because the young people were themselves already on unsure ground. The perturbation was very great because every inidividual burst out with his exaggerated demands, unsatisfied passions, and imaginary sorrows. The public cannot be expected to receive an intellectual work intellectually. Nothing was really considered but the contents, the subject matter, as I had already seen with my friends; and in addition the old prejudice arose again, based on the dignity of a printed book, namely that it has to have a didactic purpose. However, the true work of art has none. It neither approves nor censures, but instead develops sentiments and actions in sequence, and thereby illuminates and instructs.

I took slight notice of the reviews. For me the matter was completely settled, and now it was up to those good people to see how they could come to terms with it. But my friends did not fail to collect these items, which furnished them much amusement since they were more privy to my views. (p. 433)

Since I was prepared for whatever protests would be made against **Werther,** all these objections did not upset me in the least. But I had hardly thought I would be so intolerably tormented by sympathetic well-wishers. Instead of saying anything complimentary to me about my little book as it stood, every single one of them wanted to know, for once and all, how much of the affair was actually true. Then I would grow very annoyed and usually return a very rude reply. For I had meditated a long time about this little work in order to give poetic unity to its various elements, and to answer their question I would have been obliged to pick it to pieces again and destroy its form, with the result that its true constituent parts would have been, if not annihilated, at any rate scattered and dispersed. However, on second thought I could not blame the public for its demand. Jerusalem's fate had caused a great sensation. A cultivated, amiable, reputable young man, the son of one of the most prominent theologians and authors, healthy and wealthy, had suddenly, for unknown reasons, departed this life. Now everyone wondered how that could happen, and when word went out about an unhappy love, the whole younger generation grew excited, as did the whole middle class when it was said that he had encountered some small annoyances in higher society. Everyone wanted to learn the details. Then *Werther* appeared with an elaborate description which, it was believed, reflected the life and character of this particular young man. The locale and personality held true, and since the portrayal was also very realistic, people now felt fully informed and satisfied. On the other hand, a closer inspection showed that much did *not* fit, after all, and the truth seekers were faced with an intolerable task, since critical analysis cannot but raise a hundred doubts. It was impossible to get to the bottom of things, for the portions of my own life and sorrows used for the composition could not be deciphered. As an unnoticed young person, I had not gone about my business in secret, but certainly in private.

While at work I had not been unaware of how greatly advantaged that artist had been who was given the opportunity to fashion a Venus from his combined studies of several beauties; so I also took the liberty of forming my Lotte out of the figures and characteristics of several pretty girls, even though her chief traits were taken from the dearest of them. Therefore the inquisitive public could discover similarities with various young women, and these ladies themselves were not altogether indifferent about passing for the right one. But these multiple Lottes caused me endless torment, because everyone who just looked at me would insist on knowing where the real Lotte lived. Like Nathan with his three rings I tried to rescue myself with an evasion; but while this may be suitable for higher personages, it cannot satisfy either the devout public or the reading public. I hoped to be rid of these awkward inquiries after a while, but they have accompanied me through my entire life. On journeys I tried to escape them by traveling incognito, but even this expedient unexpectedly failed me, and so the author of that little work, if he had indeed done something wrong and hurtful, was sufficiently, nay, excessively punished for it by these unavoidable importunities.

Being oppressed in this way, he grew only too aware that a vast gulf separates authors and their public, although, fortunately for them, neither has any concept of it. He had long realized that all introductions are consequently in vain, for the harder one tries to explain one's intentions, the more confusion results. Furthermore an author may write as long an introduction as he pleases, the public will still continue to make the very demands of him he was trying to avert. Likewise I soon became acquainted with a related peculiarity of readers, which strikes us as being particularly comic when their criticism is printed. Namely, they suffer from the delusion that, by having accomplished something, one becomes their debtor, who will always be far in arrears of their real wants and wishes, although shortly beforehand, when they had not yet seen our work, they had not the slightest notion that such a thing existed or was

even possible. And aside from all this, the greatest good fortune or misfortune was that everyone wanted to meet this strange young author who had emerged so unexpectedly and boldly. They wanted to see him, speak to him, hear something about him even at a distance, and so he had to experience a most remarkable onrush of people that was sometimes pleasant, sometimes disagreeable, but always distracting. For the beginnings of many works lay before him, indeed enough to occupy him for several years if he had been able to keep at them with his usual devotion. But he had been dragged from the quiet dusk and darkness, which is the only atmosphere that fosters pure works of art, out into the noisy daylight, where other people demand one's attention, where one is confused both by their interest and the lack of it, by praise and by censure. These outward contacts never conform to the stage reached by our inward culture, and since they cannot help us, they must of necessity hurt us. (pp. 434-36)

Johann Wolfgang von Goethe, in his From My Life: Poetry and Truth, Parts One to Three, *edited by Thomas P. Saine and Jeffrey L. Sammons, translated by Robert R. Heitner, Suhrkamp Publishers New York, Inc., 1987, 518 p.*

J. W. GOETHE [CONVERSATION WITH JOHANN PETER ECKERMANN] (conversation date 1824)

[*The following is taken from the volume of conversations with Goethe transcribed and collected by Johann Peter Eckermann, the author's secretary and companion during the last decade of his life. Here, Goethe shares his thoughts on* Werther, *emphasizing the intense effect of the novel on young readers. For additional commentary by Goethe, see excerpts dated 1774 and 1814.*]

The conversation now turned on *Werther.* "That," said Goethe, "is a creation which I, like the pelican, fed with the blood of my own heart. It contains so much from the innermost recesses of my breast that it might easily be spread into a novel of ten such volumes. Besides, I have only read the book once since its appearance, and have taken good care not to read it again. It is a mass of congreve-rockets. I am uncomfortable when I look at it; and I dread lest I should once more experience the peculiar mental state from which it was produced."

I reminded him of his conversation with Napoleon, of which I knew by the sketch amongst his unpublished papers, which I had repeatedly urged him to give more in detail. "Napoleon," said I, "pointed out to you a passage in *Werther,* which, it appeared to him, would not stand a strict examination; and this you allowed. I should much like to know what passage he meant."

"Guess!" said Goethe, with a mysterious smile.

"Now," said I, "I almost think it is where Charlotte sends the pistols to Werther, without saying a word to Albert, and without imparting to him her misgivings and apprehensions. You have given yourself great trouble to find a motive for this silence, but it does not appear to hold good against the urgent necessity where the life of the friend was at stake."

"Your remark," returned Goethe, "is really not bad; but I do not think it right to reveal whether Napoleon meant this passage or another. However, be that as it may, your observation is quite as correct as his."

I asked whether the great effect produced by the appearance of *Werther* were really to be attributed to the period. "I cannot,'' said I, ''reconcile to myself this view, though it is so extensively spread. *Werther* made an epoch because it appeared—not because it appeared at a certain time. There is in every period so much unexpressed sorrow—so much secret discontent and disgust with life, and in single individuals there are so many disagreements with the world—so many conflicts between their natures and civil regulations, that *Werther* would make an epoch even if it appeared to-day for the first time.''

''You are quite right,'' said Goethe; ''it is on that account that the book to this day influences youth of a certain age, as it did formerly. It was scarcely necessary for me to deduce my own youthful dejection from the general influence of my time, and from the reading of a few English authors. Rather was it owing to individual and immediate circumstances which touched me to the quick, and gave me a great deal of trouble, and indeed brought me into that frame of mind which produced *Werther*. I had lived, loved, and suffered much—that was it.

''On considering more closely the much-talked-of *Werther* period, we discover that it belongs, not to the course of universal culture, but to the career of every individual who, with an innate free natural instinct, must accommodate himself to the narrow limits of an antiquated world. Obstructed fortune, restrained activity, unfulfilled wishes, are the calamities not of any particular time but of every individual man; and it would be bad indeed if everybody had not, once in his life, known a time when *Werther* seemed as if it had been written for him alone.'' (pp. 26-7)

> *J. W. Goethe, in a conversation with Johann Peter Eckermann on January 2, 1824, in his* Conversations with Eckermann (1823-1832), *translated by John Oxenford, North Point Press, 1984, pp. 25-7.*

HENRY WADSWORTH LONGFELLOW   (lecture date 1838)

[*A poet, novelist, and critic, Longfellow was one of the most popular American writers of the nineteenth century. However, his reputation suffered a serious decline after his death. The very characteristics that made his poetry popular in his own day— gentle simplicity and a melancholy reminiscent of the German Romantics—are those that fueled the posthumous debate regarding his work. Despite the continuing controversy over Longfellow's merit, he is credited with having been instrumental in introducing European culture to the American readers of his day. In this excerpt from a lecture dated 1838, Longfellow shares his reactions to* Werther, *considering both its artistic and moral worth.*]

I have read [*Werther*] several times, both here and in Germany. The effect was different. The state of society in Germany lifts one up near to a level with the book. But in this country the difference between our daily feelings and those described in the book is far greater. Above all the work should not be read in a translation. One of its great charms is its style; and the sentiment seems less factitious when seen through the dim veil of the German language. . . .

Looked upon as a work of art merely, the book deserves high praise, particularly when we remember that a young man of twenty-four wrote it in the short space of a single month. The workings of the hero's mind are truly and powerfully sketched, and the insight into human life and character, altogether remarkable in so young an author.

As to the moral effect of the book, I cannot think it is bad, unless upon minds weak and willing to err. It is a portrait, no more, and though in the days of popularity many young people became infected with its hypersentimentality, or what Franz

Horn called *Wertherismus*, the blood-stained and evil death of the hero rather terrifies than attracts.

> *Henry Wadsworth Longfellow, in an extract in* Studies in Honor of John Albrecht Walz, *by O. W. Long and others, Lancaster Press, 1941, p. 113.*

W. M. THACKERAY   (poem date 1853)

[*A famed Victorian author, Thackeray is best known for his satiric sketches and panoramic novels of upper- and middle-class English life.* Vanity Fair: A Novel without a Hero *(1848) is generally regarded as his masterpiece. In this brief poem, Thackeray offers an ironic view of Werther's love for Charlotte.*]

> Werther had a love for Charlotte,
>   Such as words could never utter,
> Would you know how first he met her?
>   She was cutting bread and butter.
>
> Charlotte was a married lady,
>   And a moral man was Werther,
> And for all the wealth of Indies
>   Would do nothing that might hurt her.
>
> So he sighed and pined and ogled,
>   And his passion boiled and bubbled;
> Till he blew his silly brains out,
>   And no more was by them troubled.
>
> Charlotte, having seen his body
>   Borne before her on a shutter;
> Like a well conducted person
>   Went on cutting bread and butter.

> *W. M. Thackeray, '' 'Sorrows of Werther','' in* The Southern Literary Messenger, *Vol. XIX, No. 11, November, 1853, p. 709.*

GEORGE HENRY LEWES   (essay date 1864)

[*Lewes was one of the most versatile men of letters in the Victorian era. A prominent English journalist, he was the founder, with Leigh Hunt, of the* Leader, *a radical political journal that he edited from 1851 to 1854. He also established and served as the first editor of the* Fortnightly Review. *Scholars often credit him with critical acumen in his literary commentary, most notably in his dramatic criticism. Lewes was also the author of the first comprehensive biography of Goethe, excerpted below. Here, he comments on the connection between Goethe and Werther and praises Goethe's artistic representation of reality in the novel.*]

[*Werther* was] composed out of a double history, the history of its author's experience and the history of one of his friends.

The story of Jerusalem, whom he met in the Wetzlar circle, furnished Goethe with the machinery by which to introduce his own experience. He took many of the details from Kestner's long letter, sent shortly after the catastrophe [see Additional Bibliography]. . . . (p. 146)

The sensation produced in Wetzlar by [Jerusalem's] suicide was immense. People who had scarcely seen Jerusalem were unable to quiet their agitation; many could not sleep; the women especially felt the deepest interest in the fate of this unhappy youth; and *Werther* found a public ready for it.

With these materials in hand, let us take up the novel to see how Goethe employs them. Werther is a man who, not having yet learned self-mastery, imagines that his immense desires are proofs of immense superiority: one of those of whom it has been wittily said that they fancy themselves great painters because they paint with a big brush. He laughs at all rules, whether they be rules of Art, or rules which Convention builds like walls around our daily life. He hates order—in speech, in writing, in costume, in office. In a word, he hates all control. Gervinus remarks that he turns from men to children because they do not pain him, and from them to Nature because she does not contradict him; from truth to poetry, and in poetry from the clear world of Homer to the formless world of Ossian. Very characteristic of the epoch is the boundless enthusiasm inspired by Ossian, whose rhetorical trash the Germans hailed as the finest expression of *Nature's* poetry. Old Samuel Johnson's stern, clear sense saw into the very heart of this subject when he said, 'Sir, a man might write such stuff for ever if he would but *abandon* his mind to it'. It is abandonment of the mind, throwing the reins on the horse's neck, which makes such writing possible; and it was precisely this abandonment to impulse, this disregard of the grave remonstrances of reason and good sense, which distinguished the Werther epoch.

Werther is not Goethe. Werther perishes because he is wretched, and is wretched because he is so weak. Goethe was 'king over himself'. He saw the danger, and evaded it; tore himself away from the woman he loved, instead of continuing in a dangerous position. Yet although Werther is not Goethe, there is one part of Goethe living in Werther. This is visible in the incidents and language as well as in the character. It is the part we see reappearing under the various masks of Weislingen, Clavigo, Faust, Fernando, Edward, Meister, and Tasso, which no critic will call the same lay figure variously draped, but which every critic must see belong to one and the same genus: men of strong desires and weak volitions, wavering impressionable natures unable to attain self-mastery. Goethe was one of those who are wavering because impressionable, but whose wavering is not weakness; they oscillate, but they return into the direct path which their wills have prescribed. He was tender as well as impressionable. He could not be stern, but he could be resolute. He had only therefore, in imagination, to keep in abeyance the native force of resolution which gave him mastery, and in that abeyance a weak wavering character stood before him, the original of which was himself.

When a man delineates himself, he always shrinks from a complete confession. Our moral nature has its modesty. Strong as the impulse may be to drag into light that which lies hidden in the recesses of the soul, pleased as we may be to create images of ourselves, we involuntarily keep back something, and refuse to identify ourselves with the creation. There are few things more irritating than the pretension of another to completely understand us. Hence authors never thoroughly portray themselves. Byron, utterly without self-command, is fond of heroes proud and self-sustaining. Goethe, the strongest of men, makes heroes the footballs of circumstance. But he also draws from his other half the calm, self-sustaining characters. Thus we have the antithesis of Götz and Weislingen—Albert and Werther—Carlos and Clavigo—Jarno and Meister—Antonio and Tasso—the Captain and Edward; and, deepened in colouring, Mephistopheles and Faust.

Werther is not much read nowadays, especially in England, where it labours under the double disadvantage of a bad name and an execrable translation. Yet it is well worth reading in the original, where it will be found very unlike the notion of it current among us. I remember many years ago reading it in the execrable English version with astonishment and contempt; this contempt remained, until accidentally falling in with a Spanish translation, the exquisite beauty of the pictures changed my feeling into admiration, and Goethe's own wonderful prose afterwards fixed that admiration for ever. It is a masterpiece of style; we may look through German literature in vain for such clear sunny pictures, fullness of life, and delicately managed simplicity. Its style is one continuous strain of music, which, restrained within the limits of prose, fulfils all the conditions of poetry; dulcet as the sound of falling waters, and as full of sweet melancholy as an autumnal eve.

Nothing can be simpler than the structure of this book, wherein, as M. Marmier well remarks, every detail is so arranged as to lay bare the sufferings of a diseased spirit. Werther arrives at his chosen retreat, believing himself cured, and anticipating perfect happiness. He is painter and poet. The fresh spring mornings, the sweet cool evenings, soothe and strengthen him. He selects a place under the limes to read and dream away the hours. There he brings his pencil and his Homer. Everything interests him—the old woman who brings his coffee, the children who play around him, the story of a poor family. In this serene convalescence he meets with Charlotte, and a new passion agitates his soul. His simple uniform existence becomes changed. He endeavours by bodily activity to charm away his desires. The days no longer resemble each other: now ecstatic with hope, now crushed with despair. Winter comes: cold, sad, gloomy. He must away. He departs, and mingles with the world, but the world disgusts him. The monotony and emptiness of official life are intolerable to his pretensions; the parchment pride of the noblesse is insulting to his sense of superiority. He returns to the peaceful scene of his former contentment, and finds indeed Charlotte, the children, his favourite woods and walks, but not the calmness which he seeks. The hopelessness of his position overwhelms him. Disgusted with the world—unsatisfied in his cravings—he dies by his own hand.

Rosenkrantz—in the true spirit of that criticism which seeks everywhere for meanings more recondite than the author dreamt of—thinks that Goethe exhibits great art in making Werther a diplomatist, because a diplomatist is a man of *shams (Scheinthuer)*; but the truth is, Goethe made him precisely what he found him. His art is truth. He is so great an artist that the simplest realities have to him significance. Charlotte cutting bread and butter for the children—the scene of the ball—the children clinging around Werther for sugar, and pictures of that kind, betray so little inventive power, that they have excited the ridicule of some English critics, to whom poetry is a thing of pomp, not the beautiful vesture of reality. The beauty and art of Werther are not in the incidents (a Dumas would shrug despairing shoulders over such invention), but in the representation. What *is* Art but Representation? (pp. 150-53)

George Henry Lewes, in his The Life of Goethe, *second edition, 1864. Reprint by Frederick Ungar Publishing Co., 1965, 578 p.*

THOMAS CARLYLE   (essay date 1864)

[*A noted nineteenth-century essayist, historian, critic, and social commentator, Carlyle was a central figure of the Victorian age in England and Scotland. In his writings, he advocated a Christian work ethic and stressed the importance of order, piety, and spiritual fulfillment. Known to his contemporaries as the "Sage of Chelsea," Carlyle exerted a powerful moral influence in an era of rapidly shifting values. An admirer of Goethe, Carlyle also translated* Wilhelm Meisters Lehrjahr *(1795-96;* Wilhelm Meister's Apprenticeship*). Here, he applauds Goethe's ability to articulate in* Werther *his generation's sense of unease and discontent.*]

That nameless unrest . . . , the blind struggle of a soul in bondage, that high, sad, longing discontent which was agitating every bosom, had driven Goethe almost to despair. All felt it; he alone could give it voice. And here lies the secret of his popularity; in his deep, susceptive heart he felt a thousand times more keenly what every one was feeling; with the creative gift which belonged to him as a poet, he bodied it forth into visible shape, gave it a local habitation and a name; and so made himself the spokesman of his generation. *Werther* is but the cry of that dim, rooted pain under which all thoughtful men of a certain age were languishing: it paints the misery, it passionately utters the complaint; and heart and voice all over Europe loudly and at once respond to it. True it prescribes no remedy; for that was a far different, far harder enterprise, to which other years and a higher culture were required; but even this utterance of pain, even this little, for the present is grasped at, and with eager sympathy appropriated in every bosom. If Byron's life weariness, his moody melancholy, and mad, stormful indignation, borne on the tones of a wild and quite artless melody could pierce so deep into many a British heart, now that the whole matter is no longer new—is indeed old and trite—we may judge with what vehement acceptance this *Werther* must have been welcomed, coming, as it did, like a voice from the unknown regions: the first thrilling peal of that impassioned dirge which, in country after country, men's ears have listened to till they were deaf to all else. For *Werther,* infusing itself into the core and whole spirit of literature, gave birth to a race of sentimentalists who have raged and wailed in every part of the world, till the better light dawned on them, or, at worst, exhausted Nature laid herself to sleep, and it was discovered that lamenting was unproductive labour. These funereal choristers, in Germany, a loud, haggard, tumultuous, as well as tearful class, were named the *Kraftmänner,* or Powermen; but have long since, like sick children, cried themselves to rest. (pp. 153-54)

> *Thomas Carlyle, in an extract in* The Life of Goethe *by George Henry Lewes, second edition, 1864. Reprint by Frederick Ungar Publishing Co., 1965, pp. 153-54.*

GEORG BRANDES (essay date 1916)

[*Brandes, a Danish literary critic and biographer, was the principal leader of the intellectual movement that helped to bring an end to Scandinavian cultural isolation. He believed that literature reflects the spirit and problems of its time and that it must be understood within its social and aesthetic context. Brandes's major critical work,* Hovedstrømninger i det 19de aarhundredes litteratur *(1871;* Main Currents in Nineteenth Century Literature*), won him admiration for his ability to view literary movements within the broader context of all European literature. In the following excerpt from the 1916 edition of his biographical and critical study of Goethe, Brandes comments on several aspects of Werther's character, including his suicidal impulses, his feeling for nature, his psychology, his love for Lotte, and his attitude toward society.*]

If we look back over the leading male characters in the works of Goethe's youth, it is quite difficult to escape a distinctly unfavorable impression—that of the unmanliness of these young men. In all of them, in Werther, and even more so in Clavigo and Fernando, not to speak of Weislingen, there is a pronounced element of weakness. We detect this indeed in Faust himself. In the case of Werther, this impression is strongest at the close of the book, a close that casts a cloud over the beginning. Modern ethics, the temperaments and sensibilities of the present, are repelled: A young man takes his life out of despair at being separated from a woman who seems quite satisfied in and with her union with another man, and who in any event can endure life without him.

Modern critics have taken to jeering Goethe because he did not commit suicide on finding himself in Werther's situation. No derision could be more absurd. Why in the name of all that is reasonable should Goethe have taken his life? People affect to feel nowadays that it was a sort of belated duty he owed himself. They refuse to believe that any great seriousness is to be attached to the suicidal thoughts by which he portrays himself as having been plagued at that time [see excerpt dated 1814]. They insist that he never really thought of sending the well-polished dagger, which he kept suspended at his bedside during those days, through his heart. What are we to understand here by "seriousness"? If the term connotes only and entirely the dwelling on such ideas of suicide as eventually lead to death, then he was not "serious." But Goethe wrote very explicitly to Zelter in 1812 (he was then sixty-three years old): "I am fully conscious of the decisions, resolutions and exertions that it cost me to escape from the waters of death." He told the whole truth when he said he wrote the novel in order to liberate himself from these feelings. Moreover, he never pretended that he felt precisely as did Werther. (pp. 193-94)

Werther in the first part, where Goethe alone is still the model, is entirely too wholesome and strong to be thought of as a suicide. His nature sense is especially healthy. Such a feeling for nature had hitherto never been detected in a German novel. Werther does not describe nature, nor does he exploit such designations as Luna and Zephyr (as Goethe did in his oldest poems). Everything is steeped in feeling. He feels life pulsating in nature, and he feels its echo in his own breast:

> When the lovely valley round about me exhales its vapor, and the sun rests at midday on the upper surface of the impenetrable darkness of my forest and only individual rays steal down into its sanctuary, when I lie then in the high grass by the babbling brook and nearer down to the earth a thousand different grasses of smaller kind become visible, when I feel the swarming of the little world between the blades, and countless and unfathomable little figures of the insects and gnats closer to my heart, and feel the presence of the Almighty who created us in His image, the fluttering of the All-Loving through space who bears us up and holds us in light eternal, my friend, when my eye becomes wrapped in dusk and the world about me and the heaven in my soul rest like the figure of a beloved—then I am seized with longing and this thought comes to me: Oh, if you could only express, if you could only breathe into the paper, all this that lives so warm and full in your soul so that it would be the mirror of your soul, just as your soul is the mirror of the infinite God! My Friend! But I court ruin in the desire; I succumb quite to the power of the glory of all I have seen.

This is the extent of his intimacy with nature; he has confidence in her; she becomes confidential and precious to him; he strives to reproduce nature.

That the feeling is Goethe's own is proved by the fact that it returns, expressed in the same way, only with less theological coloring, in Faust's monologue, *Erhabener Geist, Du gabst mir, gabst mir Alles.* The Spriit gave him Nature in all its glory as his kingdom, the power to feel it, to enjoy it, and the gift to look deep down into it as he would look into the heart of a friend. He feels like Adam: Thou leadest the files of the living by me, and teachest me to recognize my brothers in the peaceful bush, in the air, and in the water.

Werther who, as an artist, wishes to reproduce nature and is grieved when he cannot find the right word, wishes to feel divine, superhuman; he wishes to have nature arise from within his own heart; he would feel the instinctive joy in life that other creatures have, particularly that of the birds in their flight:

> How often have I longed to fly far away to the shores of the unmeasured sea on the wings of a crane which had flown above me, so that I might drink the swelling, seething joy of life from the foaming beaker of the infinite! How I have longed to feel even for a moment that there was in the pent-up enclosure of my bosom one drop of the happiness of that being which creates all things in itself and through itself.
>
> (pp. 201-03)

Goethe has made Werther's impressions of nature conform to his own momentary feelings; and he has done this with uncommon delicacy. Suffering from an unhappy love affair, he sees (August 18) in nature only the powers of destruction; in heaven and earth he sees only "an eternally swallowing up and eternally ruminating monster." But he is healthy for all that.

Deep down in his soul Werther is not an unmanly youth; and he is above all not a whimperer. The fact is, Goethe had to have a tragic end, for the strong passion which had thus far prevailed would lose its poetic interest if the conclusion were primarily idyllic. This being the case he took up with a new model at the very last, and introduced a few confusing facts from the world of reality, such as Werther's reading Lessing's *Emilia Galotti,* one of the clearest, most rational dramas in existence. In a letter to Herder Goethe himself criticises it as being "only thought."

He accommodated everything to this tragic close: He had the bright summer mood of the first part supplanted by the melancholy of autumn in the second; he dropped Homer and Homer's wholesome views of nature and took up Ossian. Homer is a distinct force in the first part. When Werther cooks his own green peas in the public kitchen at Wahlheim, his mind reverts at once to Penelope's haughty wooers who roasted their own oxen. Now the hazy, restless Ossianic pictures, which corresponded to the increasing morbidity, uncertainty, and lyrical passion, gradually gain control of the theme, until Ossian's songs—which Goethe had translated for Friederike, and which are interpolated just before the final decision—prepare the way for death and downfall.

The degree in which he estimated Ossian at this period of his life is revealed by the beautiful passage in which Werther expresses his indignation at the individual who asks him whether he likes Lotte. Like her? One might as well ask him whether he likes Ossian.

There is no one definite taste in *Werthers Leiden.* The natural and fascinating alternate with the super-sentimental and exaggerated; ingenious similes and perspicacious soul studies vie with an extravagance which could not help but seem antiquated even during Goethe's own life; indeed it made this very impression on him himself. It is fortunate that in a later edition he contented himself, on the whole, with some addenda that greatly enrich, and did not undertake another of his confusing revisions. (pp. 204-06)

In [some] places Werther represents, to be sure, a point of view which the author of the book was soon to discard, though a point of view that was justified for a quite different reason: the proclaiming of artistic naturalism as a matter of principle. By making an exact copy of nature, Werther has produced a sketch which is entirely successful, and which seems to interest him. This strengthens him in his determination to hold fast to nature alone in the future; for it is infinitely rich; it alone creates the great artists. Nature is here contrasted with the rules and not, as later in Goethe's life, with the ideals. Quite in the spirit of *Sturm und Drang* he writes: "One can say about as much to the advantage of the rules as one can say to the advantage of established bourgeois society." It does not yet occur to Goethe that it is not so much fidelity to rules that contradicts an imitation of nature. We read, to be sure, later on in his own works:

> Nachahmung der Natur
>   —der schönen—
> Ich ging auch wohl auf dieser Spur;
>   Gewöhnen
> Möcht' ich wohl nach und nach den Sinn,
>   mich zu vergnügen.
> Allein sobald ich mündig bin—
>   Es sind's die Griechen.

The poet who, in course of time, was to relegate all strong feelings to their proper limit, so much so that in the eyes of many he appeared secretive, dry and unimaginative, takes not the slightest offense at the manifestation of any type of emotional outburst in Werther. When Lotte dotes on her little sister, who is terrified by Werther's kiss and fears lest she may grow a beard because of it, Werther almost has to do violence to himself in order to keep from falling down and adoring her. Lotte takes the child to the well and washes the kiss off. Werther exclaims with undisciplined sentimentality:

> I never attended a christening with greater reverence. When Lotte returned, I would have liked to throw myself down before her as I would before a Prophet of old who had atoned for the sins of an entire people.

Had Goethe not had the poor taste to prefer, at this period of his life, the Swiss Rousseau to native French writers, he would have avoided such an outbreak.

Flaws of this kind, however, are rare; they vanish in the enraptured portrayal of Werther's infatuation. How dainty is the description of his uncertainty as to whether Lotte was trying to see him when she leaned her head out of the carriage as they drove away! And equally charming is the confession that he would gladly have kissed the boy who brought him a note from her simply because this boy had recently seen her. Beautiful and apt is also the comparison (July 26) in which he says he is drawn to her as the ships are drawn to the magnetic mountain in the fairy tale. The nails fly to the peaks and the poor wretches are shipwrecked amid falling boards and floating planks.

By means of a number of delicate touches that are eventually blended into a unified whole, the psychology of Werther is delineated with force and grace. Lotte upbraids him, for example, for his "all too passionate participation in everything." We have also a significant touch when (August 12) Albert's nature is described as being the antipodes of Werther's. The occasion of this remark—in a fine and careful preparation for the close of the novel—is Albert's well-founded objection to Werther's playing with his pistols, even when they are not supposed to be loaded, and Albert's commitments on the foolish element in suicide. It is in this connection that Werther makes use of the superbly phrased sentence that shows us the real Albert: *"Nun weisst du, dass ich den Menschen sehr lieb habe bis auf seine Zwar."* It is to be assumed as a matter of fact, says Werther, that there are exceptions to all generalities. But so would-be wise is Albert, that when he feels that he has made an over-hasty remark, or has said something that is too general or only half true, he delimits it and verifies it beyond recognition. A long conversation is spun out during which Werther first defends the actions undertaken in passion, and then, when suicide is touched upon, contends that there are certain degrees of torture which can no longer be endured and which consequently justify self-annihilation.

The figure of Lotte is introduced in a naïve and natural, and in the most original, way for the heroine of a love story. When Werther sees her for the first time she is surrounded by six children between two and eleven years old. Though beautifully dressed for the ball, in a white gown with pink scarf, she is holding a huge piece of rye bread in her hand and cutting for each of her small brothers and sisters a slice dietetically adapted to the age and appetite of the recipient in question.

Though extremely young, she is maternal and domestic; the children love her and obey her. The two oldest boys, having received permission to run along behind the carriage for a short distance, kiss her hand tenderly and cordially on leaving her.

Immediately after this we see her whirling about in the waltz with address and charm. She is beautiful, good, modest, wholesome, and without affectation.

The second part of the novel has a wholly different character from the first. The first part is plastic and living, the second is psychopathic. We hear precious little about Charlotte. It is well known that Goethe no longer uses himself as a model; he has substituted the other. It is the situation and the incidents in the life of young Jerusalem that are here portrayed. Werther is now interested more or less in another woman, who, according to the intolerable custom of that time, is referred to as Fräulein von B.

The new motive to Werther's former self-abandonment, the prejudice namely against which he as a private citizen has to fight and the humiliation to which he is exposed, are now introduced. The arrogance of the nobility is attacked and ridiculed, but from an essentially conservative turn of mind: Class differences are necessary; Werther does not forget what advantages they have brought to him himself. And now, after having been ejected from the Count's house on that afternoon because he, as an ordinary citizen, is not tolerated in the society of the nobility, the idea of suicide arises in his mind for the first time. "Ah, hundreds of times have I seized a knife in order to give air to my agonized heart. It is said of thoroughbred horses that, after they have been heated up and driven about in a fearful manner, they bite open a vein in order thereby to get air."

On the twenty-fourth of March Werther asks for his release as attaché of the legation. His mother had hoped to see him as a *Geheimrat* and *Hofmann*—a position which Goethe in actuality secured not much later.

A prince, who is without knowledge of men and talks only of what he has heard and read, takes an interest in Werther. This man places a higher value on Werther's reason and ability than on his heart, which—in accord with the spirit of that age—is his "sole pride." The melancholy youth thinks of going to war; he gives up the idea however when a general under whom he wished to serve shows him that this wish is more a matter of caprice than passion. In the beginning of July he changes his place of abode; he wants to visit a neighborhood apparently in order to study some mines, in actuality to be nearer to Lotte.

On the twenty-sixth of October he is again, and all of a sudden, near her. When he returned we are not told. In marked contrast to the circumstantiality with which everything is related, we have here not a word on the meeting at the end of a year. But Werther feels quite at home in her town; he seems to be welcome; indeed he cannot be imagined anywhere else. And the question arises in his mind, or rather in his soul: Suppose I went away, would they miss me, and if so, how long? By the fifth of November he has already lost his spirit; he has lost what he exaltedly calls "the sacred, inspiring power with which he created worlds about him."

The nearer we approach the end the more emphasis is laid on Werther's peculiarity as a being of nature and his estrangement from Christianity: "Has not the Son of God Himself said that they should be around Him whom the Father has given Him? But if I am not given to Him?" Werther wishes to be dissolved in nature. He would gladly renounce his human character in order, with the storm, to tear the skies asunder and move the waters.

The unhappy love affair and the social slight are taken up together. Werther's jealousy grows. Albert feels dissatisfied with the youth's advances to his wife. He is out of humor. The relation between the consorts is growing darker and darker. Werther feels moreover that his honor has been irreparably wounded through the social jilt he suffered. At the same time Charlotte is forced to ask him not to come to the house again for three days.

Suicidal instincts arise in his lacerated soul. He dreams of murdering her husband, her, himself. As to his criminal intentions the reader is skeptical. It is not set forth in a sufficiently convincing way. Then come, as a mood-awakener, the Ossianic poems. As an insertion they are too long. These are followed by the last meeting. For the first time in his life Werther feels that Charlotte loves him. In the final letter, written in the spirit of that age, we read of *milleniums* (as in *Götz, Clavigo, Faust*): "Lotte, milleniums can never efface these impressions." And finally the beautiful note: "Nature, thy son, thy friend, thy lover draws near—near to the infinite end!"

Rousseau's *La nouvelle Héloise* had appeared in 1761. This is the book without which Goethe could not have written his *Leiden des jungen Werthers* thirteen years later. Rousseau's hero, Saint-Preux, changed his clothes, donned the famous costume, the blue coat and yellow vest which Werther wears, and which Goethe himself had worn in Wetzlar. *La nouvelle Héloise* had enraptured France, indeed the whole of Europe. The story of Werther's passionate and unhappy love affair likewise received its significance from the fact that it did more than portray the casual passion and incidental misfortune of a single individual: It treated the theme in such a way that the passions, yearnings, and torments of an entire age found their expression therein.

The age saw itself visualized in this book. **Werther** depicted the right and the wrong of the full heart in its relation to workaday rules, its striving after infinity, its impulse to freedom, that freedom which reacts to the dividing lines of human society as it would to the bleak walls of a prison. In the course of a few months, the author of **Werther** became the most famous personality in German literature. (pp. 208-14)

Georg Brandes, in his Wolfgang Goethe, Vol. I, *translated by Allen W. Porterfield, Frank-Maurice, Inc., 1924, 503 p.*

WILLIAM ROSE   (essay date 1924)

[*In this excerpt from his study of Weltschmerz in German literature, Rose examines how Werther exemplifies this attitude.*]

Werther is the analysis of a soul that comes to grief through inability to attain harmony with the outer world. It was written at a time when the young spirits of Germany were in a moral ferment, and intensely dissatisfied with both the spiritual and material conditions of existence. The natural consequences were an inclination to melancholy and revolt against convention. The younger generation, with its irrepressible longing for the simplicity of Nature as opposed to the petrified and antiquated conventions of the age, found in **Werther** its most profound and complete expression, the first plastic representation of the new individualistic tendencies.

The story is simple and there is but little action. It is written in letter form, with a few interpolations by the editor. Werther is a simple, unambitious youth who is contented with the in-active life he is leading in the country when the story opens. Then one day he meets Lotte, for whom he conceives a deep passion, and only when her fiancé, Albert, returns, does he begin to realise that she is beyond his reach. From now on his condition of morbid despair grows more and more intense, until he goes away to a diplomatic post where he hopes to forget. A social snub, to which he exposes himself, only makes him brood the more, and he throws up his post to return to the town where Lotte, now married to Albert, is living. His mind becomes more and more unbalanced, until his relations with the married couple culminate in a scene in which he loses his self-control and embraces Lotte in the absence of her husband. He returns home and shortly afterwards shoots himself with a pistol which he has borrowed from Albert.

It has been said that **Werther** closed the period of sentimentality and depression, but that is not so. On the contrary, the latter received an added impulse, for it was in **Werther** that this spiritual condition of the seventies of the eighteenth century first found adequate expression. In a conversation with Eck-ermann, on January 2nd, 1824 [see excerpt above], Goethe agrees that the novel would have been epoch-making at any period, but he certainly underestimates the sentimental mood, the "Schwärmerei," of the time. He asserts that the much-discussed Werther-epoch has its place not in the general history of civilisation, but rather in the development of the individual, who, with his innate and independent natural instincts, has to learn to conform to the circumscribed and antiquated conven-tions of society. Happiness unattained, ambition unfulfilled and desires unsatisfied are the weaknesses not of any particular age, but of every single individual. Goethe in his old age was sometimes liable to slight astigmatism in viewing certain as-pects of his youth, and though his remark in the above con-versation is perfectly true, and Weltschmerz has always been a characteristic of certain types of humanity, yet he does not bring into line the almost universal prominence of this "path-ological condition," as he himself calls it, at the time when he wrote his novel. It is significant that he merely describes the malady without making any attempt to suggest a possible cure.

Werther's outstanding characteristic is a thorough lack of will-power, whose immediate consequence is a disinclination for action. He is unpractical and passive, and these negative traits derive from his intensified individualism. He says of himself "I turn in upon myself and find a world! But a world more of presentiment and obscure desire than of plastic living power. And everything swims before my senses, and I wander on my way with a dreamy smile." He is a receptive artist, but lacks creative power, which cannot exist when the soul is so entirely out of harmony with the world. He does not fight against his passion, but even when he can coolly and logically discuss the subject of suicide, which he justifies by argument, he asserts that where passion rules, man is helpless. "Man is man, and the little reason that one may possess does not come much into calculation, when passion rages and the bounds of humanity close one in." This can hardly be called fatalism; it is a weak yielding to the senses. It is obvious that Lotte is not Werther's fate, but that he carries the seeds of destruction in his own breast. The important factor of the novel is the hero's spiritual condition, and this stands behind and overshadows the meagre action of the love-episode. All action is reaction of the inward against the outward, and is not an object in itself. Werther's world is in his own breast, and the tragedy is one of suscep-tibility and not activity. Life in **Werther** is merely a psychic state. He is driven undecided hither and thither by his heart. On November the 24th he hovers between two decisions in a state of utter despair, unable to make up his mind, and on the 26th he utters the half-terrible, half-childish cry: "Have men before me been so wretched?" He possesses in a high degree the sense of isolation, of being misunderstood by his fellow-men. "To be misunderstood is the destiny of a person like me."

It has been said that the victim of romantic melancholy is at times tender and elegiac, at other times a heaven-defying titan. Werther is often tender and often elegiac, but it is difficult, in spite of [Friedrich] Gundolf's eloquent claim, to see any ti-tanism in his character. The latter sees as Werther's funda-mental characteristic the universally intensified susceptibility and sensitiveness which enable him to sympathise with the impulse of the animated universe.... To call a man a titan, who lives in an imaginary world, however ideal, and succumbs without a struggle the first time he comes up against a brutal reality is to weaken the force of the word. Gundolf admits that Werther differs from Prometheus, Götz, etc., and even from Faust by his *passivity*, but this distinction is vital. Goethe himself might be called a titan, because though he also longed to burst the bonds which hemmed his spiritual and corporeal self, yet he *did* fight and conquer. The desire to overstep the limits of society is not a specifically Weltschmerz character-istic; it becomes Weltschmerz when combined with *inaction*. Goethe depicted in **Werther** his own potentiality as reality, and in representing it concretely, his good sense prevailed. Werth-er's place is rather among the men of unsteady purpose, such as Weislingen, Clavigo, Fernando, Tasso and Eduard, though these have their origin in the same discord, viz. the irrecon-cilability of the desire with the power to fulfil, as the titans.

The diseased side of Werther's character is seen best in the way he derives a deep-seated pleasure from his melancholy brooding. He recognises himself this brooding tendency and promises in his very first letter to cure himself of it. He will reform, and no longer chew the cud of his misfortunes as he has hitherto done. He recognises that there would be less suf-fering in the world, if people did not occupy their power of imagination in recalling the evils of the past, rather than endure an indifferent present. It is this very power of imagination which causes his ruin. Goethe says himself that Werther undermines his existence by introspection. There is a draft of a revision of the prologue which was probably intended for the second edition, and which contains the significant phrase: "Schöpfe nicht nur wollüstige Linderung aus seinen Leiden." Werther sank into his ego and drew exquisite pain from his own mental sufferings.

His egotism is enormous. He says that a man who wears himself out in the struggle for money or honour or anything else for the sake of others, without its being his own need or passion, is a fool. In his last letter to Lotte, left on his writing-table to be found after his death, he admonishes her to think of him when she climbs the hill, and to gaze across at his grave in the churchyard. The thought of the distress and scandal he is about to cause does not enter his mind, but he intoxicates himself with self-pity as he thinks of the grass on his grave waving in the rays of the setting sun. "On Christmas Eve you will hold this paper in your hand, you will tremble and moisten it with your sweet tears."

There is something of the theatrical poseur about him. The pistol with which he shoots himself must be one of Albert's. He imagines himself lying stretched out on the floor, and sits down to add a postscript to his last letter to Lotte. He casts a romantic halo round his grave. "Oh, I would wish to be buried by the roadside, or in a lonely valley, that priest and Levite should cross themselves as they pass by and the Samaritan shed a tear." Such theatricality is childish.

Werther's propensity for philosophic speculation leads him in the direction of fatalism, which yet does not seem sincere; all effort is vain and life a dream. When he sees the limitations to which the active and speculative powers of man are subject, and when he sees how all activity is directed towards the satisfaction of needs, which themselves have no other object than the lengthening of our wretched existence; when he realises that the only result of certain speculations is a dreamy resignation—all this makes him dumb. It appears to him obvious, though nobody wants to believe it, that grown-ups, like children, tumble about on this earth, and like children, do not know whence they come nor whither they are going. His only consolation is the thought that he can quit this "prison" at will. When he complains of the impotence of reason, it is not fatalism that stands behind the words, but inability to resist the passions. His philosophic speculation is mixed up with dreamy "Schwärmerei," and it is this which has undermined his nature.

In spite of the fact that Werther invokes the deity as a personal God, he is essentially pantheistic. He knows that God is not exterior to the world, but that He is immanent in the universe, and that is why his love of Nature bears a religious character, so that when he feels his world falling around him, he despairs at the same time both of Nature and of God. His religious feeling is not profound or definite. He regards himself as the central figure of the universe, is interested in God and Nature only in so far as they affect himself, and his religious emotion manifests itself in a vague yearning. The only support he derives from religion is the consolation he finds in Nature.

The outer world is not a mere frame for the picture, as is generally the case with Rousseau, but the appearance of Nature is interwoven with the mood of the hero. His changing humour is always in harmony with changing Nature, or, in other words, he always sees Nature as coloured by his own varying moods. In the second book (no longer finding a mirror for his own soul in Homer) he plunges into the gloomy, misty world of Ossian. He reads Ossian, because the latter appeals to his mood, and under the influence of the dissolving sentimentality of these songs, his melancholy becomes ever more acute. He transfers the despair consuming him to surrounding Nature, which even before his departure to take up his diplomatic post appears to him a yawning grave, as formerly it reflected his surging joy in life. His soul is undermined by the consuming power which lies hidden in the universe of Nature; the power which has formed nothing that has not destroyed its neighbour and itself. "I see nothing but a monster, eternally devouring, eternally chewing the cud." He sees the hopelessness of his position and yet has power for nothing but tears for the sinister future. It is important to notice the way in which the novel opens with Werther happy in the sunny countryside of May, and the development of his ever-growing despair in late autumn and winter until he finds eternal peace with the close of the year. (pp. 19-29)

> William Rose, "Goethe," in his From Goethe to Byron: The Development of "Weltschmerz" in German Literature, George Routledge & Sons, Ltd., 1924, pp. 19-51.

BARKER FAIRLEY (essay date 1932)

[*Fairley has written prolifically on Goethe and is considered a major scholar of his works. Here, he explores Werther's relationship to the outer world of reality and the inner world of the spirit, identifying their significance to his suicide.*]

To the world at large the Goethe who went to Weimar in 1775 was the author of **Werther** and **Götz von Berlichingen,** and the rest of him was unknown or subsidiary. Coming as these two works did in fairly quick succession and just when the time was ripe, they have been closely associated from the start, and the most has been made of their similarity—their informal style, their love of the simple life, their joint protest against the conventions. Yet the difference, the psychological difference, is startling, as we can see from Werther's reaction to the pictorial mood so joyfully evidenced in **Götz von Berlichingen.** If in the writing of this play Goethe delighted in the colour and the panorama of life, in **Werther** he turns from it with a tragic revulsion. And the old peep-show comparison, never far from Goethe's mind in these early years, is there to point the transition. "What is life without love?" asks Werther in an early letter; "it is a magic-lantern without light. As soon as you bring in the lamp you see the gayest of pictures on your white screen. And even if they are nothing but passing phantoms, they can be a joy to us when we stand in front of them like happy boys and revel in the wondrous shows." Here, though the mood is comparatively serene, the clouds are gathering. Werther, we feel, has lost his first delight in the world of appearance, and the comfort it gives him is precarious. The sense of transience is already hanging over him, and before long it dominates him. "If you could see me," he writes a little later, "in the throng of distractions, how stagnant I am. Never for a moment does my heart overflow, never an hour's real happiness. Nothing! Nothing! I seem to stand before a raree-show (Raritätenkasten) and see people and horses jerked this way and that, and often I ask myself if it is not an optical illusion. I play my part too, or rather I have to play it, like a marionette, and many a time I seize my neighbour by his wooden hand and shrink back in horror." This passage occurs early in the second book, under the date of 30th January, after Werther has obtained his remove and exchanged the dear companionship of Lotte and Albert for the conventional life at the embassy. He is at the point of closest and most unwelcome contact with the practical world, and he uses the raree-show—symbol of Goethe's youthful delight in Shakespeare little more than two years before—to express his disgust at it.

These passages serve to remind us how unpictorial is the art of *Werther* as compared with its less reflective predecessor. In *Götz von Berlichingen* all seems visually circumscribed—unless we except the Adelheid adventure which broke its bounds in the first draft—each scene-picture being as clearly contained and filled as if it were a painter's canvas framed in its rectangle. *Werther,* on the other hand, has no statable dimensions and is perpetually out of focus. "Dämmernd" is Werther's word for this, and he is never weary of using it.

The gradual loosening of Werther's hold on the phenomenal world is finely illustrated by the shifting of his interest from Homer to Ossian. Homer—perhaps the clearest in profile of great poets—is at first his sole companion. Sitting in summertime by the well, Werther watches the girls who come from the town to fetch water—"the most harmless," he says, "and the most necessary of occupations which aforetime was done by the kings' daughters"—and in this patriarchal spirit, half Old Testament and half Odyssey, he solaces himself with his beloved Homer. His birthday present—on the twenty-eighth of August, Goethe's birthday—is the little Wetstein Homer—"two little volumes in duodecimo"—which he has long desired in place of the heavy Ernesti edition. And a little before this date he writes: "You ask if you are to send me my books. My dear fellow, I pray you for God's sake, spare me them. I do not wish to be guided, encouraged, stimulated. This heart of mine is turbulent enough. What I need is a lullaby, and I find plenty of this in my Homer."

The reader of Homer who can extract a lullaby from him is reading him strangely, and is in danger of deserting him. When this finally happens—"Ossian has supplanted Homer in my affections," he writes after an interval—we realize that it had to come. Werther is enraptured now with the grey mists and the moonlight of Ossian's shadowy world. And it is Ossian, the vague and featureless, who is with him to the end.

This is the instinctive movement of his mind, traceable even in his happiest moments. When he sees the spring blossom—this is from the earliest of the letters—he exclaims that "every tree and every hedge is a nosegay," and that he "would fain become a mayfly to float in the sea of odour and find his nourishment there"—a typical impulse which closes up the outer world and substitutes a fervent, unvisual activity for the shrewder activity of seeing and watching. Werther is not observant of the natural beauty about him, he must shut his eyes and drift hither and thither in it like the mayfly. Whatever is specific or formal, be it in thought or act, he puts from him with an uncanny thoroughness. The decent logic of his friend Albert incenses him. "You know," he writes, "that I like him well, except for his 'but' (bis auf seine Zwar), for does it not go without saying that every general statement admits of exceptions? The fellow is so precise. If he thinks he has said anything hasty, general, or half true he is never done with his qualifying, modifying, adding, and subtracting, until there is nothing left." So intense, so absolute is his passion for the illimitable, that he prefers what men call inactivity to any tangible occupation. "I could not draw now, not a line, and I was never a greater painter than at these moments."

Having forfeited all sure hold upon the outer world, Werther will brook none within. He will have no mentor but his own heart, and it is without a tether. In this chosen world of inti-

mations and vague desires he is like one lost in a spaceless sea. With growing alarm we watch the fluctuations of his mind from the near to the far, from the minute to the unbounded. More even than by the vehemence of his emotions, which makes Lotte fear that his excessive sympathy with everything will be his death, we are dismayed by his incalculable oscillations from high to low, from rapture to despair. It is with an imminent sense of catastrophe that we hear him exclaim at one moment that the might and splendour of the world will destroy him, and at another that there is no end to all this misery but the grave, or that Nature, once a nurturing mother and a paradise, is suddenly become "an engulfing and ruminating monster" (ein ewig verschlingendes, ewig wiederkäuendes Ungeheurer).

Werther's suicide is merely the outcome of this extreme way of living. He relinquishes or loses all contact with the outside world, all formal control of the mind within, all discipline of occupation and routine. His spirit arrogates to itself the freedom of the universe, and in due course the body follows and we lose sight of him for ever.

Werther can still be read with absorption. It is as near to our humanity now and as exciting as when it was first written, and it is likely to remain so. What we experience is not so much a suicide as the elimination of a personality, but the process is one that we could not have foreseen. Our individual profiles, this book tells us, must be preserved by usage, or they will disappear. For most of us the daily round and common task—the superficial concern with ourselves, with our particular wants and pleasures, the mere outward activity of our lives—preserves our outlines, our visible exteriors, until the physical processes are undermined by disease or decay, and we die. Until then the boundary line which hedges us off from the universe is trodden daily and hourly, and the pathway is clearly marked. But Werther is so incessantly, so passionately occupied with the essential, universal, absolute life which he finds deep down in himself and in things, that he neglects his personal boundaries, fails to tread the pathway, or to repair the fences which delimit his personal estate and mark him off from the vasty deep, and in due course he pays the price of this incaution and disappears beyond recall. To read his story is like watching an artist's study of a head, which by virtue of some unique and consuming vitality erases itself mysteriously before our eyes and leaves us staring at the blank sheet.

This is the real meaning of Werther's story. Unlike the suicide of Brutus or Anna Karenin, or any other in literature, it is essentially unmotived, and takes us rather to metaphysical poetry than to drama or prose fiction. Its counterpart in Goethe's works is the assumption of Ganymede in a burst of springtide exaltation or the all-but-suicide of Faust, who at the crucial moment forgets his impulse of despair at a supernal rebuff and sees only the limitless vista that awaits him beyond the narrow door; the difference being that these two are the responsible agents of the deed while Werther is the victim of it. His death is the inevitable consequence of his habit of life, not a separate act of will. It might have come earlier or later, the song of the angels which Faust heard might have deferred it or hastened it, but could never have averted it.

It is true that in another light the suicide can be ascribed to hopeless love, a thwarted career, and a case of pistols, and that Napoleon, for whom seven readings of *Werther* were apparently not enough, censured the mixing of the motives and, if we can trust the accounts of their somewhat disingenuous conversation, extracted from Goethe his concurrence in this censure. But the fact is, and Goethe must have known it, that in the deeper life of the work there was no need of specific motives; the suicide of Werther was not dependent on his meeting Lotte or on public disappointments or access to fire-arms. Give Werther his way of inner life, and a private paradise will not prevent his vanishing. For such a state of mind as his anything and everything is a motive for the last release.

There is nothing in the text of *Werther* to indicate that Goethe was closely interested in the external motives of the catastrophe, or was even careful of them. We know that when he revised his text for a later edition he modified his conception of Albert, but the story had nothing to gain by the change, and it had something to lose, since by removing a certain invidiousness from Albert's character he made Werther's relations with him and Lotte less exasperating than before and thus tended to weaken the central situation. If Goethe had been primarily concerned with the dramatic psychology of his three characters, conceived as a group, he might have been reluctant to tamper with the text at this point. He seems instead merely to have accepted the Wetzlar material—chiefly his own intimate relation with Kestner and Lotte—as a suitable basis or stiffening for his theme, and to have devoted his main attention to the mind of Werther.

Not that he was unmindful of narrative technique, as his use of Homer and Ossian shows. If Goethe has a place among the masters of prose fiction it is as much on the strength of *Werther* as of any other work. But his skill as a story-teller shows up better in his management of the invented episodes than in his use of autobiography. Prominent among these is the episode—added later when the text was revised—of the love-lorn peasant lad who murders his supposed rival in an onset of jealousy, an episode which we instinctively connect with that of the idiot youth whose year of confinement in the madhouse is remembered by him as his lost happiness. These are the two figures in the story who bear most directly on Werther and best explain his mind to us. In one sense—the sense in which everything that happens to Werther is a motive for his final resolve—they thrust him on to his doom. He is aghast at a world in which the worthiest love can culminate in crime and murder, and he is not less aghast at the dreadful case of one whose happiness is indistinguishable from his insanity. ''God in heaven, hast Thou decreed that men should only know happiness before they come to their understanding, and when they lose it again?''

But these figures serve chiefly for contrast. In Goethe's eyes Werther is neither a criminal nor a lunatic. Or if he is a criminal he is only technically so. The Law or the Church may hold him guilty, but our common humanity repudiates the charge. Werther is buried without funeral rites, but simple workfolk carry him to the grave. And if he is insane it is with the insanity of genius, not of disease, the insanity of those who see too deeply and pay the tragic penalty. ''I have been beyond myself more than once,'' says Werther, anticipating a famous passage in *Faust,* ''my passions were never far from madness, but I do not regret it. For I have come to see in my fashion that extraordinary men who do something great and seemingly impossible have always been called fanatical and insane.''

We have only to listen closely to Werther to hear a clear mind speaking. If there must be a pathological view of him there is also a normal one. Werther is remote from conventional life and he abhors it, but he is close to the man of genius, to the child, to nature. His suicide is not so much an offence against nature as an exemplification of that law of nature which says that if we venture too far and too frequently from the shores of the finite into the deeps of infinity we shall sooner or later be caught by the deeps and never return. This is a law which Nature is seldom called upon to enforce. Werther alone, it may be, has succeeded in provoking her to the enforcement, but the law remains and is not less valid for being seldom broken. For Werther the outer world of particular things and particular horizons which calls the rest of us into action and gives us our so-called liberty, is irksome and imprisoning. He can only endure it so long as it lets him sense the eternal life behind it, and it often fails him in his need. But the door, the ever-open door, to this eternity is in the depths of the heart. Here, where others are cabined and confined, he is as free as a bird, and here he takes his long flight at the last. (pp. 40-8)

Barker Fairley, in his Goethe as Revealed in His Poetry, *1932. Reprint by Frederick Ungar Publishing Co., 1963, 210 p.*

GEORG LUKÁCS (essay date 1936-37)

[*Lukács, a Hungarian literary critic and philosopher, is acknowledged as a leading proponent of Marxist thought. His development of Marxist ideology was part of a broader system in which he sought to further the values of rationalism (peace and progress), humanism (Socialist politics), and traditionalism (Realist literature) over the countervalues of irrationalism (war), totalitarianism (reactionary politics), and modernism (post-Realist literature). The subjects of his literary criticism are primarily the nineteenth-century Realists—Balzac and Tolstoy—and their twentieth-century counterparts—Gorky and Mann. Here, in remarks written in 1936-37, Lukács briefly comments on Goethe's reworking of autobiographical elements into material for the novel. For additional criticism by Lukács on* Werther, *see excerpt dated 1936 in NCLC, Vol. 4.*]

The important modern historical novels show a clear tendency towards *biography*. The direct link between the two in many cases is most probably the contemporary fashion of historical-biographical *belles lettres*. But in the really important cases this is barely more than a formal link. The popularity of the biographical form in the present-day historical novel is due rather to the fact that its most important exponents wish to confront the present with great model figures of humanist ideals as examples, as resuscitated forerunners of the great struggles of today. (pp. 300-01)

[Let us] examine how the great writers of the past went about the problem of biography, how far they used a biographic method or presentation in their art. Goethe's practice is perhaps the most instructive here. In particular, because Goethe portrayed certain problems of his own life both as straight biography and as material for his novels. *Dichtung und Wahrheit (Poetry and Truth)* contains the material of both *Werthers Leiden (Sorrows of Werther)* and *Wilhelm Meisters Lehrjahre ((Wilhelm Meister's Apprenticeship)*. Now if one follows through these works from their inception, one sees that they verge away from the biographical. (p. 301)

If one compares *Werther* with the Lotte Buff episode in the autobiography, one can see clearly what Goethe has added in the novel, where as a writer he has left the autobiographical behind. In *Werther* he has introduced the social element into the conflict and lifted the love collision onto a tragic plane. In a word, everything which gives *Werther* its lightning effect and eternal freshness is biographically untrue. No biographical account of the Lotte Buff episode could have remotely attained to the poetic greatness of *Werther;* for the elements of this poetry lay in Goethe's experience of this episode, but not in the episode itself as it actually occurred. But even then these were only elements and germs in Goethe's experience. It still required an enormous amount of poetic *invention*, the supplementing, extending and deepening work of generalization, before the story and the characters of *Werther* could take shape in the form we know them today. (p. 302)

> *Georg Lukács, "The Historical Novel of Democratic Humanism," in his* The Historical Novel, *translated by Hannah Mitchell and Stanley Mitchell, Merlin Press, 1962, pp. 251-350.*

E. L. STAHL   (essay date 1942)

[Stahl analyzes the main character, style, and form of the novel to uncover its underlying themes. For additional commentary by Stahl, see excerpt dated 1949.]

Werther cannot accept standards of life and thought prescribed by the Rationalists. Some of his most decided antagonisms are those directed against the prescriptions, in law, religion, aesthetics and social conduct, of reason and the intellect. He is a child of that epoch of the eighteenth century, in which the rejection of Rationalist standards was heralded by Rousseau himself, and in Germany by Klopstock, Hamann and Herder.

Title page to the first edition of Die Leiden des jungen Werthers.

He is the disciple of all these and goes even farther than they do in his concentration on the irrational values of life, on standards (if such there can be) to be established by imagination, intuition and feeling. He is happy only when this "finer" aspect of his nature can be brought into action. He is unhappy, above all, when he finds no scope for his store of feeling, no outlet for his sympathies, no object for his love.

If we piece together the elements of his sympathies and antipathies, we can sum up by saying that what he longs for most is unity in existence. For him the intellect distinguishes and separates, while the heart senses the whole. Behind his aspirations is the voice of Giordano Bruno, whose Renaissance feelings live in him, but shorn of their spirit of adventure.

For Werther is a spiritual revolutionary who possesses convictions, but no power of will to put them into practice. He finds himself in the impasse which is typical of the eighteenth century in Germany. There is no practical outlet for the zeal which burns in him. He is an individualist searching for that whole in which he can merge. But his individualism on the one hand, and contemporary society on the other, are such, that he is driven in upon himself—not outward towards the world. His zeal becomes a malady from which there is no escape but self-annihilation. All his passions and desires are sickened by this cast of inaction.

Fundamentally, Werther's search is a quest for a society which could not be found in his day—a society in which the individual could be preserved in his rights, yet also merge with others. This ideal community is one of Goethe's main preoccupations in the years which precede and follow the writing of *Werther*. He found it in Weimar and . . . expressed his views concerning the relation between the individual and this society in his later novels. In *Werther* the social aspect of the problem of individualism is not yet clearly stated. The elements are there—Werther's relations with the peasants and simple people of Wahlheim, and his experiences in higher society. But they are pointers and nothing more. The problem is as yet stated in the widest terms, not as the relations between the ego and the social whole, but as those between the ego and the universal whole. Goethe's preoccupation between the years 1770 and 1775 concerned this embracing problem, the philosophical basis of this later development. (pp. xiv-xvi)

It is . . . a human problem viewed in terms of religious, rather than social, difficulties which, in the last resort Goethe presents in *Werther*. It is the relation between Werther and his God rather than between him and his fellow men that gives us the clearest indication of his malady.

If we listen carefully to Werther's voice, we shall see that God is the ultimate centre of his thought. In the last stage of his life, when his distress has become insurmountable, he calls out to God as frequently as to Wilhelm. The friend to whom he had confessed his earthly joys and sorrows is replaced by the Father when the limits of earthly existence begin to recede for him. And in what is perhaps the most remarkable letter of the whole work (Part II, November 15), astonishing for the audacity of its utterance, Werther approaches God directly, rejecting the mediation of the Son. The far-reaching nature of this position can only be indicated here. It is, according to Kassner, an attitude adopted by Rilke. Werther's surmise that God claims him directly for Himself, that he is not of the world of the Son, is an explanation of his earthly life which must strike us as presumption; and perhaps this presentation of himself, as well as the image of the Prodigal Son, that other Wanderer, which he adopts for himself (Part II, November 30), are intended by Goethe to indicate the extent of Werther's spiritual disintegration. But the poignancy of his words is too strong to elicit merely censure. They are the words of one who, through suffering, finds himself driven beyond the sphere of humanity.

At an earlier stage, when suffering has not yet dimmed his vision and diminished his will to live, Werther is able to feel, subtly and keenly, the presence of God within himself, in nature, and in every other manifestation of existence. He has found what Faust seeks, what Mahomet and Prometheus also seek. . . . Werther's kinship with these figures is unmistakable; they speak the same language. They all believe, against the prevailing conception in the age of Rationalism, that God is not an "artificer" who controls the world from outside as a watchmaker might regulate a clock, but that He is the eternal creator working within nature, the living force inherent in, though not identical with, the world. They have all read their Spinoza, but also agree with Leibniz that God embraces the world and is not embraced by it. God and nature are ultimately one for them, in the complicated sense thus established, and in seeking union with God, they seek at the same time contact with nature, and in seeking it they reject intermediaries of even a divine order. Werther is perhaps a greater and more tragic figure in this respect than even Faust, because he has come nearer to finding this union, and then loses it through his suffering. (pp. xvi-xviii)

Some critics have discovered a contradiction between Werther's earlier and later conceptions of God, between the Pantheistic, or nearly Pantheistic, notions of Part I and the (approximately) Christian notions of Part II. It is a contradiction only if one denies a development in Werther's attitude. It is Werther's fate that he loses the sense of harmony, of oneness with God and nature in which he had found his greatest happiness. It is his supreme tragedy, too, that God and nature are rent asunder for him. When we hear him describe nature as a ruminating monster, we witness his greatest disillusionment. Contrary, perhaps, to our expectations, it is God in whom he continues to believe when nature is thus rendered devoid of divinity for him. When he has arrived at this point, there is nothing to hold him back on earth, and, as he says, not even the silence of God will keep him there.

One of the most remarkable features of his resolution to die is the knowledge, which he clearly expresses, that he must wait for the right moment to leave the world. It is with him not a rash decision, but a coldly deliberate and carefully prepared plan, at once a sign and the product not of weakness but of strength. But this hour of triumph is also the moment of his moral defeat. In his suffering, when he is maintaining himself against a world which he considers cruel and narrow, he has our full sympathy. But when he prepares the steps which are to lead him out of this world, he reveals a measure of harsh indifference towards Lotte's feelings which antagonises us. We cannot read his last letter to her without resenting his display of callous, almost vindictive, torturing.

This is the point at which we are compelled to consider the whole of Werther's life, and to ask ourselves whether his misfortune is not, after all, his own fault. We remember his extreme sensibility, his unhappy relations with his mother, his first love for a woman older than himself who helped him to realize for the first time the fullness of his being, the emptiness of his life after she had died, the turbulence and instability of his emotional life until he finds in Lotte another and more congenial object of his love. We remember, too, his failure to

find other consolation or to obtain relief in practical activity. But we also know, as Lotte knew, that his love for her is so tenacious because he can never possess her, and that his inability to lead a useful life is largely due to his aversion to regular work. Is Goethe not portraying a man diseased by his own introspectiveness, rendered impotent by extreme self-esteem? Werther himself knows that he is guilty. . . . [It] is hardly possible to judge him by absolute standards of conduct. Perhaps we can explain his behaviour by his own justification of suicide, namely that it is a result of a disease which is beyond the scope of ethical blame.

Werther's disease affects the whole of his being and hampers his freedom of action, in his artistic as well as his emotional life. He has potentialities as an artist, but he is not capable of sustained effort or impersonal expression. Potentially his creative powers are greatest when his heart is filled with sweet emotion. But precisely in such moments of fullness he is least able to draw and paint. Of this, too, he is well aware. A feature of his malady is his self-knowledge, the clear recognition of his own failings as an artist and a man. But there is lacking in him the knowledge of a potent source of personality, knowledge of which might have saved him.

What Werther does not understand, is the power of the subconscious, so that in the last resort his self-knowledge is insufficient. He could hardly be expected to have made any advance on Leibniz' *Nouveaux Essais* which had appeared in 1765, and in which the subconscious is defined rationalistically as *petites perceptions*. There is a good deal of rationalism in the mixture of elements composing the cult of emotions in the eighteenth century, and if sentimentality can be defined as studied emotionalism, Werther is sentimental in the manner of the later eighteenth-century bourgeois, but unlike him, Werther does not prosper by his sentimentality. Goethe saw the danger of this attitude and indeed throughout his life preserved a healthy repugnance towards it, based on a shrewd analysis of its true meaning. That Werther should end in a state of complete pessimism, in which he despairs of the possibility of true knowledge and learns from the example of the madman that we are happy only when our cognitive faculties are in abeyance, is only an apparent paradox. It is another sign of his spiritual disintegration, a disintegration through lack of balance in the exercise of both rational and emotive powers.

It is the story of this disintegration of character that forms the theme of Goethe's novel, a story of failure in more than love. (pp. xviii-xx)

[The events at Wetzlar are relatively unimportant], so far as an explanation of the main theme of **Werther** is concerned. The resemblance between Werther and Goethe is indeed striking, and it is not difficult to identify the other chief characters, as well as some of the minor ones. But the parallels are not exact, since Goethe's experiences in the home of the Brentanos in Frankfurt are an important subsidiary source for the depiction of the relation between Albert and Lotte in Part II. Furthermore, despite chronological and other difficulties, Werther can be said to have been drawn in the likeness of Jerusalem, whom Goethe hardly knew, but whose life and death, details of which he solicited from Kestner, he incorporated in the novel. But even when due weight has been given to these correspondences between fact and fiction, **Werther** cannot be called a drawing from life. When the sources are of so divergent and composite a nature, reality ceases to be of value as the starting point of an explanation. The author must have had his reasons for replacing one set of events by another, and behind these reasons lies the impetus to the work as a whole. The spiritual theme of *Werther,* which is its real content, is not connected with this or that external experience of Goethe, but is the product of his imagination at the stage which he had then reached.

Werther is the last product of the youthful stage of Goethe's development as a poet. The difficulties which had beset him for some years, intensified if not occasioned by his attachment to Charlotte Buff, were as nearly as possible written off his mind in this rapidly composed work. *Werther* presents the negative solution of some of his greatest problems. For the last time, perhaps for the only time in his literary career, he gave free vent to a sense of tragic inevitability, of the possibility of which in life, however, he remained fully conscious. The depiction of tragic events of this kind was henceforward not given a prominent place in his literary work. It is often recognized that he avoided the full impact of tragic circumstance and that his philosophy is not concerned with the ultimate reality of death. Among the writers of a nation pre-eminently given to treating the problem of death, Goethe occupies a place apart.

This is true even of his *Götz von Berlichingen* and his *Egmont,* dramas in which Goethe minimizes tragic implication of the heroes' deaths by allowing them to appear in the light of transfigurations. It is even more true of *Iphigenie, Tasso* and *Die Wahlverwandtschaften,* in each of which the tragedy of death is either not considered or else mitigated, and if *Faust* can with reason be called a tragedy, it is the life and not the death of Faust that is tragic, a life, moreover, which receives divine sanction in death. In *Werther* alone Goethe faced the full reality. Werther's death is an act of liberation from a life which was a failure, but this death does not ennoble his life, nor does it arouse anything but pity and regret.

The uncompromising realism of Goethe's account of Werther's death, taken in part literally from Kestner's description of Jerusalem's suicide, is something quite unusual in his work. Such realism Goethe could only adopt when he was not personally involved, and he appears singularly detached in the case of Werther's suicide. Werther's solution of his problems is not that of Goethe; it is a negative solution and as such it does not reappear in Goethe's work. Faust is tempted to commit suicide, but he is prevented from doing so by his memories and by a coincidence. Fate is kinder to him than to Werther and he has something to live for in this world. The works which Goethe wrote after *Werther* reveal a very different attitude on his part to life and the problem of the individual's place in the world and in society. (pp. xxi-xxii)

[In his] later works we see Goethe's philosophy of the necessity for renunciation, self-limitation and moral conduct supplying the positive solutions of the problem of the relation between the individual and the whole, which he had only begun to face in *Werther.* This is true, at any rate, of the first version of *Werther,* written in 1774. Between the years 1782 and 1786 Goethe revised the text and introduced alterations which, although they did not change the principal content of the work, certainly reveal an advance on his original position.

The alterations were made during the crucial years when Goethe was evolving his "classical" philosophy of life and art, when moreover the first six books of *Wilhelm Meister* in its early form were already being written. The influences of Weimar were perhaps at work in this revision of the text, for considerations of meeting the wishes of Kestner, who had protested against certain indiscretions and misrepresentations in the published first version, seem to have played only a minor part.

Goethe, it is true, now tries to remove ambiguities in the character of Albert, and to cover up the misunderstandings between Lotte and her husband by stating reasons for Albert's brusque behaviour on the eve of Werther's suicide. Furthermore, he now only surmises, and does not, as in the first version, state with certainty that Lotte's excitement on the fatal evening was due not to a premonition of impending disaster, but to Werther's embraces and a growing estrangement from Albert. . . . (p. xxiv)

But there is another reason for this alteration, one certainly unconnected with any consideration of Kestner's feelings. The greater detail with which Lotte's state of mind is portrayed, the concentration on psychological analysis in the place of factual occurrence, reveals an interest on Goethe's part, which is of some importance for an estimate of the form and style of the novel.

The careful reader cannot but feel a difference between the manner in which Werther presents his own state of mind, and that in which the "editor" presents it. Werther's presentation throughout the greater part of the work is not strictly a psychological one, which demands a detached point of view quite beyond his power. For lack of a better word we must call Werther's presentation lyrical, the expression of states of mind without the least attempt to arrive at truth in any but a subjective, personal sense. Against this the "editor" from the beginning of his special account tries to see what has really taken place, to see both, or, towards the end, even three, sides of the question. It can be shown that it is this latter manner, the objective, "epic" presentation which, in conformity with developments in the eighteenth century generally, Goethe came to regard as the main field of the novelist. By altering his descriptive method in the second half of the "editor's" account, Goethe is thus seen to introduce into his work the detached and objective manner of treatment that he was to develop fully in *Wilhelm Meister,* which, as we have seen, was begun during the years when he was altering the design of *Werther.* In doing so he brings to a logical conclusion a tendency which characterises final passages of *Werther* itself, even in the first version. There is evidence to show that he had intended at an early stage of writing *Werther* to give the final events not in an editorial account, but by means of Werther's letters alone. A fragment has been preserved in which Werther tells what is now told by the editor. The whole work may at one time have been conceived as a diary. When he changed his plan, by assuming the rôle of an editor, Goethe thus began a recast, which he carried even farther in the second version. Here, we can say, he altered the "lyrical" style of the work in the interests of a more objective presentation.

The other additions made by Goethe in the second version confirm the view that it was his changing conception of the character of the novel which was his main reason for altering the work. The most important of these additions is the insertion, in its entirety, of the episode of the *Bauernbursch.* The infatuation and the desperate deed of this hapless youth serve as a mirror to reflect a distorted image of Werther's own unhappiness. A parallel, though distorted, event of this kind relieves Werther's sorrows of some of that uniqueness upon which is based his "lyrical" presentation of them, and the novel has thereby gained in objectivity and depth.

Another important alteration is of a different kind. In the first version prominence had been given . . . to Werther's unhappy experience in the house of Graf C. It had been mentioned as a reason for his suicide, or at least for the state of mind which urged him to commit suicide. It is believed that Herder, as after him Napoleon (who read the work seven times, though probably only in its first form), drew Goethe's attention to this inconsistency, or rather redundancy of motivation. By toning down the effects of this insult in the second version, Goethe certainly made his work more homogeneous, but also made possible the one-sided interpretation of the novel by which it was considered to be in the first place the story of unhappy love.

It has been seen that *Werther* can be characterized as possessing two styles, a lyric and an epic style. There is a third. If we agree that the style of drama derives from the arrangement of incidents according to principles of conflict and crisis, leading gradually, but inevitably, to a final catastrophe, then *Werther* can be said to possess the dramatic quality to an exceptional degree. Also, the letter-form of the novel, while it supplies the basis of the lyric style of the work, is at the same time a dramatic device, since Goethe can allow Werther to speak directly to us, as do the figures of a drama. (pp. xxv-xxvii)

If we can thus analyse the style of *Werther,* this does not mean that the work is lacking in uniformity. It is, on the contrary, like *Iphigenie,* one of the most homogeneous of Goethe's creations. Whereas *Tasso, Wilhelm Meister* and *Faust* suffer as works of art because the author's change of purpose in the writing has irreparably damaged their unity, not even the alterations in the second version of *Werther* endanger the main design. (pp. xxvii-xxviii)

Goethe's artistry is also shown in his handling of episodes and digressions, all of which bear intimately on the revelation of Werther's character; in his mastery of the technique of intimation, by which events are foreshadowed without detriment to their later significance; and in his command of symbolism by means of which he weaves a pattern as intricate as it is homogeneous. Goethe shows himself supremely equal to the task, enjoined upon him by the use of the letter-form, of connecting the past life of Werther with his present experiences, of conveying information about his personality not consecutively, but on widely separated, yet apposite occasions, so that a unified picture results. We can search in vain for a similar achievement in German literature until Hölderlin wrote his *Hyperion.*

The style and the language of *Werther* are equally without parallel. Never before had the German language shown itself capable of being used with such effect of rhythm and cadence in prose. No mood, however violent, however subtle, no feeling, however passionate or intimate, but found its true expression in the adroit succession of Goethe's cadences. In the first version of *Werther* his youthful style is seen at its most expressive in his use of rhythmic variations, of significant and colourful verbs, and of colloquial, archaic and dialectal words and phrases. In the second version Goethe, who in Weimar sought to promote the development of a standard literary language, toned down or removed a large number of these expressions.

Werther, however, remained essentially the work of a young man, and it is significant that it was the first version which aroused the immediate interest of contemporary readers. It already contained that treatment of psychological problems and that revelation of character which were the outstanding contribution of *Die Leiden des jungen Werthers* to the development of the novel.

This singular product of Goethe's youth, however, so remarkable because it stands as the epitome of one important aspect of the age in which it was written, possesses an intrinsic value transcending mere historical interest. It is easier to accept in this work than in many others written during the eighteenth century in Germany the thoughts and sentiments characteristic of that age, and that age alone. Goethe's *Werther,* the first modern product of German literature to win recognition beyond the frontiers of Germany, is also the first to evoke more than contemporary interest. The qualities which gave it lasting value are indeed not easy to define. Is it Werther's situation, which experience has shown to be an endlessly recurring one in the modern world? Is it the novel perception of nature, and the keen appreciation of her influence on human life, for good as well as for ill, which have entered so deeply into the consciousness of modern man as to be an ineradicable part of it? Is it the voice of youth, rebellious yet devout, capable alike of the harshest condemnations and the most heedless acceptances, that enraptures a world made newly aware of the beauty of immaturity? Is it Goethe's language, ageless in its supple vigour, its measured melodiousness, and its variety and polyphony? We know that analysis is a vain endeavour to unravel the secrets of composition. The disturbing and appealing quality of Goethe's work derives not from an aspect or an element, but from the composition as a whole. (pp. xxviii-xxx)

> *E. L. Stahl, in an introduction to* Goethe's "Die Leiden des Jungen Werthers"*by Johann Wolfgang von Goethe, edited by E. L. Stahl, Basil Blackwell, 1942, pp. v-xxx.*

E. L. STAHL   (essay date 1949)

[Stahl analyzes the character and personality of Werther in his progress toward spiritual dissolution. For additional criticism by Stahl, see excerpt dated 1942.]

In the account which Goethe gives of *Werther* in Book 13 of *Dichtung und Wahrheit* [see excerpt dated 1814], he clearly shows that his first novel was a compound of personal and impersonal elements and that he strove to fuse the variegated material on which it is based into a "poetic unity", to transmute "reality" into "poetry". He recalls how his own friends and the reading public at large sought a didactic purpose behind the work, or else condemned it as immoral. But, he replies, an artistic representation is never didactic: "Die wahre Darstellung aber hat keinen (didaktischen Zweck)". Indeed, although in his short preface to *Werther* Goethe, as the "editor" of Werther's papers, calls upon the reader to pity and admire his hero, it is manifestly a special kind of reaction that he aimed to arouse. Both the admiration and the sympathy that we are asked to expend on Werther are emotions excited by a pathological case, by a man who is doomed to destruction even before we make his acquaintance. In his parody of the work, says Goethe, Nicolai failed to see that the canker was destroying Werther in his youth, that his "Jugendblüte schon von vornherein als vom tödlichen Wurm gestochen erscheine", and he gives a masterly analysis of the mentality which we find in Werther.

Goethe points out that misanthropy is the result of an inability to take a reasonable interest in the ever recurring events of life and nature: "Alles Behagen am Leben ist auf eine regelmässige Wiederkehr der äusseren Dinge gegründet . . . wälzt sich aber die Verschiedenheit dieser Erscheinungen vor uns auf und nieder, ohne dass wir daran teilnehmen, sind wir gegen so holde Anerbietung unempfänglich, dann tritt das grösste Übel, die schwerste Krankheit ein.'' This is the root of Werther's malady. He perishes because he is tormented by the instability of life. Instead of participating in its constant ebb and flow, he is detached from the life-giving force, and remains a mere spectator of the great cycle of change. . . . Werther does not grow. He merely moves with ever-increasing inevitability towards his appointed end. The only real action of which this passive spectator of life is capable is to abolish his own existence. He is not able to persuade himself that order rules in the universe; the universe falls to pieces in his mind. God, nature, society and the individual—Werther desires their fusion into an embracing unity, but feels himself thrust into the periphery of existence, where he dwells in isolation. . . . Werther seeks satisfaction in the recesses of his being. He exclaims in his letter of May 22nd: ''Ich kehre in mich selbst zurück, und finde eine Welt!''

This letter reveals his spiritual malaise. Life, he says, is a dream because the active and the speculative powers of man are in bondage. For him even the hope of immortality, the prospect of a freer existence in the beyond, is merely a form of resignation, ''eine träumende Resignation'', a brightly-coloured vista painted on the walls that hold us imprisoned. Here we see how advanced Werther's malady is at an early stage in the novel. He is out of tune with the external world and his only refuge is his ''inner world'', the realm of his imagination. But even in this world disappointment awaits him; his imagination is not plastic and productive, but merely intuitive: ''Ich kehre in mich selbst zurück, und finde eine Welt! Wieder mehr in Ahnung und dunkler Begier als in Darstellung und lebendiger Kraft''. The essential difference between Werther and his creator becomes clear when we take heed of these words. Goethe survived his own playful attempts to commit suicide, not only because he had a sense of humour (''So lachte ich mich zuletzt selbst aus . . . und beschloss, zu leben''), but also because he was able to transmute reality into poetry. This he was able to do since he possessed what both he and Novalis called creative imagination, ''produktive Einbildungskraft'', the power to embody moods in concrete images. He described this faculty when accounting for the letter-form of *Werther* in *Dichtung und Wahrheit*. Among his accomplishments Werther also possesses artistic sensibility. But he is a dilettante in Goethe's sense of the term, an impressionist lacking the capacity of productivity. . . . (pp. 48-51)

In his artistic predilections, as elsewhere, Werther is a passive spectator rather than an active participator. Even in his enthusiasm for Homer and Ossian he betrays his fatal weakness of relating things to himself, without entering truly into their being. He reads Homer while he strings peas and turns to Ossian to find there a reflection of his own moods. This reveals his lack of real empathy. To deny this quality to Werther may seem a paradox, particularly when we remember his attitude to nature as he expresses it in the letter of May 10th. Certainly he is attuned to nature; he shows what Goethe in *Dichtung und Wahrheit* calls ''ein inniges Anklingen, ein Mitschwingen ins Ganze'', but Werther's empathy is a purely passive affair. The concluding sentences of that letter are a remarkable proof of this defect. He yearns to express in his drawing the feeling which the beauty of nature has aroused in him, but fails to do so: ''Ich gehe darüber zu Grunde, ich erliege unter der Gewalt der Herrlichkeit dieser Erscheinungen''. He lacks the power of an inward organization of impressions, which every true artist must possess. . . .

This vagueness is characteristic not only of Werther's artistic efforts, but also of his attitude to nature and to life. It is a weakness which, like his fundamental egotism, his inability to transcend the limitations of his own personality and experiences, explains the hopelessness of his situation. His vague longings are necessarily doomed to disappointment. (p. 51)

Werther's weakness is nowhere shown more strikingly than in his relation to Lotte. His love for her is profound, but it is by no means a unique experience for him. Goethe's account in *Dichtung und Wahrheit* contains an illuminating paragraph on the recurrence of love, ''die Wiederkehr der Liebe'', one of the causes of misanthropy, and it is clear from the novel itself that he desired Werther's love for Lotte to partake of this quality of disillusionment. When we consider Werther's relationship not only with her, but also with Lenore's sister and with ''die Freundin meiner Jugend'' (cf. letters of May 4th and 17th), we see that what he really seeks in his friendship with women is an enhancement of his own self-esteem. In his elation he thinks only of himself. . . . Goethe has drawn the stages of Werther's relationship with Lotte from gay companionship to sentimental attachment, infatuation, obstinate passion and cruel self-assertion. This love he described in *Dichtung und Wahrheit* as a product of the separation of Werther's sensual desires from his moral instincts, the divorce between his appetite for love and his sense of devotion. Werther's capacity for true love, if he ever possessed such a gift, perishes in egotistic sensuality long before he commits suicide.

Accompanying this moral disintegration is his physical decline. At the beginning of the novel he speaks of his turbulent emotions, of his ''oft schauderndes Herz'', his ''empörtes Blut'', and later on of his feeling of suffocation, his ''gepresstes Herz'', ''innere unbehagliche Ungeduld'', and ''Beklemmung''. With remarkable originality, considering the time when the work was written, Goethe gives a convincing picture of the physiological symptoms attending spiritual decay. Only occasionally does Werther find relief from his growing sense of oppression. A calming effect is produced upon him by a spectacle of idyllic domestic happiness, such as that offered by the peasant woman and her children. His attachment to Lotte is likewise inspired by his admiration for domestic bliss. Tormented by his isolation, he cannot find any collective unit to which he may cling, except the family, and, significantly, it is not his own family. Every other form of organized society, whether at Wahlheim, at the University or at the Embassy, irks him. ''Die patriarchalische Idee'' is the ideal form of social organization for him, and it is based on the principle of family relationships.

Werther's high evaluation of the family is perhaps due to the fact that since the death of his father in the days of his childhood he had not enjoyed the benefits of family life. We hear of quarrels between different branches of the family and Werther defends his aunt against his mother's accusations. His relationship with his mother is clearly an unsatisfactory one; she does not possess his confidence and he blames her for leaving the idyllic village where he was born in order to live in an ''intolerable'' city. From this remark and other observations made by Werther we gain the impression that his maladjustment was caused by his need of that kind of sheltered existence which the family provides. His idealization of domesticity and the patriarchal state, and his love for children as well as the ''simple folk'', may represent an over-compensation for his own missed opportunities.

In *Dichtung und Wahrheit* Goethe makes a perspicacious observation which offers another explanation of Werther's malaise and permits us to recognize the social significance of this novel. Speaking of the misanthropic feelings engendered in Germany when he wrote the work, he points to the influence of English literature where a similar tendency prevailed. But, he goes on to say, an Englishman who in his youth protested the vanity of life could later overcome his pessimism by playing his part in the world of affairs in "Weltgeschäften . . . und im Parlament, bei Hofe, im Ministerium, auf Gesandtschaftsposten". In Germany, on the other hand, no relief for private disabilities could be obtained from public service. In the eighteenth century a young German like Werther lived a dreary existence "in einem schleppenden, geistlosen, bürgerlichen Leben". His suicide was the result not merely of maladjustment, but also of a total lack of opportunities for adjustment. A finely-tempered, sensitive and gifted youth who was not artistically creative, when he was born into such a void, was easily driven to the resolve to take his own life.

When Goethe, speaking as the "editor", appealed for our admiration and our sympathy, he was thinking of these aspects of Werther's character and his fate. He presents a situation which makes it impossible for the reader to maintain a censorious attitude. Werther's self-destruction is inevitable from the moment when his story begins to unfold. As early as the 22nd of May he thinks of suicide as a means to escape from the "prison" of life. It has been said, however, that the point when he does commit this act is chosen arbitrarily, since it might have occurred earlier or later. This is not the whole truth, for Goethe's novel is a masterpiece of artistic economy. Werther's suicide becomes an inescapable necessity only when every other avenue of redress has been tried by him and found wanting, and when the balance of his emotional life has been irretrievably disturbed. Werther's story is the tale of one of life's dilettantes, whom life has maimed and whom it destroys because his crippled faculties cannot be restored to health either by nature or by society or by creative artistic activity or even by faith in God.

Step by step we are taken along the path that leads to his inescapable end. The story, as it is developed before our eyes, exhibits every mark of an inevitable occurrence. *Werther* is a novel possessing greater tragic power than Goethe later permitted for this genre in his theory and it is written in language of unprecedented tragic range and beauty. But it is a novel of an exceptional kind, since it presents the hero's fate in a series of self-revealing letters which resemble the monologues and the dialogues of a drama. (pp. 52-5)

> E. L. Stahl, "Goethe as Novelist," in Essays on Goethe, *edited by William Rose, Cassell & Co. Ltd., 1949, pp. 45-73.*

KARL VIËTOR (essay date 1949)

[*Viewing* Werther *in a historical and literary context, Viëtor explores the protagonist's inner life.*]

"I am weary of bewailing the fate of our generation of human beings, but I will so depict them that they may understand themselves, if that is possible, as I have understood them." It is the state of his generation's soul which Goethe sets forth in *Werther;* the extreme character of the case affords a complete diagnosis. "Look you, the end of this disease is death! The goal of such sentimental enthusiasm is suicide!" The disease of which Goethe speaks threatened the young intelligentsia

everywhere in Europe, but nowhere more than in Germany. It was the softening and the excess of emotion which we call sentimentality. A tense and idealistic youth found itself cut off from the world of great action, worthy achievement, and lofty striving by an antiquated social order. In all cultural matters, in science, art, philosophy, the bourgeoisie had assumed leadership and justly felt that it possessed the highest moral cultivation. But in politics and society the middle class was still under constraint, still subject to the domination of princely absolutism and feudal caste. The storm clouds of revolutionary change had just begun to appear on the horizon. In the sultry calm which preceded the great storm shortly to break in France, there developed a state in which spiritual energies were pent up within and active striving was flung back upon itself. Idealistic feeling and will languished ineffectually. "Here we have to do with men living in the most peaceful of circumstances whose lives have been spoiled for them by want of deeds and by their exaggerated demands upon themselves." Where the inner life was intensified to such a pitch, any accidental passion that arose must lead to a crisis which could only be resolved by the most fatal means. "Look you, the end of this disease is death!" (pp. 28-9)

Die Leiden des jungen Werthers (The Sorrows of Young Werther), as the title of the anonymously published first version of 1774 reads, is a romance in letters. (p. 30)

In their origin as in their effect these are no true letters but highly intimate confessions which a lone man makes to himself, monologues of a suffering soul. Only Werther's voice is heard; the friend to whom he writes appears only in the reactions which his replies evoke. This new form gave psychological depth to the epistolary novel and at the same time supreme artistic simplicity. Nowhere and at no time has it been surpassed. The models for the descriptive parts, with their objectively faithful portrayal of rural life, idyllic and patriarchal conditions, and simple folk, were the new novels of the English—those of Sterne, and above all the books of Oliver Goldsmith. Goethe gratefully calls them his teachers, and says that they are "as interesting, as affectionate," as their own domestic life. In them Goethe found confirmation for the realistic tendency of his own narrative style: "Proceed from the domestic, and spread yourself, if you can, over the whole world."

Among European novels *Werther* is the first in which an inward life, a spiritual process and nothing else, is represented, and hence it is the first psychological novel—though naturally not the first in which the inner life in general is seriously dealt with. The conflict between an immoderately burgeoning passion and the ordered world of society is here described, as it were, "from within." The scene is the soul of the hero. All events and figures are regarded only in the light of the significance they have for Werther's emotion. All that happens serves but to nourish the absolutism of Werther's emotion—a fatal propensity which swells to a demonic possession and engulfs all other inward forces and possibilities.

The germ of the disease is already present in Werther before he is attacked by his passion; his passion only serves to aggravate it. As Werther describes himself at the beginning of the book, he is already a lonely man who seeks refuge from life in the bosom of nature because nothing will satisfy his insatiable heart. He speaks of nothing as frequently as of this heart, which he spoils like an ailing child. For him it is the epitome of his worth, the source of his personal life. "Ah, what I know, anyone may know. My heart is mine alone." His inner being appears capable of satisfaction only by an emotional realization of the infinity of the universal. But this is an experience which increasingly alienates him from life. Only idyllic landscapes give him inward peace; only with children and simple folk can he associate on terms of friendship; the patriarchal world of the *Odyssey* is to him a "lullaby." But his soul is filled with dark premonitions and yearning, and he sinks into his twilight dreams. This man could be healed, could be saved only by a transformation which would force him to move among the realities of life, to expend his pent-up inner riches in plans and deeds. But this transition from the sentimental state of youth to the sphere of adult activity does not come about.

The encounter with Lotte gives his searching emotion an object to which it can fasten. Now begins the spiritual event constituting the inner action of this book, which, by the standards of literary composition, is rather a lyrical drama than a novel. Goethe himself has referred to this psychic process as an illness, since every great passion is a sort of disease. As we look on, the passion of love tightens its grip upon the unresisting sufferer; we see how its effect is the more disruptive because it draws to itself all the forces which constitute Werther's greatness: his gifts of unqualified feeling, his demands for the fullness of existence, his readiness to devote himself wholly to the great thing which has seized upon him. The hero is destroyed by what is noble and good in him. Later Goethe once said: "Man's longing for the ideal, when deprived of its objectives, or when these are spoiled, turns back on itself, becomes refined and intensified until it seems to outdo itself." Werther is ruined because of and in spite of his possession of a great heart, an ideal soul. He suffocates by the abundance of his inward life. Qualities which might have raised his being to a pinnacle in friendlier times and under more favorable circumstances become his doom.

Goethe's expressions leave no doubt as to what he considers the cause of Werther's ruin in the outer world. The cause lies in the fatal conditions under which the intellectual young men of the age had to live. Since the age denied them opportunity to act greatly, they were left with no other satisfaction than to dream and to feel greatly. The fulfillment which they could not find in active life they were forced to seek in inward existence. Mme de Staël has described this situation excellently:

> Since the form of their governments afforded them no possibility to win fame and serve their country, they devoted themselves to every sort of philosophic speculation and sought in heaven a field for the activity which narrow limitations denied them on earth. They found satisfaction in ideals because reality offered them nothing to occupy their imagination.

Because the world had no room for them, they wished to expand their egos to infinity. "I turn back into myself and discover a world" (Ich kehre in mich selbst zurück und finde eine Welt).

To the motive of inward passion grown rank there was added another, which explained why the pent-up dynamism could not unburden itself outwardly. Even the modest activity which was permitted to bourgeois officials was made impossible for Werther by the painful scandal which thrust him out of a society composed of the gentry. Now every path to the sphere of action was barred to him; after a vain attempt at flight he submitted without resistance to his "endless sorrow through which any vital force that was in him must eventually be extinguished." Could a man be more lonely than he now was? Things went so far that he lost even his communion with nature. The pantheistic feeling for the "unmeasured sea," the ever-creating abun-

dance of the universal spirit in which his ego, suffering in its limitations, sought self-forgetfulness, was now displaced by the picture of an "ever-devouring, ever-regurgitating monster," an unfeeling destructive power with no concern for the survival of the individual. In the composition of the book the alternation of seasons corresponds to the transformation of inward mood. The month is May when Werther's love begins; it is December when his end comes. So, too, in the first portion his companion is the vital and energetic Homer; in the second the melancholy, unbelieving Ossian, whose gloomy pathos introduces the fateful moment when Werther locks the unattainable in his arms for a single time and so loses her forever.

Nothing in this book, not even its truth of expression unparalleled at the time, so deeply stirred Goethe's contemporaries as the self-destruction of the hero. Without charity, but also without reproach (as is appropriate to "true representation"), the suicide is here presented as the necessary consequence of a passion whose power transcended the "bounds of humanity." Christians found it immoral; rationalist skeptics and libertines thought it ridiculous to take passion so seriously. But among young men who themselves suffered from Werther's malaise there were many to whom his example gave courage to put a period to their suffering as he had done. The poet found it necessary to admonish such readers, who did not understand that the book was to be read, so to speak, against the grain, in a motto affixed to the second edition in Werther's name: "Be a man, do *not* follow me."

Then and later Goethe was accused of having provoked the "Werther fever" by his "dangerous book." He replied quite justly that he had not originated the disease but had only uncovered the evil which was latent in the young men of his time. The nature of such an epidemic of soul sickness Goethe could report correctly, inasmuch as he had with difficulty succeeded in saving himself from a similar crisis. Outbreaks of world-weariness, he says, recur in the history of civilized nations periodically. Byronism was a somewhat analogous phenomenon. In the life history of the individual something of the same sort occurs. In all ages *taedium vitae* is a problem in the development of high-spirited young people. "Frustrated fortune, hampered activity, unsatisfied wishes are not the lesions of a specific age but of every individual man. It would be too bad if everyone did not go through a period when **Werther** struck him as if it were written for him alone" [see excerpt by Goethe dated 1824]. Otherwise, for all of its artistic excellence, **Werther** would be nothing more than a document in the spiritual history of Europe and not the great work it is—the exemplary representation of a tragic conflict arising out of the situation of the modern individualist. Idealism of feeling, which demands complete realization, founders here on the reef of social usage as it is established by the formal order of civilization and by fate. (pp. 31-4)

> *Karl Viëtor, in his* Goethe: The Poet, *translated by Moses Hadas, Cambridge, Mass.: Harvard University Press, 1949, 341 p.*

VICTOR LANGE   (essay date 1949)

[*In this interpretation of the novel as "the account of a complex psychological crisis," Lange examines Werther's underlying motivations. For additional criticism by Lange, see excerpt dated 1952-53.*]

[In **Werther,** Goethe's] combination of truth and fiction was, of course, part of a specific artistic intention: transcending his own personal role in the drama which he hoped to relate, he would convey with all immediacy possible the condition of a supremely sensitive, but supremely unstable human being. *Werther* was to represent the history, not only of an unhappy lover, but of a young man who is crushed and destroyed by the unbearable weight of his own passions. That this highly perceptive youth also found himself sadly, even tragically, in conflict with an insensible society, that he could not maintain himself in a world which persisted in its conventional social and emotional habits, must be regarded as a subsidiary though essential dramatic theme of the novel. No one knew better than the young Goethe how paralyzing such conflicts could be. In his life and in his poetry he had found no better way in which to show the extraordinary strength of his own youthful feeling and imagination than by a series of emphatic, even fanatical assertions of the creative freedom of the individual. Goethe's letters of that time, his dithyrambic poetry, and the enthusiastic passages in praise of Shakespeare's genius, are sufficient evidence of his rebellious faith.

But the stirring effect of the book was by no means due only to its social theme or the sentimental and emotional revelations of a private individual. As soon as the novel was published, it seemed to release, as Goethe himself later recognized, a latent disposition among his contemporaries to melancholy and crippling introspection. What was begun as the portrait of a gifted man of feeling turned into a tragedy of sensibility. Yet, Werther is no Hamlet, even though the paralysis of the will and the overtones of despair, of "sickness unto death" may seem to be shared by both: Werther, unlike Hamlet, seeks fellowship. Throughout his early days in the country he finds himself enchanted by images of the simple life which, in contrast to his disappointing experiences among society, he discovers in the world of Homer and the plain folk of the village. And what appeals to him in Charlotte is not the fire of her love for him, but the natural kindness of her whole being. His growing attachment to her, self-centered, demanding and naïve as it is, is hardly the kind of love which counts on reciprocity. It is rather an expression of his craving for a relationship which allows him to live wholly (if egotistically) out of the exuberance of his own emotions. Surely we must not conclude that he gradually surrendered to despair and thoughts of suicide because he realized that there was no hope of his marrying Charlotte.

The true reasons for the crisis in Werther's life and the cause of his collapse lie not ultimately in the circumstances of this unfulfilled love but in the incongruities of his own paradoxical nature. With an extravagant faith in the intensity of his feelings, he defies the society of his fellow men. As he realizes the hopelessness of his attempts at communication, he is compelled by a series of inner and outer circumstances to turn from the world. In his despair he dares altogether to deny its validity and relevance and eventually knows no other escape but to draw ever closer to the domain of nature, which is below man as well as above. More than once he declares himself outside the pale of what seems to him the meaningless and disgusting show of society, and by another short step he hopes to achieve a religious (or pseudo-religious) identification of man, nature and God.

There is yet another philosophical paradox in Werther. In the process of realizing his own exaggerated vision of human potentialities, he loses all confidence in the hopeful image of man such as the eighteenth century had created. He finds himself moved by the enviable figures of outcasts and lunatics who need no longer, as he sees it, to maintain the deceptive disguise of social pretenses. The idyllic and humane world of Homer soon gives way to the violent universe of Ossian. As the benevolently deistic God of the best of all possible worlds loses meaning for Werther, there emerges for him the terrible image of a nature-deity whose grand indifference to the petty concerns of man seems the only attitude of the godhead which the palpable imperfection of man's earthly career will reasonably permit.

In the experience of human insufficiency lies, ultimately, the key to Werther. The freedom of the human heart, which he so ardently declared at the beginning of his career and which he continued to assert with such uncompromising faith, is in the end used to accomplish the act of surrender, of voluntary submission to nonhuman, Godlike nature. In terms of this dilemma, Werther's suicide only completes the deliberate extinction of the last vestiges of the human personality. It is an act by which the freedom of man to recognize his own frailty and thus to deny the very meaning and validity of his life, is dramatically asserted.

Read in the light of such ideas, *Werther* becomes a work of extraordinary importance to our own time. We, too, readers of Joyce and Kafka, are profoundly moved by Werther's ever-repeated question after the essence of man. "What is the heart, what is the destiny of man?"—this is the memorable phrase which recurs throughout the book. Werther has no simple and no comforting answer to it. His jubilant faith in the passionate resources of the human being gives way to dejection and despair.

There is in *Werther* much of the cultural pessimism of his age and much of the temperamental impatience of Goethe's own youth. But it is not a document of academic interest only; its issues are universal: "The much talked about 'age of Werther,'" said Goethe in a famous conversation with Eckermann on January 2, 1824 [see excerpt above],

> is not, strictly speaking, a mere historical event. It belongs to the life of every individual who must accommodate himself and his innate and instinctive sense of freedom to the irksome restrictions of an obsolescent world. Happiness unattained, ambition unfulfilled, desires unsatisfied are the defects not of any particular age, but of every individual human being. It would be a pity indeed if everyone had not once in his life known a period when it seemed to him as if *Werther* had been written especially for him.

If, then, we take *Werther,* not as a sentimental love story, but as the account of a complex psychological crisis, we shall all the more clearly recognize how deliberately Goethe conveyed its ramified theme.

It is not a "novel" in the sense which we attach to the great specimens of nineteenth century fiction: the area of its action is circumscribed and whatever "happens" in the slight story derives its importance almost solely from its significance for the psychological drama within Werther. None of the figures surrounding him, not even Charlotte, seem to have anything like the firmness of outline or the vitality of telling detail which are the essential ingredients in Fielding, Dickens and Balzac. As Werther loses his grasp of the world, as he longs in the true spirit of the romantic for immersion in the nonhuman universe, his own mastery of the world, whether in relation to others or to his skill in sketching, decreases and vanishes. "I have lost," he confesses in the letter of November 3, "the only joy of my life; that active, sacred power with which I created worlds around me, it is no more." It is at the point where for Werther all tangible reality collapses that Goethe carefully reinforces the narrative structure: he introduces the informed comments of the narrator and thereby gives substance and credibility to what might otherwise evaporate in the effusive monologues of the letters. With remarkable technical mastery, he weaves from beginning to end a distinct pattern of poetic motifs which mirror, as they recur, not only the passing seasons but the emotional attitudes of Werther himself.

Whatever literary examples may have been in Goethe's mind, they were carefully absorbed and transformed into a work of striking originality. Certain of its features: the epistolary form, the mixture of lyrical and melodramatic elements, the precision of psychological observation, the exactness of its pathological data, even, at times, the irony with which Goethe could not help contemplating the self-pitying utterances of Werther, are, of course, foreshadowed in the great writers of the earlier eighteenth century. Without the contemporary vogue of the melancholy poetry of James Thomson and Edward Young, without Rousseau, Richardson, Goldsmith and Sterne, the novel would not have struck its readers with equal force.

But its most enchanting quality lies in its lyrical prose which is incomparably fresh and musical and which has hardly been excelled by any other German poet. (pp. vi-xi)

> *Victor Lange, in an introduction to* The Sorrows of Young Werther. The New Melusina. Novelle *by Johann Wolfgang von Goethe, translated by Victor Lange and Jean Starr Untermeyer, Rinehart & Company, 1949, pp. v-xviii.*

VICTOR LANGE   (essay date 1952-53)

[*Lange examines* Werther *as a novel within the European tradition of fiction, focusing on Goethe's literary craftsmanship. For additional criticism by Lange, see excerpt dated 1949.*]

In his reflections on the writing of **Werther,** Goethe stresses the historical perspectives from which the mood and climate of the book can best be understood. He offers in **Dichtung und Wahrheit** [see excerpt dated 1814] an extraordinarily detailed picture of that spiritual dilemma in which the sentimental mind found itself—to live in an obsolescent and confined society in which yet here and there new and revolutionary energies of feeling and speculation emerged—energies, however, which with all their intensity remained inarticulate because suitable and generally intelligible terms for them had not yet evolved. In the social as well as the literary realm the persistent presence of empty forms demanded a constant testing of the available modes of life and art, and an effort at the creation of a fresh and usable idiom. We know that the experience of this discrepancy between a new substance of feeling and a painful sense of the inadequacy of current attitudes was unusually lively in Goethe; the letters of the years 1772-1773 reveal it as one of his central themes. But what distinguishes him from his contemporaries was his concern with turning this experience into poetic form. It may seem as we compare **Werther** to what we know of Goethe himself, that the line between life and art is remarkably thin; there is little in **Werther** that is not experienced, little indeed, that we cannot verify and document in its original biographical context. But in a work of art life, whether as motivating impulse or incident of experience, is never merely reported: it is subordinated to a compelling central intention. There can be no doubt that the manner in which Goethe here turns life into art, the achievement, for the first time in his career, of a closely motivated narrative, and the poetic demonstration of an intricate spiritual process was the

result of unmistakable artistic deliberation; and we shall not do justice to the kind or the degree of this deliberation if we overemphasize Goethe's reference to the lack of any preliminary scheme, or if we take literally his own hint as to the ''somnambulist'' state in which the book was written, ''ziemlich unbewusst, einem Nachtwandler ähnlich. . . .''

For several months in 1773 Goethe had experimented most effectively with the powerfully personal idiom of the hymn, a form peculiarly suited to that ambiguous state of mind in which elegiac and aggressive attitudes were inextricably mixed. In so far as this mood of heroic exultation is appropriate to **Werther** the hymnic technique is effectively carried over into the novel: the similarity between **Ganymed** and several of Werther's letters is familiar enough. Yet, now, early in 1774, he decided—and it was no casual decision—to experiment in an altogether different medium, the medium of fiction. Fiction, we must remember, was, in spite of its enormous popular appeal, a form of dubious critical respectability, even though it had, for various reasons, recently attracted a number of distinguished minds: Wieland had turned to it, Herder was an avid consumer of novels, and what drew Goethe to Sophie La Roche was, beyond a passing and somewhat amused interest in her rôle as ''sentimental'' confidante (and in the pretty eyes of her daughter Maximiliane), above all her acknowledged success as a writer of effusive tales. He must have felt that only fiction of one sort or another could provide the kind of vehicle, the objectivity that was needed to make a nearly incomprehensible state of inner disturbance tangible and credible. For it was certainly not only his love for Lotte Buff in Wetzlar that caused the imbalance of his mind that we have come to accept as characteristic of this period. Yet from this love, brief and strangely artificial as in many respects it actually was, he now drew the symbols of his first exercise in sustained imagination.

When, ''nach so langen und vielen geheimen Vorbereitungen,'' he began writing, he cannot have been sure precisely what form the narrative would take. His choice of letters was a fairly obvious one, though they were not to be, they could not be, of the dramatic kind that Richardson and the vogue of epistolary novels had made familiar. Werther's correspondence is one-sided, a monologue that only at first seems eager for an echo and gradually ceases to pretend that anyone can share in what is said. At the same time these letters suggest whatever attachment to the world of concrete yet increasingly insufficient reality this radically introspective mind could possibly maintain. If we read the first two or three of them carefully, we come to realize Goethe's reliance upon the devices of the contemporary novel—especially as he attempts to lay out, somewhat tentatively, the suitable elements of plot and motivation. But in spite of his initial dependence on the figures and incidents of the European sentimental novel—Werther's separation from his friend, his memories of a curiously unreal love, a contested will, etc.—Goethe moves forward almost at once to his real poetic purpose: to describe, without resorting to the shopworn tricks of satire or caricature, the inadequacies of a world in which, not the mere sentimental ''man of feeling,'' but the man of irresistible if irrational emotional energies, cannot find his way. He develops, step by step and with a prodigious sensitiveness for poetic rhythm the portrait of an eccentric in a world that has itself lost its centre. He provides examples of those current and accepted modes of life into which Werther, if he had been more obtuse, might have translated his spiritual energies; but he dismisses them all: the community of village and family, the aristocratic society, politics, organized religion, even the pattern of love as a satisfying human relationship—none of these is adequate for him. The insufficiency of all props, the discovery of an inevitable sense of loneliness, the recognition of the void which he must bring himself to accept—these are motives which beyond any mere unhappy involvement in love Goethe wanted to convey.

I do not here wish to enter into this astonishingly rich web of meaning. It is important only to insist upon the immense difficulties, the technical difficulties, that must have faced Goethe as he wrote. Far from having to deal with recognized and clearly pointed social conflict such as he might have remembered from Rousseau's *Nouvelle Héloise,* he was confronted by a situation that was incomparably more elusive and complex. He was not a purveyor of argument such as Rousseau or Lavater, and he knew that this barely definable situation had to be rendered not only with the fullest awareness of the underlying sense of the ambiguity of life, but with an array of the sharpest possible detail. Where could he go among contemporary masters to find the kind of imagery, the poetic gestures, that would be familiar to his readers? The language of his poetry and that of his generation had derived its freshness and strength from Klopstock, and Goethe acknowledges his immeasurable debt to him in that famous scene where the name of the venerated poet takes on the force of a poetic symbol.

But for the more particular ingredients of fiction he had to turn to the English novelists, and among these to the one congenial mind and craftsman that was constantly before him as he wrote: Laurence Sterne. Herder had in Strasbourg praised him, and long after Goethe had disavowed the facetious rituals of sentimental worship in Darmstadt, Sterne remained for him the most memorable among the English novelists. In Sterne he recognized the same Wertherian experience of a dissolving universe, held together only by the intensity of a restless mind, clinging, not to dubious reality, but to remembered, filtered, and reassociated fragments of feeling, observation, and learning. There are striking differences, of course, between Sterne's manner and Goethe's, and their fiction is related to different historical and social conditions. But there is, surely, in **Werther** as well as in *Tristram Shandy,* that predominant element of abysmal loneliness from which only torrential speech offers relief: broken bits of monologue, endlessly insisting, garrulous and Irish in Sterne, impassioned, lyrical, and at times a little ponderous, in Goethe.

Above all, even here in this seemingly impulsive account of Werther's sufferings, the carefully established element of irony must not be missed: no one could be a more incongruous recipient of Werther's letters than the sober friend Wilhelm; how often do we not feel amused rather than moved by Werther's solemnity, as aggravating in its way as the pedantry of Albert; does he not at times seem to display an exasperating preoccupation with his own eccentricity, aware, so to speak, of the mirrors at both ends of the room? The others, Werther complains again and again, waste their time; the others take themselves too seriously; they, not he, are indifferent to the troubles of their fellow-men. ''Sometimes I could implore them on bended knees not to be so furiously determined to destroy themselves.'' The narrator's irony alone could make the telling of Werther's incredible experience tolerable, and it was precisely by this quality so seldom fully recognized in the critical discussion of the novel, that Goethe hoped to save the book from being as maudlin and self-indulgent as many a hasty reader was later to think. This ironic attitude enabled him to transpose the experienced reality from a mere confession to a symbolic design; it permitted him, not only in the transparent

figure of the editor but in the narrative itself, to maintain himself as a trustworthy story-teller and allowed him to preserve in this account of a crumbling world a perception, a perspective, that remains steady and credible.

It is not minimizing Goethe's achievement if we say that for this first work on a large scale he invented little and borrowed nearly every detail, if not from his own experiences—either remembered, or recorded in letters to his friend Merck—then from the stock of contemporary fiction. He took many of the figures and situations, motifs and scenes from Richardson, from Goldsmith, from Rousseau and others; he used the familiar device of interpolated references to sermons and literary reminiscences; he marshalled Homer and Ossian, Shakespeare, Klopstock, and Lessing as poetic representatives of states of mind that could not be more tellingly elaborated. He employed his lively sense for the revealing scene, the anecdote, the episode, that remained so characteristic of all his later work. His portraiture, it is true, is not specific, he builds his figures by circumstantial evidence: in their physical features nearly all the characters remain indistinct. But it was not Goethe's way, certainly not, as a rule, in his fiction, to produce creatures of fresh and topical authenticity. Even in 1774 he experienced life with the preconceptions of a literary mind; and artistic notions and forms tended, here and later, to determine, sometimes even to anticipate, his observations. It seems to me clear from all we know of his stay in Wetzlar that he there superimposed a set of literary costumes upon reality; now, many months later, he could recall and use them in a poetic design almost without further inspection.

We must not forget that the often described creative unrest which inspired **Werther** was only one of its sources; the other and the more tangible was Goethe's desire to prove himself, as at that time he often confesses, in the rôle of an author; and as the author of a successful piece of fiction he remained famous for the rest of his life. (pp. 34-41)

Victor Lange, ''Goethe's Craft of Fiction,'' in Publications of the English Goethe Society, n.s. Vol. XXII, 1952-53, pp. 31-63.

RONALD GRAY   (essay date 1967)

[*In this excerpt from an introductory study of Goethe's works, Gray discusses the implications of* Werther's *sentimentality to the artistic success of the novel.*]

[Goethe] had been deeply involved in a tragic renunciation akin to Werther's, but had scarcely intended Werther to be taken as a model in all his deeds and moods. He had meant to write a novel, not a tract, a portrayal of a possible fate, not a desirable way of life; so, at least, he felt afterwards—his precise attitude at the time of writing is probably impossible to define.

Seeing the disastrous consequences for so many readers, Goethe was inclined, when speaking in his old age, to agree with the Roman Catholic authorities who had banned the book in Italy. Despite the words counselling the reader who felt as Werther did to 'draw comfort' from his sorrows, the book remained dangerous, as indeed Goethe's opponents had predicted; it continued to have the words printed at the beginning, in the address to the reader: 'Whatever I have been able to glean of the story of poor Werther I have eagerly gathered together, and present it to you here, knowing you will thank me for it. You cannot deny his spirit and character your admiration and love, or his destiny your tears. . . .' So long as Werther continued to be thought worthy of admiration, the effects Goethe deplored were likely to continue too.

For us, today, the question is not so much of the book's dangerousness, as of its qualities as a novel. It is clear now, if it was not then, that Goethe had no firmly conceived intention of justifying and thereby encouraging suicide, however close he may have been at times to taking his own life. He had rather intended to move his readers with the story of a young man so irrevocably and hopelessly in love, as any one of them might have been, that no other course but suicide seemed open to him. At the same time, he had drawn a picture of a youth of his day, overjoyed at the emotions aroused in him by the scenes of Nature, wide open to every impression, living from moment to moment at an intensity almost unbearable.

Some critics see the value of **Werther** rather in this expression of a new irrationalism, than in the story itself. 'The important thing, about **Werther** from an artistic point of view', writes Ernst Merian-Genast, 'is not the subject-matter, however sensational it may have been in its day; not the suicide from unhappy love of a talented and noble youth, but the human content, the new relationship to nature and art, to passion and reason, death and eternity, and its fashioning by the poet.' Yet it may be questioned whether the subject-matter can be so divided from the themes: Werther's 'relationship to death and eternity' may be new, but that says nothing about its value. The 'new relationship' is after all Werther's relationship, and will hold our attention and sympathy to the degree that he does.

Here lies the difficulty, for it has been recognized for a long time now that Werther's feelings are those of an extreme sentimentalist. His way of weeping floods of tears at most of his meetings with Lotte, of throwing himself on the floor at her feet, trembling and shuddering when he kisses her hand, even grinding his teeth, could seem insane if we did not have the feeling that it is merely melodramatic. Yet a certain real imbalance is there, as the prose style sometimes shows. As Emil Staiger says, many readers would agree with Albert when he accuses Werther of often talking random nonsense ('Radotage').

It is of course possible to suppose, as does Goethe's most prominent champion in England today, Philip Toynbee, that Goethe was unaware of his hero's apparent insanity, and to conclude that **Werther** is 'one of the most preposterous books ever written by a great writer'. The very name, suggesting 'worthy one', and the invitation to the reader to admire Werther, suggest a large measure of sympathy, and the *mores* of the day may well have influenced Goethe more than we would readily suppose. . . . As Walter Bruford says, 'there was a strong sentimental strain in evidence, not peculiar of course to Germany at this time, but particularly pronounced there'. In such a society Werther could well appear more normal than he does now.

But if there is to be any lasting interest in this novel it must be because of the artist's handling of his matter, rather than as a document of an age of sentimentalism. We must suppose that Goethe is detached from Werther at least to some extent, and that he is as concerned as we are to fathom the strange nature which unfolds itself in these letters. Werther's malady does emerge very clearly from his letters. He sways violently from extreme self-depreciation to extreme self-assertion, and is never able to call a halt, despite his awareness of this condition. At the same time, he has a tenacity in believing himself in the right which accepts both extremes in his character as equally proper. Thus, when an acquaintance to whose sweet-heart Werther has been too openly attentive offers a protest, Werther delivers a long homily on the need to avoid 'bad humour'. One should rejoice with one's friends, prosper their happiness, not display resentment which can only diminish another's pleasure: in short, the acquaintance should not have tried to spoil Werther's innocent enjoyment. On another occasion, shortly after, Werther is reproved by Albert, the betrothed of Lotte, for thinking of suicide even so far as to put an empty pistol-barrel to his forehead. To this Werther retorts, with many implied snubs to Albert, that those who really know the misery of being alive will never fail to see the greatness rather than the weakness of those who choose to die by their own hand: in short, Albert should not intervene in Werther's misery. On each occasion, Werther is convinced of the pharisaism of the man who opposes him: the course of his argument, however, depends entirely on his mood and needs of the moment. All-important for him is 'pleasure in oneself', 'a true feeling of oneself'. 'Taking what one wants is the most natural impulse in man!' he writes to his friend Wilhelm. 'Do not children grasp at whatever they have a mind to?—And I?' Again, 'I treat my heart like a sick child, and grant it every wish.' Being in love is one further way, perhaps the most valuable of all, towards strengthening his self-esteem: 'how I worship myself, since she loves me'; and even self-knowledge is no hindrance: 'I laugh at my heart—and do whatever it wants.'

Werther does not quite live up to his intentions here. He is always careful, until his last meeting with Lotte, to refrain from any open declaration of love despite his heartfelt desires. But he admires the young man who, in similar circumstances, offers even violent love to an unwilling mistress-employer. Again, he stifles the temptation to murder Albert, but takes what seems a masochistic delight in procuring from him the pistols with which he shoots himself, a delight which is heightened by the knowledge that the pistols were given with a trembling hand by Lotte herself. He denies any erotic feeling, but thrills at the touch of her foot beneath the table and revels in the thought of the canary which touched his lips after touching hers. Almost always his yielding to the promptings of his heart are passive rather than active, negative rather than positive. He would like to woo Lotte but does not, would like to oppose Albert but does not; instead he puts himself passively between them, making society intolerable for all three, and finally kills himself in a manner which might have been calculated to cause them the most pain.

All this must harm the reception of the serious themes of the novel, the sense in Werther that Nature, to which he is so passionately devoted, is both a creator and a destroyer:

> Mighty mountains surrounded me, abysses lay at my feet, and cloudburst-torrents hurtled downward, the rivers flooded past beneath me, and woods and mountain-chains resounded; and I saw them interweaving and intermoving in the depths of the earth, all those unfathomable forces; and now above the earth and under the heavens throng the families of countless creatures, all, all peopled with a thousand shapes; and mankind makes itself secure in its huts and builds its nests, and rules according to its own lights over all the wide world! . . . Ah, then, how often have I longed to fly with the wings of the crane that passed over my head, to the shores of the unmeasured ocean, to drink that swelling bliss of life from the foaming goblet of the infinite and to feel, though only for a moment and in the limited power of my bosom one

drop of the blissfulness of the Being which produces all this in itself and through itself.

. . . And now it is as though a curtain had parted before my soul, and the scene of infinite life transforms itself before me into the image of the eternally open grave. How can you say 'This is!' when all this passes by, when all rolls past with the speed of a thunderstorm, when the whole power of its existence so seldom endures, alas, and is swept away by the stream, plunged beneath the waves and smashed against the rocks? Not a moment passes without consuming you and those about you, not a moment when you are not, when you cannot help being, a destroyer. The most innocent walk costs the life of a thousand poor insects, one step shatters the laborious buildings of the ant, and stamps down a little cosmos into a shameful grave. Ah, it is not the great, rare disasters of the world that move me, not the floods which sweep away your villages, or the earthquakes that swallow up your cities; what tunnels beneath my heart is the consuming power that lies hidden in the whole of Nature, that has fashioned nothing that does not destroy its neighbour and itself. And thus I stagger, trembling, the heavens and earth and all their weaving forces about me, and see nothing but an eternally devouring, eternally redevouring monster.

This is the really important issue which Goethe might have treated with more effect. Despite the headiness of the emotion (which may be contrasted with Hamlet's on 'this goodly frame the earth' in Act II, scene ii—a speech which may well have inspired Goethe) here is a theme which was close to his deepest concerns, as we see from the repetition of it in Faust's encounter with the Earth-Spirit. But it is not realized at its deepest, even here. There is something grandiose and vague about this passage, a sense that the writer is very conscious of the effect he is creating—there is no 'throwaway' self-critical humour in it, as there is at the end of Hamlet's speech.

The sentimentality and egoism of the central character affect even the picture of Werther in his happier moments, playing with children, refusing to admit class distinctions between himself and the peasantry or the nobility, sending alms to the poor, attempting to be just to his enemies and his rival. There is always the sense that Werther is over-conscious of himself at such times, that, as in the consciousness of Lotte's love, he is really worshipping himself when he writes to his friend of these events.

However, this is a novel almost entirely in the form of letters written by Werther, and it is a feature of such novels, unlike novels told by a narrator, that the reader's view is restricted to the standpoint of the main character. In adopting such a form, Goethe was able to give more immediate expression to thoughts and feelings which must at least have passed through his mind, while he still remained, as author of the novel rather than as writer of the letters, uncommitted to them in their entirety. In a sense, he was trying them out, seeing how they might develop if he were not himself, but a man more closely identified with Werther. That he does stand outside the events though not as a judge or critic, is clear from the re-introduction of a narrator, in the final pages, who has collected together all the remaining letters of the hero and who pieces the story together at a time when no letters could possibly have been written. Yet this narrator is not a really satisfying novelistic device. While he does, at times, retain a matter-of-fact tone, he imagines himself so vividly in Werther's situation that many of the scenes he relates might have been related by Werther himself. The narrator appears to know far more of the most intimate feelings both of Werther and of Lotte than he could possibly have discovered by inquiry, and his implicit purpose seems rather to be that of persuading his readers of the just necessity for Werther's suicide than of giving a full picture of the events from a point of view other than Werther's.

It is this merely apparent objectivity of the narrator which makes the final catastrophe difficult to accept as a moving conclusion. When Werther himself speaks of his floods of tears, it is one thing; when the narrator imagines them, it is something different. He, the narrator, becomes bathetic in a passage such as that immediately following Werther's reading of Ossian to Lotte, when the emotion becomes purely melodramatic and 'stagey'. The mood is disturbed in other ways. There is not only the long passage from Ossian, which the narrator quotes near the climax, and which is, today, so difficult even to read through that a serious break in our sympathy must occur. There is also the extremely unfavourable light cast on Lotte and Albert by the events just before Werther's death. Werther himself could not, of course, be present during the scene when his messenger called at Lotte's house for the pistols, on the pretext that they were needed for a journey. Had he imagined at all vividly what emotions his request might arouse in Lotte, who had often heard him speak of his intention to kill himself, he might have desisted. But the reader is given no insight into Werther's mind at this vital moment in the novel. Instead, he has the narrator's account of how Lotte, fearing to tell her husband of Werther's recent passionate embrace, did not dare even to oppose the lending of the pistols, which Albert offers so brusquely as almost to make it appear that he is willing for Werther to use them against himself. Indeed, when Lotte slowly goes towards them, takes them down from the wall with a trembling hand, and delays so long that Albert has to urge her on with a questioning glance, we can only suppose that Albert does mean them to be so used— he could not possibly fail to see what Lotte's slowness meant. In all this, it is not Werther's mind into which we gain insight, but that of the narrator, who, despite his apparent neutrality, is evidently bent on arousing every possible sympathy with Werther, rather than allowing the tragic consequences for all parties to emerge more clearly.

This is ultimately the weakness of the novel; not that it presents a sentimental character or an ending liable to encourage melancholia, but that it is too closely an outpouring of self-expression on Werther's part: there is not enough of the moulding hand of the novelist in it, and where such a hand appears to be present, it is deceptive, for it serves only to support Werther's view, not to place it in a true perspective. Yet, like almost everything that Goethe wrote, the importance of **Werther** in European history, as a novel in the tradition of Rousseau's *Nouvelle Héloïse*, cannot be denied. (pp. 48-55)

Ronald Gray, in his Goethe: A Critical Introduction, *Cambridge at the University Press, 1967, 289 p.*

HANS REISS (essay date 1969)

[*Reiss is the author of the first full-length English-language study of Goethe's novels. In this excerpt from his wide-ranging analysis of* Werther, *Reiss outlines the differences between the first and second versions of the novel, examines several of its literary features, and demonstrates how Goethe reveals the novel's themes and clarifies its characterization.*]

To study [**Werther**], we must first decide which of the two versions of the text we shall use; we must choose between the first version of 1774, which made the novel famous, and the second version of 1787, which was thoroughly revised and amended. Goethe had made important changes, which were, however, in the main the result of Goethe's maturity gained through his poetic work and administrative experience during the decade which had elapsed since his arrival in Weimar in 1775. Furthermore, he must have recognized that, as an author, he had to avoid any possible identification of himself with the hero, for he had been deeply disturbed by the impact of the novel, in which many had found a justification of suicide.

Goethe, it is true, was as amused by some of the reactions to the novel as he was irritated by others. He was, however, bound to take notice of Kestner's, even if he judged it irrelevant. Kestner, who may well have been the first reader of the novel as a whole, thought it contained an inaccurate, indeed untruthful, portrait of himself and his wife. He disapproved of the characterization of Albert and Lotte, and particularly objected, it would appear, to Lotte's emotional response to Werther's passion [see excerpt from a letter to Goethe dated 1774]. Goethe had sent the novel to Kestner who, as his complaints prove, was the first of a long line of readers to approach the work in the wrong way. Goethe answered these protests by seeking to calm his perturbed friend, promising revision at a later stage, and emphasizing the necessity of his writing the novel:

> Believe me, believe me; your worries, your *gravamina*, they will disappear like nocturnal phantoms if you are patient, and then—within one year I promise to cut out everything that a public keen on gossip has retained of suspicion, misinterpretation, etc. I shall do this just as the north wind drives away mists and odours, although the public is like a herd of swine. Werther must—must be. You do not feel *him*. You feel only me and yourselves [see excerpt dated 1774].

Yet when the public did not eschew the biographical fallacy, he still did not hasten to revise the novel. Only eight years after its appearance, in 1782, did he set out to prepare a second edition. Not until 1787, in a volume of his collected works published by Göschen, did the revised edition appear. The second edition differs from the first on some important points.

The examination of **Werther** in this . . . [essay] is based on the second edition. To do justice to the work and to unfold its implications, it is necessary to outline the principal differences between the two editions, and to establish the principles underlying the alterations.

Firstly, the language differs. The changes are of detail, not of substance, and produce not a wholly altered impression but a somewhat different flavour. In the first edition, Goethe, under the influence of his own local Frankfurt dialect, did not use the standardized eighteenth-century German finally stabilized by Gottsched. In the second edition, he reverted to standard German, and to a large extent erased the traces of dialect and colloquial speech. He replaced unusual prefixes and prepositions by common ones. Above all, he softened the tone of Werther's letters. In 1774 he wrote a powerful, frequently unrestrained language characteristic of the *Sturm und Drang*. In 1787, after the first decade in Weimar, this tempestuous, exuberant tone no longer appealed to him. He struck out the drastic expressions of colloquial usage, which might offend conventional taste, and tidied up the syntactical structure to achieve smoother and more correct reading.

So much for changes in language. They all reveal the desire to be more factual, to be more objective, to let the characters speak simply and forcibly without linguistic frills which might distract attention from what they mean. They may make the work somewhat less spontaneous and its realism a shade less stark, but it is no less forceful. This 'improved' version bears the marks of a greater artistry, consciously employed to heighten the poetic effect of the novel.

Similar principles underlie the changes in content. In both editions, Werther dominates the work, but in the second, the editor's account takes up more space. It comes earlier in the novel, after the letter of 6 December instead of that of 17 December, which itself is re-dated 14 December. Several letters which preceded the editor's account now follow it. This interruption of the flow of Werther's letters, and thus of the crescendo of passion, retards the action by putting it in a slightly more distant perspective: the earlier the editor's voice is heard and the greater the space given to his detached point of view, so much the less is the immediacy of Werther's letters. But detachment implies objectivity. This change is, of course, in line with Goethe's own development, for he revised **Werther** at a time when he no longer cared to portray personal feeling directly in narrative prose, but reserved it for lyric poetry. The early years in Weimar had taken their toll of extreme subjectivity; a more objective attitude made it imperative to criticize unrestrained feeling and to insist on a balanced portrait.

The main changes, however, affect both Werther's relations to the other two main characters, Lotte and Albert, and the relationship between these two characters. In the first version, Lotte's feelings become involved with Werther to a greater degree than in the second. She appears, to some extent, emotionally torn between Werther and Albert. Certainly, in the end, she follows the dictates of duty, but it almost appears as if it were duty rather than love which makes her side with Albert. In the second version, there are a number of additional touches which emphasize Lotte's ignorance of Werther's emotions, as well as her naïveté and innocence. For instance, there is her displeasure at Werther's thinking that a letter which she had written to Albert was addressed to him. Then there is the incident where she plays with the canary which she allows to peck at her mouth. Werther has difficulty in controlling his passion, as he finds this scene so suggestive, but Lotte is totally unaware of the impression it makes on Werther. In addition, in the first version Lotte's distress is much greater after Werther has embraced her. She dreads the return of Albert whose coldness then inhibits every conversation. She feels guiltier than in the second version. Here, indeed, Lotte is never fully conscious of the conflict, nor can it be said that she has fallen passionately in love with Werther. In the first version her relations with Albert become truly strained. She is afraid of the tone of voice in which he might refer to Werther. In turn, he appears suspicious of her; he virtually quarrels with her and leaves his disapproval of Werther's frequent visits in no doubt. Albert is to a much greater extent seen through the eyes of Werther. It is not an attractive portrait, for he appears to him a philistine who does not deserve Lotte. Albert even goes so far as to tell Lotte not to go on seeing Werther, at least for the sake of appearances and so as to avoid arousing comment. Lotte is also much more moved when Werther calls on her towards the end of the novel. In the second version, however, she is to a much greater degree unaware of any impact which Werther may have made on her. Albert too acts in a more kindly manner. He always welcomes Werther. He is much calmer in the final stages of the novel, while in the first version he appears at this juncture expressly hostile to Werther, and even shows impatience with Lotte.

The greatest single addition, apart from the expanded account of the editor, is the story of the young farm labourer who has fallen in love with a widow for whom he works. He is encouraged by her, but is later disappointed because she prefers another servant to him. In his disappointment and despair he kills his rival. Werther feels akin to a man who feels desperate enough to commit murder to achieve his aim, or rather, to prevent someone else enjoying the love of his beloved. In reality, however, the situation is different, because the widow encouraged the boy, who had some reason to believe that his love was returned. His passion is, so to speak, grounded in fact and not in his own imagination. The episode makes the difference between Werther's hopes and Lotte's reaction stand out. It makes it plainer that Lotte does not, in fact, love Werther, but genuinely loves her husband.

There is, however, another deepening of perspective in the second version which results from Werther's greater self-awareness. We learn only in the second version, for instance, that he keeps a diary, the reading of which brings forth the lucidity of his mind and his weakness of will in face of passion.

The first version gives us a more one-sided and passionate account of Werther's sorrows. It should be given prominence if the primacy of feeling and the immediate impact of the novel were under review. In 1824, Goethe summed up its effect in retrospect:

> It was really the first publication of the novel, through its violent, unconditional character, which achieved the great impact; I do not wish to decry the later editions, but they are mellowed and lack the same spontaneous life.

But since this account is concerned with Goethe's achievement as a novelist, the aesthetically more satisfying second version must be discussed, although the earlier version is perhaps somewhat livelier.

Goethe succeeded in carrying out his intention as defined in a letter to Kestner:

> In hours of leisure I again took up my Werther without changing what had aroused the original sensation. I intend to raise it a few steps higher. It was also my intention to characterize Albert in such a way that the passionate youth [Werther], but not the reader, was able to misunderstand him.

In addition, it was the second version to which Goethe gave authoritative approval by including it in the standard edition of his collected works, published in his lifetime. The second version, therefore, will be the basis of our study.

• • • • •

If we wish to consider the novel as a work of literature, we must first take into account the impression which the work as a whole leaves on us. Concentration on the inner life of one individual in **Werther** makes this task easier than would be the case with a longer novel. The wealth of imagery and the power of the language may be obstacles to a detached consideration because they stir up the reader's emotions, but it is precisely in its imagery and its language that the inner coherence of the novel is found.

Die Leiden des jungen Werthers is an epistolary novel, following a prevailing fashion in fiction. Yet as an epistolary novel it is quite different from its immediate predecessors: Richardson's *Pamela* and Rousseau's *Nouvelle Héloïse*. It is much more compact, and it is the more powerful for its compactness.

Confronted with one person's letters, the reader's interest is focused on him alone; Werther, indeed, does not possess a proper antagonist. Concentration on one person alone affords a much deeper insight into his feeling and thinking than into the inner life of the other characters. We gain an impression of Albert, of Lotte and of Wilhelm, but we learn very little about their emotions. According to some critics, the novel is a diary in disguise; yet to be precise, it is neither the one nor the other; for the editor has the last word in the decisive moment of the action. Of course, Werther's letters often resemble diary-entries. Nonetheless, they constitute only one half of a correspondence, the other half of which we are not given. They present replies to letters received, and in turn demand replies. But they are letters which always centre round their author's inner life. Werther soliloquizes; often he speaks not so much to Wilhelm as to his own heart. He is concerned more with his own experience than with the effect of his outpourings on the recipient. His letters resemble a confession. He notes down thoughts at the very moment of experiencing them, and never attains any distance from the occasion that moves him. Since Werther, however, notes only the heights of his experience, the novel gains in power and coherence. It approximates to drama, to tragedy, for in drama, a more economical literary form, the plot is concentrated on what is essential. It moves within narrower confines than the novel.

The most obvious feature of the novel's structure is the division into two parts. This division is significant. The first book spans the period from 4 May to 10 September 1771, from the time of Werther's arrival in the small town to his departure. It takes him from the unsettled mood of his first letters, through the beginning and growth of his passion for Lotte, to his attempt to free himself from his passion by leaving. It prepares the catastrophe, but the crisis is as yet averted. In the second book, Werther has turned his back on the place and on the cause of his sorrows, but this detachment is only an apparent one: distance does not liberate him from his passion. He returns only to become more enslaved. The second book thus spans the period from the months of his self-chosen exile, when he seeks to live the life of an ordinary man, to his death. This division into books clearly reveals two cycles, one ending in an escape to freedom, the other in an escape by death, even if the latter be an escape conceived in a misguided way; for Werther believes that death leads to freedom.

The first impression leaves no doubt at all about the main issue of the novel. The centre of the work is Werther's inner experience, and his experience is determined by his emotions. Werther's own language proves this. He often writes sentences of an explosive nature, following the pattern of *Sturm und Drang* writing. His sentences are frequently ungrammatical, or they are mere exclamations, or only half-completed. Much of the narrative indeed consists of lyrical outbursts, which is certainly appropriate, since their purpose is to reveal the tale of Werther's emotional life.

Parallels in the structure of the two books can be perceived. Each book can conveniently be divided into three parts. In the first book, there are three periods of almost forty days each: firstly, the time before Werther comes to know Lotte (4 May-16 June 1771), secondly, the happy time of his friendship with her from 16 June to 30 July 1771, the day of Albert's arrival, and thirdly, the time before his departure on 10 September 1771. In the second book, a similar tripartite division can be noticed: firstly, the period which Werther spends at the court, secondly, the time covering his return to his home town, and finally, the last months between his return and his death. His farewell to Lotte at the end of the first book and his death at the end of the second book also afford a parallel. Although there are other similarities, there are not enough of them to permit a detailed comparison of the structure of the two books.

Each of them, in fact, corresponds to a phase in Werther's emotional life. The two books do not cover an equal length of time. If, however, we measure time not quantitatively or conceptually—i.e. by the clock—but qualitatively or perceptually—i.e. by duration or intensity (to use either Henri Bergson's or Karl Pearson's term respectively)—we are confronted with two parts of equal emotional import briefly interrupted by an interlude not belonging to either. Each of them corresponds to the seasons which it mainly describes; the first to spring and summer, the second to autumn and winter. The illusion is almost conveyed that the whole action took place within one year. The first part represents the growth and height of Werther's passion, the second its decline and Werther's final isolation and death. It is true that the interlude lasts almost a year, but the reader does not pay much attention to it in terms of the emotional course of the story. A number of events take place during this period between 10 September 1771 and 4 September 1772, but it is passed over lightly without any explicit reference to the seasons; the hero's emotional life is in the doldrums. The time of narration thus appears much shorter than the time which is narrated. Economy of presentation provides a concentrated picture. About the mood of the action there is no doubt. It is intimated by the title, the preface and the first letters. Werther carries within himself the seeds of self-destruction, which can be detected from the very beginning by the careful observer. Werther is thus doomed to death, and Goethe tells his story with irony and detachment. He has to give a psychological explanation for the hero's suicide, to portray Werther's end as a necessary consequence of his life, and to mould the material at his disposal into a work of literature.

Werther's very first words ('How glad I am to be away! My dear friend, what a thing is the human heart!') point to his predicament, the cue being given by the word *Herz* (heart), a word the meaning of which differs slightly, however, at times, according to the context. Here is Werther's habit of reflecting on his feelings, of combining his reflections into a definite point of view, and of projecting this personal point of view as a generalization about life. Werther views the world exclusively from his own angle. His own feeling is, for him, the criterion for judging mankind as a whole, but he is incapable of sustaining general reflections for long. His thoughts, as if under compulsion, revert to himself. Repetition of the word 'I' in the first sentences confirms this tendency which runs through the whole work. Werther is egocentric. For him, as for many egocentrics, his own past experiences are much more important than the presence of others. His promises to mend his ways are not convincing. No one is likely to believe him when he writes:

> I will, dear friend, I promise you, I will mend my ways; I will no longer ruminate over what little misfortunes Fate doles out to us, as I have always done. I will enjoy the present and have done with the past. You are quite right, my dearest friend, men's sufferings would be less if they did not occupy their imagination so intensely—God knows why they are made like that—in recalling the memory of bygone ills instead of trying to bear an indifferent present.

Yet later on in the same letter we read of the tears which he sheds for Count M because he is moved when thinking back upon the Count's sensitivity.

Similarly, his proficiency in practical matters must be doubted. He writes with assurance that he will settle a business matter of his mother's most expeditiously, yet no proof is forthcoming that he is really doing so: all we learn is that he finds it tedious to write about it.

He does not wish to discipline his emotions; on the contrary, he wants to surrender to the moment without restraint. Action is not prompted by circumspection or order; his actions and thoughts are motivated by the claims of the heart. Thus he does not want to stay in the town, but wishes to flee into nature. We sense that any environment which would offer him fruitful practical activity would be repugnant to him.

These indications become more prominent in the next letters. Emotion dominates Werther's thought and activity. He is neither able nor willing to master his feelings. He thus begins the letter of 10 May with the following words: 'My whole soul is filled with a wonderful serenity, like the delightful spring mornings which I enjoy with all my heart.' He abandons himself so completely to the feeling of serenity that it is hardly accurate to call his state of mind serene. He holds nothing back; his whole heart is given up to feeling. He is lost in it and never attains that detachment which can be acquired through clarity of mind and emotional stability alone. His enthusiastic attitude towards nature confirms this; he feels that he is an artist, a painter, but forgets that it is not feeling but creative achievement which alone makes a man an artist. He is able to express his emotion only by writing letters. He is an artist as a writer of letters, but certainly not as a painter. He indeed senses the power of nature, but his attitude, whether it be towards religion, nature or the past, is always unrealistic. His language indicates this; the very image which Werther uses in speaking of art, the image of the mirror, betrays the inadequacy of his point of view. Art is not, as he maintains, a mirror of the soul. Just because he is incapable of detaching himself from experience and of recreating God and nature in the mirror of art does he end his confession with the exclamation: 'My friend—but it brings about my ruin, and I am crushed by the power of this glorious vision.'

These themes are further developed in the next letter of 12 May. Although Werther wallows in his feelings, he is able to describe them with powerful intensity. He does not understand them, but he knows how to depict them. The external world appears to him unreal. He must ask himself whether this sense of unreality is brought about through 'delusive spirits' or through 'the divine and ardent fancy of his heart'. Emotion overcomes him when he sees girls fetching water from the well; for him, this scene immediately becomes an image of patriarchal existence. Since he feels deeply, he demands a similar depth of experience from others; this claim is upheld with moral power.

In order to protect his feelings, Werther also desires to protect himself against external interference. He rejects ideas, if they do not guide, encourage or inspire him. He finds criticism disagreeable and hence undesirable. He is aware of the instability of his feelings, for he writes: 'You have not seen anything so restless, so changeable as this heart.' On the one hand, he expects Homer to calm his feelings; on the other, he does not want to cure himself of this inner disquiet, but only wants to lull it for the moment. Frequently it looks as if he actually enjoys his own self-torture (another parallel to Rousseau).

Just as Werther is disinclined to fit into the normal pattern of life, so is he unwilling to see the world in a traditional, accepted manner. His radical views are intelligible as those of a young rebel—but at the same time he loves what is old and admires a patriarchal mode of living. Within him conflicting tendencies, which he is unable to control, struggle with one another. The letters of 13 and 15 May are therefore dictated by various moods. Again, these moods are given the status of universal laws, because for Werther the world of his private emotion is a symbol of the whole cosmos. Each time his mood changes, the change is reflected in a changing view of the world. At times the world appears monotonous and full of constraint and man unworthy of his freedom: in the letter of 22 May, for instance, he emphasizes that concentration on his own emotions cannot be fruitful or creative for him. The world appears dream-like, his vision is impaired. Nonetheless, he asserts that others are mistaken, while he, in all humility, claims to know the purpose of life. Strange humility! For does he not believe that he can look down proudly on others because he has retained inner freedom, the courage to leave the world while all other men cling to life?

In the next letter (of 26 May), however, we find him expressing a different point of view, which though not absolutely incompatible with, is at least completely opposed to, the view upheld in the previous letter. This time, confined existence is welcome. The image of the hut, which, for Goethe, always means restriction in domesticity, in the narrow sphere, symbolizes this view. Yet how far away Werther is from an ordered, placid life! His attitude to nature shows this; he rejects all rules in favour of nature and forgets that nature has its own rules. Similarly, he savagely caricatures the love of the ordinary man who realizes that, in practical life, the pursuit of love cannot be an activity which consumes all his time and energy. He condemns this sensible view as that of a philistine. He is moved by seeing a peasant leading a quiet, simple life, but immediately afterwards passionate feeling, and not tranquillity, arouses his enthusiasm. His lack of detachment becomes even clearer when he mistakenly believes that he is a poet because he merely experiences the desire to describe a poetic scene. He mistakes recognition of the potential raw material of poetry for the act of poetic creation itself. His one-sided vision stems from his desire to retain the emotions caused by sense-impressions. So when he hears of a young farm-labourer's love for a farmer's widow, he immediately espouses his point of view, because it is the point of view of passion.

Such is the portrait of Werther before he meets Lotte. In him are all the tendencies which make it inevitable that his passion will drive him to ruin. They are typified by the confusion and imprecision of his mind, by his indecision and his longing for the absolute. Werther refuses to accept the external world and loses himself in the apparent fullness of his inner life. The contrast between his inner life and external reality eventually becomes greater and greater, until it finally destroys him. Not love, but his unfortunate temperament destroys him. Goethe said as much himself in a letter written at the time when he was writing *Werther:*

> I have done many new things. I have written a story with the title *Die Leiden des jungen Werthers* in which I depicted a man who, endowed with a deep and pure sensibility and genuine lucidity of mind, loses himself in speculation until at last an unhappy passion overwhelms him and he puts a bullet through his head.

The features of Werther's character which render the final disaster inevitable are intimated, but intimated to the careful observer only. For in the eyes of his friends, of whom Wilhelm is the prototype, Werther is perhaps excessively sensitive or

passionate, but by no means diseased. Of course, Wilhelm cannot really be expected to have scrutinized Werther's letters as if he were a psychiatrist. Werther himself does not entertain any doubt as to the essential rightness of his mode of living. Wilhelm sees contradictions in his thought, but they do not appear to alarm him. Werther is accepted in middle-class society without any difficulty. Lotte's father, an official (*Amtmann*) and a man of experience, welcomes him in his home; the minister, a man of wide practical knowledge, invites him to join the diplomatic service; and even the Prince treats him benignly. From the first Werther contains the germs of the disease, but it is only when his emotions become involved in a situation which denies him all satisfaction that they break out, so that other people slowly begin to suspect his condition, even if they never fully grasp it. The petrifaction of his emotions, his refusal to accept the external world as it is and to learn from it what it can teach him, his unswerving reliance on his inner life—all this destroys him. (pp. 18-30)

• • • • •

To gain for his work a new reading public and to express the ambitions and hopes of this reading public, Goethe forged a new style. This style was not all of a piece; it was thus able to appeal to different levels of readers. Above all, Werther's own language speaks to all men who feel, and there are very few whose emotions have never been stirred and who have never felt the power of passion.

There are, apart from passages from *Ossian*, two styles in the novel: firstly, that of the editor, who tells his story with objective calm and sovereign superiority, and secondly that of Werther himself, whose tone is passionate. The editor's language is perhaps best described by the words which he applies to the story of Werther. 'It is simple. . . . What can we do except carefully set down what we have been able to collect through persistence.'

The editor's use of words is economical. He concentrates on what is essential to Werther's story, and we are led to believe that he confronts us only with carefully selected documents. Only when he depicts extreme emotions does he heighten his language by the accumulation of sentences containing rhetorical questions and exclamations. Only then does the language instil in us a sense of passion. This is particularly effective, as it frames the action in sober prose which never loses its detachment, even when recounting the climax of Werther's passion and his suicide. Nonetheless, it is never monotonous.

Conveying the immediacy of experience is the foremost function of Werther's own epistolary style. We can, however, detect two distinct modes in his writing: the quasi-lyrical and the epic. The quasi-lyrical predominates. The opening sentences of the first letter set the tone, with alternate exclamatory and interrogative sentences separated by statements which interrupt the flow of lyrical speech and represent an intrusion of the intellect. By combining these three kinds of sentence, a compound is created which brings Werther's increasing unrest into the open. Suppressed feelings explode in an exclamation which interrogative sentences have led up to: repetitions are skilfully used to indicate the intensity of feeling, the unremitting emphasis on emotional experience.

The fourfold repetition of 'I will' in the first sentences of the first letter is a verbal equivalent of Werther's desperate attempt to assert his own ego and to convey the impression that he wants, at all costs, to overcome his inner self-doubt. This mode of writing is employed again and again.

A depiction of Lotte cutting bread for her sisters and brothers.

Another device of Werther's style is the interruption of orderly speech. There are more and more incomplete sentences towards the end of the novel which are interrupted by exclamations. They also refute Werther's own contention that he does not like the use of the *Gedankenstrich* (the dash). They reveal a passionate inner movement. Within a single sentence there can be a shift from one type of sentence to another, as if reflecting the changing tensions of a highly-strung mind. The very abruptness of the change indicates that Werther's speech is determined by emotion, not by reason, that it is spontaneous, not reflective, that it bursts into immediate expression without thought. Only after he has spoken does he examine what he has said.

Closely related to this is another sentence structure, revealing yet another side of Werther's character and outlook, of which the letter of 13 May 1771 provides the first complete example (although instances may be found earlier). Here the sentences balance one another like two equal weights in a pair of scales. Their antithesis reveals the contrast between the outer and inner worlds which in the end imposes so great a strain on Werther. For he confronts the outer world with the claims of his own inner being. When Wilhelm reminds him that the external world cannot be ignored, Werther vehemently protests his agreement. Yet he gives in to the urging of his heart at the expense of his reason. He proposes his own solution to his problem: he will protect himself from his dependence on the outward world by excluding himself from it. A precarious balance between the inner life and the outer world is thus created, but it is a balance that does not last.

Yet another sentence is the long period beginning with a large number of subsidiary clauses. The first sentence of this kind is found in the letter of 10 May 1771.

> My whole soul is filled with a wonderful serenity, like the delightful spring mornings which I enjoy with all my heart. I am alone and am completely happy with my life in this spot which was made for souls like mine. I am so happy, my dearest friends, so absorbed in the feeling of tranquillity, that my art is suffering. I could not draw a line at the moment, and yet I have never been more of a painter than I am now. When the mist is rising from the lovely valley and the sun rests upon the impenetrable shade of my forest, so that only now and then a ray steals into the inner sanctuary; when I lie in the tall grass by the rushing brook, and discover a thousand different grasses on the ground, when I feel nearer my heart the teeming little world among the stalks, the innumerable, unfathomable creatures, the worms and insects, and when I feel the presence of the Almighty Spirit, who created us all in His image, the breath of the All-loving One who sustains us as we float in illimitable bliss—Oh! my friend, when the world then grows dim before my eyes and earth and sky are absorbed into my soul like the form of a beloved, I am consumed with longing and think, ah! would that I could express it, would that I could breathe on to the paper what is wholly alive and warm within me, so that it might be the mirror of my soul as my soul is the mirror of the eternal God. My friend—but it brings about my ruin, and I am crushed by the power of this glorious vision.

This type of sentence too, is imbued with deep feeling, but it gives it a different form. The subordinate clauses overshadow the main clause almost completely; they could hardly 'humiliate' it more. A powerful urge drives the speaker onward, moving at a tremendous pace, which ends in a final explosion with the exclamation: 'Ah, would that I could express it, would that I could breathe on to the paper what is wholly alive and warm within me.' This exclamation, however, is only an interlude; there is a new intensification which, on a sharply rising note, leads to a new exclamation: 'My friend'. Suddenly another note is struck, starting with the word 'But', as if exhaustion makes further speech impossible. The sentence then falls suddenly as if from a great height; after a weary sigh, 'My friend—but it brings about my ruin', it ends in a final brief reflection: 'I am crushed by the power of this glorious vision'. Werther's yearning, the urge of his feeling and the demands of his nature, and his passion to grasp the absolute in this finite world, gain strength as his feelings burst forth.

This celebrated letter presents 'a genuine diagram of passion' [according to Gerhard Storz]. A poetic illusion is created which may serve as a symbol expressive of feeling. Although the style is new in German fiction, it derives from a long tradition going back to the patristic rhetoric of the fourth century, and in particular to Gregory of Nyssa. Goethe may or may not have been conscious of its ancestry, but this type of sentence was known in Herder's circle as a 'homiletic battle-order'. To quote the perceptive description of two eminent critics [Elizabeth M. Wilkinson and L. A. Willoughby], it is:

> a sustained, swelling and elaborately incapsulated protasis (actually there are eleven clauses, but the impression is of nine arranged in a group of three) followed by the dying fall of a far briefer apodosis. By this means, Goethe created the very semblance of the Neo-Platonic soaring of the soul towards its creator and its sighing despair of ever being able to

express the divine affinity it feels. Embedded as it is here in the language of confession the figure foregoes its 'rhetorical' fervour and becomes a pure analogue of the felt life within. An analogue of its movements and contours—and of its ambivalences, too. For without benefit of narrator, by the sheer rise of the words put into the mouth of this as yet unsuspecting hero (it is the reader's prescience, not his, that makes, the 'Ich gehe zugrunde' at the end of the letter so ominous) Goethe lays bare the seeds of self-destruction in this particular mode of ecstasy.

Werther's feeling springs from the dark caverns of his subconscious. His ego cannot resist it; for even when he makes an attempt to do so in a main clause, his attempt is overridden by another elemental outburst in the subsequent subsidiary sentences. In the end, Werther is forced to succumb to this power; he becomes a prisoner of his inner life. The power of his emotions is too great; they dominate the outer world, just as the pressure of the subsidiary clauses overwhelms the main clause. His intellect is at the mercy of his feelings; it does not provide a counterweight to them.

Dialogue is, on the whole, sparingly used in the novel. Since it is simple and spontaneous, its effect is natural. The first dialogue, in the letter of 15 May, is typical. Simple sentences tell us how immediate the impact of the outer world is on Werther's mind. Another more abstract kind of dialogue found in Werther's heated controversy with Albert reveals his inability to accept contradiction. His reaction to the objections of others makes him more and more tense as the argument proceeds.

The second style used by Werther is completely different. It is epic. If emotional sentences represent the lyrical part of the novel, showing its closeness to the lyric poetry of Goethe's *Sturm und Drang,* his epic style strikes a different note. The language is not so excited. There are few lengthy subsidiary clauses, but the preponderance of main clauses never becomes awkward or heavy. Short sentences, interrogative sentences without predicates, and dialogue give the language a liveliness of its own. Again this liveliness results from Werther's inner participation in the events, and the language reveals it. Very often Werther's first, balanced sentences reflect an attempt to be objective, but he cannot sustain this mood. His epic descriptions do not last. He is moved, and his language again betrays the rise of passion. Frequently sentences occur where there is an accumulation of subsidiary clauses or where the main clauses burst into exclamation. This epic, or semi-epic, style does not occur towards the end of the second book. By that time Werther is too greatly disturbed to be capable of using a more leisured, objective style of writing. The function of the objective observer is taken over by the editor.

Werther's own words do not suffice to exhaust the whole scope of his vision of the world. To extend the scope of his feeling he alludes to poetry which conveys more than he is able to say. He refers to Homer, to a poem of Klopstock's, and, finally, he and Lotte read from *Ossian.* The function of these passages translated from *Ossian* is to emphasize Werther's spiritual disease for, as Goethe is reported to have said to Henry Crabb Robinson, 'while Werther is in his senses he talks about Homer and only after he grows mad is in love with Ossian'. For him, then, the language of *Ossian* stands for savagery and extravagance of feeling, which he himself delights in. The tragic note of *Ossian*'s poetry prepares for Werther's suicide. The passages from *Ossian* also confront Werther, and even more Lotte, with the latent implications of their relationship;

at the same time, they serve as a poetic parallel to Werther's own experience.

The style of the novel is not only expressed in Werther's language, but also in the structure of his letters. If we consider the structure of the individual letters, we see that Werther does not write according to a plan; his letters are too natural for that. Their structure varies, and a consistent principle of composition does not emerge. But structural variation follows a rhythm which gives life to the letters. Description, exploration of feeling, objective statements and reflective generalizations follow one another, though there is no definite, immutable order of the different parts. All combinations and permutations are possible. They vary just as the tempo of some of the letters varies. The latter variety reflects Werther's youthful, emotional unrest. No letter is without feeling. His heart is never silent even when it sounds in a minor key.

Similarly, there is no distinct design in the sequence of letters as a whole. But here, too, are definite rhythmic changes. An impression of strong emotional movement is conveyed by the change from letters describing idyllic scenes to those charged with emotion. At the beginning there is a balance between these two types of letters. Near the end of the first book, Werther's emotions master his pen, though the book ends with a letter which is mainly descriptive. In the second book, there are a number of descriptive passages, corresponding to Werther's absence from Lotte, but towards the end, the upsurge of his feeling prevents his continuing in this manner. The last letters present a pathological intensification of feeling.

Stylistic analysis makes it quite clear that Werther's language reflects his highly emotional inner life, but also leaves no doubt that his inner life is affected by his language. The power and manner of his speech allow him to enslave his reason, to make it a servant of his passion. His language reveals and furthers his confusion of mind and progressive disintegration.

There are some individual words which in themselves illuminate the nature of Werther's suffering. From among them one word—*Einschränkung* (restriction)—may be singled out as revealing Werther's temperament and thought most distinctly. It recurs again and again in a significant context and can thus be termed a key-word. Unlike other expressions which he uses to express his sense of spiritual aridity, this word does not come from the language of Pietism, the great religious movement of the seventeenth and eighteenth centuries in Germany, a movement which emphasized and sought to cultivate the inner life. Pietism also inculcated personal piety and a highly emotional attitude to the scriptures. From its strong inward religiosity, Werther's sensibility is largely derived.

Undoubtedly Werther's emotions are genuine. He does not suffer silently, but delights in pouring out his feelings into his letters. These letters do not help him to regain his composure, but raise his emotional temperature even further, for writing about his feelings corroborates his belief in his approach to life; at times, Werther gives the impression that he is seeking to enslave his mind by his words. He is, after all, a precursor of Romanticism, a movement in which language was frequently no longer the servant, but became the master of the writer. Werther's monomaniac delight in recording his suffering by virtual soliloquy, the emotional flavour of his thought, the lyrical intensity of his passion, all point to an impact of language on his mind and emotion, for it requires more detachment than Werther is capable of to be entirely unaffected by the words which we use, to escape from the interaction between style and thought. Language can be a powerful moulder of minds; it is rarely content to remain an expression of a man's inner life.

This word *Einschränkung* emphasizes the polarity which determines Werther's inner life, the conflict between the limitations imposed upon man and his urge for freedom. Werther sees himself as a wanderer whose striving will not admit of any restraint. Life appears monotonous and intolerable. He does not want to accept the limits imposed by his senses. Yet at the same time he delights in the experience of his senses so unconditionally that he becomes even more limited than is necessary or wise. His inability to reconcile these polar conflicts into a harmonious mode of being is at the root of his misfortune. His vacillating attitude towards this problem is reflected in the various shades of meaning which this word *Einschränkung* possesses in the novel. Sometimes he delights in it and rejoices in the pleasure of a restricted way of life. At the other extreme, the restrictions appear to him an absolutely unbearable imprisonment. Finally, the word is used to condemn his mode of living, as he enmeshes himself in the cocoon of his own narrow, though intense, vision of the world. (pp. 30-7)

· · · · ·

Werther's personality and his relationship to society allow us to understand his attitude towards reality. In this respect, **Werther** belongs to the tradition of the modern European novel which, since Cervantes' *Don Quixote*, can be seen as an attempt to define our view of what is real, to determine the relation between appearance and reality. In **Werther,** we encounter two views of reality—that of Werther and that of the editor. Werther after all cannot tell the story of his suicide—it is the editor's function to alleviate the tragic effect of the story.

It would, however, be a critical fallacy to believe that Goethe's views are those of the editor. Goethe attempted in this novel to attain a satisfactory view of reality. Werther's view is characterized by his refusal to adapt himself to reality. His enthusiasm presages his later failure. His enthusiastic letters, however, have their counterpart in the editor's objective report. The whole story is grasped only by taking both styles into consideration. For if we base our assessment of the import of the novel on one style only, we take a one-sided view. To side with or against Werther is equally mistaken; both modes of speaking are legitimate, and may exist side by side, even if they appear to create an irreconcilable conflict.

Werther believes that what is felt is alone real. He contemptuously rejects other interpretations of the world, whether those of Albert or of Herr Schmidt, as mistaken. Werther's conception of reality is, as the novel implies, unsatisfactory. By interposing the editor, Goethe intimates that he does not share Werther's conception and that another is possible.

The editor's account is to be objective. At first, the reader is merely assured that an event has been accurately reported. It is not suggested that a view of reality is being developed. But this very objectivity contains the whole essence of another view of the world. To describe the sorrows of Werther without any expression of sentiment is to suggest that reality is not what is felt, that feeling has to be subordinated to reason, that external events take precedence over the movement of the inner life.

What view of reality does Goethe himself take in **Werther**? Goethe's own experience was close to the events of the novel, and a later comment of his brings this out:

> It is difficult to imagine how any one could survive for another forty years in a world which appeared so absurd in early youth.

But Goethe speaks with two voices which contradict one another: each demands to be recognized as the only right one. The two versions of the novel are, apart from slight stylistic changes and from the interpolation of the young farm-labourer episode, distinguished from one another above all by the different character of the editor's account. In the second version, the editor interposes his account at an earlier stage, after the letter of 6 December, while in the first version, he does so after the letter of 12 December. His opening remarks (relating to his activity as editor of the letters) which are missing in this first version create a greater detachment.

> How I could have wished that enough evidence of our friend's remarkable last days had survived in his own hand to make it unnecessary for me to interrupt the sequence of the letters he did leave behind!
>
> I have set myself the task of collecting exact accounts from the lips of those who were in a position to know his story: it is a simple one, and all the accounts agree about it down to the smallest details; it is only over the attitude of mind of the leading characters that opinions differ, and judgements diverge.
>
> What remains for us except to relate accurately all we have found out, with a great deal of trouble, to interpolate the letters the dying man left behind, and to pay scrupulous regard to the slightest note which has come to light, especially since it is hard, indeed, to discover the true, individual motives of even a single action which takes place among people of no common sort.

The editor is detached, but he is not hostile. From the beginning of the novel, he enjoins us to regard Werther with understanding and not to deny him admiration, love and sympathy. He does not rebuke him, a view echoed almost forty years later by Goethe when he wrote to Zelter that 'if the *taedium vitae* overwhelms man, he is only to be pitied, not to be reproached.' Indeed, the editor hopes that the book may be a comfort.

The mention of the activity of collecting information serves a double purpose. It diverts the reader's attention from Werther to the problem of editing his papers. It thus makes detachment a factor in the novel, in accordance with Goethe's later classical conception, and secondly it emphasizes the genuine quality of the documentation. On the one hand, it points out that we are reading a novel; on the other, that we are confronted with a most topical action.

Goethe then does not side with any specific view of reality. He was still, at this stage of his life, uncertain of his development. He had not yet come to terms with the world he had to live in. This uncertainty or lack of adjustment is reflected in the novel. The result is conflict, destructive to a man as sensitive as Werther. For Goethe himself, this mode of behaviour appeared the only possible way of looking at the world. Only as he grew older and more mature was this conflict within him resolved and contained in a homogeneous style. In fact, both modes of writing, that of Werther and that of the editor, had their precursors—Brockes, Gessner, Gellert, Klopstock; all these poets had appealed to the sensibility, of which, indeed, a cult had been made. At the same time, the editor's matter-of-fact voice recalls the dominant tradition of the *Aufklärung*. Goethe's vision, even at the time of his youth, was related to the centre of his being. This concentration is reflected in the compactness of his novel and the carefulness of its design.

Whatever mastery, whatever careful design the novel reveals, Goethe has nonetheless here described a world in conflict. The conflict appeared to him too real, too immediate for him to be able, at that stage, to resolve it through the medium of a homogeneous style. He was only at the beginning of his search for the mode of expression suited to him. He did not consider it his task to resolve the conflict; it was his aim merely to present it. (pp. 48-50)

Werther is the work in which Goethe sought to come to terms with the role and function of feeling in life. Werther's insistence on the absolute priority of the emotional side of life may be mistaken. The novel, however, would never have attained its enormous success if it had not expressed a claim that apparently could be justified.

Inevitably, a psychological interpretation of the novel tends to over-emphasize the diseased element in Werther's character. It can easily be seen as an attempt to attack Werther's view, to disparage it as a psychological aberration. But to do so . . . is to do an injustice to *Werther*. It produces a one-sided reading. The warning against the mistaken assumption that one style, one voice in the novel is the only right one, must be repeated. For this would amount to looking at the novel from the lop-sided standpoint of Albert or Herr Schmidt, without the sympathy for Werther insisted on by the editor in his preface. But even the editor's sympathy is not enough, as the dry tone of his narrative betrays. For to appreciate *Werther* fully, we must be able to participate in the fervour with which Werther approaches life, a fervour of an almost religious kind. From one angle, indeed, it is a delusion to read *Werther* as a psychological novel at all. On the contrary, it should be read as a panegyric on the strength of feeling, a very extreme case which typifies an attitude that was felt to be new at the time (though, in fact, it was not new at all): it was the claim of feeling to have precedence over reason. This claim may appear, at first sight, to be quite unbalanced, yet it is based on an inner necessity; for we can only eschew the claim of feeling at our peril. On the other hand, to grant it priority at any price is equally dangerous. But for this praise of feeling, the novel would not have had its stupendous impact. For feeling comes here to the fore much more vehemently and more profoundly than in any earlier German novel. It feeds on a new conception of the value and capacity of man. In this Goethe was a pioneer. The *Sesenheim* lyrics and the great hymns of the *Sturm und Drang* are the first achievement in this vein. These works share with *Werther* a more vital vision, more vital since it penetrates more deeply the inner experience of life. Because *Werther* so fully conveys this vision it can claim a greater artistic worth than previous novels. The title of the novel recalls that there is talk of mental pathology, for there is explicit reference to suffering. This suffering would, however, not be positive if it were not based on the power of feeling which sweeps across the boundaries imposed by normal life, springing, as it does, from the primordial depths of inner life.

On the basis of his feelings, Werther believes that he possesses a right to liberate himself from the burden of tradition. But he does not realize that, in fact, his emphasis on feeling stems from a tradition, namely that of Pietism. Like the Pietists, he makes extreme demands, and is prepared to stake his life on them. He wants to follow his heart even if this course runs counter to the customs of the world. He refuses to accept the restrictions of social life. In this respect, he is to some extent a follower of the social and political tendencies of his time. *Werther,* indeed, is not primarily a social novel; it deals rather with the fate of an individual. (pp. 52-4)

Werther is the champion of feeling. The exalted tone of his speech, the force of his lyrical incantation may make him appear in the right. But this is just as mistaken as to side with the editor or to treat Werther as a medical case. A sound reading of the novel involves a wider view. Both the vitalizing and destructive forces of feeling must be recognized. Emotion is necessary, but it must not step beyond its limits. Werther's emphasis upon feeling is excessive, but this does not mean that feeling itself is invalid. Goethe has, indeed, written a polemic against an over-estimation of feeling, but he would not have done this if he had not also been aware of the creative qualities of emotion. Contemporary readers read *Werther* mainly as a novel of sentiment. They considered Werther a tragic victim of circumstances beyond his control, and believed his attitude and even his action justifiable.

The novel's intensity and range of emotional power are still capable of moving a reader today. The problem of canalizing a primordial force, the claims of emotion to direct our actions, are still with us. They are the problems of civilization itself. (p. 54)

Hans Reiss, in his Goethe's Novels, *Macmillan and Co. Ltd., 1969, 309 p.*

W. H. AUDEN (essay date 1971)

[*An Anglo-American man of letters, Auden is a major poet and an influential literary figure. His early poetry and criticism are informed by the psychological and political theories of Sigmund Freud and Karl Marx; his later work is heavily influenced by his conversion to Christianity. While some critics charge that the radical change in Auden's aesthetic philosophy is inconsistent and contradictory, Auden believed that an artist's work is by its nature evolutionary and responsive to the changing moral and ideological climate of the age. Among his best-known critical works are* The Enchafèd Flood; or, The Romantic Iconography of the Sea *(1950),* The Dyer's Hand and Other Essays *(1962), and* Forewords and Afterwords *(1973). In the following excerpt, he depicts Werther as an egotist unconcerned with the feelings of others.*]

So far as I know, Goethe was the first writer or artist to become a Public Celebrity. There had always been poets, painters and composers who were known to and revered by their fellow artists, but the general public, however much it may have admired their works, would not have dreamed of wishing to make their personal acquaintance. But, during the last twenty years or so of Goethe's life, a visit to Weimar and an audience with the Great Man was an essential item in the itinerary of any cultivated young man making his Grand Tour of Europe. His visitors in his old age were innumerable, but most of them had actually read only one book of his, written when he was twenty-four. What Goethe felt about this may be guessed from his first version of the Second Roman Elegy.

> Ask whom you will, I am safe from you now, you fair ladies and fine society gentlemen! "But did Werther really live? Did it all really happen like that? Which town has the right to boast of the lovely Lotte as its citizen?" Oh, how often I have cursed those foolish pages of mine which made my youthful sufferings public property! If Werther had been my brother and I had killed him, I could scarcely have been so persecuted by his avenging sorrowful ghost.

The biographers tell us that *Werther* was the product of Goethe's unhappy love for Charlotte Buff, but this is certainly an oversimplification. When writing a novel, an author naturally often makes use of his personal experiences, but a novel is not an autobiography. Goethe, for instance, did not, like his hero, commit suicide. Again, Goethe makes Werther an idle dilettante, who sketches a bit, reads a bit, but is incapable of seriously concentrating on anything. There is an element of self-portraiture in this: all his life, partly out of a temperamental impatience and partly because he was interested in so many things, he found it difficult to finish a work, but idleness was never one of his vices. When he wrote **Werther** he was probably in a disturbed state, for, a year after its publication, he wrote: ''I am falling from one confusion into another.'' The novel seems to me to be one of those works of art in which the conscious and unconscious motives of the creator are at odds. Consciously, that is, Goethe approved of his hero, but his unconscious motive was therapeutic: by cultivating to the extreme, but only in words, the indulgence in subjective emotions typical of the *Sturm und Drang* movement, to get it out of his system and find his true poetic self, just as Byron, after *Childe Harold,* was able to put humorless gloom behind him and realize his true talent as a comic poet. Certainly, the admirers of **Werther** would have been bewildered by these lines written in Goethe's middle-age.

> Vergebens werden ungebundne Geister
> Nach der Vollendung reiner Höhe streben.
> Wer Grosses will, muss sich zusammenraffen;
> In der Beschränkung zeigt sich erst der Meister,
> Und das Gesetz nur kann uns Freiheit geben.
>
> (Unfettered spirits will aspire in vain to the pure heights of perfection. He who wills great things must gird up his loins; only in limitation is mastery revealed, and law alone can give us freedom.)

Living in the twentieth century, not the eighteenth, and knowing, as most of his contemporaries did not, Goethe's later work, **Werther** can still fascinate us, but in a very different way. To us it reads not as a tragic love story, but as a masterly and devastating portrait of a complete egoist, a spoiled brat, incapable of love because he cares for nobody and nothing but himself and having his way at whatever cost to others. The theme of the egoist who imagines himself to be a passionate lover evidently fascinated Goethe, for, thirty years later, he depicted a similar character in Edouard, the husband in *Elective Affinities.*

Had Goethe, from the bottom of his heart, really wanted his readers to admire Werther, why did he introduce the story of the servant who is in love with his widowed mistress? After nursing his love in secret for some time, he finally makes a pass at her, is surprised in the act by her brother and, of course, fired. Shortly afterwards, he shoots the servant who had taken his place, though he has no grounds whatsoever for supposing that the latter had succeeded where he had failed. Goethe not only introduces this character but also makes Werther, the future suicide, identify the murderer's situation with his own, thereby making it impossible for the reader to think of suicide as ''noble.'' Again, if Goethe really wished us to be Werther's partisan in the erotic triangular situation Werther-Lotte-Albert, one would have expected him to make Albert a coarse philistine to whom Lotte is unhappily married, but he does not. Albert is, to be sure, a ''square'' who does not appreciate Klopstock or Ossian, but he is presented as a good man, affectionate, hard-working, a good provider, and Lotte as a contented wife. Never once does she show any signs of wishing she had married Werther instead. She is very fond of him, but evidently thinks of him as a ''brother'' with whom she can have interesting conversations. Her weakness, which is in part responsible for

the final catastrophe, is a dislike of admitting disagreeable facts: she keeps on hoping that Werther will get over his passion and become just a good friend, when she should have realized that this would never happen, and that the only sensible thing for her to do was to show him the door.

To escape from his own emotional confusion, Goethe became a civil servant at the court of Weimar, where he soon had important responsibilities. Similarly, in a moment of lucidity, aided by the good advice of his friend Wilhelm, Werther realizes that the only sensible thing for him to do is to give Lotte up, go away, and take a job, also, apparently, as some sort of civil servant. The society he now finds himself in is stuffy, snobbish, and conventional, but the Count, his boss, takes a great liking to him, and he seems all set for a successful career. Then a disagreeable but trivial incident occurs.

> [Count C.] had invited me for dinner at his house yesterday, on the very day when the whole aristocratic set, ladies and gentlemen, are accustomed to meet there late in the evening. I had completely forgotten this fact; and it also did not occur to me that subordinate officials like myself are not welcome on such occasions.

The ''set'' arrive and he senses that the atmosphere is chilly, but, instead of leaving, defiantly remains, is openly snubbed, and finally has to be asked by the Count to leave.

About this several things may be said. In the first place it is the professional duty of anyone in diplomacy or civil service not to forget the habits of the society in which he is living. Secondly, Werther is already well aware that the aristocratic set consider themselves superior to everyone else and, therefore, to himself, for he is not of aristocratic but bourgeois origins. Lastly, if a man thinks the social conventions of his time and place to be silly or wrong, there are two courses of behavior which will earn him an outsider's respect. Either he may keep his opinions to himself and observe the conventions with detached amusement, or he may deliberately break them for the pleasure of the shock he causes. He makes a scandal, but he enjoys it. Werther, by staying on when it is clear that his presence is unwelcome, defies the company, but his precious ego is hurt by their reactions, and he resigns from his post, returns to Lotte and disaster for all, destroying himself and ruining the lives of Lotte and Albert. What a horrid little monster! (pp. ix-xiii)

> *W. H. Auden, in a foreword to* ''The Sorrows of Young Werther'' *and* ''Novella'' *by Johann Wolfgang von Goethe, translated by Elizabeth Mayer, Louise Bogan, and W. H. Auden, Random House, 1971, pp. ix-xvi.*

ERIC A. BLACKALL (essay date 1976)

[*Blackall is the author of the important study* Goethe and the Novel. *In the following excerpt from that work, he discusses the role of the editor/narrator in the two versions of* Werther, *investigating the artistic implications of the types of narration Goethe employed.*]

We have an important piece of evidence that, in composing the last section of **Werther,** Goethe had reflected on what sort of narrative technique to adopt, and had considered various possibilities. Among the papers of Goethe's friend Frau von Stein there was a single sheet in Goethe's handwriting, which is now preserved in the archives at Weimar. . . . The German is somewhat bumpy but the meaning is clear enough. Here is a literal translation:

> They have gone through her hands, she has cleaned the dust from them, I kiss them a thousand times, she has touched you. And thou, spirit of heaven, dost favor my decision. And she gives you the implement, She from whose hands I wished to receive death and ah! now receive it. She quivered said my servant when she gave him the pistols. O Sir said the good fellow your departure makes your friends so sad. Albert stood at the desk without turning round he said to Madame: give him the pistols, she stood up and he said: I bid [you] wish him a happy journey, and she took the pistols and cleaned off the dust carefully and wavered and quivered as she gave them to my fellow and the farewell stuck in her throat [literally, "on her palate"]. Farewell, farewell!

> Here I have the fleshcolored ribbon before me which she had on her bosom when I made her acquaintance, which she gave me with so much friendliness [lovableness]. This ribbon! Ah then I did not think that the path would lead me thither. I beg you be calm.

The passage refers to the pistols, with one of which Werther shot himself. Apart from a few minor substitutions for individual words, every phrase of this passage occurs in the completed novel. But not as here presented. In the novel this material reappears partly in Werther's last letter to Lotte, and partly in the third-person account of the narrator. As presented on this individual sheet, the form is puzzling. It could be part of a letter from Werther to someone other than Lotte, for instance to Wilhelm, the recipient of Werther's other letters. But if so, to whom is the final admonition addressed, "I beg you be calm"? To the recipient of the letter? To himself? Or to Lotte? In the novel the words are addressed to Lotte. It is also possible that this is not from a letter at all, but represents an entry by Werther in his own diary. . . . It would seem therefore that this is a first sketch for the climax of the novel; but that it represents a form of communication, probably diary-entry, which was abandoned in favor of the alternation between narration by the anonymous editor of Werther's paper (the *Herausgeber*) and Werther's own last letters.

The reason for this change of form might seem obvious: Goethe needed a third-person narrator to relate the circumstances of Werther's death, because for all his epistolary genius Werther could hardly do this himself. Yet even leaving aside such extreme cases as Moses (who gave a third-person account of his own death) or Schnitzler's Fräulein Else (who dies in the middle of the last word of her stream of consciousness), this argument appears tenuous if not irrelevant. For the novel could have ended with Werther's last letter to Lotte and the announcement in it of his being about to shoot himself. Or the circumstances could have been described in a letter by someone else—by the Magistrate, for instance. The need for a third person to narrate Werther's death does not therefore in itself account for Goethe's abandonment of the epistolary form at this point in the novel, and it becomes even less likely an explanation when we consider the fact that the switch comes some time before Werther's death. Can there be some other reason? Let us examine the structural function of this switch of standpoint in the novel.

In the first published version of the novel the switch occurs after that letter of Werther's which ends with the words: "I am nowhere well and everywhere well. I wish nothing, demand nothing. It would be better if I went" [*Mir wäre besser ich gienge*]. The letter sequence is then broken by the "editor"

[*Herausgeber*], who says the break is necessary to provide an account of Werther's last days and proceeds to tell us how Werther's passion had gradually undermined the relationship between Albert and his wife.

So far everything that has been told us could have been conveyed by Werther in a letter. He would probably not have said that he was disrupting the life of the married couple, but a report of Albert's changed behavior would have implied this. Strangely enough, the narrator's account of Albert's behavior is weighted in favor of Werther. Albert is ill-humored, he speaks with "rather dry words" to his wife of Werther's "all too frequent visits." This is hardly dispassionate narration. The narrator then tells us that the idea of leaving this world was taking ever firmer hold on Werther's mind, *but that it was not a new idea to him*. Indeed it was not, as we know from Werther's letters. It would seem probably, therefore, that this "editor" is in fact Wilhelm, the recipient of Werther's letters. But he then offers an explanation for Werther's suicidal tendencies: that his honor had been offended by what happened in the society surrounding the Ambassador. It was this vexation, the narrator suggests, which gave him such distaste for all business affairs and political activity, and this, together with his debilitating passion for Lotte, had extinguished whatever life force there was in him. The attentive reader must question this "explanation": for Werther's suicidal tendency can be attested before the period at the Ambassador's, his distaste for affairs—or indeed for any activity—has been apparent from the very beginning, and he had never spoken of his honor being offended. And Wilhelm, as recipient of the letters, should have known this. Is then this "editor" someone other than Wilhelm?

It would seem that Goethe is here using the anonymous narrator, whether he be Wilhelm or not, to provide a rational explanation of Werther's melancholy and suicide. Or at least to suggest a *possible* explanation. The reason for the switch to the editor appears therefore to lie in Goethe's desire to get outside the standpoint and feelings of Werther. But is this narrator a person at all, or merely a narrative device? Is he intended to be a real reporter (possibly Wilhelm) or is this just a mechanism for ending the story? He asserts that he collected his material from those persons who were closest to Werther. In part this is a switch to the device of the omniscient narrator, but in part it is simulation of reliability through the claim that every available piece of evidence from all available witnesses is being given us. Every detail of the events of Monday, 21 December is indeed meticulously documented by this editor-reporter. Werther starts writing his letter very early; he calls his servant at 10 to tell him he is going away, he eats (presumably soon after), visits the Magistrate, is back at 5, goes to Lotte at 6:30, leaves as the maid is laying dinner, walks out through the town gate and returns home without his hat around 11. Each stage has its witness—his servant, the Magistrate, his maid (who stokes the fire at 5), Lotte, Lotte's maid, the guards at the town gate, and finally again his servant. But the only witness who could have given the narrator the details of what happened in Lotte's house is Lotte herself. The fiction of the painstaking reporter breaks down here, and we are back with the omniscient narrator. The person has yielded to the device.

Many of the details of the death scene and some of those in the material leading up to it were taken by Goethe from a real-life occurrence. A young theological student named Jerusalem had recently shot himself in similar circumstances. He had been in love with a married woman and, like Werther, had suffered a social rebuff at an aristocratic gathering and also at the hands of an ambassador. The great number of details taken over into the death scene can be seen from Goethe's friend Kestner's long account of the catastrophe in his letter to Goethe of 2 November 1772 [see Additional Bibliography]. Technically the interesting thing about this letter is that Kestner (a legation secretary who certainly must have had legal training) carefully indicates the person from whom he got each particular piece of information. The effect is of a character as he appeared to many people. This undoubtedly appealed to Goethe as a method of getting outside the character of Werther, or at least of attempting—or pretending—to do so. There is, however, no information in Kestner's report about the woman whom Jerusalem loved, except that she was the wife of the Secretary H—. Jerusalem never spoke about this, not even to his closest friend. But Kestner says he is "reliably informed" *(zuverlässig unterrichtet)* on this point. There is a reference to Secretary H— taking Jerusalem home after a dinner to drink coffee with his wife, of Jerusalem's saying that this would be the last coffee which he could drink with her. But apart from this, "no one knows what happened there," says Kestner. Jerusalem then *seems,* says Kestner, to have made careful preparations for his death; he wrote letters, including *perhaps* one to the ambassador which the ambassador *perhaps* destroyed. Such juridical caution is not maintained by the narrator in **Werther,** for some things in his narrative, notably his description of Lotte's feelings after Werther's last visit, are the work of the fictive omniscient narrator, who also "knows" precisely the several points at which Werther interrupted the writing of his last letter to Lotte.

This oscillation between a person and a device, between a well-informed reporter and the conventional omniscient "narrator" is, however, not the only disturbing feature of the final section of this first version of the novel. If the report of the editor is intended to be a distancing structural feature, then this purpose is belied by Werther's long letter, interrupted and resumed four times, which throws us right back into the tumult of Werther's own struggle for resolution. The letter is given us in five sections: the first contains the decision to die, the second the determination to see Lotte once more, the third his knowledge of her love; the fourth concerns the pistols and the last his farewell. The visit to Lotte comes between sections two and three, and the request for the pistols between sections three and four. But narration and letter are so neatly combined that one hardly notices the transitions. It is as though Werther himself were the narrator. The switch to the narrator in this first version of the novel comes at the point where the tension in Werther is too great for the epistolary fiction to be convincingly maintained. But it is not a switch away from Werther. Almost everything that is reported is colored by Werther's own viewpoint: Albert is unpleasant, Lotte unwilling to commit herself. Only after Werther is dead does the narration become really objective.

Goethe had found himself faced with an interesting structural problem. The final narration, after Werther's death, had to be objective. When was the transition to come? If the letters had continued right up to his death, the final narration would have become a coda, a footnote almost. This seems to have been unsatisfactory to his artistic sense. He breaks at Werther's exclamation that it would be better for him "to go," and moves seemingly into a well-documented protocol of what happened after that. But the objective unity of presentation is broken by Werther's letter to Lotte and by the necessity to describe, in terms that only Werther could have used, his last two meetings with Lotte, and Lotte's state of mind after the second. And so Goethe, by rejecting a continuous letter sequence and also possibly the switch to diaries, has not achieved an objective transition to the final narration.

When Goethe came to revise the novel for the second version, he seems to have realized this. He worked on it in the 1780s, and it is the revised version of 1787 that most of us read. Most of the revisions come after the switch to the editor, and those that come before seem preparatory to the changes in the editor section. The main addition before the switch is the story of the peasant lad, his passion for the widow and his committing murder out of jealousy. This is told in three sections, the last of which comes *after* the switch to the editor, which now comes even earlier, after the letter of 6 December, describing Werther's obsession with Lotte's dark eyes and the contrast between ecstasy and reality. And the editor's report begins differently: not with the cool statement that it is *necessary* to depend, from here on, on the testimony of others, but with the regretful wish that there *had* been preserved sufficient written documents by Werther so that it would *not* have been necessary to interrupt the sequence of his letters by narration. He then goes on to say that he has collected testimony from those who *could* have been acquainted with Werther's story, but this time gives *no* names and adds significantly that opinions varied, depending on the moods of the persons involved. All he can do, he says, is to report conscientiously and insert those of Werther's letters that have remained, not neglecting the smallest piece of paper because "it is difficult enough to uncover the real motivating forces in any characters, especially in such unusual persons as these." He begins by describing Werther's inner turmoil: "The harmony of his mind was completely destroyed, an inner heat and violence which drove all forces of his nature into confusion, produced the most unpleasant effects and finally left him only with a certain lassitude out of which he strove to lift himself even more anxiously than he had fought against all evils before." This state of mind made him unjust to others. Albert did *not* change, he was *not* cool towards Lotte or Werther—at least that is what Albert's friends told this narrator.

This narrator seems to be disagreeing with the narrator of the first version. The second narrator emphasizes Werther's mental state, and indicates that it alone was responsible for what followed. Lack of balance, violence, anxiety made him "a sad companion who became more and more unhappy, and more and more unjust as he became more and more unhappy." He was rapidly losing contact with the outside world, and did so completely after his attempt to defend the peasant lad, the final section of whose story comes at this point. In the peasant lad he saw himself. This apparent interest in something outside himself was therefore really just another aspect of self-obsession. In his revision Goethe plays down the idea that external events or persons had any effect on Werther's final resolve. The objective frame of reference, suggested hopefully but very tentatively in this second version (in contrast to the definiteness with which the narrator had begun in the first version), has receded immediately. It is already gone when the narrator describes Werther's lack of harmony, which follows immediately on his statement of the difficulty of ascertaining motives. And when the narrator gives us an account of what Werther was saying to himself as he fetched Lotte from her father's home, the whole spuriousness of the third-person narration is revealed. We have not gotten outside of Werther. The idea of a dispassionate, objective narrator has been abandoned, partly because it didn't work, but mainly—and this seems to me the really important point—because it was undesirable.

In the first version Goethe may have been attracted to the idea of a narrator in order to seek a transition to the necessary objectivity of the final reportage. He was undoubtedly also influenced by the form of Kestner's report on the death of Jerusalem. It seemed to be a way of getting outside the character of Werther, of breaking the tension in the letters when this had reached a point of climax, of achieving some degree of distance. But the device had not only broken down technically, as we have seen, because of the undistanced material which, for other reasons, Goethe had included in this seemingly distanced section of the novel. It had also resulted in Lotte and Albert emerging as characters outside of and independent of Werther's feelings, and to the transference of some responsibility to them. The result was that the unified, single standpoint of the book had been broken. In his revision Goethe remodeled his presentation of Lotte and Albert, leaving out that certain edginess which both of them were said, in the first version, to have shown towards Werther. He did this partly in answer to protests from his friends the Kestners on the way in which their married life had been presented in the first version of the novel. But not only for this reason, because there is artistic gain in the preservation of a unified standpoint despite the apparent distancing by the narrator. For this *is* only apparent; Werther and his point of view are still dominant. Albert's words to Lotte, definitely called "sharp" [*spizz*] in the first version, now only *seem* "cold or even hard" *to Werther;* it is now Werther who is cold to Albert, not vice versa. If the narrator of the first version may have been intended by Goethe to represent Wilhelm, but emerged as a Wilhelm who became so involved in things which only Werther could know that he ended up as Werther, this second narrator is Werther himself from the very start, a Werther trying, or perhaps we had better say *pretending,* to achieve distance toward himself, to be his own narrator.

At the time of the revision Goethe spoke of his desire to "tighten up" the book. By his treatment of the narrator section he has done this. We are deluded into a sense of having been elevated to a plane from which we can see Werther himself in a wider perspective. We feel that we have dissociated ourselves from this terrifyingly fascinating character. We say that we can now see what was wrong: we can now see how his death stemmed from his absorption in his own mental state: we feel that, now we have achieved this point of vantage, we would not ourselves succumb to such a situation, we would surely be able to rise above it, to work ourselves out of it because we recognize it for what it is. Werther is no model, no ideal character. He is a man gone wrong, but a man destroyed by himself. The "tightening up" of the narrator section in the second version reinforces this picture of Werther. We see that he is *not* badly treated, that he is not even misunderstood: but that on the contrary he is sympathetically understood and loved by both Albert and Lotte. Goethe is most anxious, in this second version of his novel, that we shall see the sickness of Werther and not identify him with his author, nor ourselves with him *totally.* This amount of distance Goethe desires: not, however, so much distance that we shall not identify with Werther *at all.* We must feel the common ground. We must understand and share Werther's anguish to the utmost, and to the very end. But we must also be able to see it as something askew. The second narrator brings us to this viewpoint and, unlike the first narrator, reveals that Werther's situation springs only from inside himself. In order to see Werther's malady we must get outside

of him; in order to sympathize with its origins we must to a certain extent remain inside his world. The second narrator serves this double function in that we remain with Werther's point of view and yet see it *as a point of view,* not as absolute. The book now maintains its single-mindedness right through to the end, and thereby gains in strength. This second narrator is no more able to get outside of Werther than Werther was able to get outside of himself. The narrator's inability to achieve distance therefore somehow provokes distance in us. (pp. 44-54)

What Goethe has done in **Werther,** and done brilliantly, is to intensify the sense of reality by combining the three techniques of first-person narration, epistolary exchange, and third-person narration by "informed observer." This observer is the recipient of the letters as well, but, in his function as editor, he suppresses his own answers. What we have is reported first-person narration without the voice of the reporter, and then when the novel later switches to third-person narration, the account given is built around Werther's last letter, so that the confessional aspect is maintained up to the very end. Even the account of Werther's death and burial makes all the points that Werther's ghost would have made. (pp. 54-5)

Eric A. Blackall, in his Goethe and the Novel, *Cornell University Press, 1976, 340 p.*

E. KATHLEEN WARRICK   (essay date 1978)

[*Warrick appraises the character of Lotte, questioning her feelings for Werther and her role in his suicide.*]

In reading **The Sorrows of Young Werther** we seem led to view Werther's love, Lotte, as a passive, innocent woman. Her goodness and sincerity appear irreproachable, and the multitude of kind deeds she performs help to create a most favorable impression of her in the reader's mind. Because readers of **Werther** have perpetuated this image of Lotte for two hundred years, the suggestions that she is not what she seems to be, that indeed she is far less innocent and far more actively participating in Werther's fate, may be greeted with suspicion. Consider, however, that the received notion of Lotte has persisted partially because Goethe presented her through two highly biased perspectives: Werther's own idealized view of her and the Editor's quite different perspective, one which reveals her conscious involvement in tempting Werther and strips away the veil of innocence Werther spreads over her actions. In addition to these contrasting views, sufficient clues within the novel suggest that there is more to Lotte's character than either of the two narrators admits. Of special importance are the two ways Lotte chiefly reveals herself, through the specific words she speaks to Werther and through the numerous touches she places upon him. These provide substantial evidence that the past image of Lotte as the embodiment of innocence and passivity needs to be reassessed. A close study of what she actually does and the motivation for her actions reveals her character to be far more complex than has heretofore been granted.

In general, the question of Lotte's role in causing Werther's suicide has received little critical attention. The assumption has been that various traits in Werther himself or in the society in which he lives are entirely responsible for Werther's desperate pursuit of Lotte's love. Lotte herself has been dealt with critically in basically three ways. First, her role in the novel is treated as irrelevant to Werther's actions. . . . Next, she is viewed as merely an innocent observer of Werther's tragic fate, a woman who has no sense of self. (p. 129)

Finally, she is considered as an actual lover in Goethe's private life, and his own relationship with her is discussed. Much has been written about Lotte as if she represented Charlotte Buff, a woman for whom Goethe had an unhappy and unrequited love. Multiple similarities between Goethe's writings to or about Charlotte Buff and Werther's statements about Lotte can be cited. (p. 130)

I would like to suggest a fourth viewpoint which recognizes that the past critical interpretation of Lotte's role as the innocent, blameless friend of Werther is inconsistent with many passages in the text itself, and that she indeed is responsible for encouraging and perpetuating Werther's love for her. Such a re-evaluation of Lotte's involvement in Werther's suicide necessarily has implications for re-evaluating the actions of Werther who, according to studies such as Peter Salm's entitled "Werther and the Sensibility of Estrangement," moves toward self-destruction, like Oedipus, merely ruled by an obsession; and, had he "shown common sense about Lotte, there would have been no suicide" [see Additional Bibliography].

Werther's representation of Lotte reveals his overwhelming need to innocentize her. Therefore, when Lotte is introduced into the novel through the words and hence the perceptions of Werther, her description is a paradigm of virtue. He portrays her as a seemingly perfect woman of innocence, whose intelligence, firmness, and inner serenity blend with her active life. He recalls upon preparing to go to the ball: "Ich bot einem hiesigen guten, schönen, übrigens unbedeutenden Mädchen die Hand. . . ." ["I asked a good, pretty, but otherwise uninteresting girl to be my partner. . . ."] Enroute to the affair, this escort describes Lotte as a beautiful girl. Filtered through Werther's vision and due to his insistence upon seeing her ideally, the image of Lotte as perfect womanhood begins to be created.

Lotte's words, considered objectively apart from Werther's innocentizing bias, belie her actual involvement in his increasing romantic vision of her as his unattainable love. However subtle her first compliment to Werther as a "Vetter" ["uncle"] may seem, she adds that she would be pleased to find he was among her relatives: "und es wäre mir leid, wenn Sie der schlimmste drunter Verwandte sein sollten." ["I should be sorry if you were to be the worst among them."] Such flattery is not an isolated incident in the story. The seeming naiveté with which Lotte conveys compliments to Werther needs to be questioned, for the frequency and overtness of such flattery betrays the sweet-lady-of-innocence role Werther persists in claiming for Lotte. Her attentions to Werther at the ball were so apparently more than a friendly acquaintance would extend that at least one woman "die mir wegen ihrer liebenswürdigen Miene auf einem nicht mehr ganz jungen Gesichte merkwürdig gewesen war" ["who had caught my attention before, because of the amiable expression of a face not exactly young"] shakes her finger at Lotte and reminds her of her engagement to Albert "zweimal . . . mit viel Bedeutung" ["twice with much emphasis."] Lotte hesitates in revealing to Werther Albert's identity, as an "einiges Nachdenken" ["thoughful shadow"] passes over her brow. This reinforces the strong implication that Lotte has been behaving towards Werther in an aggressively intimate manner.

Though Lotte at times seems offended with Werther's behavior, we consistently find her plying him with compliments and finding excuses to express personal affection to him. When Lotte begins to discuss her memory of her mother, she brings the issue to rest upon Werther quite intimately: "Wenn Sie sie gekannt hätten" ["If you had only known her"], she whimpers to Werther, and adds a compliment which could have no effect other than increasing his sense of Lotte's desire for him: "Sie war wert, von Ihnen gekannt zu sein!" ["She was worthy to be known by you."] At the same moment she, the aggressor, presses his hand into hers.

Lotte's words reveal her exuberant interest in Werther's emotional well-being. Shortly after we read a passage in which Werther accompanies Lotte on a visit to the pastor of St. ___ during which they take a walk with the pastor's daughter Friederike and her young man, we hear Lotte expressing her eager concern for Werther's well-being. She scolds him all the way home for having indicated too warm a sympathy with everything. Her words emphasize her concern that he not allow such emotions to ruin him and her wish that he would spare himself. Her involvement with Werther on a most personal level seems manifest here. What must not be overlooked is that Werther's response to her, believing that he beholds in her dark eyes "wahre Teilnehmung" ["genuine sympathy"] for his destiny, does have some basis in fact.

Werther himself helped to create the fiction of Lotte's innocence which has been so readily accepted by critics. In Werther's letters we often see Lotte making intimate advances toward Werther. She talks personally to him, places her hand on his, moves closer to him—so close that her breath reaches his lips. However, Werther credits "ihre Unschuld, ihre unbefangene Seele" ["her innocent, candid soul"] with the impossibility of understanding how she is tormenting him. She repeatedly behaves toward Werther in a fashion which indicates that she is as intelligent and aware in this aspect of her behavior as she is in her selection of reading material or involvement in philosophical discussions. What is being developed from the initial pages of the novel is not Lotte's role as a virtuous, blameless woman, but rather Werther's need to avoid life and reality by fictionalizing the nature of the person with whom he is interacting most intimately. However, Werther's illusion that his love for Lotte can be reciprocal is, as are most of his illusions throughout the novel and particularly with reference to Lotte, not merely precipitated by his imagination, but rather does have a factual basis.

Words are not the only means by which Lotte communicates her libidinal desires. Touch also speaks, perhaps louder than words, to Werther's feelings. . . . Goethe presents the reader with many examples of Lotte touching Werther. Early in the story, when the lightning and general confusion brought the dancing at the ball to a stop, many of the ladies present displayed their anxiety and distress. Lotte, in contrast to the distraught ladies, calmly began to arrange the chairs for parlor games. After her leadership and organization helped to divert the attention of the guests from the thunderstorm, "sie legte ihre Hand auf" ["she laid her hand on"] Werther's and said "Klopstock!" Both her words and her touch are here blatantly intended to arouse intense feelings in Werther, whether one argues that her actions were free of seductive motivation or not. She succeeds in touching his deepest emotions and, in the midst of this moving scene, he tearfully kisses her hand and stares into her eyes. The next scene portrays an intimate time of touching, a morning together watching the sunrise during the early hours after the ball. It is Lotte who suggests to Werther that they doze together, tenderly adding "ihrentwegen sollt' ich unbekümmert sein" ["he should not take any notice of her"]. They did not sleep, however, and we are led to believe that their wakeful hours were most enjoyable for, when Werther asked to see Lotte again that same day, she granted his request without hesitation.

Lotte's touching Werther, her body nestled close to his and her hand pressed upon his, which is mentioned repeatedly throughout the novel, suggests the power of her erotic stimulation stirring the depths of Werther's creative being as he anguishes in desire for her. Lotte's reaching out from her body to contact Werther's body attests to her aggressive sexuality. In addition, her action suggests that Werther was not merely imagining her desire for him. However, he continued to suppress, in his wish to flee reality, any conscious knowledge of her advances and to fictionalize a woman of ideal innocence.

Though Werther's own interpretation of her deeds has tried to absolve Lotte of all responsibility, both her words to Werther and her frequent touch betray her intentions. Lotte's sexual aggressiveness is revealed further when the Editor narrates the final section of the novel. The Editor pretends to tell the contents of the letters from an objective stance. However, his selection of details not only reinforces that Werther's former need was to innocentize Lotte, but Lotte herself is revealed, more blatantly than ever, to be the initiator of much of the passion Werther must cope with.

The Editor describes Lotte as appearing to miss Werther's company after his departure: "Unterwegs sah sie sich hier und da um, eben als wenn sie Werthers. Begleitung vermiβte." ["On the way Lotte now and then looked back, as though she missed Werther's company."] However, she ceased to speak of him often, realizing that Albert declined to converse with her when she did. The Editor halfheartedly explains Lotte's motives for trying to break the ties with Werther as being based

The last meeting of Werther and Lotte.

on a "herzliche, freundschaftliche Schonung" ["warm feeling of pity"] and wanting to reassure Albert of the worthiness of her love for him. This incomplete interpretation by the Editor suggests that questions purposely remain regarding Lotte's real motives. That her desire to hold onto Werther's love is still strongly controlling her actions and that she has not been able to face the possibility of parting with Werther forever, is made explicit by the Editor's descriptions. Lotte's speech to Werther encouraging him to seek another woman and to forget her at first seems laudable. However, only superficially does she appear to be making a genuine effort to part with Werther, for the Editor clues us that her gesture lacks authenticity. As she verbally discourages Werther from pursuing her further, "Sie hielt seine Hand." ["She kept his hand in hers."] Though she encourages Werther to travel and find new interests, her insincerity is starkly revealed by the Editor when, shortly thereafter, he describes Lotte's deep feelings for Werther. Here we are not hearing Werther's interpretation of Lotte which eternally cloaks her actions in innocence and purity. Rather we are learning the Editor's observation of what Lotte was saying, doing, and feeling. He tells us: "Auf der anderen Seite war ihr Werther so teuer geworden, gleich Vom ersten Augenblick ihrer Bekanntschaft an hatte sich die Übereinstimmung ihrer Gemüter so schön gezeigt." ["On the other hand, Werther had become very dear to her heart; from the very beginning of their acquaintance the harmony of their minds had showed itself in the most pleasant way."] She sensed the great gap which would be left in her existence if she should not be able to converse with him: "Alles, was sie Interessantes fühlte und dachte, war sie gewohnt mit ihm zu teilen. . . ." ["She had become accustomed to share with him everything of interest she felt or thought. . . ."] The inner struggle in Lotte's mind and the lust for possession of Werther (symbolized by her touching earlier) is revealed finally by the Editor's description of Lotte confronting the thought that she wants to keep Werther for herself. Her prevailing actions both by touch and word throughout have indicated her desire to encourage and to keep his affection. Now she confronts her desire directly.

As Lotte's battle with her feelings is openly portrayed to the reader, we see her suggesting that Werther read to her the songs of Ossian. As he reads they begin to identify their own misery with the fate of the Faels. It is Lotte who initiates the action, consistent with her previous gestures, who takes his hands, presses them against her breast, and bends her cheek toward his. Werther succumbs, of course, to her sensuous advance and showers her with kisses. We are told it was "mit schwacher Hand" ["with a feeble hand"]—the struggle of her inner turmoil weakening—that Lotte pushed Werther away. The Editor further describes her facial expression was "mit dem vollsten Blick der Liebe" ["with a look full of love"] when she told him good-bye. The Editor reveals through sharing Werther's last note that Lotte has done yet one more deed to encourage his emotional attachment to her: in order to convey that tactile sensation so representative of her erotic desire for Werther, she had sent him flowers when she had been unable to speak to him or to give him her hand at the party.

Lotte's inner struggle to possess Werther became confused with her feelings of grief, pity, selfishness, futility, and a genuine love for Albert and the life-style which he represents. A mixture of all these emotions prompted her to hand the guns—which she knew Werther would use for his self-destruction—to the young man sent for them. This action was not performed in innocence; rather it was immediately accompanied by her own sense of guilt, as the Editor observes:

Ihr Herz weissagte ihr alle Schrecknisse. Bald war
sie im Begriffe, sich zu den Füßen ihres Mannes zu
werfen, ihm alles zu entdecken, die Geschichte des
gestrigen Abends, ihre Schuld und ihre Ahnugen.

["Her heart prophesied to her the most terrible possibilities. Her first thought was to throw herself at
her husband's feet and to tell him the whole truth
about last night's events, as well as her own guilt
and her forebodings."]

At last she could possess him more passionately and completely
than ever before. He could never fully acquire the innocent
ideal whose existence depended solely upon his creative powers, so he chose to commit suicide rather than to continue the
pursuit of a woman who tempted him, but would not have him.
The description of Lotte's realization of Werther's death is
presented by the Editor as an understandable emotional response, which is also suggestive of orgasmic imagery. When
she awakens to hear the death bell "ein Zittern ergreift alle
ihre Glieder" ["a tremor seized all her limbs"], he reveals.
In her reception of Werther's death, her final possession of
Werther, the language of Eros prevails over Lotte's actions.
She becomes Eros passionately fulfilled. Is this the response
of an innocent, virtuous woman who is reacting to a terrible
event motivated by a guiltless concern or surprise? Or rather
is this the extreme response of a woman who has assertively
sought a man's passion and bears much of the responsibility
for his suicide? (pp. 130-34)

E. Kathleen Warrick, "Lotte's Sexuality and Her
Responsibility for Werther's Death," in Essays in
Literature, Vol. 5, No. 1, Spring, 1978, pp. 129-35.

JEAN H. HAGSTRUM (essay date 1980)

[Examining Werther's love for Lotte in association with four motifs—nature, death, regression to childhood, and the Oedipal triangle—Hagstrum links the novel to the sentimental tradition.]

[In his] expressions of love Goethe has fully realized the meaning of "sentiment" at the moment of its greatest richness and
ambiguity: he has united carnal delight and spiritual transcendence. But at the same time he has entered deeply into the
implications of "sensibility" in its postmeridian developments,
imbuing ideal forms with the inescapable features of morbidity
and even perversion. The last are insistently, though by no
means grossly or obviously, present in that amazing work which
was written hastily in 1774 and thoroughly revised in 1787,
Die Leiden des Jungen Werthers, a product of *Sturm und Drang,*
the German equivalent of sensibility and a potent influence on
subsequent life and letters. This work merits our attention not
simply because . . . it is a fascinating *Schlüsselroman* based on
its author's own youthful experiences of life, but also because
it shines in the Rousseauist afterglow and powerfully explores
and extends the nature of love-sensibility. These backward-
and forward-looking qualities will emerge if we consider the
love of Werther for Lotte in four connections: with (1) *nature*
(2) *death,* (3) *regression to childhood* and the childish, and
(4) the shadowy but hauntingly real presence of an *Oedipal
triangle.* This fourfold approach is intended to modify, if not
reject outright, the traditional view that Werther's suicide represents an intense but understandable response to the frustration
of a normally passionate, though deeply poetic, love for a
woman—a frustration made unavoidable by her obligations to
the state of matrimony. (pp. 260-61)

1. *Nature* does seem to proffer a Rousseauist nest at Wahlheim,
an hour's walk from town, a sequestered, homelike place. But
Werther cannot derive from it the intense, if somewhat troubled, delights which the Confessor drew from Les Charmettes
because of his taste for what Burke called the sublime of terror
and Freud the "oceanic" feeling, both real menaces to adulthood, however exploitable they may be by the creative artist.
Werther wants to lose himself in the distant hills and valleys,
which are vast and dim: he longs for the rapture of one great
emotion. But his feeling is as unspecific and undifferentiated
as the details of reality (developed in the course of the novel)
are concrete and sensuous. Early one morning Werther experiences in the presence of nature a piercing sense of Coleridge's
"vain endeavour": he is winning nothing but despair from the
outward forms he contemplates. Very soon the soft, sexual,
maternal feelings mediated by nature (these predominate at
first) are drowned in a growing din of torment as nature becomes a devouring monster: the grave gapes, streams dash
themselves to pieces on the rocks, storms flood the valley and
ruin the summer arbor; and Cowper's frightening vision in *The
Castaway* is repeated. Not quite at once: there are a few re-
missions, which, however, only accentuate the dryness and
emptiness that contact with nature now produces.

2. The theme of nature—and its ultimate disappointments—is
fatally accompanied by whispers of *death*. These adumbrations
of mortality are so carefully, consistently, and increasingly
suggested by the natural scene and also by the developing
human relationships that the careful reader does not regard
Werther's suicide as gratuitous or melodramatic. One senses
danger early on when the "oceanic" in nature blurs Werther's
perceptions as a painter and weakens his sense of form, as
everything external swims and sways before his inner being.
This loss of shape is a sure sign of *Dumpfheit* (dullness of soul)
and makes us appreciate more Blake's insistence on the
"bounding line," the "hard and wirey line of rectitude and
certainty." Feeling lethargy within, Werther finally sees a dark
abyss in the outside world and only one welcoming presence,
that of an all-encompassing death. And this is precisely the
union that Werther seeks when the mutually rapturous love
embrace with the now married Lotte is perceived to be tragically ultimate. The suicide is grimly presented: Werther shoots
himself above the eye and spills his brains, achieving death
only after lingering from midnight to noon of the next day.
(pp. 261-62)

3. If, then, as moderns using critical tools now available to
us, we examine closely the nature of Werther's desire, his
frustration, and his life process, we find that it bears close
resemblances to *the regressive* and the primal. When Werther
became a man, he simply did not heed the Apostle Paul's advice
and put away childish things. Quite the contrary. He seems to
have tightened his hold upon the childish and become one of
the longish list of pre-Romantic and Romantic children. It is
of course no sign of regression that he should love the child
or even that children he met should, of all living and inanimate
beings, be the closest to his heart. He felt that we are all children
under God—and that idea certainly has a venerable history and
should not give us pause; but when he conceived of God as
one who allows his children to live in pleasant illusions, we
perhaps have a right to be disturbed and to think ahead to how
brilliantly the first part of **Wilhelm Meisters Lehrjahre** disposes
of that notion as the hero grows up to become a man. During
the first summer in the time scheme of the novel Werther
continues to indulge this fantasy—that we are all children and
that he too is a child, even as suicidal fancies are being born.

And when the novel nears its shattering climax, during the Christmas festivities when the whole environment reverts to worshiping the Child and reaffirming the beauty and value of childhood, Werther becomes less an earthly than an everlasting boy *(das Ewig-Kindliche)*, begging for forgiveness of his Heavenly Father and promising, while awaiting Lotte in the next world, to seek out her mother, now a redeemed facsimile of the one he has loved on earth as an angel and thus consolatory as nothing terrestrial can possibly be.

4. If Werther has become a child, who is the father? Not the natural father he lost in death. Who is his mother? Not the one he visits briefly—without noteworthy emotion—after he has lost his position at court. No, the "parents" of the "child" Werther are Albert, the husband, and Lotte, his wife, whom Werther adores. Goethe thus adapts to his purposes the *Oedipal triangles* of Rousseau, Claude Anet, and Mme de Warens in *The Confessions* and of Saint-Preux, Wolmar, and Julie in *La nouvelle Héloïse*. Each of these "arrangements" is broken— by the departure of Rousseau the "son," by the death of Julie the "mother," and by the suicide of Werther the "child"— for the same reason: the situation in each instance approximates the Oedipal and so falls under a deep and ineradicable taboo that may indeed operate below the level of consciousness in the participants.

Like Saint-Preux vis-à-vis Wolmar and the Confessor vis-à-vis Claude, Werther's relations with Albert are so free of normal sexual jealousy that one is invited to treat the two as "father" and "son" rather than rival lovers. At least in the central sections, Albert's role as husband and father, as mentor and guide, supersedes his position as Lotte's suitor and lover. He is a force for law and order, particularly familial order. Like a stereotypical father, he is undiscriminatingly on the side of established value and insensitive to the individual suffering that custom and tradition entail. Toward him Werther feels only the jealousy of the child, mixed with admiring love. The lover, almost like Rousseau, who helped establish the pattern, looks to the husband as to the embodiment of stern duty from whom he half expects the ministrations of the rod.

The Werther-Albert relationship does not, however, exhaust the father-son implications that this rich novel possesses. Additional ones arise from the persistent religious metaphor which underlies much of the thought and action. About to take his life, Werther writes, "O Lotte! I shall go before you! go to my Father, to your Father. To him I will make my complaint, and he will comfort me, until you come." At the moment of his climactic action the hero is more a child than ever—now a kind of cosmic child ready to act sub specie aeternitatis. One might well ask, Why does he have a sense that he goes directly to the Father without the mediation of the Son? The reason is surely not that Goethe is making a point so often raised in Catholic-Protestant polemics about the intermediary nature of Jesus but, rather, because Werther *is* Christ in his fevered and distorted fancy. The young man has, as it were, replaced him and therefore no longer needs him. When he says he will "go to my Father, to your Father," he is not only quoting the words of Christ but assuming the Messianic role, as he does when he utters the cry from the cross: "My God! My God! why hast thou forsaken me?" He can in fact regard the sacrifice of his life not as an act of despair but as a sacrifice for another, resulting from "the certainty that my sufferings are complete." Like Christ, he is about to make a perfect sacrifice that will avail to the salvation of their loving hearts. What does this large identification mean? Not, one would guess, that Werther

is a Romantic maniac, swollen with overweening pride, about to fall into the abyss like the original Son of the Morning. He is, rather, the eternal, archetypal son, even usurping the place of the Son, so demanding is the role which he assumes—or which his nature and circumstances have thrust upon him—in his human relationships.

Lotte, both before and after her marriage, is more a mother than a fluttering girl or a trembling bride. She is at the very outset surrounded, like a Victorian child-mother in nineteenth-century novels and paintings, by eight brothers and sisters. Kindly, intelligent (she reads Goldsmith), avant-garde in her taste (she sighs the name of the *Sturm und Drang* writer Klopstock during a tempest), controlled and calm when others whimper in fright, she is a leader as well in the festivities, the establisher of arrangement at the dance. Fresh, young, healthy, she nevertheless likes older people and is liked by them. In her relations with Werther she is more often like an older woman than a beloved. She gives him sweets as though he were her little boy, and Werther kneels before her, like another Rousseau; toward her white form he stretches out his arms, like the Blakean child toward a lamb. Until the climax she remains sacred, untouchable, an "angel," as she is obsessively called by him and others.

The climax of this relationship—a passionate embrace, the only one in the novel—is followed by a gory suicide, which would perhaps be considered sensational and insufficiently motivated had Werther loved conventionally. But as a member of an Oedipal triangle, he has violated a dark taboo big with vengeance, and he must reject himself with finality. And Lotte too must reject him—with as much finality. She brushes the dust from the pistols owned by Albert and hands them to Werther's servant. Instruments of death belonging to the "father" are transmitted by the "mother" to an Oedipally infatuated boy, who uses them to remove himself from the "family" in the most decisive way imaginable. On the eve of his act Werther cries out: "Sin?. . . I am punishing myself for it. . . . I shall go before you!. . . And see your mother! I shall see her, shall find her, ah, and pour out my whole heart to her! Your mother, your image." In love-sensibility from Shakespeare to Rousseau and Keats, immortality is regarded as a prolongation of the present—but without pain, frustration, and death. And so Werther projects onto a future beyond the grave the same image he has adored here and gives to it and indeed to the whole configuration in which it grew up and flowered the ultimate sanction of the Heavenly Father. (pp. 263-66)

What Werther prizes in himself more than intelligence, artistic ability, or imagination, is his *coeur sensible:* he complains that the Prince, a candid and simple person whom the hero by no means dislikes, "prizes my intelligence and my talents more than he does this heart, which is after all my sole pride, which is the only source of everything I have, of all my force, all my bliss, and all my misery. Oh, anyone can know what I know—only I possess my heart." No further evidence is needed to show that the largest affiliation of **Werther** is not nascent Romanticism or German *Sturm und Drang* but the whole development of Western sentiment, with its profound emphasis upon the human affections. (pp. 267-68)

Jean H. Hagstrum, "The Aftermath of Sensibility: Sterne, Goethe, and Austen," in his Sex and Sensibility: Ideal and Erotic Love from Milton to Mozart, *The University of Chicago Press, 1980, pp. 247-77.*

DAVID E. WELLBERY　(essay date 1988)

[*Wellbery emphasizes the essential subjectivity of Werther's character and his experience of romantic love.*]

It is difficult today to realize that Goethe's *The Sorrows of Young Werther*—still the most popular of his works—represents an act of artistic audacity. First published in 1774 (a second version . . . appeared in 1787), it boldly transformed the conventions of the sentimental epistolary novel and in doing so elaborated a new form of novelistic discourse. Its major generic predecessors, Richardson's *Clarissa* (1747) and Rousseau's *Julie ou La Nouvelle Héloïse* (1761), are compendious books, disquisitional even in their emotionality. Both resemble slightly a moral tract. The compact *Werther,* however, unfolds its fictional world without tendentious moralizing and achieves in the shaping of its letters a lyrical intensity previously unknown in narrative prose. Whereas the earlier novels are built around intricate plot structures, Goethe's juxtaposes discrete, mutually resonant moments, a structural principle which he called, in the visual vocabulary he always favored, 'mirroring' *(Spiegelung)*. The traditional epistolary novel is dramatic; its letters are conceived with a view toward possible responses and consequences. What Werther writes to the distant Wilhelm, by contrast, plays no role in furthering the action; even the few letters addressed to Charlotte, among them the protagonist's last, do not seek to elicit an answer. The writing takes place in what might be called a pragmatic vacuum. Its function is not to communicate something to someone, but rather to make imaginatively accessible the tonality of a unique subjective experience. *Werther* is the first European novel in which subjectivity *per se* acquires aesthetic concretization.

This radical generic innovation emerged from an intense period of creative labor. In his autobiography *Poetry and Truth,* Goethe claims to have written the novel in four weeks [see excerpt dated 1814], a figure which, although certainly too small, suggests that the older poet remembered the compositional process as a consuming one. We do know that the novel was begun in early February, 1774, and in May of the same year was sent to the publisher. During this period Goethe worked through (much as one 'works through' something in psychoanalysis) a complex of experiences which had occurred for the most part a year and a half earlier during the poet's service as a practicing attorney at the Imperial Court in Wetzlar. Those experiences are essentially two: Goethe's passion for a woman named Charlotte Buff who was engaged to, and soon married, an official called Johann Kestner with whom Goethe had a friendship; and the poet's identification with a young suicide, the writer Carl Wilhelm Jerusalem, also caught in the anguish of an amorous triangle. Imaginatively repeating these events eighteen months after their occurrence, Goethe achieves for his novel a unique blend of immediacy and distance. Intimately sensed desires and anxieties are cast in an aesthetic structure so rigorous that the novel can dispense with the legitimation of official moral discourse.

Few contemporary readers were adequate to the combination of empathy and reflective distance *Werther* demanded. Such enlightened literati as Lessing were disturbed by the novel's moral reticence, but affirmative identification with the protagonist on the part of youth was sometimes disastrously total. The same split is discernible within the fiction. On the one hand the novel has its superficial moralizers, incapable of grasping the complexity of psychic conflict; one thinks especially of Albert's remarks on suicide as reported in the important letter of August 12, 1771. On the other hand, Werther, who narcissistically projects himself into books as well as the destinies of other individuals, provides the prototype of an uncritical, identificatory type of reading. The crisis of understanding and comprehension, which the reception of the novel reveals, is a phenomenon internal to the fiction itself. *The Sorrows of Young Werther* articulates a subjective experience which is both entirely compelling (leading, for instance, to acts of psychic identification) *and* opposed to the prevailing moral code. The name which our culture has since given to that experience is romantic love.

Two major shifts in the life of Western Europe during the last third of the eighteenth century engender this new form of eros. First of all, the social sphere of intimate relations becomes functionally differentiated within the society as a whole. Whom one loves and marries is decided independently of such non-amorous considerations as economic gain and the formation of family alliances; or at least these matters are not at the forefront of awareness. The subjective correlate of this is that one no longer desires in the beloved such general qualities as virtue or public esteem; love no longer borrows its values from other functional spheres. Rather, what one loves in the beloved is the particularity of that person, his or her absolute difference from everyone else. This is why, when Werther attempts to describe Charlotte to Wilhelm, the predicates he reaches for are so unsatisfying; what ultimately enchants him is not some ideal she embodies, but her unique, and inexpressible, individuality. The second cultural change which brings forth the phenomenon of romantic love is the crystallization of that social structure which today is referred to as the nuclear family: the family unit reduced to parents and children. It is within this structure that childhood, conceived as a domain of experience *sui generis,* emerges. And this sphere, in turn, assumes enormous importance in the formation of psychological identity: childhood becomes a kind of emotional cocoon in which the subject's patterns of affection and aversion, the orientation and nuances of his desire, first come into being. The dominant figure of this phase is, of course, the mother, who assumes the role of primary educator and caretaker within the new family structure. To love romantically is therefore always to act out what Freud called the family romance *(Familienroman,* literally: family novel), the plot of which binds the male subject's desire to the figure of the mother and at the same time requires that he renounce that desire. This is precisely the contradiction Werther suffers through in his impossible and yet inescapable love for Charlotte.

One of the most magnificent letters in the novel, that of June 16, 1771, recounts the sudden formation of this love. Entering the house where Charlotte reigns as virtual mother to her siblings, Werther beholds a spectacle, the epiphany of his desire's radiant object: at the center of the image is Charlotte herself, in virginal white except for the pink colored ribbons at her arms and breast (one of these will become a fetish for Werther); surrounding her are six of her siblings, all expressing with outstretched hands their childish demand; finally, linking the two components of the image, the gift of nourishment in its most basic form, the bread of life. This scene lends Werther's love for Charlotte its unique character. The paradigm of his passion is the child's longing for the nourishing maternal presence. Indeed, even the erotically most charged letter of the novel, that evoking the image of the bird at Charlotte's lips, is focussed on the oral register and the experience of feeding. It is no accident that throughout the novel Werther identifies so strongly with the children, for his desire draws its pathos from early childhood phantasies. He confesses as much himself to Wilhelm on one occasion, writing that he relates to his "heart" as if it were a sick child needing spoiling.

Beyond this anchorage in childhood, Werther's love for Charlotte is correlated with two other domains, literature and nature.

Thus, the memory of a particular poem by Klopstock triggers the flood of feeling that overcomes Werther in the climactic scene of the letter of June 16. And just as this remembered poem, an ode in celebration of Spring, has as its theme the presence of the divine in nature, Werther's own experience of nature throughout the first phase of his love is jubilantly pantheistic. One might say that for Werther love, literature and nature become all-consuming experiences; they absorb him into an imaginary world in which the constraints of social obligation seem completely erased. This is one of the novel's most fascinating and innovative features, its exploration of emotional experiences which shatter the contours of the responsible self. *The Sorrows of Young Werther* is built around a series of ecstatic transgressions that carry the protagonist beyond the limits of the social. This is why the letters often tend toward the lyrical; such extremity of experience can only be conveyed in a discourse that pushes expression outside the sayable.

The extrasocial, extralinguistic region into which Werther ventures affords him the experience of an unconditioned oneness, a state without difference and alterity which might be termed the romantic absolute. The most salient feature of this absolute is its extreme ambiguity. Unmoored to any set of stable social norms, it shifts abruptly from a positive, euphoric value to a bleakly disphoric one. Thus, the letter of May 10, 1771, describes an experience in which Werther, lying in the grass, feels himself taken up within the eternal life that animates all of nature. By the 18th of August, however, nature is sensed (no less ecstatically) as the abyss of an infinite grave, as a monster which second by second consumes itself. Werther's joyous sense of at once containing within himself and being contained within the cosmos yields to a desire to annihilate himself by plunging into something he experiences as chaos, a kind of active nothingness. In the same way, the idyllic scenery of his Wahlheim retreat transforms itself into the image of a surging flood. The literary world of the novel is no less polarized: whereas Klopstockian praise of the divine presence suffused throughout nature provides the impetus to Werther's and Charlotte's first moment of intimacy, their last, openly transgressive embrace issues from the unending lament of the Ossian poems and their monotonous evocation of absence. Even Charlotte vacillates for Werther between radically opposed imaginary values, much as the memory of her eyes appears to him now as radiance, now as gaping blackness. It is in this sense that Werther is the first romantic hero in European literature: in art, love and nature, he seeks an absolute which—precisely because it exists outside any system of differentiation—appears to the subject both as Being itself, divine presence, and as Nothingness, the radical absence of divinity.

Because it is the absolute which, in all its ambiguity, the romantic subject *desires,* the position that subject takes vis-à-vis the differentiated world of society is necessarily that of the transgressor. Certainly this is the case with Werther, whose love for Charlotte is marked from the beginning by the fact that, by law, she is forbidden him. But in addition to the obviously Oedipal situation in which he finds himself, it can be said that for Werther all social regulations, from norms of appropriately 'adult' behavior to conventionalized religious beliefs, are essentially negative: proscriptive and punitive. A forceful example of this is provided by the scenes which open Part Two of the novel and which involve Werther's employment at court. In these scenes the protagonist suffers the negativity of the social in two of its aspects, first as the pedantry of bureaucratic power and then as the exclusionary force of class distinction. Both these aspects reappear in the figure of

Albert, who is on the one hand a dutiful bureaucrat, tediously moderate in everything, and on the other the sovereign husband whose right it is to forbid contact between Werther and Charlotte. The social problem this novel articulates is one which violently affects the protagonist in every dimension of his experience. Perhaps one could say it is the problem of socialization as such; that is: of the traumatic and tenuous inscription of the child (Werther's ideal till the end) into the social order.

In addition to Werther, the novel knows three other transgressor figures whose stories function as reduced models of the hero's own. There is the clerk dismissed from the office of Charlotte's father because of his amorous interest in Charlotte and now wandering the heath, madly searching for flowers for his beloved; there is the young peasant whose love for his widowed mistress is blocked by her deceitful brother, eliciting a desperately violent act of revenge; and finally there is the girl who, betrayed by the lover for whom she had sacrificed everything, takes her own life. Like Werther, all these figures experience a desire, which, however natural it appears, is nevertheless socially unacceptable; all three suffer an enforced separation from the beloved object as soon as they bring their illicit desire to expression; and all three end by throwing themselves (or being cast) into a form of radical otherness: madness, crime, suicide. The destinies of these three unfortunates prefigure for Werther the possible outcomes of his own dilemma. The romantic subject can choose no other end than a mode of total exclusion from the social. As this becomes clear to Werther, he begins to identify his passion with that of Christ, an identification which, it should be mentioned, is suggested in the novel's title. But this must not be construed as a religious act. On the contrary, it is Christ's moment of doubt on the Cross, His sense that the Father has turned away from Him, which Werther reenacts. Werther's imitation of Christ testifies only to the absence of any religious belief he might share with a community. No clergyman, the novel's last sentence notes, accompanies him to his grave.

From the beginning Werther's desire aimed for an experience inaccessible to common parlance, unthinkable in the categories of common sense. His suicide, the most radical form of excommunication, is the culmination of this tendency. It is an act fundamentally different from the self-willed death of Emilia Galotti, the heroine of the drama by Lessing which Werther apparently reads in before taking his own life. Emilia's death occurs for the sake of a moral idea: after all she commits suicide in order to save her virtue from the debauchery of the Prince's court. Her death generates a meaning, a tragic meaning, that can become a jointly held cultural value. Werther, by contrast, dies for the sake of an imaginary construct which has reality only in his assertion of it. In other words, his feverish dream of an eternal love to Charlotte within the space of a reintegrated family bears the purely subjective significance of phantasy. The brilliant audacity of *The Sorrows of Young Werther* is to accord this significance an independent legitimacy within its fictional universe. The novel refuses every explanatory solution, be it psychological or moral. Not even the "editor's" intervention near the end of the work provides a final and, as it were, official judgment regarding the unhappy sequence of events. On the contrary, what the reader senses most acutely in this juxtaposition of objective narrative with the personal utterances of the protagonist is the sheer and utter incommensurability of the two modes of discourse; they know no common measure. If, as I mentioned at the outset, Goethe's is the first novel which aesthetically renders subjectivity *per se*, then it accomplishes this by lending Werther's speech the status of an enigma. Werther is the first romantic subject to the degree that he cannot be fully understood. However empathetic our response to his experience, he remains for us ineluctably strange. (pp. 283-88)

> *David E. Wellbery, in an afterword to* The Sorrows of Young Werther. Elective Affinities. Novella *by Johann Wolfgang von Goethe, edited by David E. Wellbery, translated by Victor Lange and Judith Ryan, Suhrkamp Publishers New York, Inc., 1988, pp. 283-96.*

ADDITIONAL BIBLIOGRAPHY

Atkins, Stuart Pratt. "J. C. Lavater and Goethe: Problems of Psychology and Theology in *Die Leiden des jungen Werthers.*" *PMLA* LXIII, No. 2, Part 1 (June 1948): 520-76.
  Investigates Lavater's influence on the novel.

———. *The Testament of "Werther" in Poetry and Drama.* Cambridge, Mass.: Harvard University Press, 1949, 322 p.
  Thoroughly explores the novel's influence on English, German, and French poetry and drama, thereby elucidating its vast effect on European literature.

Bennett, Benjamin. "*Werther* and Montaigne: The Romantic Renaissance." *Goethe Yearbook* III (1986): 1-20.
  Explores parallels between *Werther* and Michel de Montaigne's *Essais* (1580-95) in a discussion of Goethe's relation to Renaissance thought.

Brenkman, John. "Aesthetics of Male Fantasy." In his *Culture and Domination*, pp. 184-227. Ithaca, N.Y.: Cornell University Press, 1987.
  A sociological and psychoanalytical interpretation of *Werther*.

Bullock, Walter L. "On Re-Reading Three Thwarted Romances: *La nouvelle Héloïse, Die Leiden des jungen Werthers, Iacopo Ortis.*" In *Goethe Centenary Papers*, edited by Martin Schutze, pp. 65-74. Chicago: Open Court Publishing Co., 1933.
  Compares *Werther* with Jean-Jacques Rousseau's *La nouvelle Héloïse* (1761) and Ugo Foscolo's *Jacopo Ortis* (1802).

Butler, E. M. "The Element of Time in Goethe's *Werther* and Kafka's *Prozess.*" *German Life & Letters* n.s. XII, No. 4 (July 1959): 248-58.
  Contrasts the handling of time in *Werther* and Franz Kafka's *Der Prozess* (1925; *The Trial*).

Clark, Robert T., Jr. "The Psychological Framework of Goethe's *Werther.*" *The Journal of English and Germanic Philology* XLVI, No. 3 (July 1947): 273-78.
  A systematic analysis of *Werther* as a psychological novel based on the theories of Johann Gottfried von Herder.

Diez, Max. "The Principle of the Dominant Metaphor in Goethe's *Werther.*" *PMLA* LI (1936): 821-41.
  Examines Goethe's use in *Werther* of imagery depicting physical and mental suffering, which Diez considers the novel's main theme.

Duncan, Bruce. "'Emilia Galotti lag auf dem Pult aufgeschlagen': Werther as (Mis-) Reader." *Goethe Yearbook* I (1982): 42-50.
  Discusses several literary texts that Werther reads and questions their function in the novel.

———. "Werther's Reflections on the Tenth of May." In *Exile and Enlightenment: Studies in German and Comparative Literature*, edited by Uwe Faulhaber and others, pp. 1-9. Detroit: Wayne State University Press, 1987.
  Argues that the letter of 10 May functions as a paradigm for the whole novel.

Faber, M. D. "The Suicide of Young Werther." *The Psychoanalytic Review* 60, No. 2 (Summer 1973): 239-76.

A psychoanalytic interpretation of the novel that stresses Werther's failure to fully separate from his mother.

Fairley, Barker. *A Study of Goethe.* Oxford: Clarendon Press, 1947, 280 p.
  A comprehensive modern biography by a noted Goethe scholar. Fairley sets out his approach in the opening chapter, proposing to focus on Goethe's "inner biography, the account of what went on in his mind in its progress from immaturity to maturity." For commentary by Fairley on *Werther*, see excerpt dated 1932.

Feuerlicht, Ignace. "Werther's Suicide: Instinct, Reasons and Defense." *The German Quarterly* LI, No. 4 (November 1978): 476-92.
  Examines the reasons behind Werther's suicide.

Funke, Maurice R. *From Saint to Psychotic: The Crisis of Human Identity in the Late 18th Century—A Comparative Study of "Clarissa," "La nouvelle Héloïse," "Die Leiden des jungen Werthers."* New York: Peter Lang, 1983, 215 p.
  A comparative analysis of *Werther*, Samuel Richardson's *Clarissa Harlow* (1747-48), and Jean-Jacques Rousseau's *La nouvelle Héloïse* (1761).

Graham, Ilse. "Goethe's Own Werther: An Artist's Truth about His Fiction." In her *Goethe: Portrait of the Artist*, pp. 7-33. Berlin: Walter de Gruyter, 1977.
  An examination of Goethe's artistic imagination in *Werther*.

Huff, Steven R. "Lotte's Klavier: A Resounding Symbol in Goethe's *Die Leiden des jungen Werthers.*" *The Germanic Review* LIX, No. 2 (Spring 1984): 43-8.
  Discusses the symbolic role of the *klavier* (pianoforte) in the relationship between Werther and Lotte.

Kestner, Johann Christian. Letter to Goethe. In *The Life of Goethe*, by George Henry Lewes, pp. 146-50. New York: Frederick Ungar Publishing Co., 1965.
  Reprints extracts from a letter dated 2 November 1772 in which Kestner detailed the circumstances leading up to Jerusalem's death. Goethe based much of the description of Werther's death on Kestner's information.

Kieffer, Bruce. "Goethe: Chasms of Language in Society and Self." In his *The Storm and Stress of Language: Linguistic Catastrophe in the Early Works of Goethe, Lenz, Klinger, and Schiller*, pp. 27-57. University Park: Pennsylvania State University Press, 1986.
  Looks closely at the language employed by Werther and the editor.

Leppmann, Wolfgang. *The German Image of Goethe.* Oxford: Clarendon Press, 1961, 220 p.
  A thorough study of Goethe's reputation in Germany through the 1950s.

Mann, Thomas. *Lotte in Weimar.* Translated by H. T. Lowe-Porter. Harmondsworth, England: Penguin Books, 1976, 331 p.
  A novel, first published in 1939, that depicts Goethe's meeting with Charlotte Buff Kestner in Weimar in 1816, over forty years after the events portrayed in *Werther*.

Maugham, W. Somerset. "The Three Novels of a Poet." In his *Points of View*, pp. 1-55. London: Heinemann, 1958.
  Explores the relationship between *Werther* and the author's own experiences.

Maurois, André. "The First Circle of Mape; or, The Creator: *The Sorrows of the Young Werther.*" In his *Mape: The World of Illusion*, translated by Eric Sutton, pp. 11-88. New York: D. Appleton & Co., 1926.
  A fictional account of Goethe's life in Wetzlar and the composition of *Werther*.

Muenzer, Clark S. "Goethe's *Werther* and Kant's Aesthetics of Failure." *MLN* 98, No. 3 (April 1983): 492-99.
  Examines *Werther* in relation to Immanuel Kant's aesthetic of the sublime in his *Kritik der Urteilskraft* (1790; *Critique of Judgement*).

———. "Turning toward the Sublime: Reflexivity and Self-Worth in *Die Leiden des jungen Werther.*" In his *Figures of Identity: Goethe's*

Novels and the Enigmatic Self, pp. 5-36. University Park: Pennsylvania State University Press, 1984.

Considers *Werther* in light of Muenzer's thesis that Goethe's novels represent an ongoing effort to define the self.

Pascal, Roy. *The German Sturm und Drang*. Manchester: Manchester University Press, 1967, 347 p.

An extensive analysis of the German Sturm und Drang movement that contains frequent references to *Werther*.

Paulin, Roger. "'Wir werden uns wieder sehn!': On a Theme in *Werther*." *Publications of the English Goethe Society* n.s. L (1979-80): 55-78.

Examines the influence of the *Empfindsamkeit* (sentimental) tradition on *Werther*.

Plenzdorf, Ulrich. *The New Sufferings of Young W.* Translated by Kenneth P. Wilcox. New York: Frederick Ungar Publishing Co., 1979, 84 p.

A recent East German novel that retells the story of *Werther* in a modern form.

Prawer, Siegbert. "Werther's People: Reflections on Literary Portraiture, in Memory of William Robson-Scott." *Publications of the English Goethe Society* n.s. LII (1982-83): 70-97.

Relates Werther's verbal portraits of the other characters in the novel to Goethe's efforts in the fine arts.

Reiss, Hans. "*Die Leiden des jungen Werthers*: A Reconsideration." *Modern Language Quarterly* 20, No. 1 (March 1959): 81-96.

Discusses *Werther*'s structure, narration, and style, identifying how they contribute to the worldview presented in the novel. For further criticism by Reiss on *Werther*, see excerpt dated 1969.

Robertson, J. G. *The Life and Work of Goethe: 1749-1832*. New York: E. P. Dutton & Co., 1932, 350 p.

A detailed biography containing brief critical commentary.

Rose, William. "The Historical Background of Goethe's *Werther*." In his *Men, Myths, and Movements in German Literature: A Volume of Historical and Critical Papers*, pp. 125-55. Port Washington, N.Y.: Kennikat Press, 1964.

A thorough exploration of the historical background of *Werther*. This essay was originally published as an introduction to the novel in 1929.

Ryder, Frank G. "Season, Day, and Hour—Time as Metaphor in Goethe's *Werther*." *Journal of English and Germanic Philology* LXIII, No. 3 (July 1964): 389-407.

Elucidates the importance of images of time in the novel.

————. "Poetic Prose: A Suggested Approach by Way of Goethe's *Werther*." *Style* 21, No. 3 (Fall 1987): 427-38.

Considers *Werther* as poetic prose, scanning the novel for rhythm and meter.

Saine, Thomas P. "The Portrayal of Lotte in the Two Versions of *Werther*." *Journal of English and Germanic Philology* LXXX, No. 1 (January 1981): 54-77.

Traces the changes in the character of Lotte in Goethe's revision of the novel.

Salm, Peter. "Werther and the Sensibility of Estrangement." *The German Quarterly* XLVI, No. 1 (January 1973): 47-55.

Explores the tragic dimensions of *Werther*.

Steinhauer, Harry. Afterword to *The Sufferings of Young Werther*, by Johann Wolfgang von Goethe, edited and translated by Harry Steinhauer, pp. 101-25. New York: W. W. Norton & Co., 1970.

Treats the novel as "a profound character study of a psychological type . . . : the disillusioned or frustrated man, who cannot find a place for himself in society."

————. "Goethe's *Werther* after Two Centuries." *University of Toronto Quarterly* XLIV, No. 1 (Fall 1974): 1-13.

Commemorates the two-hundredth anniversary of the publication of the novel by reviewing its background and sources, its critical reception, and its enduring qualities.

Thorlby, Anthony. "From What Did Goethe Save Himself in *Werther*?" In *Versuche zu Goethe: Festschrift für Erich Heller*, edited by Volker Dürr and Géza v. Molnár, pp. 150-66. Heidelberg, Germany: Lothar Stiehm Verlag, 1976.

Ponders the difference between real and imagined life for the author, the reader, and the main character of *Werther*.

Tisch, J. H. "The Significance of the Homeric World in Goethe's *Werther* and Moravia's *Il Disprezzo*." *Canadian Review of Comparative Literature/Revue canadienne de litterature comparée* 10 (March 1983): 23-30.

A comparative study of the influence of Homer on *Werther* and Alberto Moravia's *Il Disprezzo* (1954; *A Ghost at Noon*).

Wellbery, Caroline. "From Mirrors to Images: The Transformation of Sentimental Paradigms in Goethe's *The Sorrows of Young Werther*." *Studies in Romanticism* 25, No. 2 (Summer 1986): 231-49.

Outlines the ways in which *Werther* departs from the tradition of the sentimental novel.

Geraldine (Endsor) Jewsbury

1812-1880

English novelist, critic, and author of children's stories.

A controversial literary figure in nineteenth-century England, Jewsbury is primarily remembered today for her outspoken condemnation of Victorian conventions that limited the independence of women. In her novels, including her most frequently discussed works, *Zoe: The History of Two Lives*, *The Half-Sisters*, and *Marian Withers*, Jewsbury stressed that every person needs useful and challenging work to achieve fulfillment. Jewsbury used this concept, derived from the writings of the prominent philosopher Thomas Carlyle, to denounce both the traditional educational system, which she believed prepared women for little more than parlor conversation and domestic chores, and the Victorian ideology that marriage was the most suitable objective for women. In documenting Jewsbury's ideas, recent critics have examined not only her novels but also her numerous book reviews and her letters to Carlyle's wife, Jane, with whom she had an intimate friendship. In spite of inconsistencies in Jewsbury's beliefs, her radical social commentary is valued for anticipating the concerns of modern feminists.

Jewsbury was born in Measham, England, to a cotton manufacturer and his wife. Shortly after the family moved to Manchester in 1818, Jewsbury's mother died and her nineteen-year-old sister, Maria Jane, assumed responsibility for raising Jewsbury and their four brothers. Maria Jane, herself a moderately successful writer, encouraged Jewsbury to read, and in school she revealed a talent for composition. When her sister married in 1832, Jewsbury began managing the household. She continued to read prolifically, particularly the works of Percy Bysshe Shelley and George Sand, the latter of whom is recognized as an influence on her writing. About 1840, the year of her father's death, Jewsbury suffered an attack of religious anxiety; in a letter to a friend she described her despair: "My God! I would give the rest of the years of my life to be able to know why life is given us, and I would say it and leave it behind me." Jewsbury found consolation in Thomas Carlyle's writings, in which the philosopher asserted that spiritual contentment could be achieved through devotion to duty and hard work of any kind. She wrote him an appreciative letter, which resulted in an invitation for her to visit him at his home. There, in 1841, she met Jane Carlyle, beginning a long and important friendship. The letters Jewsbury wrote to her have provided scholars with many insights into Jewsbury's character and into the ideas she expressed in her novels. In 1842, she began the first of these, *Zoe*, in collaboration with Jane Carlyle and Betsey Paulet, both of whom quickly tired of the project, leaving Jewsbury to complete it on her own. When Jewsbury finished *Zoe* three years later, Jane Carlyle used her influence to obtain a publisher for it. This novel, with its explicit portrayal of romantic passion and controversial theme of religious doubt, outraged many Victorian critics, who found it not only indiscreet but morally offensive. Nonetheless, the novel made Jewsbury a well-known writer, and she became a member of the literary circle she met through the Carlyles, a group that included such prominent writers as Elizabeth Gaskell and Charles Kingsley. Jewsbury's second novel, *The Half-Sisters*, appeared in 1848, and the

following year, she joined the staff of the London literary magazine the *Athenaeum*, to which she contributed approximately 2,300 book reviews over the next thirty years. During the 1850s, Jewsbury wrote four more novels as well as two children's stories, which are virtually ignored by critics. In 1859, Jewsbury quit writing fiction because of the strain it put on her health. In the succeeding years, apart from her work for the *Athenaeum*, she was employed by two firms—Hurst and Blackett, and Bentley and Son—as a publisher's reader, an influential position that very few women held at the time. Late in the 1870s, Jewsbury discovered that she had cancer, and in 1880 she gave up her literary activities. She died the same year.

The themes of Jewsbury's novels were important issues in her own life. One of these themes, religious doubt, is set forth in her first novel, *Zoe*, in which the protagonists, a priest named Everhard Burrows and the woman he loves, Zoe, each struggle to find personal fulfillment. As Jewsbury later explained in a letter, she put her "own religious botherations" into Everhard, whose search for contentment leads him to become a priest but whose faith in Christian doctrine fails to pacify him. While some critics now praise *Zoe* as one of the first Victorian novels to deal with the subject of religious doubt, its chief importance today rests on its concern with the condition of women in the nineteenth century. Through *Zoe*'s title character, Jewsbury argued that societal conventions prevented women from leading useful and productive lives. She contended that traditional female education was one of the greatest barriers to improving the situation of women because it was solely meant to prepare them for marriage. Thus, Jewsbury allows Zoe to be educated as if she were a man and Zoe is determined, as the novel states, "to make for herself, in spite of all obstacles, a destiny equal to all her vague dreams." Despite her education and abilities, Zoe marries to escape the stigma attached to spinsterhood. Critics assert that Zoe's indifference to her marriage and her experiments with lovers reflect Jewsbury's belief that marriage alone was an inadequate outlet for women's energies and talents. To combat their discontent, Jewsbury maintained, women needed stimulating employment. She further elaborated upon this idea in her next novel, *The Half-Sisters*, by contrasting the happiness of the successful actress Bianca with the dissatisfaction of her half-sister, Alice, who has no worthwhile occupations and is stifled by marriage. In her third novel, *Marian Withers*, Jewsbury succinctly pointed out what she saw as the major problem facing women without challenging work: "the women of England of the present day are eaten up with *ennui* to a much greater extent than suspected; the devouring activity of their minds has been stimulated by the general increase of higher culture, but they find no adequate employment for it." In her last three novels, *Constance Herbert*, *The Sorrows of Gentility*, and *Right or Wrong*, Jewsbury continued to press for reforms, although critics note that in the latter two works she is considerably less outspoken.

Despite the many unorthodox opinions presented in Jewsbury's novels regarding the place of women in society, critics stress that she retained some conventional attitudes towards her sex. For example, while she appears to undermine the convention of marriage, the title character of *Marian Withers*, an exceptionally educated woman like Zoe, finds relief from her restlessness by marrying; in *The Half-Sisters*, Bianca ultimately gives up her acting career to marry; and in *Constance Herbert*, in which the title character sorrowfully refuses a proposal of marriage because she fears that her children would inherit the insanity that runs in her family, Jewsbury provides Constance with the consolation that her suitor was unworthy, while neglecting to describe any benefits a single life might offer women. The seeming ambivalence of Jewsbury's opinions is regarded by many recent commentators as an indication of her inability to resolve tensions in her own life that arose from her conflicting roles as a professional writer and as a woman who, in fact, wanted to marry.

Most of Jewsbury's contemporary reviewers censured her opinions as unorthodox and her presentation of her ideas as obtrusive, remarking that when she did not state her views openly in narrative digressions, she contrived unbelievable characters and incidents to demonstrate them. In a review of *Constance Herbert*, George Eliot expressed the opinion of most early critics when she wrote, "Miss Jewsbury is so emphatic in the enunciation of her moral, that she forces us to consider her book rather in the light of a homily than of a fiction—to criticise her doctrine rather than her story." According to many commentators, her emphasis on ideas also weakened her characterization, particularly in her last three novels, where her didacticism resulted in a one-sided depiction of the sexes focusing on the virtues of women and the vices of men.

After the publication of her last novel, *Right or Wrong*, Jewsbury's works inspired little commentary until the early 1970s, when feminist critics began to discuss the radical ideas expressed in her novels, book reviews, and letters. These critics have praised Jewsbury for demonstrating, both through her works and her career, the potential women could realize if granted greater freedom and educational opportunity. Recent commentators have also underscored the historical significance of Jewsbury's writings, emphasizing the surprising modernity of her views. Thus, despite inconsistencies in her beliefs, Jewsbury is remembered, in the words of Monica Correa Fryckstedt, "as one of the most outspoken and progressive fighters for women's rights during Victorian times."

(See also *Dictionary of Literary Biography*, Vol. 21: *Victorian Novelists before 1885*.)

PRINCIPAL WORKS

Zoe: The History of Two Lives (novel) 1845
The Half-Sisters (novel) 1848
Marian Withers (novel) 1851
The History of an Adopted Child (juvenile fiction) 1852
Angelo; or, The Pine Forest in the Alps (juvenile fiction) 1855
Constance Herbert (novel) 1855
The Sorrows of Gentility (novel) 1856
Right or Wrong (novel) 1859
Selections from the Letters of Geraldine Endsor Jewsbury to Jane Welsh Carlyle (letters) 1892

JANE WELSH CARLYLE (letter date 1842)

[*A close friend of Jewsbury, Jane Carlyle is perhaps best known as the wife of philosopher Thomas Carlyle. However, she is also recognized as the author of numerous letters that have provided vivid and insightful commentary on the literary and social life of Victorian England. In the following excerpt from a letter to her younger sister, Carlyle comments upon an early draft of* Zoe *written by Jewsbury in collaboration with Betsey Paulet (Carlyle had by this time dropped out of the project). While praising the work, Carlyle expresses misgivings about its "indecency." For additional commentary by Carlyle, see excerpts dated 1845 and 1848.*]

I have read [*Zoe*] and, as was to have been anticipated, with a feeling little short of *terror!* So much power of genius rushing so recklessly into unknown space! Geraldine, in particular, shows herself here a far more profound and daring speculator than even I had fancied her. I do not believe there is a woman alive at the present day, not even George Sand herself, that could have written some of the best passages in this book—or would have had the courage if she had had the ability to write them—but they must not publish it, "decency forbids"! (as they write at the street corners). I do not mean decency in the vulgar sense of the word—even in *that* sense they are not always *decent!* but then their *indecency* looks so purely *scientific* and so *essential* for the full development of the story that one cannot, at least I cannot get up a feeling of outraged modesty about it—nay I should feel as if *I* were the indecent person should I find anything to blush at in what *they* seem to have written just *for fact's sake* without a consciousness of wrong—but there is an indecency or want of reserve (let us call it) in the spiritual department—an exposure of their whole minds naked as before the fall—without so much as a fig-leaf of conformity remaining—which no respectable public could stand—which even the freest spirits among us would call "coming it too strong"! I wish a clear day would dawn for me that I might give them a full and faithful deliverance upon it—for it is a difficult task they have put on me to criticise such an extraordinary jumble of sense and nonsense, insight beyond the stars, and blindness before their own nose! One thing I feel no doubt about that this Geraldine will either "make a spoon or spoil a horn"—she is far too clever to do nothing in her day and generation. (p. 66)

> *Jane Welsh Carlyle, in a letter to Jeannie Welsh on December 25, 1842, in* Jane Welsh Carlyle: Letters to Her Family, 1839-1863, *edited by Leonard Huxley, Doubleday, Page & Company, 1924, pp. 64-7.*

[HENRY FOTHERGILL CHORLEY] (essay date 1845)

[*Chorley considers* Zoe *worth reading but faults Jewsbury's diffuse narrative technique, complaining that she emphasizes ideas rather than plot. For additional commentary by Chorley, see excerpt dated 1848.*]

Though years of separation—and the chasm which no earthly love or solicitude can bridge over—have intervened between *The Three Histories* of [Maria Jane Jewsbury], and the *Zoe* of [her] younger sister, it was natural to expect that the latter might bear traces of precept and direction, nay even of modes of expression, originated in the former. At all events, we could not look for a mere circulating-library novel from one bearing the name of our authoress.

Zoe proves, in good part, that our general theory does not lack examples to illustrate it, and that our particular anticipation was anything but baseless. Without any of the parrotting which is impossible to the sincere speaker, we find in it some unconscious imitation;—something of the late Miss Jewsbury's predilection for aphorism, analysis, and definition; though less of that fervid and poetical eloquence to which she could rise when the subject was important enough to absorb her personality. Miss Geraldine Jewsbury, too, as her sister did before her, plays with her story rather than tells it. We doubt whether *Zoe* was commenced with any settled plan or purpose;—whether its writer's mind itself, as well as her creative instincts, may not have changed betwixt the commencement and the close of her labours. Too little of the tale-teller's art is visible: and sense without a story in a novel satiates as much as story without sense is apt to weary the reader. Further, we observe in our authoress that tendency to fly at every game, which, though courageous, is indiscreet. A supper at the Baron d'Holbach's, to be rightly novelized, demands a writer as witty as Diderot,—must we not add, as fearless as an Encyclopedist? Neither is Mirabeau, even when sketched in a phase of his lovership, quite as manageable as the Mandeville and Montmorency tribe of Lovelaces, in whom all the lady-novelists, from Mademoiselle de Scuderi down to Mrs. Gore, have so delighted. In brief, Miss Geraldine Jewsbury seems to us to have perilled her fiction from that besetting malady of such young writers as are thoughtful rather than impulsive,—a feverish apprehension of quiet pages. Yet such are often "landing-places," to adopt one of Coleridge's quaint designations, where the mind of the reader rests agreeably, ere preparing for a fresh start.

Perhaps, in place of these general observations, some notice of the "works and days" commemorated in *Zoe,* might by some be found more acceptable. . . . Suffice it to say, the heroine is a lady strangely born, tossed about from hand to hand rather than educated, who becomes, in the end, one of those bewitching, exceptional, incomprehensible creatures, so dear to novelists,—so murdering to the peace of mankind, their own inclusive. She gets married, by accident rather than choice, to a man older than herself, and whose character is as misty in its narrower circle as her own in the eccentric superabundance of its fascinations. Subsequently, Zoe is thrown into the company of an interesting Catholic priest, who has also become a priest by accident rather than conviction; has oscillated between implicit and devout trust and that tempting scepticism which goes far to question every act and canon of faith, and who only wants the disturbing influence of mundane passion, to break from the routine of clerical habits, and to disown a creed, of the truth of which he never felt assured. But Miss Jewsbury—worthily resolute to avoid tampering with excitements more enticing than wholesome—permits Everhard's love to be returned and disclosed, with no darker consequences than an irrevocable parting, and the impression that two existences are thereby destroyed for ever. Zoe and Everhard meet once again, it is true, but under awful circumstances, by which all rebel passion is extinguished. The secondary characters of the tale are numerous; but, like the principal ones, they are somewhat purposelessly manœuvred, and too often made the channel for speculation and opinion, in place of agents towards the carrying on the main or episodical action of the plot.

Let it not be supposed, however, that the favourable predisposition which we have acknowledged, has induced us to lavish space on what is unworthy, or to make the best of what is inferior. *Zoe* contains matter enough to demand attention, and to indicate an original mind, though it may not ultimately prove the mind of a novelist. We should imagine Miss Jewsbury better qualified to succeed in essays and speculative papers, than in descriptions of character as it is, or society as it has been.

> [*Henry Fothergill Chorley*], *in a review of "Zoe: The History of Two Lives," in* The Athenaeum, *No. 901, February 1, 1845, p. 114.*

JANE WELSH CARLYLE (letter date 1845)

[*Once again writing to her sister, Carlyle remarks upon contemporary reaction to the recently published* Zoe. *For additional commentary by Carlyle, see excerpts dated 1842 and 1848.*]

. . . It is quite curious to see the horror excited in some people (and these the least moral) by Geraldine's book [*Zoe*] while the moralest people of my acquaintance either like it or are not at the pains to abuse it. Even Miss Wilson to whom I dared to lend it—tho' she confessed to never having "ventured on reading a line of George Sand in her life" brought it back to me with *a certain equanimity*—"It is *avowedly* the book of an audacious *esprit forte*, and so of course you did not expect *me* to *approve* of it, nor do I, but I think it very clever and amusing"—voilà tout! While old and young *roués* of the Reform Club almost go off in hysterics over—its *indecency*.

> *Jane Welsh Carlyle, in a letter to Jeannie Welsh on February 26, 1845, in* Jane Welsh Carlyle: Letters to Her Family, 1839-1863, *edited by Leonard Huxley, Doubleday, Page & Company, 1924, p. 236.*

JANE WELSH CARLYLE (letter date 1848)

[*In this excerpt from a letter to John Forster, Carlyle denounces the as yet unpublished,* Half-Sisters *after having read a chapter from it. For additional commentary by Carlyle, see excerpts dated 1842 and 1845.*]

[Jewsbury] desired me to send the chapter on to *you,* and so I send it, tho' it will just have to travel back to her. This is worse than anything in *Zoe,* to my judgement, in fact perfectly disgusting for a young Englishwoman to write,—and from Chapman's point of view, quite ''unfit for circulation in families.'' I would not have such stuff *dedicated to me* as she proposed, for any number of guineas. But I am done with counselling her,—her tendency towards the unmentionable is too strong for *me* to stay it.

> Jane Welsh Carlyle, in a letter to John Forster in January, 1848, in New Letters and Memorials of Jane Welsh Carlyle, Vol. I, *edited by Alexander Carlyle, John Lane, The Bodley Head, 1903, p. 242.*

[HENRY FOTHERGILL CHORLEY]   (essay date 1848)

[*Chorley considers Jewsbury's* The Half-Sisters *a significant improvement over* Zoe *but disagrees with her depiction of the condition of women of genius in society, arguing that her novel focuses too much on the societal conventions that oppress genius. For further criticism by Chorley, see excerpt dated 1845.*]

The Half Sisters is, in every point of view, a welcome advance upon *Zöe.* The story is simpler, better-contrived and more interesting; the characters are more decidedly marked and steadily maintained; the writing is evener;—the passages of reflection are less forced and those of sentiment less freaked with eccentricity.

The tale may be added to the list of works devoted to the condition of women of genius in the midst of a world that loves to profit by the pleasure they afford, yet despises and keeps at a distance those affording it. Bianca, the heroine, is a born actress; who works her way up by her brilliant talents and remarkable worth to a high marriage. This, it will be seen, is a familiar invention. Similar combinations will be found in one of Miss Martineau's stories,—in other English novels of more recent origin (*Violet the Danseuse,* Mr. Chorley's *Conti* and *Pomfret* among the number);—and in the *Consuelo* of George Sand: not to speak of the hundred German tales owing their origin to the well-thumbed, yet dearly-loved *Corinne.* In most of these, when the Delight of ''shining theatres'' is handed over the threshold of domestic life by Love, the career of the Artist comes to its close. What a light on the peculiarity of Woman's position is shown in this unconscious coincidence! It it not introduced merely because novels usually cease with the marriage ceremony;—but because the wife or the mother on the stage is imagined, by retaining her position, to be rendered more or less unfaithful to love, duty, or delicacy,—because it has never been admitted that Art can be the main business of her life, as of Man's. This, indeed, is emphatically marked out by the provisions of Nature:—and hence, in some degree, she is liable to disturbing influences of far more powerful distraction than any which he can prove. She moves under the shadow of impending sacrifice (supposing her love of her art genuine) from the moment that she allows herself to indulge in Woman's most impassioned and purest hopes. And not merely by the ordinance of society, but also by the apportionment of her duties in the scheme of creation, is her place in the Temple rendered transient and her service there a divided one—surrounded by perils not easy to legislate for, and perplexing to contemplate.

Miss Jewsbury has looked at the picturesque side of her subject rather than solved its difficulties. Like Madame Dudevant [George Sand] in her exquisite fancy-piece of the singing-girl of the Corte Minelli, she has endowed her Bianca with preternatural grace, sobriety and intellectual development:—permitting reason to aid genius whenever it is wanted. Like other philanthropic novelists bent on social reform, she somewhat paradoxically proves it to be unnecessary, by exhibiting a heroine stronger and more admirable than any advantages of education or environments of sympathy could have made her. Of the real traces which early struggle, imperfect cultivation, public exhibition and inequality in private intercourse leave on most of the ''favourites'' of the world we here hardly find one. While Miss Jewsbury aspires to do battle with ''Conventionalism'' as a Dagon which is to be pulled down by every strong man and earnest woman, she adorns her heroine with most of its graces. Miss Edgeworth did not endow her Caroline Percy and Leonora with more moral strength and righteous prudence, nor more nicely apportion for them trials and supports, than Miss Jewsbury has done by her heroine. The story will please the novel reader all the more for this manner of managing it;—but as a piece of philosophy it is impaired so as almost to lose the value and virtue intended.

A young friendless girl—whose Italian mother, having reached England in quest of the father of her child, loses her senses—is compelled by necessity to earn her bread as a mime at a Circus. While doing this, she is befriended and generously shielded from evil by a young enthusiastic collegian. The two fall in love: but then comes the old tale of ''Mrs. Grundy's prejudices;''—and Bianca is wiser than Conrad, and sends him away from her, to prove his constancy. She rises from the Circus to the legitimate theatre, ripens into a distinguished actress, comes to London, and succeeds as *Juliet*—finding, alas! at the very moment of her triumph that her *Romeo* had returned from his travels without having made an effort to seek her. (pp. 288-89)

The actress marries a nobleman, who, of course, takes her off the stage. Madame Dudevant was more true to her text in making *her* Comtesse de Rudolstadt never quit the arena in which the exercise of her talents became to her a duty.

But Bianca has a half sister, her father's legitimate daughter, brought up by a housekeeping English mother, married to a man whose character she imperfectly apprehends, and whose ''ill stars'' throw her also in the way of the above-mentioned fickle Conrad. He finds in her the genius which fascinates his imagination, and the delicate qualities which satisfy his fastidiousness—and lays siege to her accordingly. How this adventure terminates we will not divulge; desiring to forestall no readers's pleasure in a story full of interest and undertaken with honest purpose. But in the whole position and character of Alice Miss Jewsbury has again allowed herself to be seduced into an error very nearly as vulgar as those which she so incessantly reprobates.

We dwell for a while on the fallacy adverted to—seeing that it is common to a large family of books. The sneer against ''respectability''—the complaints against it as at variance with and oppressive of Genius, have become too frequent and are too foolish not to call for animadversion. Doubtless, Genius *has* much to suffer in its intercourse with society; something from material neglect,—something from imperfect appreciation,—something (this trial being rarely counted) from false friendship or injudicious kindness. But this is the lot of superiority; bad as an influence if dwelt upon in a pharisaical or rebellious spirit—good if admitted simply as a condition of humanity. Much is conveyed in the fine line of the poet,—

> When is Man strong, until he feels alone?

albeit to court a haughty or cynical isolation is perhaps the most poisonous affectation into which a gifted person can fall. From the time when Genius begins to stir within its human tenement, a feeling of revolt is apt to arise and increase against all the cautions and maxims and observances by which "the many" are governed. To point out why this should be struggled against, not yielded to, is not the present duty. But one reason for toleration may be here advanced: to wit, that a crusade against "Dulness in a gig" (to adopt Mr. Carlyle's vehicle for satire) is a waste of bow and spear. Does any one suppose that Dulness can be dragooned into vivacity of fancy, largeness of mind, nobility of aim,—into becoming *Genius* in short. If the "respectability" so perpetually groaned against were stripped from all persons moderately provided with imagination or originality of thought, is it to be assumed, therefore, that Genius would fare the better? Would the great be secure of a more honourable entertainment from the small because the latter were deprived of their sole balance, their distinctive individuality? Would there be no danger of such things as impudent licence, clumsy imitation, or ridiculous fopperies bred of a restless frivolity and impertinent assumption? It is idle—it is *mechanical*—in any person of genius to expect from his contemporaries a mathematically-graduated allowance for his past temptations and present disturbing influences—to imagine they will strike a balance betwixt his public and his private career, and in gratitude for the favour which he has rendered in the one afford him absolution for faults which he obtrudes in the other. Supreme Wisdom can do this, sympathetic Genius *may*: but till those railed against for falling short shall prove themselves supremely wise or sympathetically gifted, are they not exposed to a harder injustice from their superiors who denounce them than they show towards those whom they comprehend imperfectly? What right have the strongest, the most high-minded, the most indifferent to conventionalisms to expect renunciation of conformity in established usage on the part of those who are nothing when not conforming? Their own very impatience is worldliness after its kind; a testimony that there is a principle in this "respectability" in which even they believe with trembling,—and from the consequences of which they would escape for their own selfish indulgence. Too much, in short, is said, year by year, book by book, of the sufferings of Genius,—too little of its responsibilities—too little of its pleasures, which no commonplace censor can take away—too little of its superiority to repayment by "purple and fine linen"—too little of its inherent dignity, to which crown and sceptre can add no state. Let Mind rule Mankind. It must—and it *will*. We, of all people, can never be accused of ranging ourselves among the shutters-up and the darkeners. We are proud of Genius, but we are as proud *for* it; ashamed to see it specked and flawed—humbled when it assumes the wallet and the whine of the mendicant—when it appeals against human justice on the plea that it has been ill-nurtured, or is weak, or should have privileges. Inasmuch as we would have it rule, are we bold to assert that its supremacy can only be assured when it clothes itself with "the form and the order,""the charities"—nay, and with the "respectabilities"—which it has been too much the habit to satirize.

These are truths which should be pondered by none more earnestly than by women of genius. How have they risen in the scale of authority and influence in proportion as they have ceased to order their affections after Tom Sheridan's famous

principle when advised to "take a wife"! How do they gain in power as artists when they no longer restlessly desire, or in the nervousness of vanity dread, being stared at as "conspicuous"! That there are many social evils which it is Woman's express province to see diminished we have again and again pointed out. Her feelings may be too warm for her to be ever an efficient satirist, but her powers of persuasion are almost without a limit. It becomes of first consequence that their direction should be healthy and simple—their exercise uninfluenced by small personalities. We would have Miss Jewsbury, as a gifted woman,—with a career of activity, literary distinction and social usefulness opening before her,—examine herself closely. We would have her calmly distinguish between random exhibitions of passion and invective such as befit the insane Prophet, and those no less earnest utterances of feeling and sympathy which (implying considerateness for all ranks and orders of humanity—the commonplace as well as the lofty) bespeak a Poet of the highest order. It rests with herself to do good service to the wide world of workers and dreamers. (pp. 289-90)

> [Henry Fothergill Chorley], in a review of "The Half Sisters: A Tale," in The Athenaeum, No. 1064, March 18, 1848, pp. 288-90.

THE SPECTATOR   (essay date 1848)

[*In this excerpt from a review of* The Half-Sisters, *the critic praises Jewsbury's descriptive abilities but finds her attention to detail inappropriate for fiction.*]

As far as outward forms are concerned, Miss Jewsbury's *Half Sisters* would seem to differ widely from her former novel, *Zöe*. The elements, however, are essentially the same. The principal characters in the *Half Sisters* as in its predecessor, are peculiar in their own nature, and operated upon by peculiar circumstances. The fiction is also of the metaphysical kind: the story is not in itself striking, and is slow in movement; the incidents, with a few exceptions, are subordinate to the exhibition of passion, feeling, or mere mental operations in singular characters rather singularly placed. The interest we take in it is not that of action, but of dissection or "demonstration." There is, indeed, more of common life in the novel before us than in *Zöe*; shown in some very clever sketches of life and character in manufacturing districts, in some scenes with Mr. Simpson and his company of equestrians, and at the provincial theatre that rejoiced under the management of Mr. Montague St. Leger. But these are mostly incidental, and are not intended to excite the deeper interest of the fiction; which rests, as we have said, upon psychological exhibition of character and passion, or at least emotion.

The Half Sisters contains a narrative of two lives, designed, so far as we can trace design, to exhibit the blessings of a resolute will and an active purpose although accompanied by external disadvantages, over a timorous and feeble spirit surrounded by the blessings of fortune but incapable of using or enjoying them through weakness of character. Under the circumstances assumed by Miss Jewsbury, her conclusions are sufficiently coherent; but the circumstances are so forced and extreme, the characters so rare, and the influences that govern them so exceedingly unlikely, that nothing is enforced by the novel itself, though the lesson is incidentally impressed by the writer. (p. 278)

[The] merits of *The Half Sisters* are technical, the defects popular: the book is more likely to receive critical perusal and praise than popular reading. The first great merits are force of composition, with clearness and strength of delineation. Whatever be the subject of the writer—whether the images of a description, the traits of a person, the emotions of the mind, or the author's observations or speculations—all is distinctly conceived, and as distinctly presented. Miss Jewsbury also exhibits great skill in the analysis of character: there is perhaps less ability in maintaining the consistency of her dramatis personæ than was shown in **Zöe**. On the other hand, the very closeness of the style gives a ponderosity if not a heaviness to the composition, which will be retarding to mere novel-readers. As little will they care for the metaphysical or philosophical remarks which are freely scattered through the pages or put into the mouths of some of the persons; and Miss Jewsbury's strong point—her power of accounting for mental changes and other idiosyncracies—is not attractive to the multitude; nor, indeed, is it altogether appropriate to fiction, which should by means of structure and incident enable the characters to account for themselves. But the great fault of *The Half Sisters,* popular as well as critical, is moral. In particular things there is an improvement upon **Zöe;** but we have little of sympathy with the characters, and take not much concern in their fortunes. The English mind cannot turn an "equestrian*ess*" and actress into the heroine of a love-romance. Alice's weakness and self-created misery are overdone, and are also unlikely. The character of a man is soon appreciated by those who live constantly with him: love is felt where it exists, and can be shown without speechifying. In the early part, Conrad is little more than a goodnatured but rather vain youth; afterwards his selfishness and profligacy inspire no other interest in the reader than a desire to see him punished; which is done by getting him under the influence of a sectarian preacher and making him turn Methodist. The artistical character of Bianca, her struggles as a provincial actress, and her love for her art, have the most interest; but it ceases with her London success; and the marriage with the lord spins out the work and flattens the conclusion. (p. 279)

> *"Miss Jewbury's 'Half Sisters',"* in The Spectator, *No. 1029, March 18, 1848, pp. 278-79.*

THE LEADER (essay date 1851)

[*This reviewer discusses the merits and limitations of* Marian Withers.]

Some time ago, among the *on dits* of literary gossip, there was one purporting that Miss Jewsbury was writing an answer to *Mary Barton*—a novel of Manchester life, which should restore the figure of the manufacturer to that pedestal from which *Mary Barton* had, as it was supposed, so sternly smitten it. *Marian Withers* is the novel in question; but such a design as the one alluded to, if ever it actuated the authoress, must early in the composition have given place to a larger and truer design, that, namely of portraying Lancashire life in its varieties of good and bad, coarse and elegant, serious and frivolous, hard-hearted and considerate.

As a picture it has many merits: first and foremost that of presenting the *realities*, not ideals and lay figures. But partly from the extent of her design, and partly from deficient attention to composition, the novel has become sketchy and straggling, to the detriment of the general effect. The various episodes are independent sections, hooked together, not related to each other; and this scattered mode of composition produces

an unsatisfactory impression compared with the excellence of the separate portions.

In John Withers we have the struggle of Genius with Circumstance. Placed on the lowest step of the social scale, he raises himself by manful toil and inventive genius to the position of a master manufacturer, respected by all and loved by his men. This is a fine type, and well studied. Miss Jewsbury has told his story with marvellous intuition into the inventor's feelings. But having given him a position she leaves him there, and throughout the rest of the novel he occupies but an insignificant place. This we cannot help regarding as a mistake. John Withers the workman is a man of genius; one of those who willingly submit to the tyranny of Great Ideas, who are martyrs or victors. But John Withers the victor is simply a sturdy, honest man—that is all. Why is this?

In Marian Withers, his daughter, we have the simple-minded girl of our day, raised above her parents and her parents' friends by a more refined education and the desires springing therefrom. She serves to bring out the characteristics of the two classes of manufacturers: the coarse rusticity of the one, and the imitation of metropolitan elegance of the other. Very vividly this is done, though at somewhat too great length. It has not enough influence upon the heroine's character or fortunes to occupy so large a space in her story.

In Hilda and Glynton and the figures grouped around them, we have the odious picture of "a good match." Youth, beauty, life, hope, all *sold* to age, decrepitude, and a fortune! Other aspects of married life are presented in Mrs. Arl and Lady Wollaston. The story of Albert Gordon's flirtation with Lady Wollaston growing into a mutual passion and ending in such ignoble tragedy is, after the story of John Withers, the most deeply interesting portion of the book. She is a glorious creature, painted with a loving and a cunning hand; Albert is somewhat indistinctly drawn, but his position is intelligible enough. (p. 825)

Marian Withers claims attention for its eloquence, its knowledge of life, its originality, its straightforward dealing with *realities*, and general elevation of tone; but it is deficient in breadth and unity, and is not equal in depth or in interest to **The Half Sisters**, which, however, was a work of unusual power. (p. 826)

> *A review of "Marian Withers," in* The Leader, *Vol. II, No. 75, August 30, 1851, pp. 825-26.*

[GEORGE HENRY LEWES] (essay date 1852)

[*Lewes was one of the most versatile men of letters in the Victorian era. A prominent English journalist, he was the founder, with Leigh Hunt, of the* Leader, *a radical political journal that he edited from 1851 to 1854. He served as the first editor of the* Fortnightly Review *from 1865 to 1866, a journal that he also helped to establish. Critics often cite Lewes's influence on the novelist George Eliot, to whom he was companion and mentor, as his principal contribution to English letters, but they also credit him with critical acumen in his literary commentary, most notably in his dramatic criticism. Here, Lewes classifies novelists according to their powers of observation and capacity for sentiment, arguing that, while both observation and sentiment are evident in Jewsbury's novels, the two qualities are not adequately unified.*]

[One] might class novelists thus—1st, Those remarkable for Observation. 2nd, Those remarkable for Sentiment. 3rd, Those remarkable for the combination of the two. Observation without Sentiment usually leads to humour or satire; Sentiment without

Observation to rhetoric and long-drawn lachrymosity. The extreme fault of the one if flippant superficiality; that of the other is what is called "sickly sentimentality." (p. 137)

[Geraldine Jewsbury should be classified as a writer] in whom Observation and Sentiment were about equal; but although she possesses, in an eminent degree, both qualities, she does not work them harmoniously together. Her keen womanly observation of life gives to her novels the piquancy of sarcasm, and her deep womanly feeling of life gives to them the warmth and interest of sentiment; but—there *is* a but!—the works seem rather the offspring of *two* minds than of one mind; there is a want of unity in them, arising perhaps from want of art. Curious it is to trace the development of her mind in the three novels she has published at wide intervals: *Zoe,* in which the impetuous passionate style clearly betrays the influence of George Sand; *The Half Sisters,* in which the style is toned down to a more truthful pitch; and *Marian Withers,* in which there is scarcely any trace of the turbulence and fervor of *Zoe.* If we look closely we shall find that age and experience have had their customary influence, and while subduing the exuberance of Sentiment, have brought into greater prominence the strong characteristics of Observation. Miss Jewsbury excels in subtle and sometimes deep observation of morals as of manners; and we look to her for still finer works than any she has yet written. (pp. 140-41)

[George Henry Lewes], "The Lady Novelists," in The Westminster Review, *Vol. LVIII, No. CXIII, July 1, 1852, pp. 129-41.*

THE ATHENAEUM (essay date 1855)

[*Citing the unrealistic aspects of* Constance Herbert, *this reviewer argues that the work succeeds as a "prose poem" but fails as a "picture of life."*]

Duty is an old theme with the moralist and the preacher. At first thought, a sermon on an abstract merit—a story in illustration of a rule of life—may not seem very attractive to the worn reader or the idle man in search of an excitement. But all themes are alike to the true artist. Granted the wizard's gift—the power to stir emotion, to arouse the sense, to hold the blood in check,—and the barren waste shall be quickened into life, the shadiest spot shall flush like a rose-garden, as the spell works and the enchanter wills. *Constance Herbert,* the new homily on "Duty," is a poem in its beauty and its lofty purpose—a romance in its variety and its fascination.

Miss Jewsbury began her career as romancer with *Zoe,*—an original and daring tale, through which a tide of passionate experience seemed to surge and roll, most curious to consider when its source was no other than the heart of a very young girl, to whom such emotions as filled it must have answered to the mere call of a creative instinct.

Ten years have gone since *Zoe* startled the ardent and amazed the stern,—calling forth worship from one and anathema from another; and Time, we infer, has come to Miss Jewsbury, as he comes to all who seek to live an earnest life, with balm and healing on his wings. At least, we find that the romancer who once delighted in bold speech and deep analysis,—in questions which disturb the timid and unnerve the wavering,—has settled down into a sober frame, has grown more reconciled to the world and accepted a serene and chastened view of life. (p. 343)

We will not spoil the reader's pleasure by a premature disclosure of the plot [of *Constance Herbert*]. The tale, as a tale, is deeply interesting: full of quiet pathos and a calm and beautiful

morality. But it is a prose poem rather than a picture of life. The characters are ideal,—the scenery is ideal,—and the moral is ideal. Were we to accept it as a picture of life, we should have to refuse our assent—not to the angelic virtues, the unfaltering constancy, the sublime devotion of the ladies, or to the unmitigated weakness, vanity and rascality of the gentlemen, so much as to the clear and absolute division of the human race into good and bad, worthy and unworthy, at the precise line which divides the two sexes. Trap's famous division of the human race into those born to be hanged and those born not to be hanged was not more absolute than Miss Jewsbury's classification. We will not quarrel with our author's old maids, however gloriously endowed with beauty, wit, and wealth. But why, to so much sugar, may there not be a little honest sack? Surely it is so in life. Art, however, is selective;—and having a poetic theme in hand, Miss Jewsbury had a perfect right to choose her drolls to suit it. . . . Our last word, however, ought not to be, and shall not be, a word involving any kind of censure. *Constance Herbert* will be read with rare pleasure, and remembered with healthful interest. (p. 345)

A review of "Constance Herbert," in The Athenaeum, *No. 1430, March 24, 1855, pp. 343-45.*

[GEORGE ELIOT] (essay date 1855)

[*Eliot was one of the greatest English novelists of the nineteenth century. Her work, including* The Mill on the Floss *(1860) and* Middlemarch: A Study of Provincial Life *(1871-72), is informed by penetrating psychological analysis and profound insight into human character. Played against the backdrop of English rural life, Eliot's novels explore moral and philosophical issues and employ a realistic approach to character and plot development. In the following excerpt from a review of* Constance Herbert, *Eliot censures Jewsbury's method of illustrating the novel's moral.*]

Miss Jewsbury has created precedents for herself which make critics exacting towards her. We measure [*Constance Herbert*] by her own standard, and find it deficient; when if measured by the standard of ordinary feminine novelists, it would perhaps seem excellent. We meet with some beauties in it which, coming from the author of the *Half Sisters,* we take as a matter of course, but we miss other beauties which she has taught us to expect; we feel that she is not equal to herself; and it is a tribute to her well-attested powers if we dwell on what has disappointed us, rather than on what has gratified us. An easy, agreeable style of narrative, some noble sentiments expressed in the quiet, unexaggerated way that indicates their source to be a deep spring of conviction and experience, not a mere rain-torrent of hearsay enthusiasm, with here and there a trait of character or conduct painted with the truthfulness of close observation, are merits enough to raise a book far above the common run of circulating library fiction; but they are not enough to make a good novel, or one worthy of Miss Jewsbury's reputation. *Constance Herbert* is a *Tendenz-roman;* the characters and incidents are selected with a view to the enforcement of a principle. The general principle meant to be enforced is the unhesitating, uncompromising sacrifice of inclination to duty, and the special case to which this principle is applied in the novel, is the abstinence from marriage where there is an inheritance of insanity. So far, we have no difference of opinion with Miss Jewsbury. But the *mode* in which she enforces the principle, both theoretically in the *Envoi* and illustratively in the story of her novel, implies, we think, a false view of life, and virtually nullifies the very magnanimity she inculcates. "If," she says in the *Envoi,* "we have succeeded in articulating any principle in this book, it is to entreat our readers to have boldness to act up to the sternest requirements that duty claims as right. Although it may at the time seem to slay them, it will in the end prove life. *Nothing they renounce for the sake of a higher principle, will prove to have been worth the keeping.*'' The italics are ours, and we use them to indicate what we think false in Miss Jewsbury's moral. This moral is illustrated in the novel by the story of three ladies, who, after renouncing their lovers, or being renounced by them, have the satisfaction of feeling in the end that these lovers were extremely ''good-for-nothing,'' and that they (the ladies) have had an excellent riddance. In all this we can see neither the true doctrine of renunciation, nor a true representtion of the realities of life; and we are sorry that a writer of Miss Jewsbury's insight and sincerity should have produced three volumes for the sake of teaching such copy-book morality. It is not the fact that what duty calls on us to renounce, will invariably prove ''not worth the keeping;'' and if it *were* the fact, renunciation would cease to be moral heroism, and would be simply a calculation of prudence. Let us take the special case which Miss Jewsbury has chosen as her illustration. It might equally happen that a woman in the position of Constance Herbert, who renounces marriage because she will not entail on others the family heritage of insanity, had fixed her affections, not on an egotistic, shallow worldling like Philip Marchmont, but on a man who was fitted to make the happiness of a woman's life, and whose subsequent career would only impress on her more and more deeply the extent of the sacrifice she had made in refusing him. And it is this very perception that the thing we renounce is precious, is something never to be compensated to us, which constitutes the beauty and heroism of renunciation. The only motive that renders such a resolution as Constance Herbert's noble, is that keen sympathy with human misery which makes a woman prefer to suffer for the term of her own life, rather than run the risk of causing misery to an indefinite number of other human beings; and mind influenced by such a motive will find no support in the very questionable satisfaction of discovering that objects once cherished were in fact worthless. The notion that duty looks stern, but all the while has her hand full of sugar-plums, with which she will reward us by-and-by, is the favourite cant of optimists, who try to make out that this tangled wilderness of life has a plan as easy to trace as that of a Dutch garden; but it really undermines all true moral development by perpetually substituting something extrinsic as a motive to action, instead of the immediate impulse of love or justice, which alone makes an action truly moral. This is a grave question to enter on *à propos* of a novel; but Miss Jewsbury is so emphatic in the enunciation of her moral, that she forces us to consider her book rather in the light of a homily than of a fiction—to criticise her doctrine rather than her story. On another point, too, we must remonstrate with her a little, chiefly because we value her influence, and should like to see it always in what seems to us the right scale. With the exception of Mr. Harrop, who is simply a cipher awaiting a wife to give him any value, there is not a man in her book who is not either weak, perfidious, or rascally, while almost all the women are models of magnanimity and devotedness. The lions, *i.e.*, the ladies, have got the brush in their hands with a vengeance now, and are retaliating for the calumnies of men from Adam downwards. Perhaps it is but fair to allow them a little exaggeration. Still we must meekly suggest that we cannot accept an *ex parte* statement, even from that paragon Aunt Margaret, as altogether decisive. Aunt Margaret tells us that in the bloom of youth and beauty, with virtues and accomplishments to correspond, she alienated her husband

by pure devotion to him. ''No man,'' she says, ''can bear entire devotion.'' This reminds us of a certain toper, who after drinking a series of glasses of brandy-and-water one night, complained the next moring that the water did not agree with him. We are inclined to think that it is less frequently devotion which alienates men, than something infused in the devotion— a certain amount of silliness, or temper, or *exigeance*, for example, which, though given in small doses, will, if persevered in, have a strongly alterative effect. Men, in fact, are in rather a difficult position: in one ear a Miss Grace Lee, or some such strong-minded woman, thunders that they demand to be worshipped, and abhor a woman who has any self-dependence; on the other, a melancholy Viola complains that they never appreciate devotion, that they care only for a woman who treats them with indifference. A discouraging view of the case for both sexes! Seriously, we care too much for the attainment of a better understanding as to woman's true position, not to be sorry when a writer like Miss Jewsbury only adds her voice to swell the confusion on this subject. (pp. 294-96)

[*George Eliot*], *''Belles Lettres,'' in* The Westminster Review, *Vol. LXIV, No. CXXV, July 1, 1855, pp. 288-307.*

THE ATHENAEUM   (essay date 1856)

[*This critic recommends* The Sorrows of Gentility *to readers but considers Jewsbury's portrayal of men inaccurate.*]

In a tale, extremely simple in idea and perfectly natural in execution, Miss Jewsbury has contrived to exhibit a choice moral, with her accustomed grace and power. *Sorrows of Gentility* is a bad title for a book in which the interest is less social than human; and we warn all readers of a high caste not to reject these volumes under the wrong impression that here is another tale of vulgar pretension and pompous poverty aping wealth, such as Mesdames Gore and Trollope have told us by the score. Gertrude Morley, Miss Jewsbury's heroine, aspires, it is true, to desert her class—runs away from honest parents with a handsome and worthless rake—and suffers most severely and for many years for her fault. But her fault springs from a mistake not of her own making; she bears her sufferingss, when they come, with dignity and patience, redeeming the one error of her early life by a display of virtues truly celestial. She shows no insolence in her rise and no baseness in her fall. Her sorrows are sorrows of the heart; but the interest of the reader in her tale is not a sentimental interest. It is almost wholly intellectual and poetic.

Shall we once again venture to object to Miss Jewsbury's presentation of her *men*? Of course an author has a right to choose her own fairy land:—in Barataria very queer people sometimes live and rule. But Fairy Land is not the common world; and there is so much of worldly observation and of the wisdom which comes from experiment only in *The Sorrows of Gentiliy* that Miss Jewsbury would feel most justly offended if we said her work was unreal. Why, however, will she people her stories with unreal beings of one sex while she crowds them with life-like creatures of the other? In *Sorrows of Gentility* there is scarcely one man introduced who has the merit of a single virtue. Old Morley is a brutal savage. Young Morley is weak and contemptible. Donelly is a heartless blackguard. Lord Southend pinches and brands his lady. Hutchins is ''bad in every way.'' And so throughout: the ladies possess all the virtues, as they ought to do, perhaps, in the works of a lady,— but the men are not *manly*. Cannot Miss Jewsbury conceive a husband who neither beats his wife nor fears her tongue? Has she never known a man who is a friend to his wife and a master to his household, ruling in kindliness and strength, because it is his nature to do so, without timidity and without fuss? Her novels contain a great deal of shrewd appreciation and subtle analysis; but we think they scarcely represent both sides of the social question with the same fullness and fairness.

Such an observation, however, falls in only by the way; and the absence of higher character in the male puppets, though it may reduce the completeness of the book as a picture of human life, detracts nothing from the interest of the story. We advise our readers to send for *The Sorrows of Gentility*.

A review of "The Sorrows of Gentility," in The Athenaeum, *No. 1492, May 31, 1856, p. 675.*

THE ATHENAEUM   (essay date 1859)

[*While admitting that* Right or Wrong *is original and interesting, this reviewer objects to the story on moral grounds and faults Jewsbury's depiction of men.*]

In one of the volumes of that strange magazine of human vice and weakness, the French *Causes Célèbres,* is told the story of a married monk. He lived in Paris, and had once been a soldier. His life divided itself between the duties of a citizen and the duties of an ecclesiastic; six months of the year he was a staid physician, wedded, honoured, and employed; the other six he spent in prayer, processions, and religious exercises. For twenty years this fraud went undiscovered. At length he became Prior of his convent, and his duties within the walls no longer suffered him to absent himself for such very great

A photograph of Jewsbury taken in 1855.

lengths of time. Love may have cooled as ambition warmed. The physician died, at least report so had it, in the country; the wife wore her widow's weeds; and a world of stern denial divided the two who had been man and wife. Justice, however, overtook the Prior; his marriage was proved against him, and the awful chastisement of the Church descended upon his head. Such is the theme on which Miss Jewsbury has this year chosen to lavish all the wealth of her imagination and her style. We cannot say that she has succeeded as a writer of her powers and practice ought to succeed. The theme is ungrateful and out of her line of observation. What could a good and pure-minded lady make of a rascal like Father Paul? With the daring or the eccentricity so often found in our feminine writers, Miss Jewsbury clings with a kind of love to Paul—as though she saw some good in him to redeem that which is openly mean and obtrusively vile. But the rogue is a rogue in spite of her affection. Had she herself created this character, we should have fancied her smitten for a moment with a moral squint; but she found it to her hand in the old books; and as an artist she fell into the temptation of appropriating it, along with its sad story and bad moral, for the purposes of her own art. We are sorry for it. We must be allowed to tell her that the Vicomte, whose easy, unabashed viciousness she has placed in contrast to Paul's virtue, is far less of a scoundrel than the pretentious monk. All the male figures of her story are, moreover, shadows. How few of our lady-writers have shown the power to delineate a man. We have dreams done in sepia, in water-colour, in sugar-candy; but not one creature that by its acts, conversation or set of character might not pass, under petticoats and a pretty name, for a woman more or less good or bad. How is this? More, how far would male critics be justified in asking, whether ladies in general take us to be the boneless, fluid, imponderable things that female writers paint?

There are mistakes, too, of chronology and manners in *Right or Wrong* which the antiquaries may wrangle over in the coming generations. And there is one blunder of so very singular a character for a woman to make that we hold ourselves excused from a more precise reference to it. No reader will miss it. (pp. 148-49)

Let us hasten to add that this story, if less than might have been expected from Miss Jewsbury working on a happier ground of fact, is, nevertheless, as a story, very interesting and fresh. Once taken up, it will not be laid down. We may quarrel with it, but we must read it. (p. 149)

A review of "Right or Wrong," in The Athenaeum, *No. 1631, January 29, 1859, pp. 148-49.*

THE SPECTATOR   (essay date 1892)

[*While noting the intrinsic literary charm of* Selections from the Letters of Geraldine Endsor Jewsbury to Jane Welsh Carlyle, *this critic contends that the chief interest of Jewsbury's letters lies in their revelation of the author's character.*]

[The] interest in Miss Jewsbury's letters [*Selections from the Letters of Geraldine Endsor Jewsbury to Jane Welsh Carlyle*] is . . . seriously diminished by the absence of Mrs. Carlyle's; we have but one side of the correspondence, and can only dimly guess at the other; and it says much for their intrinsic value that, even under such disadvantages, the ordinary reader, who knows little or nothing of the writer, can still find considerable pleasure in their perusal. The exact cause of this interest is difficult to define. Possibly their chief value consists in affording a very curious and interesting study of character, for, as far as any woman can reveal herself by her own words, Miss Jewsbury did so lay bare her inmost thoughts and feelings to her friend. The letters are obviously honest and genuine, written without any attempt at literary or any other form of effect, full, as such a woman's letters would be, of apparent contradictions and discrepancies, and yet presenting, to anyone who has eyes to see, a very complete and interesting portrait of an uncommon but very human personality. The virtues and the failings that are supposed to be especially feminine were writ large in Miss Jewsbury, and she, in her turn, wrote them large for the edification of her friend. . . . We have said that there is no striving after literary style in the letters; but we should add that they possess, nevertheless, a literary charm of their own. Miss Jewsbury, even when her thoughts and sentiments are commonplace, finds an original mode of expressing them, and some of her phrases are quite as felicitous in their effect, as they are evidently spontaneous. It is hardly fair to quote them, as taken away from their context they can only sound unmeaning. (pp. 684-85)

There is very little reference in the correspondence to contemporary life, literary or otherwise. Of *Jane Eyre* Miss Jewsbury speaks very disparagingly. *Hide and Seek,* a novel by Wilkie Collins, excites her warm admiration, and she is disposed to be enthusiastic over *Alton Locke.* Of Kingsley, as a preacher, she also speaks with some enthusiasm, and recounts, in this connection, an extraordinary scene which took place after one of his sermons. An amusing reference is made to a very distinguished author of our own day. "I am going out to-night," she writes, "to meet the author of *Nemesis of Faith,* a very nice, natural young man, though rather like a lost sheep at present." But the chief interest of the book lies, as we have said, not in the matter of which it treats, but in the curious insight that it gives into a character which is more than usually worthy of study. . . . Miss Jewsbury's confessions to her bosom friend were not intended for the public eye; they are altogether free from self-consciousness, absolutely genuine in their profession of feeling. (p. 685)

"Miss Jewsbury's Letters," in The Spectator, *No. 3359, November 12, 1892, pp. 684-85.*

VIRGINIA WOOLF (essay date 1929)

[*A British novelist, essayist, and short story writer, Woolf is one of the most prominent literary figures of the twentieth century. Like her contemporary James Joyce, with whom she is often compared, Woolf is remembered as one of the most innovative of the stream-of-consciousness novelists. She was concerned primarily with depicting the life of the mind, and she revolted against traditional narrative techniques, developing her own highly individual style. Woolf's works, noted for their subjective explorations of characters' inner lives and their delicate poetic quality, have had a lasting effect on the art of the novel. She was a discerning and influential essayist as well as a novelist. Her critical writings, termed "creative, appreciative, and subjective" by Barbara Currier Bell and Carol Ohmann, cover almost the entire range of literature and contain some of her finest prose. In the following excerpt from "Geraldine and Jane," an essay exploring the unusually close friendship between Jewsbury and Jane Carlyle, Woolf comments upon* Zoe. *Woolf's remarks were written in 1929.*]

[When Jewsbury sent Mrs. Carlyle] the manuscript of her first novel, *Zoe,* Mrs. Carlyle bestirred herself to find a publisher ("for", she wrote, "what is to become of her when she is old without ties, without purposes?") and with surprising success. Chapman & Hall at once agreed to publish the book, which,

their reader reported, "had taken hold of him with a grasp of iron". The book had been long on the way. Mrs. Carlyle herself had been consulted at various stages of its career. She had read the first sketch "with a feeling little short of terror! So much power of genius rushing so recklessly into unknown space" [see excerpt dated 1842]. But she had also been deeply impressed.

> Geraldine in particular shows herself here a far more profound and daring speculator than ever I had fancied her. I do not believe there is a woman alive at the present day, not even George Sand herself, that could have written some of the best passages in this book . . . but they must not publish it—decency forbids!

There was, Mrs. Carlyle complained, an indecency or "want of reserve in the spiritual department", which no respectable public would stand. Presumably Geraldine consented to make alterations, though she confessed that she "had no vocation for propriety as such"; the book was rewritten, and it appeared at last in February 1845. The usual buzz and conflict of opinion at once arose. Some were enthusiastic, others were shocked. The "old and young roués of the Reform Club almost go off into hysterics over—its *indecency*" [see Carlyle excerpt dated 1845]. The publisher was a little alarmed; but the scandal helped the sale, and Geraldine became a lioness.

And now, of course, as one turns the pages of the three little yellowish volumes, one wonders what reason there was for approval or disapproval, what spasm of indignation or admiration scored that pencil mark, what mysterious emotion pressed violets, now black as ink, between the pages of the love scenes. Chapter after chapter glides amiably, fluently past. In a kind of haze we catch glimpses of an illegitimate girl called Zoe; of an enigmatic Roman Catholic priest called Everhard; of a castle in the country; of ladies lying on sky-blue sofas; of gentlemen reading aloud; of girls embroidering hearts in silk. There is a conflagration. There is an embrace in a wood. There is incessant conversation. There is a moment of terrific emotion when the priest exclaims, "Would that I had never been born!" and proceeds to sweep a letter from the Pope asking him to edit a translation of the principal works of the Fathers of the first four centuries and a parcel containing a gold chain from the University of Göttingen into a drawer because Zoe has shaken his faith. But what indecency there was pungent enough to shock the roués of the Reform Club, what genius there was brilliant enough to impress the shrewd intellect of Mrs. Carlyle, it is impossible to guess. Colours that were fresh as roses eighty years ago have faded to a feeble pink; nothing remains of all those scents and savours but a faint perfume of faded violets, of stale hair-oil, we know not which. What miracles, we exclaim, are within the power of a few years to accomplish! But even as we exclaim, we see, far away, a trace perhaps of what they meant. The passion, in so far as it issues from the lips of living people, is completely spent. The Zoes, the Clothildes, the Everhards moulder on their perches; but, nevertheless, there is somebody in the room with them; an irresponsible spirit, a daring and agile woman, if one considers that she is cumbered with crinoline and stays; an absurd sentimental creature, languishing, expatiating, but for all that still strangely alive. We catch a sentence now and then rapped out boldly, a thought subtly conceived. "How much better to do right without religion!" "Oh! if they really believed all they preach, how would any priest or preacher be able to sleep in his bed!" "Weakness is the only state for which there is no hope." "To love rightly is the highest morality of which mankind is capable." Then how she hated the "compacted, plausible theories of men''! And what is life? For what end was it given us? Such questions, such convictions, still hurtle past the heads of the stuffed figures mouldering on their perches. They are dead, but Geraldine Jewsbury herself still survives, independent, courageous, absurd, writing page after page without stopping to correct, and coming out with her views upon love, moralilty, religion, and the relations of the sexes, whoever may be within hearing, with a cigar between her lips. (pp. 209-11)

> Virginia Woolf, ''Geraldine and Jane,'' in her The Second Common Reader, *Harcourt Brace Jovanovich, 1932, pp. 200-17.*

IVAN MELADA (essay date 1970)

[*Melada discusses the influence on* The Half-Sisters *of Thomas Carlyle's concept of the relationship between fulfillment and duty.*]

In ***The Half-Sisters,*** Geraldine Jewsbury reveals the extent of her discipleship to the author of *Sartor Resartus* [Thomas Carlyle] by taking as her themes, work versus idleness and the relation of both to the reality of the spirit. These themes are developed through the characters of William Bryant, an ironmaster, his wife Alice, and her half-sister Bianca.

The late Phillip Helmsby, father of Alice and Bianca, was an ironmaster from Newcastle who, having been sent on business to Genoa, fell in love with an Italian woman. They took matters into their own hands and Bianca was born illegitimate. Upon his father's death, Helmsby came home to take over the ironworks; and the affairs of business left no room for thoughts of love which ''can thrive only in idleness.'' Blotting out his Italian dream, he married his partner's daughter, a sensible if prosaic woman. Shortly after Alice was born, he died; and the iron works were sold. To her eventual regret, Alice did not lose touch with the world of business. She and her mother continued to move in the circle of her late father's business acquaintances. But Alice, who seemed to have inherited the nature that her father exhibited at Genoa before he entered the real world of work, was unhappy with her existence. One of the reasons for this was that the men of her acquaintance, occupied with business, had no interest in the graces and refinements of feminine society:

> Society in a prosperous commercial town is a raw material not worked up into any social or conventional elegances. . . . Labour has never yet been made to look lovely, and those engaged in labour have nothing picturesque or engaging in their manners. . . . The men engaged all day in business operations on a large scale, frequently with several hundred workpeople to manage, were not likely to feel any interest in small refinements and elegances for which there was no tangible use. Consequently, female society went for very little. To manage the house well, and to see that dinner was punctual and well appointed; to be very quiet and not talk nonsense, or rather to talk very little of anything; were the principal qualities desired in wives and daughters. . . .

Alice, on the point of suffocation from boredom and given to reverie, is captivated by William Bryant, an ironmaster many years her senior. As Othello did to Desdemona, he tells her of his business travels on the Continent and of the strange races of people he had encountered, with the result that, ''William Bryant became the hero of her desert.'' Bryant thought Alice ''charmingly romantic'' but, believing that she would outgrow

it and become the sensible woman her mother was, he married her.

Nevertheless, Alice's new station did not alter her existence. She was depressed by the idleness expected of her as the wife of a prosperous man, and Bryant did not perceive her state of mind. (pp. 134-36)

Engrossed in business activities which required all his energy, Bryant, a kind and affectionate man, loved Alice, but had no leisure to provide companionship or occupation for her. She wished to please him in some way and he desired only that she amuse herself: ''Constantly occupied himself with affairs of deep importance, he had no idea of the weight of *ennui* which was eating the life out of Alice. He was not in the least insensible to Alice's demonstrations of affection, although it was not in his nature to be demonstrative himself; and he sometimes wished his wife to be a little less sensitive and romantic.'' Unaware that idleness can take a mischievous turn, Bryant invites a young gentleman without occupation, Conrad Percy, to spend a few days at his home. On one occasion when they are alone, Alice, offering a glimpse into the despondency of soul in a woman without a regular occupation or duties, discusses with Conrad the employment of her time. When Conrad asks her what she does all day, Alice replies that she does nothing, that every day, like an unstrung bead, has no connection with the one before or after, that each does not transcend the Actual by being a part of a larger goal or Ideal:

> I hardly know . . . I have nothing to do that seems worth doing. I am depressed under a constant sense of waste, a vague consciousness that I am always doing wrong, and yet I can find out nothing that I ought to do. . . . I used to think that I should be so happy, if I might have all my time to improve myself, and spend as I like; but now that I have it, I do not know what to do with it. My whole life is one cloud, and I have a sense of responsibility which I can neither adequately discharge nor deliver myself from. I have nothing to look forward to. When I get up in the morning, I know all that is likely to happen before night; one day is like another, and the weight of life that lies upon me is intolerable.

Bryant's unceasing preoccupation with business, which makes him blind to Alice's soul's need, leads to her taking the fatal step of running away with Conrad, who has insinuated himself into the family by becoming an investor in Bryant's concern. The climactic moment arrives when Bryant must leave home to look into the failure of one of his correspondents. He is silent and abstracted by business anxieties. Alice, not trusting herself with Conrad, appeals to her husband to take her with him. The harassed Bryant tells her not to be childish, to be reasonable, and to stop making such scenes: '''I should be in the way,' sobbed she, as soon as she was alone, 'he is quite tired of these scenes—business, business, always business—I am nothing, or at best of secondary importance. Well, be it so, be it so; I need feel no more remorse; he has lost me by his own fault.''' Overcome by guilt, however, Alice collapses in the midst of the preparations for her departure and dies of a seizure shortly afterwards.

Because of her lack of spiritual resources, Alice had been unable to transcend the world of the Actual in which she was trapped by the inertia of idleness. She had never attained the state of mind with which she could respond to Carlyle's dictum that, ''Doubt of any sort cannot be removed except by Action,'' or to his other precept, '''*Do the Duty which lies nearest thee,*' which thus knowest to be a Duty! Thy second Duty will already have become clearer.'' Though not concerned with states of unbelief, Geraldine Jewsbury seems to have applied to Alice's predicament Carlyle's notion that the Ideal, a contemplation of which brings spiritual peace, exists only in the Actual. The following passage from *Sartor* seems to suggest what Alice was unable to perceive. Writing about the moment of ''Spiritual Enfranchisement,'' Carlyle explains: ''The Situation that has not its Duty, its Ideal, was never yet occupied by man. Yes here, in this poor, miserable, hampered, despicable Actual, wherein thou even now standest, here or nowhere is thy Ideal: work it out therefrom; and working, believe, live, be free. Fool! The Ideal is in thyself, the impediment too is in thyself: thy Condition is but the stuff thou art to shape that same Ideal out of. . . .'' Carlyle then exhorts the ''tempest-tost Soul'' who is imprisoned in the chaos of the Actual to create a world out of chaos by following his well-known advice, ''Whatsoever thy hand findeth to do, do it with thy whole might.''

Alice's husband, Bryant, though having found something to do and having done it with all his might, has not performed his whole duty. Working with Mammon as his god, he too has, like Alice, been living a day-to-day existence confined to the Actual, for him the practical world of business. The death of Alice is a profound experience that liberates him from a totally material existence. His new found belief in the Ideal is expressed in a fusion of the Christian concept of a life after death with Carlylean transcendentalism:

> Men must lose some dear object by death before they can realise the invisible world: we must have a stake in it before we can believe it.
>
> Sitting there, beside his dead wife, Bryant was admitted to the threshold of the unseen state. What now to him was the dream of life, with all its highly-coloured appearances? Hope and fear were alike dead: he sat in the presence of the Invisible and calmness came gradually to his soul.
>
> Alice's weakness—Conrad's treachery—his own wounded pride—all seemed now hushed to insignificance in the presence of the great mysterious fact of Death; even his grief seemed small and idle. What was he that he should complain? The tumult and glare which had surrounded all things subsided before the cold, colourless light of death.
>
> He left that chamber in the early dawn of the next morning with some portion of the eternal calmness on his soul.

The spiritual experience of a glimpse into the invisible world transforms Bryant into Carlyle's noble captain of industry who renounces a Mammonish for a God-like spirit. He reveals his future plans to a Lord Melton:

> As long as I live, I must be doing something. I do not care for making money now; it is the work I care for. I shall live in the mountains among the miners. Since I have been in sorrow, I have thought of many things that never struck me before, especially since I have been lying here. We have many hundred workmen in our employ—we paid them their wages—they did our work—the rest was their concern. I think we should have considered something more than making money out of them. They are a sad wild set. I have not much faith in benevolent schemes, but I shall see what can be done about them.

Bryant continues his work with the sole object of ameliorating the condition of his working men.

In contrast to Alice's complete failure to perceive the Ideal and Bryant's realization that came too late, Bianca is successful from the start. Arriving penniless in England, she meets with a company of actors. Faced with the necessity of working, she struggles to make good as an actress. Far from considering her profession solely as a livelihood, Bianca, inspired by an old actor who loves his work, aspires to an ideal of her art:

> I care for perfecting myself in my art more than for any praise or credit. Oh! to be able to realize the idea of which you gave me a glimpse when I beheld you acting for the first time! To enter into that world, which, as it were, lies unseen around us, and bring out thence the thoughts and conceptions that are hidden there, and force them into a visible shape, a bodily expression, I would consent to dwell in darkness my whole life.

She is also encouraged by Lord Melton's advice on the insufficiency of happiness as a life's goal. Thus having found her work, Bianca achieves a transcendent spiritual peace.

In all, *The Half-Sisters* is a curious novel even for its time. Though it is permeated by the spirit of the Everlasting Yea, it successfully embodies philosophical states of mind into characters without making those characters into abstractions. Alice, Bryant, and Bianca work out their separate destinies with a minimum of intrusion of philosophic ideas. Carlyles' notions aside, the novel might be called an antomy of boredom, a subject that has not been searchingly treated by other novelists of the time. Even Charlotte Brontë who published *Shirley* in 1849 does not so much examine the agony of female ennui as describe female annoyance at having no serious work to do in a man's world. We may remember in that novel Caroline Helstone's aunt, who passes much of her time straightening the contents of her bureau. The world of *The Half-Sisters,* with its busy ironmasters living in an atmosphere where workmen must be managed and schedules and bills of exchange must be met, does not permit women fulfilment through any avenue other than the kitchen or dining room. Nor does it allow them a share in the feeling of engrossment in work that pervades such an atmosphere. Next to the highborn ladies of the fashionable novel who spend their time reciprocating morning calls, Alice Bryant stands uneasily. We have entered the modern world in which idleness for the wealthy woman of sensibility is no longer a badge of class status but a curse. (pp. 136-39)

> *Ivan Melada, ''Plugson of St. Dolly Undershot,'' in his* The Captain of Industry in English Fiction: 1821-1871, *University of New Mexico Press, 1970, pp. 118-39.*

MEREDITH CARY   (essay date 1974)

[*Focusing on* Zoe *and* Constance Herbert, *Cary underscores Jewsbury's unconventional attitudes toward the role of women in Victorian society.*]

Feminine passion and feminine dependency are not unheard-of topics in Victorian fiction, being most often the unspoken ingredients of the Woman Question, which received considerable airing. Yet, when considered by women as well as by men, they tended to occur as problems with results rather than as solutions. For example, even George Eliot, whose private life suggests a more independent approach, wrote within the usual pattern: Maggie Tulliver is punished for her drift toward passion, Gwendolyn Harleth is severely chastened for her will to dominate, and a suitable marriage constitutes Dorothea Brooks' reward for her eventual self-knowledge and self-control. In the context of such conventions, Geraldine Jewsbury's remarkable attitudes toward the Woman Question take on considerable importance.

In some ways, Jewsbury's early fiction seems deceptively conventional. Her first novel typically enough involves marriage, motherhood, and eternal as well as sexual passion. Yet from the beginning she absorbed herself in references to the problems implicit in these ordinary views of women. She represented the ill effects of the dependency of women, of their lack of recognition, their lack of freedom, the ''deliberate sensuality'' of the training which replaced education for them. In addition, she described herself as lacking the contemporary stock responses on the subject of the relation between the sexes—a complex she referred to [in her letters to Jane Carlyle] as the Moral Sense—and the unconventionality of her private life suggests the accuracy of her judgment. She was therefore free to change her novel pattern as she gradually perceived a discrepancy between her real experience and the theoretical standard.

Growing up in Manchester in a manufacturing family, Jewsbury learned to respect ability more than position and effort more than ''blood.'' Such an attitude complicated her view of marriage. Mere social position could not impress her, and where was she to find a man who could outshine her emotional and intellectual intensity—who would be ''high enough to rule''? She pursued her search with vigor and method, ''offering herself on paper'' to various men who caught her fancy. She despaired of an English husband because of British ''respectability.'' But although she turned first to a Mussulman and then to a New Zealander to be ''safe,'' and although she prolonged her search considerably beyond the usual period for such anxiety, she was destined to die unmarried. (p. 201)

[She] began to compare her reluctant spinsterhood with the marriages of her friends, among them the Thomas Carlyles. Her increasingly cynical inspection discovered in marriage a gradually accumulating bitterness which, added to her own unreconciled frustration, provoked her vow to set aside sentimental convictions and tell the truth about the female situation.

The shift from hope to anger . . . is important in her novels. In contrast to the vigor and optimism of her early work, many of the details of her later novels are dictated by her growing disillusionment. Nevertheless, an examination of *Zoe* and of *Constance Herbert,* the novels which most clearly illustrate her crisis in morale, reveals that her basic analysis of the Woman Question did not importantly change. Her method was consistently to deal not so much with men and women as with a variety of personalities responding to the ramifications of intellectual, social, and emotional choices.

In *Zoe, A Study in Two Lives,* Jewsbury analyzes the life histories of two individuals engaged in the universal human search for freedom and self-fulfillment. In each instance, the account includes the adolescent choices which help to determine the mature life—the vocational choice in the case of the man, the choice of a husband in the case of a woman. The novel evaluates the implications of these choices in the economic, social, intellectual, and emotional lives of each character. And because Jewsbury judges the relative success of the two against an identical measure, the novel becomes an examination of different personality types—the ''believer'' as opposed to the ''heretic''—rather than of sexual roles.

Jewsbury's procedure is not unexpected in the case of the man. She shows Everhard choosing to enter a monastic school rather than become the heir and understudy of a distant relative. That he is a ''believer'' in more than religious terms is revealed by his assumption of a kind of mystic brotherhood in the cloister. He is accordingly appalled by the cynicism he finds there: one of his old friends turns up for economic reasons, and his superiors dismiss Everhard's religious questionings as adolescent maunderings. Because he is shocked by them, he is emotionally remote from his fellow priests. His vows divide him from such non-believing friends as Zoe, and his intellectual doubts divide him from believers such as his own students. He is finally forced to an admission of the inutility of his belief by the heart-wrenching discovery that, not only has he been unable to convert Zoe, the heretic wife of one of his parishioners, but, to the contrary, she has both undermined his faith and attracted his love.

His response is characteristic: rather than reexamining his idealism, he shifts the image of his devotion. He solves his economic and social problems by undertaking a medical and technological mission to the primitive peoples of Wales. In his spare time there, he writes a philosophical treatise intended as a guide to readers facing his own crisis of faith, thus accommodating his intellectual needs. And he dreams of the distant Zoe in order to exercise his emotions.

But reality intrudes again. He loses even his bare living and his limited social mission when the Welsh reject his emotionless advice in favor of some itinerant religious demagogues. His hope of an attenuated dialogue through publication ends when his book provokes only vilification from the reviewers who object to the arrogance and blasphemy of his position. And when, in his final illness, he struggles back to the country estate where he first met Zoe, he finds the family gone. In a churchless man's equivalent of a final confession, he painfully writes, explaining to Zoe his love and silence. But since Zoe does not arrive until after he has slipped into a final coma, his devotion produces no response which he can register.

Everhard, the believer in secular as well as religious terms, has been a man of rules throughout. He deserts the church not because it exists by rule but because he discovers the particular rule to be sometimes useless. He retreats from monasticism not to become free but to devise a better code. In the meantime, he continues to live by rule. For example, his vows of chastity are not cancelled, he decides, despite his defection from the agency exacting the vow. His personal mission in Wales is hampered by his new regulations, for he considers that since he is no longer operating as an agent of the church, his social service must be totally religionless. Therefore he cannot face down the irresponsible missionaries who appeal to a peasant population which unwarily craves emotion as well as money and medicine. The public repudiation of the intellectual project whereby he attempts to set up a new method of coping with universal and eternal problems also symbolizes the dubiousness of substituting a personal system for a system which has, at a minimum, the authority of centuries of meditation. The social and physical neglect in which his life ends suggests the condition of a hermit in a saintless world: unable to devise a system suitable both to himself and to society, he dies unfulfilled in every area.

To compare Everhard's life with Zoe's is to be reminded that defining freedom is not the same as being free. In contrast to Everhard's retreat from daily life, Zoe is only slightly concerned with theory. She makes comfortable use of existing systems when they offer something she wants without losing sight of them as generalities which may not, untailored, fit a particular individual.

Her approach to marriage is characteristic. If she stays with her uncle in England she enjoys considerable tolerance of her independent spirit, whereas in France, social expectations regarding the proper behavior of maidens render her a virtual prisoner in her father's tiny apartment. On the other hand, in England she will have to look forward to permanent dependence upon her uncle because of a shadow on her legitimacy—a taint which does not exist to the less exquisitely squeamish French eye. Having surveyed her options, Zoe undertakes the first of the pragmatic acts which culminate in her being called a heretic. She guarantees her economic position by taking advantage of the French attitude in order to marry a kindly friend of her father, toward whom she feels a rather dispassionate amiability. He is, she thinks, ''very good-natured; and he is not so very ugly either.''

Although Zoe has proceeded rationally in an area where emotion is the more usual vehicle, the results of her choice are excellent. She discharges her obligation to her husband through the production of two excellent sons. As a hostess of considerable charm and influence, she is able to satisfy her own impulse toward social service by offering a second home to a variety of young relatives and temporarily deracinated friends. Further, through her social contacts, she is able to fulfill her intellectual cravings, for the intellectual men she meets stimulate her to pursue and develop her ideas. And she enjoys a number of friendships in which a central element is a pattern of serious conversations on responsible topics.

The keys to Zoe's success, then, are her ability to perceive her own needs and her willingness to be rational about the facts of her options. Unlike Everhard, at no time does she fall into empty obedience to forms. Her consistent refusal of the stereotyped response is most clear in her emotional life. It is not surprising that her marriage should leave her emotionally unencumbered since she did not pretend it to be other than a practical arrangement. However, her relation with Everhard is revealing. Upon the termination of their flirtation, Everhard withdraws into the self-repressive attenuation of unconsummated but unflagging distant adoration whereas Zoe seems to feel at liberty to reoccupy her emotions elsewhere. She is, accordingly, free to reciprocate when, as a recent widow, she attracts the eye of Mirabeau—a libertine of international fascinations.

The resulting *grande passion* proves to be the supreme test of her character, although not in the usual sense. The attraction is clearly both mutual and profound. But Mirabeau has been divorced under French law, which does not permit remarriage. He can therefore do no more than demand that she prove herself above the law by living with him on the basis of passion rather than ritual. Her failure to acquiesce convinces him that she is centrally conventional, after all.

Thinking of the moral expectations of the time the novel was written, one might be inclined to agree, if it were not for the implications of the courtship. Until Mirabeau's electric advent, Zoe had been very much the dominant figure in her own life, deferred to by husband, sons, relatives, and friends. But in Mirabeau she encounters a will as strong as her own. He literally drags her to the theater after she has broken an engagement to go with a mutual friend. He impugns her motives in withdrawing from society in order to nurse one of her sons through an attack of scarlet fever. He insults her for insincerity and lack of courage when she seems to expect a conventional settlement from him. The entire courtship is, in fact, a contest of wills. After the introspective and self-denying love of Everhard, expressed in hints and renunciations, Mirabeau's intense passion seems doubly overpowering. Her existence as a kind of private saint in Everhard's lonely reveries requires nothing of her. But Mirabeau's demands—that she become flamboyantly a sinner—would submerge her life in his. . . . Except for the aura of glamor which sin and vigor give, these demands are no different from those of any English husband. Accordingly, in choosing to relinquish Mirabeau's passional intensity, Zoe is maintaining her individuality. And her occasional glimpses of his later activity satisfy her of the correctness of her choice, for his growing importance in French politics clearly suggests the extent to which she would have been eclipsed in his larger arena.

In thus rejecting what is unquestionably the passion of her life, Zoe is not engaged in a self-repressive gesture: she is protecting her independence rather than her morals. And when she retires to a convent in the throes of the devastating aftermath of her involvement with Mirabeau, she seeks a return to peace not through the conventional development of a religious vocation but through the recovery of her old life energy. Therefore, as she slowly rouses from her sense of loss, she returns her attention to her sons, the narrower lives where she dominates.

As would be expected if she were a man, Zoe has throughout her life judged her situation in terms of what she is herself capable of rather than of whom she can attract to her as spouse or lover. And her orientation regarding other social conventions is equally independent. For all her choices suggest that when she finds them convenient she makes use of such social structures as marriage and convents without imagining that any generalized agency or system will prove consistently either appropriate or inappropriate for any private life. The value of her pragmatism is suggested in the extent to which the same social and religious codes which hamper Everhard, the believer, tend to help Zoe, the heretic, make herself free and useful.

On the basis of these overlapping life histories, one concludes that a sense of freedom and fulfillment for any individual results not from speculation in isolation but from finding some socially useful task appropriate to his capabilities. It is an idea which pervades Jewsbury's work. She depicts the problem in a variety of forms. In *The Sorrows of Gentility* the drone works out his destructive fate in the portrait of the elegant young husband who has too much gentility to be more than a sponge of declining grace. In *The Half-Sisters* there is the ''ideal English lady,'' a wife so unassertive as to become too vacant to perform even household tasks. *Marian Withers* includes a representation of the unvarnished implications of the ''good match,'' in which a young woman sacrifices all personal and social considerations for the sake of an imagined establishment which is, predictably, not forthcoming.

Not always content with portraiture, Jewsbury sometimes comments directly on the problems of boredom, dependency, and greed. For example, she intrudes into the narrative of *Marian Withers* to observe that

> the women of England of the present day are eaten up with *ennui* to a much greater extent than is suspected; the devouring activity of their minds has been stimulated by the general increase of higher culture, but they find no adequate employment for it. . . . In the days of our grandmothers, what superfluous energy was not worked off by domestic employment,

broke out in gambling; this has, in our day, given place to a craving for emotion,—a more refined but still more dangerous resource.

(pp. 202-07)

For people of talent, the solution to all these problems seems obvious. In addition to Zoe, with her abundance of energy and courage, there is Bianca [from *The Half-Sisters*] . . . , whose dedicated cultivation of a musical talent provides her with both a sense of identity and a livelihood. But Jewsbury does not commit the common novelistic mistake of offering success only to the superlative. In *The Sorrows of Gentility* the humble wife contracts for needlework to gain self-respect and independence from her degenerating husband. And Marian Withers, whose assets seem limited to an unpretending sincerity, finds fulfillment in giving up false "social" goals in favor of kindly offices among the neighborhood mill hands.

In thus evaluating the destiny of all types of women as well as men always in terms of work, Jewsbury was quite deliberately countering the usual female "solution" of a demure evanescence into love and marriage. She consistently represents passion, no matter how soul-engulfing, as unjustifiable, not particularly on moral grounds, but because of the extent to which it usurps the subject's attention from more important matters. Thus, when even Bianca would be willing to abandon her art for a worthless passion, her old mentor scolds: "When you women get hold of a love affair, you make that your business, and the most important things which concern your real interest, you make your play." (pp. 207-08)

If passion is often degrading and always delusive, a marriage even for love cannot constitute a feminine solution—it only obscures the obligation of self-development. Mr. Cunningham, the avuncular man who eventually marries Marian Withers, gives her a "good scolding" on this subject when he finds her in the throes of a miserable youthful passion:

> Self-control, self-discipline, is the first law for both man and woman, from which no power can give a dispensation. Your present suffering arises mainly from having failed in this duty towards yourself. My dear child, it is only God himself who is entitled to say, 'Give me thine heart,'—and on him alone can we fling ourselves with all our weakness and our dependence. . . . You are not yet competent to be the life-long companion of such a man as you desire to belong to: think rather of deserving than of enjoying; begin to live worthily *now*.

With such an understanding it becomes clear that marriage for women should be viewed in exactly the same terms as for men; it may or may not prove supportive but it cannot in itself prove to have been an adequate goal.

This approach to both men and women as human beings rather than sexes was so arresting to Jewsbury's contemporaries that members of the Reform Club were reported to have read *Zoe* to titillate themselves. And although Jane Carlyle eventually could offer the suspiciously ambiguous comment that *Zoe* was "the cleverest Englishwoman's book I ever remember to have read," she responded to the "indecency" and the "want of reserve" of an early draft of the work with a feeling "little short of terror!" [see letter dated 1842].

But by the time *Constance Herbert* was published, the public response to Jewsbury's work had changed. For example, the *Westminster Review* missed the meaning of this later novel in order to complain that Jewsbury "only adds her voice to swell the confusion" on the subject of women since she might just as well have offered a heroine who would have "fixed her affections, not on an egotistic, shallow worldling like Philip Marchmont, but on a man who was fitted to make the happiness of a woman's life, and whose subsequent career would only impress on her more and more deeply the extent of the sacrifice she had made in refusing him" [see excerpt by George Eliot dated 1855]. So dogged an insistence on the natural supremacy of the male must cast a doubt on the review rather than on the novel. Nevertheless, it identifies the difficulties to be faced by a writer departing from the conventional settlement between men and women.

Although her later work offered a less-balanced presentation, Jewsbury had, from the beginning, addressed the problem of the condition of women either in the voices of her strong characters or in auctorial asides. A dowager admonishes a young girl [in *Zoe*]: "You have nothing in you to attract him in the way of conversation, so if he talks to you it is for no good." In describing another character [in *Constance Herbert*], Jewsbury observes that her "very deficiencies were her charms," since her "intelligent passivity" constituted her "intense attraction" to her lover. Although she is unyielding in her insistence that women must develop some merit of their own, she also is concerned with the sources of female vacuity. Thus, feminine education frequently provokes Jewsbury's "editorials." A good measure of Zoe's remarkable character is to be attributed to the fact that her guardian has "a theory of my own about education, and I will try it upon her; she shall be taught just as if she were a boy, and I will not have her plagued with sewing and darning any more."

Few women were so fortunate as Zoe. A more usual male attitude appears in *Constance Herbert*:

> "No girl could learn even what the boys on the lowest form have to do; they could never stand caning without crying out, and no boy cares for that."
>
> "I have always thought," said Margaret . . . "that it would be an excellent thing if girls had, as far as practicable, the education of boys; everything is diluted and prepared for the use of women, even facts. So much fuss is made about their learning the most trifling branches of common knowledge, that they learn nothing naturally or thoroughly; they are not taught to aim at the severe exactness demanded from men in their studies, and I think any rational being has reason to regret when the faculties and qualities which God has given him are not called out to the utmost; when anything *less* than the *best* of which he is capable is accepted from him, either in matters of morality or intellect."
>
> "But my dear madam, you would have women much less charming, if you entailed upon them the headaches of severe study. They were not made to carry the heavy metal of scientific information; they would be much too formidable."
>
> "My dear sir . . . I have no wish to entail either headache or science on women who have no vocation that way. I only protest that they shall not have 'learning made easy'; that what they acquire shall be learned thoroughly, and without the flattering stimulus of a superficial facility. A great deal of patient labour produces very moderate results, and I do not see any danger of women becoming more 'formidable' than the generality of men."

The concept of education expressed in this dialogue has not changed from that of Jewsbury's earlier work, but the bigotry of the boy and the pointed wit of the woman emphasize the extent to which the tone of *Constance Herbert* is different. Jewsbury had become convinced that, if women were allowed to lead "normal" lives, there would "not be so many marriages" and women would be "taught not to feel their destiny *manque* if they remain single. They will be able to be friends and companions in a way they cannot be now."

It is in terms of such an understanding that this later novel is unmistakably a feminist document. It represents the upbringing of the daughter of a compulsive gambler and a woman confined to a madhouse with inherited insanity. The child's situation constitutes an excellent justification for stating the case against marriage. The aunt who raises Constance, the Margaret of the above conversation, is not so summary as to rest her case with the fact of a tainted inheritance. She cannot feel she has done her job unless she can convince Constance that her necessary celibacy is a blessing, no matter how it may seem to a conventional view of a woman's destiny.

Margaret brings up Constance on tales of the virgin saints alternated with disillusioning observations on the marriages in the surrounding society. Rather than helplessly endure the demoralizing presence of Marchmont, the unscrupulous lawyer to whom Constance's father, Charles, has lost his property, she so impresses Marchmont with her grace and integrity that he appoints her the hostess of a combined household, in which position she is able to set a tone of dignity and self-control pointedly unavailable to either the scheming Marchmont or the demoralized Charles. When Marchmont's shallow son becomes interested in Constance, Margaret wards off disaster through discussions of the disillusionments of love.

Margaret's educational activities are considerably assisted by Charles, whose life constitutes almost a reverse illustration of her theme. When his gambling finally results in his seeming to be the receiver of stolen goods, his general lack of integrity contributes to his snowballing abjectness: too frightened to go to the police with the truth, he becomes implicated in the crime of hiding the money and identifiable jewels in his possession. Finally dying of guilt and apoplexy while the police search the bedroom around him, he serves as a shocking emphasis to Margaret's parables of self-indulgence and self-control. One concludes that since everyone's life is controlled by someone, the happier man controls his own.

As in *Zoe,* this novel's underlying idea serves to measure both men and women. Yet in the case of *Constance Herbert,* its application proves to be by no means dispassionate. If in this later novel, Jewsbury is discussing the human condition, she is doing so in a world where only women are human: except for a nonentity and a dead boy, there are no "men" in the novel, so degraded are most of the males. There is, centrally, the spectacle of Charles: "He had got a fixed idea that he should die in a workhouse, and he had become penurious in his habits, dirty and sordid in his person. Gambling was the only means in which he had any faith for getting money, and it was, besides, the ruling passion of his life—the only point of vitality that still remained in activity."

In addition to Charles' story, there is the sad chronicle of Margaret's youth. In love with a man whose parents disapprove, she refuses a conventional secret marriage but insists instead on a Catholic marriage which, not legally binding in England, should result in a wholly voluntary emotional union. Margaret is punished for her idealized notion of love when her extra-legal husband eventually contracts a legal marriage with someone else. Recalling her past for Constance, Margaret sums up the case for love: "My dear Constance, that self-abandonment, self-devotion, becomes dreadfully fatiguing and wearying to the object of it in a very short time—no human being can be made an idol with impunity." In the context of Charles' life and Margaret's story, Kate's lunacy becomes symbolic: a woman must be mad to marry.

Such an attitude created a technical problem. Jewsbury had described the growth of a young girl to the age when the usual novelistic options would be either a happy marriage or a decline into self-sacrifice or tragedy. If Constance's failure to marry was to seem an advantage rather than a self-repressive response to her tainted genes, something more positive than a catalogue of worthless males was required. The alternative was complicated. Constance's economic problems are solved by the suicide of one of her hopeless young suitors. His will defines and solves one female problem, for he bequeaths his entire estate to Constance "to have and hold in her own right, independent of father, husband, or any other relation or connection."

Constance is provided with a social role as well. The conventional ambiguity of social position of the single woman is rendered unimportant by the creation of a female society: the friendship of the three women is a sufficient group.

Even progeny are supplied. Margaret is more to Constance than her biological parents have been, and Constance in turn acquires an heir by adopting one of the girls born to Miss Wilmot's belated marriage. Therefore, in her final situation, Constance has sacrificed nothing and has gained independence.

Miss Wilmot's apparently happy marriage may be the final bitterness of Jewsbury's feminist vision, for Miss Wilmot's husband is so shadowy a figure that he seems to exist only to provide children. He appears to be a male version of the role reserved for women in a male society. And like those biological receptacles, he approves the freedom of the individualists he serves, for he "thought Constance one of the most enviable women in the world, to be able to manage her estate for herself, and have all her own way as though she were a man."

That Constance is finally able to "have all her own way" is a major testimonial to Margaret's effectiveness, for originally Constance could scarcely have been less free. The child of a madwoman, a girl in a society which males control, and at the economic and moral mercy of a father who gambles away the home she should have inherited and exposes her to the advances of a worthless suitor, she has biology, tradition, and man against her. As she gradually develops a character in contrast to the utterly uncontrolled Kate, in straightjacket and padded cell, and the increasingly fearful and abject Charles, she emerges as the embodiment of the kind of freedom this novel considers. She triumphs over all her handicaps through self-control.

In thus insisting on Constance's independence Jewsbury is suggesting an evaluation of Constance's life on the same basis as that used for a man. The idea of graceful inertness is specifically set aside: Constance is to be independent and has something to do. To be sure, her happy ending constitutes on the one hand a feminist's answer to marriage—she is provided with financial security, a social position, a child. But the insistence on work—not after all surprising in a friend and admirer of Carlyle—returns this novel to the broader concerns of Jewsbury's earlier novels.

If, in the throes of her own bitterness, Jewsbury fails to deal fairly with the men in *Constance Herbert,* she is still in this novel judging her women on the same basis as that she had before consistently used for all her people. Drawing illustrations from both sexes she decries throughout her work the solitary, the dependent, the idle, who neither contribute to society nor explore their own private potential. She condemns excessive individualism, which fosters withdrawal, marriage, which offers dependence, and passion, which triggers idle brooding. Fulfillment is offered only to those individuals who govern themselves within her conviction that every person needs work he or she can do and a social context within which to do it.

It is true that she addresses herself more urgently to women than to men. But her greater absorption in the feminine predicament is understandable in view of her conviction that, although the goals should be the same for everyone, women start from a position of disadvantage. In a letter to Jane Carlyle she sums up the problem, insisting that neither

> you or I are to be called failures. We are indications of a development of womanhood which as yet is not recognized. . . . I regard myself as a mere faint indication, a rudiment of the idea, of certain higher qualities and possibilities that lie in women, and all the eccentricities and mistakes and miseries and absurdities I have made are only the consequences of an imperfect formation, and immature growth. . . . A 'Mrs. Ellis' woman is developed to the extreme of her little possibility; but I can see there is a precious mine of a species of womanhood yet undreamed of by the professors and essayists on female education, and I believe also that we belong to it.

The crux of her plea is that women should be creatures of the "larger possibilities" which result from freedom and learning. Social strictures should not limit all but "superior women" to immaturity and dependency. Neither should distinctions in educational opportunity condemn even superior women to remain no more than sketches of their true potential. Instead she calls for equality in all these matters so that women legitimately could be expected to compete with men on an equal basis in the same arena. This concept pervades her novels in the form of her concern to judge all individuals of any sex or talent on a single basis. When society at large could be prevailed upon to follow this lead, she believed the Woman Question would be answered. (pp. 208-13)

> *Meredith Cary, "Geraldine Jewsbury and the Woman Question," in* Research Studies, *Vol. 42, No. 4, December, 1974, pp. 201-14.*

ROBERT LEE WOLFF   (essay date 1977)

[*Wolff views* Zoe *as one of the first novels of religious doubt in nineteenth-century England.*]

[*Zoe: the History of Two Lives* was] perhaps the first serious effort to deal with the subject [of Christian doubt in Victorian fiction]. "Modesty and reserve" are wholly absent from *Zoe,* set in the eighteenth century and dealing with a handsome married woman, a friend of Dr. Johnson and his circle (all of whom appear), who falls in love with a Catholic priest, Everhard Burrows. But Everhard is not just an ordinary Catholic priest: he is a friend of the eighteenth-century sceptics in both France and England, has taken priestly orders with no profound conviction, and thereafter grows steadily more convinced that the *evidence* for the truth of Christianity is unsatisfactory. Questioning the truth of revelation, he finds himself "in utter ignorance, without a hope or a belief to guide him."

What was Miss Jewsbury to do with him then? She wrote to Jane Carlyle that she could not provide Everhard with "new doctrines to begin to lead the remainder of his lifetime. . . . What can any of us do? What do any of us know?" Having resigned from the priesthood, Everhard first goes in for social work among the Welsh coalminers, but is forced to leave by Wesleyan revivalists who are more popular than he. He writes a book about religion which precipitates a scandal, retreats to Germany, and in that more congenial atmosphere writes a learned philosophical history that makes him famous.

But before Everhard had abandoned the priesthood, he had fallen in love with Zoe. He has never told her so until the night he rescues her from a fire. "A warm palpitating weight," she lies on his bosom (she is in her nightclothes at the time), and soon he "who had never touched a woman" experiences a "whole life of passion" in a single moment. "He crushed her into his arms with ferocious love,—he pressed burning kisses upon her face, her lips, and her bosom; but kisses were too weak to express the passion that was in him. It was madness like hatred,—beads of sweat stood thick on his forehead, and his breath came in gasps." At once, Zoe's own "burning arms were round his neck, and her long hair fell like a veil over him." After a few moments of "delirium," Zoe recovers first, and she begs Everhard to tell her that he has not "lost the esteem" he had had for her. It is this torrid episode that leads directly to his resignation of the priesthood, and so it should. Later on in the novel, Zoe has another love affair with Mirabeau himself, and Everhard dies in poverty.

The love affair between Zoe and Everhard harks back to such famous "Gothic" novels as M. G. Lewis's *The Monk* (1796), in which Catholic monks or priests press unwelcome sexual attentions on fair young women, usually in a vaulted chapel. The only difference is that Zoe welcomes Everhard's embraces (which also take place in a chapel, immediately before the altar). In all other respects *Zoe* is a truly pioneering effort. It is the first novel to sound the notes which novelists were so often to repeat. Scepticism of Christian evidences, sublimation of doubt in sex, social service among the poor as a substitute for faith, the importance of German biblical criticism in undermining belief: all these—entirely new in 1845—[were to be found in later, more famous novels of doubt]. (pp. 403-04)

Little wonder that, despite its glaring faults, *Zoe* struck Jane Carlyle with a "feeling little short of terror! So much power of genius rushing so recklessly into unknown space!" [see letter dated 1842]. She added that the "old and young roués of the Reform Club almost go off into hysterics over its indecency" [see letter dated 1845]. Though *Zoe* did not even have "a figleaf of conformity," though its publisher was deeply worried about its outspokenness, and though its reviewers protested against its "fling at the resonableness as well as the purifying influence of the Christian faith" or found it—quite rightly—"feverish" or "most dangerous," it made a great noise. Had Everhard been an Anglican priest instead of a Roman Catholic (who were, as we know, rather expected to be seducers), the scandal would have been far worse. And, one must emphasize, the doubts that Everhard felt about Christian evidences were Geraldine Jewsbury's own, even as early as 1845. Her cry of "What can any of us do? What do any of us know?" justifies us in regarding *Zoe* too as a kind of autobiography. (pp. 404-05)

> *Robert Lee Wolff, "Spiritual Agonizing Bellyaches," in his* Gains and Losses: Novels of Faith and Doubt in Victorian England, *Garland Publishing, Inc., 1977, pp. 389-417.*

J. M. HARTLEY   (essay date 1979)

[*Hartley argues that in her works, Jewsbury attempted to reconcile her own conflicting roles as a professional writer and as a woman. According to the critic, Jewsbury established an antithetical relationship between the protagonists in most of her novels, using the opposing characters to represent her contradictory roles.*]

The middle of the nineteenth century was recognized at the time as 'distinctly the age of female novelists', a golden age distinguished not only by writers still much admired today—the three Brontës, Mrs. Gaskell, George Eliot—but also by many minor writers who dominated the best-seller lists of the season. However good or bad they were as novelists, these women all shared and had to confront the same problem: that of being simultaneously women and novelists. . . . Geraldine Jewsbury . . . provides an interesting, almost stark illustration of the effects that such a struggle could have, and it is in this light that I would like to offer a brief analysis of her fiction, and of her presentation of the heroine. While attempts to draw general conclusions from her work must falter in the face of her own proud warning to her friend Jane Carylye—'It is of no use your getting up a theory about me. . . . I was born to drive rules and theories to distraction'—the way in which Jewsbury divided her protagonists and progressively diminished their stature and scope does seem to provide a particularly striking example of the way in which the struggle to be both woman and writer could shape the fiction that was in its turn born out of this very conflict. (p. 137)

It is no coincidence that aspects of Jewsbury's life read like one of her own early novels, for by bringing life and literature closer together in her own life she could attempt some resolution of her anomalous roles. Thus she obtruded literature into life, and although she might have appeared unconventional as a woman she was nevertheless behaving very much in the convention of the woman novelist, as she interpreted 'George Sandism', and very much in the convention of her own first heroine, the exotic Zoe. In the approximation of life to literature the real dissolves into the fictional and *vice versa;* in the process each validates the other. In Jewsbury's rhetoric Jane Carlyle is transmuted into fiction: 'She is a *heroine* and right or wrong makes a prescription for herself'. However, the only heroine who really interested Jewsbury, in literature as in life, was herself; in both we can see her embodying Geraldine Jewsbury as heroine.

Jewsbury's first novel, *Zoe: The History of Two Lives,* was her most famous, or perhaps notorious would be a better word since it provided the scandal and the circulating library success of the season. That Jewsbury was conscious of violating female literary convention is clear from her desire for anonymity:

> I had rather not have my name stuck to the thing. First, because there are many things said in it that I don't want to walk about amongst some of my reputable friends as being guilty of holding. . . . Another reason is, that I myself have a general sort of prejudice against women's novels, with very few exceptions. I mean, I would not on any account take up a woman's novel at a venture, unless I knew something about the writer.
>
> (p. 142)

According to Jewsbury, Zoe 'puzzled everyone', and this seems to have included her creator. The puzzle has obvious personal relevance since it concerns the nature and the problems of the woman of genius: what is she and what can she do? Jewsbury's account extends to many pages of confused justification and generalization; it includes a defiant apology which seems to refer both to her heroine and to herself, for

> the eccentricity which generally makes women of strong energetic character . . . chafe against the harmless conventionalities which are a law to their weaker or better broken-in companions.

The title alerts us to Jewsbury's method of confronting this puzzle: in this *History of Two Lives* she has split herself into Zoe, the thwarted brilliant woman, and into Everhard, the religious conscience of the age—'I put *my own* religious botherations into him'. Zoe and Everhard share the same simple problem: what to do. The author expounds her theme directly in passages such as the following:

> If we once could discern what was required of us exactly to do, it is not the greatness of the task that would frighten us (for we are capable of immense drudgery of labour); but it is left to us to discover our own work, and to set our hands to it as best we can, and this makes the weariness of life. We spend half our strength in beating the air, and we seldom have the satisfaction of feeling that we have wisely and adequately bestowed our labour; that which we ought to have done still remains undone; and we are devoured by unrest and vague remorse.

The writing of this first novel provides Jewsbury with the fulfilling kind of labour which she and her characters seem to need so intensely. The personal application of this preoccupation within the book was noticed by a reviewer who described *Zoe* as 'a strange and striking book, the vehement protest of a young, clever, susceptible Englishwoman against the thousandfold dullness of her narrow sphere of provincial life'.

In Everhard's life Jewsbury can present someone actively seeking out a suitable sphere for fulfilment (he tries religious, intellectual and social work) which she cannot do with Zoe, for ever-hard—as the masculinity of the name so clearly indicates—is what a woman cannot be. Jewsbury does not step so far out of line as to say that women should devote their 'genius' to other than womanly enterprises; hence the paradox at the heart of the book. A genius must do something to prove him or herself, but a true woman can do little, except marry. Femininity and genius are almost by definition irreconcilable, and Zoe retains her femininity only at the expense of her genius. She must forfeit her independence and strength, because according to the author:

> The most exalted female nature requires some visible manifestation to cling to: they are by the very constitution of their being, passive, receptive; in proportion as a true feminine disposition is developed, the positive, the active becomes uncongenial to their nature; and in exact proportion as a woman becomes active, self-sufficing, subjective instead of objective, she is a grander character, of a stronger and more heroic mould, but she approaches the nature of a man, and loses her feminine empire over the hearts of men. With all her elevation of nature, Zoe was a thorough woman.

In this passage and throughout the presentation of Zoe, Jewsbury is exploring the nature of 'genius' in women, and its relation to conventional images of femininity. Must feminine excellence differ from masculine excellence? The answer seems to be yes: a woman must excel only in being womanly. The only arena open is that of the emotions, and Zoe enters it with zest.

This theme, together with Jewsbury's concern with female education, makes comprehensible the remarkably slow opening of the book. The whole of the first volume is split into the two separate stories of the childhood and adolescence of the two protagonists, who do not meet until the second volume. Before Zoe appears the ground for her characterization is prepared in a conversation about women and genius. The wits of the brilliant Parisian society in which Everhard dallies decide that the talented woman's sphere should be that of the feelings rather than either action or intellect:

> 'Whenever a woman attempts to throw herself into the mêlée of action, and to contend with men on a footing of equality, she is always seen in the end to commit either some grave fault, or some signal folly. No woman has ever succeeded in gaining lasting fame, but many have lost their reputation in the attempt.'

The truth of this is acknowledged, and explained by a male wit to the satisfaction of all:

> 'Women are never engrossed by any object sufficiently to forget to display themselves; unless indeed, the object be a lover, and then they can be sublime. When a woman's affections are engaged, all her littleness disappears; women have been grand, almost superhuman, through the strength of love, but the moment they desire to distinguish themselves, they become stripped of the "divinity that doth hedge" a woman.'

Zoe's arena is thus already established before her entrance, and this conversation acts as a signpost throughout the ensuing descriptions of Zoe's childhood and education. The inadequacies of traditional female education preoccupied Jewsbury throughout her novels. Since this education is rigidly devised to ensure results of one unexceptional pattern, the exceptional Zoe must be exempt. To this end she is given a Greek mother and hence a 'tropical organization and . . . strong passions . . . lying latent within her'. This exotic temperament naturally rebels against the homely curriculum that her kindly English cousins prepare for her, and tempts her uncle to experiment in progressive education. 'Taught just as if she were a boy', Zoe develops into a woman of unspecified 'genius'. As such she cannot be accommodated within her mundane environment, and accordingly emerges as a *femme incomprise*, the misunderstood, unfulfilled type of heroine later to be developed so successfully by Charlotte Brontë and George Eliot. An early version of this type, Zoe unfortunately lacks interest and conviction because of the vagueness and extravagance of her characterization. (pp. 143-44)

Inadequate employment for women joins inadequate education as a major preoccupation; the weak plots of this and subsequent novels exploit the scrapes, usually romantic, in which women embroil themselves because they have nothing better to do. The only course clearly open to Zoe is marriage, a state of affairs which provokes a tart comment from Jewsbury about 'false maxims instilled betimes, which could mould the feelings of a hot-blooded, passionate young creature into the semblance of those of a cold, calculating merchant'. The use—or rather misuse—of marriage affords no solutions for the passionate heroine; Zoe is unfulfilled and indeed almost unaffected by her experiences as a wife and mother. After brilliant society has been tried and found wanting, Zoe's quest for fulfilment leads her to take two lovers, one for the passions and one for the soul: one lover it seems, cannot meet all the demands of Zoe's turbulent nature. Her love for the priest Everhard is religious

and spiritual: to her he appropriately appears as 'a thing apart . . . an angel from Heaven'. The peace he brings her is, however, soon challenged by the satanic Count Mirabeau, over whose face a 'radiant intelligence . . . gleamed like lightning'. He successfully reawakens Zoe's passionate nature, but his failure to make her his mistress (he is already married) demonstrates that Zoe has eventually managed to combine within herself the characteristics of both her lovers and now needs neither. Finally she is strong enough to exist alone without support from either husband or lover, but at the cost of that brilliance which had so fascinated and confused her creator. Zoe 'went through life' we are told at the end of the book, 'with a composed and chastened spirit'. The resolution offered to the problems of the exceptional woman entail the modification of her 'genius' into something more ordinary, more suited to everyday life. To be successfully extraordinary one has to be ever-hard and a man. The problems raised by Zoe are resolved in Everhard; the division of Jewsbury into male and female evades the issues posed by Zoe, especially since Jewsbury is unwilling to jeopardize the 'womanliness' of her heroine in quite conventional terms.

In her next novel, *The Half Sisters: A Tale,* Jewsbury attempts a different division. She again pursues the problem of fulfilling employment, this time with exclusive reference to women. Jane Carlyle thought that by taking this theme so explicitly Jewsbury was moving on to dangerous ground and indulging her 'tendency towards the unmentionable'. What Jane Carlyle found 'disgusting for a young Englishwoman to write' [see letter dated 1848] was probably not only the outspokenness but the obvious personal application of the book. For in it Jewsbury is justifying her own professional career and her own activity by portraying other women's, and those other women as heroines. The main profession in the book is acting, but the argument (of which there is a great deal) always includes the other professions. . . . (p. 145)

From her first novel and from her own life Jewsbury knew that the question of employment for women was difficult. In her second novel she approaches the problem through the division manifest in the title of the book. The *Half* refers to the actual relation between the two heroines—Bianca is the illegitimate daughter of Alice's father. It could also perhaps refer to Jewsbury's attempt to resolve contradictions through splitting the heroine into the two halves which have proved incompatible in her first heroine and in her own life. One half is the traditional, feminine figure of the provincial Alice, who has to marry, because that is the only career open to her; the other half is the orphaned Bianca who becomes a successful actress, adopting her career out of necessity rather than choice. This devices enables Jewsbury to evade some knotty problems. While Bianca is working she does not marry, so that the two roles of work and marriage do not co-exist in one character. The ordinary Alice, for whom a profession would have been so much more out of the ordinary, does not work. And by stressing the economic pressures on Bianca, Jewsbury blurs the issues at stake in the employment question, issues which centred not upon the necessity of work for middle-class women but upon their need for something worthwhile to do.

The incompatibility between work and marriage, as embodied in the separation into the two halves of Alice and Bianca, structures the book, divides it and provides much of its subject-matter. The stories of the two heroines do not coalesce for almost 200 pages, as Jewsbury lengthily pursues her interest in female education. Before the heroines meet and the arguments begin, the presentation of each heroine seems to indicate that the opposition might not be an easy clean antithesis of career-girl and traditional young lady. The first words of the book introduce us to Bianca:

> On a bed, scantily hung with faded print, lay a woman apparently in extreme suffering. A girl of about 16 stood over the fire, carefully watching the contents of a small pan; at length it seemed sufficiently prepared, and she poured it into a tea-cup, and approaching the bed where the sick woman lay moaning and restless, she addressed her in Italian, and endeavoured to raise her up.

Thus the first image of the career-girl shows her performing the traditional feminine task of tending the sick. Bianca as career-girl *and* traditional woman could afford scope for showing the possibility of women combining both these roles, were it not that in these early sentences Jewsbury is already providing herself with an escape route: Bianca speaks in Italian, and this exotic heritage (like Zoe's) gives her special qualities and special latitude. She can do with impunity what young English ladies cannot, as the picture of Alice's narrow and frustrated lot is used to show. Furthermore, Bianca's career impinges little on her characterization as a traditionally feminine figure, which is over-emphasized in compensation. Here Jewsbury's treatment parallels Mrs. Gaskell's treatment of Ruth 5 years later: just as Ruth's one lapse from idealized feminity is to be an unmarried mother, so Bianca's one lapse is to be (forced by necessity) a brilliant actress. In both cases the drive behind this characterization is towards audience acceptance, hence the heavy stress on the traditionally acceptable and admirable qualities of womanhood. It would have been much more difficult to create a sympathetic heroine out of a more professional woman—and a less successful one, since success carries with it its own vindication. But the 'strong-minded' woman was a contemporary anathema even to strong-minded women novelists. While we should not underestimate the progress marked by Bianca in having a career at all, we can regret the way in which Jewsbury shuffles over some of the central issues involved in employment for women.

Our introduction to Alice, the other half of the antithesis, shows her in rebellion against the kind of traditional task in which she and not Bianca should be delighting:

> After being for some time diligently occupied with her work, the young lady exclaimed with vivacity: 'There, thank Heaven! This tedious work is finished at last. I have taken the last stitch, and now one can go out. It is quite a sin to be in the house on such a beautiful day.'

The young lady as rebel is an interesting proposition, especially when her mother reprimands her for her unfeminine literary preoccupations:

> 'Your life will be domestic; you are neither to be a fashionable woman nor an authoress; therefore your excessive devotion to books and accomplishments will bring no useful results, but only unfit you for your duties, and fill your mind with fancies'.

These discordancies, however, are undeveloped, and this might be attributable to Jewsbury's two-fold purpose in the characterization of Alice. On the one hand she must ensure that her heroine stands out from the herd of provincial girls who:

> were pretty, trifling, useless beings, waiting their turn to be married, and in the meanwhile, doing their worsted work, and their practising, and their visit-

ings; and were on the whole nicely-dressed, quiet, well-conducted young women, with as little enthusiasm as could well be desired.

As heroine Alice must be distinguished from these women, hence the minimal traces of the *femme incomprise* in her characterization: 'None of those around her could understand the vague, undefined, restless aspirations that filled her heart.' On the other hand, in her antithetical relation to the exceptional Bianca, Alice represents a standard of ordinariness, a standard based firmly on traditional notions of femininity. Jewsbury stresses Alice's typicality and its nature:

> Alice was a type of a very numerous class of English women, whose fine qualities, with lack of wise guidance, evaporate amid the common material details of household life, leaving them ineffectual and incomplete—grown children without the grace of childhood.

The repeated analyses of Alice, and her sad marital progress through the book, underline the flaws which Jewsbury sees as necessary but debilitating elements in traditional notions of femininity. According to Jewsbury, Alice's 'feminineness' renders her 'negative and useless; which, however, most men seem to regard as the peculiar type of womanly perfection'. Alice has become the victim of her perfections:

> The intense yearning after sympathy, and the habit of fancying all to be wrong which did not come with the sanction of other people's opinion, was the weak part of Alice's character, although the source of much in her that was delicate and graceful; it gave that confiding, clinging beautiful helplessness, which was the fascination of her manner. But still it is *strength*, and not graceful weakness, that is to be desired.

This 'strength' Jewsbury attempted to infuse into Zoe and Bianca, and into her own life, in order to invigorate and revitalize the 'negative' conventions of traditional femininity, while never wanting to abandon those conventions completely. It is this attempt to redefine femininity to include strength which links Jewsbury firmly with her more successful contemporaries, Charlotte and Anne Brontë, Mrs. Gaskell and George Eliot.

The long arguments about employment for women prominently placed at the beginning of the second volume of ***The Half Sisters*** (and conducted for the most part by men) debate conventional notions of femininity. Bianca's champion, Lord Melton, elaborates repetitiously and sententiously points that Jewsbury has already made: she unfortunately seems to think they carry more conviction from a man, and a lord. The solution he offers is, however, unsatisfactory: having extolled the life of independent action, all that he can advocate is that 'all the women of England should be shut up in what Catholics call RETREAT . . . to sit down and consider . . . what is a real matter of conscience, and what is only a matter of convention'. The major argument lies in the person of Bianca, intended to unite within herself the virtues of strength and femininity. This combination enables her to escape that 'ennui' which is the mortal disease threatening all Jewsbury's women who are inadequately educated and hampered by convention. In a long speech Bianca reiterates the main statement of the book:

> 'Look, for instance, at the great body of unmarried women in the middle classes—they spend their days in the same kind of trifling that slaves in the east amuse themselves with, till some one comes to put them in a harem. They want an object, they want a strong purpose, they want an adequate employment.'

Bianca charmingly concedes to her (and Jewsbury's?) detractors that she has 'become in some degree hard and coarse from my contact with the harsh realities of life'; there is of course absolutely no evidence for this. For Bianca employment is a 'blessing':

> 'I have had a purpose, and have endeavoured to work it out; and I say that if you could furnish women with a definite object, or address motives in them fit to animate rational beings, you would have a race of wives and daughters far different from those which now flourish in your drawing-rooms; the quality of their nature would be elevated; they would be able to aid men in any noble object by noble thoughts.'

This speech reveals the reasoning behind Jewsbury's plea for female employment: not that women will become better in themselves or closer to equality with men, but that they will make better 'wives and daughters'; i.e. they will serve their men better. That this was not an argument that Jewsbury subscribed to wholeheartedly herself can be seen in her encouragement to Jane Carlyle to write, despite Mr. Carlyle's disapproval. But Jewsbury had in mind readers less enlightened that Jane Carlyle, and this might account for the ending of the book: both a failure of nerve and a logical consequence of this line of argument. Having demonstrated that she can be both independent and delightfully feminine, Bianca is now worthy of the conventional prize, the hand of a lord. The status of her hitherto brilliant career as an actress pales in the prospect of becoming Lord Melton's wife, the career for which she has really been in training throughout the book. The prize won, the function of Bianca's career no longer exists, and she can rapidly accede to the request of her future sister-in-law:

> 'My dear Bianca will not, I am sure, refuse the first request made by her sister; which is, that she will not again appear on the stage, now that she belongs to us.' 'So be it then,' said Bianca gracefully; 'arrange all as you wish it to be, and I will be comfortable.' 'That is being a good child,' said Lady Vernon.

By dividing the heroine into two, and by softening and idealizing Bianca, Jewsbury has clouded the issues at stake in the book, issues which have to be reinforced through overt statement and through other professional women who are not heroines. The 'enlightened' Lady Vernon is engaged in producing such women, in giving middle-class girls an adequate education. She is motivated not by feminist ideals which, although historically probable in 1848, might have alienated Jewsbury's audience, but by her desire to prevent more Alices, who, according to Lady Vernon,

> 'belong to a class which . . . needs thoroughly educating a great deal more than the children of the actual poor. . . . Where any reverse happens as the death of their parents, misfortunes in business, or what not, such as deprives them of their means of living, shoals of these young women are thrown on the world utterly incapable of work.'

Arguing from pragmatism rather than principle, Lady Vernon emphasizes the unrevolutionary nature of her scheme, that all the occupations taught in her establishment 'may be followed by young women in their own houses—a great advantage'. Later she does allow one of her pupils to train professionally as a singer under Bianca's guidance, giving reasons common at this time among progressive thinkers:

> 'I cannot help thinking women are happier and better when they are the centre of a home, and can live

there contented amongst their duties. . . . Still, if God is pleased to give a woman faculties, I suppose she must cultivate them.'

This is the argument used by Mrs. Gaskell in discussing Charlotte Brontë, and it applies well to creative talents such as writing and acting; not quite so well perhaps to other interesting but non-creative work. Finally, lest readers should misinterpret the crusade for female employment as a self-regarding enterprise, we have the contrasting example of La Fornasari, the Viennese opera singer. Although she looks like Bianca she differs totally in that 'music, singing, acting, all seemed nothing but so many vehicles for the glorification of *herself*'. Thinking of 'self' is the great crime in Jewsbury's novels, unsurprisingly since most of her leading characters are either women or priests, and both groups are traditionally associated with submission to and consideration of others.

Although much in *The Half Sisters* shows that it is intended as a courageous crusade for female employment, the antithesis between the heroines is not fully exploited to this end. We learn far more about what Bianca does not forfeit than about what she gains through work. We could perhaps find reasons for this in the powerful symbolic apparatus prescribing the heroine's qualities and functions and prohibiting innovation; we might also find reasons in the author's relation to her heroine, in Jewsbury's romanticized, fictionalized notions of what a heroine is, and in her desire to justify herself in rosy fictional terms.

Jewsbury's concern for the position of women does not appear again so directly in her subsequent novels; and concomitant with this change is a dwindling of vitality. Perhaps Jewsbury now recognized the contradictions inherent in her fragmented portrayals of the heroine as genius, worker, feminine woman and conventional wife, and realized that these images were irreconcilable, whether in fiction or in her own life. This might have been honest but was also unfortunate as the tensions between these types of the heroine had energized her first two novels. The change in direction was not, at first, of her own choice, since her next novel, *Marian Withers,* was commissioned after the publication of *The Half Sisters* by the *Manchester Examiner and Times,* although what they commissioned and what she produced turned out to be two different things. They asked for an industrial novel and she gave them a domestic novel. This might have happened because of a misunderstanding over the nature of *The Half Sisters.* The editors of the Manchester paper probably hoped that she would tackle the industrial situation in Manchester much as she had presented the issue of employment for women in her previous novel: with energy, sympathy and progressive interest. This, however, did not happen. Although Jewsbury was clearly familiar with the terrain involved, her enthusiasm was not sparked by industrial issues: she was interested in Marian Withers rather than John (Marian's father, a self-made mill-owner) and certainly not at all in John's employees. From the resulting book we can infer that Jewsbury's interest in employment for women sprang not from social concern so much as personal involvement. The industrial element in *Marian Withers* serves mainly to provide a setting for the female characters; but in doing so it prescribes their presentation. For the problems confronting these women concern the flux induced in the social hierarchy by the new industrialism; in this unstable world women must devote their attention not to personal fulfilment but to survival in and manipulation of their economic context. In contrast with the vibrant Zoe, Marian is a blank page, to be written upon by her environment. Her father exploits her as an item of conspicuous consumption, 'a high-water mark which showed how much he had risen'. Other women show her how to manipulate the value of marriage in a market where 'Every woman is bound to make the best bargain she can'. Marian's young friend Hilda explains the currency of her innocence in this market set up by men who

> 'look upon us as women as so much property, to be laid out as it please them to have us, not as it is good for us to be'.

Hilda is about to marry an aging wealthy ex-roué with a 'fancy for little innocent shepherdess-sort of girls, in white muslin'. Marian is saved from this world not by her own volition—she is fascinated by the shallow, socially-ambitious Albert—but by the paternal Mr. Cunningham. Women apparently need guidance, and he gives it to her in sermons about the worthiness of marriage to men like himself. His wedges of Victorian pietism are the magic kiss to Marian, who feels 'like one roused from a slumber'; she dutifully fulfils Mr. Cunningham's precepts about 'living worthily' and qualifies as his wife. But the blank page has been written on by others; Marian has no life of her own. While she is perhaps more realistic and less ridiculous than Jewsbury's earlier heroines, her plight as passive victim is ultimately less optimistic.

In her next novel, *Constance Herbert,* Jewsbury returns to some of the questions raised in *The Half Sisters.* But whereas the earlier novel juxtaposed conventional marriage with employment, *Constance Herbert* juxtaposes marriage with spinsterhood *without* a career. Bianca never considers the idea of remaining single in order to pursue her career; this would have been sinfully selfish. In *Constance Herbert,* where there are no marriages, there are no careers either, and the women remain single not from selfish choice but from selfless renunciation. An absurd plot is constructed, involving family curses, hereditary madness, compulsive gambling and machiavellian social opportunism, in order to force women into the position of having to renounce marriage, even though, as Jewsbury herself well knew, many women remained single without this strange coercion of circumstance. The story deals with three women who 'each . . . had the hope of their lives struck down when they trusted most securely that it would endure'. They each refuse an offer for what are originally seen to be higher motives; however, sacrificial renunciation appears to bring its rewards, since all three men in question turn out to be weak or bad. George Eliot was one of the contemporary reviewers who rebelled against this version of renunciation, with criticisms relevant to her own later portrayals of the renouncing heroine:

> It is not the fact that what duty calls on us to renounce, will invariably prove 'not worth keeping'; and if it *were* the fact, renunciation would cease to be moral heroism, and would be simply a calculation of prudence [see excerpt dated 1855].

This flaw, together with the wild absurdity of the plot, led another woman critic, Mrs. Oliphant, always quick to criticise her feminine rivals, to comment that 'we have seen few books so perfectly unsatisfactory as *Constance Herbert*'.

The reasons why Jewsbury should have written such a 'perfectly unsatisfactory' book can be traced, I think, to the theme of the single woman. For in dealing with this theme unresolvable difficulties arise from Jewsbury's refusal to take the questions of employment and spinsterhood together. This means that the women in the book do not do anything, or if they do they create surrogate families, such as Margaret's school and Constance's estate in Yorkshire. The problem of what spinsters

can or should do is blurred by Jewsbury's predictable device of dividing the heroine into two—the third woman, Miss Wilmot, is peripheral to most of the book. Although the ostensible heroine is Constance Herbert, her aunt Margaret is almost as important: she educates Constance and prefigures her future. Margaret has learnt the lesson of renunciation, and teaches Constance by example and indoctrination:

> She willingly told her stories of the noble women and saints of long ago, who gave up all manner of greatness and grandeur for the sake of leading a noble and holy life. She endeavoured to invest the idea of renunciation and self-denial with an heroic attraction beyond any personal gratification.

As the book recounts the birth of Constance and the death of Margaret we might expect that between them these two women will span the whole life of a Lady of Renunciation. But the lives of the two women do not overlap: by the time Margaret enters the book she already has a past full of romantic activity (including a secret 'Romish' marriage), a past which is now over. When we leave Constance at the end of the book she is only about 19, with her future all before her, although it presages to be a quiet one. This, however, we do not see; thus there is a gap of about 20 years between Margaret as we find her, and Constance as we leave her. This 20-year gap, between approximately 20 and 40, is the period that would be occupied with marrying and having children. Neither Constance nor Margaret have any training for anything but marriage, glorying as they do in all the traditional home-making feminine tasks. Hence the recourse to surrogate families, and to the division of the heroine into two, so that Jewsbury can avoid confronting directly the problem of showing what single women do when they should be marrying.

The fragmentation of the heroine into two in *Constance Herbert* indicates particularly clearly the tactics Jewsbury evolved to cope with the 'contradictions' she described within herself. Each heroine, in this and her other novels, represents one aspect of her life or character, but Jewsbury never presented herself fully in any one character. Her method of dividing herself into a series of heroines becomes an evasion, a device for maintaining irreconcilable elements, both within a novel and successively from one novel to another. Jewsbury as Heroine develops into an amorphous, contradictory disunity. She reproduces herself as Zoe, the exceptional woman and romantic lover; as Bianca, the successful professional woman; as Marian, the victim of materialist society, and as Constance, the renouncing spinster. These versions contract in their scope and optimism, and this contraction continues in her two last novels.

The Sorrows of Gentility reiterates Jewsbury's preoccupations with the inadequacies of female education, but from a significantly altered perspective. Where such education was earlier reviled for its constriction of women's potential, there is now little evidence of the novelist's faith in this potential. The heroine emerges as a smaller, blanker page than even the null Marian Withers, a provincial inn-keeper's daughter with social pretentions instilled through misdirected education above her station. Gertrude's aspiration is condemned as folly; she is forced to learn the 'dignity of fulfilling her duties in the station of life in which she had been placed'. The flaccid Gertrude redeeming herself through her commitment to her embroidery compares sadly with the flamboyant Zoe. The earlier search for grand answers to grandiose questions about the nature of womanhood is replaced by minimal characterization and small gestures towards duty and domesticity; the book as a whole appears thin and dispirited. That this diminishment corresponds

Jewsbury's intimate friend, Jane Carlyle.

with Jewsbury's decreasing faith in womanhood seems all the more probable in the light of her next, last and worst novel, **Right or Wrong**. . . . Here Jewsbury attempts her last division of herself, for the first time *within* one character, and for the first time the major protagonist is a man. Jewsbury seems to be exploring the possibility of a man succeeding where she herself has failed, in combining contradictions within himself. In order to explore this possibility Jewsbury forces her plot into bizarre absurdity. Father Paul leads a literal double life for 20 happy but illegal years: half the year a dutiful monk in a 'convent', the other half a respectable doctor, husband and father. . . . Not even the divinely-aided Father Paul, however, can sustain the exigencies of a dual existence. His failure is attributed partly to pragmatic considerations—his law-breaking is discovered—and partly to moral weakness. Father Paul has been guilty of excessive self-regard:

> 'Self-consciousness, the desire to bring my *me* to perfection that *I* might be beautiful or grand, was the rock on which I split.'

Thus Father Paul splits into two and provides Jewsbury with her answer to the question posed by the title of the book: the attempt to divide one's life is proved to be both illegal and wrong. (pp. 146-53)

The retrenchments of the later novels, the progressive retreat of her heroines from freedom and grandeur into duty, domesticity and diminishment, might have been due to the natural processes of aging; as she got older Jewsbury saw her life in a less romantic and optimistic light. Read chronologically, the novels can be seen to reveal a sad personal statement of failure. If writing the novels had provided Jewsbury with a means for the expression and justification of her various selves, as well as with a means with which to unite the apparently disunitable, these possibilities are foreclosed in the pessimistic conclusion of her last novel. (p. 153)

> J. M. Hartley, *"Geraldine Jewsbury and the Problems of the Woman Novelist,"* in Women's Studies International Quarterly, *Vol. 2, No. 2, 1979, pp. 137-53.*

MONICA CORREA FRYCKSTEDT   (essay date 1983)

[*Fryckstedt examines the numerous reviews of feminist books that Jewsbury wrote for the* Athenaeum, *documenting the author's opinions on the situation of women in Victorian society.*]

Between 1849 and 1880, one of mid-century England's most important literary magazines, the *Athenaeum*, published anonymously over 2300 reviews by Jewsbury, its most prolific woman-contributor. Whereas Jewsbury's novels are being subjected to increased examination, this vast body of her reviews has received no attention because of their inaccessibility. Impressive as Jewsbury's reviews are by sheer volume alone, one category of them is of particular interest—her reviews of feminist books. Obviously, anonymity affected Jewsbury's freedom of expression in these reviews. Knowing that the identity, sometimes even the sex, of the reviewer was unknown to the reader, she could pronounce her views with a frankness unparalleled in her novels. As a result, the *Athenaeum* reviews offer new insights into Jewsbury's stance on the woman question. (p. 51)

Jewsbury's novels reflect the author's concern with the woman question, first seriously debated in England in the 1840s and 50s. They advocate improved female education, expose the negative effects of prevailing marriage conventions and plead for meaningful occupations and a wider sphere of action for middle-class women. As Meredith Cary has shown, the heroines of Jewsbury's *Zoe* and *Constance Herbert* are remarkably unconventional [see excerpt dated 1974]. . . . What do the *Athenaeum* reviews then reveal that causes us to reconsider Jewsbury's attitude to the woman question, so perceptively examined by Cary? They show that although ahead of her time in creating unusual heroines, Jewsbury was very much a product of her age: her candid comments in reviews on influential mid-nineteenth century writers enable us now to relate her to the feminist movement and see her in a historical context. Furthermore, these new sources provide a more diversified picture of Jewsbury's state of mind than we have hitherto possessed, proving, for instance, that there was a time gap between her private and public positions and manifesting at times perplexing contradictions and dilemmas.

It is hardly a coincidence that 1855, the year that saw Jewsbury's first reviews of feminist books, also became a turning-point in her private life. Like Elizabeth Barrett Browning, Harriet Martineau, and Elizabeth Gaskell, she openly committed herself to the cause of women: she signed the petition to Parliament, requesting reform of the married women's property law. Jewsbury's involvement in the woman question gathers momentum in the late 50s and 60s, decades when responsible people witnessed with alarm the growing number of "surplus" women, the inability of "reduced gentlewomen" to earn their living and the inefficient training and limited range of employments available to women. So intense was the public debate that in 1862 Jewsbury complains that "every schoolboy seems to think he can solve all the difficulties of the Woman-question," and she even wishes that "women were *let alone* for a little while." But her weariness is apparent rather than real. For what she objects to is the condescending tone of the discussion; she deplores the fact that women are "talked at, lectured on, treated as curiosities of psychology" and regarded as "exceptional phenomena."

Jewsbury's objections arise from her convictions that women are rational beings endowed with immortal souls, and not, as many saw them, "a race of beautiful zebras," the mere "'property' of men, along with riches, houses, horses, and ancestral estates." Her argument that any amelioration of the plight of women is impossible until they learn to "consider themselves as rational beings," aligns her with Mary Wollstonecraft, and her praise of Emily Shirreff's *Intellectual Education and Its Influence on the Character and Happiness of Women* (1858) for treating women "as rational beings, with souls of their own to be saved," establishes her close kinship with this writer as well as with Margaret Fuller, who had given expression to this fundamental belief.

With an excess of nearly half a million women over men and with a work force comprising 3 million women in mid-nineteenth century England, the Victorian stereotype of woman as wife, mother, and guardian of the home gradually gave way to new ideas. Jewsbury's reviews show an acute awareness that women had to adapt themselves to a changing world and to seek wider spheres of action. "It is," she writes, "not a question whether it is a better or worse state of things, it is a fact." With a tinge of bitterness, she regrets that many women confronted the new conditions with such pain as to make them yearn for their traditional role: "God knows how thankful the majority of women would be, in these days, for homes to keep!" (pp. 52-3)

The preponderant number of women brought about a change of attitude towards spinsterhood: to be an "old maid" in the old days, Jewsbury writes, "was the consequent penalty for being either intensely ugly or extremely disagreeable," but, she continues, "all that is now changed." Her observation finds support in Frances Power Cobbe's claim that the "'old maid' of 1861 is an exceedingly cheery personage, running about untramelled by husband or children."

The surplus of women focused the attention of Victorians on marriage, and a growing frankness entered the discussion of marriage as an institution, the so-called marriage market and the prescribed role of the wife. . . . In view of the criticism of marriage manifest in Jewsbury's novels, it is hardly surprising that she should praise Margaret Fuller for representing ideal marriage as "the true heart union and life companionship between man and woman," and admire Fredrika Bremer for depicting the humiliation of marrying just to be supported. Evidently, Jewsbury's views on marriage are very similar to Shirreff's theory that "fear of poverty . . . and the want of definite occupation and station in society . . . drive many women to look to marriage as their only resource." (pp. 53-4)

Jewsbury's novels champion what might be termed the gospel of work and blame the lack of meaningful occupations for leading women into flirtation, unhappiness and even suicide. Unlike the novels, however, the reviews provide a detailed analysis of the problems facing women at work. Like other rights, Jewsbury says, women's right to work "must be redeemed." The reduced "gentlewoman" without any training

constitutes a pathetic figure whose "genteel, ineffectual labour" arouses contempt, she claims, because in her wages is "the element of *alms-giving*." Incapacity and inefficiency are seen as "the cause and the sting of humiliation." When the "amateur element" disappears from women's work, she argues, and "unemployed women take seriously to work it will bring about a social and political change, the extent of which cannot be foreseem or calculated." It sounds a modern note, reminiscent of our century's women's liberation movement, when Jewsbury demands that "women be brought up to work for their living" since "money is power." Moreover, in a curiously modern way she argues that women must be prepared to compete on equal terms in order to acquire recognition:

> . . . women should test what they can do by the same standard and the same tests that are applied to men. . . . Human beings can only thrive in an element of veracity. Protection is as fatal to moral and intellectual prosperity as it is to commercial development.

The *Athenaeum* reviews indicate that for Jewsbury work constituted the road to female emancipation. She predicts that "the two million and a half of women who earn their own bread are the leaven which is working a change in the whole state and condition of women." Acceptance of women's right to labour will indeed herald a new era: it will initiate a liberation that in Jewsbury's mind becomes their enfranchisement:

> . . . the "right to labour" is the noblest franchise that women have yet conquered. We speak of the right to labour on their own account as human beings, not to drudge as squaws and slaves. This is the true key to their "enfranchisement"; all the "privileges" will follow in their proper places—in their due season. It will be a great social revolution when women accept the fact, that when they earn their own living they rise . . . "from virtual pauperism to actual participation in the substantial benefits of society."
>
> (pp. 54-5)

Jewsbury's reviews manifest a strong moral bias on [the question of educating women]. Like Wollstonecraft, Mme de Staël and Fuller, she favoured the free development of women's talents and intellects. Education would be a means of strengthening the female mind and eradicating the code that prescribed, as Wollstonecraft put it, "gentleness, docility, and a spaniel-like affection" as cardinal virtues for women. It is evident, however, that on educational matters Jewsbury was, above all, a supporter of Emily Shirreff, whose *Intellectual Education* she acclaims for suggesting that "girls should be educated, not as though marriage was 'their beings' end and aim,' but as though marriage were to be the exception, and a single life the rule." Shirreff's method of education, Jewsbury claims, would "put an end to that 'eye service as men pleasers,' which has hitherto so spoiled and falsified the motives on which women have been brought up."

Jewsbury believed that in order to benefit from higher education, girls must be trained from childhood to regard work "as a natural condition, and not as a voluntary or exceptional state of things 'for a woman'." Only greater self-discipline and moral stamina would enable them to attain the same goals as men. Jewsbury's vision of the future of women is remarkable for its time, even if twentieth-century career women are beyond her horizon:

> The higher education of women will make a greater change in the habits of society than foreseen. If women are resolved to go in for thorough education like men, they must give up the triumphs of vanity. . . . Love,

marriage, and even flirtations, must be postponed: hard work and hard study must be the first consideration. Whether women will be sufficiently "strong-minded" to incur this cost remains to be seen.

In contrast to the novels, Jewsbury's reviews reveal her attitude to the legal status of women. The married women's property law, which classed married women together with "criminals, lunatics, and minors," gave husbands legal possession of their wives' property and destroyed not only their independence but their self-respect. As we have seen, Geraldine Jewsbury's was one of the 26,000 signatures on the petition which initiated the struggle resulting in the Married Women's Property Acts of 1870 and 1882. She agreed with Caroline Norton, whose *Letter to the Queen on Lord Chancellor Cranworth's Bill* (1855) she reviewed, that "the laws relating to the personal property of women call for alteration." Curiously enough, the reviews show that the customary link between women agitating for property reforms and those demanding female suffrage found no advocate in Jewsbury. In fact, she was averse to agitation for female suffrage and confessed in 1869 that "the franchise for women is that aspect of the question about which we feel least anxiety." She believed that as a result of adequate education, the franchise would come "at the right time, and as a matter of course." Jewsbury's gospel of work would eventually bring about the necessary changes: in the two and a half million unmarried working women lay "the germ of the 'enfranchisement'." Thus, while on the married women's property law she advocated interference, she envisaged a laissez faire solution for female suffrage; "like all questions," she argues, it "must work itself clear from *within,* it cannot be legislated from without."

Jewsbury's support of the laissez faire principle brings us to another topic of which there is no trace in the novels: she maintained that women had only themselves to blame for their oppression and should only look to themselves for redress. With such notions she tried to account for the reasons underlying the plight of innumerable Victorian women. They could only be free on the same terms on which nations acquire freedom, she claimed, "that of showing themselves capable of obtaining and holding it." For when women have manifested "strength of character" and "sound judgment," they have had, just like men, "power and influence and reverence accordingly." (pp. 55-6)

That Jewsbury, like Wollstonecraft and Fuller, blamed the lack of solidarity among women for preventing them from attaining their goals is also illustrated in the *Athenaeum* reviews. Time after time they strike the same note: women "are divided against themselves"; "they all seek their own"; the greatest obstacle for improving the status of English women "arises from the levity and egotism of women themselves." (p. 56)

A comparison between Jewsbury's letters to Jane Carlyle, written between 1841 and 1852, and her *Atheneaum* reviews reveals that a considerable time gap existed between her private and public positions. While public criticism of marriage hardly occurred until the 1860s, Jewsbury confessed her dreams of a better future as early as 1849 in a letter to her friend:

> . . . I believe we are touching on better days, when women will have a genuine, normal life of their own to lead. There, perhaps, will not be so many marriages, and women will be taught not to feel their destiny *manque* [sic] if they remain single. They will be able to be friends and companions in a way they cannot be now. All the strength of their feelings and thoughts will not run into love; they will be able to

associate with men, and make friends of them, without being reduced by their position to see them as lovers or husbands. Instead of having appearances to attend to, they will be allowed to have their virtues, in any measure which it may please God to send, without being diluted down to the tepid "rectified spirit" and "feminine grace" and "womanly timidity"—in short, they will make themselves women, as men are allowed to make themselves men. . . . I do not feel that either you or I are to be called failures. We are indications of a development of womanhood which as yet is not recognised.

In the 1860s, however, not only had "the utility, freedom, and happiness of a single woman's life . . . become greater," as Frances Power Cobbe asserted, but the Divorce Court had revealed so many appalling atrocities inflicted on English wives that "the *knowledge* of the risks of an unhappy marriage" had become "more public," and the concept of English domestic felicity was beginning to vanish. By 1869 such drastic changes had taken place in the climate of opinion that Jewsbury's public voice had caught up with her private one: she warns married women that submissiveness will lead to moral bondage: "They dare not and cannot stand upright; they are under a perpetual moral *courbature.* 'To avoid being blamed' is the great article of their code; they dare not and do not develop their faculties." (p. 57)

Another instance of this time gap is her views on education. Educated at school in the late 1820s, she rejected the traditional educational system she had been exposed to which stressed accomplishments rather than intellectual pursuits. In 1849 she wrote to Jane Carlyle:

> . . . I hope and believe that in a generation or two, women will be very different to what they have ever been yet . . . [rather than] being born and educated, having their manners and characters flavoured with certain qualities, . . . just to the point which may make them fancied as wives (for the tendency of all the training they get is just adapted to the prevailing fancy of men . . . a sort of ornamental ring-fence to their virtue, and . . . not for the saving of their own souls . . .).

Again, it took two decades until she could openly express similar convictions in the *Athenaeum*:

> The one deep, strong, intelligible cry that has arisen . . . is the demand of women for Education—to be taught thoroughly, to be taught well—to have the tools of work put into their hands that they may work like reasonable beings at skilled labour, and not like beasts of burden. Education has ceased, for women, to be ornamental: a mere additament to their powers of pleasing, they demand a thorough education, as a means to enable them to . . . earn their living with credit and reality, not to work to be paid for as disguise for alms.

In spite of Jewsbury's outspoken advocacy of women's rights, her reviews, unlike her novels, display at times what can only be called vacillation, almost as if she were torn by inner doubts about her role as a feminist. So, for instance, she will on occasion show a curious nostalgia for the past, for a time when the home constituted women's natural shelter. . . . While Jewsbury appreciated that the *Athenaeum* had "always done justice to the right of women to become all that heaven has made them capable of being and doing," she paradoxically mourned in another contribution "the misfortunes of women . . . who are exhorted to make themselves cooks, artists, architects, doctors of every degree, carpenters, painters, glaziers, apothecaries, chemists, printers.''

The modern reader is also puzzled by Jewsbury's contradictory statements on education. To say in 1860 that ''nobody . . . throws the smallest impediment in the way of any woman becoming as wise and well instructed as her nature will admit . . . nor have any women reason to complain that they are cramped 'by old traditions and rules of conventionality','' runs counter to the picture she eloquently draws in 1869, when she states that ''at present it is a thorough Education for women, the deliverance from all restrictions on learning, which is much more pressing than the inauguration of political privileges.''

Similarly, in view of Jewsbury's crusade against the legal oppression and undue submission of women, how are we to interpret her cryptical question: ''What *is* the emancipation of women?—what is it proposed to emancipate them from?'' Equally paradoxical is a review in which she approved of men who rejected ''strong-minded . . . emancipated females'' because they were ''disagreeable,'' while privately she mocked at a traditional English husband she had met for having no idea of ''what an 'emancipated woman' he was showing off to.''

It is true that these inconsistencies in Jewsbury's reviews are few, but they cannot be ignored and do not lend themselves easily to a satisfactory explanation. It is possible that, at times, they are a concession to pressures from a male dominated society, an attempt perhaps to palliate editor and reading-public with confirmations of their conservative opinions, something she had no reason to do in her private correspondence. It is equally conceivable that Jewsbury's vacillating attitude stems from inner personal conflicts which this emotional woman is likely to have experienced when she had to face the contradictory and deeply disturbing social problems that afflicted women in mid-nineteenth century England. Perhaps the closest we can come to an explanation is Jewsbury's own admission, in a letter to Jane Carlyle, that when women ''with literary reputations of their own . . . are recognised—their specialty spoils them as women'' and that she herself is at a loss to ''reconcile the contradictions into anything like a theory.'' Yet, these occasional inconsistencies and inner doubts can hardly detract from our overall picture of Geraldine Jewsbury as one of the most outspoken and progressive fighters for women's rights during Victorian times, and it is only now, one hundred years later, that we can fully appreciate what must have been a hard and lonely struggle. (pp. 57-9)

> *Monica Correa Fryckstedt, ''New Sources on Geraldine Jewsbury and the Woman Question,''* in Research Studies, *Vol. 51, No. 2, June, 1983, pp. 51-63.*

SHIRLEY FOSTER (essay date 1985)

[*Foster views Jewsbury's novels as overt challenges to conventional ideas regarding woman's place in society but emphasizes the ambivalent nature of many of her ideas on the woman question.*]

Victorian women novelists, . . . writing in the context of growing protest about the position of their own sex, echo the anxieties, anger, and ambivalence which . . . constitute the voice of mid-century feminism. The protesters, Janus-fashion, looked both ways: most of them genuinely believed that wifehood and motherhood represented the apotheosis of womanly fulfilment, yet they also recognised that since it was impossible that all women should achieve this fulfilment, society should stop promoting delusive ideologies and instead equip women to deal

with the changed circumstances; they acknowledged, too, that spinsterhood had its own rewards and that it was reprehensible to deny this. The novelists also looked both ways, reflecting the attitudes of their more overtly propagandist contemporaries. Their challenge is wide-ranging, from a tentative assertion of womanly independence to a celebration of the blessings of the single life, from muted dissent from the ideology of matrimonial bliss to an outright attack on masculine deficiencies and tyrannies, but underlying all of it is an awareness of the profound tensions between new visions of womanhood and the old traditions upon which their lives were founded and to which they still in part adhered. (p. 15)

Geraldine Jewsbury is an example of a novelist who expresses her dissent . . . overtly. As a recent article has argued, Jewsbury's fiction reflects the contradictions she herself experienced: the conflict of roles which . . . troubled many Victorian women writers, is expressed in her work through 'split' characters who enact the contrary pulls of womanly 'normality' and professional or spiritual independence [see excerpt by J. M. Hartley dated 1979]. (p. 27)

She delighted in her own unorthodoxy; she smoked cigars, used slang, relished the fact that her first novel *Zoë,* which treated sexual passion and religious apostasy, was widely regarded as 'outrageous', and upheld 'George Sandism' as her model of female authorship. She enjoyed informal friendships with the men encountered in her literary work—. . . perhaps vindicating her belief in future comradeship between men and women in which the women's feelings would not all run to love, and they would not be 'reduced by their position to see them [men] as lovers or husbands'. She was particularly critical of romantic creeds which forced women into undesired roles. Her strong sympathy for wronged wives, including Jane Carlyle, whom she regarded as the victim of a selfish husband and whose 'patience and endurance' had done nothing but perpetuate her wifely misery, is based on indignation at male attitudes towards women. She is highly scornful of the 'civility, or the sort of gallantry (God save the mark!) that adulterates all the little bit of straightforward dealing women meet with from men, and is the reason they do so little that is really worth anything!' Like the early feminist theorists, she views idealising images of womanhood as the creation of male fantasy; at present, she argues scathingly, 'the tendency of all the training they [women] get is just adapted to the prevailing fancy of men—a strong taste of housewifery in one generation, a dash of delicate 'feminine' stupidity in another, a gentle flavour of religion'. One of her dearest hopes for the future is that women will be released from constricting ideologies:

> I believe we are touching on better days, when women will have a genuine, normal life of their own to lead. There, perhaps, will not be so many marriages, and women will be taught not to feel their destiny *manqué* if they remain single.

(pp. 27-8)

Despite this vision of a new species of womanhood, Jewsbury retained many of the traditional assumptions about her sex. . . . Jewsbury sees that love will always be central in women's lives, and though she is wry about her own love affairs—'I don't think I ever shall have luck with my lovers'—she clearly lived on her emotions, and suffered considerable pain from her romantic involvements, including her stormily passionate friendship with Jane. She also acknowledges the importance of the mother/child relationship, and accepts that home duties, such as looking after a sick brother, must come before literary activities. . . . Like other Victorian women novelists, Jewsbury experienced the stressful dualities involved in being both woman and writer. . . . (p. 29)

What a phrenologist observer of Jewsbury termed her 'inconsistencies', but what may more accurately be called her ambivalence, plays a direct part in her novels. . . . [In *Zoë*, the] eponymous heroine diverges from feminine normality: educated like a boy and rebelling against social values, she is determined 'to make for herself, in spite of all obstacles, a destiny equal to all her vague dreams', but because she is a woman subject to parental and societal restraints she has no employment for her energies. Marriage comes to seem her only possible release, the only way of finding the freedom of a 'rational being'. Jewsbury's stance is, however, ambiguous. She shows how an aspiring woman is driven into the delusive bonds of matrimony because she can find nothing to satisfy her artistic or intellectual impulses, yet she also argues that female sublimity can be achieved only through romantic passion, which, as one character expresses it, 'in its highest manifestations, ceases to be a mere passion; it becomes a worship, a religion; it regenerates the whole soul'. Zoë falls in love with an apostate Roman Catholic priest, Everhard, who also has unfulfilled aspirations but who as a man can implement his unorthodoxy in an active vocation (he helps in a Welsh community, then goes to continue his work in Germany). Everhard's male achievement is contrasted with Zoë's female helplessness, while his love becomes a redeeming force, softening and purifying her and teaching her real 'moral beauty'. Yet because such passion tarnishes the traditional image of sinless womanhood, it cannot stand as the apotheosis of womanly fulfilment. Everhard has to be rejected; and when Zoë's second lover, the masterful Byronic Mirabeau, urges her to flee with him, she refuses on grounds of self-respect (like Jane Eyre, she is not prepared to accept the insecurity of an illegal liaison) and of maternal responsibility (she will not abandon her children). She is finally left a chastened and disappointed woman, embodying a stereotypical female resignation.

In *Zoë*, Jewsbury directly expresses the same ambivalence about female roles that we saw in her letters:

> [women] are by the very constitution of their being, passive, receptive; in proportion as a true feminine disposition is developed, the positive, the active, becomes uncongenial to their nature; and in exact proportion as woman becomes active, self-sufficing, subjective instead of objective, she is a grander character, of stronger and more heroic mould, but she approaches the nature of a man.

The dualities of the novel indicate her inability to resolve this paradox. She wants to assert the primacy of female individuality, but cannot envisage it divorced from emotional satisfaction; she recognises the inadequacies of conventional marriage, but cannot propose a more radical alternative of 'free' womanhood.

In *The Half Sisters*, Jewsbury breaks away from the impasse of defining womanly fulfilment solely in terms of idealised sexual passion. The two heroines—the half-sisters of the title—represent contrasting ways of confronting the restrictiveness of conventional female existence. Both aspire beyond trivial domesticity and both reject standard ideologies about female roles. But whereas the one's rebelliousness is positive and energetic, the other's is aimless and self-destructive. Alice Helmsby's aspirations are 'vague, undefined, restless', and she cannot free herself from the small-town attitudes which teach that wives should be quiet, efficient housekeepers and that spinsters are poor dreary creatures. She marries Bryant—a respectable, preoccupied businessman who does not understand her—and is stultified by matrimony; able to conceive of no higher goal than an exclusive, adoring love, she indulges in an undutiful passion for the fickle Percy Conrad, the strains of which finally kill her. The half-Italian orphan, Bianca, on the other hand, aims beyond merely emotional gratification by resolutely embarking on an acting career. Her high goal is art, the 'sacred necessity', and her professionalism confers on her a kind of supra-personal individuality. Consecrated by the nobility of her aim, she finds her own voice through creativity.

This sharpness of contrast is not maintained. Alice's dismal fate highlights the predicament of a woman who wants to achieve self-identity but is too feeble to escape from the interlocked alternatives of restrictive matrimony or unlicensed passion. Yet Bianca, apparently triumphing over this predicament, herself returns to female conventionality when she accepts a marriage proposal from her admirer, Lord Melton; she willingly accedes to his request that she leave the stage, now recognising her emotional needs and convinced that dedication to art is not woman's highest vocation. This apparent inconsistency in the novel is directly examined, and the duality it represents becomes a central theme. In a lengthy discussion, Melton and Conrad debate the issue of wifehood versus careers for women. Conrad's complacent male egotism is revealed in his uncompromising assertion that

> 'A woman who makes her mind public, or exhibits herself in any way, no matter how it may be dignified by the title of art, seems to me little better than a woman of a nameless class. . . . The intrinsic value of a woman's work out of her own sphere is nothing.'

For him, the ideal wife must have 'rational, though inferior intelligence . . . a gentle, graceful timidity . . . a sense of propriety . . . purity and delicacy of mind . . . she is the softened reflex of her husband's opinions—she does nothing *too* well!' Melton's scornful refutal clearly represents Jewsbury's own rejection of such chauvinistic conservatism. In contrast to Conrad, Melton believes that women 'never were intended to lead a purely *relative* life . . . I believe in the possibility of finding women who pursue art, for the love of art, and not for the glorification of themselves'. His arguments are expanded in a later chapter in which he, his sister (who sponsors model educational schemes for lower-middle-class girls), and Bianca discuss 'the condition of women'. As Bianca sees it, 'the true evil' is the purposelessness of unmarried women's lives; they need 'definite employment' such as she has had, which has given her 'a sense of freedom, of enjoyment of my existence, which has rendered all my vexations easy to be borne'.

Though no credence is given to Conrad's views, it is significant that both Melton and Bianca temper their protest with more conservative opinion. Melton claims that all women need 'wise guidance and government' in order for their aspirations to succeed, and Bianca, arguing for purposefulness in women's lives, resorts to the standard justification of early feminists:

> 'if you could furnish women with a definite object, or address motives in them fit to animate rational beings, you would have a race of wives and daughters far different from those which now flourish in your drawing-rooms . . . they would be able to aid men in

any noble object by noble thoughts, by self-denial,
by real sympathy and fellowship of heart.'

The second area of debate in the novel considers how far female artistic expression should be divorced from emotional feelings. Bianca believes that the 'unutterable mysteries' of the dramatic impulse are consecrated only by dedication to an object of love; though she momentarily accedes to the view of an old actor friend that art must be its own inspiration, she soon reasserts her conviction that to live 'a calm, self-sustained existence . . . like that of a priestess, cold, strong and pure . . . would not do, she needed some more human motive to sustain her'. The danger of an outer-directed woman's becoming 'cold' and unfeminine, touched on in *Zoë*, is illustrated here in the actress La Fornisari, who is egotistical and manipulative, and whose corrupted womanhood is symbolised by her guilty secret of a lost child. Bianca is saved from this fate: she retains true femininity through marriage and service to men. As in *Zoë*, Jewsbury reveals, but does not resolve, the dichotomies. She challenges limiting ideologies, but ultimately resorts to traditional images of womanhood—at the end, Bianca is merely a more successful version of Alice. As a contemporary reviewer sardonically observes [see excerpt by Henry Fothergill Chorley dated 1848], 'while Miss Jewsbury aspires to do battle with "Conventionalism" as a Dagon which is to be pulled down by every strong man and earnest woman, she adorns her heroine with most of its graces'; Conrad's fallacies with regard to womanly genius may be punctured, but 'the consolation which she accords to the unkindly used Bianca is a tacit admission of the justice of many of his—comments'.

Jewsbury's later novels rely even more heavily on the conventionalism which she is apparently trying to undermine. In *Marian Withers,* for instance, she both directs a quizzical look at marriage, especially when it is viewed merely as an escape from dreariness or a means of social elevation, and takes up her previous complaint that womanly genius can find no outlet or stimulation in a life of wearisome ennui. Her heroine, Marian, feels 'buried alive' as she struggles to realise her unfocused aspirations. But Jewsbury's solution is to provide Marian with a good husband, who gives her a purpose in life and a healthier moral outlook, which in this case means recognising that true womanly fulfilment is attained through duty and service. Female individuality here is asserted not through challenge to traditional roles (a professional career or ennobling passion) but through the orthodoxies of wifehood and Christian self-discipline.

One of her last novels, *Constance Herbert,* which George Eliot rightly criticised for its 'copy-book morality' and its confused approach to the subject of 'woman's true position' [see excerpt dated 1855], leaves its heroine unmarried at the end, but far from championing female singleness it aims to illustrate the familiar Victorian female ethic that obedience to duty is more blessed than personal emotional fulfilment. The novel's extraordinarily confused and unconvincing plot is built around the central issue of inherited insanity: Constance, her future determined by the unlikely coincidence of madness in both parents' families, nobly rejects an offer of marriage from the only man she could ever love, so as to save future generations from her doom; she is strengthened in her resolve by the comforting notion of moral rectitude as well as by the knowledge of her aunt's unhappy matrimonial experiences. Despite Jewsbury's assurance that for a woman it 'is no ignoble destiny to be allowed to sacrifice her hopes of a happy marriage, and of being the mother of children' for such a good cause, and that her heroine 'had not made the sacrifice of her life needlessly',

Constance's final state is distinctly dreary. Having nursed her father through his last illness—predictably involving mental collapse—she is left to run her own estate alone, having sacrificed her ideas of being loved to an acknowledgement of higher obligations than personal happiness; her only comfort (the false morality objected to by Eliot) is the realisation that the man she gave up was worthless anyway. Spinsterhood here takes on the sterotypical formulations of spiritually ennobling deprivation. Jewsbury's apparent increasing reluctance to confront openly the dichotomies she observes in women's experience is probably the result of the growing conservatism of middle-age. Her ultimate conventionality may seem disappointing, but she is nevertheless to be admired for directly voicing her more radical attitudes in her fiction and for allowing her novels to accommodate, if not satisfactorily to resolve, her own dualities. (pp. 30-4)

> *Shirley Foster, "Introductory: Women and Marriage in Mid-Nineteenth-Century England," in her* Victorian Women's Fiction: Marriage, Freedom and the Individual, *Croom Helm, 1985, pp. 1-39.*

ADDITIONAL BIBLIOGRAPHY

Cruikshank, Margaret. "Geraldine Jewsbury and Jane Carlyle." *Frontiers* IV, No. 3 (Fall 1979): 60-4.
>   A study of Jewsbury's relationship with Jane Carlyle from a lesbian feminist perspective.

Fahnestock, Jeanne Rosenmayer. "Geraldine Jewsbury: The Power of the Publisher's Reader." *Nineteenth-Century Fiction* 28, No. 3 (December 1973): 253-72.
>   An examination of Jewsbury's reports to Bentley and Son Publishers on the acceptability of submitted manuscripts. Fahnestock contends that Jewsbury's criteria for good fiction changed over the years, citing the liberal nature of her own novels and the conservativeness of these later reports.

Fryckstedt, Monica Correa. "Geraldine Jewsbury and *Douglas Jerrold's Shilling Magazine*." *English Studies* 66, No. 4 (August 1985): 326-37.
>   A discussion of six essays on social topics that Jewsbury wrote for *Douglas Jerrold's Shilling Magazine*. In the essays, Jewsbury considers such contemporary concerns as the unfair treatment of servants, women, and the lower classes in Victorian England.

——. *Geraldine Jewsbury's "Athenaeum" Reviews: A Mirror of Mid-Victorian Attitudes to Fiction.* Studia Anglistica Upsaliensia, edited by Gunner Sorelius, Sven Jacobsen, and Rolf Lunden, no. 61. Uppsala, Sweden: S. Academiae Ubsaliensis, 1986, 163 p.
>   Studies the 2,300 book reviews Jewsbury contributed to the *Athenaeum,* asserting that her tastes in fiction reflected those of the mid-Victorian reading public.

Griest, Guinevere L. "Readers, Reactions, and Restrictions." In her *Mudie's Circulating Library and the Victorian Novel,* pp. 120-55. Bloomington: Indiana University Press, 1970.
>   An analysis of Jewsbury's publishers' reports.

Howe, Susanne. *Geraldine Jewsbury: Her Life and Errors.* London: George Allen & Unwin, 1935, 236 p.
>   The only book-length biography of Jewsbury. This work also summarizes most of her novels and documents their critical reception.

Ireland, Mrs. Alexander. Introduction to *Selections from the Letters of Geraldine Endsor Jewsbury to Jane Welsh Carlyle*, by Geraldine Jewsbury, edited by Mrs. Alexander Ireland, pp. v-xviii. London: Longmans, Green, and Co., 1892.

    A biographical sketch.

Maison, Margaret M. "The Tragedy of Unbelief." In her *The Victorian Vision: Studies in the Religious Novel*, pp. 209-41. New York: Sheed & Ward, 1961.

    Examines *Zoe* as a novel of religious doubt.

Thomson, Patricia. "Georgy Sandon." In her *George Sand and the Victorians: Her Influence and Reputation in Nineteenth-Century England*, pp. 137-51. New York: Columbia University Press, 1977.

    Marks the influence of George Sand on *Zoe* and *The Half-Sisters*.

(Conte) Giacomo (Talegardo Francesco di Sales Saverio Pietro) Leopardi

1798-1837

Italian poet, prose writer, translator, and editor.

Recognized as the foremost Italian poet of the nineteenth century, Leopardi is primarily known for his formulation of a profoundly pessimistic philosophy. In the majority of his poems, Leopardi expressed his feelings of anguish and his bleak view of the human condition. These despairing works, like his patriotic *canzoni,* or songs, lamenting the loss of national pride and heroism in nineteenth-century Italy, are widely acclaimed for their exquisite lyricism. Leopardi also composed a number of prose works in which he set forth his philosophy of pessimism. Most notable among these are the *Operette morali (Essays and Dialogues),* a series of prose poems, essays, and fictional dialogues between historical and imaginary figures, and his *Zibaldone,* or daily notebook, containing his informal jottings on such subjects as his theory of poetry and the development of his art. In addition to these achievement, Leopardi is recognized for his accomplishments as a classical scholar, translator, and linguist. Though not widely known in his lifetime, Leopardi has since been heralded as the greatest Italian poet since Dante. Not only is he recognized as an important figure in Italian Romanticism, but he is also regarded as a masterful stylist, one of the most distinguished scholars of his era, and an eminent Italian patriot.

Leopardi was born into a family of the lesser Italian nobility. His father, Count Monaldo Leopardi, dabbled in literature, philosophy, and politics, amassing a substantial library that reflected his wide interests. His impractical nature and inability to manage finances led to losses in the family fortune; consequently, Leopardi's mother, the Marquess Adelaide Antici, took control of their money. Described as a domineering and unemotional woman, she established an austerely religious home, encouraging her children to renounce worldly activity and devote themselves to an ecclesiastical calling. Leopardi, the eldest child, proved a precocious student, and by the age of fourteen he had surpassed the learning of the itinerant priest who was his tutor. Thereafter, he was allowed to freely use his father's extensive library, where he studied classical literature, the sciences, philosophy, and linguistics, and taught himself English, French, Spanish, and Hebrew. He read hundreds of pages daily, wrote commentaries on the ancient texts, and translated Moschus's lyrics and Homer's satires, among other works. At the age of fifteen he wrote "Storia dell' astronomia" (A History of Astronomy), an exhaustive survey based on a bibliography of over three hundred works, followed in 1815 by *Saggio sopra gli errori popolari degli antichi* (Essay on the Popular Errors of the Ancients), an exposition on superstitions and popular culture of the past. While still a teenager, Leopardi achieved such a degree of proficiency in classical Greek literature that a work of his own composition, "Hymn to Neptune," was mistaken for an ancient text by the most respected scholars of his day.

While Leopardi was successful in scholarly pursuits, he suffered from numerous physical ailments (many attributed to his

excessive study and lack of physical activity) and from a profound sense of isolation, melancholy, and boredom, which he described as *noia,* that was to plague him throughout his life. Early disappointments in love added to his dejection, leaving him bitterly aware of his hunched back, failing vision, and general ill-health and further emphasizing his isolation. In 1817 he began to record his thoughts and feelings in a daybook, later published as *Pensieri di varia filosofia e di bella letteratura* but better known as the *Zibaldone,* which he was to maintain until 1832. Between 1817 and 1821 Leopardi initiated correspondences with a number of prominent writers, including the Swiss classicist Louis De Sinner, the publisher Antonio Stella, and the Italian patriots Pietro Giordani and Antonio Ranieri. In 1818, after a visit with Giordani, Leopardi was inspired to compose two of his best-known poems, the patriotic "Al' Italia" ("To Italy") and "Sopra il monumento di Dante" ("On the Projected Monument to Dante"), in which he urged his countrymen to reestablish the glory of Italy's past. Leopardi's correspondents also fueled his desire to escape the restraints of his birthplace, Recanati, an isolated rural village, and in 1819, with the help of his younger brother, he attempted to run away from home, only to be detained when his parents discovered the endeavor. Compelled to remain in the family home due to his lack of money, Leopardi continued his studies, but came to place a greater emphasis on his own writing, composing at this time several of his most admired poems, including "L'infinito" ("The Infinite"), "Alla luna" ("To the Moon"), "Alla primavera" ("To the Spring"), and "Bruto minore" ("Brutus"). When in 1822 Leopardi had the opportunity to travel to Rome, he was disappointed by the lack of stimulating society he found there and thought the urban atmosphere generally oppressive. Furthermore, he was unable to find congenial employment: an avowed agnostic and Italian patriot, Leopardi was ideologically, as well as physically, unsuited for the clerical and academic posts available to him in his Roman Catholic and politically suppressed surroundings. He therefore determined to pursue his ambitions of literary greatness. After a few months in Rome he returned to Recanati, where he devoted much of his time to composing the works that constitute the *Operette morali*. Following the publication of his first collection of poetry, *Canzoni*, in 1824, Leopardi once again left his hometown, returning only intermittently for the rest of his life. Traveling first to Milan and Bologna, he supplemented his income by editing the works of Cicero, writing a commentary on Petrarch, and compiling two anthologies of Italian literature. In the early 1830s, while living in Florence, Leopardi was forced to accept the aid of friends, for he was unable to support himself by his writings despite the publication of a new collection of poems, *Canti*. In Florence he fell in love with Fanny Targioni-Tozzetti, and his hopeless passion for her inspired three of his saddest poems—"Il pensiero dominante," "Amore e morte" ("Love and Death"), and "Consalvo." In 1833, aided by a stipend from his family, Leopardi was able to move to Naples, where he lived in the company of his friend and confidant, Ranieri, and Ranieri's sister, Paolina. In his last years, Leopardi became increasingly ill and despondent, particularly discouraged by his failed romance with Fanny and by the suppression of his works by the pro-Austrian government then in control of Italy. Leopardi died in 1837 of pulmonary failure resulting from his long-standing illnesses.

The concept of *noia* pervades all of Leopardi's works, and scholars have studied both his poetry and prose in documenting his philosophy. At first convinced that others enjoyed the happiness he himself never experienced, Leopardi later came to believe that happiness, love, and beauty are mere illusions and that all human life is meaningless and filled with sadness. According to Leopardi, true happiness can exist only for children, whose illusions have not yet been destroyed by reason, science, and knowledge. Leopardi denied the possibility of hope and the existence of God; to him nature was hostile, progress led to evil, and death was the only escape from the anguish of life. In such a world, he concluded, it was better never to have been born. Nonetheless, he was unable to advocate suicide, and he acknowledged the necessity of beauty and joy to human existence. For Leopardi, great works of literature were a source of beauty: "the very recognition of the irremediable vanity and falseness of all things great and beautiful is itself a great and beautiful thing which fills the soul, when the recognition comes through works of genius." The anguish of Leopardi's outlook is fully expressed in his poems, notably in such important works as "Canto notturno di un pastore errante dell'Asia" ("Night Song of a Wandering Shepherd in Asia"), which describes the absolute isolation of a nomadic shepherd whose alienation from nature leads him to contemplate the meaninglessness of the universe, and "La sera del dí di festa" ("Eve of the Holiday"), a lament contrasting the boredom of everyday life with the excited anticipation surrounding an annual village celebration. Other poems regarded

among Leopardi's masterpieces include "The Infinite," in which he contemplates the vastness of the universe in relation to human limitations, "A Silvia" ("To Silvia"), an elegy on the early death of a peasant girl, and his final poem, "La ginestra" ("The Broom"), in which he explores nature's hostility to humanity. In addition to studying Leopardi's ideas, critics have devoted considerable attention to his style. A painstaking, careful writer, Leopardi valued straightforward language. His poetic style is frequently praised for its simple, classical elegance, linguistic grace, and vivid imagery; indeed, some critics consider the lucidity of his lyric expression to be his greatest poetic achievement.

Leopardi's prose works deal with many of the same concerns examined in his poetry. The writings contained in his *Operette morali* are marked by a melancholy, disenchanted outlook. His tone ranging from sardonic satire to light irony, Leopardi expresses his views on death, the essentially hostile nature of the universe, the impossibility of happiness, illusion and reality, and the search for truth. His "Storia del genere umano" ("History of the Human Race"), one of the better-known *operette morali*, chronicles the disillusionment of humanity: happiness and beauty evaporate when confronted by truth, and the human race is left in complete misery, its only hope being the attainment of love, a pursuit the poet views as illusory and futile. In another of the *Operette morali*, "Dialogo di un venditore d'almanacchi e di en passegere" ("Dialogue between an Almanac Peddler and a Passer-By"), Leopardi concludes that intelligence and reason only contribute to unhappiness, for those with greater understanding are more fully aware of their misery. One of his most outstanding fictional dialogues, "Dialogo di Federico Ruysch e dell sue mummie" ("Dialogue between Frederick Ruysch and His Mummies"), likens death to a pleasurable slumber.

During his lifetime Leopardi was highly respected by his contemporaries and acclaimed for his scholarship, although most of his works were not widely known. After his death, Ranieri edited a collection of his writings, declaring in his introduction that Leopardi was unquestionably the greatest Italian poet since Dante. During the remainder of the nineteenth century, Leopardi enjoyed the high regard of his compatriots; not only was he the most beloved Italian lyric poet, his patriotic works were adopted as expressions of Italian nationalism. Outside his homeland he was acclaimed by such diverse readers as Henry Crabb Robinson, George Henry Lewes, William Ewart Gladstone, and James Thomson. Nineteenth-century English-language critics, reading Leopardi's works either in Italian or in translation, typically praised Leopardi's style, his expression of emotion, and the beauty of his imagery. Nonetheless, most reviewers felt compelled to decry his agnosticism and pessimism.

A number of modern critics have attempted to document the development of Leopardi's philosophic system, looking not only to his poetry and the *Operette morali* for insights, but also to the *Zibaldone*, his letters, and the *Pensieri*, a miscellany of aphorisms he composed between 1834 and 1837. Some scholars, while acknowledging that Leopardi's philosophy is thoroughly pessimistic, have concluded that he eventually came to espouse a humanistic outlook in his belief that people should be united through their common bond of suffering. Others, however, have questioned the validity of his thought, suggesting that his pessimism was merely a reflection of the unhappy circumstances of his own life rather than a coherent, fully developed philosophy with universal application. In addition to examining the development of Leopardi's pessimism and analyzing his themes as they relate to his philosophy, twentieth-century critics have considered his writings in relation to classicism and European Romanticism. While Leopardi had little or no contact with the key figures of English and German Romanticism, his career demonstrates parallel developments in both form and subject matter. He ultimately rejected the classical forms of his early poetry in favor of the personal lyric, and many commentators have also cited his subjectivity and his belief that imagination, not reason, is the source of poetic inspiration as evidence of Romantic inclinations. In addition, Leopardi's key themes—alienation, nationalism, heroism, and the negative aspects of progress—link him with the Romantic outlook. Yet many critics point out that, in terms of language, his style remained essentially classical, noting that he vehemently attacked the excessive and overblown manner he associated with the Romantics, preferring instead simple, clear diction.

Leopardi is recognized as one of the greatest writers in the history of modern Italian literature. For their influence on Italian Romanticism, for their forthright expressions of personal despair, and for their simple, polished style, Leopardi's poems are considered his most notable achievement. His prose works, however, also continue to be studied and admired for their masterful style and for the light they shed on his poetic themes. Not only have Leopardi's works inspired a large body of Italian and English-language criticism, they continue to appeal to readers in the twentieth century as explorations of timeless themes. As Ottavio M. Casale remarked, "Leopardi reminds us of what it is to be a poet and what it is to be human."

PRINCIPAL WORKS

Saggio sopra gli errori popolari degli antichi　(prose) 1815

Canzoni del Conte Giacomo Leopardi　(poetry)　1824; also published as *Versi del Conte Giacomo Leopardi* [enlarged edition], 1826

Operette morali　(essays, fictional dialogues, and prose poetry)　1827; enlarged edition, 1836
　[*Essays and Dialogues of Giacomo Leopardi*, 1882; also translated as *Essays, Dialogues and Thoughts of Giacomo Leopardi*, 1905]

I canti　(poetry)　1831; enlarged edition, 1835
　[*Canti*, 1962]

Paralipomeni della Batracomiomachia　(satire)　1842
　[*The War of the Mice and the Crabs*, 1976]

Opere di Giacomo Leopardi. 6 vols.　(poetry, essays, fictional dialogues, aphorisms, and letters)　1845-49

Pensieri di varia filosofia e di bella letteratura—("*Lo Zibaldone*"). 7 vols.　(prose)　1898-1900

The Poems of Leopardi　(poetry)　1923

Epistolario di Giacomo Leopardi. 7 vols.　(letters) 1934-41

Tutte le opere di Giacomo Leopardi. 5 vols.　(poetry, prose, fictional dialogues, essays, aphorisms, prose poetry, and letters)　1937-49

Poems from Giacomo Leopardi　(poetry)　1946

Giacomo Leopardi: Selected Prose and Poetry　(poetry, prose, and fictional dialogues)　1966

A Leopardi Reader　(poetry, prose, aphorisms, and letters) 1981

GIACOMO LEOPARDI　(letter date 1817)

[*In this excerpt from the letter that initiated his correspondence with the notable Italian patriot and anti-Romantic writer Pietro Giordani, Leopardi briefly expresses his literary aspirations. For additional commentary by Leopardi, see excerpts dated 1817 and 1820.*]

I have known you only through your writings, for here where I live, not a soul discusses literary men. But I do not know how one can admire a writer's qualities—especially when they are great and striking—without coming to like the person too. When I read Virgil, I fall in love with him. And I do so even more with the great contemporaries, who are so few, as you rightly point out. . . .

I possess an extremely great, perhaps immoderate and insolent, desire for glory, but I cannot stand it when people praise things of mine which do not please me, nor do I know why they reissue them with more damage to me than profit to those who do so without my knowledge. . . . (p. 30)

As a teacher, you say that translating is very rewarding at my age, a sure proposition which my own practice has made most clear to me. For when I read one of the classics, my mind seethes and grows confused. So then I begin to translate as best I can, and those beauties, by necessity scrutinized and mulled over one by one, fix themselves in my imagination, enrich it, and bring peace to me. Your judgment renews me and encourages me to continue.

Do not speak to me of Recanati. It is so dear to me as to suggest ideas for a dissertation on "Hatred for One's Birthplace." . . . But my country is Italy, for which I burn with love, thanking heaven for making me an Italian, for ultimately our literature, even though little cultivated, is the only legitimate daughter of the only two truly great ancient ones. . . . You can rest assured that if I live, I will do so for literature, because I cannot live for anything else, nor do I wish to. (p. 31)

> Giacomo Leopardi, in a letter to Pietro Giordani on March 21, 1817, in his A Leopardi Reader, *edited and translated by Ottavio M. Casale, University of Illinois Press, 1981, pp. 30-1.*

GIACOMO LEOPARDI　(letter date 1817)

[*In this excerpt from a letter to Pietro Giordani, Leopardi complains of his poor health and uncongenial surroundings before discussing his preference for poetry over prose. For further material by Leopardi, see excerpts dated 1817 and 1820.*]

You recommend moderation in my studies with such warmth and evident concern that I wish to open my heart to you and let you know the feelings that reading your words has awakened in me, feelings which will never, never die unless the heart changes form and substance. To answer as best I can to such affection, I will tell you that my health is not just weak but excessively so; and I will not deny that it has been a bit affected by the labors to which I subjected it the last six years. But now I have reduced them considerably: I do not study more than six hours a day, often less; I write almost nothing; I regularly read the classics of the three languages in small volumes easily carried about, so that I must always study in the mode of the Peripatetics; and—*quod maximum dictu est*—I often endure for hours and hours the torment of sitting with my hands in my lap.

Who would have dreamed Giordani would leap to the defense of Recanati? . . . The cause is too desperate for a single good advocate—or a hundred. It's all very well to say that Plutarch loved his Chaeronea and Alfieri his Asti. They loved them but did not live there. So I too shall love my birthplace when I am far away from it; meanwhile, I say I hate it because I am in it, since this poor town is guilty only of not having offered me one good thing besides my family. It is sweet and beautiful to remember the place where one has spent his childhood. Yet it is too easy to say: "Here you were born and here Providence wants you to stay." Say to a sick man, "If you try to heal yourself, you are fighting Providence." . . . These maxims verge on Fatalism. "But here you are a large fish in a small pond; in a larger city it will be otherwise." This seems to me a low form of pride, one unworthy of a noble spirit. One wants to excel in virtue and genius, and who can deny that these qualities shine infinitely more in great cities than in small? . . .

"But here you could be more useful than elsewhere." In the first place, I do not like the thought of spending my life on this little group, of renouncing everything else to live and die for them in a cave. I do not think nature made me for this, nor that virtue requires of me such a fearsome sacrifice. Second, do you really believe that the Marches and southern Italy are like Romagna and northern Italy? There the word "literature" is often heard. There they have papers, academies, discussion groups, and bookshops in great number. Gentlemen read a little. Ignorance is for the masses, who wouldn't be the masses without it. But many try to study and many fancy themselves poets and philosophers; they may not really be such but they at least try. . . . Here, my dear Sir, everything is dead, everything is foolishness and stupidity. Foreigners are amazed at this silence, this universal sleep. Literature is a sound unheard of. The names of Parini, Alfieri, Monti, Tasso, and Ariosto have to be explained. There is no one who wants to be something else, not a one for whom the name of ignorant seems strange. They call each other that sincerely and know they speak the truth. Do you think a great mind would be esteemed here? As a pearl in a dung-heap. . . . Indeed, I will tell you without any boasting that our library has no equal in the province and only two inferiors. On the door it is written that this library is for citizens too and all are welcome. Now how many do you think frequent it? Never a one. . . .

In my early days, my head was full of modern principles and I scorned and loathed studying our language. All my first scribblings were translations from French; I disdained Homer, Dante, and all the classics; I would not read them; and I gloried in reading what I now detest. What made me change my tune? The grace of God, but no man certainly. Who urged me to learn the languages necessary to me? The grace of God. Who keeps me from blundering at every turn? No one. But let's suppose all of this means nothing. What is there that is beautiful in Recanati that a man would care to see or learn? Nothing. Now God has made this world of ours so lovely, men have created so many beautiful things, there are so many men who anyone but an insensate would long to see and know, and earth is rich with wonders—and should I, at eighteen, say that I will live and die in this pit where I was born? Do you think that one can restrain these desires? That they are wrong, excessive, wild? That it is madness not to content oneself with seeing nothing, not to content oneself with Recanati?

Someone has misinformed you that the air of this town is healthy. It is most changeable, damp, salty, hard on the nerves, and because of its thinness unsuitable to some constitutions.

Add to this the stubborn, black, horrendous, barbarous melancholy that wears away and devours me, and grows and grows whether I study or not. I well know, for I used to experience it, the sweet melancholy, sweeter than happiness, which gives birth to beauty. That kind of melancholy is, if I may speak so, like twilight whereas this one is densest night and horrible; it is a poison, as you say, that destroys the powers of body and soul. Now how shall I free myself from it while I do nothing but think and feed on thinking, with no distractions in the world? And how should the effect cease if the cause does not? And what do you mean by amusements? The only diversion in Recanati is studying: the only distraction is that which kills me—everything else is *noia*. . . .

You say that when one's intellect has matured to enough firmness so as to know with some surety where nature is calling it, one must necessarily begin writing prose rather than poetry. With this I must take issue. One can easily err when analyzing one's self, but I will tell you what I think has happened and is happening to me.

From the time I began to recognize a little what beauty is, only the poets aroused in me the keen desire to translate and make my own what I read; only nature and passion have led me to that rage to compose, but to compose in a forceful and elevated way, making my soul expand in all its parts and say within me: "This is poetry indeed, and I need verse, not prose, to express what I feel." And so I gave myself to poetry. Won't you allow me now to read Homer, Virgil, Dante and the other sublime poets? I do not think I could abstain, because I taste in reading them a pleasure beyond words; and very often, when I have been quiet, alone, and thinking of something entirely different, a verse of a classical author, by chance recited by a member of my family, makes me catch my breath and compels me to follow it. And when, in an hour friendly to the Muses, I have been alone in my study with my mind placid and free, and have picked up Cicero so as to try by reading him to lift my mind, I have been so distressed by the slow heaviness of that prose that I could not continue but took up Horace instead. And if you concede me these readings, can you expect me to recognize their greatness, to savor and analyze each separate beauty, without launching out after them?

Whenever I look at nature here in these truly pleasant surroundings (the only good thing my birthplace has), and in this time of year especially, I feel myself so completely transported that it would be a mortal sin to pay no heed, to let the ardor of youth go by, to wish to be a good prose-writer, and to postpone poetry a score of years—after which, first, I will not exist; second, these thoughts will have fled; or my mind will have grown colder or cooler than it is now. I need scarcely add that if nature calls one to poetry, one must ignore everything else to follow it; indeed, I think it manifest that poetry demands infinite toil and study, and that poetic art is so profound that the more one advances the more one realizes that perfection exists somewhere beyond what one had imagined. . . . (pp. 31-4)

Giacomo Leopardi, in a letter to Pietro Giordani on April 30, 1817, in his A Leopardi Reader, *edited and translated by Ottavio M. Casale, University of Illinois Press, 1981, pp. 31-4.*

GIACOMO LEOPARDI   (essay date 1820)

[*Leopardi describes the progress of his creative development in this excerpt from his* Zibaldone. *For further commentary by Leopardi, see excerpts dated 1817 and 1820.*]

In my poetic career my spirit has followed the same course as the human spirit in general. At first imagination was my strong point, my verses were full of images, and I always sought in my reading of poetry to profit in terms of the imagination. I was also very sensitive to emotions, but I knew not how to express them in poetry. I had not really thought about things, and of philosophy I had only a glimmer (a vague one at that), and I shared the usual illusion we have, that in life and the world there must always be an exception in our favor. I have always been unfortunate, but my misfortunes then were full of life and made me despair only because I felt (not reasonably but in my active imagination) that they deprived me of happiness, something others enjoyed. In sum my state was thoroughly like that of the ancients. . . .

The total transformation in me, and the passing from the ancient to the modern condition, occurred more or less in one year, 1819, when deprived of the use of my eyes and of the constant absorption of reading, I began to feel my unhappiness much more darkly; to abandon hope; to meditate deeply about things. (In these writings, for example, I wrote in that one year almost twice as much as I had in the preceding year and a half, and on subjects regarding our nature, as opposed to the generally literary thoughts of my earlier efforts.) I began to become a philosopher instead of the poet I used to be; to feel the certain infelicity of the world instead of just recognizing it—and this was partly due to a lethargic physical state which all the more distanced me from the ancients and brought me closer to modern men.

My imagination then was greatly enfeebled, and as much as the inventive faculty actually grew larger in me (indeed seemed to be born), it inclined chiefly toward either prose matters or sentimental poetry. And if I set myself to writing verses, the images came with great difficulty. Although my verses overflowed with sentiment, my fancy was in fact nearly dried up (even apart from poetry, such as in contemplating beautiful natural scenes, etc., as now when I remain hard as stone). Thus it can be fairly said in all rigor that the ancients were, above all, poets, and now none are as poetic as children or the young, and the moderns who take this name are but philosophers. And I, in fact, did not become sentimental until I had lost my imagination and had become insensitive to nature, totally dedicated to reason and truth—in sum, a philosopher. (pp. 49-50)

> *Giacomo Leopardi, in an extract from a journal entry on July 1, 1820, in his* A Leopardi Reader, *edited and translated by Ottavio M. Casale, University of Illinois Press, 1981, pp. 49-50.*

GIACOMO LEOPARDI   (essay date 1820)

[*In the passage from his* Zibaldone *excerpted here, Leopardi describes the state of mind necessary for poetic composition. For additional material by Leopardi, see excerpts dated 1817 and 1820.*]

[The] period of enthusiasm, heat, and agitated imagination is not right [for poetic creation]; indeed it works against it. One needs a time of intensity, but tranquil intensity, a time of real genius rather than real excitement . . . , an impression of past or future or habitual emotion rather than its actual presence—one could say its twilight rather than its bright noon. Often the best moment occurs when, the feeling or impulse being over, the mind though calm surges up again after the storm, as it were, to pleasurably recall the past sensation. That is perhaps the aptest time for conceiving an original subject or the original

parts of it. We can say generally that in poetry and the fine arts, demonstrations of excitement, imagination, and sensibility are the direct fruit of the author's memory of the enthusiasm rather than of the enthusiasm itself.

> *Giacomo Leopardi, in an extract from a journal entry on October 2, 1820, in his* A Leopardi Reader, *edited and translated by Ottavio M. Casale, University of Illinois Press, 1981, p. 55.*

GIACOMO LEOPARDI   (essay date 1820?)

[*In this excerpt from* Zibaldone, *most likely written in 1820, Leopardi outlines his view of the role of art as it relates to his pessimism. For further remarks by Leopardi, see excerpts dated 1817 and 1820.*]

Works of genius have this in common, that even when they vividly capture the nothingness of things, when they clearly show and make us feel the inevitable unhappiness of life, and when they express the most terrible despair, nonetheless to a great soul—though he find himself in a state of extreme duress, disillusion, nothingness, *noia*, and despair of life, or in the bitterest and *deadliest* misfortunes (caused by deep feelings or whatever)—these works always console and rekindle enthusiasm; and though they treat or represent only death, they give back to him, at least temporarily, that life which he had lost.

And so that which in real life grieves and kills the soul, opens and revives the heart when it appears in imitations or other works of artistic genius (as in lyric poems, which are not properly imitations). Just as the author, in describing and strongly feeling the emptiness of illusions still retained a great store of illusions—which he proved by so intensely describing their emptiness—so the reader, no matter how disenchanted *per se* and through his reading, is pulled by the author into that very illusion hidden in the deepest recesses of that mind the reader was experiencing. And the very recognition of the irremediable vanity and falseness of all things great and beautiful is itself a great and beautiful thing which fills the soul, when the recognition comes through works of genius. And the very spectacle of nothingness presented seems to expand the soul of the reader, to exalt it, and reconcile it to itself and to its own despair. (A tremendous thing and certainly a source of pleasure and enthusiasm—this magisterial effect of poetry when it works to allow the reader a higher concept of self, of his woes, and his own depressed, annihilated spirit.)

Moreover, the feeling of nothingness is that of a dead and death-producing thing. But if this feeling is alive, as in the case I mean, its liveliness dominates in the reader's mind the nothingness of the thing it makes him feel; and the soul receives life (if only briefly) from the very power by which it feels the perpetual death of things and of itself. Not the smallest or least painful effect of the knowledge of great nothingness is the indifference and numbness which it almost always inspires about that very nothingness. This indifference and insensibility is removed by reading or contemplating such a work: it renders us *sensible* to nothingness. . . . (pp. 55-6)

> *Giacomo Leopardi, in an extract from a journal entry in 1820? in his* A Leopardi Reader, *edited and translated by Ottavio M. Casale, University of Illinois Press, 1981, pp. 55-6.*

[GEORGE HENRY LEWES]   (essay date 1848)

[*Lewes was one of the most versatile men of letters in the Victorian era. A prominent English journalist, he was the founder, with Leigh Hunt, of the* Leader, *a radical political journal he edited from 1851 to 1854. He also served from 1865 to 1866 as the first editor of the* Fortnightly Review, *another journal he helped to establish. Critics often cite Lewes's influence on the novelist George Eliot, to whom he was companion and mentor, as his principal contribution to English letters, but they also credit him with critical acumen in his literary commentary, most notably in his dramatic criticism. In the following excerpt from an introductory overview of Leopardi's life and works, Lewes outlines Leopardi's literary career, his place in the tradition of European Romanticism, and his philosophy of despair and pessimism.*]

Giacomo Leopardi is a name which makes the heart of almost every cultivated Italian beat with a certain sorrowful pity and a noble pride. To English ears it is a mere sound signifying nothing. It calls up no sweet memories of harmonious verse; it brings with it no compassion for the sufferings of a sad and struggling spirit. The first occasion an Englishman ever mentioned the name in print was, we believe, in a recent novel. Yet Germany has long known and cherished Leopardi. Even France, generally so backward in acknowledging a foreigner, has, on several occasions, paid tribute to his genius. (p. 659)

Leopardi's mental history is crowded with striking contrasts. We see him learned even among the erudite, and, at the same time, a great poet; at one period grubbing like an archæologist, covered with the dust of folios; at another, borne away on the irresistible wings of upward-soaring imagination. Nor is this all. The man who, with exquisite taste, appreciated the severe simplicity of the great works of Grecian art, first learned to know Greece through the tawdry rhetoric of the Fathers; and the bard who, of all others, deserves to be called the 'poet of despair'—whose scepticism exceeds that of *Manfred* or even *Lélia*—began by planning sacred hymns of fervent piety.

Leopardi was self-taught. The limited instruction which he gained from two ecclesiastics was insignificant by the side of that which he acquired for himself. Unaided, he studied French, Spanish, English, Greek, and even Hebrew; the latter sufficiently to enter upon disputations with some learned Jews at Ancona. His studies had not, however, that desultoriness which is usually noticeable among self-taught men, but were almost exclusively philological. Thus, before he attained maturity, we find him compiling commentaries on the rhetoricians of the second century; writing his erudite little treatise on the vulgar errors of the ancients; collecting the fragments of the Fathers of the second century; translating and dissertating on the *Batrachomyomachia;* throwing new light upon the life of Moschus, and translating the *Idylls;* translating the *Odyssey,* Hesiod's *Theogony,* and the second book of the *Æneid.* A strange preparation for a poet! As examples of mere erudite industry, such exploits would have done honour to a long career; as the productions of a boy, they excite unmingled astonishment.

The love of mystification joined to a consciousness of power, which dictated the forgeries of Chatterton, Macpherson, and Allan Cunningham, seduced Leopardi into the scholar's trick of publishing a pretended Greek hymn to Neptune. The translation was accompanied by notes, in which erudite dust was thrown in the eyes of the public, so as to deceive the most suspicious. This production is included in his works; as well as the two *Odes* of Anacreon, which he published at the same time, and which were said to have been found in the same place. These odes are capital imitations. The first is but another

variation of the old theme, Love crowned with Roses, but it has the true Greek *naïveté* in it. The second, "To the Moon," is longer, and generally preferred; but, to our taste, though a better ode, it is not so happy an imitation. He was only nineteen when he played this trick, a circumstance which must be taken in extenuation of the offence.

Although so ardent in pursuit of learning, his faculties were not wholly engrossed by it; for amidst these dry recondite studies he was groping his way in a far more arduous and important path—the study of his own being. The seeds of decay had early been sown in his constitution; and now a hump grew out on his back, adding a source of moral anguish to his physical pains. It is easy to understand the poignant humiliation which every sensitive nature must endure from such a deformity; but by one other cruel contradiction in Leopardi's fate, this grief was heightened beyond the common lot; the energetic nature of his soul prompted him, above all things, to a life of action. To such a spirit deformity would have operated only as one stimulus the more; but accompanied as it was with acute suffering and bodily debility, it made Leopardi feel that he was powerless and despised. Nevertheless, the chained eagle is an eagle still—his thoughts are with the sun. Leopardi could say of himself, in seriousness, that Nature had made him for suffering:—

> A te la speme
> Nego, mi disse, anche la speme; e d'altro
> Non brillin gli occhi tuoi se non di pianto:

for she had thrown him helpless upon the world; but the eagle was only chained, not subdued.

Unfitted for a life of action, he sought activity in burrowing amidst the dust and obscurity of the past. He lived a life of Thought; and at his side sat Sorrow, as a perpetual enigma and as a constant monitress,—'La parte più inesplicabile dell' inesplicabile mistero dell' universo.' He suffered and asked himself if others suffered in the same way,—asked himself whether it was just that he should suffer, having done no wrong. He looked abroad in the world, and saw sadness painfully legible on its face; he looked far into the past, and still the same mournful aspect met his eye. Of his own soul he asked the explanation of this mystery, and he became a poet.

His two first canzoni were published in 1818. They are on the same theme—the degradation of Italy; and it would be idle to speak of the author's youth, because no trace of youth or inexperience is to be found in them. At twenty, Leopardi was old,—at least, in thought and suffering. We wish we could, without too great a sacrifice of the original, translate the first of these canzoni. Often as her poets have reproached Italy—from Dante downwards, there have been no more piercing, manly, vigorous strains, than those which vibrate in the organ-peal of patriotism sent forth by Leopardi. Felicaja mourned over the fatal gift of Beauty in a passionate music which has stirred all hearts; but his sonnet is many degrees below the ode by Leopardi, the irregular but rhythmic march of which seizes hold of your soul and irresistibly hurries you along with it. Utter the name of Leopardi before any Italian, and he instantly bursts forth with,—

> O patria mia, vedo le mura e gli archi
> E le colonne e i simulacri e l'erme
> Torri degli avi nostri,
> Ma la gloria non vedo,
> Non vedo il lauro e il ferro ond'eran carchi
> I nostri padri antichi. Or fatta inerme,
> Nuda la fronte e nudo il petto mostri.

Oimè quante ferite,
Che lividor, che sangue! oh qual ti veggio
Formosissima donna! Io chiedo al cielo
E al mondo: dite, dite
Chi la ridusse a tale? E questo è peggio
Che di catene ha carche ambe le braccia;
Si che sparte le chiome e senza velo
Siede in terra negletta e sconsolata,
Nascondendo la faccia
Tra le ginocchia, e piange.

The sustained yet musical vehemence of this opening is continued throughout. Leopardi does not join the cry of those who exclaim against Italy's fatal gift of Beauty. He feels that Italy's greatness is *not* the cause of her abasement; but that her sons are no longer worthy of her: their ancient courage and manliness have deserted them.

But these men, so supine in their country's cause, are invincible when fighting for another, and this thought wrings from the poet a cry of anguish. He then turns from the degeneracy of his age to those happy antique times when men gloried in dying for their country; this leads him to think of the Thessalian passes, where a handful of men were stronger than the might of Persia, stronger than fate itself; and then as St. Beuve says, 'il refait hardiment le chant perdu de Simonide.'

The second canzone, that on the proposed monument to Dante, is in the same strain; or, let us rather say, it pours forth the same indignant sorrow: for, in point neither of thought nor expression, is it a reproduction of its predecessor. In its patriotic hatred towards France, the despoiler of Italy, we read the effects of that same spirit which animated a Körner and an Arndt; with this additional motive, that while the Germans only hated a cruel enemy, Leopardi hated the enemy who, having conquered his country, sent her sons to perish amidst the distant snows of Russia. (pp. 659-61)

It was in 1822 that Leopardi left Recanati and first went to Rome. His reputation as a *savant* had preceded him, and he was employed to draw up a catalogue of the Greek MSS. in the Barberini Library. (p. 661)

While at Rome he published some of his most important philological researches; and had to endure the jealousies and *tracasseries* of a certain Mangi, the librarian, whom he lashed in two satirical sonnets under the name of *Manzo* (an ox). But to a poet the Eternal City could not be made vulgar by any petty jealousies; Rome was one continued inspiration to Leopardi. He walked amidst its ruins, and felt that even in its ruins it was sacred ground. . . . No one ever felt more thoroughly the real grandeur of Rome, and he saw, in the recent discovery of Fronto's *Letters* and Cicero's *Republic*, the signs of a complete resuscitation of ancient writers, which would force the moderns to catch something of their spirit. In the first Revival of Letters, how great was Italy! Shall there be a second Revival, and no response be heard? The first produced a Dante, a Petrarch, an Ariosto, a Tasso, a Columbus; the second will produce a new race, of whom Alfieri is the chief.

Nothing can be more natural than that a poet and a scholar should look to literature as the regenerator of his country; and, consequently, to a second Revival of Letters as the one thing needful. So long as the love of letters survives, he says, Italy will not be dead; and, as a commentary on this text, we refer to his noble ode to Angelo Maï. The lines in it on Dante, Ariosto, and Tasso, are worthy of the names they commemorate.

The date of this canzone, as St. Beuve pertinently remarks, is the same as that of Manzoni's *Carmagnola* (1820). 'Le drapeau d'une réforme littéraire flottait enfin, toute une jeune milice s'ebranlait à l'entour;' and this period will form one of the most instructive epochs in the history of literature, characterised as it is by the rising of five great nations against the despotism of a system, and the spontaneous recurrence of each to its early writers. The court of Louis XIV. had long domineered over the literature of Europe. Taste in the fine arts was religiously accepted from French critics, and the critics could see nothing but *le grand siècle*. The rude strength and healthy vigour of the early poets were universally pronounced barbarous, because they were (undeniably) against 'good taste.' . . . Certain it is, that wherever you cast your eyes during the close of the seventeenth and throughout the eighteenth centuries, the perruque of Louis XIV. is before you stiff and pompous. The trees and groves are not allowed their natural proportions, but are trimmed into rigidity. The Muses are wigged.

The reaction came. Lessing, the brilliant, restless, irregular, but intrepid captain of his age, harassed the imperial forces on all sides, routed, and finally drove them ignominiously from the field. Germany began to have a literature of her own. England returned to Shakespeare, Spenser, and her ballad literature; so great was the reaction, so strong the feeling against the French school, that even eminent poets could discuss, and without final agreement too, the astonishing question,—Was Pope a poet? Spain made an effort to throw off the yoke of France, and began to inquire about Lopes de Vega, Calderon, and the *cancionero*. France rose up against her own glory, and the *école romantique* sounded the tocsin of revolt. In Italy the standard was as openly raised. Everywhere men fought in this quarrel as if their liberties were inseparably connected with the abrogation of the unities, as if on the permission to use familiar and even trivial language in poetry was staked the whole interests of society.

The outlines of the history of this reaction have often been sketched, but one point has not, we believe, hitherto been insisted on, and it is this: not only was the reaction against *le grand siècle* felt throughout Europe, but in each country the tendency of the New School was the same. This identity of principle is suggestive, and nothing can be easier than the proof of its universality. A strong predilection for the early national literature—a blind reverence for the great Immortals who had early thrown around the nation the lustre of their genius—a pre-eminence given to Nature and the so-called Natural above all conditions of Art—such were the characteristics of the New School in each country. (pp. 662-63)

It is to be noted that, though belonging to the new school, Leopardi has his place apart in it. While the Manzonis, Berchets, and others, were agitating theories of dramatic art, discussing the unities as a vital problem, he paid no attention whatever to the question. Moreover, while Italy, as well as England and France, was greatly influenced by Germany, there is not a trace of that influence on Leopardi. This is a point to be insisted on, because it lets us into the secret of his poetic nature. He was not ignorant of Germany; his friendship with Niebuhr, Bunsen, and Sinner, must have been the means of rendering him acquainted with its best writers: but they were evidently uncongenial to him. His clear, southern nature, could ill sympathise with the mysticism, reverie, and absence of precision and beauty which belong to the north. Even Göthe seems to have made little or no impression on him. '*The Memoirs of Göthe*,' he says in a letter to Puccinotti, 'contain much that is new and excellent: all his works, and a great proportion of the works of other Germans, do so. But they are written with such wild confusion and obscurity, and evince such *bizarre*, mystical, and visionary sentiments and ideas, that I cannot say they really please me much.' Thus partly, no doubt, from early culture and familiarity with the masterpieces of antiquity, but greatly also from the bias of his own mind, he received no durable impression from the literature of Germany.

The distinctive characteristic of Leopardi's poetry is despair over the present, accompanied with a mournful regret for the past. His sympathies are with Greece and Rome; his deep compassion with Italy. His mind seems to linger with touching mournfulness over the remains of the antique world, to recall which for his beloved Italy he would have gladly laid down his life. It was an error, perhaps, but a generous and poetic error.

From Rome, where all things spoke to him of the days he regretted, he returned to the 'abhorred and inhabitable Recanati.' There his health becoming worse and worse, his studies were almost entirely interrupted; and in his pain and solitude he had no resource but poetry. 'Io cercava,' he says, 'come si cerca spesso colla poesia di consacrare il mio dolore.' He poured his sorrows into song, which immortalised him and them. His was no fictitious grief: it was a malady of the body and of the mind—disease and despair. Never free from pain, he had not mental peace to soothe him. He was a stoic-sceptic. In every thing he wrote, verse or prose, dedication or familiar letter, you may see the traces of a deep sense of the nothingness of life, a poignant feeling of its unhappiness, and a stoic contempt for the suffering which bowed him to the earth. Listen to this passage, taken from a calm letter to his friend Brighenti:—

> Aged twenty-one, having commenced while yet a child to think and to suffer, I have run the round of a long life, and am morally old and decrepit; especially now that the enthusiasm, which was the companion and aliment of my life, has passed away in a manner which alarms me. It is time to die—it is time to yield to fortune: the most horrible thing that a youth can do—youth, so full of hope as it usually is; but it is the only pleasure that remains to one who has long convinced himself he was born with the sacred and indelible malediction of Fate.

A gloom was on the world; he had neither the faith, which is a ray of light even in the darkness of death, nor that happy elasticity of mind which could say to the passing moment, 'Stay, thou art fair,' and with it be content. At times, indeed, as in the **"Bruto Minore,"** his scepticism rouses him to defiance:—

> O miserable life! we are but the merest trifles. Nature is not troubled at our wounds, nor do the stars darken at the sight of human agony. Dying, I appeal not to the deaf kings of Olympus or Cocytus—to the contemptible Earth—nor to Night—nor to Thee, O last ray in the darkness of Death, the belief in a Future State. Let the winds take my name and memory.

Elsewhere he asks, 'Of what use is life? to despise it.'

> Nostra vita che val? solo a spregiarla.

Do not suppose these things were said out of bravado or poetic caprice. His letters are sadder even than his poetry. 'La calamità,' he once wrote to a friend, 'sono la sola che vi convenga, essendo virtuoso.' In one of his dialogues he makes Nature, addressing a soul about to enter a human frame, say, 'Vivi e tu sii grande e infelice;' for he could not understand how hap-

piness was possible, unless man was too stupid to apprehend his own fate. Suffering, deep and constant, was Leopardi's individual lot; and the condition of his nation seemed to him little better: for it was to the many one of cowardly submission, of galling servitude to the few, who felt their chains, and knew that liberty was hopeless. The time was out of joint. Leopardi, quoting the verse of Petrarch,—

> Ed io son un di quei che'l pianger giova
> (And I am one of those whom grief delights),

adds, 'I cannot say this, because grief is not my inclination, but a necessity of the time, and the will of Fate.'

As the 'poet of despair,' we know of no equal to Leopardi. But he is too limited ever to become popular. His own experience of life had been restrained within a small sphere by his misfortunes: it was intense but not extensive; consequently his lyre had but few strings. He had thought and suffered, but had not lived; and his poems utter his thoughts and sufferings, but give no image of the universal life. Yet he is never tiresome, though always the same. His grief is so real and so profound, that it is inexhaustible in expression; to say nothing of the beauty in which he embalms it. Something of the magic of his verse he, doubtless, owes to that language which ennobles the most trivial thoughts, and throws its musical spell over the merest nothings; but more to the exquisite choice of diction, which his poet's instinct and his classic taste alike taught him. It is worthy of remark, that while Italian is, perhaps, of all languages the easiest for the composition of poetry, all the great Italian poets have been slow and laborious composers: they have had to combat against the fatal facility of their tongue, as the French do against the enormous difficulty of theirs. We are not, therefore, surprised at Leopardi's account of his own slow and elaborate mode of composition, which is very similar to that recounted by Alfieri of himself: the conception of the poem was the result of a momentary inspiration or frenzy (*un ispirazione o frenesia*); the execution always demanded time. He was no master of the accomplishment of verse, and able to write at a given moment on a given theme; if the poetic enthusiasm seized him he could write, not otherwise. 'Se l'ispirazione non mi nasce da se, più, facilmente uscirebbe acqua da un tronco, che un solo verso dal mio cervello. Gli altri possono poetare sempre che vogliono; ma io non ho questa facoltà in niun modo.'—*Opere*.

The years 1825-26 he passed at Bologna, during which time he published more canzoni. Among them is one entitled **"First Love,"** from which, and from some of the other poems, 'il resulterait,' says St. Beuve, 'que Leopardi n'a connu de ce sentiment orageux que la première et al plus pure, la plus douloureuse moitié, mais aussi la plus divine; et qu'il n'a jamais été mis à l'epreuve d'un entier bonheur.' Alas! the poor, sickly, humpbacked poet, could expect to find no favour in a woman's eyes, and found none; the heart to love was not cased in a form to be loved. That his devotion was ill received is unquestionable; and we have no doubt but that he translated the satire by Simonides, "On Women," with cruel sincerity. That he was deeply hurt may be gathered from his strange outburst in one of his letters, wherein he writes, 'L'ambizione, l'interesse, la perfidia, l'insensibilita delle donne che io definisco *un animale senza cuore,* sono cose che mi spaventano.'

As love poems, Leopardi's have one merit above their class; we mean their truth. They are the transcripts of real emotions, and not the ingenious caprices of a man at ease playing with regrets. One example is worth citing. Poets have told us, till we are heartily tired of hearing it, that the moment they loved,

Nature wore a new and brighter aspect to their eyes,—that, in fact, they were awakened to a sense of Nature's beauties by the keen delight within them. It never occurred to us that this rhapsody might be false, till we read in Leopardi the true feeling. Directly he loved, Nature became no longer the delight she had been. Fame was a bubble, Knowledge was idle; for one passion swallowed up all the rest.

Verses to the moon are suspicious, for, though one of the most melancholy and poetical objects in existence, she has had the discredit of so many and such wretched poems that one begins to doubt her power of inspiring; yet who that ever looked on her sad face can help being charmed with the delicate pathos of these lines?—

"Alla Luna"

O graziosa luna, io mi rammento
Che, or volge l'anno, sovra questo colle
Io venia pien d'angoscia a rimirarti:
E tu pendevi allor su quella selva
Siccome or fai, che tutta la rischiari.
Ma nebuloso e tremulo dal pianto
Che mi sorgea sul ciglio, alle mie luci
Il tuo volto apparia, che travagliosa
Era mia vita: ed è, nè canzia stile,
O mia diletta luna. *E pur mi giova*
La ricordanza, e il noverar l'etate
Del mio dolore.

This reads like a chapter of the heart's memoirs, and not like a 'copy of verses' to the moon. The same may be said of the charming poem which precedes it **"La Sera del dì di Festa,"** . . . and of several other pieces in the volume; and this quality, far beyond the mere art of verse, will render them durable. Only that which is vital and issues out of life can hope to live; and Leopardi will not pass away from the fashion of a day, because his poems are the expressions of real emotions. (pp. 663-66)

Among the works written [during his residence in Florence from 1826 to 1831] we must not pass over without mention his *Dialogues,* the style of which a great judge, Manzoni, declared had never been surpassed; and a collection of detached thoughts, not at all in the Rochefoucauld strain. We must confess, however, that, to us, his prose derives much of its interest from his poetry; it is not satisfactory in doctrine, nor happy in tone. The learned essays on philological subjects are more to our taste,—that is, when we are in a philological mood; but as that mysterious entity, the 'general reader,' can hardly be expected to be often in such a mood, we spare him some tiresome pages on the matter. (p. 666)

The erudite essays, which the pious love of Leopardi's friends has collected together in one curious volume, may be commended to the attention of scholars; the public will not heed them, or heeding, will think of them, with a certain interest, only as the productions of one born with a spirit for great achievements, to whom all achievements were denied. It was not an age for action, and the most energetic of his countrymen were powerless. To the absence of a fitting theatre whereon to play an heroic part, there was added the want of a physical organisation capable of supporting even the humblest part; and the soul of the poor, emaciated hunchback, felt itself doubly imprisoned,—first, in a prostrate, nerveless country; secondly, in a feeble, helpless body. What, then, remained for him? Incapacitated for action, unable to incarnate his thoughts in deeds, he incarnated them in poems and essays. And if in this lower sphere of human activity, as he regarded it, he sometimes

frittered away his time in the scholar's fascinating researches, no one who knows the temptation will blame him. Philology, to most a dry and fruitless study, was with him an early passion; and in the sadder earnestness of manhood it was indulged, because it kept him in closer familiarity with that Past which was the Golden Age of his credulous imagination, when, as he was wont emphatically to say, men *lived* and *acted*.

There is a tendency among modern writers to overvalue Thought and to undervalue Action. This is partly, no doubt, as a set-off against the coarse depreciation by the mass of men of those conquests that are merely intellectual; but partly, also, in consequence of authors living more secluded lives than when Æschylus stormed upon the dark-haired Persian at Marathon, or Cervantes lost his arm at Lepanto. In Germany, we see this error pushed to an extreme; and the vices of her literature arise mainly from this, that literature is cultivated for its own sake, as a means, not as an end. What a contrast is presented by these German writers, shut up in their studies, breathing an atmosphere thick with tobacco smoke and the dust of ponderous volumes, and squandering their lives in sterile speculations, or in laborious researches into matters of no human importance, to the free and active lives of the Greek and Roman writers, or even those of our Chaucers, Spensers, Shakspeares, Miltons, Clarendons, Burkes, &c.,—writers who were *men,* not thinking machines! And it is interesting to read the excuses Cicero frequently puts forward for his pursuit of literary fame, as in no way interfering with his active duties, but simply as dignifying his leisure. Leopardi thought with Cicero. If human life, he says, be the principal subject of literature, and if the regulation of our actions be the first intention of philosophy, there can be no doubt that *to do* is more dignified than to mediate or to write; inasmuch as the end is more noble than the means,—and things and actions than words and syllogisms.

> . . . [No] mind is by nature created for studies; no man is born to write, but to act. Therefore do we see that the greatest writers and the most illustrious poets of our own times, such as Vittorio Alfieri, were, from the first, intensely inclined to *do* great things; but Time and Fate forbidding this, they *wrote* great things. Only those capable of executing great things are capable of writing them.
>
> [**"Il Parini, ovvero della gloria"**]

So little was Leopardi of a mere bookworm! Forced to find in study a refuge against sorrow and *ennui,* he never exaggerated the part which study should occupy in man's life. Literature in his eyes was but a *pis aller* for action,—the mimicry of a life that could not be really lived. His great hope in literature was, that by means of it men would be stimulated to action. It angered him to see his countrymen reducing it to an amusement. 'It can have but one solid principle,' he said, 'and that is the regeneration of our country.'

Leopardi's sense of helplessness was very keen; that he was useless in the world, where so much sorrow attended him,— that he only expected peace on quitting it, is evident in all his poems. The beauties of nature seem but to deepen his sadness; his very style is painful. When not roused to indignation, his Muse has but one low plaint—a yearning for release from life. In one of his smaller pieces this is delicately touched; every reader who has known the luxury of reverie when contemplating a setting sun will recognise the yearning for the Infinite Silence in his lines, **"L'Infinito."**

But it is in the poem on **"Love and Death"** that he most undisguisedly expresses that desire for release which the brilliant Frenchwoman uttered when she said, 'I sometimes feel the want to die, as the wakeful feel the want to sleep.' (pp. 667-68)

Leopardi did not long survive this appeal to Death. He lingered out his few remaining years at Naples, secluded from the world, secluded even from study, but somewhat consoled by the sympathy of his friend, Antonio Ranieri, and by that of Count Platen, a kindred spirit, who, in a rapid decline, had come from his cold Germany to linger out a few months longer at Naples. In the brief intervals of his respite from pain, Leopardi amused himself with composing a satyrico-political continuation to the *Batrachomiomachia* (*Paralipomeni della Batrach*), in eight cantos, which may, probably, be amusing to Italians, but has little attraction for foreigners. On the 14th of June, 1837, in his thirty-ninth year, just as Ranieri was about to remove him to Portici, the cholera having burst out at Naples, his sufferings ceased. A few hours before his death, says St. Beuve, he wrote some verses in the style of Simonides or Minnermus, 'et dont voiçi le sens: Mais la vie mortelle, depuis que la belle jeunesse a disparu, ne se colore plus jamais d'une autre lumière ni d'une autre aurore; elle est veuve jusqu'à la fin, et à cette nuit qui obscurcit tous les autres âges, les dieux n'ont mis pour terme que le tombeau.' To the very last, the same despair!

Our task is done. We have introduced the name of a great writer and most unhappy man, and, in a general way, indicated the nature of his genius and the cast of his thoughts. It remains for those who can appreciate and enjoy the one, without being ungenerous towards the other,—who can admire the writer while condemning his opinions, and who, in the calm serenity of their own minds, can still recognise a corner of doubt, and believe that, so long as doubt and sorrow shall be the lot of mankind, the poet whose lyre vibrates powerfully with their accents will deserve a place amongst the musical teachers,— it remains for them to seek in Leopardi's works a clearer, fuller knowledge, of the man. (p. 669)

> [*George Henry Lewes*], *"Life and Works of Leopardi," in* Fraser's Magazine for Town & Country, *Vol. XXXVIII, No. CCXXVIII, December, 1848, pp. 659-69.*

[WILLIAM EWART GLADSTONE]   (essay date 1850)

[*An English statesman and orator, Gladstone is remembered for his classical scholarship in* Studies on Homer and the Homeric Age *(1858) and* Juventus Mundi *(1869) and for such political writings as* The State in Its Relations with the Church *(1838) and* Belgian Horrors and the Question of the East *(1876). In the following excerpt from a review of* Opere di Giacomo Leopardi, *a six-volume edition of the author's collected works, Gladstone discusses Leopardi's varied achievements, praising his scholarship and polished style, yet lamenting his agnosticism, relative lack of imagination, and pessimism.*]

Genius, unless guided by a malignant spirit, has an indefeasible claim to our sympathy in its reverses, and in its achievements to our fervid admiration: nor is there any more touching, any more instructive lesson, than such as are afforded by its failures in the attempt to realise, out of its own resources and without the aid of Divine revelation, either intellectual contentment or a happy life.

In the writings of Leopardi there are other sources of pathetic interest: the misfortunes of his country, both its political and social, and its religious misfortunes, and his own personal

difficulties and calamities, have stamped their image indelibly upon his works, and may be traced, not only in the solemn and impassioned verses, or in the mournful letters, of which they are more or less directly the theme, but in the tone which pervades the whole.

We believe it may be said without exaggeration, that he was one of the most extraordinary men whom this century has produced, both in his powers, and likewise in his performances, achieved as they were under singular disadvantage. For not only did he die at thirty-eight, almost *nel mezzo del cammin di nostra vita,* and at the time when most great men are but beginning the efforts which have stamped them with that character; but likewise, 'Heaven's unimpeached decrees' in his case nearly—

> Made that shortened span one long disease.
>
> (p. 295)

[Leopardi's] literary life divides itself into two great periods: the first of them occupied by his philological labours and by translations from the classical poets, the second chiefly by poetry and philosophy. The division is not minutely accurate; but his first poem of any note was written in 1817: he only published three of his odes before the year 1824, and he had then written but little poetry; he had for some years before that, from the state of his sight as we suppose, almost entirely ceased from his philological labours, and had already designated them as the studies of his boyhood. And all his efforts in philosophy belong to the later division of his life, which begins about the last-named year.

The earliest composition among his published works is the **"Essay on the Popular Errors of the Ancients,"** dated in the year 1815, and written therefore in his 17th or early in his 18th year. It is remarkable not only for the quantity of erudition, classical and patristic, which he had even then accumulated— his editor has appended a list of near four hundred authors whom he cites—but for the facility with which he handles his materials, and with which also he philosophises upon them. Homage is emphatically rendered in this work to the Christian religion: the youthful author tells us that unbelief had generated worse prejudices than had ever sprung from credulity, and that the name of philosopher had become odious with the sounder part of mankind; he declares Christianity to be the second mother of our race, and asserts that the true Church had ever condemned superstition, against which she is the true and the only bulwark. And yet we see a baleful shadow projected even at this early period over his future, where he eulogises Voltaire as 'that standard—bearer of bold minds, that man so devoted to reason and so hostile to error.' The time was too near at hand when he would be prepared to subscribe that scoffer's words:—

> O Jupiter, tu fis en nous créant
> Une froide plaisanterie.

But what strange idea and stranger practice of education must prevail, where the admiration of Voltaire as an apostle of true reason grows up peacefully in the mind of a boy, side by side with the admiration of the Church of Rome as the unsparing foe of superstition!

The only specimens of original composition in Greek verse (in Latin there are none) which these volumes afford, are two Anacreontic odes, written in 1817. We doubt whether they justify the panegyric of Giordani, *Per verità neppure esso Anacreonte le potrebbe discernere tra le sue proprie figliuole.* They would, we suppose, when cleared of some inaccuracies, probably due to defective typography, be termed good exercises at Eton, but no more; and this is among the easiest descriptions of Greek composition. More remarkable, we think, were his translations from the Greek. In 1815 he published a complete translation of Moschus, with a learned and acute discourse prefixed to it, containing among other things a severe criticism upon the affected and licentious manner of certain French translations of his works and those of Anacreon. He was, however, at all times a sharper critic to himself than to any other author. He says, while yet a youth, *Sono io di tal tempra, che nulla mi va a gusto di quanto ho fatto due o tre mesi innanzi.* And he soon became dissatisfied with this work, which, nevertheless, appears to be extremely well executed.

In 1816 he went on to publish a translation of the first Book of the *Odyssey*; and in 1817 the second Book of the *Æneid.* He was himself sensible of the great difficulty of translating Virgil, and his own effort must be admitted to be a failure; the spirit of the original evaporates in the operation, and the work is dead and flat.

Leopardi, however, had a most exalted conception of the function of a translator. He says he translated the second book because *he could not help it;* that after reading it, as was commonly the case with anything that he read and thought really beautiful, he was in an agony until he had cast it in the mould of his own mind. . . . Every translation of a great work, to be good, must have great original qualities. We must not confound the subject by assimilating the work of the translator to that of the copyist in painting. In that case the problem is to construct an image of the picture, given the same materials. But in the case of pure mental products the material form is the language, and the very condition of the work is that this be changed, as the workman must reproduce in another tongue; and in proportion as the original to be rendered is a great one, the union between the thought of the writer and his language is more intimate: at every step as the translator proceeds, he feels that he is tearing asunder soul and body, life and its vehicle; so that in order to succeed in his task, he must, within certain limits, create anew.

To create anew was Leopardi's idea of translating, and such he very clearly showed it to be in his later efforts of this description, which are prose translations from Xenophon, Isocrates, Epictetus, and others; executed in the latter part of his life, and only published after his death. It is evident that while he was engaged upon them, the idea and aim of reproduction predominated over that of mere representation. And so far as we have been able to examine them in close comparison with the original text, we have found them not sufficiently precise in their character—their secondary character, as we readily admit—of copies, to satisfy a scholar of the English type: but admirable in their force and spirit; and, if viewing them with a foreign eye, we may presume to say so much—although only re-echoing the judgments of native and skilled Italians—faultless as compositions; bearing that stamp of freshness and of power, which realizes Leopardi's idea of a translator's function in its normal state. (pp. 298-301)

As we have seen, his first efforts were applied to philology; and it was not till he was seventeen and a half—rather an advanced period in his early-ripened mental life—that he gave himself to literature in its ordinary sense. It was probably not so much choice as necessity that threw him upon the former line of study. Not that he had great advantages for it, but the reverse. The merits of his father's library have apparently been exaggerated by Ranieri; it did not, for example, contain a

Xenophon. Still it was a library, and it had no modern books; and being thus thrown upon the dead languages, and having for the most part to learn them by means of reading their authors, his acquisitive mind was naturally drawn to their speech and its laws.

We are inclined to trace to this circumstance the accuracy and beauty of his own diction and his admirable style. He had handled early and familiarly those among all the instruments for the expansion of thought, which are the most rigorously adapted to its laws, and had also deeply considered the mode and form of the adaptation. Yet it is certainly wonderful that he should have issued from these studies not only a refined scholar and philologian, but a powerful and lofty poet; as well as that he should have carried to maturity in the most fervid and impatient period of life pursuits which are commonly considered rather dry. But it is a cardinal truth, that no study whatever can be dry to such a mind when earnestly embracing it. (pp. 309-10)

When we regard Leopardi in his character of a poet—in which no Italian of the present generation, we conceive, except Manzoni even approaches him, and he in a different order, and perhaps but in a single piece—it is not difficult to perceive that he was endowed in a peculiar degree with most of the faculties which belong to the highest excellence. We shall note two exceptions. The first is the solid and consistent wisdom which can have no other foundation in the heart of man than the Gospel revelation: without which, even while we feel the poet to be an enchanter, we cannot accept and trust him as a guide: and of which Wordsworth is an example unequalled probably in our age, and unsurpassed in any age preceding ours. Nor let it be said that this is not properly a poetical defect; because the highest functions of the human being stand in such intimate relations to one another, that the want of any one of them will commonly prevent the attainment of perfection in any other. The sense of beauty enters into the highest philosophy, as in Plato. The highest poet must be a philosopher, accomplished, like Dante, or intuitive, like Shakspeare. But neither the one nor the other can now exist in separation from that conception of the relations between God and man, that new standard and pattern of humanity, which Christianity has supplied. And although much of what it has indelibly impressed upon the imagination and understanding, the heart and life of man, may be traceable and even prominent in those who individually disown it—although the splendour of these disappropriated gifts may in particular cases be among the very greatest of the signs and wonders appointed for the trial of faith—there is always something in them to show that they have with them no source of positive and permanent vitality: that the branch has been torn from the tree, and that its life is on the ebb. There is another point in which Leopardi fails as compared with the highest poets. He is stronger in the reflective than in the perceptive, or at any rate than in the more strictly creative powers. Perhaps these latter were repressed in their growth by the severe realities of his life. It is by them that the poet projects his work from himself, stands as it were completely detached from it, and becomes in his own personality invisible. Thus did Homer and Shakspeare perhaps beyond all other men: thus did Goethe: thus did Dante when he pleased, although his individuality is the local centre, to so speak, of his whole poem; which is only to say in other words that by this gift the poet throws his entire strength into his work and identifies himself with it; that he not only does, but for the time being is, his work; and that then, when the work is done, he passes away and leaves it: it is perfect in its own kind, and bears no stamp or trace of him—that is of what in him pertains to the individual as such, and does not belong to the general laws of truth and beauty. Thus all high pictorial poetry is composed: thus every great character in the drama or romance is conceived and executed.

It is the gift of imagination in its highest form and intensity which effects these wonderful transmutations, and places the poet of the first order in a rank nearer to that of creative energies than anything else we know. (pp. 310-11)

Leopardi, though he had abundance both of fancy and of imagination, either was not possessed of this peculiar form of the latter gift or had not developed it: his impersonations are beautiful, but rather after the manner of statues: they have just so much of life as is sufficient to put his metaphysical conceptions in motion; but we always seem to discover his hand propping them up and moving them on: they have not the flesh and blood reality: he is eminently a subjective poet, and the reader never loses him from view. But he is surely a very great subjective poet, and applies to his work, with a power rarely equalled, all the resources of thought and passion, all that his introspective habits had taught him: he has choice and flowing diction, a profound harmony, intense pathos: and he unites to very peculiar grace a masculine energy and even majesty of expression, which is not surpassed, so far as we know, in the whole range of poetry or of eloquence, and which indeed gives the highest evidence of its prerogative by endowing sentiments, now become trite and almost vulgar through use, with perfect freshness of aspect and the power to produce lively and strong impressions. . . . His gift of compression, in particular, is one which seems, not borrowed, for such things no man can borrow—they are marked 'not transferable'—but descended or inherited from Dante himself.

Although it has appeared that his first poetical efforts were relatively late, yet they were as early as those of most poets who have acquired particular celebrity for juvenile productions, and they will bear, we imagine, favourable comparison with those of Pope or of Milton. Indeed, as their beginning and maturity were almost simultaneous, he is really no less remarkable as a youthful poet than as a youthful scholar and critic, and holds one of the very first places in the troop of beardless Apollos. (pp. 311-12)

To speak plainly . . . [of Leopardi's] abstract philosophy of life and action, paganism is Gospel light and the Great Desert a *pays riant* in comparison with it. The falseness, misery, and hopelessness of life are the burden of his strain in the familiar letters of his early youth under his father's roof, as often as they become subjective. And as soon as the year 1819 he wrote to Giordani that he had not spirit remaining to conceive a wish, not even for death: he had indeed no fear of it in any respect, but it seemed so little different from life, from life in which now not even pain came to sustain him, but an intense weariness both exhausted him and tormented him as if it had been the extreme of pain, and drove him beside himself in his incapacity to feel that even his despair was a reality. In his happier moods he had just strength enough to weep over the miseries of man and the nullity of all things. This looks like mere rhapsody, and in ordinary cases one would say, it is a love-sick or brain-sick boy, and the very violence of the fit is the best assurance that it cannot last. But with him it was a settled and habitual tone of thought; and only on rare occasions throughout the whole course of his letters or his works will the reader find even a transient expression that is not in unison with it. In common life we are sometimes astonished and appalled at the

power of the human frame to endure protracted nervous agony; and the records of this extraordinary man constantly suggest a similar feeling with respect to the capacity of the mind both to suffer and to heighten and inflame the causes of its torture. Doubtless, as regarded his practical life, there are deductions to be made from the extreme breadth of these statements. Even while he told Giordani that he could not *conceive a wish,* and even had ceased to understand the meaning of friendship and of affection, he also begged for letters, and said he would always love him. But what we have said is too strictly true of his speculative man—and although his speculations are in reality illogical and incoherent, and cannot be said to form a system further than as universal destruction is a system in a negative sense, yet speculation was in his case the master-key of life.

The child, he says, is happy, but happy only because he is blind. True life ends where manhood begins; none live longer, except those who continue to be children after they are grown up. Study has value because it is the most secure source of forgetfulness, and a more durable illusion than most others. The only exertions conformable to truth and reason are those founded upon the recognition *che tutto è nulla,* and, as we here arrive at the *apex* of all paradox in the shape of a contradiction in terms, it seems not easy to carry this part of the description further in detail. Pain, again, is cruel to us: but tedium, weariness, and disgust are even worse. Sometimes he tells us there is nothing real except pain. Sometimes that not even pain is real. Truth and reason are our implacable foes; they do nothing but reveal misery and hopelessness. Nature it is true resists, but then nature lies. As to a future state, it was a most mischievous invention; because before men thought of it, they might, at any rate, have had an undisturbed hope of escape by death.

If in his letters this be declamation, it is earnest and deliberate enough in his philosophical writings. It is impossible to escape from the natural conclusions by pleading the form of Dialogue: first, because the reasons of its adoption are patent; next, because in the *Pensieri,* to quote no other case, he passes out of that form and speaks in the first person. There are places, indeed, where he seems as if he had been trying earnestly, though hopelessly, to keep a slippery hold upon some fragment of belief; but the end is, always and obviously, conscious failure. . . . [The] dark and hopeless doctrine blackens nearly every page, and the marks of high and noble gifts with which it is mixed serve to make the gloom more palpable and thick. Those who desire, without the pain of traversing so dreary a course at length, to see his miserable no-creed summed up, will find it in the verses (a poem they can hardly be called) **"A Se Stesso,"** anticipating death. (pp. 318-20)

It may be thought that, if such be the real character of Leopardi's philosophy, we should have done better to pass it by than to expose it to the reader's eye. But in the first place there can be no more futile, no more mischievous conception, than that faith is to be kept entire by hiding from view the melancholy phenomena of unbelief. And, secondly, the kind of unbelief which is really unworthy of any notice except simple denunciation, is that which attacks us through the sense of ridicule, or insinuates itself by bribing the passions. It is not so with Leopardi. His philosophy, and his frame of mind in connexion with it, present more than any other that we know, more even than those of Shelley, the character of unrelieved, unredeemed desolation. The very qualities in it which attract pitying sympathy deprive it of all seductive power. Antecedently to confutation by reasoning, it carries with it its own antidote. It was not a voluptuous, a scoffing, a frivolous, a wanton infidelity, but one mournful and self-torturing; one that, in hiding from view any consolatory truth, consumed all enjoyment, peace, and hope in the mind that harboured it. Unbelief was to him the cannon-ball:

> Shattering that it may reach, and shattering what it reaches.

Religion took its flight from him like the fabled deities from Troy, when Destruction had begun, and in order that Destruction might proceed. There was left to Leopardi this melancholy distinction, that he has brought more nearly than any other person to uniformity, if not to consistency, the philosophy of nullity, misery, and despair. (pp. 320-21)

But he was not commonly a Capaneus bidding defiance to the thunders of heaven, nor a Prometheus who drew moral strength from the great deeds that he felt he had done for man, but he resembled rather the Hercules of the Trachiniæ, or Philoctetes in Lemnos, when under the agony of his wound he

> made the welkin ring again,
> And fetched shrill echoes from the hollow earth;

or like Œdipus when he recoiled from the discovery of the terrible enigma, bowed his head to the strength of Destiny, and was driven by its tempest, homeless and hopeless, through the earth.

As, therefore, no case has ever existed in which the claim to pity and sympathy was stronger, so never was there one in which it could more safely be indulged. His scepticism, at least, did not stoop to baseness, did not drive its bargain with the passions: nor had he the presumption of those who, having hidden from their view the sun of the Gospel and created a darkness for themselves, light some farthing candle of their own in its stead. The place from which he had driven the 'sacred mother of humanity,' the Catholic faith, he would not attempt to occupy with any inferior scheme. In the vacant shrine he set up no idol. For common speculative liberalism, and for the opinions of the day, he had a contempt as energetic even as his revulsion from theology, and as deeply imprinted on his whole mental constitution.

It is indeed true that scarcely any notice of Christian doctrine is to be found in his works. . . . His quarrel seems less with his Church (he tells us he observed *novenas* and *triduos* to obtain the grace of a speedy death) than with Christianity; and not so much with Christianity as with the whole ground—not only of revelation but—of natural religion in its first and simplest elements. Wonderful as it may seem, his writings in their general effect go as near as human language well can go to evincing a total disbelief in God, the Soul, and Immortality. And yet there is a passage, even in his speculative essays, which bears a touching, would to God it were an intentional, resemblance to the great primordial idea of Christianity. It is the **"Storia del genere umano,"** and is as beautiful in language as in thought. (pp. 321-22)

Rapidly surveying the character of Leopardi as a writer, we cannot hesitate to say that in almost every branch of mental exertion, this extraordinary man seems to have had the capacity for attaining, and generally at a single bound, the very highest excellence. Whatever he does, he does in a manner that makes it his own; not with a forced or affected but a true originality, stamping upon his work, like other masters, a type that defies all counterfeit. He recalls others as we read him, but always the most remarkable and accomplished in their kind; always by conformity, not by imitation. In the Dorian march of his

terza rima the image of Dante comes before us; in his blank verse we think of Milton (whom probably he never read); in his lighter letters, and in the extreme elegance of touch with which he describes mental gloom and oppression, we are reminded of the grace of Cowper; when he touches learned research or criticism, he is copious as Warburton, sagacious and acute as Bentley: the impassioned melancholy of his poems recalls his less, though scarcely less, deeply unhappy contemporary Shelley: to translation (we speak however of his prose versions) he brings the lofty conception of his work which enabled Coleridge to produce *his* Wallenstein; among his 'Thoughts' there are some worthy of a place beside the *Pensées* of Pascal or the Moral Essays of Bacon; and with the style of his philosophic **Dialogues** neither Hume nor Berkeley need resent a comparison. We write for Englishmen: but we know that some of his countrymen regard him as a follower, and as a rival, too, of Tasso and of Galileo in the respective excellences of verse and prose. Some of his editors go further, and pronounce him to be a discoverer of fundamental truths: an error in our view alike gross, mischievous, and inexcusable. Yet there are many things in which Christians would do well to follow him: in the warmth of his attachments, in the moderation of his wants, in his noble freedom from the love of money, in his all-conquering assiduity. Nor let us, of inferior and more sluggish clay, omit to learn, as we seem to stand by his tomb beside the Bay of Naples in the lowly church of San Vitale, yet another lesson from his career; the lesson of compassion, chastening admiration, towards him: and for ourselves, of humility and self-mistrust. (p. 336)

> [*William Ewart Gladstone*], *"Works and Life of Giacomo Leopardi," in* The Quarterly Review, *Vol. LXXXVI, No. CLXXII, March, 1850, pp. 295-336.*

HENRY T. TUCKERMAN   (essay date 1857)

> [*In this excerpt, Tuckerman examines Leopardi's skeptical outlook, basing his discussion on the fable "Storia del genere umano," the essay "Detti memorabili di Filippo Ottonieri," and several of Leopardi's fictional dialogues. Tuckerman also briefly discusses Leopardi's patriotic verse.*]

Leopardi was born at Recanti, on the twenty-ninth of June, 1798, and died at Naples, on the fourteenth of June, 1837. The restraint under which he lived, partly that of circumstances, and partly of authority, both exerted upon a morbidly sensitive and lonely being, kept him in his provincial birthplace until the age of twenty-four. After this period he sought a precarious subsistence in Rome, Florence, Bologna, and Naples. Of the conscious aim he proposed to himself as a scholar, we may judge by his own early declaration: "Mediocrity frightens me; my wish is to love, and become great by genius and study." In regard to the first desire, he seems, either from an unfortunate personal appearance, or from having been in contact with the insincere and the vain, to have experienced a bitter disappointment; for the craving for sympathy, and the praise of love, continually find expression in his writings, while he says of women, "L'ambizione, l'interesso, la perfidia, l'insensibilità delle donne che io definisco un animale senza cuore, sono cose che mi spaventano." He translated, with great zest, the satire of Simonides on women. Elsewhere, however, there is evinced a remarkable sensibility to female attractions, and indications appear of gratified, though interrupted, affinities. Indeed, we cannot but perceive that Leopardi belongs to that rare class of men whose great sense of beauty and "necessity of loving" is united with an equal passion for truth. It was not, therefore, because his taste was too refined, or his standard too ideal, that his affections were baffled, but on account of the extreme rarity of that sacred union of loveliness and loyalty, of grace and candor, of the beautiful and the true, which, to the thinker and the man of heart, alone justifies the earnestness of love.

Nature vindicated herself, as she ever will, even in his courageous attempt to merge all youthful impulse in the pursuit of knowledge, and twine around abstract truth the clinging sensibilities that covet a human object. He became, indeed, a master of lore, he lived a scholar, he kept apart from the multitude, and enacted the stoical thinker; but the ungratified portion of his soul bewailed her bereavement; from his harvest-fields of learning went up the cry of famine; a melancholy tone blended with his most triumphant expositions; and an irony that ill conceals moral need underlies his most vivacious utterance.

In his actual life Leopardi confesses himself to have been greatly influenced by prudential motives. There was a reserve in his family intercourse, which doubtless tended to excite his thoughts and feelings to a greater private scope; and he accordingly sought in fancy and reflection a more bold expansion. His scepticism has been greatly lamented as the chief source of his hopelessness; and the Jesuits even ventured to assert his final conversion, so important did they regard the accession of such a gifted name to the roll of the church; but his friend, Ranieri, in whose arms he died, only tells us that he "resigned his exalted spirit with a smile." He presents another instance of the futility of attempting to graft religious belief externally, and by prescriptive means, upon a free, inquiring, and enthusiastic mind. Christianity, as practically made known to Leopardi, failed to enlist his sympathies, from the erroneous form in which it was revealed, while, speculatively, its authority seemed to have no higher sanction than the antique philosophy and fables with which he was conversant. Had he learned to consider religion as a sentiment, inevitable and divine; had he realized it in the same way as he did love—as an experience, a feeling, a principle of the soul, and not a technical system, it would have yielded him both comfort and inspiration.

Deformed, with the seeds of decay in his very frame, familiar with the history, the philosophy, the languages, of the earth, reflective and susceptible, loving and lonely, erudite, but without a faith, young in years, but venerable in mental life, he found nothing, in the age of transition in which he lived, to fix and harmonize his nature. His parent was incapable of comprehending the mind he sought to control. Sympathy with Greece and Rome, compassion for Italy, and despair of himself, were the bitter fruits of knowledge unillumined by supernal trust. He says the *inesplicabile mistero dell 'universo* weighed upon his soul. He longed to solve the problem of life, and tried to believe, with Byron, that "everything is naught"— *tutto è nulla;* and wrote, *la calamità é la sola cosa che vi convenga essendo virtuoso. Nostra vita,* he asks, *che val? solo a spregiarla.* He thought too much to be happy without a centre of light about which his meditations could hopefully revolve; he felt too much to be tranquil without some reliable and endeared object to which he might confidently turn for solace and recognition. The facts of his existence are meagre; the circle of his experience limited, and his achievements as a scholar give us no clue to his inward life; but the two concise volumes of prose and verse [*Opere di Giacomo Leopardi*] are a genuine legacy; a reflection of himself amply illustrative to the discriminating reader.

As regards the diction of Leopardi, it partakes of the superiority of his mind and the individuality of his character. Versed, as he was, both in the vocabulary and the philosophy of ancient and modern languages, he cherished the highest appreciation of his native tongue, of which he said it was *sempre infinita.* He wrote slowly, and with great care. In poetry, his first conception was noted, at once, and born in an access of fervor; but he was employed, at intervals, for weeks, in giving the finishing touches to the shortest piece. It is, indeed, evident that Leopardi gave to his deliberate compositions the essence, as it were, of his life. No one would imagine his poems, except from their lofty and artistic style, to be the effusions of a great scholar, so simple, true, and apparently unavoidable, are the feelings they embody. It is this union of severe discipline and great erudition with the glow, the directness, and the natural sentiment, of a young poet, that constitutes the distinction of Leopardi. The reflective power, and the predominance of the thoughtful element in his writings, assimilate him rather with German and English than modern Italian literature. There is nothing desultory and superficial; vigor of thought, breadth and accuracy of knowledge, and the most serious feeling, characterize his works.

His taste was manly, and formed altogether on the higher models. In terse energy he often resembles Dante; in tender and pensive sentiment, Petrarch; in philosophical tone he manifested the Anglo-Saxon spirit of inquiry and psychological tendency of Bacon and Coleridge; thus singularly combining the poetic and the erudite, grave research and fanciful speculation, deep wisdom and exuberant love. Of late Italian writers, perhaps no one more truly revives the romantic associations of her literature; for Leopardi "learned in suffering what he taught in song," as exclusively as the "grim Tuscan" who described the world of spirits. His life was shadowed by a melancholy not less pervading than that of Tasso; and, since Laura's bard, no poet of the race has sung of love with a more earnest beauty. He has been well said to have passed a "life of thought with sorrow beside him." The efflorescence of that life is concentrated in his verse, comparatively limited to quantity, but proportionally intense in expression; and the views, impressions, fancies, and ideas, generated by his studies and experience, we may gather from his prose, equally concise in form and individual in spirit. From these authentic sources we will now endeavor to infer the characteristics of his genius.

His faith, or rather his want of faith, in life and human destiny, is clearly betrayed in his legend or allegory, called **"Storia del Genere Umano."** (pp. 270-73)

In a note to this fable, he protests against having had any design to run a philosophical tilt against either the Mosaic tradition or the evangelists; but it is evident that he did aim to utter the convictions which his own meditations and personal experience had engendered. Nor is the view thus given of the significance and far-reaching associations of human love, when consecrated by sentiment and intensified by intelligence, so peculiar as might appear from his manner of presenting it. In Plato, Dante, and Petrarch, in all the higher orders of poets and philosophers, we find a divine and enduring principle recognized under the same guise. The language in which Leopardi expresses his faith on the subject is not less emphatic than graceful:

> Qualora viene in sulla terra, sceglie i cuori piu teneri
> e piu gentili delle persone piu generose e magnanime;
> e quivi siede per alcun breve spazio; diffondendovi
> sì pellegrina e mirabile soavità, ed empiendoli di
> affetti sì nobili, e di tanta virtù e fortezza, che eglino

allora provano, cosa al tutto nuova nel genere umano,
pinttosto verità che rassomiglianza di beatitudine.

The satire of Leopardi is pensive rather than bitter; it is aimed
at general, not special error, and seems inspired far more by
the sad conviction of a serious mind than the ascerbity of a
disappointed one. In the dialogue between Fashion and Death,
the former argues a near relationship and almost identity of
purpose with the latter; and the folly and unwholesome effects
of subservience to custom are finely satirized, in naïvely showing how the habits she induces tend to shorten life and multiply
the victims of disease. So in the proposal of premiums by an
imaginary academy, the mechanical spirit of the age is wittily
rebuked by the offer of prizes to the inventor of a machine to
enact the office of a friend, without the alloy of selfishness
and disloyalty which usually mars the perfection of that character in its human form. Another prize is offered for a machine
that will enact magnanimity, and another for one that will
produce women of unperverted conjugal instincts. The imaginary conversation between a sprite and a gnome is an excellent
rebuke to self-love; and that between Malambruno and Far-
farello emphatically indicates the impossibility of obtaining
happiness through will, or the agency even of superior intelligence. Leopardi's hopelessness is clearly shown in the dialogue of Nature and a Soul, wherein the latter refuses the great
endowments offered because of the inevitable attendant suffering. In the Earth and Moon's interview, we have an ingenious satire upon that shallow philosophy which derives all the
data of truth from individual consciousness and personal
experience.

One of the most quaint and instructive of these colloquies is
that between Frederico Ruysch and his mummies, in which the
popular notion of the pain of dying is refuted by the alleged
proof of experience. The mummies, in their midnight song,
declare the condition of death to be *lieta no, ma sicura*. Phys-
iologically considered, all pleasure is declared to be attended
with a certain languor. Burke suggest the same idea in reference
to the magnetical effects of beauty on the nervous system; and
this agreeable state is referred to by the mummies to give their
inquisitive owner an idea of the sensation of dying. The philosophy of this subject, the vague and superstitious fears respecting it, have recently engaged the attention of popular
medical writers; but the essential points are clearly unfolded
in this little dialogue of Leopardi.

In his essay entitled **"Detti Memorabili di Filippo Ottonieri,"**
we have apparently an epitome of his own creed; at least, the
affinity between the maxims and habits here described and
those which, in other instances, he acknowledges as personal,
is quite obvious. Ottonieri is portrayed as a man isolated in
mind and sympathies, though dwelling among his kind. He
thought that the degree in which individuality of life and opinion in man was regarded as eccentric might be deemed a just
standard of civilization; as, the more enlightened and refined
the state of society, the more such originality was respected
and regarded as natural. He is described as ironical; but the
reason for this was that he was deformed and unattractive in
person, like Socrates, yet created to love; and, not being able
to win this highest gratification, so conversed as to inspire both
fear and esteem. He cultivated wisdom, and tried to console
himself with friendship; moreover, his irony was not *sdegnosa
ed acerba, ma riposata e dolce*.

He was of opinion that the greatest delights of existence are
illusions, and that children find everything in nothing, and
adults nothing in everything. He compared pleasure to odors,
which usually promised a satisfaction unrealized by taste; and
said, of some nectar-drinking bees, that they were blest in not
understanding their own happiness. He remarked that want of
consideration occasioned far more suffering than positive and
intentional cruelty, and that one who lived a gregarious life
would utter himself aloud when alone, if a fly bit him; but one
accustomed to solitude and inward life would often be silent
in company, though threatened with a stroke of apoplexy. He
divided mankind into two classes—those whose characters and
instincts are overlaid and moulded by conformity and conventionalism, and those whose natures are so rich or so strong as
to assert themselves intact and habitually. He declared that, in
this age, it was impossible for any one to love without a rival;
for the egotist usually combined with and struggled for supremacy against the lover in each individual. He considered
delusion a requisite of all human enjoyment, and thought man,
like the child who from a sweet-rimmed chalice imbibed the
medicine, according to Tasso's simile, *e dal' inganno sus vita
riceve*. In these, and many other ideas attributed to Ottonieri,
we recognize the tone of feeling and the experience of Leopardi;
and the epitaph with which it concludes breathes of the same
melancholy, but intelligent and aspiring nature: *"Nato alle
opere virtuose e alla gloria, vissuto ozioso e disutile, e morto
sensa fama non ignaro della natura nè della fortuna sua."*

The **"Wager of Prometheus"** is a satire upon civilization, in
which a cannibal feast, a Hindoo widow's sacrifice, and a
suicide in London, are brought into vivid and graphic contrast.
To exhibit the fallacy which estimates life, merely as such, a
blessing, and to show that it consists in sensitive and moral
experience rather than in duration, as color is derived from
light, and not from the objects of which it is but a quality, he
gives us an animated and discriminating argument between a
metaphysician and a materialist; and, in illustration of the absolute mental nature of happiness when closely analyzed, he
takes us to the cell of Tasso, where a most characteristic and
suggestive discussion takes place between him and his familiar
genius. The tyranny of Nature, her universal and inevitable
laws, unredeemed, to Leopardi's view, by any compensatory
spiritual principle, is displayed in an interview between her
and one of her discontented subjects, wherein she declares
man's felicity an object of entire indifference; her arrangements
having for their end only the preservation of the universe by
a constant succession of destruction and renovation.

His literary creed is emphatically recorded in the little treatise
on **"Parini ov vero della Gloria"**; and it exhibits him as a true
nobleman in letters, although the characteristic sadness of his
mind is evident in his severe estimate of the obstacles which
interfere with the recognition of an original and earnest writer;
for to this result, rather than fame, his argument, is directed.
As a vocation, he considers authorship unsatisfactory, on account of its usual effect, when sedulously pursued, upon the
animal economy. He justly deems the capacity to understand
and sympathize with a great writer extremely rare; the preoccupation of society in the immediate and the personal, the
inundation of books in modern times, the influence of prejudice, ignorance, and narrowness of mind, the lack of generous
souls, mental satiety, frivolous tastes, decadence of enthusiasm
and vigor in age, and impatient expectancy in youth, are among
the many and constant obstacles against which the individual
who appeals to his race, through books, has to contend. He
also dwells upon the extraordinary influence of prescriptive
opinion, wedded to a few antique examples, upon the literary
taste of the age. He considers the secret power of genius, in
literature, to exist in an indefinable charm of style almost as

rarely appreciated as it is exercised; and he thinks great writing only an inevitable substitute for great action, the development of the heroic, the beautiful, and the true in language, opinion, and sentiment, which under propitious circumstances would have been embodied, with yet greater zeal, in deeds. He thus views the art in which he excelled, in its most disinterested and noblest relations.

There is great naturalness, and a philosophic tone, in the interview between Columbus and one of his companions, as they approach the New World. In the **"Eulogy on Birds,"** it is touching to perceive the keen appreciation Leopardi had of the joyous side of life, his complete recognition of it as a phase of nature, and his apparent unconsciousness of it as a state of feeling. The blithe habits of the feathered creation, their vivacity, motive power, and jocund strains, elicit as loving a commentary as Audubon or Wilson ever penned; but they are described only to be contrasted with the hollow and evanescent smiles of his own species; and the brief illusions they enjoy are pronounced more desirable than those of such singers as Dante and Tasso, to whom imagination was a *funestissima dote, e principio di sollecitudini, e angosce gravissime e perpetue.* With the tokens of his rare intelligence and sensibility before us, it is affecting to read his wish to be converted into a bird, in order to experience a while their contentment and joy.

The form of these writings is peculiar. We know of no English prose work at all similar, except the *Imaginary Conversations* of Landor, and a few inferior attempts of a like character. But there is one striking distinction between Leopardi and his classic English prototype; the former's aim is always to reproduce the opinions and modes of expression of his characters, while the latter chiefly gives utterance to his own. This disguise was adopted, we imagine, in a degree, from prudential motives. Conscious of sentiments at variance with the accepted creed, both in religion and philosophy, the young Italian recluse summoned historical personages, whose memories were hallowed to the imagination, or allegorical characters, whose names were associated with the past, and, through their imaginary dialogues, revealed his own fancies, meditations, and emotions. In fact, a want of sympathy with the age is one of the prominent traits of his mind. He was sceptical in regard to the alleged progress of the race, had little faith in the wisdom of newspapers, and doubted the love of truth for her own sake, as the master principle of modern science and literature. Everywhere he lauds the negative. Ignorance is always bliss, and sleep, that "knits up the ravelled sleeve of care," the most desirable blessing enjoyed by mortals. He scorns compromise with evil, and feels it is "nobler in the mind to suffer" than to reconcile itself to error and pain through cowardice, illusion or stupidity. He writes to solace himself by expression; and he writes in a satirical and humorous vein, because it is less annoying to others, and more manly in itself than wailing or despair. Thus, Leopardi's misanthropy differs from that of Rousseau and Byron in being more intellectual; it springs not so much from exasperated feeling as from the habitual contemplation of painful truth. Philosophy is rather an available medicament to him than an ultimate good.

Patriotism, learning, despair, and love, are expressed in Leopardi's verse with emphatic beauty. There is an antique grandeur, a solemn wail, in his allusions to his country, which stirs, and, at the same time, melts the heart. This sad yet noble melody is quite untranslatable; and we must content ourselves with an earnest reference to some of these eloquent and finished

lyrical strains. How grand, simple, and pathetic, is the opening of . . . **"Al' Italia"**!

> O patria mia, vedo le mura e gli archi
> E le colonne e i simulacri e l'erme
> Torri degli avi nostri,
> Ma la gloria non vedo,
> Non vedo il lauro e il ferro ond'éran carchi
> I nostri padri antichi. Or fatta inerme
> Nuda la fronte e nudo il petto mostri.
> Oimè quante ferite,
> Che lividor, che sangue! oh qual ti veggio,
> Formosisiima donna! Io chiedo al cielo
> E al mondo: dite, dite,
> Chi la ridusse a tale? E questo é peggio,
> Che di catene ha carche ambe le braccia,
> Sì che sparte le chiome e senza velo
> Siede in terra negletta e sconsolata,
> Nascondendo la faccia
> Tra le ginocchia, e piange.

In the same spirit are the lines on the **"Monument to Dante,"** to whom he says:

> Beato te che il fato
> A viver non danno fra tanto orrore;
> Che non vedesti in braccio
> L'itala meglie a barbaro soldato.
>
> . . . . .
>
> Non si conviene a sì corrotta usanza
> Questa d 'animi eccelsi altrice a scola:
> Se di codardi é stanza,
> Meglio l'è rimaner vedova e sola.

The poem to Angelo Mai, on his discovery of the Republic of Cicero, is of kindred tone—the scholar's triumph blending with the patriots grief. An identical vein of feeling, also, we recognize, under another form, in the poem written for his sister's nuptials. Bitterly he depicts the fate of woman in a country where

> Virtù viva sprezziam, lodiamo estinta;

and declares—

> O miseri o codardi
> Figliuioli avrai. Miseri eleggi. Immenso
> Tra fortuna e valor dissidio pose
> Il corrotto costume. Ahi troppo tardi,
> E nella sera dell 'umane cose,
> Acquista oggi chi nasce il moto e il senso.

"Bruto Minore" is vigorous in conception, and exquisitely modulated. In the hymn to the patriarchs, **"La Primavera,"** **"Il Sabato del Villaggio,"** **"Alla Luna,"** **"Il Passaro Solitaria,"** **"Il Canto notturno d' un Pastore errante in Asia,"** and other poems, Leopardi not only gives true descriptive hints, with tact and fidelity, but reproduces the sentiment of the hour, or the scene he celebrates, breathing into his verse the latent music they awaken in the depths of thought and sensibility; the rhythm, the words, the imagery, all combine to produce this result, in a way analogous to that by which great composers harmonize sound, or the masters of landscape blend colors, giving birth to the magical effect which, under the name of tone, constitutes the vital principles of such emanations of genius.

But not only in exalted patriotic sentiment, and graphic portraiture, nor even in artistic skill, resides all the individuality of Leopardi as a poet. His tenderness is as sincere as it is manly. There is an indescribable sadness native to his soul, quite removed from acrid gloom, or weak sensibility. We have already traced it in his opinions and in his life; but its most affecting and impressive expression is revealed in his poetry. **"Il Primo Amore,"** **"La Sera del Dì di Festa,"** **"Il Risorgimento,"** and other effusions, in a similar vein, are instinct with this deep yet attractive melancholy, the offspring of profound thought and emotion. *"Uscir di pena,"* he sadly declares, *"é diletto fra noi; non brillin gli ochi se non di pianto; due cose belle ha il mondo: amore e morto."* (pp. 277-84)

> Henry T. Tuckerman, *"Giacomo Leopardi: The Sceptical Genius," in his* Biographical Essays: Essays, Biographical and Critical; or, Studies of Character, *Phillips, Sampson and Company, 1857, pp. 267-84.*

[MARGARET OLIPHANT] (essay date 1865)

[*Oliphant was a prolific nineteenth-century Scottish novelist, critic, biographer, and historian. A regular contributor to* Blackwood's Edinburgh Magazine, *she published nearly one hundred novels, many of them popular tales of English and Scottish provincial life. Here, Oliphant ranks Leopardi a second-rate genius, but nonetheless offers a highly sympathetic account of his life, career, and pessimistic outlook.*]

The works of Leopardi are so little known in England, that it is scarcely presumption to fancy that it is a new poet whom we are about to introduce to a large number of our readers; and though it would be vain to pretend that they are of an order which can be called popular, they express at least the emotions of a mind of our own century, whose thoughts run in a more modern channel than those of the greater poets of Italy, and by means of whom the reader may perhaps ascend more easily to those great and solemn heights. Leopardi has neither the breadth nor the depth of the great masters of Italian song. Perhaps no favourable combination of circumstances could have qualified him to take his place in the first rank among those supreme intelligences, whose first and greatest qualification is the largeness of their nature and power of comprehending and embracing all the lesser individualities. He is, on the contrary, all individual—one of those marked, distinct, and separate souls, who in themselves are more interesting, by right of being less great, than the Shakespeares and Dantes. (p. 459)

[For] itself and by itself the secondary development of genius is perhaps the more interesting of the two. It has light enough to reveal in full relief the human character and career of the individual who possesses it; while, at the same time, it has not sufficient light to dazzle the spectator, and fill his eyes with motes and discs of shadow, as happens to a man who takes to gazing at the sun. What we call the temperament and peculiarities of genius—attributes which critical imbecility would fain attach to the greatest—are infallibly drawn from those men in the second rank who alone can come fully under our observation. The great poet, if he is not lost in the infinite heights like a mountain-top, is probably lost in those depths of universal nature, which are not less infinite, where the man who is manifold and many-sided and in sympathy with all men, presents few inequalities for the curious to grasp at. He is too broad, too large, too all-embracing to be peculiar: and the eye loses itself in his greatness as in the sea, the sky, the light, and all unfathomable things.

But a man of the second rank is altogether different. He is neither too high, nor too deep, nor too broad to be inspected round and round. And his genius, instead of cloaking him in an excess of light, betrays him, and makes all his irregularities,

his weaknesses, his heights and hollows, visible to the spectator. It is to this class that Leopardi belongs. The two small volumes [*Opere di Giacomo Leopardi*] which are all that he has left behind him, are full of clear landscapes and rural scenes done at a touch, fresh and dewy as are the evenings and the mornings which they preserve for ever. They abound with those touches of nature that go to the heart, and with pathetic reasonings full of restrained fire and power, and detached thoughts of the most subtle beauty. But still the great thing in them is not so much the poems or the philosophy as the singular human soul, clearly defined and apparent against the confused background of the world from which he has separated himself, and amid the peaceable nature which is external to him. It is not his to walk like Dante over the burning sands below, or to mount the celestial degrees above, with calm eyes open and ears intent, and a soul never so much preoccupied as to be unaware of the call of any miserable shadow in the gloom, or serene spirit in the light. Leopardi, in hell or in heaven, would have seen none of these things; he would have seen with the most wonderful intensity his own sufferings or delights, and a dim crowd surrounding him, whose pains or joys were naturally the reflex of his; but that would have been all. To the greater poet humanity was infinite, and the sky and the deeps teemed with living creatures, with whom he himself might or might not have distinct relations, but who existed, and whom he saw. But to the lesser there are only two unmistakable existences in heaven and earth, himself and another—who may be God, or Chance, or Fate, or Joy, or Misery, as a harder or happier education may decide. Of such was Leopardi, whom we think we are justified in calling one of the greatest of modern Italian writers. It is impossible to read his works—we might almost say, so strong is the personal impression they convey, to look at him—without the profoundest, almost painful, sympathy and pity; nor without, at the same time, the most earnest interest and a kind of hope, which may all orthodox theologians forgive us, that instead of his harsh stepdame Nature, Leopardi might wake up in the other existence with a wonderful and joyful surprise to find a Father-God putting some sense and reason into life. It is possible to imagine that after such a discovery the poor soul would make his way even down to Hades, if that were needful, with a certain content. One does not concern one's self particularly about Dante's experiences (who knew so well all about it) in the other world—which is a proof of what we have been saying, that the lesser genius, being the more distinct individual, is, in a certain sense, more interesting. For, to tell the truth, for our own part, we cannot prevent our imagination from following Leopardi out of the profound darkness of his life into the hereafter which he did not believe in, with a curious sense of watching the amazement, and shock of unfamiliar joy, of his awaking there.

Affixed to the volumes which contain his collected works, one of his friends has given us a brief biography—the story of a life without any events—valuable only as a kind of exposition and elucidation of his own utterances. Leopardi was one of the men who are born to struggle with pain and bodily suffering, and condemned to a forced renunciation of everything that in the world is called happiness. Signor Ranieri, his biographer, treats with a certain magnificent indistinctness, which is perhaps natural to the flowing and redundant Italian, the nature of Leopardi's malady. But it was such as to render life a continual agony, and to cut him off from all the happier ties which a man can form for himself. Everybody has known instances of such involuntary martyrdom, and most people have seen examples in which the hard lot was conquered by a patient spirit, and made into something sublime; but Leopardi's spirit was not patient, nor had it the natural softness which helps resignation. Sick and helpless and suffering, his impotent body contained a fiery, impetuous, Italian soul. He had it in him to do and dare, and love and enjoy, with all the force and fulness of his race; and he found himself fettered and feeble, forbidden the joys of existence, and even its labours, which might have made him forget its joys. When he found this out—which does not seem to have been until after all the hopes and plans of youth had formed in his mind—bitterness and despair filled his heart; and thereafter he affords the strange and pitiful spectacle of a man struggling to convince himself, since he cannot be happy, that happiness does not exist. In almost everything he has written, the stamp of this conflict is impressed. In the depths of his heart he believes in love and in joy, with a strength of conviction all the more deep that he is continually asserting to himself their nonexistence; and when he breaks into song, or falls into those minute and subtle trains of thought which are even more poetic than his poetry, it is not so much the world as himself whom he addresses. If he could but make sure that not he only, but *all* are miserable; and yet he can never make sure; and the more boldly he asserts it, the more evident is the doubt underneath, and sense, after all, that it is he who is the shadow in the landscape, and that joy exists though he cannot find it. Nature is cruel to him, and yet he clings to her; love is forbidden to him, and yet an infinite love of love possesses his spirit; his mind burns with activity and vital force, and yet to him all spheres of activity are closed.

For such a lot it should have been a patient feminine soul open to the smaller compensations of an incomplete life; and it was the fiery spirit of a man, impatient, exacting, thirsting for enjoyment and progress. Nothing can be more terrible than such a conjunction of strength and weakness; and his suffering continually intensifies his individuality, and keeps his eyes more and more fixed upon himself. He asks the heavens and the earth to tell him why it is, and he can find no answer. Life has no reason, no meaning, in the eyes of a man to whom it is a perpetual dying, and who has no religious hope to inspire him with expectation of another life to set matters right. There are many good people who would doubtless say that his misery was the due recompense of his infidelity, and leave the unhappy poet with composure to his fate; but it is hard to leave him in his suffering and yearning and despair, or to hear without a pang of sympathy the cry that comes out of his heart. This is the interest which gives a double power to his minute and melancholy philosophy, and to his outbreaks of tender and plaintive song. His life and his productions afford a picture terribly intense and full of a sad unity, of a condition of being which every thoughtful mind must one time or other have passed through, but which with Leopardi endured always. Few are the men who do not come to a pause one time or other in their existence, stricken with the hopelessness, the powerlessness, the mockery of life, and with a sense that somehow the reason of it must be demanded from God, who is responsible; but most men are beguiled from that great question by the softer solacements of humanity, the tenderness of friends, the stir of occupation, the tranquillising flow of time itself, and that strange sustaining force of mere existence which can endure and surmount a thousand deaths. But to Leopardi these secondary consolations were wanting; he was kept for ever face to face with that grand question which nobody can answer. Existence for him was a feeble current wanting the tide and force of health. Occupation he had none of any absorbing or compulsory character; and the question was all the more bitter and absolute since life was limited, in his eyes, by the grave. A man without hope for the hereafter may yet derive a certain

philosophic satisfaction from the thought that life, circumscribed as it is, still has had its share of joy, its natural delights, and exhilarating sense of being; but with Leopardi life was but a cheat, a lie, an inexplicable hard necessity, which some cruel unknown power had imposed upon him. There is a sonnet among his poems ["**To Myself**"] which expresses in the most striking manner his final abandonment of the idea of immortality. (pp. 460-62)

[However, this sonnet] is the only distinct utterance of that grand final despair to which Leopardi gives vent. His want of hope shows itself more in the utter absence of all light, except that of his bitterly-regretted youth, upon the lovely little sketches of nature and rural life, which are all rounded with a sigh, and upon his close and acute studies of men and thought, than in any direct statement. In the East there linger still the traces of that glory by which he was once attended; but neither above him is there any sun shining, nor from the western wilderness before is there any symptom of the evening light. The light comes all from behind, and projects his shadow drearily over the unresponsive earth; and in bitterness, with a sense of wrong and injury and injustice, he recalls to himself the unrealised hopes and vain imaginations of his youth.

Giacomo Leopardi was born in Recanati, in the March of Ancona, in 1795, of a noble, well-regulated (*costumata*), and religious family. It was perhaps the moment when the fortunes of Italy were at their lowest ebb, and when least of all she had any career to offer to her children. He was not false to the universal tradition of all the poets and writers of Italy who have kept up since Dante's time an unfailing and fervent protest against the dismemberment of the *patria* and the presence of the stranger. But his genius was not political, nor had any such gleam of revival arisen as that which inspired and justified the fiery eloquence of the Florentine Guisti, born later when the patience or disgust of despair had changed into the fury of hope. It would be well for those who still doubt the reality and stability of the Italian kingdom to study a little the unfailing and unanimous sentiment of all the minds that have in her bitterness and depression given utterance to Italy. Such a study might teach even the narrow spectator who still talks of Piedmont to believe that perhaps the Italians know better what they want and is good for them than he does. Leopardi was not false to this universal sentiment; but the effect of his country's downfall and bondage upon him was characteristic and individual, like that of every other great influence of his life. The sentiment of national prostration aggravated the gloom of everything that surrounded himself. He was a soul bound hand and foot in a country bound hand and foot, the one completing the other's misery—and, naturally, the view that he took of her position agreed with the general tenor of his mind and thoughts. It was not in his way to gnash his teeth at the *stranieri*. What he saw and mourned, and chafed over with the bitterness of shame as well as grief, was her submission to her fate, and the supineness of the race under their yoke. At one time, indeed—but the poem bears traces of being one of his earliest—he finds his country seated on the ground, with hair dishevelled and unveiled, hiding her face on her knees; and calls upon heaven and earth to tell him why—who has brought her to this? "Do none fight for thee?" he asks; "do none of thine own defend thee?"

> Where are thy sons? I hear the sound of arms,
> Trumpets, and chariots, and the voice of war,

On foreign coasts afar
Thy children fight. Listen, oh Italy,
Listen . . . . . . in foreign lands thy children fight—

. . . . .

Oh hapless he who thus in war is spent,
Not for his native shores encountering death,
For babes nor wife—but unto strangers lent,
For strangers slain; who with his dying breath
Can never say, Dear land, to thee
I render back the life thou gavest me.

But it is not under this picturesque form that he generally
regards the prostration of his country. For the most part he
upbraids her and her people with it, with lofty indignation and
shame. "Turn thee behind and look at that infinite host of
immortals, and weep and disdain thyself," he says. "For once
take thought of thine ancestors, and of thy children"—and then
he blesses passionately the fate of Dante, who did not live to
see these miseries:—

Blessed art thou whom fate
Gave not to live among so many harms,
Who seest not thy Italy for mate
Grasped in the barbarous soldier's arms,
Nor how the pilgrim's frenzy and vile sale,
Ravage and waste our hills and cities fair,
Nor of Italian genius rare
The works divine dragged over hill and vale,
Beyond the Alps to wretched slavery.

Still more bitter is the bridal song with which he hails the
marriage of his sister Paolina . . .—

My sister, who in grave and troublous times,
Wilt give increase to the unhappy race
Of Italy unhappy,

"Thy sons will be," he says to the bride, "either wretched or
codardi—choose for them to be wretched;" and then he breaks
forth into the following appeal:—

Women, from you I claim
Of our estate the reason true.
Is, then, the holy flame
Of youth extinguished by your hands? by you
Our soul diminished? yours the blame
Of slumbrous minds, unworthy wills,
And this poor mass of flesh and nerve that fills
The mould of native force and right?
To worthy deeds
Love is a spur to him who loves aright,
And beauty to high influence leads
But he whose heart ne'er leaps
Within his breast, when to the combat rise
The winds, and when the angry skies
And cloud over Olympus sweeps,
And the dull roar of tempest shakes the hill:
Let him from love be banished still.
Oh brides, oh virgins, guard
Your hearts 'gainst him whom peril moves;
His wishes and his vulgar loves
With scorn and hate reward.
If in your female race
The love of men, not babes, has place.

This will show how deep in Leopardi's heart was the sense of
national downfall—a depression which reacted upon himself. . . . There is nothing about freedom or oppression in the
following poem, written apparently in one of the many visits
paid by Leopardi to his paternal home; but it shows more clearly
than a hundred denunciations how stifling and terrible to ev-

erything that was best and most hopeful in the race, was that
period of stupor and national death now fortunately at an end:—

"Recollection"

Fair stars of Ursa, I ne'er thought to turn,
As in old times, to contemplate your light
On the home-garden glimmering, nor to talk
And reason with you at the windows where
I mused, a child—and which behold at last
The end of all my joys. How many dreams
And fancies once took life beneath your rays.
And those companion lights that shine with you!
When silent, seated on the verdant sward,
Gazing at the clear heavens, hearing afar
The distant frog croak in the dusky fields,
It was my wont to pass the lingering eve.
The glow-worm wandered by the hedge, the nets
Shrilled to the wind; the odorous alleys breathed,
And the sad cypress yonder in the wood—
And 'neath my father's roof was sound of voice
Alternate, and the servants' tranquil toil—
What thoughts immense, what gentle dreams inspired,
The sight of that fair sea, and those blue hills,
Which, one day crossing, I should swift disclose,
Thus said I in my thoughts, mysterious worlds,
Mysterious gladness feigning for my life!
For still my fate I knew not, unaware
How many times this naked, mournful life,
Glad and well pleased, for death I would have changed—
Nor did my heart e'er whisper my green age
Should be condemned to waste and pass its prime
In this wild native village, 'mid a race
Unlearned and dull, to whom fair Wisdom's name
And Knowledge, like the names of strangers sound,
An argument of laughter and of jest;
Who hated me and fled me. Not that they
Were envious; of no greater destiny
They held me than themselves; but that I bore
Esteem for my own being in my heart,
Though ne'er to man disclosed by any sign.
Here passed my years, recluse and desolate,
Without or love or life: bitter and harsh,
Among the unkindly multitude I grew.
Here was I robbed of pity and of trust,
And, studying the poor herd, became of men
A scorner and disdainful. Thus flew by
The dear days of my youth; more dear than fame
Or laurel; dearer than the limpid light
Of day; dearer than breath. Oh thou sole flower
Of arid life, here, without use or aim
Or one delight, I lost thee; 'mid a crowd
Of sorrows mean, in this abode obscure.
The wind brings softly from the village towers
The chiming of the hour; and I recall
How oft, a child, awaking in the dark,
Pursued by terrors, sighing for the morn,
That sound consoled me; nothing can I hear
Or see, but some imagination past
Returns, or some sweet memory wakes again,
Sweet for itself, but mingled with the sad
Thoughts of the present, and a vain desire
After the past; and the sad words—I was.
That balcony below, turned to the last
Rays of the day; these pictured walls; the herds
Which in my mind I see; the sun that rose
O'er the Campagna, to my leisure bore
Thousand delights, so long as at my side,
Where'er I was, my strong delusion went. . . .
But useless misery all. Though bare and void
Have been my years, though desert and obscure
My mortal state, little of fortune's gifts

I seek or heed. Ah, but by times my thoughts
To you go back, oh hopes of old—to you,
Blessed imaginations of my youth!
When I regard my life, so mean and poor
And mournful, and that death alone is all
To which so much hope has advanced my days.
I feel my heart stand still, and know not how
To be consoled of such a destiny.
When this death, oft invoked, shall be at hand,
When my misfortunes to their end arrive,
When this earth like a foreign valley lies
Behind, and when the future flies away
Out of my sight; then still, my hopes, of you,
I will bethink me, and that image still
Will come with sighs; will make it miserable
To have lived in vain; will temper with distress
Even the great sweetness of the fatal day.

Such is the profound unalterable melancholy which breathes
out of everything Leopardi has ever written. He had lived in
vain; God had refused him health and action and happiness,
and his country had no occupation for him. A foreign land
might have given him employment for his genius, and for the
vast stores of learning which his youth had accumulated; but
Italy, dismembered and without hope, Italy *infelicissima*, could
but let him go back to the garden at Recanati, to watch the
cypress trees sway in the night wind, and mourn to the stars
from the loggia, which he had once paced in the glory of his
hope. Touched by another hand than his own, the figure of the
sad and sick Italian in his ancestral house, among the frescoed
walls and stately gardens, with the blue Apennines at hand,
and the great sea, would make just such a picture as once
sentimental fancy identified with Italy. But as for the Conte
Giacomo, he finds no fitness in it. ''The same sound is in his
ears as in these days he heard,'' and those sounds and sights
go to his heart. They are so many witnesses and proofs to him
that he has lived in vain. (pp. 463-66)

Still more delicate in its mournful sentiment is the **"Sabato
del Villaggio."** The melancholy of the moment after the feast
is over, has been often enough the subject of verse; but to
Leopardi the feast itself is sad. It is the eve of the holiday, the
bloom of anticipation, undebased by any touch of reality, which
strikes his pensive fancy. That, unconnected as it is with anything actual, is the true moment of happiness—and it is to this
he turns, never without a thought that the festa of his life has
been to him disappointment and bitterness, although the eve
of that festival, the early moment of hope and anticipation,
was so sweet. Nothing can be more sweet and perfect than the
original, which, however, like almost all his poems, is in a
measure very difficult to follow, and almost impossible to
reproduce with any exactness—the arrangement of the rhymes
being entirely without rule, and occurring just as it may happen.

"The Village Saturday"

From the Campagna, when the sun is low,
   The little maiden goes,
Bearing her load of grass, her hands aglow
    With heaps of violet and rose,
With which, as she is wont, to deck her hair,
And her fair bosom to adorn,
To grace the feast to-morrow morn;
And seated with her neighbours on the stair
Where latest falls the sun,
The old woman talks and spins and tells her tale
Of her best days before her course was run;
How for the festa, decked and fair,
She danced the evening through among her peers,

Among the comrades of her fairer years.
The brown air darkens; the blue sky
Deepens; the shadows turn and lie
From hills and house tops, changing round
At whitening of the recent moon;
And lo, the bell whose sound
Tells of the festa drawing nigh,
And thou wouldst say, to hear
That voice the heart takes cheer.
And in the Piazzetta in a crowd
The children shout and cry,
Making a tumult gay and loud;
And back to his poor board the labourer goes.
Whistling, and thinking of his day's repose.
And when around all other work is done,
And all the world is still,
I hear the hammer beat, the saw's sharp tone,
The carver with his lamp alone
In his closed shop withdrawn,
Intent to end his work before the dawn.

   Of all the seven the happiest morn,
So full of hope and joy!
To-morrow sadness and annoy
Reclaim the hours, and to the accustomed toil
Each in his fancy will return.
Oh joyous boy!
Thy flowery age that so doth smile,
Is like a day of gladness rife,
A clear day and serene.
That comes before the festa of thy life.
Be glad, my child, the path is fair and green.
The season sweet to see.
No more to thee I say;
But if thy festa lingers on its way,
It will be well for thee.

These dreary philosophisings never fail to conclude the sweet
and fresh pictures which he seems to linger over with a yearning
fondness in spite of himself. Let us add another snatch of verse
without the sting, from which it can be separated without in-
juring the completeness of the picture:—

"The Quiet after the Storm"

The storm is past and gone;
I hear the birds make festa, and on high
Upon the road the fowls with clearest tone
Repeat their verse. And lo, the opening sky
Breaks to the Westward o'er the mountain's head;
   From the Campagna, all the shadows clear,
And, glimmering in the vale, the streams appear.
   Now every heart is glad; on each hand springs
The common sound and din.
The common works begin;
The artisan looks out, and sings,
His work in hand, and by the opening high
Admires the humid sky.
Forth comes the little woman to the tide,
The flowing current of new rain;
The herbalist awakes again,
From path to path beside,
His daily cry;
And lo the sun returns, and smiling glows
Upon the hills and villas; terrace fair
And loggia open wide the family throws;
And from the distant road I hear
Tinkling of bells—the waggon onward goes;
The passenger resumes his way,
   So every heart grows gay.

It is impossible not to recognise in all these sketches of song
the same landscape which is first presented to us by night in
the Recanati garden. There are always at hand the mountains

The village square depicted in "Il sabato del villaggio"; the large house on the left is the Palazzo Leopardi.

and the sea, and the balcony which faces to the sunset, and which is opened by "the family" when the sweeping rain is over, and the sky breaks over Apennine. Local affection is an Italian quality, but scarcely in this fashion; and it is curious to see how the paternal house which was to him a prison, and the sight of which made him so bitterly aware that he had lived in vain, comes in always as the central point in his landscape. His biographer gives a fanciful and pleasant description of the effect which Florence had upon his mind, with "the luxuriance of its flowers, the harmony of its language, the ineradicable grace of its women, the purity of its life, the graceful, and, so to speak, aerial curve of its architecture, the something *un non so che,* of caressing and homelike—a something Attic and light, which he had made up to that time supposed ideal, and now found palpable and existent." But whatever his personal predilections might be, it is always to the old house of the Leopardi, with its balconies and terraces, that he goes back in verse. It is there he watches the sky, and sees the morning rise and the evening fall. Perhaps because this home, in after days so monotonous and dreary, was still always enshrined in the light of his youth. It is there that he is roused from his studies by the young voice of the girl who sings perpetually at her work, to come out and regard the sea and the hills and all the "golden ways." It is from thence that he watches the shadows turn from eastward to westward as the moon rises, in that magical moment which stands for twilight in Italy; and sees the artisan come out with his work in his hand to look at the clearing of the sky, and the little woman step forth to the current of the new-fallen rain. Even the fowls that "say their verse," and the frog that croaks in the dark fields, attract his ear. From his loggia he sees all and hears all, without knowing that he either sees or hears; and thus, whenever his thoughts or his pangs leave him free for a moment, it is the old familiar landscape that rises before him—a landscape all Italian, with bird-

nets on the boughs, and frogs in the fields, and fireflies in the hedges; surveyed from that balcony, the "loggia, volta agli estremi raggi del dì," where at the same time he can hear the alternate voices indoors, and sounds of the tranquil domestic work; lighted with the light of stars, and made musical by the dark sweep of the cypress trees close at hand, the village bell in the distance, the villagers making ready for the weekly festa. His soul chafed to think that these were all; that the man had never found in his life any impressions so deep or distinct as those which had stamped themselves without his consciousness on the youth's ardent imagination. Perhaps it only required a deeper philosophy, a gentler spirit, to show to the suffering poet how much real treasure he had in these associations of his youth; perhaps a little happiness would have done it. But it is not our business to reproach Leopardi or set him right. So intense an appreciation of use and joy in a nature which God and the circumstances of his life and his country had made incapable of either, place a soul, so noble and sorrowful, almost above criticism. What can anybody say to a man, full of man's fullest energies and wishes, who is denied and unfitted for everything that makes life worth having? One can say, "God willed it so," with a sickening sense of how easy it is for others to content themselves with that ultimate certainty, and how hard for him. The only possible way of supporting such hard conditions is the belief that this life is, after all, but a fragment of life, which God, when his time comes, will clear up and set right; and in the mean time, the harder the service the more trustworthy and proved the soldier. But Leopardi was destitute of such a hope. Somehow, in a combination of circumstances so heartrending, one has not the heart to blame the sufferer. He has the infinitely Pitiful to deal with in the blindness of his misery; and is not to be judged by happier men. (pp. 467-69)

[*Margaret Oliphant*], *"Giacomo Leopardi,"* in Blackwood's Edinburgh Magazine, *Vol. XCVIII, No. DC, October, 1865, pp. 459-80.*

THE SPECTATOR (essay date 1883)

[*In this review of* Essays and Dialogues, *the anonymous critic decries Leopardi's philosophy of pessimism yet praises his literary skill.*]

[*Essays and Dialogues*] contains translations of the chief prose works of one of the most remarkable of modern Italian writers, and is, therefore, of considerable value and interest. As to its own qualities, they are not unlike those of a photograph which gives us correctly enough the outlines of some beloved face, but gives them to us so harsh and cold, that we would not have it seen by those who do not know the original. And yet [the translator and editor] Mr. Edwards is evidently an ardent admirer of his subject,—a far more ardent and uncompromising admirer than we can profess to be. "The name of Giacomo Leopardi," he says, "is not yet a household word in the mouths of Englishmen;" but he desires that it should be so, and to that end has "Englished" (according to the old phrase) the finest of the Italian's writings. We do not greatly share the desire, nor at all the hope, which has inspired his labours. For even if the extreme beauty of style which charms us in the original could ever survive the process of translation, if the delicate fancy could preserve its wings unclipped, the pure thought be unweakened, still, we would no more choose to feed the minds of our countrymen and women with the despairing utterances of the pessimist poet, than we would their bodies with hasheesh. Such melancholy as his, clothed in such eloquent words, may be the luxury of the idle; it is poison to those who have work to do in the world. It shuts out hope, the very spring of energy; it makes the cheerful, steady pursuit of duty a thing utterly beyond human powers.

For we can none of us stand alone. Either in human or divine love, we must find the mainspring of all life worth living. There must be something outside of ourselves, which we regard not with despair, but with hope. . . .

We fancy that Leopardi has given his view of himself in the dialogue between Nature and a Soul. Perhaps he did not intend to do so, but as he was unquestionably alive to his genius, he most probably found the original of the portrait in his own consciousness. . . .

> *Soul.*—Tell me, are excellence and extraordinary unhappiness the same thing? or if they are two things, cannot you separate the one from the other?
>
> *Nature.*—In the souls of men, it may be said that these two things are almost the same, because excellence in souls implies greater comprehension of their life, and this in itself implies also keener feeling of their own unhappiness, or, as I might say, greater unhappiness. . . . In the same manner, the fuller life of souls includes greater strength of self-love . . . which means greater desire for happiness, and consequently more discontent and weariness in the deprivation of it, and more pain in the adverse circumstances that hinder it. . . . Moreover, the refinement of your own intellect, and the liveliness of your imagination, will in a great measure deprive you of self-mastery. . . . Men such as you, constantly wrapped up in themselves, dominated, as it were, by the greatness of their own powers, and helpless against themselves, lie most of their time under a burden of ir-

resolution, both as regards their thoughts and their actions; and this is one of the heaviest miseries of human life. Add to this that, while by the excellency of your talents you will easily and quickly surpass others of your race in profound knowledge, and in the most abstruse studies, it will, nevertheless, be extremely difficult or even impossible for you to learn or practise a thousand things, trifling in themselves, but most necessary in intercourse with other men. All the souls of men, as I have told you, are given up as a prey to unhappiness, without fault of mine.

What wonder is it, if the soul, threatened with such a fate as this, cries out, "Place me, then, in the lowest of creatures, or give me, I implore you, death, rather than immortality!"

But though we should be sorry to see Leopardi's pessimism exercising its baneful influence over the young and imaginative natures which would be most likely to be fascinated by it, we are not blind to the truth and greatness of his genius. It is difficult to imagine a more exquisite piece of writing than the **"Cantico del Gallo Silvestro,"** more delicate humour than that of **"Copernico,"** or more beauty of thought than shines through the *Dialogues* in general. (p. 236)

"Giacomo Leopardi," in The Spectator, *Vol. 56, February 17, 1883, pp. 236-37.*

W. D. HOWELLS (essay date 1885)

[*Howells was the chief progenitor of American realism and an influential American literary critic during the late nineteenth and early twentieth centuries. Although he wrote nearly three dozen novels, few of them are read today. Despite this eclipse, he stands as one of the major literary figures of his era; having successfully weaned American literature from the sentimental romanticism of its infancy, he earned the popular sobriquet "the Dean of American letters." In the following excerpt, Howells considers Leopardi's preoccupation with death.*]

Leopardi lived in Italy during the long contest between the classic and romantic schools, and it may be said that in him many of the leading ideas of both parties were reconciled. His literary form was as severe and sculpturesque as that of Alfieri himself, whilst the most subjective and introspective of the romantic poets did not so much color the world with his own mental and spiritual hue as Leopardi. It is not plain whether he ever declared himself for one theory or the other. He was a contributor to the literary journal which the partisans of the romantic school founded at Florence; but he was a man so weighed upon by his own sense of the futility and vanity of all things that he could have had little spirit for mere literary contentions. His admirers try hard to make out that he was positively and actively patriotic; and it is certain that in his early youth, he disagreed with his father's conservative opinions, and despised the existing state of things; but later in life he satirized the aspirations and purposes of progress, though without sympathizing with those of reaction.

The poem which his chief claim to classification with the poets militant of his time rests upon is that addressed **"To Italy."** (p. 317)

His patriotism was the fever-flame of the sick man's blood; his real country was the land beyond the grave, and there is a far truer note in this address to Death.

> And thou, that ever from my life's beginning,
> I have invoked and honored,
> Beautiful Death! who only,
> Of all our earthly sorrows knowest pity:

If ever celebrated
Thou wast by me; if ever I attempted
To recompense the insult
That vulgar terror offers
Thy lofty state, delay no more, but listen
To prayers so rarely uttered:
Shut to the light forever,
Sovereign of time, these eyes of weary anguish!

I suppose that Italian criticism of the present day would not give Leopardi nearly so high a place among the poets as his friend Ranieri claims for him and his contemporaries accorded. He seems to have been the poet of a national mood; he was the final expression of that long, hopeless apathy in which Italy lay bound for thirty years after the fall of Napoleon and his governments, and the reëstablishment of all the little despots, native and foreign, throughout the peninsula. In this time there was unrest enough, and revolt enough of a desultory and un-organized sort, but every struggle, apparently every aspiration, for a free political and religious life ended in a more solid confirmation of the leaden misrule which weighed down the hearts of the people. To such an apathy the pensive monotone of this sick poet's song might well seem the only truth; and one who beheld the universe with the invalid's loath eyes, and reasoned from his own irremediable ills to a malign mystery presiding over all human affairs, and ordering a sad destiny from which there could be no defense but death, might have the authority of a prophet among those who could find no promise of better things in their earthly lot.

Leopardi's malady was such that when he did not positively suffer he had still the memory of pain, and he was oppressed with a dreary ennui, from which he could not escape. Death, oblivion, annihilation, are the thoughts upon which he broods, and which fill his verse. The passing color of other men's minds is the prevailing cast of his, and he probably with far more sincerity than any other poet nursed his despair in such utterances as this:—

"To Himself"

Now thou shalt rest forever,
O weary heart! The last deceit is ended,
For I believed myself immortal. Cherished
Hopes, and beloved delusions,
And longings to be deluded,—all are perished!
Rest thee forever! Oh, greatly,
Heart, hast thou palpitated. There is nothing
Worthy to move thee more, nor is earth worthy
Thy sighs. For life is only
Bitterness and vexation; earth is only
A heap of dust. So rest thee!
Despair for the last time. To our race Fortune
Never gave any gift but death. Disdain, then,
Thyself and Nature and the Power
Occultly reigning to the common ruin:
Scorn, heart, the infinite emptiness of all things!

Nature was so cruel a stepmother to this man that he could see nothing but harm even in her apparent beneficence, and his verse repeats again and again his dark mistrust of the very loveliness which so keenly delights his sense. One of his early poems, called **"The Quiet after the Storm,"** strikes the key in which nearly all his songs are pitched. The observation of nature is very sweet and honest, and I cannot see that the philosophy in its perversion of the relations of physical and spiritual facts is less mature than that of his later work: it is a philosophy of which the first conception cannot well differ from the final expression. (pp. 318-19)

The bodily deformities which humiliated Leopardi, and the cruel infirmities that agonized him his whole life long, wrought in his heart an invincible disgust, which made him invoke death as the sole relief. His songs, while they express discontent, the discord of the world, the conviction of the nullity of human things, are exquisite in style; they breathe a perpetual melancholy, which is often sublime, and they relax and pain your soul like the music of a single chord, while their strange sweetness wins you to them again and again.

This is the language of an Italian critic who wrote after Leo-pardi's death, when already it had begun to be doubted whether he was the greatest Italian poet since Dante. A still later critic finds Leopardi's style "without relief, without lyric flight, without the great art of contrasts, without poetic leaven," hard to read. "Despoil those verses of their masterly polish," he says, "reduce those thoughts to prose, and you will see how little they are akin to poetry." . . .

I am not wholly able to agree with him. It seems to me that there is the indestructible charm in it which, wherever we find it, we must call poetry. It is true that "its strange sweetness wins you again and again," and that this "lovely pipe of death" thrills and solemnly delights as no other stop has done. (p. 319)

I confess that [those of Leopardi's poems that] I have read leave me somewhat puzzled in the presence of his reputation. This, to be sure, is largely based upon his prose writings—his dialogues, full of irony and sarcasm—and his unquestionable scholarship. But the poetry is the heart of his fame, and is it enough to justify it? I suppose that such poetry owes very much of its peculiar influence to that awful love we all have of hovering about the idea of Death,—of playing with the great catastrophe of our several tragedies and farces, and of mar-veling what it can be. There are moods which the languid despair of Leopardi's poetry can always evoke, and in which it seems that the most life can do is to leave us, and let us lie down and cease. But I fancy we all agree that these are not very wise or healthful moods, and that their indulgence does not fit us particularly well for the duties of life, though I never heard that they interfered with its pleasures; on the contrary, they add a sort of zest to enjoyment. Of course the whole transaction is illogical. But if a poet will end every pensive strain with an appeal or an apostrophe to Death; not the real Death, that comes with a sharp, quick agony, or "after long lying in bed," after many days or many years of squalid misery and slowly dying hopes and medicines that cease even to relieve at last; not this Death, that comes in all the horror of under-taking, but a picturesque and impressive abstraction, whose business it is to relieve us in the most effective way of all our troubles, and at the same time to avenge us somehow upon the indefinitely ungrateful and unworthy world we abandon,—if a poet will do this, we are very apt to like him. There is little doubt that Leopardi was sincere, and there is little reason why he should not have been so, for life could give him nothing but pain.

De Sanctis . . . , who speaks, I believe, with rather more au-thority than any other modern Italian critic, and certainly with great clearness and acuteness, does not commit himself to spe-cific praise of Leopardi's work. But he seems to regard him as an important expression, if not force or influence, and he has some words about him, at the close of his *History of Italian Literature,* which have interested me, not only for the estimate of Leopardi which they embody, but for the singularly distinct statement which they make of the modern literary attitude. I should not, myself, have felt that Leopardi represented this, but I am willing that the reader should feel it, if he can. De Sanctis has been speaking of the romantic period in Italy, when he says,—

> Giacomo Leopardi marks the close of this period. Metaphysics at war with theology had ended in this attempt at reconciliation. The multiplicity of systems had discredited science itself. Metaphysics was regarded as a revival of theology. The Idea seemed a substitute for Providence. Those philosophies of history, of religion, of humanity, had the air of poetical inventions. . . . That reconciliation between the old and new, tolerated as a temporary political necessity, seemed at bottom a profanation of science, a moral weakness. . . . Faith in revelation had been wanting; faith in philosophy itself was now wanting. Mystery reappeared. The philosopher knew as much as the peasant. Of this mystery, Giacomo Leopardi was the echo in the solitude of his thought and his pain. His skepticism announced the dissolution of this theologico-metaphysical world, and inaugurated the reign of the arid True, of the Real. His songs are the most profound and occult voices of that laborious transition called the nineteenth century. That which has importance is not the brilliant exterior of that century of progress, and it is not without irony that he speaks of the progressive destinies of mankind. That which has importance is the exploration of one's own breast, the inner world, virtue, liberty, love, all the ideals of religion, of science, and of poetry,—shadows and illusions in the presence of reason, yet which warm the heart, and will not die. Mystery destroys the intellectual world; it leaves the moral world intact. This tenacious life of the inner world, despite the fall of all theological and metaphysical worlds, is the originality of Leopardi, and gives his skepticism a religious stamp. . . . Every one feels in it a new creation. The instrument of this renovation is criticism. . . . The sense of the real continues to develop itself; the positive sciences come to the top, and cast out all the ideal and systematic constructions. New dogmas lose credit. Criticism remains intact. The patient labor of analysis begins again. . . . Socialism reappears in the political order, positivism in the intellectual order. The word is no longer liberty, but justice. . . . Literature also undergoes transformation. It rejects classes, distinctions, privileges. The ugly stands beside the beautiful; or rather, there is no longer ugly or beautiful, neither ideal nor real, neither infinite nor finite. . . . There is but one thing only, the Living.

I began by calling Leopardi the Laureate of Death; I end by letting another proclaim him the Laureate of Life. Perhaps there is no difference, though I am not yet realist enough to affirm this. (pp. 321-22)

> *W. D. Howells, "The Laureate of Death," in* The Atlantic Monthly, *Vol. LVI, No. CCCXXXV, September, 1885, pp. 311-22.*

W. M. ROSSETTI (lecture date 1891)

[*Rossetti was an original member of the Pre-Raphaelite Brotherhood and a chronicler of the movement. He was also a literary critic and edited important editions of the works of William Blake, Percy Bysshe Shelley, Walt Whitman, and James Thomson. In the following excerpt from his study of Leopardi, which was originally delivered as a lecture on 24 November 1891, Rossetti examines the reasons for Leopardi's melancholy and asserts his preeminence as a stylist.*]

It is, I believe, not only plausible but correct to describe Leopardi by two phrases in the superlative degree of comparison: he is the *most* unhappy among men of literary genius; and he is the *most* finished master of style in Italian letters since the date of Petrarca. (p. 55)

I by no means intend to imply that he suffered outward misfortunes greater than, or at all equalling, those which several of his compeers have had to endure; to go no farther than two of his own illustrious countrymen, the external misfortunes which tried the mettle of Dante and of Tasso in the furnace of affliction were beyond comparison greater than those which beset Leopardi. . . . [By] way of external misfortunes, he had nothing severer to show than a partly uncongenial home, unappreciative townsfolk, narrow means, and . . . some disappointments in the attempt to obtain employment, or to develop on a large scale the vast resources of his intellect. Even these distresses were but partial; for his family were upright and to a large extent affectionate, and his literary reputation was, if limited in scope, very considerable in degree. But it is the man himself that was unhappy—abnormally and almost uniquely unhappy. His miserable ill-health scourged him from pillar to post, deformed his person, made him an object of derisive compassion, hampered and stunted his power of work. But physical disability and suffering served only as the ante-room to settled and profound mental gloom. Leopardi meditated upon the nature and the destiny of man, and the character of men in society; and he found scarcely anything to record except the blackness of desolation. A large proportion of his writings is devoted to enforcing the view that men and women in society are almost universally selfish, heartless, malicious, and bad; that the very idea of happiness in this world, for any human being, is a mere delusion; that there is not any other world to serve as a counterbalance or compensation to man for his unhappiness in this sphere of being; and that thus it is a universal misfortune for men to be born, and the only thing to which they can reasonably look forward with some sense of consolation, or some approach to satisfaction, is death. He allowed that the emotion of Hope, though irrational, affords some mitigation to the evils of humanity; and laid stress upon the noble aspirations of virtue, wisdom, glory, love, and patriotism, as magnificent incentives, although essentially illusions—phantasms which man does well to believe in until the paralyzing influence of Truth resolves them into nothingness. Happiness, according to Leopardi, would really consist in the sensation or emotion of pleasure, and freedom from pain; but these, especially after the season of early youth is past, are not to be attained, unless in transient and momentary glimpses: old age he regarded with peculiar repulsion. He was therefore as absolute a pessimist as any writer of whom literature bears record. It seems difficult to doubt that what compelled him into pessimism was, to a great extent, his own chronic suffering, and the lot of bitterness and self-abnegation which this imposed upon him in all his personal and social relations. He himself admitted as much, in a letter dated in 1820; but afterwards, in another letter of May, 1832, he indignantly repelled such an inference, and affirmed that his pessimism was the genuine unbiassed deduction of his own reasoning upon the nature and condition of general humankind. It is curious that, of the two poets who, by frailty of constitution and deformity of frame, most nearly resembled each other, Alexander Pope and Giacomo Leopardi, one, the Englishman, professed the extreme of optimism, 'Whatever is, is best,' while the other proclaimed an equally complete pessimism, amounting practically to the assertion, 'That speck in the universe, called man, is born to nothing but disaster in life, and extinction in death—the puppet and the mockery of fate.'

I find it somewhat difficult to account for the extremely bad opinion which Leopardi formed of the characters of men—and women he regarded as even inferior to men. It is said that in his early years he assumed that people were, broadly speaking, all good; with the lapse of time he went to the opposite pole of opinion, and considered them to be all bad. In other words, he held that human nature was so frail and faulty as to leave the good elements in it, or the good specimens of the race, in a lamentable minority. As early as 1820 (when he was only twenty-two years of age, and had never left his native town) he could write as follows to a friend: 'The coldness and egoism of our time, the ambition, self-interest, perfidy, the insensibility of woman, whom I define as an animal without a heart, are things which scare me.' He does not however appear to have ever become misanthropic, rightly speaking; he was willing to be courteous and accommodating to all, and cordial to some. Neither is it shown that he had any cause to regard his professing friends as callous or treacherous, or to complain of the treatment which he received from ordinary acquaintances, or (apart from his own townspeople) from general society. His letters to various friends—more especially Giordani, Brighenti, the ladies of the Tommasini and Maestri families, and his own sister and brother Carlo—continued to the end to be full, not only of earnest affection, but of strong asseverations of his belief in their gifts and virtues; and, if he thought so extremely well of a few persons with whom he was intimate, he might have been expected to infer that a vast number of other people, whom he had no opportunity of knowing, would prove to be similarly distinguished for character or faculty. This however was not his inference; he viewed human nature as a mean affair, human society as a hotbed of corruption, and human beings as condemnable in the lump. As to his pessimism in its more express shape—his opinion that no man is even moderately happy, and that all men, from the cradle to the grave, are an example of persistent tribulation, increasing as the years advance— it is not my business to enter into any discussion. Spite of Leopardi, a great multitude of people have believed, and will continue to believe, that their life consists of a balance between unhappiness and happiness. Some will go so far as to say that the happiness visibly predominates. To consider yourself, to feel yourself, principally or partially happy; must *pro tanto* amount to *being* principally or partially happy; and the lucky people who are conscious of that sensation will continue to entertain it, spite of the most positive assurances from the pondering or ponderous philosopher that, under the fixed conditions and adamantine bonds of human existence, they neither ought to be, nor are, nor can be, happy in any but the smallest degree. It should be added that, according to Leopardi's view, not only mankind but all living creatures drag out a life of suffering, and had better never have been born; he made a possible exception for birds, whose structure, powers, and demeanour, impressed him as showing a vivacity of temperament unknown to other animals. Men, of course, he regarded as *more* unhappy than the others, owing to their vaster aspirations, their acuter perception of the facts, and their unshared faculty of reasoning upon them, and realizing to themselves the nothingness of hope and the emptiness of things. (pp. 67-71)

I think the main trait of his character was a great personal pride. By pride I do not mean anything allied to arrogance, presumption, or conceit; but a strenuous internal self-assertion, which urged him to rise superior to whatever, in natural conditions, or in the stress of society or of the affections, seemed to threaten to bend or break his will. Pride of this sort can even take on the guise of humility, and Leopardi confessed, with a frankness emulated by few writers, those terrible problems of the dominancy and inscrutability of nature, and the impotence of man bound with the iron chain of necessity— problems which sap the very root of human pride. He confessed them, but did so with a sense that this was a bolder, a manlier course than other people were prepared to adopt—that he could do what others flinched from doing, and that to do it was one more proof, not of a submissive, but of a resolute and unconquered soul. A distinguished French writer, Edouard Rod, makes some observations on Leopardi's mental attitude which appear to me both true and acute. 'Remark', he says, 'that Leopardi never did anything to escape from the tyranny of his ideas; quite on the contrary, he cherished them. He found a sort of bitter and haughty satisfaction in proclaiming, in the name of all sentient beings, the woe of living.' And further on, 'His disposition for seeing the truth of things made him at once timid in temperament and stoical in mind.' In society Leopardi appears to have been uniformly quiet, unassuming, and free from any aristocratic prejudices; conscious indeed that he seldom or never met his peers, but not allowing this consciousness to transpire by any overt act or wilfulness of speech. He was, according to Ranieri, modest, pure in mind and in deed, just, humane, liberal, high-spirited, and upright. It is true that at a later date Ranieri wrote in a different strain—impelled perhaps by that jealous perversity which makes a man resent the commonplaces of universal praise bestowed upon a long-deceased friend to whom, in his hour of trial, only the one helping hand had been extended. He then dwelt more than enough on the poet's physical infirmities, and partly on blemishes of his mind or character. Of these blemishes, most are immediately related to those same physical infirmities, and consist of capricious, neglectful, or unreasonable habits, detrimental to his own interests as an invalid, and to the comfort of the persons whose care was lavished upon him in that capacity. Apart from this, the most substantial charge is that he was excessively and unduly sensitive to literary praise or blame; a point in which, even if we suppose the charge to be true to the uttermost, Leopardi only shared a weakness highly common among poets, and not uncommon among authors of whatsoever class. There is also the statement, well worth noting, that Leopardi detested the country and country-life as distinct from town-life. If this is entirely correct, he must have had a wonderful power of assimilating, without enjoying or liking, the aspects of natural landscape; for many most finished, touching, and intimately felt pictures and details of this kind are to be found in his poems. His love of the moon and moonlight seems at any rate unmistakably genuine. It is perhaps true that Italians generally are not such lovers of scenic nature as people are in England, where a Wordsworth and a Ruskin—not to speak of other writers—have almost made it a canon of moral obligation, or a test of spiritual rectitude, that we should admire a flower or a tree, a mountain or a river, the rolling rack or the illumined horizon and unfathomable zenith. (pp. 75-7)

[Leopardi wrote that] he would rather die to-day than enjoy the fortune and fame of Caesar or of Alexander. This is spoken in the person of Tristano, an imaginary speaker in one of his *Dialogues*; but it is plainly intended to represent the deliberate conclusion of the author himself. The idea of well-earned renown, of glory, was certainly one of those for which Leopardi had a powerful natural bias; and, if he preferred death to glory, he must have wished for death very intensely—and indeed he constantly asserted that so he did. The wish for death, combined with the highly negative opinions which he entertained regarding a revealed or peremptory rule of right, or an immortal destiny for man, might naturally have suggested the act of suicide. Nor was this thought foreign to Leopardi's mind. But practically he rejected the notion of suicide; saying, in a letter to Signora Tommasini, dated in 1828, 'the unmeasured love which I bear to my friends and relatives will always retain me in the world so long as destiny wills I should be there.' And in an elaborate dialogue which he composed, with Porphyry and Plotinus as the speakers, he develops the same conception in befitting detail. (p. 77)

The mature period of Leopardi's poetic genius and performance commences with . . . the address **"To Italy"** and the canzone **"On the Projected Monument to Dante."** As these were composed in the autumn of 1818, when he was but twenty years of age, and as both are highly finished performances, majestic in tone, exalted in style, and purged in diction, one must number Leopardi among the poets who in adolescence have produced the fruits of ripest manhood—an Ephebus worthy to take his seat among the Areopagites. Having once attained this height, he never descended from it; whatever he produced afterwards in verse is so excellent of its kind, so clearly conceived as a whole, with details so congruous and so selected, adornment so precious and so discriminate, fine literary form so constantly observed, force and depth of feeling so enhanced by strength of self-restraint, that one might almost cite any and every one of his compositions as a model of how—given the theme to be treated—the treatment should best proceed. In saying that he never descended from his original height, I do not mean to ignore the fact that a few of his pieces, especially his last and longest poem, are of a more familiar kind—they are indeed of a directly satirical or sarcastic cast, with clear touches of humorous ridicule; but these examples, not less than the others, are permeated by large ideas, and executed with a not inferior sense of style, according to their requirements. Neither do I beg the question whether the themes which he treated are always or to the full approvable; they are often the themes of a pessimist, and pessimism is a doctrine which many or most of us dissent from, and which a large number heartily disapprove.

If we leave out of count the one rather long poem, the whole of Leopardi's mature writing in verse is of extremely moderate bulk; there are about forty compositions, in the form of canzoni or other lyrics, and of blank verse; not a single sonnet is among them—a rarity for an Italian author. Their most general subject-matter is the sorrows of mortality—the mystery and nothingness of man's life, his perpetual endeavours, his ever-recurrent and sometimes sublime illusions, the fate which dogs, and the death which extinguishes him. I should incline to say that the very finest of these poems is that entitled **"Canto Notturno di un Pastore Errante dell' Asia"** (**"Nightly Chaunt of a Nomadic Shepherd of Asia"**), written chiefly in 1826; the greatest general favourites are perhaps the two latest in date, **"The Setting of the Moon,"** and **"La Ginestra"** (**"The Broom-Plant"**)—where this shrub, growing in abundance on the volcanic slopes of Vesuvius, is used as the occasion for much gloomy and far-reaching comment on the transiency and insignificance of the human generations. Leopardi continually takes some aspect of Nature as a symbol or incentive of feeling, and fuses the two things so that the feeling predominates. Apart from their general tone of philosophic or speculative meditation, always in the direction of sadness and pessimism—a sadness which is bitter without being exactly sour, and pessimism which is scornful without lapsing into actual cynicism—the poems have naturally some amount of variety in subject; some being mainly patriotic,

others tender and passionate (never erotic); others chiefly descriptive, replete with quiet yet precise observation of Nature and of ordinary life, all touched with a lingering pity, and mellowed by the light of a noble contemplative imagination. That none of these poems is in any degree 'entertaining' (if perhaps we except the **"Palinodia a Gino Capponi"**) may be admitted at once; their general tone is castigated and severe, and certainly not conciliating to such as are minded to run while they read. The epithet 'stuck-up' is about the mildest which readers of this turn would apply to the verse of Leopardi. (pp. 82-4)

Melody of sound and poetic charm are ever present, with a grace and force of words which (so far as these precious qualities are alone concerned) we may perhaps more nearly compare to that of Tennyson than of any other English writer; there are of course greater austerity of presentment, and greater detachment from the thing presented, than we find in Tennyson. The diction is very condensed, and one has to pay steady attention lest some delicacy of meaning or some shade of beauty should remain unprized. The perfection of expression is great indeed. In some of his poems Leopardi is free in mixing unrhymed with rhyming lines; and he does it with so much mastery that the ear catches a diffused sense of rhyme, without missing it where it is not. He is throughout one of the most personal of poets; all that he says he says out of himself; I use the term 'personal' rather than 'subjective,' though the latter now rather hackneyed adjective would also be quite apposite here. Not indeed that he never takes a motive or a suggestion from earlier writers; he has done so—especially in his more youthful compositions—from Petrarca, and not from him alone; but he appropriates such things, and does not merely reproduce them. His subject never overmasters him. Whatever he deals with, he seems to see round it, to impose upon it his own law of thought, to extract its quintessential virtue according to this law, and to present the result to us with a sense of superiority—no means or common achievement of volition for a writer whose continual theme is inscrutable and unappealable Fate, Nature hostile and Man the shadow of a shade.

The last and longest poem of Leopardi—he completed it only the day before his death—is of a very different class from all the others. It is named ***Paralipomini della Batracomiomachia,*** forming a kind of arbitrary sequel to the Greek *Batrachomyomachia,* of which in early youth he had produced two verse-translations. This poem is in the *ottava rima,* the metre of Ariosto and Tasso, and represents the fortunes or misfortunes of the Mice after their army had been slaughtered by the Crabs. It is the only narrative poem by our author, and the only one which professes to be amusing. And amusing it is, though rather diffuse—one may well suppose that it would have been condensed here and there prior to publication by himself. Its tone is light, pungent, and grotesque, not unmingled with serious meanings. The poem is generally reputed to be a satire on the Neapolitans, and their revolution of 1820; the Mice (so says Ranieri, who must have heard something of the sort from Leopardi) standing for the Italians, the Crabs for the Austrians, and the Frogs for the Priests. There is, however, I think, a great deal of 'chance medley' in the narrative, which does not stick close to Neapolitan or any other political events, but here glances at some actual incident, there laughs at some actual person (Louis Philippe and the French Revolution of 1830 are clearly enough implied), and there again makes merry at the weaknesses or grievances of general humankind.

From what has been said of his style it necessarily follows that Leopardi was an extremely careful writer: even such a minor matter as punctuation received considerate and precise attention from him. In conception he was rapid, in execution deliberate and fastidious. In a letter dated in 1824, after observing that he had only written few and short poems, he adds:

> In writing I have never followed anything except an inspiration or phrensy: when this arrived, I found in a couple of minutes the design and distribution of the entire composition. When that is done, my custom always is to wait until I again feel myself in the vein; when I do, and this generally happens only a month or so later on, I then settle down to composing; but with so much slowness that I cannot possibly finish a poem, short as it may be, in less than two or three weeks. This is my method: and, if the inspiration does not come to me spontaneously, more easily would water gush from a tree-trunk than a single verse from my brain.

The serious spirit in which Leopardi wrote poetry appears from another letter, dated in 1826. He there remarks that, by the mere common sort of verse-spinning, 'we do an express service to our tyrants, because we reduce to a sport and a pastime literature, from which alone the regeneration of our country might obtain a solid beginning.'

The prose works of Leopardi—apart from [his] early critical or linguistic writings . . .—consist principally of Dialogues, which he began writing towards 1820. There is also a very noticeable performance named **"Detti Memorabili di Filippo Ottonieri,"** which may be termed a mental autobiography, thinly disguised: it is imitated from the account of a real sage in Lucian's *Demonax;* and a set of scattered *Pensieri* on a variety of subjects. For acuteness and penetration, and a kind of intrinsic perception of the characters and manners of men from an extrinsic point of view, these two works are highly remarkable. The style of them, as also of the *Dialogues,* is regarded by Italians—and we may safely acquiesce in this verdict—as consummately good: straightforward, pure without mannered purism, unlaboured, and yet tempered and polished like the most trenchant steel. Leopardi considered excellent prose-writing to be more difficult than excellent verse; comparing the two to the beauty of a woman, undraped and draped. There is besides the collection of his letters, of which no fewer than 544 are given in the principal edition, and some others are to be found elsewhere. . . . [They] are full of sensibility, and contain a great deal of strong substance eloquently put. An Italian editor holds that the letters to Giordani, and to the historian Coletta, surpass all Italian letters except those of Tasso; he terms them 'tasteful, candid, affectionate, edifying, philosophical.' To an English taste the letters generally are no doubt somewhat marred by the ceremonial style which has been common among Italians: some small service or symptom of good-will is acknowledged as if it were the acme of benevolence; the acknowledgment itself pants through superlatives; the person addressed figures as the most commanding, and the writer as the least considerable, of mankind. All this is on the surface; it must be skimmed off and allowed for, and the letters then become enjoyable reading, though also—from the constant suffering of body and mind which they exhibit—saddening and poignant.

The *Dialogues* and some other prose-writings were published in 1827 under the name of *Operette Morali.* Lucian appears to have been Leopardi's chief model in the Dialogues, as in the **"Detti Memorabili di Filippo Ottonieri;"** but, while often sportive in form, and not sparing in sallies of telling wit and humour, he is a far more serious Lucian. As usual, the un-

accountableness of life, the yawning gulf between the aspirations of man and his capacities and destiny, the want of *raison d'être* for such a creature so circumstanced, the trammels which he fashions for himself so as to make his position all the more comfortless and absurd, form the burden of the strain. Leopardi here combines the weeping and the laughing philosophers. That so the thing should be is a grief 'too deep for tears': the mode in which the thing presents itself to observation, the sorry shifts adopted by these sorry beings, oscillating and staggering between a hapless birth and a death inevitable, final, and in its degree welcome, the uselessness of hope, the cruelty of Nature and of Truth, furnish the occasion for smiles frequent enough, though they come mostly on the wrong side of the mouth. 'Grin and bear it' might be inscribed as a general motto for Leopardi's *Dialogues.* Luckily he writes so well, says so many things barbed with meaning and feathered with grace, that the reader is enabled to smile along with him. After **"A History of the Human Race,"** a very pregnant and suggestive summary in a vivid imaginative form of allegory (this is not a dialogue), come the colloquies of **"Fashion and Death," "Nature and a Soul," "The Earth and the Moon," "A Physicist and a Metaphysician," "Nature and an Icelander," "Copernicus and the Sun,"** and several others, bearing titles which do not so strongly indicate the general nature of their subjects. The two which I have named last are among the very best. (pp. 84-9)

It has been [Leopardi's] privilege to convey to the reader, along with the hard and unwelcome assertions of pessimism, a large measure of sympathy with his own singularly adverse fate: we read his personal sorrows into his abstract cogitations, and those among us who have no liking and little indulgence for the latter are still touched by their all too close affinity to the former. As a poet, Leopardi holds us by a firm and thrilling grasp, and readers who have once passed under his spell recur to him again and again with a still increasing sense of its potency. I will borrow in conclusion a strong, yet no more than a just, expression of one of our best critical authorities, Dr. Richard Garnett, and say that Leopardi is 'the one Italian poet of the nineteenth century who has taken an uncontested place among the classics of the language.' (pp. 90-1)

W. M. Rossetti, "Leopardi," in Studies in European Literature: Being the Taylorian Lectures, 1889-1899 *by W. M. Rossetti and others, Oxford at the Clarendon Press, 1900, pp. 55-91.*

JOHN VAN HORNE (essay date 1907)

[*Van Horne considers the impact of European Romanticism on Leopardi, basing his discussion on both Leopardi's poetry and critical writings. Van Horne concludes with earlier critics that, while many of Leopardi's themes are characteristic of the Romantics, his treatment of them is essentially classical.*]

Many attempts have been made to explain the failure of romanticism to gain a firm foothold in Italy. In the dearth of better examples Leopardi is often cited as an exponent of this movement, so popular in other countries. This statement is always made with distinct reservations, and the conclusion is generally reached that Leopardi was a severe classicist in form, but was influenced by many elements contributing to the romantic outbreak. Much has been said in support of both contentions, and examination of the *Canti* and of the *Prose Morali* would seem to disclose a reasonable basis for both views.

The *Zibaldone* and other miscellaneous writings shed a great deal of light upon Leopardi's attitude. Although the major portion of what he writes is distinctly inimical to romanticism, it is quite often the case that he shows leanings and desires that may well be called romantic. Strongly influenced by his reading of French philosophical writers, by his own natural inclinations and by his bodily suffering, he devotes page after page of his notes to a glorification, in fact to a deification of nature and of the primitive stages of human history. His whole being is in revolt against the conditions that surround him. He builds up a system of philosophy that has as one of its elements the unavoidable misery of man in the condition of civilization and in the presence of truth.

Turning to other documents, we find among Leopardi's suppressed productions a number of efforts characterized by romanticism. Among these is the **"Diario d'Amore,"** written in 1819 at the age of nineteen years, an unfinished and extravagant conception based upon a sudden and violent fancy of the poet for his cousin Geltrude Cassi. Two *canzoni* found among the Neapolitan papers also bear testimony to his romantic leanings.

Clear as many of these indications of romantic feeling are, they are overshadowed by the evidence in favor of classical tradition. Whenever Leopardi indulged in literary or artistic criticism he left no doubt of the direction in which his preference lay. There are many attacks upon romanticism to be found among the scattered entries of the *Zibaldone*, but all are presented together in a prose article written in 1819 and published in 1910 among the *Scritti Vari*. This article is entitled **"Discorso di un Italiano intorno alla Poesia Romantica"**. It was originally intended as an answer to some observations that had appeared in *Lo Spettatore Italiano*. In fact Leopardi first called his article "Intorno alle Osservazioni del Cavaliere Lodovico di Breme sulla Poesia Moderna". Later he decided to change the title of the piece and to withhold it from publication, because others had answered the article in *Lo Spettatore*. Moreover, he did not think that Italians were sufficiently impressed by the observations he was answering to heed a simple refutation of them.

A summary of the contents of this **"Discorso"** follows:

> In theory the romanticists attempt to make poetry metaphysical; to destroy all illusions that spring from the imagination; to appeal to the intellect. They forget that in order to produce its effect poetry must deceive. Not truth but the semblance of truth—fact clothed in beautiful settings—is the object of the poet's art. In the best poetry there should also be a popular appeal. In practice the romanticists do not abide by their theories, but they adopt all sorts of bizarre and out-of-the-way conceptions.

> Genuine delight can come only from nature. This is shown by the pleasure derived from the primitive elements in the ancient poets. Modern children share the fanciful illusions of the ancients, peopling the world with beautiful creations. The romanticists are wrong to strive against these natural feelings by an appeal to reason. Reason destroys imagination; as a man grows in intellect his fancy becomes weak. Hence the poet should try not to follow the principles of science, but to release fancy from the bonds of reason.

> The romanticists wish to drag poetry from the ancient state of nature to the modern condition of civilization. "Because one of the principal differences between romantic poets and our poets, a difference in which many others are summed up, consists in this: that our poets sing of nature and of the eternal and changeless matters and shapes and things of beauty, in short, of the works of God, while the romanticists treat of

civilization, of what is transitory and mutable—of the works of men.''

Three reasons may be assigned for the undeniable popularity of romanticism. First of all, the taste of the reading public is corrupt; future critics will be amazed at the vogue of the romantic poets just as nineteenth century critics wonder at the liking for the absurdities of the *seicento*. The second reason is to be found in many men's lack of feeling, caused partly by nature, partly by civilization; let the English and the Germans write for such readers if they choose. Third and most important of the reasons for the spread of romantic poetry is its novelty; singularity and strangeness are always attractive; hence it is no wonder that the reading public is drawn to the outlandish imitations and conceptions of the romantic movement. The vagaries of the school tend to excite laughter rather than fear.

The poets of the new movement deny that the illusions of the ancient world can be used in the scientific modern age. They forget that the province of poetry is the imagination and not the intellect. Separated as he is from nature, a modern writer must study the ancient poets closely. The wholesale rejection of the stories of antiquity is absurd. By this it is not meant that the old poets must be imitated slavishly or pedantically; they must be studied for the sake of their natural point of view—so hard to attain in modern times. It is the opponents of the classics who are pedantic in their sweeping condemnation of ancient models.

Romanticists hold that sentiment belongs peculiarly to their style of poetry. This pretension is refuted by citations from Homer and Vergil. Vergil is to be considered an excellent portrayer of the feelings that are called modern. The romanticists by indicating Petrarch as an example of their poetic manner contradict themselves. Their whole position is absurd, because sentiment exists in nature. Expressed by the ancients it is spontaneous; expressed by the moderns it is artificial and overdone. The nineteenth century poets aim at psychological interpretation, at a science of the human mind. But though they know more than the ancients knew about the workings of human thought, they are unable to express their knowledge naturally.

Romantic poetry contains much that is monstrous, little that is moderate or harmonious. It is all sentiment; scorning the stories of ancient mythology, it does not hesitate to adopt artificial foreign imagery. The ancients peopled nature with many beautiful creations; they attributed life to inanimate objects; life is more attractive than death, and with all their theories the romanticists are unable altogether to refrain from the practices of ancient poets.

In imitations of nature the essential element is wonder. Romanticism loses this effect by a too literal picture of nature.

The closing pages of the **"Discorso"** contain an appeal to the young men of Italy to preserve the glorious artistic traditions of their country. As he feels that Italian literature is closer than that of any other nation to Latin and Greek literature, Leopardi urges all patriotic Italians to unite in resisting the flood of romanticism flowing from the North, which would fain destroy the stronghold of good taste and of classical tradition.

Reading of the entries in the *Zibaldone* for the years 1818 to 1823 shows that Leopardi's enthusiasm for the literature of classical antiquity was not less striking than his depreciation of modern letters. He pays tribute after tribute to Homer and to other great masters of antiquity, to the ancient languages, to ancient style. He proclaims as absurd the idea that only the moderns understand nature and can interpret her moods. He maintains that the writers of ancient times were truer to nature than those of the modern world; that the imitation and interpretation of nature have always been inevitable, and here the ancients may be esteemed to excel the moderns; that Homer and Anacreon represent the true imitation of nature, while the romantic poets often tend toward over-sentimentalism and artificiality. In short Leopardi tells us that it is only through recourse to ancient writings that we can hope to compose in a natural way, and that it is impossible really to equal the great Greek productions. He says: "The eternal sources of the great as well as of the beautiful are the writers, the works of all kinds, the examples, the customs, the feelings of the ancients; and by the ancients every remarkable mind of our times is fed."

In view of Leopardi's expressed abhorrence for romanticism, as he conceived it, it may well be asked why he typifies certain fundamental tendencies that are often, and with some reason, called romantic. The answer to this question is to be found in the fact that he had a very distorted notion of romanticism. At the time when he was forming his ideals of literary composition, and writing his first great poems, he had never left his home in Recanati, and had enjoyed very few opportunities of making the acquaintance of literary men. The library collected by his father was well supplied with classical works, but not nearly so well furnished with the output of modern authors. There is little evidence to show that Leopardi was acquainted with many of the best productions of contemporary literature. Even in later life he was not a great reader of modern works, largely because ill health prevented him from devoting much time to study.

On the other hand, he was only too well acquainted with the works of revolutionary theorizers, who typified what seemed to him worst in the writings of the modern school. We have seen in his **"Discorso"** how he chose to reply to one such production. He had a horror of display, of eccentricity, and of careless style in literary composition. Conservative by nature, he was alarmed at all efforts to break with classical tradition as far as the fundamental art of poetry is concerned. A good example of his horror of display is to be found in a criticism of Lord Byron, which runs as follows:

> The whole of the *Corsair* of Lord Byron (I speak of the translation, I don't know about the original nor about his other works) is interwoven with dashes, not only between sentence and sentence, but between phrase and phrase, and very often even the phrase itself is divided and the substantive is separated from the adjective by these dashes (he comes very near dividing single words), which say to us at every turn, like the charlatan who shows some beautiful thing: 'Pay attention, notice that this which is coming is a fine piece, observe this epithet, which is notable, linger over this expression, fix your mind on this image, etc.', a thing which is displeasing to the reader.

It may be remarked, by way of comment on the above citation, that Leopardi makes a plea for sobriety and modesty in literary composition. On the other hand, he shows clearly that he is not very conversant with the works of Byron. There is little evidence to show that he knew much about English or German literature of modern times until long after he had formulated

his artistic rules (and of course long after the **"Discorso"** was written). Even in later life, he does not indicate any very great knowledge of or interest in the best contemporary authors. There are many who are never mentioned in his notes.

We are fortunate in possessing a statement of Leopardi that reveals his lofty conception of the importance of the lyric poem. Equally valuable is the description left by him of his method of writing a poem. These two passages follow [the first from *Pensieri,* the second from *Epistolario di Giacomo Leopardi*]. . . .

> The lyric can be called the height, the culmination, the summit of poetry, which is the summit of human speech. . . .
>
> I have written in my life only very few and short poems. In writing them I have followed nothing but an inspiration (or frenzy) and when that would come upon me, I would form in two minutes the design and the distribution of the whole composition. When this has been done, I am accustomed always to wait until another moment comes to me, and when it does come (which ordinarily happens only some months later), I begin to compose, but with such slowness that it is not possible for me to finish a poem, even though extremely short, in less than two or three weeks. This is my method, and if the inspiration is not born in me of itself, water would sooner come from the trunk of a tree than a single verse from my brain. Others can write poetry whenever they wish, but I have not this faculty at all, and however much you might ask me, it would be useless, not because I should not want to accommodate you, but because I should not be able.

Perhaps the most valuable conclusions to be drawn from the utterances of Leopardi just quoted, are his appreciation of the great importance of poetry, his extreme care in composition, and his originality. If he had been a mere imitator of classical poetry, he would have felt able at any moment to grind out a few lines of respectable verse. His reverence for the sacred nature of the poetic art, and for classical poetry in particular, did not allow him to descend to such a practice. Throughout his life he never failed to recommend the most painstaking thoroughness in literary composition.

The poems of Leopardi have been classified by Carducci in a manner so satisfactory that it would be futile to endeavor to make any improvements. According to this classification there are two main divisions of Leopardi's poetic output. The first extends from 1816 to 1826, that is to say from the **"Appressamento della Morte"** to the **"Epistola a Carlo Pepoli."** It embraces the period of Leopardi's principal mental struggles and uncertainty; and is accompanied by constant progress in art. The second division extends from the **"Risorgimento"** (1828) to the author's death in 1837, embodying the period of perfection in art and of the dominion of pessimism.

The first division of poems includes the Elegiac pieces (1816-1818), the patriotic *canzoni* (1818 and January, 1820), the idyllic poems, the classic *canzoni* (1821-1823), and the **"Epistola a Carlo Pepoli"** (1826). The later group embraces the second set of idylls ("i grandi idilli", 1828-1830), the impassioned lyrics (1831-1833) and the philosophical poems (1834-1837).

The poetry composed by Leopardi between 1816 and 1823 reflects the philosophical studies that are found in the *Zibaldone;* studies resulting as has been seen, in a glorification of nature and a depreciation of civilization. These theories, joined to his feeble health, impel him to write in a pessimistic strain, and to look back with regret to the only world that he knows and loves—the ancient world. His original genius alone makes of him a truly modern poet. No matter under what form he chooses to clothe his ideas, whether he makes Brutus or Sappho his mouthpiece, he is expressing the despair and world-weariness of a nineteenth century pessimist.

When Leopardi published his first ten *canzoni* in 1825, he wrote a preamble in which he delivered his own opinion of his work. The sum and substance of the philosophy conveyed by these poems is there indicated by him as follows: "All is vain in the world except grief; grief is better than tedium; our life is good for nothing else than to despise itself; the necessity of an evil consoles common minds for that evil, but not great minds; everything is a mystery in the universe, except our unhappiness."

Before discussing the romantic or non-romantic tendencies of the earlier poems, it will be well perhaps to glance at the later ones, in order that a comprehensive outlook may be obtained over the whole of Leopardi's poetic work. The most striking change noticeable in all his later productions is the new attitude toward nature and civilization. After the year 1823 comparatively few pages were added to the *Zibaldone*. But from them and from other sources it is clear that Leopardi gradually modified his conception of nature, until at length he regarded her as the pitiless foe of mankind. At the same time his estimate of the value of civilization shows a correspondingly great divergence from that of his earlier years. As far as personal feelings are concerned, his pessimism seems deeper than ever before. No other conclusion can possibly be drawn from the reading of the majority of his later compositions.

The best insight into his philosophical views toward nature and civilization is to be obtained from a consideration of his last and most profound lyric poem, "**La Ginestra.**" It is well, however, to bear in mind that the development therein traced is not the result of a sudden shift of view-point, but that it is the culmination of a great deal of profound thought.

"**La Ginestra**" is the poem which, above all others, represents Leopardi's Neapolitan period. It is the deepest and the most philosophical of the *Canti*, and in many ways the most important. It represents the final phase of the author's thought. The late poems all evince an ever increasing horror at the remorseless cruelty of the power of nature that had formerly been so adored. "**La Ginestra**" is the final expression of dismay, an outcry against the ruthless destructiveness of nature. Living beside Mount Vesuvius, Leopardi could see and imagine the desolation wrought by a volcanic eruption. Moved to the bottom of his heart by his reflections, he urges the union of men against the forces of nature, the abandonment of war, the linking of all possible means for opposing natural harshness and cruelty. Human thought, he says, is the one power that has made any headway against the principle of destruction; this it has done by effecting civilization.

In this poem the reader discovers a point of view almost diametrically opposite to that held by Leopardi as a younger man. Thus his philosophy has completely changed since the time when he wrote the "**Discorso,**" in opposition to the extravagance of the romantic school. His artistic ideals do not show a corresponding change. Investigation serves only to confirm what Leopardi hoped and expected in early life. His literary career represents a gradual advance toward the classical perfection to which he aspired, and which he thought was to be found above all in the works of the ancients.

With this brief review of the poems of Leopardi in mind, we may notice some of his traits that can be called distinctly romantic. Without trying to pick out inconsequential minutiae, we can at once point to the deification of the natural state of humanity, contempt for material progress, strong individualism and subjectivity, and the discontent that has often been referred to in critical works under the name of "male de siècle" or "doglia mondiale."

The fact that at once forces itself upon the attention of the student of Leopardi is that the romantic tendencies just enumerated are all connected with the poet's philosophy of life, and not with his artistic theories. Futhermore, some of these tendencies inclined to become less prominent and even to pass entirely away, or to be replaced by opposite sentiments, as the poet grew older. He retained, however, his personal discontent with his surroundings, and his individuality, as long as he lived. We may say with justice that characteristics such as love of nature, defiance of environment, general unhappiness, and strong expression of personality were shared by Leopardi with prominent members of the romantic movement. Tinged with romanticism also is his attitude toward love, which he seemed to consider the sole comfort of man, and the last of the great illusions. But no treatment of these themes could be less romantic, in the ordinary sense of the word, than that of Leopardi. And the more experienced he became, the more severely classical did his poems show themselves to be.

Passing to Leopardi's own attitude toward romanticism, we see that he considered the quality of individuality distinctly classical. He believed most firmly that every author should write for his own time, that is to say, he should treat matters of contemporary interest. In this way only, he felt that the classics could be truly imitated. Therefore, the very qualities that may be picked out as romantic are the ones that Leopardi felt to constitute the genuine following of his great models. It is almost useless to say that he misunderstood the better side of romanticism. But his sincerity in attributing his individuality to classical influence and to long study is not to be doubted. His own words on this subject are as follows:

> To my mind, there is nothing that Italy can hope for until she has books suited to the times, read and understood by the reading public, and which go from one end to the other of that public; a thing that is as common among foreigners as it is unknown in Italy. And I think that the recent example of other nations shows us clearly what power really national books have in this century, to awaken the dormant minds of a people and to produce great events. But to complete our troubles, there has arisen, from the seventeenth century on, a wall between the learned class and the people, a wall that is becoming constantly higher, and which is unknown in the other nations. And while we love the classics so much, we are unwilling to see that all the Greek, all the Latin and all the ancient Italian classical writers wrote for their own time, and according to the needs, desires, customs, and especially the knowledge and intelligence of their compatriots and contemporaries. And as they would not have been classic if they had acted otherwise, so we shall never be so, if we do not imitate them in this, which is substantial and necessary, more than in a hundred other trifles to which we devote our principal study.

There is no reason found in this study of Leopardi's personal attitude toward romanticism to change the commonly accepted opinion of his general relation toward the romantic school. The most that can be done is to bring his position into better relief and to point out what he actually said and thought. The conclusion seems inevitable that no man of similar feelings and intellect, living at such a time, could have been more unsympathetic toward the movements advocated by his contemporaries. On the other hand, his very hostility illustrates that no man of his genius could escape what was really profound and valuable in the intellectual life of the times.

In conclusion, it seems established that Leopardi, in addition to being an accomplished scholar and a poet, was a profound and original thinker. For this reason the subject matter of his poems is intensely modern. Such a man could not imitate antiquity to the extent of resigning his philosophical convictions. It is natural then that he should approach and even exemplify many phases of thought found among poets of the romantic movement. But his attacks upon romanticism were directed against artificiality, extravagance and poor taste, and not against love of nature or bold originality of thought. In fact he esteemed these last qualities as characteristic of ancient and not of modern literature. His ideal of poetical composition was the treatment of modern subjects in the spirit of antiquity. (pp. 4-14)

> *John Van Horne, "Studies on Leopardi: The Attitude of Leopardi toward Romanticism," in* University of Iowa Humanistic Studies, *Vol. I, No. 4, 1907-1918, pp. 3-14.*

REMY DE GOURMONT (essay date 1910)

[*Gourmont, a French poet, novelist, critic, and essayist, was one of the founders of the influential* Mercure de France, *a journal that championed the symbolist movement in France during the late nineteenth century. Gourmont is considered one of the most perceptive and sensitive of the symbolist critics, and his work is noted for its detached and objective tone. He was an individual of broad interests and encyclopedic knowledge, as is evidenced in his essays on such diverse topics as aesthetics, biology, and religion. Gourmont is also remembered as the critic who promoted the works of Friedrich Nietzsche, Stéphane Mallarmé, J. K. Huysmans, and Jean Marie Villiers de l'Isle Adam in France. In the following excerpt, Gourmont correlates aspects of Leopardi's life and writings and evaluates the veracity of his pessimistic philosophy. This essay was originally published in 1910 in* Promenades littéraires.]

Leopardi has never been widely read in France. While Schopenhauer has achieved a certain literary popularity, Leopardi has remained, even for scholars, in the shade. This is due in large measure to the mediocrity of his translators and his commentators. . . .

Leopardi's poetry is difficult to enjoy. M. Turiello says that it is obscure even to Italians of the present generation. It is true that Leopardi is somewhat addicted to archaism and that, moreover, the Italian language has since his day undergone rapid development under the influence of French. His prose, despite its severe form, now too concise and now a trifle oratorical, is more approachable. . . . But if translation, is always a difficult task, it is particularly difficult to translate Leopardi.

In prose as in verse he is a pessimist more by nature than as a result of reasoning. It is his sensibility rather than his intellect that speaks. He constructed no system; he gathers his impressions, his observations, and attempts, not without arbitrariness, to generalize them. His philosophy is entirely physiological: the world is bad because his personal life is bad. He conceives the world in most terrifying fashion, and supposes that if all men do not judge it as he does, it is because they are mad.

Optimism, in fact, is fairly widespread. While there is life there is hope. The fable of Death and the Woodcutter is a fair symbol of humanity's outlook. On the other hand it is certain that literatures and philosophies, even those which aim to produce laughter as well as those which exalt life, are generally pessimistic. There is a tragic background to Molière's plays and a gloomy background to Nietzsche's aphorisms. Absolute, beatific optimism is compatible only with a sort of animal insensibility and stupidity: only idiots are constantly laughing and are constantly happy to be alive. Absolute pessimism, however, can develop only in certain depressed organisms: its extreme manifestations are plainly pathological and connected with maladies of the brain.

Schopenhauer affirms that life is evil, yet he loves it and enjoys it. Let fame come, and he expands with cheer. His character is by no means gloomy. He is at the same time a philosopher and a humorous writer. Leopardi never knew these expansions. He affects to despise even glory, for which he nevertheless labors. But he, too, is a keen, witty spirit, although ever bitter; and he, too, is a humorist. He certainly takes pleasure in writing. If he does not know life's other joys, he knows that of being able to impart a beautiful, puissant form to a lucid thought. Nevertheless his existence, much more logical than Schopenhauer's, is in exact accord with his philosophy. Sickly, isolated, not understood, Leopardi lacked the strength to react; but if he allowed himself to be swept along by his sadness, it was at least in full knowledge of the fact. He questions his despair and enters into discussion with it. And this questioning presented us with those fine dialogues which, together with a few thoughts, were gathered together under the title *Operette Morali*.

Leopardi died in 1837. His writings seem of this very day. Almost all the questions touched upon with unparalleled sagacity in the **"Dialogue Between Tristan And A Friend"** are such as still interest philosophers and critics. "I understand," says Tristan, "and I embrace the deep philosophy of the newspapers, which, by killing off all other literature and all other studies of too serious and too little amusing a nature, are the masters and the beacon-light of the modern age." Already, in his day, the flatterers of the crowd were saying, like the Socialists of today: "Individuals have disappeared in the face of the masses." Already sober stupidity affirmed: "We live in an epoch of transition," as if, resumes Tristan, all epochs and all centuries were not a transition toward the future!

The theme itself of the dialogues is the idea of the wickedness of life and the excellence of death. It recurs time and again and Leopardi manages to avoid monotony only by the ingeniousness of his imagination, the beauty of his style, the keenness of his wit. For example, the magnificent passage in which, after having said that although the world is rejuvenated every spring it is continually growing older, he announces the supreme death of the universe:

> Not a vestige will survive of the entire world, of the vicissitudes and the infinite calamities of all things created. An empty silence, a supreme calm will fill the immensity of space. Thus will dissolve and disappear this frightful, prodigious mystery of universal existence, before we have been able to understand or clarify it.

Without a doubt. But in the meantime we must live, or else die. And if we choose to live, it is reasonable to do our best to adapt ourselves to life. Pessimism has but the slightest of philosophical value. It is not even a philosophy; it is literature, and, too often, rhetoric. This man is a bit ridiculous, tranquilly pursuing his existence, daily adding a page to his litany of death's delights. In short, Leopardi, like many another man, humble or exalted, suffers from not being happy; his originality consists less in taking pleasure in his suffering, which is not very rare, than in finding reasons for this pleasure and expounding them logically and resolutely. His sincerity is absolute.

Considered in opposition to the base reveries of the promissors of happiness, this literature is useful. But it is good that it should be rare, for if we finally got to take pleasure in it alone, it would prove only depressing. Life is nothing and it is everything. It is empty and it contains all. But what does the word *life* mean? It is an abstraction. There are as many *lives* as there are living individuals in all the animal species. These lives are developed according to curves and windings of infinite variety. It is the height of folly to bring a single judgment to bear upon the multitude of individual lives. Some are good, others bad, the majority colorless, according to every possible degree. In this order of facts there is no justice, and the reign of justice is particularly chimerical in this case, because the joys and sorrows of a life are related far less to the events by which it is crossed than to the physiological character of the individual.

Abstractions do us much harm by impelling us to the quest of the absolute in all things. Joy does not exist, but there are joys: and these joys may not be fully felt unless they are detached from neutral or even painful conditions. The idea of continuity is almost self-negating. Nature makes no leaps; but life makes only bounds. It is measured by our heartbeats and these may be counted. That there should be, amid the number of deep pulsations that scan the line of our existence, some grievous ones, does not permit the affirmation that life is therefore evil. Moreover, neither a continuous grief nor a continuous joy would be perceived by consciousness.

Whether we deal with the transcendental theories of Schopenhauer or the melancholy assertions of Leopardi, we arrive at the same conclusion. Pessimism is not admissible, any more than is optimism. Heraclitus and Democritus may be dismissed back to back, while fearlessly and with a moderate but resolute hope, we try to extract from each of our lives,—we men,— all the sap it contains, even though it be bitter. (pp. 87-94)

"The three greatest pessimists who ever existed," said Schopenhauer one day,—"that is to say, Leopardi, Byron and myself,—were in Italy during the same year, 1818-1819, and did not make one another's acquaintance!" One of these "great pessimists," Leopardi, happened just at this time to be writing a little dialogue that might well be reprinted at the beginning of every year. It would always seem new.

Life is bad, says Leopardi, and here is the proof: nobody has ever found a man who would wish to live his life over again exactly as it happened at first:—who would wish even, at the beginning of a new year, to have it exactly the same as the year just past. What we love in life is not life such as it is, but rather life such as it might be, such as we desire it to be.

But since this **"Dialogue Between The Passer-By And The Almanac-Vendor,"** if it has ever been translated, has remained buried in unreadable volumes, here is a version of this excellent, though somewhat bitter, page:

The Almanac-Vendor.—Almanacs, new almanacs! New calendars! Will you buy some almanacs, sir?

The Passer-by.—Almanacs for the new year?

Vendor.—Yes, sir.

Passer-by.—Do you think it will be a happy one,— this coming year?

V.—Oh, yes, sir! Certainly!

P.—As happy as the one just past?

V.—Oh! Far, far more so!

P.—As happy as the one before that?

V.—Far, far more.

P.—As happy as which other one, then? Wouldn't you be glad to have the coming year the same as any one of the recent years?

V.—No, sir. No. That would hardly please me.

P.—How long have you been selling almanacs?

V.—For twenty years, sir.

P.—Which of those twenty years would you prefer the new year to resemble?

V.—I? I don't know.

P.—Can't you recall some year that seemed happy to you?

V.—Upon my word, no, sir.

P.—Yet life is a good thing, isn't it?

V.—Oh, yes indeed!

P.—You would be willing to live these twenty years all over again, and even all the years since you were born?

V.—I should say so, my dear sir. And would to God that were possible!

P.—Even if this life were to be exactly the same that you lived before,—no more no less,—with the same pleasures and the same sorrows?

V.—Oh, that! Indeed no!

P.—Then what sort of life would you wish?

V.—Just a life, that's all,—such as God would grant me, without any other conditions.

P.—A life left to accident, of which nothing would be known in advance,—a life such as the coming year brings?

V.—Exactly.

P.—That's what I, too, would desire, if I had my life to live over again,—what I and everybody else would wish for. But that means that fate, up to this very day, has treated us badly. And it is rather easy to see that the common opinon is, that in the past evil has triumphed greatly over good, since nobody, if he had to go over the same road again, would consent to be reborn. That life which is good is not the life we know, but the life we do not know,—the life ahead of us. Beginning with the new year, fate is going to deal kindly with us,—with you and me and everybody,—and we are going to be happy.

V.—Let us hope so.

P.—Well, let me see your handsomest almanac.

V.—Here you are, sir. It costs thirty cents.

P.—Here's your money.

V.—Thanks, sir. See you again. Almanacs! New almanacs! New calendars!

There is, perhaps, a slight error in Leopardi's reasoning. It is not because our life has been bad that it would be a burden to begin it all over again. Even a happy life lived twice would scarcely possess any greater pleasures. The element of curiosity must be taken into account. There is no human being, however resigned to the monotony of a becalmed existence, who does not in the bottom of his heart hope for some unforeseen event.

But is it really true that this idea is not contained in Leopardi's dialogue? It is there, although hidden, and doubtless I have taken it from there. Wherever it may come from, it is true, at least if it be applied to life as a whole. For everybody cherishes the remembrance of hours, and sometimes days, which he would gladly live over again. It is often one of the occupations of men to seek to create in their lives circumstances that plunge them for a moment back into the joys of the past, even if they must pay for this momentary resurrection with subsequent pain. . . .

Leopardi, who was a distinguished philologist, an excellent Hellenist, a great poet and an ingenious philosopher, endowed with eloquence, was unable to discover happiness or even peace in the exercise of these multiple gifts. His health was of the most wretched; his heart, left empty, sounded in his bosom at the slightest shock; he was timid and his nerves quivered at every jar, like those harps which were in fashion during his youth. He was born four years before Victor Hugo and died young, without having tasted fame, while Manzoni, who was destined to fill an entire century, had been for a long time known throughout Europe. Is the source of Leopardi's pessimism to be sought among these divers causes? That is hard to believe. The invalid, far from cursing life, is filled with hope; he is an optimist, and wishes to get well; he knows that he will recover. He is not the person with whom to speak of the infinite vanity of all things. It would rouse his fury to listen to the condemnation of those boons that are momentarily out of his reach but which he is preparing to seize and reconquer. Scarron was more sickly and more deformed than Leopardi, yet he was none the less a gay, all too gay, fellow. As for not being understood, or at least, not being received at one's proper value,—there is nothing in that to make a healthy mind pessimistic. The superior man, after all, scorns the opinion of men so long as it remains only an opinion,—that is to say, a matter without practical consequences. And this was Leopardi's situation, for he could have lived in independence upon his scant, but honorable patrimony.

Pessimism is related to character, and character is an expression of physiology. The case with writers, philosophers and poets is exactly the same as with men of other professions. They are gay, sad, witty, morose, avaricious, liberal, ardent, lazy, and their talent assumes the color of their character.

If one were to make a study of literature from this point of view,—a procedure which would not lack interest,—one would very probably discover a great number of pessimists, or, as they were called formerly, sad spirits. . . . There is no great writer without great sensibility; he is capable of keen joys, and of excessive pain as well. Now pain, which is depressive, leaves deeper traces in life than joy. If intelligence does not rule, if it does not intervene to establish a hierarchy, or an equilibrium of sensations, then the sad ideas triumph because of their superior numbers and power. Renan's serenity is perhaps only the apathy of indifference; Goethe's serenity represents the victory of intellect over sensibility.

Pessimism is neither a religious sentiment nor a modern one, although it has often assumed religious form and although the most celebrated pessimists belong to the nineteenth century. The Greeks, who knew everything, knew the despair of living: the pessimism of Heraclitus had preceded the optimism of Plato. There are few pages more bitter than those in which the naturalist Pliny summarizes the miseries of human life. Nature casts man upon the earth; of all animals he is the only one destined to tears; he cries from the moment of birth and never laughs before his fortieth day. And after having enumerated all the evils and the passions which desolate mankind, Pliny concludes by approving the ancient Greek epigram: "It is best not to be born or to die as soon as possible."

Leopardi has scarcely done more than paraphrase these elementary ideas, but this he has done with abundance and ingeniousness. So funereal is his spirit that he throws a veil of mourning over the most charming things: "Enter a garden of plants, herbs and flowers," he says,

> even in the gentlest season of the year. You cannot turn your glance in any direction without discovering traces of misery. All the members of this vegetable family are more or less in a 'state of suffering.' There a rose is wounded by the sun that has given it life; it shrivels, blanches, and withers away. Further on, behold that lily, whose most sensitive, most vital parts are being sucked by a bee. . . . This tree is infested by a swarm of ants; others, by caterpillars, flies, snails, mosquitoes; one is wounded in its bark, tortured by the sun, which penetrates into the wound; the other is attacked in the trunk or in its roots. You will not find in all this garden a single small plant whose health is perfect. . . . Every garden is, in a way, nothing but a vast hospital,—a place even more lamentable than a cemetery,—and if such beings are endowed with sensibility, it is certain that non-existence would to them be far preferable to existence.

Leopardi here commits the error of him who wishes to prove too much. His pessimism abdicates reason, and the sentence about nothingness being preferable to life, which in Pliny was beautiful and philosophic, acquires in the Italian philosopher a somewhat ridiculous sentimentality. (pp. 96-106)

But if he had possessed a more intimate knowledge of nature, and of the relations between insects and plants, what a picture at once admirable and cruel would not Leopardi have been able to draw! Those mosquitoes, upon whom he looks as allies of the caterpillars in ravaging the leaves of some cherry-tree, are ichneumons, and it is the caterpillars themselves that they have come to attack, piercing them with a long, hollow borer which permits the mosquito to lay in the very flesh of the caterpillar eggs which, when they become larvae, will gnaw the living flesh like terrible little vultures.

If Leopardi had known this and many another thing,—if he had known that every living creature is in turn prey and depredator, in turn eater and eaten, he would have considered with even greater bitterness the arrival of the new year, which hastens from the very first days of its springtime, to impart full strength and full passion to the instincts of life and devastation.

Leopardi despairs: he is, therefore, a weakling. His humble almanac-vendor is made of better clay. He hopes; he wishes to live and live happily; he possesses at least a little of that energy without which other gifts prove only too often to be blemishes and burdens. (pp. 107-08)

Remy de Gourmont, "The Pessimism of Leopardi,"
in his Philosophic Nights in Paris, *translated by Isaac*

Goldberg, John W. Luce and Company, 1920, pp. 87-108.

RADOSLAV A. TSANOFF (essay date 1920)

[*Tsanoff discusses aspects of Leopardi's philosophical pessimism that elevate it from the expression of a merely personal despair to a statement of universal melancholia.*]

Most men read Leopardi only as a poet is read, feeling with him perhaps, but not thinking. Or else, as often, his views of life are ascribed to his personal sorrows: Leopardi's message of life is agonizing, not because life is necessarily an agony, but because Giacomo Leopardi's life happened to be agonized.

The first attitude can easily be appreciated by anyone who has fallen under the spell of Leopardi's poetry. The latter point of view is not much more difficult to understand. The story of Leopardi's life is a masterpiece of black misery, irony, and despair. Rickety and hunchbacked, his body undermined by consumption and dropsy, organic and nervous overstrain and exhaustion, he was daily wracked by indefinable pains. And in this deformed and agonized body dwelt a flaming soul, intense, energetic, craving love and light and finding none. Thus to physical deformity and pain was added and superadded mental anguish. Denied parental understanding and sympathy, imprisoned in the *borgo selvaggio* of Recanati, there to be envied and mocked by a rude populace, he was forced to struggle in an alien world, experiencing what Alphonse Daudet rightly called "the worst of human miseries: to have had a childhood without tenderness."

Distinction is sometimes made between unreasoned and reasoned pessimism, or subjective and philosophical pessimism. Now, to be sure, pessimism, like optimism, is a matter of emotional no less than of intellectual temper. But, if a man's temperament and experience have enabled him to perceive and reveal more vividly some one aspect of life, his views and disclosures are nowise to be discounted by any rehearsal of his private weals or woes. The clinical, scandal-mongering method of dealing with the modern pessimists does not quite dispose of their theories of life, any more than Job's questions are to be turned to ridicule because they are the questions of a man who never asked them until he found himself atop the ash-heap. Job's presence on top of that heap is itself a most relevant fact which does not detract but rather adds to the significance of his testimony in the matter under consideration.

So Leopardi himself repeatedly protests against those who busy themselves with his maladies instead of studying his observations and reasonings. Leopardi is the true poet of pessimism, because he is also a philosopher; Carducci rightly calls him the Lucretius of Italian thought. He is not to be confused with the Byrons and the Chateaubriands, with the Werthers, the Evgeny Onyegins, and the Jacopo Ortises. These are romantic sufferers, conscious of a rare dolorous distinction by virtue of their rare griefs; of the world apart, they wrap themselves up in their melancholy mantles; they are the aristocrats of sorrow. Even of Alfred de Musset, Aulard rightly says: "It is not sorrow that he chants, but his own sorrow."

Leopardi's spirit is radically different. The misery is not that he is unhappy, but that no one can be happy. Genuinely lyrical as is the tone of his utterances, they are not mere subjective wails but convictions held on objective grounds, which Leopardi is prepared to defend also in terms of reasoned argument. The ardent lyrics of the *Canti*, the impassioned or the coldly cynical prose of the *Operette morali*, the more intimate and casual reflections in the *Epistolario*, the logical arguments and the aphorisms of the *Pensieri* are but various expressions of Leopardi's daily attitude towards life, an attitude none the less carefully thought out because it was so intensely felt. The key to his writings is not a particular personal experience, emotion, or mood; it is a process of thought. The development of this thought leads him to the theory of what he calls *l'infelicità*, the essential infelicity of existence.

Man's life is an exhausting pursuit of sublime phantoms and illusory goods, from the attainment of which he expects what he never does and never can get: felicity. Life is essentially self-defeating, a vanity and futile misery. All the roads on which men seek felicity are blind alleys. Glory is "a dear purchase;" man's every gain is vitiated by its impermanence; all the labors, all the vaunted progress of mankind only reveal to us the more clearly that vast abyss of nothingness which is life. Virtue itself is an illusory and a futile goal, *stolta virtù;* the world is getting worse:

> In peggio
> Precipitano i tempi.

> (**"Bruto Minore"**)

All ambition is vain, and vain are all the ideals for which men spend their lives, as vain as is the faith in a divine Providence that watches over us.

One phantom ideal remains, the most precious and dominant, the longest-lived of all: Love,

> Amor, di nostra vita ultimo inganno.

> (**"Ad Angelo Mai"**)

Leopardi's poetry shows a mighty effort to keep on believing that sure felicity is in love. This insistence is made manifest in a number of poems, especially in **"Consalvo"** and **"Il pensiero dominante."**

But in the depth of his spirit he recognizes that love's felicity, too, is an illusion, *sogno e palese error*, divine sovereign of man's soul, but death's own sister. This last *caro inganno* is finally renounced by Leopardi. In the short lyric **"A sè stesso"** we have pessimism unqualified and absolute:

> Omai disprezza
> Te, la natura, il brutto
> Poter che, ascoso, a comun danno impera,
> E l'infinita vanità del tutto.

This pessimistic view of life, which is poetically disclosed in the *Canti*, Leopardi undertakes to maintain in reasoned terms. The very self-consciousness which makes us at all capable of desiring felicity makes felicity unattainable. For our self-consciousness is self-seeking, and its goal, happiness, recedes as we approach it: no sooner is one desire satisfied than the very satisfaction arouses a greater desire for a further happiness. To experience real felicity we require the enjoyment of an infinite attained good. Such enjoyment is, in the very nature of things, impossible, and hence all striving after happiness is doomed to disappointment. The disappointment is the keener the more actively conscious the individual is. So D'Alembert writes: *"Soyez grand et malheureux."*

Ask a man: would he live his life over again, without any change? Who would consent to repeat the sorry tale? Yet man does crave another life. Why? Because he clings to the illusion that in the next life he would realize what he has so dismally missed in this. Therein is to be found the motive and the tragedy of the hope of immortality. In all the universe man alone is not content with himself. Are we to reason from this that man's existence is not limited to this world? Leopardi's mature thought is a consistent rejection of this notion. He does not believe in immortality, and he would not have it. Man's groping after the Beyond does not prove the reality of the Beyond, but only the miserable reality of the groping and striving after infinite unlimited satisfaction. The infinite felicity sought is illusory, even the pain is really without any foundation. Genuine and ever-present is only the ennui of existence, *noia immortale* (**"Al Conte Carlo Pepoli"**).

Immortality is a delusion; heart-breaking though it is, we must face the truth. So in **"Il sogno"** the poet, seeing his dead love in a vision, by a supreme effort brushes aside the vain hope:

> Or finalmente addio.
> Nostre misere menti e nostre salme
> Son disgiunte in eterno. A me non vivi,
> E mai più non vivrai . . .

It is unwarrantable to appeal to the *consensus gentium*. Antiquity has little to say on the subject. Indeed if men really believed in life after death, why do they mourn for the dead? Is it because they believe them to be in Hell? But Leccafondi, the *filosofo morale filotopo* of the **Paralipomeni della Batracomiomachia** finds neither rewards nor punishments in the land of the dead. Besides, if the mourner thought of the dead as being in eternal torment, horror and aversion should enter into his sorrow. No, the dead are mourned because, in their inmost hearts, men feel that the departed are really gone; the thought that really crushes us is the thought of the *caducità umana* of which death is the visible manifestation,—death *sola nel mondo eterna*, as sing the mummies of Frederic Ruysch.

So we mourn the cessation of life. But why do we mourn it? How can death be regarded as an evil? Even if life were good, the question would be open, whether the prolongation of existence would be any more desirable than a never-to-be-ended sonnet. "But if life be not happy,. . . better to endure a short term of it than a long one." Man is essentially incapable of felicity "in this world or in another." Besides, "heaven is scarcely an inviting place," and highly unreal and empty; for it can only be conceived after the fashion of this life, and like it is void of meaning. Ruysch's mummies can answer no questions save in terms of their earthly life; aside from which their existence is a void.

The disclosure that the hope of immortality is illusory reveals to us no terrifying prospect, but is really our only comfort: "death is our greatest good." Yet even if the prospect were terrifying, as indeed life is terrifying in its misery, better far to face the truth and be miserable than to seek cowardly refuge in illusion. So Leopardi declares:

> I reject every childish consolation and illusive comfort and am courageous enough to bear the deprivation of every hope, to look steadily on the desert of life. . . . This philosophy . . . gives the courageous man the proud satisfaction of being able to rend asunder the mysterious cloak that conceals the hidden and mysterious cruelty of human destiny. . . . I ardently wish for death above everything. . . . Hopes of glory and immortality are things now undeserving of even a smile.

> (pp. 549-54)

Radoslav A. Tsanoff, "Pessimism and Immortality," in The Philosophical Review, *Vol. XXIX, No. 6, November, 1920, pp. 547-70.*

BENEDETTO CROCE   (essay date 1923)

[*Croce was an Italian philosopher, historian, editor, and literary critic whose writings span the first half of the twentieth century. He founded and edited the literary and political journal* La critica, *whose independence, objectivity, and strong stand against fascism earned him the respect of his contemporaries. According to Croce, the only proper form of literary history is the* characteristica, *or critical characterization, of the poetic personality and work of a single artist; its goal is to demonstrate the unity of the author's intention, its expression in the creative work, and the reader's response. In the following excerpt from his influential appraisal of Leopardi's work, Croce discounts the validity of Leopardi's pessimistic philosophy, attributing the poet's despair to personal disappointment rather than to universal insights. Croce also identifies that portion of the author's work that may be properly termed art—that which is free of didacticism, satire, and "evil laughter." Croce's remarks were originally published in Italian in 1923.*]

The dolorous spirit of the Italian poet Giacomo Leopardi was very soon placed in the pleiad of those other tortured and disconsolate spirits who had appeared everywhere since the end of the eighteenth century and had sung the funereal song of despair to the human race bound to wander henceforth in a universe without a God. It seems impossible to avoid taking count of this furrow of sorrow and of nobility which he wore upon his forehead as a sign whereby kindred souls should know him, if we are to understand aright the rapid formation and diffusion of his glory as a poet. Leopardi was indebted above all to the emotional elements contained in his poetry for his effortless triumph over obstacles, which would otherwise have prevented a writer such as he, of classical education, of classical and learned vocabulary and of classical modesty, from succeeding in that period of fervid literary romanticism. For the tendency was then towards the popular on the one hand and on the other toward the unbridled, the disproportionate, the facile and the verbose, also in Italy. It was due to their emotional and pessimistic content that Leopardi's poems brought him European notoriety and esteem when, owing to hide-bound prejudice, it was believed that nothing of universal value could appear in provincial Italy. From that time onward his name shines among the poets and poetical personages who represent "the sorrow of the world," Werther, Oberman and René, Byron, Lénau, De Vigny, Musset and the rest; and since the systematic philosopher of pessimism paid homage to the Italian pessimist, he was ranged alongside of Arthur Schopenhauer. (pp. 111-12)

During the period of the Italian Risorgimento Leopardi was "the poet of the young men," of the youthful liberals who were preparing war and revolution. This is not to be wondered at when we consider the passionate link between emotional romanticism and national sentiment in Italy, the generous discontent and the generous longing for better days, the sorrow of the world and the sorrow of our Italy. For this reason and setting aside the properly patriotic poems of Leopardi, the young men felt that such a man as he was one of them, almost in virtue of that very pessimism of his, and that "if destiny had prolonged his life till the 1848," they would have found him at their side, "comforter and combatant." Yet the very young man of them who said this [Francesco De Sanctis], destined to become a remarkable critic in later years, after having venerated Leopardi as the bringer of the truth and a master of life, perceived, in 1850, that it was no longer a time to doubt, to imprecate and to moan, that human sorrow is the "seed of liberty," that suffering is necessary, but in acting and in hoping, and that for this reason "Leopardi must be set aside," Leopardi, master of life.

And we too must set him aside in respect of the new and attenuated form which that erroneous and deceptive notion has assumed, of Leopardi as a very great thinker, whose arguments and doctrines should have their place in the history of philosophy. The sense of delusion produced by the publication of Leopardi's *Correspondence* will be fresh in many minds. So these doctrines (it was said), to which we had attributed speculative value, were nothing but the reflection of the sufferings and unhappiness of the individual? So they were merely reflections of the infirmities with which he was afflicted, of family restrictions and cramped economic conditions, of vain longings for the love of a woman who would none of him?

But there was no true reason for awaiting these biographical or autobiographical revelations in order to become aware of the quality of Leopardi's speculation. Whenever and inasmuch as philosophy is pessimistic or optimistic, it is always intrinsically pseudo-philosophy, philosophy for private use, for the reason that everything can become the object of approbative or disapprobative judgments, good or evil can be uttered of everything, except of reality and life, which itself creates and uses for its own ends the categories of good and evil. Hence praise attributed to or blame inflicted upon reality has no other foundation than that of a movement of passion, occasioned by good or bad humour, by cheerfulness, lightsomeness, intolerance, caprice, by favourable or unfavourable happenings. True and serious philosophy neither weeps nor smiles, but is concentrated upon the investigation of the forms of being, the activity of the spirit; its progress is marked by the ever richer, more varied and definite consciousness that the spirit acquires of itself. The philosophers who call themselves optimistic or pessimistic draw their sole importance as philosophers from, let us say, the logical or ethical or other such contributions which they make to philosophy outside and beyond their pessimistic or optimistic attitudes. That is their only claim to enter into the history of thought, which is always the history of science and criticism.

But Leopardi makes only a slight contribution to philosophy thus understood, and his observations are scattered, lacking depth and system. He thus stands outside creative philosophy, being without speculative tendencies or training. He also arrived at no new, closely thought-out truth of importance in the theory of poetry and of art, although he was led to meditate more than once upon their nature. "Are the things I say" (he asked naïvely in the dialogue of Timander and Eleander about those questions of evil and suffering) "leading truths or are they merely accessories?" He replies to himself with the remark that "the substance of all philosophies is to be found in them." A like error is committed by the many who to-day deplore in solemn philosophemes life as sorrowful and life as evil and believe that they are thus philosophizing and, what is more, philosophizing as to the highest truths. Were this the case, philosophy would have accomplished its task many centuries ago, indeed ever since man was man, because such emotional propositions have always been uttered by man and belong to the common stock.

It is also well here to dispose of another exaggeration, which appeared at the moment of the publication of the *Zibaldone,* in which Leopardi was in the habit of annotating his thoughts over a period of years. There can be no doubt that much is to be learned from Leopardi in relation to the practice of the art of literature, especially in our days, when the discipline of writing has been so much neglected; but there is as much to be learned from other writers who, like him, studied their art,

and to quote one of them of equal stature, I may mention Foscolo, as well as another who abhorred him and whom he abhorred, Tommaseo, profoundly versed, however, in the secrets of style and of language. Others, too, there are of lesser build, such as Cesari and Puoti, exact and subtle-minded, as purists are wont to be, and much, too, is to be learned in other ways from Manzoni and his followers.

All were masters and models in something, none a master or model in an absolute sense, because Leopardi could not be a "model" to anyone but himself (this is clear), and anyone who wishes to avoid being merely a commonplace imitator must create of himself and for himself his own model. Utterly vain are therefore the disputes which have arisen as to the direction which Leopardi is supposed to have indicated to Italian literature, but which has not been followed and which should now be followed. Leopardi's language and style suited him well; but since they could not be adopted by his contemporary Manzoni, because Manzoni's spirit was not that of Leopardi, this proved equally impossible for the generations of Verga and of Carducci which followed. (pp. 112-15)

What was Leopardi's life? By this I mean the spiritual process through which man expresses and shapes his own feelings, defines and particularizes his own thought, asserts his aspirations in action, and in a general way develops the germ which he bears within him, realizing more or less completely, yet substantially, his own ideal. To employ a crude but expressive metaphor, his was a strangled life. (p. 116)

[The] lament for what might have been, yet might not be, for the promise that Nature had not kept, constantly inspired his work. Gradually he arrived at an intellectual judgment, which eventually took the form of a philosophical theory, as to the evil, sorrow, vanity and nullity of existence. This was itself, as we have said, really a lamentation, a sense of bitterness, a masked expression of feeling, a reasoned projection of his own unhappy state. His spiritual horizon was limited to this complaint, to this theory of lamentation and of accusation. The sole fount of inspiration of his imagination, the sole centre of his thoughts, lay in the contemplation and reflection upon this mystery of suffering.

Leopardi has sometimes been looked upon as a poet-philosopher, a point of view which we have shown to be inexact in his case, as it is always inexact in the case of every poet. His fundamental condition of spirit was not only emotional and not philosophical, but it might be defined as an emotional absorption, a vain longing of so desperate a nature, so violent and condensed, as to overflow into the sphere of thought and determine concepts and judgments. Thus, whenever that tendency of soul in him forgot its true nature and comported itself as though it occupied a reasoned doctrinal position and gave forth criticism, polemic, or satire, that part of Leopardi's work which is to be frankly recognized as vitiated made its appearance. Such are the majority of the *Operette morali* and in verse particularly "**Palinodia**" and *Paralipomeni*.

He had got himself into a blind alley as regards doctrine, engaged in a useless strife. He held that life was an evil and should be lived with the bitter consciousness of this radical evil; but he found other men around him who viewed the matter otherwise than he, because they felt in a different way and were able to dispose of their physical powers, their nerves were calm, their minds well balanced, and the joy of living dominated and animated them. They enjoyed the smiles of hope, were burning for action, drunken with love, and as for sorrows and adversities they resisted them by placing them among the inevitable difficulties to be dealt with, when they were free of them, and when they did arise faced and overcame them. They did not think of death, thus obeying the ancient saying, that death does not concern the living, because they are alive, nor the dead, because they are dead. It was such men as these that Leopardi would have wished to persuade that they were wrong and that they should join him in despairing. But there is no reasoning possible with feeling.

Years ago one might have read an inscription outside a little rustic dwelling in the Tyrol to the following effect (the German verses may still be in their place for aught I know); they ran as follows: "I am living, but for how long? I shall die, without knowing where nor when. I go I know not whither and I am astonished that I am so gay in spite of all that. Lord Christ, protect my house!"

Leopardi was not astonished, but he was angry that men should be so gay in spite of all that. He called them cowards and tried to confound, to shame and to convert them, that is to say, to infuse into them in the form of arguments his personal state of soul, having recourse, with this object in view, to irony, sarcasm and the grotesque. Those among the *Operette morali* with this mission were necessarily altogether frigid: they contain vain attempts to produce comic effects (which cheerfulness and serenity of the imagination can alone produce, not the spirit of strife and ill-humour); their characters are nothing but names; their dialogues are monologues; their language, although extremely laboured, has no depth and often smacks of academical vain parlance.

In verse and prose he mocked the faith of the new age, the incessant growth and broadening of the human spirit, progress; he mocked at liberalism and attempts at reform and revolution, at economic and social studies, and at the philosophy of the new times, which was beginning to see the light among the great thinkers of Germany; he mocked at philology, which allowed itself to break through traditional groupings and to discover relationships between Indo-European languages, and indeed at every single thing which gave signs of vitality, of ardour or of invention. (pp. 118-21)

There is something unhealthy in that prose and in those palinodes and paralipomena. De Sanctis himself was led to talk of the "evil laughter" which one hears in its pages and of the "dagger thrusts," which the writer tries to give, "with the joy of an avenger," and of "unfriendliness for the human race," in which one is "the man refused by fate."

And here we may well pause a moment to consider the wonted lack of understanding which exalts such writings as these to the position of works of pure imagination, thought and art. But let us hasten to add that the "evil laughter," the bursting forth of rage, is really to be placed to the account of that most cruel stepmother of Leopardi, Nature, to the account of Leopardi sick . . . , and if it obliges us to certain critical reservations, yet constrains us to human pity, and, in any case, is incapable of altering our already recorded admiration for the nobility of Leopardi's character. The scoffer at liberals had all his friendships among liberals, the contemner of mankind had no other longing than to love and to be loved. Ah, if one ray of sunlight had chased out of his blood the poisonous malady, dissolved the torpor which aggravated it! He would have at once gone out afoot and with astonishment yet greater than that which he sung in the **"Risorgimento,"** would have looked upon the world with new eyes and seen the dark clouds of his imagination disappear in the distance, while the powers of creative application crushed down in his sickly body, would have spread themselves abroad in generous abundance.

The library of Leopardi's home in Recanati, where he studied and wrote.

If, therefore, we wish to discover the pure, healthy Leopardi writing as an artist, we must seek him, not in his polemical, ironic and satirical moods, with their echo of evil laughter, but where he expresses himself seriously and is really moved. This Leopardi is to be found in certain places among the same *Operette,* such as, for instance, in certain pages of the Timander and Eleander, so much akin in tone to the best letters of the *Epistolario.* In this connection, we must observe that the question that has been mooted and is still in the air concerning Leopardi's "prose," which by some is held to be of classical, marmoreal quality, by others artificial, and as to which others again dispute whether it suits or does not suit Italian literature— is in the last clause without meaning and in the two former ill stated. Leopardi's prose is indubitably vicious where the conception itself and the tone are wrong, and where he is found making vain efforts and borrows false graces, but it is most beautiful where it is truly founded upon thought.

Here and there also in the *Paralipomeni,* in strident contrast with the rest of the poem, Leopardi relaxes his tone of ironic tension and forced merriment, and expresses himself with simplicity, as in the well-known octaves on Italy or in the apostrophe to the beauty of Virtue, verses which remain in the memory. Yet, in addition to the criterion of diffidence as to Leopardi polemist and ironist, we must retain yet another in mind, relating particularly to Leopardi when he is serious and moved, to the Leopardi quite full of his sorrow and of his sorrowful thought.

There can be no denying that this condition of spirit, since it is the extreme point and conclusion of an internal process, has something in it of the static. For this reason, it presents itself as a dogma believed and inculcated in its objective form, and in its subjective form, as though it were an epigraph upon his own life, henceforth closed. It would seem that here too there can be no true lyrical quality, which must always be epic and dramatic in its nature as well as lyrical, a multiplicity assembling itself to form a unity, an external world discovering itself as an internal world. The exposition of a series of thoughts, of a pessimistic catechism, and the assertion of a desperate resignation, of a renouncement or of a denial, are this side of or beyond poetry.

For this reason, there is a large amount of didacticism in Leopardi's poetry; scattered more or less everywhere with its prosaic tone, sometimes even filling an entire composition such as the "Epistola al Pepoli," or almost a whole composition, such as the "Ginestra." To compare it with Dante's didacticism in the *Paradiso* is a mistake, because it frequently resembles rather the tone of Dante's verses on nobility and other such themes, when he abandoned the sweet rhymes of love to which he was wont to attune his thoughts. Such are the verses of the "Ginestra:" "A noble nature is that which burns to rise higher," etc. At other times, the didactic tone is dropped and it is rather an oration, an indictment, a series of questions such as are put to an accused person whose place is taken by nature, virtue, the mystery of things—such as in the "Bruto" or in the "Canto notturno."

Not less frequently also, we find in Leopardi the assertion of suffering as a historical fact, a recognition or repetition that such is the case. This is manifested in a certain dryness of tone, in summary fleshless diction, which are not life itself in action, but the reflection of life as in a compendium, its reduction to the conceptual form. The brief poem "A se stesso" may serve as an instance of this epigraphical style, which it does not seem possible to describe as lyrical: "The extreme

deception of my own eternity has perished. It has perished. I am well aware of our dear self-deceptions, but now not only hope, but desire also is extinguished." Here, as elsewhere, the tone is so sorrowful, so heart-broken, so desolate, so free from all coquetry of suffering, that it cannot fail (and never has failed) to produce a profound impression and to inspire a sort of reverence. But, on the other hand, there is no gainsaying the fact that here, as in other similar cases, we have rather a notation of feelings or sentiments which do not extend beyond the sphere of the individual. On a very few rare occasions we meet with the opposite procedure, when Leopardi tries to express directly the full emotion: once in the case of the amorous emotion from which he extracted the burning desire expressed in the "Consalvo," and on another occasion when his soul is thrown open to the commotions of life, in the "**Risorgimento.**" But in the "Consalvo" there is something of those solitary ravings about love of which Ranieri was sometimes witness. In the "Risorgimento," the motion of the soul fails to finds its adequate and proper form of expression and the author allows it to run in the channels of the brooklet of Metastasio's little half descriptive half musical strophes.

Where, then, is the poetry of Leopardi? you will say: it is neither here nor there, nor in any other place either. Do you wish to suggest that Leopardi was not in any sense a poet?— Well, conscious critical opinion in general has already pointed to the places where the poetry is to be found. It received coldly the *Operette morali;* it refuted the arguments of the *Paralipomeni* and the "Palinodia"; it accused the "Ginestra" and other poems of being prosaic. With the utmost positiveness and by the mouthpiece of De Sanctis, and despite the shouts of patriotic fanatics from Settembrini to Carducci, it recognized further that the early poems are rhetoric of the schools, that of the crazy or minatory poems only a few traits are to be retained, that in the case of those that remain there are reserves to be made.

It directed admiration especially to the so-called "idylls," both early and later, and to the "great idylls." It seems to me sufficient to avoid making this statement into an exclusive and comprehensive approval of certain particular compositions and to understand it in its ideal and profound sense, in order to obtain the criterion by which to discern the true poetry of Leopardi.

Leopardi, as we have said, was "shut off from life," but not so that, in his early youth, he had not dreamed and hoped and loved, enjoyed and lamented, nor that later in life, at certain moments, he did not feel himself alive and his mind again open to the emotions of life. In these moments, when he again felt himself forming part of the world, either by remembering things of distant years or by immediate recollection, his poetical imagination was stirred: for poetry may be what you will, but it can never be cold or acosmical. Such moments of inspiration are the "**Sera del di di festa**," the "**Vita Solitaria**," the "**Infinito**," the "**Sabato del Villaggio**," the "**Quiete dopo la Tempesta**," the "**Ricordunze**," the "**Silvia.**" Then his words take on colour, his rhythm becomes soft and flexible and full of harmonies and intimate poetry, the emotion trembles as it reflects itself in the dewdrop of poetry. The effect is the more powerful, inasmuch as those moments of life, those glances at the surrounding world, not in order to reject, but to receive it sympathetically, those bursts of desire, those hopes of love, that tenderness, that suavity, have in them something almost furtive and are snatched from the jaws of a hard destiny, which presses closely in his steps, and from the chill feeling that is to come so soon. They are expressed with the reserve, the modesty, the chastity of one who says things which he is no longer in the habit of saying. Hence their particular charm, hence the slight touch of carmine on the pale cheek of this poetry, which makes much vigorous highly coloured literature seem pale indeed by comparison.

Who does not bear in mind and heart the images which come then to flower, those divine images, those girlish faces, those aspects of the country-side, of humble folk at their work? Silvia at her loom, singing in odorous May, her mind full of a beautiful dream, and of the young man who stays his writing to lend an ear to the sound of that voice, linking his dream with the girl's dream? Those evenings in the father's house, the starry sky, the song of the frogs, the glow-worms wandering among the hedges, the voices of those within the house alternating with one another, while thought and desire sail away into the infinite?—The tranquil village of a Saturday night with the girl standing there, the flowers for her adornment on the morrow in her hand, the old woman who babbles of the past, the boys jumping and shouting, the labourer returning to his frugal table as he thinks of the morrow's repose, the smith and the carpenter, who hasten to complete their work, while all the world sleeps, betrayed by the light that filters through the chinks of the workshop;—the evening of the feast-day, so full of sadness, with the memory of the song which one can still hear dying slowly away in the distance;—the solitary margin of the lake, "crowned with still flowers," near which he sat down and abandoned himself to his thoughts, becoming motionless as motionless nature;—the impression of life reviving after the tempest; and others similar, all of them eternal and ever new creations? And then there are such cameo-lines as "When beauty shone resplendent in thy laughing fleeting eyes"; and those perfect lines: "The wind comes bearing with it the sound of the hour striking on the tower of the town"; "soft and clear is the night and free from wind. . . ."

Those other moments, when Leopardi takes refuge in the intellectual world so dear to him, and, so to speak, loves love and death together, as in the most beautiful **"Pensiero dominante"** and in **"Amore e morte,"** rise to the level of poetry together with these memories of life. Although their form is meditative, they are not didactic; and the **"Aspasia"** is not didactic but dramatic, in which, after the shipwreck of his last love, he finds refuge on the firm shores of the intellect and recovers his strength by explaining to himself what had happened and in making a theory about it. The old passion still vibrates in his soul, but he believes that he has gone beyond it and is able to dominate it by means of his calm thinking.

It is true that Leopardi's work is rarely or never entirely poetic. Almost always, he becomes didactic or rhetorical, or dry and epigraphical in the way already described. In the **"Sabato del Villaggio,"** the poetic scene which should have suggested by its very poetical touches the thought of joy awaited, which is the only true joy, the joy of the imagination, is commented upon critically and weighed down with allegory, which takes the form of a rhetorical exhortation addressed to "the merry little boy." Even in the **"Silvia"** itself, which is perhaps his masterpiece, that "Hope," which appears at the close, has in it something of the abstract, and some interpreters and many readers (although they are wrong as a matter of fact) have been led to merge this Hope in Silvia, reviving her by means of this fusion, and making the poet have a young girl and not an allegory as "dear companion of his new age" and with her "so many delights at once," of love, of pleasure, of works

and of experience. These poetical passages of one tone into that of another or of poetry into what is different from poetry, these lapses into aridity could not be demonstrated otherwise than by examining each element separately. . . . It is . . . possible to see more clearly into what is called the poetic style of Leopardi by means of such an examination: language, syntax, metres. Leopardi has always the choice and exquisite style of the humanist, for whom it would be impossible to have recourse to words and modes of expression suitable to poets of other origin and formation, in the sense of being more sociable and popular in their appeal. He is, however, able to show himself simple and immediate, without abandoning that refinement of choice and solemnity of tone. Elsewhere, however, he is dominated by literary formulas as regards certain rhythmical arrangements and phraseology, even accepting Metastasio and the Arcadians as guides. See, for instance, **"Amore e Morte,"** where we find: "Things fair as these are not to be found elsewhere here below; nor in the stars," and further in the **"Sabato del Villaggio,"** where not only the "young hopeful" but the "nice little girl" and the "dainty little bouquet of roses and violets" are effeminate and unworthy of the rest.

All this goes to prove—and this shall be my last critical and methodical remark on Leopardi in these brief notes—that we must not allow ourselves to be deceived by the perfect correctness, propriety and style of Leopardi's poetry, but look beyond that and observe that if we never find emptiness of thought and feeling beneath that impeccable form, we do nevertheless find now the poetically strong and now the weak, now the complete and now the incomplete, and come to the conclusion that the poetry of Leopardi is much more subject to these variations than is generally suspected or believed. There is in it something arid, prosaic, merely literary, and something also of sweetest, purest and most harmonious; and perhaps that very obstacle, preceding or following the free movements of the rhythm and the imagination, makes us better able to experience the miracle of poetic creation. (pp. 121-30)

> *Benedetto Croce, "Leopardi," in his* European Literature in the Nineteenth Century, *translated by Douglas Ainslie, Alfred A. Knopf, 1924, pp. 111-30.*

GEORGE SANTAYANA (essay date 1935)

[*Santayana was a Spanish-born philosopher, poet, novelist, and literary critic who was for the most part educated in the United States. Although he is regarded as no more than a fair poet, his facility with language is one of the distinguishing features of his late philosophical writings. Santayana's major philosophical work of his early career is the five-volume* Life of Reason *(1905-06). These volumes reflect his materialist viewpoint applied to such areas as society, religion, art, and science, and, along with* Skepticism and Animal Faith *(1923) and the four-volume* Realms of Being *(1927-40), put forth the notion that, while reason undermines belief in anything whatever, an irrational animal faith suggests the existence of a "realm of essences" that leads to the human search for knowledge. In this excerpt, originally written as a preface to Iris Origo's 1935 biography of Leopardi (see Additional Bibliography), Santayana seeks to describe the appeal of Leopardi's poetry.*]

There is only one thing that the purely English reader may miss [in reading *Leopardi*, by Iris Origo], because it is only communicable to those who have some familiarity with the Italian language and some sympathy with the classic temperament: I mean the poignant accent, the divine elevation of this poet. The student, the writer, the sufferer, the wanderer was only Conte Giacomo Leopardi, but the poet was Orpheus himself. Long passages are fit to repeat in lieu of prayers through all the watches of the night. How shall I express their quality? Suppose you were held up in some minor Italian town where by chance an itinerant company was to perform *Il Trovatore*. Suppose that having nothing better to do you strolled into the theatre, resigned in advance to a meagre stage-setting, a harsh orchestra, a prima donna past her prime, a rhetorical little tenor saving his breath for the gymnastic prodigy of his final high note. But suppose also that, having found things in general much as you expected, suddenly you heard, coming from behind the wings, an unexampled heavenly voice, a voice pure as moonlight, rich as sorrow, firm as truth, singing *Solo in terra*. Alone on earth that voice might indeed seem, and far from earth it would carry you; and no matter how commonplace the singer might look, or even ridiculous, when he stepped before the footlights, if ever that sheer music sounded again, there would be something not himself that sang and something not yourself that listened.

I speak of voice and of music, but that is only a metaphor. What works the miracle in Leopardi is far from being mere sound or diction or the enigmatic suggestion of strange words. His versification is remarkable only when a divine afflatus blows through it, which is not always. This afflatus is intellectual, this music is a flood of thoughts. We are transported out of ourselves ascetically, by the vision of truth. Leopardi lived in a romantic tower, a dismal, desolate ruin; but through the bars of his prison he beheld the same classic earth and Olympian sky that had been visible to Homer, Pindar, and Sophocles. The world is always classical, the truth of human destiny is always clear, if only immersion in our animal cares does not prevent us from seeing it. Lifting the eyes would be so easy, yet it is seldom done; and when a rapt poet compels us to do so, we are arrested, we are rebuked, we are delivered.

The misfortunes of Leopardi were doubtless fortunate for his genius. Every classic poet has his romantic agent, corresponding with the scope of his intuition and the degree of harmony or conflict that the vision of the truth creates in his heart. In Leopardi this vision was saturated with anguish; narrowed by it, no doubt, but not distorted. The white heat of his anguish burned all anguish away, and cleared the air. Beneath the glorious monotony of the stars he saw the universal mutation of earthly things, and their vanity, yet also, almost everywhere, the beginning if not the fullness of beauty; and this intuition, at once rapturous and sad, liberated him from the illusions of the past and from those of the future. (pp. 208-09)

> *George Santayana, "Leopardi," in his* Essays in Literary Criticism of George Santayana, *edited by Irving Singer, Charles Scribner's Sons, 1956, pp. 208-09.*

THEODORE WEISS (essay date 1955)

[*Weiss addresses the duality in Leopardi's thought, noting that, while he deplored the nothingness of life, he nonetheless found pleasure in squarely confronting his despair. According to Weiss, Leopardi's greatness—and his relevance to modern readers—lies in his "ability to feel, to respond, to keep the human heart going in the midst of . . . destructiveness."*]

After well over a hundred years of comparative neglect, Leopardi's pertinency becomes increasingly clear. In his grasp of certain basic problems he looks astonishingly like us. Surely not our proudest efforts at gloom can surpass his. Beside him Eliot seems a rather weary don, even as most modern existen-

tialists seem superficial before the essence Leopardi made of many of the qualities we take for granted as unique to existentialism. For with unflagging courage he maintained a steady look at actuality in its most flagrant forms, this with an appealing pride that spurned the comforts not a few of us, bruised and frightened, have succumbed to. His prose as well as poetic matter is usually the sadness of the brevity of youth, its illusions and hopes, and the concomitant horrors of age and decay. At the same time he knew how remote most human desires are from reality; you, "tired heart," he insists in **"To Himself,"**

> . . . have the right to hate
> Yourself, the world as it is, the brute
> Energy that secretly enjoins the common fate,
> And the immense immeasurable emptiness of things.

Believing life in its common ills as in its end essentially unhappy, he fully understood the common need of consolations. Yet he despised this need (especially as it feeds on the deceits of reason, little more than a form of anesthesia) and the failure of almost all of us to live in denial of it. Eventually he found a kind of fervor and satisfaction, if not contentment, in the acid truth:

> . . . sick or well, I stamp upon the cowardice of mankind, I refuse every consolation, every childish deceit, and I have the courage to bear the deprivation of every hope, to look intrepidly at the desert of life, not to disguise any part of human unhappiness, to accept all the consequences of a philosophy that is painful, but true. Philosophy which, if it is of no other use, gives to strong men the proud satisfaction of seeing every cloak torn from the concealed and mysterious cruelty of human destiny.

Of course one can suspect him, as much as the rest of us, of casting the world in his own image. Dogged by ailments and infirmities—several self-induced by incredible rigors of study—most of his tormented life, incapable for one reason or another of the passionate fulfilment he believed in and devoutly wished, he probably could not help visiting his frustrations on the world he lived in. However, with his wonted uncommon sense plus his veneration for the Greeks, he excoriated the Christian tendency to ignore physical health for "spiritual" reasons. How much our loftiest values and acts depend on it was especially brought home to him by his feeble body; he was hardly one to deny the testimony of his own experience. Describing his feelings of contempt for mankind in its lust for consolations, he can go so far as to admit, "If these feelings arise from sickness, I do not know. . . ."

As thoroughly convinced of the nothingness of this life and the world as anyone, even he for all his clear-headedness could not wash his hands of the whole business, could not go on to conclude logically—no doubt this is one of his principal attractivenesses—that whatever distractions and illusions man seeks out to make life a little more endurable, they must be categorically accepted. For if life is truly meaningless what difference can conduct make? What standards, based as they must be on some first principle, can one allow oneself? Such the contradiction at the heart—and the heart—of his work. On the contrary, since he seems to have put his hope in man's living with man, in the human community against indifferent nature, his sense of outrage at the failure of mankind to be honest, honorable, noble (though at times he admits the emptiness of these qualities too!) was much stronger than most men's. But as we shall discover, perhaps his notion that he saw things as they nakedly, anguishingly, are comprised his final necessary illusion, the nourishment that permitted him to live at least with some ardor. As he said, despair was infinitely preferable to emptiness; though it may have been his disappointments that made him feel the whole world meaningless, at least they made him feel. Believing in youth, its uncompromisingness before evil and weakness till age overtakes it, he clung relentlessly to his own uncompromisingness to the end.

In any case, one can suggest that out of love Leopardi expected too much of man, had too much pride in him and his potentialities to be "tolerant" before his self-indulgences, his deceits. Like Pascal he asked why man, pitiable creature that he is, should be able to rack himself with such gigantic desires and torments. Pound's translation, **"Her Monument, the Image Cut Thereon,"** concludes:

> O mortal nature,
> If thou art
> Frail and so vile in all,
> How canst thou reach so high with thy poor sense;
> Yet if thou art
> Noble in any part
> How is the noblest of thy speech and thought
> So lightly wrought
> Or to such base occasion lit and quenched?

In short, Leopardi adored what he hated, hated what he adored: man's consciousness, that which, separating him from nature and the animals, enables him to recognize the wretchedness (as well thereby to complicate it) and so the superiority of his condition. Envying though he may have the lifelong free fancy of birds, like that of children and the childhood of the race, at the same time Leopardi exercised, enjoyed exercising, his intellect to the full.

Despite his own incapacities he rarely blinked the importance of high-minded aims and mighty efforts; and in his work, as **"To Italy"** well illustrates, valiantly he sought by direct appeal, by satire, by scathing comment, to rouse his countrymen to noble thinking and noble doing. Entirely aware of the potentialities of depravity (this he saw in nature; in this he saw, alas, the oneness of man and nature), he insisted that we must with utmost resolution bestir ourselves against these potentialities.

Nor did he capitulate to deterministic thinking to the point of relieving us of the responsibilities of our lives. XLV of his *Pensieri* concludes, ". . . the weak live because of the world's will, and the strong because of their own." Yet Leopardi, as his sardonic statements amply attest, was overwhelmingly aware of the hostility of the modern world to art—that is, to sensitivity, distinction, love, meaningful and realized living. No one knew better than he the grimness of the struggle. Steeped in his appetites and his expectations, naked to his surroundings, whether his little desolate native Recanati or pompous, self-infatuated Rome, he experienced it, the smothering of the spirit, with still intolerable, infuriating freshness. Like a Swift before him and a Flaubert after he must rabidly—the price of the artist in him—savor each minute revolting particular.

Animated all his life by the desire for achievement and fame, he realized the folly of this desire, particularly in an apathetic modern world, in a time characterized by him as a "century of boys." What can better convey his scorn than "even mediocrity has become extremely rare!" His age's easy bloated optimism, its naive confidence in progress and the infinite perfectibility of man, convinced him of its hopelessness. He saw through the superficial impressiveness of mass education to its very deep dangers: the thinning, the leveling, and the consequent destruction of real learning. With his customary

hawk-like fierceness he pounced on that wonderfully consolatory cliché, "this is a century of transition." It is hard to believe that his denunciation of it was written well over a century ago. How much he would consider us the infants—not to say still-borns—of the children of the 19th century. As he pointed out, it is one thing to remark the absurd in the root of life; it is quite another to elevate absurdities into root principles. How horrified he would be and how grateful for his own poor age could he see the super-fulfilment of his prophecies in the enormous ingenuity we expend to maintain and speed the life of imbecility and to hide from actuality. One can imagine his derision before our egregious efforts to develop a monetary idealism and out of it an interlocking set of ideas to insulate us against the always more vexing "facts of life." Our world seen almost entirely in the abstractions of the newspaper and the blatherskiting of politicians, we are embroiled in arguments, life and death ones, often as real as those of medievalists to us about the permissible congestion of angels on a pinhead, this ironically enough in a country particularly arrogant about its practicality, its realism, its scientific procedures, the latter in many ways the most abstract we have. The atom bomb, that monument of and to abstraction come alive, may at last, in our dedication to it, splitting us from the life that so troubles us, forever abstract us all. Naturally, as a Leopardi would say, as the truth becomes daily more clamorous, daily more unpleasant, so the noise and the rigor of our prejudices must grow.

But such challenge it is that precisely helps to underscore the size of a work of art. What is a major quality of a creative piece if not its ability to exceed its day's limitations. It is the welling up for reasons usually impossible to come by of the magic springs in the desert that makes the genius dear to us, a welling up despite—sometimes it would seem because of—brutality, depravity, destructiveness. It is the ability to feel, to respond, to keep the human reality going in the midst of this destructiveness that compels us to honor and preserve the great works of art. To ignore nothing of human and natural enormity, to meet fate on its own terms, this is the triumph we can hope for, this as well as the heroism of the noble failure persisted in. As Leopardi puts it [in the **Zibaldone** (see excerpt dated 1820?)],

> Works of genius have the peculiarity that, even when they represent the nothingness of things, even when they clearly demonstrate and make us feel the inevitable unhappiness of life, when they express the most terrible mood of despair [it is interesting to compare the despair of a *Hamlet* or a *Macbeth*, say, with that of *The Waste Land*], yet to a great mind even though it may be in a state of extreme depression, disillusionment, blankness, *noia*, and weariness of life, or in the bitterest and most paralysing misfortunes . . . they always serve as a consolation, rekindle enthusiasm; and though they treat and represent no other subject than death, they restore to such a mind at least momentarily that life which it had lost. Consequently that which when seen in the reality of things stabs and kills the soul, when seen in imitation or in any other way in works of genius . . . opens the heart and restores it to life. In any case, just as the author, while describing and feeling so strongly the emptiness of illusions, yet retained all the time a great fund of illusion, and clearly proved that he did by so eagerly describing their emptiness; likewise the reader, however much undeceived both by himself and by what he reads, is yet drawn by the author into that very deceit and illusion latent in the most intimate recesses of the spirit which he was

searching. . . . The very contemplation of nothingness is a thing in these works which seems to enlarge the soul of the reader, to exalt it and to satisfy it with itself and its own despair. . . . Moreover, the feeling of nothing is the feeling of a dead and death-inflicting thing. But if this feeling is alive . . . its liveliness prevails in the mind of the reader over the nothingness of the thing which it makes him feel, and the soul receives life, if only for a moment, from the very violence with which it feels the perpetual death of things in its own death.

It is the *greatness* of the despair that remains with us, the valor of the human effort: to dare, to persist, to know, as well as to persist in the indefatigable truth of its deepest, noblest nature: the bracing of truth whatever shape it takes. One watches a Macbeth in all the agony and negation of the human spirit and one is deepened as well as vitalized by the magnitude of the struggle, what forces—superhuman no less than natural—are required to overcome human grandeur.

Nor should we neglect the satisfaction, the independence, it occasionally affords a man, this salubriousness of wholesale denial, the ability to pierce all earthly and spiritual vanities. We know how much Leopardi like Flaubert, say, now and then envied ordinary absorptions; but basically both despised them and went on to despise all human occupations. In the words of Flaubert:

> To be unable to be satisfied by the whole of earthly good, even, so to speak, by the whole world, to accuse things of insufficiency and nothingness, and to suffer from a perpetual lack and sense of emptiness—that seems to me to be the chief sign of greatness and nobility to be found in human nature.

Leopardi in LXVIII of the *Pensieri* is even more explicit about the splendors of boredom:

> In a certain sense boredom is the most sublime of human feelings . . . that inability to be satisfied by any earthly thing, not even, as it were, by the whole earth itself, to consider the incalculable breadth of space, the number, the marvellous mass of worlds—and to find that all is slight and tiny compared to the capacity of one's own spirit; to imagine that the number of worlds is infinite, the universe infinite, and yet to feel that our spirit, our desire would still be greater than any such universe; to accuse things always of insufficiency and nullity, to suffer the lack, the void, and therefore boredom—this seems to me the finest sign of grandeur and nobility that human nature manifests. And so boredom is little known among men of small importance and slightly, or not at all, among the other animals.

Man is so constituted that he can plume himself on his capacity for finding pleasure in nothing in the universe (so he does find pleasure!) and, in the same breath, in *his* nothingness in the universe. Leopardi can write,

> Nothing demonstrates more clearly the power and greatness of the human intellect, the loftiness and nobility of man, than his power of knowing and entirely comprehending his smallness. When he, considering the plurality of the worlds, feels himself as the infinitesimal part of a globe that is the smallest part of one of the infinite systems that make up the World, and in this consideration he marvels at his smallness . . . is almost one with nothingness and almost loses himself in the incomprehensible vastness of existence, then with this act and with this thought he gives the greatest proof possible of his

nobility, of the strength and immense capacity of his mind, which, enclosed in so small and infinitesimal a being, has attained to the comprehension of things so superior to his nature, and can embrace and contain within his thought this same immensity of existence and of things.

Yet whether it be praise of man for the insatiability of his desire or praise for his magnificent sense of his nothingness (in either case mind, its power of awareness, is at the base of what Leopardi is acclaiming), the unity that runs through both positions is his insistence on nobility. His work is of this order: not a yielding to the waste land and at his maturest not a straining to escape it in cloud-cuckoo-lands, but a declaration for the noble life in the desert, of man's understanding his tragic role in the presence of unqualified knowledge, of maintaining love, friendship, the appetites, great deeds, regardless of the hostility of circumstance and the cost in self: the power men have on occasion of being more than themselves in the moment of extremity—illusions perhaps, yet real by what transpires between these illusions, our feelings, and the world. And the spectacle of such a performance cannot help waking some heroism of response in us. As De Sanctis said,

> Leopardi produces the opposite effect to that which he proposes. He does not believe in progress, and he makes you yearn for it; he does not believe in liberty, and he makes you love it. Love, virtue, glory he calls illusions, and he kindles in your breast an inexhaustible passion for them. . . .

Not that Leopardi lacked his moments of majestic and ecstatic yielding. His perhaps most famous poem, **"The Infinite,"** concludes: "in this immensity my thought is drowned; / and to be wrecked in such a sea is sweet."

Nonetheless, though Leopardi traveled the whole arduous distance of reason, as with many a good Existentialist his heart would not be denied: its truths also require attention, and the primacy of feeling asserts itself again and again, if only in despair. Long ago De Sanctis remarked,

> . . . Leopardi, amid the wreckage of principles and with so much scepticism of mind and so much faith of heart, could not and should not have given us anything but a *lyric* work—expression of internal discord, a lament for the death of the poetic world and, indeed, of poetry itself.

This is Leopardi's poetry, the new kind he and his best peers developed. For Leopardi was that oddest, most painful and extraordinary of combinations: a naturalist by intellect and a poet by heart, his poetry the offspring of their violent marriage. A much earlier poet comes to mind here, Lucretius with his passionate avowal to the point of most rigorous dogma of naturalistic doctrine. Like him Leopardi passionately asserts the emptiness, the nullity of life. But whereas Lucretius exults in this as the source of endless delight and emancipation, Leopardi is most passionate in his belief in the pleasures and passions of life and in his chief objection, not to them, though he sees their only partial satisfyingness, but to their brevity and their loss, their passing in age when we are left with our desires but no power to fulfil them. This objection we must expect to be especially acute in one most nobly endowed with capacity for love and enthusiasm, but physically denied them from the start. Man being mortal attains at best—or, better, recovers—only momentary glimpses of that beauty the hunger for which dogs him all the days of his life; and these glimpses, rare as they are, make the arid times all the worse. Yet a lifetime of agony is not too much to pay for them. Leopardi cannot, like

Lucretius, (for Leopardi would have deemed this another lie) persist in depreciating the sweet, any more than he can—except for such moments as the one with boredom above—call the bitter part of the pill sweet; but he can taste it with manly anger and with a refusal to pretend that it is other than it is.

Such conflict between heart and head in its sharpness makes much of Leopardi's might as well as much of the subject-matter of his writing: his brilliant, tenacious reason going on and on in the midst of his desire and the desire honing, rising, as it sees itself more and more gainsaid; one corroborates and deepens the other even as it gainsays it. It is his poetry, its passion, that defines with painful precision his loss, as it is his comprehension of the loss that sharpens his passion. And at least he still had the splendors of his precise, very precisely realized loss. One of the first to appreciate, for Eden was still freshly behind him, the vastness of the catastrophe of being outcast and therefore the extraordinariness of the wilderness as well as the drama, the fierceness, of one, the wilderness, up against the other, Eden, he constituted the link agonized, crucified, the angel burning, between them. For the 18th century the sense of belonging, if seriously shaken and shrunken, still persisted. But a Leopardi, by the ruthlessness of his reason and the cogency of his feeling of estrangement, could find reinforcement in no doctrine, no articulated body of beliefs. With several other early 19th century poets and thinkers, challenging this sense of belonging, contemning its casualness, its passivity and its smugness, believing that it must include all or nothing, Leopardi shattered it. Discovering nothing that could satisfy his longing and his consequent feeling of estrangement, no satisfactory objective correlative for it in the world (as the failure to find an objective correlative is *the* problem and the denial of the world *the* correlative of a Hamlet), at last Leopardi made that irrevocable feeling, the last remnant of Eden, its own objective correlative; and he found unity if only in the completeness of the break through all things, in his lightning-strong, all-things-embracing, all-things-pervading lyrical outcry. (pp. 5-11)

Intellect is of course at the heart, if not the heart, of this outcry. We know the bittersweet savor of all things, as of that apple tasted and tasting most—most painfully—sweet in the moment of knowledge it produced, paradise seen most vividly in the lightning clap of consciousness (God feared this man "become as one of us, to know good and evil") and therefore of loss. Appropriately Leopardi, employing this consciousness, its powers of memory (already an acknowledgement of loss), most often centered his poems in the image of a lovely young girl out of his youth, as in **"To Sylvia,"** or a mature woman, both as inspiration and absorption. (It was through Eve, we must remember, that Eden attained its happiest, ripest moment as well as its fall.) The young girl, contemplated, summons up the past she occupied, youth in its poignant aura of hope; the woman embodies the possibility of deep love, something Leopardi regarded as the loftiest human emotion, and of a kind of Platonic redemption. But as the girl is finally no more than a bitter mirage, a phantom existing only in the spell of the poem, so the woman he hopes to appeal to, an even crueler image, never responds, never reciprocates his passionate care. As with Poe the muse has become a real woman, but a woman dead to Leopardi who unlike Poe finds nothing but anguish in this death and so one of the several mainsprings of his poetry. As early as **"Memoirs of His First Love"** Leopardi identifies beauty and a particular lovely woman. At the same time despite his youth, with the scathing objectivity he can apply even to him-

self, he admits that any other woman might have moved him just as much.

Perhaps as important as woman in his feelings is the moon, an obviously feminine image, feminine too in its influences. For the moon is a softener, an embalmer, a rebuilder in its mildness and dreamlike quality of what time, men, and the harsher seasons mar; like music it is vision's atmosphere, emboldener of the imagination. His eyes often shine with weeping in the moonlight; yet they do shine, shed their glow on things, and see as he remembers. He speaks of "the incredible power music habitually has over me, and . . . the wringing of my heart by certain doggerel songs heard by chance. . . ." A passing singer enchants him as he listens, unseen, from some height, a balcony, a tower, a hill. The human voice, his as well as that overheard, alone in the earth, swelling out, fills all with its lament, charges the world with the poignancy of its being and its gigantic awareness of frailty. That is what one expects of a poet and his poetry, that it will translate the world into human terms and into the breath, alone godly for man, into language where we live and by its loveliness live more freely, gracefully, triumphantly, that he will give us the world according to his heart and ours. For Leopardi music, heights, and delicacy come into their consummate own in that one creature that seems to have remained in Eden—the bird. Its winged way of life, coupled with its light unstable fancy which keeps it a child all its days, permits it a superb, almost mythical harmony with nature. However, in his **"The Single Bird,"** contrasting himself with the bird he addresses, a bird happily solitary according to the dictates of its nature, he must acknowledge the misery of his hermit-like separation from the others and from the joys of youth which he can know only in his deprivation of them.

His glorification of adolescence marks Leopardi out a romantic. He saw youth's anguishes, but thought them delicious ones of hope as against cold indifference and the dying of age; in that he maintained his anguish, he maintained, he believed, some of his passion and youth. He hated society the more for its conspiracy of envy to crush youth out of its children as quickly as possible by its misbegotten forms of education (CIV of the *Pensieri*).

But very much unlike the romantics, at least our general notion of them, he was magnificently capable of incorporating, in an unsurpassed purity of utterance, the complex of feelings summoned forth by an image, event, realization: he was a master of the articulating of these feelings' juxtaposition, interdependence, their working in and through each other, their startling shifts. In his genius for evoking the past in its actual youthful shimmer, simultaneously with an adult intellectual examination of it, memory and realization, and a sense of the prosaic present, Leopardi reminds one of the Joyce of stories like "Araby." Leopardi could achieve a combination of image and idea, statement and situation, these interlacing, one as real as the other, a duet of equal convincing parts very few modern poets have been able to reach (so much so that we hardly have the language or the attitude needed to translate him successfully). This mastery appears in his prose no less than in his poetry and is perhaps for the open play of his extraordinary analytical powers, most clearly displayed in prose of the order of **"Memoirs of His First Love"** and the **"Dialogue of Tristan and a Friend."** Such work proves what mordant mind he possessed, how fierce in penetration and psychological insight—all part of his unsparing sense of truth, the rights of observation, particularly striking in a poet marked by solitude; we have had few more devastating commentators on society and its inanities. (pp. 12-13)

Theodore Weiss, "Giacomo Leopardi: Pioneer among Exiles," in Quarterly Review of Literature, *Vol. VIII, No. 1, 1955, pp. 5-14.*

DOMENICO VITTORINI (essay date 1958)

[*In the following excerpt from his survey of Italian literature, Vittorini counters the traditional reading of "L'infinito" set forth by the Italian critic Francesco de Sanctis (see Additional Bibliography), arguing that this interpretation ignores the human element in Leopardi's conception of infinity.*]

The famous critic Francesco De Sanctis, commenting upon this jewel of Leopardi's poetry ["**L'Infinito**"], reaches the conclusion that the poet romantically loses himself in the sea of infinity evoked by his thought. To us, it seems that, through this interpretation, Leopardi's "**L'Infinito**" loses the continuity of thought which is its greatest asset.

De Sanctis's interpretation shows us a Leopardi who mystically rises toward infinite space, forgetful of the earth where he is dwelling and wavering between two quite different planes: earth and heaven, finite and infinite. We feel that "**L'Infinito**" rests on three different planes: the world of nature, the concept of the infinity, and between these two worlds, a third zone where Leopardi loves to dwell, for it is a creation of his own thought. In this discussion we hope to prove that our interpretation can be supported by reconstructing the psychological mood as projected in the poetry.

Giacomo Leopardi was the victim of tuberculosis of the spine, the dread disease that brought him to an early death. One of the few pleasures that he allowed himself in the studious life that he led in his father's house was to stroll up the Tabor Hill, near Recanati. He tells us:

> Sempre caro mi fu quest'ermo colle
> E questa siepe, che da tanta parte
> Dell'ultimo orizzonte il guardo esclude.

> Always dear to me was this bleak hill
> And this hedge, that from such a large part
> Of the faraway horizon excludes my gaze.

The higher he climbed the wider the horizon became. When he grew tired and sat beneath the tall trees to rest, no longer able to see the fields in the valley and the faraway horizon, he began to dream, wondering what there was above the blue arch of the sky. His mind found that there were only "endless spaces," "superhuman silences," and "deepest quietude." The poet informs the reader that a sense of fear overcame him because he found himself face to face with nothingness. He was awakened from this awe by the murmur of the leaves of the trees, which carried him back to the world of nature that was throbbing with life, buzzing with insects, the flights of birds, human toil, and joy. But even here, suffering flesh and poor tortured heart that he was, he could not find a haven of rest, and his thoughts entered into play. The poet created his own infinite, humanized and solidified, alive with the beauty that surrounded him and touched his heart. It was only then that the previous terror turned into infinite sweetness, as he concluded the last lines of his idyll.

The central point, on which a critic must focus his attention, is the passing of the poet from his awe to the feeling of joyous intimacy, conveyed by the last line:

> e naufragar m'è dolce in questo mare

> and to be shipwrecked in this sea is sweet to me.

Had Leopardi been a normal and healthy person, he would have lived in nature. He was excluded from it by the disease that crippled his body, turning his existence into slow agony. Neither could he accept the concept of the infinite, as does a religious-minded believer, who gives a religious overtone to his musing. He had suffered too much, and his mind was too objective and cold to fill the infinite sky with dreams and visions, turning the concept of the infinite into a religious fantasy. Rejected by earth and heaven, by nature and the infinite, his mind continued to ask whether the infinite could have any meaning whatsoever. All the strength of the poem is concentrated in this attempt that ends in harmony and intimate joy.

The "**Infinito**" is a short philosophical poem. It encompasses the brief drama lived within the solitude of Mount Tabor. It is philosophical poetry, like all great poetry, especially of the last century.

We have seen that, when the poet directed his gaze toward the sky, his mind turned to the infinite. He found there only silence, opacity, and a deadly quietude: only a white, shapeless desert, vanishing into nothingness. The rustling of the leaves of the trees brought him back to nature, sensuous and serene, as it spread all around its green cloak of beauty. How could the poet abandon himself to this life, which he saw tainted by the shadow of death? If yesterday's seasons fell into the pit of the infinite, the present one, too, carried within itself that certitude. The poet reveals this philosophical musing when he confided to us:

> io quello
> Infinito silenzio a questa voce
> Vo comparando.

> I that
> Infinite silence to this voice
> Go comparing.

Thus far he has revealed two moods only: that of awe and that of the awareness of the beauty of nature in its full bloom. But, then, why the ensuing joy of the poet, when he became aware that death urges everyone toward the abyss of nothingness? At this point a third mood appeared: his joy for having infused a human element into the cold and spectral concept of the infinite. It is this third mood that superinduces joy in his heart.

In the "**Infinito**" we see only the result or consequence of this creation: the poet's thought that loses itself in the feeling that envelops his mind before nature. The poet seems to confide to the reader: Yes, tomorrow this blooming beauty will wilt, but how very beautiful it is in this fleeting moment, how touching is the greenness that every year covers the earth. The "dead seasons" fall into the grave that surrounds the earth, but, before falling, they fill man's heart with joy. This is the certitude that illumines Leopardi's concept of the infinite. The emptiness has disappeared, and the abstract concept of the infinite has acquired a new reality: that given to it by the poet's mind. This reality cannot be found in nature, which is life destined to death, nor in the concept of the infinite, which is empty, since it has filled the poet with awe.

We have said that the artist has revealed only in part the process of philosophical elaboration through which he reached the meaning that he gave to the concept of the infinite. In fact, he has told us that the thought of eternity and of the dead seasons was followed by that of the present season with its sounds and hues. If one admits De Sanctis's interpretation, one is forced to admit that the concept of the infinite was the cause of Leopardi's joy. Nor can one admit that nature itself was its cause. The very title of the poem, "L'Infinito," denies this and, if so, and we exclude that the concept of eternity could be the source of his enjoyment, we can only identify the source of his joy with the reality that his mind was able to weave upon two extreme terms: one, the concept of eternity; the other, nature, alive and beautiful, harmonizing and fusing these two concepts in the poet's own concept of beauty and goodness of life.

One could believe that this sweetness to which the poet abandoned himself was in contrast to the pessimism generally attributed to be the only chord of Leopardi's poetry. His pessimism, however, was not objective and categorical; it was not all of one color, uniformly and monotonously black. On the contrary, in all of his poetry there was a constant and painful yearning for beauty, love, and happiness. How could he have continued to yearn unless life would have, conceptually, looked beautiful to him? The poet confessed that sweet life, as enjoyed by everyone else, was denied to him. One should observe **"Il Passero Solitario"** (**"The Lonely Sparrow"**), where the unhappy destiny of the poor bird who spread his sad, monotonous song through the countryside is opposed to the other birds' lot

> a gara insieme
> Per lo libero ciel fan milli giri
> Pur festeggiando il lor tempo migliore.

> vieing with one another
> Through the free sky they make a thousand turns
> Rejoicing in the happiest time of their existence.

With a sense of harmony and clarity of form typical of him, Leopardi compared his own sadness with the happiness of healthy people:

> La gioventù del loco
> Lascia le case, e per le vie si spande;
> E mira ed è mirata, e in cor s'allegra.

> The youth of the town
> Go out of their homes and spread through the streets;
> And they look and are looked at, and rejoice in their hearts.

The essence of Leopardi's poetry is exactly in this endless oscillating between the conclusions reached by his mind, that forces upon him the outlook that life is evil, and the voice of his heart, that inexorably directs him toward nature and love.

> Primavera dintorno
> Brilla nell'aria, e per li campi esulta
> Sì ch'a mirarla intenerisce il core.

> Spring all around
> Shines in the air, and it spreads its joy in the field,
> So that, to look at it, it makes my heart grow tender.

Thus the sweetness reached by the poet in **"L'Infinito"** finds parallels in many other poems. This fact explains clearly the shift from awe to the sweetness in which his mind loses itself.

Another point, too, can help us to understand this change. We find it especially in the brief lyric **"Alla luna"** and in **"Canto notturno di un pastore errante dell'Asia."** The poet feels the limitations of his own tortured flesh, upon which death stretches its cold fingers. But he is also conscious of the strength of his painful condition. It is what only man can do, and which is denied to brute nature. The moon is regulated by the same inexorable laws as govern man, yet it is not conscious of its own condition. The sheep led by the philosopher-shepherd in Asia are subject to these same laws, but they cannot look detachedly at themselves and gaze at their own tragic destiny whose only end is death. But man can do so. Is this not a source of great and just pride? Is this not proof of man's nobility and of his superiority over animal nature? Does this not show the great wedge that separates man and brute nature? If this is so, then man finds in being conscious of his destiny and in his understanding of the infinite the reason for an inner satisfaction that consoles him for all the sadness inherent in life.

In **"L'Infinito"** the poet finds this joy in the consciousness of being able to infuse a human connotation into the empty and cold concept of eternity. Not only the joy of thinking, but the joy of having created his very own "immensity," which, being the fruit of his own mind, is indeed his very own. This is much more than the generic "living within his own thought," attributed to the romantic poets. Leopardi has in his lyric created a short drama in which, through the poet's feeling, abstract thought has become living reality. (pp. 128-33)

> *Domenico Vittorini, "Giacomo Leopardi's 'L'Infinito'," in his* High Points in the History of Italian Literature, *David McKay Company, Inc., 1958, pp. 128-33.*

JEAN-PIERRE BARRICELLI (essay date 1963)

[*In the following excerpt from an introduction to his translation of Leopardi's poems, Barricelli considers the themes of Leopardi's poetry—sorrow, nature, beauty, love, and death—in relation to his "aesthetic optimism."*]

Leopardi's drama can be explained with Amiel's remark, "The more a man loves, the most he suffers. The sum of possible grief for each soul is in proportion to its degree of perfection." In Leopardi's poems the pervasive theme of unhappiness is punctuated at every opportunity by recurring notes of consoling force: youth, love, dreams and the sweet deceptions of nature and beauty. To speak of idealism in a Platonic sense is inaccurate, for Leopardi admired physical more than ideal beauty, regardless of Kant's concern over its ephemeralness. This does not mean that Leopardi confined his notion of beauty to the flesh and bones of the feminine body and that he did not place it in loftier focus. In fact, he perceived beauty as an emanation rather than as a contained quality, or as a "ray divine" which was nonetheless the creation of his mind, rather than as the Greek philosopher's divine reflection whose source lay in an absolute realm very removed from this world. Were it not in his mind, it would no longer be an illusion. The realities which delude man into believing in a fruitful, prosperous, and peaceful outcome of his many painful occupations are ultimately useless by the very nature of that outcome, while the illusions usually characterized as useless by pragmatic calculations emerge as useful. Hartmann's attitude comes close to Leopardi's: beauty's power of consolation for life's ubiquitous misfortune, a temporary therapy that strengthens us at sporadic moments.

Pessimism becomes, therefore, a fallacious term if it is used to label Leopardi's thought in any absolute sense. Basically, as the years passed, he lamented his declining capacity for illusion, his lost youth, in other words, and the happiness that proceeds from its untried and unsoiled fantasies. The illusions he associated with his youth and caressed so fondly suggest archetypes which he sought yearningly but never attained. Hence the pessimism, a metaphysical anguish which, if one may judge from the usual disparity between his physical torments and the elevated tone of his poetry, was unrelated to bodily concerns. Beauty, as Hegel and Schopenhauer had considered it and Keats had illustrated it, was for Leopardi, too, the portrayal of an idea in a work of art. As such, Art provided the release and emancipation which made his pessimism only relative. The juxtaposition of "foundering" and "sweet" in the last verse of **"The Infinite"** is both acrid in its reality and uplifting in its illusion. Schiller and later Spencer may have regarded Art as deception divorced from the real; Leopardi preferred to esteem it for its very deception, for raising fiction to the level of a supreme reality, and for offering man a purpose. This was subjective idealism. He promoted an aesthetic optimism from lack of which the life of Werther suffered and through which Goethe survived the malaise of his own hero. Leopardi's pessimistic themes, however sharp the stings of despair and scorn, are orchestrated lyrically in serene, consoling tonalities, and are never gratingly discorded by the acrimony and psychosis of, say, a Baudelaire.

In this context, it would seem logical that Nature, which occupies a medial position between man and destiny, should command less regard than Art. If Nature is beautiful, Art is sublime. But Nature, the dispenser of illusions, is the very life-source of Art, and Leopardi loved it with all the solitary passion of a Werther or a René. In 1820, he wrote to Giordani:

> I too am warmly sighing for spring as the only medicinal hope which is left to my soul's waning; and a few nights ago, before going to bed, with my chamber window open, and seeing a pure sky, a beautiful moonbeam, feeling the lukewarm air, and hearing certain dogs barking in the distance, ancient images were awakened within me, and I thought I felt a stir in my heart, for which reason I started shouting like a madman, asking mercy of nature, whose voice I thought I was hearing after so much time. And at that moment, looking back upon my former condition, to which I was sure of returning—as did happen—I froze with fear, not being able to understand how life could be tolerated without illusions and live affections, and without imagination and enthusiasm. All my time was composed of these things a year ago, and I used to make myself so happy, in spite of my troubles.

Yet, with all this attachment, Leopardi is not a colorist or a pictorial poet in the grand sense. Unlike someone like Hugo or Lenau, his brushstrokes are light; the pigments are those of water colors rather than of oils. His scenes are rapid, accurate enough, indeed visual, in scattered details, but more often vague, like pale backdrops that give relief to the central ideas. Leopardi's geographic horizons were limited, during his lifetime, to a few Italian cities. He knew he was too frail of body to sustain the efforts required to reach the Alpine panoramas dear to Rousseau, or the more exotic vistas described by travelers like Byron, Shelly, and Chateaubriand. Although highly suggestive, he is not a poet of colorful plasticity in the manner of Leconte de Lisle, nor is he usually the scientific observer that Goethe can be. Vigny's account of the dying wolf and Swinburne's impression of the swallow betray a far stronger desire to interpret animal nature, in this instance, than Leopardi ever displayed.

The depth of the Italian poet's emotional response to Nature, however, cannot be fathomed by surface comparisons with his European contemporaries. He transcended the Alps, the desert sands, the Spanish towns, and the forests of the New World with what may best be called a cosmic view, emotionally powered by the same sense of wonder that had underscored Pascal's "the eternal silence of the infinite spaces." The sun and especially the moon recur as cosmic leitmotifs, the former with its reawakening clarity and compulsion to pursue life's labors, that latter with its preferable invitation to meditation and dream. Rather than look upward at the spectral or diabolical or grotesque moon of the English poets or of Lenau or of Musset, Leopardi, while lifting the Asian shepherd's eyes to its friendliness, seems to gaze downward from it upon the world of men, whose size hardly exceeds that of an ant-hill. This downward direction which characterizes his contemplation obviates the possibility of mysticism, to which he was temperamentally averse. In this he differed from Lamartine. And when he turns his sight away from the sky to appreciate Nature from the common vantage point of other men, there is still no mystique involved, but there is a restrained admiration for its many wonders. Leopardi sketches them accordingly, with a feeling of elegiac simplicity which contrasts with the impetuosness of Byron, the lushness of Chateaubriand, or the pomp of Hugo. Under the spacious heavens, a sunny field and a hazy mountain, a flowery shore which lines a stretch of sea, broom on a wasteland, a border of trees around a lake, a wandering hen or a thrush or a flock of sheep, attract the poet at regular intervals of relaxed approval. He must have exclaimed many times with Faust: "Stay, O moment: thou art so fair!" Love and Beauty are intimate allies.

Intellectual experiences later dampened the warmth of his affection when, like Vigny as opposed to Wordsworth and to Richter who sang of Nature's joys, he was disillusioned in discovering that his love remained unreciprocated. Leopardi's moral sensibilities were aroused at Nature's injustice, declaring her not only an indifferent, but indeed a malevolent, "stepmother" or a "harsh nurse." But while Vigny, in siding proudly with "the majesty of human suffering," gave vent to a deep-seated hatred, Leopardi, with broader vision, could not reject her categorically. Illusion would not submit completely to the dictates of reason. The value of Beauty to offset the truth, not to corroborate it in Keats' terms, was too necessary to warrant an entire repudiation on realistic grounds. Where Hölderlin confessed that Nature had died for him with the disappearance of his dreams of youth, Leopardi, even in his very last poem, continued to be captivated by the "silvered countryside and waters" and by the "dawning rise of morn." The goddess is implacable, yet, in the presence of her countless beauties, some ill-defined hope sets the poet's heart astir. Hope lives, to paraphrase Coleridge, because it has an object.

Death completes the trinity of Love and Beauty. The triple association, from which Solomon had derived such frequent inspiration, places Leopardi in a position of marked individuality in the poetic tradition of death. For the authors of ancient Greece and Rome, whether portrayed in the eerie and ugly terms of Euripides or Horace or Seneca, or simply in its relationship to Sleep and Night, Death was an integral part of the natural order. Christianity and the Middle Ages converted it from a law into a punishment, and Milton did not exaggerate this view when he made it a monster. In between, Dante's and Petrarch's ennobling experiences after the passing away of Beatrice and Laura, had led them to hail Death as gentle and desired and sweet. Novalis' experience with Sophia was no different. But Leopardi, who had put aside early the hopeful faith of the other poets, saw Death with finality, as the ineluctable "abyss" in which the personal drama of reason and illusion ends forever.

But if Death is "the sole goal of being," it is perhaps for this reason beautiful and elicits our love. What Baudelaire will fear and hate, Leopardi had adorned and deified. What Leconte de Lisle will salute as "divine," the author of **"On an Ancient Sepulchral Bas-Relief"** had already depicted as a "most beautiful young maiden." And Consalvo had said: "Two things of beauty has the world: love and death."

Death must be understood in a more universal sense than in the petty meaning given to it by suicide. While sympathizing with the nature of Brutus' and Sappho's decisions, Leopardi concluded that suicide stems from love of life rather than from a negation of living. Schopenhauer had asserted that the act is directed essentially against the accidental portion of unhappiness which creeps into existence, not against existence itself. What counted for Leopardi was the philosophical negation of life in both its effective pains and in its false felicities. Only in this way could one claim moral consistency: through the affirmation of a negative totality. Debunking life gives man no right to feel superior in Pascal's sense ("Though the universe should crush him, man would still be nobler than what kills him, for he knows he is dying, and the advantage the universe has over him; the universe does not know it at all."); on the contrary, to know and yet have to stand by helplessly makes for an abject, groveling condition to which not even plants and animals are subjected.

Suicide resolves nothing. If there is one feeling which grows, or should grow, spontaneously from universal unhappiness, it is reciprocal compassion, each man's love for all men, occasioned by the awareness of a common and inalienable destiny. Compassion and mutual assistance he calls supreme duties, caring little about the possible contradiction between this attitude and the belief in "the infinite vanity of all things." Perhaps a sense of responsibility is an illusion, but it is a beneficial one. The poet spoke out of a candid sense of goodness, and preferred to be conciliatory rather than dogmatic, humane rather than dialectic, where mankind was concerned. A profound, moral exigency prompted the author of **"Genesta"** to appeal for a heroic humanity to band together in stoic opposition to the vicious forces of nature, notwithstanding the ultimate decrees of destiny. Besides, action has the power of diverting our concentration from meditation. "Irresolution," he wrote in the *Zibaldone,* "is worse than desperation," and in **"To a Victor in a Ballgame"** we read: "To what avail our life? only to condemn it; blessed then when fraught with perils, it forgets itself, and does not count the harm of slow and sordid hours, or listen to their gliding by." Another passage from the *Zibaldone* should be quoted:

> Just as pleasures do not delight unless they have a goal beyond themselves, as I say elsewhere, so does life itself not delight, however full of pleasure, unless it has a goal in the totality. We must propose a goal to our own lives in order to live happily. Literary glory, a fortune, dignity, in short, a career. I have never been able to understand how those jobless and carefree people can be happy, how they can live, those who, though mature and old, go from pleasure to pleasure, from frolic to frolic, without ever having said to, or settled with, themselves:—of what use will my life be to me?—I have not been able to imagine what kind of a life they lead, what kind of death they are expecting.

The Leopardian ethic is composed of the theory of action and the rule of love: to act out of love of one's neighbor, to succor him in bearing the pain of his existence, and to confine one's deeds to those which are consonant with goodness. Leopardi's pessimism seeks heroically and finally achieves its own redemption.

The contest between truth and dream never caused paroxysms of extreme unhappiness, because the absence of despair permitted Leopardi to clothe his pessimism in serenity. There is something of Montaigne's calm wisdom in this serenity, thanks to its cosmic viewpoint and conscious understanding of the mind's every movement. In a way, he is a poet of distance, deliberately subtracting himself from the tyrannical cares of daily existence into the "infinite spaces" where his thought liked to roam freely. In an opposite way, he is, though not a colorist, a poet of closeness, telescoping his vision into a few town or countryside items, and seeing if not observing the most transitory motion of details with the kind of myopic pleasure one detects at times in other intellectual poets of greater scientific ability such as Lucretius, Dante, and Goethe. Illusion and reality are, after all, as much a question of optics as of metaphysics. Not a small part of Leopardi's greatness as a poet lies in his ability to fuse optics with metaphysics, or, as Schelling would have it, to express the infinite through the particular. His "Weltanschauung" which relies mainly on dreams and remembrances for anchorage has nevertheless a quality of concreteness and clarity about it not readily found in the vague moods of Lamartine or in the flowery modes of Shelley. Inspiration and reflection blend intimately for the poet whose nature was itself a fusion of idyllic and philosophical dispositions. For this reason, too, his pessimism cannot vibrate sympathetically with Heine's derisory bitterness or Byron's ostentatious tragedy, nor could it open melodramatically a pelican's breast with Musset or drive deliriously a black banner through a skull with Baudelaire. As it is sober, it is not egotistic; the fanatic and pathological concentration on the ego neither dominates nor appears. Although Leopardi is always at the base of his poem, he stands there as an example, not as a display, of man's condition. The epic view objectifies, and precludes the morbidly subjective. By comparison, Baudelaire also rises above the personal to the symbolic, but a residual sense of almost clinical aberration is strong enough to place him more in the center of his own world than Leopardi places himself in the center of his.

Leopardi never actively sought themes or moods for his poetry: they came to him without foreplanning. And when they did, they invariably were themes of sorrow, unlike those of Goethe which embraced the experiences of both sorrow and pleasure. "Our sweetest songs are those that tell of saddest thought," sighed Shelley. Whether an impression, a remembrance, or an image, the point of departure was brief: a bird, a flower, the moon, a girl, a hedge, a tomb. Each, however, developed like a Beethoven symphony into expanded statements of lament over a solitary existence, of appeal for man's solidarity against nature, of grief over a hostile destiny, of desire for the unpossessable, of fright at the insignificance of thought, of despair over irreparable losses and ruins and unlived years. In the singleness of a fleeting note, Leopardi captured the cosmic harmonies of man's history and nature's infinity.

Whether or not the themes would have been the same if Leopardi's life had favored him more than it did is a frequently asked and vain question. Aside from the purposelessness of wrenching reality out of shape for the sake of an inconclusive speculation, the fact remains that he was by nature a sensitive and intellectual poet and thinker whose lyricism perhaps was accentuated by his physical ills and whose philosophy perhaps found confirmation in his moral adversities, but nothing more. It is a matter of degree, and of marginal significance. Whatever his circumstances, he would have been as great simply because he was an artist.

Illusion, therefore, had to supplant reality by forging its own reality, a super-reality. The resulting voice is eternal, even with the demolition of every other value in life. Art as form cannot be abstracted from its content, but rather is made tangible by it. To quote the critic Gaetano Amato, "... that process of devaluation, employed in every pessimistic attitude of our spirit before the real, tends, by virtue of art, to resolve itself in a superior revaluation of what has been recently devaluated. Let life become devoid of any values: art fills it with her unique, real, infinite values. Let the world become a dark and desert place: art has the invincible power to repopulate it with images and to transfigure it in her light."

Through such aesthetic optimism, art, even in Leopardi's pessimistic garb, affirms and exalts life. Leopardi knew this, and, like every great thinker, loved his ideas. Reason and illusion surfaced in his mind in almost capricious alternation. If, on the one hand, the alternation appears as a drama, especially if one confronts his life with his poetry, on the other it seems, less pretentiously, an interplay. Not that as an interplay it has no afflictive ramifications. It has, but the culminating experience, art, endows it with a halo of accomplishment and satisfaction. When Leopardi passed from speculative analysis to lyrical creation, or from the crude and momentary image to the luminous world of visions, he attained spheres of poetic loftiness along with an undoubtedly profound and cathartical self-realization. The philosophy he molded for himself out of a background of such torment was absorbed with consummate lyricism into the godly super-reality of Art, a feat of rarity, conceded only to the supreme poetic creators—Dante, Shakespeare, Milton, Goethe, Yeats,... and the "miracle of Recanati." (pp. 25-32)

> *Jean-Pierre Barricelli, in an introduction to* Poems
> *by Giacomo Leopardi, translated by Jean-Pierre*
> *Barricelli, Las Americas Publishing Company, 1963,*
> *pp. 11-32.*

G. SINGH (essay date 1964)

[*In this excerpt from his full-length study of Leopardi's theory of poetry, Singh outlines Leopardi's critical principles, frequently comparing them to those of such other important poets and theorists as William Wordsworth, Samuel Taylor Coleridge, and Percy Bysshe Shelley.*]

No poet in the history of Italian literature occupied himself with the theory of poetry so much as Leopardi; and, indeed, [according to C. M. Bowra in *Inspiration and Poetry*] "few men have given so much hard thought to the matter." As a poetic theorist, he not only compares well with Goethe, Wordsworth, and Coleridge on the one hand, and Edgar Allan Poe and Baudelaire on the other, but in virtue of his classical learning and philological scholarship, which he brought to bear on certain aspects of the literary and poetic theory, especially the linguistic and stylistic aspects, he easily surpasses them all. Moreover, the range of the literary and philosophical reference within which his critical mind worked was not limited to ancient thought and literature; it embraced modern literature and modern thought as well. Besides French and Italian literatures, which he had thoroughly mastered, he was also fairly well acquainted with the major literary works in English, German, and Spanish. Hence for his "incomparable literary education" alone, leaving aside the still more important fact that he was [in the words of Vincenzo Cardarelli in his introduction to Leopardi's *Opere complete*] "the greatest Italian writer of modern times," Leopardi's views on the art of poetry as well as on individual authors and works deserve our serious consideration. Indeed, *Operette Morali,* **"Discorso di un italiano intorno alla poesia romantica,"** *Epistolario,* and, above all, *Zibaldone* constitute a body of criticism as remarkable for its depth and soundness as for its range and variety.

In *Zibaldone* and elsewhere not only is Leopardi uninterested in expounding any systematic philosophy of art or poetry, but he does not even pretend to throw any new light on the revaluation of any particular author or question in literary history. His main interest is to register impressions and reactions in the course of his loving study of both ancient and modern literary masterpieces and to ponder on their implications. Having little or no use for a priori rules and formulas, Leopardi considered each work of art to be itself furnishing, to a discerning mind, the very basis and criteria, according to which it ought to be judged. Invented by "poor grammarians," rules serve to produce not art but artifice; and while art "conserves the variety and delight of nature, artifice, which is the food of reason, is monotonous and it is merely the product of 'dry' curiosity." Hence his condemnation of literary academies like the Della Crusca as being detrimental to the progress of arts. All great poets among the Greeks, for instance, had written before Aristotle, as all the Latin poets before or at the same time as Horace. As against academies and systems of rules and formulas, Leopardi favors the possession or cultivation of good taste both among the individuals and the nations. Homer, who wrote before any rules were formed, did not dream, says Leopardi, that from what was so fresh and original in his work, rules and formulas would be derived that would prevent others from following his own example, i.e., from being "true, irregular, great, and original like him." Hence Leopardi's attitude to preestablished rules and canons governing creative arts, and even the very science or art of criticism, and his desire to assert the autonomy of both creative activity and the critical function is more or less the same as that of Coleridge, though he had never heard the latter's name. "Could a rule be given from *without,*" said Coleridge [in his *Biographia Literaria*], "poetry would cease to be poetry, and sink into a mechanical art." Instead of assessing the literary worth of a work merely in terms of the degree to which it measures up to certain preconceived notions or standards derived from past models, one should, Leopardi emphasized, try to enter into the very spirit of a given work, both in so far as it is different from and in so far as it is similar to other masterpieces. And this one can do not so much by analyzing the milieu or the personality of the artist, as by recreating and reexperiencing the spirit and meaning of that work of art within the bounds of one's own imagination, sensibility, and culture, or by transferring it into ourselves. For all his respect for the ancient classics, and especially for Homer, "the father and the perpetual principle of all the poets of the world," Leopardi never fails to stress the link between the reader's or the critic's inner world of sensibility and experience (both of life and of other works of art and poetry), and his ability to judge a particular work of art. It is in this sense that one can say of Leopardi that he combines the sense of tradition with the spirit of modernity. And tradition does not mean blind subservience or uncritical acceptance of the classics, any more than modernity means a cloak for inane extravagances or innovations, indulged for their own sakes. One proof of Leopardi's critical liberalism and independence of judgment is the fact that in turning to ancient critics, literary historians, and theorists he does not always follow the footsteps of Plato and Aristotle, but quotes minor poets, historians, and orators as well.

Leopardi's theory of poetry, like all theories of poetry more or less, is based on certain fundamental assumptions regarding the role of memory, imagination, sentiments, and sensibility as well as the nature and function of poetry itself. It is inseparably bound up with his particular view of life, with what may be called his philosophical system, which has its roots in eighteenth-century French thought and literature. "All great poetry," says T. S. Eliot, "gives the illusion of a view of life. When we enter into the world of Homer, or Sophocles, or Virgil, or Dante or Shakespear, we incline to believe that we are apprehending something that can be expressed intellectually; for every precise emotion tends towards intellectual formation." Not only in Leopardi's poetry, but even in Leopardi's theory of poetry we have something like this illusion. His never-failing sense of the fundamental unity between art and life happily prevented him from divorcing the aesthetic pleasure or emotion from the moral and intellectual aspects of poetry, from divorcing form from content, and contemplating them in isolation.

Some, Fubini for one, have found Leopardi's union of the aesthetic with the moral a weakness in his theory. In Leopardi, Fubini tells us, "an aesthetic problem is transformed . . . into a moral problem: the primitive spontaneity of true poetry, which Leopardi exalts, and whose unique model he sees in his Greeks, is mistaken by him for every other form of spontaneous life which reason falsifies and mortifies." The vital humanity of Leopardi's attitude to poetry lies mainly in this: that he identified poetry with every spontaneous form and manifestation of life. In other words, there is, in this attitude, something at once more human and more philosophical than one usually finds in a purely literary or critical attitude. Defining the function of a philosopher, which in his view cannot altogether be separated from that of a literary critic or a poet, Leopardi notes:

> Naturally and of necessity [a philosopher] looks for a thread in his consideration of things. It is impossible for him to be content with isolated notions and truths. If he had contented himself with these, his philosophy would have been the most trivial and the most wretched, and would not have yielded any result. The aim of philosophy (in the widest sense of the term) is to discover the causes of truths. These causes are to be found only in the inter-relationships among these truths, and they are to be found by means of generalization. Do we not know that the faculty of generalization alone constitutes the thinker? Do we not admit that philosophy consists of speculation on these relationships?

It is in relating the specific problems of literary criticism and poetic theory to the general problems of life, in deriving from the criticism of life not only the material for his poetry, but also the values and criteria by which that poetry ought to be judged, that Leopardi's merit as a philosophic critic or theorist of poetry lies. His absorbing concern is not with the form or technique of poetry, though one of the paramount qualities of his own poetry is its formal and prosodic excellence, nor even with style in the abstract sense, though his own style (both prose and poetry) is uniformly superb, but with poetry in its

purest essence. But instead of defining this essence in metaphorical terms—such as "the breath and finer spirit of all knowledge . . . the impassioned expression which is in the countenance of all science" (Wordsworth), or "the identity of all other knowledges, the blossom of all other systems of thought . . . the perfect and consummate surface and bloom of all things" (Shelley)—terms and definitions which, for all their rhapsodical charm, leave the essence of poetry as much in the vague as ever, Leopardi tries to approach this essence not in order to discover what it is *per se,* but in order to identify and characterize the qualities common to all great poetry, and, as far as possible, to try to account for them. Hence, whatever amount of interdependence there might be between Leopardi's poetry and his theory of poetry, it does not constitute exactly the same sort of relationship as one finds between, say Shelley's poetry and his *Defence of Poetry.* Of the latter, W. P. Ker says that "it is not itself poetry and Shelley would not have us think so. But it is one mode in which he expresses a theory which is expressed poetically in *Prometheus* and *Adonais.* The prose meaning of the *Defence* is the poetical meaning of Asia and Urania." Now this cannot be said of the meaning of the **Canti** and the general critical import of Leopardi's poetic theory, which consists, for the most part, of factually plain and prosaic observations concerning the art of poetry treated almost as a science. The content of Leopardi's poetic theory is largely intellectual rather than emotional, and it is constructive only in so far as it is analytical. Behind each and everything he condemns or exalts there is always the specific prose-reason why he does so; and it is his own critical sensibility, rather than any a priori rules or standards, which molds his judgments and reactions. Appreciation and criticism, evaluation and analysis are not two processes divided into tight compartments, as unfortunately they sometimes are, but two complementary aspects of the same process in Leopardi's poetic and critical theory. And the language he employs is mostly a language consisting of direct and factual remarks, and, as far as possible, shunning rather than, like Goethe or the English romantics, indulging in mystical and emotive observations.

If, however, Leopardi does sometimes use the metaphorical language while talking of poetry, it is not so much in order to adorn or mystify, as to clarify and drive home a particular truth. For instance, while differentiating between poetic vocabulary and scientific vocabulary, he observes:

> It is the duty of poets and writers (who create *belles lettres*) to cover as far as possible the nudity of things, just as it is the duty of scientists and philosophers to reveal it. Hence, precise words suit the latter, and they are extremely unsuitable for the former. . . . To a scientist the more precise and more expressive of an idea in all its nudity the words are, the more convenient they are. On the contrary, to a poet and to a man of letters the more vague and the more expressive of uncertain ideas and of a large number of ideas the words are, the better.

The metaphorical phrase, "to cover the nudity of things," makes the poet's thought and its various implications more clear and impressive than an analytically factual statement would have done, since the subject happens to be such a subtle and abstruse one as not so much the difference but the distinction between the poet's language and the language of science. Moreover, the phrase "the nudity of things" does in itself embody a very rich and very typical concept of Leopardi's. It does not mean the same thing as, for example, Tasso's phrase "the naked material" in "Discorso dell'arte poetica," material, as Tasso himself explains, "which has not yet received any quality from a poet's or an orator's artifice.'' For Leopardi, on the other hand, the phrase means the reality of things as they are in themselves—a reality that is not simply less beautiful than poetic illusions, but also more restricted in its scope and relevance than it would be if charged with the pathos and power of illusions, which confer on it almost a symbolic value. Similarly, to take another example, Leopardi's statement that an inexperienced person has always a more or less poetic character, and that he becomes prosaic with experience, sums up the opposition between worldly experience and poetic character, but not between experience and poetry, because the songs of experience are as legitimately poetry as the songs of innocence.

For all his concern with going to the very root of the problem, and for all his endowment as a thinker, which was certainly richer than that of a Wordsworth or a Shelley, Leopardi rarely strayed into the realm of metaphysical abstractions or metaphorical rhetoric while discussing poetry. To his lifelong study of poetry and his own experience as a poet, Leopardi added a long and close study of philology. This enabled him to compare the poetic validity of one word with that of another, the vocabulary of one poet or epoch with the vocabulary of another, and sometimes to distinguish between the nuances of meaning and poetic character of the same word in the same author occurring in different works or even in the different contexts of the same work. The poet's art, for Leopardi, lies not so much in the invention of new things, or in communicating original ideas or truths, as in the manipulations of words in such a way as to be able to create a new effect, a new melody, a new style. Extremely dubious of the novelty of subject-matter or content as being a very useful or important factor in poetry, Leopardi emphasizes that poetry should move us by means of those very objects that we already knew before we started reading poetry, and should delight us through those very causes and circumstances, which are already familiar to us. The poet's art consists in choosing

> the most beautiful things among the known things, in newly and harmoniously . . . arranging the known things and adapting them to the capacity of the majority, newly clothing, adorning and embellishing them by means of the harmony of verse, metaphors, and every other splendor of style, in conferring light and nobility upon the unknown and ignoble things, in giving novelty to what is commonplace, in changing, as if by some magical incantation, the aspect of anything he happens to be dealing with; in taking, for instance, persons from nature and making them talk naturally, but nonetheless in such a way that the reader, while recognizing in that language the very language he is used to hear from such persons in real life in similar circumstances, may at the same time find it new and incomparably more beautiful than the ordinary language on account of the poetic ornaments, the new style, in a word, the new form and body which the poet has given it.

This reads like a condensed but more lucid account of practically all the major arguments that parade through Wordsworth's celebrated *Preface* as well as through Coleridge's equally celebrated critical examination thereof.

Similarly Leopardi's account of the nature and function of poetic imagination is far more simple and straightforward, without being less elucidating, than, say, sometimes that of Coleridge himself. ''That synthetic and magical power,'' says Coleridge [in his *Biographia*], ''to which I would exclusively appropriate the name of imagination . . . reveals itself in the balance or reconciliation of opposite or discordant qualities . . . the sense

of novelty and freshness with old and familiar objects; a more than usual state of emotion with more than usual order; judgment ever awake and steady self-possession with enthusiasm and feeling profound or vehement.'' And the chief gifts of imagination are ''the sense of musical delight . . . together with the power of reducing multitude into unity of effect, and modifying a series of thoughts by some one predominant thought or feeling.'' In comparison, Leopardi, regarding imagination as ''the most fertile and most marvellous inventor of the most hidden relationships and harmonies,'' points out that a man endowed with such imagination ''. . . sees such connections, passes on from one proposition to another so rapidly, understands the link between them so vividly and so easily, accumulates so many syllogisms in one moment, and all so well-connected, so well-ordinated and so clearly conceived that in one leap he covers the distance of many centuries.'' As to the inventive power of imagination, Leopardi goes even further than Coleridge, in so far as he regards it as not only the fountainhead of sentiments, passions, and poetry, but of reason itself. It is imagination that makes ''great philosophers and the discoverers of great truths,'' imagination from which, when ''differently applied, differently modified, and differently determined by diverse circumstances and habits, came the poems of Homer and Dante, and the mathematical principles of the natural philosophy of Newton.''

Thus Leopardi's critical as well as interpretative pronouncements have both the edge and concreteness of a particular truth or statement and the depth and universality of what is called a generalization. In this he may be compared with Samuel Johnson, for neither he nor Johnson thought of literary criticism as being something essentially different from the general criticism of life. Leopardi's theory of poetry itself is constantly buttressed by a solid hold on the realities of human nature on the one hand, and by a full awareness of the specific problems and difficulties of practical literary criticism on the other. It is only by disassociating Leopardi's poetic theory from the general critical awareness that almost invariably informs it that one can come to the partial view of that theory as being, to quote Mario Fubini, ''rather an ideal of art than a concept of art, rather a moving celebration of poetry than a satisfactory definition of the aesthetic activity.'' As to the definition of the so-called aesthetic activity and its absence from Leopardi's theory and criticism of poetry, one can dismiss the charge by reminding oneself of F. R. Leavis's highly apt statement that ''as so often, the term 'aesthetic' signals a lack of grip.'' If while theorizing about the nature and effect of poetry, Leopardi is at times capable of soaring into what Santayana calls the ''realm of essence'' and of arriving at that ''intuition of pure Being as well as the sense of existence'' without which, as Sir Herbert Read so rightly points out, ''the highest poetry is inconceivable,'' it is mainly on account of his taking a habitual recourse to hard analytical reflection, backed up as it almost invariably is by a keen and alert sensibility and subtle perception. That is why his poetic theory convinces and enlightens us far more than all the excogitations of the aesthetic critics and philosophers; that is why [according to Vitaliano Brancati in *Societa, lingua e letteratura d'Italia di Leopardi*] ''a critical page of Leopardi's is much more firm than one of De Sanctis' . . . the richness of critical terms in Leopardi (not in the formal or extrinsic sense, but in the sense of feeling and understanding) is superior to that of De Sanctis.''

In one of his *Operette Morali*, ''**Il Parini ovvero della gloria**,'' written when Leopardi was only 26, one can trace the structure of Leopardi's major critical assumptions, in virtue of which he may be regarded as a critic who was strikingly ahead of his times. He represents, indeed, what T. S. Eliot called, apropos of Remy de Gourmont, "the critical consciousness of a generation," the literary generation in Italy from 1820 to 1837. While discussing the precariousness of posthumous literary glory, and the preference which in ancient times great writers and poets displayed for great actions rather than literary fame, Leopardi (or his mouthpiece the eighteenth-century poet Parini) tells us, echoing Buffon, that it is the force of style that may be regarded as the enduring warrant of literary fame, at least with posterity, thereby showing his tendency, which would grow stronger with years, to consider the literary merit of a given work as being very largely, if not exclusively, dependent rather on its formal and stylistic qualities than on anything else. And in order both for the reader and the critic to fully appreciate these qualities, it is necessary to recreate a work, as it were, within oneself "almost as perfectly as the author of that work himself did it." Thus criticism is considered from the very outset as not merely an act of analyzing, inquiring, and evaluating, but also one of creating. There are, however, certain pitfalls to which this subjective or personal method of criticism may sometimes be exposed. For one thing it may be unduly influenced, or even dictated "rather by blindly embraced habits than by one's own judgment"; for to be able to criticize a work of literature "with complete liberty of judgment and with no care whatsoever of others' authority" is not within the reach of the majority of readers, who even with the help of the enlightened guidance and authority are more likely to be delighted "by the gross and patent beauties than by the subtle and delicate ones, by what is bold (and prominent) than by what is subdued and bashful, by the appearance than by the substance of things; and ordinarily by what is mediocre rather than by what is best."

But if, on the one hand, Leopardi pleads for, or at least approves of, a direct approach to literary works on the part of the common reader, with an open mind and with an independence of judgment he warns, on the other hand, against the fallacy of judging literary works not so much on the basis of their qualities in themselves, as on the effect they produce on the reader. A due balance between the consideration of what the work in itself is and of what effect it produces on a certain reader, which itself may very largely depend on the literary sensibility and the general character and culture of that person, is according to Leopardi the *sine qua non* of what may be called creative criticism. Another prerequisite is the reader's ever active and vigilant passivity, so to say, his inward disposition to "follow the minimum impulse of what is being read, feel vividly every light touch" and thus create in oneself "thousands of movements and images, wandering at times in the sweetest delirium, almost transported beyond oneself."

Leopardi goes on to demonstrate that the very basis of poetry is illusions—illusions which are naturally more rife and more efficacious in youth than in old age. And just as the creative faculty generally declines with the loss of youth, so also does the critical faculty itself to some extent. It is not merely that, to paraphrase T. S. Eliot, one outgrows the majority of poems as one outgrows the majority of human passions, but also that one's capacity for the "suspension of disbelief" and (what is even harder) for belief itself or the capability of being "strongly moved by what is imaginatively grand and beautiful"—which is the most indispensable condition involved in all critical activity—perceptibly declines. Preferring as a rule, however, "the excessive to the moderate, the pretty and superb to the simple and the natural, as regards modes and ornaments, and false

beauties to the true ones," the young are generally incapable of appreciating the "mature and accomplished virtue of literary works." A true critic, therefore, is obviously one who combines in himself the maturity of judgment with the emotional vigor and liveliness of youth.

Even though young, it was by dint of long systematic study and reflection that Leopardi had come to achieve this degree of critical consciousness. Having spent all his boyhood and early youth in his father's library in an intensive study of the literary—and not merely literary—works both of classical antiquity and modern times, Leopardi had acquired that academic discipline and intellectual maturity, which are, generally speaking, the basis of critical thought. In fact his study was not that of one who is merely a scholar or an erudite; from the very earliest stage of his scholarly career—in itself precocious—one notes in him the presence of a certain critical vein which determined his reactions to everything he read or wrote about. In one of Leopardi's earliest writings, **"Discorso sopra Mosco,"** written when the poet was hardly 18, one already discerns the power of critical discrimination, coupled with an independence of judgment that enabled him to attribute a certain idyllic poem to Stobaeus, instead of as the universally prevalent opinion of his day did, to Moschus. Behind this ability to sift the evidence, which, in such cases, is bound to be internal rather than external, and to come to a more satisfactory and more convincing conclusion than the one hitherto prevalent, there lies not merely the power of reasoning, but also, and above all, the poetic sensibility in the judging critic himself—a sensibility that helps him distinguish between the characteristic merits of Moschus and Theocritus, and to indicate his own cautious preference. "In Theocritus," says the young Leopardi, "one likes the negligence, in Moschus the delicacy. Theocritus has more carefully hidden the art with which he has depicted nature. Moschus has let it come out a little, but in a way so that it attracts rather than annoys, makes us relish, without being satiated, and by showing only one part, and by hiding the rest, makes us desire to see the whole"; as regards his own preference, Leopardi characteristically remarks: "I dare not prefer Moschus to Theocritus, who has inimitable beauties, and who is, among the ancients, the poet *par excellence* of the shepherds and meadows; but I have no difficulty in saying that to some of his *Idylls*, in which there dominates that austere style, which puts before our eyes the countrymen with all their rusticity, I prefer the graceful and finished poems of Moschus." This is not merely the expression of a personal whim or liking, but the statement of well-pondered and well-balanced opinion that has in it all the elements and evidence of a degree of critical evaluation quite surprising in a boy of 18.

Leopardi's early bent for philological and literary research was itself an aid, as far as it went, to the development of his critical and reflective powers. In this research Leopardi did not merely confine himself to the compilation of data and to the sifting of factual external evidence, but he was also led to exercise his own faculty for reflection and discrimination. In **"Discorso sopra la Batracomiomachia,"** written in 1815, while examining all the scholarly evidence and the various authorities' efforts to determine the authorship of *La Batracomiomachia*, Leopardi sometimes makes pungent fun—a fun and pungency worthy of A. E. Housman—of those who on the basis of a very slender evidence, accompanied by a very specious piece of reasoning, jump to a conclusion which neither commonsense nor the scholarly conscience can ever approve. (pp. 1-18)

The same critical spirit, coupled with commonsense and equipped with erudition, Leopardi manifests in another early work of

his—"**Discorso sopra la vita e le opere di M. Cornelio Frontone.**" More than his first-hand knowledge of the material in
question, which is itself impressive for its wide range and
depth, it is Leopardi's masterly grasp of the problems that arise,
and the extremely sound and pertinent notions that he puts
forward, which renders this work so interesting. Here one can
find Leopardi's theory of style and language delineated in a
more than rudimentary form—a theory that Leopardi would
reaffirm, later, in **Zibaldone** in a more elaborate and more
detailed way. Describing Frontone's zeal for the purity of language, Leopardi tells us what is almost as true of himself:

> He was most zealous about the purity of language;
> he pondered long over single words, examined at
> bottom the propriety of terms, weighed the particular
> value of every synonym, and did not disdain the
> office of a grammarian, since he was persuaded that
> it is not enough to think, that one must also talk, that
> the Orator cannot do without words any more than
> he can do without things, that if not helped by terms,
> thought languishes, and that at the back of the cor-
> ruption of the fable [subject-matter] lies the very cor-
> ruption of eloquence itself.

A veritable master and philosopher of style, Frontone was not
desirous "of the unheard and the marvellous; he preserved his
style exempt from exaggeration, excessive exquisiteness, affected sublimity; in a word he escaped with every possible care
from the excess of artifice." Through such observations Leopardi both underlines his preference for a particular style, and
defines what his own ideal of style is. He also gives proof of
his deep involvement, from a very early age, in the problem
of style, a problem whose subtlety and complexity he realizes
just as fully as he realizes its importance. "The force and the
use of the word *style,*" says Leopardi, "are obscure and almost
fluctuating, not only in the case of the majority of people, but
in the case of the most cautious and most learned," in so far
as it is not easy to discern, as one must, "the qualities of the
form of style from the quality of the material or of the words
and the fable."

Whatever, therefore, be the intrinsic or historical value of Leopardi's juvenile writings of philological character as such, they
constitute an indisputable proof of the level of critical awareness that his mind had reached at such an early age, and that
governed his whole attitude to all he read or wrote. "No modern
poet," Cardarelli justly observes [in "La fortuna di Leopardi"], "seems to be so philologically armed and such a
master of his proper means as Leopardi." With such an arduous
training and background behind him, whatever Leopardi was
going to say henceforward about poetry and literary criticism
must at least have one infallible quality about it, that, whether
it was basically right or wrong, it was the voice of a man who
knew what he was talking about, and whose most casual observation was directly or indirectly the fruit of close study and
earnest thought. (pp. 19-20)

> *G. Singh, in his* Leopardi and the Theory of Poetry,
> *University of Kentucky Press, 1964, 365 p.*

ROBERT MARTIN ADAMS (essay date 1966)

[*An American educator and critic, Adams is the author of works
on religion, opera, and literature, including the highly regarded*
Stendhal: Notes on a Novelist *(1959). In this excerpt from his*
Nil: Episodes in the Literary Conquest of Void during the Nineteenth Century, *a study of the increasingly prevalent literary theme
of nothingness, Adams relates the idea of* noia, *or boredom, in*
Leopardi's poetry to the author's "psychological-sociological myth"
of the human condition.]

A pair of famous passages in the **Pensieri** (67 and 68) seem to
exalt boredom as a state to which only the spiritual man can
aspire. Looking across the world and through the galaxies,
Leopardi in the person of this spiritual man finds everywhere
nullity, vacancy, and insufficiency by comparison with his own
teeming soul and infinite desires. This version of boredom as
a kind of cosmic complacency gives it rank among manifestations of the egotistical sublime; but the part which the concept
plays in Leopardi's extended thought, and particularly in his
poetry, is more various and interesting. It must be prefaced by
a few words outlining the psychological-sociological myth which
he took for granted.

According to this Leopardian myth, both the individual in his
youth and society in pagan days were originally capable of
imagination, which filled life with vivid though false imagery,
making the world seem alive and sympathetic to its inhabitants.
Under these circumstances, man's senses would be quick and
unclouded, his passions vigorous. So life was in the age of our
primitive ancestors, in the golden age of mankind; so it is for
children, and so it may still be in a few surviving wildernesses
like California (*quantum mutata*, 1965!). But science and civilization have cut man off from the life of the senses, and so
from his own power of imagination; out of this inner, partial
death rises *noia*, which is essentially a disease of the civilized,
and which, in its early stages, is the simple absence of feeling.
So the poem "**Ad Angelo Mai**" contrasts those fortunate figures
of the past who were capable of authentic grief with moderns,
who can feel nothing at all:

> Ahi dal dolor comincia e nasce
> L'italo canto. E pur men grava e morde
> Il mal che n'addolora
> Del tedio che n'affoga. Oh te beato
> A cui fu vita il pianto! A noi le fasce
> Cinse il fastidio; a noi presso la culla
> Immoto siede, e su la tomba, il nulla.

[In a footnote the critic adds a prose translation: Alas,
in sorrow begins and ends Italian song. And yet less
deep and bitter the pain which stabs than the tedium
which smothers. Happy were you whose life was
sorrow. About us boredom fastens its bandages; by
our cradle and on our tomb sits motionless the Void.]

Knowledge has shrunk the world, not expanded it, and made
evident its uniformity, not its variety—has rendered it dead:

> Ecco svaniro a un punto
> E figurato è il mondo in breve carta;
> Ecco tutto è simile, e discoprendo,
> Solo il nulla s'accresce.

[The critic translates: Here, reduced to a point, the
world is represented on a bit of paper; see, everything
is the same, and from our discoveries only Nothing
is increased.]

Thus man is necessarily isolated within the universe; whether
he travels, struggles, or socializes with his own kind (as the
poem "**To Count Carlo Pepoli**" declares), he inevitably carries
within him the adamantine pillar of boredom:

> ahi, ma nel petto,
> Nell'imo petto, grave, salda, immota
> Come colonna adamantina, siede
> Noia immortale, incontro a cui non puote
> Vigor di giovanezza, e non la crolla
> Dolce parola di rosato labbro,

E non lo sguardo tenero, tremante,
Di due nere pupille, il caro sguardo,
La più degna del ciel cosa mortale.

[The critic translates: Alas, but within the breast, in
the depths of the breast, heavy, massive, motionless,
like an adamantine column sits immortal boredom,
against which even the vigor of youth is helpless; nor
will it be shaken by sweet words from rosy lips, or
the tender, tremulous glance of two black eyes, the
beloved glance, among all mortal things most worthy
of heaven.]

So heightened and sharpened, boredom passes beyond apathy;
it is metaphysical anguish and pure desire, abstracted from this
or that particular object, not directly frustrated, yet knowing
itself incapable of fulfillment. When other passions and distractions leave the mind, the ground-bass of *noia* rises to fill
it. Perhaps a cause and certainly a result of this *noia* is the
posture of hallucinated immobility and total self-abandonment
which Leopardi repeatedly describes:

Talor m'assido in solitaria parte
Sovra un rialto, al margine d'un lago
Di taciturne piante incoronato.
Ivi, quando il meriggio in ciel si volve,
La sua tranquilla imago il Sol dipinge,
E erba o foglia non si crolla al vento,
E non onda incresparsi, e non cicala
Strider, nè batter penna augello in ramo,
Nè farfalla ronzar, nè voce o moto
Da presso nè da lunge odi nè vedi.
Tien quelle rive altissima quiete;
Ond'io quasi me stesso e il mondo obblio
Sedendo immoto; e già mi par che sciolte
Giaccian le membra mie, nè spirto o senso
Più le commova, e lor quiete antica
Co' silenzi del loco si confonda.

[The critic translates: Then I sit solitary on a mound
by a lake crowned with quiet plants. There, when
noon rises in the skies the sun paints its quiet portrait,
and neither grass nor leaf bends to the wind, nor does
wave ripple nor cricket call nor bird flutter wing on
bough nor butterfly flit; neither sound nor motion
from near or far do I hear or see. Deepest quiet covers
the bank; so that, sitting motionless, I almost forget
myself and the world, and now it seems that my limbs
lie still, neither spirit nor sense moves them any
more, and their ancient quiet mingles with the silence
of the place.]

We note in this passage from **"La Vita Solitaria"** (lines 23-38)
how a soft, deep phrase like "lor quiete antica" invites the
imagination back to an original repose underlying the restless
motion of the limbs—as if in this new quiet of the place they
were merely regaining a stillness which was their immemorial
right. **"L'Infinito"** too describes a recovery of quiet at the
heart of the self, a withdrawing into interior distance. Only
when the hedge turns back his gaze from the horizon does the
poet's mind go adventuring beyond it:

interminati
Spazi di là da quella, e sovrumani
Silenzi, e profondissima quiete
Io nel pensier mi fingo.

The wind rustling through the hedge becomes the noise of the
world; and by contrast with the poet's physical immobility, the
comparison of time's rattling noise with the infinite silence of
space is a steadily deepening, advancing experience, as the
strong verbal form underlines:

io quello
Infinito silenzio a questa voce
Vo comparando.

The mind is lost in its own contemplations, drowns or is shipwrecked; yet its fate is, for unspecified reasons, "dolce":

Così tra questa
Immensità s'annega il pensier mio:
E il naufragar m'è dolce in questo mare.

The adjective implies that he has regained or rediscovered
something, and in fact the imagery of drowning is rich in tacit
implications of regeneration, cyclical return, erotic surrender,
mortal abandon, and new counterpart-worlds—all of which are
left to cluster, if they will, around the magnetic, because unexplained, word "dolce."

In the last of the **Canti**, **"La Ginestra"** poses the fragile flower
of human life against the hot lava overflowing from Vesuvius,
under the infinite perspectives of interstellar space, assures us
that under these circumstances death and only death is inevitable, and yet invokes too a chilly, almost astral vision of love.
The flower, which can only be love, grows on the edge of the
abyss, in defiance of its own Nothingness, pretending to be
only the creature of an instant; yet it returns in the teeth of
defeats, pushing continually forward

Per sì lungo cammino,
Che sembra star.

The huge cyclical indifference of which Leopardi elsewhere
accuses Nature seems here allied to an equally large impersonal
force in man—as if, for the first time, love were not a refuge
from Nature or an opponent of Nature, so much as an expression of it. Leopardi thus suggests in his last poem a Nothing
within or beneath the illusion of love, as well as at either end
of it. That this poem should be taken as an affirmative expression seems particularly wrong, since it summarizes the case
for a human love which it has already toned down to *caritas*
in terms of clear-eyed cynicism:

Così star suole in piede
Quale star può quel ch'ha in error la sede. . . .

Startled by Leopardi's bitter, unbelieving pessimism, a good
many otherwise-perceptive contemporaries tried to dismiss him
as a man who because he was a hunchback denied God. The
superficiality of this cruel and rather Latin logic is apparent;
but it seems to have been important not to let oneself look into
Leopardi's universe or admit that it might be one's own. There
is no reason to doubt that the peculiarities of Leopardi's wretched
youth and the influence of his classically misguided parents
confirmed in him a whole range of idiosyncratic attitudes. Yet
in many respects his cosmos is closer to our own than is, say,
that of his respectable contemporary Manzoni; eccentric in his
own day, he is far less so today. He first drew in the thin,
bitterly cold air of absolute Nothing with the sense that it was
both deadly and inevitable; he proclaimed *noia* the disease of
modern man and *nulla* his destiny, and did so in terms transcending the Rousseauistic primitivism which represented the
rationale of his outlook if not its real roots. By the hardness
of his style and the purity of his perceptions, he gave evidence
of a sort that man could after a fashion survive in the empty
spaces of imaginative non-existence and unbelief. Indeed, we
now know that his experience of *nulla* was more profound and
terrifying than contemporaries could have estimated from his

public writings. The correspondence and the immense *Zibaldone* or commonplace-book became public property only at the turn of the century, and in them we find passages like these:

> I was terrified to find myself in the midst of nothing, and myself nothing. I felt as if I were suffocating, believing and feeling that everything is nothing, solid nothing.

Or, from a letter to Giordani (19 November 1819):

> If at this moment I were to go mad, my madness I believe would consist in remaining seated with eyes staring, mouth open, hands upon my knees, not laughing or weeping or moving, unless compelled, from the place where I found myself. . . . This is the first time in my life when *noia* has not only oppressed and wearied me, but suffocates and tears at me like an intolerable pain, and I am so terrified by the vanity of everything and of man's condition when, as with me, every passion in his soul has been extinguished, that I am beside myself and have come to believe that my very desperation too is nothing.

These are the accents, not of spite or pose, but of extreme, direct necessity. Leopardi's triumph is to have recognized in this condition a permanent aspect of man's earthly state, and made it serve major ends in his art. As with Mallarmé, the pure simplicity of his finest lyrics is outlined against the black of void; they do not push because there is nothing for them to push against; the self-contained poise of their carriage is reflected in pools of motionless despair which lie beneath them, liquid and glittering and permanent. (pp. 224-31)

> Robert Martin Adams, "Some Instances of Boredom," in his Nil: Episodes in the Literary Conquest of Void during the Nineteenth Century, *Oxford University Press, 1966, pp. 217-38.*

JOHN HEATH-STUBBS (essay date 1966)

[*An English poet and critic, Heath-Stubbs has written studies on John Dryden, Charles Williams, and, in his* The Darkling Plain *(1950), a number of neglected Victorian authors. Here, he considers Leopardi's ties to Romanticism, classicism, and the Enlightenment, also examining key aspects of his philosophy in an attempt to underscore the modern-day relevance of his poetry.*]

Leopardi was born in 1798, ten years later than Byron, six years later than Shelley, and three years later than Keats. The year in which he died, 1837, also saw the death of Pushkin and of Georg Büchner. This chronology will serve to place him in that general movement of European literature which we may term Romanticism in the broad sense of that word. The qualification is necessary because the word Romanticism is employed in relation to continental literatures, including the Italian, in a more specialized way, to indicate a type of sensibility that draws its inspiration from the Gothic, the exotic, and the extravagant. In this sense, Leopardi is not a Romantic. He is indeed a Classicist. His poetry seeks its models in those Greek and Roman authors of whom he possessed a profound and scholarly knowledge. But one has only to think of the work of Keats and of much else in the English Romantic tradition, and of such poets as Hölderlin in Germany, to realize that a nostalgia for the clear light and the pure forms of the antique world could itself be a feature of Romanticism.

Characteristic of the whole movement was the poets' recognition of their alienation. As the nineteenth century dawned, this was borne in upon them by the new currents of political,

philosophical, and scientific thought. Everywhere the old patterns of society were in the melting pot, and long-established ideas were being challenged. The poets could no longer be certain of their role in society nor sure of their audience. They were therefore forced to rely more and more on particular inspiration, fitful and transient though it might turn out to be, and less and less on exterior sanction and occasion. Since the traditional forms of religious belief seemed largely to have lost their significance, the poets constructed their own systems, taking their symbols from revived mythologies, or from their experience of erotic passion or natural beauty. This tendency found a fairly superficial expression in the self-dramatization of such a poet as Byron, a profounder one in Wordsworth's pursuit of a solitary communion with nature, or Keats's contemplation of sensuous beauty. But Leopardi, perhaps more than any of his contemporaries, goes furthest in the exploration of his own alienation. It is this that makes him in some ways a more modern figure than they, a precursor of the existentialist thought of our own age.

All Leopardi's work presents at one and the same time both a remarkable unity and a curious duality. He is, as we have said, at once a Romantic and a Classicist. He is even, indeed, an anti-Romantic. There is both the lyrical poet of the *Canti* and the hard dry prose writer of the *Operette Morali.* Yet the poems of the former and the dialogues of the latter frequently deal with common themes and complement and comment upon one another. In his verse Leopardi often handles many of those subjects that preoccupied the Romantic poets in general. The reader familiar with English literature may particularly be struck by the number of times Leopardi's poetry suggests that of Wordsworth. This may seem a paradox, since Wordsworth is one of the most joyful of poets, and Leopardi the saddest. Yet it is nevertheless the case. For example, Leopardi's **"Le ricordanze"** presents a close parallel to Wordsworth's "Tintern Abbey" both in its theme and structure. In each poem a scene is contemplated for what it now is and also in terms of the poet's memory of it at an earlier period of his life. Wordsworth's poem reaches its final note of hope in his invocation to his sister Dorothy. She is still in communion with that natural beauty with which Wordsworth himself will lose touch. Leopardi's poem ends with his despairing lament for the lost Nerina. The one poem might almost be considered as an inversion, or mirror-image, of the other. Again, Leopardi's Sylvia and Wordsworth's Lucy are parallel figures, not only pathetic images of girls who died young but symbols of something more essential that the poet himself has lost forever. . . . **"Il Risorgimento"** examines the central Romantic dilemma of the poet's relation to his own inspiration. So also do Wordsworth's ode on "Intimations of Immortality" and Coleridge's "Dejection." Wordsworth and Leopardi were, as far as I know, entirely unaware of one another's existence. But the fact that two poets so utterly different in background and temperament should so strikingly approach each other shows to what an extent common experience underlay the European poetry of their day.

The Greek affiliations of Leopardi's poetry bring it into relation with other widely current preoccupations of his age. He is more truly a Hellenist than Shelley or Keats, more akin to André Chénier in France and Landor in England. The latter was resident in Italy during Leopardi's lifetime, and it is rather surprising that he nowhere in his writings refers to the Italian poet. For these two have more in common than their Hellenism and their employment of the dialogue form (with, in each case, a debt to Lucian). Both are aristocrats; both seem to have held a kind of Roman republicanism as their political ideal; and both possessed a contempt for the mob, as well as for the more vaporous enthusiasms of their age. When Nietzsche singled out these two, with Heine and Mérimée, as the four greatest prose writers of the nineteenth century, he divined in them more in common than their stylistic purity.

In his poem **"Alla primavera"** Leopardi laments the loss to modern man of that mythopoeic view of the world whereby the Greeks were able to humanize the natural scene and to feel at home in the universe. Thus also Keats lamented, and Wordsworth, that he could not hope to hear old Triton blow his wreathèd horn. Thus also Schiller in his famous ode "The Gods of Greece." But above all it was Hölderlin who, driven by the same nostalgia, sought to reconcile his Hellenistic neopaganism with the Protestant Christianity of his upbringing, before he was driven into the abyss of insanity. At one period of his life Leopardi made some approach to a similar attempt at a synthesis. From an early age he had been in revolt against the grim and life-denying Catholic pietism of his mother. But in later years he drafted fragments of an ode to Christ, and to the Virgin, in which he sought to rehabilitate these images in terms of his own subjective and Romantic mythmaking. But such a solution, if it might be a solution, was not for him. His universe remains, as for his own Brutus, one in which human anguish has not dimmed the stars.

For Leopardi is not only the child of the Romantic movement but also of the Enlightenment. The *Operette Morali* are essentially a product of the rationalism of the eighteenth century. Like the prose of Schopenhauer, the coincidence of whose thought with Leopardi's has often been pointed out, the *Op-*

The view from Infinity Hill, the scene that inspired Leopardi's poem "L'infinito."

erette are in the tradition of the French moralists of the preceding age—La Rochefoucauld, for example. Behind this tradition stands the figure of Pascal. Leopardi's English disciple, James Thomson (the poet of "The City of Dreadful Night"), devoted an interesting essay to a comparison of the nineteenth-century Italian and the seventeenth-century Frenchman. Of Leopardi it might indeed be said, as Baudelaire said of Pascal, that he carried his gulf with him wherever he went. Both possessed that terrifying experience of the empty interstellar spaces, which finds expression early in Leopardi with **"L'Infinito,"** one of his best-known poems. For a religious mind like Pascal's this experience may be a preliminary stage toward a mystical purgation. For a mind rendered incapable by temperament or upbringing of entering into such a state, this experience can only erect a backdrop of total despair against which the human drama is enacted. Moreover, Leopardi's universe is perhaps vaster and in a sense more terrifying than Pascal's. The universe of Newton had expanded into that of Laplace, for whom God was an unnecessary hypothesis. Thus in **"La ginestra"** Leopardi speaks not only of the stellar universe as we know it, but also of the galaxies that lie beyond it. This vision is only just beginning to be accommodated to the general educated consciousness in our own day. Even more remarkably, in his **"Dialogue between Copernicus and the Sun"** he anticipates, however playfully, what is in effect the modern theory of relativity.

These observations may serve to suggest that Leopardi's pessimism has a wider significance than has sometimes been recognized. It has too often been treated as a merely subjective romantic melancholy that had its roots in the pathetic circumstances of his life. Not, of course, that a consideration of these circumstances is irrelevant to an understanding of Leopardi's work. It does not require much acquaintance with modern psychology to see that the child's failure to love and to be loved by his mother led to the man's projecting that maternal figure upon an indifferent or even hostile nature. It is the image of this indifferent nature, which manifests itself in the colossal figure, like an Easter Island statue, that confronts the wanderer in the **"Dialogue between Nature and an Icelander."** Sometimes, indeed, Leopardi does suggest that there is a power behind the phenomena of the universe, but an actively malignant one. Besides the poems he planned to Christ and the Virgin, he drafted one to Ahriman, the power of evil in the dualistic system of Zoroastrian religion. That it remained unwritten is significant. A Satanist no less than a Christian answer would for him have been an oversimplification. It is here only that Leopardi comes near to the Byronic type of Romanticism, which in general he held in low esteem.

The characteristic setting of Leopardi's poetry is landscape transfigured by moonlight. One may surmise that his weak eyes and the fear of that scorn to which his deformed figure exposed him, gave him a preference for nocturnal excursions. But the moon, throughout Leopardi's poetry, is a recurrent symbol for that beauty which so poignantly touches the darkness of human existence. This beauty is mutable and transient. In his early **"Frammento,"** Leopardi imagines that the moon might fall from the sky; while in his last poem, said to have been composed upon his deathbed, the moon finally sets for him, leaving total darkness behind. So it is also with Nerina and Sylvia, idealized figures of young girls loved at a distance, whose early deaths symbolize for Leopardi the passing of youth and hope. In a later poem, **"Sopra il ritratto di una bella donna,"** Leopardi momentarily seems to suggest a quasi-Platonic view—that mortal beauty is a ray cast by an eternal splendor. But the poem ends with a paradox and a question mark.

For Leopardi the perpetual condition of man's existence is *noia*. This is a diffcult word to translate effectively. It may literally be rendered "boredom" or "tedium." But in Leopardi's writings it assumes the quality almost of a metaphysical absolute, which these words scarcely suggest. The French *ennui*, its etymological equivalent, gives a better idea of its scope, and it can be related to the use of the word "spleen" by English writers of the eighteenth century and also by Baudelaire. From this condition man is momentarily liberated by the exercise of his imagination and his intellect. And thus liberated he is able to apprehend the ideas of beauty, of virtue, and of love. But these are seen in the end to be mere illusions. Sappho dies an outcast from beauty, and Brutus, cursing virtue; while in the most terrible of his poems, **"A se stesso,"** Leopardi records the passing of love, the last illusion.

It is from the apprehension of these ideas, however, that Leopardi's poetry takes its life; the fact that they are seen to be illusions gives it its peculiar lyrical poignancy. In the prose **Operette Morali,** which Leopardi speaks of as if they were (what they scarcely can be said to be) systematic philosophy, he embarks on the task of liberating man by demolishing his delusions one by one. For Leopardi, the ultimate wisdom to be gleaned from experience is that men, fully conscious of their condition—that they are in a universe without God, where neither nature nor destiny is on their side—may learn to be more humane, in the solidarity of suffering. This is the moral of **"La ginestra,"** his longest and most ambitious poem, in which Mount Vesuvius stands as the symbol for the destructive potency in nature and the insecurity of man's lot. In this poem Leopardi pours scorn upon the nascent optimistic philosophy of progress. It so happened that the year in which Leopardi died ("as if unable to bear the prospect," as Ford Madox Ford put it) saw, in England, the opening of the Victorian era, in which this optimism was to be dominant. In another late poem, his **"Palinodia,"** Leopardi ironically parodies Virgil's "Messianic Eclogue" in celebrating the new Golden Age, which England and her machines are to bring about. (pp. 9-14)

The duality and the paradox then remain. To some, Leopardi's aristocratic humanism will seem sterile and reactionary; but to others he will appear the most essentially modern and clearsighted as well as one of the greatest of the poets of his time. It is too facile to dismiss his work, as it sometimes has been dismissed, as merely the product of a sick body and a sick mind. It is of the nature of poetic insight to transcend such misfortunes. In reading his poetry we cannot fail to be moved by the pathos of Leopardi, the unloved hunchback. But the impression that finally remains is rather of the gentleness and dignity of spirit that shines through all his bitterness and scorn of life. (p. 14)

> *John Heath-Stubbs, "Introduction: Leopardi as Poetic Thinker," in* Selected Prose and Poetry by Giacomo Leopardi, *edited and translated by Iris Origo and John Heath-Stubbs, 1966. Reprint by New American Library, 1967, pp. 9-14.*

NICOLAS JAMES PERELLA (essay date 1970)

[*Perella analyzes Leopardi's use of night imagery, focusing on the spiritual significance of the moon in his poetry.*]

[In considering] Leopardi's nocturnal poetry, let us first recall that the concept of night was held by the poet to be most poetical by virtue of the indistinct, incomplete, or obscure idea-sensation that it arouses in us: "Le parole *notte notturne* ec. le descrizioni della notte ec., sono poeticissime, perchè la notte confondendo gli oggetti, l'animo non ne concepisce che un'immagine indistinta, incompleta, sì di essa che quanto ella contiene. Così oscurità, profondo ec. ec."

Now this is a concept that would seem to be at odds with Leopardi's descriptions of night, especially the nocturne that opens **"La sera del dì di festa"** and the Homeric night-simile that in the **"Discorso"** of 1818 he held up as a supreme example of the sentimental or pathetic (and, in a way, of the sublime) in nature and poetry. Indeed, along with Homer's simile, as a second example of the sentimental in nature and poetry he chose yet another nocturne—the soft clear moonlit night from Virgil's *Aeneid*. These, as most of Leopardi's nocturnal landscapes which one is tempted to call southern or Mediterranean nights as opposed to the northern or "spectral" night, are unique for a remarkable clarity in which the most distant objects can be easily perceived. We must not rush into a hasty judgment of them as unreal. (p. 117)

Let us now also add that dimension of silence which is so important in Leopardi's nights. Max Picard has noted that "In no other phenomenon are distance and nearness, range and immediacy, the all-embracing and the particular, so united as they are in silence." Certainly it is the sense of vastness that predominates in the silence of night; for, indeed, at any hour, but especially at night, there is nothing like silence to suggest a sense of unlimited space. (p. 118)

[It is the] idea-sensation of vastness or immensity and deep silence in connection with a crystalline moonlit and starlit landscape that lends to the Homeric and Leopardian nocturnes their "poeticalness." The connection between such nights as those described by Homer and Leopardi and the sense of the sublime was not infrequently made. (p. 119)

Among Leopardi's thoughts is one holding that the sight of the sun or the moon in a vast and brightly lit landscape and in a deep clear sky is pleasurable because of the very vastness of the sensation it arouses in us: "La vista del sole o della luna in una campagna vasta ed aprica, e in un cielo aperto ec. è piacevole per la vastità della sensazione." It is in the light of this poetic too that we more fully appreciate in **"La sera del dì di festa"** the emotion connected with the solitary song heard at night and fading into the vastness of silence. The anguish felt by the poet on that occasion was perhaps not without something of that "delightful horror" associated with the sublime:

> È piacevole per se stesso cioè non per altro, se non per un'idea vaga ed indefinita che desta, un canto (il più spregevole) udito da lungi o che paia lontano senza esserlo, o che si vada appoco appoco allontanando, e divenendo insensibile o anche viceversa (ma meno) o che sia così lontano, in apparenza o in verità, che l'orecchio e l'idea quasi *lo perda nella vastità degli spazi....* Stando in casa, e udendo tali canti o suoni per la strada, *massime di notte* si è più disposti a questi effetti, perchè nè l'udito nè gli altri sensi non arrivano a determinare nè circoscrivere la sensazione.

[This passage from *Zibaldone*], written in October of 1821, brings us back to the **"Discorso"** of 1818, for Leopardi goes on to say that such images in poetry are always beautiful, especially when they are put down "negligentemente," and night or the image of night is the most appropriate time for increasing or creating these emotions evoked by sound. Virgil, he says, has masterfully implemented this idea; and the reference given in illustration of his point is the very scene he had quoted in the **"Discorso"** along with Homer's nocturne as proof of the pathetic in ancient writers.

Let us recall that for the author of the 1818 **"Discorso"** nature was still "la santa natura" and a source to which man could turn in order to offset the nefarious effects of reason. With this we may again consider the use in that essay of Homer's nocturne-simile which Leopardi considered exemplary of the natural in expression because, unlike the moderns who exaggerate emotions in order to evoke the pathetic, Homer gives us the image and the emotion simply and purely, "senza spasimi e senza svenimenti." But in his translation of the simile there is a clue to Leopardi's own romantic or subjective (though discreetly so) reading of Homer. It is found in the very first line when Leopardi characterizes the stars surrounding the moon as "graziosi," whereas the original refers to them as being conspicuous, that is, standing out in their brightness:

> Sì come quando graziosi in cielo
> Rifulgon gli astri intorno della luna,
> E l'aere è senza vento, e si discopre
> Ogni cima de' monti ed ogni selva
> Ed ogni torre; allor che su nell'alto
> Tutto quanto l'immenso etra si schiude,
> E vedesi ogni stella, e ne gioisce
> Il pastor dentro all'alma.

Here then we are led . . . to the affective quality that Leopardi associated with brightness and limpidness. . . . The word *grazioso* is connected in Leopardi's poetic and affective life with that something of tenderness that inheres in clearness. Semantically it is linked with "benign" with which it makes a binomial; indeed, it has something of the value given to it by Francesca when she first addressed the pilgrim Dante: "O animal grazioso e benigno" (*Inferno*). Leopardi used the same binomial in an early love diary in which he recorded the feelings and impressions aroused in him by his cousin Gertrude Cassi during a visit by the latter to the Leopardi residence in December 1817. Of this woman who was his senior by several years, he wrote: "maniere *benigne* e, secondo me, *graziose, lontanissime dall'affettato.*" Thus those qualities are in turn associated with a state of naturalness. Moreover, they are inevitably suggestive of a tender, feminine presence. And here, of course, one thinks of the lyric [**"Alla luna"** that Leopardi was soon to write, opening with the apostrophe "O graziosa luna." Strictly speaking, there is nothing in the original simile that justifies Leopardi's use of so affectively charged a word as *graziosi* for the stars. Nothing like that occurs in versions of the simile by Cesarotti or Foscolo. Even Monti's use of *vezzose* is lacking in the magic evoked by Leopardi's word. Not even Pascoli "intrudes" in his adaptation of the simile. Perhaps Tennyson in his translation of the simile comes close to what Leopardi has done:

> As when in heaven the stars about the moon
> *Look beautiful*, when all the winds are laid.

Or Shelley may be even more pertinently cited here for his lines in *Queen Mab*:

> Heaven's ebon vault
> Studded with *stars unutterably bright*,
> Through which the moon's unclouded grandeur rolls.

In Leopardi's choice of *graziosi* there is something like Shelley's "unutterably bright," but with a connotation of something tender by virtue of which he has rendered Homer's nocturne the more "pathetic." (pp. 119-21)

Certainly, Leopardi was among those who most readily identified themselves with Homer's "solitary shepherd," filled with a sense of peace and even of joy (of a sort) in the face of so "touching" a scene. The shepherd's heart is gladdened by the brightness of the night, not for the prosaic reason that such clarity enables him "to scan every hilltop and jutting cliff and valley for the sheepstealer," but because he is in fact comforted at nighttime by a light and a meteorological calm great enough to offset night's darkness and that nocturnal terror that the Greeks felt at dimly lit or pitch-black nights. He is also gladdened by the beauty of the night and by the promise of calm weather.

We may contrast the night and shepherd of this simile with . . . [another simile from the *Iliad*]: "As from his watching place a goatherd watches a cloud move / on its way over the sea before the drive of the west wind; / far away though he be he watches it, blacker than pitch is, / moving across the sea and piling the storm before it, / and as he sees it he shivers and drives his flocks to a cavern." It has been said that "in the clear-cut comparisons in Homer, the feeling for Nature is profound; but the Homeric hero had no personal relations with her, no conscious leaning towards her; the descriptions only served to frame human action, in time and space."

If not the Homeric hero, then within the context of such "idylls" as the two we are considering, the figure and reactions of the shepherd (more exemplary of ordinary humanity than is the hero) serve to establish the specific value and the particular state of sensibility the description is meant to convey. Without denying a close relevance of the similes to the epic narrative and the object or idea that is meant to be compared, we can see that it is indeed the presence of the human figure in the comparisons that allows the latter to be isolable as independent esthetic units. Homer's shepherd and goatherd, then, "humanize" the landscape in which they appear, lending to it an interest and a relevance that would be lost without them. It is significant that in the **"Discorso,"** when Leopardi takes up the question of landscape painting, he claims that scenes of nature, however well executed they may be, will always leave us dissatisfied if they are without the presence of the human figure that somehow gives a fuller meaning to the scene. In **"La sera del dì di festa"** he is himself the dominant human figure.

Like Homer's herdsmen, Leopardi as a child had a great fear of the dark, and in his early *Saggio sopra gli errori popolari degli antichi* (1815) he included a chapter on nocturnal terrors. If, at the outset of **"La sera del dì di festa,"** the night seems "tender" (*Dolce*), it is because in the midst of a vast nocturnal calm, the moon gilds everything with a soft silvery light. In the **"Discorso,"** the emotion Leopardi attributed to Homer's beautiful night scene can be glossed by what he wrote as a boy at the opening of the chapter on the stars in the *Saggio sopra gli errori popolari degli antichi:* "Lo spettacolo di un cielo stellato colpisce *ogni uomo riflessivo.* Esso avrà forse sorpresi e gettati in *una dolce estasi i primi uomini.* Ma *il popolo* non è capace di *sentimenti delicati,* nè questi possono in lui durare assai lungo, quando l'oggetto che li risveglia è affatto ordinario nella natura." It is something of this mood or emotion of a *dolce estasi* that Leopardi seems to evoke in the opening of **"La sera,"** but for all the affective value that the first word, *Dolce,* may summon up, or because of it, one senses that in that poem the contemplator of the night is somewhat more meditative, indeed, more of an ''uomo riflessivo,'' than Homer's shepherd is before a similar scene. He is, in fact, what Homer's shepherd is not: a wistful, even a melancholy man. So too he is wiser (hence, sadder) and more chastened than the young Leopardi who a few years earlier (1816) had written—in Greek and in Latin—a fairly remarkable hymn to the moon.

The latter poem is the second of the two *Odae adespotae*, ''odi greche, supposte di Anacreonte o di qualche altro antico,'' published in 1817 in *Lo Spettatore* of Milan. In it the moon is praised for her silvery face and for her dominion over the silent night. Mistress or queen of the sky to whom the stars pay homage, she guides the white chariot and horses rising from the sea. When everywhere men are weary and keep silent, she travels across the heavens, alone and softly nocturnal, over mountains and tree tops, over rooftops, paths, and lakes, showering her clear light over all. Night thieves fear her when she looks out, but nightingales celebrate her the night through in summer, singing softly amid the dense boughs. She is welcome to wanderers when she rises from the waters, and she is loved even by the gods: supreme, revered and beautiful moon of the silver face.

Two things to be said of Leopardi's early hymn are that it makes use of a classicizing mythology and that it openly emphasizes the feminine and numinous quality of the moon. The classicizing bias of the adolescent Leopardi may also be seen in the note he affixed to his translation of an idyll attributed to Moscus. Here he praises an ode to the moon by Lady Mary Wortley Montagu for its ''Grecian'' character:

> Gemella di questo Idillio può sembrare la bella ode
> alla Luna di Milady Montaigu, che è veramente, come
> dice Algarotti, di atteggiamento greco. Eccola:

> Thou, silver Deity of secret Night,
> Direct my footsteps through the woodland shade;
> Thou conscious witness of unknown delight,
> The Lover's Guardian, and the Muse's aid.
> By thy pale beams I solitary rove:
> To thee my tender grief confide;
> Serenely sweet you gild the silent grove,
> My friend, my Goddess, and my guide.

It is worth noting, then, that the nocturnes of Homer's simile and Leopardi's **''La sera del dì di festa''** are free from any mythologizing, free indeed from excessive anthropomorphic (or animated) elements, although Leopardi felt the need of addressing the moon almost as a person. By way of contrast, and without seeking out an extreme case, one may think of these lines by Keats—from the *Ode to a Nightingale*—which are meant to evoke the same kind of night:

> Tender is the night,
> And haply the Queen-Moon is in her throne,
> Cluster'd around by all her starry Fays.

In Keat's poem these lines are in a proper enough context, as they would be in Leopardi's early ode in Greek and Latin. But except for the magic of the phrase ''Tender is the night,'' which is just slightly less ''pathetic'' than Leopardi's ''Dolce e chiara è la notte e senza vento,'' this is a manner which would ill become the poet of **''La sera del dì di festa.''**

But besides the examples from Lady Montague and Keats, it may also be useful to consider here a nocturnal address to the moon by an ''ancient'' bard, in verses that would seem to have in abundance the prerequisites that Leopardi demanded for the

evocation of the pathetic; a good example, one might say, of that poetry natural to ''primitive'' man that he had extolled in the **''Discorso.''** This is the address to the moon in Ossian's *Dartula* as translated by Cesarotti, that very Ossian who was heralded by many (Cesarotti and Blair among them) as being the supreme poet of the pathetic and the sublime:

> Figlia del ciel, sei bella; è di tua faccia
> Dolce il silenzio; amabile ti mostri
> E in oriente i tuoi cerulei passi
> Seguon le stelle; al tuo cospetto, o luna,
> Si rallegran le nubi, e 'l seno oscuro
> Riveston liete di leggiadra luce.
> Chi ti pareggia, o della notte figlia,
> Lassù nel cielo? In faccia tua le stelle
> Hanno di sè vergogna, e ad altra parte
> Volgono i glauchi scintillanti sguardi.
> Ma dimmi, o bella luce, ove t'ascondi
> Lasciando il corso tuo, quando svanisce
> La tua candida faccia? Hai tu, com'io
> L'ampie tue sale? O ad abitar ten vai
> Nell'ombra del dolor? Cadder dal cielo
> Le tue sorelle? o più non son coloro
> Che nella notte s'allegravan teco?
> Sì sì, luce leggiadra, essi son spenti,
> E tu spesso per piagnerli t'ascondi.
> Ma verrà notte ancor che tu, tu stessa
> Cadrai per sempre, e lascerai nel cielo
> Il tuo azzurro sentier; superbi allora
> Sorgeran gli astri; e in rimirarti avranno
> Gioia così, com'avean pria vergogna.

To this passage Cesarotti appended a note on Ossian's naïve but beautiful belief that nature was animated by tender sentiments that the bard felt in himself. It was his blessed ignorance that allowed him to create so ''touching'' a piece, for if he had known the physical or scientific causes of the moon's phases, he would have expounded a cold doctrine. Poetry draws infinitely more from an ''interesting illusion'' than from a cold truth. However, Cesarotti counsels us, we must distinguish between illusion and absurdity.

Such a comment must have been greatly appreciated by Leopardi, and makes it all the more significant that in the **''Discorso''** he did not choose this or any like passage to represent the pathetic among the ancients. Not only are the Homeric and Virgilian passages he did choose free from all such anthropomorphism or personification of the moon and the stars, but, save for an occasional and unobtrusive allusion, his own major poetry is free from it. For he who in the 1818 **''Discorso''** had defended the use of the ancient myths in modern poetry had by 1820 ruled out that possibility for himself at least.

The truth is that already in the **''Discorso''** Leopardi warned that modern poets should make only a judicious and sparing use of the ancient myths, and even then only if the myths had been assimilated and somehow made one's own, a view that excludes not only abuse and indiscriminate appropriation but also a merely decorative implementation: ''Le favole greche sono ritrovamenti arbitrari, per la più parte bellissime dolcissime squisitissime, fabbricate come ho detto sulla natura, non naturali; perciò non sono comuni agli antichi con noi, ma proprio loro: non dobbiamo usurpare le immaginazioni altrui, quando o non le facciamo nostre in qualche maniera, o non ce ne serviamo parcamente.''

From the earliest (*Saggio sopra gli errori popolari degli antichi*), despite his attraction to the mythologized moon . . . and to the age of fable in general, Leopardi knew full well that such a poetry was no longer possible and that it could only be lamented as a lost beatitude. So it is that in **"Alla primavera"** (with its significant subtitle (**Delle favole antiche**) he nostalgically recalls that happy time in the history of mankind which was the childhood of the race, when one could think of the moon (''Ciprigna luce'') as a friendly and solicitous (''pensosa'') female companion to the traveler who gazed intently upon her chaste nudity while making his way over hills and dales in an otherwise lonely night:

> Ignuda
> Te per le piagge e i colli,
> Ciprigna luce, alla deserta notte
> Con gli occhi intenti il viator seguendo,
> Te compagna alla via, te de' mortali
> Pensosa immaginò.

The irremediable loss of that vision is accentuated by the finality of the past absolute *immaginò*. Unlike Foscolo, Keats, Shelley, and other Romantics, Leopardi did not attempt to revitalize the ancient myths. One wonders what this poet of the moon might have done with Diana and Endymion. But quite significantly, and with perfect coherence, the ancient fable he was most tempted to utilize is that of Psyche and Eros in whose story he saw a myth commensurate with and anticipatory of the true history of mankind and the human condition in the present. It was another version of the fall of man from the grace of ignorance. . . . (pp. 122-28)

It is true, of course that in his poetry the moon is at times addressed or appealed to as though it were a feminine confidante or witness to the poet's sorrow, but her virginal silence bespeaks Leopardi's basic skepticism as well as his anguish in the face of a beautiful but indifferent (when not cruel) nature.

And yet the intellectual knowledge that the moon is a lifeless satellite did not wholly keep Leopardi from experiencing what Mircea Eliade [in *Patterns in Comparative Religion*] calls the ''hierophanies'' of the moon. Eliade's remarks are so well suited to the case of Leopardi that they will not be out of place here:

> The orientation of intellectual activity from Aristotle onwards has done much to blunt our receptiveness towards the totality of sun hierophanies. What has happened in the case of the moon proves that this new intellectual orientation does not necessarily make the experience of the heirophany in itself impossible. No one, indeed, would maintain that a modern was *ipso facto* closed to the hierophanies of the moon. On the contrary, we can see as clearly as primitives how the symbols, myths and rites connected with the moon fit together. Perhaps the fact that the mentalities of the ''primitive'' and the ''modern'' respond so similarly to the sort of sacredness expressed by the moon can be explained by the *survival even in the most totally rationalist outlook* of what has been called ''the nocturnal domain of the mind.''. . . The moon would be appealing to a layer of man's consciousness that the most corrosive rationalism cannot touch.

Even in his disenchantment with truth, and despite his espousal of the rationalist's philosophy, Leopardi's relationship with the moon or night is one that often suggests an arcane if not a numinous quality about it. In **"La vita solitaria"** he announces that in his deepest despair the moon, ''*benigna* / Delle notti *reina*'' as he addresses her with a passing bow to ancient mythology, will be forever gentle to him, revealing to his eyes smiling hills and vast fields with her power of transfiguring the poet's familiar landscape. He will forever praise her, whether

she appears among clouds or in a clear sky; and she will witness his solitary nocturnal life. . . . (pp. 128-30)

But how deeply and persistently the magic of the moon worked its spell on Leopardi is best seen by comparing again the first and final versions of the opening of **"La sera del dì di festa."** It can be said that even in his disenchantment with truth, and despite his espousal of the rationalist's philosophy, Leopardi's reaction to the moon reveals a need to make of it (almost) a person rather than an object. The early version—with *Dolce* already replacing the original *Oimè*—reads:

> Dolce e chiara è la notte e senza vento
> E queta in mezzo agli orti e in cima ai tetti
> La luna si riposa, e le montagne
> Si discopron da lungi.

Here are all the elements that were to make up the final draft of the scene, but save for the first line, little of the latter's spell:

> Dolce e chiara è la notte e senza vento,
> E queta sovra i tetti e in mezzo agli orti
> Posa la luna, e di lontan rivela
> Serena ogni montagna.

Critics have been right to note the importance of the change in the order of the second line, and the still more crucial change in the third line from the heavy and somewhat opaque ''La luna si riposa'' to ''Posa la luna.'' For ''posa'' bespeaks a softer *pausing* than does the reflexive form in ''si riposa'' which creates too much of an anthropomorphized value and the impression of a plumping down. ''Posa(re)'' fixes the moon in a picture-like immobility, but at the same time, also allows us to think of it as actively but softly laying its light upon the rooftops and in the orchards.

Contributing to this, indeed, essential to it, is the new position of ''luna'' whereby it acquires greater prominence and significance. In the earlier lines 2-4, the moon is not really the radiating center of the scene. It is not even the only grammatical subject; the distant mountains reveal themselves, as it were— ''le montagne / Si discopron da lungi.'' Thus the original version had two subjects and two reflexive verbs, both of the latter happily eliminated by the changes made. By virtue of its strategic syntactical position in the poem's definitive form, the moon triumphs as the sole active subject, so that besides pausing in the sky whence it illuminates the village scene, *it* also *reveals* the far-off peaks, a function not attributable to it as long as it was bound to the verb ''si riposa.'' The moon, in short, has now become the unifying factor of the several elements of the scene, including, of course, the generic impression of the night's tender clarity announced in the first line.

But not the least important change to have taken place is the introduction of *serena*, a word whose importance is second to none in our poet's lexicon. As with ''la luna,'' its occurrence here attests to the critical nature of the collocation as well as of the choice of words in Leopardi, for the creation of both those supremely Leopardian poetic values of rhythm and semantic richness. The position of *serena* not only allows it to be referable to ''ogni montagna''—in which case we understand it to mean chiefly the clarity in which the mountains appear—but also makes it predicable of ''la luna,'' the moon itself in connection with the activity of revealing (i.e., illuminating), in which case the word is felt in its value of *serene(ly)* or *soft(ly)*, or, if we prefer, *tender(ly)*. Thus the last attribute—*serena*—confirms the initial attribute—*dolce*. It is not simply that the mountains are ''serene,'' that is, clearly discernible. The whole landscape shares in this quality of the serene, in the "tenderness" that is bestowed by the night or, more specifically, by the moon.

This reading can be supported by two Leopardian passages . . . , both of them having import for **"La sera del dì di festa."** One is the annotation that preannounces the poem's exordium: "veduta notturna colla luna a ciel *sereno* dall'alto della mia casa tal quale alla similitudine di Omero." The other occurs in the **"Discorso"** of 1818 and is directly connected with the Homeric simile therein translated by Leopardi: "Una notte *serena* e chiara e silenziosa, illuminata dalla luna, non è uno spettacolo sentimentale? Senza fallo." Here we need but substitute *dolce* for *serena* and we almost have the first words of **"La sera"**—"Dolce e chiara è la notte." Indeed, *sereno* and *dolce* are semantically equivalent in Leopardi, at least in affective value.

So too in the brief prose passage it is the entire expanse of the night scene that is said to be *silenziosa*. And in the poem the adjective *queta*, which is grammatically connected with the moon *(luna)*, is a quality applicable to the whole moonlit landscape. There is no reason then to limit such a key Leopardian word as *serena* to one alone of its possible referents and functions. The moon of **"La sera del dì di festa"** is *serenely*, that is, *sweetly* or *benignly* active (for others, if not entirely so for the poet-lover who is nonetheless not entirely free from its charm: "questo ciel, che sì benigno / Appare in vista, a salutar m'affaccio") in a manner that is not unlike that of the moon that shines "serenely sweet" in those verses by Lady Montagu that Leopardi had already praised for their "Grecian" quality:

> Thou, silver Deity of secret night,
>
> . . . . .
>
> *Serenely sweet you gild the silent grove.*

The line, I am sure, had an influence in the fashioning of the final version of **"La sera"**'s opening nocturne and in the use therein of both *dolce* and *serena*.

Leopardi's moon is, like the moon of Wordsworth's *The Excursion*, "ample"; and with like effect it seems almost to transform things into its own substance, thanks to its "power / Capacious and serene." But in his poem, the Italian poet reveals no Wordsworthian conviction that a "Like power abides / In man's celestial spirit."

The plaintive meditation of the **"Canto notturno di un pastore errante dell' Asia"** is particularly relevant at this point, for here is a solitary Leopardian shepherd who is indeed an "uomo riflessivo" gazing on the same (or a similar) night scene that Homer's shepherd beheld. Unlike Homer's shepherd who is gladdened by the brightness of a moonlit and starry night, Leopardi's reflective shepherd feels not a "dolce estasi" but a metaphysical anguish as he gazes up at the silent moon, at the stars, and into that deep, clear, infinite-like nocturnal sky:

> Spesso quand'io ti miro
> Star così muta in sul deserto piano,
> Che, in suo giro lontano, al ciel confina;
>
> . . . . .
>
> E quando miro in cielo arder le stelle,
> Dico fra me pensando:
> A che tante facelle?
> Che fa l'aria infinita, e quel profondo
> Infinito seren? che vuol dir questa
> Solitudine immensa? ed io chi sono?

The undercurrent of irony implicit in much of Leopardi's poetry is basic to the **"Canto notturno."** Contrary to what is usually held to be true of the pastoral life (in the tradition of pastoral and Arcadian poetry), Leopardi's nomadic shepherd does not lead an existence that is in harmony or in communion with nature and his flock. On the contrary, he knows and feels himself to be alien from both. How un-Wordsworthian then are his words and his situation. And how different is this shepherd from Homer's. How different is he also from that other Leopardian shepherd (a daytime shepherd) of the poem **"Alla primavera,"** nostalgically evoked in an Arcadian landscape and in a time—the Golden Age—when illusions were not yet rudely blasted by arid truth:

> Già di candide ninfe i rivi albergo,
> Placido albergo e specchio
> Furo i liquidi fonti. Arcane danze
> D'immortal piede i ruinosi gioghi
> Scossero e l'ardue selve (oggi romito
> Nido de' venti); e il pastorel ch'all'ombre
> Meridiane incerte ed al fiorito
> Margo adducea de' fiumi
> Le sitibonde agnelle, arguto carme
> Sonar d'agresti Pani
> Udì lungo le ripe; e tremar l'onda
> Vide, e stupì, che non palese al guardo
> La faretrata Diva
> Scendea ne' caldi flutti, e dall'immonda
> Polve tergea della sanguigna caccia
> Il niveo lato e le verginee braccia.

The immense starry vault of the heavens could assure Kant of an inner sublimity of a moral order. And among the many who used the argument by design was Cesarotti who went from ecstasy to ecstasy in passing from the wondrous makeup of the celestial bodies to their Author. . . . (pp. 130-34)

Leopardi, because of his philosophical beliefs, could not join with the great chorus hymning this faith. We also know that Leopardi felt and expressed that at times enthralling and at times "serening" effects of a bright, clear, nocturnal sky. But concerning what is perhaps more characteristic of him, the poetry of the nocturnal sublime and the sense of man's anguished isolation in the immensity, if not the infinity, of the universe merge into one supreme manner in various moments of his work, most notably (restricting ourselves to the poetry) in **"La sera del dì di festa,"** the **"Canto notturno,"** and lines 158-185 of **"La ginestra"** (1836).

The latter passage takes us . . . to the pronouncement in the *Zibaldone* on August 12, 1823, regarding man's miniscule presence in the incredible, incomprehensible vastitude of existence, except that now, as in the **"Canto notturno,"** the feeling of man's greatness in being able to contain this vastness within the mind gives way to an embittered sense of the meaninglessness and total nullity of man's existence:

> Sovente in queste rive,
> Che, desolate, a bruno
> Veste il flutto indurato, e par che ondeggi,
> Seggo la notte; e su la mesta landa
> In purissimo azzurro
> Veggo dall'alto fiammeggiar le stelle,
> Cui di lontan fa specchio
> Il mare, e tutto di scintille in giro
> Per lo vóto seren brillare il mondo.
> E poi che gli occhi a quelle luci appunto,
> Ch'a lor sembrano un punto,
> E sono immense, in guisa
> Che un punto a petto a lor son terra e mare

Veracemente; a cui
L'uomo non pur, ma questo
Globo ove l'uomo è nulla,
Sconosciuto è del tutto; e quando miro
Quegli ancor più senz'alcun fin remoti
Nodi quasi di stelle,
Ch'a noi paion qual nebbia, a cui non l'uomo
E non la terra sol, ma tutte in uno,
Del numero infinite e della mole,
Con l'aureo sole insiem, le nostre stelle
O sono ignote, o così paion come
Essi alla terra, un punto
Di luce nebulosa; al pensier mio
Che sembri allora, o prole
Dell'uomo?

As with **"La sera del dì di festa"** and **"Canto notturno,"** this is another moment in which the vast, which we have heard Leopardi often acclaim because it produces a pleasurable, an elevating, or even a serening idea-sensation, appears as something more like the dread abyss of nothingness that threatens to engulf us. (pp. 134-35)

[Leopardi] was tormented by the belief that infinity applied to nothing other than nothingness itself. Nonetheless, there is something of grandeur and sublimity in **"La ginestra"**; nor is it in those lines where, in describing the vast destruction wreaked on man and his world by the eruption of Vesuvius, Leopardi used a sort of manner of the sublime—the sublime of the terrible and of power—in order to indicate the fierce enmity of nature toward man. (p. 136)

In **"La ginestra,"** where man's presumptuousness is scourged equally by nature and the poet's uncompromising rationalism, we can yet acknowledge in Leopardi something other than a dejection or a sense of self-disparagement born of the knowledge of man's absolute nullity in the scheme of the universe: The sublimity or grandeur of the soul willing to unmask and gaze upon the naked truth of the human condition no matter how humiliating it may prove to be:

> Nobil natura è quella
> Che a sollevar s'ardisce
> Gli occhi mortali incontra
> Al comun fato, e che con franca lingua,
> Nulla al ver detraendo,
> Confessa il mal che ci fu dato in sorte.

Our night thoughts, however, must conclude, as did our poet's, with what was perhaps his last poem—**"Il tramonto della luna."** It is a poem which opens with a description whose length and detail are unusual in Leopardi. It is as though the poet were delaying as long as he could the setting of the moon and, in the figure of his waggoner, bidding it farewell in much the same way that, in Foscolo's poem *Dei sepolcri*, the dying are said to send their last sigh towards the fading light of the sun. For here, no less than the setting sun of **"La quiete dopo la tempesta,"** the moon's sinking behind the mountains or into the sea symbolizes the unredeemable passing of youth, of hope, and of those fortunate errors (i.e., illusions) that alone made life, in the time of childhood, "meaningful" and happy:

> Quale in notte solinga,
> Sovra campagne inargentate ed acque,
> Là 've zefiro aleggia,
> E mille vaghi aspetti
> E ingannevoli obbietti
> Fingon l'ombre lontane
> Infra l'onde tranquille
> E rami e siepi e collinette e ville;

Giunta al confin del cielo,
Dietro Apennino od Alpe, o del Tirreno
Nell'infinito seno
Scende la luna; e si scolora il mondo;
Spariscon l'ombre, ed una
Oscurità la valle e il monte imbruna;
Orba la notte resta,
E cantando, con mesta melodia,
L'estremo albor della fuggente luce,
Che dianzi gli fu duce,
Saluta il carrettier dalla sua via;
    Tal si dilegua, e tale
Lascia l'età mortale
La giovinezza.

But now the poet's own passing merged with his vision of the death of youth. And while the poem, particularly the first part, is not as weak (relative to his best poems) as some critics would have us think, this knowledge surely contributes to the pathos it evokes in us. (pp. 136-38)

> *Nicolas James Perella, in his* Night and the Sublime
> in Giacomo Leopardi, *University of California Press,*
> *1970, 151 p.*

ERNESTO G. CASERTA   (essay date 1976)

[*Caserta discusses* Paralipomeni della batracomiomachia (The War of the Mice and the Crabs), *identifying some of Leopardi's sources and explicating the satire.*]

The ***Paralipomeni della Batracomiomachia*** is Giacomo Leopardi's longest poem. Composed after the ***Canti*** and the ***Operette morali***, between 1830 and 1837, and for the most part during his residence in Naples, the work was first published in Paris in 1842, but until recent years it has enjoyed little favor among scholars due to various prejudices both moral and aesthetic. (p. 13)

Leopardi called his poem the "Paralipomena" ("Additions") of the *Batrachomyomachia* apparently because he wanted to continue the narration of the battle between the frogs and the mice of the homonymous pseudo-Homeric poem, *Batrachomyomachia*, which he had translated into Italian three times (1816, 1821, 1826). His poem, in fact, starts just where the Homeric poem ends, with the defeat of the mice caused by the intervention of the crabs, sent by Jupiter, who along with the other gods did not want the total extermination of the frogs. Leopardi relates this futile battle of mice, frogs, and crabs to the revolutionary movements of the Italians (especially those which took place in 1820-21 and in 1830-31) against the Austrians. The Italians would be the poor mice defeated by the crabs, the Austrians, described in their brutal strength and rough manners.

Besides the pseudo-Homeric *Batrachomyomachia*, which was undoubtedly a primary source and at the same time a model to emulate, Leopardi may have had in mind the *Animali parlanti* of Giambattista Casti and, in the opinion of some critics (e.g., Moroncini), Byron's *Don Juan* or *The Age of Bronze*, which is full of political allusions. The Dog, the liberal minister of the king in the *Animali parlanti*, looks like Leccafondi (Bottom-Licker) in the ***Paralipomeni***, and in both works the government, the populace, and the intrigues and cunning of the courtiers are ridiculed. In both works we find two stanzas in which virtue is exalted, the description of the prehistoric world and references to the legendary island of Atlantis, as well as the abrupt end of the narration with the pretext of the loss of the manuscript.

The *Paralipomeni* have in common with *Don Juan* the contempt for despotism (an attitude which Leopardi inherited more directly from the theater of Alfieri and from the patriotic poetry of the early Risorgimento), several digressions on philosophical, religious, and moral issues, and especially the disdain for newspapers, statistics, and political economy. In addition, the episode of the heroic deaths of the old Turk and his children before the victorious enemy is very similar to the heroic death of Rubatocchi (Chunk-Stealer). But these similarities are extrinsic and we know that the personality of Leopardi has very little in common with Byron's.

On the other hand, Leopardi knew so well the works of the ancient, medieval, and Renaissance fabulists that it would be impossible to determine precisely which sources, if any, were directly influential. Leopardi was a friend of Pietro Colletta and so we may assume that he was familiar with Colletta's *History of the Kingdom of Naples,* but even with respect to historic documents we wander in the dark since the poet may have gotten his material directly from the chronicles and newspapers of his day or from oral sources. In some characters, like Boccaferrata (Ironed-Mouth) and Camminatorto (Crooked-Walker), we find the same spirit that animated a number of contemporary journals, such as the *Voce della verità* and the *Voce della ragione.* (pp. 18-19)

Externally the *Paralipomeni* are a political satire of the Carbonari and in particular of the Neapolitan patriots, always optimistic when they were in the piazzas and open-air cafés but ready to run at the first sight of the enemy. However, the scope of the satire is much broader, including not only the Austrians (the crabs), described as barbarians, and Hegelian idealism, but the entire cultural trend of the century. To Leopardi the Italians seemed ridiculous in the way they carried out their conspiracies, with their superficial manifestations of warlike fierceness (thick mustaches and long sideburns), with their oratory and self-exaltation, because they fled at the very appearance of the dust raised by the marching enemy troops. They were daydreamers because they were hoping to receive foreign military assistance and did not realize that unless they helped themselves, unless they stopped being children and became men, foreigners would not only have contempt for them but would be ready and willing to subjugate them.

Although the political satire constitutes the dominant motive of the *Paralipomeni* it is not the only one, and many critics, racking their brains to establish precise historical allusions beneath each character and event of the narration, have, on account of this unilateral reading, missed the real poetic significance of the work. It is not our intention here to document with exact historical references every incident of the war between the mice and the crabs because we are convinced that such precise documentation would be of little value in appreciating the poem. Let it suffice to say that the poet had in mind the Neapolitan revolution of 1820-21 and those which took place in Europe and Italy in 1830-31. In the flight of the mice, described in Canto I, we can recognize the defeat of Guglielmo Pepe at Androdoco, and the general himself in Rubatocchi (Chunk-Stealer), who leads the troops to safety; but some scholars have suggested other personalities, for example Joachim Murat, whose retreat after defeat by the Austrians at Tolentino (May 2 and 3, 1815) was well known to Leopardi, since pillaging occurred around his home town. Brancaforte (Strong-Claw) is commonly identified with Marshal Bianchi, who defeated Murat, while Camminatorto (Crooked-Walker) and Brancaforte (Ironed-Mouth) have suggested to many critics the name of the shrewd

and cunning Metternich. Senzacapo (Without-Head) resembles a lot Emperor Francis I, who also liked to play the violin. Rodipane (Bread-Muncher) calls to mind King Ferdinand I of Naples, but Louis-Philippe has also been mentioned. Personifying the philosophy of history, optimism, and idealism, Daedalus may be identified with Jean-Jacques Rousseau or some German idealist. Assaggiatore (Taster), according to the most common interpretation, is the author himself.

More than a caricature of a limited group of political figures, however, Leopardi intended to give his answer to all the would-be heroes and false ideas of his time. Various historical personages are filtered through the poet's imagination and acquire their own particular identity within the poem. How ridiculous, in fact, the behavior of Leccafondi (Count Bottom-Licker)! We no longer think about the Prince of Canosa, Capponi, or Mazzini, but only about Leccafondi, the typical daydreamer, naive and superficial, as he was felt and portrayed by the poet.

Leopardi, who said that "the world is a league of scoundrels against true gentlemen, of cowards against generous people" *(Pensieri),* had no illusions concerning the success of the secret societies of the Risorgimento. There was always too great a discrepancy between what he wanted and what he thought to be historically feasible for him to hope for the social and political regeneration of mankind. Leopardi's unwavering skepticism and despair before the course of human events could not but give rise to the ironic overtones and the sense of the ridiculous which prevail in the *Paralipomeni.* The poet laughs at these new heroes who speak with so much eloquence and enthusiasm, who plan military strategies and social and political reforms from the balconies, yet face to face with the enemy tremble like leaves and flee like the wind. He ridicules all of the idealists and political visionaries who prefer to live in a dream and ignore the truth.

No one is spared the poet's ridicule, certainly not the journalists, who act like the prophets and benefactors of mankind with their predictions of progress and future prosperity, nor those who voraciously read such rubbish and base their lives upon it. And not surprisingly the populace is the object of Leopardi's laughter, screaming like a herd, "Long live the Charter! Long live Bread-Muncher!" for the royal favor of some cheese and polenta.

The satirist launches out against the prominent political theorists of the time, who after the Restoration and the establishment of the Holy Alliance spoke of European balance of power and royal successions as if they were the executors of God's will, while in practice they resorted to the law of the jungle, using force in the most brutal manner against the helpless and poor nations. The satire is particularly virulent against the absolute power of the Austrians (the crabs), who with their strongly repressive methods destroyed all semblance of freedom and human dignity. More than once Leopardi expresses his great aversion to the Austrians, calling them "an army of greedy and strange brutes," "people without brains," and very often he alludes to their ignorance, saying that education and the arts "are not dear to those countries."

Although Leopardi never explicitly formulated a political ideology, it can be said with certitude that he no longer adhered to the views of his father, Monaldo, the conservative author of the *Dialoghetti,* who favored the papal hegemony. He gives only marginal importance in the poem to the frogs, considered by some scholars to represent the army and the politics of the

Pope, and links them with the miserable destiny of the mice or even worse.

The poet's harsh invectives against foreign invaders as well as those who would debase or destroy Italy from within derived from his intense love for his country and her highly civilized traditions. To Leopardi, who firmly believed that the original human state was savage and that civilization is the gradual and heroic conquest of Humanity, the naturalistic optimism of a Rousseau and the idealism of his contemporaries seemed not only absurd but dangerous. Such a doctrine could lead mankind back to barbarism, causing it to slip from a level of culture attained by so much effort.

Describing the total indifference of the dead souls before the questions of Leccafondi, Leopardi demonstrates the futility of concerning oneself with the hereafter. In this last period he thus defined to his friend Ranieri his intellectual materialism: the thinking principle is nothing else but matter, the ideas of the soul, of immortality, of an all-providing God, etc., are deliriums of the human mind, and Nature rather than friendly to man is his principal executioner. Having lost his faith in God, Leopardi was left with only his faith in human potential, in a culture which has been tested by millenary experience and which must be conquered anew by the heroic effort, both individual and collective, of each succeeding generation. His contemporaries, instead, were preaching easy ways out, creating an illusory world which could only bring more disappointment and despair.

Leopardi's satiric attitude had its source in his detachment from others, in his refusal to espouse the ideals of his time and to adhere enthusiastically to what was going on around him. Anxious to discover the very meaning of human life, he perceived other men too attached to the materialistic and practical concerns of daily living. Preoccupied with the absolute and the universal, he found others too wrapped-up in their own immediate self-interest. He could only laugh at Man, who despite the discovery of Copernicus and the cruel evidence of Vesuvius, continued to view himself as the center of the universe, as a creature with special privileges enjoying a destiny superior to that of any other animal under the sun and favored by God with so many gifts on earth and even in heaven. The whole description of the underworld of the animals located on the fabulous island of Atlantis is a flavorful satire of human pride and man's radicated belief in his own immortality.

In the tradition of Aesop and Phaedrus, Leopardi portrayed human beings as animals, for example in the **"Dialogo di un cavallo e di un bue"** (**"Dialogue between a Horse and an Ox"**), in which a parallel is drawn between people and animals, which, after they have been fattened, are slaughtered. But by now it should be clear that the poet's reduction of man to animal form and proportion was not the simple adoption of a popular literary device. The form was a natural one for Leopardi, in whose opinion man behaves not too differently from the lower animals, like mice, crabs, frogs, birds, and fish, concerned with his own needs and resorting without pity to the law of the jungle. Like mice, men are ready to adjust to no matter what form of life or government in order to eat. Cheese and polenta were the true ideals of the majority of the mice, the rest was only rhetoric. And the crabs, endowed with the strength of their shells, were with great ferocity imposing their barbarism on the mice in the name of law and order. Leopardi saw the men of his century behaving no better than mice and crabs, yet preaching human progress and utopia, a new paradise on earth as well as in heaven. He felt instead that unless man

becomes truly civilized through a continuous endeavor to rise above his bestial instincts, unless he is willing to accept his modest place on earth and respect the dignity of his fellow men, he will either bring about the extermination of his race, as the mice were about to exterminate the frogs, or he will act as brutally as the crabs, chopping off limbs in order to maintain the so-called balance of power.

The satiric tone of the *Paralipomeni* is accompanied and at times overwhelmed by the poet's desolation before the wretchedness of the human condition. The utter vanity of the war of the mice against the crustaceans reflects this disheartened attitude of the poet towards humanity, doomed to a blind and painful existence. In the figure of Daedalus, the only human being in the animal epic, we may perceive very clearly the anguish of mankind. Disgusted by the superficiality of his fellow men, Daedalus prefers to live alone, and he prefers the languages of the animals to human dialogue. More than representing Rousseau, as Boffito has suggested, Daedalus personifies many of the ideas and feelings of Leopardi himself. In his visit to the underworld, we may well see that Daedalus, like the poet, preferred the world of the dead to the world of the living, which can have meaning only if there is mutual understanding and fraternal collaboration.

In the poetry of his youth Leopardi sang of his personal sorrow before the gradual vanishing of his "speranze" and his "ameni inganni." Now in his maturity he chants the miserable destiny of the whole of mankind blindly in search of an illusory progress. The individual sadness that permeated the lyrics of his youth has been universalized, and in the satire of the reactionary crabs and the liberal mice lives an awareness of a deeper and more virile drama, whose terms surpass the easy optimism and humanitarianism of Leopardi's contemporaries as well as of the "new believers" of any age. (pp. 24-9)

> *Ernesto G. Caserta, in an introduction to* The War of the Mice and the Crabs *by Giacomo Leopardi, translated by Ernesto G. Caserta, U.N.C. Department of Romance Languages, 1976, pp. 13-29.*

OTTAVIO M. CASALE (essay date 1981)

[*In this excerpt, drawn from Casale's introduction to a selection of Leopardi's works in English translation, the critic considers the importance of language to Leopardi; his critical standing; the growth of his philosophical system in relation to the development of his art; his view of the imagination; and finally, the reasons for his appeal and continuing relevance.*]

Giacomo Leopardi was one for whom words were special, primal, and chaste. In a life which reads like a devastating textbook on alienation, words were the instruments for reaching out, for tracing truth, creating beauty, affirming love, trying to touch other people, other times. And if no one else were listening, which was most of the time, he wrote to and for himself.

The urgency of Leopardi's desire to express is understandable. His body hunched and ruined by illness ("a walking sepulchre," as he phrased it), he knew early that the life of heroic action preferred by him and led by many of his cherished Greeks was out of the question. Indeed, a normal social existence including sexual love, marriage, and children was not possible. Words were a way to break through these limitations and those imposed by his parents' house, his parents' provincial town, the "abhorred" Recanati, and, worst of all, his parents' ideas. Besides the prisons of Leopardi's body, birthplace, and intellectual environment, there is another fact with implications for his expression: he denied to himself belief in God or any other comforting numinous reality, and he evolved as exclusively a humanistic and skeptical worldview as we encounter in the history of letters. This rejection may have taken a deep psychological toll of one who had been groomed to be defender of the faith (it certainly affected his reputation), but it also contributes to the deep and vulnerable humanity of his utterance. We see everywhere in Leopardi—explicit or implicit, direct or paradoxical—the importance of humans, their kinship, and their discourse; and this is so despite Leopardi's own frequent arguments to the contrary. Denied supernal aid, as he felt, he reaches out for humans, to learn from and teach, to feed off and to feed. (p. 3)

When at the age of twenty-four he finally escaped Recanati for a few months at Rome, he was bitterly disappointed by the intellectual vacuum he found there, only to revive at discovering the learned German philologer-diplomats Niebuhr and Bunsen. The letters especially reveal the need for emotional and intellectual contact. Leopardi usually initiates a correspondence; he keeps track of answers and often asks explicit questions to insure response; and he always tries to answer promptly, even lengthily, himself. If his closest siblings, Carlo and Paolina, fail to write, he scolds them. Above all, when the correspondent leans psychologically on him, he temporarily suspends his own problems and tailors the topics and tone to the correspondent's needs.

Perhaps more impressive than Leopardi's words aimed at immediate communication, however, are those devoted to expressing himself to or about inert or distant realities, which come alive and close through his attention. Much of this utterance is melancholy, but undeniably he took pleasure in his solitary reading and writing. Leopardi had the literary intellectual's bent of being fascinated by linguistic facts, poetic and philological relationships, and sociological and philosophical connections, and he squirreled away his notations in a notebook for future use. The number of allusions in the *Zibaldone* to literatures and languages is in itself staggering. What is even more striking is that the erudition is in no way postured (as in Poe, for example). Rather it seems a vital outreaching for nutrition badly needed and for an objective world providing health and continuity to a mind worried over the precariousness of both. During the moments when Leopardi waited for a manuscript page to dry, it is said he would memorize the definition of one or two English or German words so as not to waste time. Even when he saw almost no personal future before him, he was projecting a *Letter to a Young Man of the Twentieth Century*. A good deal of the enormous amount of writing he did was obviously on deposit for his own future use and ours, but just as clearly he wrote to express a hermetic journey of the mind, a journey wherein the *process* of mind itself was as important as the discoveries made, the points achieved.

Nowhere is the hermetic aspect of Leopardi's commentary seen more sharply than in the poems, where he created an existential landscape all his own. Even the despairing conclusions of the dialogues in the *Operette Morali* seem tempered by the fact of conversation between humans or their surrogates. The poems, however, are loneliness made palpable. The poetic voice is variously that of a lone, alienated historical figure (Brutus, Sappho), an almost mythical spokesman for grieved humanity (the wandering shepherd of Asia), or the poet himself remembering former happiness and lamenting current or timeless fate (the speaker of **"To Spring," "To Sylvia,"** or **"Memories"**).

The entities addressed do not answer. They are usually mute forces or things in or behind the cosmos: nature, fate, the moon, the stars, a flock. If Leopardi does address individual humans, it is the departed Sylvia or Nerina (even the names indicate their unreality), symbols of his and perhaps everyman's lost vibrant youth. And, of course, there is the poem with the most barren landscape of all, **"To Himself."** It is not only *"la donna che non si trova"* in these works, it is basic human contact we miss. If it were not for the exquisite language, the desire implied, and the beauty craved, these would be stark experiences indeed.

Leopardi expressed himself well enough to be considered one of the eminent writers in western literature (except possibly in our United States, where language barriers seem higher than elsewhere). Even if we were to set to one side his countrymen's opinion, which generally places him, with Tasso, Petrarch, and a few others, second only to Dante in the Italian tradition, there is the admiration of the greats from other lands. Sainte-Beuve seemed awed equally by the erudition and the art Leopardi displayed. Nietzsche was taken by the prose, estimating Leopardi one of the four great prose writers of the nineteenth century, along with Emerson, Merimée, and Landor [see Additional Bibliography]. George Santayana, while acknowledging (as one must) that Leopardi's vision was narrowed by suffering, said of the poetry, "Long passages are fit to repeat in lieu of prayers through all the watches of the night" [see excerpt dated 1935]. Matthew Arnold, that arbiter of touchstones, thought Leopardi one of the very greatest "modern" poets and compared him with Goethe, Wordsworth, and Byron [see Additional Bibliography]. Schopenhauer, naturally enough, thrilled to the pessimism, bemoaning the fact that he and Leopardi never met.

But the opinions of the great cannot make or keep a writer great. That prize can only be conferred by numberless readers over time, each confronting the literature on his own. In the confrontation with Leopardi, a problem instantly arises: how do we deal with the explicit pessimism or melancholy? The question is especially important to Anglo-American readers habituated for centuries to aggressively optimistic writing. And the issue is aggravated when the reader is at the mercy of translations of the poetry, when inevitably the bare idea communicates much more sharply than other poetic values. Consider how we might react to Keats's great opening line, "When I have fears that I may cease to be," if we were reading it for the first time in a translation beginning, "Every time I think I might not live long. . . ." There are other questions too. How much of Leopardi's darkest substance has universal, objective force, and how much should we ascribe to individual and therefore untypical woe? (He himself was paradoxical on the issue, resenting the *ad-hominem* equation but also admitting to his Tuscan friends that with his poems he sought "to consecrate my pain.") And how do we explain the seeming anomaly of a writer whose style sometimes approaches the sublimity traditionally associated with the most enraptured religious vision but which is linked in Leopardi to death, transcience, and negation? After all, we expect our Miltons to be Miltons and our Jobs Jobs.

At the start of an essay on Leopardi, Francesco De Sanctis said, "Everyone forms his own God; and everyone forms his own Woman." We can add that every reader forms his own Leopardi, approving or not, being moved or unmoved, fascinated or bemused, selective and even censoring, according to the different aesthetic and metaphysical tastes of the reader and his times and even according to the texts available. For example, whereas the publication of the complete letters generally invigorated interest in Leopardi, Croce admitted to being depressed at looking into what he saw as the personal workshop of a poetry he had thought objective [see excerpt dated 1923]. The history of Leopardi's reputation is almost unique for the extent to which commentators reveal as much or more about themselves as they do about their subject. The relativist Leopardi might have shrugged his shoulders at the fluctuating spectacle.

Frequently, readers with a cause, religious or secular, theistic or atheistic, have simplified Leopardi and then discussed, rejected, or accepted their image whole. In addition to Schopenhauer, the English poet James Thomson, the author of "The City of Dreadful Night," admired the pessimism and devoted months of his life to learning Italian so as to translate the **Operette Morali**. The patriot Giuseppe Mazzini, on the other hand, bent on carving out a new Italy and world, relegated Leopardi to the school of backward-looking classicists and aesthetes of no use to the struggle for nation and brotherhood. The school of Lombrosian scholars in Italy accounted for Leopardi's darkness deterministically in terms of the physiological type to which he belonged. The most summary view of Leopardi, however, was probably that of his contemporary Niccolò Tommaseo, an ardent Catholic and also the scholarly annotator of a Cicero edition crisply dismantled by Leopardi. For Tommaseo, Leopardi was a little count who croaked like a frog, "There is no God because I am a hunchback, I am a hunchback because there is no God." (Hell hath no fury like that of a professor scorned.)

Perhaps the most tension-filled criticism of Leopardi is that of commentators excited by certain qualities and depressed by others. The complexity and paradoxes in Leopardi have bred their analogues in readers. The Italian biographer Ferretti, for example, agrees with Leopardi's priest friend, Vincenzo Gioberti, that Leopardi's denunciations paradoxically revealed his religious yearning, and says that Gioberti "understood the inner torment and the unconfessed need of God." At the other ideological pole, the Italian Marxist critic Cesare Luporini, made somewhat uncomfortable by the more despairing ideas of his author, argues that Leopardi was actually "vitalistic" and "progressive" in his vision for humanity. In a famous judgment, Croce found Leopardi's pessimism reprehensible, "a reasoned projection of his own unhappy state." To Croce, Leopardi was a great idyllic poet whose "pseudo-philosophy" vitiated many poems. (pp. 4-7)

In the building of his *sistema,* Leopardi drew nurture from his vast reading. From his study of ancient "superstitions," Leopardi learned to identify with the ancients; from reading ancient and modern rationalists and materialists in order to refute them knowledgeably, he grew to admire them. A mere listing of influences would take pages, as the **Zibaldone** index would show. Suffice to say that Leopardi's poetry and poetic theory owed much to Homer, Longinus, Virgil, Horace, Dante, Tasso, Petrarch, Burke and the English "graveyard poets," Alfieri, and Foscolo. Among the materialist or skeptical philosophers he respected deeply were Lucretius, Epictetus, Hobbes, Montaigne, Locke, Rousseau, Voltaire, Condillac, Chateaubriand, Helvétius, and d'Holbach. The tragic writings of Sophocles, Euripides, and of the authors of *Job* and *Ecclesiastes* played a part in his development, as did the speculations of Pascal, Vico, and Leopardi's beloved Madame de Staël. If one were forced to reduce this list to names of those who had the greatest impact on Leopardi's mind, one might choose Homer, Lucretius, Locke, Rousseau, and de Staël.

Like other romantics, Leopardi inherited the problem of belief, of "placing" man in a post-Cartesian universe where matter and spirit seemed at odds. The problem for Leopardi was probably exacerbated by personal factors. For figures like Blake, Coleridge, Emerson, and Shelley, the answer lay in differing versions of transcendental idealism which invested their worlds with benign spiritual presence and meaning. Even Poe, apparently such a materialist, held that the goal of poetry was supernal Beauty, and in his *Eureka* he outlined a cosmogony merging the physical and spiritual dimensions. As for Leopardi, many have attempted to idealize or spiritualize his meanings, but he himself attempted unblinkingly to create a system or mythos which would deliberately exclude the numinous. During and after his philosophical conversion, he embraces Locke and rejects absolutes: "There is hardly any absolute truth except that *All is relative*." And he self-consciously adopts the posture of Montaigne, asserting that "I by nature am not far from doubt even about things regarded undoubtable." With almost a dread of accepting supernal causation or facile explanations, no matter how attractive, Leopardi seeks to analyze man's practical and mental life in terms of a material cosmos. In a fallen world, with man uprooted and God gone or *"absconditus,"* as Pascal feared at times, Leopardi tries materially and systematically to justify the woes of man to men.

Such a task is not easy even for a great philosopher, which Leopardi was not, and the reader approaching Leopardi should arm himself with fruitful reservations about the ambiguities and tensions in the scheme at any point of Leopardi's development. In the first place, no system or program has ever accounted for the greatness of an artist, no matter how fond certain writers have been of their mythos. The riches and paradoxes of Yeats and Zola transcend gyres and chromosomes. With Leopardi, the philosophical ideas only begin to set up the impact of the art. Second, although for the sake of tidiness I will discuss the phases of Leopardi's thought, the truth is that for Leopardi almost no important idea or attitude is exclusive to one period; rather, a complex of attitudes bulges prominently in one phase of his life or another.

Leopardi's early system, heavily conditioned by Rousseau, is sometimes described as his "historical" pessimism because of the linear fall he ascribes to man, from a state of nature to one of civilization. In nature, man felt a unity with his cosmos, and though he was unhappy at times, nature supplied him with a rich imaginative life. The saving illusions granted to man tempered his pain sporadically, lifted him beyond self-love and self-immersion, fended off tedium and despair, and fulfilled his ingrained yearnings toward beauty, meaning, happiness, and the infinite. In the "denatured" or civilized condition, man has fallen into a world dominated by intellect, science, and truth, and he has no sure, continuing access to those "sacred" and vivifying illusions. The twin horrors which make modern life nearly unbearable are the vision of *nulla* and the experience of *noia*. Using his intellect or reason, man inevitably peers into the abyss of *nulla,* or nothingness, the void of his and the universe's purposelessness. More biting even than this vision is the enduring of *noia*, an untranslatable concept, indelibly associated with Leopardi, to which the English words "tedium" and "spleen" and even Baudelaire's "ennui" are inadequate. As the reader will see, Leopardi kept on expanding and refining the idea. (Words for things and states we constantly experience are, after all, the ones that become irregular or complicated in their usage.) At its root, *noia* is the *"taedium vitae"* described by countless writers over time, but Leopardi goes further. It is the psycho-spiritual paralysis which makes all physical, moral and intellectual activity or affirmation impossible and undesired, a kind of becalming reminiscent of Carlyle's "Center of Indifference." Taking the idea even further, as Leopardi does in some of his *Zibaldone* entries and *Pensieri, noia* is the state in which life-energy or desire pulsates for engagement but there is no goal or journey to occupy it. Put another way, it is desire, having no object, eating away at its own psychic container—a kind of mental or spiritual ulceration. Add to these ideas the fact that Leopardi eventually came to consider the experience of *noia* not only as a curse but as the paradoxical badge of a person's sensitivity and capacity to be regenerated and exalted, and one begins to appreciate his meanings. . . . As to the cause of man's fall from the natural Eden, Leopardi is quite ambiguous. Refusing to blame the devil or cite the abhorrent idea of original sin, he is left to shadowy references to the passage of time and the pursuit of truth. While this myth of a decline may be philosophically untidy, Leopardi does no worse than other thinkers on the problem of evil. Besides, the myth is imaginatively productive, suggesting as it does a parallel between the life of the race and that of each human who falls from childhood.

There is, of course, a large fly in the Rousseauvian broth: Leopardi could not explain through this scheme the recorded misery of the ancients, and the more he read and pondered Theophrastus, Pindar, Sophocles, the writers of *Job* and *Ecclesiastes,* and other tragic ancient authors, the more the pressure mounted on him to discard Rousseau. In mid-career, therefore, and certainly by the time he wrote most of the *Operette Morali* in 1824, Leopardi began to stress what is often called his "cosmic" pessimism. In this view, the inevitable suffering of man has not developed historically but has always been. The "unhappy truth" is that man's undeserved pain, unfulfillable longing, and monumental insignificance are not anomalies caused by his alienation from nature but features built into his existence by nature herself. Nature is conceived as an abstract force whose surface beauty masks a core sometimes indifferent, usually hostile, always inscrutable. As the Icelander of the dialogue puts it, she is the "executioner" of her own children. Since being means pain, emptiness, and *noia*— the more sentience the more *noia*—it would have been better for man, as Leopardi and Job agree, had he not been born. Failing that, the existence of the zoophyte is preferable. If one is condemned to life as a human, then one might as well prefer to be great rather than puny, reasons the soul in one of Leopardi's dialogues; to which nature responds with an amen: "Live then, and be great and unhappy." At this rock-bottom of Leopardi's despair, there are only a few explicit avenues of temporary escape for humans; the conscious pursuit of illusions and diversions and the occasional burst of beauty afforded by love or the aesthetic experience. The ruling principle, however, is *male*. If in Italian the word means more than "evil"—the ideas of hurt and wrongness may also be implied—that is little compensation for suffering man in Leopardi's system.

Leopardi expresses this full-fledged cosmic pessimism in the *Operette Morali,* the works which (Carducci noted) Dante would have described as "eating away layer by layer at the heart and mind producing them. . . ." Although there are still holdovers of attraction toward the ancient state, it is significant that in the *Operette Morali* Leopardi places characters over a wide spectrum of real or mythic time and space so as to generalize their woe. There are real historical persons (Plotinus, Columbus, Copernicus, Tasso, Parini), figures from traditional mythology (Prometheus, Momus, Atlas), and more or less mythic personae of his own creation who exist timelessly (the Icelander, Nature). In any case, it is these *Operette,* on the surface so disenchanted, which came to identify Leopardi as an unwavering pessimist to be grouped, and sometimes dismissed, along with Schopenhauer, Hartmann, and the Buddha.

If Leopardi's vision consisted only of the negative lessons of his cosmic pessimism there would be little further to say about him or to experience through him. One who courts or studies nonbeing can only repeat himself and wait. But Leopardi does not end there and we cannot; his works have redemptive and energetic values which invite attention.

Sporadically through Leopardi's writings and then emphatically after 1828-29, a different explicit attitude emerges toward nature, man, and civilization. Call this posture what we will— titanism, heroism, humanism, existentialism—the fact is that Leopardi gradually clarified a stubborn positive belief in man's ability to move with relative grace in a world where the odds are against him. As far back as the June 23, 1823, letter to his Belgian friend Jacoppsen, Leopardi mused that men might be happier if they could be loving, enthusiastic, and virtuous, important words to him. If to love virtue and each other ardently is to indulge in illusions, so be it: the trick of life then is to agree on our shared illusions (Wallace Stevens was to call them the "supreme fiction") and to pursue them. Here, as Whitfield observes, is the motif which will grow pronounced in works like the **"Dialogue of Plotinus and Porphyry"** and swell majestically in Leopardi's late poetic testament to man, **"La ginestra,"** or **"Broom."** Leopardi's final and humanistic position, which is clear even though he did not live to articulate it completely, rests on our distinguishing limitations from capabilities, creative illusions from destructive ones, wishes from realities, friends from foes. In his thinking, nature is the chief enemy. Although she brings us forth, we are to her as children to a mindlessly destructive stepmother; or, to change the image, we are as expendable as the broom-plant is to Vesuvius, on whose desert slopes it briefly lives. Leopardi argues—in a sweeping attack on nineteenth-century idealisms—that we should reject the false myth-makers and illusion-weavers: those who would teach us that we are perfectible either in this world or another; that through religion or socio-scientific engineering, or some combination, we can achieve, regain, or create paradise. In the satirical and awesomely entitled *Paralipomeni della Batracomiomachia* (his "additions" to the pseudo-Homeric *War of the Mice and the Crabs*), Leopardi strongly attacks the idea that man has fallen from anything; there never was a glorious primitive state (*pace* Rousseau). As Leopardi says in a startling metaphor, the city did not precede the citizens, the citizens came before the city.

This concept of existential citizenry is the heart of Leopardi's humanism. If we are to live with dignity on the volcano's edge with no aid from without, we must become ever more civilized. This means recognizing that *we* are all we have, that against our common doom we must pit the force of fraternal love. We can do this because despite our weakness, vulnerability, and lamentable tendencies toward self-love and self-deception, humans are flexible and can learn through necessity and habituation (the Lockean attack on innate ideas served Leopardi till the end). Leopardi suggests something even more important, if quite sacrilegious—that despite our smallness relative to the vast impersonal cosmos, we are potentially more decent and civil than anything else in that cosmos. Some aspects of this position look back to Lucretius, others to *Candide,* although the garden Leopardi urges us to cultivate is even more modest, dry, and besieged than Voltaire's. Furthermore, the reader may see anticipations here of the Sartre who could write that "life begins on the other side of despair" and the Camus who could recreate the toil of Sisyphus for us.

As important to Leopardi as the nature of existence was the nature of poetry, and not surprisingly there are connections between his reflections on both subjects. The young Leopardi tended to see art the way Aristotle and most neoclassical writers had, in terms of imitating the objective experiences and truths *there* in nature. The older Leopardi was much more romantically oriented in stressing the creativity of the individual human imagination. In short, nature or the outer world cedes some power and authority to man and the subjective faculties. One element that remains constant is Leopardi's stubborn attempt to root the aesthetic experience within the material dimension.

Leopardi's early view of poetry is linked essentially to his schematic interpretation of the ancient state's superiority over the modern. The imagination of the ancient poet, Homer being the supreme example, was intimately activated by a benign nature. His goal was to imitate nature directly, to capture beauty and sublimity, the proffered illusions, clearly, simply, and with a kind of natural ease or negligence *(sprezzatura).* The ancient could be truly imaginative because he was closer to nature, the source of imagination, and he was not as intellectually prone "to murder to dissect" as the modern poet is. The modern, distanced from nature and living in an age of "truth," science, and prose, substitutes the sentimental for the imaginative; the pathetic for the sublime; the analysis of self for the presentation of nature; emotion about things for the things themselves; the willed for the inevitable. If the modern occasionally rises to imaginative heights, it is usually through evoking childhood, the state wherein his vision approximates the ancient's. Common to poets of any era is the imaginative craving for the infinite despite the tendency of the intellect to shrink perception and deny the infinite. Influenced by Longinus and such English theoreticians as Burke and Akenside, Leopardi dwells lovingly on the subject of how certain words and things can electrify the imagination to contemplate the sublime and seemingly raise us above the sphere of earth and reason.

This ancient-modern aesthetic is not unique, most of it resting on neoclassical doctrine and on the ideas of earlier writers who had exalted the naive and the primitive (e.g., Vico, Rousseau, Schiller). As Leopardi matured, however, his aesthetic ideas shifted like his general philosophy and took on a more romantic and personal character. It is striking that just as he came to distrust the intentions and validity of objective nature and to put a greater faith in man's active creating and controlling of illusions, so in his criticism there grew a greater respect for the most subjective of poetic forms—the lyric—and for the creative, not imitative, power of the imagination. René Wellek points out that in the privacy of his *Zibaldone,* Leopardi eventually urged "more radically than anybody else in contemporary Europe" the cause of the lyric, which he came to consider the "summit" of literary expression [see Additional Bibliography]. Simultaneously, he grew to deprecate the more objective genres like the drama and epic; indeed his comments on the epic sound much like Poe's attacks on the essential prosiness of *Paradise Lost.* The essence of the lyric poem for Leopardi is the initial emotional-imaginative surge or impulse *(impeto),* which when processed in tranquility through the poet's memory could result in good poetry. As for the imagination,

it does not merely record or combine, but rather it invents or makes *(fabbrica);* and the imagination's product not only can stir our sense of beauty but can also lift us morally, no matter how dark the substance. Here Poe is left to one side, and Leopardi draws closer to Shelley and Wordsworth.

Even though the imagination can ennoble and *seem* to carry us beyond, Leopardi is usually careful to locate the source of beauty *within* the universe. Those who attempt to idealize or supernalize his attitude or diction must reckon with a pervasive caution he himself shows. For example, there is a passage from the early **"Discourse of an Italian on Romantic Poetry"** where Leopardi describes an unearthly experience: "I myself remember in my childhood my imagination's seizing upon the sensation of a sound so sweet it was never heard on earth." It would be easy to read this as evidence of a Shelleyan affirmation of supernal beauty—until we grow accustomed to Leopardi and recognize his belief in the illusory force of the imagination and his tell-tale inclusion of words like "sensation" in such texts. Again, in his late poem **"On the Likeness of a Beautiful Woman,"** Leopardi notes how humans are vile and weak but seemingly "in part of nobler birth." Some translators render the word "nobler" as "divine," but that is not what Leopardi said. Indeed, when Leopardi actually uses the word "divine" in his writing, he seems very conscious that he is using time-honored but loose and hyperbolic language, and we should be similarly conscious in order to understand him fully. Elsewhere in **"On the Likeness"** Leopardi explicitly cites the natural rather than supernatural derivation of beauty, its apparent rather than its real quality:

> The dazzling light which pulses from the heart
> Of timeless nature falls
> Upon these lower sands,
> Seeming to give the index and sure hope
> Of more than human possibilities,
> Of realms more fortunate and golden worlds.

The writer who penned those lines seems clearly to be at the same time a yearning idealist *and* a careful rationalist. Reading such passages exclusively one way or the other denies to Leopardi his tensions and his agony.

Whatever the period of Leopardi's thoughts on poetry, he remains constant to certain ideas. He continually dwells on the special power in certain words to shimmer in the imagination and lure us beyond our too-definite reality. His ideas on style greatly shaped by ancient languages (especially Greek) and the habits of Greco-Roman and Italian poets, he deplores the obscurity and complexity of moderns like Goethe and applauds instead the classical virtues: clarity, naturalness, and the demand on poets to hide their art. Needless to say, Leopardi always preferred classical writers to his own contemporaries: "Everything has improved since Homer, but not poetry."

Leopardi's poems are usually thought to be, especially by those who read Italian, the high point of his achievement. Indeed, the vortex of appreciation has at times threatened to swallow up the varied riches of Leopardi's other expressions. Some critics have tried to break down Leopardi's poems into exclusive types—idyllic, elegiac, heroic, philosophical, and the like. But this tendency often throws more darkness than light over the poems, and could lead as sensitive a reader as Croce to rebuke Leopardi for getting too philosophical in poems where he should have remained idyllic. What rigidly categorical readers may fail to recognize is that Leopardi himself was much more supple and iconoclastic about poetry than his admiration of the past would lead us to think. That flexibility led him to chafe increasingly against needless strictures to form and expression (including rhyme). Leopardi began by trying to make sharp distinctions between his idylls, *canzoni*, and *odi-canzoni*, but he ended by calling nearly all his poems simply **Canti**. He consciously experimented with lyric poetry, trying to expand the scope of what could be done in it. Less consciously, perhaps, he was taking part in a striking poetic development which cut across national boundaries and linked romantic poets—the evolution of what M. H. Abrams has called "the greater romantic lyric." According to Abrams, who focuses on the English romantics, this new poetic form mixed lyrical nature description and internal meditation; it featured an "out-in-out process, in which mind confronts nature and their interplay constitutes the poem." In examining such poems as "**Memories**" and "**The Village Saturday**," we can see how Abram's acute induction applies beyond *Tintern Abbey* and the English romantics. We can also caution ourselves against *a priori* labels and admire the way in which the isolated, classically leaning Leopardi could be so attuned to the romantic frequencies of his time.

In the early patriotic *canzoni* of 1818 "**To Italy**" and "**On the Monument of Dante**", Leopardi showed his attraction to ancient heroic ideals and adopted the posture of the national bard trying to tongue-lash the consciousness of Italians to the level of that of their Greco-Roman forebears. Quickly, however, Leopardi found his own personal stride and by 1819-20, with the writing of "**The Infinite**" and "**To the Moon**," he is creating subjective lyrics stamped with his own style and substance. Although the slightly later "**Brutus**," "**To Spring**," and "**The Last Song of Sappho**" refer on the surface to ancient myth and history, the speakers are projections of Leopardi, and the personal statements reveal his characteristic preoccupations. Except for possibly "**The Infinite**," the lonely poet or persona of the early poems etches the tragic perceptions of one caught between two dimensions or times: time and self *then* as against time and self *now;* the world as seen through illusion, memory, hope, and the affections compared to the world grasped by the disenchanted reason; the desire for love, life, fame, and virtue as opposed to the reality of our transience, pain, and ignominy. These themes repeat again and again in Leopardi. As Figurelli observed, "Leopardi is never the poet of immediate experience, and when he tried it he became inferior to himself. He does not chant his life, but the memory of it. . . ." We could add that Leopardi must have approved of Dante's celebrated words, "No greater sorrow than to remember happy times in present misery."

One reason scholars can speak so confidently of Leopardi's later poems as a group is that they are set off by a long dry period in the middle of his career. During the 1823-28 period, Leopardi, seemingly convinced that a premature aging process had sapped his poetic abilities, devoted himself to the "truth" of existence and to the genre he then thought appropriate to it, prose. It is the period dominated by the **Operette Morali**, and although the latter have a poetry of their own—indeed in a few of them he pushed toward the prose poem—the only important independent poem he produced at this time was the wistful and almost tired "**To His Lady**." When the thaw came, however, it came decisively. Under the balmy influence of Pisa in the spring of 1828, Leopardi wrote "**The Reawakening**," a description of the return of feeling and imagination to the dried-up mind, and "**To Sylvia**," perhaps his perfect lyric. From this point on Leopardi was definitely a poet again, producing what most readers believe to be his greatest verse, for example, "**Memories**," "**Night-Song of a Wandering Shepherd of Asia**,"

and ultimately "**Broom**." Although his earlier tragic themes persist (so that in a way one must read outside the poems to taste the complete author), the late poems show a tougher, more confident, at times heroic, cast of mind. Even at the psychological low points of the later poems—which I take to be the poems of the "Aspasia" cycle inspired by the unfortunate love for Fanny Tozzetti—there is an irreducible core of flinty strength and pride. The poem "**To Himself**" ends with Leopardi staring down at deceiving nature as if he held her in great scorn. And in the not completely successful "Aspasia" poem, he can describe the passage through the burning rites of unreturned love and willed deception to that purified point where he can lie at ease upon the grass, "gaze at ocean, earth, and sky, and smile."

Almost inevitably, the later poems are leaner in imagery, metaphor, and diction than the earlier ones, and they have less color. Increasingly Leopardi indulges in philosophical discourse in the poems, as if he were questioning the beauty-truth, poetry-prose distinctions and moving toward a master concept of expression which would shatter the old polarities. (Perella says that the late Leopardi saw poetry "as the expression of the human spirit no longer able to wander freely in a rich illusory world and so reduced to a poetry that has more in common with 'philosophy.'") Just as noticeable in the later verse is the almost complete abandonment of classical mythology and any ornament extrinsic to Leopardi himself. Some of the later poems are extremely intimate evocations of personal history against the background of man's fate ("**To Sylvia**" or "**The Calm after the Storm**.") Others involve mythic but not mythological figures; that is, "characters" such as the wandering shepherd and the broom-plant take on the mythic size and intensity of the Icelander of the prose piece, but all these mythic creations come from within not without. They arise not from the escape from reality but from the personal encounter with it, not from the opposition of beauty and truth but from the attempt to ground one in the other. That is why we often get the sense in Leopardi's late works of being in the presence of an ancient tragic Greek or Hebrew come again to speak in modern yet timeless terms.

Once we have sketched the explicit features of Leopardi's life, system, and art, we have still not accounted for those qualities which have sent readers away inspired rather than depressed, expanded rather than belittled. Depression comes from reading Leopardi's biography, not his work.

One of the positive appeals of Leopardi is the sheer display of and concern for morality. Many have pointed out that Leopardi was not a complete philosopher; rather, he was interested in the problem of wrong in the world and how we should act to right it, a problem which forms only part of a metaphysician's concern. In a world he perceives to be dominated by mystery and pain, he searched for ways to act. The German scholar Vossler framed some of the essential Leopardian questions as these: "Why do men sympathize so much with each other while at the same time they hate each other? How is it they are sociable while each seeks his self-interest? Why are they so bold while each is so attached to life? Why is life so monotonous when once it was so varied? Why are joy, art, poetry, love, faith, and hope receding from the world? Why is happiness always more rare while everything tends toward it?" Some Italian scholars have even tried to link this eudaemonistic questioning on Leopardi's part to the development of nineteenth-century Anglo-American pragmatism, the view that the justification of belief is in our action.

This moral quest may seem quaint to the reader who expects moral sensibility to be based on a theistic view of the world. Such a reader must solve that problem on his own, for despite Leopardi's materialism the moral dimension is undeniably and crucially present, and it reveals itself in rhetorical as well as substantial ways. Consider what Leopardi's fundamental criticism of nature and life is. At bottom he attacks in an almost childlike way the failure of justice, virtue, and honesty. He cannot accept the idea of original sin because to him that means accepting the idea of unfair punishment for something one did not do. He will not entertain the idea of an ideal Platonic dimension because belief in such a world does not really solve the problem of hurt in this one. He will not trust in a Christian afterlife because it is too little and too late; for him, to use contemporary terms, "Justice delayed is justice denied." And he sees no reason to expect less moral behavior from nature (often seemingly invoked as a codeword for some higher force) than from men. Furthermore, the virtues Leopardi demands from actions in this life extend to *thinking* about life. Bickersteth correctly said that "scrupulous honesty both of heart and head was throughout life Leopardi's greatest moral quality" [see Additional Bibliography]. While we must acknowledge the possibility of a totally corrupt person writing beautifully, nonetheless when we read Leopardi we have the inescapable sense that morality of mind and purity of style in this case do reflect each other. Leopardi is everywhere in his verbalization preoccupied with rightness. He labors to be as lucid, logical, and precise as he knows how at the moment. Except when he uses an "etcetera" to remind himself to fill in later, he is ruthlessly complete and clean in his discussion. If three elements are introduced in the premises of a paragraph or essay, those three will, almost tediously at times, reappear in the summary or conclusion. Often in his prose, Leopardi does something surprising for a poet: he apologizes for hyperbole or metaphor by inserting the words "in a sense" or "so to speak." This is partly the usage of the scholar he was, but it is also the caution of a mind that does not wish to distort, even to itself. Just as in the strictly active sphere, Leopardi demands justice and honesty—a proper relation between causes and effects, actions and results, behavior and fate—so in the sphere of words he illustrates sincerity, logic, precision, clarity, and balance. Perhaps there is only one word which can cover Leopardi's concern for verbal and ethical rightness. It is integrity.

Connected to this essential decency of Leopardi's mind, there is the central paradox that no matter how hard Leopardi works to present his disillusioned version of man's real position, his positive values shine through. Whitfield argues convincingly that "Leopardi's dismay is the gauge also of his affirmation. . . . No statement of Leopardi is greater than its opposite, and if the tragedy in which man is involved is immense for Leopardi, it is because the stature of man partakes of that immensity." In the **"Night-Song"** he affirms the pain and *noia* of life while at the same time revealing his awed appreciation of the universe's stunning swirl. In **"The Setting of the Moon,"** that somber elegy on the death of man and the seeming triumph of darkness, he exhilarates us by describing the sun continuing to suffuse the world. What kind of atheist is this who takes such comfort in the stars? Even in the *Operette,* supposedly his unadorned attack on man and nature, if not more, the words "magnanimous," "virtuous," "noble" continually pop up to disclose the true value system. The ideas of pain, hatred, *noia,* disillusion, and nonbeing take their ultimate meaning in terms of joy, love, vitality, wonder, and being—the desiderata of Leopardi's heart. De Sanctis, who had the pleasure when a

boy studying at Naples of meeting Leopardi, described Leopardi's ambivalent impact this way:

> . . . Leopardi produces an effect opposite to the one he proposes. He does not believe in progress and he makes you crave it; he does not believe in liberty and he makes you love it. He calls love, glory, and virtue illusions, and he kindles in your breast an insatiable desire for them. And you cannot lay him down without feeling better for it; and you cannot approach him without first collecting and purifying yourself so that you will not have to blush in his presence. He is a skeptic and he makes you a believer. . . . He has so low an opinion of humanity, and his lofty, pure, and gentle spirit honors and ennobles it.

The essential Leopardi does lie in the search for these qualities and in the way that search is expressed by words and art. At all moments of his career, no matter how he struggles against self-deception, no matter what his personal or philosophical torment, Leopardi shows an enduring trust in literature; in the power of well-chosen words to clarify our being and even for a time to make us whole instead of riven. That is what he is getting at in the *Zibaldone* paragraphs where he describes the exalting effect of great imaginative works, no matter how tragic. And Leopardi's spokesman in the **"Dialogue of Timander and Eleander"** phrases it even more explicitly:

> If any moral book could be useful, I think that poetic books could be most so. I say "poetic" in the broad sense, that is, books aimed at moving the imagination. And I mean prose works as well as verse. Now I am not impressed by that poetry which when read and meditated fails to leave in the reader's mind for half an hour a feeling noble enough to prevent him from harboring a mean thought or doing an unworthy act. But if the reader breaks faith with his best friend one hour after the reading, I would not therefore blame that poetry—for then I would have to scorn the most beautiful, the most impassioned, the most noble poems of the world.

Despite the pervasive melancholy in Leopardi (especially in the poems) and his occasional self-pity and querulousness, many of his utterances have the feature he describes. It is a function of a style and address, for want of a better word, that is dimmed by translation and is only faintly describable in any language. Perhaps Croce came close when he said that certain Leopardi passages "express themselves with the reserve, the modesty, the chastity of one saying things he is no longer used to saying." Whether the words are those of an idealist *manqué,* a supreme rationalist, a proto-existentialist, a true believer or true skeptic, are issues with which we must wrestle. Suffice to say that Leopardi reminds us of what it is to be a poet and what it is to be human. (pp. 13-25)

> *Ottavio M. Casale, "General Introduction: The Mind and Art of Giacomo Leopardi," in* A Leopardi Reader, *edited and translated by Ottavio M. Casale, University of Illinois Press, 1981, pp. 1-25.*

GIOVANNI CECCHETTI　　(essay date 1982)

[*In the following excerpt from his introduction to a translation of Leopardi's* Operette morali, *Cecchetti reviews the themes and style of the work, summarizes early critical appraisals of it, and assesses Leopardi's overall importance.*]

On January 5, 1821, Leopardi wrote to his literary friend and elective mentor Pietro Giordani:

Leggo e scrivo e fo tanti disegni, che a voler colorire e terminare quei soli che ho, non solamente schizzati, ma delineati, fo conto che non mi basterebbero quattro vite. Se bene io comprendo anzi sento tutto giorno e intensamente l'inutilità delle cose umane, contuttociò m'addolora e m'affanna la considerazione di quanto ci sarebbe da fare, e quanto poco potrò fare. Massimamente che questa sola vita che la natura mi concede, la miseria me la intorpidisce e incatena; e me la vedo sdrucciolare e sfumare tra le mie mani; in guisa che laddove ai miei disegni si richiederebbero molte vite, non ne avrò quasi neppur una.

I am busy reading and writing and thinking of so many projects that to bring to completion even those I have drafted, not to mention those I have only sketched, would, I am sure, take me four lifetimes. Although I continuously understand, in fact I intensely feel, the futility of everything human, I am still grieved and distressed by the thought of how much there is to do—especially because this one life granted me by nature is benumbed and shackled with misery; and I see it slipping through my fingers. So while my projects would require many lifetimes, I shall hardly have even one.

He had already mentioned one of those projects to that same friend four months earlier and had also noted it down in a long list of future works: "**Dialoghi satirici alla maniera di Luciano**" ("**Satirical Dialogues in the Style of Lucian**"). This was, of course, a reference to that series of shorter prose works that were to become the *Operette morali.* But their actual writing began in January 1824 and lasted until the middle of November of the same year, when Leopardi completed the "**Cantico del gallo silvestre**" ("**Song of the Great Wild Rooster**"), which concluded the original group of twenty essays and dialogues. Many of the innumerable observations that had crystallized in the thousands of pages of his *Zibaldone* were thus finally organized and reworked into what Leopardi thought would become a philosophical book but instead turned out to be, as he himself realized some years later, a book of poetic myths.

The title, *Operette morali,* points to his philosophical intention, but it can in no way be understood literally. The *operette* are "moral" in the sense that they proclaim the true nature of life itself and ultimately advocate facing it for what it is. They are also "moral," therefore, in the sense that every real work of art is moral: a translation of the perpetual desires and disappointments of man into images of permanent value and thus an exalted, universal objectification of such desires and disappointments.

His vast humanistic background caused Leopardi to find an example in Lucian, the Greek master of satirical prose, with whom he felt he could compete. The term *satirical* was, in fact, the one most often mentioned in the planning stages of the book. But, notwithstanding the original intention, very few of the dialogues and not a single one of the essays can be said to have any precedent in Lucian. Moreover, very little in them can be considered satirical. Whenever Leopardi wants to chide his contemporaries, he is serious and direct in his condemnation. Like Dante, he is much too convinced of their folly and of his own righteousness to be able to laugh with detachment. There are indeed times when he tells us that he is laughing, but it is the laughter of bitterness and derision, not the Socratic smile of the sage who stands above human foibles.

At the center of Leopardi's meditations and writings lies an incessant dialectical struggle between illusion and reality. It is conceived as the very nucleus of the inner world of man—a

world in which, from one day to the next, man hopes for fulfillment, for a happiness that will come in the future, when present dreams are finally realized. But then reality unfailingly reveals itself as inferior to all hopes and expectations. Thus, the only good moments are those in which man imagines happiness to come. The only desirable and acceptable part of life is early youth, when man dreams without any knowledge of reality; and the only desirable part of the day is the morning—the day being the concentrated image of life. In a famous poem, "**Il sabato del villagio**" ("**Saturday Evening in the Village**"), written five years after the *Operette morali,* Leopardi maintains that the best hours of the week are those when people look forward to, and prepare themselves for, the holiday, not the holiday itself, which brings nothing but tedium and the thought of the coming work days. Life then is possible only as long as man can overcome, or rather forget, that reality, or that truth, which destroys all dreams.

This concept runs through the *Operette morali* from the first page to the last. It is developed in all its ramifications and regularly leads to inevitable conclusions. The opening piece, "**Storia del genere umano**" ("**History of the Human Race**"), which is intended as a vast overture to the series, is rooted in this theme. The "**Storia**" was the first essay to be written—itself an amazing fact, for it demonstrates that when, in January 1824, Leopardi sat down to compose his initial *operetta,* he already had clearly in mind the structure and contents of the whole book, if not in all its details then certainly in the general design.

In the "**Storia del genere umano**" the poetic presence of dreams, hopes, and expectations is quickly transformed into man's indefatigable search for "happiness"—a word that is constantly woven into the narrative texture so that it appears more and more elusive, a mirage growing more and more unreal. In fact, no one knows whether it exists or if it has any substance. Jove himself, the great creator who can strew the night with stars and make provisions to uplift the spirit of man, at least temporarily, does not have the power to satisfy the insatiable yearnings of his creatures. All he can do is to distract them by complicating life. He even sends them powerful illusions, or phantoms, which give life itself the semblance of meaning and purpose. But mankind, possessed by an irrepressible desire for knowledge, wants Truth. When Truth does come to earth, all illusions disappear, leaving the human race feeling more miserable than ever. At this point Jove and the other gods, in their infinite compassion, send Love, who dwells in the hearts of only a few, but "negli animi che egli si elegge ad abitare, suscita e rinverdisce . . . l'infinita speranza e le belle e care immaginazioni degli anni teneri" (in those he elects to inhabit, he revives and restores . . . the infinite hopes and the cherished fantasies of their tender years). Love is the ultimate illusion, as Leopardi had written four years earlier in his *canzone* to Angelo Mai, and lovers can find a measure of happiness only because they revert to childhood, the age of illusions and expectations. Thus, the "**Storia del genere umano**" ends with the rediscovery of its own beginning.

As can be said of many of the *Operette morali,* the "**Storia del genere umano**" is a history of mankind from within, not from without. It relates and reinterprets the eternal myths of man—from the Golden Age to the age of philosophers to the Romantic era—by translating them into man's own perpetual spiritual needs and turning them into a greater and more comprehensive myth. This continuous unveiling of the spirit of man and then clothing it in man's own dreams and fantasies—whether de-

XXXIII.

Il tramonto della luna.

Quale in notte solinga,

Sovra campagne inargentate ed acqua,

Là 've zefiro aleggia,

E mille vaghi aspetti

E ingannevoli obbietti

Fingon l'ombre lontane

Infra l'onde tranquille

E rami e siepi e collinette e ville;

Giunta al confin del cielo,

Dietro Apennino od Alpe, o del Tirreno

Nell'infinito seno

Scende la luna; e si scolora il mondo;

Spariscon l'ombre, ed una

The manuscript copy of the beginning of Leopardi's poem "Il tramonto della luna."

rived from classical literature or modern history, or personally invented—is the method Leopardi adopts in his book. It is also what makes him one of the great humanists of modern times and one of the few writers who can legitimately stand side by side with the classics.

Happiness, as the incessantly frustrated purpose of life, is presented again in the **"Dialogo di un Fisico e di un Metafisico"** (**"Dialogue Between a Scientist and a Philosopher"**). It often assumes other names. There are cases, for instance, when it is called "piacere" (pleasure), by which Leopardi means fulfillment in the most complete sense of the word. In the **"Dialogo di Torquato Tasso e del suo Genio familiare"** (**"Dialogue Between Torquato Tasso and His Familiar Spirit"**), Leopardi theorizes on the very essence of pleasure: "è un desiderio, non un fatto . . . un concetto, e non un sentimento" (it is a desire, and not a fact . . . a concept, and not a feeling), and he reaches the conclusion that it belongs to the sphere of "dreams." A somewhat modified restatement of the same concept permeates the **"Dialogo di un venditore d'almanacchi e di un passeggere"** (**"Dialogue Between an Almanac Peddler and a Passer-By"**), which concludes with these striking words: "Quella vita ch'è una cosa bella, non è la vita che si conosce, ma quella che non si conosce, non la vita passata, ma la futura" (The life that's beautiful is not the life we know but the life we don't know; not the past life but the future one). This relates to another fundamental Leopardian conclusion: if reality destroys dreams,

hopes, and illusions and if the understanding of reality is more likely to come to the intelligent than to those with limited mental powers, it follows that intelligence is indeed a calamity. In the **"Dialogo della Natura e di un'Anima"** (**"Dialogue Between Nature and a Soul"**), Nature develops this concept with such cogent arguments that the Soul asks to be stripped of all intellectual gifts and be made the most stupid and senseless human spirit who ever lived on earth.

The consciousness of reality and the state of inert suspense between disappointment and new hopes produce a condition of tedium, boredom, or ennui—that same feeling that leads the men of the **"Storia del genere umano"** and the Englishman of **"La scommessa di Prometeo"** (**"The Wager of Prometheus"**) to suicide. It is a Romantic motif that Leopardi grasped at the very beginning of the century, before it was defined as *le mal du siècle*. He gave it what was probably the most penetrating and suggestive expression of his time.

Boredom is the neutral condition of the human spirit, like the lull between two storms, creating a state of mind that is difficult to sustain. In the **"Dialogo di Torquato Tasso e del suo Genio familiare"** Leopardi says that boredom "is of the same nature as the air" and occupies all the intervals between pleasures and pains; and since pleasures are made of the same substance as spider webs—extremely thin, tenuous, and transparent—boredom permeates and fills them just as air permeates and fills webs. Finally, he declares that boredom is the pure desire for happiness, which is neither satisfied by pleasure nor openly troubled by pain. In the **"Dialogo di Plotino e di Porfirio"** (**"Dialogue Between Plotinus and Porphyry"**), one of the two interlocutors asserts that boredom is sufficient reason to end one's life voluntarily. This theme of boredom recurs in a celebrated poem, the **"Canto notturno d'un pastore errante dell'Asia"** (**"Night Song of a Wandering Shepherd in Asia"**), written in 1830. Leopardi also offers some remedies for boredom. In the **"Storia del genere umano"** they are the continuous difficulties of survival, the necessity of hard work to find food, and especially all kinds of diseases; and in the magnificent **"Dialogo di Cristoforo Colombo e di Pietro Gutierrez"** (**"Dialogue Between Christopher Columbus and Pedro Gutierrez"**), the unavoidable risks faced by sailors and by soldiers, who hold life particularly dear because they are in constant danger of losing it.

But we find other themes in the *Operette* as well. Among them stand out the anti-Romantic demonstration of the eternal cycles of Nature and of her resulting total disregard for man and his needs and the insignificance of earth and of man on earth.

A special place must be assigned to the **"Dialogo di Federico Ruysch e delle sue mummie"** (**"Dialogue Between Frederick Ruysch and His Mummies"**), generally considered one of the most astonishing treatments of the theme of death in all literature. Profoundly poetic in itself, it begins with one of the most essential and austere of Leopardi's poems, suddenly sung at the same time by the dead of all ages. This extraordinary vision is followed by a discussion of the moment of death, which is likened to the relaxing process of falling asleep. Presenting death as pleasurable rather than painful was indeed revolutionary in a culture in which the last hours of life were—and still are—called "agony." But the image of sleep bringing the ultimate escape is still more significant. The escape of death is presented in the **"Storia del genere umano"** and the escape of sleep in the **"Dialogo di Torquato Tasso e del suo Genio familiare."** In the **"Dialogo di Federico Ruysch e delle sue mummie"** Leopardi unifies these two escapes—as he does again in the justly celebrated **"Cantico del gallo silvestre,"** where, after stating that in the morning we must revert from the false to the real, he contemplates a world without sound and without movement, perpetually asleep, and then he loses himself in the vision of the disappearance of the entire cosmos, with universal sleep and universal death having become one and the same thing.

The gullibility of man is deplored in the **"Dialogo della Moda e della Morte"** (**"Dialogue Between Fashion and Death"**). But the "dialogues" Leopardi wrote in defense of his own ideas and of his own book are still more significant: the **"Dialogo di Timandro e di Eleandro"** (**"Dialogue Between Timander and Eleander"**) and the **"Dialogo di Tristano e di un amico"** (**"Dialogue Between Tristan and a Friend"**), where he engages in open and hopeless battle against the stubborn delusions of his own century, until he finds a haven in death.

To survey the main themes of the *Operette morali,* as I have partly done so far, necessarily reduces them to little more than a collection of skeletons. The truth is that every page pulsates with quiet excitement like the surface of an ocean. In a book that intends to strip life of all those ornaments that make it bearable and to reveal its bareness, there is remarkably little despair. Human life, Leopardi tells us, is what it is, and it would be cowardly to delude ourselves and to live by false beliefs. Yet "il nostro fato, dove che egli ci tragga, è da seguire con animo forte e grande" (our fate, wherever it might lead us, must be followed with great strength and courage). This is what we read at the end of the lengthy **"Il Parini, ovvero della gloria"** (**"Parini's Discourse on Glory"**). And at the conclusion of the **"Dialogo di Plotino e di Porfirio"** Leopardi states that life should be lived so that we may at least "keep each other company" and "help and support each other." Ultimately, then, our association and communion with others is what gives meaning to human existence.

Although great works of art are generally the distillate and the rejuvenation of an entire tradition, they are also projected toward the future; they speak a new language and present newly formulated perceptions of the world and of man, thereby offering what will be part of a new tradition. For this reason many important products of the human mind are not fully appreciated by their contemporaries and often meet with outright rejection. For us, at the end of the twentieth century, it is difficult to understand that the first and main objections even to printing the *Operette morali* came from opposition to its philosophical content, which was dubbed totally negative and destructive. Leopardi managed to convince his Milanese publisher and friend Antonio Stella to bring out the book in 1827. But the reviews were mostly unfavorable. They praised the consummate artistry of the style but could not accept the ideas. In 1829 Leopardi entered his volume into competition for the prestigious Accademia della Crusca prize, which was given every five years to the best new literary work. This time it was awarded to the bulky and undistinguished *Storia d'Italia* by Carlo Botta because of the "importance of the subject matter." Again the judges praised Leopardi's style but deplored his ideas. After 1827 no printing of the *Operette morali* appeared until 1834. In 1835 Leopardi asked a Neapolitan publisher to issue a new, enlarged edition of the book, but the printing was soon interrupted by order of the local authorities. The first complete text was published in Florence in 1845, eight years after the poet's death. In 1850 it was placed on the index of forbidden books by the Roman Curia.

Leopardi had not expected his ideas to meet with such general disapproval, for most of them were already present in the poetry and prose of the ancient Greeks. He proved this point by quoting from Homer as well as from other authors in the central part of the **"Dialogo di Tristano e di un amico,"** written eight years after the original *operette* published in 1827. During those eight years, he also composed a number of letters, containing statements that are quite significant, for they tell us his personal opinions and his intentions concerning his book. Early in 1826 he wrote to Stella about the manuscript: "In quel ms. consiste, si può dire, il frutto della mia vita finora passata, e io l'ho più caro de' miei occhi" (This ms. is, so to speak, the result of my past life, and I hold it dearer than my very eyes). Later he worried about the possibility that the Milanese censors might not return the manuscript, and he declared: "Mi contenterei assai più di perder la testa che questo manoscritto" (I would rather lose my head than this manuscript). Such expressions of attachment to his *Operette* occur in several other letters. They all indicate that he was profoundly conscious of having written an important book.

When Stella passed on to him the opinion of a noted writer and critic, Niccolò Tommaseo, who had called the contents of the *Operette* "gratuitous, nauseatingly cold, and desolatingly bitter," Leopardi answered that this judgment did not surprise him and that he wished Tommaseo were right. Similar comments were offered by nearly all the critics of the time. Leopardi could not defend himself, nor did he try to do so. He knew that he had written the truth about life and that man can never accept the truth. Therefore, if rejection of facts is characteristic of human nature, no one can be expected to accept those facts. When his father, Monaldo, who had literary ambitions of his own, urged him to make some changes, he answered that he would seriously consider doing so, but to counteract his father's criticism, he simply added that his intention had been "di fare *poesia in prosa*" (to write *poetry in prose*). Soon after, Monaldo published his *Dialoghetti* (Little Dialogues) based on a rather conventional view of human life and of contemporary society but in title and structure vaguely reminiscent of the *Operette morali.* A number of readers thought that Giacomo had authored them, and he had to deny publicly having done so.

But the assertion that he had intended to write "poetry in prose," freely adapting all kinds of myths, brings us back to the most intimate substance of the *Operette morali.* Undoubtedly, the book had a philosophical intent in the general sense that it was to present the essence and the purpose of life as Leopardi saw it. Like the writers of antiquity, he considered poetry the ideal vehicle for a message, a mirror reflecting eternal truths. Ancient prose itself, such as the *Dialogues* of Plato, could not be regarded as anything but poetry. He was so convinced of this fact that several years before writing the *Operette,* he had stated in his diary that prose was more suitable than verse to modern poetry ("pare che la prosa sarebbe più confacente del verso alla poesia moderna"). Obviously, he applied this principle when he wrote his essays and dialogues. Interestingly enough, at the beginning of our century the critics and poets who gathered around the journal *La Ronda* maintained that the *Operette morali* was a great work of poetry, though written in prose—their judgment thus coinciding with Leopardi's own intentions.

The *Operette morali* is written in an extremely elaborate prose style that has deep roots in the entire tradition of Italian literature as well as in Latin and Greek models. Leopardi had developed his style after many years of study and through profound feeling for the specific harmonious combination of words that at once reflects and produces images. He knew that ideas carry very little weight unless they are expressed with consummate artistry—an artistry that he called "stile" (style). In **"Il Parini, ovvero della gloria"** he insists on the "perfection of style" as the very substance of literature, and then he adds: "Spessissimo occorre che se tu spogli del suo stile una scrittura famosa, di cui ti pensavi che quasi tutto il pregio stesse nelle sentenze, tu la riduci in istato, che ella ti par cosa di niuna stima" (It very often happens that if you take a famous writing that you thought important mostly for its ideas and deprive it of its style, you reduce it to such a state that it seems of no significance whatsoever). It is on style, he says, that the future life of a work of literature depends.

Leopardi's sentences are complex, full of incidental phrases, of suggestive-sounding adverbs, and of verbs and nouns and adjectives that generally appear in pairs, producing a form of binary melody that stays with the reader. The creation of the echo in the **"Storia del genere umano"** and the last paragraph of the **"Cantico del gallo silvestre"** are examples of such a melody. Leopardi was fascinated by visions of space, by the mystery of time, by the sense of eternity remaining silent after the disappearance of the universe. His prose creates this world of vastness and places it before our eyes in the same way the poetry of Homer and Virgil creates the vast movement of the sea. It is a prose that does indeed approach the perfection he sought with so much passion. He wrote in his diary that the most suggestive words are the unusual ones and those indefinite in meaning, for they offer special possibilities to our imagination. In the **Operette morali** he utilizes words of this type particularly in the more poetic parts of his essays where he establishes a musical and visionary background for his thoughts.

But the prose of the **Operette morali** varies with the situation. It is more solemn, closer to Leopardi's own poetry, in such works as the **"Storia del genere umano,"** the **"Elogio degli uccelli,"** and the **"Cantico del gallo silvestre"**; and it is more fluid, spoken (but generally on a high level) in many dialogues. The reader experiences these differences; he also realizes that in some dialogues, such as the **"Dialogo di Cristoforo Colombo e di Pietro Gutierrez,"** and the **"Dialogo di Tristano e di un amico,"** the spoken continuously intermingles with the poetic, thus creating the feeling that, through words, ideas can indeed become music.

Memorable are the definitions Leopardi gives of his **Operette morali** in the book itself. In the **"Dialogo di Timandro e di Eleandro"** not only does he bare his philosophical intentions— by stating that the most useful, and therefore moral, books are the "poetic" ones ("libri destinati a muovere l'immaginazione" [books destined to move the imagination])—but he searches deeply into himself to disclose the very nucleus of his personal meditations and of all his writings:

> Lodo ed esalto quelle opinioni, benché false, che generano atti e pensieri nobili . . . quelle immaginazioni belle e felici, ancorché vane, che danno pregio alla vita; le illusioni naturali dell'animo.

> I praise and exalt those beliefs, though untrue, which produce noble actions and thoughts . . . those beautiful and happy images, which, though empty, make life worthwhile, the natural illusions of the mind.

In this dialogue, originally viewed as both a conclusion to and a justification of the **Operette morali,** Leopardi speaks to his future readers. He is, in fact, the Socrates of the **"Detti me-** morabili di Filippo Ottonieri" ("**Memorable Sayings of Filippo Ottonieri**")—a Socrates, however, who can speak, not to the ancient Athenians but to his own contemporaries.

Soon after, he was to discover that neither critics nor readers would understand him. In fact, they would reject his "negative" philosophy. Thus, in 1832 he decided to write another conclusion to his book, the **"Dialogo di Tristano e di un amico,"** where he bitterly condemned the blindness of his contemporaries. As to the **Operette morali** he said that it was to be considered merely "come un libro di sogni poetici, d'invenzioni e di capricci malinconici, ovvero come un'espressione dell'infelicità dell'autore" (as a book of poetic dreams, of inventions, and of melancholy whims, or as an expression of the unhappiness of its author): a work of poetry, yes, but also a totally private one, intended only for the author to give vent to his own personal feelings; no longer a work written to reveal to man "the natural illusions of the mind," which "make life worthwhile." Now Leopardi could declare that for him the "fable of life" was "concluded," that he was "ripe for death," and that death was his greatest hope.

> Se mi fosse proposta da un lato la fortuna e la fama di Cesare o di Alessandro netta da ogni macchia, dall'altro di morir oggi, e che dovessi scegliere, io direi, morir oggi, e non vorrei tempo a risolvermi.

> If I were offered, on the one hand, the fortune and the fame of Caesar or of Alexander, pure of all stains, and, on the other, to die today, and if I were to make a choice, I would say to die today; and I would not want time to think it over.

He was to live another five years and to berate again the blindness of his contemporaries, but that last definition of the **Operette morali** and that page of the final dialogue remain as the testament of a great poet who has finally withdrawn into total isolation.

Pietro Giordani, in his epitaph for Leopardi's tomb in Naples, defined him as a "Scrittore di filosofia e di poesia altissimo / da paragonare solamente coi Greci" (A supreme writer of philosophy and of poetry / to be compared only with the ancient Greeks). But this acknowledgment of greatness remained without audible echoes until Francesco De Sanctis published his first essays in the 1850s. De Sanctis examined again various aspects of the "poet of [his] youth" in the late 1870s and in the early 1880s. His essays, though generally emphasizing only the verse at the expense of the prose, were of fundamental importance in establishing the position of the poet in the development of Italian literature. Thus, not only did Leopardi join his two famous contemporaries, Ugo Foscolo and Alessandro Manzoni, to constitute the great Romantic triad of Italy—all three of them rooted in the classical past and at the same time initiating modern literary traditions—but he was also accorded his rightful place among the most celebrated authors of Romantic Europe.

By the end of the last century Leopardi had become the best-loved poet of Italy. If, because of De Sanctis's reservations, some critics still had doubts concerning the greatness of the **Operette morali,** no one expressed any uncertainty as to the purity of the poems. It was left to our own century to produce a new understanding of Leopardi's essays and dialogues and to place them, in their own genre, on the same level as his poetry.

As a result of this widespread recognition, Leopardi's influence on modern Italian literature has been immense. Not only such good but minor figures as Vincenzo Cardarelli, but poets of acknowledged international significance such as Umberto Saba, Eugenio Montale, and especially Giuseppe Ungaretti, have found in him a model and a master. And outside of Italy his fame has been steadily growing. At long last Giordani's words are felt to be a true definition of the writer and are beginning to be taken for granted. (pp. 2-18)

Giovanni Cecchetti, in an introduction to Operette Morali: Essays and Dialogues *by Giacomo Leopardi, edited and translated by Giovanni Cecchetti, University of California Press, 1982, pp. 1-18.*

ADDITIONAL BIBLIOGRAPHY

Alexander, Foscarina. "Studies in Genius I: Leopardi." *Horizon* XV, No. 87 (April 1947): 195-214.
    A discussion of Leopardi's philosophy that identifies his idea of illusion as central to the themes of his works.

Arnold, Matthew. "Byron." In his *The Complete Prose Works of Matthew Arnold*. Vol. IX, *English Literature and Irish Politics*, edited by R. H. Super, pp. 217-37. Ann Arbor: University of Michigan Press, 1973.
    Identifies Leopardi, with Lord Byron and William Wordsworth, as among the most important authors of the nineteenth century. This essay was originally published in 1881 as a preface to Arnold's selected edition of Byron's poetry.

Barricelli, Gian Piero. *Giacomo Leopardi*. Twayne's World Author Series: Italian Literature, edited by Anthony Oldcorn, no. 753. Boston: Twayne Publishers, 1986, 231 p.
    A biographical and critical study of Leopardi.

Beardslee, Clarence. "Giacomo Leopardi: Patriot-Poet." *Italy America Review* II, No. 3 (July 1937): 1-5.
    An appreciative retrospective of Leopardi's life and works written on the centenary of his death.

Bickersteth, Geoffrey L. *Leopardi and Wordsworth*. London: Oxford University Press, H. Milford, 1927, 34 p.
    A comparison of the poetic achievements of Leopardi and William Wordsworth building on Matthew Arnold's criticism (see entry above).

Bini, Daniela. *A Fragrance from the Desert: Poetry and Philosophy in Giacomo Leopardi*. Stanford French and Italian Studies, edited by Alphonse Juilland, vol. XXVII. Saratoga, Calif.: Anma Libri, 1983, 188 p.
    A study designed "to show the presence in Leopardi of a dialectical inner relationship between philosophy and poetry, seen not as separate moments which exclude each other, but as mutually necessary."

Bonadeo, Alfredo. "Death in Leopardi's Prose." *Italian Quarterly* XVIII, No. 70 (Fall 1974): 3-19.
    Identifies three responses to the reality of death in the *Zibaldone*: acceptance of suicide, faith in the Christian doctrine of the soul's immortality, and belief in the idea that immortality can be attained through artistic achievement.

Brose, Margaret. "Leopardi's 'L'Infinito' and the Language of the Romantic Sublime." *Poetics Today* 4, No. 1 (1983): 47-71.
    Examines "L'infinito" in the context of European Romanticism, focusing on Leopardi's linguistic orientation.

Caesar, Michael. "Poet and Audience in the Young Leopardi." *The Modern Language Review* 77, No. 2 (April 1982): 310-24.
    Explores Leopardi's conception of his audience as revealed in the works written in 1818.

Carne-Ross, D. S. "Leopardi: The Poet in a Time of Need." In his *Instaurations: Essays in and out of Literature, Pindar to Pound*, pp. 167-92. Berkeley and Los Angeles: University of California Press, 1979.
    An appreciative introduction to Leopardi's prevalent themes focusing on such well-known poems as "Alla primavera," "Le ricordanze," and "Il passero solitario."

Carsanigo, Giovanni. *Giacomo Leopardi: The Unheeded Voice*. Edinburgh: Edinburgh University Press, 1977, 129 p.
    A study of the poet's life and writings focusing on his philosophical concerns.

Casale, Ottavio M. "Leopardi: The Poet of Paradox." *Italica* XXXIX, No. 1 (March 1962): 44-53.
    Identifies the central paradox in Leopardi's thought as the dichotomy between beauty and illusion on the one hand, and reality on the other. Casale discusses numerous instances of paradox in Leopardi's philosophy, poetic themes, and language, offering a close reading of "La sera del dí di festa" as evidence of the importance of recognizing these paradoxes.

Cecchetti, Giovanni. "An Introduction to Giacomo Leopardi's 'History of Mankind'." *Italian Quarterly* 5, No. 19 (Fall 1961): 3-15.
    Reviews the circumstances surrounding the composition of *Operette morali* before focusing on "The History of Mankind." In his examination of the "History" Cecchetti stresses Leopardi's interrelated themes of illusion and reality, humanity's unsatisfied yearning for happiness, and the power of love.

Chomel, Luisetta Elia. "Extratemporality in Leopardi's Major Idylls: 'La rimembranza' and 'Le temps retrouvé'." *Italica* 63, No. 2 (Summer 1986): 161-70.
    Studies Leopardi's themes of time and memory.

Cotten, Lyman A. "Leopardi and 'The City of Dreadful Night'." *Studies in Philology* XLII, No. 3 (July 1945): 675-89.
    Analyzes the influence of Leopardi and his writings on the Scottish poet and translator James Thomson, author of "The City of Dreadful Night," which was dedicated to Leopardi.

Del Greco, Arnold Armand. *Giacomo Leopardi in Hispanic Literature*. New York: S. F. Vanni (Ragusa), 1952, 285 p.
    Chronicles the course of Leopardi's critical reputation in Spanish-speaking countries and demonstrates his influence on Hispanic writers.

Enrico, Harold. "Shipwreck in Infinity: Leopardi, Coleridge, and Wordsworth on the Imagination." *Proceedings: Pacific Northwest Conference on Foreign Languages* XXI (1970): 93-101.
    Examines parallels and differences between the theories of poetic inspiration set forth by Leopardi and the English Romantic poets Samuel Taylor Coleridge and William Wordsworth.

Fleming, Ray. *Keats, Leopardi, and Holderlin: The Poet as Priest of the Absolute*. Harvard Dissertations in Comparative Literature, edited by James J. Wilhelm. New York: Garland Publishing, 1987, 159 p.
    A study of three Romantic poets who, having rejected traditional religion, endowed poetry with religious and philosophical significance.

Foster, Kenelm. *The Idea of Truth in Manzoni and Leopardi*. Proceedings of the British Academy, vol. LIII. London: Oxford University Press, 1967, 257 p.
    Compares the philosophies of Leopardi and his contemporary, the Italian novelist and poet Alessandro Manzoni, focusing on their quests for truth.

Garofalo, Silvano. "The Tragic Sense in the Poetry of Leopardi and Unamuno." *Symposium* XXVI, No. 3 (Fall 1972): 197-211.
    A discussion of similarities between the two poets dealing principally with their shared sense of the tragedy of life.

Koffler, Richard. "Kant, Leopardi, and Gorgon Truth." *The Journal of Aesthetics and Art Criticism* XXX, No. 1 (Fall 1971): 27-33.
    Compares Leopardi's and Immanuel Kant's approaches to discovering truth.

Kroeber, Karl. "The Reaper and the Sparrow: A Study in Romantic Style." *Comparative Literature* X, No. 3 (Summer 1958): 203-14.

Examines William Wordsworth's "The Solitary Reaper" and Leopardi's "Il passero solitario" as a way of defining the meaning and concerns of Romanticism.

————. *The Artifice of Reality: Poetic Style in Wordsworth, Foscolo, Keats, and Leopardi.* Madison: University of Wisconsin Press, 1964, 235 p.

Explores the movement from revolutionary to visionary ideals in the works of four Romantic poets. Kroeber also examines the functions assigned to poetry in the nineteenth century and studies the techniques developed to achieve these aims.

Kuhns, Oscar. "The Nineteenth Century." In his *The Great Poets of Italy, Together with a Brief Connecting Sketch of Italian Literature,* pp. 284-342. Boston: Houghton, Mifflin and Co., Riverside Press, 1903.

Includes a discussion of Leopardi in a survey of nineteenth-century Italian literature.

Leo, Ulrich. "'Il passero solitario': Study of a Motif," translated by Kurt L. Levy. In *Petrarch to Pirandello: Studies in Italian Literature in Honour of Beatrice Corrigan,* edited by Julius A. Molinaro, pp. 131-49. Toronto: University of Toronto Press, 1973.

A reading of "Il passero solitario" using the poem's title as the key to interpreting the work.

Maurois, André. "Giacomo Leopardi." In his *The Art of Writing,* translated by Gerard Hopkins, pp. 174-211. London: Bodley Head, 1960.

Examines Leopardi's tragic life as the inspiration for his poetry.

Nelson, Lowry, Jr. "Leopardi First and Last." In *Italian Literature, Roots and Branches: Essays in Honor of Thomas Goddard Bergin,* edited by Giose Rimanelli and Kenneth John Atchity, pp. 333-62. New Haven: Yale University Press, 1976.

Studies Leopardi's early work "Al' Italia" and his last poem, "La ginestra," in relation to the Italian poetic tradition.

Nietzsche, Friedrich. "Book Second." In his *The Complete Works of Friedrich Nietzsche.* Vol. 10, *The Joyful Wisdom ("La Gaya Scienza"),* edited by Oscar Levy, translated by Thomas Common, pp. 93-148. New York: Macmillan Co., 1924.

Includes a brief, complimentary reference to Leopardi's preeminence as a prose stylist.

Norman, Hilda. "Leopardi and the Machine Age." *Isis: An International Review Devoted to the History of Science and Civilization* XXXIV, No. 96 (Spring 1943): 327-37.

A study of Leopardi's attitudes toward the scientific advances of his day.

Origo, Iris. *Leopardi: A Study in Solitude.* London: Hamish Hamilton, 1953, 305 p.

The first and most reputable full-length biography of Leopardi in English. This work originally appeared in 1935.

Robb, Nesca A. "Leopardi." In her *Four in Exile,* pp. 55-81. London: Hutchinson & Co., 1948.

A study of the poet including a brief biography. Robb's commentary largely centers on her own personal impressions of Leopardi.

Rogers, Stephen. *Classical Greece and the Poetry of Chénier, Shelley, and Leopardi.* Notre Dame, Ind.: University of Notre Dame Press, 1974, 233 p.

Demonstrates the importance of classical antiquity to the thought and writings of André Chénier, Percy Bysshe Shelley, and Leopardi.

Sanctis, Francesco de. *Giacomo Leopardi.* Edited by Walter Bini. Scrittori d'Italia. Bari, Italy: n.p., 1953, 356 p.

Influential criticism of Leopardi in Italian.

Singleton, Charles S. "Italian Literature: Three Masters, Three Epochs." In *World Literatures,* pp. 154-69. Pittsburgh: University of Pittsburgh Press, 1956.

Identifies the three dominant figures of Italian literature as Dante Alighieri, Giovanni Boccaccio, and Leopardi.

Sowell, Madison U. "A Comparative Interpretation of Leopardi's 'La vita solitaria'." *Rocky Mountain Review of Language and Literature* 38, Nos. 1-2 (1984): 44-54.

Explicates the poem, examining its unity of structure and demonstrating Leopardi's "spiritual communion" with other poets. Sowell describes "La vita solitaria" as "a highly original fusion of wide-ranging sources, from classical poets to Petrarch to Parini, to Thomas Gray, and a skillful elaboration of a familiar Romantic theme."

Tsanoff, Radoslav Andrea. "The Poetry of Pessimism: Giacomo Leopardi." *The Rice Institute Pamphlet* IX, No. 4 (October 1922): 214-46.

Examines Leopardi's philosophy, focusing on such key points as his thoughts on nature, morality, happiness and illusion, imagination, the meaning of *noia,* and humankind's ability to sublimate sorrow and find value in life.

Vanasco, Rocco R. "Concept of Nature in Leopardi." *Proceedings: Pacific Northwest Conference on Foreign Languages* XX (1969): 85-7.

Describes four stages of development in Leopardi's concept of nature.

Van Horne, John. "Studies on Leopardi: Giacomo Leopardi and Classical Antiquity." *University of Iowa Humanistic Studies* I, No. 4 (1907-18): 15-31.

A discussion—based primarily on the *Zibaldone*—of the importance of classical antiquity to the development of Leopardi's thought and writings.

Wellek, René. "The Italian Critics." In his *A History of Modern Criticism, 1750-1950.* Vol. 2, *The Romantic Age,* pp. 259-78. Cambridge: Cambridge University Press, 1955.

Includes a discussion of Leopardi in a study of Italian Romanticism. Wellek praises the depth and originality of Leopardi's critical insights.

Whitfield, J. H. "Poetry and Patriotism in Leopardi." *The Modern Language Review* XLII, No. 2 (April 1947): 215-22.

Builds on the comments of the Italian critic Francesco de Sanctis (see entry above) in examining Leopardi's patriotism in "Al' Italia."

————. *Giacomo Leopardi.* Oxford: Basil Blackwell, 1954, 268 p.

A respected critical appreciation of Leopardi's writings.

Wilkins, Ernest Hatch. "Leopardi." In his *A History of Italian Literature,* pp. 399-410. Cambridge: Harvard University Press, 1954.

A general survey of Leopardi's life and works.

Williams, Orlo. "Ecclesiastes and the Poetry of Disillusionment." *The Cornhill Magazine* LXII (April 1927): 446-61.

Considers Leopardi's melancholy outlook with reference to other pessimistic poets, including Lucretius and the biblical author of Ecclesiastes.

Woodbridge, Benjamin M. "The Role of Illusion in Leopardi's Pessimism." *Italica* XXII, No. 4 (December 1945): 196-204.

A discussion of illusion as a key issue in Leopardi's philosophy of pessimism.

Ippolito Nievo

1831-1861

Italian novelist, poet, essayist, and dramatist.

Nievo is known primarily as the author of *Le confessioni di un italiano (The Castle of Fratta),* which is considered one of the greatest Italian novels of the nineteenth century. His other works, including earlier novels, poetry, essays, and dramas, remain untranslated and have received comparatively little attention from English-language critics. *The Castle of Fratta,* however, has been widely praised as a stirring historical novel and is recognized as a vivid portrayal of life in Italy during its struggle for cultural rebirth and independence from French and Austrian domination in the late eighteenth and the first half of the nineteenth century.

Nievo was born in Padua, the son of a doctor and a Venetian noblewoman. After attending various primary and secondary schools in Pisa and Mantua, Nievo entered the University of Padua at age twenty-one. He graduated in 1855 with a law degree and subsequently resided in Milan, where he was involved in literary and political circles and wrote a number of novels, poems, and plays, many of them based on patriotic themes. Although critics sometimes regard Nievo's *Angelo di bontà* and *Il conte pecoraio* as significant contributions to the development of realism in Italian fiction, these novels are not considered as important as *The Castle of Fratta,* which he began in December 1857 and finished in August of the next year. Following the outbreak of war in 1859 between Italian patriots and the Austrian army, Nievo joined the rebel forces under Giuseppe Garibaldi. In 1860 he served as one of Garibaldi's famous "Thousand" who attacked Sicily and overthrew the Bourbon government, an experience he chronicled in the poetry collection *Gli amori garibaldini.* The following year, while en route from Naples to Palermo, Nievo disappeared when his ship vanished without a trace, presumably in a storm. He was only thirty years old.

Although Nievo made sporadic efforts during his lifetime to publish *The Castle of Fratta,* his political and personal concerns prevented him from devoting his full energies to the project. The novel was not printed, therefore, until 1867, when, to avoid the political implications of its original title, the publisher decided it should appear as *Le confessioni di un ottuagenario* (Confessions of an Octogenarian) rather than *Le confessioni di un italiano* (Confessions of an Italian). Despite the change in title, it was the novel's patriotic spirit and themes that made it immediately popular with readers, gaining Nievo a level of renown that none of his previously published works had brought him.

The Castle of Fratta traces in semi-autobiographical fashion the life of its narrator, Carlino Altoviti, during Italy's fight for unification and freedom from French and Austrian rule in the first half of the nineteenth century. Beginning with Altoviti's boyhood at the ancient and picturesque Castle of Fratta, the novel follows his adventures in love and politics for over eighty years, blending history, fiction, and autobiography. Critics have pointed out that Altoviti's evolution from youth to old age is paralleled in the novel by different stages in the history of Italy's emergence as a sovereign nation. The major occurrences

in Altoviti's life are thus directly connected with the social and political changes taking place in Italy from the time of the Napoleonic invasions in the late eighteenth century up through the close of the story in 1855. At the center of Nievo's depiction of this momentous period in Italian history is his portrayal of the spirit and events surrounding the revival of Italian culture and national identity known as the *Risorgimento,* or "resurrection." This movement, which began in the early nineteenth century as a social and intellectual force, eventually found expression in armed revolt against the foreign powers occupying Italy and represented both a renewal of national pride and the revitalization of Italian politics.

The initial popularity of *The Castle of Fratta* is attributed by scholars to its nationalistic tone and patriotic subject matter, and during the nineteenth and early twentieth centuries critics focused largely on the political and biographical aspects of the novel, extolling Nievo as a gallant soldier-poet whose works reflected his heroic life. Modern critics have given less attention to the extra-literary aspects of *The Castle of Fratta,* concentrating instead on Nievo's strengths and weaknesses as a writer. Lovett F. Edwards's partial English translation of the novel in 1954 brought the work to the attention of numerous critics and reviewers, and recent commentators have acclaimed many aspects of *The Castle of Fratta.* Critics cite in particular Nievo's vivid descriptions of scenery and customs, his skillful blending of fictional events with a dramatic historical setting, and his astute characterizations. In discussing Nievo's characters, commentators have given particular attention to the psychological insight displayed in his portrayal of Pisana, Altoviti's lively and mercurial cousin with whom he shares an enduring romantic attachment. Most critics judge the relationship between the two lovers to be the most engrossing aspect of the novel. Yet, commentators have found fault with various facets of *The Castle of Fratta:* there is widespread agreement that the novel suffers from inordinate length and a lack of sufficient revision. Some have argued that the second book of the novel·is greatly inferior to the first precisely because Nievo never properly revised it. Despite these and other reservations concerning *The Castle of Fratta,* critics generally concur with literary historian Ernest Hatch Wilkins in describing it as the "one really great novel" of mid-nineteenth-century Italian literature.

PRINCIPAL WORKS

I versi (poetry) 1854
Angelo di bontà, (novel) 1855
Il varmo (novella) 1856
Il conte pecoraio (novel) 1857
Le lucciole (poetry) 1858
Gli amori garibaldini (poetry) 1860
*Le confessioni di un ottuagenario (novel) 1867; also
    published as *Le confessioni di un italiano,* 1931
    [*The Castle of Fratta* (partial translation), 1954; enlarged
    edition (partial translation), 1957]
Poesie di Ippolito Nievo (poetry) 1883
Teatro (dramas) 1962

Scritti politici e storici (essays) 1965
Tutte le opere narrative di I. Nievo. 2 vols. (novels,
    novellas, and short stories) 1967
Tutte le opere di I. Nievo: Poesie (poetry) 1970

*This work was written in 1857-58.

JOSEPH SPENCER KENNARD (essay date 1906)

[*In his commentary on Nievo and* The Castle of Fratta, *Kennard
emphasizes the connection between the novelist's life and his art,
praising his ability to capture an era in Italian history and his
skill at characterization and description.*]

Seldom has it been granted a man to so represent his age and
to be so identified with his environment that it is impossible
to separate his personality from that of his time and country.
The very name of Ippolito Nievo is an evocation of the romantic
and rebellious, heroic and imprudent, Italy of the early half of
the nineteenth century.

Whether we see him defying the rigour of an Austrian tribunal,
or donning the red shirt to follow Garibaldi and his thousand
heroes in search of a soldier's death, his was ever the same
heart, his was ever the same faith, that rang in his verse and
quivered in the romance wherein he revealed himself as he
would have wished to be! Nievo sang of that period as a poet,
lived through it as a soldier, and described it in a masterpiece.
His life, his novel, and his Italy are typical; each explains the
other.

Like a hero of some legend, like a personage of romance, to
utter a cry, to wield a sword, to love and to be loved; and then
in the fulness of joy on the morrow of victory and eve of glory,
his head crowned with war-like laurel and the halo of martyrdom, he made his exit, wrapt in a death that lends immortality
to his youth. The blue waves of the reconquered sea piously
concealed his agony, and kept the secret of that mysterious
shipwreck.

To depict this double evolution of the man and his environment
was Nievo's purpose in writing his romance, ***The Memoirs of
a Man of Eighty.*** Doubtless, too, he was impelled to reveal to
the world, in words vibrating with pathos, passion, and sincerity, the birth, growth, and fruition of that wonderful love
which had absorbed and inspired his own life. Marvellously
has he succeeded in both intentions.

Nievo begins:

> "I was born a *Venetian* in the year 1775; I will die
> an *Italian* whenever it please an overruling Provi-
> dence. This narrative," he continues, "of an indi-
> vidual life does not presume to be the history of a
> nation, but rather a foot-note pinned at the bottom
> of an official document. . . . The private activity of
> one individual, who has been neither so selfish as to
> live apart, entrenched against public troubles, nor so
> stoical as to ignore them, nor so wise as to spurn
> them, will, methinks, represent the general activity
> of his fellow creatures as correctly as the falling of
> one drop represents the drift of a shower."

In order to succeed in this double purpose, of presenting in a
complete and harmonious whole both the psychological study
and the historical picture, Nievo required not only to thoroughly
possess his subject, but also intuitively to know those profound

affinities that determine human relations. His imagination must
soar to embrace the whole scheme and return earthward to
reconstruct the details.

This Nievo accomplishes in his novel, where each phasis in
the life of Carlo Altoviti answers to an historical period; each
stage of the national evolution corresponds with a crisis in his
life. His childhood is spent in the midst of the obsolete feudal
Venetian world, in the Frioul; his boyhood is stirred by the
warlike tumult of the French invasion, is fascinated by the
glamour of revolutionary principles; his youth blossoms during
the early storms of the first risings and the tempests of Romanticism; his manhood ripens during the ensuing lull; his
quiet and smiling old age gazes on the first dawn of Italian
life, and rejoices in the prosperity and in the grandeur of his
country.

The synchronic evolutions of Carlo and of the national life each
completes, each explains the other; each is felt as a reciprocal
immanent force. Always in the torrent of social progress, we
are shown this atom impelled by the flood, yet in his turn
directing and transforming the society of which he is a part.

The first ten chapters of the novel are the strongest. They have
been written with abounding love and with intimate knowledge;
they are pages from Nievo's own life. The action takes place
in the Castle of Fratta and in the surrounding Frioul, a part of
the Venetian state. It is a wonderful picture of feudal Venetian
life at the close of the eighteenth century, mouldering in such
sloth that nothing could save it from ruin. (pp. 159-62)

No history could present a more accurate or more vivid description of the political and social life in the Italian Venezia,
during [the] early years of the nineteenth century, than this
romance of Nievo's. . . . But it is more than a history of a
political movement, more than a vivid picture of the social life
of the times. It is a marvelous revelation of personality; a
psychological study; full of reality, power, and modernity. It
lives! That double duo, Pisana and Carlo, Clara and Lucilio,
chant a wonderful hymn to the master passion—Love.

Here Nievo's youth, the passionate romanticism of his time,
the sensuous vitality of his race, quiver and throb. Here poet's
imagination, lover's emotion, hero's passion are all presented.
Here is complete analysis, penetrating observation.

Nievo's story starts at the beginning of [the lives of his char-
acters] and continues to the end. He avoids no difficulty, disguises no contradiction, scorns petty artifice. He encompasses,
understands, and relates everything about these people, and
suggests that indefinite, intangible something which is the very
soul of living, throbbing humanity.

Other psychologists generally limit their efforts to introducing
people whose personalities have already attained their development; they play their *rôle,* then step from the stage, and the
curtain drops. At best the more conscientious resume in a few
preliminary pages the personal experiences, the thousand influences, that have enlarged or restricted the mental and moral
growth of their characters; just enough to illumine the passing
crisis of life which is described, and on which our attention is
expected to converge. But Nievo's personages from the very
first moment stand out as a whole. No sooner are they evoked
than they live, live intensely, both individually and also as part
of the universal life.

In the work of a writer so athirst with sincerity, one of the
personages should be a portrait of the author and the confession
of his soul. Carlo Altoviti is what Ippolito Nievo would have

been had he lived the life he narrates. The dream of the one is the reality of the other. Nievo's short life was filled with activity, but his psychic activity becomes even more wonderful when we consider that his thirty years have contained the whole evolution of Carlo's eighty. He has not only plucked out of himself the whole matter, feelings, emotions, thoughts, and opinions, all the mental and passionate life of this literary creation, but he has had something of his own personality left over for other characters. (pp. 170-72)

Nievo has successfully analyzed [many passions]. . . . La Rochefoucauld has not depicted with more pitiless reality the thousand disguises of ambition. Patriots of all shades, braggarts, bullies, rogues—all are comprehended, all keenly observed.

Although the evolution of Carlo Altoviti is the echo of Nievo's evolution, still there are rebellious doubts, failings, which other personages are called to represent. Lucilio echoes ambitious and calculating Positivism. The suicidal despair of Leopardo Prevedoni has been a part of Nievo's passionate nature, else he could not have told in such heart-breaking accents this sad story.

Yet this powerful subjectivism is only a part of Nievo's talent. Alternating with these numerous passages, all throbbing with his own personality, we find by hundreds descriptions, portraits, reflections that are the outcome of the most modern objectivism. Then we have an exact and impressive reproduction of reality. Nievo draws back, conceals his own personality with an intuition of the literary formula which has since been discussed, but which no one had then foreseen.

Nievo can equal the best of our landscape painters, and with a poet's soul reproduce the great pantheistic soul of the world. There are pages about the sea that might have been worded by Maupassant, descriptions of the Fratta countryside which would not disparage Theuriet's best, and everywhere broadcast he has scattered with princely prodigality little sketches spontaneous and bright with exquisite colour and graceful outline. (pp. 186-87)

The rippling streamlet, the thickets alive with the chirping of birds, the marshes that slope down to a low seashore. As in a Fragiacom's canvas are the light and shade that play about that fountain of Venchieredo, complaisant to lovers. Like some picture by an old Dutch master are those scenes in the sooty, cavernous, mysterious kitchen at Castle Fratta.

Yet is there a flaw in Nievo's objectivism, a deficiency characteristic of the Italian genius of the time. His personages cannot talk. Their conversations are monotonous, colourless. Passion grows declamatory and good sense preaches heavily. These people have been speaking in a dialect which has moulded their habits of thought, the tenor of their feelings. In Nievo's effort at transposing this into pure Italian, the poignancy, the terseness of speech have stiffened, frozen, and become colourless.

Nievo's language has no accent, his style has no distinction. The pen trained by journalism to make readers understand that which the *censura* would punish if spoken plainly, can no longer reproduce primitive and familiar forms of speech.

Real humour, with its undercurrents of scepticism, despondency, vanity, and egoism, is not among Nievo's chords. His ideal of greatness is too high, his love of beauty too real, his emotion too genuine, for him to joke about them. Even at the moment when he depicts some meanness of life, he admires, worships Life, and is sure that grand and beautiful things may be accomplished. If he sometimes doubts, faith soon recovers

full possession; though he somewhat resembles Don Quixote, he still believes that the dream is more true than vulgar reality; though he whimpers with poor Yorick on caged birds, he rushes to set them free.

The most obvious objection to Nievo's romance is that it is too long. Events are too numerous, personages so crowded, that we have matter for a dozen ordinary novels. Few works of fiction have attained such dimensions without being divided into parts. Shakespeare's plays, that often embrace whole existences in ample historical pictures, are separated into acts. *La Divina Commedia* is repeatedly divided with subtle art. But Nievo's novel is so intemperate in style, so abounding in detail and in superfluity of material, that it intimidates the reader and perplexes the critic; yet it is easy to understand its purpose.

Under all this prodigality of invention, amidst all this abundance of accessory adornment, Nievo never loses sight of his purpose. Sometimes he seems to wander from his plan, but it is only seeming; he knows his path and his goal.

These [*Memoirs of a Man of Eighty*] have been compared to *War and Peace* of Tolstoi, to *The Sentimental Education* of Flaubert, to *Wilhelm Meister* of Goethe, and to *Gil Blas* of Lesage. The list could easily be lengthened. All the writers who have adopted the same conception of the novel, who have endeavoured to separate the individual from the mass and converge the divers elements into one central action, must agree in the general execution of their plan.

It would be interesting to study together these great landmarks of the human mind. Across the temperament of artists that have resumed a collective soul we could discern the disparities and the similarities, and thus better comprehend some of the great problems that these superior minds have investigated from diverse points of view and in varied ways and in different climes.

Nievo, whom fame has long ignored and now condescends to praise, is not one of the world's greatest writers, yet does he possess some of all the qualities for which other great artists have been admired: some of Flaubert's penetration softened by some of Tolstoi's pity, enlarged by some of Goethe's philosophy, and enlivened by much of Lesage's good sense. Though thoroughly Italian, Nievo's education, under Austrian obscurantism, took the form of the worship of abstract ideas, a dogmatism affected by French *"ideologues et faiseurs de programmes."*

The principles which have inspired the great Romanticists of northern Europe also penetrated the Italian conscience, putting forth spreading roots, sprouting pregnant buds. The wind of Romanticism blew, and this Romanticism, because it had spoken of rebellion against all fetters, because it aspired towards new horizons, and because in the beginning it set free imagination, this Romanticism seduced the Italian youth. But though Nievo owes to Classicism of the French pattern his first education, though he owes to Romanticism many of his best qualities and some of his failings, it is to the philosophers of the eighteenth century that he owes the substance of his thought.

He has fed his mind on the doctrines of the *Encyclopédie*; he has assimilated as much as he could of Rousseau's genial folly, Voltaire has taught him the art of darting the winged shaft, feathered with some serious idea, and Montesquieu has enlarged his social horizon.

But it is from Diderot, the untiring workman, the intellectual iconoclast, that Nievo has received his most fundamental conceptions.

From him too came that blending of materialism and poetry. Their manner of work is the same. In both there is exhaustive preparation through observation of facts and examination of documents. In both there is deep penetration, winged imagination, enduring labour, the imperious impulse to mix in life's strife. Their aims differ because they represent the evolution of different societies, and they are prompted by unlike motives.

Nievo is a fervid patriot, because his people aspire for a country. Humanitarian Diderot might have sacrificed his country to his dream of universal brotherhood. Then Nievo is constructive, Diderot is destructive. But to both we can apply these words of Carlo Altoviti:

> He who by disposition and by character will be always and in all things just towards himself, towards others, towards the whole humankind, that man will be the most innocent, the most useful, who has ever lived. His life will be a blessing to himself and to humanity; he will leave behind a deep and honourable trace in the story of his country. This example of victorious humanity will point out to all what Nature grants to her well-situated atoms.

It is because Nievo was one of those examples of victorious humanity, one of those "well-situated atoms" that fulfill the obligations entrusted to them, that his life and his novel deserve our consideration. (pp. 188-92)

Joseph Spencer Kennard, "Ippolito Nievo," in his Italian Romance Writers, *Brentano's, 1906, pp. 159-92.*

THE TIMES LITERARY SUPPLEMENT (essay date 1932)

[*In this excerpt from a centenary tribute to Nievo, the anonymous critic describes the major strengths and weaknesses of* The Castle of Fratta, *focusing on the author's characterization of Pisana, his portrayal of history, and the differences between the two volumes of the novel.*]

[There are] two general grounds on which *Le Confessioni di un Italiano* can be called a great novel—vividness and amplitude of human and historical delineation, penetration and psychological force as a study of a romantic passion. . . .

[The first volume] has a unity of interest and execution that is not to be found in the sequel. In spite of digressions and a certain romantic garrulity in the manner of its time, it presents a vivid scene of actual life, a number of sharply and humorously drawn characters, a variety of incident, some episodes of passion and a sufficiency, though not an excess, of that moralizing upon human conduct in general which is the avowed aim of the whole novel. The events described in this volume are typical rather than dramatic or directly historical; and the scene, from the opening description of the great kitchen in which the whole feudal family of Fratta lived, is set with that copiousness of detail that gives the great romantic novelists their permanent attraction. Those who love Scott and Dickens will at once feel at home in the castle of Fratta, whether it be at the solemn midday meal of the household, the general slumbers that followed it, the congregation in the kitchen till the light was lit, the intoning of the rosary at half-past eight, or some more solemn occasion, such as the review of the local militia by that hideous old fire-eater Captain Sandracca. It is a picture of the feudal system at its last gasp, a little world of antiques gathered within the walls of one castle with local religion, justice and soldiery all complete—the Count in his bagwig, a stiff and stilted tyrant, the Countess a shrew, the chancellor corrupt, the

canon a glutton, the captain a braggart, the sacristan a spy. The angelic Clara and the coquettish Pisana are the only beings that shed any light in this stuffy and murky old keep.

In the second volume this unity of scene is left behind: the castle and domain of Fratta simply decay in the background while every kind of vicissitude without illustrates the chequered history of modern Italy, from the fall of the Venetian Republic, in which Carlo Altoviti, aided by his father's money, becomes a patrician, through the Napoleonic regime to the typical exile of a patriot who has fallen into the hands of Austria and been freed after a harsh imprisonment. Portions of this long panorama are quite indigestible, it must be confessed, while others, which present the more dramatic or passionate episodes in the hero's experience are full of life and energy. Almost the final episode, as English readers may be interested to hear, takes place in London, the natural refuge of every exiled Italian. It is Lord Byron's heyday. Carlo is practically blind as the result of his imprisonment, and is tended by Pisana, who has left her husband to perform this service of devotion. She even supports him by begging in the streets, till help comes along in the shape of the young doctor who had hopelessly loved her sister Clara and now counts Byron his patient; and then, after a touching and eloquent scene, she dies in Carlo's arms. Unfortunately Nievo, never having been to England, was unable to give any colour to the London episode, which is only redeemed by the long passages of magnificent dialogue that bring it to a close, particularly by the speech of Lucilio Vianello, the doctor, on the reasons for continuing to live although in spiritual misery.

Indeed, if there were space, it would be interesting to follow the speeches that Nievo puts into the mouth of this Lucilio, a character almost terrifying in his disillusioned strength, who seems to embody the Promethean resistance of the human consciousness to all powers, human and superhuman, outside itself. Looking at Nievo's portrait, that of a young man in uniform with a most uncompromising nose, an alarming brow under a high forehead, and a sharp, decisive chin, we have little difficulty in seeing where the conception of Lucilio came from. Nobody, however, seems to know whence came, for certain, the conception of La Pisana, unless it was from Bice Melzi, his correspondent and friend. Had her creator been able to endow her with a little more charm, La Pisana might have been a rival to some of the favourite heroines of romance, to a Duchesse de Sanseverino or a Diane de Maufrigneuse; and the fact that he stinted her in this respect may be a proof that Nievo never knew, or at least never loved, her in the flesh. All through the novel we follow her, as Carlo followed her, from childhood to death, now loving her, now hating. She is the passionate, unstable coquette, spoiled by her upbringing, incorrigible in her innate duplicity, heartless to those who loved her, yet capable of any sacrifice that her heart or her caprice dictated, and saved from the taint of ignobility by her strength of will and her ability to judge, if not to correct, her own waywardness. It has been suggested that Pisana is an allegorical presentation of Italy, for obvious reasons; but if this idea was present in Nievo's mind he kept it to himself. What the reader finds in the character of Pisana—and it is surely enough—is a very remarkable psychological study of a passionate woman's nature, though conducted at times with an exaggerated gravity. The fiery young creature in the course of the novel runs the whole gamut of virtues and vices; now mad with jealousy of her sister, now coldly heedless that a man is dying of her disdain; now marrying a rich old nobleman for his money, and yet leaving her vicious mother all the enjoyment of it; capable of promising a young French officer that she would be his mistress if he would desert Napoleon and set Venice free, but also of slapping his face soundly when he refused, and of running off to live with Carlo as his mistress into the bargain. And a merry, heedless, spendthrift little witch she proves herself for the enchanting month they spend together in Venice. Not long afterwards Carlo surprises her as the mistress of his commanding officer in the Cisalpine army—a treachery which she redeems by rescuing him more than once from captivity. Devoted but unfaithful, she leaves him to tend the sick bed of her old husband; capricious, even in her love, she forces a wife on him, and then resents his display of conjugal affection; and finally, almost impossibly devoted, she begs in the London streets for him, content, for his wife's sake, to let him believe that she no longer loves him.

Those who have once made the acquaintance of Nievo's Pisana will certainly never forget her, and nobody, indeed, who has read the *Confessioni di un Italiano* will forget its vigor and humour, its strength of characterization and its power of impressing a scene upon the reader's mind. The largeness of its sweep, its vivid illustration of stirring historical events, its passionate patriotism and its political interest lift it high above the purely picaresque novel. (p. 18)

"Ippolito Nievo," in The Times Literary Supplement, *No. 1563, January 14, 1932, pp. 17-18.*

THE TIMES LITERARY SUPPLEMENT   (essay date 1957)

[*This critic reviews Lovett F. Edwards's translation of* The Castle of Fratta, *offering a positive appraisal of the novel.*]

Ippolito Nievo's novel, best known under the title *Le Confessioni di un Italiano,* is a celebrated work in the catalogue of Italian fiction. In spite of a generally acknowledged inferiority, as an artistic and literary performance, to Manzoni's masterpiece *I Promessi Sposi,* that is the only other single Italian novel with which it can legitimately be compared. It is of immense length, it has a tremendous vigour, it abounds in striking descriptions, it contains—especially in its earlier parts— a gallery of unforgettable portraits drawn with an incisive humour, a passionate love-story runs through it, it purports to cover eighty years of Italy's chequered history from 1775 onwards, and it is pervaded by a fervent faith in high moral and political principle which, though it occasionally leads the author into excessively long dissertations, not only redeems the often rambling garrulity of the narration but stamps upon the whole work the impressive character of Nievo himself, of the unswerving, self-sacrificing patriot, one of Garibaldi's Thousand, in contemplating whose lofty nature, as Benedetto Croce remarked, one feels a little intimidated but also uplifted. . . .

From a purely artistic point of view this vast narrative would bear a considerably closer pruning; for the second book, being largely concerned with the miserable history of the last days of the Venetian Republic and the diverse incidents of the vexed Napoleonic era in Italy, has by no means the compulsive power over the reader that the first book exercises. It is this first book, all the events of which take place in or near the ancient castle of Fratta in the Friuli, which has given this novel its lasting place in literature. Here, as Mr. Edwards writes, is depicted "the decay of a feudal society, drawn with swift touches of malignant wit, saved from caricature by the deep feeling for the pitiful and the absurd" [see Additional Bibliography]. The domestic life of the narrow community, the figures and actions of the old Count, the Countess, the timid Chancellor, the braggart captain of militia, the idle and greedy Monsignore, the

old servant Martino, and the two young girls, Clara and Pisana, who come to play leading parts in the subsequent story, are presented with irresistible spirit through the eyes of Carlo Altoviti, the narrator, then nothing but an ill-treated, neglected and unwanted poor relation.

Not only the daily round of the family life, centred on the vast, smoky kitchen, but such episodes as the siege laid to the castle by another noble and the uprising of the populace as the first French troops appear in the vicinity, have long been favourites of Italian readers. Moreover, the portrait of Pisana, whom we first meet as a little impetuous child, and to whom we only bid farewell on her deathbed towards the end, is justly famous not only as the counterpart to the hero Carlo, her devoted lover whom she led a life-long dance and yet begged for him in exile in the streets of London, but also as a consummate psychological study of a woman cursed from childhood by the tyranny of the senses which, in spite of many lovable qualities and great capacity for devotion, she is never able to withstand.

"A Great Novel of Italy," in The Times Literary Supplement, *No. 2907, November 15, 1957, p. 694.*

MARC SLONIM   (essay date 1958)

[*Slonim was a Russian-born American critic who wrote extensively on Russian literature. In this excerpt from a review of the first English-language translation of* The Castle of Fratta, *Slonim lauds the novel while expressing the common judgment that it suffers from a lack of revision.*]

Passions and tempestuous love affairs give a romantic tinge to his biography, but Nievo possessed a cold, analytical mind and a sharp sense of reality that made him abhor rhetoric and pretense. This combination of romantic externals with a hard core of rationalism and irony offers a key to the understanding of his main work, *Confessioni di un Italiano,* published posthumously in 1867 under the title of *Confessioni de un Ottuagenario,* now offered for the first time in an English version as *The Castle of Fratta.*

Nievo wrote the eleven hundred pages of this novel (abridged in the present English translation) between two campaigns, from December, 1857, to August, 1858, and never revised or pruned the original text. Hence the obvious defects of the book: uneven composition, wrong shifts of tonality and idiom, long-winded passages, verbose details and arid moralistic digressions.

Despite all its shortcomings, this epic, which so happily unites an unhurried pace of exposition with pulsating vitality, is a fascinating work. The 26-year-old novelist, who merged personal experience with creative inventiveness in a truly Goethian mixture of *Wahreit* and *Dichtung,* presents his imaginary hero, Carlo Altoviti, as an octogenarian bent on writing his autobiography. In the opening sentence of his confessions Carlo says; "I was born a Venetian, 18 September, 1775 . . . and I shall die, by the Grace of God, an Italian."

This defines the historical range of the novel: it unfolds a panorama of Italian life from the end of the eighteenth to the second half of the nineteenth century, with special emphasis on the disintegration and downfall of the Republic of St. Mark, the Napoleonic invasion and the patriotic struggle for Italy's unity and liberty. Within this general framework Nievo paints an ironical picture of feudal customs at the Castle of Fratta, near Venice, where the hero has spent his youth.

The description of the dying and corrupt world of Italian gentry, swept away by the new order emerging from wars and revolutions, belongs certainly to the best specimens of Italian prose. Not less masterful is another level of the chronicle, the adventurous love of Carlo and Pisano, Countess of Fratta, a capricious and tender, courageous and wanton woman, all contradictions and whims, equally capable of devotion and betrayal. Had Nievo created only this superb feminine character, perhaps unique in all Italian nineteenth-century literature, he would deserve a place of honor in European fiction of the romantic era.

The captivating relationship between Carlo and Pisana, with its alternation of submission and torture, of surprising leaps from sensuousness to spirituality, supplies the dynamics of the plot, but the story is continually expanded on various other planes. It is both a family chronicle and a historical narrative, and it includes a wonderful gallery of characters whose careers are traced with powerful realistic strokes from the cradle to the grave. Their diversity is truly amazing: excellently drawn noblemen and noblewomen of Fratta with all their retinue and servants, dissolute Venetian magistrates and grim Examiners of the Inquisition, Carlo's exotic father and sister who come from Turkey, peasants and landowners, officials and generals, priests and bandits, respectable matrons and girls of easy virtue.

What confers unity on this abundant historical and psychological canvas is the surprising maturity of the young author. He follows the tradition of the historical novel, set by Alessandro Manzoni, his older contemporary, but he is miles away from the enlightened catholicism and resignation of Manzoni's *The Betrothed.*

Nievo, a representative of a new generation, had an unquenchable vitality and belief in human happiness, a happiness that could be achieved by struggle, within the environment of national independence, political freedom and moral dignity. One may object to Nievo's rationalizing and didactic statements, but the immediacy of emotions he translated into his images and his central idea imparts a spirit of modernity and significance to that rambling, old-fashioned and yet charming *Castle of Fratta.*

> Marc Slonim, "The Making of Italy," in The New
> York Times Book Review, *January 5, 1958, p. 5.*

ALFRED F. ALBERICO   (essay date 1960)

[*Alberico explores the complex and occasionally disturbing elements of Pisana's character in* The Castle of Fratta.]

No matter what each reader of Ippolito Nievo's *Le Confessioni d'un Italiano* may conclude about the book as a whole, he inevitably joins the chorus of the admirers of Pisana, the heroic companion in the weaknesses, errors, and victories of the life of the unheroic protagonist of the novel, Carlino Altoviti. His esteem for this remarkable creation of Nievo's poetic imagination, however, is not essentially a constant, serene attitude. It is, in fact, a more complicated reaction on the part of the reader, characterized by a subtly permeating feeling of uneasiness. Such has been Pisana's power that she has evoked in the minds of her devotees the figures of some of the most adorable and provocative women of fiction (Manon Lescaut, Natacha, Albertine) while in the field of Italian letters, she has been hailed as the first female personage to break the long established mold which, through the centuries, had produced characters who were less than women because of the fact that

they were more than women. Pisana has been cited, therefore, not only as the "angelized" Beatrice, or the apotheosized Laura, or the Aurora of death, Silvia, but, first and foremost, as a real, accomplished woman in her senses and affections.

Much has been written about the vital part which Pisana plays in the structure of *Le Confessioni d'un Italiano* and about her effecting the final and most important step in the formation of Carlino's moral code and religious faith. It would be worthwhile now to attempt to understand more fully the nature of the disquieting element in Pisana's character, which determines an apprehensive note in the admiration inspired by this apparently fickle woman, who is always cloaked in the mystery and impenetrability which often surround powerful beings. Such a consideration and the conclusion to which it leads serve to elucidate further Nievo's art and his intellectual position which has justly been defined as being somewhere between the rationalistic ideal of the *Settecento,* as it was rendered turbid and complicated by early Romanticism, and the confining definition of reality proposed by verism and naturalism.

In 1855, some two years before the composition of *Le Confessioni d'un Italiano,* Nievo wrote concerning the realistic trends of his day the following condemnation, which appears to contain the aesthetic guide he was to follow in writing the novel and, in particular in creating Pisana.

> Stolta filosofia, che lacera il velo ideale onde la vita si copre naturalmente al giudizio degli uomini; e credendo indagare la vera natura dei fatti, li discarna di quella loro insita e comprensibile bellezza che è l'idealità! Stolta veramente, come colui che a negare la femminile avvenenza, deformasse col coltello anatomico il cadavere d'una vergine, e sotto la pallida rotondità delle guance, sotto le pudiche palpebre ed il candido petto mostrasse i muscoli recisi, il sangue grumato nelle vene, e i nervi sfibrati e tremolanti. Propongonsi taluni di cercare e conoscere la verità; ma già prima di accingersi a tanta impresa si figgono in capo che costei sia la più truce e sozza cosa del mondo, e ad ogni bellezza che incontrano, si la gettano via come cosa falsa o dappoco, e quando trovano del marcio, stropicciansi allor solo le mani e mostranlo a tutti, . . . Ma la verità è il tutto e non una parte; la verità comprende il grande ed il piccolo, il generoso e l'abbietto, il bello ed il brutto, come cosa terrena ch'ella è; chè se per verità si volesse intendere la corruzione dell'umana progenie, allora non è duopo di tanto affanno per provarla oscena e vituperevole; ma converrà pur trovare un altro vocabolo che significhi quella ragione immutabile posta da Dio nelle cose create, per la quale esse, come frazioni decimali, si raccostano perpetuamente alla perfezione senza toccarne la pienezza.

Pisana, *"come cosa terrena ch'ella è,"* is made up of the great and the small, of the generous and the abject, of the beautiful and the ugly. As a fusion of these qualities, she represents for Carlino that beauty which is ideality, the immutable force placed by God in his creatures, which perpetually incites them to approximate perfection even though they are not able to attain its fullness. In fact, the novel, in its most successful parts, is a depicting of the various elements of Pisana's personality as they motivate Carlino and an artistic description of the process of their fusion. This melding is attained only upon her deathbed and results in the concretizing of Carlino's courageous, if humble, ideal: to raise a family and through his own unheroic life, to give an imitable example to future citizens of a free and united Italy.

So it is that Pisana is the cause of Carlino's most intense happiness while she is at the same time the reason for his constant restlessness and for his most disconsolate moments of despair. As in their childhood, when Pisana would alternately lead Carlino from the height of innocent glee to the depth of a precocious anguish by her unpredictable acceptance or refusal to partake in his games, so throughout their lives, it is Pisana, or her memory, that instigates Carlino's important sentiments and actions. It is as a direct result of the intervention of Pisana that Carlino takes every important decision and makes every decisive move: from his first faint conception of a rational Providence at the Bastione di Attila, to his accepting the simple and austere moral code of the dead Martino, to his blissful oblivion of the shameful fall of the Venetian Republic, to his marriage to Aquilina, to his twice-repeated rescue from prison, to the indigent London exile, when the consumptive Pisana uses her last reserves of strength to beg for the temporarily blind Carlino, to the finding of courage and strength in her memory to strive to raise a family and live positively in the difficult years which, throbbing with restive suppression, preface the unification of Italy.

Because of his convictions concerning the real and the ideal, Nievo has given us a very complex Pisana. The reason for her continued success among the readers through the years lies in the fact that she is not presented to us as an ideal force, which, self-contained, evaporates from the realm of reality and, in the most generous of opinions, must be adjudged to the role of a well-assembled motor in the machinery of the plot. Instead, we follow the vicissitudes of la Pisana, child, adolescent, and woman, completely absorbed in her private drama as she, sometimes most cruelly and always unwittingly, becomes for Carlino *"il velo ideale onde la vita si copre naturalmente al giudizio degli uomini."*

The necessity of creating Carlino's ideal from the Nievian reality is a delicate task, and there are times when Nievo loses his artistic balance. Then the reader confronts the often decried moments of romantic farrago. On the other hand it is Nievo's adherence to reality which is responsible for the instilling and analyzing at the very core of his Pisana an aspect of the human personality which was later to be investigated more extensively and, at the same time, in a more limiting manner by Freudian psychology. Throughout the course of the novel, Pisana reveals certain traits, which would be labeled today as masochistic and sadistic, and these traits form the subconscious motivations for many of her actions, which otherwise remain unexplainable or even implausible unless one attributes to her creator highly questionable romantic devices.

It is the conceiving of these tendencies, never clearly recognized by Nievian criticism, as the center of a personal drama that renders la Pisana a passionate, fascinating character and accounts for the disquieting note manifest in the modern reader's feelings toward her.

Needless to say, Nievo does not refer to masochism or sadism in giving expression to his Pisana since such terms and the concepts implied by them were not in vogue in the middle of the *Ottocento*. Perhaps, it is Nievo's unawareness of such a thesis in developing Pisana and in portraying her love shared by Carlino that has caused her to be one of the most original and striking females of Italian literature. Furthermore, in the light of Nievo's wholesome and moral purpose in writing the **Confessioni d'un Italiano** and in view of his concept of reality, it should be quite obvious that he cannot wield the "anatomical knife" and depict his Pisana in a morbidly perverted manner.

Her personality having been deformed in childhood, Pisana is amoral rather than immoral; rather than perverted, she is represented as struggling against a threatening, incipient perversion instigated by an uncontrolled desire as a child to satisfy her whims and to seek and to accept only her own pleasure. Rapidly, she loses whatever sense of measure she may have had, and the rest of her life is spent in a discontented search for more and more pleasures until she finds that she can realize herself through service to others even if her spoiled nature causes her to administer such assistance in a way which is often agonizing to the receiver. Until the last few days of her life, Pisana (and perhaps the reader too) is not fully aware of the nature of her personal struggle; yet, she struggles successfully to keep the attainment of this strange pleasure from becoming the prime factor of her existence.

Pisana was endowed by nature with a sensitive soul capable of strong sentiments, with intelligence, and with beauty. It was the duty of society, through education, to nourish, refine, and bring forth these gifts. Her rare intelligence *"le si veniva viziando . . . fra le frivolezze e le vanità in cui era lasciata in balìa,"* and her sensitive soul was corrupted and drawn toward sensuous passions because her senses had been stimulated before her sentiments by the shoddy examples of the maids in whose care she had been neglectfully thrust by her mother, the Countess of Fratta. (pp. 13-16)

Carlino, writing many decades after the death and apotheosis of Pisana, solemnly warns,

> Dalla vita che le si lasciò menare essendo bimba e zitella, sorsero delle eroine; non mai delle donne avvedute e temperanti, non delle buone madri, non delle spose caste, nè delle amiche fide e pazienti: sorgono creature che oggi sacrificherebbero la vita ad una causa per cui domani non darebbero un nastro. E' presso a poco la scuola dove si temprano le momentanee e grandissime virtù, e i grandi e duraturi vizii delle ballerine, delle cantanti, delle attrici e delle avventuriere.

On the other hand, Pisana was also endowed by nature with a strong will bordering on stubbornness and with an unusually fine skill in using female wiles and coyness. At the age of three she has shown these traits to such a remarkable degree that Carlino exclaims,

> . . . conosceva già certe sue arti da donnetta per invaghire di sè, e avrebbe dato ragione a coloro che sostengono le donne non esser mai bambine, ma nascer donne belle e fatte, col germe in corpo di tutti i vezzi e di tutte le malizie possibili.

It is in considering Pisana as an illustration of what poor education and training can do to human nature that Nievo addresses many admonitions such as the following to the reader.

> E così le circostanze dell'infanzia, se non governano l'intero tenore della vita, educano sovente a modo loro quelle opinioni che formate una volta diventano per sempre gli incentivi delle opere nostre. Perciò badate ai fanciulli, amici niei; badate sempre ai fanciulli, se vi sta a cuore di averne degli uomini. Che le occasioni non diano mala piega alle loro passioncelle; che una sprovveduta condiscendenza, o una soverchia durezza, o una micidiale trascuranza non li lascino in bilico di creder giusto ciò che piace, e abbominevole quello che dispiace . . . Un grano di buona esperienza a nove anni val più assai che un corso di morale a venti . . . Il germoglio è nel seme,

e la pianta nel germoglio; non mi stancherò mai di
ripeterlo; . . .

The dangers of the development of an abnormal personality
are quite obvious in these facets of the character of the child
Pisana. The likelihood of a warped adulthood is greatly increased if there is not the tempering and coordinating effects
of a loving but disciplined guidance. There is, however, the
redeeming factor in Pisana's nature: an inborn generosity. At
first a haughty and almost disdainful generosity (*"qual sarebbe
d'una regina che dopo aver schiaffeggiato e avvilito per bene
un troppo ardito vagheggino, intercedesse in suo favore presso
il re suo marito"*), quite rare in its manifestations, it develops
until it purifies her and transforms her at the moment of her
death into the Pisana whom the readers of the *Confessioni*
cannot help but admire. For it is only then, after the absolutely
unselfish sacrifice of her life for Carlino, that she finds the
strength to openly avow her faults and to acknowledge a tardy
but not fruitless victory over them.

The faults in Pisana's make-up, which current taste would
prefer to label as sado-masochistic, appear at a very early age.
A very alarming note, for instance, is sounded by an incident
which occurs when Pisana is about eight years old and Carlino
about ten. Because of Pisana's mistreatment of him in their
games, Carlino runs away from the Castle of Fratta and returns
long after night has fallen. The final phase of a long, agonizing
punishment for such an action is imprisonment in a barren,
isolated room. In the middle of the night, Pisana comes to see
and console him, but the visit takes a strange turn when she
demands that he pull her hair as a punishment for her wickedness toward him. As Carlino refuses, she threatens to arouse
the whole household with her cries and to submit herself to
the beatings of her mother. Finally she herself performs the
punishment by suddenly and violently jerking her head and
thereby leaving in the hands of Carlino a lock of hair which
he has been fondling.

Poor Carlino is left somewhat disturbed by the outcome of
Pisana's visit, which at first had promised to bring him so
much comfort and joy.

> Scommetto che se la sua mamma nel castigarla le
> avesse strappato uno di quei capelli, ella ne avrebbe
> strepitato tanto da metter sottosopra la casa ed anche
> ora mi maraviglia che la sopportasse quel dolore senza
> batter palpebra; tanto potevano in lei la volontà e la
> bizzarria infin da bambina. Io poi non so se quei
> momenti mi fossero più di piacere o di rammarico.

There are many other points about this episode which might
be noticed: Pisana's kissing and sucking a wound on Carlino's
forehead *"con tal forza che non pareva una bambina di otto
anni."* Yet, the whole incident might be dismissed as the *mal-
izia* of children if it were not for the uneasiness created in
Carlino, also a child.

> . . . sentiva (dico sentiva, perchè a nove o dieci anni
> certe cose non si capiscono ancora) sentiva, ripeto,
> che l'immaginativa e la vanagloria di mostrare un
> piccolo portento di prodezza, c'entravano più assai
> dell'affetto in un tale eroismo. M'era dunque raum-
> iliato d'alquanto dal primo bollore d'entusiasmo. . . .

If Carlino (Nievo) can at one time attribute her extravagances
and disquieting cruelty to *"vanagloria," "immaginativa,"* or,
even more tellingly to *"una sfrenata bramosia di piacere,"*
there comes a moment when he is obliged to apologize for not
being able to explain the disturbing whimsicality of his companion. Pisana decides that Carlino should marry Aquilina just

as he seems to have attained his ideal happiness in living with
Pisana in their beloved, intimate Friuli.

When Pisana announces her decision to Carlino, Nievo allows
the reader to surmise a moral purpose in the marriage. Pisana,
loving Carlino more than herself, wants to give him a guarantee
of happiness in a marriage which will produce children. She
cannot have children, *"e così cosa rimane una moglie?"* The
sacrifice of their love, moreover, is an act of charity since it
will create the happiness of Aquilina, who, so Pisana feels,
cannot live without Carlino.

The marriage is successful, and the happiness it produces is
the children. One is tempted to ask Pisana *"cosa rimane una
moglie"* if she is only an instrument to give legality to offspring. When the period for producing children has passed,
there is no great sense of companionship or love between Carlino and his wife. In fact, as the years pass, they drift farther
and farther apart, and poor Aquilina, never equal to the mental
and spiritual capacity of her husband, becomes more and more
of a shrew and a bigoted old woman.

The reason behind Pisana's matchmaking, as well as the explanation of her tormenting attitude toward the blind Carlino,
whom she nurses and saves from starvation by going out to
beg in the streets, is made evident by Pisana herself in the
conversations with Carlino a few days before her death in
London. (pp. 17-19)

After [her] revelation, the reader can more fully appreciate the
almost voluptuous connotations of some of the remarks of
Pisana at the time when she exposed the marital plans she had
concocted for Carlino: *"e io unirò le vostre mani e benedirò
le vostre nozze,"* where there is a strange dwelling upon painful
moments. The reader also recalls and understands more readily
the striking inconstancy of the adolescent Pisana, who, one
day dressing and acting like Mary Magdalene, was apt to behave as an Amazon the next and who was always as ready to
shower her generosity upon anyone who directed a plea to her
as she was to abandon herself to a sensation of voluptuous
passion.

> Il suo volto aveva l'espressione più voluttuosa che
> mai scultore greco abbia dato alla statua di Venere
> o di Leda; una nebbia umida e beata le avvolse le
> pupille, e la sua personcina s'accasciò con tanta mol-
> lezza che Lucilio dovette circondarla con un braccio
> per sostenerla.

Unless her abnormal traits are acknowledged, Pisana, in many
instances, must be reduced to a mere device to advance the
plot, and it is as such that Luigi Russo judges her in the second
part of the novel. On the other hand, if such traits and the
important part they play in her actions are admitted, Pisana
emerges as a more complex and lifelike figure than even the
most favorable criticism of the past has recognized. Then the
reader realizes why Pisana's presence inspires a feeling of
discomfort at certain moments. Moreover, Pisana can be understood as a convincing example of Nievo's blending of realism
and idealism whereby a sublimating love is inspired by a struggle and victory over unhealthy desires, which never once are
permitted to dominate the narration or to become *per se* the
object of sordid curiosity. (pp. 20-1)

*Alfred F. Alberico, "Nievo's Disquieting Pisana,"
in* Italica, *Vol. XXXVII, No. 1, March, 1960, pp.
13-21.*

NICOLAE ILIESCU (essay date 1960)

[*Iliescu examines* The Castle of Fratta *within the context of nineteenth-century Italian fiction, demonstrating the ways in which Nievo's novel departed from tradition.*]

[When Ippolito Nievo wrote *Le confessioni di un italiano,* he] had already published two previous novels and two volumes of poetry, and he had written two tragedies, as well as a number of stories, sketches, and articles which appeared in various reviews in Udine, Milan, Brescia, and Mantua. But all the assiduous activity of the young Nievo failed to produce a work of positive literary value. His earlier work remained raw material, reflecting only the several cultural influences which the writer underwent successively as he came into contact with various authors. His efforts included tales of country life which exhibit a certain fashionable air (Giulio Carcano, Caterina Percoto, Francesco Dall'Ongaro, and George Sand had all published such works); poems in which the satiric spirit of Giusti is clearly felt; and Manzonian imitations, especially the two novels. Although these first publications do not have a value beyond that of pure experiment, they do reveal—together with Nievo's correspondence—the direction in which the writer was developing and which was to find a more felicitous expression in the thousand pages of the *Confessioni.*

Born in Padua in 1831, Nievo lived during the most troubled period of the Risorgimento, participating actively in that historic movement and meeting his death as one of Garibaldi's intrepid *Mille*. A combative spirit, he nonetheless remained cheerful always, and was continually given to joking, as his letters, his verses, *Gli amori garibaldini,* and even the reports he wrote on the expedition of the *Mille* testify. But his daring disposition and the cheerfulness of his temperament did not blind him to serious problems. These he approached with an open and meditative mind, intending to inquire deeply into them. While he did not profess to be a Catholic and showed no sympathy for ecclesiastic hierarchy, Nievo yet understood the social role of the priest and realized that to take the support of religion away from the peasants would mean the destruction of the foundation of their happiness. If one compares his tranquility with the grossly exaggerated imprecations of Guerrazzi, with the heartfelt hatred of the Church which Mazzini nourished, or with the deep-seated anticlericalism of Luigi Settembrini, one is struck not only by a difference in attitudes toward the problems of life, but also by a clear distinction on the level of the realism of their thought. Whereas Mazzini and the others proceed from more or less theoretical concepts in their antipathy to or rebellion against the Church, Nievo draws his conclusions from an examination of everyday reality. Thus to the theoretical and literary socialism of the times he opposes the observations made during his long wanderings in Friuli and through the countryside around Mantua. *La nostra famiglia di campagna, dipinture morali e di costume* constitutes the best documentation of the seriousness of his views. Here he presents the serenity of the peasants in the face of a life full of cares. He then contrasts this picture with the concept of class struggle. Nor is he satisfied with Mazzini's notion of a generic humanity, which in essence turns out to be a confused pantheism of secret societies. ''L'umanità è una nel tempo e nello spazio,'' he writes to his friend Francesco Rosari, ''bellissima idea, ma quest'idea che può consolare il mio cervello finchè esso lavoracchia o bene o male, nelle cellette del cranio, qual ristoro darà a me ridotto a nulla o, se vogliamo, anche disciolto nell'universo?'' In the same letter, he writes gravely: ''Non so, ma mi pare che il mondo sia diviso ormai fra gaudenti e ipocondriaci, impotenti quelli per difetto, questi per eccesso di sensibilità; i primi vigliacchi, i secondi disperati.'' He concludes, addressing himself once more to his friend: ''Un calore d'amicizia che confonda i dolori, e li tolga dal martirio di restar sordomuti! In ciò vive quest'ultimo barlume di bene che ci resta.'' Such words reveal Nievo's generous mind and the enthusiasm of his youthful spirit which, steadfast in all the actions of his life, colors as well *Le confessioni di un italiano.* It is with this disposition of mind that the author, after unsuccessful attempts to give life and artistic form to his moral world, poured out the [*Confessioni*].

The reader or critic faces several problems at the end of a reading of Nievo's novel. On the one hand, a reading of the novel leaves no doubt that in the author's eyes life has value only if it is conceived within the compass of moral and social justice. ''La vita fu da me sperimentata un bene, ove l'umiltà ci consenta di considerare noi stessi come artefici infinitesimali della vita mondiale, e la rettitudine dell'animo ci avvezzi a riputare il bene di molti altri superiore di gran lunga al bene di noi soli,'' says the hero of the novel, Carlo Altoviti, at the close of his memoirs, thus voicing a thought which enters into the ethical vision of life proper to romanticism. And it is in the name of the ideal of Italian unity that the *Confessioni* opens: ''Io nacqui veneziano ai 18 ottobre del 1775, giorno dell'evangelista San Luca, e morrò per la grazia di Dio, italiano quando lo vorrà quella Provvidenza che governa misteriosamente il mondo.''

On the other hand, seen in the light of the history of the novel prior to Nievo, the book strikes us with the thought that the treatment of the problems of life and literature has undergone a change, and that the conclusions arrived at are clearly different from what we find in the works of Manzoni, D'Azeglio, and Guerrazzi. In order to establish, therefore, the position and importance of *Le confessioni di un italiano* within the limits of the nineteenth-century Italian novel, we must first of all clarify further the relationship between Nievo and the literary tradition of which he is the natural heir. Only then can we consider what is new in the novel.

Besides the aforementioned literary influences, which characterize Nievo's works previous to his major novel, and in addition to the moral conception of life discussed above, several other elements in the *Confessioni* link Nievo to the nineteenth-century writers who preceded him. Among these, the element of adventure is of primary importance.

Conceived as a vast fresco which takes in more than half a century of Italian history and life, *Le confessioni di un italiano* becomes defective at a certain point in the narration when there occurs a change of subject matter and of tone. While the first half of the novel draws its inspiration from the ''ultimo e ridicolo atto del gran dramma feudale,'' seen through the vicissitudes of a family of country squires of Friuli, the second part, which begins with Chapter xv (after the episode dealing with the fall of Venice), is built upon the innumerable political and military events of the first half of the Italian nineteenth century. The protagonist takes part directly in these events. And it is precisely in the second part of the book that the subject matter becomes dispersed and fragmentary and the reader finds himself in the presence of an ''adventure'' in the manner of D'Azeglio and Guerrazzi. The story of Aglaura, for example, gives rise to a succession of extraordinary events, and the reader is made to follow the exploits of a character who is given to mysterious flights, leaps from high cliffs, attempts passionately to avenge betrayed love, and is given to astounding misunderstandings. None of this belongs organically to the structure of the work. Like the story of the courtesan Selveggia in D'Azeglio's *Niccolò de'Lapi*, this is a spurious element in the *Confessioni.*

The same thing must be said of the mysterious life of the hero's father, Todero Altoviti. His appearances and disappearances come about by way of certain strange and unaccountable coincidences at the most dramatic moments of the protagonist's adventures. Of a strongly romantic flavor also are the well-known episodes of the fire of Velletri and the rescue *in extremis* of the hero by way of Pisana's almost miraculous intervention.

Such elements, stuck haphazardly together in the novel, destroy the equilibrium and the unity of the narration, and constitute the greatest defect of the work, creating as they do a serious unevenness between the first and second parts of the novel. It is interesting to observe how the poetic vein of the author diminishes precisely in that part of the novel where he most relies on the traditional techniques of the historical novel. Desiring to impart a character of historical reality to his work, Nievo fails to contain his subject matter within a single focus.

Benedetto Croce severely charged this lack of unity in the tone and manner of the book's narration, but he considered it inherent in the autobiographical form to which the novel belongs. But surely Nievo's is not, as Croce asserts, an error of literary genre. The explanation is an obvious one; the writer is simply held too firmly by the literary and patriotic ideals of his time to be able to find in himself the spirit or time for meditation on his historical material. If we then add the fact that the historical novel exercised in his time an almost absolute control over narrative, we are better able to understand the nature of the error which Nievo, a youth of scarcely twenty-seven years, makes. Not even Verga could escape the predominance of the historical novel and wrote three Guerrazzi-style novels of the worst quality.

From the literary climate of his century Nievo also drew his method of interweaving civil history with the depiction of the passions of his protagonist. From the time of Foscolo's *Ortis*, through *I promessi sposi* and all the novels of D'Azeglio and Guerrazzi, such a method had been adopted repeatedly.

Even more direct ties may be established between Nievo and Manzoni. The situation in which Carlino finds himself during the Portogruaro uprising calls to mind Renzo in the midst of the Milanese riots. Similarly, the "pathetic" (Nievo's word) farewell to youth with which the twelfth chapter opens may be considered a reminiscence of the well known passage from *I promessi sposi* which begins "addio, monti . . ." Also undoubtedly inspired by Manzoni is the scene between Clara and Padre Pendola, in which the family history of Gertrude is recounted. Other comparisons could no doubt be made with Goldoni, himself a native of the Veneto region. But instead of literary derivations, it would be better to speak of the native comicality which is characteristic of the *Veneti* and of the identical temperaments of Nievo and Goldoni. Further traditional elements in the novel include references to proclamations, historical documents, and official acts.

In the sphere of moral attitudes and literary derivations, Ippolito Nievo may, then, be studied along with the writers who preceded him. This sphere, however, is composed of relatively external elements which are inherent in every writer, while *Le confessioni* does contain new material even if it is not entirely realized artistically. The novel is based, on the whole, on

presuppositions considerably different from those which the nineteenth-century Italian novel could offer. (pp. 275-77)

[The] novel's plot is sufficient to show that, from the initial positing of the subject, it is possible to draw a line of demarcation between the *Confessioni* and antecedent historical novels. The myth of distant history, present even in Manzoni's tragedies and to a certain extent in *I promessi sposi*, is nowhere to be found in Nievo's novel. The lofty history of the past, which had permeated the novels of D'Azeglio and Guerrazzi, holds no attraction whatsoever for Nievo. Its place is taken by the everyday happenings of contemporary times, recalled in autobiographical form by one of the living protagonists of those times. The story of the *Confessioni* is the story of Carlino Altoviti, felt and lived in a real setting, not merely constructed in accordance with some didactic intent. We are offered here a provincial and commonplace world from which the great civil dramas of Manfredi, Ferruccio, and Michelangelo have disappeared, along with the great injustices suffered by Carmagnola, Beatrice, and Ermengarda; gone also is the sense of *nulla* which accompanies Adelchi. A world of little people and ingenuous country squires takes the place of Niccolò de'Lapi and Ettore Fieramosca. The great figures in the novels of D'Azeglio and Guerrazzi and even *l'innominato* in *I promessi sposi* are surrounded by a kind of majestic light; they are all exceptional people and dignitaries, in one sense or another. It is through them that history takes on form and content. There is nothing of this in the *Confessioni*. At the close of the novel, Carlo Altoviti barely succeeds in putting together his memoirs, from which, in any case, there can be drawn no great lesson for posterity. At the very most, the protagonist succeeds in becoming a little more aware of himself, in discovering, if anything, himself, precisely as eighty-five years of life have formed him.

With the triumphant entrances of the great characters of the historical novel in mind and with almost a touch of irony directed at the noble figures of history, Nievo makes the following comment: "Il maggior effetto prodotto nei lettori del capitolo primo, sarà stata la curiosità di saper finalmente chi fosse questo Carlino." Thus the author finds a justification for Altoviti's appearance:

> Mia madre aveva fatto, com'io direi, un matrimonio di scappata coll'illustrissimo signor Todero Altoviti, gentiluomo di Torcello: cioè era fuggita con lui sopra una gallera che andava in Levante, e a Corfù s'erano sposati. Ma parve che il gusto dei viaggi le passasse presto, perchè di lì a quattro mesi tornò senza marito, abbronzata dal sole di Smirne, e per di più gravida. Detto fatto, partorito che la ebbe, mi mandò senza complimenti a Fratta in un canestro; e così divenni ospite della zia l'ottavo giorno dopo la mia nascita. Quanto gradito, ognuno lo può argomentare dal modo con cui ci capitavo. . . . La signora Contessa, fin dalla prima occhiata, sentì per me l'odio più sincero, e non tardai a provarne le conseguenze. Primo punto si giudicò inutile, per un serpentello uscito non si sapeva di dove, prender in casa o assoldare una balia. Perciò fui consegnato alle cure della Provvidenza, e mi facevano girare da questa casa a quella, dove vi fossero mammelle da succhiare, come il porcello di Sant'Antonio, o il figlio del Comune. Io sono fratello di latte di tutti gli uomini, di tutti i vitelli e di tutti i capretti che nacquero in quel torno nella giurisdizione del castello di Fratta; ed ebbi a balie oltre tutte le mamme, la capre e le giovenche, anche tutte le vecchie e i vecchi del circondario. Martino infatti mi raccontava che, veden-

domi qualche volta innaspato per la fame, aveva do-
vuto compormi un certo intingolo di acqua, burro,
zucchero e farina, col quale m'ingozzava finchè il
cibo giunto alla gola mi impedisse di piangere.

The reader understands at once that there is no place for great
actions in the life of such a character. If we remember that
D'Azeglio's Ettore Fieramosca had as preceptor no less a figure
than the humanist Pontano, we realize that the difference could
not be greater. In this respect, one should note the tremendous
irony which is evident in Altoviti's comments upon Foscolo's
delusions of grandeur and his pompous way of speaking, as
well as the passages containing the drama of the will of Lucilio,
a character who incarnates the conception of life objectified in
a single ideal.

At the conclusion of the memoirs, when the hero must supply
a reason for his confessions, the only words he finds are these:

Nè il mio semplice racconto rispetto alla storia ha
diversa importanza di quella che avrebbe una nota
apposta da ignota mano contemporanea alle rivela-
zioni di un antichissimo codice. L'attività privata di
un uomo che non fu nè tanto avara da trincerarsi in
se stessa contro le miserie comuni, nè tanto stoica
da opporsi deliberatamente ad esse, nè tanto sapiente
e superba da trascurarle disprezzandole, mi par debba
in alcun modo riflettere l'attività comune e nazionale
che l'assorbe; come il cader di una goccia rappresenta
la direzione della pioggia. Così l'esposizione dei casi
miei sarà quasi un esemplare di quelle innumerevoli
sorti individuali, che dallo sfasciarsi dei vecchi or-
dinamenti politici al rafforzamento dei presenti com-
posero la gran sorte nazionale italiana. Mi sbaglierò
forse, ma meditando dietro essi potranno alcuni gio-
vani sbaldanzirsi dalle pericolose lusinghe, e taluni
anche infervorarsi dell'opera lentamente ma dure-
volmente avviata, e molti poi fermare in non mutabili
credenze quelle vaghe aspirazioni che fanno loro ten-
tar cento vie prima di trovar quell'una che li conduca
nella vera pratica del ministero civile. Così almeno
parve a me. . . ."

This generic language, delivered here with the exact tone of
an aged provincial, and this philosophy of *aurea mediocritas*
indicate, on the one hand, the fact that "eran passati i tempi
degli impeti generosi ma inconsiderati," to use the words of
one critic [D. Mantovani]. It reveals as well a sudden reopening
of the Italian novel to the real world after thirty years of infatuation with the attempt to restore life to the distant and dead
past.

This return, as it were, to the manner of the humble Manzonian
character is in itself a sign of the great maturity of Nievo. A
character of no merit whatsoever who begins a cycle of history
and concludes it in the same fashion, moralizing and scribbling
his confessions in a remote village of an even more remote
corner of the country, is indeed a great novelty in the midst
of all the fuss and hyperbole of Guerrazzi, D'Azeglio, and
Mazzini. Nievo understood, just as Manzoni had, that in order
to infuse new life into a narrative it was necessary to return to
a living, contemporary, and emotionally experienced reality,
and to abandon stereotyped noble characters and the practice
of digging up past events and making them look majestic.

This was Nievo's assumption when he set about retracing the
life of his octogenarian, setting the scene in Friuli and Venice.
These were the places Nievo knew and loved best and which,
therefore, he could feel most sincerely and reproduce most
artistically. In this assumption lies as well a second reason for
the poetic rupture of the *Confessioni* at a certain point. We

have said earlier that when Nievo attempts to play the role of
historian, following in the wake of his predecessors, his capacity for recollection is diminished. It should now be added
that the world of Friuli is the world lived by the writer, and,
consequently, a part of his innermost emotions (almost all the
locales of the action are of an autobiographical nature), while
the world of history is somewhat foreign to him, illuminated
by a point of view more problematic than sentimental.

But Manzoni's characters, while always supremely human,
move, in a certain sense, within a well-defined scheme of
thought; they respond to a design of the author and justify a
dialectic, which is that of man's responsibility with regard to
his own destiny. In Nievo, instead, each character, with the
exception of Lucilio and Clara (who incarnate a polemical
concept), moves in a spacious field of actions, thoughts, and
sentiments without that sense of rational inevitability which
gives importance and singularity to Manzoni's personages. The
protagonists of the *Confessioni* act only in the human world,
in history, and they lack Christian transcendence. They are
simply caught up in the unceasing flow of events, and it is
only with respect to such events that they achieve their destiny
or fail, as, in a way, with Verga's characters. The absolute
truth, the truth which contains "un effetto definitivo," which
was Manzoni's objective, acquires in Nievo a relative character; from generation to generation, the value of life is effected
in an immeasurable progression. When Manzoni moves Renzo
and Lucia from Lecco and develops around them an entire
period of history and a multiplicity of events, he does so with
the sole intention of shedding light on "the condition of mankind" from the point of view of man's ultimate destiny. And
one realizes that there is no other alternative.

This is not the case with Nievo. The ideals of Carlo Altoviti
live on in his children, who carry them into Greece and America; one period runs into another, and the past opens the way
to the future in a perpetual concatenation and in a progressive
widening of horizons. Altoviti says:

La mia esistenza temporale come uomo, tocca ormai
al suo termine: contento del bene che operai, e sicuro
di aver riparato per quanto stette in me al male com-
messo, non ho altra speranza ed altra fede senonchè
essa sbocchi e si confonda oggimai nel gran mare
dell'essere . . . Ma il pensiero prima di tuffarsi in
quel tempo che non avrà più differenza di tempi, si
slancia ancora una volta nel futuro degli uomini; e
ad essi lega fidente le proprie colpe da espiare, le
proprie speranze da raccogliere, i propri voti da
compiere.

It is no longer "la fiducia in Dio" which "raddolcise e rende
utili per una vita migliore i guai" of this world, according to
Lucia's conclusions. Life is "sperimentata un bene" by Altoviti, insofar as men are "artefici infinitesimali della vita
mondiale."

The reality to which the author adheres is that of the protagonist, a reality made up of mistakes and simple pleasures,
recollected only in what it contains that is human and varied.
Manzoni's pessimism, which is the real source of irony in *I
promessi sposi,* has as its counterpart in Nievo's novel a vigorous faith in life and in the future (which is consciousness of
time), leading Carlo Altoviti to tranquility, indulgence, and an
even temperament. Croce errs badly when he asserts that the
recollection of life in the castle of Fratta is presented in a tone
"quasi costante di caricatura e di beffa." Just the opposite is
true. The author's presence in the story (through his hero) is
actually a sentimental involvement in the various vicissitudes

of his characters, especially in those events which take place at the castle of Fratta. This involvement is evident in the vivacious picture which Altoviti renders of that "piccolo areopago di buon temponi" which is the community of the castle and of that "intrecciarsi di contese di frizzi, di reticenze e di racconti che somigliava un mosaico di parole" which characterizes that community. One may even go so far as to say that when the protagonist, after the many misadventures of his life, turns his thoughts to the castle of Fratta, the comparison of the present with the world reawakened by his emotions results in heartfelt melancholy:

> Dov'era Amilcare, dov'erano Giulio del Ponte, Lucilio, Alessandro Giorgi, e dov'ero finalmente io, benchè meno di essi trasportato da furore d'indole a imprese arrischiate? Profughi, esuli, morti, vaganti qua e là, come servi cacciati a lavorare sopra campi non nostri, senza tetto certo, senza famiglia, senza patria sulla terra stessa della patria . . . Bruto (the only one of the Hero's companions who, invalid, returns to Fratta) era ormai escluso dall'agone dove noi andavamo giostrando alla cieca senza sapere quale sarebbe stato il premio di tanti tornei. Almeno aveva ritrovato il focolare paterno, il nido della sua infanzia, una sorella da amare e da proteggere! Il suo destino gli stava scritto dinanzi agli occhi non glorioso forse nè grande, ma calmo, ricco di affetti e sicuro.

Nievo's own dual character of cheerfulness and meditation thus finds artistic fulfillment in the waggish and recollective aspect of the narration in *Le confessioni di un italiano*. Between Manzoni and Verga, Nievo's novel is the only literary work in which the life of the protagonist is constructed with true elements of human sensibility: emotions, mistakes, enthusiasms, defeats. But precisely because of his inclination to regard life more from a sentimental than a rational point of view it would seem that Altoviti is more an anticipation of Padron 'Ntoni in *I Malavoglia* than a continuation of Fra Cristoforo. Altoviti may further be considered an ancestor of Verga's characters in that he habitually recovers his equilibrium in the midst of the most terrible misfortunes by virtue of a kind of inertia which precludes any daring flight: "Tutti mi verranno addosso con baie e con rimbrotti, ma io lo confesso senza vergognarmene, ebbi sempre gli istinti della lumaca, ogniqual volta il turbine non mi portò via con sè." (Verga in turn will speak of "l'ideale dell'ostrica" in *Fantasticheria*.) And again: "Fare, lavorare, sgobbare mi piaceva per prepararmi una famiglia, una patria, una felicità; quando poi questa mèta della mia ambizione non mi sorrideva piú nè vicina nè sicura, allora tornavo naturalmente col desiderio al mio orticello, alla mia siepe, dove almeno il vento non tirava troppo impetuoso, e dove sarei vissuto preparando i miei figliuoli a tempi meglio operosi e fortunati." This is the moral philosophy of a utilitarian with good sense; it also represents resignation in the face of life. "Vi sarete accorti," Altoviti continues, "che di tutte le professioni cui io mi dedicai, a nessuna mi aveva condotto il mio libero arbitrio, e che la volontà degli altri, o la necessità del momento, o un concorso straordinario di circostanze m'avevano dato in mano il partito bell'e fatto, senza ch'io potessi pur ragionarci sopra."

How far this is from the spirit of the historical novel! One should simply live from day to day, be satisfied with whatever the moment happens to offer, and count upon this only; such is the philosophy of the spit-turner turned sage. It is as good as any, for one proceeds "pian piano scendendo verso la vecchiaia, mentre il paese riacquista la sua gioventù"; because

"padri e figliuoli sono un'anima sola"; and the world "cambia sempre e sempre vive." The concept of incessant renewal thus reappears in a different guise. Giovanni Verga (*Fantasticheria*) makes use of an analogy with the world of ants to express this same notion of the unnoticed passing of things and their constant rebirth. Earlier, Nievo's protagonist spoke in this fashion: "Ebbi la pazienza della formica, che, capovolta dal vento, cento volte perde la sua strada e cento la riprende per compiere a passi invisibili il suo lungo sammino." However, while Verga is always tragic, Nievo remains idyllic even in the face of fate:

> Nel riandare la mia storia, io penso sempre alla margheritina, a quel modesto fiorellino dal bottone d'oro e dai raggi bianchi, sul quale le zitelle traggono il pronostico d'amore. Una per una le cavano tutte le foglie, finché resta solo l'ultima; e così siamo noi, che dei compagni coi quali venimmo camminando lungo i sentieri della vita, uno cade oggi, l'altro domani, e ci troviamo poi soli e melanconici nel deserto della vecchiaia.

But it is in the love story of Altoviti and Pisana that Nievo fully reveals his power and originality. In the Italian literary tradition there had been but one type of woman. Whether her name was Beatrice or Laura, Simonetta or Angelica, Clorinda or Sofronia, Lucia, Silvia, or Nerina, she had always had symbolic value. She had always been seen and situated in a light of superior goodness or beauty, always singularly fascinating, but without a completely human life of her own. This applies even to Ermengarda in Manzoni's tragedy *Adelchi*, although she remains the most feminine of the heroines of this gallery. The type appears in Nievo, too, here she is called Clara—but by now it is almost as if the obituary of the woman as symbol were being written.

Le confessioni di un italiano is the novel with which the *donna angelicata* disappears from Italian literature. Clara represents the beauty, sweetness, and purity of an entire series of exceptional women, but with her are buried all of these abstract qualities. The place of such women is taken by Pisana, and it is from her that the women of Verga, D'Annunzio, and modern Italian novelists stem. Pisana seems exceptional today only when we look to the past. In this sense, the representation of her character is the result of a supreme test of courage on the part of the author who conceived her and gave her life in literature. She is a woman who no longer has a "function" and who does not represent moral concepts, neither *per se* nor in contrast with someone else. She lives entirely through her own emotions and her own impulses, and has no history; she is a grown woman right from childhood. She defies all definitions; she is "una creatura siffatta," says the protagonist, "che soltanto chi nacque, si può dire, e crebbe con lei, e pensò sempre a lei, e non amò che lei, può averla interamente indovinata." In the *Confessioni* the author does not place her in an idyllic environment, as he does with the lovers Clara and Lucilio or Doretta and Leopardo Provedoni. Indeed, genteel surroundings would hardly be in keeping with her restless disposition. Pisana is "volubile come una farfalla che non può restare due minuti sulla corolla d'un fiore," says Carlo Altoviti, and the definition is to be taken literally, not merely as a commonplace poetic expression. The hero says of her: "Un andare, ora quieto ed eguale, come di persona che discerna poco, ora saltellante e risoluto, come d'una scolaretta in vacanza; adesso muta, chiusa pensierosa, di qui a poco aperta, ridente, se volete anche ciarliera." The critic Dino Mantovani describes her in the following manner: "Negli scatti di indole imperiosa, nella seduzione carezzevole, nella fiamma di vita che emana da tutto l'esser suo . . . donna che sa mescolare il male col bene, che può apparire matta e sconsigliata, accarezzare e ferire e amare sempre.''

Confronted with such a character, upon whom the author imposes no censure of a moral nature, another critic [M. Filograsso] believes that she does not represent Nievo's feminine ideal. The question in itself is an idle one, but merely stating it suggests how deeply rooted in Italian literature is the figure of the woman of superior virtues. The same question reveals the singularity of Nievo's position in the patriotic and civil narrative of the last century. At the center of the *Confessioni* stand Pisana and Carlo Altoviti; around them is woven the narration of a love story in which the sundry other threads of the plot meet to create the unity of the novel. The author removes from his stage all other female figures, creating space for Pisana alone; the hero opens his memoirs with her, one may say, and completes them while remembering only her at the very end.

In summation, one might say this of Pisana: she leaves the ancestral feudal castle, where everything is anachronistic, to live a passionate life, free from questions of etiquette or morals and guided exclusively by her own disposition, with the identical kind of violence with which she opens the way for the contemporary novel, situating herself well on this side of any angelic ideal, in the world of tormented and contradictory creatures.

As for the language of the novel, we need only say that it flows slowly and smoothly, as the language of memoirs ought to; it is far from the rhetoric of post-Manzonian novels and is unified in its totality, without overt reworkings of old models. Indeed, in contrast with such rhetoric, there are here and there expressions in the dialect of Veneto which best convey certain nuances of Nievo's humor.

It remains an exceptional fact that the author of *Le confessioni di un italiano,* at twenty-seven years of age, without ever having the opportunity to revise his text, could find the proper tone and language for the emotions of both childhood and old age. Bright colors, immediate and yet tenuous images for the world of children; and for the octogenarian's world, a discursive language, recollective, conciliating, but never bombastic or declamatory.

Even in this respect, then, Nievo's novel holds a special place between the realism of Manzoni and that of Verga. It is the sole work, after *I promessi sposi* and before *La vita dei campi* (1880), in which the language reflects directly the minds of the characters and the world in which they live. (pp. 278-82)

> *Nicolae Iliescu, ''The Position of Ippolito Nievo in the Nineteenth-Century Italian Novel,'' in* PMLA, *Vol. LXXV, No. 1, March, 1960, pp. 272-82.*

SERGIO PACIFICI (essay date 1967)

[*In this excerpt from his survey of the modern Italian novel, Pacifici focuses on various aspects of* The Castle of Fratta, *including the progress of its reputation, its place in nineteenth-century Italian letters, and the literary value of the novel's characterization and historical atmosphere.*]

[*The Castle of Fratta* is] one of the truly engaging, colorful, and adventureous novels of the nineteenth century. Its author was Ippolito Nievo who, at the age of thirty (at the time of the completion of his book) had already behind him a promising

literary production and a distinguished career as a civil servant. In his historical narrative, *Dal Quarto al Volturno*, Cesare Abba describes him with these telling words: ''A Venetian poet, who at the age of twenty-eight has written novels, ballads, and tragedies. He will be the poet-soldier of the expedition. Sharp profile, genius shining on his brows. A striking figure. A fine soldier.'' The epithet of poet-soldier eventually stuck and, as Miss Olga Ragusa correctly remarks, ''critical opinion on Nievo, the writer, thus crystallized on non-literary elements'' [see Additional Bibliography entry dated Summer 1958]. Anyone who has studied him is bound to feel attracted by Nievo's ability to feel intensely, with a mixture of joy and sadness, about life, or by his seemingly inexhaustible appetite for the tragicomedy of existence. Indeed, it must have been this side of the novelist's personality that impelled Sergio Romagnoli to write, in his splendid Introduction to the 1952 Ricciardi edition of Nievo's *Opere:* ''there is no Italian writer who, within a thirty-year span, accomplished an equal amount of work, without denying himself life itself—that is, family affections, love, study, friendships, walks, fighting in politics and in wars alike.''

For all the dash and exuberance informing his masterpiece, and despite its originality and worth as a historical novel encompassing events of great magnitude and drama, neither the book nor its author have commanded steady attention among the critics and readers. Although the first monograph on Nievo was brought out at the turn of the century, even an acceptable edition of his main literary production had to wait until the early fifties before appearing. Interest in Nievo seems to have gained considerable momentum shortly before the outbreak of World War II. Part of this interest was generated by the reappraisals of past works that take place periodically as the result of changes in taste; but much of it probably is traceable to the magnetism of *The Castle of Fratta*. After all, what is unusual about being absorbed by a book that speaks to us about consequential matters—what we are, how did we become this way, and where are we going? The main purpose of his book is to give us a feeling of the anguish, the struggles, and the combination of victories and setbacks experienced by a nation on its way to independence. But the political-historical theme of the book is closely interwoven with a love story, the grand passion of the protagonist for his elusive cousin Pisana. It is easy to see, even on the basis of such general characterization, why *The Castle of Fratta,* much like Pasternak's *Doctor Zhivago* and Lampedusa's *The Leopard,* should be enjoying a favorite position in today's Italy. The extraordinary success encountered by this particular type of narrative, which according to critical consensus often gives a distorted or at best a partial interpretation of history, must simply be ascribed to an all too-human longing to read a story set in less complex, if only deceptively less painful, times than the ones we live in. This is even truer, I believe, when as in the case of Nievo, the writer exhibits what Miss Ragusa calls ''a nostalgia of a dead world,'' accompanied by ''fervent hopes for the future.'' The pathos of the novel is always restrained and nicely balanced by the engaging vitality of the adventureous tale it tells. It is no wonder that some critics, notably the late Ernest H. Wilkins, have considered *The Castle of Fratta* ''the one great novel of the [post-Manzoni] period'' [see Additional Bibliography].

Two main reasons have been offered as partial explanations, if not justification, of the neglect long endured by Nievo: the inordinate length of his chief novel, which runs close to a half million words, thus ranking as one of the longest single stories ever written by an Italian, and the adverse evaluation offered by the influential Benedetto Croce, whose objections to our author and his work proved to be effective enough to influence an entire generation of readers. The notable shortcomings of the Nievian masterpiece—its length, its grammatical flaws unpardonable in a country that places a heavy premium on stylistic elegance, the rambling character of the entire second part— may have been due less to the author's sensitivity or temperament than to what we may simply call his working habits. Nievo composed his book at an almost compulsive pace, writing it feverishly between December 1857 and mid-August 1858. He refused to allow enough time to elapse so that he might refashion his novel into something more tightly constructed. Internal evidence indicates that he revised only the first half of his manuscript, without bothering to eliminate a good many pages that make his story unwieldy, distracting the reader's interest from the central themes and figures. He poured entirely too much into his book (at least one critic has complained that it contains enough material for several novels), and the richness of his story possibly contributed both to "the bad design of the book" (the words are Croce's) and to the unevenness of the narrative. The complexity of the tale is unquestionably the factor that caused the insufferable *coups de scène* and the numerous *deus ex machina,* without which the tangled plot could never be resolved. Finally, Nievo was unable to see his novel through the press, for the work that was to consign his name to posterity did not appear until six years after his death.

It is clear that Nievo never allowed his artistic ambitions to interfere with the demands of practical life. Indeed, what we know about him points to a man unwilling to trade action for meditation, incapable of abandoning the field of battle for the tranquillity and safety of his ivory tower. . . . "He sang of his period as a poet," notes Joseph Spencer Kennard, "lived through it as a soldier, and described it in his masterpiece. His life, his novel, his Italy, are typical; each explains the other" [see excerpt dated 1906].

The very richness and variety of content to which I have alluded would not, in themselves, be reasons enough to single out *The Castle of Fratta.* The originality of the book, whose sweeping quality makes one think of *War and Peace, La Chartreuse de Parme,* and *The Betrothed,* lies in quite another direction. More freely than others, and with a more authentic personal stamp, the book fuses autobiographical and invented material to give us a picture that has a human and a historical significance. It is irrelevant to discuss, in the present context, the similarity of the hero and heroine of the story with the author and his cousin Bice Melzi, for what matters is that they are believable, and entirely captivating figures, endowed with a personality that permits them to live independently of their author. The novelty of the book is, first of all, in the vivacity and realism of its characters, but also, and perhaps principally, in the way in which they assume the role of protagonists in the drama that is political and human. To be sure, even without being Romantic in the strictest sense, Nievo implicitly accepted the notion of fiction as a vehicle to inculcate a moral truth, and as demonstration on the level of poetry of a way of life that could be just and compassionate at the same time. But he also transcended his literary tradition in several important respects. Firstly, he shows us a man of humble birth who becomes the Italian who narrates his own story as well as that of his country; secondly, he identifies his narrator protagonist with the citizen of the new Italy, capable of detachedly looking at recent past history and extracting a lesson from it for future action; thirdly, he endows his creatures with enviable strength and courage of conviction to fight their own battles. Of the dozens of historical

novels written in the nineteenth century, and justly consigned to oblivion, *The Castle of Fratta* has withstood the test of time, because, as the literary historian Natalino Sapegno observes, "the historical theme is no longer born out of the impulse of fashion, it does not respond to external reasons or aesthetic preferences, [but] is, rather, the expression of a new and active culture that wants to acquire an awareness of itself and of its tradition." Unlike his predecessors, Nievo was candid enough to deal with the truth as *he* saw it, as a patriot and as a novelist, debunking, whenever necessary, public or private myths. In his novel, both Napoleon and the poet-novelist Ugo Foscolo, at once the idols and the devils of public imagination, find themselves satirized and justly cut down to size, as it were. Of course, it is true that the irony and effectiveness of the book are due to the fact that the hero of the story is the narrator, protagonist, and recorder of past events, and therefore amply entitled to a multiplicity of perspective possible in such cases. This permits a certain amount of moralizing, or commentary, on events being described, but the reader finds himself more willing to tolerate them since they come from the mouth of one who has undergone the experience narrated. We might notice that, when compared with his most illustrious predecessor, Manzoni, what is striking about Nievo, in terms of his attitude, is his willingness to show how history is the true product of man, his blunders or foresight, not of Providence. Therefore, history can neither be exalted nor disparaged, for the hope it generates is determined only by the men who are its architects. But what is particularly novel is Nievo's emphasis on the possibilities of change through wars and revolutions, through which the individual will gain greater freedom and his country will achieve new dignity in the family of nations.

Nievo's choice of the historical setting for his novel was suggested, on the one hand, by his life experiences (the story is set in the author's native ground and covers at least a portion of a period he had witnessed), and, on the other hand, by his strong commitment to his times. In *The Castle of Fratta* we are not transported into the world of a past more or less wretched, or a world whose remoteness enables the novelist to take certain liberties with history, distorting it when necessary to sustain the cogency of the plot. Nor are we asked to see and study his characters from afar, with the objectivity possible when the narrator is not one with the protagonist. On the contrary, we mingle with them in the privacy of their abodes; we travel in their company, journeying to far away cities or nations; we constantly feel the pulsation of their activities. History, to be sure, remains quite important for Nievo, as it had been for Manzoni and the majority of his followers and epigones. But history as he presents it shows people in an earthly pilgrimage, during which they experience love, war, sorrow, pain, sickness, and loneliness before they fulfill their human destinies. When we reach the end of the hero's long confessions, we are not at all surprised to find, as in Manzoni's novel, that the protagonist gives us a summation of the lesson he has learned through his experiences. What we do not find in Carlino's words, however, is an expression of his faith in the power of a benevolent God who, acting through Divine Providence, has either punished or rewarded His children. Without being religious, Carlino accepts the inevitability of good and evil in the world, while at the same time he points out man's capacity to work out his destiny by exercising his free will. Nowhere better than in the respective attitudes of Manzoni's and Nievo's principal characters do we get a feeling of their world view: thus, where Renzo [in Manzoni's *I promessi sposi*] would imply that noninvolvement is the safest path to perfect happiness (his final words are nothing less than a promise to stay out of trouble, not to make speeches in the streets, and "a hundred things of the kind"—advice that if followed could only lead down the path of servitude and tyranny), Carlino, by his words and deeds, upholds the necessity of being committed. "Happiness is in our consciences," he humbly states toward the end of the book, and we must accept his words as yet another expression of the individual attempt each man must make to reach it, as best as his powers permit. Carlino is sufficiently wise to be aware that he has attained only an imperfect understanding of himself (and therefore a limited amount of happiness and fulfillment), for the world is inscrutable, a large enigma to the mind of a finite being. Moreover, whatever he has learned by the end of his long and rich life, replete with all sorts of experiences, can hardly transcend its private significance, even when the lessons he has mastered gave an undeniable degree of universal applicability.

If, as I have hinted, the spirit of the novel is distinctly Romantic, so obvious is Nievo's penchant for adventure, color, and love-story telling, his sensitivity is more modern than chronology would normally lead us to believe. Carlino's remembrance of things past, his vivid recreation of the life in his native town which has since his birth decayed and all but died (something that permits him to repeat the *où sont les neiges d'antan* motif) has inclined some critics to speak of him as a kind of Proust *avant la lettre*. Nievo's harking back to his childhood experiences as vital to a valid understanding of the complexity of his existence and the inexorability of his loneliness may make us think of the later psychological novelists. Even in his attitude toward history . . . Nievo's stance is more modern than that of the majority of his contemporaries. "Nothing of all this would be unusual or worth telling," he frankly confesses at one point, except "that an account of my experience will serve as an example of those countless individual destinies that, from the breaking up of old political orders to the refashioning of the present one, together compose the great national destiny of Italy." Not until De Roberto, almost forty years later, will we find an equal eagerness to study seriously recent historical events as one possible way to understand the present, thus gaining some insights into the problems brought about by the Risorgimento and by the eventual unification of the country.

Both in terms of treatment and theme, *The Castle of Fratta* is an ambitious book. It purports to give us an incisive, accurate, and complete (at least insofar as the memory of its protagonist permits) picture of pre-Risorgimento Italy, and of the first wars of independence. Within the limitations of the fictional story it tells, it also analyzes the political maneuverings and deals, as well as the military defeats that bore their fruit only in the second half of the nineteenth century. The novel spans from 1780 to 1858, and passes in review the central historical events of that period. Nonetheless, by virtue of the fact that the protagonist is also the narrator-author, his figure occupies a focal position, from which everything that happens is observed and interpreted. More convincingly than in Manzoni's *The Betrothed*, history becomes in Nievo's novel the very stuff of the lives of the characters, the experience that involves them all, if in varying degrees. Indeed, in this respect Nievo is considerably more successful than his predecessor, for he makes history the very fabric of the book, and at last the characters have the opportunity to operate in and upon it, less by accident or fate than choice. Stated in another way, the novel might be characterized as a journey from the sheltered world of the castle to the chaotic, but infinitely rich world of history, a method that permits the author to depict the collapse of an era, and

the slow, painful but inevitable emergence of another. Throughout this journey, that takes Carlino Altoviti from boyhood to old age, most of the characters fulfill their destinies as lovers and as protagonists in the historical drama of their era: indeed, history and love serve as the elements of tension without which the tale would be deprived of its effectiveness and interest.

In the last analysis, the novel's special character is the profoundly moving and intriguing richness of human experience it recounts, so that its pace is determined not by history itself, but by the love story of three couples, all of whom are destined to meet with a different fate: Carlino and Pisana; her sister, Countess Clara, and doctor Lucilio Vianello; and Leopardo Provedoni and Doretta. As befits the character of the book, which is of the confessional variety, the three couples do not receive an equal amount of attention, even if their stories are masterfully developed to their resolution. The destiny of each character is followed strictly from the perspective of the protagonist, and whatever happens to them is seen and evaluated in terms of Carlino's and Pisana's lives. (pp. 58-66)

The novel is too stuffed with historical facts for me to do it justice; its episodes are both varied and diverse, and Nievo succeeds in recreating a stormy period less as a historian than as a poet. For his book, unlike history, gives us a real feeling for things as they were and how they have changed. It enables us, above all, to see the unfolding of momentous events from a perspective that is at once subjective and objective, since the action is viewed in retrospect by a man who was part of it. And the tone, for the same reasons, is discursive, intimate and, not infrequently, lyrical. It would be inconceivable, of course, to think of a Nievo without Manzoni preceding him, yet . . . the differences by far outnumber the similarities. Thus, for example, Carlino and Pisana differ from Manzoni's Renzo and Lucia by seeming to be capable of leading a fully authentic life, buffeted by fate, to be sure, but never its willing victims. They are enterprising, imaginative, and resourceful; endowed with a strong character, they can be realistic or idealistic as the case requires. "Everyone knows that Providence matures her designs through our own thoughts, our own sentiments, and our own works," Carlino comments wisely at one point, "and to hope to receive food from her already cooked was either a dream of the desperate or the flattery worthy only of street women." Man, as the novelist seems to assume, is put on earth to fulfill a mission he shall never fully comprehend until the curtain is about to fall for the last time on the stage. Yet he, and he alone, must work that mission out for himself, fighting against all odds, if necessary, so as to conquer his own dimension and place in history. "Manzoni's characters," writes Nicolae Iliescu, "while supremely human, move, in a certain sense, within a well-defined scheme of thought. . . . In Nievo, instead, each character . . . moves in a spacious field of action, thoughts and sentiments without that sense of rational inevitability that gives importance and singularity to Manzoni's characters" [see excerpt dated 1960].

As a novelist working within a young and unadventurous narrative tradition, Nievo depends for his effort purely on characterization and plot. It has often been observed that, had he had the time and opportunity to revise his manuscript, he might have produced a book with a more limpid story, less marred by occasional awkwardness or confusion, or by stylistic gracelessness. It is doubtful that additional time or work could have improved the collection of characters he created to inhabit his book; they constitute indeed a veritable gallery of human beings who are as real as any that sprung from the pen of an Italian.

The two major figures of Carlino and Pisana are drawn with the depth, sympathy, and completeness possible to a novelist who models his creatures on himself and on people he has intimately known and understood. Both are vivaciously and coherently developed. Perhaps one of the notable qualities of the narrative is to be found precisely in the manner in which Nievo transforms Carlino, a playful and dreaming boy, into an idealistic, brave, and adventuresome man, at once reflective and generous; Pisana, a fickle, capricious, and spoiled young girl, on the other hand, matures into a woman capable of great passion and sacrifices, never losing her thirst for happiness to be found outside conventions. The supporting cast is equally colorful; but more than that, it lends a special dimension to the narrative through its variety. Clara and Vianello, together with Leopardo and Doretta, for example, aptly complement the two protagonists's romantic and idyllic love. To be sure, as Natalino Sapegno remarks, Leopardo's passion for Doretta betrays its literary inspiration; still, it lends to the novel a pathetic, almost tragic, note that adds further resonance to the tale.

The lesser characters filling the huge canvas of the Nievian world are as large in number as they are memorable: there is the old, kind Martino, who exerts considerable influence upon the young Carlino; there is also Spaccafumo, Captain Sandracca (the commander of an outdated and ineffectual militia), the Dowager Countess (it is impossible to forget her quasi-royal descents to the castle's cavernous kitchen to give the orders for the day), her old husband, the Signor Count, with his boots, spurs, and sword dangling at his side; there is also his fat, hypocritical gourmand brother, Monsignor Orlando, embodying the worst features of a politically reactionary and morally corrupt church; there is Carlino's father, a clever yet generous merchant who seems to make his entrances at the right moment; and, finally, there is a myriad of soldiers, servants, politicians, captains, administrators—all of them enable the story to proceed at its almost impetuous pace, giving it a brio that adds to the warmth of its composition.

Through the action of Carlino, who finds himself in the midst of history and accepts his role in what is clearly a new society, Nievo also conveys a sense of the passing of time, the changes it brings to the seasons of mankind, altering its directions, shaping its sensibility. At the end of an extraordinarily long, and equally rich book, no reader can possibly doubt that Nievo's avowed intention of dealing with "the live and boiling matter . . . of a man's life" has amply been fulfilled. As Carlino himself looks back to a life that has known action and reflection love and suffering, comedy and tragedy, now that he has reached the end of his adventurous pilgrimage, he can serenely declare, "The calm of my soul is forever undisturbed, like the calm of a sea where there are no winds; I march towards death as towards a mystery, obscure and inscrutable, yet deprived for me of menaces and fears." We should look to such a declaration if we wish to find the secret of Nievo's modernity; for here we find a man with the courage of his convictions, at peace with himself and even happy as he examines his past, for he knows he has done his best—and his best is equated not with withdrawal from life for the sake of personal safety, but with a strong determination to be himself, never refusing to be engaged in the challenges, variety, and surprises life has in store for man. (pp. 69-72)

Sergio Pacifici, "Ippolito Nievo: History as Confessions," in his The Modern Italian Novel: From Manzoni to Svevo, *Southern Illinois University Press, 1967, pp. 57-72.*

ADDITIONAL BIBLIOGRAPHY

Edwards, Lovett F. Foreword to *The Castle of Fratta,* by Ippolito Nievo, translated by Lovett F. Edwards, pp. ix-xv. 1958. Reprint. Westport, Conn: Greenwood Press, Publishers, 1974.

   Describes Edwards's first reading of *The Castle of Fratta* while a prisoner of war, the reasons why he was attracted to the novel, and his subsequent decision to translate it into English. Edwards also provides a brief biographical sketch of Nievo.

Katz, Giuliana Sanguinetti. *The Uses of Myth in Ippolito Nievo.* L'interprete, vol. 23. Ravenna, Italy: Longo Editore, 1981, 225 p.

   A psychoanalytic study of Nievo's works.

Ragusa, Olga. "Nievo Now in English." *Italian Quarterly* 1, No. 4 (Winter 1958): 90-2.

   A brief review of Lovett F. Edwards's edition of *The Castle of Fratta.* Ragusa devotes a major portion of her remarks to assessing Edwards's skills as a translator.

———. "Nievo, the Writer: Tendencies in Criticism." *Italian Quarterly* 2, No. 2 (Summer 1958): 20-34.

   A history of Italian-language criticism of Nievo's works.

Wilkins, Ernest Hatch. "Contemporaries of Mazzini." In his *A History of Italian Literature,* pp. 429-35. Cambridge: Harvard University Press, 1954.

   Contains a brief discussion of Nievo's life and *The Castle of Fratta.*

Thomas Love Peacock

1785-1866

(Also wrote under pseudonym of P. M. O'Donovan, Esq.) English novelist, poet, critic, and essayist.

Peacock is chiefly remembered for his innovative, satirical novels scrutinizing the political, scientific, artistic, and philosophical movements of the Romantic and early Victorian eras. Especially noted for their erudite, classical style and comic characters, Peacock's novels, particularly his five novels of conversation, are considered unique in their emphasis on the expression of ideas through dialogue rather than through traditional plot and character development. Although Peacock also wrote poetry, literary criticism, and other essays for which there has been moderate praise, the focal point of popular and critical interest remains his novels. These have never lacked an audience nor failed to elicit critical commentary, even though his unusual use of character, plot, and scholarship has kept his readership relatively small. Most commentators agree that Peacock's satirical fiction is difficult to categorize in conventional literary terms, yet invaluable to an understanding of his age.

Peacock was born in Weymouth, the son of a London glass merchant who died when Peacock was three. Peacock and his mother subsequently moved to a village outside of London where they resided with Peacock's maternal grandfather. Until the age of thirteen Peacock attended school at Englefield Green, and it was there that he learned Latin and Greek, beginning a lifelong interest in classical studies. After a brief sojourn as a clerk in London, Peacock, encouraged by his well-educated mother, spent several years in self-directed study, writing poetry and reading classical literature, French, and Italian. Throughout his life he often sought his mother's opinion of his works and remained a self-taught man of letters; biographers note that his writing reflects the personal, idiosyncratic interests of his private scholarship. In 1800 Peacock's first published poem appeared in a children's magazine, followed four years later by *The Monks of St Mark,* a poem containing comic situations similar to those in his later novels. These writings attracted little notice, however, and it was not until the publication of *Palmyra, and Other Poems* in 1806 that Peacock's work drew critical attention. The reviews of this volume were extremely favorable, encouraging Peacock to take himself seriously as a poet and to publish several other books of poetry in the following years.

In 1812 a mutual acquaintance introduced Peacock to the Romantic poet Percy Bysshe Shelley, who became a close friend and influenced Peacock's literary aspirations. Recognizing the genius of the younger man, and stimulated by the varied opinions of Shelley's liberal and eccentric circle of friends, Peacock began to produce works of fiction reflecting his reaction to the ideas and behavior of his new acquaintances. During the next few years, *Headlong Hall,* the prototype of his novels of conversation, *Melincourt,* and *Nightmare Abbey* appeared in quick succession. Critical reaction to these works was enthusiastic. Shelley, in particular, admired Peacock's writing despite conjecture that Peacock had satirized Shelley's radical ideas through one of his characters. In 1819, in an effort to supplement his income, Peacock became an employee of the East India Company; he did not retire from the firm until 1856, and the friend-

ships he formed there with the Utilitarians Jeremy Bentham, James Mill, and John Stuart Mill influenced the ideas represented in his fiction. In 1820, Peacock wrote "The Four Ages of Poetry," an ironic essay denouncing contemporary poetry that provoked Shelley's more well-known response, *A Defence of Poetry.* Peacock also married during 1820, but his home life, while quiet, retired, and comfortable, did not prove untroubled. Several circumstances, including the death of a favorite daughter and the poor health of his wife, marred his happiness. Yet he continued to write, publishing *Maid Marian* and *The Misfortunes of Elphin* in the 1820s and one of the best known of his satirical novels, *Crotchet Castle,* in 1831. Peacock wrote little fiction during the next three decades, concentrating instead on essays and criticism. His lengthy essay "Memoirs of Percy Bysshe Shelley" appeared in *Fraser's Magazine* from 1858 to 1862, and in 1861, he published the last of his satirical novels, *Gryll Grange.* By this time, however, Peacock was no longer widely known as an author, and, when he died in 1866, only one obituary notice mentioned his literary career.

Among Peacock's lesser works, which include poetry, essays, and criticism, *Rhododaphne,* a long poem based on classical subject matter, is generally considered one of his best, although it has never been widely studied. Commentators agree that

Peacock's poetic gifts are best expressed in the shorter poems and drinking songs composed for his novels. For instance, Mr. Cypress's song from *Nightmare Abbey,* which lampoons Lord Byron's introspective melancholy, is often cited as evidence of Peacock's poetic talent. Peacock's essays and criticism have received relatively little attention. Even "The Four Ages of Poetry," the best-known example of Peacock's criticism, is usually considered of more importance for having stimulated Shelley's famous response than as a work in its own right.

Peacock's seven novels, on the other hand, are generally agreed to be his most noteworthy contribution to English literature. Although they have common elements of satire and romance, the novels fall roughly into two groups, the romances and the novels of conversation. The romances, *Maid Marian* and *The Misfortunes of Elphin,* are distinguished by Peacock's use of legendary settings and more traditional plot and narrative devices. These novels are of less critical importance, even though *Maid Marian* was Peacock's most popular work during much of the nineteenth century. Based on the Robin Hood tales, this novel contains many of Peacock's best-known short poems. Its satire is evinced in the comparison between an idealized past age and contemporary society. By portraying characters from a distant era who behave much like modern men and women, Peacock was able to expose universal human foibles. *The Misfortunes of Elphin,* set in ancient Wales, also makes its satirical points by comparing two civilizations; commentators note, in particular, its attack on parliamentary systems through the powerful characterization of Prince Seithenyn, who makes speeches echoing those of contemporary politicians.

It is in his novels of conversation or ideas that critics find the essence of Peacock's artistry. Commentators point out that Peacock first developed his formula for these novels in *Headlong Hall,* and to a greater or lesser extent the other four novels of conversation share the same elements. In *Headlong Hall,* a number of guests assemble at a country house in an idyllic Welsh setting. Each character embodies in his own peculiar way an intellectual trend of the day. Mr. Escot, a "deteriorationist," Mr. Foster, a "perfectibilist," Mr. Panscope, a character whose literary thought parodies that of the poet Samuel Taylor Coleridge, and others interested in such topics as craniology and landscape gardening are gathered by the host, Squire Headlong, around his dinner table. The ensuing dinner conversations, in which no one ever agrees, allow the characters to exhibit the full force of their ideas or crotchets with humorous and satirical effect. Many of the ideas satirized—medievalism, for example—are associated with the Romantics, although Peacock himself did subscribe to aspects of the movement. Characterization is slight and the only vestige of plot in the novel is pure romance: the satisfactory conclusion of a love affair between Cephalis Cranium and Mr. Escot. Eating, drinking, and farcical episodes are the mainstay of the action. Commentators also identify other typical Peacockian elements in this first novel, particularly his elegant, classical style with its roots in the eighteenth century, his scholarly footnotes, his coinage of unusual words and character names, and the presence of some characters meant as caricatures of real persons. Scholars note that a prominent theme in these novels, as in the romances, is the contrast between the contemporary world of scientific progress and a simpler, more natural life based on Peacock's interpretation of the ideals of classical Greece. Yet, scholars also comment on differences between the novels: *Nightmare Abbey* has an uncharacteristically cohesive plot, *Gryll Grange* more highly developed characters than the other novels. In addition, critics find a progression in Peacock's

satiric purpose from the early to the late novels. *Melincourt* advocates social reform movements associated with Utilitarian thought, while *Crotchet Castle* and *Gryll Grange* develop a more Epicurean concern for the happiness of the individual.

Contemporary critical reception of Peacock's works was mainly positive and concentrated almost exclusively on the novels, though several reviewers hesitated to use that term because of the emphasis on conversation and the lack of plot and characterization in his fiction. Many praised Peacock's elegant style and originality of form and content, but some objected to his innovations and esoteric, haphazard scholarship. In the late nineteenth and early twentieth centuries, Peacock's readership was small, a circumstance commentators attributed to the novels being too scholarly, satirical, and unusual for a popular audience. Critics, however, applauded Peacock's style, with some positing that style alone made him an important writer. Others, however, found his imagination weak and his characters unconvincing. From the mid-twentieth century onward, criticism has focused on plot, characterization, style, and form, and attempts have been made to place Peacock within the tradition of English literature. Some reviewers have noted similarities between his work and Jane Austen's in satirical purpose and precision of style, while a few scholars have discarded the label satirist in favor of caricaturist or critic. In addition, Peacock's literary influence has been traced in the works of such writers as George Meredith, Aldous Huxley, and Evelyn Waugh. Most conclude that Peacock's importance as a writer lies in his development of an original satirical form ridiculing the intellectual foibles of his day. For this reason, his works are considered an important contribution to the study of nineteenth-century culture.

PRINCIPAL WORKS

The Monks of St Mark (poetry) 1804
Palmyra, and Other Poems (poetry) 1806
The Genius of the Thames (poetry) 1810
The Philosophy of Melancholy (poetry) 1812
*Sir Hornbook; or, Childe Launcelot's Expedition: A
    Grammatico-Allegorical Ballad* (poetry) 1814
Sir Proteus: A Satirical Ballad [as P. M. O'Donovan, Esq.]
    (poetry) 1814
Headlong Hall (novel) 1816
Melincourt (novel) 1817
Nightmare Abbey (novel) 1818
Rhododaphne; or, The Thessalian Spell (poetry) 1818
"The Four Ages of Poetry" (essay) 1820; published in
    periodical *Ollier's Literary Miscellany*
Maid Marian (novel) 1822
The Misfortunes of Elphin (novel) 1829
Crotchet Castle (novel) 1831
Paper Money Lyrics, and Other Poems (poetry) 1837
"Memoirs of Percy Bysshe Shelley" (memoir) 1858-62;
    published in periodical *Fraser's Magazine for Town &
    Country*
"Recollections of Childhood: The Abbey House"
    (memoirs) 1859; published in periodical *Bentley's
    Miscellany*
Gryll Grange (novel) 1861
The Works of Thomas Love Peacock. 3 vols. (novels,
    poetry, letters, and essays) 1875
The Collected Prose Works of T. L. Peacock. 10 vols.
    (novels, essays, and unfinished novel) 1891
The Poems of Thomas Love Peacock (poetry) 1906

THE MONTHLY REVIEW, LONDON (essay date 1806)

[*In this excerpt from a review of* Palmyra, and Other Poems, *the critic offers a mostly positive appraisal of Peacock's poetry.*]

Fenced and barricadoed as Helicon is, according to the report of some persons, against the approach of the moderns,—and as we have indeed melancholy evidence in the quantity of trash, called poetry, with which we are incessantly pelted,—a few individuals occasionally contrive to clamber over the inclosure, and to get a sip from the sacred fountain. Mr. Peacock appears to be one of this favored minority; and even those who are somewhat fastidious will receive pleasure from the vigor of his conceptions, the elegance of his expressions, and the harmony of his numbers [in *Palmyra, and Other Poems*]. Palmyra, whose splendid ruins of white marble, in the midst of an extensive sandy desert, present so striking a spectacle to the traveller, illustrative of the transitory nature of human glory, is a fine subject for a poem; and if our expectations were raised on this occasion, we are bound in gratitude to Mr. P. to report that we were not disappointed. With a boldness and a fire which belong to the Ode, he sings the fate of this once magnificent city, its rulers and inhabitants, and introduces those awful reflections which are a lesson to the proud and a consolation to the humble. Notes, illustrative of the allusions in the text, are subjoined: but we think that, though Mr. P. can adduce good authority for the omission, the names of the persons, viz. of *Zenobia, Longinus,* &c. to whom he refers, should have been woven into the stanzas appropriated to them; for, as Dr. Johnson observes, "An Epitaph and a history of a nameless hero are equally absurd, since the virtues and qualities so recounted in either are scattered at the mercy of fortune to be appropriated by guess. The name, it is true, may be read on the stone; but what obligation has it to the poet, whose verses wander over the earth, and leave their subject behind them, and who is forced, like an unskilful painter, to make his purpose known by adventitious help?" This remark on the omission of the name in an epitaph applies also to other poems. We mean not to discourage the addition of explanatory notes: but authors should consider that poems, and odes in particular, are intended for recitation, and that the necessity of illustration should be sedulously avoided. The bard amply avails himself of the scanty records respecting Palmyra, but the name of its celebrated queen Zenobia never occurs in the whole ode. (p. 323)

A review of "Palmyra, and Other Poems," in The Monthly Review, *London, Vol. XLIX, March, 1806, pp. 323-25.*

THE ECLECTIC REVIEW (essay date 1816)

[*This anonymous reviewer briefly assesses* Headlong Hall.]

It is truly refreshing to meet with a production of chaste and genuine humour. Our satirists are for the most part of that saturnine complexion, that forbids their relaxing into the easy hilarity which characterizes the pleasantry of Goldsmith or of Addison; while our professed comic writers seem to have no other notion of humour than that of caricature or broad farce. (p. 372)

We will not extend our approbation of [*Headlong Hall*] to every expression which it contains. The character of Dr. Gaster will be considered as falling under the same objection as that to which Dr. Syntax, and similar caricatures, are justly exposed. That such characters exist in real life, is an insufficient excuse for their being brought out on the canvass. The general design of the volume is however so unexceptionable, the execution is so spirited and good-humoured, and the satire in general so well-directed, that we cannot but accord to it, on the whole, a high measure of commendation. (p. 379)

A review of "Headlong Hall," in The Eclectic Review, *n.s. Vol. V, April, 1816, pp. 372-80.*

THE MONTHLY REVIEW, LONDON (essay date 1817)

[*This critic provides a short, complimentary critique of* Headlong Hall, *emphasizing the variety of ideas that Peacock satirizes.*]

[*Headlong Hall* is a] clever little burlesque on all the favourite *hobbies,* whether of men of science or taste, of amateurs or professors, of sciolists or philosophers, of perfectionists or deteriorationists, of maintainers of the rectilinear, circular, or ziz-zag progress of the human mind,—of the optimists, in a word, or the pessimists, or the *stationers,* of all descriptions. Advocates of every system, and examples of every fancy, meet together at the Christmas table of a convivial Welsh esquire, and their conversations form the principal business of the book. A spice of adventure seasons the conclusion of the volume; which, however, does not profess to depend on *story* for its interest. To all curious or even careless observers of the solemn and important whims of the day, it will afford a pleasant evening's amusement; and we recommend it as a very harmless care-killer to a numerous class of readers.

A review of "Headlong Hall," in The Monthly Review, *London, n.s. Vol. LXXXII, March, 1817, p. 330.*

THE LITERARY GAZETTE, LONDON (essay date 1817)

[*In the following essay, the critic reviews* Melincourt, *focusing on form and characterization in the novel.*]

Though with the most inveterate Novel-name that we have latterly found in a title-page, [*Melincourt*] cannot well be denominated a Novel. It contains little love, less incident, and, if we remember right, not even the common etiquette of a single swoon. The whole plot consists in a visit paid by some match-making ladies and speculating gentlemen, to Anthelia Melincourt, a young heiress of Westmoreland; and in one or two abortive schemes for forcing her into matrimony. All the rest is conversation and character.

With such slender materials, it would require no small portion of wit, knowledge, and acumen, to rouse and to sustain interest, through three thick volumes: and, indeed, we most cheerfully confess, that the writer has not shown himself deficient in any of these qualifications. His dialogue abounds with humour and learning, and though his Antisaccharine fête has become obsolete by the abolition of the Slave-Trade, and though the election of an ape to the Borough of Onevote, is rather an outrageous improbability, yet still the poignant burlesque of both, compelled us to laugh most heartily. In truth, this ape, originally introduced to our acquaintance as an estated baronet, Sir Oran Haut-ton by name, is the most conspicuous character in the work, and we should almost say, the hero of it. He was caught young in the woods of Angola, and purchased by the Captain of a frigate, who had him dressed and educated in all the external accomplishments of a gentleman. Amidst "the fashionable world, he seemed to be particularly comfortable, and to feel himself completely at home."

Such a personage, brought forward and passed off as a human being, must needs startle the reader, who has seen only our own sketch of him; but in the work itself, due pains are taken to reconcile probabilities; and there are abundant extracts from Lord Monboddo, Buffon, and Bontius, for the purpose of proving his pretensions to humanity; still, we must think, that the case is not sufficiently made out, and that a pair of gloves, at least, and paint, or perhaps a mask, might have assisted the deception. But, with all our critical fastidiousness, we would not, for a doubtful violation of probability, consent to expunge this honorable Baronet from the red-book, inasmuch as he has proved the source of much exquisite sarcasm, both on those brainless fops, who would degrade men into monkies by their example, and on those over-brained philosophers, who would exalt monkies into men by force of theory.

There is, likewise, in some other characters, rather more of fancy than of reality. They are a species without a genus; or at least their peculiarities do not appear such as men acquire, who mix with the world; and, therefore, are not such as often fall under common observation. This is always a disadvantage in the delineation of particular character; for it is here as with portrait painting; we cannot enjoy the imitation, unless we have already seen the original. On the contrary, narratives of fact, like historical pieces, tell their own stories themselves, and are not dependant upon our personal acquaintance with their prototypes.

Whoever the author of *Melincourt* may be, (for he has not thought proper to affix his name, though he might surely have done so, without fear of its suffering by the announcement), we think we may venture to congratulate him, by anticipation, on the success of his singular, and we may add, original work. We should not even be surprised if it led the way to a new species of humourous writing; which, taking the novel for its foundation, and the drama for its superstructure, should superadd to both, the learning and enquiry of the Essay. Fortunately, the sheer, downright novel is growing out of repute every day. Miss Edgeworth was the first who moralized it, Miss Porter endowed it with historical strength, the author of *Waverley* gave it national interest, and the author of *Melincourt* may fairly be said to have advanced it another degree higher, in the moral and intellectual scale of literature.

A review of "Melincourt," in The Literary Gazette, *London, No. IX, March 22, 1817, p. 132.*

THE BRITISH CRITIC   (essay date 1817)

[*The following excerpt is drawn from a negative review of* Melincourt *in which the critic faults Peacock's scholarship, politics, and religion.*]

Melincourt is written by the author of *Headlong Hall,* a novel which appeared about two years ago, of the same cast and character with the present tale; which, though we read and disapproved, we did not think of sufficient consequence to expose. Not that we think *Melincourt* of any more importance in itself, nor are we afraid of any serious mischief arising from such miserable trash; the powers of the author are not equal to his intentions.

The author is evidently a scholar; but one of that order who mistakes sound for sense, and taking the leading idea in a passage for the whole, quote it boldly, without troubling themselves with the meaning or construction of any particular word, much less with the bearing of the passage as relating to the context. As far then as the *Hurlothrumbo* sort of citation is to be accounted scholarship, the author of *Melincourt* is a scholar. The story (if such it may be called) is contained in a few words. Miss Melincourt, a lady of ten thousand a year, is resolved to choose for her husband a man of "disinterested, energetic, and chivalrous generosity," and so she chooses Mr. Forester, the author's *beau ideal,* or philosopher, reformer, and infidel; in the relation of whose vagaries, and the commendation of whose absurdities, the principal part of three volumes is consumed. Among other notions of this aforesaid gentleman, is one which he has borrowed from Lord Monboddo, of introducing an Ourang Outang into human society. (pp. 430-31)

We shall not tire the patience of our readers with the *reforming* notions of our author, as they will see them much better done in Cobbett, Hunt, or Hone. . . . Who the [author] may be, we know not, as he has wisely chosen to conceal his name. Were he a poor man writing for bread, we might pity him; were he a young man, discharging the scum of an enthusiastic brain, we might pardon him. We suspect him to be neither. From a certain dictatorial slang observable throughout, we imagine that he has been accustomed to lay down the law to a circle of dependents; from his citations we know him to be sonorous, rather than a solid scholar; from his ludicrous perversions of Holy Writ, we should suppose he was an adept in blasphemy. He has chosen the form of a novel, to disguise his venom, and to vent his bitterness with the more effect: but never was poison more innocent, nor malice more impotent. It wants but the name of the author to consign it to hopeless and fearless oblivion. (p. 441)

A review of "Melincourt," in The British Critic, *n.s. Vol. VIII, October, 1817, pp. 430-42.*

THE LITERARY GAZETTE, LONDON   (essay date 1818)

[*This reviewer provides an enthusiastic assessment of Peacock's* Nightmare Abbey, *lauding such aspects of the novel as the humorous conversations between characters and the songs they sing on memorable occasions.*]

The author of this work, and of several similar productions, is, we understand, a Mr. Peacock. It would be difficult to say what his books are, for they are neither romances, novels, tales, nor treatises, but a mixture of all these combined. They display a sort of caricature of modern characters and incidents; executed with greater license than nature, and with more humour than wit.

The contrivance is to group together a number either of persons, whose originals are easily recognized in the literary or political world, or of individuals who are made the representatives of some fashionable folly or doctrine; and from their collision to elicit a laugh at the actors or at their opinions. Thus in *Nightmare Abbey,* its proprietor, Christopher Glowry, Esq. is a gentleman of highly atrabilarious temperament, and a prey to gloom and blue devils; his only son, Scythrop, is a transcendentalist, filled with a grand plan for rendering mankind perfectly happy. At the ancient mansion, which gives the name to the publication, assemble as visitors, Mr. Hilary, a gay and lively relative, with his niece Marionetta O'Carroll, a blooming coquette; Mr. Flosky, a morbid personage of some note in literature, and a disciple of Kant (we suppose aimed at Mr. Coleridge;) a Mr. Toobad, "the Manichæan Millenarian," who is constantly asserting the predominancy of the evil principle; the Rev. Mr. Larynx, an accommodating divine, "always most obligingly ready to take a dinner and a bed at the house of any country gentleman in distress for a companion." To these are afterwards added the Hon. Mr. Listless, a dandy, with a disposition suitable to his name; Mr. Asterias, (quasi that worthy baronet Sir J. Sinclair) a believer in, and hunter after Mermaids; Mr. Cypress, a Lord Byron bard; Miss Toobad, the daughter of the Manichæan, herself a philosopher of the independent school; and one or two others of less notoriety.

The principal parts of the volume are occupied with conversations, in which these parties figure, generally in a whimsical and amusing manner. Scythrop becomes attached to Marionetta and Miss Toobad, and is so enamoured of both, that he knows not to which to give the palm. After some curious adventures an eclaircissement ensues, and both ladies renounce a lover who finds it so difficult to make up his mind. (p. 787)

There are several pretty little poems introduced, of which we select a song by Mr. Cypress, who maintains that "having quarrelled with his wife, he is absolved from all duty to his country."

> There is a fever of the spirit,
> The brand of Cain's unresisting doom,
> Which in the lone dark souls that hear it
> Glows like the lamp in Tullia's tomb:
> Unlike that lamp, its subtile fire
> Burns, blasts, consumes its cell, the heart,
> Till, one by one, hope, joy, desire,
> Like dreams of shadowy smoke depart.
>
> When hope, love, life itself, are only
> Dust—spectral memories—dead and cold—
> The unfed fire burns bright and lonely,
> Like that undying lamp of old:
> And by that drear illumination,
> Till time its clay-built home has rent,
> Thought broods on feeling's desolation—
> The soul is its own monument. . . .

Upon the whole, we think this little volume cannot fail to be read with pleasure throughout, and with the delightful adjunct of several hearty laughs in turning over its most farcical pages. (p. 788)

> *A review of "Nightmare Abbey," in* The Literary Gazette, *London, No. 99, December 12, 1818, pp. 787-88.*

HENRY CRABB ROBINSON   (diary date 1818)

[*Robinson is remembered as an insightful and outspoken commentator on the literary world of nineteenth-century London. Chronicled in his* Diary, Reminiscences, *and* Correspondence, *his recollections provide an astute assessment of literary trends and society during his lifetime. In the following excerpt, Robinson disparages* Headlong Hall.]

I read, beginning of the week, *Headlong Hall*—satirical dialogues—an account of a visit to a Welsh squire's seat. The interlocutors represent certain literary parties in the country. There is one who is an optimist, another a deteriorist, who obtrude their speculations on every occasion; there are reviewers, a picturesque gardener, etc.; but the commonplaces of the literators of the day are not preserved from being tiresome by original humour or wit, so that the book is very dull.

> *Henry Crabb Robinson, in an extract from a diary entry on December 31, 1818, in his* Henry Crabb Robinson on Books and Their Writers, Vol. I, *edited by Edith J. Morley, J. M. Dent and Sons Limited, 1938, p. 226.*

PERCY BYSSHE SHELLEY   (essay date 1818)

[*Regarded as a major English poet, Shelley was a leading figure in the English Romantic movement. He wrote his famous* A Defence of Poetry, *considered a powerful statement of the Romantic ideal of art and the artist, in response to Peacock's "The Four Ages of Poetry." While Peacock had argued that poetry had lost its force and relevance in contemporary society, Shelley countered with an affirmation of the vital moral importance of poetry in all ages. Shelley viewed poetry, as he did human society, as a continuing evolution of ideas—in his words, as a "fountain forever overflowing with the waters of wisdom and delight." Thus poets, the "unacknowledged legislators of the world," contribute to the spiritual and political development of mankind. In this excerpt from a review written in 1818, Shelley offers high praise for Peacock's poem* Rhododaphne, *expressing admiration for its classical subject matter and the breadth of its classical scholarship. For further commentary by Shelley, see excerpts dated 1819 and 1820.*]

Rhododaphne is a poem of the most remarkable character, and the nature of the subject no less than the spirit in which it is written forbid us to range it under any of the classes of modern literature. It is a Greek and Pagan poem. In sentiment and scenery it is essentially antique. There is a strong *religio loci* throughout, which almost compels us to believe that the author wrote from the dictation of a voice heard from some Pythian cavern in the solitudes where Delphi stood. We are transported to the banks of the Peneus and linger under the crags of Tempe, and see the water lilies floating on the stream. We sit with Plato by Old Ilissus under the sacred Plane tree among the sweet scent of flowering sallows; and above there is the nightingale of Sophocles in the ivy of the pine, who is watching the sunset so that it may dare to sing; it is the radiant evening of a burning day, and the smooth hollow whirlpools of the river are overflowing with the aerial gold of the level sunlight. We stand in the marble temples of the Gods, and see their sculptured forms gazing and almost breathing around. We are led forth from the frequent pomp of sacrifice into the solitudes of mountains and forests where Pan, "the life, the intellectual soul of grove and stream," yet lives and yet is worshipped. We visit the solitudes of Thessalian magic and tremble with new wonder to hear statues speak and move and to see the shaggy changelings minister to their witch queen with the shape of beasts and the reason of men and move among the animated statues who people her enchanted palaces and gardens. That wonderful overflowing of fancy, the *Syria Dea* of Lucian, and the impassioned and elegant pantomime of Apuleius, have contributed to this portion of the poem. There is here, as in the songs of ancient times, music and dancing and the luxury of voluptuous delight. The Bacchanalians toss on high their leaf-interwoven hair, and the tumult and fervor of the chase is depicted; we hear its clamor gathering among the woods, and she who impels it is so graceful and so fearless that we are charmed—and it needs no feeble spell to see nothing of the agony and blood of that royal sport. This it is to be a scholar; this it is to have read Homer and Sophocles and Plato. (pp. 311-12)

> *Percy Bysshe Shelley, in a review of "Rhododaphne; or, The Thessalian Spell," in his* Shelley's Prose; or, The Trumpet of a Prophecy, *edited by David Lee Clark, The University of New Mexico Press, 1954, pp. 311-13.*

PERCY BYSSHE SHELLEY   (letter date 1819)

[In the following excerpt from a letter to Peacock dated June 1819, Shelley comments favorably on Nightmare Abbey. *For additional criticism by Shelley, see excerpts dated 1818 and 1820.]*

Enough of melancholy. **Nightmare Abbey** though no cure is a palliative. I have just received the parcel which contains it, and at the same time the 'Examiners' by the way of [?Malta]. I am delighted with **Nightmare Abbey**. I think Scythrop a character admirably conceived and executed, and I know not how to praise sufficiently the lightness, chastity and strength of the language of the whole. It perhaps exceeds all your works in this. The catastrophe is excellent,—I suppose the moral is contained in what Falstaff says *'For God's sake talk like a man of this world'* and yet looking deeper into it, is not the misdirected enthusiasm of Scythrop what J C calls the salt of the earth? My friends the Gisbornes here admire and delight in it exceedingly. I think I told you that they (especially the lady) are people of high cultivation; she is a woman of profound accomplishments and a most refined taste.

> *Percy Bysshe Shelley, "On 'Nightmare Abbey'," in* Peacock: The Satirical Novels, a Casebook, *edited by Lorna Sage, The Macmillan Press, Ltd., 1976, p. 37.*

PERCY BYSSHE SHELLEY   (poem date 1820)

[In an excerpt from his poem "Letter to Maria Gisborne," composed in 1820, Shelley describes the effect of Peacock's artistry. See excerpts dated 1818 and 1819 for additional commentary by Shelley.]

> —his fine wit
> Makes such a wound, the knife is lost in it;
> A strain too learned for a shallow age,
> Too wise for selfish bigots; let his page,
> Which charms the chosen spirits of the time,
> Fold itself up for the serener clime
> Of years to come, and find its recompense
> In that just expectation.

(pp. 37-8)

> *Percy Bysshe Shelley, "A Strain Too Learned for a Shallow Age," in* Peacock: The Satirical Novels, a Casebook, *edited by Lorna Sage, The Macmillan Press, Ltd., 1976, pp. 37-8.*

[ALBANY FONBLANQUE]   (essay date 1831)

[In the following excerpt from a review of Crotchet Castle, *Fonblanque focuses on Peacock's satirical intentions.]*

The author of **Headlong Hall** is a bitter persecutor of the singularities and excrescences of science. He is a prose Peter Pindar, writing however with a vast deal of knowledge on the topics about which he is occupied, but with the keenest eye upon the absurdities of all who come under his cognizance. Dr. Walcot represented sir Joseph Banks as boiling fleas, in order to ascertain whether they turned red like lobsters; and the traveller Bruce as cutting his beefsteaks from a living animal, and then sending the bullock to graze. Who now doubts at this time of day that sir Joseph Banks and Bruce were benefactors of society; there will be as little hesitation on the question, whether the phrenologists, the conchologists, and the political economists, with numerous other tribes of scientific devotees, who are described by the Greek termination ιοτη, of the present day, are to be considered as the patrons of human happiness, and the benefactors of their race by our successors in the next age, and in coming centuries. We do not mean, that all who boast the name of science will be so considered; for, as soon as any science or branch of knowledge has made a certain progress, it necessarily follows, that it will be professed by numerous pretenders, who will probably greatly magnify its importance, and at any rate possibly make an outcry, of which the real originators are heartily ashamed. We believe, sincerely, that it is not the warriors, but the followers of the camp, against which Mr. Peacock levels his shafts; he would probably be himself the first to regret his prowess if he thought he had put the whole army to the rout, and we are quite certain that he would much grieve, did he know, that by his very able sharpshooting upon the stragglers he was mistaken for the advance corps of the enemies of all improvement, whether in science or politics.

It is a pity, that men are most inclined to satirise that of which they know the most. Juvenal, hot from the stews, Petronius Arbiter, fresh from the garden of Epicurus, in the first moments of re-action employed their genius upon the exposers of their partners in vice: it is thus with Mr. Peacock, he does not satirize the boroughmongers, for he is not of their click; he does not attack the money-brokers, for he is not a regarder of pelf; were he of the Stock Exchange he would rail against waddlers and men of straw; were he of the Universities, a fellow of some musty college, he would run down the malappropriation of testamentary funds, and the misdirection of the courses of instruction; the idleness which passes under the name of learned ease, the ignorance which is called erudition. Had he been a lawyer or a police magistrate, the chicaneries of the law, or the absurdities of society would have been his food. We should, perhaps, have laughed as much, but not so wisely. Mr. Peacock happens to be well acquainted with those studies on which men at the present day chiefly pride themselves, he consequently detects more acutely than others the hollowness and emptiness of the pretensions of the trainbearers of these particular sciences. Being himself a master of the art, he can instantly discover the clumsy efforts of a sciolist—having a great susceptibility of the ridiculous, he is forced upon comparisons of the most laughable description. In order to be understood, however, he aims at the most distinguished representatives of the science, where others would have satirized the pretenders.

The most conspicuous personage of **Crotchet Castle** is Mr. Mac Quedy, the economist; he is represented in colours not to be mistaken; and it is very possible that they who are incapable of understanding the writings of the author satirized, are quite equal to the comprehension of the satire. Political Economy has enemies enough in the ranks of those who are ignorant of it; weapons are now supplied from its own arsenal. Under the name of Mr. Skionar, the professor of the transcendental school of poetry is ridiculed, and we have no objection. We can also forgive the vagaries of the antiquary, Mr. Chainmail, who lives in the twelfth and thirteenth century. Dr. Folliot is the representative of Common Sense, according to the author's idea of it. Common Sense, then, is a divinity doctor, of a great wine capacity, a parson of uncommon pugilistic force, as clever at knocking down an antagonist with a classical quotation, as with his cudgel. Mr. Peacock's notion of love is of the same quality as that of his idea of Common Sense. Mr. Chainmail finds a romantic beauty in Wales, hanging over a water-fall; she turns out to be a model of accomplishment and amiability in disguise; a London banker's daughter, in a russet boddice, her name is Touchandgo—the only point about her, which is not well adapted to the meridian of the Minerva Library. (pp. 208-09)

It is impossible to deny the exquisite humour of . . . *Crotchet Castle:* and it is pleasant to laugh without, at the same time feeling the twitchings of reason and conscience, sensations which we do not hesitate to say, have presented very considerable drawbacks on the amusement which we cannot help taking in all the writings of our author. He is learned and he plays with his erudition, he is well acquainted with modern discoveries and he laughs at them, he is liberal in all his political opinions, and he attacks liberals only. The hero of the church and the ring, Dr. Folliott is precisely the jovial and narrow-minded athletic grammarian, whom *Blackwood's Magazine* would deify as the model of men, a pattern for all Christendom in religion, politics, and morals, a gormandizer of sensual things, a wielder of the fist, a knocker-down of arguments. It is true that he is the antipodes of cant, which implies professions of disinterestedness: the model of men despises all generosity, and does not pretend to a virtue which no hypocrisy could procure him credit for. It does not become us to assume the direction of the efforts of a man of Mr. Peacock's genius, more particularly after suffering ourselves to be so greatly entertained by the perusal of one of his works, nevertheless we cannot help beseeching him to apply his most trenchant qualities to the extirpation of the greater nuisances which prey upon the well being of society, and impede the future improvement of mankind. (p. 218)

> [*Albany Fonblanque*], *in a review of "Crotchet Castle," in* The Westminster Review, *Vol. XV, July, 1831, pp. 208-18.*

FRASER'S MAGAZINE FOR TOWN & COUNTRY   (essay date 1831)

[*Disputing the favorable assessment of* Crotchet Castle *offered by Albany Fonblanque (see excerpt above dated 1831), this reviewer dismisses the novel as "conceited nonsense."*]

We were sorry to see the *Westminster Review* praising such a budget of conceited nonsense as

Crotchet Castle.

Peacock is one of the people

> Marked with the indelible d—d cockney blot;

and that perhaps may account for the panegyric lavished upon him by Bowring. By the way, it is a shame that so very clever a fellow as Bowring should not emancipate himself totally from the herd of Arcadians, of ears beyond the usual dimensions of asinity asinine. *He* cannot think that Peacock is any thing else but a blockhead, whatever he may write to the contrary.

The name of Rabelais has been mentioned in connexion with that of Peacock by the *Examiner. O Maître Alcofribas!* if it were possible that you should revive—if you could return now that you have solved (as we opine) the *grand peut-être,* of which you doubted so especially before you died—what a kicking would you not give the comparer! What! the author of the trial of Bridlegoose, of the Lecture on the early experiments of Gargantua—the fabricator of Panurge—the creator of Friar John—the author of the story of the fox and the lion, the young devil of Papemany, the adventure of Frère Roidymet, the miracles of the Decretals, the voyage to the holy bottle, the consultation on the case of Panurge's wedding—the one—the only one—the Rabelais himself, compared with an ignorant, stupid, poor devil, who has no fun, little learning, no facility, no *easiness*—a fellow whose style of thought is in the very contrary vein of the Rabelaisian—a dolt who thinks that the daily nonsense vomited up by all sorts of asses is something of moment, something worthy of even being satirised, instead of being spoken of in the same tone that we speak of the contents of nightmen's carts. What would the unsparing Doctor of Chinon,

Petite ville, grand renom,

have thought of one who spoke *seriously* of the political eonomists?

How differently Rabelais would have handled Macculloch! Instead of talking the precious stuff here put into the mouth of Mr. Macquedy (what a name! but we shall have occasion to say a few words about Peacock's name-giving before we conclude)—instead of this precious stuff, Rabelais would have hitched the great doctor of absenteeism into an immortal chapter, as probably one of the consulting advisers of Panurge, "when he had the flea in his ear," and set forth his rugged ribaldry as a jest for ever.

Dr. Folliott is avowedly in imitation of Friar John. The especial foolery of Peacock is visible in his nonsense about the doctor's name.

> In a village in the vicinity of the castle was the vicarage of the reverend Doctor Folliott, a gentleman endowed with a tolerable stock of learning, an interminable swallow, and an indefatigable pair of lungs. His pre-eminence in the latter faculty gave occasion to some etymologists to ring changes on his name, and to decide that it was derived from Follis Optimus, softened, through an Italian medium, into Follē Ottimo, contracted poetically into Folleotto, and elided Anglicè into Folliott, signifying a first-rate pair of bellows.

Now this is not learning, nor any thing like it—it is nonsense, and nonsense only. Equally remote from scholarship are the petty scraps of Greek culled out of Pindar and Aristophanes. . . . (p. 17)

Ignorance manifested in ninety-nine pages is not to be palliated by bits of out-of-the-way Greek, scraped out of a lexicon, in the hundredth. Such was not the scholarship of Rabelais, whose learning breathes forth in every page, and who quotes it in none. (pp. 17-18)

The story is stuff—there is nothing of the slightest interest about it; the philosophy is rubbish, the wit trash. Of its name-making, which is evidently a matter on which Peacock prides himself, it is quite sufficient to say that the heroine, who is all perfection, is a Miss Touchandgo. Her father is a swindler, and writes her a letter from America, in which he avows the most rascally principles, and receives a most flattering answer from the honourable young lady. She marries a Mr. Chainmail, who is in love with the twelfth century. The economist is Mr. MacQuedy, *i.e.* Mr. Mac Q.E.D. (which was to be demonstrated)—and so forth.

Some years ago it entered the imagination of Hunt and Keats, and some others of that coterie, to crown themselves with laurel, and take off their cravats. This was the janty thing, and quite poetical. While the coroneted and uncravated company were sitting thus one day, "with their singing robes about them," Peacock came in. "Do," said a lady, who officiated as coronet manufacturer, "do, dear Mr. Peacock, let me weave you a chaplet, and put it on your head; then you will sit as poets altogether."

"No, ma'am," said Peacock, wiping his head, "no, ma'am; you may make a fool of your own husband, but there is no need of your making a fool of me."

This anecdote is authentic, and we agree, after reading his books, that there is no need of making a fool of Peacock, by crowning him with a laurel chaplet, or any more convenient utensil, because it is evident that he is blockhead enough already. It is quite refreshing, as his squad say, to find him apeing Sir Walter Scott—the sign painter has very naturally a contempt for Raphael.

Peacock, however, *is* a poet, and it is only fair that we should give a specimen of his song.

> In the days of old,
> Lovers felt true passion,
> Deeming years of sorrow
> By a smile repaid;
> Now the charms of gold,
> Spells of pride and fashion,
> Bid them say good morrow
> To the best-loved maid.
>
> Through the forests wild,
> O'er the mountains lonely,
> They were never weary
> Honour to pursue:
> If the damsel smiled,
> Once in seven years only,
> All their wanderings dreary,
> Ample guerdon knew.
>
> Now, one day's caprice
> Weighs down years of smiling,
> Youthful hearts are rovers,
> Love is bought and sold:
> Fortune's gifts may cease,
> Love is less beguiling;
> Wiser were the lovers
> In the days of old.

The peacock does not sing exactly as the swan. (pp. 19-20)

A review of "Crotchet Castle," in Fraser's Magazine for Town & Country, *Vol. IV, No. XIX, August, 1831, pp. 17-20.*

[JAMES SPEDDING]   (essay date 1839)

[*An English editor and writer, Spedding was chiefly known for editing the works of Francis Bacon. In this excerpt from a review commonly regarded as the first important examination of Peacock's novels, Spedding evaluates Peacock's satirical methods.*]

[Peacock] stands, among the disputing opinions of the time, a disengaged and disinterested looker-on; among them, but not of them; showing neither malice nor favour, but a certain sympathy, companionable rather than brotherly, with all; with natural glee cheering on the combatants to their discomfiture, and as each rides his hobby boldly to the destruction prepared for him, regarding them all alike with the same smile of half compassionate amusement. Of all the philosophies which are encouraged to expose themselves in these pages, we have endeavoured in vain to conjecture which enjoys the largest, or which the smallest share of his sympathy. Could we find one constantly associated with more agreeable personal qualities, or with more brilliant conversation, or with sounder argument than any other;—were there any which he seemed to handle with peculiar tenderness, or in the showing up of which he appeared to take peculiar pleasure; we might suspect that we had discovered the secret of his preference or aversion. But no such clue is offered to us. The instances of the kind which we have been able to detect serve only, when rightly understood, to baffle us more completely. It might certainly seem that his respect for the good old times of roast-beef and quarter-staff, and his contempt for the 'march of intellect,' have a touch of earnestness in them;—that of all theories of human life, that which maintains the superiority, in all that concerns man's real welfare, of the twelfth century to the nineteenth, has most of his secret sympathy; and, that that which is advocated in broken Scotch by certain imaginary members of our own fraternity, and which may be called the politico-economical theory, is most to his personal distaste;—that of all characters his favourite is the worldly man who boldly proclaims and acquiesces in his infirmity; his aversion, the worldly man whose weakness is disguised by himself under the affectation of something better, or protected from the censure of society by the sanctity of his profession or his order. But, rightly considered, these apparent sympathies and antipathies are not to be taken as an index to his real feelings. It is not their greater or less conformity to his own tastes, but their greater or less acceptance in the world, by which he is repelled or attracted. We see in them only the working of a scepticism truly impartial and insatiable, which, after knocking down all the opinions which are current in the world, proceeds to set up an opinion made up of all that is *not* current in the world, that when that falls too, the desolation may be complete. (pp. 438-39)

Assuming the legitimacy of his general design, the praise of great skill in the execution will hardly be denied him. He shows a free delight and a prevailing thirst for excellence in his art, which places him, in our estimation, decidedly among men of *genius,* properly so called; men, that is, whose minds are moved and controlled by an inner spirit, working restlessly towards some end of its own, in the simple attainment of which, independently of any use to be made of it, and in that alone, it finds satisfaction. Hence his rare accomplishment in the use of his weapons, which he wields with a grace, a dexterity, and (excepting a few cases, in which, not content with public conduct and opinions, he undertakes, not very happily, to interpret motives and exhibit personal qualities) with a gay good-humour which takes away all offence from his raillery, and secures for him a free toleration in the exercise of his privilege. The spirit of frolic exaggeration in which the characters are conceived,— each a walking epitome of all that is absurd in himself,—the ludicrous felicity of self-exposure with which they are made to talk and act,—and the tone of decided though refined caricature which runs through the whole, unite to set grave remonstrance fairly at defiance. And while the imagination is thus forced into the current of his humour, the taste is charmed by a refinement of manners, and by a classical purity and reserved grace of style, which carries all sense of coarseness or vulgarity clean away; and the understanding is attracted and exercised by the sterling quality of the wit, the brilliancy, fulness, and solidity of the dialogue, the keenness of observation, the sharpness and intelligence, if not the delicacy or philosophical depth, of satire; and a certain roguish familiarity with the deceitfulness of human nature, from which we may derive many useful hints, to be improved at pleasure. Add to this, that although he dwells more habitually among doubts and negations than we believe to be good for any man, he is not without positive impulses,—generous and earnest, so far as they go,—which impart a uniformly healthy tone to his writings. There are many things both good and bad which he does not recognise; but the good which he does recognise is really good; the bad really bad. Explicit faith of his own he seems to have none; the creeds, systems, and theories of other men he treats alike as toys to play with; his humour, though pure, is shallow; his irony covers little or none of that latent reverence and sympathy,—rarely awakens within that 'sweet recoil of love and pity,'—which gives to irony its deepest meaning, and makes it in many minds the purest, if not the only natural language of tender and profound emotion; his general survey of life has something of coldness and hardness, so that much good seed falls in vain and withers on the surface. But his nature bears no weeds, and the natural products of the soil are healthy and hardy. Inhumanity, oppression, cant, and false pretensions of all kinds are hated with a just hatred; mirth, sunshine, and good fellowship are relished with a hearty relish; simplicity, unassuming goodness, and the pure face of nature never fail to touch him with natural delight. It is most pleasant and encouraging to observe these better qualities gradually prevailing and exercising in each successive production a larger influence. The humour seems to run deeper; the ridicule is informed with a juster appreciation of the meaning of the thing ridiculed; the disputants are more in earnest, and less like scoffers in disguise; there is more of natural warmth and life in the characters; and, altogether, there is a humaner spirit over his later works, and a kindlier sympathy with his subject.

A corresponding improvement may also be observed in the management of his plots—in the skill with which the incidents are interwoven with the conversations, and made to assist in developing the humours of the dialogue. In the two earliest of them, indeed, *Headlong Hall* and *Melincourt,* the whole story might be stripped off, so as to leave a series of separate dialogues scarcely injured by the change. We should miss only, what, indeed, we should be very sorry to miss, the picturesque grouping and lively satirical narrative by which they are accompanied and relieved. In *Nightmare Abbey* this could not be so easily done. Without the successive situations which form the story, the humour of *character* (which is more considerable in this than in the two foregoing tales) could hardly be brought out. Scythrop, the gloomy and mystical regenerator, who builds morbid hopes for the future upon a morbid discontent with the present;—Mr Glowry, the large-landed misanthropist, to whose table all men are welcome, who can find nothing in the world for a reasonable man to enjoy;—and Mr Toobad, the Manichean millennarian, who can see nothing there except the devil himself, having great wrath—could hardly have been displayed in full character without the loves, jealousies, and contradictions which it is the business of the narrative to develope. In *Maid Marian* and *Crotchet Castle,* the interest lies in a kind of running commentary on the action; which would lose its meaning if the scene and story were taken away. In *Crotchet Castle,* the incidents are employed to bring out the humours of individual character, and are so well wrought into the texture of the work, that, slight as they are, they could not be separated

from it without material injury. It is not that truth to nature is more strictly preserved in the later than in the earlier tales, for the spirit of exaggeration and caricature is still kept up; but that the caricature is deeper and more pervasive, and better harmonized. In the latter, the characters *live* upon their hobbies; in the former, they only mount them to dispute upon.

But though the management of the plots is in this respect very skilful, the author has wisely abstained (except in one instance, which we shall notice presently) from attempting to give them any independent interest as stories. They are of the simplest construction, and the incidents are taken from everyday life. A hospitable house, a variety of guests, and an occasion which may bring them together on easy terms, are all he wants: no matter whether it may be a Christmas party, a wedding party, a party of speculators in philosophy or in the stocks, or a party of rival suitors to an attractive heiress. The course of true love cannot run too smoothly; virtue cannot triumph with too little help from accident or superhuman effect,—need not indeed triumph at all; the true heir cannot be in too little danger of losing his inheritance; the meeting of the guests cannot be too easily brought about, or the parting cause too few tears. The business of the fiction lies in the dialogues, and would only be injured and embarassed by any independent interest that might be combined with it of an exciting or pathetic nature. (pp. 443-45)

> [*James Spedding*], *in a review of "Headlong Hall" and others, in* The Edinburgh Review, *Vol. LXVIII, No. CXXXVIII, January, 1839, pp. 432-59.*

THE SPECTATOR   (essay date 1861)

> [*In an excerpt from a review of* Gryll Grange, *this critic examines the plot, setting, and tone of the novel.*]

Among the numerous benefits which the invention of novels has conferred upon the human race, not the least is to be reckoned that of enabling certain men to convey their ideas to the public who would otherwise be considerably puzzled to devise an appropriate vehicle for their expression. Some persons, no doubt, feel aggrieved at the intrusion of one sort of literature into another; it confuses their minds, like having soup at the conclusion of dinner; they like novels to be novels, comedies to be comedies, and treatises on matters in general— if there must be such things—to be divided into their appropriate heads and published in the organ properly devoted to each species of observation. But it would be an intolerable world if we were obliged to conform to the boundaries of our literary departments with the exact formality of the extracts in a "Speaker," and we should lose a great deal of amusing and genial stuff simply for want of a place to put it in. To disfranchise a writer unless he could show that his work would fit into some recognized pigeon-hole, would be like the mistake of people who send fowls on board ship without a due supply of earthy matter to mix with their food. They lay eggs all the same, but the absence of shells causes a certain degree of inconvenience to the consumer. Much of the wit, humour, and learning which now find a place in fictitious literature would be reabsorbed into the writers' systems, or dissipated in the melancholy form of "adversaria," if some ready method did not exist of stimulating an author who has something in him by the appeal to an extended audience, comprising those who can appreciate his more recondite merits, as well as the larger class for whom his livelier faculties are, not unhealthfully, called into activity.

The reappearance of the author of *Headlong Hall* produces a feeling like that with which we await a bottle of wine that we recollect in its "relish fiery-new," but which we have reason to believe calculated to improve by a twenty years' sojourn in the cellar. No one who had read Mr. Peacock's early novels was likely to forget that he had made the acquaintance of a thoroughly original writer, whose conceptions of character might often be crude, and his notions of incident forced, but whose frankness, freshness, love of letters, and cultivated *bonhomie* would make him always welcome, however far he might deviate from received models in the form he had chosen for embodying his observation of society. About a man as to whom one is uncertain what he will say or do next, yet certain that he will do nothing disagreeable or ungentlemanly, there is the charm of curiosity and often of real liking; and there is the absence of the one unpardonable fault—dulness.

Mr. Peacock's **"Recollections of Shelley"** showed that he had lost none of his former vigour and freshness, and the book before us proves that his other qualities have ripened in their seclusion into a full-flavoured though not too rich a maturity. Mellow is the word which perhaps most adequately expresses the tone of thought which pervades *Gryll Grange,* and the kind of associations it awakens. Most readers will probably be aware that it is republished from *Fraser's,* and, though it is as far as possible from realizing the idea popularly, and justly, entertained of a "magazine story," its first medium of appearance was not the less appropriate. Next to a thrilling romance which leaves the hero hanging over a bottomless pit by his eyelids at the close of each number, nothing is so good for magazine fiction as a story which does not pretend to be any story at all, but in which one is always sure of some pleasant reading without the labour occasioned by the tepid intermediate class of novels, of recollecting their last imaginary difficulty or psychological dilemma. Mr. Peacock's characters being simple, distinct, and few in number, cause no such trouble; and as some of them are remarkable rather for what they say than for what they do, and are only interesting while they are saying it, there could not possibly be an easier piece of reading. The thread of the tale is as slight as possible, and though every one who takes it up will be interested in seeing how it ends, its principal purpose seems to be that of forming a vent for the author's opinion of the nineteenth century in general, and for his store of scholarship in particular. The events are told in a sort of textual narrative, and to the conversations, which are in smaller type, the names of the speakers are prefixed, which gives the whole story the aspect of a genteel comedy, with what Mr. Carlyle would call "connecting elucidations." It is useless to appeal to magazine readers, possibly also to severer critics, without a love affair, and thus the various conversations and incidents tend to the ultimate tying of nine matrimonial nooses, which for so small a book would be extravagant, but that seven girls go, as auctioneers say, "in one lot." Mr. Gryll is an epicurean country squire in the New Forest, who boasts a descent from some of the sailors of Ulysses whom Circe turned into swine, and is blessed with a congenial friend in Dr. Opimian, the neighbouring vicar, equally devoted with himself to classic lore and the cultivation of a refined taste for gastronomy. Mr. Gryll has a niece, whom he has named after Morgana, in the "Orlando Innamorato," and who has rejected almost as many suitors as Penelope. Dr. Opimian, in one of his country rambles, unearths a young gentleman named Falconer, who lives in a tower at the top of a hill in the middle of the forest—a sort of innocent-minded Beckford—with an excellent library in which he spends most of his time, a stock of equally good Madeira, and seven young, pretty, and ac-

complished housekeepers, whom he regards as his sisters. To avoid scandal they never move about the house except in pairs, and always finish the evening by performing for their master's solace a hymn to Saint Catherine, whom he has adopted as the object of a kind of ideal worship. Through an accident which obliges Mr. Gryll and his daughter to stay some time at his retreat, this fascinating hermit is brought out and induced to join a party at the Grange, where the germs of an attachment between him and the young lady begin apparently to develop themselves. Matters, however, are complicated by the arrival on the scene of two other persons—a brilliant young nobleman, Lord Curryfin, whose only steady pursuit is that of occasionally delivering a lecture on fish at most of the coast towns, and who diversifies his leisure by taking up every pursuit of the day in turn, with equal success and inconstancy—and a young lady, Miss Niphet, graceful as a Greek statue, but almost as reserved. Which of these four persons shall pair off with which forms the plot, or what stands in place of one. There would be no especial difficulty about matching the two couples in some way or other, but Mr. Falconer is averse to leave his poetic retreat, and does not know what is to become of his seven young Pleiads if he allows them to turn into planets. So he remains irresolute, and goes home occasionally to refresh his taste for solitude. Lord Curryfin, on the other hand, is uncertain of which young lady he prefers, and as Miss Gryll is also wavering in her choice, while Miss Niphet is alternately attracted and repelled by the varying aspects of Lord Curryfin's rather Protean character, the materials are presented for a problem of which it may be left to the reader's curiosity to investigate the solution. The *motif* of the book is not a tragic one, and we therefore know we are safe from any harrowing up of our feelings in a manner inconsistent with the genial and comfortable spirit in which all the other business is carried on. "You will find bream-pie," says Dr. Opimian, in one of the earlier conversations, "set down as a prominent item of luxurious living in the indictments prepared against them [the monks] at the dissolution of the monasteries. *The work of destruction was too rapid, and I fear the receipt is lost.*" This sort of thing is evidently incompatible with blighted hopes. So, too, is the production of a miniature Aristophanic comedy on the subject of table-turning and other follies of the day, which is described as being written and performed with appropriate scenery, dresses, and decorations in a Greek theatre built for the purpose, with a chorus of clouds, represented by the most charming female performers. Various translations and poems are introduced as part of the evening's amusements, the former of which are so spiritedly done as to make us hope that Mr. Peacock will undertake to introduce us to Bojardo in a more extended form. (pp. 222-23)

The spirit of the book is not one of satisfaction with the nineteenth century, and would please both Dr. Sewell by its satire on Pantopragmatic societies (*i.e.* "Social Science" and the like), and Mr. Ruskin by its denunciation of the rapid pace at which people now-a-days think it necessary to live. . . .

There is not a dull page anywhere, and the few descriptions of scenery which occur are complete and picturesque without being overloaded, and just in the right tone. The poems are peculiar, because the highest note of imaginative feeling is not struck; yet there is a nameless charm, resulting partly from their having an unusual amount of pity and substance, partly from their very high finish, which is likely to make many of them favourites. The lyric called **"Youth and Age,"** reminds us of some of Mr. Thackeray's poems, but without any of the cynicism which the latter sometimes show on similar subjects.

In the set manner in which the characters are presented, the aesthetic, epicurean tone which pervades the book, the utter improbability of the incidents, the romantic haze which is thrown round them, and the conspicuous position which dramatic affairs occupy, we are reminded of Goethe's *Wilhelm Meister* more than of any other book. The German work is like a great, confused, half epic, half allegoric sketch in which there is little proportion, and no unity of impression, if of meaning; Mr. Peacock's is a cabinet picture, with every part equally elaborated, with a lower aim satisfactorily realized. The philosophy of things in general has never appeared in a more genial guise. It is not a book of which it would be worth while to criticize the opinions, nor would the most staunch upholder of the superiority of ourselves over our ancestors care to prove the author an obstructive or an obscurantist. His ideas are to be enjoyed rather than questioned, and any one who takes up the book in such a belligerent spirit may be assured that he is not looking at it from the right point of view. We cannot get out of the nineteenth century even if we try, so Mr. Peacock's antagonists, if he has any, are safe in their position. But it is pleasant, sometimes, to lapse into a dream of other things, as one drops down to Burnham Beeches to lose the roar of cab and omnibus in one's ears. It is in some such place that the book should be read—not at railroad speed, or, indeed, anywhere near a railway. There is a time for swallowing Swindon soup, and there is a time for sipping Amontillado sherry. Mr. Peacock's volume has an almond-like flavour, which renders it a fit concomitant of the latter process, and we feel instinctively that it is under such circumstances that he would wish it to be taken up by those best able to appreciate it. (p. 223)

A review of "Gryll Grange," in The Spectator, *Vol. 34, No. 1705, March 2, 1861, pp. 222-23.*

[JAMES HANNAY] (essay date 1866)

[*Hannay was a British novelist and journalist and the author of* Lectures on Satire and Satirists *(1854). In this excerpt from an article published shortly after Peacock's death, Hannay describes the chief characteristics of the Peacockian novel.*]

Thomas Love Peacock [is the] author of **Headlong Hall, Crotchet Castle,** and other pleasant and clever books—all bearing that *cachet* of a distinctive character and intellect in the writer, which is the unfailing accompaniment of really superior parts. In these days, when so many 'twaddling essays' are written, and when the pleasantry of our younger wags is too often mere Cockney garbage, we recur with delight to the vivid satire, manly sense, and brilliant scholarship of this distinguished, but not sufficiently known author. (p. 85)

We know what the fashionable novel of 1866 is—either a photograph of commonplace life by an artist who sets up his camera at the drawing-room door as mechanically as his brother artist at Mayall's; or a literary Chinese puzzle, made up of all imaginable complications of crimes committed by stupidly unnatural puppets fobbed off on us for characters. The Peacockian novel is something quite different. It is a sort of comedy in the form of a novel, making very little pretension to story, or to subtle character-painting, but illustrating the intellectual opinions and fashions of the day in capital dialogues; natural even in its most comic freedoms, and full of wit, satire, literature, and playfulness of every kind. Peacock had a favourite set of *dramatis personae*, who reappear with more or less variety in most of his books. There is a cultivated squire, whose mansion forms a rendezvous for the company, and whose

daughters or lady visitors supply occasion for the only half-serious love-making of the story. There is a parson of the old school, sometimes merely remarkable for eating and drinking, but generally a classical scholar and wit into the bargain. There is a Scotch philosopher of the *Edinburgh Review* type. And there are representatives of all the pet schools of speculation and sentiment in his day: the phrenologist; the Byronic misanthrope; the Coleridgian mystic; the perfectibility of the species man; and so forth. These people all get very fair play, even when ridiculed, and are brought to the test of sound common sense, and of that kind of wit which has been described in the *Pall Mall Gazette* as 'only sense sharpened till it shines.' The politics of the author are not easily defined. Like many men who are literary rather than political, he seems to have been Conservative on one side of his mind, and Liberal on the other. He laughed at the 'March of Intellect;' the glorification of the physical sciences; the worship of the multitude; and the novel schemes of education; of one class of his contemporaries. But he laughed also at the defences of rotten boroughs, and the high-flying Toryism of another class. He quizzed Brougham. He more than quizzed Southey, whom he somewhere calls 'a Priapus set up to guard the golden apples of corruption.' In short, he was a satirist, without being a partisan, and thought himself entitled to satirize whatever exaggerations he pleased, no matter in what directions the exaggerations tended. With regard to his place in the great schools of satire, just as we trace the pedigree of Churchill, through Dryden, to Juvenal, and that of Pope, in spite of grave differences, to Horace, so we call Peacock a child of Aristophanes. He had the gaiety; the dramatic freedom; the lively wit; the feeling for nature; the turn for song; all of which were possessed by

The merry Greek, tart Aristophanes,

of course on a greater and more brilliant scale. (pp. 87-8)

[*James Hannay*], *in a review of "Headlong Hall," in* The North British Review, *n.s. Vol. VI, No. LXXXIX, September, 1866, pp. 85-8.*

EDMUND WILLIAM GOSSE (essay date 1875)

[*A distinguished English literary historian, critic, and biographer, Gosse wrote extensively on seventeenth- and eighteenth-century English literature. His commentary in* Seventeenth Century Studies *(1883),* A History of Eighteenth Century Literature, 1660-1780 *(1889),* Questions at Issue *(1893), and other works is generally regarded as sound and suggestive, and he is also credited with introducing the works of the Norwegian dramatist Henrik Ibsen and other Scandinavian writers to English readers. In the following excerpt from a review of Henry Cole's 1875 edition of Peacock's works, Gosse emphasizes the impartial and all-inclusive nature of Peacock's satire.*]

A commonplace of conversation, which is only too sadly true, is for ever reminding us that the activity and energy of this age, with its quenchless thirst for physical and mental movement, has swept off the face of the earth a certain very interesting type of the human individual. All English generations before our own have had time to produce a race of men who, without much creative power, have possessed a passion for learning, a craving for reflective intellectual exercise, a faculty for the successful cultivation of *belles-lettres,* which, indeed, have added little to the stores of our literature except some verses, some scholia, or some reflections, but which have done inestimable service in making broad and solid the culture of the educated minority. A quiet practical life, without strain and without the possibility of poverty, has enabled them to cultivate what was called a hundred years ago 'an elegant retirement.' Now the fever of business and the widening of all intellectual interests, the fight for life and the claims of society, conspire to reduce to a minimum the numbers of those who are able and willing to devote themselves to the study of letters for its own sake. The 'people of quality' who did so much in a quiet way for poetry, classical learning, archaeology, and music in the eighteenth century are either tempted into the wasting circle of the politics of the hour, or if they give themselves to intellectual exercise at all, it is rather in the channel of experimental science. The gentlemen who met seventy years ago to quote Pindar over their wine, or to discuss Lord Byron's poems over a cup of green tea with my lady, now flock, with geological specimens in their pockets, to the meetings of the British Association, or argue about the acoustic transparency of the atmosphere with scientific ladies from Girton. It would be idle to discuss the advantage or disadvantage of the new state of things. The times change, and we change with them. No doubt the port-wine was heady, the classic quotations monotonous, the criticism dreary and stupid, in the old-world days of elegant retirement. Possibly the present fashion for the anatomy of phenomena may one day seem to have been a scraping among dry bones. The fact is indisputable that the race of gentlemen who combined ease and the *belles-lettres* with an affectionate study of the classics has completely passed away. And Thomas Love Peacock was the last and by no means the least worthy of them.

Many of the characteristics of a 'last man' clung about Mr. Peacock. He was suspicious, resentful and dolorous in his aspect towards the world in general, hopeless for the future, regretful of the past, using satire as punishment, not as correction, and saved only by his affectionate and generous inner nature from the moroseness of disappointment and despair. Born in a generation full of the ferment of new hopes and aims, stirring with fresh intellectual stimulus towards all kinds of literary revival, a generation, too, remarkable for its ardent friendships and partizanships, Peacock remained, like Rogers, quite aloof, and, in this most unlike Rogers, without personal communion with the men of his time. Shelley is almost the only literary friend his granddaughter mentions in her recently-published biography of him, and his antagonism to all the other poets is ludicrously patent in his writings. It was not that he was envious of their success; his nature was altogether too noble for so base an emotion as envy to take root in it; but he conscientiously disapproved of their innovations, and would have been content to find all modern literature destroyed, and the latest attainable verse to be the tragedies of Seneca. There was something beautifully impartial in his disdain for his contemporaries; the Lake School, the Cockney School, the Satanic School, all alike to him were heretics of the deepest dye. Walter Scott the Enchanter of the North? Mr. Peacock averred that the man who arranged the pantomimes at Drury Lane was a much greater enchanter! Southey was a god 'of the garden of the golden apples of corruption,' and the deity was rudely and most inaptly named! Coleridge is the 'self-elected laureate of the asinine king,' and all the poets of the day, even Byron, fall under the lash of this unlimited invective. Of course, with such singular and unconciliatory tastes, Peacock's own books were not likely to have much success.

> Quis leget haec? Nemo, hercule, nemo;
> Vel duo, vel nemo!

might appropriately have been asked and answered in sight of such books as these; and yet, as what is intrinsically good will never wholly lack readers, in spite of all their author did to

make them unpopular, *Headlong Hall, Crotchet Castle*, and the rest of Peacock's novels have never been without admirers, and now seem destined to enjoy a fresh lease of immortality. (pp. 496-97)

Edmund William Gosse, "Thomas Love Peacock," in London Society, *Vol. XXVII, No. CLXII, June, 1875, pp. 496-509.*

[ALEXANDER I. SHAND]   (essay date 1875)

[*Shand discusses reasons for Peacock's limited audience in this excerpt from a review of the first collected edition of his works.*]

Fourteen years ago a novel made its appearance which was more favourably reviewed than generally read. Moreover, *Gryll Grange* puzzled the critics, and many of them had the candour to own as much. It set at defiance the received canons of the craft, and was in flat contradiction to the prevailing fashions of the day. Its plot was loose and wild, its incidents were incoherent or extravagant, and its characters anything rather than the commonplace individualities one is in the habit of meeting in everyday life. But it bore upon every page the marks of a vigorous idiosyncrasy; it showed comprehensive acquaintance with men and things, with social theories and political systems, although it regarded them almost invariably through an eccentric medium. It was clear that the writer had read much and reflected deeply; that the studies of his predilection had been among the classical authors of Greece and Rome, until the cast of his thought had taken its tinge from them, and he had insensibly imbued himself with the very spirit of their literature. A critic by temperament with the gifts of a poet, perhaps his strength lay in satire and irony. But he was absolutely brimming over with humour that was sometimes kindly though often sarcastic. No subject came much amiss to him, though it was plain that he had marked preferences, and it might be assumed that his opinions were as decided as his prejudices. But it was difficult to surmise what his opinions really were, for sometimes when his characters seemed to be delivering his mind and you were submitting your ideas to the dexterity of his arguments, he would turn short upon you with a grave smile and demolish by the breath of another of his mouth-pieces the ingenious structure it had pleased him to rear. It was impossible to say where jest began and earnest ended. You read in constant mistrust lest you might be the victim of a mystification when you least expected one. Nor did deliberate afterthoughts always tend to reassure you, and when you laid down the book the impression was confirmed that it was seldom safe to be sure he was serious. No wonder that the reviewers had a difficulty in dealing with him—that the most appreciative of them, for the most part, were inclined to keep to generalities, and heartily recommend a novel they scarcely professed to interpret. Nor was it strange that their recommendations were by no means very universally attended to, for when *Gryll Grange* was christened a novel, it was launched on the libraries under delusive pretences. The very qualities that attracted men of taste and cultivation were likely to deter the ordinary run of subscribers. It demanded sustained thought and careful reading: to most people it was an effort to enter into its spirit, to many it was an absolute impossibility. In order to enjoy it, your mind had to be always on the stretch, guessing at riddles, seeking out the key to paradoxes, or following the author in subtle processes of reasoning from strange premises. Many of its readers too must have had an uneasy consciousness that foibles of their own were being reproduced or caricatured for their delectation; while at every page they were unpleasantly convicted of ignorance and inferiority by allusions that were as much Greek to them as the abounding quotations from Aristophanes or Athenaeus.

Yet with all its defects from the popular point of view, it was clear that the author of **Gryll Grange** could be no novice either in life or literature. Indeed a reference to the title-page showed that the book was but one of a series, bearing signs of the marked idiosyncrasy of their writer in a generic eccentricity of title. But most of those that had gone before it had been written in the very beginning of the century; there had been a hiatus in the series, of the better part of an ordinary lifetime, and **Headlong Hall, Crotchet Castle,** and **Nightmare Abbey** had scarcely been heard of by the present generation. Mr. Peacock had lived long enough to have some depressing experience of the ephemeral nature of literary fame, for he might undoubtedly have flattered himself, at one time, that he had made a mark in the literary world. Those earlier writings of his had won respectful consideration from thinkers who cared nothing for the productions of the Minerva Press, and gentlemen whose ideas he abused most heartily had heaped coals of fire on him by being lavish of their praise. Nay, a firm of enterprising publishers had thought his books contained sufficient promise of popularity to make it worth while reprinting them in collected shape as one of the volumes of the Standard Library of Fiction. We do not know, however, that the reprint did much to redeem either the works or the memory of their author from the oblivion to which time seemed surely consigning them; and **Gryll Grange** threatened to go the way of its predecessors, without having revived any permanent interest in them. With a very hearty admiration for Mr. Peacock, we can scarcely profess to be surprised at this. He chose deliberately to follow out his bent, inclining to qualify for a visitor to his own **Crotchet Castle.** He was as uncompromising in his mannerisms as in his opinions, and he wrote with almost defiant independence for the few rather than the many. He paid the inevitable penalty in suffering from the neglect he may be said to have courted; yet the better you know him the more thoroughly you appreciate him, and to know him even fairly well, you should be conversant with the whole series of his writings. We know no works that gain so greatly by being studied in their chronological order, or lose more by being taken separately. We use the word 'studied' advisedly. To get to the bottom of his mind, he must be read in constant reference to parallel passages that occur in his writings *passim*, as well as to the previous conversations in which he has been originating and developing his ideas. There can be no doubt, then, that his present editors have judged wisely in publishing this complete edition of his works [**The Works of Thomas Love Peacock**]. It gives him precisely the artificial help he needed towards obtaining the limited appreciation he would have coveted, and men of humour and intellect may be grateful to Lord Houghton and Sir Henry Cole. For not only have they done the best for the separate works by uniting the set in appropriate setting, but by collecting Peacock's more fugitive pieces they have shown the scope of his versatile powers as poet and dramatist, essayist and critic. (pp. 110-13)

> [Alexander I. Shand], in a review of "The Works of Thomas Love Peacock," in The Edinburgh Review, Vol. CXLII, No. CCLXXXIX, July, 1875, pp. 110-44.

MRS. OLIPHANT   (essay date 1882)

[Oliphant was a prolific nineteenth-century Scottish novelist, critic, biographer, and historian. A regular contributor to Blackwood's Magazine, *she published nearly one hundred novels, many of them popular tales of English and Scottish provincial life, including her best-known work, the series of novels known as the* Chronicles of Carlingford. *In the following excerpt from commentary first published in 1882, Oliphant discusses the uniqueness of Peacock's novels.*]

Peacock's reputation . . . rests upon the curious series of novels, if novels they can be called, **Headlong Hall, Nightmare Abbey, Crotchet Castle,** etc., which he has left behind him, books which are scarcely stories, though there is an artificial and whimsical thread of narrative to link their often brilliant conversations and discussions together. These, we were about to say, are unique in literature; but they have served as a model in our own day to other productions of a similar character, not so incisive and terse, and far from being so amusing. But Peacock was for many years alone in the curious vein of satire which he discovered. His method is somewhat artificial; and we can imagine the dismay of the ordinary novel-reader who should suddenly find himself confronted by the caustic fun and amusing dialogue of **Headlong Hall** or **Nightmare Abbey** when in search of an innocent romance. Perhaps it requires the zest of a consciousness, that were we not somewhat superior ourselves, we should not enjoy them, which has disposed such as have come under his spell to regard Peacock with something like enthusiasm. (p. 151)

In . . . ironic banter and *reductio ad absurdum* Peacock has no superior. His books themselves will probably seem tedious to the hasty reader, but even he will find in them innumerable suggestions which subsequent writers have made capital of. His wine and beasts have helped us to many feasts since his day. (pp. 155-56)

> *Mrs. Oliphant, in an excerpt in her* The Literary History of England, Vol. III, *Macmillan and Co., 1886, pp. 151-56.*

GEORGE SAINTSBURY   (essay date 1886)

[Saintsbury was an English literary historian and critic of the late nineteenth and early twentieth centuries. A prolific writer, he composed several histories of English and European literature as well as numerous critical works on individual authors, styles, and periods. In the following excerpt, Saintsbury provides a descriptive survey of Peacock's novels and examines the scope of his literary appeal.]

Although there are few novelists who observe plot less than Peacock, there are few also who are more regular in the particular fashion in which they disdain plot. Peacock is in fiction what the dramatists of the school of Ben Jonson down to Shadwell are in comedy—he works in "humours." It ought not to be, but perhaps is, necessary to remind the reader that this is by no means the same thing in essence, though accidentally it very often is the same, as being a humourist. The dealer in humours takes some fad or craze in his characters, some minor ruling passion, and makes his profit out of it. Generally (and almost always in Peacock's case) he takes if he can one or more of these humours as a central point, and lets the others play and revolve in a more or less eccentric fashion round it. In almost every book of Peacock's there is a host who has a more or less decided mania for collecting other maniacs round him. Harry Headlong, of Headlong Hall, Esquire, a young Welsh gentleman of means, and of generous though rather unchastened taste, finding, as Peacock says, in the earliest of his gibes at the universities, that there are no such things as men of taste and philosophy in Oxford, assembles a motley host in London, and asks them down to his place at Llanberis. The adventures of the visit (ending up with several weddings) form the scheme of the book, as indeed repetitions of something very little different form the scheme of all the other books, with the exception of *The Misfortunes of Elphin,* and perhaps *Maid Marian.* Of books so simple in one way, and so complex in others, it is impossible and unnecessary to give any detailed analysis. But each contains characteristics which contribute too much to the knowledge of Peacock's idiosyncrasy to pass altogether unnoticed. The contrasts in *Headlong Hall* between the pessimist Mr. Escot, the optimist Mr. Foster, and the happymean man Mr. Jenkison (who inclines to both in turn, but on the whole rather to optimism), are much less amusing than the sketches of Welsh scenery and habits, the passages of arms with representatives of the *Edinburgh* and *Quarterly Reviews* (which Peacock always hated), and the passing satire on "improving" craniology and other manias of the day. The book also contains the first and most unfriendly of the sketches of clergymen of the Church of England which Peacock gradually softened till, in Dr. Folliott and Dr. Opimian, his curses became blessings altogether. The Reverend Dr. Gaster is an ignoble brute, but not quite life-like enough to be really offensive. But the most charming part of the book by far (for its women are mere lay figures) is to be found in the convivial scenes. *Headlong Hall* contains, besides other occasional verse of merit, two drinking songs—**"Hail to the Headlong,"** and the still better **"A Heel-tap! a heel-tap! I never could bear it"**—songs not quite so good as those in the subsequent books, but good enough to make any reader think with a gentle sigh of the departure of good fellowship from the earth. Undergraduates and Scotchmen (and even in their case the fashion is said to be dying) alone practise at the present day the full rites of Comus.

Melincourt, published, and indeed written, very soon after *Headlong Hall,* is a much more ambitious attempt. It is some three times the length of its predecessor, and is, though not much longer than a single volume of some three-volume novels, the longest book that Peacock ever wrote. It is also much more ambitiously planned; the twice attempted abduction of the heiress, Anthelia Melincourt, giving something like a regular plot, while the introduction of Sir Oran Haut-ton (an orang-outang whom the eccentric hero, Forester, has domesticated and intends to introduce to parliamentary life) can only be understood as aiming at a regular satire on the whole of human life, conceived in a milder spirit than *Gulliver,* but belonging in some degree to the same class. Forester himself, a disciple of Rousseau, a fervent anti-slavery man who goes to the length of refusing his guests sugar, and an ideologist in many other ways, is also an ambitious sketch; and Peacock has introduced episodes after the fashion of eighteenth century fiction, besides a great number of satirical excursions dealing with his enemies of the Lake school, with paper money and with many other things and persons. The whole, as a whole, has a certain heaviness. The enthusiastic Forester is a little of a prig, and a little of a bore; his friend the professorial Mr. Fax proses dreadfully; the Oran Haut-ton scenes, amusing enough of themselves, are overloaded (as is the whole book) with justificative selections from Buffon, Lord Monboddo, and other authorities. The portraits of Southey, Coleridge, Wordsworth, Canning, and others, are neither like, nor in themselves very happy, and the heroine Anthelia is sufficiently uninteresting to make us extremely indifferent whether the virtuous Forester or the *roué* Lord Anophel Achthar gets her. On the other hand, detached passages are in the author's very best vein; and there is a truly delightful scene between Lord Anophel and his chaplain Grov-

elgrub, when the athletic Sir Oran has not only foiled their attempt on Anthelia, but has mastheaded them on the top of a rock perpendicular. But the gem of the book is the election for the borough of One-Vote—a very amusing farce on the subject of rotten boroughs. Mr. Forester has bought one of the One-Vote seats for his friend, the Orang, and going to introduce him to the constituency falls in with the purchaser of the other seat, Mr. Sarcastic, who is a practical humourist of the most accomplished kind. The satirical arguments with which Sarcastic combats Forester's enthusiastic views of life and politics, the elaborate spectacle which he gets up on the day of nomination, and the free fight which follows are recounted with extraordinary spirit. Nor is the least of the attractions of the book an admirable drinking song, superior to either of those in *Headlong Hall,* though perhaps better known to most people by certain Thackerayan reminiscences of it than in itself:—

"The Ghosts."

In life three ghostly friars were we,
And now three friendly ghosts we be.
Around our shadowy table placed,
The spectral bowl before us floats:
With wine that none but ghosts can taste
We wash our unsubstantial throats.
Three merry ghosts—three merry ghosts—three merry ghosts
    are we:
Let the ocean be port and we'll think it good sport
        To be laid in that Red Sea.

With songs that jovial spectres chaunt,
Our old refectory still we haunt.
The traveller hears our midnight mirth:
"Oh list," he cries, "the haunted choir!
The merriest ghost that walks the earth
Is now the ghost of a ghostly friar."
Three merry ghosts—three merry ghosts—three merry ghosts
    are we:
Let the ocean be port and we'll think it good sport
        To be laid in that Red Sea.

In the preface to a new edition of *Melincourt,* which Peacock wrote nearly thirty years later, and which contains a sort of promise of *Gryll Grange,* there is no sign of any dissatisfaction on the author's part with the plan of the earlier book; but in his next, which came quickly, he changed that plan very decidedly. *Nightmare Abbey* is the shortest, as *Melincourt* is the longest, of his tales; and as *Melincourt* is the most unequal and the most clogged with heavy matter, so *Nightmare Abbey* contains the most unbroken tissue of farcical, though not in the least coarsely farcical, incidents and conversations. The misanthropic Scythrop (whose habit of Madeira-drinking has made some exceedingly literal people sure that he really could not be intended for the water-drinking Shelley); his still gloomier father, Mr. Glowry; his intricate entanglements with the lovely Marionetta and the still more beautiful Celinda; his fall between the two stools; his resolve to commit suicide; the solution of that awkward resolve—are all simply delightful. Extravagant as the thing is, its brevity and the throng of incidents and jokes prevent it from becoming in the least tedious. The pessimist-fatalist Mr. Toobad, with his "innumerable proofs of the temporary supremacy of the devil," and his catchword "the devil has come among us having great wrath," appears just enough, and not too much. The introduced sketch of Byron as Mr. Cypress would be the least happy thing of the piece if it did not give occasion for a capital serious burlesque of Byronic verse, the lines, "There is a fever of the spirit," which, as better known than most of Peacock's verse, need not be quoted. Mr. Flosky, a fresh caricature of Coleridge, is even less like the original than Mr. Mystic, but he is much more like a human being, and in himself is great fun. An approach to a more charitable view of the clergy is discoverable in the curate Mr. Larynx, who, if not extremely ghostly, is neither a sot nor a sloven. But the quarrels and reconciliations between Scythrop and Marionetta, his invincible inability to make up his mind, the mysterious advent of Marionetta's rival, and her abode in hidden chambers, the alternate sympathy and repulsion between Scythrop and those elder disciples of pessimism, his father and Mr. Toobad—all the contradictions of Shelley's character, in short, with a suspicion of the incidents of his life brought into the most ludicrous relief, must always form the great charm of the book. A tolerably rapid reader may get through it in an hour or so, and there is hardly a more delightful hour's reading of anything like the same kind in the English language, either for the incidental strokes of wit and humour, or for the easy mastery with which the whole is hit off. It contains, moreover, another drinking-catch, **"Seamen Three,"** which, though it is like its companion, better known than most of Peacock's songs, may perhaps find a place:—

> Seamen three! What men be ye?
> Gotham's three wise men we be.
> Whither in your bowl so free?
> To rake the moon from out the sea.
> The bowl goes trim, the moon doth shine,
> And our ballast is old wine;
> And your ballast is old wine.
>
> Who art thou so fast adrift
> I am he they call Old Care.
> Here on board we will thee lift.
> No: I may not enter there.
> Wherefore so? 'Tis Jove's decree
> In a bowl Care may not be;
> In a bowl Care may not be.
>
> Fear ye not the waves that roll?
> No: in charmèd bowl we swim.
> What the charm that floats the bowl?
> Water may not pass the brim.
> The bowl goes trim, the moon doth shine
> And our ballast is old wine;
> And your ballast is old wine.

A third song sung by Marionetta, **"Why are thy looks so blank, Grey Friar?"** is as good in another way; nor should it be forgotten that the said Marionetta, who has been thought to have some features of the luckless Harriet Shelley, is Peacock's first lifelike study of a girl, and one of his pleasantest.

The book which came out four years after, *Maid Marian,* has, I believe, been much the most popular and the best known of Peacock's short romances. It owed this popularity, in great part, no doubt, to the fact that the author has altered little in the well-known and delightful old story, and has not added very much to its facts, contenting himself with illustrating the whole in his own satirical fashion. But there is also no doubt that the dramatisation of *Maid Marian* by Planché and Bishop as an operetta, helped, if it did not make, its fame. The snatches of song through the novel are more frequent than in any other of the books, so that Mr. Planché must have had but little trouble with it. Some of these snatches are among Peacock's best verse, such as the famous **"Bramble Song,"** the great hit of the operetta, the equally well-known **"Oh, bold Robin Hood,"** and the charming snatch:—

> For the tender beech and the sapling oak,
>   That grow by the shadowy rill,
> You may cut down both at a single stroke,
>   You may cut down which you will;

> But this you must know, that as long as they grow,
>   Whatever change may be,
> You never can teach either oak or beech
>   To be aught but a greenwood tree.

This snatch, which, in its mixture of sentiment, truth, and what may be excusably called "rollick," is very characteristic of its author, and is put in the mouth of Brother Michael, practically the hero of the piece, and the happiest of the various workings up of Friar Tuck, despite his considerable indebtedness to a certain older friar, whom we must not call "of the funnels." That Peacock was a Pantagruelist to the heart's core is evident in all his work; but his following of Master Francis is nowhere clearer than in *Maid Marian,* and it no doubt helps us to understand why those who cannot relish Rabelais should look askance at Peacock. For the rest no book of Peacock's requires so little comment as this charming pastoral, which was probably little less in Thackeray's mind than *Ivanhoe* itself when he wrote "Rebecca and Rowena." The author draws in (it would be hardly fair to say drags in) some of his stock satire at courts, the clergy, the landed gentry, and so forth; but the very nature of the subject excludes the somewhat tedious digressions which mar *Melincourt,* and which once or twice menace, though they never actually succeed in spoiling, the unbroken fun of *Nightmare Abbey.*

The Misfortunes of Elphin, which followed after an interval of seven years, is, I believe, the least generally popular of Peacock's works, though (not at all for that reason) it happens to be my own favourite. The most curious instance of this general unpopularity is the entire omission, as far as I am aware, of any reference to it in any of the popular guide-books to Wales. One piece of verse, indeed, the **"War-song of Dinas Vawr,"** a triumph of easy verse and covert sarcasm, has had some vogue, but the rest is only known to Peacockians. The abundance of Welsh lore which, at any rate in appearance, it contains, may have had something to do with this; though the translations or adaptations, whether faithful or not, are the best literary renderings of Welsh known to me. Something also, and probably more, is due to the saturation of the whole from beginning to end with Peacock's driest humour. Not only is the account of the sapping and destruction of the embankment of Gwaelod an open and continuous satire on the opposition to Reform, but the whole book is written in the spirit and manner of *Candide*—a spirit and manner which Englishmen have generally been readier to relish, when they relish them at all, in another language than in their own. The respectable domestic virtues of Elphin and his wife Angharad, the blameless loves of Taliesin and the Princess Melanghel, hardly serve even as a foil to the satiric treatment of the other characters. The careless incompetence of the poetical King Gwythno, the coarser vices of other Welsh princes, the marital toleration or blindness of Arthur, the cynical frankness of the robber King Melvas, above all, the drunkenness of the immortal Seithenyn, give the humourist themes which he caresses with inexhaustible affection, but in a manner no doubt very puzzling, if not shocking, to matter-of-fact readers. Seithenyn, the drunken prince and dyke-warden, whose carelessness lets in the inundation, is by far Peacock's most original creation (for Scythrop, as has been said, is rather a humorous distortion of the actual than a creation). His complete self-satisfaction, his utter fearlessness of consequences, his ready adaptation to whatever part, be it prince or butler, presents itself to him, and above all, the splendid topsy-turviness of his fashion of argument make Seithenyn one of the happiest, if not one of the greatest, results of whimsical imagination and study of human nature. (pp. 417-20)

Crotchet Castle, the last but one of the series, which was published two years after *Elphin* and nearly thirty before *Gryll Grange,* has been already called the best; and the statement is not inconsistent with the description already given of *Nightmare Abbey* and of *Elphin.* For *Nightmare Abbey* is chiefly farce, and *The Misfortunes of Elphin* is chiefly sardonic persiflage. *Crotchet Castle* is comedy of a high and varied kind. Peacock has returned in it to the machinery of a country house with its visitors, each of whom is more or less of a crotcheteer; and has thrown in a little romantic interest in the suit of a certain unmoneyed Captain Fitzchrome to a noble damsel who is expected to marry money, as well as in the desertion and subsequent rescue of Susannah Touchandgo, daughter of a levanting financier. The charm of the book, however, which distinguishes it from all its predecessors, is the introduction of characters neither ridiculous nor simply good in the persons of the Rev. Dr. Folliott and Lady Clarinda Bossnowl, Fitzchrome's beloved. "Lady Clarinda," says the captain, when the said Lady Clarinda has been playing off a certain not unladylike practical joke on him, "is a very pleasant young lady;" and most assuredly she is, a young lady (in the nineteenth century and in prose) of the tribe of Beatrice, if not even of Rosalind. As for Dr. Folliott, the author is said to have described him as his amends for his earlier clerical sketches, and the amends are ample. A stout Tory, a fellow of infinite jest, a lover of good living, an inveterate paradoxer, a pitiless exposer of current cants and fallacies, and, lastly, a tall man of his hands, Dr. Folliott is always delightful, whether he is knocking down thieves, or annihilating, in a rather Johnsonian manner, the economist, Mr. McQuedy, and the journalist, Mr. Eavesdrop, or laying down the law as to the composition of breakfast and supper, or using strong language as to "the learned friend" (Brougham), or bringing out, partly by opposition and partly by irony, the follies of the transcendentalists, the fops, the doctrinaires, and the mediaevalists of the party. The book, moreover, contains the last and not the least of Peacock's admirable drinking songs:—

> If I drink water while this doth last,
>   May I never again drink wine;
> For how can a man, in his life of a span,
>   Do anything better than dine?
> We'll dine and drink, and say if we think
>   That anything better can be;
> And when we have dined, wish all mankind
>   May dine as well as we.
>
> And though a good wish will fill no dish,
>   And brim no cup with sack,
> Yet thoughts will spring as the glasses ring
>   To illume our studious track.
> O'er the brilliant dreams of our hopeful schemes
>   The light of the flask shall shine;
> And we'll sit till day, but we'll find the way
>   To drench the world with wine.

The song is good in itself, but it is even more interesting as being the last product of Peacock's Anacreontic vein. Almost a generation passed before the appearance of his next and last novel, and though there is plenty of good eating and drinking in *Gryll Grange,* the old fine rapture had disappeared in society meanwhile, and Peacock obediently took note of the disappearance. It is considered, I believe, a mark of barbarian tastes to lament the change. But I am not certain that the Age of Apollinaris and lectures has yet produced anything that can vie as literature with the products of the ages of Wine and Song.

Gryll Grange however, in no way deserves the name of a dry stick. It is, next to *Melincourt,* the longest of Peacock's novels,

and it is entirely free from the drawbacks of the forty-years-older book. Mr. Falconer, the hero, who lives in a tower alone with seven lovely and discreet foster-sisters, has some resemblances to Mr. Forester, but he is much less of a prig. The life and the conversation bear, instead of the marks of a young man's writing, the marks of the writing of one who has seen the manners and cities of many other men, and the personages throughout are singularly lifelike. The loves of the second hero and heroine, Lord Curryfin and Miss Niphet, are much more interesting than their names would suggest. And the most loquacious person of the book, the Rev. Dr. Opimian, if he is somewhat less racy than Dr. Folliott, is not less agreeable. One main charm of the novel lies in its vigorous criticism of modern society in phases which have not yet passed away. "Progress" is attacked wth curious ardour; and the battle between literature and science, which nowadays even Mr. Matthew Arnold wages but as one *cauponans bellum,* is fought with a vigour that is a joy to see. It would be rather interesting to know whether Peacock, in planning the central incident of the play (an "Aristophanic comedy," satirising modern ways), was aware of the existence of Mansel's delightful parody of the *Clouds.* But *Phrontisterion* has never been widely known out of Oxford, and the bearing of Peacock's own performance is rather social than political. Not the least noteworthy thing in the book is the practical apology which is made in it to Scotchmen and political economists (two classes whom Peacock had earlier persecuted in the personage of Mr. Mc-Borrowdale, a candid friend of Liberalism, who is extremely refreshing); and besides the Aristophanic comedy, *Gryll Grange* contains some of Peacock's most delightful verse, notably the really exquisite stanzas on **"Love and Age."**

The book is the more valuable because of the material it supplies in this and other places for rebutting the charges that Peacock was a mere Epicurean, or a mere carper. Independently of the verses just named, and the hardly less perfect **"Death of Philemon,"** the prose conversation shows how delicately and with how much feeling he could think on those points of life where satire and jollification are out of place. For the purely modern man, indeed, it might be well to begin the reading of Peacock with *Gryll Grange,* in order that he may not be set out of harmony with his author by the robuster but less familiar tones, as well as by the rawer though not less vigorous workmanship of *Headlong Hall* and its immediate successors. The happy mean between the heart on the sleeve and the absence of heart has scarcely been better shown than in this latest novel.

I have no space here to go through the miscellaneous work which completes Peacock's literary baggage. His regular poems, all early, are very much better than the work of many men who have won a place among British poets. His criticism, though not great in amount, is good; and he is especially happy in the kind of miscellaneous trifle (such as his trilingual poem on a whitebait dinner), which is generally thought appropriate to "university wits." But the characteristics of these miscellanies are not very different from the characteristics of his prose fiction, and, for purposes of discussion, may be included with them.

Lord Houghton [see Additional Bibliography] has defined and explained Peacock's literary idiosyncrasy as that of a man of the eighteenth century belated and strayed in the nineteenth. It is always easy to improve on a given pattern, but I certainly think that this definition of Lord Houghton's (which, it should be said, is not given in his own words) needs a little improvement. For the differences which strike us in Peacock—the easy joviality, the satirical view of life, the contempt of formulas and of science—though they certainly distinguish many chief literary men of the eighteenth century from most chief literary men of the nineteenth, are not specially characteristic of the eighteenth century itself. They are found in the seventeenth, in the Renaissance, in classical antiquity—wherever, in short, the art of letters and the art of life have had comparatively free play. The chief differentia of Peacock is a differentia common among men of letters; that is to say, among men of letters who are accustomed to society, who take no sacerdotal or "singing-robe" view of literature, who appreciate the distinction which literary cultivation gives them over the "herd of mankind," but who by no means take that distinction too seriously. Aristophanes, Horace, Lucian, Rabelais, Montaigne, Saint Evremond, these are all Peacock's literary ancestors, each, of course, with his own difference in especial and in addition. Aristophanes was more of a politician and a patriot, Lucian more of a freethinker, Horace more of a simple *pococurante*. Rabelais may have had a little inclination to science itself (he would soon have found it out if he had lived a little later), Montaigne may have been more of a pure egotist, Saint Evremond more of a man of society, and of the verse and prose of society. But they all had the same *ethos,* the same love of letters as letters, the same contempt of mere progress as progress, the same relish for the simpler and more human pleasures, the same good fellowship, the same tendency to escape from the labyrinth of life's riddles by what has been called the humour-gate, the same irreconcilable hatred of stupidity and vulgarity and cant. The eighteenth century has, no doubt, had its claim to be regarded as the special flourishing time of this mental state urged by many others besides Lord Houghton; but I doubt whether the claim can be sustained, at any rate to the detriment of other times, and the men of other times. That century took itself too seriously—a fault fatal to the claim at once. Indeed, the truth is that while this attitude has in some periods been very rare, it cannot be said to be the peculiar, still less the universal, characteristic of any period. It is a personal not a periodic distinction; and there are persons who might make out a fair claim to it even in the depths of the Middle Ages or of the nineteenth century.

However this may be, Peacock certainly held the theory of those who take life easily, who do not love anything very much except old books, old wine, and a few other things, not all of which perhaps need be old, who are rather inclined to see the folly of it than the pity of it, and who have an invincible tendency, if they tilt at anything at all, to tilt at the prevailing cants and arrogances of the time. These cants and arrogances of course vary. The position occupied by monkery at one time may be occupied by physical science at another; and a belief in graven images may supply in the third century the target, which is supplied by a belief in the supreme wisdom of majorities in the nineteenth. But the general principles—the cult of the muses and the graces for their own sake, and the practice of satiric archery at the follies of the day—appear in all the elect of this particular election, and they certainly appear in Peacock. The results no doubt are distasteful, not to say shocking, to some excellent people. It is impossible to avoid a slight chuckle when one thinks of the horror with which some such people must read Peacock's calm statement, repeated I think more than once, that one of his most perfect heroes "found, as he had often found before, that the more his mind was troubled the more madeira he could drink without disordering his head." I have no doubt that the United Kingdom Alliance, if it knew this dreadful sentence (but probably the study of the United Kingdom Alliance is not much in Peacock), would like to burn all the copies of *Gryll Grange* by the hands of Mr. Berry, and make the reprinting of it a misdemeanour, if not a felony. But it is not necessary to follow Sir Wilfrid Lawson, or to be a believer in education, or in telegraphs, or in majorities, in order to feel the repulsion which some people evidently feel for the Peacockian treatment. With one sense absent and another strongly present it is impossible for any one to like him. The present sense is that which has been rather grandiosely called the sense of moral responsibility in literature. The absent sense is that sixth, seventh, or eighth sense, called a sense of humour, and about this there is no arguing. Those who have it, instead of being quietly and humbly thankful, are perhaps a little too apt to celebrate their joy in the face of the afflicted ones who have it not; the afflicted ones, who have it not, only follow a general law in protesting that the sense of humour is a very worthless thing, if not a complete humbug. But there are others of whom it would be absurd to say that they have no sense of humour, and yet who cannot place themselves at the Peacockian point of view, or at the point of view of those who like Peacock. His humour is not their humour; his wit not their wit. Like one of his own characters (who did not show his usual wisdom in the remark), they "must take pleasure in the thing represented before they can take pleasure in the representation." And in the things that Peacock represents they do not take pleasure. That gentlemen should drink a great deal of burgundy and sing songs during the process appears to them at the best childish, at the worst horribly wrong. The prince-butler Seithenyn is a reprobate old man, who was unfaithful to his trust and shamelessly given to sensual indulgence. Dr. Folliott, as a parish priest, should not have drunk so much wine; and it would have been much more satisfactory to hear more of Dr. Opimian's sermons and district visiting and less of his dinners with Squire Gryll and Mr. Falconer. Peacock's irony on social and political arrangements is all sterile, all destructive, and the sentiment that "most opinions that have anything to be said for them are about two thousand years old" is a libel on mankind. They feel, in short, for Peacock the animosity mingled with contempt which the late M. Amiel felt for "clever mockers."

It is probably useless to argue with any such. It might, indeed, be urged in all seriousness that the Peacockian attitude is not in the least identical with the Mephistophelian; that it is based simply on the very sober and arguable ground that human nature is always very much the same, liable to the same delusions and the same weaknesses; and that the oldest things are likely to be best, not for any intrinsic or mystical virtue of antiquity, but because they have had most time to be found out in, and have not been found out. It may further be argued, as it has often been argued before, that the use of ridicule as a general criterion can do no harm, and may do much good. If the thing ridiculed be of God, it will stand; if it be not, the sooner it is laughed off the face of the earth the better. But there is probably little good in urging all this. Just as a lover of the greatest of Greek dramatists must recognise at once that it would be perfectly useless to attempt to argue Lord Coleridge out of the idea that Aristophanes, though a genius, was vulgar and base of soul, so to go a good deal lower in the scale of years, and somewhat lower in the scale of genius, everybody who rejoices in the author of **"Aristophanes in London"** must see that he has no chance of converting Mrs. Oliphant [see excerpt dated 1882], or any other person who does not like Peacock. The middle term is not present, the disputants do not in fact use the same language. The only thing to do is to recommend this particular pleasure to those who are capable of being pleased by it, of whom there are beyond doubt a great number to whom it is pleasure yet untried. (pp. 421-25)

George Saintsbury, "Thomas Love Peacock," in Macmillan's Magazine, Vol. LIII, No. 318, April, 1886, pp. 414-27.

RICHARD GARNETT (essay date 1891)

[*Garnett was an English literary historian, poet, critic, and biographer. In this excerpt from the introduction to his 1891 edition of Peacock's works, Garnett assesses the author's importance to literary history.*]

Peacock's . . . place in literature is pre-eminently that of a satirist. This character is not always a passport to goodwill. Satirists have met with much ignorant and invidious depreciation, as though a talent for ridicule was necessarily the index of an unkindly nature. The truth is just the reverse: as the sources of laughter and tears lie near together, so is the geniality of an intellectual man usually accompanied with a keen perception of the ridiculous. Both exist in ample measure in Peacock, whose hearty and sometimes misplaced laughter at what he deemed absurd is usually accompanied with a kindly feeling towards the exemplars of the absurdity. The only very noticeable instance of the contrary is the undoubtedly illiberal ridicule of the Lake poets in his earlier writings; still there is sufficient evidence elsewhere of his sincere admiration of their works. Brougham he certainly abhorred, and yet the denunciation of him in **Crotchet Castle** has hardly more of invective than the gibes at the "modern Athenians." Add to this geniality a bright fancy, a lively sense of the ludicrous, a passion for natural beauty, strong sense, occasionally warped by prejudice, genuine tenderness on occasion, diction of singular purity, and a style of singular elegance, and it will be allowed that, *prima facie*, Peacock should be popular. That he has nevertheless been only the favourite of the few is owing in a measure to the highly intellectual quality of his work, but chiefly to his lack of the ordinary qualifications of the novelist, all pretension to which he entirely disclaims. He has no plot, little human interest, and no consistent delineation of character. His personages are mere puppets, or, at best, incarnations of abstract qualities, or idealisations of disembodied grace or beauty. He affected to prefer—perhaps really did prefer—the pantomimes of "the enchanter of the south" to the novels of "the enchanter of the north"; and, by a whimsical retribution, his own novels have passed for pantomimes. "A queer mixture!" pronounced the *Saturday Review*, criticising **Gryll Grange**, and such has been the judgment of most. It will not be the judgment of any capable of appreciating the Aristophanic comedy of which, restricted as their scale is in comparison, Peacock's fiction is, perhaps, the best modern representative. Nearly everything that can be urged against him can be urged against Aristophanes too; and save that his invention is far less daring and opulent, his Muse can allege most of "the apologies of Aristophanes." When he is depreciated, comparison with another novelist usually seems to be implied, but it would be as unfair to test him by the standard of Miss Austen or Miss Edgeworth, as to try Aristophanes by the rules of the New Comedy. A master of fiction he is not, and he never claimed to be; a satirist, a humourist, a poet he is most undoubtedly. Were these qualities less eminent than they are, he would still live by the truth of his natural description and the grace and finish of his style: were even these in default, the literary historian would still have to note in him the first appearance of a new type, destined

to be frequently imitated, but seldom approached, and never exactly reproduced. (pp. 280-82)

Richard Garnett, "Thomas Love Peacock," in his Essays of an Ex-Librarian, 1901. Reprint by Books for Libraries Press, 1970, pp. 239-82.

A. MARTIN FREEMAN (essay date 1911)

[*Freeman's* Thomas Love Peacock: A Critical Study *is considered one of the best analyses of Peacock's art. In the following excerpt from this work, Freeman explores the elements of the Peacockian novel and surveys his major writings.*]

In style and manner, in the more restricted sense of the words, [Peacock] still belongs to the eighteenth century, Fielding being his most obvious influence, especially noticeable in his careful and lucid accounts of unheroic events, in the epic style; while Sheridan perhaps inevitably influenced his arrangement of the witty sayings of his characters, though he owes more to Cicero than to either of them. The stateliness and restraint of his language in description also belongs to a previous age. But any likeness between Peacock's style and that of the older authors is the outcome of strong and original sympathy, not of imitation. He belongs, in style and language, to a school, but he borrows from no master. He lived intellectually and, it is not too much to say, emotionally in ancient Greece and Rome and in England of the "classical" period. The style which he inherited and absorbed from the great writers of the past became his own favourite and familiar mode of expression. He made use of it in his books, prefaces, articles, letters to the papers, and in all but the most trivial scrawls among those to his intimate friends. He certainly conversed in it at times; and there can be little doubt but that it decorates many official communications in the archives of the East India House.

If verbal criticism assigns Peacock to a previous school or period, an examination of the conduct of his stories, if they are to be so called, will show that his method is all his own. It is indeed the most drastic, the most economical of time and trouble that was ever adopted by a reputable author. The recipe is simple: Let there be a country house (described); let there be a gathering of numerous guests therein (catalogued); let the various opinions of the party be as opposite and irreconcilable as possible (opinions briefly but adequately sketched); invent a slight plot for form's sake, bring your characters together at the dinner table, and conversation will follow as a matter of course, leading to amusing scenes and revelations. When you have written enough, disperse the guests and add a formal Conclusion. Such is the general scheme of the Peacockian novel. **Headlong Hall** adheres very closely to this type. Some of the others depart from it in varying degrees, but they gain little or nothing by such divergence. In **Crotchet Castle,** for instance, the harmony and cohesion of the work suffer considerably owing to the unusual amount of importance assumed by the plot; the book consequently challenges a criticism from which it would otherwise have been safe and which can only be destructive. **Melincourt** is a more pronounced instance of divergence from type and consequent diminution of interest and weakening of effect. The true genial atmosphere, with the author at his best, is to be found in **Headlong Hall, Nightmare Abbey** and **Gryll Grange,** and in parts only of **Crotchet Castle** and **Melincourt,** where the company gathers round one or at most two hospitable tables, and the conversation, now amicable, now acrid, now uproarious, but always formal and complete, furnishes the main interest.

Peacock was at no pains to conceal his neglect and scorn of the usual methods of the full-sized novel. *Headlong Hall,* typical in this as in all other respects, is deliberately calculated to flout and disgust the habitual reader of fiction in his own or any other age. The stage-coach with the four passengers, who "it appeared, to the surprise of every one, though perfect strangers to each other, were actually bound to the same point," and were to be the guests of the same eccentric individual, is not incredible: but the details immediately added to this remarkable circumstance, sufficient in itself to satisfy as much credulity as is usually demanded by a first chapter, give a series of shocks to the sensibility nurtured in the conventionalities of well-ordered fiction. When it is discovered that the four interlocutors are incapable of agreeing on any point, such a reader feels that the author is trifling with him; the derivation of their names—Escot, ες σκότον in tenebras, scilicet, intuens, and the rest—is little less than an insult to the stiff-necked intelligence. The categorical method is pursued in the introduction of the guests on their arrival, each with an appropriate description or a speech in character. But the chapters are short, and the true value of the book soon becomes apparent: if the reader's heart has not been won by Mr. Milestone and the "finger of taste," it cannot long hold out against Mr. Escot, with his calm and dispassionate manner in analysing the opinions of his opponents, until they are all given off in vapour, leaving nothing behind. All must follow him with sympathy, in his series of victorious conflicts with his enemies, clerical, literary and scientific; for never was there a hero for whom favour was so openly and yet winningly canvassed by the author.

There is little characterisation in this early work. The men and women are types, and exaggerated types, whose only duty is to amuse. Peacock's progress in this respect continued steadily throughout his life, until in *Gryll Grange* he created living beings, whose personality may be viewed in various aspects. But this was never a strong point with him, and even his last book will not bear comparison with the works of the artists in character-drawing. The desideratum of a Peacockian character is that he shall be able to talk. The best in the early novels are good disputants: in the later, they are good conversationists. The talk in *Headlong Hall* is formal, finished, precise, witty, learned, possessing all the qualities, in short, in which conversation in England is invariably lacking. Over their wine the speakers make dissertations, trespassing by their length alone on the forbearance of the listeners. Each man is allowed to state his case to the bitter end, and is similarly answered. They grow heated, but not careless. They wrangle, and even quarrel violently, in rigidly grammatical and accurately punctuated sentences of perfect balance. Yet we read it all with avidity, for the sake of the wit, the neatness and ingenuity in the manner of stating the various points of view, and for the ridiculous picture of the discomfited and enraged theorists. Perhaps the only one whom we would fain hear no more of is Mr. Jenkinson, the equable philosopher who will countenance neither optimism nor pessimism. The plot, such as there is, is amusingly brought to a point by means of the skull of Cadwallader, and a happy ending given to a most felicitous *jeu d'esprit.* More than any other author perhaps, Peacock interests us himself throughout the book. To all the characters he has given qualities to amuse and hold our attention; his partiality for Escot arouses curiosity about his own personality. We have enjoyed his method and, above all, his style. But is this all? Does he care for nothing but the logical faculty, generally used in confuting whatever statement is made in his presence? From this book he does indeed seem to be an arch-antagonist and disbeliever. His style is his chief virtue. (pp. 229-35)

A simple criterion, too seldom applied in criticism, will reveal at once the technical and spiritual faults of *Melincourt.* The removal of its dullest portions will reduce the book to a reasonable compass, while leaving the plot intact, and will moreover restore a true balance between the relative importance allowed to the characters. Mr. Forester is a ponderous and gullible person, easily led astray, and dragging the wearied reader with him, into the more arid pastures of the intellect. Greater blame attaches to his subjugator, the merciless and prosy Mr. Fax. Most of their conversation together should be torn out of the book, including the episode of Desmond, the paper money scenes, and one or two more chapters of the peregrination in search of Anthelia, who, to tell the truth, was not worth so much trouble. Lightened by the jettison of these passages, together with all the notes from Buffon, Rousseau, Lord Monboddo and other sources, *Melincourt,* reduced in bulk by one fifth, would have been well able to bear comparison with the author's best books. As it stands, it is the easiest to abuse and decry.

Peacock's conduct in this story is indeed reprehensible. He basely neglects the legitimate hero and devotes pages and chapters on end to the sermons and disputations of the pretender. An effort of memory is constantly needed to enable the reader to realise that Sir Oran is in the company of Mr. Fax and Mr. Forester during the whole of their expedition. His is but a too typical case of the sacrifice of the higher to the lower type. His instincts are so much in excess of the chivalric rules of courtesy that though he is eager to avenge an insult to the weak and unprotected a personal affront seldom touches him at all. He trudges along, mile after weary mile, making no protest at

A portrait of Peacock at age eighteen.

the ill-mannered neglect with which he is treated by his companions. Poetic justice, of which he is so able a dispenser, would demand that he should extend his powerful fingers to comprise the necks of the garrulous offenders and, receiving at the same time the gift of speech, flourish his cudgel and cry, like the innkeeper of old, "No more of this, by Goddes bones!" But he is silent and gives no sign of impatience. It is noticeable that the excision of the passages above mentioned would restore to Sir Oran his due prominence in the story.

In thus leaving his work disfigured by unessential and uninteresting excrescences Peacock is guilty of the sin of incontinence, comparatively trivial and pardonable. But its grave blemish is in the characters of Anthelia and Forester. These priggish and pretentious young people, with no humanising inconsistencies, whose disapproval of the rest of mankind is unenlivened by any spark of humour, can excite no sympathy. Their courtship and marriage fail to interest. They are undoubtedly made—and too obviously!—for each other; though it seems a pity that they should be allowed to perpetuate their kind, it is as well that they should be out of the way together. Could damaging criticism go further? The story, sufficiently long in its essential features, eked out with dull interpolated disquisitions; the hero apparently forgotten for long stretches together; three of the four principal personages insufferable: how many legs has the book left to stand on? is it in any degree readable?

That it is eminently so, is a striking proof of the rare quality of Peacock's genius. The faults, which damn it as a novel, do but detract from its value as a Peacockian novel, a literary genus by itself with no satisfactory name to distinguish it from apparently similar forms. The personal incidence of the satire has already been discussed. Directed, now against mankind in general, now against the representative system, now against a parliamentary or literary group and now against some private fad or enthusiasm, it ranges from the broad and boisterous to the sly and subtle manner. Sir Oran Haut-ton has been most unjustly treated and the author accused of endowing an ape with human qualities in order to heap ridicule on mankind. Such a procedure would indeed be but a laboured piece of burlesque. A similar method had been adopted by Swift, and legitimately used for the most bitter and misanthropic satire. His is a weapon of wholesale slaughter; in his use of it he may command admiration but can evoke little sympathy. Horses, he cries, are nobler animals than men, and men more debased than monkeys. If you protest, you do but assert your kinship with these despicable beings. Peacock's method is essentially different. "An ape" is precisely what Sir Oran is not. The scientists and philosophers have described him, and Peacock, collecting and welding their statements, shows that they have discovered an almost ideally perfect man, a human being who though unacquainted with the arts of civilisation has all the instincts and puts into practice all the precepts of true nobility. He is the ever-ready champion of innocence against oppression and villainy. Gentle, unobtrusive, dignified, he is an ornament to the most polished society: powerful and impulsive, he always submits to the ruling of those whose reason and familiarity with the circumstances he feels to be superior to his own. Every detail of the picture, his graces and accomplishments, his social adaptability, the propriety of his table manners, his taste and capabilities in music, all these had been vouched for by the learned authorities. Had Peacock added anything to what was already common property, the shafts of his satire would have been blunted and retarded. By his reticence and skilful handling of the character he presented to contemporary civilisation its own scientific discovery, the outcome of its own wisdom and

research, to hold up the mirror to it. He mocks simultaneously at human credulity and incredulity; for while he pursues with his ridicule the believers in *homo sylvestris* he has Parthian shots for those who follow after him protesting their unbelief. The incredibility of a being in whom are united all these ideal qualities arises, not from the supremacy of reason, but from the decline in morals.

The lyrics in *Melincourt* are uninspired. The best and most appropriate is the absurd character song by the members of the secret committee at Mainchance Villa, giving a neat finish to the scene and summing up the political attitude of the conspirators in the imaginary crisis. **"The Ghosts"** is a jovial drinking song; **"The Magic Bark,"** the most ambitious attempt, is elaborate but conventional. But if the book is thus deprived of a subsidiary interest, regularly expected in these novels, it is rich in a few passages of fine classical prose. The first chapter may be cited as an example of the author's style at its best. Short, simple in language, admirably smooth and perfectly articulated, it is made up of twelve small paragraphs and is crystallised into eight distinct points of irony. In strikingly few words an adequate and interesting description of the Castle and its surroundings is conveyed and this without any effort of emphasis or picturesque diction. To read it is to be present at one of the occasional exhibitions of eloquence by a man of reserved nature. His habitual continence and dread of verbiage are a guarantee against the tedium which is almost inevitably a result of the outpourings of those whose enthusiasm lies nearer to the surface and is less under control. His disclosures of feeling possess a charm by no means to be accounted for entirely by their rarity: this only adds to their value by making them more concentrated and personal. For on ultimate analysis it is the personality of the speaker that is the source of delight; not the accurate or vivid presentment of the scenes, but his suppressed emotion in contemplating them. The same departure from a consistently jesting or critical mood was noticed in the description of the prospect from the Traeth Mawr embankment. The passionate love of scenery again lures the author from his cave of concealment in the chapter called "The Torrent," relating the setting forth of Anthelia for a country ramble, the suddenly bursting storm and the swelling torrents which cut off her retreat from her perilous position. In an entirely different style, but of equal merit, are the descriptive passages in the two chapters telling of the elections at the borough of Onevote. Though obviously comparable with many pages of Fielding, in style and language they are intensely individual. Heroic incidents are in the author's mind as he writes; but he does not, like Fielding, make use of epic diction and tags of ancient verse to produce a mock-heroic effect. In plain and almost scientifically exact language it is shown how a small cause led to a greater effect, which in turn proved to be but an early link in the chain of consequence. The comedy is thus objective and cumulative, arising from a clear and faithful report of an incident, by one standing as it were on an eminence overlooking the scene, and thus able to explain what was unintelligible to the excited participants. (pp. 244-51)

Headlong Hall and *Melincourt* had been mainly satirical: *Nightmare Abbey* and *Maid Marian* are made up primarily of comedy and romance. Both pleasant and light-hearted tales, they are in many respects Peacock's best book and his worst. The first is in strict continuation of the lines laid down in *Headlong Hall,* and shows development and improvement in almost every particular. Its length is precisely the same; but in spite of the initial boldness and compression of the earlier work, *Nightmare Abbey* is fuller and more satisfying. It is a perfect miniature. Within its small compass it is many-sided and complete. The interest is more evenly divided between the characters, and each is allowed adequate expression, and with a wonderful impartiality each one is made, while he is speaking, to appear the best in the book. With more right than Mr. Flosky, Mr. Escot might be called a spectator of shadows; but he follows them up in order to discover and expose the bodies responsible for them, and bid mankind have no faith in the delusive shade. Hilary, his more genial successor, has no impostors and perverts to expose: as the author's advocate, he mingles pleasantly and most unobtrusively in the company, and only lodges an official protest against the tendency of some of the members to introduce an unnecessary and exotic misery into the lot of mankind, instead of trying to make the best of it.

In form this is certainly Peacock's most perfect work. The romantic plot, worked out in the lonely tower, is skilfully brought into contact with the choice band of conversational experts who frequent the more cheerful parts of the house, and whose talk is its accompaniment and commentary. It is a Tale of Mystery, unfolded amidst a company of all the latter-day types of humanity, the credulous, the sceptical, the fashionable, the scheming, the common-sense, the frivolous and the mono-maniacal doctrinaire, and receiving from each in turn indirect and provisional illumination. Wit, wisdom and folly come bubbling forth from the nine abundant springs of conversation in a rippling, dancing stream. The farcical confrontation of the unsuspecting rivals and relatives is effected by the most natural means, and causes an inevitable break-up of the house-party, bringing the story automatically to an end. To this technical perfection of outline is happily united a brilliance and vivacity of writing, the high-water-mark of Peacock's style in this . . . period. (pp. 259-60)

Crotchet Castle, an essentially middle-aged production, is entirely non-constructive. It is a criticism, and its main drift is an exposure of cant in all its manifestations. Sentimental cant, philosophical, philanthropic, economic cant, the cant of literary people and scientific specialists, is here represented by the usual set of typical personages. In opposition to these at various points are ranged three characters, far more individually and closely studied, who do undoubtedly express between them a large measure of Peacock's personal attitude, though they air his dislikes more freely than his likes. Lady Clarinda, the keen scrutineer of persons, and Mr. Chainmail, who regrets the ages of greater simplicity, when there was less opportunity for cant to flourish in the great variety of its present day activities, each has his marked sympathy. Yet Lady Clarinda passes sentence on her own professed philosophy by marrying a poor man; while Mr. Chainmail is convicted of the possession of illusions, approaching very near to cant, and finally violates one of his strongest principles by uniting himself with the daughter of a moneylender, "one who in the twelfth century would have been plucked by the beard." The Rev. Doctor is the most logical and, as things are, the most powerful enemy of cant. Having himself no illusions or ideals, he does not believe in those sincerely or falsely professed by others. Peacock attributes to him many of his own traits—his classical proficiency and partiality for Nonnus, his hatred of Brougham and all his works, his aversion to the Scotch and the political economists. But it is noticeable that he does not credit him with superior spiritual qualities. He lends him, not a wittier tongue, but a louder voice than the rest. He does not scruple to ridicule him. The Doctor becomes drunken and passionate at table, and has to be called to order; in the argument on the Venuses he is overcome by a self-taught merchant, and left with a decidedly

unintellectual side presented to the company. He is a favourite with the author and the reader, and rightly so. Most happily the Comic Spirit triumphed among the claimants to the patronage of this book. Cant is not to be seriously outpreached or philosophically dissected, but boisterously shouted down. Its arch-enemy is found not in a sermonising Forester, nor even in a stern and logical Escot, but in this worldly, dogmatic, exclusive scholar. Some of his jokes and repartees belong to a type new in Peacock's writings, showing the humour of character rather than of pure intellect. (pp. 311-13)

The frank non-morality of the Doctor, the economic philosophy of Mr. Macquedy, the sentimentality of the Captain, the airy cynicism of Lady Clarinda, the absurdity of the scientists; in the interplay of these lies the main interest of the greater part of *Crotchet Castle.* In these conversations and comments Peacock is certainly seen at the height of his brilliance as satirist and stylist. They have the perfection of maturity—strength without violence, confidence and precision, all the old keenness with the added mellowness of time. With a wantonness peculiar to himself he has, by the mere subterfuge of an excursion up the Thames and Severn and the Ellesmere Canal, tacked on to these studies in scholarly idiosyncracy a love story, threatening every now and then to become a pastoral romance, taking place in North Wales and entirely unconnected with the beginning and end of the story. With this as with all his wayward deeds, it is useless to ask how Peacock could have permitted himself so flagrant a violation of the proprieties. If we like this quarter of the book, let us thank him for it; if its presence offends us, our capacity for enjoyment is sadly limited. (pp. 314-15)

Like Peacock at Halliford, [the characters of *Gryll Grange*] live a secluded life on the borders of the New Forest, where echoes from the outside reach them, though faintly, just often enough to remind them that they are better off in their rural peace than in a world where most things are going wrong. Where ambition and greed have not falsified men's outlook there is in human nature a preponderance of good. Life is eminently enjoyable to the man who prizes its really valuable aspects, and men and women both estimable and lovable:

> *The Rev. Dr. Opimian.* "No doubt, of the recorded facts of civil life some are good, and more are indifferent, neither good nor bad; but good and indifferent together are scarcely more than a twelfth part of the whole. Still, the matters thus presented are all exceptional cases. A hermit reading nothing but a newspaper might find little else than food for misanthropy; but living among friends, and in the bosom of our family, we see that the dark side of life is the occasional picture, the bright is its everyday aspect. The occasional is a matter of curiosity, of incident, of adventure, of things that really happen to few and may possibly happen to any. The interest attendant on any action or event is in just proportion to its rarity; and, happily, quiet virtues are all around us, and obtrusive vices seldom cross our path. On the whole, I agree in opinion with Theseus, that there is more good than evil in the world."
>
> *Mrs. Opimian.* "I think, Doctor, you would not maintain any opinion if you had not an authority two thousand years old for it."
>
> *The Rev. Dr. Opimian.* "Well, my dear, I think most opinions worth maintaining have an authority of about that age."

Here speaks the author of *Headlong Hall:* the old preferences, the old dislikes, the old criticism is here, but the tone has been mellowing since 1815, until the violence and bitterness have disappeared, leaving a greater discrimination, if less incisive force; more human interest, if less sparkling comedy. The political misdemeanours of the Lake poets even have been forgotten, and only their beauties remembered: exception is now taken, though how soberly! to Tennyson's misconceptions and Longfellow's want of scholarship. Within the frame of the actual novel, discussion has taken the place of argument—there is not a single dispute in *Gryll Grange*—tolerance of intolerance; satire is still present, but satire of a kind that springs more from love than from hate: Peacock has not even the heart to ridicule Lord Curryfin without more than compensating for it by making him interesting and socially popular, accomplished and courageous. Can this be the author who last wrote of Mr. Henbane and Dr. Morbific? And so with all the rest. Can the creator of Mr. Maclaurel actually bring himself to describe a Scotch economist as Mr. Macborrowdale is here described? Can he admit that the old physician who was called to attend Miss Gryll at the Tower was good as well as clever? Can it be that in his happier social surroundings he has forgotten the Hon. Mrs. Pinmoney and discovered Miss Ilex? Ay, this and much more he tells us in his last talk. Not only is there more good than evil in the world, but good may come out of evil; misfortune is sometimes half a blessing, and disappointment often not so final as it seems at the time. (pp. 327-28)

Compared with the rest [of the novels *Gryll Grange*] is more subdued and reflective, and even more personal and idiosyncratic. Already in *Crotchet Castle* it is noticeable that Peacock is introducing more of himself and less of other people than in his earlier books. In this epilogue to all his works—in poetry, fiction, criticism—the tendency to write about himself is seen to have grown strong enough to become the leading element of the book. This is accompanied, perhaps necessarily, by a remarkable artistic carelessness and by a supreme neglect of his public. He is now writing purely and simply to please himself. . . . (p. 338)

> *A. Martin Freeman, in his* Thomas Love Peacock: A Critical Study, *Mitchell Kennerley, 1911, 348 p.*

CLIVE BELL   (essay date 1918)

[*Bell was a critic of art and literature and a member of the Bloomsbury group, an early twentieth-century circle of English writers and intellectuals whose most prominent member was the novelist Virginia Woolf. His book* Art *(1914) is credited with having created widespread interest in modern art. In the following excerpt from another work, Bell explains why he considers Peacock a writer of originality and importance.*]

In calling Peacock a great writer we [raise] a claim that needs some support. His exquisite style with its Tacitean flavour, the perfection of his lyrics, his wit, and that intellectual brilliancy which sparkles from all the facets of his satire, parody, and epigram, suffice to endear him to the small, fastidious world whose approval is best worth having, and also, perhaps, to justify our opinion. But, unless we mistake, the appeal of his novels goes farther than the frontiers of good taste. Peacock's mind was original; he thought about many things and he did his own thinking. He is the other side to every question; his way of looking at life is a perpetual challenge; and a man without a vestige of humour or taste may read him with profit for his point of view.

Peacock belongs to no school or age. He has been called a man of the eighteenth century living in the nineteenth; nothing

could be farther from the truth. He loved the sense and dignity of the Augustans, just as he loved the fire and romance of the Renaissance, and the mysterious gaiety of the Middle Ages; but he could have criticized any of them with as good a will as he criticized the age of machinery and "the march of mind," and, had he been born in any one of them, would doubtless have done so. He was a student of bardic poetry who yet admired Ariosto; his passion for classical literature was uncommonly wise and sincere; he read Sophocles for pleasure. So remote was he from the eighteenth-century Grecians that he could perceive and enjoy the romantic element in Greek life and art; yet it is a mistake to call him a Greek. An Athenian of the time of Pericles was, he thought, the noblest specimen of humanity that history had to show, and of that nobility he assimilated what he could. He acquired a distaste for cant, prudery, facile emotion, and philanthropy; he learnt to enjoy the good things of life without fear or shame; to love strength and beauty, and to respect the truth. For all that, he was a modern too; sharp eyes can see it in his verse. A touch of gloating and uninquisitive wonder, a suspicion of sentiment for sentiment's sake, the ghost of an appeal from the head to the heart, from the certainty of the present to the mystery of the past and the future, betray the descendant of Shakespeare and Sterne. The very culture that he inherited from a Graeco-Roman civilization, his bookishness, his archaeology, his conscious Paganism, would have looked queer in an Athenian of the fifth century B.C. The author of **"Love and Age"** was no Greek; but he was Greek enough to stand out above his fellows, from whom he is most honourably distinguished by his Athenian open-mindedness. (pp. 54-6)

The truth is, Peacock had standards tested by which the current ideas of almost any age would be found wanting. Without being a profound thinker, he was one of those people who "bother about ends" to the extent of being unwilling to approve of means unless they are satisfied that the end in view is good—or at least that there is some end in view. With a self-complacent age, in which every one was shouting "Forward!" and no one was expected to inquire "Whither?" he was necessarily out of sympathy. To the shouters he seemed irrational and irrelevant. They called him "immoral" when they were solemn, and "whimsical" when they were merry; and "whimsical" is the epithet with which we are tempted to label him, if labelled he must be. Genius makes strange bedfellows; and Peacock's intellectual candour finds itself associated with the emotional capriciousness of Sterne. Truly, he is always unexpected, and as often as not superficially inconsequent. To state the three parts of a syllogism is not in his way; and by implication he challenged half the major premises in vogue. His scorn of rough-and-ready standards, commonplaces, and what used to be called "the opinion of all sensible men" made him disrespectful to common sense. It was common sense once to believe that the sun went round the earth, and it is still the mark of a sensible man to ignore, on occasions, the law of contradictions. To that common sense which is compounded of mental sluggishness and a taste for being in the majority Peacock's wit was a needle. He was intellectual enough to enjoy pricking bladders, and so finished a performer that we never tire of watching him at his play.

He was, in fact, an artist with intellectual curiosity; and just as he lacked the depth of a philosopher so he wanted the vision of a poet. That he possessed genius will not be denied; but his art is fanciful rather than imaginative and of creative power he had next to none. His life was neither a mission nor a miracle. But he was blessed with that keen delight in his own sensations which makes a world full of beautiful and amusing things, charming people, wine, and warm sunshine seem, on the whole, a very tolerable place, and all metaphysical speculation and political passion a little unnecessary. He made an art of living, and his novels are a part of his life. He wrote them because he had a subtle sense of the ludicrous, a turn for satire, and style. He wrote because he enjoyed writing; and, with a disregard for the public inconceivable in a man of sense, he wrote the sort of books that he himself would have liked to read. They are the sort, we think, that will always be worth reading. (pp. 59-61)

Clive Bell, "Peacock," in his Pot-Boilers, *Chatto & Windus, 1918, pp. 50-73.*

J. B. PRIESTLEY (essay date 1927)

[*A highly prolific English man of letters, Priestley is the author of numerous popular novels that depict the world of everyday, middle-class England. In this respect, Priestley has often been likened to Charles Dickens. His most notable critical work is* Literature and Western Man *(1960), a survey of Western literature from the invention of movable type through the mid-twentieth century. In the following excerpt from his study of Peacock, Priestley describes the imaginary world of Peacock's novels, his characters, and his style.*]

Let us admit . . . that the personages in [Peacock's] novels do little but talk and that most of them—the Milestones and Sir Simon Steeltraps and Henbanes and Feathernests—are not creatures of this world but simply so many personified ideas or interests. Does this mean that *Headlong Hall* and the rest cannot really be considered novels at all? Are they best approached as so many comic dialogues? So some critics would seem to think, and one of them has described the Peacock novel as "a Platonic dialogue as Aristophanes might have caricatured it" [see entry by Osbert Burdett in Additional Bibliography]. This is an excellent description so long as we are allowed to assume that Aristophanes (who was certainly Peacock's greatest master) would have turned his dialogue into what we now call fiction. Otherwise it is misleading. Peacock's critics have been so anxious to point out that he did not write conventional fiction that they have frequently driven him away from the novel altogether. This, however, is a mistake because Peacock is, in his own queer way, a novelist, and his five tales of talk are just as far removed from philosophical dialogues and the like as they are from ordinary realistic fiction. They occupy a position—perhaps a unique position—between the two. It is one of the secrets of their appeal, this curious intermediate character of theirs, which makes them less concrete and documented than novels proper and yet far less abstract than such things as dialogues and allegories. Indeed, they are far less abstract, are nearer the earth, than a great many of the old artificial comedies. If these novels of his do not give us fully human records, neither do they transport us entirely to some abstract region of ideas. Their action passes in a world, even though it is a world at some remove from the one we know. It is easily recognised and quite unlike any other, so that we can say there is a Peacock world just as we say there is a Dickens world. Peacock, so unlike the great original novelists in almost every particular, at least resembles in this, that he has created a world of his own. And whatever difference there may be between *Headlong Hall* and *Gryll Grange, Melincourt* and *Crotchet Castle,* one and all take us to the same Peacock world.

It is of course a world of talk and talkers. Its personages are almost completely themselves when they are happily seated

behind the decanters, each hammering away at his own theory. But there are also some women, fair and pleasant-spoken, and some romantic young lovers. Moreover, this world is provided with the scenery of romance. Consider this passage in the best of these novels, *Crotchet Castle:*

> One day Mr. Chainmail traced upwards the course of a mountain-stream, to a spot where a small waterfall threw itself over a slab of perpendicular rock, which seemed to bar his farther progress. On a nearer view, he discovered a flight of steps, roughly hewn in the rock, on one side of the fall. Ascending these steps, he entered a narrow winding pass, between high and naked rocks, that afforded only space for a rough footpath carved on one side, at some height above the torrent.

> The pass opened on a lake, from which the stream issued, and which lay like a dark mirror, set in a gigantic frame of mountain precipices. Fragments of rock lay scattered on the edge of the lake, some half-buried in the water: Mr. Chainmail scrambled some way over these fragments, till the base of a rock, sinking abruptly in the water, effectually barred his progress. He sat down on a large smooth stone; the faint murmur of the stream he had quitted, the occasional flapping of the wings of a heron, and at long intervals the solitary springing of a trout, were the only sounds that came to his ear. The sun shone brightly half-way down the opposite rocks, presenting, on their irregular faces, strong masses of light and shade. Suddenly he heard the dash of a paddle, and, turning his eyes, saw a solitary and beautiful girl gliding over the lake in a coracle. . . .

There is a passage that any romance might wear as a jewel. Nor would it be difficult to find companion passages, in which remote and beautiful places are described in a style that is vivid in spite of its obvious restraint. Even the comic debaters and crotcheteers are always provided with a charming or wild and picturesque background, far removed from bustle and noise and dirt. Thus the opening paragraph of *Crotchet Castle* takes us to an Arcadian countryside:

> In one of these beautiful valleys, through which the Thames (not yet polluted by the tide, the scouring of cities, or even the minor defilement of the sandy streams of Surrey) rolls a clear flood through flowery meadows; under the shade of old beech woods, and the smooth mossy greensward of the chalk hills (which pour into it their tributary rivulets, are pure and pellucid as the fountain of Bandusium, or the wells of Scamander, by which the wives and daughters of the Trojans washed their splendid garments in the days of peace, before the coming of the Greeks); in one of those beautiful valleys, on a bold round-surfaced lawn, spotted with juniper, that opened itself in the bosom of an old wood, which rose with a steep, but not precipitous ascent, from the river to the summit of the hill, stood the castellated villa of a retired citizen.

And Headlong Hall is in the romantic Vale of Llanberis; Anthelia Melincourt has an old castle "in one of the wildest valleys in Westmoreland", where daily she sees "the misty mountain-top, the ash-fringed precipice, the gleaming cataract, the deep and shadowy glen, and the fantastic magnificence of the mountain clouds"; Nightmare Abbey very naturally has a more dismal setting, being situated somewhere between the sea and the Fens in Lincolnshire, but is equally picturesque and remote; and Gryll Grange, "on the borders of the New Forest, in the midst of a park which was a little forest in itself, reaching nearly to the sea, and well-stocked with deer'', is clearly only a stone's throw from Arden itself. This world of Peacock's, then, though it would seem a world of intellectual comedy, is filled with Arcadian countrysides and wildly romantic solitudes. The droll debates and the bumpers of Madeira are set against a background of quiet rivers and green shades, of the gleaming cataract and the deep and shadowy glen. It is the poet, the romantic, the idealist, in Peacock who has touched in this background purely for his own good pleasure.

If satire pure and simple—political, literary, social satire— were his object, then it is curious that he should have given us these idyllic or romantic settings instead of taking us to London, that he should have assembled all his characters in these remote places instead of displaying them in their native haunt, the Town. It is true that his house-party method, bringing all his people under one roof and leaving them to entertain one another, gives him a certain advantage, but this is far outweighed by the advantage offered by the London scene, which obviously is far richer in possibilities for the satirist. But being something more than satirist, being also a poet and humorist, Peacock preferred to set his scene against these backgrounds because, we repeat, their creation gave him pleasure. His imagination took refuge in these idyllic or romantic settings, which represent one side of his mind just as the intellectual farce that is played there represents another. The poet in him, who once wrote *The Philosophy of Melancholy* and *Rhododaphne,* now finds satisfaction in idealising the scenes of the novels, and this he could do quite safely, without any fear of being laughed at, because he was already protected by the mockery in their action and characterisation. If the foreground in his fiction is mostly filled in with a caricature of what actually goes on in the world, its background gives us a sketch of what ought to go on in the world, of the author's ideal realm. There is something very piquant in the contrast, and piquancy, so welcome to sophisticated minds, has long been noted as one of Peacock's characteristics. If its presence has been noted, however, it has not been explained, simply because no explanation is possible so long as the satirist in him is allowed to hide completely the poet in him, so long as he is seen as a writer of comic dialogues only and not as a novelist, creating a world of his own in which his imagination can happily play. It is a very queer world, but it suited Peacock, whose novels were primarily a recreation, and, in spite of its obvious limitations, it is capable of providing rest and refreshment for any reader who brings to it a sense of humour.

It certainly provides rest and refreshment for its own creatures. For them it shows meat and drink. They are only asked to bring out their pet theories, hold fast to them and remain entirely unconvinced by other people's arguments, slake their thirst and pass the bottle. However wildly different their views may be, they are all alike in their passion for talk and conviviality, in the gusto with which they give and take hospitality. Even the weirdest of them do not fail in these particulars: Mr. Mystic's life at Cimmerian Lodge is like a metaphysical nightmare, but nevertheless he puts before his guests a good dinner and ''some superexcellent Madeira''; the gloom of Nightmare Abbey does not prevent the rapid circulation of the bottle; and not one of the crotchets that are produced at the table in Crotchet Castle suggests any possible abstinence from the hock and champagne, the salmon and chicken and asparagus, to be found there. The worst reactionary and the wildest rebel of them all do not hesitate to fill a bumper or join in a chorus. All these persons, in spite of their completely different opinions, have a strong likeness to one another, and are clearly inhabitants of the same world, in which the really strange visitors, the monsters who never make their appearance, would be ascetics, skinflints, water-drinkers, people who like to go to bed early, people who refuse to talk. Here again there is idealisation, a droll kind of poetical heightening. If you are fond of ideas and debate and conviviality (as Peacock himself was and as most of his admirers are), then this fantastic world, in which every one seems to talk and dine for ever, in which all those things that interfere in base reality with argument over the bottle are stoutly kept at bay, is a paradise, even though a comic little paradise. That Peacock used this world of his for purposes of satire is a fact so obvious that it is not worth stressing, but the ideal elements in it, by means of which he achieves humour rather than satire, have been so generally overlooked that they must be thrown into relief at the outset.

The characters in these novels . . . can be roughly divided into three classes; the crotcheteers in general, each with his dominating interest or theory; the caricatures of actual persons; and the more rounded and normal characters (including practically all the women), who range from mere faint sketches to complete individuals. All the novels, except *Gryll Grange,* are filled with crotcheteers. Some of them merely represent a dominating interest. Thus, Mr. Chromatic in *Headlong Hall* and Mr. Trillo in *Crotchet Castle* care about nothing (with the usual exceptions, applying to all these people, of hearty eating and drinking) but music. These personages are not amusing and are nothing but supers in the scene. On a slightly higher level are such characters as Mr. Cranium, with his phrenology, Mr. Asterias, who spends his life looking for a mermaid, Mr. Firedamp, who thinks that water is the evil principle, Mr. Henbane, with his passion for poisons and antidotes, and Mr. Philpot, who ''thinks of nothing but the heads and tails of rivers''. A little above these, because they play a larger part in their respective novels, are the three debaters from *Headlong Hall:* Mr. Foster, the perfectibilian; Mr. Escot, the deteriorationist; and Mr. Jenkinson, the statu-quo-ite; and such personages as those two medieval enthusiasts, Mr. Downderry and Mr. Chainmail. One of the best of these crotcheteers is Mr. Toobad in *Nightmare Abbey.* This character . . . shares some of the grotesque opinions of Peacock's Bracknell friend, Newton, but in spite of that he can hardly be classed with the caricatures of actual persons. He believed that the supreme dominion of the world was given over for a while to the Evil Principle, hence his favourite quotation from Revelations: ''Woe to the inhabiters of the earth and of the sea! For the devil is come among you, having great wrath, because he knoweth that he hath but a short time.'' Peacock makes this absurd person pop up, crying, ''The devil is come among you'', throughout the story, and is clever enough to make just sufficient use of him. There is something very droll in the way in which, triumphantly riding his hobby-horse, he contrives to find solid satisfaction in any disastrous event, which may injure him as a man but does at least flatter him as a theorist. But these crotcheteers, hanging the world on one interest or one opinion, are not very entertaining by themselves but only in the mass, when we see one after another following his nose and discovering in every statement of fact or event only a further proof of the truth of his opinion. As characters they are not important, but they are useful as a kind of chorus, hinting at wilder and wilder absurdities and antics of the human mind.

We now come to the second class of characters, made up of what we have called caricatures of actual persons. . . . [When] we say, for example, that Mr. Feathernest and Mr. Mystic in *Melincourt* represent Southey and Coleridge, what do we mean?

In exactly what sense can they be said to represent them? Only, it is clear, in a very restricted sense. Mr. Feathernest and Mr. Mystic are obviously not creatures of this world at all but are typical inhabitants of Peacock's own Cloud-Cuckoodom. And even there, where every person is inevitably strangely transformed, they are not really Southey and Coleridge. Peacock never disavowed deliberate caricature as, for example, Dickens did, yet Dickens's Harold Skimpole is far more like Leigh Hunt than any of Peacock's characters are like their victims. This is because Peacock did not represent Southey and Coleridge in his two characters, but merely created two fantastic creatures out of their opinions. With these characters and the scenes in which they display themselves at length, he does what he maintained that all the great comic writers did, he creates fiction out of opinions. Although at times he may go too far, for the most part he deals with his victims simply as public persons and does not try to represent them in their private life or make any reference to it. Thus, Mr. Feathernest is not the actual Southey of Greta Hall, Keswick, the unselfish, industrious, upright man of letters, but simply some of Southey's more reactionary opinions endowed with Peacockian humanity. (pp. 136-45)

The chief figures in the third class of characters are the various hosts, the women, and the parsons. There is little to be said about the hosts, Squire Headlong, Mr. Glowry, Mr. Crotchet, Squire Gryll. Their part is to issue invitations to all the eccentrics of their acquaintance and then to see that the bottle is kept moving. Squire Headlong and Mr. Crotchet, we are told, had a passion for learned persons and disputation, and we try hard to believe that such indeed was the fact. Mr. Glowry has a point of view of his own, and Squire Gryll is not without learning and opinions, but they are little better than lay figures. The women begin by being lay figures, but gradually come to life with the development of Peacock's art. Thus the female characters in *Headlong Hall* are merely so many names and scraps of dialogue, but those in *Crotchet Castle* are lively and attractive individuals. Most critics have dismissed these women characters with a brief word, but Raleigh, in his notes on Peacock, has gone to the other extreme and given them the place of honour [see Additional Bibliography]. Peacock's young ladies, he notes,

> are real, perhaps because they are pleasant and sensible (which few of the men are), perhaps because the author takes fewer freedoms in the portraiture. It is difficult to say exactly how they make so pleasant an impression—probably by their freedom from censoriousness, and by the good will of the other characters towards them.

And he goes on to suggest that Meredith, "who learned more from Peacock than from any other writer", was especially indebted to his father-in-law for his characters of women. When we remember the proud position of Meredith's heroines, we can only regard this as a very great compliment indeed. Raleigh is too generous, however, though he is nearer the truth than those critics who dismiss all Peacock's women as so many ornamented sticks.

Anthelia Melincourt, who is more of a conventional heroine than any of the others, never contrives to catch hold of our imagination at all. If she can be regarded as a human being, then she must be considered an incredibly stiff and priggish creature. Even when all allowances have been made for the conventions of dialogue in the old novel, it is difficult to feel any interest or even believe in a young lady who always talks in this way:

> Both sexes, I am afraid, are too much influenced by the spirit of mercenary calculation. The desire of competence is prudence; but the desire of more than competence is avarice: it is against the latter only that moral censure should be directed: but I fear that in ninety-nine cases out of a hundred in which the course of true love is thwarted by considerations of fortune, it will be found that avarice rather than prudence is to be considered as the cause. . . .

The thought of her marital dialogues with her equally priggish and long-winded Mr. Forester makes us shudder. Yet there is in Anthelia the faint outline of a new and very attractive type of heroine, for she is represented as being intelligent, cultivated, independent, a distinct individuality, and yet not at all unfeminine. Here perhaps is the protoplasm out of which Meredith, bringing his own bright sunshine and strong air, evolved his glorious women. There could have been little development in Peacock's own comic world, which is pre-eminently a masculine world, through which his women lightly pass, smiling and singing. In *Nightmare Abbey,* Celinda Toobad, who, as Stella, becomes Scythrop's esoteric beloved, is merely a droll sketch of feminine high-falutin', but her rival, Marionetta, pretty, vivacious, coquettish, has a fluttering life of her own, and her scenes with her fantastic lover are sufficiently convincing and are good comedy. Better still, however, is Lady Clarinda, whom we may consider the leading lady of *Crotchet Castle,* though its author would probably prefer the claim of his Miss Touchandgo, a romantic figure in spite of her name. Lady Clarinda is a delightful woman of the world and reminds us of the great ladies of artificial comedy; she has their cool sparkle, their good sense and wit and teasing airs. In the chapter that describes the various eccentrics who are gathered round the dining-table of Crotchet Castle, Peacock uses Lady Clarinda as his mouthpiece, and this change from direct to indirect description is a considerable gain. Moreover, Lady Clarinda, at once amused and detached and filled with fine feminine common sense, is the ideal person to describe these oddities. And Peacock has given her an individual tone of voice, as it were, and it is just the right tone of voice. (pp. 153-56)

The best of all these general characters, however, is not Lady Clarinda but her companion in the same volume, the Rev. Dr. Folliott. We are told that Peacock described this character as his *amende honorable* to the Church of England, which had cut a very poor figure in his earlier novels in the persons of Dr. Gaster, of *Headlong Hall,* the Reverend Mr. Grovelgrub, in *Melincourt,* the Mr. Larynx of *Nightmare Abbey.* Whether all the members of that Church would care to accept Dr. Folliott as an adequate apology is not a question that Peacock discusses. There is nothing very spiritual about the Doctor, who would have remained much the same man if Christianity had never come into existence. But unlike his clerical predecessors, he is the very best of company. In the Peacock world of dining, wining, and debating, he is an ideal figure, for he dines and drinks and talks both learnedly and enthusiastically. If there is ever an Epicurean Church, he should be one of its saints. Here again, and to a higher degree, Peacock contrives to blend character and satire. Dr. Folliott is his creator's mouthpiece at every other moment, and his talk is a mine of satire. Nevertheless, there is nothing of the lay figure about him; we see him as a real person; he has an attitude of mind and a tone of voice of his own; and though Peacock put a great deal of himself into him, he is not to be taken for a mere mask, but is a genuine creation. He might be shortly described, however, as a projection and heightening of one side of Peacock's mind, the Tory, Greek-loving, Epicurean, anti-reform, unromantic side.

This explains why he is portrayed with such gusto, but every reader must be warned against carrying the identification of author and character too far, a mistake made by many critics, who imagine they have been describing Peacock when in reality they have been describing Dr. Folliott. The romantic Peacock, with his idylls among the Welsh mountains and so forth, is worlds away from Dr. Folliott, and there are times when Peacock is laughing at his worthy Doctor's limitations and prejudices just as heartily as he laughs at those of his lesser figures.

Dr. Folliott is as crotchety as any of the other people at Crotchet Castle, but having more gusto and wit and pugnacity, he carries it off better than the others. He is a scholar and an epicure and, being very comfortable himself, he wants everything to be left untouched so that he can enjoy his Greek and his dinner in peace. As old things are obviously the best, old books, old wine, old customs, it is therefore monstrous folly to want to chop and change. People who desire such changes, who come disturbing the peace, are either rascals, feathering their nests, or idiots, who have not the sense and taste to see that no real improvement is possible, that the golden age was in the past and that therefore all innovations are disastrous. This is the secret of his intense conservatism, and it is well to remember that Seithenyn in *The Misfortunes of Elphin,* with his absurd defence of his policy of leaving the crumbling embankment to look after itself, is only Dr. Folliott seen, as it were, from the reverse side. With a mind so constituted, and with humour, wit, learning, and polemical acuteness to aid him, Dr. Folliott is a dangerous if genial adversary. He has a lightning eye for the absurd pretensions of too complacent reformers and cranks in general, and as his company consists for the most part of such persons, he deals execution right and left. Peacock deliberately brings most of the cant of the age before him, and very little of it escapes. He reminds us of Dr. Johnson in his ready and sometimes unscrupulous repartee and in his ability, when such methods are obviously of no avail, to use other weapons, notably his bamboo, with which he lays out the footpads. But his manner and talk are all his own and have the Peacockian sparkle and salty tang. (pp. 158-60)

It should hardly be necessary now—for even those readers who do not know their Peacock must have made the discovery for themselves—to indicate where his strength lies in these novels. They consist for the most part of talk, and it will have been noticed that when the talk is in full swing, the narrator withdraws himself altogether, being content, like a dramatist, to let the dialogue carry him on. It is obvious that the talk must have a special quality of its own, and indeed, that the whole narratives must have some unusual appeal to compensate us for their narrow scope and lack of ordinary interest. This special quality, this compensating appeal, is found, of course, in Peacock's style. "I know not how to praise sufficiently the lightness, chastity, and strength of the language of the whole," wrote Shelley, of *Nightmare Abbey* [see excerpt dated 1819]. This may be said of Peacock throughout his work, though his style is seen at its best, having gained in ease and piquancy, in *Crotchet Castle* and *The Misfortunes of Elphin*. To the latter we will return in the next chapter: our present concern is with *Crotchet Castle* and its companions, the novels of talk. The secret of Peacock's success in these odd productions is chiefly to be found in the piquantly flavoured dialogue. His manner, like that of all genuine ironists, is nearly always grave and restrained. He does not try to be playful, facetious. His writing always seems almost colourless and stilted. Yet his style has a distinct flavour of its own, and he is really just as personal a stylist as a Lamb or a Carlyle. All his people, in spite of

individual differences, which are more marked in the later novels, talk in the same way, like members of one closely united family. They all talk in crisp phrases, delicately balanced and full of antithesis, and with a precision that is at once admirable and droll. However wild their opinions and arguments may be, their actual statements of them are all given an epigrammatic brevity and ring. Thus the maddest of them is something of a stylist and a wit. But this very fact gives all their speeches, which usually put forward some ridiculous notion, a curious undercurrent of irony. They explain themselves, as it were, only too well: there is mockery in the very precision of their language and the crisp rhythm of their phrases. If, setting aside the obvious absurdities, you miss this constant undercurrent of irony, this faint mockery in the very neatness of the dialogue, this grave mischievousness in the style itself, a style like an old dry wine, you will probably fail to understand, as so many excellent persons have failed to understand, the enduring appeal of Peacock. The idea, sometimes put forward by his critics, that he cannot be enjoyed by readers unacquainted with the notions and persons he satirised, is quite untrue, although a knowledge of his age undoubtedly heightens the comedy. What he certainly does demand, however, is both a sense of humour and a fine literary palate. (pp. 165-66)

J. B. Priestley, in his Thomas Love Peacock, *The Macmillan Company, 1927, 215 p.*

VIRGINIA WOOLF   (essay date 1929)

[*A British novelist, essayist, and short story writer, Woolf is among the most prominent literary figures of the twentieth century. Like her contemporary James Joyce, with whom she is often compared, Woolf is remembered as one of the most innovative of the stream-of-consciousness novelists. She was concerned primarily with depicting the life of the mind, and she revolted against traditional narrative techniques to develop her own highly individual style. Woolf's works, noted for their subjective explorations of characters' inner lives and their delicate poetic quality, have had a lasting effect on the art of the novel. She was a discerning and influential essayist as well as a novelist. Her critical writings, termed "creative, appreciative, and subjective" by Barbara Currier Bell and Carol Ohmann, cover almost the entire range of literature and contain some of her finest prose. In an excerpt from her 1929 essay "Phases of Fiction," Woolf discusses the strengths and limitations of Peacock's style.*]

When we open *Crotchet Castle* and read that first very long sentence which begins, 'In one of those beautiful valleys, through which the Thames (not yet polluted by the tide, the scouring of cities or even the minor defilement of the sandy streams of Surrey)', it would be difficult to describe the relief it gives us, except metaphorically. First there is the shape which recalls something visually delightful, like a flowing wave or the lash of a whip vigorously flung; then as phrase joins phrase and one parenthesis after another pours in its tributary, we have a sense of the whole swimming stream gliding beneath old walls with the shadows of ancient buildings and the glow of green lawns reflected in it. And what is even more delightful after the immensities and obscurities in which we have been living, we are in a world so manageable in scale that we can take its measure, tease it and ridicule it. It is like stepping out into the garden on a perfect September morning when every shadow is sharp and every colour bright after a night of storm and thunder. Nature has submitted to the direction of man. Man himself is dominated by his intelligence. Instead of being many-sided, complicated, elusive, people possess one idiosyncrasy apiece, which crystallizes them into sharp separate characters, colliding briskly when they meet. They seem ridiculously and gro-tesquely simplified out of all knowledge. Dr. Folliott, Mr. Firedamp, Mr. Skionar, Mr. Chainmail, and the rest seem after the tremendous thickness and bulk of the Guermantes and the Stavrogins nothing but agreeable caricatures which a clever old scholar has cut out of a sheet of black paper with a pair of scissors. But on looking closer we find that though it would be absurd to credit Peacock with any desire or perhaps capacity to explore the depths of the soul, his reticence is not empty but suggestive. The character of Dr. Folliott is drawn in three strokes of the pen. What lies between is left out. But each stroke indicates the mass behind it, so that the reader can make it out for himself; while it has, because of this apparent sim-plicity, all the sharpness of a caricature. The world so happily constituted that there is always trout for breakfast, wine in the cellar, and some amusing contretemps, such as the cook setting herself alight and being put out by the footman, to make us laugh—a world where there is nothing more pressing to do than to 'glide over the face of the waters, discussing everything and settling nothing', is not the world of pure fantasy; it is close enough to be a parody of our world and to make our own follies and the solemnities of our institutions look a little silly.

The satirist does not, like the psychologist, labour under the oppression of omniscience. He has leisure to play with his mind freely, ironically. His sympathies are not deeply engaged. His sense of humour is not submerged.

But the prime distinction lies in the changed attitude towards reality. In the psychologists the huge burden of facts is based upon a firm foundation of dinner, luncheon, bed and breakfast. It is with surprise, yet with relief and a start of pleasure, that we accept Peacock's version of the world, which ignores so much, simplifies so much, gives the old globe a spin and shows another face of it on the other side. It is unnecessary to be quite so painstaking, it seems. And, after all, is not this quite as real, as true as the other? And perhaps all this pother about 'reality' is overdone. The great gain is perhaps that our relation with things is more distant. We reap the benefit of a more poetic point of view. A line like the charming 'At Godstow, they gathered hazel on the grave of Rosamond' could be written only by a writer who was at a certain distance from his people, so that there need be no explanations. For certainly with Trol-lope's people explanations would have been necessary; we should have wanted to know what they had been doing, gath-ering hazel, and where they had gone for dinner afterwards and how the carriage had met them. 'They', however, being Chainmail, Skionar, and the rest, are at liberty to gather hazel on the grave of Rosamond if they like; as they are free to sing a song if it so pleases them or to debate the march of mind.

The romantic took the same liberty but for another purpose. In the satirist we get not a sense of wildness and the soul's adventures, but that the mind is free and therefore sees through and dispenses with much that is taken seriously by writers of another calibre.

There are, of course, limitations, reminders, even in the midst of our pleasure, of boundaries that we must not pass. We cannot imagine in the first place that the writer of such exquisite sentences can cover many reams of paper; they cost too much to make. Then again a writer who gives us so keen a sense of his own personality by the shape of his phrase is limited. We are always being brought into touch, not with Peacock himself, as with Trollope himself (for there is no giving away of his own secrets; he does not conjure up the very shape of himself and the sound of his laughter as Trollope does), but all the

time our thought is taking the colour of his thought, we are insensibly thinking in his measure. If we write, we try to write in his manner, and this brings us into far greater intimacy with him than with writers like Trollope again or Scott, who wrap their thought up quite adequately in a duffle gray blanket which wears well and suits everything. This may in the end, of course, lead to some restriction. Style may carry with it, especially in prose, so much personality that it keeps us within the range of that personality. Peacock pervades his book. (pp. 131-33)

Virginia Woolf, ''Phases of Fiction,'' in her Granite and Rainbow, *The Hogarth Press, 1958, pp. 93-145.*

JEAN-JACQUES MAYOUX   (essay date 1932)

[*In the following excerpt from commentary first published in 1932, Mayoux offers a series of general observations on Peacock and his works.*]

1. Is it necessary once more to indicate Peacock's limits? He belongs to a human type which, on the whole, only rarely makes its voice heard: the type of the sage. Not the philosopher or the lover of wisdom, but 'the sage'. Without doubt, this type at its highest level is the richest and most comprehensive of all. The most precious and rare wisdom is that which, far from avoiding life, involves itself in life in its most various and intense aspects. Such is the wisdom of certain great poets—of Goethe, for example; and (though I dare to say it is less evident) of Shakespeare. As all wisdom consists of mastering an experience, the supreme form of wisdom is that which masters, or is capable of mastering, all experience. The wisdom of Peacock is of another sort. It consists of surveying the possibilities of experience, of measuring it. Its natural and preferred milieu is calm and composure; it does not master the storm. It is Epicureanism.

Epicureanism—and we discount here the vulgar notion of it—is far from always achieving wisdom. A doctrine solely and of itself never makes for wisdom; this is the outcome of a combination of a doctrine with a temperament. Now a many-sided temperament—and there are plenty such—chooses its doctrine, I venture to say, by adhering to the predominant trait. Those tendencies which are not incorporated take their revenge. The life of Sainte-Beuve, to cite only one example, presents the curious spectacle of an Epicureanism painstakingly built on the dangerous and false basis of his natural hedonism (it is a mistake to confuse hedonism with Epicureanism) and hence of a repression of the strength of the will. His Epicureanism is a mongrel of weak constitution, vulnerable to the sharp and painful pricks of life. For all that he may be one of the most fervent pupils of the school, an Epicurean so readily given to perfidy and venom as the worthy Sainte-Beuve is remote from the master Epicurus and from the true disciples, such as Montaigne.

A modern Epicureanism, drawing strength from the ancient original, which it perhaps purifies and certainly enriches, has about it, as an effect of the long perspective of time, a kind of Romanticism. One calls to mind the Romantic outlook so delicately formulated by Pater and attributed to his Marius. That of Peacock is also partly blended with what we may term (in an admittedly arbitrary identification) the Hellenic concep-tion of life: a harmonious individualism, governed by the ap-preciation of beauty in things, in acts, in thinking, and by a religious feeling about the real and material world.

Peacock exhibits the links between Utilitarianism and Epicureanism: the endeavour to rationalise pleasure and to create, out of rational enquiry into pleasure, a personal and social morality. Reason imposes on the individual an awareness of the universal, and it impels Peacock towards democratic doctrines, the logic of which is immediately apparent if one is convinced both of the universality of egoism and of the universal legitimacy of pleasure—that is, if one is at once a Hobbesean and a rational Epicurean.

2. Peacock's development can be summarised fairly briefly. There are two periods—the first combative, the second defensive—in the lives of almost all thoughtful men, though these periods are sometimes disguised by insincerity or, most frequently, by illusion. In the first they conceive, and tend to believe achievable, a world fashioned to their tastes and inclinations; in the second they are concerned with protecting their tastes and inclinations from the world as it actually is or as it threatens to become.

By nature sceptical and wary, delighting in the game of dialectics, but perceiving beyond this the individualism of the human intellect and the wholly relative character of its conclusions, Peacock nevertheless found in the Utilitarianism of Bentham a doctrine to sustain him. This is his first period. But soon enough the anarchism which Benthamism encourages makes for something quite different from the position of Bentham himself, who was ever preoccupied with absolute verities and smitten at not finding them in human affairs. Peacock, in compensation, begins to strike out his own comic and philosophic path in pursuit of imposture and the Proteus of illusion. At the same time he perceives that to rationalise the world requires the world's co-operation. The world reveals itself as incapable of emerging from an anarchic confusion of values—anarchic and also oppressive. From this point Peacock's development is logical. As he turns away from the attempt to rationalise individualisms or to justify social oppression on grounds of Utility, he recovers his own individuality which, at the outset of his Utilitarian phase, he had bravely thrown into the common stock in the interests of social-contact theory. The artist in him, his sensibility to beauty and to the good things of body and mind, reawaken. He had earlier proclaimed the downfall of the poet who voluntarily departed from the city, but he now feels increasingly ill at ease in face of the choice of values presented by the city, and he confronts in his own terms, implicitly, our contemporary problem of the day-to-day position of the intellectual and his culture in the modern city. To the value systems suited to unpretentious and ordinary individualities, the numerical majority, there is opposed a system, aristocratic in character, which sustains the notion of a hierarchy of intellect, and does not regard numbers as of prime importance—indeed, on the contrary, is apprehensive of their hostile pressure. Isolated by circumstance, Peacock chooses to increase the isolation by renouncing the city and withdrawing to his own version of Thélème. It is the conclusion of a curious endeavour.

Generally speaking, Peacock's evolution corresponds to the trend of his epoch—or, more precisely, to a fairly broad revulsion from the trend. The subjective causes of his development —the principal one being, as he himself realises, the simple elapse of time together with the withdrawal into himself—are mingled with objective causes, among which the main one is a pessimistic, or at least bitter, reaction against materialism and the mechanistic notion of progress. There is about Peacock something of a nineteenth-century Montaigne: an intellect critical, ironic, pyrrhonian, applied to the gradual liquidation of the idea of progress.

3. In seeking wisdom in the modern world, Peacock's path needs must follow mechanistic progress or Romantic escapism, or some systematisation which runs counter to these two routes. It is fascinating to observe his relationship with Romanticism, for what it has to tell us concerns not only Peacock.

In poetry and prose he deploys many of the Romantic themes; in the main these are the most obvious, 'exterior' themes, the prime catch-all categories which captivate the Romantic mind: Nature, Solitude etc. Peacock comes soon enough—after ***Melincourt***—to have a sage's view of *wild* nature, to master it and to counter the sublime terrors of Burke by a brave pantheism. As for Solitude: it is throughout his life the regulator of his thoughts and his feelings—albeit far remote from him is the wilderness where the passions swell. Can he have had more than a hazy notion of the true solitude, he who thought to find it by leaving London for the English countryside?

There is only one Romantic theme for which this friend of Shelley (here wavering in his allegiance to Epicurus) has a full appreciation, if not a deep feeling: the theme of Absolute Love; for he was, in this respect at least, a Platonist. It figures prominently in his work, right up to that moving culmination in the autumn of his life, ***Gryll Grange***. Even so, he is for ever striving to make even Platonism rational.

Admittedly, it is only in ***Nightmare Abbey*** that Peacock makes a frontal attack on Romanticism, as being unwholesome. But in all his writings he is campaigning against the subtle disguises, the metamorphoses, of Romanticism. For unbridled individualism, that is Romanticism. The passionately held system of thought and action, the grand personal idea offered to others for their salvation or well-being, and the huge endeavour to convert men—these also are elements in Romanticism. The idea of progress itself—so absurdly debased into the reign of the machine, the frenzy for production, for speed and so on—is for him the collective and, so to say, organic Super-Romanticism of modern times. Confronting it, Peacock becomes one of the first of a paradoxical race (though well established by our day): that of the Rousseauan rationalists.

And even in regard to material progress his position is not a simple one, for his rational, reasonable mind and his sense of proportion modify the Rousseauan critique. He is far from being a remote and ineffectual desk-bound censurer; he designs and successfully builds steam-engines, to show he knows what he is talking about when depreciating steam-power and seeking to keep it in its place.

4. The two stages of Peacock's thought are translated into comedy, and thereby is revealed, under this transformation, the profound and substantial unity of his spirit. Within all his comedy—***Gryll Grange*** excepted—there is an individualism making mock of individualism. It is an individualism moderated and self-aware, accepting the conditions necessary for universalising itself; and it ridicules the individualism of the immoderate, encroaching and proselytising kind, seeing in this nothing other than the desire for power masked by illusions.

We find in Peacock a strong sense of comedy—of the comic spirit even—and very little of the satiric spirit. The things he mocked at most often were those close to himself, the frenzies or disorders of a kind of individualism which clearly fascinated him: the individualism of the eccentric, the deviser of theories, the discoverer of panaceas, the enthusiast, the man with a saving mission—in short, the 'crank'. (This English word is the only exact designation of the type for, despite the example of Fourier and others, it is a type essentially English.) The crank, the individual who has attained certitude, is borne along by a Romanticism of the brain. It is among seekers after the Absolute that our author found his favourite subjects, and it is with such materials that his dialectical mind fashioned what I would term his intellectual comedies. And yet, for all the derision with which he explores the fantastic by-ways of the Idea, we feel that he loves it for itself, as one may love a woman without any need to possess her.

He makes jest of the unconscious alliances between thinking and private fantasy (we say fantasy, not imagination, for this latter merits respect as the supreme faculty of mind; and be it noted that Peacock prefers as a subject the second-rate system-builder, the proponent of the preposterous). But these he replaces by a conscious alliance. If he decks thinking with cap and bells, it is to enable him to frisk about more freely, more gaily. The originality of Peacock lies in his setting up a post in the frontier zone of thought, imagination and fantasy, and in helping to bring a rather arid terrain into the demesne of the literary art. He animates, with the charms of an amateur's naïveté and awkwardness, some very bizarre puppets. And yet, as this or that one performs, not a few of us will say, smilingly (for it is all in the mind only): 'Mon semblable, mon frère'.

In the strong maturity of his intellectual life, Peacock was much mistrustful of poetry, which most of us would regard as the highest form of literature. As a good Epicurean and an optimist by temperament, he put life itself in first place. This characterises all his writing.

5. Peacock's comic spirit shows itself at many points in the concurrence of a cathartic, secondary function (a little akin to the symbolic function of a poem or a drama) with a form of fantasy which is directly expressive and jocund. This, I believe, is the essential characteristic of the role of wine at his fictional dinner-parties. Wine makes for joy in a wholly different manner from the other sources of sensuous pleasure. The mutual bottle goes round the table; it is the visible, tangible and collective source of personal feelings which are not only happy but quasi-fraternal. Hence wine—together with good food, of course—is not only the symbol of all the vivid, yet not extreme, pleasures of the life of the body; it is also the type of a communion in these pleasures, opposing to the solitude of the mind and spirit the sociability of the body. For Peacock—by intention—is the most sociable of individualists; and it is perhaps this touch of contradiction that imparts such sureness to his aim and such success to his humourous critique of individualism.

The bottle always stands, even if some see it waveringly double, as a figure of objective reality among the table-companions—more real than the lucubrations of more temperate, but solitary, moments (let us remember that it is all a matter of symbols). With the admirable exception of Seithenyn in *The Misfortunes of Elphin,* Peacock chooses to ignore drunkenness and its unreality.

6. The well-known epigram of Horace Walpole tells us that the world is a comedy to those that think, a tragedy to those that feel. This is at the least a gross simplification; it is all a question of a difference of proportion. The remarkable thing about Peacock, the thing which keeps him away from the highest peaks of comedy, is not that his head overrules his heart, but that head and heart are so blithely separate in their functioning. The greatness and profundity of Molière's comedy

come from their interaction. When the critical and comic spirit is quiescent in Peacock, he sentimentalises; thus it is with his heroines, and with his Nature.

7. Stendhal remarks somewhere: 'We say that a man has genius when he has invented his *genre.'* Dialectical comedy, such as is blended with a fantasy so diverse and subtle, is pretty well Peacock's invention.

A classicist by temperament, he displays nothing of the sad sense of imperfection, though he almost always evinces a great concern for formal finish. This makes him appear, in the broad day of the nineteenth century, a remotely classical spirit. Herein Peacock is an anomaly, and this has governed his literary reputation right up to our own day. A disillusioned imagination such as Peacock's receives worthy appreciation only in an age of disillusionment.

8. His life, personality and character are compounded of greatness and littleness. Beneath the gaiety and the jesting we discern a massive and compact strength; and we watch him over the years in proud pursuit of his solitary course. But shall we call it grand or petty, this olympian, non-comic mask which he wears as a protection from fully human experience?

Judgement of Shelley has often been based on the Shelleyans, the lanky young men with high-pitched voices and missionary zeal for their idol. It would be quite as unfair to judge Peacock by the Peacockians who cherish him solely as he was in his old age: the quizzical man of letters, the Hellenistic gourmet, the squat and staid Epicurean. (pp. 160-66)

> *Jean-Jacques Mayoux, "Radical and Epicurean,"*
> *translated by D. Mirfin, in* Peacock: The Satirical
> Novels, a Casebook, *edited by Lorna Sage, The Mac-*
> *millan Press, Ltd., 1976, pp. 141-68.*

DOUGLAS BUSH   (essay date 1937)

[*Bush was a Canadian-born American educator, literary historian, and critic. In this discussion of* Rhododaphne, *he compares Peacock's use of classical mythology with that of contemporary Romantic poets.*]

Rhododaphne is an attractive if not important poem, and it partly expresses an element in Peacock which the reader of his lively prose might overlook. Though his literary career covered the first two thirds of the nineteenth century, Peacock was always an eighteenth-century aristocrat. His mellow (and sometimes belligerent) classical scholarship, his Epicurean creed, which was both gustatory and philosophic, his infinite common sense, his skeptical mockery of all forms of irrationality and "enthusiasm," these things are of the eighteenth century, and, along with his mental agility and high spirits, they give to his books their unique sanity and sparkle and tang. As a largely self-trained classic, Peacock united to more than donnish crotchets the more than donnish passion for Greek with which he endowed such fine old pagan clerics as Dr. Folliott. In temperament he was closer to Lucian than to Plato, and, like most satirists, he attacked his own age because he had visions of a better one. But he was no martyr or crusader because, again like most satirists', his visions were of the past, not of the future. Greece, however, is not a mere refuge from reality, it is reality; it is the touchstone of truth and simplicity, of rational wisdom. In the Aristophanic comedy in *Gryll Grange,* Peacock, like Spenser, makes use of Plutarch's Gryllus, the victim of Circe who preferred to retain his hoggish nature; for the man of the Renaissance such porcine contentment is an affront to the dignity of the human soul, in Peacock it expresses a resolute Tory's contempt for modern boasts of progress. If Gryllus belongs to the backyard of the Pantheon, Peacock employs mythology proper, along with medieval romance, in the prose fragment *Calidore*. In this fantasy, which reminds us of Heine's *The Gods in Exile*, we learn that the Olympian deities were happy in their relations with humanity until men degenerated and began to call the gods Beelzebub and Astaroth, to sigh and groan and turn up the whites of their eyes. The Nonconformist conscience, as Mr. Beerbohm would say, had made cowards of them all, and the gods, disgusted with so unpleasant a race, retired to an undisturbed island.

The harmony which soon prevailed between the Olympians and their Arthurian visitors might be taken, allegorically, as a symbol of Peacock's combination of Hellenic rationalism with a genuine romantic strain. When in **"The Four Ages of Poetry"** he says, "We know too that there are no Dryads in Hyde-park nor Naiads in the Regent's-canal," he is not a rationalist rejoicing in the march of mind but a romantic mourning the decay of the spirit of wonder and mystery that progress has brought about. He feels, like Arnold thirty years later, how unpoetical the age is. And at the end of his life he was not merely the "whiteheaded jolly old worldling" whom Thackeray saw. The confession of faith that he put into the mouth of Mr. Falconer may stand as essentially his own; Peacock himself, strange as it seems, was a devotee of St. Catherine. Mr. Falconer feels the need of believing in some local spiritual influence, genius or nymph, to link him with the spirit of the universe, for the world of things "is too deeply tinged with sordid vulgarity."

> There can be no intellectual power resident in a wood, where the only inscription is not "*Genio loci*," but "Trespassers will be prosecuted"; no Naiad in a stream that turns a cotton-mill; no Oread in a mountain dell, where a railway train deposits a cargo of vandals; no Nereids or Oceanitides along the seashore, where a coastguard is watching for smugglers. No; the intellectual life of the material world is dead. Imagination cannot replace it. But the intercession of saints still forms a link between the visible and invisible. . . .

If this complaint has a touch of elderly sentimental peevishness—like "By the Ilissus there was no Wragg, poor thing"—Peacock's fundamental attitude, like the much more philosophic Arnold's, was sincere. His half-primitive and pagan belief, or desire to believe, was the closest approach to religious sentiment that his irresponsible intelligence permitted. But while in mythological poems Keats and Shelley, with their larger vision, did not lose sight of the modern world, Peacock did in *Rhododaphne*. The critic of modernity who wrote the novels owed much to his commerce with the ancients; the Hellenism of the poem is wholly a romantic dream, a way of escape.

The fable of the seven cantos can be briefly summarized. The maiden Calliroë suffers from a strange disease, and her lover Anthemion goes to a festival in honor of Love to make an offering on her behalf. He is enthralled by the beauty and magical power of Rhododaphne. He escapes to his own home, to find Calliroë well and radiant, but when he kisses her with the lips that have been kissed by the enchantress, she swoons, apparently in death. The stricken Anthemion rushes away. He is recaptured by Rhododaphne, who passionately insists that she holds sway over all things but his heart, and she must possess it. They live together in a magic palace, until Rhododaphne is slain by Uranian Love for profaning his altars. The palace vanishes, and Anthemion awakens to find himself at home in Arcadia, with the dead Rhododaphne beside him. But Calliroë appears, alive and lovely, to be reunited with him, and to weep for the fate of the loving Rhododaphne.

Peacock's main interest was in a tale of ancient magic and mystery and beauty. His imagination was too concrete, too simply romantic, for the symbolism that Keats and Shelley instinctively found in the antique, yet he went some way in that direction. The poem commences with a differentiation of threefold love, creative, heavenly, and earthly, and at the beginning of the last canto we are reminded that "Love's first flame," Anthemion's love for Calliroë, is "of heavenly birth," while the passion between him and the enchantress is earthly. The story of a young man torn between a supernatural and a human love will have recalled Keats's *Endymion*, which appeared a few months after *Rhododaphne*, and which Peacock did not like. But Peacock did not work out his parable with anything like Keats's seriousness, so that his critics have generally failed to observe that he has one. The episode of the magic palace reminds us at once of *Lamia*, and . . . Keats apparently gathered some hints from Peacock.

Rhododaphne contains, as Shelley said, "the transfused essence of Lucian, Petronius, and Apuleius," and the author's classical learning appears, unobtrusively, in and between the lines. In comparison with *Endymion* and *Prometheus Unbound*, if not in an absolute sense, the poem deserves Shelley's epithets, not yet overworn, of "Greek and Pagan," although, as Shelley went on to say, the love story is more modern than the spirit and scenery. The "strong *religio loci*" is partly in the substance of the tale, and so far may be called Hellenic, and partly it is in the way of modern and nostalgic comment. The most genuine emotion in the poem is felt in the expressions of wistful regret for the passing of the infant world and its divinities:

> The life, the intellectual soul
> Of vale, and grove, and stream, has fled
> For ever with the creed sublime
> That nursed the muse of earlier time.

Peacock's classical taste is everywhere apparent, not merely in the use of local color but in the crystalline clarity, definiteness, and objectivity of his narrative method, style, and imagery. We have no vagueness or fumbling, no Keatsian lapses in taste, no beating of Shelleyan wings. That is a merit, and it belongs partly to the ancients and partly to the eighteenth century; one may say of the poem what the East India Company's officials said of the author's examination papers, "Nothing superfluous and nothing wanting." But one is compelled to add that Peacock is not struggling to utter anything of much difficulty or importance. If we happen to begin *Rhododaphne*, we yield at once to its melodious charm and the freshness of its bright water-color pictures, but we retain no memory of it, and we may forget to pick it up again; the story of human love stirs no emotion, the diablerie causes no *frisson*. If we compare the description of Rhododaphne in the moonlit grove with parallel scenes in *Christabel*, we feel at once what the former lacks, or avoids. When Peacock uses the simile "like the phantom of a dream," it has in its context something of Greek externality and distinctness which is quite different from the inwardness, the suggestion of reverie, in Shelley's "As suddenly Thou comest as the memory of a dream." There seem to be echoes of the poem in Shelley's work, and it was doubtless association with Shelley that kindled a genuine poetic flame from the ashes of *Palmyra* and *The Genius of the Thames*. Yet Peacock remained himself, a modern Ovid. (pp. 180-86)

Douglas Bush, *"Minor Poets of the Early Nineteenth Century,"* in his Mythology and the Romantic Tradition in English Poetry, *Cambridge, Mass.: Harvard University Press, 1937, pp. 169-96.*

V. S. PRITCHETT   (essay date 1940)

[*Pritchett, a modern British writer, is respected for his mastery of the short story and for what critics describe as his judicious, reliable, and insightful literary criticism. He writes in the conversational tone of the familiar essay, approaching literature from the viewpoint of an informed but not overly scholarly reader. In his criticism, Pritchett stresses his own experience, judgment, and sense of literary art, rather than following a codified critical doctrine. In the following excerpt, Pritchett offers some general comments on Peacock's novels as seen from a personal perspective.*]

Nowadays, the Peacock novels, as they come fragmentarily into focus, have the farcical atmosphere of the surrealist dreams. Their slapstick and their unexpected transitions, their fancy and the burlesque discussions, lead through *Alice in Wonderland* to the present. It is amusing to find present parallels for the deteriorationist and the rational economist, and Peacock chose eternal types; but without the farce and the romance, that amusement would soon become bookish and musty. Scythrop concealing his lady in the tower and lying about the movable bookcase, Mr. Toobad jumping out of the window at the sight of the "ghost" and being hooked out of the moat by the dreary scientists who are down there with their nets fishing for mermaids, Squire Headlong's experiments with explosives, Dr. Folliott's adventures with the highwaymen—this picaresque horseplay is the true stuff of the English comic tradition from Sterne and Fielding, a new gloss on the doings of the Pickwick Club. And Peacock can alternate the perfunctory or the heroic manner which our tradition especially requires. Gradually, as he perfected his genre, progressing from the Hall to the Abbey, from the Abbey to the Castle—I have never got as far as the Grange—Peacock balanced his extremes. Here romantic love plays its part; not the wild stuff of course, but a romance which infuses an artificial sweetness, that *faux naturel* of the eighteenth century which at once suggests the formal and the untutored. In the mad brainy world the women alone—if one expects the highbrow Poppyseed and the awful Mrs. Glowry—have the sense and sensibility. Peacock cuts short the sighs; marriages are arranged, not made in Heaven; dowries are not forgotten, but what a delightful convention (the India clerk reminds us), marriage is.

One might expect more broadness in so keen a reader of Rabelais, but Peacock (unless my memory is bad or my ear for *double entendre* dull) appears to share the primness of Dr. Folliott, a primness one often finds among the drinkers. There is only one smoke-room remark in *Crotchet Castle*—and a very good one it is. It occurs after the cook has set her room on fire when she has fallen asleep over a treatise on hydrostatics in cookery:

> Lord Bossnowl: But sir, by the bye, how came your footman to be going into your cook's room? It was very providential to be sure but . . .

> Revd. Dr. Folliott: Sir, as good came of it, I shut my eyes and ask no questions. I suppose he was going to study hydrostatics and he found himself under the necessity of practicing hydraulics.

I suppose it should be argued that Dr. Folliott's quarrel later on about the exhibition of an undraped female figure on the stockbroker's mantelpiece was grounded less in the prudery of

the bibulous than in the general Peacockian dislike of popular education. He was against putting ideas into his footman's head. An act of benevolence, for no one knew so well as Peacock, how funny a man with an idea in his head can be. (pp. 42, 44)

V. S. Pritchett, *"Mr. Peacock,"* in The New Statesman & Nation, *Vol. XX, No. 490, July 13, 1940, pp. 42, 44.*

RONALD MASON   (essay date 1944)

[*Mason assesses Peacock's satire, exploring his creativity, critical methodology, characterization, central goals, and other facets of his art.*]

This opinionated and Epicurean eccentric has found himself a niche. He is appreciated especially by a cultivated, rather restricted set of readers who find an instinctive response in their temperaments to his dogmatic and often arbitrary assertions. Lawyers read him, liberal clergymen, higher civil servants, the professional classes, the older men of letters. The values that he proclaims satisfy their relaxation very well. He is a bit of a curiosity, an isolated specimen, a writer whom it tickles their fancy to read and their vanity to have read. A little nervous about the form society is to take and the place they are going to take in it, they are very much heartened by the gusto with which Peacock's violent common sense reinforces their innermost articles of faith. He pleases this class immensely, in the same way that Trollope pleases them, by his implicit insistence on the foundations on which they themselves are based, and by his bull-like activities in the china-shop of Idiosyncrasy. They sense in idiosyncrasy a threat to stability; and Peacock's invigorating forthright satire smashes to their satisfaction the idiosyncrasy and the threat. Thus he is read by them appreciatively, not critically. Outside this circle he has no very wide public.

Yet it is undoubtedly worth the effort to break through this crust of prejudice to find out what there is in him besides this protective aggressiveness. Nowadays when critics are apt to seize mercilessly upon a writer's confessed or implied ideology before deciding whether his creative work is to be admitted to criticism or not, it is not so easy as it used to be to disinter the secret of the durability of a man like Peacock from the wreckage of his social or political heresies. It is time we were reminded that neither Peacock nor Trollope have lived so long as they have on the strength of comfortable conservatism alone. There was a period of literary criticism—it is all over now—when books and their authors were judged almost solely on their capacity for imparting enjoyment. Of this school of critics Saintsbury was the sanest and most appreciative; and if you want to read a full and fair recital of Peacock's richness, his abiding attraction, you will find Saintsbury's introductions to the novels, reprinted in his *Prefaces and Essays*, unequalled in their own class as a benevolent appreciation of the man and his work. A very important job was done by the appreciative school of critics; they whetted the immediate appetites in a way that no access of sophistication has been able to improve on; and the limitation of that school is not that their criticism lacked acuteness or even profundity, but that the standards they set and the methods they employed could not readily take into account just those factors of historical and social relevance that are essential to the adjustment of the author's literary importance. Had he relevance to his age? If so, how? If his age is in any way related to our own, how may he be helpfully aligned to that relation? And so on. Questions of this sort set a figure more solidly in the round, when adequately answered, than any amount of appreciative quotation can do. The appreciative critics provide a very valuable, but only a partial, answer to the general inquisitiveness which we feel about a good writer. Peacock has been well enough served by them; it is time he was examined in a perspective which they did not afford him; and a recent second reading of the novels has suggested to me that the isolation and comparative obscurity in which he exists today is mainly referable to the lack of any serious attempt to discuss him objectively. He has been left to his circle of willing appreciators, a circle which for social and historical reasons is growing narrower. This is a tentative attempt to break out of it. (pp. 238-39)

It is true enough that what is left of his fame today is not a residue of great creations, separate works of art, but of a personality expressing itself through arbitrary incidental forms. His books are not entities, independent once the navel-string has been severed. We don't say, 'Ah, that reminds me of something in *Nightmare Abbey*', as we might say, 'That reminds me of something in *Esmond,* or *Treasure Island,* or *Moby Dick,* or *Mr. Polly*'. We say instead, 'That reminds me of something in Peacock'. And although that doesn't amount to a final criticism, one way or the other, it cannot help indicating the essential subordination of the work produced to the character of the author producing it. In this way a man may perpetuate character, but not art. And when from this premiss we turn to examine the several novels, it becomes only too evident that the essential individuality, which a single work must have if it is to exist in its own right at all, is present in the temper of his work but absent from the forms in which he expressed that temper. There is none of that dramatic progress from a given point to a given point which is part of the minimum requirement of the novel; and deprived of the *shape* without which separate existence is not possible, these novels remain random lengths of sample Peacock, and do not amount to art.

This does not, of course, invalidate Peacock; it limits our field of search, that is all, since as a pure novelist we can write him off. It becomes clear that his appreciative readers are appreciating him, not the books he has written. But it would also be misleading to suggest, as I may have seemed to be suggesting, that because his novels are shapeless conventionalities it is his thought alone that makes him worth reading. His peculiar liveliness came from other sources as well as from the philosophical ones. Refer back to the class I have indicated as echoing his sentiments. They are generally impatient of novels of ideas. Henry James, for example, E. M. Forster, Edward Upward, Rex Warner, find little response from them. Using these readers as a touchstone, there must be some quality we can find in Peacock which enables him to transmit his own very definite vitality to them other than through the medium of the interplay of ideas. Take away shape from a novel, take away all but the most conventional plot, and what have you left? With Dickens, at any rate, miraculous characters. With Peacock it is not so easy to give an answer. Good satire needs more than naked ideas, and their effectiveness depends a lot on the sort of flesh and blood they are dressed up in.

It is therefore a little disconcerting to find that Peacock does not push his characters much beyond the type stage. These distinctive but obedient puppets do not vary from book to book, any more than the arbitrary antics through which they are put vary either. For the most part the novels are animated *causeries* prinked out with lively comment: the similarity of most of the

titles, *Melincourt, Headlong Hall, Nightmare Abbey, Crotchet Castle, Gryll Grange,* reflects inevitably the similarity of theme and treatment. Peacock assembles his characters in a convenient collection under one roof, hustles them as quickly and as often as he can into the presence of food and drink, and simply leaves them to talk. The author retires; each protagonist is permitted to speak under the bare signpost of his name in capitals, and in each speech we find displayed in caricature a different humour. All the old tricks of Jonsonian or Restoration comedy are resurrected, and each character is named and invested with the minimum of individuality required for the exercise of the foible he is embodying. Foster, Escot and Jenkison in *Headlong Hall* represent the three standards of optimism, pessimism and the complacent halfway conservatism between the two, and none of the three utters a word throughout to conflict with, or even significantly to amplify, the doctrine which is his only source of existence. Furthermore when Peacock extends his satire to individuals rather than to types, the frequency of his success, as in the delicious Flosky caricature of Coleridge in *Nightmare Abbey,* has rather obscured the essential similarity between his use of 'humours' and his use of individual caricature. Escot is the deteriorationist and nothing else, and nobody gains or loses by his deteriorationism; Flosky is Coleridge and nobody else, and nobody gains or loses by his Estesianism. He is in as complete a vacuum as Escot. He performs for our diversion his ordained and patterned idiosyncrasy, and stops when he is turned off. He is funny in his own vacuum, as Escot, more soberly, is funny in his. The tragedy of Peacock's characters is that not one of them ever hears one word that any other one is saying. They are little isolated bits of Peacock himself, or of Peacock's enemies, and they enunciate their forthright monologues, pause for breath, and resume at the correct interval. Nothing that has passed meanwhile interests or affects them. In this they differ from the protagonists in Restoration drama, who are at least aware of the complex convention in which they are employed, are in fact breathlessly anxious to conform to it, like earnest participants in the lancers; and also from characters in such drama as Shaw's, where 'types' who are introduced do at least play an integral part in the development of the play and often end by being seen in the round, contributing idiosyncrasy to the action and deriving independence from the drama. All this is foreign to Peacock; his art lacks this creative integration. His plots do not affect his characters; his characters do not affect his plots. The characters spin independently, on their own individual axes; the stories, such as they are, proceed unobtrusively without them. The development shown in *Gryll Grange,* where the plot is in part managed by the characters themselves, is noteworthy but elementary; and the story by itself would not arrest attention in a women's magazine. (pp. 240-42)

It is not his characters, then, or even his types, that give Peacock life; they are too occasional and spasmodic for that. His work, if it were sustained by their presence alone, would be much more uneven than it is; in fact, its quality has a consistency about it that would be remarkable if it were not simple to account for it by the salutary rigour that a real knowledge of the classics imparts to self-criticism. The name of A. E. Housman rises spontaneously as a parallel. A true classical scholar turning to creative work will never, assuming him to have genuine talent, write rubbish. Peacock never did, and that helps to preserve safely all that is valuable in his achievement.

There is only one more way to turn now that his characters have failed us, as they do in all but memorable isolated actions, and that is to the ideas embodied in his books. Here we are on rather more rewarding ground, as a personality emerges; a personality whose positive value, once we can gauge it, will help to measure the validity and extent of his position and influence in literature. The prescription is simple: accept the *dicta* of Peacock's favourite characters as corresponding to his own opinions, and for the rest reckon generally that the more far-fetched and ridiculous he makes a set of postulates appear, the more violently he is opposed to them. Flosky's transcendental obscurantism and that of Mr. Mystic in *Melincourt,* also drawn off Coleridge, Cranium's craniology, Seithenyn's *laisser-faire* conservatism, the toadyism of the particular character in nearly every novel who is intended to represent Southey— all these are contrasted understandably with the more acceptable qualities of Peacock's favourite divines, among whom Friar Michael of *Maid Marian* (that neglected but refreshing exercise in satiric romance) occupies a place less pontifical, not to say parasitical, than his black-coated brethren. The distinctions of doctrine are broad enough to enable us to extract from these contrasts a fairly comprehensive set of conclusions on Peacock's general outlook, and if we set him in the context of his age we can better judge whether that outlook had any constructive result when he translated it into words.

You have to remember that this man lived through one of the most turbulent periods in history and chose to write satire as his expression of his considered opinions. He lived as a conscious contemporary of the French Revolution, the Napoleonic Wars, the Romantic Revival, the Corn Laws, the Reform Act, Chartism, the Communist Manifesto, the Great Exhibition, the Crimean War, *The Origin of Species,* the rapid development of the internal combustion engine, the Oxford Movement and the first faint suggestions of Pre-Raphaelitism. Of very few of these things does he appear to be aware. Now Jane Austen, writng in the middle of the Napoleonic Wars, was perfectly justified in sticking to her drawing-room so long as she was consistent about it; but Peacock, swivelling a baleful eye on developments in modern society which happened to displease him, laid about him on a national scale while retaining the prejudices and the predilections of a Regency buck like Creevey. And Peacock, who had ten times the learning and ten times the wit of Creevey, and a capacity for satiric and humorous writing that placed him for short passages in the company of Dickens, lost half his value by this stubborn parochialism. It is not difficult to accuse and convict him of deliberate ignorances.

Yet his awareness shows up startlingly at times, like sudden clear patches in fog. Nothing could be better than the election racket in *Melincourt,* where the gentlemanly orang-outang gets safely returned to Parliament; there is a savour of Gilbert in this, and more than a savour of Dickens again. Eatanswill was not conceived for another twenty years, nor the election in *Middlemarch* (whose more rational realism does not blunt its telling effectiveness) for another fifty or so. Peacock was wide awake to the rotten state of the franchise, and in *Melincourt* he ran the topic neatly in harness with a genial bullyragging of Monboddo's surprisingly perceptive theories on the descent of man and Rousseau's commonly misrepresented conception of the noble savage. Sir Oran Haut-ton is a brilliant idea and a deftly managed character, being in fact the biggest spot on Peacock's most tedious novel; and as there is no reason to suppose that Peacock trusted Darwin any further than he trusted Monboddo, we need not chuckle over Peacock's presumptive loss of countenance on the publication of *The Origin of Species.* . . . [There] could be no neater summary of articulate Toryism, as lively (or as deadly) in the 1820s as in the 1940s,

than in Seithenyn's bibulous defence of the policy of the guardians of the embankment in face of the rising floods:

> The parts that are rotten give elasticity to those that are sound; they give them elasticity, elasticity, elasticity. If it were all sound, it would break by its own obstinate stiffness; the soundness is checked by the rottenness, and the stiffness is balanced by the elasticity. There is nothing so dangerous as innovation. . . . This immortal work has stood for centuries and will stand for centuries more, if we let it alone. It is well; it works well; let well alone. . . . It was half rotten when I was born, and that is a conclusive reason why it should be three parts rotten when I die.

That is, of course, magnificent; I suppose it has its equal in Falstaff, but not in many other contexts that I can think of. The piercing sanity that could evolve that devastating comment has its obvious application to our far more perilous plight today; and as a parallel piece of clear good sense I would refer you to the doctrines of Mr. Forester in *Melincourt,* who as a character in fiction is an unholy bore, but who seems to represent an earnest and almost crusading seriousness in Peacock that commends him rather to the social reformer than to the lover of satire.

> If in any form of human society any one human being dies of hunger, while another wastes or consumes as much as would have preserved his existence, I hold that second man guilty of the death of the first. . . . What would you think of a family of four persons, two of whom should not be contented with consuming their own share of diurnal provision, but, having adventitiously the pre-eminence of physical power, should either throw the share of the two others into the fire, or stew it down into a condiment for their own?

Here are the beginnings of a healthy critical disgust with what at that time was only just about to be called capitalism. Forester is an example of the solitary and sincere crusader who, endowed with a little more vision and a little more conscientious indignation than the next man, becomes a burden to his fellows through his martyr-like insistence on carrying through his theories to a practical conclusion. It led him in *Melincourt* to eschew slave-produced sugar and to inaugurate the rather misleadingly named Anti-Saccharine Fête—activities paralleled by the efforts of Brailsford and Nevinson in their persuasive onslaught on the cocoa trade in 1908; it might have led him a century or so later to the uncompromising community-life of the pacifist who weaves his own clothes out of his own sheep's wool rather than align himself with a profit-making and war-waging society. Given the change in contexts, it is not too far-fetched to see in Forester the sign that Peacock had a glimmering of the ghastly alternative facing the modern sensitive mind—kill or die; and in the light of our experience Forester's sugarless tea is as noble and futile as the renunciation of ration-books by his modern successors.

But Peacock did not pursue the transitory gleam; he retired among his favourite wines, weighing his postulates blandly over the beakers and not sparing anyone whose eccentricity jarred upon him. Canning is flagellated, but so is Brougham; the man who wished to return to medievalism gets a gentle beating, but the progress of scientific invention, represented especially by the energies of steam, gets one too, and not so gentle. He wastes on the barren question of paper-money nearly as much paper as was consumed by the misuse he complained of; and anyone who showed himself a connoisseur of claret or the classics was all that Peacock could desire. At times he seems to be using his admirable clarity of expression, his forth-right inimitable critical prose, to gratify a splenetic whim engendered by over-indulgence. He hits, and hits hard, not for the reason that the object of his attack has offended against any canon of taste or morals, but because it has happened in the eccentricity of his own mood to annoy him personally. The manifestly unfair attacks on Southey and Wordsworth, and one ill-tempered reference to Burke, are representative examples of this habit. His invective never fails to entertain, but it lapses from the standard of good satire.

For the value of a good satirist is akin to the value of a good critic; it depends on more than his insight or his power of expressing that insight. It varies in the ratio of the consistency of his central critical creed. 'He who frees criticism from the moral duty of placing itself in the service of a general, recognized and pursued life-task is treading the path that leads to nihilism and anarchy.' I feel this to be broadly true, though perhaps a little heavily expressed, and no less true because it happens to be by Hitler and meant in a rather specialized sense in the context in which he used it. Hitler insists on the subordination of critical honesty to a central policy; whereas I am stressing the co-ordination of critical insight with philosophical or moral standards. Criticism without a central set of values is not valuable criticism; it is as worthless as the armament of a battleship without anchor or steering-gear. Peacock wallowed in the heavy seas of the nineteenth century, his magnificent guns superbly manned and mounted. To port lay the fleet of progress, to starboard the fleet of reaction; and so irresponsible was the steering of this formidable vessel that when it let off a broadside it was a toss-up which of the opposing fleets took the weight of it. The models from whom in large part his form and effectiveness were derived, Aristophanes, Lucian, Marmontel and Voltaire, all possessed a central control foreign to Peacock's quicksilver temper, and the damage done by the satire of at least three of these was all the deadlier for the uncompromising consistency of their standards. By their side, and especially by Voltaire's, Peacock is an easy-going old reactionary with a hot temper and a talent for expressing it: he is not favoured by the comparison.

So his ideas do not give him the 'shape' we are looking for, any more than his creation of character or plot did. It is not easy, looking round, to see why he is any more than an attractive story-teller. There is, indeed, a genuine and rather moving consistency and beauty in the expression of his love for the various types of English scenery—the Thames in *Crotchet Castle*, the Lake District in *Melincourt*, the Fens in *Nightmare Abbey*, Wales almost everywhere, the New Forest in *Gryll Grange*; and the bitter note at the beginning of this last book on the subject of enclosures is echoed more than once in other parts of his work not discussed here, and is typical of this real enlightenment in him. There is, of course, one outstanding factor that assists his permanence out of all proportion to his narrative or persuasive ability—his style. It is classic. His immence erudition in Latin and Greek studies had ingrained in him a fastidiousness which was a sure shaper of as clean and clear a prose as his century can offer us. By comparison Macaulay is repetitive and turgid, even Newman frigid and remote; the involved excitabilities of Ruskin and Carlyle are hot air beside him, the classical artificiality of Pater as shallow as the romantic artificiality of Stevenson. His satiric temper, like Voltaire's before him, ground his style to a fine edge. It has orotundities and, as cannot easily be avoided when a classic treats a romantic subject, flatnesses at unexpected places where the emotional intensity required by the context puts too great

a strain on the emotional vocabulary at his command—contrast his treatment of wild Nature with his son-in-law Meredith's: the comparison is valuable as it aligns Peacock conspicuously with the eighteenth century, and invests him with a sculptured dignity which gives Meredith with all his red-blooded romanticism the air of an upstart crow, even although he has succeeded where Peacock has failed. And failure and all, Peacock's style is an admirable weapon; and often it is more than a weapon; it is, in the same way as Sterne's, a verbal embodiment of a personality. Firm, trenchant, economical, it accommodates itself to all moods and carries with it into all of them its pervading satiric essence. This gives it an immunity from bathos and bombast alike, and at times an irresistible humour. The strength and precision of his characters' assertions are frequently the chief origins of the characters' life; which is a clear example of how a style formed primarily for criticism can in the process become truly creative. This style has several notable modern descendants; Shaw is not unreminiscent of it even when he is most like Shaw; Belloc at his more pontifical (consciously pontifical, I mean, and hence very slightly self-satirical, as in *The Path to Rome* and *The Four Men*) provides startlingly faithful echoes. A number of our older moderns, revolting in the flush of youth from the crushing incubus of the three-decker, snatched with enthusiasm at Peacock's novel-form and gave it an exhilarating renewal of life. The gap had been partly bridged by Mallock's *New Republic*, but this had been even more of a retreat from the novel than Peacock's; the newer writers sought to manipulate their ideas within the conversation-piece framework and yet to retain the imaginative quality inherent in the novel. Generally they failed; but *South Wind*, *Crome Yellow* and *Those Barren Leaves* were incidental justifications of the attempt.

The style goes for much, then; but it cannot prolong a man's value into succeeding generations with nothing to back it. And it is because I believe Peacock to be of real value, and not so much because I believe him to have gained at the enthusiastic hands of Saintsbury and Priestley more than his due of praise, that I believe it time for a reassessment of him. Entertainment value must not be under-rated, and he has that in full enough measure. We shan't come to much harm if we read him simply for fun, although we shall then lay ourselves open to the danger of swallowing him whole, as even Saintsbury did, for the sake of the taste of the jam round the satiric pill. I have sought to show that his abiding value is neither creative nor truly critical, since his characters are not fully formed, his central purpose neither constructive nor consistent, and his satire irregularly aimed; he is Mr. Facing-both-ways, and today when he who is not for us is keenly suspected of being against us, Mr. Facing-both-ways is on unsafe ground. Yet there is one salutary quality in his satire: it is, if absorbed warily, a splendid corrective. Classical to the core, he steered his middle course throughout. Retrogressive reaction he bullied until it was over-ruled, hot-headed idealism he pricked until it burst. He was a man who hated extremes, and while it is not easy to see in these days whether anything but a considered extremism will ever infuse the necessary recreative faith into a collapsed society, it will be well for the hot-heads to correct themselves in mid-venture with a dose of this thermostatic humour of which Peacock is so efficient and delightful a provider. To regard his aggravating inconsistencies in this light may help us to come to easier terms with this excellent minor novelist. The restricted circle who read him now will, I hope, continue to do so; but I hope, too, that they will be joined by others whose critical discrimination will examine his satire against a wider background and his importance in relation to deeper and more enduring values; and it will be these who will come in time to give him his due. (pp. 244-50)

Ronald Mason, "Notes for an Estimate of Peacock," in Horizon, London, Vol. IX, No. 52, April, 1944, pp. 238-50.

HUMPHRY HOUSE   (lecture date 1949)

[In the following excerpt from commentary originally delivered in a radio broadcast, House asserts that Peacock's literary achievement lies in his role as critic of his age.]

It has often been said that Thomas Love Peacock has suffered because he has been too much regarded as the friend of Shelley and too little regarded as a person and author in his own right. It is certainly true that some idolators of Shelley have maligned Peacock, thinking to do their idol a good turn. But Mr. David Garnett has recently spoken out to redress the bias of his grandfather's judgments and to direct our attention to Peacock himself and to his works [see Additional Bibliography]. Even when this is done, there does remain a man with a place in history, the man who was the friend of Shelley and lived to be the father-in-law of George Meredith. He spans the generations, and his last novel is curiously like his first, though there is a gap of forty-four years between them. Peacock is a man whose true value cannot be seen apart from this context in history. His books are unintelligible without it. For he was not primarily an artist or a novelist, but a critic, a critic abnormally sensitive to the important movements of the mind and spirit in his age.

Though the title of this talk has been announced as 'Peacock's Novels' I do not mean to say anything about *Maid Marian* or the *Misfortunes of Elphin,* but to keep to what are called the novels of talk; for these are Peacock's most characteristic works and they are in fact scarcely novels at all by most people's standards, and were not meant to be. They are dialogues set in a slight frame of narrative; and though the narrative bears a greater part in some than in others, and is sometimes more and sometimes less closely knit to the talk, nobody would ever pretend that it is the narrative that gives them their value or interest. The coincidences and absurdities in the narratives are too flagrant in many instances even to deserve mention. They are books about opinions and not about events; and it is the expressed opinions in them that matter.

The major strain and drift of opinion running through them all is the critique of romanticism; the critique of romanticism in many different moods and different phases, represented in a great many different people. Of course there is also the critique of a great deal else besides. Political economists, Malthusians, charity commissioners, high-and-dry clergy, quarterly reviewers, borough-mongers, dons, popularisers of science, chemists, all come in for their share and all recur. But in all the books the talk turns mainly on one variety or other of romanticism, ranging from the most trivial skeleton business to the analysis of personality in the ironic rejection of suicide. In this sense it is the true focus in thinking of Peacock to think of him as the friend of Shelley; he was the man who was the intimate friend of Shelley and also kept his head. He was the adviser to whom Shelley turned even when he knew Peacock did not approve. Peacock was neither bewitched nor angry; he did understand. Not only in his reading, but in this friendship most of all, Peacock lived through the major phases of romanticism, and he speaks of it with that intimate knowledge.

It is a mistake, of course, to suppose that Scythrop Glowry in *Nightmare Abbey* is Shelley any more than Forester in *Melincourt* is Shelley. They are not portraits, and portraiture was not Peacock's method. He took elements from the Shelley situation and explored the thoughts that accrued round them.

The general critique of romanticism can well be illustrated by the discussion of Sir Walter Scott in chapter nine of *Crotchet Castle.* It is part of the conversation on the water-voyage from the Thames to North Wales. They have just gathered hazel on the grave of Rosamond at Godstow. Dr. Folliott the clergyman is talking to Lady Clarinda, with one short interpolation from Mr. Trillo the musician:

Lady Clarinda: History is but a tiresome thing in itself; it becomes more agreeable the more romance is mixed up with it. The great enchanter has made me learn many things which I should never have dreamed of studying, if they had not come to me in the form of amusement.

The Rev. Dr. Folliott: What enchanter is that? There are two enchanters: he of the North, and he of the South.

Mr. Trillo: Rossini?

The Rev. Dr. Folliott: Ay, there is another enchanter. But I mean the great enchanter of Covent Garden: he who, for more than a quarter of a century, has produced two pantomimes a year, to the delight of children of all ages, including myself at all ages. That is the enchanter for me. I am for the pantomimes. All the northern enchanter's romances put together would not furnish materials for half the southern enchanter's pantomimes.

Lady Clarinda: Surely you do not class literature with pantomime?

The Rev. Dr. Folliott: In these cases I do. They are both one, with a slight difference. The one is the literature of pantomime, the other is the pantomime of literature. There is the same variety of character, the same diversity of story, the same copiousness of incident, the same research into costume, the same display of heraldry, falconry, minstrelsy, scenery, monkery, witchery, devilry, robbery, poachery, piracy, fishery, gipsy-astrology, demonology, architecture, fortification, castrametation, navigation; the same running base of love and battle. The main dif-

East India House, headquarters of the East India Company, around 1825.

ference is, that the one set of amusing fictions is told in music and action; the other in all the worst dialects of the English language. As to any sentence worth remembering, any moral or political truth, any thing having a tendency, however remote, to make men wiser or better, to make them think, to make them even think of thinking; they are both precisely alike: *nuspiam, nequaquam, nullibi, nullimodis.*

Lady Clarinda: Very amusing, however.

The Rev. Dr. Folliott: Very amusing, very amusing.

There is a whole view of Scott, presented, left poised for consideration; it is not tediously thrashed-out; but at once Mr. Chainmail rides in on his own particular hobby-horse and picks up the talk with: 'My quarrel with the northern enchanter is, that he has grossly misrepresented the twelfth century.' 'He has misrepresented everything,' says Folliott, 'or he would not have been very amusing.'

I have the thankless task of doing what Peacock never did, the task of underlining what is said and remarking that it is ultimately serious and important to declare in such a way that Scott is not ultimately serious and important, and that there is a distinction to be drawn always between amusement literature and literature with higher claims. The 'amusement' side of medievalising romanticism has there been caught once and for all; and even if there is scope for disagreement about its application to Scott, the terms of reference are apparent. It is in this art of presenting a point of view that Peacock excels, presenting it so that it is pointed and memorable and stays in the mind as a sort of critical touchstone; and he nowhere does it better than in his views of the Romantics. Perhaps the best place of all is the famous passage in the eleventh chapter of *Nightmare Abbey.* The Byronic view is put by Mr. Cypress in a speech which is an acknowledged paraphrase of parts of Canto Four of *Childe Harold:*

> *Mr. Cypress:* Human Love! Love is not an inhabitant of the earth. We worship him as the Athenians did their unknown God: but broken hearts are the martyrs of his faith, and the eye shall never see the form which phantasy paints, and which passion pursues through paths of delusive beauty, among flowers whose odours are agonies, and trees whose gums are poison.

> *Mr. Hilary:* You talk like a Rosicrucian, who will love nothing but a sylph, who does not believe in the existence of a sylph, and who yet quarrels with the whole universe for not containing a sylph.

A whole long chapter of Professor Irving Babbitt says little more.

Then a little further on comes the Litany of Melancholy from all the party:

> *Mr. Toobad:* How can we be cheerful with the devil among us?

> *The Hon. Mr. Listless:* How can we be cheerful when our nerves are shattered?

> *Mr. Flosky:* How can we be cheerful when we are surrounded by a *reading public* that is growing too wise for its betters?

> *Scythrop:* How can we be cheerful when our great general designs are crossed every moment by our little particular passions?

The mind is suddenly held up and stops: it is the one question of Shelley's life.

But this quotation has also brought to light one of Peacock's failures. He hit the nail on the head again and again in dealing with the forms of Romanticism he observed in Shelley and Byron, he was sometimes well on the head with Wordsworth and Southey; but he always mis-hit over Coleridge. His instinct forbade him to leave Coleridge alone, and he recurs to him in book after book as if he were always determined to obliterate his last failure. There are four distinct attempts to put something of the Coleridge point of view—in the mouth of Mr. Panscope in *Headlong Hall,* in Mr. Mystic in *Melincourt,* in Mr. Flosky in *Nightmare Abbey* and in Mr. Skionar in *Crotchet Castle;* there is not much to choose between them, though perhaps Mr. Mystic is the worst; there are a few good verbal jokes round Mr. Flosky, as when he is made to speak 'in a tone of ruefulness most jeremytaylorically pathetic', but the joke is so monotonously directed against Coleridge's transcendental 'obscurity' that we are forced to the conclusion that Peacock had never really tried to understand one of his works; he was writing too plainly from hearsay. It is a serious failure, and points plainly to Peacock's limitations. He did not really understand or care about philosophy; he never dealt with the deeper and more exacting struggles of thought but only with thought as it emerged into opinion or emotional attitude. Or it is perhaps fairer to say that he was temperamentally better able to follow the processes of empirical thought, with the result that his utilitarians and economists declare more of themselves than his Coleridges; the opinions of Mr. Fax do reveal something of the means by which they have been reached; but Mr. Mystic's never do.

This means that Peacock was disqualified from apprehending all the significant features of his age; but much can be forgiven him because of his alertness to so much; he was doing in his own medium the same sort of thing that Hazlitt was doing in the essays that were published as *The Spirit of the Age;* and Hazlitt is the best introduction to Peacock. What neither of them could do was done by John Stuart Mill's two essays on Bentham and Coleridge. Between the three of them there was the material for a great analytical satire that none of them ever wrote; yet in a way Peacock was nibbling at it all his life. *Headlong Hall, Melincourt* and *Nightmare Abbey* are all products of a single impulse and have very little separate artistic being—even those who know them well find it hard to remember exactly which characters come in which, and many are interchangeable; it seems an accident that these should have been written and published as three separate works. And *Crotchet Castle,* coming thirteen years later than *Nightmare Abbey,* is a sort of admission that the original impulse had not achieved its proper expression. Peacock needed some one big work on the scale of Rabelais'. Recurrent all through his books are quotations from Rabelais, references to him and even long imitations of him. It is, of course, no more possible to say that Peacock was consciously modelling his whole work on Rabelais than to say that he was modelling it on Aristophanes, or on *Hudibras* Butler or on Voltaire; there are a number of contributory streams of influence, and there is plenty of evidence that Peacock was aware of them all. But I mean to suggest that the proper fulfilment of his purposes would have been a work more like that of Rabelais than like that of anyone else, a huge, voraciously inclusive satire, ranging everywhere and getting its unity from its energy and range. For he was a viewer of a phase of civilisation, the recorder of its moods and idioms and opinions; and he switches his point of view with each of his talkers. The point for a moment is Mr. Toobad's:

> The devil has come among us, and has begun by taking possession of all the cleverest fellows. Yet,

forsooth, this is an enlightened age. Marry, how? Did our ancestors go peeping about with dark lanterns, and do we walk at our ease in broad sunshine? Where is the manifestation of our light? By what symptoms do you recognise it? What are its signs, its tokens, its symptoms, its symbols, its categories, its conditions? What is it, and why? How, where, when is it to be seen, felt, and understood? What do we see by it which our ancestors saw not, and which at the same time is worth seeing? We see a hundred men hanged, where they saw one. We see five hundred transported, where they saw one. We see five thousand in the workhouse, where they saw one. We see scores of Bible Societies, where they saw none. We see paper, where they saw gold. We see men in stays, where they saw men in armour. We see painted faces, where they saw healthy ones. We see children perishing in manufactories, where they saw them flourishing in the fields. We see prisons, where they saw castles. We see masters, where they saw representatives. In short, they saw true men, where we see false knaves. They saw Milton, and we see Mr. Sackbut.

This whole comparative view—it is like Pugin's *Contrasts*—never quite has its scope in Peacock; it seems asking for something bigger than he is able to give it, and for an energy that he has not quite got. He never quite becomes a satirist; he hasn't the anger and he shirks the bawdry; but within his limits he goes, as a critic, to the spots that others have only reached since by more laborious means. He saw that the symbol of one side of his age was the workhouse, of another the steamboat, of another the skull. His own preference was for a skull full of Madeira. (pp. 997-98).

> Humphry House, *"The Novels of Thomas Love Peacock," in* The Listener, *Vol. XLII, No. 1089, December 8, 1949, pp. 997-98.*

EDMUND WILSON (essay date 1950)

[*Wilson is generally considered twentieth-century America's foremost man of letters. A prolific reviewer, creative writer, and social and literary critic endowed with formidable intellectual powers, he exercised his greatest literary influence as the author of* Axel's Castle *(1931), a seminal study of literary symbolism, and as the author of widely read reviews and essays in which he introduced the best works of modern literature to the reading public. In the following excerpt from a revised version of a 1947 review of* The Pleasures of Peacock, *a newly published sampler of Peacock's work, Wilson examines both the unique appeal and the substantial limitations of the satirist's novels.*]

An omnibus of Thomas Love Peacock, under the title *The Pleasures of Peacock,* has been brought out by a New York publisher. It is a good thing to have these novels reprinted, and Mr. Ben Ray Redman, who has edited the volume, contributes a well-informed introduction that touches briefly on almost every side of Peacock. But this book has what seems to me the serious defect of being mainly a collection of excerpts. Only two novels are given complete: *Nightmare Abbey* and *Crotchet Castle.* The other five appear merely in selections. Now, it is true that from one point of view Peacock lends himself easily to anthologizing: his plots are not usually important, and his narrative is a loose series of episodes. Yet each of his books as a whole shows the same delicate sense of form as each of the episodes and each of the sentences, and it is a pity to take them to pieces—especially since they are all so short that it was possible, in a thin-paper edition published

some years ago, to include the complete novels in one pocket-size volume. It is also rather unfair, it seems to me, to shear off, as Mr. Redman has done, all the quotations that head Peacock's chapters, and to trim away a part of his learned notes. The main text can stand without them, but they do represent the soil out of which that text has grown and help to situate Peacock's mood in an early-nineteenth-century library, where the Greek and Latin classics are mingled with Italian light comedies and the wild folk ballads of Wales. Surely anyone who can care for Peacock would prefer to have him intact.

The Pleasures of Peacock, however, serve to remind us, in any case, of a very fine writer and to offer a pretext for talking about him. We have already seen one revival of Peacock—during the twenties, when J. B. Priestley did a book about him [see excerpt dated 1927] and when Aldous Huxley gave him some vogue by deliberately imitating him. The element that Huxley exploited was the characteristic Peacock symposium: the conversation in a country house, with much passing of port and claret, among highly intellectual guests, each of whom appears as the exponent of some current tendency or doctrine reduced to its simplest terms and carried to its most absurd lengths. This is the critical side of Peacock, for which he is now perhaps most famous because Huxley has seized upon it, injected into it moral earnestness and transposed it into a peevish key. But it is by no means the whole of Peacock, as one can see by comparing him and Huxley. With the later as with the earlier writer, the opinions of the various philosophers more or less cancel one another out; but for Huxley this leads to bitterness and a demand for religious certainties, whereas in Peacock it leads to a final drink and a song in which everyone joins. And this fencing by Peacock's cranks with rigid contradictory ideas—excellent sometimes, of course, but not always remarkably clever—is hardly enough to have preserved him so long. What is it, then, that makes Peacock live? Why is it that Mr. Redman believes that we can still enjoy reading his novels?

Another critic, Mr. Ronald Mason, asked this question three years ago in the English review *Horizon,* and, after discounting almost every source of interest that one may expect to find in a novel, came to the conclusion that Peacock's strength lay mainly in his firmness as a nipper of extremes and in his admirable prose style [see excerpt dated 1944]. Both these merits Peacock certainly had. It was a godsend that in the early nineteenth century, with its seraphic utopianisms, its attitudinizing anti-social romanticisms and its cannibalistic materialisms, one man who had the intelligence to understand and the aesthetic sensibility to appreciate the new movements and the new techniques that were going to people's heads, should have been able to apply to their extravagances a kind of classical common sense; and Peacock's value, as Mr. Mason suggests, should by no means be less today, at a time when extreme ideas are being violently put into practice. As for his style: to the mature reader, whom mere sonority and movement and color do not intoxicate as they did in youth, it seems one of the best in English. Light, lucid, neat and dry, it is as far from the prose of his own period, mossily clogged or grassily luxuriating, as from the showy upholstery of the later age. It redeems him from insipidity at the moments when he is running thinnest; it gives charm to his most telling jokes by slipping them in with a minimum of emphasis. "Nothing superfluous and nothing wanting" was the comment of India House on the papers that won Peacock his job there. If one compares him, particularly, with Thackeray, who liked his work and who is sometimes praised for qualities similar to his, one is struck by the relative coarseness of the texture of the Victorian's writing, with its dilutions and its repetitions, and by the relative commonplaceness of his mind, with its worldly preoccupations and its embarrassing exhibitions of benevolence. When we come to Peacock from this, we are aware of his restraint and distinction, of the spareness and sureness of the pencil which he uses for his prose line-drawings.

This brings us to an aspect of Peacock which Mr. Mason leaves out of account. The fact that Peacock's *imagination* is not vigorous, varied or rich has, I believe, rather kept people from realizing how exquisite his effects sometimes are. It is usual to treat him as a satirist whose power is more or less weakened by his scoring off both sides of every question; but the truth is that Peacock is an artist the aim of whose art is to achieve not merely a weaving of ideas but also an atmosphere—an aroma, a flavor, a harmony. You get closer to what Peacock is trying to do by approaching him through his admiration for Mozart—"There is," he wrote, "nothing perfect in this world except Mozart's music"— than by assimilating him to Lucian or Voltaire. His books are more like light operas than novels (it was quite natural that *Maid Marian* should have been made into one) and the elements of fantasy with which they play— the civilized orangutan of *Melincourt*, who is chivalrous with the ladies, the seven lovely maidens of *Gryll Grange* who keep house for the young man in the tower—as well as the landscapes of mountain streams, the drives and rides in the New Forest, the boating and skating parties, are as important as the conversations. It all makes a delicious music, at the same time sober and gay, in which the words fall like notes from a flute, like progressions on an old-fashioned pianoforte, lighted by slim white candles. In *Gryll Grange,* when we come to the snowstorm, we almost have the illusion that these pale and sifted words of Peacock's are dropping on the page like snowflakes and that they melt away as we read. Even the openings of Peacock's unfinished novels—so sure is his touch on the keyboard to convey us at once to his realm—may be enjoyed as little works in themselves, like the "preludes" of Debussy or Chopin.

It seems to me, too, that the nonchalance of Peacock in dealing with political and moral systems has been given a wrong meaning by his critics—for he is always, in some way, on the *human* side, and he shared the generous ideas of the romantic and utopian generation to an extent that his conservative encomiasts are sometimes reluctant to recognize. I have a suspicion that the relative indifference of the typical Peacockian to *Melincourt* may be partly due to the fact that the hero of this early novel gives expression to such ideas with an eloquence which can almost be called glowing and which suggests real conviction on Peacock's part. The book does go on a little too long, for Peacock has not yet quite found his form; but it is certainly one of his best—with its gentleman anthropoid, its beautiful blue-stocking oread, its forthright and very funny satire on rotten-borough politics and the publishing business, and its admirable discussion, at the end, under the title *The Hopes of the World,* of the future of civilization. Mr. Redman could not have remembered *Melincourt* when he wrote in his introduction in such a way as to give the impression that Peacock's friendship with Shelley is only to be explained on the ground of the attraction of opposites. The creator of the Rousseauist Mr. Forester had no difficulty in sympathizing with the poet's utopian yearnings toward a happier and freer society. It was only that he could not help kidding his friend in the skit of *Nightmare Abbey*—the dry diagnosis of which is a corrective to more impassioned portraits—for the self-delusions of Shelley in his childish relations with women; and that the cool human sympathy I have spoken of compelled him to defend Harriet—in his **"Memoirs of Percy Bysshe Shelley"**—against the slanders of the Shelley-worshippers.

The mountain-loving Anthelia of *Melincourt* is one of Peacock's most attractive versions of his ideal young Englishwoman—always a strongly positive element in his stories. These girls of his—frank, independent, brave, intelligent and rather intellectual—stand somewhere between the heroines of Shelley and the heroines of Jane Austen. I find them a great deal more attractive, as well as a great deal more convincing, than the women of Victorian fiction. That these latter could not have been found particularly sympathetic by Peacock may be concluded from the unfinished *Cotswold Chace,* in which he is careful to explain that his heroine "wears no crinoline, and, if I might venture to divine, no stays." It is obvious that Peacock's young girls—witty, athletic and fresh—are the mothers of the anti-Victorian goddesses of his son-in-law George Meredith's novels.

The later Peacock was less interested in reformers, less "progressive" and less optimistic. But it is true, as Mr. Redman reminds us, that he had already in the sixties lived long enough to see a great many reforms accomplished but life rendered rather less agreeable than it had been in the early years of the century, and to foresee the mechanical developments—prophesied in *Gryll Grange*—which were to increase men's productive powers and at the same time to reduce them to bondage. When he had retired from his job at India House, he took his family to live in the country, where he spent most of his time with books—though he liked to go to visit Lord Broughton, who, as John Hobhouse, had been Byron's friend and who could give Peacock the good entertainment and the free-ranging conversation with which he had filled his novels. Thackeray met Peacock once in 1850 and called him "a white-headed jolly old worldling"; but he was never really a Thackeray character. He was not worldly in Thackeray's sense. The world he loved was the world of his library—to which he fled when, at the age of eighty, he was warned that the house was on fire, declaring, when they tried to get him out: "By the immortal gods, I will not move!" He was upset when his favorite daughter, who had been educated, on the model of his heroines, both in literature and in outdoor sports and who is said to have been both brilliant and beautiful, married the young George Meredith. Meredith wore a beard, which Peacock could not abide; and, though the young man respected his father-in-law and was influenced in his own work by Peacock's, his ardors, energetic and uneasy, annoyed the old man and made him nervous. It was quite a different thing from Shelley.

Nor did Meredith and his bride get along together. They were both sharp-tongued and self-willed, and they had very little money to live on. They tormented one another unbearably. Mary Meredith, at the end of nine years, ran away to Capri with another man, but soon came back to die in England. Peacock, then seventy-nine, did not go to her funeral, but he composed for her an epitaph in Latin and Greek, which was never inscribed on her grave. Meredith published soon after, as a commentary on his tragic marriage, the great sequence of sonnets called *Modern Love,* full of self-probings and passionate frustrations of a kind that must have been inconceivable to Peacock; and when one glances back on this mid-century Peacock from the point of view of *Modern Love,* one seems to see an old man in a bottle, whose unshakable poise and calm depend on his not coming out.

For when we look back on Peacock from Meredith's time instead of seeing him in the dawn of the century, he seems to us less mobile and cooler. Peacock's father was a dealer in glassware, and there is sometimes a glint of glassware in the clear, sound and smooth work of Peacock. The editors of the Halliford Edition of Peacock have included in his last novel, *Gryll Grange,* a peculiarly appropriate frontispiece which shows a spun-glass bust of Homer that Peacock had hung in his library. It makes us reflect that the classics in Peacock's hands do a little take on the aspect of having been deftly spun into glass; and his own work may look to us at moments like a fine antique sideboard display, with rows of graceful flower-calyxed goblets all ready for the very best wine—which you will have to buy from somebody else: somebody like Meredith or Shelley. In the meantime, however, Peacock can elicit from them a very pretty music by delicately moistening the rims and rubbing them with the tips of his fingers. (pp. 404-11)

> Edmund Wilson, *"The Musical Glasses of Peacock," in his* Classics and Commercials: A Literary Chronicle of the Forties, *Farrar, Straus and Company, 1950, pp. 404-11.*

KINGSLEY AMIS (essay date 1955)

[*A distinguished English novelist, poet, essayist, and editor, Amis was one of the Angry Young Men, a group of British writers of the 1950s whose writings expressed bitterness and disillusionment with society. Common to the work of the Angry Young Men is an antihero who rebels against a corrupt social order in a quest for personal integrity. Amis's first and most widely praised novel,* Lucky Jim *(1954), is characteristic of the school and demonstrates his skill as a satirist. Amis has since rejected categorization or alliance with any literary group and maintains that he is only interested in following his artistic instincts. In his review of a modern reprint of* Maid Marian *and* Crotchet Castle, *Amis calls for a revaluation of Peacock's novels.*]

Until about twenty years ago, Peacock was still getting his fair share of literary attention, in quantity at any rate: the big scholarly Halliford edition was still coming out in the 1930s, and at that time the belletristic belt was kept rolling merrily along with stuff about his connections with Wales and his friendship with Shelley. More recently there has been a recession in this line, while no modern critic that I know of has thrown more than a passing glance towards Peacock's work. It may be that the obvious joviality of most of that work, coupled with an absence of complexity and of the dark night of the soul, has put off some possible investigators; others may have decided, with some show of reason, that any friend of Shelley's could be no friend of theirs. However this may be, when we pick up the nice new Macmillan reprint of *Maid Marian* and *Crotchet Castle,* we find old George Saintsbury still occupying the Introduction, just as he did in the printing of sixty years ago.

Now there is clearly much to be said for this arrangement and for Saintsbury himself, who was debarred by nature from writing anything not worth reading, and is typically judicious here in his account of Peacockian ingredients and formulas. He goes as far and as amiably as most university students, and many general readers, will probably require. Talents far more extraordinary than his, on the other hand, would have been needed to prevent much of what he says from dating, in particular a mysterious remark about Peacock's letters to Lord Broughton being inaccessible 'for another half-dozen years,' which time has robbed of topicality. And talking of dating, was it really necessary to reproduce here F. H. Townsend's truly horrible

illustrations to the old edition, with their olio of Rossetti and 1890s *Punch*? If book-illustration is coming back, as some signs indicate, surely someone on the pay-roll of the *Radio Times* or of some hot-drink manufacturer could have been called in to replace Townsend? It wouldn't have been much trouble, any more than it would have been much trouble to announce the identity of the 'G.' who indefatigably footnotes the anachronisms of *Maid Marian.*

It may reasonably be objected that this doesn't really matter, that this reprint has made two of the novels more easily available (in a pleasant binding) and that's what counts. I agree in a way. At the same time, if criticism is any use at all, I do feel that the expense of printing a new Introduction, at any rate, could reasonably have been borne and that a small cheque could have coaxed somebody a bit younger than Saintsbury into turning out a few thousand words which might have done something towards re-examining Peacock, towards seeing how he stands up to recent changes in taste and critical approach. Such an effort, such a revival of interest, would be worth while, I think, if only because its subject is almost the only nineteenth-century novelist free of what one might call the puffing and blowing so sadly common in the fiction of his age—and of our own.

The first thing, of course, would be to throw out the notion, popular with Saintsburyite devotees of the printed word, that all Peacock's novels are good, that although *Maid Marian* may not be everybody's cup of tea and *Melincourt* drags here and there, the whole thing is much of a muchness. It would be more reasonable to argue that what we really have is a wild disparity between different books and sometimes between parts of the same book, and an uncertainty on Peacock's part, never resolved or else resolved in the wrong way, about what he was trying for and what he was good at. There is no point, at this date, in glossing over the tedium of a great part of his work, in failing to recognise straightaway, for example, that *The Misfortunes of Elphin* is not superior enough to *Maid Marian* to make much odds and that both are fatally injured by whimsy and quaintness, by cumbersome ironising on modern life and, especially in *Elphin,* by those erudition-exercises which will wring a repeated groan from any but the most addicted reader. This last defect, no doubt the result of Peacock's being what we have been taught to call an autodidact, comes near to ruining whole areas of nearly all the novels, not only through the mouths of those awful old gasbags the Reverend Doctors Folliott and Opimian, but in the author's personal commentary as well. It could be suggested, though, that none of this is really radical, and that the real trouble is to be found somewhere in Peacock's very conception of his own talents. He was never at his best, I think, as a pure satirist, or anyway not as the sort of satirist he spent most time on trying to be: the persecutor of learned fools who condemn themselves by their own utterances.

A line must be drawn somewhere between the living and the faded parts of his work, but merely to draw that line between living and faded targets of ridicule—between, say, the Shelley bits in *Nightmare Abbey* and Mr. MacQuedy's political economy in *Crotchet Castle*—would not be quite adequate. To throw in a reflection on Peacock's inordinate capacity for simple diffuseness and repetition would have the advantage of helping to get *Melincourt* and *Gryll Grange* out of the way (where they belong), but would be little use on the harder questions. What can we turn to next, then? To plot *versus* no plot? No: the answer that appeals to me is that Peacock was only at his best in farcical-sentimental comedy with a satiric background. The moment the satirist holds the stage he makes a dive for the lectern, and the reader, unfortified with cold fowl and Madeira, spreads a handkerchief over his face.

With *Headlong Hall,* accordingly, the obvious point to make is not that there is something intrinsically absurd about picturesque gardening which helps on the satire, but that the whole business leads up to, and is justified by, the demolition which blows Mr. Cranium into the lake; similarly, Mr. Escot is not just a deteriorationist, but a deteriorationist comically in love. And in *Nightmare Abbey,* again, although all the raillery about romanticism has the advantage of bearing on something fairly durable in ideas and conduct—and Mr. Hilary's objections to the ideology which 'quarrels with the whole universe for not containing a sylph' are much more penetrating than most raillery—yet we can all agree that it would have little force if it were not made to focus upon Scythrop, whose antics are constantly being pulled across the border into farce, the domain where the amatory and moral themes of the book, remaining recognisable and indeed perfectly serious, are finally clinched. And in *Crotchet Castle*—who wouldn't consent to liquidating that whole tribe of after-dinner lecturers for the sake of a few more pages of the matchless Clarinda taking the stuffing out of Captain Fitzchrome? Those scenes show Peacock in possession of something he never quite found again: a delightful airy felicity which looks back to Congreve and forward to Wilde:

> Do you know, though Mammon has a sort of ill name, I really think he is a very popular character; there must be at the bottom something amiable about him. He is certainly one of those pleasant creatures whom everybody abuses, but without whom no evening party is endurable. I daresay, love in a cottage is very pleasant; but then it positively must be a cottage *ornée:* but would not the same love be a great deal safer in a castle, even if Mammon furnished the fortification? . . . A dun is a horridly vulgar creature; it is a creature I cannot endure the thought of: and a cottage lets him in so easily. Now a castle keeps him at bay. You are a half-pay officer, and are at leisure to command the garrison: but where is the castle? and who is to furnish the commissariat?

Passages like that, together with almost the whole of *Headlong Hall* and *Nightmare Abbey,* entitle Peacock to his place as a minor master—and as somebody far more energetically original than the chorus of drowsy Victorian and Edwardian eulogy would imply. That enchanting urbanity, which gave him command of a whole range between witty seriousness and demented knockabout, was something which disappeared from the English novel almost before it had properly arrived. (pp. 402-04)

Kingsley Amis, "Laugh When You Can," in The Spectator, *Vol. 194, No. 6614, April 1, 1955, pp. 402-04.*

A. E. DYSON (essay date 1965)

[*Dyson is an English editor and literary critic who once described himself as a "liberal humanist," but now considers himself a "Christian." During the 1970s he said, "The great need for the times, as I see it, is a Christian critique of our civilisation, to challenge secularism, and restore confidence in love, and hope, in a darkening world." In the following excerpt, Dyson examines the clash between realism and idyllic fantasy in Peacock's novels.*]

Peacock's frivolity is central . . . [to his] works; but is it incompatible with the serious ironic intention which we sometimes discern? The problem is forced upon us by the very nature of Peacock's method, which is to collect a number of individuals with interesting hobby-horses, and to race them against one another in a kind of caucus-race of the mind. The detached amusement with which this race is commented upon suggests a certain superior reasonableness in the author; whose pose may be less Olympian than Gibbon's, yet has an urbane self-assurance of its own. What we appear to be offered is the reassertion of commonsense over wild intellectualism, a two-sides-to-every-question geniality, steering all sharp exchanges towards the safety of sport. The very setting is attuned to this kind of resolution. In *Headlong Hall* Squire Headlong drinks his Burgundy in rural intactness, his Horatian well-being an ambience where all crankiness is baptised and absorbed. In *Crotchet Castle* the 'schemes for the world's regeneration' evaporate 'in a tumult of voices', as Mr Crotchet's 'matchless claret' has its destined effect.

All of which is abundantly pleasant; and surely too pleasant to be intruded upon by any morose reflections which the sober moralist may entertain? Yet the moralist has his right to be heard, and indeed must be heard, if the right kind of claim for Peacock is in the end to be made. The 'wand of enchantment' which Mr Milestone flourishes is Peacock's also; he creates a world for our pleasure, more idyllic, for all its irony, than the world as it actually is. We submit to his spell as we read, and are properly grateful; yet if we submit too completely, we may overlook how much is surrendered by the admirably genial tone. The mental sharpness which any totally satisfying irony must have is surrendered; and so is the radicalism from which this irony, in particular, often pretends to spring. Peacock's characters are not 'good' or 'bad' in any serious sense . . . ; they are morally neutral in themselves, whatever the implications for good or ill in their ideas. They are more-or-less eccentric, more-or-less loveable cranks; or alternatively, more-or-less eccentric, more-or-less loveable cynics, resisting crankiness in the name of common sense, good humour and port. Peacock's own *persona* veers in different novels between the two: in Mr Hilary of *Nightmare Abbey* he puts himself in the latter camp, but in Dr Folliott of *Crotchet Castle* and the Reverend Dr Opimian of *Gryll Grange* (both part *personae*) he moves somewhat the other way. A revealing remark about Dr Folliott is made by Lady Clarinda: 'He is of an admirable temper, and says rude things in a pleasant, half-earnest manner, that no-body can take offense with.' This 'manner' is one which Peacock clearly admired; yet how much complacency, how much insensitivity, how much intransigent reaction, must it have sanctioned in its time?

The setting is attuned, then, to Peacock's temperament; and so is his characteristic handling of ideas. He hardens ideas towards absurdity, as politicians harden one another's policies in election year. There is little regard for truth, and none for fairness. To make the ideas amusing, and therefore impossible, is the sole intent. (pp. 61-2)

[The ideas] need, for Peacock's purpose, to be both simplified and arrested: simplified so that original notions sound wildly eccentric; and arrested so that one simplified idea can clash with its opposite to the greatest effect. The result falls far short, one need scarcely add, of synthesis; and still further short of the point where any meaningful action might occur. It guarantees that no synthesis or action will ever be possible—not, that is to say, while Peacock's geniality can keep its hold.

In itself, the technique can be amusing, and not unsubtle—as in this exchange in *Nightmare Abbey,* when Scythrop and his father clash over a choice of bride (Mr Glowry speaks first).

> 'Sir, I have pledged my honour to the contract—the honour of the Glowries of Nightmare Abbey: and now, sir, what is to be done?'

> 'Indeed, sir, I cannot say. I claim, on this occasion, that liberty of action which is the co-natal prerogative of every rational being.'

> 'Liberty of action, sir? there is no such thing as liberty of action. We are all slaves and puppets of a blind and unpathetic necessity.'

> 'Very true, sir; but liberty of action, between individuals, consists in their being differently influenced, or modified, by the same universal necessity; so that the results are unconsentaneous, and their respective necessitated volitions clash and fly off in a tangent.'

> 'Your logic is good, sir; but you are aware, too, that one individual may be a medium of adhibiting to another a mode or form of necessity, which may have more or less influence in the production of consentaneity; and, therefore, sir, if you do not comply with my wishes in this instance (you have had your own way in everything else), I shall be under the necessity of disinheriting you, though I shall do it with tears in my eyes.' Having said these words, he vanished suddenly, in the dread of Scythrop's logic.

Ostensibly, this is an intellectual discussion depending on logic; obliquely, it is a clash of wills, conveyed to us precisely through the exuberant irrelevance of the ideas. The fun is beautifully managed, with Peacock's usual side-glances at transcendental long-windedness, yet the ideas are totally sacrificed to the humour of the situation itself. And why not, when Peacock writes as amusingly as this?—except that one would like to be sure that the author realises the limits, as well as the possibilities, of his technique. Our suspicion is that he does not realise the limits; that he mistakes his skill in having fun with ideas for serious satire against the ideas themselves. He misunderstands, it sometimes seems, his actual target—which is not a variety of ideas, but one kind of person: the person who talks rather than acts, and is superficial in his talk. The various incarnations by which Shelley and Coleridge are pursued through his writings are always amusing; but does he realise that they are not Shelley and Coleridge? Does he see that they are, rather, undergraduates talking Shelley and Coleridge?—talking fluently and pretentiously, and with all the major ideas just slightly askew?

Did Peacock realise, in fact, that Shelley really was an exceptional man, for all his absurdities, and that Coleridge (to use Mill's tribute) was one of the two great seminal minds of his age? This matter is clearly important, for though there is nothing objectionable in caricature recognised as caricature, there is certainly something objectionable in caricature parading as satiric truth. And Peacock himself may not have known this; there is no evidence that he understood the nature of a truly original or speculative mind. He had little understanding of which questions were really worth asking, or of which kinds of enquiry might lead towards truth. He had no insight into which kinds of originality might be productive. The charlatan and the scientist, to him, were entirely the same.

Mr Cranium in *Headlong Hall* is an interesting instance; Mr Cranium's theory, it will be remembered, is that our behaviour is largely determined by bumps. He lectures on this theme with amusing pedantry, and what he says, one agrees, is almost self-evidently absurd. Yet *is* it as absurd as we think it?—or is it the kind of absurdity which might be a growing pain for truth? Mr Cranium was wrong about bumps, and human behaviour cannot be related to them; it can, however, be related to genes, though Mr Cranium was naturally in no position to know about these. His search for some physical link was, however, inherently plausible. Might we not see him in retrospect as a transitional figure between magic and science—a necessary link, even, between the astrologer, and the molecular biologist of today?

My contention is not that there are no Mr Craniums in the world we live in, for clearly there are, and every bit as silly as Peacock makes out. It is, rather, that there are also geniuses who superficially resemble Mr Cranium, and that Peacock makes no distinction whatever between the two. In *Nightmare Abbey* the scientific butt is Mr Asterias; and of course Mr Asterias *is* very funny, with his theory that all life evolved from the water, and his search for mermaids and tritons as a missing link. But would Peacock have seen a Mr Asterias in Darwin? It is virtually certain that he would. In *Crotchet Castle* Mr Firedamp's remedy for malaria is remarkably funny, and it is no doubt unfortunate, for Peacock at least, that it also turned out to be true. And Mr Toogood's political theories are 'the strangest of the lot', as Captain Fitzchrome points out: 'He wants to parcel out the world into squares like a chess-board, with a community on each, raising every thing for one another.'

If Peacock had lived in the twentieth century, Freud would have been a godsend to him, while Professor Fleming's early experiments with penicillin would have exhibited just the kind of absurdity he relished most. And this, really, is why a moral point about him cannot be evaded: he makes his cranks representative of the men who shape destiny, as cosy reactionaries nearly always do.

I have suggested that Peacock failed to distinguish between genius and crankiness. He failed also, from his own point of view more disastrously, to distinguish between complacency and common sense. You have only to compare him with Johnson, whom he sometimes paraphrased and obviously admired, to make this failure almost embarrassingly clear. In the writings of Johnson there is always a vital distinction between ills such as death, which we must learn to accept, however painfully, and ills such as poverty, against which we must never cease to campaign. From the former we can learn fortitude, from the latter justice; and the two together form part of a true 'commonsense'. Common sense, as Johnson conceives it, is a kind of wisdom: a distillation of human experience over the ages, a codification of all that is fine. To turn from this concept to Peacock's is to turn from human greatness to the smug complacency which 'commonsense' usually is. Peacock sees little difference, as facts that must be accepted, between death and poverty; since both are part of the world we live in, to protest against either would be somewhat absurd. His acceptance of class distinctions is everywhere apparent, in the early and more 'radical' works like *Melincourt,* as well as in *Crotchet Castle* and *Gryll Grange*, where resistance to social change has turned into a major theme. And with the acceptance of class distinctions, there is acceptance of the social *status quo*. In *Melincourt*, it is true, a corrupt clergyman is satirised for his attacks on education, but in *Crotchet Castle* the pendulum has swung the other way. This time it is Lord Brougham who is satirised, for his efforts to spread education to the workers. It has dawned upon Peacock that if you educate people they might get ideas above their station. They might even be disruptive to the people who have educated them: and this, Peacock's brand of radicalism cannot be expected to endorse.

Exactly here, I think, we have a clue to our ambivalence about Peacock: I speak for myself, of course, but I fancy that many modern readers might feel the same. The more realistic he is, the less we like him; for the more realistic he is, the more conscious we become of basic assumptions with which it is impossible to agree. The nearer he moves, however, to idyll and fantasy, the greater his hold on our imagination, and indeed on our affection, becomes. As a realist he is reactionary, and his tone, when it fails to be genial, can sound harsh and false. As a writer of idyll and fantasy, he is a great entertainer; and the entertainment has its own pleasantness, its own validity, its own proper tone.

I want in conclusion to develop this distinction, and to suggest that Peacock is a reactionary writer whom his greatest opponents can still, however, enjoy. Even in *Melincourt,* reactionary habits of mind proliferate, despite the attack on slavery, which Peacock vigorously and honestly launched. The Anti-Saccarine Fête, it will be remembered, is part of a boycott; sugar is a West Indian product, and Mr Forester sees the boycott as a means of resisting slavery from home. But the Fête, though launched as a boycott, turns into a feast; and the manner in which even Mr Forester thinks of it suggests something less than wholehearted commitment to a cause. When ills nearer home are mentioned, the radical impulses appear to have expended themselves. The chapters on Desmond and his family are a *locus classicus* for anyone wishing to assimilate benevolence to the political right. Desmond is driven by poverty nearly to desperation, but is rescued by the private charity of a benefactress—in this case, by the heroine of the book. The payment for charity is, of course, heartfelt gratitude; and this Desmond offers, in company with the wife and children who have been rescued along with himself. Mr Forester's approval of the whole episode is also Peacock's, and his words are worth quoting in full.

> I am no revolutionist. I am no advocate for violent and arbitrary changes in the state of society. I care not in what proportions property is divided (though I think there are certain limits which it ought never to pass, and approve the wisdom of the American laws in restricting the fortune of a private citizen to twenty thousand a year), provided the rich can be made to know that they are but stewards of the poor, that they are not to be the monopolisers of solitary spoil, but the distributors of general possession; that they are responsible for that distribution to every principle of general justice, to every tie of moral obligation, to every feeling of human sympathy: that they are bound to cultivate simple habits in themselves, and to encourage most such arts of industry and peace, as are most compatible with the health and liberty of others.

How, one wonders, can this not be ironic? But in Peacock no irony is intended, not even, I think (though I am less sure of this) in the very peculiar parenthesis about 'the wisdom of the American laws'. Mr Forester is no revolutionist, certainly, as he admits: he is, rather, the exponent of that brand of optimistic Toryism which can afford to be good-humoured and genial, as long as 'simple habits' are not interpreted in too austere a sense. A radical's irony would be certain to be at the opposite pole to this with Oscar Wilde: 'the virtues of the poor may be readily admitted, and are much to be regretted.' Has any radical

ever been able to consider the gratitude of the poor without dismay?

Crotchet Castle is altogether the harshest and least pleasing of Peacock's novels, no doubt because here the threat to benevolent Toryism is most pressingly felt. 'I am out of all patience with this march of the mind,' announces Dr Folliott. 'My cook must read his rubbish in bed; and as might naturally be expected, she dropped suddenly fast asleep, overturned the candle, and set the curtains in a blaze.' 'His rubbish' is Lord Broughams' *Observations on Education of the People,* and the effect on the cook ('naturally to be expected,' says Mr Folliott) combines the literal and symbolic dangers of education in one. Lady Clarinda, the heroine of *Crotchet Castle,* is strangely egotistical and cynical; her wit has the glitter and hardness of Restoration Comedy, yet Peacock seems to endorse it in the course of the tale. The element of farce in this novel becomes more violent. For once, someone is actually killed in the course of a brawl, but since he is only a robber, and a lower-class robber at that, we are made to feel that his death hardly counts. The attack on America, moreover, is surprisingly lacking in the urbanity we have come to expect. We are reminded, naturally enough, of *Martin Chuzzlewit,* but the similar content merely underlines the dissimilar tone. Dickens's satire originated in disappointed idealism; Peacock's is more like the stay-at-home's 'I told you so'.

In the early novels Peacock's serenity rested in the unchanging pattern of English life; given this, radicalism was a luxury he could well afford. Only later, when social change turned out to be in full flood, did he see the threat contained in it to all that he valued most. The ideas he had played with so amusingly seemed somehow less funny; they had taken hold—or some of them had—and the very world where one could laugh at them was being destroyed. In *Crotchet Castle* Peacock seems just to have made this discovery, and there is a corresponding rawness in his tone. But by the time *Gryll Grange* was written, much later in his life, he had assimilated the change, and was able to wave his wand of enchantment once again. This last novel is both his mellowest and his most purely delightful, even though his reactionary sympathies are here most openly displayed. And this, if I am right, is because he has returned from realism, or near realism, to fantasy. Once more, the mood of idyllic seclusion is fully established; the mood of Dr Opimian, indulging in his country retreat the four tastes which were so much Peacock's own: 'a good library, a good dinner, a pleasant garden, and rural walks.' Dr Opimian is not so much a benevolent Tory as a reconciled Canute; confronting the incoming tide which cannot be halted, he enjoys present good fortune all the more fully in such time as is left. His views on science are famous, and one hundred years later sound less eccentric, perhaps, than they may have done at the time:

> Science is one thing, and wisdom is another. Science is an edged tool, with which men play like children, and cut their own fingers. If you look at the results which science has brought in its train, you will find them to consist almost wholly in elements of mischief. See how much belongs to the word Explosion alone, of which the ancients knew nothing. . . . See collisions and wrecks and every mode of disaster by land and by sea, resulting chiefly from the insanity for speed, in those who for the most part have nothing to do at the end of the race, which they run as if they were so many Mercuries speeding with messages from Jupiter. . . . Look at our scientific machinery, which has destroyed domestic manufacture, which has substituted rottenness for strength in the thing

made, and physical degradation in crowded towns for healthy and comfortable country life in the makers. The day would fail, if I should attempt to enumerate the evils which science has inflicted on mankind. I almost think it is the ultimate destiny of science to exterminate the human race.

Whereas the doctrine of regress was once, for Peacock, one eccentric extreme to be played off against its opposite, it now speaks fairly directly for himself. And there are other interestingly prophetic passages in this last of the novels: Dr Opimian already foresees the pattern of Britain's declining influence in a changing world

> . . . the time will come when by mere force of numbers, the black race will predominate, and exterminate the white.

But alas for radicalism—and alas for the hope that Peacock's England might submit gracefully to the drift of world events. In the face of the threat, all Dr Opimian's reactionary prejudices float to the surface: the inferiority of foreigners (especially coloured foreigners) and the inferiority of peasants, both self-contained categories, whose emergence from obscurity can be expected to cause nothing but harm.

Yet geniality in **Gryll Grange** has re-established itself; and not least in the plot, with its total defiance of these gloomy forebodings about the great world outside. In the plot, nothing is changed: the old order is arrested at its most idyllic point, and celebrated in strains of high romance. The main frame of the novel presents us, in fact, with a choice of two idylls; the Horatian contentment of Dr Opimian in his rural seclusion, and the fairy-tale contentment of Mr Falconer, secure and studious in his 'enchanted palace', with seven chaste young ladies to order his life. The idyll of Mr Falconer, longingly though Peacock toys with it, is the one that has to yield. Peacock will believe, himself, in the bare possibility, but he knows that it is 'too good for this world'. The world will disbelieve in Mr Falconer's purity; and Mr Falconer's seven virgins *are* lower class, despite the superior education they have had. This 'superior education' is, at a more realistic level, the problem: it has unfitted the seven young ladies for their normal station, so what is a novelist responsible for them to do? If they are not to devote themselves chastely to Mr Falconer they must find other employment; but Peacock finds it hard to see what this could possibly be. Fortunately, when realism is powerless, idyll comes to the rescue. Seven virtuous young men of the virgins' own class appear, rugged and healthy, admiring and true. These young men know that the young ladies are too good for them, but are prepared to marry and cherish them just the same. 'They are so like young ladies,' as one of them puts it, 'they daze us, like.' Any italics that a modern reader is tempted to insert here are entirely his own.

With the intervention of the seven providential peasants, the other complications of personal relationship are also solved. The novel can move to its last major statement in the Aristophanic Comedy, a showing forth of the truth that for nearly two thousand years nothing has changed but for the worse. Modern music, modern cities, modern inventions, all conspire against us, in a shadowy regress which only mirth and present laughter can hold at bay.

And is this not a fitting apotheosis for Peacock himself, as well as for the last of his works? If irony cannot stop ideas and customs from changing, at least it can extract humour from them in the present that we have. To enjoy the present, to swallow up foreboding in geniality, to feast and to celebrate—

these are Peacock's gifts as a writer, the wand of enchantment which he, like his own Mr Milestone, has. And in his hands, too, the wand is a genuine magic, whether we respond to its owner's vision or not. For why should we not respond, even though our own vision may be a different one? If a man has reasonable taste and reasonable wealth; if he loves the good things of life, yet is by temperament reclusive; if he enjoys the play of ideas, but mistrusts their meanings; if he can forget the encroachments of change, and lay social conscience by: is this not a possible way for him to live, even today?

If, like Peacock, he can also amuse and entertain us, making some part of his good fortune vicariously ours, there seems every reason to accept unchurlishly what he gives. (pp. 62-71)

> *A. E. Dyson, "Peacock: The Wand of Enchantment," in his* The Crazy Fabric: Essays in Irony, *Macmillan and Co. Ltd., 1965, pp. 57-71.*

PHILIP PINKUS   (essay date 1969)

[*Pinkus explores Peacock's satire, distinguishing between his approach to the genre and that of his Augustan predecessors.*]

Thomas Love Peacock wrote in the shadow of the great satires of the Augustan age. His novels attack the same Augustan targets, make almost the same satiric comment, use an imagery that is surprisingly similar, and this one hundred years after the Augustan period. Even the tone and some aspects of the style remind one of Augustan satire. Yet the effect of Peacock's satire is very different. It has neither the thrust, nor the intensity, nor the heights and depths that give Augustan satire its enormous range, and one might well conclude that it is simply Augustan satire manqué—it has no teeth. In such situations, Swift has recommended, the satirist should "revenge that Defect with [his] Breath," and this is what Peacock appears to have done. His satire seems to exhale a kind of nitrous oxide, wafting clouds of whimsy and Arcadian tra-la-la over the reader. The effect is sometimes so gentle and disarming compared with the lacerating edge of Augustan satire, that we might question if the novels are indeed satire. But they are satire, a delicate and complex kind of satire almost unique in English literary history. Seldom has so profound a satire been so charming.

The fact that the satire of one period resembles the satire of another, in itself is not surprising. In Aristophanes' *The Clouds*, there is an image of Socrates suspended in a basket; the image is repeated in Swift's orators suspended in their oratorical machines in *A Tale of a Tub*, and in the modern egghead suspended in his ivory tower, which suggests that satiric images and targets can persist over 2500 years. There is, in fact, a remarkable similarity in the targets and images that satirists have used through the ages. It is the nature of the genre. But Peacock's satires seem to have a special relationship to the eighteenth century. He makes numerous allusions to Butler, Swift, and Pope. He quotes or sometimes playfully misquotes from a wide variety of sources, but particularly from *Hudibras* and Butler's *Miscellaneous Thoughts*, from *A Tale of a Tub* and *Cadenus and Vanessa*, from Dryden and Pope, and from two of the great inspirations of Augustan satire, Rabelais and Horace. He seems continually to be looking over his shoulder at the great satiric masters of the previous age, almost self-consciously aware that he is writing within a clearly defined satiric tradition. In effect, he assumes a familiar satiric stance that his contemporaries must have recognized instantly, despite the Peacockian manner, making them feel that they were on familiar ground.

Peacock satirized Augustan targets, however, not merely to invoke the satiric tradition but for the obvious reason that the same evils that disturbed the Augustans disturbed him also. The targets undergo a slight sea-change after a journey of one hundred years and Peacock's Romantic criteria alter the perspective considerably, but in many respects it must have seemed to Peacock that society had moved one hundred years along the path that the Augustan satirists had predepicted. The Augustan satirists dealt with a wide range of targets, including stock butts like the philosopher-pedant, the lawyer, the doctor, the soldier, the fop, the politician, and a whole army of hypocrites who are the staple diet of all satirists. Peacock took his share from the general satiric storehouse. The most persistent of all his targets is the philosopher-pedant. In fact, most of his satire is directed at the philosopher, making the traditional comment that he lives in a cloud-cuckoo land, spinning his theories out of air. The lawyer, the doctor, the soldier, and the fop, those Augustan favourites, all are found in Peacock's novels, though they are only peripheral to the satire. But Peacock's satiric comment on these targets is traditional. The lawyer's concern is only for his fee; the doctor kills more than he cures—Peacock names one of them Dr. Killquick; the soldier is a hired killer; the fop is merely a bundle of fashionable clothes and gestures; the politician is concerned with faction rather than truth, with feeding his own interests rather than those of the community. The politician is one of the main objects of Peacock's satire, as we see, for example, in *Melincourt* with the attack on Canning (Mr. Anyside Antijack) and the whole system of rotten boroughs. But it is the army of hypocrites which, in effect, is the generalized target of all satire, that becomes Peacock's most persistent centre of interest. A pervasive theme of all his satire is the difference between theory and practice. All these targets, however, are traditional to satire, and the fact that they may be found in Augustan satire as well does not in itself indicate Peacock's link to the Augustan period. They form part of the ritual of the satiric genre, inviting the reader to partake of the satiric experience.

But what gives satire its specific direction is not so much the target, nor even the usual associations of the target—for example, Dr. Killquick, the physician—but the philosophic framework in which they are put. This frequently takes the form of a comparison between the old world which the satirist proclaims and the new world which threatens to overrun the values of the old. Since the old world is usually some golden world that never existed, it does not mean that the satirist is always a conservative but that these values represent an ideal which becomes his ultimate criterion. Juvenal looked back to a Rome of heroic virtue, Horace to a world with the Stoic simplicity of his Sabine farm, Swift to a humanist world whose virtues are guarded by the early Christian fathers. The watershed which divided the old world from the new for the Augustan satirists like Swift, Pope, and Gay, is the new philosophy and the advent of science, together with a new commercial ethic. That is, they referred to a world before science and after science, before the City (the middle-class business values) came to Westminster, as we witness in Pope's *Dunciad*, and after. Peacock's satire also seems to accept the same watershed. Even though the nature of his golden world is Romantic rather than neoclassical and seems to stress a healthy, Rousseauistic primitivism rather than the Christian humanist restraint of the Augustans, it is controlled by Peacock's strong belief in the classical values of Greece and Rome which makes his criterion not very different in its satirical emphasis from that of the Augustans. That is, despite the difference in criteria,

the philosophical framework is sufficiently similar for Peacock to be making almost the same satiric comment. (pp. 64-5)

Peacock's attitude is not precisely Augustan. He obviously was absorbed in the humanist tradition of the Greek and Roman classics—his novels are filled with classical allusions—but he is influenced as much by Rousseau as by the classical moralists. He is religious only in the wildest sense of the word. He does not believe in the doctrine of original sin implicit in most Augustan satire, nor in society's institutional restraints to promote goodness. What man needs, according to Peacock, is disinterested benevolence, a value he refers to repeatedly. His novels reveal an exuberant interest in ideas, in the cultural traditions of his society, the mark of a refined sense of civilization, order, and harmony that he must have derived from his classical reading. These are some of the values he feels are threatened. They are only partially Augustan. As for the satiric targets, the new natural philosophy of the Augustan period was no longer new. Science had become a familiar and even spectacular part of Peacock's world. The new philosophy for Peacock was German transcendentalism, with its exponent, Coleridge. It seemed to Peacock to be the reverse of rationalism, to be, in fact, the abdication of all reason for the worship of mystery, jargon, and superstition. Nor is Peacock concerned with the loss of an aristocratic heritage—this is not the Romantic way. The other aspect of Augustan satire, the commercial ethic, was for Peacock not so much a matter of the City coming to Westminster, of an aristocratic heritage being overrun by the middle class, as it was of civilized values being overrun by considerations of profit and loss.

But having said this, it is worth repeating that there are sufficient similarities to justify linking Peacock with the Augustans, if only to show how from a similar base so different a satire can evolve. Though Peacock's perspective is not Swift's, his world is menaced by the same dehumanizing rationalism, the same quantitative attitude of the scientific method. In his later satires, especially *Crotchet Castle* and *Gryll Grange*, Peacock dwells on "the march of mind" and its dubious fulfillment in the Industrial Revolution. The disturbing message of *Gryll Grange* is that man is transformed by a Circean science and scientists progress into a pig, which is another Augustan equation. In his treatment of the philosophers, Peacock includes scientific rationalism within the same absurdity as German transcendentalism. (The Augustans had linked the mystical meanderings of Behmen, Paracelsus and the Rosicrucians to the Royal Society.) As in Augustan satire, rationalism is linked to the commercial ethic by the science of political economy. Peacock calls it "interest" or "persuasion in tangible shape." Mr. Mac Quedy, the political economist in *Crotchet Castle*, "turns all the affairs of this world into questions of buying and selling." Disinterested values are denied: "It is na admitted, sir, amang the pheelosophers of Edinbroo', that there is only sic thing as desenterestedness in the warld, or that a mon can care for onything sae much as his sin sel." In effect, a whole society, its literature, its aesthetics, its justice, its government, becomes for Peacock a matter of buying and selling. Man is looked upon as a marketable product, responding to no other values but his own interests. This raises the question in *Melincourt* whether or not man is significantly better than the orangutan, Sir Oran Haut-ton, M.P., and the matter is left in some doubt. Throughout all his novels Peacock is constantly discussing the opposing theories of perfectibility and deterioration, progression and regression, scientific advancement, the values of political economy, and the simple joys of the unsophisticated life with the moral and aesthetic restraints of classical learning—in effect, the new world and the old. The scale, however, is constantly tipped towards the old. Even though Peacock's golden world seems more pagan than religious, it helps create the same kind of antithetic pattern of Ancients and Moderns that we find in Augustan satire, hinged on the same targets, moving in the same satiric direction.

From the repeated allusions to Augustan satire in his novels it is obvious that Peacock knew he was continuing the same attack on the same targets. One would expect, therefore, that his satire be at least as indignant. But as I already have suggested this is not the case. It is mild, gentle, diffuse. Even in *Gryll Grange,* where he comments on the excesses of the Industrial Revolution, there is hardly a trace of *saeva indignatio.* He links the Industrial Revolution to the advance of science and the new rationalism, to the fashionable idolatry of progress and political economy, all sound Augustan targets, but he scarcely dramatizes their effects. He even manages to establish a comparison between men and pigs without sounding very angry. For an Augustan satirist, the Industrial Revolution would have been a heaven-sent opportunity to draw a powerful satiric image and drive home with corrosive force the horrors of scientific rationalism. Peacock, however, does not seem to be interested in these kinds of effects, he is writing a different kind of satire. He uses a variety of techniques, but his main device is to have his characters sit around the table over good food and good wine and have them talk. With only a few exceptions, each character represents a particular point of view or theory, based on the principle outlined by the Reverend Dr. Folliott in *Crotchet Castle:* "[The mass of mankind has] a fixed direction to their stupidity, a sort of incurable wry neck to the thing they call their understanding. So one nose points always east, and another always west, and each is ready to swear it points due north." This is the principle of the crotchet, characteristic of Peacock's novels. An item of conversation is seized upon; it might be the wine or the weather or whether or not one should dance, or it might be a somewhat loftier subject, such as the nature of man, or what constitutes human progress, or the designing of a garden, or the purpose of literary criticism. Each conversationalist approaches the subject from the point of view of his own crotchet: for example, the political economist discusses the dinner wine in relation to the national economy, the craniologist in relation to craniology. In this way Peacock can create his satire either by dramatizing the speaker's intellectual position or by examining the target argumentatively. An issue is raised, turned over, and attacked from so many different directions that the argument almost collapses of its own weight. At times it may be difficult to determine what Peacock is satirizing, or whether he is satirizing anything at all, yet the argument itself becomes a kind of madness. Peacock seems to be reasoning you into his satiric position: it is satire as dialectic.

It is a strange kind of satire, very different from our usual conception of it. Conventional satire is essentially ironic. In its simplest form, structurally, there is one sustained image of evil, growing in intensity until it reaches monstrous proportions. We see this in Dryden's poem *Mac Flecknoe.* By the time Dryden has completed the Shadwell image it is far removed from the historical fact of Shadwell, yet there is sufficient resemblance to show the connection. The satire develops through an increasing ironic divergence between what Shadwell pretends to be—a good poet—and the frightening actuality that Dryden perceives. The satiric target, therefore, is increasingly split on the two poles of the irony. (It is this incongruity which gives satire its grotesque force and makes the satiric experience so unsettling.) But in Peacock's satire the target and the image,

the two poles of the irony, are deliberately obscured, and we are less aware of a sustained ironic movement. Except for *Nightmare Abbey,* which is clearly a satire on the Gothic novel and the gloomy excesses of transcendentalism, the satiric target seems out of focus and the image of the target's evil is correspondingly blurred. Even in *Nightmare Abbey* Peacock weakens the satiric force of the image by a discursive plot, irrelevant narrative elements, and outpourings of song and verse. But in his other novels Peacock seems to scatter his satiric shots, and though there is a discernible pattern (that is, a general target can be perceived), the effect is diffuse so that we get even less sense of a developing image than in *Nightmare Abbey.* Peacock seems deliberately to avoid powerful satiric images. Where he does use imagery with satiric potential, such as the swine image in *Gryll Grange* or Sir Oran Haut-Ton, M.P., the orangutan in *Melincourt,* his treatment is almost playful, as if he does not wish to intrude emotional unpleasantness into his satires. In fact, he seems to go out of his way to muffle any cumulative satiric effect, often stopping the action abruptly for a song or a love scene or a descriptive passage of sheer romantic beauty. But it is the conversation technique itself, Peacock's major satiric device, that creates most of the diffuseness in both target and image. Whatever satiric point Peacock is trying to make is bounced on the seesaw of his dialogue, and though by the end of the novel we may know what end is up, it has been a vertiginous experience and not conducive to sharpness of irony.

One of the main purposes of satire is to show that what the satirist attacks is accepted or even admired by society. He makes his point by revealing what society actually is admiring, the evil beneath the target's respectable pose. Therefore the satirist usually casts his satire in such a way that the satiric evil is acclaimed, as Pope celebrates the coming of Dulness in *The Dunciad,* or shown to be eminently reasonable as in *A Modest Proposal,* or the logical conclusion to the social values of the moment, as in *Brave New World.* In other words, there is a prevailing pattern of what is called blame-through-praise irony, which is characteristic of most satire since 1660. But Peacock tends to avoid this kind of irony also. There are isolated instances of it, and the mock seriousness of Peacock's tone contributes to the feeling that all the idiocy he presents is profound wisdom, but in general this irony is not the effect that dominates.

All these elements in this negative definition of Peacock's satire lead to one final difference. Because there is little sense of a growing image of evil in Peacock's satires, there is no "satiric scene" as Alvin Kernan describes in *The Cankered Muse.* The "satiric scene" is Mr. Kernan's attempt to abstract, as it were, the common metaphoric elements of all satire, the overall satiric picture that satire presents. Insofar as it is possible to make such a generalization, this concept of satire has considerable validity. Mr. Kernan saw the essential elements of the satiric scene in Hieronymus Bosch's "The Carrying of the Cross," a group of peasants, almost more animal than human, thrusting into the foreground, and behind them, all but hidden by the animal congestion, is the cross itself. Many of Hogarth's sketches with their dirty, deformed humanity almost blocking out a lone church steeple on the skyline, create the same effect. To describe this effect in terms of satiric action rather than pictorially, we might say that in satire good is crowded out by the forces of evil. Despite the illusion of ridiculing the evil away, if we examine the text of satire we notice that this is not the case: the dragon kills St. George. Satire does not have a happy ending. Yet Peacock's novels do.

There are novels like Jane Austen's *Pride and Prejudice* where a sustained satiric theme is absorbed into a comic framework and everything ends happily. But the happy ending is prepared for, it is the consequence of Jane Austen's characterization and of the values the novel asserts, and we therefore call the novels comic. Other novels, like Fielding's *Jonathan Wild*, also end happily, but the ending is obviously contrived. In fact, it is so improbable, given the world that Fielding creates, that it derisively reinforces the satiric point that the villainous Jonathan Wilds of this world usually do win out. The happy endings in Peacock's novels, however, seem almost irrelevant to the satire. They do not follow from the characterization. There is scarcely enough psychological depth in most of his characters even to consider the point. It is true the happy endings seem to reinforce a consistent, positive theme in Peacock's novels which has an ironic relationship to the satire. But the link is tenuous because the ending is part of a romantic framework so artificial that it seems to be merely a structural excuse for the main burden of the novel. Ostensibly, Peacock's novels are satiric romance with the happy ending required by romance. For the most part, however, the romantic structure is barely visible. The happy ending itself becomes an ironic counterpoint to the main thrust of the satire and at the same time creates the further irony that happy endings are likely to occur only in a world of romance. Peacock never lets us forget this distinction between an artificial romantic world and the real world outside. Even though our awareness of the real world is largely implicit, it is a part of Peacock's satiric machinery, and it is in this sense that Peacock provides the traditional pattern of satire where there are no happy endings and the dragon kills St. George.

All Peacock's novels are set in some remote part of Britain, virtually isolated from the rest of the world. The setting is usually an old castle surrounded by a wild, natural beauty that one could imagine in a poem by Byron. The very titles of Peacock's novels suggest the setting: *Headlong Hall, Melincourt, Gryll Grange, Nightmare Abbey, Crotchet Castle.* (pp. 66-9)

The idyllic quality of the setting seems reflected in some of the action. In all of his novels Peacock creates a kind of peasant pastoral centered around the rustics in some isolated village near the castle. Their wants are few, their attitude to life has a simple wholesomeness untroubled by the speculations of the philosophers in the castle. In effect, they live a form of romantic primitivism, with a healthy common sense and a lusty vitality that show their delight in being alive. Even Peacock's philosophical characters share something of this joy of living. Their lives seem to be a continual round of dining well and drinking with gusto, bursting into drinking songs and love songs, which have a startling irrelevance to their rambling cerebrations. In effect, side by side with the satiric theme, Peacock asserts his romantic criterion: life is good, provided that the eternal talkers, intellectualizers, system-mongers, do not try to shape society in their image; there is joy in life, and beauty, even human affection and warmth, the closer one gets to the tranquillity of the romantic ideal. We are not accustomed to such an emphasis on positive values in modern satire. In the Roman *satura* and formal verse satire in general, the satiric criterion is an explicit part of the structure. But Peacock is not writing formal verse satire.

Satirists usually isolate their characters in some fantasy world in order to show the satiric evil more effectively. Both setting and characters combine to form one powerful satiric image. But Peacock seems to reverse the satiric process. His setting

and his characters frequently are at odds. In this remote world of beauty and archaic charm, Peacock's characters are not only isolated, they are rendered harmless. They talk endlessly, often fatuously, while the world goes on as if they had never spoken. The beauty of the setting seems to stress their irrelevance. What makes them even more innocuous is that Peacock focuses not on their actions but on their ideas, which they expound on all occasions and at the slightest excuse. The implications of their theories are seldom shown directly, seldom dramatized in action. Therefore, on the surface at least, they can be dismissed as talk. Even though the issues are argued cogently, each character pushing home his own point of view, the isolation of the characters in Peacock's romantic world seems to reduce their possible danger to an after-dinner entertainment.

But Peacock's characters have two dimensions. In the romantic dream world they are merely attitudes and postures, the mechanical reflex of their crotchets, a puppet show designed to make us laugh. In the world outside, however, the attitudes represent real people, people like Coleridge, Wordsworth, Byron, Shelley, Malthus, Canning, the critics of the *Edinburgh Review* and the *Quarterly Review;* or they are fictional figures representing serious issues that threaten society, such as scientific rationalism, "the march of mind," the political economic approach to man's problems. On almost every page of his novels there are elaborate footnotes and direct quotations drawing our attention to the real world and the significance of his characters. All satire, of course, directs the reader away from the author's fantasy world to the actual society which is being satirized. But in Peacock's novels, because his romantic world seems so delightful and the characters so harmless, his footnotes are more than an engaging supplement to the satire as in Pope's Variorum edition of *The Dunciad*. They are a necessary adjunct to make the link with society explicit so that we are constantly aware that beyond the charm of the romantic dream there is the ugly fact of man's world. To the degree that the fatuous crotchets of his characters directly influence the shape that society takes, the satire becomes more disturbing. But this very fatuousness makes almost all his characters dangerous because it suggests that a new Dulness is spreading over the land, infesting the political, economic and cultural patterns of an entire society.

The structure of Peacock's novels, except for the two romantic tales, puts them more in the tradition of Menippean satire than of the novel itself. If one can assume a characteristic structure to the novel—a risky business at best—it would be some variation of Aristotle's remarks on tragedy, that it is an imitation of an action that is complete and entire. By action, as Francis Fergusson suggests in *The Idea of a Theater,* I mean the entire thrust of the novel towards its conclusion, giving it focus and direction. By imitation I mean that recreating of human experience expressed through the novel's various elements, such as plot, characterization, imagery—the shape that the novel takes. By "complete and entire" I mean, with Aristotle, that which has a beginning, a middle, and an end, a compelling progression in which all the structural elements coalesce. In Menippean satire, however, we do not get the same tightness of form. There is, of course, an overall direction which might be called the action; and to the degree the satire has artistic unity, its various elements contribute to the action. But there is no sense of an inevitable progression. Menippean satire, as Dryden points out, is a mixture of prose and verse. But more to our purpose, it is a series of incidents, many of which could be arranged in a different order; it includes various digressions which usually have an overall relationship to the whole, but the point is that they stop the action; it contains abrupt shifts in plot, tone, and characterization. Often we are not sure what the action is until we reach the end of the satire. This is the form that Peacock's novels take.

The plot of the novels, we have seen, is almost incidental to the action. At times, it is apparent that Peacock does not even take the plot seriously. At the climax of the romance in *Headlong Hall,* for example, where the hero finally wins the heroine, her father begins to sympathize with the losing rival. But "Mr. Panscope [the rival] begged him not to distress himself on the subject, observing, that the monotonous system of female education brought every individual of the sex to so remarkable an approximation of similarity, that no wise man would suffer himself to be annoyed by a loss so easily repaired. . . ." This is hardly romance as we ordinarily understand the word. It is apparent that Peacock's interest is elsewhere and the romantic plot is largely a framework around which to hang the satire. Even the word "framework" overstates the case because the plot often disappears for long intervals, emerges again with virtually no connection to what has gone before, vanishes again, only to rise triumphantly at the end with the hero and heroine joined in the usual connubial expectations. Between these snippets of plot there are long philosophic discussions, self-contained episodes, formal digressions, and song, totally irrelevant to the romantic thread. There is seldom a sufficient link between these various elements to call them a logical sequence. But there is a connection between the parts. Since most of the characters are hardly more than personified intellectual crotchets, they approach every issue and incident with the same squint, making the same argument, so that they provide a continuity of theme with the same ideas turning over and over again. That is, there is a dialectical thread of argument running through each novel, and it is this which ties together the novel's scattered elements. The dialectic provides whatever conflict the novels contain—there is little of it in the romantic plot. But it is a sporadic conflict, there is no sense of an unfolding drama as you have in Bernard Shaw's drama of ideas. Yet from this seemingly haphazard structure with its revolving themes, a kind of dialectical synthesis emerges, which is Peacock's satiric point. (pp. 70-2)

If we examine Peacock's use of dialogue, the nature of his satire becomes more clear. There is no logical direction to the dialogue except for the ding-dong exchange of a particular argument. The beginning is usually accidental and the ending may be signalled by a dinner-gong or an explosion or the lateness of the evening, or the start of a fresh chapter. The discussion comes out of nowhere and ends nowhere. Irrelevance is its supreme characteristic. As for the disputants, they make no dramatic conversions, "each party continuing firm in his own opinion, and professing his profound astonishment at the blindness and prejudices of the other."

If Peacock's dialogue has any form, it is musical: "You . . . get up a discussion on everything that presents itself," Miss Gryll remarks to Doctor Opimian in *Gryll Grange,* "dealing with your theme like a series of variations in music." A good example of this is Chapter XI of *Nightmare Abbey* where Mr. Cypress (Byron) announces his intention to leave England. There is first a short, rhythmic response from the eight characters present, each in his own crotchet, each line beginning with, "It is the only. . . ." It is stychomythia. Then the responses get larger, then shorter, then another stychomythia, to the lyrics of "How can we be cheerful . . ."; and then the reply:

> Mr. Glowry. Let us all be unhappy together.
>
> Mr. Hilary. Let us sing a catch.
>
> Mr. Glowry. No: a nice tragical ballad. The Norfolk Tragedy to the tune of the Hundreth Psalm.
>
> Mr. Hilary. I say a catch.
>
> Mr. Glowry. I say no. A song from Mr. Cypress.
>
> All. A song from Mr. Cypress.

And Mr. Cypress sings a song, one of the most melancholy of the Byronic mood.

> Mr. Glowry. Admirable. Let us all be unhappy together.
>
> Mr. Hilary. Now, I say again, a catch.
>
> The Reverend Mr. Larynx. I am for you.

Mr. Hilary and the Reverend Mr. Larynx sing a drinking song, **"Seamen three,"** and all of the party join in the chorus, "each raising a bumper to his lips," and the chapter ends.

Few of Peacock's discussions are so musical, but it is not surprising for the characters to burst into song, which they frequently do. The musical structure is sufficiently apparent for the reader to suspect a pun on the word "crotchet": It is not merely a whimsical notion but a musical quarter note that separates one character from another. That is, the crotchet makes the character respond in the same mechanical way to every stimulus, play the same musical note, so that his profound arguments emerge as a leitmotiv in some Wagnerian opera written by Gilbert and Sullivan. The ideas of each character have such a narrow and predictable range that they can be matched against each other as in a chorus. Consequently, even where the argument is profound and the subject the evils of the universe, what emerges is not a serious debate but a duet or a quartet. It is easy for Peacock to slip into full chorus with all the characters ensemble bursting out, "The church is in danger! The church is in danger!"; move from there to a succession of speeches rhythmically balanced against each other; rise to the crescendo of a stychomythia and the Hallelujah chorus of a quintetto, sung to the tune of "Turning, turning, turning, as the wheel goes round," with alternate recitatives by the five members of the chorus. In a discussion on electoral reform, the effect is madness. But in varying degrees this kind of madness seems implicit in almost all the discussions.

Peacock's continual use of the discussion method—*Headlong Hall* is almost entirely discussion—suggests the main emphasis of his satire. The point he consistently makes is that each character rides his own crotchet, regardless of the logic and the reasons massed against him, almost as if no one else has spoken. Since none of the disputants is concerned with his opponents' arguments except as a springboard for his own rhetorical flight, we have a kind of disconnected dialogue different only in degree from the effect we get in the plays of Ionesco. Despite the pretense to discourse, his characters do not listen to each other; despite the powerful reasoning of their own theories, they are not amenable to reason. Continually they discuss the immense problems of civilization, the nature of man, the questions of universal values, and they are not even aware of what stares them in the face. They seem impervious to the simplest facts of experience. "I stand here as the representative of general reason," said Mr. Fax (Malthus's crotchet of excess population) to the rustic bride and groom "to ask if you have duly weighed the consequences of your present proceeding?"

The Bridegroom. . . . General Reason! I be's no so-
ger man, and bea'n't countable to no General what-
zomecomedever. We bea'n't under martial law, be
we? Voine toimes indeed if General Reason be to
interpole between a poor man and his sweetheart.

Peacock seems to enjoy showing that their theories are not
merely remote from life but remote from their own lives. Continually he demonstrates the distance between their theoretical
principles and their practice.

Nothing, you well know [said Mr. Sarcastic in *Melincourt*], is so rare as the coincidence of theory and
practice. A man who "will go through fire and water
to serve a friend" in words, will not give five guineas
to save him from famine. A poet will write Odes to
Independence, and become the obsequious parasite
of any great man who will hire him. A burgess will
hold up one hand for purity of election, while the
price of his own vote is slily dropped into the other. . . .

What motivates a man, usually, is not his elaborately reasoned
argument but his selfish interests. Peacock makes this point
frequently. And here, perhaps, is one of the main justifications
for the discussion method of satire. The philosophers reason
and speculate and spin out their theories, and the result is
irrelevance. The more serious, the more profound, they appear,
the greater is the irrelevance. And Peacock stresses its irrelevance by the lofty, almost mock epic, tone that he adopts,
especially when the subject matter is trivial, larding his prose
with pedantic jargon and obscure classical allusions. Where
his characters do practice as they preach—apart from those
who clearly are intended as a criterion and appear quixotic and
a bit foolish—they preach a theory devoid of human sympathy
and warmth, and therefore become another example of the
distance between abstract reasoning and the experience of living.

In general, Peacock seems to be arguing that life cannot be
comprehended by speculative systems or, in fact, by the reasoning process, because essentially life is not rational. Man is
not a rational creature. This does not disturb Peacock as much
as it did Swift. Of course, man should be a reasoning creature,
but in order to evoke the warm instincts of his humanity, man's
life should be intuitive and responsive to the flow of nature.
To put human experience in logical straitjackets such as political economy, to develop machines and factories at the expense of man's humanity, is to degrade life into an abstraction
and man into a beast of burden to serve an abstraction.

Behind the eighteenth-century façade of Peacock's satire is a
nineteenth-century substance with all the overtones of the romantic movement. His satire is not excremental, nor bestial,
nor sharply derisive, but a satire which gently invites his reader
to sit down and reason while he cheerfully saws away the floor
beneath the chair (pp.74-6)

*Philip Pinkus, "The Satiric Novels of Thomas Love
Peacock," in* Kansas Quarterly, *Vol. 1, No. 3, Summer, 1969, pp. 64-76.*

CARL DAWSON   (essay date 1970)

[*Dawson analyzes Peacock's use of irony in "The Four Ages of
Poetry" in the following excerpt from a book-length study of his
works.*]

To what extent Peacock was serious in his diatribe against
poetry and what he actually intended are matters about which
there has been little agreement, ever since Shelley responded
to the essay ["**The Four Ages**"] with slightly disingenuous

horror. George Saintsbury, who admired Peacock and who
admitted the brilliance of the essay, could find no place for it
in his *History of Criticism*. More recently, M. H. Abrams has
acknowledged its relevance to early nineteenth-century criticism, at the same time maintaining 'it is idle to inquire about
the exact boundaries of irony in this essay. . . . Peacock cannot
be pinned down' [see Additional Bibliography]. The essay
certainly is enigmatic, apparently with intention, and Peacock
cannot perhaps be pinned down—if the phrase is appropriate.
But much of his irony can and should be clarified, for it tells
a great deal. Granted there is a risk of tilting at windmills.
(pp. 83-4)

[The] argument in "**The Four Ages**" is almost entirely of the
sort that is scattered through the novels. Like the characters in
the novels, the voice in "**The Four Ages**" is the voice of a
travestied proposition, not unconnected with its author, but by
no means his direct outlet. Peacock's method of dialogue is to
force two or three spokesmen to ever more extreme positions,
so that each casts doubt on the others. In "**The Four Ages**",
the author himself argues as though he had an antagonist—and
perhaps he did have Shelley in mind. That his thesis is largely
a spoof can be seen in the survey of the literature of the
Renaissance.

From these ingredients [love, battle, and fanaticism]
of the iron age of modern poetry, dispersed in the
rhymes of minstrels and the songs of the troubadours,
arose the golden age, in which the scattered materials
were harmonized and blended about the time of the
revival of learning; but with this peculiar difference
[this is one of Peacock's favourite rhetorical devices],
that Greek and Roman literature pervaded all the
poetry of the golden age of modern poetry, and hence
resulted a heterogeneous compound of all ages and
nations in one picture; an infinite licence, which gave
to the poet the free range of the whole field of imagination and memory. This was carried very far by
Ariosto, but farthest of all by Shakespeare and his
contemporaries, who used time and locality merely
because they could not do without them, because
every action must have its when and where: but they
made no scruple of deposing a Roman Emperor by
an Italian Count, and sending him off in the disguise
of a French pilgrim to be shot with a blunderbuss by
an English archer. This makes the old English drama
very picturesque. . . .

If some of the writing here—such as 'This was carried very
far by Ariosto, but farthest of all by Shakespeare'—reads like
an anticipatory parody of T. S. Eliot's essay style, most is
clearly burlesque of neo-Aristotelian or Horatian dicta of the
Rapin/Boileau/Rymer family. Obviously Peacock does not accuse Shakespeare of any real breach of propriety, nor does he
confuse the paraphrased nuggets of earlier poetic credos with
Shakespeare's actual achievement. His method is to compress
judgments into the briefest compass, to state them in parallel
with other distorted judgments, and to develop the resulting
mixture into a final climactic piece of nonsense. The passage
above ends by comparing the literature of Shakespeare's time
to nothing more than a 'Venetian carnival'.

The argument of the essay is engagingly simple, comprising
in its few pages an indictment of apparently wholesale proportions. Possibly its most remarkable quality is the nudity of
its statement, the absence of what, in an attack upon poetry,
one would expect to find prominent. Peacock's essay prompted
Shelley to write the *Defence*, and since Shelley himself clearly
turned to Sir Philip Sidney's classic apology for poetry, one

naturally thinks of **"The Four Ages"** in connection with Stephen Gosson's tract, *The School of Abuse,* an angry diatribe that served to provoke Sidney. Peacock uses as his motto a line from Petronius, to the effect that he who works in the kitchen must smell of food and hence lose all sense of discrimination. Gosson had written, 'For Hee that goes to Sea must smell of the Ship'. Like Gosson, Peacock directs his censure at the poets—though on intellectual rather than moral grounds—and his main thrust similarly concerns the undesirable effects of verse on the reader. But as it is in tone detached, supercilious, calmly assertive, his essay has little in common with Gosson's heated outburst. 'He that sitteth in the heavens', according to the psalm, 'shall laugh'; Peacock writes here as though his place aloft were assured:

> A poet in our times is a semi-barbarian in a civilized community. He lives in the days that are past. His ideas, thoughts, feelings, associations, are all with barbarous manners, obsolete customs, and exploded superstitions. The march of his intellect is like that of a crab, backward. The brighter the light diffused around him by the progress of reason, the thicker is the darkness of antiquated barbarism, in which he buries himself like a mole, to throw up the barren hillocks of his Cimmerian labours.

The allusiveness—he echoes *Hamlet* and refers to the *Odyssey*—the quiet overstatement, the careful building to the final metaphor, reveal a sophistication and wit far different from anything in Gosson.

Nor is the difference chiefly that of tone. Whereas Gosson's approach had been a sort of puritanical and derivative Platonism, Peacock's is surprisingly un-Platonic. Surprisingly so, because Plato offered the strongest traditional authority for an attack on poetry. To the extent that Peacock asserts the ill effects of verse, especially modern verse, and argues the need for another type of discourse, his argument might be Platonic. On these grounds, however, he had been anticipated by Bentham and Bentham's followers. Many of the standard Platonic arguments he leaves largely untouched. He does refer to various sorts of inspiration, among them that from 'vinous spirits', that *ascribed* to poets by the ignorant, as well as three more predictable 'ingredients': 'the rant of unregulated passion, the whine of exaggerated feeling, and the cant of factitious sentiment'. Knowing quite well what Plato had done with comparable assertions, Peacock remains content with a few, undeveloped feints. On the matter of imitation he is also remarkably silent. Since he charges poets with letting loose undesirable emotions, and therefore imitating the worthless—their own morbid souls—one would have expected echoes of Plato's discussions of imitation in the *Ion* and *Republic*. It is curious that neither Peacock nor Shelley in his 'antidote' seems to recall that Plato had anything whatever to say at the expense of poetry. Shelley's reasons need no comment. One can only begin to understand Peacock's by asking about the intent of his essay. A man familiar with Plato, appreciative of his writings, who seriously wanted to denounce poetry, would surely have invoked both the name and the central arguments in an effort to buttress his case.

The usual estimate of Peacock is, to twist Shelley's words, that he would have preferred to 'be right with Horace' than to 'err with Plato'. But underlying **"The Four Ages"**, as it underlies most of his writing, is a respect for Plato and for Plato's ideas. The difference between Shelley and himself lies in allegiance to final answers, for Peacock refused to, or perhaps could not, commit himself to either speculative hypotheses or inclusive systems. Nevertheless, there is a great deal of Plato in his works, as **Rhododaphne** has made clear; and a great deal of admiration, as a number of his letters testify. Many details of his fiction are drawn from Plato. It was not by accident that Peacock entitled chapters 'Symposium', or that he fabricated his witty dialogues in mock-Platonic fashion, as though they were Socratic without an enlightening Socrates.

On receiving a copy of **"The Four Ages"**, Shelley suggested to Peacock that he should read the *Ion* again, implying that the counter to his argument could be found there. Ironically, Peacock had introduced Shelley, not only to less popular Greek writers, but even to parts of Plato. He probably knew the *Ion* as well as Shelley did. Was he then inviting a rebuttal to his argument based on Plato or on neo-Platonic grounds or, more precisely, did he expect his reader to see in **"The Four Ages"** the other side to his arguments, so that the attack would be recognized as ironic? It seems more than likely.

While maintaining the charges against modern poetry, **"The Four Ages"** becomes an implicit apology for the literature of older and largely, though not entirely, classical times. Because Peacock burlesques his own arguments as much as he mocks the poets, he excludes Plato from unflattering company. In any case, the ostensible argument of the essay is neither puritanical nor Platonic, but rather Utilitarian on the one hand and primitivistic or Viconian on the other. Both arguments overlap, and both contain Platonic elements, but they are also to an extent distinct. Peacock insists that poetry is inferior to various scientific and philosophical disciplines; he also introduces a historical and dialectical scheme, which at once points to the rise and fall of poetry and offers him a convenient organizational pattern.

Essentially the scheme underlying **"The Four Ages"** is the old primitivistic view of history, common to dozens of earlier writers, and first known to us in Hesiod, significantly altered in order to make 'primitive' and modern poets—or primitive modern poets—appear ridiculous. 'Poetry', then, 'like the world, may be said to have four ages, but in a different order: the first age of poetry being the age of iron; the second, of gold; the third, of silver; and the fourth, of brass'. It develops that poetry has not four but eight ages, four modern corresponding—as the shadow to the real thing—to four ancient. The effect is merely to emphasize the decline of poetry in modern times. Sentence pronounced, we can only wait, and perhaps with surreptitious glee, until the guillotine descends on Wordsworth and Byron. But again the scheme is too rigid, too pat, to be taken in earnest.

The idea of the cyclical scheme, though common to writers as different as Hesiod and Hegel, had found its fullest exponent in Giambattista Vico, whose *The New Science* had appeared almost a century before **"The Four Ages"**. Peacock describes, like Vico, the cycles of poetry and comes to the same intolerable conclusion that the expiration of the modern cycle—beginning for both men in the Middle Ages—has led to the virtual death of poetry. Since what remains to be written can no longer and should no longer be written in verse, and since science has eclipsed poetry, the poet has become a barbarian in a civilized community. The state of mind requisite for the creation of poetry having disappeared, it is idle to versify. When Peacock says, 'We know too that there are no Dryads in Hyde-park nor Naiads in the Regent's-canal', his argument parallels Vico's. And the absurd associations and apparent glibness mask a nostalgia comparable to Vico's own.

Just as the ancient cycle of poetry concluded with Nonnus, he writes, so the modern, in its early dotage, results in the Lake Poets and other 'confraternities of rhymesters'; but 'with a difference'—the phrase is Peacock's, and he uses it often. Nonnus, to his credit, could write occasionally beautiful passages, and he never expressed pernicious ideas. Modern poets are not so harmless. They are all

> wallowing in the rubbish of departed ignorance, and raking up the ashes of dead savages to find gewgaws and rattles for the grown babies of the age. Mr. Scott digs up the poachers and cattle-stealers of the ancient border. Lord Byron cruises for thieves and pirates on the shores of the Morea and among the Greek islands. Mr. Southey wades through ponderous volumes of travels and old chronicles, from which he carefully selects all that is false, useless, and absurd, as being essentially poetical; and when he has a commonplace book full of monstrosities, strings them into an epic. Mr. Wordsworth picks up village legends from old women and sextons; and Mr. Coleridge, to the valuable information acquired from similar sources, superadds the dreams of crazy theologians and the mysticisms of German metaphysics, and favours the world with visions in verse, in which the quadruple elements of sexton, old woman, Jeremy Taylor, and Emanuel Kant, are harmonized into a delicious poetical compound.

What these poets have in common is a scornful disregard of lucid thought and clear language. Peacock's criticism is an orthodox one, reapplied to new conditions. His charge echoes that of Pope and Swift; it also anticipates those of Arnold, Irving Babbitt, and George Orwell. He sensed the political dangers as well as the dangers for literature in what he considered to be a misuse of the language. And he suggested that the misuse resulted from a new conception of the sources and purposes of poetry, recognizing in the poetry of his time the seeds of a cryptic and private communication. The new poets also compound their mischievous distortions of language and their misguided views of nature by theoretical defences. In parody of Wordsworth, Peacock writes: 'Poetical impressions can be received only among natural scenes: for all that is artificial is anti-poetical. Society is artificial, therefore we will live out of society. The mountains are natural, therefore we will live in the mountains'.

A more central charge against Wordsworth's theories concerns Peacock's notions as to the public responsibilities of the poet. . . . He accuses Wordsworth of a penchant for self-indulgence, of putting into his verse some inevitable 'phantastical parturition of the moods of his own mind'. Again, he had nothing but contempt for expressive theories of art, for theories based upon 'the overflow of feelings', in part because he tended to confuse the object of imitation with the imitative work, in part because he found a Wordsworth's effusion less interesting than a Pope's craft.

Modern poets, in short, having lost the original function and the legitimate models of poetic writing, have also perverted what small role might have remained for them. If Peacock does attack poetry, it is largely these inheritors of the muse who receive his blows; Homer and Virgil, Milton and Pope, remain unmolested. (He calls Milton 'the greatest of English poets'.) The argument, of course, includes an ironic complication, because if history follows a prescribed scheme, and poetry necessarily conforms to it, any condemnation of individual poets must be gratuitous. And if poetry becomes the victim of the times, the times themselves are to blame; in which case the real import of the essay becomes an unvoiced complaint about those factors making poetry impossible. To explore this question we need to glance at the utilitarian assertions within **"The Four Ages"**.

Like his Platonism, Peacock's Utilitarianism tended to be a part-time commitment. There is no doubt about his acceptance of some of Bentham's principles, nor about his affiliation with Bentham and Mill, his professional connection with the new intellectual establishment. Peacock succeeded James Mill as Examiner in the India House. (He was himself succeeded by John Stuart Mill, whom he also knew.) He is said to have been fairly intimate with Bentham, at any rate intimate enough to dine with him on a regular basis. Several of his major periodical essays were written for the *Westminster Review,* a Utilitarian journal. If guilt by association cannot demonstrate Peacock's toleration of the Utilitarians, his correspondence makes it clear. In letters to Shelley and to his friend and publisher Edward Hookham, Peacock expresses hope in a future conditioned by Bentham, who has laid 'a mighty axe to the root of superstition'.

In his lectures *On Bentham and Coleridge,* John Stuart Mill was to make his well-known distinction between what he called negative and positive philosophers, those who attack and tear down, and those who found new systems. Bentham, he said, had both capacities. Peacock, as his statement about the 'axe to superstition' indicates, seems to have appreciated Bentham's attack on 'superstitions'. He could not respond to what he considered to be Bentham's own superstitions.

His objections to certain assumptions of the Utilitarians are best illustrated in Mr. MacQuedy of *Crotchet Castle.* MacQuedy is a Utilitarian, what Cobbett would call a 'scotch feelosopher', the new breed of social scientist from the 'New Athens', or Edinburgh. This 'son of a demonstration' proves a relatively amiable though essentially narrow thinker, far too certain of his own logic, and too sure of progress, especially technological progress. He is both contemptuous of history and smug about his systems, and for his errors Peacock trusses him up for sacrifice. MacQuedy's host, Squire Crotchet, whose intellect elsewhere is seldom keen, clearly speaks for Peacock when he defends an alternative point of view: '. . . where the Greeks had modesty, we have cant; where they had poetry, we have cant; where they had patriotism, we have cant; where they had anything that exalts, delights, or adorns humanity, we have nothing but cant, cant, cant'. To say that Crotchet speaks for Peacock in this instance is not to imply that Peacock subscribed to all of Crotchet's charges. The squire is involved in a dialectic, of which he is at once the perpetrator and the victim. Yet his general indictment holds. We are inferior to the Greeks; we have too much faith in social amelioration; and we subscribe to meaningless verbal systems.

If he distrusted the social and political assumptions of Bentham, then Peacock strenuously objected to his aesthetic conclusions. For, like Squire Crotchet, he could not and did not want to reject the past, and he did not find the 'cant' of political scientists any adequate substitute for the sweetness and light of earlier literature. Whatever Bentham's virtues as a thinker in other respects, his understanding of poetry was hopeless. His notorious comparison of poetry with 'push-pin' characterizes his almost quaint denigration of poetry to a minor, and far too aristocratic, source of pleasure. In this judgment Bentham was merely borrowing from certain empirical thinkers, notably John Locke, who on different grounds had argued similarly a century earlier. But Bentham extended the argument. He suggested that poetry may actually be harmful. 'The game of push-pin is always innocent; it were well the same could be asserted of poetry. Indeed, between poetry and truth there is a natural opposition.' This combination of half-truths and unqualified overstatement is a quality of **"The Four Ages"**, and one object of Peacock's humour is evidently Bentham himself.

Peacock reduces to absurdity a number of stock Utilitarian ideas, at the same time poking fun at the 'superstitions' of modern poets. He argues that *all* poetry is Utilitarian in the crudest sense: poets are flattering and self-flattering Tommy Tuckers, singing for their suppers. The categorical absoluteness of the following passage might be a travesty of any page from Bentham—though the spectre of Adam Smith also creeps in:

> The natural desire of every man to engross to himself as much power and property as he can acquire by any of the means which might makes right, is accompanied by the no less natural desire of making known to as many people as possible the extent to which he has been a winner in this universal game. The successful warrior becomes a chief; the successful chief becomes a king: his next want is an organ to disseminate the fame of his achievements and the extent of his possessions; and this organ he finds in a bard, who is always ready to celebrate the strength of his arm, being first duly inspired by that of his liquor. This is the origin of poetry, which, like all other trades, takes its rise in the demand for the commodity, and flourishes in proportion to the extent of the market.

His other objection is more centrally Utilitarian and more of a real charge against poetry. Concluding his argument, Peacock writes that in an age of 'mathematicians, astronomers, chemists, moralists, metaphysicians, historians, politicians, and political economists'—the Swiftian, polyglot list is itself damning—'who have built into the upper air of intelligence a pyramid, from the summit of which they see the modern Parnassus far beneath them . . .', poetry can find only an inferior place. Several types of irony, or at least directions of the irony, can be seen here. Peacock may, for example, have been responding specifically to a letter from Shelley, who had asserted—in a passage that reflects oddly on his *Defence*—that he found poetry 'very subordinate to moral & political science'. And he wrote after reading **"The Four Ages"** that he would rather, 'for my private reading, receive political geological & moral treatises than this stuff in terza, ottave, & tremilesima rima, whose earthly baseness has attracted the lightening of your undiscriminating censure . . .'. Peacock's censure included the very kind of 'stuff' for which Shelley confessed a preference; he failed to see the burlesque.

Thomas Carlyle was to speak about the 'cold voice of science' and the readiness of many writers of the previous generation to find poetry emasculated by science. The idea, if not commonplace, had been fairly widely invoked even before **"The Four Ages"**. Peacock probably did not know that Keats speculated about the adverse effects of science—as well as of critics—on poetry, but he might have known the public statements by Francis Jeffrey and William Hazlitt. One could read **"The Four Ages"** as a travesty of Hazlitt's *Lectures on the English Poets,* with its remarks on the climate necessary for poetry and its historical survey of the major writers. Hazlitt says, for example, that poetry 'is not a mere frivolous accomplishment . . . the trifling amusement of a few idle readers or leisure hours'. Leave out the 'not', and one has Peacock's essential charge. But Peacock's arguments as to the present decline of poetry sound like echoes of Hazlitt, and they are in fact close in sentiment. Hazlitt writes: 'It cannot be concealed . . . that

the progress of knowledge and refinement has a tendency to circumscribe the limits of the imagination, and to clip the wings of poetry. . . .' And: 'It is not only the progress of mechanical knowledge, but the necessary advances of civilization that are unfavourable to the spirit of poetry.'

Implicit in Peacock's 'pyramid' of knowledge, with its suggestion of Babel and islands in the sky, is that haunting question of the time: Was there, indeed, any purpose left for poetry? Keats and Hazlitt, despite grave doubts, managed to arrive at an affirmation. Peacock skirts the issue by irony. But it is clear that his sympathies came closer to those of Keats and Hazlitt than to those of Bentham. If one remembers how Mr. Cranium of **Headlong Hall** and other specialists in Peacock's novels topple from their 'pyramids'—a tower in the case of Mr. Cranium—it becomes clear that Peacock chastises society itself, or these its representative intellectuals. Of the professions he lists as examples of an emergent common sense, nearly all are scourged in the course of the novels. That some prig should set himself up, whether as phrenologist or metaphysician, is to Peacock, as earlier it had been to Swift, at once the height of absurdity and the occasion for satire.

Just as he bemoans the passing of an intelligent audience for poetry and condemns those who insist on crying in the wilderness, so Peacock finds intolerable the fact that poetry succumbs to a false progress. Boileau is reported to have said about Descartes that he cut the throat of poetry: that rational inquiry and systematizing had made fancy obsolete. Peacock's ultimate irony is not so much that we have a Wordsworth where we ought to have a Milton, or a Byron where we might have had a Pope; it is that while we have a decline in poetry, we do not have any genuine corresponding 'march of mind'. In modern times it is learned barbarians in the guise of philosophers who cut the throat of poetry. (pp. 86-96)

> *Carl Dawson, in his* His Fine Wit: A Study of Thomas Love Peacock, *University of California Press, 1970, 330 p.*

MARILYN BUTLER (essay date 1979)

[*In the following excerpt from the introduction to her full-length study of Peacock's satire and its historical background, Butler investigates Peacock's reputation as a detached, laughing observer and links the underlying principles of his work to the neoclassical tradition.*]

There is some justification . . . for the received picture of Peacock as a laughing bystander; but at the same time it is profoundly misleading. To some extent, the aristocratic attitude—cynical, reserved, exaggeratedly independent—is no more than the upper-class posture of the day. Taking it as special to Peacock saddles him with a coldness and emotional detachment which the facts contradict. Equally, the manner has been translated into intellectual indifference, and here there is much more evidence that Peacock's true attitudes were of quite another kind.

On one occasion, Peacock appears to give countenance to those who see him as intellectually frivolous, the caricaturist of anything amusing that catches his eye. He is describing the circle Shelley introduced him to at Bracknell, probably in 1813:

> I was sometimes irreverent enough to laugh at the fervour with which opinions utterly unconducive to any practical result were battled for as matters of the

highest importance to the well-being of mankind:
Harriet Shelley was always ready to laugh with me.

There is, after all, a potentially significant phrase in this account—'unconducive to any practical result'. Peacock could
have meant—in fact, his writings will suggest he did mean—
that the Bracknell circle was ridiculous not because it was
enthusiastic but because it was impractical. But the passage
has been cited in evidence, far beyond its intrinsic significance,
and out of its context, to sustain an impression of Peacock as
a universal scoffer, an inveterate sketcher of eccentricity in all
its forms, and a man who laughed at people simply because
they had opinions.

The same rather too memorable glimpse of life at Bracknell
supports an even more pervasive conception, which is at the
very heart of the image of frivolity and intellectual detachment.
Peacock is taken for a caricaturist of people in real life whom
he knew or had read about. Again, 'identifications' of characters in fiction were very much in keeping with the person-
ality-mongering spirit of the age. Some guesses at Peacock's
originals were soon believed in Peacock's own circle, and got
back to the author himself. But, surprising though this will
seem, there is no sound evidence that Peacock drew what can
fairly be called *portraits* of real-life individuals. In fact, the
best testimony, Peacock's own, is directly to the contrary. In
the Preface he wrote for **Melincourt** when it was reprinted in
1856 he specifically denies any attempt to represent anyone's
'private' character. 'Of the disputants whose opinions and public characters (for I never trespassed on private life) were shadowed in some of the persons of the story, almost all have
passed from the diurnal scene.' Peacock's careful phrasing
concedes that in some of his novels the name of a minor character is deliberately meant to bring a real-life thinker or public
figure to mind. It will usually be a public figure, rather than
someone Peacock knew personally. But it is important to realise
that, even when a specific connection can be made, the individual concerned is not one man, not as it were himself, but
a public persona, which is in turn the representative of a type.
Even this practice, of using real-life exempla, is rarer than has
been supposed, for with his major figures Peacock is careful
to blend characteristics in such a way as to frustrate identification with real people.

The most celebrated instance of an apparent portrait is Scythrop
Glowry in **Nightmare Abbey,** who has been universally taken
to 'be' Shelley. The steady growth of this belief follows a
typical enough pattern: its first known appearance in print was
in the 1840s, and after Peacock's death it was alluded to as a
more or less established fact by Medwin and Buchanan. And
yet, when the references Shelley make to Scythrop in his letters
are checked, it will be found that Shelley nowhere states unequivocally that Peacock intended to portray him as Scythrop—
while Peacock himself (who is seldom unequivocal) avoids a
clear statement both about his own intention, and about what
Shelley felt his intention to be—'he took to himself the character of Scythrop'.

At a period when he already saw that his comic kind was no
longer liked or understood, Peacock defined that tradition as
he saw it, a comedy of ideas rather than of character. He was
reviewing a French comic writer of the 1830s, Paul de Kock,
and finding him interestingly different from Pigault le Brun,
a predecessor of the French Revolutionary period. Le Brun had
belonged to an older, classic, tradition of French comic writing,
one which 'embodied opinion in a very cogent and powerful
form':

Peacock by Henry Wallis.

Rabelais, one of the wisest and most learned, as well
as wittiest of men, put on the robe of the all-licensed
fool, that he might, like the court-jester, convey bitter
truths under the semblance of simple buffoonery . . .
It would be, we think, an interesting and amusing
enquiry to trace the progress of French comic fiction,
in its bearing on opinion, from the twelfth century
to the Revolution; and to show how much this unpretending branch of literature has, by its universal
diffusion through so many ages in France, contributed to directing the stream of opinion against the
mass of delusions and abuses which it was the object
of those who were honest in the cause of the Reformation, and in the causes of the several changes
which have succeeded it to the present time, to dissipate and destroy.

Peacock concedes that the liberal causes for which such writers
have worked have often been only partially successful:

we shall find, nevertheless, in the first place, that
every successive triumph, however perverted in its
immediate consequences, has been a step permanently gained in advance of conscience and freedom
of inquiry; and we shall find, in the second place . . .
that comic fiction has contributed largely to this result.

It was a comic tradition which was ultimately European rather
than only French, for it embraced Aristophanes, Petronius,
Cervantes, Swift, the Fielding of *Jonathan Wild,* as well as
Rabelais and Voltaire. It aimed to intervene in affairs, a general
aspiration which made it quite distinct from the less ambitious
comedy of character. Though Peacock is too modest to say so,
it is impossible to believe that this article does not contain a
manifesto for his own purposes and methods as a writer of
comedy.

But, if this is the case, there is a certain perversity in the
favourite contribution of Peacock's critics, and above all his

editors: the note, footnote or introductory essay identifying the originals of Panscope and Escot, Philomela Poppyseed and MacLaurel. This was a process begun, needless to say, in Victorian times, by Richard Garnett and Saintsbury among the editors, but it is a vein which has by no means run out. A good recent editor of Peacock, David Garnett, added considerably to the number of identifications in his edition of 1948 [see Additional Bibliography]. Eleanor L. Nicholes has provided [in *Shelley and His Circle* (1961), edited by K. N. Cameron] a by now almost traditional list, in a passage which begins confidently, 'Peacock's novels are all in some measure *romans à clef*'.

It is a scholarly guessing-game which cannot have contributed to Peacock's readability, or not at least as far as the general public is concerned. As time has gone on, rendering most of the supposed originals shadowy—who now knows Amelia Opie or J. F. Newton, or even Jeffrey and Gifford?—the slowly growing corpus of annotation has given the satire an increasingly antiquarian air. Readers of Peacock remain fixed in much the position of readers of Pope in the 1920s and 1930s. The clutter of obscure personalities is confusing and wearisome: a world peopled with cranks, not richly caricatured (as in Dickens) but thinly announced by a single governing attribute (as are most of the minor figures in the *Dunciad*).

The difference between his characterisation and that of the novelist Dickens is significant. Analysis of a speech uttered by one of Peacock's figures tends to reveal a rich texture: sentence by sentence, allusion to a specific text, a pre-existent *locus;* while the speech in its entirety, and still more the attitude of the speaker, call to mind in the most literal sense *opinion*—that is, a familiar contemporary controversy. Here, of course, is the centre of the problem concerning Peacock, the real reason why he became, and has remained, so profound a puzzle. While he is offering ideas, he appears to deal with character, and for this his modern readers have elaborate training, and expectations. Like the Victorians, we have a set of assumptions derived from novel-reading and, supported by the professional expertise of the psychiatrist, we have what is in a sense an even more developed interest in personality. By the standards of either the novelist or the psychiatrist, Peacock's characters are disappointing. In fact his dislike of his period's taste for personality is maintained in his work, and he does not deal in character at all. Of all his unorthodoxies, his humorous gestures of intellectual sabotage, it has been perhaps the most uncomfortable, the hardest to forgive.

It is no new discovery that Peacock's writing is in one sense or another learned and traditional. He was prodigiously well read in Greek and Latin, French and Italian, as well as in English literature, and takes a special pleasure in confounding the reader by allusion to an esoteric favourite, such as the *Dionysiaca* of the fifth-century poet Nonnus. His friend and fellow-Platonist Thomas Taylor no doubt intended a compliment when he christened him Greeky-Peaky, but the attainment has been found largely rebarbative since. Shelley's lines about Peacock have proved apt and prophetic, except that (as in other spheres) the better times Shelley anticipated have not yet arrived [see excerpt dated 1820]:

> ... his fine wit
> Makes such a wound, the knife is lost in it;
> A strain too learned for a shallow age,
> Too wise for selfish bigots; let his page
> Which charms the chosen spirits of the time,

> Fold itself up for the serener clime
> Of years to come, and find it[']s recompense
> In that just expectation.

And yet, it is not necessary to know as much Greek as Peacock did, or indeed any Greek at all, to understand in general terms what he took Greece to signify. Men have been known to lose themselves in a past era, or in its literature, out of some kind of nostalgia, or rejection of the present. Sentimental antiquarians of this type were at large in Peacock's day; in Folliott and Chainmail of *Crotchet Castle* he was to satirise some of them. But such an attitude to the past, far from being his own, was peculiarly alien to the Greek spirit as he understood it.

When Greek literature was revived in the Renaissance, it was initially a study to which arcane matter, the accretions of the Dark Ages, adhered. Plotinus was as much a name to conjure with as Plato: the neo-Platonism of the sixteenth century is a curious growth, divorced from a clear historical sense, reminiscent of the Near East and Alexandria as much as of Periclean Athens. The tradition lingers on in the eighteenth century. It is present, for example, in the work of Thomas Taylor, that 'pagan Methodist', as Southey called him, who, like Blake, was the denizen of a tradesman or artisan world of esoteric religious cults. In the 'Preliminary Dissertation' to his *Mystical Initiations: or, Hymns of Orpheus* (1787), Taylor undertook to interpret the Orphic religion, through the commentaries 'of the latter Platonists, as the only sources of genuine knowledge, on this sublime and obsolete enquiry'. Coleridge, whom Lamb long afterwards recalled at Christ's Hospital in the later 1780s, mouthing 'the mysteries of Jamblichus, or Plotinus (for even in those years thou waxedst not pale at such philosophic draughts), or reciting Homer in his Greek, or Pindar', had probably come by his impressively arcane knowledge via Taylor. But this is not Peacock's Greece, even though Peacock liked Taylor for preferring the pagan pantheon to Christianity. Nor was Peacock primarily interested in another flourishing tradition of classical scholarship, that of the great editors. Earlier in the century, the greatest of English scholars, Richard Bentley, had led the modern movement towards establishing sound texts. But, though Peacock all his life was interested in questions of language, grammar and metre, he was always more interested in content; and in this above all perhaps he differed from the mere specialist in ancient literature or art or antiquities. To be 'Greek', one need not become a pedant. One did not even have to know the language. Keats did not, and as late as 1817 Shelley was happy to read difficult works in translation, or to gather their meaning imperfectly, without using a dictionary. When Peacock thought of running a school in 1813 or 1814, he stated firmly in the prospectus that the Greek he meant to teach was no more than the means to an end.

His classicism developed notably original features, especially in collaboration with Shelley, but it was also in origin part of a movement of the second half of the eighteenth century. For the arts as a whole the era has been called a period of 'sharp action and innovation' (as opposed to the first half of the nineteenth century, the period of 'response and reflection'). Typically, the Enlightenment implied for the arts the democratisation of content, and the drastic simplification of style. From mid-century, the visual arts especially tend to reject the charming, the detailed, the decorative—the rococo, a style for an aristocratic coterie—in favour of something grander, graver and more universal. Artforms which flatteringly mirror an advanced society give way to primitivism: to the ancient Rome of Piranesi, the Greece of Winckelmann, or, in literature, the Celtic twilight of Ossian or Gray. In simpler times, the feeling runs, Man was nearer to Nature, and also freer to be himself. Architects pursue the essential, by evoking the Roman or the Doric, or by the even more brutal simplification of triangle, circle and cube. Painters turn away from the finicky, and implicitly affectionate, representation of colour, clothing, and texture; they prefer to represent the middle-class family in the course of common daily life, or a motionless nude figure, recalling the *Apollo Belvedere*, drawn in pure outline against a minimal background.

For post-Romantic art critics, and even more for literary critics, 'neo-classicism' has commonly been a pejorative term. Invented in the 1880s, it still reflects that period's lack of sympathy with the eighteenth century, and especially its belief that eighteenth-century art was academic and derivative. But the real impulse behind the 'true style' advocated during the Enlightenment was not antiquarian. For Winckelmann, Diderot, Reynolds, the idea of copying the ancients was anathema. The study of the ancients they proposed was meant to recover a primal simplicity, free from the accretions of a too elaborate modernity. So Gluck, in his dedicatory epistle to *Alceste* (1769), rejects the 'florid descriptions' of the libretti of Italian opera, for his own librettist's 'strong passions' in 'heartfelt language'; or Joseph Warton complains of Pope's cleverness and artifice. The movement back to Nature to which the early Rousseau gave an impetus is perfectly neo-classical, as are Burns' poetry of mice and ordinary men, Cowper's divine chit-chat, Blake's drawings and Wordsworth's *Lyrical Ballads*.

The art of the Enlightenment was radical in its rejection of previous styles, but not necessarily radical in its politics. Its confident individualism, its dignity and idealism, was perfectly echoed, for example, in the parliamentary oratory of the *anciens régimes:* it was the international language of the European aristocracy. The American and French Revolutions neither caused radicalism in art nor were created by it, but were further manifestations of underlying social pressures, a deeper pattern of change. However, political revolution, especially the French, had a profound effect upon attitudes to the arts: what had been natural and a-political before the fall of the French monarchy became charged with meaning. Cowper's *Task* was loved by readers of all shades of opinion. Even Burns' obvious egalitarianism, and impropriety, caused relatively little outrage. But the reputations of Cowper and Burns were established before the Terror. Wordsworth's *Lyrical Ballads*, poems professing to be for and about the people, appeared at the height of the French Republic's military success. They were censured for their political unsoundness even by the liberal Whig Francis Jeffrey (who in private admitted to being moved by them); even, in retrospect, by Wordsworth's friend and co-author, Samuel Taylor Coleridge.

As neo-classicism in its broader, artistic sense had to change after the Revolution—to become more defensive, less bold in its assertions and less universal in its appeal—so too the vogue for the Greek. In the eighteenth century, both republican Rome and ancient Athens could be used, unselfconsciously and more or less interchangeably, as models of freedom. Aristocrats engaging in ideological warfare against a monarch were particularly prone to idealise this kind of republic, along with modern oligarchies like Venice and Switzerland. So Gibbon exalts the memory of the Roman Republic, in *The Decline and Fall of the Roman Empire,* or Thomson of Athens in his *Ode to Liberty*. Ancient art, though praised in the language of taste, is valued above all as an advertisement for personal freedom. 'Only liberty', declares Winckelmann in the 1760s, 'has ele-

vated art to its perfection.' By the end of the century, this kind of sentiment had a very different ring.

The French Revolutionaries make the common motifs of late eighteenth-century polemic their own. Their painter, J. L. David, takes classical subjects like *The Oath of the Horatii,* and the simple, severe setting, the idealised human figures, the noble gestures become the expression of revolution. The cropped revolutionary haircut, the sudden simplification in the lines of women's dress, help to legitimise the new republicanism, by making it seem older and more prestigious than monarchy. English sympathisers with the French Revolution in the 1790s adopt the republican style, both of dress and of language, but this kind of classicism, naive and propagandist, does not outlast the decade. In France, by a grim historical irony, it gives way to the heavy institutional grandeur of Napoleon's Imperial style. In England, neo-classicism survives for another generation as the dominant mode, in painting, in architecture, in formal criticism, but after the turn of the century its assertions are far less bold and universal. Blake's glorious or tortured human figures, which dominate his prints up to 1795, are succeeded by his obscurer and more detailed illustrations to the Bible. Sir John Soane's powerful geometric Bank of England (1798) is followed by the Regency terrace. The *Lyrical Ballads,* also 1798, are one kind of neo-classical statement; *English Bards and Scotch Reviewers,* 1809, is another. What is lost in the Counter-Revolution is the confident public gesture.

The classicism of the wartime radical necessarily takes on a special tone. In the later eighteenth century, republican Rome had been more fashionable in England than Greece. Italy, especially Rome itself, was more accessible. British artists like Gavin Hamilton and Robert Adam studied at Rome. Fuseli, Swiss-born but Rome-trained, settled in London. Piranesi became a strong influence. After England had fully absorbed the shock-waves of the Revolution, from about 1800, it was the cultural influence of Greece which seemed to advance, and some of the explanation for this is surely psychological. With the Revolution compromised—by the Terror, by French expansion, and now by Bonaparte's dictatorship—the beleaguered English intellectual needed something other than David's republican Rome as a cultural model. Liberals like Godwin could not now pin their hopes on radical action, or parliamentary reform; the alternative was an inward process, freedom not in action but in thought. Here Athens had the advantage. The Roman republic was an inspiring example of civic co-operation and personal responsibility, but its citizens were not blessed with (in the eighteenth-century phrase) enlarged views, and they had left few texts to keep alive the flame of liberty. Athens was the home of the Academy, of Socrates, Plato, and Epicurus.

The Greek was, after all, an intellectual, and characteristically an isolated one, in a world always dominated by men of action. Even in Athens's heyday this was so. Plato, Socrates and Aristophanes appealed to Peacock because their times, he thought, like his own, called upon them to be critics. The long Greek twilight, when Athenian arts were overtaken by Roman practicality and progress, threw up other congenial iconoclasts. One of Peacock's particular favourites was the prose satirist Lucian, who satirised established religion, in graceful, witty dialogues, in the second century AD. Among Latin writers he tended to prefer those who acknowledged a debt to the Greek tradition. He shared with Shelley a veneration for Lucretius, who had substituted for the state religion of Augustus Epicurus's bleak, necessitarian concept of a universe of speeding atoms. Virgil, whose *Aeneid* grandiloquently canvassed the official view, was by contrast the court-flatterer *par excellence*. Shelley preferred to the *Aeneid* Lucan's *Pharsalia,* an account of the inception of the Empire which was firmly republican in its sympathies. But Peacock, typically, liked a comic, scurrilous variant, Petronius's *Satyricon,* in which the action apparently turns on an impudent inversion of the *Aeneid:* instead of a solemn hero of epic times whose life is complicated by his unintentional affront to Juno, we have a vulgar hero of modern times whose adventures are brought about by his accidental insult to Priapus. This cluster of works which clearly refer to public affairs, and also wittily to one another, evidently fascinated Shelley and Peacock. On the one hand, Virgil's epic, the great Latin poem according to the received view; on the other hand, more or less offensive counter-epics by a group who seem to constitute an intellectual resistance movement. In Peacock's *Melincourt* and Shelley's *Prometheus Unbound,* the structure and the exalted intention of genuine epic appears to co-exist with the critical spirit, the iconoclasm, of early imperial counter-epic. It is a tone, and above all an example, which has far more to do with a dialectical conception of classical literature than with the mock-heroic of the English Augustans.

Peacock shares the original principles of the neo-classicism of the Enlightenment: so, partly through Peacock, does Shelley. The basis of this classicism is liberal, intellectual and humanist. Certain kinds of art are appropriate vehicles for a belief in man and in a regenerated society. But altered circumstances have drastically affected which works best seem to represent Greece for the new age. Humanism, individualism, universality—the abstractions which the Enlightenment found epitomised in Greek statuary—are all politically suspect. Without faith in Man, the *Apollo Belvedere* is no longer a fit model. Instead of proclaiming a common ideology for an upper-class world in various phases of radicalism, the progressive artist now finds himself in a minority. His target is not the effete, exploded cultural habit of the previous age, but the dominant orthodoxy of his own. Hence the paradox, that Peacock preaches activism, but is obliged to adopt the stance of a wry onlooker; the popular cause, through a terminology that becomes increasingly esoteric. It is not personal eccentricity, but a representative experience for the English intellectual of his age-group and the next. (pp. 15-25)

> *Marilyn Butler, in her* Peacock Displayed: A Satirist in His Context, *Routledge & Kegan Paul, 1979, 361 p.*

BRYAN BURNS (essay date 1985)

[Burns, in an excerpt from his book on Peacock's fiction, disputes the notion that Peacock's approach to his novels was static and failed to evolve over time.]

[Interesting] and sometimes excellent though his non-fiction may be, Peacock's reputation must always rest with his novels. These books present to the reader a facade which is curious and enticing but also rather misleading. Apart from the two romances, they constitute a group which has every appearance of homogeneity. Their concentration on dialogue, their high comedy, the fabling nature of their effects, their wit and irony and the slightness of their story-telling and characterization all set them apart from the mainstream of contemporary fiction. Not only are they unlike the works of other writers of Peacock's own time, formally at least: they are also unlike most books that have appeared before or since. Their organization is unique, and, in order to refer to them, we have to invent a classification

of 'conversation novel' in which we can convincingly admit only Peacock as author. Evidently, the fact that these works bear such limited and sometimes perverse similarities to other works which we also call novels has encouraged us to see them as a unity, offering us clever variants on a single, unchanging pattern. In some ways, this is correct. The ingredients and most of the techniques are not strikingly different as between *Headlong Hall* and *Gryll Grange,* although in time they span almost half a century.

But one of the things that has become plain to me is that the unity of Peacock's conversation novels cloaks a surprising diversity and development in feeling and procedure. Their themes remain fairly constant, but these are dialectical works, putting doubts into motion and revolving nervously around contrasting poles of optimism and pessimism. Frequently, Peacock's festive cheerfulness is subdued: in a book like *Melincourt* it seems overwhelmed. However, it always makes itself felt, and always suggests some counterbalance to his fears of mutability and constraint. Even in a world largely given over to oppression, misdirection and folly, he can perceive hope, especially in love, in Nature, in freedom, and in the pleasures of music, food and wine. In the later novels, from *The Misfortunes of Elphin* onwards, it is this hope which predominates, though a due sense of difficulty and a distaste for the most disagreeable manifestations of the public life of the time accompany it to the end. Thus, if Peacock's career in fiction begins with the frail joviality and hectic glitter of *Headlong Hall,* it concludes with the reasserted warmth and solace of *Gryll Grange.*

One should resist the impulse to derive too neat a pattern from any *oeuvre,* no matter how small, and I hope I am not being unduly systematizing here. But it seems to me that it is hard to avoid an impression of roundedness when one looks at Peacock's writing as a whole, and not to see it in terms of a greater comic richness and a more charged emotional involvement than it has often been seen in the past. In addition, I find that Peacock moves towards a fuller rendition of character and circumstance than one might expect from the fabling quality of his materials, and that in *Nightmare Abbey* and *Crotchet Castle,* but above all in *Gryll Grange,* he creates an ambience that may not unfairly be compared with those in more orthodox novels of his time.

Peacock has been mistakenly presented as a tranquil Epicurean whose accomplished art merely applies the chaste standards of the Augustans to the intemperacy of the Romantic period. In fact, everything about him is bound up with the problems of the age in which he lived. Political and economic unrest, the growth of a radical new literature and the rapid erosion of certainties incumbent upon a time of change all influenced him as profoundly, if not as directly, as his contemporaries. As Kiely has said, the Romantic novel, the form most immediately engaged with the dilemmas of its world, 'at best and at worst, is an almost continuous display of divisive tension, paradox, and uncertain focus' [see Additional Bibliography]. . . . I have had occasion to compare Peacock with Jane Austen, the greatest novelist of the early nineteenth century in England, and to remark on the gulf which separates them in spite of their shared concern with social health and personal concord. But although they are very different, comparable doubts underlie their books and give notice of the disturbing circumstances of which both writers are the product. An attentive reading of either *Pride and Prejudice* or *Nightmare Abbey* could produce no impression of serenity; the success of Jane Austen and Peacock rests not upon security but upon an engrossing accommodation with anxiety. I do not pretend that Peacock achieves this with Jane

Austen's extraordinary pertinacity and technical expertise, but it seems to me that his novels respond as freshly as hers to the problems not only of their own time, but of all times. They are taut and moving; they may be diversions, but they have a serious point; they do not evade pressing difficulties, but manage them subtly and pleasingly, at one remove; above all, they are works of conflict, not repose. Mayoux, I think, captures them precisely when he says, 'Il y a quelque chose de contradictoire—c'est le centre de force de Peacock'.

Given his dislike of the society he saw around him, his lack of religious belief and his susceptibility to feelings of transience and alienation, it is obvious that Peacock would need powerful compensations if he were not to produce books of undiluted gloom and ill-omen. He finds the strongest of these compensations in the notion of love, which becomes for him a guarantor of the freedom and fulfilment which his own world signally failed to provide. All his novels end with weddings, among the sophisticated as well as the simple, and we feel these to be hopeful portents for the future; they indicate that man and woman may still achieve liberation from the mood of fracture by which the books are often governed. In *Headlong Hall* the love element in the story is slight, and our interest is directed more at crotcheteers than at sweethearts. In succeeding novels, its encouraging counterpoint to the follies of public life grows in importance and affect. In *Nightmare Abbey,* emotions take on a human charge and the major characters are developed with fullness and sympathy; as a result, romantic intrigues acquire both vigour and depth. This process advances in *Maid Marian* and *The Misfortunes of Elphin,* where the lovers are seen in a legendary light which adds greatly to our sense of the representative, torch-bearing quality of their situation. It is consummated in *Gryll Grange,* a book saturated with romantic feeling and one in which love is brought to stand nobly against the forces of death and disruption. Associated with love are the power of Nature, and the delights of food, drink and music which are regularly used by Peacock to recall his characters from separateness, prescription and obsession to the truer satisfaction of their communal, sensuous natures. In every novel, music produces harmony, and eating and drinking cut short disputes and import cheerful gratification into the companionable groupings that they foster. This is a matter of comedy and a relish for the good things of life, especially as these are seen, like love, to offer prospects of camaraderie far more attractive than the empty systems-making of figures such as Mr Escot or Flosky. Although beef, Madeira and Old English songs are to be found from first to last in Peacock, and always engagingly perform the reassuring function I have ascribed to them here, one notices again that their significance increases, and their incidence becomes greater, as one moves to *Crotchet Castle* and *Gryll Grange.* In these latter-day works of retrenchment and consolidation, Peacock's concentration on music and dinners is expressed with extravagant insistence; it is as if, towards the end of his life, his need for alleviation was even stronger than before. Also, it is only in *Gryll Grange* that the recondite classicism of Peacock's reading is thoroughly organized for an artistic purpose. Previously, it was an omnipresent constituent of texture, conducted an unstressed, nostalgic campaign against the modern world, and injected curious enjoyments into his prose. But, in this final novel, references to Greece and Rome add a visionary perspective to the love stories with which he is dealing, and we come to feel the real romantic warmth, nourished by Petronius, Lucian and Apuleius, which underlay their earlier, quiet use. When we unearth the positive elements of Peacock's books, as I have done here, it is hard not to feel that their basic congruity is more striking than their superficial disparity. Together, they give an impression that mankind's happiness is to be discovered principally in the joys of the flesh, broadly conceived, and in circumstances far from the constraint of the public and fashionable spheres of life. Peacock distrusts our civilization and all its manifestations both personal and institutional; in his writing, he moves out among the beauties of the countryside and to country-houses largely segregated from the town, and there he builds up his imaginative celebration of the private, liberated, loving and sensuously satisfied existence which he valued above all others.

Peacock's conviction, which in one way or another is shared by many of his contemporaries, is that an existence such as he evokes is not only natural to man, but would also free him from the bonds in which he has been trapped by his society. The basis of Peacock's approach lies in his Old English, but at the same time Romantic, trust in man's innate capacity for a life of love and pleasure. In some respects this is primitivistic and pastoral, and very much of its time, and it certainly relates Peacock to Wordsworth and Scott as well as to the Jacobin novelists and Utilitarian thinkers with whom he is commonly associated. Although its context is dreamy, this is neither trivial nor evasive; in most of his books, it is not that he is fleeing a public world of which he disapproves, but rather that he is seeking to accommodate and redeem it in the easier alternative realm of his fiction. His works cope with difficulties not directly but by amusing, consoling obliquity; in the face of disorder, they assert as best they can the affirmative, comic values of love, kinship and bodily delight. As Able says, Peacock's is a serious interest in the human spirit, 'whose cultivation he saw increasingly neglected in an age devoted to a mere material progress'. But with his hopefulness goes an inescapable scepticism as to the possibility of an actual change for the better. I do not think that his novels express any immediate, reforming urge, except in the case of *Melincourt;* they expose our true natures and indicate the misdirection of many of our efforts, but they do not urge us towards revolution. Instead, they offer refreshment, and return us to everyday life with a surer trust in our more resilient selves and a sharper awareness of the forces of pro and contra in our experience. Their aim is clarification and compensation; they encourage us not to act but to understand.

It must be evident from what I have said that Peacock, except perhaps in *Crotchet Castle,* is not at all concerned with giving indulgent triumphs to the positive elements in life and neglecting the more threatening, contrary aspects of his world. In fact, he shows a distaste not just for his own society, but for many features of society *tout court;* corrupt institutions and authoritarian procedures are detected and opposed as keenly in the Arthurian Wales of *The Misfortunes of Elphin* as in the present-day literary milieu of *Nightmare Abbey.* I think it is a mistake to restrict the satirical application of Peacock's fiction merely to overt, contemporary targets, though these are clearly important. He goes out of his way to demonstrate that most of the follies about which he complains are to be seen in all civilizations, only the Greek offering a partial exception. He really has no faith in the state or in the systems by which man attempts to regulate and organize his behaviour; acutely, Able compares him with de la Rochefoucauld, 'persuaded that the selfish interest of the individual is . . . the cause behind every social institution' [see Additional Bibliography].

In view of the turmoil and rootlessness of his period and his own disenchantment with public life, it is easy to imagine that Peacock would suffer from no shortage of targets at which to direct his irony. I think there are four main ways in which his scepticism is felt by the reader. First, there are the Peacockian crotchets casting aspersions on Scotsmen, paper money and the universities which reappear in book after book. There is a substratum of censure to these remarks, but in principle they affect one in a playful, jokey way rather than as requiring solemn consideration. They are almost aspects of character and tone instead of theme; it is as if they were pointing out Peacock's own good-natured identification with the crotcheteers in his fiction, and inviting us to extend to him the same tolerance he reaches out to them. These are entertaining matters of texture, I suggest, and need not be taken *au sérieux*. Second, in most of his novels Peacock occasionally casts aside the clever relativism and refraction of his approach, and speaks openly to some question in hand. This is particularly the case in *The Misfortunes of Elphin*, where crude, high-pitched belligerence sometimes juts through the urbane indirection of the prose, with disastrous effects on the usually elegant ordonnance of Peacock's writing. I see this as evidence both of the strength of his disapprobation of certain features of his own age, and of the necessity of subtle stratagems for the mastering and expression of this feeling. Certainly it disrupts the tone of the books, and I can see no way in which we could regard this as other than an error of tact on Peacock's part. Third, we have the vivid, and intermittently not so vivid, crotcheteering for which Peacock is best known. Figures like Mr Asterias are creatures of a single obsession around which they try to arrange their whole experience of the world; they are reductionists, replacing multifariousness and liberty with singleness and authority. In general, these figures have a pronounced contemporary colouring; their hobby-horses may derive from the controversies of Peacock's day, or they may incorporate features of characters who attracted the author's attention during the composition of his novel. It is only rarely, it seems to me, that the crotcheteers can be taken as simple, parodic transpositions from life into literature. Mostly, they put together material cunningly annexed from different sources, and rearrange it in the interests of artistic vivacity rather than of convincing, authentic commentary. Mr Cranium, for example, is a charming creation whose relevance goes far beyond a mere ironic rebuttal of the claims of craniologists. Thus, although the neat systems by which they operate are shown to be unnatural impositions on the diverse fabric of life, and their energetic discussions, inevitably futile, get them nowhere near agreement or conclusiveness, the crotcheteers are far from negative. Their fads and prescriptions do not work, but they themselves are treated with indulgence; as producers of comedy and animation, they are superb. There is no bitterness in their handling; they are in error, as we all may be, and Peacock is tolerant of quirks which give so much pleasure and so rich a liveliness and brio. Some, such as Mr Cypress and the Hon Mr Listless, also reach heights of poetry and extravagance whose effect is almost purely attractive, and which compensate for the leadenness of figures like Flosky. The problem with Flosky, I think, as with Mr Forester and a number of others, is that they exist in a disconcerting state mid-way between developed character and satirical marionette, and that it is difficult for a reader to accommodate the veerings of presentation that this involves. But in principle Peacock's crotcheteers are hard to fault, combining criticism with amusement in a way that had not previously been well explored and has not since been used with anything like equivalent success. Fourth, and encompassing and arising from the forms of reproof which I have just been describing, is the larger political and ethical dimension of Peacock's antipathies. Although his works are full of contemporary reference, it seems

to me that their vision is more universal than particular; they are comedies, not only satires. They are really about mankind in general, about the problems which it has always faced and will go on facing in the future: the follies of his own time provide Peacock with impetus and example, but his substance comes from a wider-ranging, cool perspective on the activities of man. Peacock has a constant preference for the freedom of the individual, and constantly rejects authoritarianism and constraint, in public and private matters alike. If there is a single core to Peacock's thematic concerns it is this attack on the brash, prescriptive patterning which impedes the joy, openness and warmth that ought to form the true kernel of existence. (pp. 219-26)

Given the drama, conflict and irresolution of Peacock's writing, it is evident that the mood of his novels cannot be simple or single. Since in most cases its basis is not bland assertion but rather a complex balancing of forces, each doing battle with the others for supremacy, the result can only be a matter of dividedness and shifting half-tones of feeling. In his best work, Peacock marvellously presents the poignant strivings towards happiness and truth which are characteristic of his time, and in a context which does justice to the unsettlement of his circumstances. He is far from the frivolous escapism and classical tranquillity of which he has been accused, and his Epicurean accommodation of the problems of his time is anything but irresponsible. It is important that so much of his writing derives from the tradition of the debate; composure or predication is neither its aim nor its effect. A note of disturbance is heard throughout, and it is about this core of anxiety, this long-term collision between the claims of hopefulness and despondency, with its attendant qualities of animated equivocation and restlessness, that the books are organized. As I have said, there are variations between the novels, as in any process of change there would have to be. *Melincourt* is the blackest, its Italianate romance submerged in political satire and direct attack; *The Misfortunes of Elphin* has the most jovial *bonhomie*; *Crotchet Castle* is agreeable, but determinedly supine; *Gryll Grange* has the greatest charge of emotion and the fullest rendering of the power of love.

A wide range of moods is found in Peacock's works, from the warmth of satisfied love through the comic tautness of crotcheteering to the exasperation of political complaint, and our overall feelings are mingled and intricate. Absolute affirmation or negation does not exist; every element of every book is presented with a subtle threading of approval and disapproval. The consequence of this is that straightforward views and complacent acceptances are thoroughgoingly forbidden the reader; he is not permitted to sit back in conventionality and ease. Instead, alertness is enjoined at the same time that witty entertainment is provided. Peacock is humorous but sceptical, and prevents us from tolerating black and white notions or from looking thoughtlessly on any topic that comes within his purview. I have often had occasion to compare Peacock with Diderot . . . , and it is Mayoux who best defines their similarity when he talks of them as 'deux esprits dialectiques, incapables de se tenir à une position sans apercevoir la force de la position inverse, et donc incapables d'orthodoxie'. Thus, Peacock's irony is not just a matter of witty qualification: it is the necessary instrument of a probing sensibility alive to contrariety and nuance more than to the reassurance of simple outlines. A limp acquiescence in the status quo is allowed nowhere in his writing, apart perhaps from *Crotchet Castle*; his fiction is open-eyed and mercurial and, with the exception I have noted, emanates risk and liveliness rather than settlement. I think this awareness of fracture, this sense of the refractory nature of experience, is central to the success of Peacock's novels. It is what gives the lie to complaints about the evasiveness of his treatment of important notions. In fact, Peacock is a writer of serious concern and ingenious cleverness as well as a great entertainer, and . . . the value of his work derives substantially from the fusion within it of anxiety and reassurance to produce a comedy which pays proper heed both to the gloomy and to the more hopeful aspects of the world he presents.

I have so far been describing the tenor of Peacock's novels as a whole, and have not registered the changes that occur between **Headlong Hall** and **Gryll Grange**. In principle, teasing doubts and hesitancies make room, over the decades, for surer optimistic feelings, but there is no schematic progression from first book to last. In the earliest novels good cheer is more vulnerable than later, though an elegant balance and clarity is achieved in **Nightmare Abbey.** The romances move towards a freer enjoyment of positive emotion, though it is shadowed by a powerful undertone of political disquiet. **Crotchet Castle** and **Gryll Grange** cast off the cares of the outside world and pass concentratedly towards a celebration of love and pleasure from which the most burdensome import of the public sphere and its activities has been expunged. As I have said, I think there may be doubts about the integrity of the former of these novels, but of the latter, none: it is a genuinely noble piece of writing and loses nothing from the comparative narrowness of its scope and the personal quality of its regard.

Peacock's work is, then, less static than it may seem, and offers a range of feelings which alter from book to book but in which a pertinacious general direction may be seen. Equally, in every work, though in a framework of comedy, he is at pains to sharpen our minds to the ambiguity of experience and to prevent us from sinking gullibly into a mere submission to received opinion. In his career *in toto,* one therefore sees Peacock simultaneously true to a central core of interest, and exploring this core in different and developing ways, and one can hardly fail to be impressed by the richness of this process.

Clive Bell has written well and appreciatively about Peacock, but concludes his discussion on a downbeat note, remarking that 'He had stood for many great causes but for none had he stood greatly'. In this ringing apothegm I would take exception to the implication of the words 'great' and 'greatly'; it does not seem to me that the heroic endeavour they appear to predicate is a necessary, or often even a desirable, quality for the fostering of literary success. In fact, I have several times noted situations in which Peacock's attempts to cope with the problems of his day are half-hearted or rather compromising. I do not think that he was at all gladiatorial in his relations with the difficulties he saw both particularly around him and also attendant on life in general. But this does not detract from the high intelligence, entertainment and acute enquiry of his novels. Their merit is the cool, witty way in which they accommodate at one remove certain fears which are relevant to the novelist and to the world at large; they are not grand, and do not need to be. Their essence is better caught by Price, I think, who says of Peacock that 'He has his own world as much as Dickens, a fantastic place, strangely unreal, and yet strangely serious'. That mention of Dickens is apposite, and Price is fair to the cunning blend of comedy and satire which only Peacock has achieved so well. (pp. 228-31)

Bryan Burns, in his The Novels of Thomas Love Peacock, *Croom Helm, 1985, 250 p.*

ADDITIONAL BIBLIOGRAPHY

Able, Augustus Henry. *George Meredith and Thomas Love Peacock: A Study in Literary Influence.* 1933. Reprint. New York: Phaeton Press, 1970, 142 p.
 A discussion of Peacock's influence on George Meredith that explores sentimentalism, characterization, and other subjects.

Abrams, M. H. "Varieties of Romantic Theory: Shelley, Hazlitt, Keble, and Others." In his *The Mirror and the Lamp: Romantic Theory and the Critical Tradition,* pp. 125-55. New York: Oxford University Press, 1953.
 Interprets Peacock's "The Four Ages of Poetry" as a parody of Wordsworth's poetic theory.

Black, Sidney J. "The Peacockian Essence." *Boston University Studies in English* III, No. 4 (Winter 1957): 231-42.
 Identifies fundamental aspects of Peacock's satirical fiction.

Brett-Smith, H. F. B. Introduction to *Peacock's "Four Ages of Poetry," Shelley's "Defence of Poetry," Browning's "Essay on Shelley,"* by Thomas Love Peacock, Percy Bysshe Shelley, and Robert Browning, edited by H. F. B. Brett-Smith, pp. vii-xxv. Boston: Houghton Mifflin Co., 1921.
 A historical discussion of Peacock's essay, Shelley's response, and Browning's appreciation of Shelley.

————, and Jones, C. E. Introduction to *The Works of Thomas Love Peacock.* Vol. I, *Biographical Introduction and "Headlong Hall,"* by Thomas Love Peacock, edited by H. F. B. Brett-Smith and C. E. Jones, pp. xii-ccxii. London: Constable & Co., 1934.
 Generally considered an authoritative account of Peacock's life.

Brogan, Howard O. "Romantic Classicism in Peacock's Verse Satire." *Studies in English Literature, 1500-1900* XIV, No. 4 (Autumn 1974): 525-36.
 Labels Peacock a Romantic classicist and discusses his satirical poetry.

Buchanan, Robert. "Thomas Love Peacock: A Personal Reminiscence." *New Quarterly Magazine* IV (April-July 1875): 238-55.
 An admiring biographical portrait used by later biographers as a source of information.

Burdett, Osbert. "Thomas Love Peacock (1785-1866)." *The London Mercury* VIII, No. 43 (May 1923): 21-32.
 A sketch of Peacock's life and a survey of his works.

Campbell, Olwen W. *Thomas Love Peacock.* New York: Roy Publishers, 1953, 104 p.
 Provides an unfavorable assessment of Peacock's life and works. Scholars sometimes fault this study for inadequate research.

Crabbe, John K. "The Harmony of Her Mind: Peacock's Emancipated Women." *Tennessee Studies in Literature* XXIII (1978): 75-86.
 Traces the development of the independent heroine in Peacock's fiction.

Dawson, Carl, ed. *Thomas Love Peacock.* The Profiles in Literature Series, edited by B. C. Southam. London: Routledge & Kegan Paul, 1968, 116 p.
 A collection of extracts from Peacock's novels with critical commentary.

Dodson, Charles B. Introduction to *Thomas Love Peacock: "Nightmare Abbey," "The Misfortunes of Elphin," "Crotchet Castle,"* by Thomas Love Peacock, edited by Charles B. Dodson, pp. vii-xxviii. New York: Holt, Rinehart and Winston, 1971.
 A critical overview of three of Peacock's novels focusing on, among other topics, theme, fictional technique, characterization, and prose style.

Draper, John W. "The Social Satires of Thomas Love Peacock: Parts I and II." *Modern Language Notes* XXXIII, No. 8 (December 1918): 456-63; XXXIV, No. 1 (January 1919): 23-8.

Outlines Peacock's attitudes toward the social issues of his day.

Fain, John T. ''Peacock on the Spirit of the Age (1809-1860).'' In . . . *All These to Teach: Essays in Honor of C. A. Robertson*, edited by Robert A. Bryan and others, pp. 180-89. Gainesville: University of Florida Press, 1965.
Explores Peacock's treatment of commercialism in his works.

Fedden, Henry Romilly. ''Thomas Love Peacock.'' In *The English Novelists: A Survey of the Novel by Twenty Contemporary Novelists*, edited by Derek Verschoyle, pp. 125-38. London: Chatto & Windus, 1936.
A critical introduction to Peacock's life and works.

Felton, Felix. *Thomas Love Peacock*. London: George Allen & Unwin, 1973, 319 p.
A detailed study of Peacock's life and works covering such topics as his early and late writings, his friendship with Shelley, and his daughter's relationship with George Meredith.

Frye, Northrop. ''Rhetorical Criticism: Theory of Genres.'' In his *Anatomy of Criticism: Four Essays*, pp. 243-340. 1957. Reprint. New York: Atheneum, 1966.
An influential critical work that divides literature into several broad categories and analyzes the way in which these categories relate to their sources in myth and ritual. Frye includes a brief description of the form of Peacock's satires.

Garnett, David, ed. *The Novels of Thomas Love Peacock*, by Thomas Love Peacock. London: Rupert Hart-Davis, 1948, 982 p.
Contains critical introductions to each of Peacock's novels.

Hewitt, Douglas. ''Entertaining Ideas: A Critique of Peacock's *Crotchet Castle*.'' *Essays in Criticism* XX, No. 2 (April 1970): 200-12.
Concludes that *Crotchet Castle* is flawed by Peacock's refusal to treat the ideas it contains seriously.

Hoff, Peter Sloat. ''The Voices of *Crotchet Castle*.'' *The Journal of Narrative Technique* 2, No. 3 (September 1972): 186-98.
Examines narrative voices in *Crotchet Castle*.

————. ''*Maid Marian* and *The Misfortunes of Elphin*: Peacock's Burlesque Romances.'' *Genre* VIII, No. 3 (September 1975): 210-32.
Describes the principal features of Peacock's romances and asserts that they are as successful as his satirical fiction.

Houghton, Lord. Preface to *The Works of Thomas Love Peacock, Including His Novels, Poems, Fugitive Pieces, Criticisms, Etc.*, by Thomas Love Peacock, edited by Henry Cole, Vol. 1, pp. vii-xxiii. London: Richard Bentley and Son, 1875.
A critical introduction to Peacock's works.

Jack, Ian. ''Peacock.'' In his *English Literature: 1815-1832*, pp. 213-24. Oxford: Oxford University Press, Clarendon Press, 1963.
Examines Peacock's novels, exploring similarities and differences in plot, character, and theme.

Kiely, Robert. ''*Nightmare Abbey*: Thomas Love Peacock, 1818.'' In his *The Romantic Novel in England*, pp. 174-88. Cambridge: Harvard University Press, 1972.
Examines Peacock's treatment of the ideas of the English Romantics in *Nightmare Abbey*.

Madden, Lionel. *Thomas Love Peacock*. Literature in Perspective. London: Evans Brothers, 1967, 160 p.
Asserts that the attitudes underlying Peacock's satire are positive and charts the development of Peacock's thought through an examination of his poetry, novels, and other writings.

————. ''A Short Guide to Peacock Studies.'' *The Critical Survey* 4, No. 4 (Summer 1970): 193-97.
A critical history of works by and about Peacock.

Millett, Fred B. ''Thomas Love Peacock.'' In *Minor British Novelists*, edited by Charles Alva Hoyt, pp. 32-58. Carbondale: Southern Illinois University Press, 1967.
An analysis of Peacock's novels centering on character and plot and interspersed with biographical detail.

Mills, Howard. *Peacock: His Circle and His Age*. Cambridge: Cambridge University Press, 1969, 257 p.
Argues that Peacock's friendship with Shelley was crucial to his development as an artist, and that Peacock's work must be read not as the product of a major imagination but as a comment on his age.

Mulvihill, James D. ''Thomas Love Peacock's *Crotchet Castle*: Reconciling the Spirits of the Age.'' *Nineteenth-Century Fiction* 38, No. 3 (December 1983): 253-70.
Claims that Peacock is more successful at synthesizing the disparate ideas in *Crotchet Castle* than is generally supposed.

————. ''Peacock and Perfectibility in *Headlong Hall*.'' *Clio* 13, No. 3 (Spring 1984): 227-46.
An examination of the theme of progress in *Headlong Hall*.

Nicolls, Edith. ''A Biographical Notice of Thomas Love Peacock.'' In *The Works of Thomas Love Peacock, Including His Novels, Poems, Fugitive Pieces, Criticisms, Etc.*, by Thomas Love Peacock, edited by Henry Cole, Vol. 1, pp. xxv-lii. London: Richard Bentley and Son, 1875.
An account of Peacock's life by his granddaughter that is often relied upon by later biographers.

Paul, Herbert. ''The Novels of Peacock.'' *The Nineteenth Century and After* LIII, No. 314 (April 1903): 651-64.
A survey of Peacock's novels. Paul notes that despite his limitations, ''there are few more fascinating novelists than Peacock.''

Praz, Mario. ''Thomas Love Peacock.'' In his *The Hero in Eclipse in Victorian Fiction*, translated by Angus Davidson, pp. 87-101. London: Oxford University Press, Geoffrey Cumberlege, 1956.
Labels Peacock a bourgeois satirist with roots in the eighteenth century and finds his works destructive because they fail to expose underlying truth.

Prickett, Stephen. ''Peacock's 'Four Ages' Recycled.'' *The British Journal of Aesthetics* 22, No. 2 (Spring 1982): 158-66.
Contends that in his essay Peacock was not attacking particular schools of poetry, but examining the nature and purpose of poetry in the modern age.

Priestley, J. B. ''Prince Seithenyn.'' In his *The English Comic Characters*, pp. 178-97. New York: Dodd, Mead and Co., 1925.
A character study of Prince Seithenyn in Peacock's *The Misfortunes of Elphin*.

————. Introduction to *''Nightmare Abbey'' and ''Crotchet Castle''*, by Thomas Love Peacock, pp. vii-x. The Novel Library. London: Hamish Hamilton, 1947.
A short overview of *Nightmare Abbey* and *Crotchet Castle*.

Raleigh, Walter. ''On Some Writers and Critics of the Nineteenth Century: Peacock.'' In his *On Writing and Writers*, edited by George Gordon, pp. 151-54. 1926. Reprint. London: Edward Arnold & Co., 1927.
Finds Peacock a lover of ideas and praises the realism of his female characters.

Read, Bill. *The Critical Reputation of Thomas Love Peacock with an Annotated Enumerative Bibliography of Works by and about Peacock from February, 1800, to June, 1958*. Ann Arbor, Mich.: University Microfilms, 1960, 285 p.
An evaluative study of Peacock criticism including an annotated bibliographical list of works by and about Peacock.

Sage, Lorna, ed. *Peacock: The Satirical Novels, a Casebook*. London: The Macmillan Press, 1976, 253 p.
Contains nineteenth- and twentieth-century critical appraisals of Peacock's work.

Salz, Paulina June. ''Peacock's Use of Music in His Novels.'' *Journal of English and Germanic Philology* LIV, No. 3 (July 1955): 370-79.
Establishes Peacock's love of classical music, especially opera, and discusses its effect on the style and structure of his novels.

Tillyard, E. M. W. "Thomas Love Peacock." In his *Essays Literary and Educational*, pp. 114-29. London: Chatto & Windus, 1962.
> A general survey of Peacock's life and novels.

Van Doren, Carl. *The Life of Thomas Love Peacock*. 1911. Reprint. New York: Russell & Russell, 1966, 299 p.
> One of the first major biographical studies of Peacock. It describes the rational foundation of Peacock's satire, and assesses his style and the lasting value of his works.

Vidal, Gore. "Thomas Love Peacock: The Novel of Ideas." In his *The Second American Revolution, and Other Essays (1976-1982)*, pp. 115-31. New York: Random House, 1982.
> A favorable review of Marilyn Butler's *Peacock Displayed* (see excerpt dated 1979) in which Vidal discusses the political, religious, and philosophical content of Peacock's novels.

William Makepeace Thackeray

1811-1863

(Also wrote under pseudonyms of Michael Angelo Titmarsh, Samuel Titmarsh, George Savage Fitz-boodle, Mr. Snob, Yellowplush, Ikey Solomons, The Fat Contributor, and Jeames de la Pluche, among others) English novelist, essayist, short story, fairy tale, and sketch writer, poet, critic, and editor.

The following entry presents criticism of Thackeray's novel *The History of Henry Esmond, Esq., a Colonel in the Service of Her Majesty Q. Anne, Written by Himself* (1852). For a discussion of Thackeray's complete career, see *NCLC*, Vol. 5; for criticism devoted to his novel *Vanity Fair: A Novel without a Hero,* see *NCLC*, Vol. 14.

The History of Henry Esmond is at once a colorful historical novel of eighteenth-century battles and political intrigues and the absorbing private memoirs of its title character, who reminisces about his earlier life from the perspective of old age. Shocking to most early reviewers due to its unconventional love theme, *Henry Esmond* later came to be viewed as Thackeray's most accomplished work because of its historical verisimilitude and unified construction. Today, while the novel is no longer considered his best—that superlative is usually reserved for *Vanity Fair*—*Henry Esmond* is generally regarded as Thackeray's most provocative book for the ambiguity of its resolution and the complexity of its characters.

Thackeray was a popular and well-established author by the time he wrote *Henry Esmond.* He had capped a successful career as a satirical writer for various periodicals with the serial publication of several novels, including the widely acclaimed *Vanity Fair,* which appeared in 1848. Now rivaling Charles Dickens as a marketable author, Thackeray signed a contract in 1851 with the publishing firm of Smith, Elder, which offered him 1,200 pounds for a novel to be published in book form rather than serially. Probably begun in September of 1851, *Henry Esmond* grew out of two circumstances in Thackeray's life—one professional and the other personal. Shortly before beginning the novel, he had finished a series of lectures called *The English Humourists of the Eighteenth Century;* his interest in the eighteenth century and its literature suggested the idea of making his new work a historical novel of the period. The writing of *Henry Esmond* also coincided with a turbulent time in his personal life. Thackeray—whose wife, Isabella, had years earlier suffered a severe mental breakdown from which she never recovered—was deeply in love with Jane Brookfield, the wife of his old and close friend William Henry Brookfield. Both Brookfields were aware of Thackeray's attachment and unconcerned about it; however, about the time he began work on *Henry Esmond,* Thackeray argued with Brookfield about his friend's treatment of his wife, and was forbidden her company as a result. Thus, *Henry Esmond* was written while the author was despondent over his separation from the woman he idolized, a circumstance that contributed, biographers believe, to the melancholy tone of the book. Scholars also surmise that Jane Brookfield is figured to some extent in *Henry Esmond* in the character of Rachel Castlewood while Thackeray himself wrote that Esmond was, in part, a "handsome likeness" of himself.

Henry Esmond was published in three volumes in the fall of 1852. At the time, several critics doubted the wisdom of an author whose past successes lay in his incisive satire of contemporary society undertaking a historical novel. The work showcases some of the most noteworthy and dramatic events of the period through the hero's involvement in the War of the Spanish Succession, including his participation in the Duke of Marlborough's 1704 campaign against the French and Bavarians, the Battle of Blenheim. The protagonist of *Henry Esmond* also becomes involved in the Jacobite cause, intending to secure the throne for the Pretender James Edward Stuart upon the death of Queen Anne. Indeed, even in its appearance and language the work was imbued with the flavor of the eighteenth century: it was set in old-fashioned type and sprinkled with archaic diction and spelling. While a variety of historical figures appear in the novel, they are of secondary interest in comparison to the fictional characters, the chief of whom is the narrator, Henry Esmond himself. Esmond tells his autobiography primarily in the third person, though he occasionally lapses into first, usually at moments of great emotion or crisis. The history he reveals begins when he is twelve years old, the orphaned son, supposedly illegitimate, of the third viscount of Castlewood. He comes to live with his late father's kinsman, the fourth viscount, his 20-year-old wife, and their two young children, Beatrix and Frank. From the start, Esmond loves, indeed, worships, Lady Rachel Castlewood for her beauty and kindness. As time goes on, Esmond notes increasing disharmony in the household: Lord Castlewood drinks and philanders, Rachel is jealous and demanding. When her beauty is marred by smallpox, the break between the Castlewoods is complete. Nonetheless, after the villainous Lord Mohun assails his wife's honor, Castlewood engages him in a duel. Fatally wounded, Castlewood reveals to Esmond, now a young man, that he is not illegitimate but is in fact the rightful heir to Castlewood. Esmond chooses not to act on this information out of his regard for Rachel and her children. Imprisoned for a year for acting as Castlewood's second in the duel, Esmond is visited in jail by Rachel, who, in a passionate scene, holds him responsible for her husband's death and also accuses him of causing their earlier estrangement. Esmond is devastated by this unexpected and unfair treatment from the woman he has, as he frequently emphasizes, loved as a mother and worshipped as a goddess. Upon his release from prison he becomes a soldier and leaves England immediately.

Eventually, Rachel relents and Esmond is again received by the family. On a visit to Castlewood after an absence of some duration, Esmond falls in love with the woman who will haunt him and taunt him for the next ten years. In one of the novel's most famous scenes, Beatrix descends the staircase to greet him and Esmond is suddenly aware that she has become a desirable woman. Willful, capricious, ambitious, and utterly enchanting, Beatrix repeatedly rejects Esmond, intending to marry for position and money. Esmond, who confides his passion to Rachel, is persistent, nonetheless, and continues to pursue a career as a soldier, hoping always that any recognition he earns will endear him to Beatrix. It is his love for Beatrix, rather than any political conviction, that induces Esmond to join her and Frank in their involvement in the Jacobite cause. Their plans fail, however, because at a crucial moment in the intrigue the Old Pretender, James Edward Stuart, is at a tryst with Beatrix. Seeing this, Esmond relates that his love for Beatrix vanished on the spot. In the novel's denouement, briefly narrated rather than presented in detail, Esmond marries Rachel and the two emigrate to Virginia.

A single aspect of *Henry Esmond* has dominated criticism of the novel: Esmond's relationship with Rachel. While early reviewers did discuss such topics in the novel as its artistic unity, which was generally praised, and its historical ambience, which elicited mixed responses, it was the unexpected marriage at the novel's conclusion that overshadowed all other critical concerns. Thackeray himself, asked by an acquaintance why he had married Esmond and Rachel, reportedly answered: "My dear lady, it was not I who married them. They married themselves." Many of the book's earliest reviewers were horrified by the suggestion of incest implicit in Esmond's marriage to a woman toward whom he had stood in the relationship of a son throughout the rest of the story. Such an occurrence was "a perversion which sickens the heart," according to one critic. George Eliot said simply, "*Henry Esmond* is the most uncomfortable book you can imagine." A related objection concerned Rachel's moral character, as her obvious flaws of jealousy, emotionalism, and possessiveness, coupled with her harboring of an illicit, "unnatural" passion for Esmond, seemed to many readers to render her an inappropriate and unacceptable heroine. That Thackeray could make his hero marry such a woman was seen as a fresh example of the unpleasant and chronic cynicism, the inability or unwillingness to distinguish standards of right and wrong, that reviewers had detected in his previous works. One dissenter from this opinion was George Brimley, who argued that the delicacy of Thackeray's handling of his love theme and the human truth of it kept the union from being offensive. Brimley also defended Thackeray's characterization of Rachel, claiming that her faults only contributed to the veracity of her portrayal. Despite the vehemence and superior numbers of Thackeray's detractors, it was Brimley's view that prevailed. By 1864, the year after Thackeray's death, reviewer Richard Simpson could refer to *Henry Esmond* as the author's "best novel" as though this were an accepted judgment, and in 1879 Anthony Trollope enthusiastically commended *Henry Esmond* as "the greatest work that Thackeray did." Every aspect of the novel now came to be praised: the authenticity of its historical atmosphere, the unity of its plot, the verisimilitude of its characters, even, in a dramatic reversal of earlier opinion, the moral goodness of Esmond and Rachel. While uneasiness over the novel's denouement continued—William Dean Howells remarked in 1900 that the marriage did not seem "either nice or true"—on the whole such objections were few.

Although *Henry Esmond* has been overshadowed in modern criticism by *Vanity Fair*, which has come to be viewed as Thackeray's greatest work for its incisive satire and panoramic vision of English society, *Henry Esmond* nevertheless has elicited a large body of commentary in the twentieth century. The exact relationship between Esmond and Rachel remains a central concern of the novel's modern critics, and discussion of the issue invariably involves speculation regarding a prominent and difficult question of *Esmond* criticism: since the narrator is himself a character rather than an omniscient, impartial recorder of events, to what degree is Esmond aware of the implications of his own story, and, indeed, how reliable and truthful a narrator is he? In particular, scholars debate how seriously the reader is to take what Ioan Williams has called Esmond's "closing hymn to domestic bliss." Some commentators unhesitatingly accept Esmond's assessment of the wisdom of his marital choice and the happiness that resulted from it; they thus see *Henry Esmond* as a sort of *Bildungsroman*, the tale of a youth's growth to an emotional maturity symbolized by his rejection of Beatrix and his marriage to Rachel. Other commentators, contending that Esmond's own explicit statements regarding his happiness are subtly and ironically undermined by the novelist himself, suggest that Esmond's marriage to Rachel is no conventional happy ending because his love for her remains fundamentally filial rather than sexual, because her jealousy and possessiveness are sure to poison her second marriage as they did her first, and because Esmond is still in love with Beatrix. The novel's characters no less than its conclusion spark disagreement because of their ambiguity. Esmond has been viewed at any point along the spectrum from moral hero to emotional sadist; Rachel from self-sacrificing martyr to demanding shrew; Beatrix from misunderstood victim to heartless coquette.

Henry Esmond is in some respects an anomaly in Thackeray's canon. His only novel to be completed before publication, it is usually credited with possessing a unity and cohesion lacking in the author's other works. Further, in *Henry Esmond*, Thackeray employed the generally un-Thackerayan techniques of a single narrative perspective and a historical setting. Nonetheless, the novel is considered vintage Thackeray in the equivocality of its resolution and the complex ambiguity of its characters. While rarely regarded by modern scholars as his finest work, *Henry Esmond* remains Thackeray's most perfectly constructed novel as well as an intriguing and provocative creation.

(See also *Something about the Author,* Vol. 23, and *Dictionary of Literary Biography,* Vol. 21: *Victorian Novelists before 1885,* and Vol. 55: *Victorian Prose Writers before 1867.*)

CHARLOTTE BRONTË   (letter date 1852)

[*An English novelist, Brontë broke with the traditional portrayal of women in fiction by introducing intelligent, self-confident female protagonists. Her admiration of* Vanity Fair *prompted her to dedicate to Thackeray the second edition of her own most famous novel,* Jane Eyre *(1847). Thackeray's publisher, George Smith, gave Brontë the first volume of* Henry Esmond *to read before the novel's publication. In the following excerpt from a letter to Smith acknowledging the favor, she appraises both the historical and moral atmosphere of* Henry Esmond, *critiquing also Thackeray's depiction of women in the novel.*]

It has been a great delight to me to read Mr Thackeray's work [*Henry Esmond*]; and I so seldom now express my sense of kindness that, for once, you must permit me, without rebuke, to thank you for a pleasure so rare and special. Yet I am not going to praise either Mr Thackeray or his book. I have read, enjoyed, been interested, and, after all, feel full as much ire and sorrow as gratitude and admiration. And still one can never lay down a book of his without the last two feelings having their part, be the subject of treatment what it may. In the first half of the book what chiefly struck me was the wonderful manner in which the writer throws himself into the spirit and letters of the times whereof he treats; the allusions, the illustrations, the style, all seem to me so masterly in their exact keeping, their harmonious consistency, their nice, natural truth, their pure exemption from exaggeration. No second-rate imitator can write in that way; no coarse scene-painter can charm us with an allusion so delicate and perfect. But what bitter satire, what relentless dissection of diseased subjects! Well, and this, too, is right, or would be right, if the savage surgeon did not seem so fiercely pleased with his work. Thackeray likes to dissect an ulcer or an aneurism; he has pleasure in putting his cruel knife or probe into quivering living flesh. Thackeray would not like all the world to be good; no great satirist would like society to be perfect.

As usual, he is unjust to women, quite unjust. There is hardly any punishment he does not deserve for making Lady Castlewood peep through a keyhole, listen at a door, and be jealous of a boy and a milkmaid. Many other things I noticed that, for my part, grieved and exasperated me as I read; but then, again, came passages so true, so deeply thought, so tenderly felt, one could not help forgiving and admiring.

I wish there was any one whose word he cared for to bid him God speed, to tell him to go on courageously with the book; he may yet make it the best he has ever written.

But I wish he could be told not to care much for dwelling on the political or religious intrigues of the times. Thackeray, in his heart, does not value political or religious intrigues of any age or date. He likes to show us human nature at home, as he himself daily sees it; his wonderful observant faculty likes to be in action. In him this faculty is a sort of captain and leader; and if ever any passage in his writings lacks interest, it is when this master-faculty is for a time thrust into a subordinate position. I think such is the case in the former half of the present volume. Towards the middle he throws off restraint, becomes himself, and is strong to the close. Everything now depends on the second and third volumes. If, in pith and interest, they fall short of the first, a true success cannot ensue. If the continuation be an improvement upon the commencement, if the stream gather force as it rolls, Thackeray will triumph. Some people have been in the habit of terming him the second writer of the day; it just depends on himself whether or not these critics shall be justified in their award. He need not be the

second. God made him second to no man. If I were he, I would show myself as I am, not as critics report me; at any rate I would do my best. Mr Thackeray is easy and indolent, and seldom cares to do his best. (pp. 314-15)

> *Charlotte Brontë, in a letter to George Smith on February 14, 1852, in* The Brontës: Their Lives, Friendships and Correspondence, *Vol. III, Basil Blackwell, 1980, pp. 314-15.*

THE ATHENAEUM   (essay date 1852)

[*In the following excerpt from a mixed review of* Henry Esmond, *the critic finds that the novel displays Thackeray's characteristic eloquence and insight into human nature, but complains that it is too similar to his previous works and that it lacks a satisfactory plot.*]

Many reasons combine to invest the re-appearance of Mr. Thackeray as a fictionist with interest. His admirers who saw in *Pendennis* to a considerable extent a reproduction of the materials which compose the admirable qualities of *Vanity Fair* will desire to know if on the new ground which he has here broken [in *Esmond*], he has produced new views of life and characters not described before. Again, in his two former works Mr. Thackeray laboured under the artistic disadvantages of serial writing,—from which in the present one he has freed himself. He comes now before his audience with the opportunity of shaping his story in due form, and giving consistency to its parts. Then, if both these conditions be fulfilled, his novelists have still to be tried in other respects by the very high standard of *Vanity Fair*.

As regards the first of these questions,—we fear that we must adopt the title to the second chapter of the third of the volumes before us—"I harp on the same string"—as a reply. *Vanitas Vanitatum* is still the text on which Mr. Thackeray everywhere moralizes. Admirably worked up as are many of the brilliant passages of *Esmond,* much of it reads like a monologue in the author's peculiar manner on the hollowness of the world as seen in Queen Anne's time. There is in this work a wide display of mastery over the rhetoric of fiction, and a copious exhibition of the writer's hoarded knowledge of men and books. Once more we feel that we have before us a masculine and thoroughly English writer, uniting the power of subtle analysis with a strong volition and a moving eloquence. But no fresh fount of thought is touched in *Esmond,*—no new characters are exhibited,—no novel forms of life are introduced. The emotions stirred are the same as of old,—and after the old fashion.— On the other hand, the author's eloquence has gained in richness and harmony,—his pathos is now sweeter, less jarred against by angry sarcasm, but perhaps scarcely so powerful. The conception of Esmond's life is somewhat unnatural,—at the least, extremely improbable; and for a writer whose *forte* is the description of common nature, the plot is too romantic, and not sustained by sufficient colour. A man with the martyr-like moral heroism of Esmond could be best painted by a writer with a sanguine glow of enthusiasm, and with more faith in human nature than the author of *Vanity Fair* avows. In the hands of Mr. Thackeray Esmond wants vital heat. We read of his trials,—but do not feel them.

Though the story, costume, incidents, and diction of *Esmond* are different from those of *Vanity Fair,* there is such resemblance between the views of Human Nature shown in each, that we cannot accept *Esmond*—with all its ability and its various display of literary power—as a new triumph for the author. If he sustains, he certainly does not extend his reputation by it. If we had never read *Vanity Fair* this work would have struck us on the ground of indisputable originality. New scenes and a language artificially varied (however skilfully the latter feat may be performed) do not constitute essential novelty. When an author in fiction desires to open a fresh vein, he can do so only by inventing novel characters or by describing fresh nature. . . .

In *Esmond*—as we have said—we find no new creations of fiction. By many degrees the finest character in the book is Viscountess (Francis) Castlewood;—but Mr. Thackeray's readers know her well already—differently dressed. Beatrix is but another Becky,—more brilliant in costume, less sparkling in talent. Esmond, a more original sketch, is of a dull morality. He is called *Don Dismallo* by his comrades,—quizzed by Beatrix as "Knight of the Rueful Countenance,"—and named by the Pretender *"Le Grand Ennuyeux."* The various historical persons introduced are sketched rather than described. It is felt by the reader, that they do not contribute to the action, except in the case of the Pretender,—who is ingeniously enough introduced towards the end of the third volume. The picture of Marlborough is the best historical portrait in the whole work. We know nowhere a better likeness of this unheroic hero than is here presented. But when we tell our readers that the incidents of the story extend from the battle of the Boyne to after the battle of Blenheim, they will feel that there could not be space to manœuvre a third of the crowd of celebrated persons who are introduced within three volumes. Of the wits of the period Steele fares best, and is the most lifelike figure. The attempts at portraying Swift and Bolingbroke are decided failures,—the portrait of Addison is not much better. As an historical novel this cannot be accepted.

Esmond must, then, be read, not for its characters—which are all cases of metempsychosis,—but for its romantic though improbable plot, its spirited grouping, and its many thrilling utterances of the anguish of the human heart. While the plot fails to satisfy as an artistic whole, its incidents are startling and bold, but somewhat unreal-looking. As we have said, Esmond himself wants life. We can form from his own narration no distinct conception of him,—and the artifice of making his daughter describe him in the Preface reads coldly. The *finale* of the piece is painfully disappointing. The reader who has been hoping throughout that Beatrix would at last flower into virtue for Esmond's reward, is shocked to find her finally flung away like a withered weed, and Esmond's affections abruptly transferred from the daughter to the mother. To this latter lady Esmond has stood in such relations throughout the story that his sudden appearance with her at the altar affects us somewhat like a marriage with his own mother. All the previous emotions of the piece return to taunt us,—and the sympathies which Mr. Thackeray has been kneading and compounding through the whole of his previous pages are mockingly tossed out of the window like Dr. Kitchiner's salad.—We must add, that the display of literary art is too strong in every chapter of these volumes. There is too much of the retrospective wisdom of the nineteenth century—and too frequent an interposing of the writer as a sentimental moralist in his own peculiar way,—not to disturb the illusion of the narrative. Many of the passages in which the author moralizes are among the best and most highly finished, as well as the most pathetic, that have come from Mr. Thackeray's pen;—but, as in *Vanity Fair,* there is often a curious and not quite satisfactory conjunction of the sarcastic and the sentimental,—as if a cynic were resolving to chastize with his satire, and relenting into tears. The antique diction

does not hide the peculiar *manière de penser;* while it produces sometimes a *bizarre* effect, as if we were reading a speech of the Premier in blank verse, or a chapter of Mr. Macaulay's *History* in pentameters. (p. 1199)

We advise our readers to begin by carefully mastering the chapter showing the pedigree of the Castlewood family,—else they will not understand the plot, and will be compelled repeatedly to turn back. The number of Lords Castlewood and the very intricate inter-relationship of the family give an appearance of confusion in the commencement of the story,— and it is not until the middle of the first volume that it clears itself away. Having reached that point—"Forward" will be the wish of every reader of this highly-wrought work. (p. 1201)

A review of "Esmond: A Story of Queen Anne's Reign," in The Athenaeum, No. 1306, November 6, 1852, pp. 1199-1201.

[GEORGE HENRY LEWES] (essay date 1852)

[*Lewes was one of the most versatile men of letters in the Victorian era. A prominent English journalist, he was the founder, with Leigh Hunt, of the* Leader, *a radical political journal that he edited from 1851 to 1854. He served as the first editor of the* Fortnightly Review *from 1865 to 1866, a journal that he also helped to establish. Critics often cite Lewes's influence on the novelist George Eliot, to whom he was companion and mentor, as his principal contribution to English letters, but they also credit him with critical acumen in his literary commentary, most notably in his dramatic criticism. In the following excerpt from a favorable review of* Henry Esmond, *Lewes praises the originality and moral seriousness of the novel.*]

It is to show us some reflected image of [Queen Anne's] time that [*The History of Henry Esmond*] is written; and therefore, unless duly warned, the reader may feel some disappointment when he finds that "Thackeray's new novel" is not a comic novel, scarcely a novel at all, and in no sense a satire. It is a beautiful book, not one sentence of which may be skipped; but it is as unlike *Vanity Fair* and *Pendennis* as a book written by Thackeray can be.

To those who look beyond the passing hour, and see something more in literature than the occupation of a languid leisure, *Esmond* will have many sources of interest. One of these may be the purely biographical one of representing a new phase in Thackeray's growth. Tracing the evolution of his genius from the wild and random sketches which preceded *Vanity Fair,* we perceive an advancing growth, both as a moralist and as an artist. In *Vanity Fair* the mocking mephistophelic spirit was painfully obtrusive; to laugh at the world—to tear away its many masks—to raise the crown even from Cæsar's head, that we might note the baldness which the laurels covered—to make love and devotion themselves ridiculous, seemed his dominant purpose; and had it not been for the unmistakeable kindliness, the love of generosity, and the sympathy with truth which brightened those mocking pages, all that has been ignorantly or maliciously said of Thackeray's "heartlessness" would have had its evidence.

In *Pendennis* there was a decided change. The serious and nobler element, before subordinate, there rose to supremacy; the mockery withdrew into the second place. A kinder and a juster appreciation of life gave increased charm to the work. Although, perhaps, not on the whole so amusing, because less novel, and, in some respects, a repetition of *Vanity Fair,* it was, nevertheless, an advance in art, was written with more care, and, as before hinted, was less sarcastic and sceptical.

That vein of seriousness which ran like a small silver thread through the tapestry of **Vanity Fair**, has become the woof of **Esmond**; the mocking spirit has fled; such sarcasm as remains is of another sort—a kind of sad smile, that speaks of pity, not of scorn. Nor is this the only change. That careless disrespect, which on a former occasion we charged him with [in an 1850 review of **Pendennis**], is nowhere visible in **Esmond**. If as a work of art **Esmond** has defects, they are not the defects of carelessness. What he has set himself to do, he has done seriously, after due preparation.

Seeing, as we do, such evidences of growth, and of growth *upwards,* and remembering that he is only now in his forty-second year, may be not form the highest hopes of such a mind? Considered as a landmark on his career, **Esmond** is of peculiar significance. But we have here to consider it in another light; the reader impatiently asks, "What am I to think of it?"

Little Sir, you are to think *this* of it: An autobiography, written in the autumn light of a calm and noble life, sets before you much of the private and domestic, no less than of the public and historic activity of the reigns of William and Anne. The thread which holds these together is a simple and a touching one—the history of *two* devotions. All who have *lived* will feel here the pulse of real suffering, so different from "romantic woe;" all who have loved will trace a real affection here, more touching because it has a quiet reserve in its expression; but we shall not be in the least surprised to hear even "highly intelligent persons" pronounce it "rather a falling off." But you, good sir, who follow your *Leader,* will honestly declare that it touched and delighted you; that from the first page to the last you loved the book and its author.

Without pretending to that minute knowledge of the period which could alone justify an authoritative opinion, we may say that this book has so much the air and accent of the time, it would impose on us if presented as a veritable History of Colonel Esmond; and this verisimilitude is nowhere obtruded; the art has concealed the art.

In structure and purpose it reminds us of Leigh Hunt's *Sir Ralph Esher,* to which justice has not been done, because it has been read for a novel. The men of those days, no less than the events, move across the scene, and we get hasty yet vivid glimpses of Addison, Steele, Swift, Bolingbroke, Marlborough, Atterbury, Lord Mohun, and the Pretender.... [These] historic persons have none of the "dignity of history"—they walk before us "in their habit as they lived."

The characters are numerous, but are rather "sketched in," as one would find them in memoirs, than elaborately developed, as in a fiction. Lady Castlewood and Beatrix are, indeed, full-length portraits; both charmingly drawn, from the same originals, we suspect, as Mrs. Pendennis and Blanche Amory. The attentive reader will note, however, that in the portrait of the coquette, Beatrix, he has thrown so much real impulsive goodness, that she becomes a new creation—and, let us add, a true one. She is not bad—she is vain; and her fascination is made very intelligible.

What novel readers will say to Lady Castlewood's love, and to Esmond's love for the woman who calls him "son," we will not prophecy; for ourselves we feel, that although *vrai,* it is not always *vraisemblable.* (pp. 1071-72)

[*George Henry Lewes*], "Thackeray's New Novel," in The Leader, *Vol. III, No. 137, November 6, 1852, pp. 1071-72.*

[GEORGE BRIMLEY]   (essay date 1852)

[*Brimley is unusual among early reviewers in his praise of Rachel's character and her marriage to Esmond.*]

There is abundance of incident in [**Henry Esmond**], but not much more plot than in one of Defoe's novels: neither is there, generally speaking, a plot in a man's life, though there may be and often is in sections of it. Unity is given not by a consecutive and self-developing story, but by the ordinary events of life blended with those peculiar to a stirring time acting on a family group, and bringing out and ripening their qualities; these again controlling the subsequent events, just as happens in life. (p. 1066)

[Mr. Thackeray] has selected for his hero a very noble type of the Cavalier softening into the man of the eighteenth century, and for his heroine one of the sweetest women that ever breathed from canvass or from book since Raffaelle painted Maries and Shakspere created a new and higher consciousness of woman in the mind of Germanic Europe. Colonel Esmond is indeed a fine gentleman,—the accomplished man, the gallant soldier, the loyal heart, and the passionate lover, whose richly contrasted but harmonious character Clarendon would have delighted to describe; while Falkland and Richard Lovelace would have worn him in their hearts' core. Lucy Hutchinson's husband might have stood for his model in all but politics, and his Toryism has in it more than a smack of English freedom very much akin to that noble patriot's Republicanism. Especially does he recall Colonel Hutchinson in his lofty principle, his unswerving devotion to it, a certain sweet seriousness which comes in happily to temper a penetrating intellect, and a faculty of seeing things and persons as they are, to which we owe passage after passage in the book, that it requires no effort to imagine Thackeray uttering himself in those famous lectures of his, and looking up with his kind glance to catch the delighted smile of his audience at his best points. Nor is there anything unartistic in this reminder of the author; for this quality of clear insight into men and things united with a kindly nature and a large capacity for loving is not limited to any particular time or age, and combines with Colonel Esmond's other qualities so as to give no impression of incongruity. But besides the harmonizing effect of this sweetly serious temperament, the record of Colonel Esmond's life is throughout a record of his attachment to one woman, towards whom his childish gratitude for protection grows with his growth into a complex feeling, in which filial affection and an unconscious passion are curiously blended. So unconscious, indeed, is the passion, that, though the reader has no difficulty in interpreting it, Esmond himself is for years the avowed and persevering though hopeless lover of this very lady's daughter. The relation between Esmond and Rachel Viscountess Castlewood is of that sort that nothing short of consummate skill could have saved it from becoming ridiculous or offensive, or both. In Mr. Thackeray's hands, the difficulty has become a triumph, and has given rise to beauties which a safer ambition would have not dared to attempt. The triumph is attained by the conception of Lady Castlewood's character. She is one of those women who never grow old, because their lives are in the affections, and the suffering that comes upon such lives only brings out strength and beauty unperceived before. The graces of the girl never pass away, but maturer loveliness is added to them, and spring, summer, autumn, all bloom on their faces and in their hearts at once. A faint foreshadowing of this character we have had before in Helen Pendennis: but she had been depressed and crushed in early life, had married for a home, certainly without passion; and her nature was chilled and despondent. Lady Castlewood has the development that a happy girlhood, and a marriage with the man she devotedly loves, can give to a woman; and her high spirit has time to grow for her support when it is needed. Even the weaknesses of her character are but as dimples on a lovely face, and make us like her the better for them, because they give individuality to what might else be felt as too ideal. Nothing can be more true or touching than the way this lady demeans herself when she finds her husband's affection waning from her; and Mr. Thackeray is eminently Mr. Thackeray in his delineation of that waning love on the one side, and the strength and dignity which the neglected wife gradually draws from her own hitherto untried resources, when she ceases to lean on the arm that was withdrawn, and discovers that the heart she had worshiped was no worthy idol. But to those who would think the mother "slow" we can have no hesitation in recommending the daughter. Miss Beatrix Esmond—familiarly and correctly termed "Trix" by her friends—is one of those dangerous young ladies who fascinate every one, man or woman, that they choose to fascinate, but care for nobody but themselves; and their care for themselves simply extends to the continual gratification of a boundless love of admiration, and the kind of power which results from it. If Miss Rebecca Sharpe had really been a Montmorency, and a matchless beauty, and a maid of honour to a Queen, she might have sublimated into a Beatrix Esmond. It is for this proud, capricious, and heartless beauty, that Henry Esmond sighs out many years of his life, and does not find out, till she is lost to him and to herself, how much he loves her "little mamma," as the saucy young lady is fond of calling Lady Castlewood. Beatrix belongs to the class of women who figure most in history, with eyes as bright and hearts as hard as diamonds, as Mary Stuart said of herself; and Mary Stuart and Miss Esmond have many points in common. Of her end we are almost disposed to say with Othello, "Oh! the pity of it, Iago, oh! the pity of it." Unlovely as she is because unloving, yet her graces are too fair to be so dragged through the dirt—that stream is too bright to end in a city sewer. But the tragedy is no less tragical for the tawdry comedy of its close. Life has no pity for the pitiless, no sentiment for those who trample on love as a weakness. (pp. 1066-67)

> [*George Brimley*], "Thackeray's 'Esmond'," *in* The Spectator, *Vol. 25, No. 1271, November 6, 1852, pp. 1066-67.*

GEORGE ELIOT   (letter date 1852)

[*Eliot is considered one of the greatest English novelists of the nineteenth century. Her work, including* The Mill on the Floss *(1860) and* Middlemarch: A Study of Provincial Life *(1871-72), is informed by penetrating psychological analysis and profound insight into human character. Played against the backdrop of English rural life, Eliot's novels explore moral and philosophical issues and employ a realistic approach to character and plot development. In the following excerpt from a letter to her friends Mr. and Mrs. Charles Bray, Eliot describes her unfavorable reaction to* Henry Esmond.]

Esmond is the most uncomfortable book you can imagine. You remember, Cara, how you disliked *François le Champi* (George Sand's). Well, the story of *Esmond* is just the same. The hero is in love with the daughter all through the book, and marries the mother at the end. (p. 67)

> *George Eliot, in a letter to Mr. and Mrs. Charles Bray on November 13, 1852, in her* The George Eliot Letters: 1852-1858, *Vol. II, edited by Gordon S. Haight, Yale University Press, 1954, pp. 67-8.*

[SAMUEL PHILLIPS]   (essay date 1852)

[*In the following excerpt, Phillips remarks upon Thackeray's success as a satirist of contemporary society and decries his decision to write a historical novel. Phillips also disapproves of* Henry Esmond's *resolution and its author's jaundiced view of human nature. Although Thackeray later wrote that Phillips's review "absolutely stopped" the novel's sales, this is generally held to be an exaggeration.*]

We were gratified with the announcement which reached us about a twelvemonth since, that the author of *Vanity Fair* had resolved to eschew the serial form of publication and to make his next venture [*The History of Henry Esmond*] under the circumstances best calculated to display a writer's powers and to achieve permanent success. Month to month writing is but hand to mouth work, and satisfies neither author nor reader. But the announcement was accompanied by another not altogether so agreeable. Mr. Thackeray had entertained the town with some lively lectures upon the humorists of the days of Queen Anne, and had grown so familiar and fascinated with the period during the interesting process, that he resolved not only to write a Queen Anne novel, but positively to write it with a Queen Anne quill, held by a Queen Anne penman. In other words, the distinguished novelist, whose very breath of life is the atmosphere in which he lives, and whose most engaging quality is his own natural style, had suicidally determined to convey himself to a strange climate and to take absolute leave of his choicest characteristic. We confess that a more desperate venture we could hardly conceive it possible for a popular writer to make. We have a great respect for Queen Anne and for the writers of Her Majesty's Augustan age, and when we read Addison and Swift we are charmed with the classic grace of the one, and made strong by the bold English of the other. But why lose our genuine Thackeray in order to get a spurious Steele or Budgell? Having made up his mind to write a novel in monthly parts no more, and to do as Scott and Fielding did before him, why, Mr. Thackeray, in the name of all that is rational, why write in fetters? Why have your genius in leading strings? Why have the mind and hand crippled? Why pursue the muse under difficulties? Garrick must have been a great actor: so was John Kemble; but what would our fathers have said to Kemble had he undertaken to destroy for a season his own identity, in order to present a counterfeit of his great predecessor? We decline to judge Mr. Thackeray's powers from his present exhibition. He shall have justice from us, though he has none from himself. We reserve our opinion whether or not Mr. Thackeray is equal to a masterly and complete work of fiction until he attempts the labor with the energies of his spirit free. . . .

The inconvenience of the plan to which Mr. Thackeray has chained down his intellect is made manifest in every part of his work. It is no disparagement to say that his disguise is too cumbrous to be perfect. That it is maintained so well is marvellous. The patience and perseverance of the writer must have been incessant, and infinite skill has been thrown away, which we feel with vexation and disappointment might have been devoted to the noblest uses. But, in spite of all the cleverness and industry, discrepancies and anomalies are inevitable: and one discrepancy in such a work is sufficient to take the veil from the reader's eyes, and to put an end to the whole illusion. That Steele should be described as a private in the Guards in the year 1690, when he was only fifteen years old, and a schoolboy at the Charterhouse, is, perhaps, no great offence in a work of fiction; but a fatal smile involuntarily crosses the reader's cheek, when he learns, in an early part of the story, that a nobleman is "made to play at ball and billiards by sharpers, who take his money;" and is informed sometime afterwards that the same lord has "gotten a new game from London, a French game, called a billiard." It is not surprising that for a moment Mr. Thackeray should forget that he is Mr. Esmond, and speak of "rapid new coaches" that "*performed* the journey between London and the University in a single day," when he means to say "*perform*;" neither is it astonishing that the writer of 1852 should announce it as a memorable fact, that in the days of Queen Anne young fellows would "make merry at their taverns, and call toasts," although it is quite out of place for the writer of 1742 to marvel at the same custom, seeing that Colonel Esmond must have known the fashion to be in vogue in the times of George the Second. A less pardonable oversight certainly occurs in the second volume, when the reign of William III. and that of Queen Anne seem unaccountably jumbled together in the same paragraph; but were such faults as we have indicated to present themselves with tenfold frequency, it would be idle and unfair to insist upon imperfections inseparable from such an effort as that to which Mr. Thackeray has doomed himself for no better reason that we can discern than that of demonstrating how much more amusing, lively, and companionable he is in his easy attire, than when tricked out with the wig, buckles, and other accoutrements of our deceased and venerated ancestors.

The History of Henry Esmond, Esq., is not a very striking one. The most remarkable fact connected with it is, that it proves, beyond a doubt, that folks very like our contemporaries lived and prospered in the days of Queen Anne. All our friends that entertained us for so many months in *Vanity Fair* and *Pendennis* have their *fac-similes* in Mr. Esmond's volume. The colonel himself is just such another creature as Dobbin—as kind-hearted, as self-denying, as generous, as devoted, and, must we add, almost as weak and simple. Captain Crawley, the *roué,* belongs to the same family as Castlewood, for all the lords of that name indulge in his propensities. Miss Amory is the very embodiment of intrigue and selfishness; so is Beatrix Castlewood, who sets her cap at great people without caring a straw for them, precisely like the other lady. It must have been generally remarked that Mr. Thackeray is morbidly fond of reproducing his old creations upon the scene. The *dramatis personae* of *Pendennis* bore not only a great resemblance to the characters of *Vanity Fair,* but some of them were actually reproduced in the second production, or referred to by name. In like manner, our old friends, the Crawleys, are familiarly spoken of in Colonel Esmond's history. It is well to have a natural affection for your offspring, but there may be occasions when to obtrude them upon the notice of your visitors is to betray want of tact, of breeding, and good sense.

Infinite pains are taken to beguile us into the notion that we are reading a book written and printed upwards of a century ago. Mr. Thackeray has done his part in the matter, and the printers and publishers have done theirs; but perfect contentment, after all, does not dwell upon the mind of the reader. The style is an admirable imitation, and would be charming if it were not tedious; the type is most delusive, even to the title-page, which acquaints us that the book is printed by "Smith and Elder, over against St. Peter's Church, in Cornhill;" but the vital part of the work is no more a representation of the spirit and soul of the time, than it is of the age that preceded or followed it. The depths of society are not probed, and the merest glimpses of its outward shape are vouchsafed. There are two great faults in the volumes, and this is one of them. Had the book really proceeded from the pen of an officer in the service of Queen Anne, he would unquestionably have written in the quaint fashion of this work, but he would have done a great deal more. He would not in the substance of his production have imitated Mr. Thackeray as Mr. Thackeray has imitated him in the form. He must have displayed in a domestic story something like a social picture of his time, and afforded his present readers infinite amusement from the comparison of two widely separated epochs. Even *Tom Jones* and *Pamela* are most instructive in this respect, for both reveal a condition of society very different indeed from that in which we play our part. How much more different and interesting the domestic proceedings of the loyal subjects of Queen Anne! If any one will take the trouble to translate Mr. Esmond's language into modern English, he will be surprised to find how much of the book applies with as much force to men and manners in 1852 as to men and manners in 1792. It is very true that Mr. Esmond tells us that he went to the theatre to witness the performance of Mrs. Bracegirdle; but he might have said that he went to listen to Mrs. Kean for anything that follows from his visit. Mr. Esmond proceeds to Cambridge University, and, to our astonishment, we discover that University life in the days of Queen Anne differed in no respect whatever from University life in the happier times of our gracious Queen Victoria. We learn, indeed, that Mr. Esmond's friends drink, fight, quarrel with their wives, intrigue, and are very selfish and good for nothing, or good for something and very stupid, but precisely this account reached us of the friends of Mr. Pendennis and of Mr. Osborne, so that, indeed, Mr. Esmond is quite as much indebted to the author of *Vanity Fair* as the author of *Vanity Fair* is to him. We say again, Mr. Thackeray is not to be too harshly dealt with for not accomplishing a feat which a life-long and exclusive study of one peculiar period of his nation's history would hardly enable him to achieve with unqualified success. But he is to be remonstrated with for presenting us with a very questionable and cracked specimen of old China when he had it in his power to offer us sound and genuine British porcelain. Our foremost writers must not become the venders of sham curiosities.

The second grave fault in Colonel Esmond's narrative is one for which Mr. Thackeray must be prepared to answer in his own proper person. He has inflicted a stain upon the good taste and feeling of the worthy colonel, of which that gentleman has every reason to complain. Nothing can be more amiable than Mr. Esmond's character as described in every incident of his story, yet the sentiment with which we take leave of him is one of unaffected disgust. No hero of any age ever finished his career less heroically than Mr. Esmond. . . .

Henry Esmond, the importunate and high-souled, the sensitive and delicate-minded, marries his own "dear mother!" Lady Castlewood has been in love with the youth throughout; has been jealous of her daughter; feigned hatred of the boy after her husband was slain, when most she doated upon him, and was "making eyes" at him all the while she was hypocritically pretending to advance his suit with his so-called "sister"— her own much-envied and at length defeated daughter. Yet Lady Castlewood is the heroine of this story, is held up page after page to our admiration and respect, and Colonel Esmond is the immaculate hero! Strange are Mr. Thackeray's notions of human perfection!

We repeat, we will not accept the present novel as an evidence of Mr. Thackeray's powers as a writer of fiction. We desire to see a complete novel from his pen, but he must give himself an unencumbered field, and allow the reader as well as himself fair play. That he is capable of greater efforts than any he has hitherto made, we believe; that he has a potent pen for description of character, is manifest from the very striking portraiture of Marlborough that appears in these volumes; and that he may make a permanent impression upon the literary character of his times, is quite possible if he will only trust to his better impulses and survey mankind in the spirit of trust, affection, and belief, rather than of doubt, incredulity, and contempt.

[Samuel Phillips], "Mr. Thackeray's New Novel,"
in The Times, London, December 22, 1852, p. 8.

THE ECLECTIC REVIEW (essay date 1853)

[This anonymous critic objects to Henry Esmond on both aesthetic and moral grounds.]

Mr. Thackeray, the author of [The History of Henry Esmond], is already known to the public as a writer of fiction, chiefly through his Pendennis and Vanity Fair,—works which, though marked by some defects, have obtained a wide and deserved popularity. This, we are inclined to think, will not be much augmented by the work before us. Not only does the same author manifestly re-appear in these pages, but with him the prominent characters of his former productions with nothing changed but their dress, while some peculiar defects make their first appearance in Esmond.

There are not many novelists who, like Godwin, have been ambitious enough to produce a work, the interest of which is made to turn on some other central point than that of youthful love. To such an attempt, however, Mr. Thackeray has, as nearly as possible, committed himself; for although all his characters are not of one sex, and although his hero does not escape the snares both of love and marriage, yet the author has ingeniously contrived to alienate the sympathies of the reader from his hero in both, and mischievously to combine with the sweets of love an extract of 'poppy and mandragora,'—an element of tedium and nausea. (pp. 37-8)

When he presents youth and beauty, it is passionless and frivolous, and when he depicts the ardour of woman's love, he associates it with mature years and fading charms. Indeed, the reader might be almost tempted to suppose that Mr. Thackeray is seeking to solve the problem of how much popular interest can be attracted to a novel from which all the beauties most proper to that class of literature are excluded; in which the plot is a puzzle, and the development of it an ever-increasing disappointment.

As a mere narrative of facts it is clumsy and unintelligible, and its complexity is increased by the narrator most commonly speaking of himself in the third person, but not unfrequently in the first. Nay, even the style in which the whole merit of the book consists, is open to serious objection. The antiquated forms of expression in which it abounds, are quite unnecessary to mark the age of Addison. The quaint typography, too, looks very much like a clap-trap. Nor is the mind drawn into illusion by reading on the title-page, immediately above the date 1852, 'printed for Smith, Elder, & Company, over against St. Peter's

Church in Cornhill,' nor by discovering from the next page, that Messrs. Bradbury and Evans prosecute their laudable vocation in the 'precinct of Whitefriars.' But this is not all; just in proportion as Mr. Thackeray assumes this adopted style do his sentences become stiff and unnatural, and whenever he rises to real eloquence, as he frequently does, it is quite evident that he has come home from his chronological wanderings to his proper location in the middle of the nineteenth century.

Indeed, if we could forget the lumpy, insulated haths and doths, which make a progress through his paragraphs somewhat like walking along a road newly subjected to the first operations of MacAdam, the involution of the sentences would render it a wearisome book. Long parentheses here and there suspend the progress of thought, while the mode of punctuation would seem to have been adopted for no other purpose than to perplex and annoy. So, too, the narrative itself presents the most slovenly inconsistencies. Thus, in describing an accident which befel one of the characters, who leaped from a carriage, the horses of which were running away, the author says: 'His large periwig and feathered hat had fallen off, and he was bleeding profusely from a wound on the forehead, and looking, and being, indeed, a corpse!' Of course, the reader dismisses this gentleman from his attention with a mental requiescat in pace. But in a few lines he finds his mistake, and reads: 'He was half an hour before he came to himself, by which time Dr. Tusher and little Frank arrived, and found my lord not a corpse, indeed, but as pale as one!' (pp. 38-9)

One or two general criticisms must close our notice of a work which we believe is already obtaining a very wide circulation. In spite of all the defects of this particular work, the author has a freshness of fancy and a vividness of style which must ensure his popularity; but he appears to be drawn, by a natural preference, to portray the inconsistencies, failings, and vices, rather than the excellencies of human nature. In his pages we meet rarely or never with an animated exhibition of exemplary virtue. His best characters are unworthy of imitation, while the rest are too low to be infectious either by their proximity or their moral influence. This study of the morbid anatomy of character is, in the hands of Mr. Thackeray, utterly unprofitable. If he associated the exhibitions which he makes with profound views of moral and religious truth; if he had the spiritualized fancy of Bunyan, the voice of a modern Ecclesiastes, or even the didactic pencil of a Hogarth, we might wish him to addict himself to what appear to be his favourite subjects of contemplation. But in his exhibitions of human infirmity there is no tone of dehortation. Amidst the shoals and quicksands of immorality, too truly charted, he erects no warning beacon, and he crowns no portraiture of heroic virtue with the 'immortal palm.' Passing by for a moment his propensity to exhibit chiefly the darkened hemisphere of human nature, we cannot help observing that his delineations of modern good and evil, lose all their influential effect through a perpetual silent omission of that great standard of right and wrong, the recognition of which alone can regulate the morals of mankind. We may concede to fiction the uses which have been attributed to it by general convention and consent; grant that the heart may be purified by the influence of terror and pity, and softened by even fictitious representations of generosity and tenderness; we still contend that exhibitions, whether of virtue or of vice, apart from those eternal laws which sanctify the one and condemn the other, can work only moral mischief by tacitly representing as unnecessary those great principles in the absence of which Christianity is a fable and a name.

In conclusion, we would urge a friendly admonition on a writer of great intellectual power, and of equal literary facility and skill, to abstain from profanity. The repast which from time to time he provides for the public, needs no such coarse and vulgar condiment. The soldiers, statesmen, and gentlemen of the age of Addison might be identified without their oaths. To take no higher ground, they are silly and empty expletives, and only remind us of the habit of illiterate letter writers of scoring an unmeaning emphasis under every alternate word, or of the efforts of a man to shout under the nightmare of dyspepsia, which issue in a voiceless gasp, and only indicate the irregularities of his diet over night. (pp. 48-9)

> *A review of "The History of Henry Esmond, Esq.,*
> *a Colonel in the Service of Her Majesty Queen Anne,"*
> *in* The Eclectic Review, *n.s. Vol. V, January, 1853,*
> *pp. 37-49.*

[C. W. RUSSELL]   (essay date 1853)

[*The following excerpt is drawn from an essay censuring contemporary novelists for their failure to inculcate Christian morals in their works. Here, Russell objects strenuously to Esmond's "contemptible" character and to Rachel's unvirtuous love for him.*]

It is true . . . that, in the works of our popular novelists, there is no stint of the purely natural virtues, honour, generosity, benevolence, delicacy of sentiment, disinterestedness. Perhaps, indeed, the ideal of these is generally too high to be practically available as a model; and we have little doubt that the excess to which this ideal perfection had been carried, was the cause of the reaction on the opposite side, which has been the distinguishing characteristic of the new and most influential school of fiction, founded by Mr. Thackeray. His conception of human nature, (we are speaking now of his earlier works,) is the very reverse of all this. Far from idealizing its great and good qualities to form his heroes, he may rather be said to have blotted them out from his portraits altogether. In his sketches of life we look in vain for those perfect beings which it was the fashion of older novelists to draw. It is not merely that in his pages we lose sight of that perfect disinterestedness which seems to live solely for the happiness of others; that we meet no more of that utter disregard of self which (whatever may be the minor peculiarities of individual conception), forms the common basis of the character assigned to the hero of a popular novel. Mr. Thackeray is not content with suppressing all this; he has absolutely reversed the picture, and the axiom from which he starts in his conceptions of character is, that self, the love of self, the interest of self, the gratification of self, and the exaltation of self, constitute for all, rich and poor, high and low, men and women, the main-spring of action, and the guiding and controlling principle of conduct. For him life is one vast "Vanity Fair;" and, if we be content to accept his delineations, we must believe that there is no single human being exempt from its influence. All is hollow, insincere, sham. The degree of sham may vary, but the difference is only in degree; and the principle of action is the same in all his characters, from the professional adventurer who swindles for his daily bread, to the doating and (as far as meets the eye,) self-denying lover who sacrifices all for the happiness of the object of his affection. Under all the best and most generous actions which he pourtrays, Mr. Thackeray never fails to place the same unvarying under stratum, and sooner or later we are sure to see it cropping up from below. If there be any exceptions to this rule among the many personages whom he has sketched, their good qualities are marred in our eyes by the weakness,

simplicity, and utter want of dignity, with which they are coupled. There is not a single generous or unselfish character in Mr. Thackeray's novels, who is not almost a simpleton, at least in those things in which this generosity is displayed. Certainly there is not a single one of whom it could be said that Mr. Thackeray's delineation of generosity is calculated to render that virtue respectable or attractive. The generosity of a hero, in his hands, degenerates into the weakness of a muff.

Thus the direct tendency of the writings of Mr. Thackeray and his imitators, is to create a painful scepticism, if not an utter disbelief, in the existence of genuine virtue among men. In this point he is evidently himself a hearty unbeliever. Hence it is that among the whole host of satirists, ancient and modern, there is not one who is more earnest or more scathing in his denunciations of vice in all its forms, and especially of the master-vice of the world, hollowness and sham. Nevertheless we do not hesitate to say, that we regard Mr. Thackeray's writings as more dangerous to virtue in certain temperaments than, if this be possible, the most inflammatory production of the modern French school. No man is more successful in denouncing vice and laying bare its turpitude. But while he does so, he exhibits it as universal, and by a natural inference unavoidable. If all the world around us is corrupt, how can we hope to maintain ourselves pure? Other writers undermine virtue by a process of seduction. Mr. Thackeray withers it up by the ordeal of despair. (pp. 182-84)

Mr. Thackeray's novel *Esmond,* is in the form of the autobiography of a Colonel in the service of Queen Anne—a form which the author, although with occasional slips and anachronisms, has taken every pains to maintain in all the details of language, style, sentiment, and manners. Esmond is (as it is supposed,) the illegitimate son of Lord Castlewood, the head of one of the old Catholic Cavalier families. On the death of his father, he has been taken under the protection of the new Lord Castlewood and his lady. He is educated along with the Castlewood children, Frank and Beatrix, is loved and cherished especially by Lady Castlewood, with all the tenderness of a parent. Lord Castlewood, though warm-hearted and generous, and blest with a wife's love, by far the purest and most devoted which Mr. Thackeray has yet pourtrayed, becomes a drunkard, an indifferent, and ultimately an unfaithful husband. He is estranged from his wife, and notwithstanding his own infidelities, becomes jealous of her. In a duel, which is the result of this jealousy, and in which Esmond, after vainly endeavouring to prevent it, acts as his second, Lord Castlewood is slain; not, however, until after he has learnt that the supposition as to the illegitimacy of Esmond's birth is without foundation, and that he is in reality the rightful heir of the title and estates, which he had himself been enjoying. Lady Castlewood resents the share which Esmond has had in the fatal duel which cost her husband's life, and for a time withdraws her protection from him, so that he is thrown upon his own resources, and forced to battle single-handed with fortune.

The history of his subsequent but little career is, we must say, exceedingly tedious and uninteresting, and is enlivened by his passion for the fair Beatrix, the daughter of his former patron and protector. Still there is much in his story which it is impossible not to admire. He is made aware of the secret of his birth and his rights, and yet, in delicacy to the living and the dead, he sacrifices all, and refuses to avail himself of the knowledge to their humiliation. We had hoped, as we read Mr. Thackeray's powerful and thrilling description of the struggle between, on the one side, ambition and love, (for his hopes of the hand of Beatrix are wound up in the decision,) and on the other, friendship, affection, and respectful consideration for the feelings of those whom he loves, that he had become a convert from his old sceptical and misanthropic theories, and had learned to understand and appreciate true generosity of heart. But we are sorry to say that the illusion was speedily dissipated. Esmond is generous, disinterested, self-denying, it is true. But the effect of these noble qualities is marred in him, precisely as it was marred in the heroes of Mr. Thackeray's former stories. Dobbin, in *Vanity Fair,* possessed the same qualities in a high degree. Yet the character of Dobbin rises but little beyond what is familiarly termed a "spooney." And we are almost tempted to say, that weak and mawkish as Dobbin is, we should pronounce him a more respectable character than the hero of the present tale. The weakness and blindness of Esmond's passion for Beatrix, (a heartless and unprincipled coquette, who is but a reproduction of Blanche Amory in *Pendennis,*) is a blot on his character which no amount of high qualities could redeem, and which has the effect of rendering all the certainly great qualities of Esmond contemptible, if not repulsive. It is not merely that his love is proof against all her indifference; that it survives the assurance on her mother's part that she will not accept him, and that she is not worthy of him. It is proof against *his own* knowledge of her worthlessness; his conviction of her worldly and ambitious character; against his knowledge of her having made and unmade engagements of marriage in which her heart had no concern; even against her still more questionable schemes to win what never could be a lawful love. Through all this, weakly, blindly, and against every principle of manly dignity and self-respect, he persists, not alone in loving on, but in suing meanly for a love the worthlessness of which is but too plain to every eye.

The character of Lady Castlewood, too, is equally disappointing. In the earlier period of the history she is very loveable indeed; and we were especially gratified to find that in her, for the first time, Mr. Thackeray had fully recognized the religious element of the female character as a main source of the true charm of the sex. Yet, here again, it is all marred, and more than marred. This Lady Castlewood, who has been as a mother—if not in years at least in position—to Esmond; who has lived for years with him in that character, addressing him and being addressed by him in the endearing terms of such relationship; who has been the confidante and depository of his love for her daughter; this Lady Castlewood—the soul of matronly honour—the paragon of Christian piety—the pattern of a wife—the impersonation of all womanly delicacy—turns out to have been in love with this adopted son from his boyhood; to have been cherishing this passion during her husband's life; yielding to low and unwomanly jealousy of her own daughter; and blindly clinging to her ill-placed love through all the changes of Esmond's fortune! And in the end, when she has long passed the age (at least in novel life) for marrying or giving in marriage, she actually marries the foolishly fond and oft rejected suitor of her heartless daughter!

Where is the young female mind, we ask, whose impressions of true female virtue, and of that sentiment which is akin to virtue, and its best natural preservative, would not be weakened, if not utterly destroyed, by such a picture as this? (pp. 185-87)

> [*C. W. Russell*], *in a review of "The History of Henry Esmond, Esq., a Colonel in the Service of Her Majesty Queen Anne," in* The Dublin Review, *Vol. XXXIV, No. LXVII, March, 1853, pp. 182-87.*

THE CHRISTIAN EXAMINER AND RELIGIOUS MISCELLANY (essay date 1856)

> [*The reviewer praises the artistic unity and historical verisimilitude of* Henry Esmond, *but labels the character development of Rachel and Beatrix "a perversion which sickens the heart."*]

That Mr. Thackeray can produce, when he likes, a harmonized and complete work of literary art, is made evident by his *History of Henry Esmond.* With the exception of the heroine and her mother, whose incongruous shifting of relations towards the hero and the painful development of whose respective endurance and deviltry is a perversion which sickens the heart, this story meets the essential claims of an historical romance in the skill and consistency with which it is evolved. The spirit of the times, the military, social, and literary characteristics of Queen Anne's palmy days and closing reign, are felicitously reproduced; we hear the din of arms from the Flemish camp, partake of the *éclat* of Marlborough's victories, read the *Spectators* with contemporary eyes, behold Addison oracular at Wills', Steele personified as the successful wit and lover, and Lady Churchill dominant at court. The very language, tinctured as it is with the olden construction, the very print, adopted from obsolete type, impart to the whole a mellow tone and a *vraisemblance* which render the illusion complete. The minor and historical personages, the incidental scenes, the still-life, and the refrain caught from the past, are admirably blended; from the State Trials, the current literature, the military and civic annals, and the private memoirs of the period, an effective and reliable work is thus elaborated, which indicates a capacity, on the part of the author, for something besides modern caricature and local satire. (pp. 114-15)

> *H. T. T.,* "*Mr. Thackeray as a Novelist,*" *in* The Christian Examiner and Religious Miscellany, *Vol. LX, January, 1856, pp. 102-21.*

THE CHRISTIAN EXAMINER (essay date 1864)

> [*This anonymous critic considers* Henry Esmond *a successful work, but notes the novel's "obvious" defect: Rachel and Esmond are victimized by their own passions.*]

The History of Henry Esmond is an attempt to look at the age of Queen Anne through the eyes of a contemporary, and to record the result of the inspection in the style of the period. It is, on the whole, successful. The diction of the book is exquisite; pleasant glimpses are given of the memorable men of the era,—literary, political, and military; and the languid pace with which the story rambles to its conclusion provokes just that tranquil interest with which Esmond himself recalls in memory the incidents of his career. Both persons and scenes have the visionary grace and remoteness which objects take when seen through the thin and shining mist of recollection. Beatrix Esmond, the heroine, is another of Thackeray's studies in perverted feminine character, and is worthy of the delineator of Becky and Blanche. The picture of the old age of this pernicious beauty, given in *The Virginians,* is equally skilful and true. The defect in the plot of *Henry Esmond* is obvious to every reader. Lady Castlewood, whom the author intends to represent as the ideal of a noble woman, loves the lover of her daughter, and is swayed by passions and placed in situations degrading to womanhood; while Esmond himself, put forward as a high-toned gentleman and chivalrous man of honor, is so demoralized by his passion for a jilt, that he enters into a conspiracy to overturn the government, and involve England in civil war, simply to please her, and with a profound disbelief in the cause for which he is to draw his sword. The atrocious villany of such conduct, from which a Marquis of Steyne would have recoiled, appears to Thackeray simply the weakness of a noble nature. (pp. 219-20)

> *"Thackeray," in* The Christian Examiner, *Vol. LXXVI, No. 11, March, 1864, pp. 211-22.*

[RICHARD SIMPSON]   (essay date 1864)

[*Simpson designates* Henry Esmond *Thackeray's best novel.*]

Several causes conspire to make *Esmond* [Thackeray's] best novel. . . . [One is] the value of its autobiographical form. Another reason is its thoroughly literary character. Alone of his larger works it was not given to the world in monthly parts, but all at once. Its laborious imitation of the style of the writers of Anne's age, its circumstantial exactness to the costume, the manners, and the feelings of those times, were voluntary fetters, which only increased the agility and grace of the athlete. It will not be so valuable to the antiquarian of the next century as a contemporary painting; but it will be proportionately more valuable to the poet as a picture of human nature. Pegasus never exhibits his mettle so well as when he is checked with the brake; nothing makes the reader yawn more than an art which flew down the writer's mouth while he was yawning. Labour sharpens the mind and polishes the wit; its benefit is not confined to the single detail on which it is expended; it reacts on the workman, and through him on his whole work and all its parts. To aim at clearness of expression is also to seek clearness of thought, logical arrangement of parts, and unity of the whole. *Esmond* has Thackeray's best plot, some of his best characters, his most subtle reflections, his most delicate pathos, and his most poetic language. There are single sentences in it which contain more poetry than all his ballads, the best of which are the funniest and most nonsensical. (pp. 508-09)

> [*Richard Simpson*], *"Thackeray," in* The Home and Foreign Review, *Vol. IV, April, 1864, pp. 476-511.*

ANTHONY TROLLOPE   (essay date 1879)

[*Trollope was a prolific and popular Victorian novelist who is praised for his perceptive, vital characterizations. His most important works include two series of novels, the Palliser series, which portrays London political life, and the Barsetshire series, which depicts middle-class life in an English cathedral town. Trollope's was one of the earliest book-length critical studies of Thackeray. In this excerpt, he discusses characterization in* Henry Esmond, *as well as the work's unity, style, and mood.*]

The novel with which we are now going to deal I regard as the greatest work that Thackeray did. Though I do not hesitate to compare himself with himself, I will make no comparison between him and others; I therefore abstain from assigning to *Esmond* any special niche among prose fictions in the English language, but I rank it so high as to justify me in placing him among the small number of the highest class of English novelists. Much as I think of *Barry Lyndon* and *Vanity Fair,* I cannot quite say this of them; but, as a chain is not stronger than its weakest link, so is a poet, or a dramatist, or a novelist to be placed in no lower level than that which he has attained by his highest sustained flight. The excellence which has been reached here Thackeray achieved, without doubt, by giving a greater amount of forethought to the work he had before him than had been his wont. . . . [In *Vanity Fair,* in *Pendennis,* and

in *The Newcomes,* the] richness of the author's mind, the beauty of his language, his imagination and perception of character, are all there. For that which was lovely he has shown his love, and for the hateful his hatred; but, nevertheless, they are comparatively idle books. His only work, as far as I can judge them, in which there is no touch of idleness, is *Esmond. Barry Lyndon* is consecutive, and has the well-sustained purpose of exhibiting a finished rascal; but *Barry Lyndon* is not quite the same from beginning to end. All his full-fledged novels, except *Esmond,* contain rather strings of incidents and memoirs of individuals, than a completed story. But *Esmond* is a whole from beginning to end, with its tale well told, its purpose developed, its moral brought home—and its nail hit well on the head and driven in.

I told Thackeray once that it was not only his best work, but so much the best, that there was none second to it. "That was what I intended," he said, "but I have failed. Nobody reads it. After all, what does it matter?" he went on after awhile. "If they like anything, one ought to be satisfied. After all, Esmond was a prig." Then he laughed and changed the subject, not caring to dwell on thoughts painful to him. The elbow-grease of thinking was always distasteful to him, and had no doubt been so when he conceived and carried out this work.

To the ordinary labour necessary for such a novel he added very much by his resolution to write it in a style different, not only from that which he had made his own, but from that also which belonged to the time. He had devoted himself to the reading of the literature of Queen Anne's reign, and having chosen to throw his story into that period, and to create in it personages who were to be peculiarly concerned with the period, he resolved to use as the vehicle for his story the forms of expression then prevalent. No one who has not tried it can understand how great is the difficulty of mastering a phase of one's own language other than that which habit has made familiar. To write in another language, if the language be sufficiently known, is a much less arduous undertaking. The lad who attempts to write his essay in Ciceronian Latin struggles to achieve a style which is not indeed common to him, but is more common than any other he has become acquainted with in that tongue. But Thackeray in his work had always to remember his Swift, his Steele, and his Addison, and to forget at the same time the modes of expression which the day had adopted. (pp. 119-22)

It was this that Thackeray tried in his *Esmond,* and he has done it almost without a flaw. The time in question is near enough to us, and the literature sufficiently familiar to enable us to judge. Whether folk swore by their troth in the days of King Richard I. we do not know, but when we read Swift's letters, and Addison's papers, or Defoe's novels, we do catch the veritable sounds of Queen Anne's age, and can say for ourselves whether Thackeray has caught them correctly or not. No reader can doubt that he has done so. Nor is the reader ever struck with the affectation of an assumed dialect. The words come as though they had been written naturally—though not natural to the middle of the nineteenth century. It was a *tour de force,* and successful as such a *tour de force* so seldom is. But though Thackeray was successful in adopting the tone he wished to assume, he never quite succeeded, as far as my ear can judge, in altogether dropping it again. (p. 123)

It is not my purpose to tell the story here, but rather to explain the way in which it is written, to show how it differs from other stories, and thus to explain its effect. Harry Esmond, who tells the story, is of course the hero. There are two heroines who equally command our sympathy—Lady Castlewood, the wife of Harry's kinsman, and her daughter Beatrix. Thackeray himself declared the man to be a prig, and he was not altogether wrong. Beatrix, with whom throughout the whole book he is in love, knew him well. "Shall I be frank with you, Harry," she says, when she is engaged to another suitor, "and say that if you had not been down on your knees and so humble, you might have fared better with me? A woman of my spirit, cousin, is to be won by gallantry, and not by sighs and rueful faces. All the time you are worshipping and singing hymns to me, I know very well I am no goddess." And again: "As for you, you want a woman to bring your slippers and cap, and to sit at your feet and cry, O caro, caro! O bravo! whilst you read your Shakespeares and Miltons and stuff." He was a prig, and the girl he loved knew him, and being quite of another way of thinking herself, would have nothing to say to him in the way of love. But without something of the aptitudes of a prig the character which the author intended could not have been drawn. There was to be courage—military courage—and that propensity to fighting which the tone of the age demanded in a finished gentleman. Esmond, therefore, is ready enough to use his sword. But at the same time he has to live as becomes one whose name is in some degree under a cloud; for though he be not in truth an illegitimate offshoot of the noble family which is his, and though he knows that he is not so, still he has to live as though he were. He becomes a soldier, and it was just then that our army was accustomed "to swear horribly in Flanders." But Esmond likes his books, and cannot swear or drink like other soldiers. Nevertheless he has a sort of liking for fast ways in others, knowing that such are the ways of a gallant cavalier. There is a melancholy over his life which makes him always, to himself and to others, much older than his years. He is well aware that, being as he is, it is impossible that Beatrix should love him. Now and then there is a dash of lightness about him, as though he had taught himself, in his philosophy, that even sorrow may be borne with a smile—as though there was something in him of the Stoic's doctrine, which made him feel that even disappointed love should not be seen to wound too deep. But still, when he smiles, even when he indulges in some little pleasantry, there is that garb of melancholy over him which always makes a man a prig. But he is a gentleman from the crown of his head to the sole of his foot. Thackeray had let the whole power of his intellect apply itself to a conception of the character of a gentleman. This man is brave, polished, gifted with that old-fashioned courtesy which ladies used to love, true as steel, loyal as faith himself, with a power of self-abnegation which astonishes the criticising reader when he finds such a virtue carried to such an extent without seeming to be unnatural. To draw the picture of a man, and say that he is gifted with all the virtues, is easy enough—easy enough to describe him as performing all the virtues. The difficulty is to put your man on his legs, and make him move about, carrying his virtues with a natural gait, so that the reader shall feel that he is becoming acquainted with flesh and blood, not with a wooden figure. The virtues are all there with Henry Esmond, and the flesh and blood also, so that the reader believes in them. But still there is left a flavour of the character which Thackeray himself tasted when he called his hero a prig.

The two heroines, Lady Castlewood and Beatrix, are mother and daughter, of whom the former is in love with Esmond, and the latter is loved by him. Fault has been found with the story, because of the unnatural rivalry—because it has been felt that a mother's solicitude for her daughter should admit of no such juxtaposition. But the criticism has come, I think, from those who have failed to understand, not from those who have understood the tale; not because they have read it, but because they have not read it, and have only looked at it or heard of it. Lady Castlewood is perhaps ten years older than the boy Esmond, whom she first finds in her husband's house, and takes as a *protégé;* and from the moment in which she finds that he is in love with her own daughter, she does her best to bring about a marriage between them. Her husband is alive, and though he is a drunken brute—after the manner of lords of that time—she is thoroughly loyal to him. The little touches, of which the woman is herself altogether unconscious, that gradually turn a love for the boy into a love for the man, are told so delicately, that it is only at last that the reader perceives what has in truth happened to the woman. She is angry with him, grateful to him, careful over him, gradually conscious of all his worth, and of all that he does to her and hers, till at last her heart is unable to resist. But then she is a widow;—and Beatrix has declared that her ambition will not allow her to marry so humble a swain, and Esmond has become—as he says of himself when he calls himself "an old gentleman"—"the guardian of all the family," "fit to be the grandfather of you all."

The character of Lady Castlewood has required more delicacy in its manipulation than perhaps any other which Thackeray has drawn. There is a mixture in it of self-negation and of jealousy, of gratefulness of heart and of the weary thoughtfulness of age, of occasional sprightliness with deep melancholy, of injustice with a thorough appreciation of the good around her, of personal weakness—as shown always in her intercourse with her children, and of personal strength—as displayed when she vindicates the position of her kinsman Henry to the Duke of Hamilton, who is about to marry Beatrix;—a mixture which has required a master's hand to trace. These contradictions are essentially feminine. Perhaps it must be confessed that in the unreasonableness of the woman, the author has intended to bear more harshly on the sex than it deserves. But a true woman will forgive him, because of the truth of Lady Castlewood's heart. Her husband had been killed in a duel, and there were circumstances which had induced her at the moment to quarrel with Harry and to be unjust to him. He had been ill, and had gone away to the wars, and then she had learned the truth, and had been wretched enough. But when he comes back, and she sees him, by chance at first, as the anthem is being sung in the cathedral choir, as she is saying her prayers, her heart flows over with tenderness to him. "I knew you would come back," she said; "and to-day, Henry, in the anthem when they sang it—'When the Lord turned the captivity of Zion we were like them that dream'—I thought, yes, like them that dream—them that dream. And then it went on, 'They that sow in tears shall reap in joy, and he that goeth forth and weepeth shall doubtless come home again with rejoicing, bringing his sheaves with him.' I looked up from the book and saw you. I was not surprised when I saw you. I knew you would come, my dear, and saw the gold sunshine round your head." And so it goes on running into expressions of heart-melting tenderness. And yet she herself does not know that her own heart is seeking his with all of women's love. She is still willing that he should possess Beatrix. "I would call you my son," she says, "sooner than the greatest prince in Europe." But she warns him of the nature of her own girl. "'Tis for my poor Beatrix I tremble, whose headstrong will affrights me, whose jealous temper, and whose vanity no prayers of mine can cure." It is but very gradually that Esmond becomes aware of the truth. Indeed, he has not become altogether aware of it till the tale closes. The reader does not see that transfer of affection from the daughter to the mother which would fail to reach his sympathy. In the last page of the last chapter it is told that it is so—that Esmond marries Lady Castlewood—but it is not told till all the incidents of the story have been completed.

But of the three characters I have named, Beatrix is the one that has most strongly exercised the writer's powers, and will most interest the reader. As far as outward person is concerned, she is very lovely—so charming that every man that comes near to her submits himself to her attractions and caprices. It is but rarely that a novelist can succeed in impressing his reader with a sense of female loveliness. The attempt is made so frequently—comes so much as a matter of course in every novel that is written, and fails so much as a matter of course, that the reader does not feel the failure. There are things which we do not expect to have done for us in literature, because they are done so seldom. Novelists are apt to describe the rural scenes among which their characters play their parts, but seldom leave any impression of the places described. Even in poetry how often does this occur? The words used are pretty, well chosen, perhaps musical to the ear, and in that way befitting; but unless the spot has violent characteristics of its own, such as Burley's cave or the waterfall of Lodore, no striking portrait is left. Nor are we disappointed as we read, because we have not been taught to expect it to be otherwise. So it is with those word-painted portraits of women, which are so frequently given and so seldom convey any impression. Who has an idea of the outside look of Sophia Western, or Edith Bellenden, or even of Imogen, though Iachimo, who described her, was so good at words? A series of pictures—illustrations—as we have with Dickens' novels, and with Thackeray's, may leave an impression of a figure—though even then not often of feminine beauty. But in this work Thackeray has succeeded in imbuing us with a sense of the outside loveliness of Beatrix by the mere force of words. We are not only told it, but we feel that she was such a one as a man cannot fail to covet, even when his judgment goes against his choice.

Here the judgment goes altogether against the choice. The girl grows up before us from her early youth till her twenty-fifth or twenty-sixth year, and becomes—such as her mother described her—one whose headlong will, whose jealousy, and whose vanity nothing could restrain. She has none of those soft foibles, half allied to virtues, by which weak women fall away into misery or perhaps distraction. She does not want to love or to be loved. She does not care to be fondled. She has no longing for caresses. She wants to be admired—and to make use of the admiration she shall achieve for the material purposes of her life. She wishes to rise in the world; and her beauty is the sword with which she must open her oyster. As to her heart, it is a thing of which she becomes aware, only to assure herself that it must be laid aside and put out of the question. Now and again Esmond touches it. She just feels that she has a heart to be touched. But she never has a doubt as to her conduct in that respect. She will not allow her dreams of ambition to be disturbed by such folly as love.

In all that there might be something, if not good and great, nevertheless grand, if her ambition, though worldly, had in it a touch of nobility. But this poor creature is made with her bleared blind eyes to fall into the very lowest depths of feminine ignobility. One lover comes after another. Harry Esmond is, of course, the lover with whom the reader interests himself. At last there comes a duke—fifty years old, indeed, but with semi-royal appanages. As his wife she will become a duchess, with many diamonds, and be Her Excellency. The man is stern, cold, and jealous; but she does not doubt for a moment. She is to be Duchess of Hamilton, and towers already in pride of place above her mother, and her kinsman lover, and all her belongings. The story here, with its little incidents of birth, and blood, and ignoble pride, and gratified ambition, with a dash of true feminine nobility on the part of the girl's mother, is such as to leave one with the impression that it has hardly been beaten in English prose fiction. Then, in the last moment, the duke is killed in a duel, and the news is brought to the girl by Esmond. She turns upon him and rebukes him harshly. Then she moves away, and feels in a moment that there is nothing left for her in this world, and that she can only throw herself upon devotion for consolation.

> "I am best in my own room and by myself," she said. Her eyes were quite dry, nor did Esmond ever see them otherwise, save once, in respect of that grief. She gave him a cold hand as she went out. "Thank you, brother," she said in a low voice, and with a simplicity more touching than tears; "all that you have said is true and kind, and I will go away and will ask pardon."

But the consolation coming from devotion did not go far with such a one as her. We cannot rest on religion merely be saying that we will do so. Very speedily there comes consolation in another form. Queen Anne is on her deathbed, and a young Stuart prince appears upon the scene, of whom some loyal hearts dream that they can make a king. He is such as Stuarts were, and only walks across the novelist's canvas to show his folly and heartlessness. But there is a moment in which Beatrix thinks that she may rise in the world to the proud place of a royal mistress. That is her last ambition! That is her pride! That is to be her glory! The bleared eyes can see no clearer than that. But the mock prince passes away, and nothing but the disgrace of the wish remains.

Such is the story of *Esmond*, leaving with it, as does all Thackeray's work, a melancholy conviction of the vanity of all things human. *Vanitas vanitatum,* as he wrote on the pages of the French lady's album, and again in one of the earlier numbers of *The Cornhill Magazine*. With much that is picturesque, much that is droll, much that is valuable as being a correct picture of the period selected, the gist of the book is melancholy throughout. It ends with the promise of happiness to come, but that is contained merely in a concluding paragraph. The one woman, during the course of the story, becomes a widow, with a living love in which she has no hope, with children for whom her fears are almost stronger than her affection, who never can rally herself to happiness for a moment. The other, with all her beauty and all her brilliance, becomes what we have described—and marries at last her brother's tutor, who becomes a bishop by means of her intrigues. Esmond, the hero, who is compounded of all good gifts, after a childhood and youth tinged throughout with melancholy, vanishes from us, with the promise that he is to be rewarded by the hand of the mother of the girl he has loved.

And yet there is not a page in the book over which a thoughtful reader cannot pause with delight. The nature in it is true nature. Given a story thus sad, and persons thus situated, and it is thus that the details would follow each other, and thus that the people would conduct themselves. It was the tone of Thackeray's mind to turn away from the prospect of things joyful, and to see—or believe that he saw—in all human affairs, the seed of something base, of something which would be antagonistic to true contentment. All his snobs, and all his fools, and all his knaves, come from the same conviction. It is not the doctrine on which our religion is founded—though the sadness of it there is alleviated by the doubtful promise of a heaven?

> Though thrice a thousand years are passed
> Since David's son, the sad and splendid,
> The weary king ecclesiast
> Upon his awful tablets penned it.

So it was that Thackeray preached his sermon. But melancholy though it be, the lesson taught in **Esmond** is salutary from beginning to end. The sermon truly preached is that glory can only come from that which is truly glorious, and that the results of meanness end always in the mean. No girl will be taught to wish to shine like Beatrix, nor will any youth be made to think that to gain the love of such a one it can be worth his while to expend his energy or his heart. (pp. 124-33)

> *Anthony Trollope, in his* Thackeray, *Harper & Brothers, 1879, 206 p.*

WILLIAM DEAN HOWELLS (essay date 1900)

[*Howells was the chief progenitor of American realism and an influential American literary critic during the late nineteenth and early twentieth centuries. Although he wrote nearly three dozen novels, few of them are read today. Despite his eclipse, however, he stands as one of the major literary figures of his era; having successfully weaned American literature from the sentimental romanticism of its infancy, he earned the popular sobriquet "the Dean of American Letters." The following excerpt is drawn from two essays, "Thackeray's Bad Heroines" and "Thackeray's Good Heroines." Howells considers Beatrix and Rachel, finding both to be unbelievable characters.*]

[Beatrix Esmond] is never directly seen, but always through the eyes of that intolerable prig Henry Esmond, which are fixed mainly upon his own perfections. Even if she had been directly seen, however, I doubt if there would have been much real drama in her, though plenty of theatre. Several *coups de théâtre* there are in her career, and chiefly that when Esmond and her brother find her at Castlewood with the young Pretender, and prevent her for the time from giving her worthlessness to his worthlessness. If one reads the story in cold blood it is hard to believe in it at all, it is at every moment so palpably and visibly fabricated; and perhaps Beatrix is no more a doll than those other eighteenth-century marionettes; but compared with Becky Sharp a doll she certainly is. It is only in her avatar of Madame Bernstein, in **The Virginians**, that she begins to persuade you she is at best anything more than a nineteenth-century actress made up for her part. She suffers, of course, from the self-parade of Esmond, and has not, poor girl, half a chance to show herself for what she is. Her honest, selfish worldliness is, however, more interesting than her mother's much-manipulated virtues; but it is to be remembered in behalf of Lady Castlewood that Beatrix has at no turn of her career such a false part to play as that of a woman who falls in love with a boy, and then promotes his passion for her daughter, and at last takes him herself when her daughter will not. Indeed, I do not know why she should be so much blamed for her heartlessness; people cannot go and have heart unless nature has provided them the means; and after all the heartlessness of Beatrix is shown chiefly in her not loving Mr. Esmond, who is not an unprejudiced witness. The solemn scolding he gives her when he breaks the Duke of Hamilton's death to her seems to me quite preposterous; but then he is at all times preposterous. When he interferes in her intrigue with the Stuart whom he is helping put on the English throne, it is no wonder she

hates him: mischief for mischief, hers is far the less. Esmond, it will be remembered, scolds the prince in much the same temper that he has scolded Beatrix, for running down into the country after her, when he ought to have been waiting Queen Anne's death in London. He burns up the patent of Marquis which the Stuarts had given his father, and once more renounces his right to the title of Castlewood—he does it half a dozen times in all—and then the prince gives him and Lord Castlewood the satisfaction of a gentleman for his pursuit of their sister and cousin, by crossing swords with them.

> The talk was scarce over when Beatrix entered the room. What came she there to seek? She started and turned pale at the sight of her brother and kinsman. . . . "Charming Beatrix," said the prince with a blush that became him very well, "these lords have come a-horseback from London, where my sister lies in a despaired state, and where her successor makes himself desired. . . . Mademoiselle, may we take your coach for town?" "Will it please the king to breakfast before he goes?" was all Beatrix could say. The roses had shuddered out of her cheeks; her eyes were glaring; she looked quite old. She came up to Esmond, and hissed out a word or two. "If I did not love you before, cousin," says she, "think how I love you now." If words could stab, no doubt she would have killed Esmond. She looked at him as if she could. But her keen words gave no wound to Mr. Esmond; his heart was hard. And as he looked at her he wondered that he could ever have loved her.

This, I will confess, seems to me great rubbish, of the true historical-romance sort, the mouthing and the posing and all; and of the whole group it is Beatrix alone who seems natural. But doubtless one ought not to praise her, and I will allow that she is preferable only to the good people of the story. (pp. 1802-04)

· · · · ·

Thackeray imagined his things better than he represented them. . . . I think that sometimes he changed his mind about them, and "fought" them, as the actors say, to a conclusion different from that which he originally had in view. This appears to me particularly true of the situation in **Henry Esmond,** where (without knowing the "inside facts") I believe that when he first imagined Esmond in love with Beatrix, he meant him to be either fortunate or unfortunate in his love of her with no ulterior view for him. His love for Lady Castlewood and hers for him affects me as an afterthought; and though Thackeray achieved a novelty by it, he did not create beauty, as one always does when one follows the line of probability. It is, of course, *possible* that a man may fall in love with a woman ten years his senior, after he has been in love with her daughter; and of course such a woman *may* have cherished a passion for him, at first unconscious, and always silent, and having promoted his love for her daughter by every means in her power, may end by marrying him herself. I say the thing is possible; but it is so ugly, so out of nature, that it is not less than revolting; and therefore I cannot believe that the case was first imagined so.

Having finally imagined it so, Lady Castlewood's creator begins well back in her duplex personality to prepare the reader for the unhandsome dénouement. The story is told by Esmond, and very early in it he dwells upon the beauty of his "sweet mistress," his "dear mistress," and more and more repeats his sense of it, with an increasing emphasis upon the surprising youthfulness which survives in the mother of a married son

Rachel's visit to Esmond in prison.

and grown-up daughter. Apart from this perfunctory admiration of her charms, however, Esmond shows her a most interesting and noble character, with those limitations which best realize her virtues. It is altogether in character that a beautiful and serious girl should fall in love with a dashing young nobleman like Castlewood; that she should be devoted to him, and then with just cause resentfully jealous; that she should turn in her despair of him to the friendless little Esmond who has come to live with them, and should spend her wounded and outraged love in motherly tenderness upon him; that she should rely increasingly upon his truth and courage, and love him as an eldest son; that later, when he has become a man, and has been wounded in her husband's fatal quarrel, she should come to him, sick and in prison, to upbraid him for her loss. It is a great scene, where she does so, and much admired, though I doubt if it is always admired for what is finest in the subjective drama, namely, her wish to punish herself in him for the fact that she had really ceased to love her husband. She does not really suspect Esmond of failing Castlewood or abetting him in his quarrel; but somehow she must take out her remorse, and womanlike she takes it out of the creature she loves best.

Sometime she must begin to be conscious that she no longer loves Esmond quite as a mother; of a young girl it could be supposed that she might continue ignorant of the nature of her feeling, but Lady Castlewood is a mature woman, with all the experience of a wife. The false note is first sounded when in this necessary consciousness she tries to promote his passion for her daughter, which would be impossible. I know that all sorts of idiotic and detestable self-sacrifice is preached in fic-

tion, but this is a little too repulsive for belief. The imagination of the reader refuses to join with that of the author, who is left henceforth to manage the affair alone. . . . (p. 1946)

Lady Castlewood, in fine, seems to me a beautiful creation of which too much is asked. If she could have been left quietly a widow, and Esmond been allowed, or required to console himself for Beatrix with some other, or no other, if need be, she would have remained one of the most perfect figures in fiction. But as it is her loveliness is blotted, her perfection is marred by the part so improbably attributed to her. Women marry a second time, and they are not unapt to marry men younger than themselves in such cases, but Lady Castlewood is apparently the only woman who brought up a boy as her son, and after she had witnessed his unrequited love for her daughter, whom she tries to have marry him, marries him herself. It does not seem either nice or true; if it were true that would go a great way toward consoling one for its not being nice. (p. 1948)

> *William Dean Howells, "Thackeray's Bad Hero-*
> *ines" and "Thackeray's Good Heroines," in* Har-
> per's Bazar, *Vol. XXXIII, Nos. 46 and 48, November*
> *17 and December 1, 1900, pp. 1799-1804, 1945-50.*

CHARLES WHIBLEY (essay date 1903)

[*Whibley assesses the naturalness of Thackeray's treatment of his historical theme, focusing on his language, characters, and dramatic method.*]

Esmond is a deliberate attempt to reconstruct the past in word, in fact, in feeling. The scene is laid in the England of Queen Anne, and Thackeray puts his curious knowledge of the period to the best advantage. But he is never dominated by history; as in the Lectures, so in **Esmond,** it is the novelist who always keeps the upper hand. Nor does he indicate his period by any trick of phrase or artifice of diction. His style is no affair of old trappings, made in Wardour Street. You will search his pages in vain for strange words or strangely constructed sentences. It is true that he makes a few concessions to an ancient fashion of spelling: he writes Peterborow, for instance, and Bruxelles; but for the rest he gives a very liberal interpretation to archæology. How, then, does he produce the effect of another century? Merely by keeping his style at a higher level than it usually attains. From beginning to end he writes with a restraint which you will vainly seek in **Pendennis.** He has thrown over the story a veil of solemnity, through which his personages appear far away like the distant shapes of another age. The critic who declared that there is no page of **Esmond** but might have been written by a contemporary of Queen Anne was manifestly deceived. Examine the text narrowly, and you will find both words and phrases essentially modern. Indeed, it is the cadence rather than the phrase that is of the eighteenth century, and Thackeray's ear seldom misled him. In other words, the author of **Esmond** has reproduced the effect, not the actual language, of the past, an achievement at once more subtle and convincing than the ransacking of some *Gradus ad Parnassum* for musty names and otiose epithets.

The truth is, Thackeray's knowledge was profound enough to be held in check. He had not crammed the period up in a night to answer a popular demand. There was no need for him to cloak a too obvious ignorance with a parade of hastily acquired knowledge. He did not attain local colour, after the fashion of to-day, by admitting nothing into his novel that was not obsolete. The heroes of modern romance do not live in a real world; they are ticketed in a museum of antiquity; they make love beneath trees whose branches are haunted by stuffed birds; the very words they use belong not to human speech, but to a time-worn phrase-book. But Thackeray's method, far happier than that of his successors, was also an indirect reproof to those of his contemporaries who pursued the art of historical fiction. He swept away at a stroke all the conventions of G. P. R. James and his school, of Bulwer and Harrison Ainsworth. In *Esmond* you will find none of the catch-phrases, once so popular. He does not tell you that "as dawn was breaking a solitary horseman might be seen" and the rest of it. The best of his characters are real men and women, although they belong to the past, and it might be said that the shining merit of *Esmond* was its naturalness. At the same time, while Thackeray is not enslaved by archaeology, he makes the period clear by a thousand light and incidental touches. When Esmond writes his verses to Gloriana, "Have you never read them?" he asks. "They were thought pretty poems, and attributed by some to Mr Prior." And so, while he scrupulously avoids pompous description and fine writing, he creates an atmosphere at once consistent and just.

When, in *Vanity Fair,* Thackeray chose a great historical setting for his characters, he made no attempt to introduce Napoleon or Wellington upon the mimic scene. He allowed his readers to hear no more than the echo of the guns which swept the plain of Waterloo. In *Esmond* he was less wisely counselled, and though the temptation to let Steele, Addison, and the others speak for themselves was strong, the novel would have been all the better had he resisted it. He had sketched these personages, for good or evil, in his Lectures, and there he might have left them to the judgment of posterity. But he must needs ask them to play their part in the drama of *Esmond*; and it may be said that his characters are never further from reality than when they bear real names.

Now, if a novelist admits famous men into his romance, he lays upon himself a double burden. For the famous men must not only be picturesque and consistent with the creatures of the writer's imagination—they must also be consistent with their own history. That is to say, the author's fancy is, or should be, hampered by truth, and the difficulty of the problem is seen by the rarity of its solution. The invention of imaginary characters carries with it no such responsibility: to attempt an artistic presentation of historical facts is doubly dangerous, because not only does it control the author's imagination, but it admits the reader into the workshop. The material being known, the treatment of it can be more narrowly scrutinised; and *dramatis personæ* bearing the names of Richard Steele and Joseph Addison challenge a criticism which Tom Smith and John Brown escape. Thackeray, being a man of letters, has succeeded in a difficult task far better than the most of his rivals. The heroes whom he borrows from real life are never ridiculous. Though they often speak with a voice which is not their own, their accent is not inhuman, and even if you forget their names, you might still deem them men. Nevertheless the author is not at his ease with them. They neither move nor speak with the naturalness which distinguishes Esmond and Castlewood, and whenever they appear they enwrap the story in another atmosphere.

The positive errors may be passed over lightly. It is superfluous, for instance, to ask why Thackeray should have dressed up Prue Steele in the garb of Mrs Malaprop, or why he should insist that Roger Sterne was an Irishman. Nor need we do more than refer to the repeated and monstrous outrage upon Jonathan Swift. Let us take Richard Steele and Joseph Addison, who are drawn with the deepest sympathy and the greatest elaboration. They are both a trifle bibulous. Dick the Scholar always "imparts a strong perfume of burnt sack along with his caress," and Addison drinks too deeply of my Lord Halifax's burgundy. Again, they both speak like books. Steele quotes copiously from his own *Tatlers,* and Addison cannot keep off the subject of his own poems. And since men of letters have a life and character apart from their printed works, this restriction indicates a certain timidity in Thackeray's treatment. For the rest, they are both amiable fellows, even though they do some violence to their own characters. They are bound together by that tie of schoolboy loyalty which united Lamb and Coleridge, and which Thackeray illustrated again and again. Steele is a pleasant trifler, even when sober; Addison is not guiltless of pomposity even in his cups. The scene wherein Esmond visited Addison at his lodging, pictured the famous battle, and "drew the river on the table *aliquo mero*," is admirably managed; but the dinner of the wits is as forced as Mr Bungay's party, and *Esmond* is never at its best when these miracles of wit and learning are on the stage. However, Thackeray himself realised their subordination; he knew that they were merely incidental to the action—mere painted trappings in the background; and he makes it clear that his essential interest is in his own characters. Had he suppressed all his great men, his own story would still have been complete.

But there is one personage, the great Duke of Marlborough, whom Thackeray has sketched with peculiar rancour, and against whom, in the person of Esmond, he brings the most fantastic charges. It is unnecessary to say that the portrait is inconsistent with history as with itself. The Duke, indeed, as Thackeray paints him, is no man but a monster, a mere epitome of the vices, a proper pendant in inconsequent ferocity to the Dean of St Patrick's, painted by the same hand. Being Commander-in-Chief, he traitorously accepts bribes from the French king, and loses battles that he may fill his own pocket. His personal sins are worse even than those which sully his public reputation. In cowardice and hypocrisy he almost outdoes Swift himself. "He would cringe to a shoeblack," we are told, "as he would flatter a minister or monarch; be haughty, be humble, threaten, repent, weep, grasp your hand (or stab you whenever he saw occasion)." These words are strangely applied to a hero, at whose feet all Europe knelt, and who never cringed to man or woman save to Sarah, his own implacable Duchess. Nor is this the worst. The Duke lied, we are told, cheated fond women, and robbed poor beggars of halfpence. And these charges are brought not by the villain of the piece, but by Esmond himself, who is not merely the hero of the romance, but who may, without injustice, be accepted as the vehicle of Thackeray's own opinion.

Of course a writer of fiction is not upon oath: he may handle history with a certain licence; but he oversteps his privilege when he paints white black, and breathes the very soul of meanness into a hero or a patriot. (pp. 180-86)

But when Thackeray deserts the great ones of history for the personages of his own creation, there is no fumbling nor faltering. In none of his books does he keep so firm a grasp upon his characters as in *Esmond,* which is as consistent in portraiture as it is in style and effect. Nor was the task which he set himself a light one. Not only is the scene laid in the England of Queen Anne, but the action covers many years, and the actors grow up under the reader's gaze. Yet they are never false either to their time or to themselves. What Esmond was, when he first came to Castlewood, so he remained until the last chapter, when his dear mistress's "eyes of meek surrender yield to his respectful importunity." He may not realise an ideal of all that is noble in mankind. Some may detect in him the signs of a nascent priggishness. Some may object that now and again he resembles the author of his being too nearly to be a true Augustan,—that his essentially modern tirade upon the horrors of war, for instance, belongs more intimately to Thackeray himself than to a soldier of the eighteenth century. (Perhaps it was not for nothing that Esmond, when he went to Cambridge, kept in Thackeray's own rooms, "in the great court close by the gate.") Nevertheless he is a man of blood and bone, who acts always in accord with his own qualities. And in his dear mistress he is well matched. Lady Castlewood, an odd mixture of caprice and devotion, of kindliness and anger, is always the same and always herself. She, also, has certain traits which we could dispense with in our friends. She is almost as lachrymose as Mrs Pendennis! She carries devotion too far, when she says to Esmond: "Let me kneel and worship you." But our preferences do not affect the truth of an exquisite portrait, subtly conceived and finely drawn.

Again, the main theme of the book is treated with the utmost delicacy. The transference of a man's love from daughter to mother is not a sympathetic motive for romance. But Thackeray insists so gravely upon Esmond's admiration and my Lady's gratitude, that her surrender is not surprising, is even inevitable. Mrs Beatrix is not so successful. She, indeed, does not come into her own, until she appears in later life as Madame de Bernstein. Her caprices are too vain for belief; her rejections too heartless. Yet how picturesquely she is brought upon the scene! Who will ever forget her descent of the stairs, and the scarlet glint of her stocking? (pp. 186-90)

But if Beatrix is a picturesque apparition rather than a real woman, the world of Castlewood, through which she walks a magnificent shadow, is admirably depicted. The vague background of rebellion and jesuitry gives an air of added gaiety and peace to the gay or tranquil inhabitants. My Lord Castlewood himself is one of those warm-hearted, foolish, shiftless gentlemen whom Thackeray knew so well how to draw. He is a Rawdon Crawley, more happily mated, and when the crisis of his destiny arrives he bears himself, as did Rawdon, like a man. Nothing could be better than his conduct of the duel with Lord Mohun, a duel most artfully composed from the records of the time. Nor is the son, Francis the Younger, unworthy his brave, spendthrift, debonair father. Though he is as vain as his sister, his vanity is tempered by an amiable disposition. . . . And while the principal actors in the drama are well understood and well drawn, *Esmond* is singularly free from those stock-characters with which few novelists can dispense. True, the jesuit Holt, with his strange comings and goings, his secret hiding-places, and his inaccurate information, is a type rather than a man. True, also, the old Marchioness, the wicked Dowager of Chelsey, is but Miss Crawley artfully disguised, and more thickly coated with paint. But, when all deductions are made, Thackeray has achieved a success granted to few novelists besides Sir Walter Scott: he has peopled an unreal world with real men and women, for though the age is Anne's, Esmond and my Lady and Frank Castlewood and human enough to have lived at any time and under any sky.

But it is not merely for its characters that we esteem *Esmond*, nor for its many passages of dignified, even elevated, prose. The book will ever be memorable also for one or two scenes of haunting beauty, or dramatic intensity. Who can ever forget

Esmond's visit to Walcote after his return from Vigo? It is in Winchester Cathedral that he sees my Lady Castlewood and Frank after his estrangement, bringing back with him, in Tom Tusher's phrase, "Gaditanian laurels." "And Harry's coming home to supper. Huzzay! huzzay!" cries my lord. "Mother, I shall run home and bid Beatrix put her ribands on. Beatrix is a maid of honour, Henry. Such a fine set-up minx!" The passage expresses the sentiment, not the sentimentality, of home-coming, without a word too much, without a note falsely struck. Still better is the last chapter of all, wherein Esmond and the young lord pursue the Prince to Castlewood. These dozen pages are, I think, Thackeray's highest achievement. The three men are perfectly realised—Esmond dignified and austere, as becomes the head of the house; Frank chivalrous and impulsive, like the sound-hearted boy he is; and his Majesty, when once his rage is mastered, every inch a king. "Eh, bien, Vicomte," says the young Prince, who was a boy, and a French boy, "il ne nous reste qu'un chose à faire: embrassons nous." It is a brave picture, bravely painted, without a stroke awry, without a superfluous touch.

Since *Esmond* many hundreds (or is it thousands?) of historical novels have been published; yet *Esmond*'s supremacy is still unchallenged. (pp. 190-93)

Charles Whibley, in his William Makepeace Thackeray, *William Blackwood & Sons, 1903, 262 p.*

LORD ROSEBERY [ARCHIBALD PHILIP PRIMROSE] (lecture date 1911)

[Primrose expresses his distaste for the plot of Henry Esmond. *His remarks were first presented in a lecture delivered on 30 June 1911.]*

Esmond is a great effort, a wonderful revival, a triumphant masquerade. So marvellous is the skill of the master in reproducing the words, the thoughts, and the manners of a past age that some have placed this remarkable book as high as *Vanity Fair*. I must frankly own myself a dissentient. The plot to me is simply repulsive. The transformation of Lady Castlewood from a mother to a wife is unnatural and distasteful to the highest degree. Thackeray himself declared that he could not help it. This, I think, only means that he saw no other than this desperate means of extricating the story. I cannot help it, too. One likes what one likes, and one dislikes what one dislikes, and so I must face the just indignation of Thackeray idolaters by declaring that, much as I admire this masterpiece in one respect, it is to me a story with a painful blot. (pp. 68-9)

Lord Rosebery [Archibald Philip Primrose], "Thack-eray," in his Miscellanies: Literary & Historical, *Vol. I, edited by John Buchan, Hodder and Stoughton, 1921, pp. 59-76.*

JOHN W. DODDS (essay date 1941)

[In this excerpt from his respected critical study of Thackeray, Dodds analyzes the major characters of Henry Esmond, *also commenting on the difficulty of determining the exact nature of Rachel and Esmond's love for one another.]*

It has always been recognized that *Esmond* is the best constructed of Thackeray's novels. It was the only one to be planned and written as a whole before it appeared in the full dress of three volumes. This helps to explain why it is only half as long as *Vanity Fair, Pendennis,* and the later novels. It has fewer characters and therefore less elaboration of minor collateral figures, as well as fewer loose ends. Nor does Thackeray indulge so freely in his customary whimsical digression and comment. Esmond tells his own story, and the point of view, which in the previous novels had suffered moments of uncertainty, is here steadily maintained. Although Esmond tells the story in the third person, the voice is unmistakably his throughout. Thackeray reminds us of this from time to time when with a cunning artlessness he makes Esmond drift easily into the first person. Any comments or philosophical or pious generalizations, therefore, appear to be Esmond's own. Although the melancholy hero has a definite infiltration of Thackeray's own temperament ('a handsome likeness of an ugly son of yours,' Thackeray told his mother), the disquisitions seem more natural because the showman is in the background. (pp. 164-65)

Henry Esmond himself is quite properly the hero of the novel, and yet not quite all a 'hero' in the historico-romantic sense. He is brave, capable of quick and decisive action in a crisis, sensitive, a 'pattern of moral behaviour,' quixotically generous in his refusal to claim the title which was his by rights. His daughter, writing the preface to his memoirs, pictures him as a Virginia country gentleman who is a very paragon of courtesy and grace and refinement. Yet he is not good looking, is moody and lonely, and given to pious moralizing. Trollope called him 'a gentleman from the crown of his head to the sole of his feet' [see excerpt dated 1879], and Thackeray wrote to his mother that the hero of his new novel was 'as stately as Sir Charles Grandison.' But he is capable, as Thackeray admitted, of being a most unheroic bore. His natural melancholy becomes at times merely a moody gloom; Beatrix calls him 'Don Dismallo' and he even refers to himself as the Knight of the Woeful Countenance. (Perhaps that is the reason the comedy he wrote ran only three nights and sold but nine copies.) His typical moods alternated between an exalted grief and a highly charged sentiment. The art comes, of course, in Thackeray's making Esmond thus reveal himself in his own words, and our impatience with Esmond cannot hide the fact that he is a real if sometimes irritatingly dreary person. There is little satire in *Henry Esmond*, but there is much of the deep irony which permeates Thackeray's best work—an irony blended with pity. It is not merely that we find a mixture of good and evil in all people, or that worldly persons are their own punishment. It is found in Esmond's tone of high regret and in the recognition of the irreconcilable contradictions of character in the noblest people. Of such contradictions Esmond has his share; the most intricate, however, belong to Rachel, Lady Castlewood.

Many readers have come away from *Esmond* feeling not a little uncomfortable about the relation between Esmond and Rachel. Rachel is sufficiently real—pious, tender, sweet, moving in an aura of sanctity and unpretentious benevolence. Esmond declares that she has great powers of intellect (which are not made clear in the novel) and that she is wittier than Beatrix (the only testimony for this being one sickly pun). When she was cheerful, says Esmond, she 'said the finest things.' It is our misfortune to see her when cheerfulness has difficulty creeping in. The fact is that she is too much like Esmond himself, stricken with a passionate sadness which envelops her and gives even her scenes of tenderness a curious hectic quality. She lives for affection, feeds on raptures, and is happiest when she can immerse herself in ecstasies of adoration or reconciliation. 'Don't raise me,' she would say to Esmond in a wild way, sinking to her knees, 'let me kneel, and—and—worship you.' There is, to be sure, nothing vulgar or offensive in Thackeray's presentation of this, nor is there any hint that Esmond

is distressed by the highly charged sentiment. Quite the contrary. But Thackeray sets himself the hard task of showing, through Esmond's eyes, how this goddess is less than divine in her jealousy, which is just as passionate as her affection. She could be hard and unyielding, relentlessly sinless and just as relentlessly stern—as for instance when she blames the lad Esmond for bringing small-pox into the house, or when she overwhelms him with recriminations for not preventing Mohun from killing her husband, though Esmond has really tried to avert the quarrel.

This phase of her character is pointed up sharply in her daughter's preface to the book, which represents, presumably, Thackeray's final reflections on the people he had created. There Rachel is shown to have been so insistent, as long as Esmond lived, upon absorbing every bit of his love that she was jealous of his fondness for their own daughter; and Esmond, under her watchful eye, was unable to express his real fondness for the child. It is not much wonder that the earlier Lord Castlewood tired of such adoration; it took a Henry Esmond to live with it and like it.

Now it is not impossible that a woman of Rachel's high-strung and devotedly passionate temperament, whose idolization of her coarse husband was just as unreasoning as was her later devotion to Esmond, should after her husband's death transfer her affection to the lad whom she had protected. Nor is it unlikely that she would be jealous of Esmond when he is mooning after her daughter Beatrix. This is all within the bounds of human probability and need be neither ridiculous nor repugnant; although one feels a little uneasy at the spectacle of the mother who, as Mrs. Jameson put it, 'for years is the confidante of a man's delirious passion for her own child, and then consoles him by marrying him herself!' But we watch the love grow until Thackeray's comment, when he was taken to task for marrying them at the end, is perfectly plausible: 'I didn't make them do it; they did it themselves.' Very credible, too, is Rachel's wavering between instinctive jealousy and a determined martyrdom. At one moment she will warn Esmond against Beatrix, saying that the man who marries Beatrix will never be happy. But at another time she tells Esmond: 'I wish she would have you,' and Esmond, at the height of his love-sickness, reposed all his dreary confessions with his 'dearest mistress' Rachel, 'who never tired of hearing him and pleading for him.'

The difficulty with a situation like this is that its delineation requires an absolute certainty of touch, and it is at just such moments that Thackeray is likely to be confused by conflicting impulses. We are never sure, during the growth of this strange affection, just what it means at any given moment. It is not improbable that Rachel and Esmond themselves should at certain stages be uncertain of the exact nature of their feelings for each other, but certainly Thackeray should know, and it is not clear that he did.

The relationship begins with a generous protective impulse on the part of the young wife towards the lad who is seven or eight years her junior, and with a rapt worship of his benefactress on the part of the lonely Esmond. His sustained tone is one of awed rapture that such a pure devotion as Rachel's should be poured out on him. A little later young Frank Castlewood tells Esmond bluntly that his mother is in love with him, but the word 'love' is a confusing one in this book, and Esmond seems not to get the full significance of Frank's remark. After a year's separation Esmond returns home and "his mistress . . was his dearest mistress again . . . 'Twas happiness to have seen her: 'twas no great pang to part; a filial tenderness, a love that was at once respect and protection, filled his mind as he thought of her; and near her or far from her, and from that day until now, and from now until death is past, and beyond it, he prays that that sacred flame may ever burn.' Come now, Esmond, *what* flame? Your 'filial tenderness,' long before this writing, must have been sublimated at the marriage altar. And in that famous scene in which Esmond returns home to Rachel, 'bringing his sheaves with him,' and swears eternal devotion to her, he is a confused blend of son and lover. Rachel, for her part, speaks 'with a mother's sweet plaintive tone and look.' But here is what she *says*: 'Yes, there is no sin in such a love as mine now; and my dear lord in heaven may see my heart.'

Still later, when Esmond has been pouring out to Rachel his love for Beatrix, she says: 'I am your mother, you are my son, and I love you always'; and Esmond's comment is on 'that amazing and constant love and tenderness with which this sweet lady ever blessed and pursued him.' It is impossible to tell at what point, or even how, this attachment turns into what it ultimately becomes. All we know is that immediately following the *débâcle* of the Pretender episode and Esmond's sudden wonderment, as he looked at Beatrix, that he could ever have loved her, comes the record of Rachel's marriage to Esmond, amid some supercharged transports of wonder and gratitude.

One comes to the conclusion that his perplexity as far as *Esmond* is concerned stems, as in previous instances, from Thackeray's inability at certain times to reconcile and justify the characterization and the comment on the characterization. Here, to be sure, Esmond is making the comments, but it is clear that Thackeray does not sense the strange mixture of feelings. Esmond is by no means blind, for example, to Rachel's hard jealousy. 'If my mistress was cruel,' he says 'at least she never could be got to own as much. Her haughtiness quite overtopped Beatrix's, and, if the girl had a proud spirit, I very much fear that it came to her by inheritance.' Against such passages as these one has to set off the 'devotional ceremonials' which would indicate that Rachel is almost too fragile a spirit to endure the terms of our mortality. The reader retires in some confusion. (pp. 167-71)

There is no such uncertainty in the characterization of Beatrix. As Rachel is to Amelia Sedley, so Beatrix is to Becky Sharp; and Beatrix, like Becky, would save any novel. So far does she cast her shadow over *Henry Esmond* that it is hard to believe that the story is half over before we see her in anything except occasional flashes. The explanation is, of course, that it takes her 250 pages to grow up. Yet from almost the beginning she is the vivacious bright-eyed coquette—pert, vain, bright, mischievous—who makes eyes at Esmond, and who, indeed, would make eyes at anything in breeches. Her haughty beauty captivates Esmond as it captivated her long line of devotees from the Marquis of Blandford to Lord Ashburnham to the Duke of Hamilton to the Pretender. Esmond knew her faults well, knew that she was imperious, light-minded, flighty, false, and he loved her with a humiliated desperation. She is blandly unmoved by his protestations. Even her delight in conquest and her passion for admiration, so primary in her nature, could not keep her from being fatigued by the raptures of the noble but dullish young man. 'She was a princess, though she had scarce a shilling to her fortune; and one of her subjects—the most abject and devoted wretch, sure, that ever drivelled at a woman's knees—was this unlucky gentleman; who bound his good sense, and reason, and independence, hand and foot; and submitted them to her.' She once explains to Esmond that he might

have fared better if he had not been so humble and down on his knees.

Thackeray makes of this character, however, more than a brilliant coquette. Behind her magnificent vanity was a hard ambitious purpose which she confessed to with a worldly cynicism: she wanted a wealthy husband and she knew that her face was her fortune. She demanded what Esmond could not give her—flattery, compliments, diamonds, a coach-and-eight. But as Charlotte Brontë pointed out, Beatrix is pursued by a terrible destiny. Her suitors die, or are killed, or drop away from her. Her heart had not been touched by any of them, and at length this dazzling creature discovers that she shares the fate of all such worldlings: she no longer has any heart to be touched. In a terribly candid and self-revealing passage she tells Esmond that had she found the man she could love 'I would have followed him in rags had he been a private soldier, or to sea, like one of those buccaneers you used to read to us about when we were children . . . I was frightened to find I was glad of his [her betrothed, Lord Hamilton's] death; and were I joined to you, I should have the same sense of servitude, the same longing to escape.' Her last game at high stakes was to lure the impressionable Pretender away from Kensington to Castlewood at the time when he should have been active in the plot for the throne. At this point Esmond's love dies within him, and he is free. (pp. 171-72)

Henry Esmond is not, in spite of its many delights, 'the greatest of all novels.' It is not even Thackeray's best or most penetrating. But it has warm brilliant spots and it tells a rattling good tale. It is more than a *tour de force*; it is a great artistic achievement. (p. 178)

John W. Dodds, in his Thackeray: A Critical Portrait, *1941. Reprint by Russell & Russell, Inc., 1963, 257 p.*

HOWARD O. BROGAN   (essay date 1946)

[*Brogan discusses the simultaneous presence of virtue and vice in Rachel's character, questioning why Thackeray depicted her sympathetically despite her faults.*]

How are we to account for the disparity between Thackeray's praise of Rachel and his acute awareness of her very serious faults?

In the first place, we must not be too certain that we always have Thackeray's true opinions. He writes with something of the detached irony of Thomas Mann, never totally identifying himself with any of his characters, and not above practicing upon the gullibility of the reader. Henry Esmond, not Thackeray, is writing the story, and we have Thackeray's own word for it that Henry is a prig. Just as Dobbin's idealization of Amelia in *Vanity Fair* is by no means in complete agreement with the opinion of Thackeray (who refers to her playfully as "an over-rated woman"), so the encomiums which are heaped upon Rachel by the priggish Henry are hardly to be taken as coming directly from the author. Often enough, in all probability, he is laughing up his sleeve both at Henry and at those overly serious readers who take at face value everything that Henry says. Yet I think nobody can doubt that, with minor reservations, Thackeray was in essential agreement with Henry. . . . Thackeray clearly admires and respects Henry, in spite of his priggishness, and while Henry's blind adulation of Rachel may sometimes verge on the ridiculous in the author's eyes, we are quite justified in assuming that a woman whom Henry is allowed to worship throughout the book must be thought even by Thackeray to possess very real virtues. The paradox of Thackeray's idolization of a faulty woman cannot be explained away by the hypothesis that his praise is not to be taken seriously.

In the second place, we must not underestimate the seriousness of Rachel's faults. The paradox is not to be escaped by assuming that Victorian ladies may have been shocked by defects which would not appear serious to this enlightened age. Her major fault is the unpleasant vice of jealousy. So unbridled is this passion in her that through its excess she either loses or strains to the breaking point the love of all those closest to her except Henry.

She is introduced to us as a very "exacting" wife, "perfectly tolerant and kindly" toward the other sex, but "invariably jealous of her own." When Rachel is enraged at Henry for associating with Nancy Sievewright, a village girl, whereby he brought smallpox into the house, her Lord consoles the boy by drunkenly exclaiming that

> "the very notion of a woman drives her mad. I took to liquor on that very account, by Jove, for no other reason than that, for she can't be jealous of a beer-barrel or a bottle of rum. . . ."

Rachel will hear nothing of a reconciliation while her husband continues to keep a mistress. Only his death at the hands of Mohun in a quarrel over her can bring her to a contrite admission that God is punishing her for her "wicked, jealous heart."

The same jealousy is transferred with her affections from her husband to her son. In his childhood she is never separated from her son if she can avoid it, fusses as much over his minor ailments as she previously had over those of her husband, and brings him in on her side in the quarrel between the parents. The consequence is that Lord Castlewood does not love his own son. We are specifically told that young Frank's early revolt from maternal authority, to which he never again submits, is an escape from his mother's possessiveness; so that it is by reason of her jealousy that Rachel finds herself at the end of the novel unwelcome in her son's home.

Most shocking of all, however, is the effect of her jealousy upon her daughters. Conflict with Beatrix becomes evident when the daughter sides with her father in the quarrel between the parents. The unnatural contest of mother and daughter over the affections of Henry—who stands to them almost as son and brother respectively—is of course the central interest of the novel and the chief reason for condemnation of it by strict Victorians. Rachel's jealousy of Beatrix is all the more unpleasant because she is the confidante of Henry's mad passion for her daughter. Though loyally supporting his suit, she with difficulty represses her anxiety that he may succeed. Both Henry and Beatrix are conscious of her attitude; and when Beatrix says that Rachel is waiting jealously outside the room in which they are conferring together, Henry can offer no other defense than this, that she did not show her jealousy, having among "other feminine qualities . . . that of being a perfect dissembler." At last the submerged struggle breaks into the open in the scene in which Beatrix is being removed from the temptation of the Pretender. Rachel cruelly humiliates her daughter before Henry, who says merely that his Lady was not often harsh, "but there are some moments when the tenderest women are cruel, and some triumphs which angels can't forego." Beatrix retaliates by asserting most significantly that she had always had to struggle against her mother's jealousy: "You

never loved me, never—and were jealous of me *from the time I sat on my father's knee*." That this state of affairs is not solely Beatrix's imagination is indicated by the complaint of Mrs. Warrington, Rachel's daughter by Henry, that her mother's love of her father was "so passionate and exclusive" that "before her, my dear father did not show the love which he had for his daughter. . . ." Since Rachel's jealousy estranged her from husband, son, and daughters, the least prudish contemporary reader can hardly look upon her flaw as a trivial one.

If Rachel's weakness is so great a blemish on her character, and yet we have good reason to think that Thackeray wished his readers to love and admire her, we must inevitably ask ourselves what virtue she can possibly have to overbalance her fault. Examination of the story shows at once that her passionate jealousy is the excess of a love even more passionate, that her possessiveness, overwhelming in her youth, is increasingly restrained by a strongly developing spirit of self-denial.

As a young wife her possessiveness is inescapable. She is utterly absorbed in her Lord, upon whose looks she lives, whose continued favor is the summit of her hopes. So urgent and unceasing is her worship that her Lord soon wearies of the restraint put upon him as a household divinity. She is already beginning to lose him even before the smallpox, by spoiling her beauty and driving him away to renewed escapades in gaming and with women, makes a breach in their nuptial love. Yet in spite of his neglect and of that unconsciously developing interest in Henry into which his neglect is driving her, we are told that she would do anything, even chop up "the Dean, her old father, in order to bring her husband back again." The continuance of possessive love is what makes reconciliation with her husband impossible while he persists in keeping a mistress. The strength of a living passion is part of the force behind her unreasonable anger at Henry's part in the fatal duel, and the catastrophe of her Lord's death awakens within her for the first time genuine repentance and a desire to be forgiven by the soul of the man from whom her love had selfishly tried to exact too much.

The lesson in self-sacrifice which the tragedy of her first love had begun is continued by her unhappy relations with her children. Her great venture in happiness having gone down, "she laid out all upon her children, indulging them beyond all measure, as was inevitable with one of her kindness of disposition. . . ." Here, too, her love is exclusive, so much so that for a time she deprives her Lord of the affection of both children. She begins to love Henry when he saves the life of young Frank. She is careful to swear him to Frank's service, thereby saving the title for her son. She interferes with her husband's gambling for fear he may ruin her children's inheritance; and after the catastrophe of his death, stoops to the pity of her old rival, the Dowager, and resorts to undignified scrimping in order to restore the estate for her son's sake. Her devotion to her son is unswerving. Frank sows his wild oats with the certain knowledge that she will forgive him anything. She does forgive him unhesitatingly his extravagance, his imprudent marriage, and his conversion to the Catholic religion, and she bears even estrangement from him with anguished resignation. In spite of the incipient jealousy of Beatrix which she can never quite overcome, she also pursues her daughter's best interests, going even to the extent of begging her to marry the man with whom Rachel herself is secretly in love; and, when Beatrix is endangered by the Pretender, Rachel attempts to save her daughter from shame, though certain that Beatrix, if saved, will continue to be a rival for Henry's affections.

The self-denial of Rachel, forged in the tragic fires of her first love and tempered in the bitter tears of her grief for her children, meets its supreme tests in her love for Henry. She fell in love with him unawares, her motherly affection for a waif deepening imperceptibly into gratitude to the savior of her son, but never being suspected of unlawful strength until her jealous anger over his innocent pursuit of Nancy Sievewright reveals the full force of her feelings to herself. Struggling against her fate, she utilizes her little inheritance to send Henry off to college, with the laudable purpose of avoiding temptation. Not until later does she realize that her secret desire had been, by making him chaplain at Castlewood, to keep him permanently by her. The death of her Lord ends her self-deception. She breaks decisively with Henry, not merely from anger at his part in the duel, but from a clear perception that she is secretly in love with him. Her taking a button from his coat, which she afterward wears in her bosom, shows plainly enough that she is now conscious of her passion.

Her self-denial now meets its greatest trial. Henry falls madly in love with Beatrix. Rachel wavers "between instinctive jealousy and a determined martyrdom," but in the end she voluntarily embraces the martyrdom. Though hoping Henry may recover from his infatuation (as she fondly believes she has done), she presses his suit for him, even begging Beatrix on her knees to reward Henry with her hand for the saving of young Frank from Mohun. Beatrix may guess her jealousy, but with iron self-control Rachel prevents herself from showing it to Henry.

Revelations of her love are always involuntary, the effect of surprise, naïveté, or enormous emotional pressure. What affection she does show is at least half sublimated, so that neither the characters nor the reader can be quite certain how to take it. Thus her jealous fit over Henry and Nancy Sievewright is able to masquerade as concern over the danger of smallpox to her children, and her fainting at the news, "here's poor Harry killed," could apply as well to Mohun as to Henry. Her reconciliation with him after the duel makes of Henry "a confused blend of son and lover." . . . Yet when Henry proposes to take her away to Virginia with him—one is not certain whether in the capacity of mother or wife—she firmly assumes the role of mother, disavows all other sentiment for Henry, and gives him up to Beatrix without a struggle.

She customarily speaks of her love for him in a most ambiguous manner. Naïvely she admits that she knew he would return, fondly remarks that "Henry is very good to look at," and cannot help showing a cheerful face as she sends him away from Beatrix, even though he goes to the wars. In the belief that she is only expressing gratitude for his sacrifice to Frank, she kisses Henry's hand and kneels in the very extravagance of passion to worship him. At times indeed her great emotion forces a vent, as when she breaks into hysteric laughter following Henry's kissing of Beatrix's foot, but she immediately passes it off as reproof to her daughter: "it is your hand, my dear, and not your foot he wants you to give him. . . ." Though she is sarcastic over Henry's eagerness to separate Beatrix and the Prince, still her cruelty to her daughter is disguised as moral reproach, and she does not go to Henry until he has given Beatrix up as hopeless and Rachel herself is left without a home.

Had Rachel competed openly and consciously with her daughter, she would have been monstrous; but despite all the hints listed above—which seem conclusive enough when brought together, despite the natural growth of their affection and the premature aging by which Henry is fitted for a woman who remains much younger than her years, and despite the fact that her Lord, Mohun, the Dowager, Frank, and Beatrix all half suspect the truth, still the nature of her love for Henry is doubtful right to the end. The reader is surprised fully as much as he is shocked when Rachel finally marries the man who had so long been to her almost another son.

If critics with reason could complain of Rachel's conduct, Henry could praise it with reasons just as strong. From one point of view she represents the Victorian ideal of womanhood. She is the fanatically devoted wife, submissive and uncomplaining even under the ruins of her love, the doting mother, whose every thought is of her children's welfare, and the perfect older feminine friend, whose seemingly platonic affection and disinterested advice are the mainstays of a young man's life. She successfully represses her natural desires as a woman when they conflict with her conventional duties as a wife and mother. She is always and eagerly sacrificing her own interests to those of the people whom she loves. Moreover, she does not marry Henry until every other course has become impractical.

Where Thackeray departed from the ideal was in his clear-sighted perception that such virtues can easily be carried to excess. He saw into the heart of the dilemma, realizing that the intense concentration upon domestic affections required by Victorian morality inevitably resulted in selfish possessiveness. In no other character is this dilemma given such tragic force as in that of Rachel, torn between Victorian martyrdom and primordial jealousy, deceiving herself as well as others by a chameleon-like concealment of secret desire, and against her better will leaving behind her a trail of frustrated loves and broken lives. No wonder those Victorian critics who were less able to transcend their age than Thackeray was rebelled against his unsparing, half unconscious exposure of these feet of clay beneath the gleaming marble of their ideal. (pp. 224-32)

> *Howard O. Brogan, "Rachel Esmond and the Dilemma of the Victorian Ideal of Womanhood," in ELH, Vol. 13, No. 3, September, 1946, pp. 223-32.*

JOHN E. TILFORD, JR.   (essay date 1952)

[Tilford closely analyzes the progress of Esmond and Rachel's love and speculates as to why the nature of their love has been obscure to readers.]

The first chapter of *Henry Esmond* opens with the meeting of young Henry and Rachel Esmond, Viscountess Castlewood, and their complex relations provide the major thematic integration of the novel. For most readers, however, the love interest centers in Henry's chronic courtship of Beatrix, Rachel's daughter. In modern criticism of the novel, allusions to the love of Henry and Rachel are usually perfunctory, often indicating little more than that, after the decline and fall of Beatrix, they were wed—a union which distressed many Victorian critics because of its disquieting implications of incest. For a century there has been no widespread perception of Thackeray's intentions regarding this pervasive love theme. (p. 684)

Many readers today, like the Victorian reviewers, are agitated when Henry Esmond announces his marriage to his "dear mistress." They have not clearly seen that he "had been in love with the mother, as well as with the daughter, all along," that "she did not exactly wait to be a widow before she fell in love with him," and particularly that Thackeray had long foreshadowed the eventual marriage. Pelham Edgar observes [see Additional Bibliography] that even the first meeting of the pair in Chapter I "has more value than appears on the surface, for it adjusts our point of view at the outset to the charm and graciousness of Rachel, and to the precocious gravity of the boy . . . The author's problem will be to lead us through the subsequent years of Esmond's infatuation for the daughter to his marriage with the mother; and infinite and almost successful are the pains he takes to accommodate us to this strange adjustment of his affections." Actually, Thackeray begins adjusting our point of view in the Preface to the memoirs, supposedly written by Henry's daughter. There, besides revealing much that Henry could hardly tell, the daughter presages some of the most important elements of the story—the extraordinary youthfulness of Henry's wife ("At sixty . . . she still looked young"); her "extreme devotion" to him, "passionate and exclusive"; her pathological jealousy; and even the end of the "future bishop's lady" (i.e., Beatrix). We are not told that Henry's wife is named Rachel (though his daughter's having the same name is a broad hint); still, her most apparent characteristics are emphasized, and her final relations to Henry implicit. The crucial question is whether Thackeray's pains are only "almost successful" in accommodating us to "this strange adjustment."

Though it is not possible here to trace all the ramifications of the love theme, Thackeray's intentions and methods can be clarified by focusing attention on two key scenes. In each there is crisis, and from each the love theme takes a new turn. The first of these is at Castlewood when Henry brings smallpox to his benefactors. To prepare specifically for this revelation of Rachel and Henry's relations, Thackeray allows only two of the first seven chapters. The first (I, i) sets forth Rachel's kindness to young Henry and his wholehearted gratitude. (The following five chapters deal with the Esmond family and Henry's unhappy childhood.) The second (I, vii) stresses Henry's nature: "He . . . had a fond and affectionate heart, tender to weakness, that would fain attach itself to somebody"—the somebody of course being Rachel, for whom he soon feels "a devoted affection and passion of gratitude, which entirely filled his young heart. . . . It cannot be called love, that a lad of twelve . . . felt for an exalted lady, his mistress: but it was worship." Then follows a summary of the next three years, during which their associations and sympathies grow ever closer, and hints of her marital troubles appear. Thackeray again gives one of his countless foreshadowings of the end: Henry vows "that no power should separate him from his mistress," and adds, "Now, at the close of his life . . . , he can think, not ungratefully, that he has been faithful to that early vow." Thackeray also has Henry occasionally hint at Rachel's feelings—for instance, she sighs apprehensively at the idea of his eventually leaving Castlewood, divining "his thoughts with her usual jealous watch and affection."

The reader who has noted such preparations is better able to interpret Rachel's almost hysterical vituperation of Henry in the first key scene (I, viii), which reflects both her natural fears of the smallpox and her jealousy of Henry (now sixteen), who has been seeing Nancy Sievewright. "Revelations of her love," says Howard O. Brogan, "are always involuntary, the effect of surprise, naïveté, or enormous emotional pressure" [see excerpt dated 1946]. Thackeray carefully insinuates not only Rachel's inner tensions but also her recognition of their nature and danger. This is notably seen in her apologies to Henry—the first a tacit admission of her jealousy:

"I beg your pardon, Henry," she said; "I spoke very unkindly. I have no right to interfere with you—with your"—My Lord broke into an oath. "Can't you leave the boy alone, my Lady?" She looked a little red, and frankly pressed the lad's hand as she dropped it.

Later she apologizes again "in a hard, dry voice," and her entire speech, though ostensibly innocent, is an ironic intimation of her feelings. Henry must perceive, she says, that he cannot "continue to stay upon the intimate footing in this family" he has enjoyed and should go on to the university:

"... I did not press this matter, thinking you a child, as you are, indeed, in years—quite a child; and I should never have thought of treating you otherwise until—until these *circumstances* came to light. And I shall beg my Lord to dispatch you as quick as possible: and I will go on with Frank's learning as well as I can (I owe my father thanks for a little grounding, and you, I'm sure, for much you have taught me),—and—and I wish you a good night, Mr. Esmond."

The strangely formal behavior ("Mr. Esmond"), the repetitions and hesitations, the double meanings ("these *circumstances*"), all signify awareness of her passion for Henry—even, perhaps, the acknowledgment for what he has taught her, which is not only languages but the fact that her love for him is no longer innocent. (If one thinks too much is being read into this dialogue, let him recall that later—II, vi—Rachel indicates that she deliberately sent Henry away in order to thrust temptation from her.)

Thackeray's methods of conveying this intelligence to the reader need emphasis, for they are his principal means of setting forth Rachel's central problem hereafter. Because Henry is the narrator, Thackeray is restricted to dramatic presentation: the hero must report Rachel's dialogue and actions, but his interpretive comment must be carefully controlled, or, for one thing, the story would be given away directly. Thus Henry's memoirs must show, as Brogan puts it, that Rachel's love gradually changes from "motherly affection for a waif" into love of "unlawful strength"—a love which she recognizes but which few others do, including Henry (and many readers). And while other characters in time "half suspect the truth" about their love, says Brogan, "the nature of her love for Henry is doubtful right to the end." But however doubtful it may be to others, *it is never doubtful to Rachel herself.* Hence Thackeray must try to make clear Rachel's private conflicts, which the hero-narrator does not then fully comprehend himself; and he must make the hero, at the same time, indicate his own mixed feelings.

Following the first key scene are many events, culminating in Viscount Castlewood's death and Henry's imprisonment. But these are primarily significant with relation to the love theme, which Thackeray never allows us to forget. Henry matures, and the sympathies between him and Rachel increase because of various circumstances (including the Viscount's philandering). Henry observes "that a secret care . . . was weighing upon her"—apparently her concern about her crumbling marriage, which was really no secret, but implicitly her anxiety about her attraction to Henry. When she donates a small inheritance to send him to the university, the feelings of both are pointed up (I, ix). She looks at Henry "with sad penetrating glances," while he hangs back "abashed," protesting that if she wished he would stay forever. Her agitation and ambiguous utterances make even the simple Viscount uneasy:

"Curse me, Rachel, if I know now whether thou art in earnest or not," said my Lord.

"In earnest, my Lord! . . . Is there much subject here for joke?"

She gives "a stately look to Harry Esmond, which seemed to say, 'Remember; you understand me, though he does not'." She seems "rejoiced to lose him" and cuts short "his protests of love and his lamentations." "'Indeed, you are best away,' said my Lady, laughing, as she put her hand on the boy's head for a moment." And her calling him her "knight" makes him blush, for that is his thought too. So, by such word-play and hinting, otherwise gratuitously meaningless, Thackeray continually suggests her struggles and Henry's own nebulous feelings.

Often, however, Thackeray's methods are more apparent. For example, Henry's attempt to reconcile his patrons is met with inexplicable sarcasm from Rachel. (I, xii).

> ". . . What wrong have I done you that you should wound me so, cruel woman?"
>
> "What wrong!" she said, looking at Esmond with wild eyes. "Well, none—none that you know of, Harry, or could help. Why did you bring back the small-pox," she added, after a pause, ". . . You could not help it, could you? Which of us knows whither fate leads us? But we were all happy, Henry, till then."

Her first exclamation, her "wild eyes," her "none that you know of, Harry," her pause, the allusions to fate and unhappiness—all these could only signify her continuing spiritual perturbation, his innocence of its causes, and her recognition of that innocence. And there is no doubt of Thackeray's desire to keep us mindful of the theme when he makes Mohun say to Henry (I, xiii): "By the Lord, I believe thou hast an eye to the pretty Puritan thyself, Master Harry. . . . Whisper, Harry, art thou in love with her thyself? . . ." Harry protests that he loves her as a mother and worships "her as a devotee worships a saint," which, we must believe, is what he honestly thinks, at the time. A few minutes later, when her husband cries that "Harry" (Mohun) has been killed, she, thinking of Harry Esmond, screams and faints.

To one who has overlooked these implications of Rachel's emotional state in Book I, her behavior toward Henry in prison, as Book II opens, would be almost meaningless. For her speech here is that of one profoundly distraught for reasons greater than the loss of a husband she no longer loved (though she now protests adulation of him). She says that her misfortunes are "a just judgment on my wicked heart—my wicked jealous heart," but, as in the smallpox scene, blames Henry for everything. "And, young as you were . . . there was evil, I knew there was evil, in keeping you," she says, and again reproaches Henry for bringing the smallpox, presumably because it injured her beauty and alienated the Viscount. But it is altogether clear now that, undone by a tragedy for which she feels responsible, she is overwhelmed by a profound feeling of guilt, though she distorts the reasons for that feeling. Thus is explained her obsession with the smallpox, which had the important dual effects on her life not only of increasing her husband's lack of interest in her, but of bringing into the open her passion for Henry. Her feeling of guilt, we now know, is not due to jealousy; it is due to loving Henry beyond maternal bounds. The "evil" in him is not that he brought smallpox but that he aroused fearful desires in her. (In this scene Thackeray employs a clumsy little device to indicate, finally, that even as she

harangued Henry she really loved him: while he is unconscious she purloins from his sleeve a button, which, the last line of the novel tells us, "she wore ever after . . . on the tenderest heart in the world.") And Thackeray again emphasizes Rachel's feelings of guilt when Steele reports to Henry her remarks (II, ii): religious counsel, she tells Steele, bids her "to part from [Henry], and to see him no more," though in future years, "when our knees and our tears and our contrition have changed our sinful hearts, we may meet again." Such counsel could follow only from confession of her "guilty" love. And when she adds that "Mr. Esmond will find other—other friends," her hesitation, as usual, signifies.

Thus throughout the episodes following the first manifestation of the love theme, Thackeray continually implies how things stand with his principals. He emphasizes Rachel's problems; but he does not neglect to remind us that Henry has some too, if less excruciating. And again as a pointer, he makes the Dowager Viscountess, like Mohun, suspect Henry of being in love with Rachel (II, iii), though Henry merely replies that he takes no shame in loving and honoring her "before all the world."

The second key scene presents the reunion of Henry and Rachel at Walcote (II, vi). With respect to the love theme, it is the most significant event in the novel. In this intensive short chapter Thackeray attempts three important things which must be understood before much can be made of the major characters or of the ensuing narrative. Using the dramatic technique, he clarifies much of what has gone before, indicates the present feelings of Rachel and Henry, and prepares for what is to come.

The scene is set with masterly skill. Henry has been driven to Walcote, despite Rachel's interdiction, by indignation (though it looks more like jealousy), for he has heard that Tom Tusher might marry her. The date is the 29th of December, memorable for both Henry and Rachel (who celebrate it as his "birthday"; on it long ago he saved young Frank's life, for which, she said, "she would love him all her life"—I, xi). They meet at Winchester cathedral, a solemn and suggestive setting. More than half the chapter is dialogue, with almost no interpretive comment by Henry; and though the conversations seem to move naturally, the matter is highly compressed, as in a play.

"It was a rapture of reconciliation," says Henry, and Rachel weeps with gladness. After summarizing his past attitudes toward her, Henry introduces a mutation that prepares for what happens later in the chapter and beyond:

> Brighter eyes there might be, and faces more beautiful, but none so dear—no voice so sweet as that of his beloved mistress, who had been sister, mother, goddess to him during his youth—goddess now no more, for he knew of her weaknesses; and by thought, suffering, and that experience it brings, was older now than she; but more fondly cherished as woman perhaps than ever she had been adored as divinity.

During the talk Rachel says much that enlightens. It was her "selfishness" that made her wish Henry to be the chaplain at Castlewood, so that he might be near her. She elaborates on her feelings of guilt and sin, and, though by indirection and pointed ellipsis, makes clear the nature of that sin. She says "it was God's will that [she] should be punished," and acknowledges "how wicked [her] heart has been" and how she has suffered. "I confessed to Mr. Atterbury—I must not tell any more." To do so would be to declare openly her love for Henry and its effect on her life. Her religious counselor's advice (to which she refers here) that she should try to see Henry no more could be meaningful only in this implied context.

Besides furnishing a striking background, the cathedral reflects Rachel's strong religious nature (she is the daughter of a clergyman) and gives Thackeray a means of leading to another of her revelatory outbursts. The symbol for this is Psalm 126, which is being chanted when she first sees Henry. Overcome with emotion after the service, she smiles "an almost wild smile" and recalls the date: "She burst into a wild flood of weeping as she spoke; she laughed and sobbed on the young man's heart, crying out wildly, 'bringing your sheaves with you—your sheaves with you!'" By now even Henry, who has hitherto been made to be rather dully oblivious of her deeper feelings, is allowed to comprehend what is going on; and he remarks that "the depth of this pure devotion (which was, for the first time, revealed to him) quite smote upon him, and filled his heart with thanksgiving." His next speech specifies this revelation (and foreshadows much), for here he first proposes to her—hesitantly and obliquely, but nonetheless proposes:

> "If—if 'tis so, dear lady . . . why should I ever leave you? If God has given me this great boon—and near or far from me, as I know now, the heart of my dearest mistress follows me, let me have that blessing near me, nor ever part with it till death separate us. Come away—leave this Europe. . . . Begin a new life in a new world. . . . that land in Virginia. . . . Frank will give us that. . . ."

Marriage, it is true, has not been named, and Brogan thinks that "one is not certain whether Henry wishes to take her away in the capacity of mother or wife"; but the wording of the proposal, with its echo of the marital vows, and especially the context seem clearly to imply "wife" (Henry's cherishing her as a "woman," his recognizing "the depth" of her "devotion," and the way he presses the matter and her reasons for refusing). Her immediate objections show understanding of his meaning: "And my children—and my duty—and my good father, Henry? . . ." When he wonders why, if he "would leave all to follow" her, she cannot "be as generous," she suddenly retreats back to her maternal role, for the first time in the chapter: "'Hush, boy!' she said, and it was with a mother's sweet plaintive tone and look that she spoke." Moreover, she says, again bringing up the subject, she has "been so weak and sinful" she must "pray out an expiation." Then Thackeray has her add, by way of emphasis:

> ". . . But I would love you still—yes, there is no sin in such a love as mine now—and my dear lord in heaven may see my heart; and knows the tears that have washed my sin away—and now—now my duty is here, by my children, whilst they need me, and by my poor old father, and"—

> "And not by me?" Henry said.

> "Hush!" she said again, and raised her hand up to his lip.

Once more she refers to her sin and its horrors, and when Henry seeks to interrupt, she gives the final reason for her refusal: ". . . Be silent! let me say all. You never loved me, dear Henry—no, you do not now, and I thank heaven for it. I used to watch you, and knew by a thousand signs that it was so." Thus Rachel, realizing that Henry has never "loved" her, i.e., erotically, believes that his proposal was inspired rather by strong feelings and his duty as a gentleman than by a sincere desire to have her to wife. She thanks heaven, perhaps, because she knows that if his love were erotic, she would likely yield.

And that would involve her sense of sin again, as her next words indicate: because she sent him (i.e., temptation) away to college, she received "absolution" from two clergymen—Mr. Atterbury and her father.

Henry comprehends the general tenor of this enigmatic dialogue, for as the chapter ends he rather easily acquiesces to her apparent desire to re-establish the old relationship: "'I think the angels are not all in heaven,' Mr. Esmond said. And as a brother folds a sister to his heart; and as a mother cleaves to her son's breast—so for a few moments Esmond's beloved mistress came to him and blessed him." Because of the relations tacitly agreed upon, the way is left open not only for Henry's pursuit of Beatrix (beginning in the next chapter), but for the continuation of Rachel's conflicts in considerably modified circumstances. Whether Henry really comprehends her terrible struggles is not certain—presumably he does so only dimly. But when John W. Dodds complains that in this scene Henry "is a confused blend of son and lover" [see excerpt dated 1941], he is overlooking the fact that that is just the point.

The focus of the chapter, however, is not Henry but Rachel. Her speeches not only clarify her feelings but prepare for her future behavior and, ultimately, for her acceptance of Henry as her husband. Her momentary loss of control and her preoccupation with her sin manifest attempted suppression, but by no means eradication, of her passionate desire for Henry. It is difficult, as Dodds points out, to reconcile her speaking "with a mother's sweet plaintive tone and look" and her saying that "there is no sin in such a love as mine now." In one sense, indeed, she could mean: "Because I have repented loving you before my husband died, my (erotic) love is not now sinful." But both her deliberate behavior and her speech seem rather to make the meaning: "As I have exorcised my passion for you, my love is maternal now and hence sinless." She seems to be attempting to convince Henry, as well as herself, that her love is and will be henceforth maternal (or sisterly); and certainly what she later says and does is meaningful only in the light of this inner struggle.

As if to make sure that his reader does not overlook the significance of this unusual scene, Thackeray accentuates its major ideas in the several following chapters. For instance, just after Beatrix has smitten Henry with her beauty (II, vii), Thackeray has Frank, in the midst of a long speech, say to Henry: ". . . mother's in love with you,—yes, I think mother's in love with you. She was always praising you, and always talking about you; and when she went to Southampton, to see the ship, I found her out. But you see it is impossible. . . ." And a few pages later (II, viii) Rachel, warning Henry ("my son") of Beatrix's weaknesses, alludes to the now familiar subject: "I know you both, and love you: need I be ashamed of that love now? No, never, never. . . ."

This chapter (II, viii) ends with a statement of Henry's unsettled feelings about Rachel: "and as for his mistress, 'twas difficult to say with what a feeling he regarded her. 'Twas happiness to have seen her; 'twas no great pang to part; a filial tenderness, a love that was at once respect and protection, filled his mind as he thought of her, and from that day until now, and from now till death is past, and beyond it, he prays that sacred flame may ever burn." This is indeed ambiguous and one feels like asking, with Dodds, "Come now, Esmond, *what* flame? Your 'filial tenderness,' long before this writing, must have been sublimated at the marriage altar." In part, at least, it should have been. But might not Thackeray have been attempting a compressed statement that moves in two dimensions of time? The first part of the passage expresses Henry's feelings at the time of action. The second suggests how those feelings, with modifications, have extended to the present time, i.e., of the writing of the memoirs. Thus the "sacred flame" may waver and even feed on different fuels, but it never goes out; so that the implication is one of transition and continuity. The closing lines of the following chapter (II, ix) deal with Henry's feelings from another angle: off to the wars again, he ponders his hopeless passion for Beatrix; then—"And as, before the blazing sun of morning, the moon fades away in the sky almost invisible, Esmond thought, with a blush perhaps, of another sweet pale face, sad and faint, and fading out of sight, with its sweet fond gaze of affection: such a last look it seemed to cast as Eurydice might have given, yearning after her lover, when fate and Pluto summoned her, and she passed away into the shades." In both passages is reflected the delicate situation: Rachel, loving Henry passionately but trying to suppress her love and sublimate it into a "sinless" one; Henry, loving Rachel in a somewhat different way (and now infatuated with her daughter), but, though outwardly conforming to the filial relation, vaguely aware of disturbing elements in his own feelings that he is as yet unable to isolate and analyze. Orpheus and Eurydice, however, were lovers.

If the remainder of *Esmond* is analyzed in terms of the Walcote scene, much that otherwise seems puzzling or irrelevant is clarified.

The most obvious part of Thackeray's design in the love theme, as Trollope and others have seen, is stressing Rachel's youthful beauty, a preparation extending from the Preface to Henry's own remark at the end that "the tender matron" was "as beautiful in her autumn, and as pure as virgins in their spring." And Thackeray concurrently disparages Beatrix. Henry constantly makes such declarations as: "Beautiful as she [Beatrix] was, he had heard people say a score of times . . . that Beatrix's mother looked as young, and was the handsomer of the two," and "my lady Castlewood, though now almost forty, did not look to be within ten years of her age." Technically more disarming are the many similar remarks of others, including those of Steele (II, ii), Bolingbroke (II, xv), the Pretender (III, ix), and occasionally even Beatrix—"Does not mamma look charming?" (III, iii). Simultaneously, Henry is being made older—"Why, you are old enough and grave enough to be our father," says Beatrix (III, iii).

More important than this assiduous "romantic adjustment" are Thackeray's continual efforts to keep the reader ever mindful of his characters' problems—by scores of references, often in dialogue and without comment, as well as by innumerable, almost hidden, allusions. Rachel's jealousy is ever present. It is shown, for example, by her impatience when she finds Henry kissing Beatrix's foot (III, ii), by her often meeting Henry when he leaves Beatrix, implicitly by anxious design, and by Beatrix's dialogue (III, vii). Likewise, Thackeray repeatedly makes Rachel manifest her suppressed love through her tender solicitousness toward Henry, her acute sensitivity to his feelings, and her keen glances at him when Beatrix is present or discussed. Sometimes her emotions break through her self-imposed maternal role, and then Henry's own bewilderment is likely to be reflected—as, for instance, when she comforts him (II, x): "'I am your mother, you are my son, and I love you always,' she said . . . : and he went away comforted and humbled in mind, as he thought of that amazing and constant love and tenderness with which this sweet lady ever blessed and

pursued him." But the love she expresses, we feel sure, is not wholly maternal. The final chapter of Book II (which is saturated with references to Rachel's beauty and charm) particularly marks the relations of the two principals. Rachel, calling Henry her son and Beatrix his sister, talks of the latter's weaknesses: "'I though you might cure yourself of your passion,' my lady added fondly." His confusion is seen in his reply, ". . . You are a thousand times better; the fondest, the fairest, the dearest of women. . . . But she is my fate . . . *Je l'aime.*" And when Rachel says, "I wish she would have you," Thackeray allows us to determine her sincerity for ourselves. But when she says, "You are such a treasure that the woman who has your love, shouldn't change it away against a kingdom, I think," who can doubt what she means? It is peculiar lovemaking, but it is a peculiar situation; and Thackeray treats it with amazing adroitness. A more obvious instance occurs when Henry formally renounces his claim to the Castlewood title (III, ii) and Rachel kneels and kisses his hands "in an outbreak of passionate love and gratitude," saying, "in a wild way": "Don't raise me. . . . Let me kneel—let me kneel, and—and—worship you." (Henry is made to report scenes like this with a straight face!)

Rachel's sense of sin is not forgotten, either. Once (III, iii) this is brought out by the candid Beatrix: "Oh, how good she is, Harry! . . . She has had a great sorrow in her life and a great secret; and repented of it. It could not have been my father's death. She talks freely about that; nor could she have loved him very much—though who knows what we women do love, and why?" His reply ("What, and why, indeed") is vapid, to be sure; but he could hardly have been allowed to remark the implications, as he could not have been a few moments later when Beatrix observes that her mother "loves you, sir, a great deal too much; and I hate you for it."

Finally, as very pointed preparation for the ending, Thackeray again selects Beatrix as a means. "You and mamma are fit for each other," she says to Henry (III, iii); and again (III, iv), "Mamma would have been the wife for you, had you been a little older, though you look ten years older than she does. . . ." And, just before the plot to restore the Pretender (III, vii), Beatrix returns the family jewels to Henry: "You will give them to your wife, Cousin. . . . My cousin, your wife has a lovely complexion and shape." The allusion to Rachel is unmistakable. But Henry, though he reflects occasionally on his own emotions, is never allowed to appear fully aware of the crucial issues between him and Rachel—as if his passion for the daughter, plus the tacit agreement at Walcote, have made him obtuse to those issues.

As the final scenes approach, Thackeray has but to fulfill what he has been so long preparing for. In the last chapter (III, xiii) he quickly kills Henry's desire for Beatrix ("The love was dead within him"); destroys her beauty ("The roses had shuddered out of her cheeks; her eyes were glaring; she looked quite old"); and makes Henry rather lamely wonder "that he could ever have loved her." Then, with a sentimental prelude about that "happiness . . . of its nature sacred and secret" and "the truest and tenderest and purest wife ever man was blessed with," Thackeray allows him to announce "that my dear mistress became my wife."

Though these few citations can hardly convey Thackeray's subtleties of technique or the cumulative effect of the whole, they indicate the nature of his "infinite pains" in developing his love theme: to keep before his readers the feelings of his characters, especially Rachel's, as the story proceeds and circumstances change, and to prepare for the marriage which, we cannot doubt, he wished to appear the natural and inevitable result of all that had gone before.

The evident pattern of the love theme makes Thackeray's intentions unmistakable. He wished, as George Brimley pretty well saw in his review [see excerpt dated 1852], to show the growth of an unusual kind of devotion, beginning as that of a dependent-son-brother of twelve and a protector-mother-sister of twenty, and ending primarily as that of lovers twenty years later. But it is not first one thing exclusively and then another thing exclusively, as is often assumed; rather it is a gradual development, with the relation continually modifying for each character until at the end it is not a simple, conventional love, but a complex one, cumulatively grown. The cohesive tension is ever Rachel's suppressed passion for Henry, attended by conflicting feelings of guilt and desire—tension continually interacting with Henry's own fluctuating and uncertain affection for her.

Yet a large number of readers have failed to see the manifestations of the theme or have appeared only vaguely cognizant of them. Hence we must return to the question of whether Thackeray was only "almost successful" in fulfilling his intentions. If we assume that he was not being wilfully obscurant, then we must admit that communication between author and readers has been imperfect.

There are several probable causes. The reader today may overlook the development of the love theme simply because he does not expect to find such an anomalous treatment of passion in a Victorian novel (though, ironically, many Victorians found it readily enough), and because he likely approaches the book as no more than a conventional "historical romance"—once Beatrix descends the stair, he understandably expects her to pair off with Henry at the end. And to the reader who has missed Thackeray's manifold preparations, the ending may well appear capriciously sudden.

There are more consequential reasons, however, in addition to Thackeray's natural restraint in treating an unusual and delicate subject. Despite the persistence of the thematic ideas, they are overshadowed by other elements of the story—the long accounts of Henry's military campaigns, the ten-year courtship of Beatrix, the elaboration of the historical background, and, finally, the excitement of the restoration plot. Moreover, the reader does not find in *Esmond* the authorial help he has become accustomed to in Thackeray and his contemporaries. With a few exceptions (like Emily Brontë) Victorian novelists oversimplified, slanted, and generally interpreted to the extent that hardly a reader could fail to understand. So it had been in *Vanity Fair* and *Pendennis*. But *Esmond*, though plain enough when it deals with Rachel's beauty or Marlborough's improbity, contains almost no interpretive comment about the love theme. Its presentation is preponderantly dramatic; the meanings are implicit rather than explicit; and the reader must do his own interpreting. The failure to appreciate this quality of Thackeray's technique in *Esmond*, I believe, is a major cause for uncertainty about his intentions.

The technical problems of Thackeray's narration are not often considered. In form *Esmond* is ostensibly a memoir, written by Henry for his grandsons and other descendants, who may be presumed to know already the general outline of the story, including the outcome. But *Esmond* is also a novel: hence there must be suspense, and information that would not in reality be withheld from the grandsons must be withheld from the reader.

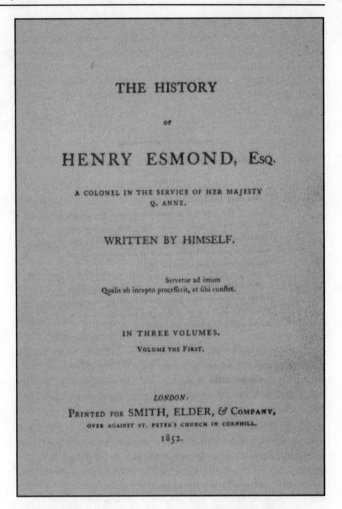

THE HISTORY

OF

HENRY ESMOND, ESQ.

A COLONEL IN THE SERVICE OF HER MAJESTY
Q. ANNE.

WRITTEN BY HIMSELF.

Servetur ad imum
Qualis ab incepto procefferit, et fibi conftet.

IN THREE VOLUMES.
VOLUME THE FIRST.

LONDON:
PRINTED FOR SMITH, ELDER, & COMPANY,
OVER AGAINST ST. PETER'S CHURCH IN CORNHILL.
1852.

Title page to the first edition of Henry Esmond.

Furthermore, Henry is writing decades after the action, when presumably he comprehends the meaning of what he reports; but simultaneously he must appear not to understand certain parts of it as of the time of action. Hence Thackeray's difficulties in keeping his work looking like an ingenuous memoir. His problems do not differ essentially from those of other novelists whose heroes tell the story, except perhaps in the unorthodox kind of love to be depicted and in the curious use of the third person, which gives the narrator the similitude of the omniscient author without his prerogatives. Henry must necessarily be limited in awareness from time to time (as Copperfield must be with respect to Agnes and to Steerforth); but he must be limited, or at least is limited, to the degree that he perforce appears naïve, a bit dull, and occasionally a little stupid. Yet if Thackeray should allow him to understand, the plot would have to be drastically altered, the narration would become extremely complicated, and much of the sense of immediacy would be impaired. Hence, even when Beatrix mentions her mother's "great secret," Henry gently passes it by.

Dodds thinks that to delineate relations like those of Henry and Rachel "requires an absolute certainty of touch, and it is at just such moments that Thackeray is likely to be confused by conflicting impulses. We are never sure, during the growth of this strange affection, just what it means at any given moment. It is not improbable that Rachel and Esmond themselves should at certain times be uncertain of the exact nature of their feelings for each other, but certainly Thackeray should know, and it is not clear that he did.'' No one would hold that Thackeray had ''an absolute certainty of touch,'' yet it is not implausible to claim that, considering his obstacles, he evinced a remarkable certainty until the very end. And as Henry himself tells the story, it would be extremely difficult for Thackeray to make clear that he, the author, knows ''the exact nature'' of his characters' feelings, particularly Rachel's. If he had ''conflicting impulses'' about the love theme, they were perhaps rather those of technique than of understanding—rather of trying to determine just how much ought to be shown and how to show it.

The depiction of Rachel is of paramount importance in an interpretation of the love theme. Indeed, the story is not so much Henry's as hers: the history of a passionate and imperfect woman who long suffers what she thinks to be a sinful love— a history told by the object of her passion. Henry's emotional problems are perplexing enough, but, except when concerning his infatuation with Beatrix, they are rarely as sharply set forth as Rachel's. Always it is Rachel who is the restrained aggressor, who has long believed that he does not ''love'' her in her sense of the word. And it is the presentation of her character, rather than Henry's, which has most disturbed readers. Especially have some been distressed by the contradiction between Henry's constant praise of her virtues (hence, they conclude, implying Thackeray's own approval) and the many less admirable qualities she displays, such as jealousy, haughtiness, and dissemblance. As Lord David Cecil says: ''Lady Castlewood . . . moves through *Esmond* to a sort of organ accompaniment of approbation; in speaking of her Thackeray's colloquial tone takes on a religious enthusiasm that makes it resemble something between a chat and a chant. . . . Yet her actions reveal her as a most unamiable character. . . .'' But Cecil credits Thackeray with no dramatic ability and seems to forget that it is Henry who is supposed to be writing his memoirs. Henry could hardly be expected to call his grandsons' attention pointedly to their grandmother's weaknesses (though he occasionally does); besides, he is a gentleman of sentimental loyalty writing about his wife, whom in his fashion he loves. Still, as Thackeray must make him portray her accurately in action and speech, in this fictional memoir the apparent discrepancy is hardly avoidable. Brogan well observes that Henry's views are not necessarily his creator's, calling readers ''overly serious . . . who take at face value everything that Henry says.'' But Brogan thinks ''that with minor reservations, Thackeray was in essential agreement with Henry,'' the dilemma being explained by the fact that Rachel's faults exemplify real virtues ''carried to excess.'' Brogan develops his argument ingeniously, but, again, the explanation minimizes Thackeray's dramatic technique and its implications. Are not Henry's praise—itself often wryly ironical—and Rachel's actions implicit commentaries on both their characters? And cannot Thackeray be given credit for deliberately using these means of character portrayal and revelation? He was no novice at fiction.

A final concern is Thackeray's treatment of the incestuous implications of the love theme, and especially his resolution of the problems involved; for it is this resolution which has helped cause misapprehension of his intentions. It would be unrealistic to complain that, writing in the 1850's, he was not highly explicit in dealing with these implications. But there is hardly doubt that they are to be understood as part of Rachel's ''sin,'' intensifying her humiliation at what happened—she not only fell in love with a poor dependent while her husband lived, but did so with one who in many ways was like a son.

Her almost pathological preoccupation with her sin, her religious adviser's belief that she should not see Henry again (otherwise, why should she not, after her husband's death and after her repentance and absolution?), and her desperate attempt to restore and maintain her maternal relation to him—all these indicate Thackeray's intention for his reader to be aware that she was troubled by some feeling of incest. Henry never speaks of similar doubts, though his own mixed feelings derive in part from the continual difficulty of adjusting his first strong love for Rachel as a ''mother'' or ''sister'' to a love for her as a desirable woman. But how does Rachel overcome her sense of sin as well as her belief that Henry does not love her in the appropriate way? And Henry's misgivings about his feelings for her—how are they dispelled? We are never told. The vague ending may have been due to Thackeray's disinclination or temperamental inability to probe openly a matter that might be distasteful to his readers, even though he had deliberately built his love story around it, or to his feeling that, because of the elaborate preparations, the reader's imagination could fill in as necessary. It may even have been that he could not decide how to handle the problem. But whatever the reason, the gap is there; and even readers who sympathetically follow the love theme will not find the conclusion satisfying and will feel that he did not carry out his responsibility to them—that of giving *his* idea of the resolution of those problems which would establish the ending as clear and convincing. He did not, therefore, completely fulfill his intentions; and his novel must take the artistic consequences. The evasive resolution—if it be a resolution at all—is the major artistic flaw, and a grave one, in the novel.

The high praise *Esmond* has received has rarely included recognition of the full significance of the love theme, though it is that theme on which the novel largely depends for meaning. The scope of this study forbids an attempt to evaluate *Esmond* as a whole—there is too much else to consider. But when the love theme, rigorously isolated here for analysis, is integrated into the full body of the novel, Thackeray's entire accomplishment can be more justly appraised; and, despite serious weaknesses, it will, I think, appear more astonishing than has been supposed. If we must admit that he did not entirely succeed in fulfilling his intentions, we must concede that his readers have not always seen what he put there for them. Those who are unhampered by presuppositions, however, and who are willing to grant *Esmond* the attention they give later symbol-fraught novels, will be rewarded by an ironically perceptive interpretation of an uncommon human relationship. They will also find one of the most provocative and subtle portraits of a lady in nineteenth-century English fiction. And they may even be willing to forgive Thackeray his final artistic blemish. (pp. 686-701)

John E. Tilford, Jr., ''The Love Theme of 'Henry Esmond','' in PMLA, *Vol. LXVII, No. 5, September, 1952, pp. 684-701.*

WILLIAM H. MARSHALL   (essay date 1961)

[Marshall suggests that the sexual nature of Rachel and Esmond's early love is more evident in Rachel than in Esmond because the latter, as narrator of the story, is intent upon justifying the righteousness of his feelings and actions.]

''The man cannot understand what I am writing'' Thackeray remarked concerning the review of *Henry Esmond* that appeared in the London *Times* [see excerpt by Samuel Phillips dated 1852]. "The man," like many other reviewers, had objected to the marriage of Henry and Rachel. Though there has been some rather pointed doubt whether Thackeray's knowledge and abilities matched his intentions, most critics have accepted as successful what has been called [by John E. Tilford, Jr. (see excerpt dated 1952)] "the major thematic integration of the novel", the account of the complex emotional relationship between Henry and Rachel, which reaches its climax with the announcement: "the great joy of my life was bestowed upon me, and . . . my dear mistress became my wife." The apparent suddenness of the narrator's revelation disturbs those readers who have at this point in the novel not become well aware of the significance of much that has been told them, for to them Henry and Rachel have at least appeared to regard each other in a maternal-filial way. Certainly the matter becomes crucial in any attempt to evaluate *Henry Esmond* as a work of literary art. It is my intention to suggest the reason that the announcement takes the form that it does, that its occurrence in this position is probably inevitable, and that within the larger structure of the novel it is evidence of complex literary achievement rather than of failure.

Rachel's long suppressed erotic love for Henry has been described [by Tilford] as "the cohesive tension" of the novel. It is suggested by Rachel's strong reaction to Henry's presumed interest in Nancy Sievewright, by her special preparation of flowers for Henry's homecoming, and by her ironic astonishment at Henry's attempt to reconcile her to her husband: "Are you come to me as ambassador—you?" Rachel's attempt to convert Lord Mohun, so easily misinterpreted by Beatrix, constitutes a kind of sublimation. Her reaction to what she thought was news of Esmond's death ("Here's poor Henry killed, my dear"), though no more than normally maternal when regarded in isolation, adds to the evidence. (pp. 35-6)

Not so persuasive, however, is the assertion that Henry's love for Rachel has long been similar to hers. In fact, all direct evidence, admittedly from Henry's own statements, points to his filial love for Rachel. "My lord, my lord," Henry replies to Mohun's suggestion that Henry is in love with Rachel, "I never had a mother, but I love this lady as one." "Indeed, I loved and honored her before all the world," he answers the Dowager after she has made a similar suggestion. "I take no shame in that." At their reunion at Walcote, the narrator recalls, "as a brother folds a sister to his heart; and as a mother cleaves to her son's breast—so for a few moments Esmond's beloved mistress came to him and blessed him"; and in parting, "a filial tenderness, a love that was at once respect and protection, filled his mind as he thought of her." (pp. 36-7)

Henry's love for Rachel during his early life is essentially filial but implicitly Oedipian and therefore of indistinguishable components. The pattern of his development is the reverse of that which the psychologists describe as expected in the normal family situation, for with Henry the erotic aspect of the Oedipian love is, rather than repressed, ultimately triumphant. The movement is gradual, almost imperceptible, and in the course of the narrative renders Henry's situation very unlike Rachel's: though her story is one of conscious development toward emotional fulfillment amid strong feelings of guilt and recurring suppression, Henry's emotional conflict as described seems never to rise to the level of consciousness. Hence, though his development may be gradual, within the frame of the narrative the revelation of its conclusion appears to be sudden. Henry's decision to marry Rachel would therefore seem unmotivated, and from the viewpoint of the narrative he would appear to be

a weak personality. Or, more severely, the very weakness of his character, the indefiniteness surrounding his decision, and the vagueness of the conclusion of the novel would seem to constitute the aesthetic flaw of *Henry Esmond.*

This view, however, neglects for the most part the essential aspect of the structure of *Henry Esmond*: the novel, though not didactic itself, is constructed in the form of a memoir by an old man, whose purpose is the explicit justification of the course he has chosen to follow. Only by recognizing the full significance of this structure can the reader discover that what appears to be an artistic flaw in the work is in reality an expression of the speaker's dilemma, which, if properly understood, contributes to the reader's ironic awareness of the tension in the work. The ostensible purpose of the aging Henry in writing his memoirs is to offer to his grandsons an example, in the form of his own biography, of ideal behavior under adverse circumstances and the rewards that this brings. In accomplishing this aim he must concern himself with the question of his marriage to their grandmother. To be posthumously assisted by his daughter, who is to understand his intention when she comes to edit his memoir, the old man casts his story in the third person, thereby implying that it possesses a quality which in reality it lacks rather strikingly—objectivity. In the titles of his chapters and in expression at moments when his recollections increase his tension, he reverts to the first person; similarly, though he frames his story in the past tense, he unconsciously falls into the present when recording moments of intensity. More pointed is the conscious tension which Esmond creates between his image of the self in the past and his view in the present: one chapter is entitled "I Am Placed Under a *Popish* Priest and Bred to That Religion" (italics mine); within parentheses he comments upon William's seizure of the Crown, "righteously taking it, as I think now"; he can describe the cause of King William's death as "that accident . . . which ended the life of the greatest, the wisest, the bravest, and most clement sovereign whom England ever knew"; and knowing as he writes what the events of history have taught him about the failings of the Pretender, he remarks, "'Tis with a sort of rage at his inaptitude that one thinks of his melancholy story." Most significant perhaps is Henry's presumably naive mention of occasions on which he has been accused of sermonizing— by the Viscount, by Beatrix, and by the Pretender—and his pointed insistence to his grandsons, in telling the story of young Frank Castlewood, "I am not going to play the moralist, and cry 'Fie!' For ages past, I know how old men preach, and what young men practise; and that patriarchs have had their weak moments too, long since Father Noah toppled over after discovering the vine." That he would be taken literally is of course what Esmond intends, but that he should be so taken, in this and in many other instances, is precisely what lies outside the frame of the novel.

Esmond *is* preaching a sermon, one filled with exempla, from the opening of his story, in which he is concerned with the value of history and the possibility of a concept of heroism, to the close with the description of idyllic life in Virginia. He is aware of course of the psychological value of his writing: "As there are a thousand thoughts lying within a man that he does not know till he takes up the pen to write, so the heart is a secret even to him (or her) who has it in his own breast." But he is essentially and unswervingly dedicated to self-justification in his decision regarding the Castlewood title and his marriage.

Henry meets the first of these responsibilities quite directly: he accounts the external facts of his life in such a way that as he passes through each experience he emerges in the image of what is clearly his own idea of the hero. His rescue of young Frank Castlewood is proleptic of his constant vigilance over his kinsman during the campaigns, which itself only reflects his crucial sacrifice of the title on Frank's behalf. Esmond attempts to intervene with Mohun to save Francis, but then, when the duel appears to be inevitable, he renders faithful service to Francis to the end. Rachel angrily blames him for Francis's death, ironically after he has just resolved to sacrifice for her his basis for identity. "If I cannot make a name for myself, I can do without one," he thinks some days later. "His cruel goddess had shaken her wings and fled: and left him alone and friendless," he comes to consider, "but *virtute sua*." At the end of his imprisonment he goes to the army, bringing not only the advantages of his university learning, he remarks, but "that further education which neither books nor years will give, but which some men get from the silent teaching of Adversity." In the English plunder of St Mary's, "this shameful campaign," his only violent act is "the knocking down an English sentinel with a half-pike, who was offering insults to a poor trembling nun." Following the day of battle at Ramillies, "Far more pleasant to him than the victory . . . it was to find that the day was over, and his dear young Castlewood was unhurt." Regarding his second encounter with Mohun, he remarks, "If Captain Esmond had put Mohun out of the world, as he might, a villain would have been punished and spared further villainies—but who is one man to punish another? I declare upon my honour that my only thought was to prevent Lord Mohun from mischief with Frank." Beatrix's rejection of him and Frank's conversion to Catholicism would seem to have intensified Henry's temptation to claim his title, but despite whatever motives might have once existed, he has in the last phase of his recalled experiences a more than sustaining sense of inner worth.

In developing the image of his own righteousness, Esmond implicitly contrasts himself with three others—Thomas Tusher, Frank, and James the Pretender. In Henry's mind Tusher, the least important of these, represents a kind of fixed position, that of one who—whether as a child arguing in support of his Church, as a student at Cambridge reading dogmatically and unimaginatively, or as a young cleric accepting the living which his father had held—is incapable of growth, a quality which by implication becomes for Henry the essence of his own character. Henry's contrast between himself and Frank is a necessary aspect of the achievement of his purpose, the justification of his decision regarding the Castlewood title. "My poor Frank was weak, as perhaps all our race had been, and led by women," Esmond remarks: Frank needs the title and all that it brings, but Henry, rejecting the claim to an old family, can become the founder of a new one. But the implications are perhaps most powerful in the contrast which he establishes between himself and James Stuart. The events of Henry's own story of the sacrifice of legitimacy are framed by the struggle of the Pretender for what has seemed his right. Henry has clear claim to a title but refuses it because he is strong and generous; James has but uncertain claim to the Throne and loses all opportunity for possession of it because he is weak and selfish. James has been the symbol of all that Henry has believed from childhood but from which, in the eyes of the old man telling the story, he had to break away. Henry's disillusionment in the Pretender, linked with his total rejection of Beatrix, is crucial, for it leaves in the place of what have been three emotional forces only one, Rachel, and in the place of his image of the Pretender as hero the sustaining image of himself. From the latter develops his mature political philosophy which

permeates his memoir, a justification of what he has found in life: "In England . . . you patch up, but you never build up anew. Will we of the New World submit much longer, even nominally, to this ancient British superstition?" The final encounter with the Pretender dramatizes the fulfillment of the didactic intention of the memoir, therefore, when Esmond simultaneously renounces his allegiance to the Jacobite cause and destroys all evidence of his claim to the Castlewood title; within the structure of the story that Esmond tells the somewhat melodramatic quality of his behavior on this occasion is perfectly justifiable.

It is significant that as Henry tells his story, developing the image of himself as triumphant, his own passiveness seems to become a necessary, though perhaps undesired, corollary. Henry simply reacts to circumstances in the way best suited to the ideal of personal nobility that the old man telling the story conceives. His central problem arises from the circumstances of birth. His decision regarding the claim seems necessary because of a somewhat confusing sequence of events between his birth and Francis's death. The exposure to smallpox at Three Castles seems circumstantial, for his intentions toward Nancy Sievewright are not as explicit as Francis jokingly suggests. He only reacts to what seems inevitable in the affair of the Mohun duel and then accepts his passive part in the separation from Rachel and her children during the following year. Grief actively wounds but does not destroy him: "Esmond thought of his early time as a noviciate, and of this past trial as an initiation before entering into life—as our young Indians undergo tortures silently before they pass to the rank of warriors in the tribe." Life becomes a test, therefore, and goodness would seem to be largely a matter of reacting to the conditions of evil. Henry goes to war and rises in the army for his valor, but he does not become an active bloodletter. He loves Beatrix and his happiness depends upon her nature, but even after his final disillusionment he can rise above bitterness to indifference. Although in his attempt to bring the Pretender to the Throne he would appear to be dominantly active, the undertaking is inspired by his love for Beatrix as much as his devotion to the Stuarts; and once established, the situation is really shaped by the personality of the Pretender, whose weakness causes the plan to fail. Only in making a marriage does Henry appear to have taken the initiative from circumstance, but even here, within the story that the old man tells, there is real doubt.

The justification of his marriage, toward which Esmond has been moving from the beginning of his narrative (when, for example, describing the effects of smallpox on Rachel's beauty, he comments upon the dangers of marrying merely for beauty), proves to be more difficult than the comprehensive task of self-justification to which it is related. Esmond must attempt to make the marriage appear to have been well motivated and at the same time clear himself of any suspicion of improper intentions toward one who had long been married to another and whom he had regarded with filial affection. The method which he follows intensifies the passivity being simultaneously developed in the image of himself: he tells the story, by suggestion rather than assertion, of Rachel's love for him, extending back to the years before her husband's death, and he offers no indication that he is aware of the beginnings of his own extrafilial love for her. But this attempt ends in a dilemma, for in order to exculpate himself he suggests the sinfulness (qualified, it is true, by the record of atonement) of a woman who is otherwise pictured as lovable and explicitly described as inspirational to him.

It is this dilemma, arising from Esmond's persistently complex motivation which gives the novel its real "cohesive tension". If we do not read *Henry Esmond* completely within its structural frame, the memoir of an old man ordering his recollections so that they reveal what is exemplary and in so doing trying to escape the trap into which they necessarily lead him, then the dilemma appears to be merely an artistic flaw. Though we may then find moral value in what Esmond says, an easily para-phrased "meaning" in the book, we fail to recognize the irony that is essential to the aesthetic achievement of *Henry Esmond*. (pp. 37-42)

> *William H. Marshall, "Dramatic Irony in 'Henry Esmond'," in* Revue des langues vivantes, *Vol. 27, 1961, pp. 35-42.*

GEORGE J. WORTH (essay date 1961)

[*Worth reads* Henry Esmond *as a* Bildungsroman *in which the hero matures in his attitudes toward love, religion, politics, and the military.*]

Henry Esmond is essentially a *Bildungsroman* in which the protagonist, through a process of trial and error, eventually attains stability and maturity. He attaches himself to one impossible or impractical cause after another, sometimes several at once, and he becomes aware of his errors of judgment, of the ways his head has been swayed by his heart, as the result of bitterly painful experience. If we look at the novel in this way, all of Henry's misguided allegiances become parts of a pattern: his unrequited devotion for Beatrix, his absorption in the flamboyant Roman Catholicism of Father Holt, his Jacobitism, even his dedication to the military life. In each case, Henry learns to renounce the spectacular and the romantic; in each case he comes to accept the sober, the prudent alternative. He learns what Scott's Jeanie Deans knew intuitively all along: that the glamorous, exciting past is past, that a realistic acceptance of the sometimes humdrum reality of the present is an essential characteristic of sane maturity.

Soon after Henry, then nine or ten years old, arrives at Castlewood, he embraces his father's Catholicism and, along with it, his Jacobitism. Characteristically, both these beliefs grow out of personal loyalties: the religious out of Henry's attachment to Lord Castlewood's chaplain, Father Holt; the political out of his attachment to his lord, patron, and father. Henry's earliest recollections were of the Huguenot people by whom he had been brought up at Ealing, in an atmosphere of pious anti-Catholicism, "psalm-singing and churchgoing," but when he falls under the spell of Father Holt, who takes him from Ealing to Castlewood, all that is soon forgotten. Holt is a man of great charm and impressive appearance, who treats the orphan boy kindly and thereby earns his profound gratitude and affection. He paints for Henry a glowing picture of Catholicism in general and the Jesuit order in particular, telling the impressionable youngster

> of its martyrs and heroes, of its Brethren converting the heathen by myriads, traversing the desert, facing the stake, ruling the courts and councils, or braving the tortures of kings; so that Harry Esmond thought that to belong to the Jesuits was the greatest prize of life and bravest end of ambition; the greatest career here, and in heaven the surest reward; and began to long for the day, not only when he should enter into the one Church and receive his first communion, but when he might join that wonderful brotherhood, which was present throughout all the world, and which num-

bered the wisest, the bravest, the highest born, the most eloquent of men among its members.

Moreover, Holt is an exceedingly colorful figure, the very sort to capture the imagination of a sensitive boy like Henry: he is deeply involved in all sorts of romantic plots and keeps disappearing and reappearing mysteriously, often decked out in strange disguises.

Father Holt and Roman Catholicism strike Henry even more favorably by contrast with the unprepossessing Doctor Tusher, the incumbent of the living of Castlewood, and his brand of Anglicanism. Tusher himself is "a horrid old man" who "had offered to kiss [Nancy Sievewright] in the dairy," and his religion appears cold and calculating in comparison with the ardent zeal of Catholics as described by Father Holt. (pp. 346-47)

Just as his Catholic sympathies grow out of his strong attachment to Father Holt, so his Jacobitism is initially a direct result of his devotion to the family of Castlewood. The third Viscount and his lady, as well as the fourth Viscount and Rachel, are fervent Jacobites, and young Henry, as is his custom, adopts the views of those who are kind to him and whom he admires. But there are some important differences between these two Lords Castlewood, and between their wives, and these are largely responsible for the first major change in Henry's views represented in the novel. For one thing, Francis and Rachel, unlike Thomas and Isabella, are Anglicans; and once Father Holt passes out of young Henry's life, after the battle of the Boyne, Henry's Catholicism very quickly fades and he adopts the religion of his new patrons. Again his religious allegiance is a direct outgrowth of a personal attachment, this time to Rachel Esmond. The unforgettable picture of the "fair young lady of Castlewood, her little daughter at her knee and her domestics gathered round her, reading the Morning Prayer of the English Church . . . the sun shining upon her golden hair until it made a halo round about her" affects him powerfully, "and before a couple of years my Lady had made a thorough convert." "It did not require much persuasion to induce the boy to worship with his beloved mistress."

Although the fourth Viscount and Rachel are Jacobites, their advocacy of the Stuart cause is not as rashly passionate as Thomas's and Isabella's. Francis, like Thomas, engages in some Jacobite plotting, but he is not as deeply involved as his cousin had been. . . . Both he and his wife, however, persist in their Jacobite sympathies and Henry follows them, particularly Rachel. (pp. 348-49)

Under the influence of Francis and especially Rachel, then, Henry's religious and political views are moderated: he forsakes the romantic Catholicism of Father Holt and reconciles his Jacobitism with his admiration of King William and his service under Queen Anne. Catholicism is to have no more attractions for him, but it is replaced by no deeply felt adherence to Anglicanism: Henry's faith while he is at Cambridge is admittedly weak and vacillating and he prepares to take holy orders solely to please the family of Castlewood. Much later in the novel, when he is a battle-scarred veteran of several campaigns, he resists Father Holt's attempts to convert him back to Catholicism, defending his Anglicanism not on emotional or doctrinal but on nationalistic grounds. . . . This is his final position on the religious question: the wise man worships as his fellow countrymen do. Religion is not a means to personal glory or self-immolation, but one of the strongest ties holding a people together. Henry has come a long way since his dreams of suffering martyrdom in the service of the Jesuits.

Esmond persists in his modified Jacobitism until he actually meets the Pretender. Then, as in the case of his conversion from Father Holt's Catholicism to a Laodicean version of Rachel's Anglicanism, personal relations play a powerful part in changing his views. For the Pretender soon proves thoroughly unworthy of Henry's allegiance: he is an idle, dissipated, irresponsible skirt-chaser. Henry's disenchantment is shared by young Frank, at moments Beatrix, and, significantly, Rachel. . . . (pp. 349-50)

The final break with Jacobitism comes in the last chapter of the novel when Prince James proves his unworthiness beyond any shadow of a doubt by running off to Castlewood with Beatrix just when decisive action might have gained him the crown. When Henry breaks his sword and denies the Pretender, he is not renouncing a merely personal loyalty: he is retracting the visionary political creed which had centered on his now-fallen idol.

Of course, the Henry Esmond who hatches the plot to bring the Pretender to England to claim his throne is no longer the ardent idealist he had been while living at Castlewood. He has known bitter disillusionment in his experience with love—the long, futile yearning for Beatrix—and his military service. In both spheres he has come to recognize the falseness of romantic aspirations and the dreariness and harshness of life as men have to live it. The climactic exposure of the Pretender's criminal weakness, linked as it is with a particularly flagrant example of Beatrix's amorality, is merely the *coup de grâce*.

Almost from its beginnings in childhood, Henry's feeling for Beatrix has been marked by a powerful ambivalence. He is irresistibly drawn to her, all the while realizing the hardness of her character and the hopelessness of his suit. Beatrix is perfectly frank about her attitude toward Henry: she has never been able to feel real love, she tells him, least of all for a man like Henry. "You were ever too much of a slave to win my heart . . .". But Henry, although aware of her unworthiness, persists, his reason paralyzed by the icy glitter of her magnificence. His suit drags on till his discovery of Beatrix with the Pretender at Castlewood. On this occasion, her flirtatiousness, which always seems to draw her into doomed love affairs, has dashed the hopes not only of Henry but of all the Pretender's adherents. "As he looked at her he wondered that he could ever have loved her. His love of ten years was over. . . . I have never seen her from that day."

Henry's military service has been as disenchanting as his suit of Beatrix. He had originally joined the army, after the death of Francis and his own quarrel with Rachel, to make a name for himself, to escape from his ennui and to learn something of the world. At the outset of his career as an officer, he is full of enthusiasm. . . . But Esmond soon discovers that combat involves more than heroism on the battlefield. Again and again, he sees troops indulging in barbaric atrocities, and he is sickened by the spectacle. (pp. 350-51)

Again, painful experience has shown Henry that the romantic view of the world is inadequate and distorted. Again, too, a personal relationship is involved in the disillusionment. His hero General Webb is repeatedly overshadowed and humiliated by the much more glamorous Duke of Marlborough, who turns out to be, in Thackeray's portrait, an unscrupulous trimmer of questionable military competence, willing to resort even to treason to advance his own ends.

We see, then, not only in what John E. Tilford, Jr. [see excerpt dated 1952] has called the "love theme" of *Henry Esmond*, but also in the religious theme, the political theme, and the military theme, a fundamental change overtaking the protagonist. He comes to recognize the falseness and ineffectuality of the glittering, the colorful, the romantic alternative—whether it goes by the name of Beatrix, Father Holt, James Stuart, or John Churchill, Duke of Marlborough. He comes to accept the less exciting and glamorous but more stable and solid alternative in each case—the love of Rachel; a quiet, unspectacular Anglicanism; allegiance to the eminently unexciting House of Hanover; a retreat to the rural peace of Virginia from the social battlefields of Augustan London as well as the military battlefields of the Continent. Perhaps this is only another way of saying that in the course of the novel Henry Esmond grows up—grows up into Thackeray's ideal of a gentleman. (pp. 352-53)

George J. Worth, "The Unity of 'Henry Esmond'," in Nineteenth-Century Fiction, *Vol. 15, No. 4, March, 1961, pp. 345-53.*

JULIET McMASTER (essay date 1971)

[*McMaster approaches* Henry Esmond *as "a sustained piece of dramatic irony," illustrating the equivocality of Esmond's moral goodness.*]

[Among Thackeray's 'good' characters, Henry Esmond] seems to me to be a special case. Thackeray's qualifications about his goodness are expressed not so much in terms of his effect on others, as in terms of his own inner perception and motivation; and to discover these involves a certain amount of detective work, and some scrutiny of Thackeray's use of the limited point of view. The other saints tend to be mainly passive beings, more characteristic in their suffering and their tears and their deaths than in their doing: and when they do take the initiative they are likely to suppress a letter, like Helen, or lead their friends into financial disaster, like Colonel Newcome. It is easier to see the limitations of such goodness. But Henry Esmond is both active, and noble in his action. Where then is the qualification? It would seem that here at last we have a good man. And though critics have frequently found him dull, and somewhat sententious, they have seldom thought him anything but the '*noble cœur*' of Father Holt's description. Attention has in fact been focussed on the relative merits of Esmond's women: Beatrix had her day when the novel was read as a historical romance, and Rachel, who shocked some contemporary readers, has since Tilford's reexamination [see excerpt dated 1952; see also Additional Bibliography] most fascinated modern ones. But the moral claims of Esmond himself have usually been taken for granted. Thackeray after all called him 'a handsome likeness' of himself.

But we know enough of Thackeray to realize that an element of the self-portrait, even a 'handsome' one, is no guarantee of extraordinary goodness. And what emerges from an examination of Esmond is that for Thackeray there *is* no extraordinary goodness, if the motive as well as the effect is taken into account. Like Pendennis, and Clive and Ethel, and Kew, and all of Thackeray's prodigals, a human being can only do his best, without much hope of outstanding merit, in a world whose claims are not reducible to simple moral alternatives.

The point of view is of major importance in *Henry Esmond*, because it is the main vehicle of Thackeray's irony. The events of the narrative show the protagonist to be a noble character, but the fact that they are narrated by Henry himself introduces an ambiguity, just as the same situation does, say, in *Pamela*. But the point of view in Thackeray's novel is more complicated than in Richardson's, for Esmond recounts his life in the third person—that is, he tells the story without appearing to do so. His own motives for this procedure would no doubt be conscientious enough, had he formulated them: he might be trying to distance himself from the experience in order to be less biassed in his reporting; or he might use the third person from motives of modesty, to avoid the appearance of boasting. But to boast without the appearance of boasting is perhaps more vain than the unmuffled blowing of one's own trumpet; and as the attempt to attain the truth by distancing can be more delusive than a frankly subjective account, so such modesty is closely related to a deep self-centredness.

The reader should not allow himself to be put off his guard by that third person, or to suspend his usual practice of weighing a statement according to who makes it. For it makes a considerable difference that we are hearing Esmond's story from Esmond himself. His account is very definitely biassed in his own favour, both in the information that he gives and, even more, in the information that he withholds.

A crucial question in our moral assessment of Henry is 'did he know Rachel was in love with him?' If he does not know, comparatively little blame can attach to him. But a man of honour does not remain in a household where he knows his presence is destroying a marriage, or make a woman the confidante of his passion for her daughter if he is aware that she loves him herself. The older Esmond evidently learned from her stealing of the gold sleeve button that Rachel had been in love with him at least since immediately after her husband's death; but on the key issue of the extent of his younger self's knowledge, Esmond is silent. He does however manage to suggest his innocence by omitting to record his inner thoughts at certain times.

There are constant hints, and even direct statements made by other characters, of the love between Harry and Rachel. Both Mohun and the dowager Isabel suggest that he is having an affair with 'the pretty Puritan.' 'Mother's in love with you,— yes, I think mother's in love with you,' says Frank; 'You and mamma are fit for each other. You might be Darby and Joan,' says Beatrix; and so on. It is noticeable that Esmond very seldom shows his own reaction to these suggestions, either in his immediate reply or in his commentary. He apparently chooses not to understand them, or not to take them seriously.

It becomes necessary to postulate that Harry maintains a sort of wilful ignorance about the question, or some intermediary state where he can have the advantage of both the blamelessness of ignorance and the satisfaction of knowledge. In the crucial scene of Harry's reunion with Rachel at Walcote, for instance, she is almost explicit about the sexual nature of her love for him: 'I would love you still—yes, there is no sin in such a love as mine now; and my dear lord in heaven may see my heart; and knows the tears that have washed my sin away'; but she is not *quite* explicit, and this leaves just a possibility for Harry not to know. Certainly his answer, 'I think the angels are not all in heaven,' is singularly inept for a man who has just heard a confession of adulterous love.

The novel is of course mainly about Esmond's emotional and domestic life, of which his military and political activities are extensions rather than interruptions. It is worth examining in some detail his part in the two main emotional situations of the book, which take the shape of two, interlocking, triangle relationships. In the first Harry is one of the two men in the affections of a lady, and in the second he is himself the apex of the triangle, while mother and daughter are rivals for his love.

The first is a courtly love situation: the lord of the castle, or 'Castlewood,' is Harry's beloved patron, and Harry is the lady's faithful worshipper and 'knight,' who longs for a dragon to slay so that he might prove his devotion: 'it pleased him to think that his lady had called him "her knight," and often and often he recalled this to his mind, and prayed that he might be her true knight, too.' All the usual tensions of conflicting loves and loyalties are in operation in this situation, with the added irony that the 'knight' seems ignorant of his role as lover. It seems that the narrating Esmond, too, is not aware of the full significance of the situation, for his account of what happens in the marriage is heavily biased.

He describes the deterioration of the marriage with an authority which his limited knowledge does not warrant; and according to his analysis the main fault lies with the husband. What happens by his account is that Francis, Lord Castlewood, first shows his moral weakness to his adoring wife when he deserts her at the time of the smallpox, and that he ceases to love her when she loses her beauty. Then he further betrays her by taking a mistress. So, as he ceases to love Rachel, she finds how little worthy he was to be loved himself. Once a woman has found out her idol's feet of clay, 'what follows?' asks Esmond, and confidently answers his own question: 'They live together, and they dine together, and they say "my dear" and "my love" as heretofore; but the man is himself, and the woman herself: that dream of love is over, as everything else is over in life.' Esmond speaks with the detachment of a mere observer of the situation, when in all probability he is the cause of it. Similarly, when Harry returns from Cambridge to find a 'secret care' preying upon his mistress, he finds no difficulty in diagnosing her sorrow—'his affection leading his *easily* to penetrate the hypocrisy under which Lady Castlewood generally chose to go disguised.' '*No doubt*,' he says, the sorrow is the loss of her husband's love. The reader, however, can divine that it is more likely the lack of Harry's. There is much that is penetrating about his analysis of the situation; but he still does not tell us the whole truth.

If we consider the situation from the husband's point of view, it emerges that it is he who has lost his wife's love, not she who has lost his; and we can infer that the reason is that Rachel has transferred her adoration to Harry. As we have seen, Castlewood has some cause to feel that it is his wife who is to blame. There are several hints that, after that complex incident of the smallpox, when she betrayed to herself if not to others her love for Harry, Rachel actually denies her husband sexually. He constantly talks of her coldness, and in his cups he contrasts her previous warmth of love with what she has become: 'hands off, highty-tighty, high and mighty, an empress couldn't be grander.' If he takes a mistress, he might have some excuse: 'Her coldness blights my whole life, and sends me to the punch-bowl, or driving about the country,' he justifies himself. And his assertions are to some extent dramatically confirmed by Rachel's behaviour to him, for she frequently rejects his demonstrations of affection. When she announces her decision to spend her legacy on sending Harry to Cambridge, her husband, after a moment of sulkiness, bursts out impulsively, '"By G—d, Rachel, you're a good woman!" says my lord, seizing my lady's hand, at which she blushed very much, and shrank back, putting her children before her.' When Francis abuses Rachel as a jilt, Esmond says piously, 'so a man dashes a fine vase down and despises it for being broken.' His narration, then, always suggests that it was the husband who deserted the wife; but we have evidence that it was just as likely the wife who deserted the husband.

In this courtly love triangle the lady is the most aware of what is going on, and has most to conceal. Even the husband seems to know more of Rachel's feelings for Harry than Harry, or even the mature Esmond, does himself. Harry would convince us that Rachel 'never thought of or suspected the admiration of her little pigmy adorer'; but Castlewood knows better than this: 'Why, when you was but a boy of fifteen I could hear you two together talking your poetry and your books till I was in such a rage that I was fit to strangle you.' And he has his momentary deep suspicions of Harry, even when he is on a false scent in suspecting Mohun: the young man tries to exonerate Rachel by saying she was thinking of him, not of Mohun, when she fainted at the news of 'Harry's' accident.

> 'But my lord, *my* name is Harry,' cried out Esmond, burning red. 'You told my lady, "Harry was killed!"'
>
> 'Damnation! shall I fight you too?' shouts my lord, in a fury. 'Are you, you little serpent, warmed by my fire, going to sting—*you?*—No, my boy, you're an honest boy; you're a good boy.' (And here he broke from rage into tears even more cruel to see.)

'Honest, honest Iago' comes momentarily to mind.

Harry himself tells us singularly little of *his* reactions when his patron voices such a suspicion, although his blushes show his consciousness; and it must surely be a subject that would be much in his thoughts. Does the boy miss the constant hints about Rachel's love for him as completely as his silence suggests? Is even the mature Esmond, who has for years been married to Rachel, ignorant of the implications of the blushes and suggestive words and gestures which he reports? It seems more likely that the boy Harry knows a good deal more than his older self is prepared to admit; that he is closer to being the 'little serpent' than at first appears; and that Esmond is omitting to tell us a good many things which he knows, or at least suspects, well enough, but which might make his young self appear in a discreditable light.

The next triangle situation is still more complex, when we consider the part the hero plays in it. The situation appears to be that he is hopelessly pursuing a disdainful Beatrix, while confiding in her mother and relying on a maternal sympathy from her. But, as we know from the last sentence of the book, where he mentions the gold button, the mature Esmond at least must be fully aware of Rachel's sexual love for him at this time. And he is again reticent about this awareness.

At one point it does sound as though he admits to a full knowledge of the suffering he is causing Rachel:

> This passion [for Beatrix] did not escape—how should it?—the clear eyes of Esmond's mistress: he told her all; what will a man not do when frantic with love? To what baseness will he not demean himself? What pangs will he not make others suffer, so that he may ease his selfish heart of a part of its own pain? Day after day he would seek his dear mistress, poor insane hopes, supplications, rhapsodies, raptures, into her ear.

This sounds as though he knows the full extent of the suffering which he is causing Rachel; and, with some part of him, indeed he must do. But he immediately annuls what looked like an admission by suggesting that 'compassion' is the only pang he is causing her. And he is all too ready to believe her when she

re-asserts the purely maternal nature of her love for him. . . . Only towards the end of the book, where Harry the protagonist and Esmond the narrator begin to merge into a single consciousness, does he seem ready to admit a knowledge of her sexual jealousy: after his tête-à-tête with Beatrix, 'Esmond's mistress showed no signs of jealousy when he returned to the room where she was. She had schooled herself so as to look quite inscrutably, when she had a mind.'

Beatrix's part in the triangle is also more complex than a single reading makes apparent. For Esmond again appears greatly to underestimate his place in her feelings. As he says that Rachel cared little for the worship of her 'pigmy adorer,' when she was just betraying an adulterous love for him, so he says deprecatingly of his place in Beatrix's estimation:

> Beatrix thought no more of him than of the lackey that followed her chair. His complaints did not touch her in the least; his raptures rather fatigued her; she cared for his verses no more than for Dan Chaucer's, who's dead these ever so many hundred years; she did not hate him; she rather despised him, and just suffered him.

But we should be as wary in one case as the other of taking Esmond's words at face value. Beatrix is by no means as unattainable as he likes to suggest. Harry makes himself unacceptable by wooing her in the guise of 'the knight of the Woeful Countenance,' when what she wants is an impetuous lover who will sweep her off her feet. In her long self-examination, at Harry's last abject proposal, she says that he was 'ever too much of a slave to win my heart,' but that had she found the man she loved she would have followed him in rags. It is not for his poverty or his bar-sinister that she rejects him, but for his lack of resolution.

Esmond seems to have a knack of proposing in such a way as to determine a refusal. Even Rachel, who confesses to loving him, meets his first proposal that she should go away with him to Virginia with a sad refusal: 'You never loved me, dear Henry—no, you do not now.' The manner of his proposals evidently gives Beatrix the same conviction. And perhaps in being refused Harry feels the same mixture of satisfaction and chagrin that Pen experienced after his half-hearted proposal to Laura: 'Was he pleased, or was he angry at its termination? He had asked her, and a secret triumph filled his heart to think that he was still free. She had refused him, but did she not love him?'

Beatrix often gives Harry opportunities to win her. In the scene where Rachel leaves the two alone so that Beatrix can break the news of her engagement to the Duke of Hamilton, Beatrix leads instead to the subject of Harry's feelings for her. But he moons in his usual manner about his despair, and she tries to provoke him into being more demonstrative and determined: 'I feel as a sister to you,' she tells him:

> 'Isn't that enough, sir?' And she put her face quite close to his—who knows with what intention?
>
> 'It's too much,' says Esmond, turning away.

Esmond may be telling us of the hopelessness of his love; but the image here is one of the woman who, within the bounds of propriety, is wooing the man, while the man is rejecting her. That he never really wanted her to accept him is suggested by his relief when he knows of her engagement.

> 'I have been hankering after the grapes on the way,' says he, 'and lost my temper because they were beyond my reach; was there any wonder? They're gone

now, and another has them—a taller man than your humble servant has won them.' And the colonel made his cousin a low bow.

'A taller man, cousin Esmond!' says she. 'A man of spirit would have scaled the wall, sir, and seized them! A man of courage would have fought for 'em, not gaped for 'em.'

Such a hint suggests that, even at this stage, if Harry had been really resolute he could have made her break off her engagement: he could have become the man she would follow in rags. But his reply shows not only lack of resolution, but a good deal of pique as well: 'A duke has but to gape and they drop into his mouth.' Beatrix at this can only reply, with justifiable exasperation, 'Yes, sir . . . a duke *is* a taller man than you.' (pp. 109-17)

Beatrix, the cynosure of all eyes, the sun that eclipses all other luminaries, etcetera, can be seen as a lonely and rejected woman. If Harry puts Rachel to the torture by making her watch him with Beatrix, so he torments Beatrix by making her watch him with her mother. Neither loves Beatrix, it seems, as much as she loves them. 'Is it mamma your honour wants, and that I should have the happiness of calling you papa?' she asks Harry banteringly; but the tone is only half playful, and leaves the impression that the spectacle of the absorption of these two in one another gives her more pain than she is prepared to admit. She foresees their marriage long before either of them, and by her own confession (she is franker than Rachel) she is not immune from jealousy:

'She loves you, sir, a great deal too much; and I hate you for it. I would have had her all to myself; but she wouldn't. In my childhood, it was my father she loved . . . And then, it was Frank; and now, it is Heaven and the clergyman. How I would have loved her! From a child I used to be in a rage that she loved anybody but me; but she loved you all better—all, I know she did.'

And when she is banished from the prince's presence by a conspiracy between her brother, her mother, and Harry, she has the last word, and it is not calculated to make us think the better of the 'saintly' Rachel: 'I always said I was alone; you never loved me, never—and were jealous of me from the time I sat on my father's knee. Let me go away, the sooner the better; I can bear to be with you no more.' Far from being proud, self-sufficient, and disdainful, as Esmond seems to depict her, Beatrix, as she appears in an alternative picture, is finally a pathetic figure. She is not deficient in love, like Becky, but she cannot reconcile her love with her pride. When in *The Virginians* she dies an old woman, in her delirium she is still complaining of her mother's rejection of her, and calling on Henry to kill his royal rival.

Beatrix tells Harry, explicitly and repeatedly, that he is the only man who has touched her heart, that 'you might have had me,' even that she loves him. But he continues to regard her as beyond his reach, and persists in offering the wrong price to buy her—military glory, diamonds, the restoration of the Stuart dynasty—when what she wants is to be not bought but taken. As he prefers to believe that Rachel's love for him is only maternal, so he prefers to think Beatrix is unattainable, and that she loves the world better than him. But at the same time, perhaps, he has a secret satisfaction in the half-knowledge that he could take either woman whenever he wishes. He loves to be on his knees and yet worshipped at the same time.

There is a similar ambivalence in his behaviour with the family title. There is no doubt that his action in forgoing the title, to which he has a just and legal claim, in gratitude to the family that befriended him, is generous and heroic. And yet how he enjoys the situation! In a moment of genuine self-examination, he admits that he is 'perhaps secretly vain of the sacrifice he had made, and to think that he, Esmond, was really the chief of his house, and only prevented by his own magnanimity from advancing his claim.'

As he enjoys underestimating his place in the feelings of women, while having a secret knowledge of his own importance, so he enjoys being thought a bastard in society, while having a secret knowledge that he is legitimately head of the family. He likes to be on his knees before Beatrix, with a knowledge that he is the stronger; and he likes to be patronized by Frank, knowing that the right to patronize is really his. (pp. 117-19)

The subtle masochism which Harry shows in his emotional life has its parallel in his social attitude, which is that of the inverted snob. In his way, he is a refined Bounderby, parading his menial origin while enjoying his actual power. His encounter with Swift has been taken as just another instance of Thackeray's animus against the Dean, who of course appears in no very gracious light. But it is characteristic of Esmond, too, that he should first lead Swift to believe he is a menial, and a 'poor broken-down soldier' (as he has before called himself pigmy adorer, lackey, and bastard), and then humiliate him with his mistake when they are both guests at the table of General Webb, with Esmond taking the precedence. (pp. 119-20)

If we take Esmond's memoirs at face value, we have a picture of a man who may be grave and melancholy, but who is possessed of the virtues of courtesy, honesty, courage, wisdom, love, and humility. He renounces a title from pure generosity; and though he contributes to the failure of a marriage, and causes some suffering to a woman who loves him by confiding in her while he woos her daughter, he does these things unwittingly. He hopelessly loves an unworthy woman, but finally learns to reject her and marry the elder and more worthy one. Through his life he grows to wisdom and maturity, not only in knowledge of the world, but emotionally and morally as well. There is something god-like about so much virtue and self-abnegation.

If, on the other hand, we read the novel as a sustained piece of dramatic irony, we notice not so much the god-like attributes as the wish to appear god-like. His humility is inverted pride, and his self-abnegation an elaborate glorification of self. He renounces a title because he finds more satisfaction in the debt than the ownership. He keeps two women at his feet by maintaining a pose of being at theirs, and he takes a secret pleasure in his knowledge of their adoration while pretending to be unaware of it. And, far from growing to maturity, he finally fulfils the infantile impulse to marry his mother.

My interpretation has suggested the second reading because critical emphasis has usually been the other way. But I do not mean to exclude the first: there is again that double focus which is part of the complexity of Thackeray's moral vision. As usual, Thackeray's interest turns on the psychology that is the basis of the morality: Esmond's suffering is real, even if there is part of him that enjoys it, and his actions are noble, even if he has himself a rather exaggerated sense of their nobility. Generosity *is* akin to selfishness, and humility to pride, and knowing and not knowing one's place in another's feelings is of the essence of any deep relationship. Esmond (as he would be the first to say himself) is no hero; but he is certainly not a wicked man either, only a human being whose very goodness is necessarily tainted by a somewhat selfish enjoyment of appearing selfless. But judge every man according to his ulterior motives, and who should 'scape whipping? (pp. 124-25)

Juliet McMaster, in her Thackeray: The Major Novels, *University of Toronto Press, 1971, 230 p.*

JOHN HAGAN (essay date 1972)

[*Hagan regards* Henry Esmond *as a "masterpiece of irony," contending that Esmond's life is fundamentally unhappy because his love for Rachel remains filial throughout their marriage.*]

Although frequently praised by Thackeray's seasoned admirers as his masterpiece, **The History of Henry Esmond** is a novel that still awaits a fully convincing interpretation. Perhaps the most persuasive formulation of the novel's theme is George J. Worth's [see excerpt dated 1961]. . . . Yet even this reading is finally unsatisfactory—not because it fails to see what is the centrally important action in the novel, but because the account it gives of that action is incomplete.

There is a startling and extraordinarily revealing discrepancy between Worth's picture of Esmond contentedly taking up his patriarchal duties on his plantation in the "rural peace of Virginia," calm of mind, all passion spent, and the picture of Esmond in his declining years presented by Thackeray himself as omniscient narrator in chapter 3 of the sequel to **Esmond,** **The Virginians**:

> At one period, this gentleman had taken a part in active life at home and possibly might have been eager to share its rewards; but in latter days he did not seem to care for them. A something had occurred in his life, which had cast a tinge of melancholy over all his existence. He was not unhappy—to those about him most kind—most affectionate, obsequious even to the women of his family, whom he scarce ever contradicted; but there had been some bankruptcy of his heart, which his spirit never recovered. He submitted to life, rather than enjoyed it, and never was in better spirits than in his last hours when he was going to lay it down.

Between this poignant version of Esmond's fate and Worth's bright one there is simply no accord. Yet this is not the result of a change which took place in Thackeray's attitude toward his protagonist between the writing of the two novels. The vision presented in **The Virginians** is already before us, subtly and obliquely, in **Henry Esmond.** For the Esmond whose story of youthful errors and misplaced allegiances ends on the last page is not finally the only Esmond, or even the most important Esmond, on whom this complex novel is focused. Thackeray also implicitly invites us to concern ourselves with the Esmond who has lived well beyond this point and has had time not only to reflect on all which he is in the process of telling us about his earlier life, but to have married Rachel, to have lived with her for many years, to have fathered their daughter, and to have measured the full impact made on his life by Beatrix. This Esmond has discovered that the vanity of his human wishes did not end with his disillusionments in Father Holt, in Marlborough, in the Pretender, or in Beatrix, but went beyond these to take in the whole of his life's quest for meaning and fulfillment. He is extremely careful, of course, in his reserved, decorous, and gentlemanly fashion, never to admit this in so many words or in any way to give it central prominence in his

narrative. But the hints are all there for the attentive reader to pick up and piece together. **Henry Esmond** is thus a masterpiece of irony, not merely in the obvious sense that it employs irony to expose the vanities Worth speaks of, but in the sense that it requires us to penetrate the disguises, the understatements, and the indirections of the narrator, Esmond himself, and to discover the truth of his feelings which his own narrative so effectively in part conceals both from his readers and very probably even from himself.

To grasp the full implications of Esmond's career we have to perceive, in addition to the pattern of allegiances and rejections which Worth describes, the underlying pattern of Esmond's motivation. For what is so striking about these allegiances and rejections is that none of them is the result of a reasoned decision; none is an intellectual choice based on principle. All of Esmond's decisive actions rest on emotional rather than doctrinal grounds and are an expression of his domination by a single imperious need. This is the need to love and be loved, which is rooted deep in the sad experiences of his childhood—in his alienation from his scapegrace of a father, who, in order to make a mercenary marriage, placed between himself and his son the barrier of a fictitious illegitimacy, and, most decisively, in his separation from his mother. . . . (pp. 293-95)

Early in the novel Thackeray establishes the key fact that Esmond "was a docile child, and of an affectionate nature." To say that he was "always touched by a kind face and a kind word" is, indeed, a considerable understatement. Because of the emotional deprivations of his earliest years he has a seemingly boundless capacity for devotion, and becomes at once the staunchest hero-worshiper of whoever shows him the smallest kindness or love. . . . This is obviously the impulse behind the first major commitment of his life, the decision to become a Jesuit. No process of intellection leads to this decision—Esmond is not even ten years old when he makes it. He is inspired solely by his devotion to Father Holt, to whom he "gave himself up with an entire confidence and attachment" and whose "willing slave [he became] almost from the first moment he saw him," simply because the latter shows a fondness for the boy which his natural father displays only intermittently. Ironically, after the death of his father and Holt's disappearance, the same process of responding to love with reverence and dedication leads Esmond to renounce Holt's religion entirely and make the second major decision of his life, to become a convert to Anglicanism, once he falls under the affectionate care of the kind and beautiful Rachel. (pp. 296-97)

His quest for love is also the decisive factor shaping his political opinions and actions as well as his decision to enter the army and the value he comes to place upon his career there. Jacobitism has been a tradition in the Esmond family, of course, since the time of the First Viscount, and thus when the boy is first brought to live at Castlewood he witnesses from the sidelines the intrigues of both his father and Holt. Because he is too young to understand much of what is going on, however, his own adoption of the cause occurs only later, and once again the chief influence is his love for Rachel. His "eager devotion for his mistress" also plays its part in leading him to become a soldier, for when that devotion is slighted by her cruel and unjust repudiation of him at the time of her husband's death in the duel with Mohun, he turns to the army in "a bitter feeling of revolt." Equally important in directing his political and military commitments is the subsequent development of his violent passion for Beatrix. At first, knowing how hopeless his love for such an ambitious coquette is likely to be, he takes advantage of his life in the army to keep out of her dangerous influence. But eventually he attaches a wholly new value to this life, developing a full-blown "desire for military honour," when he comes to imagine that it "might raise him in Beatrix's eyes." The same hope induces him later to embark on the foolish, foredoomed plot to restore the Pretender. As for his eventual rejection of Jacobitism for Whiggery, that too comes about no more through rational deliberation than did his adoption of Jacobitism in the first place because of his love for Beatrix's mother. For even before the Pretender's flight to join Beatrix at Castlewood causes the plot to fail, Esmond's old allegiance to the Stuarts has been shattered by his jealousy. Just as Rachel's rejection prompted him to renounce the Anglican priesthood for the army, so the mere prospect of her daughter's rejection of him prepares him to renounce the Tories for the Whigs.

It is clear, then, that no description of the theme of *Henry Esmond* solely in terms of Esmonds's "misguided allegiances" to and renunciations of the vanities described by Worth can be complete. The real dynamic of the book lies deeper. From beginning to end the primary focus is upon Esmond's search for love—a love that can compensate or substitute for the maternal love of which he was deprived almost from the time of his birth. The various vanities which he pursues and rejects are not ends in themselves, but only means to the satisfaction of his profound emotional need.

But, if this is true, the question which naturaly arises is whether this need *is* ever satisfied. The answer to that will bring us to what the novel is finally all about.

The problem is posed, of course, by Esmond's marriage. Are we not supposed to understand that his marriage to Rachel in the final chapter, by representing his attainment at last of sound values, brings his disillusionments to an end, and sets him henceforth on a course leading to what Worth calls "stability and maturity"? Certainly, this is the way that Esmond himself—at least in one of his moods—would have us see it. The novel approaches its conclusion on a note of glowing eulogy:

> That happiness, which hath subsequently crowned it [his life], cannot be written in words; 'tis of its nature sacred and secret, and not to be spoken of, though the heart be ever so full of thankfulness, save to Heaven and the One Ear alone—to one fond being, the truest and tenderest and purest wife ever man was blessed with. As I think of the immense happiness which was in store for me, and of the depth and intensity of that love which, for so many years, hath blessed me, I own to a transport of wonder and gratitude for such a boon—nay, am thankful to have been endowed with a heart capable of feeling and knowing the immense beauty and value of the gift which God hath bestowed upon me. Sure, love *vincit omnia; is* immeasurably above all ambition, more precious than wealth, more noble than name. He knows not life who knows not that: he hath not felt the highest faculty of the soul who hath not enjoyed it. In the name of my wife I write the completion of hope, and the summit of happiness. To have such a love is the one blessing, in comparison of which all earthly joy is of no value; and to think of her, is to praise God.

Esmond's daughter, Madam Rachel Esmond Warrington, also tries to give an idyllic impression of her father's married life in both her Preface and a footnote in Book 3, chapter 10.

These assertions by father and daughter are very imposing, to be sure, and the assumption of readers and critics alike has apparently been that we must accept the picture they present at face value. There is no doubt, of course, about Esmond's goodness; the question concerns the degree of his marital happiness, and on this point there is room for suspicion. (pp. 297-99)

The language of [Madam Warrington's] remarks is so stereotyped . . . as to present a picture of Esmond in the role of the benign and happy patriarch of a Southern plantation, surrounded by happy family, happy friends, and happy Negro slaves, which is little more than a caricature—especially when we juxtapose it ironically with Esmond's own Prefce, which demands that historians deal in the "familiar rather than [the] heroic," and with his express desire that "his grandsons believe or represent him to be not an inch taller than Nature has made him." Madam Warrington's account is, all too obviously, a highly circumspect, "official," "public" version of things, designed not to teach these grandsons the truth, but to create and perpetuate a myth. Part of the circumspection lies in its ambiguity. Although her account certainly gives the impression that one of the sources of Esmond's alleged contentment in his later years was a happy marriage, she never actually asserts this. Nowhere does she either state or give evidence that her mother's "extreme devotion" for Esmond was at all reciprocated. What she stresses is only that the blessing he bestowed on his immediate family was one of "*fatherly* love and protection", (italics mine). The adjective seems not to have been chosen casually.

Esmond himself, however, has affirmed the depth of his love for Rachel. Or has he? If we reexamine the highly eulogistic passage I have quoted from the novel's final chapter, we are likely to be startled to discover that what he is speaking about is only Rachel's *love for him*. And it is solely on this that he dwells even in the novel's famous last sentence, the purpose of which is simply to adduce as further evidence of her devotion the fact that the gold sleeve button she stole from him when he was in prison many years earlier has been worn "ever after . . . on the tenderest heart in the world." When he speaks of his response to this devotion, his emphasis is exclusively on his gratitude for having been made its object. There can be no doubt, of course, that the closing paragraphs of the novel do explicitly assert that his marriage has brought him a great deal of happiness. What is troublesome about this assertion, however, is that it is overinsistent, strained, smacking of merely formal rhetoric. Like the tone and manner of Madam Warrington's eulogies, it seems to have too palpable a design upon us. It is also much too close for comfort to the wonderfully comic-pathetic passage in chapter 67 of *Vanity Fair,* in which Thackeray ironically celebrates the reunion of Dobbin and Amelia. To conclude that Esmond is being as consciously ironical about himself as Thackeray is about Dobbin would, of course, be a mistake. Esmond is not so self-aware or so self-detached as that, or if he is, he is so only intermittently and reluctantly. But neither is he a calculating hypocrite, cynically setting himself up as an idol for his grandsons' worship. He is too much of the Christian gentleman for that. The fact of the matter is, I would argue, that when Esmond sings the praises of his marriage to Rachel, the stridency of his affirmations measures not an achieved happiness but a will to achieve it in the face of the dreadful alternative of squarely confronting the truth—and perhaps even a guilty feeling that, in not having achieved it, he has betrayed his wife's love for him. If he is not really happy, he urgently wants to be.

The main evidence for this interpretation of Esmond's ambivalent feelings toward Rachel and his marriage is an extraordinary passage in Book 1:

> Who does not know of eyes, lighted by love once, where the flame shines no more?—of lamps extinguished, once properly trimmed and tended? Every man has such in his house. Such mementos make our splendidest chambers look blank and sad; such faces seen in a day cast a gloom upon our sunshine. So oaths mutually sworn, and invocations of Heaven, and priestly ceremonies, and fond belief, and love, so fond and faithful that it never doubted but that it should live forever, are all of no avail towards making love eternal: it dies, in spite of the banns and the priest; and I have often thought there should be a visitation of the sick for it, and a funeral service, and an extreme unction, and an *abi in pace*. It has its course, like all mortal things—its beginnings, progress, and decay. It buds and it blooms out into sunshine, and it withers and ends. Strephon and Chloe languish apart; join in a rapture: and presently you hear that Chloe is crying, and Strephon has broken his crook across her back. Can ye mend it so as to show no marks of rupture? Not all the priests of Hymen, not all the incantations to the gods, can make it whole!

The immediate context of these remarks, of course, is Esmond's discussion of the breakdown of the marriage between Rachel and Frank. But what is so remarkable is that the language rises to a level of generality which is far in excess of the ostensible occasion; Esmond extends his observations of Rachel and Frank to include "every man" and to speak of *all* lovers and *all* marriages. If his intention were to limit the

Jane Brookfield.

application of his remarks merely to the situation of his benefactors, such unqualified expressions would be pointless. The fact, we are forced to conclude, is that Esmond is also reflecting upon his own marriage—that his secret feelings about it, which he is trying to conceal at the end of the book by an insistent and hyperbolic rhetoric of celebration, are here forcing themselves to the surface. Certainly, the "poetic," personal, and urgent quality of the prose in the earlier passage and the comparatively stilted, abstract, public, ceremonial language of the later stand in the sharpest contrast. The earlier is nothing less than a cry of the heart, which here, for once, proves irresistible, breaks through his censorship, and cracks the elaborately wrought facade he is working so earnestly to erect not only for others to believe in but for himself. It is the complete giveaway to the fact he does not want to face: the fact of his unfulfilled life.

This impression that his marriage has left him unfulfilled is confirmed when we examine its nature more closely. . . . I shall consider the major flaw in Rachel's character and Esmond's explicit or implicit reactions to it, and . . . [then] I shall look more fully at the precise sort of "love" he feels for her.

Rachel is by no means the paragon Esmond frequently seems to be insisting she is. One of her most conspicuous weaknesses is her proneness to idolatry: she is always seeking a hero whom she can bow down before and worship. From a certain point of view, no doubt, this is an admirable quality; it is the one for which we have seen Esmond expressing the deepest gratitude. But, as in the case of his similar penchant which leads him onward in his pursuit of vanities, it can also have grave disadvantages, as her first husband, Frank, finds to his sorrow. For the fanatical devotion with which she originally regards him brings with it "a penalty . . . : and, in a word, if he had a loving wife, had a very jealous and exacting one." "'The very notion of a woman,'" Frank complains, "'drives her mad.'" Her jealousy even goes so far as to make her resentful of her husband's love for their own daughter and of his friendship with Esmond. Eventually, by driving Frank to drink and then into the arms of a mistress, it sets in motion a chain of events that shatters their marriage.

Nor do her marital disillusionments bring Rachel's jealousy to an end. She simply transfers her hero-worship from her husband to Esmond and reacts in the same way to the new idol as to the old. After her husband's death, she makes strenuous efforts to stifle this idolatry in accord with the dictates of her guilty conscience, for she feels that in having loved Esmond while Frank was still alive she committed adultery in her heart. To expiate her "sin" she even promotes his suit with Beatrix (with whom he has fallen in love after his visit to Walcote), although she knows the girl will inevitably cause him suffering. But, in spite of her efforts to keep her passion suppressed and hidden, it becomes only too clear that she regards Beatrix as a rival. Indeed, so far as Thackeray's portrayal of Rachel is concerned, this conflict between conscience and jealous passion is the principal substance of the novel's second and third Books.

The point to which all this is leading, of course, is the fact that the same combination in Rachel's character of idolatry and inordinate jealousy that poisoned her first marriage is ironically repeated in the second. The novel comes full circle. (pp. 300-03)

Beatrix asserts at one point that the only woman who could make Esmond happy is one who worshiped him. Rachel is exactly this kind. But, given the "penalty" her idolatry always exacts, his happiness is far from a certainty. Obviously, Rachel's jealousy does not destroy her marriage to Esmond as it destroyed her marriage to Frank, for Esmond is a far different kind of man and thus does not react to the provocation in the same way. Frank was unwilling "to defray" the penalty because his nature was coarse; he was a sensualist who married "for mere *beaux yeaux*." Esmond, who scorns "household tyrants," is more patient, more refined, more gentlemanly. But that the separation which Rachel has placed between him and his daughter must be causing him pain is distinctly hinted. He tells us that he has always felt great love for children in general, and Rachel Warrington has herself testified to how much he loved her in particular. Given these feelings, it is almost impossible to believe that he would react to the tyranny of Rachel's jealousy with indifference. Indeed, when we consider the circumstances of his own childhood, such a reaction becomes inconceivable. For, ironically, Rachel's rejection of their daughter and the barrier she places between her and her father are a grim reminder of exactly what Esmond himself experienced in his youth at the hands of Madame Pastoureau— to whose cruelty he explicitly attributes his sympathy for children—and, above all, to the Dowager. Had it not been for the interference of the latter, his life with his father would have been far different.

But the causes of Esmond's dissatisfaction with his marriage also lie at a deeper level than the one I have considered so far. Even if Rachel were not flawed in the ways I have suggested, there would still be difficulties arising from the very nature of Esmond's "love" for her. That her love for him is deeply erotic from beginning to end is perfectly clear. After her first husband's death, she masks it as motherly and sisterly love only because she feels she must expiate the "sin" of having felt sexual passion for Esmond while she was still married to another. Esmond's feelings, however, are quite different; that he and Rachel do not love one another in the same way is, in fact, one of the centrally important and most poignant features of their story.

Throughout Book I of the novel Esmond's feelings for Rachel are a blend of three different attitudes: he sees her as a sister, as a mother, and as a kind of lofty being whom he variously calls "an exalted lady," a "saint," and "angel," and a "goddess." In all three roles he literally "worships" her (the word appears many times), and what leads to this extravagance of devotion is his gratitude for the love and kindness she has bestowed upon him in his abandonment and loneliness. Nowhere in all these pages is there the slightest hint that he regards Rachel as a sexual object. His response to her is essentially no different in kind from what it was earlier to Father Holt: she has appeared at a critical juncture in his life to satisfy his imperious need to find a substitute for the love of which he was deprived by the deaths of his mother and father. When he first meets her, of course, he is only twelve years old, and therefore erotic passion cannot be expected of him; he sees her physical beauty through a haze of juvenile idealization. But even after he has reached adolescence and returned from the university, he feels the same way: as he says to Mohun, whom he suspects of having sexual designs on Rachel, "'I worship her as a devotee worships a saint. To hear her name spoken lightly seems blasphemy to me. Would you dare think of your own mother so, or suffer anyone so to speak of her! It is a horror to me to fancy that any man should think of her impurely.'" When, at this period, his heart begins "throbbing with desires undefined," they are directed entirely at Beatrix.

In Book 2 all this appears to change. After his rejection by Rachel at the time of her husband's death, the halo fades away, and he is able to see her much more realistically as a flawed human being. As a result, when they are reconciled at Walcote a year later, he discovers that she can be "more fondly cherished as woman perhaps than ever she had been adored as divinity." The obvious temptation is to read this as an assertion of sexual passion which has presumably developed in the interim as Esmond has grown older and more experienced. But the context makes clear that this is not what Esmond means at all. The sentence which immediately precedes his remarks is as follows:

> Brighter eyes there might be, and faces more beautiful, but none so dear—no voice so sweet as that of his beloved mistress, *who had been sister, mother, goddess to him during his youth—goddess now no more* for he knew of her weaknesses; and by thought, by suffering, and that experience it beings, was older now than she.... (italics mine)

The language of this important passage is very carefully considered: while making clear that Esmond no longer loves Rachel as a "goddess," it does not exclude the possibility that he still loves her as a "sister" and a "mother," and, indeed, that in saying he cherishes her "as woman" he means this and nothing else.

But there is also the fact that a few paragraphs later he proposes marriage to her and urges her to embark with him to the Virginian plantation. Furthermore, we recall that he hurried to Walcote in the first place because he had heard it rumored that Rachel was planning to marry Tom Tusher and he hoped to interdict the banns. Do not these actions prove that he is now able to love her erotically, after all? Not in the least. His objection to her marrying Tusher is not the result of sexual jealousy, but is based merely on the disparity between their social positions. Even more important are quite explicit indications that the primary motive for his proposal is nothing more than gratitude. Nowhere in the proposal scene does Esmond speak of *his* love for Rachel; what he emphasizes is his thankfulness for *hers*. This is shown in his proposal itself by his use of the words "this great boon" and "blessing" and in equivalent terms which appear in the paragraph immediately preceding:

> ... the depth of this pure devotion ... smote upon him, and filled his heart with thanksgiving. Gracious God, who was he, weak and friendless creature, that such a love should be poured out upon him? Not in vain, not in vain has he lived—hard and thankless should he be to think so—that has such a treasure given him.

This, of course, is only an intensified version of that "devoted affection and passion of gratitude," that "passion of grateful regard" which Esmond has felt for Rachel from the very beginning. There has been a change in the degree of his feelings, but not in their kind. What prompts the change at this specific moment is only the impassioned way in which Rachel has welcomed him, which reveals the full extent of her "devotion" to him "for the first time." But if he perceives what the reader of the scene can hardly miss—namely, its frenzied sexuality— he shows no willingness to reciprocate it.

That there is no erotic content in the proposal is further confirmed by the very strange scene which immediately follows it. Rachel refuses Esmond's offer, and gives as her reason that she has a "duty" to stay behind in England and take care of her children and aged father. It becomes clear from her response to Esmond's protest, however, that this is only a rationalization. Her talk here about "sin" makes clear that she is still dominated by her old guilty feeling about having loved Esmond during her husband's lifetime. To be sure, she asserts that this sin has been "washed . . . away" by her "tears," that "it has been forgiven" her, and that she has received "absolution"; but, obviously, she is confused, for in another breath she says, "'I have been so weak and sinful that I must leave it [the world], and pray out an expiation, dear Henry. Had we houses of religion as there were once . . . I often think I would retire to one and pass my life in penance.'" This is the real reason for her refusal of Esmond's proposal. Why, otherwise, would she speak to him with the look and tone of a "mother"? Just as later she will try to cope with her guilty conscience by promoting his suit with Beatrix, so here (and subsequently, until she finally accepts his second proposal at the end of the novel) she also tries to cope with it by transforming her erotic passion into an exalted, morally acceptable maternal love. The crucial point in all this, however, is Esmond's reaction. Since he never asks Rachel what she means by her rather enigmatic remarks, we can only conclude that he understands them: he could hardly have failed to see, moments before, the significance of her display of sexual frenzy, and from that perception to a recognition of what she means by a desire to "expiate" her "sin" there is the easiest of inferences.

But, if Esmond does understand the nature and the cause of Rachel's guilt feelings, and if he also loved her erotically, his natural response would be to try to reason or persuade her out of those feelings—to reject a purely mother-son or brother-sister relationship as an insult and an injury to the erotic passion of both of them. But he does not do this. The scene and the chapter end with his accepting Rachel wholly on her terms: "'I think the angels are not all in heaven,' Mr. Esmond said. And as a brother folds a sister to his heart; and as a mother cleaves to her son's breast—so for a few moments Esmond's beloved mistress came to him and blessed him." The only possible interpretation is that Esmond welcomes this sort of relationship because it relieves him of any need to respond to Rachel's erotic passion in kind. She herself charges him with being unable to requite this passion ("'you never loved me, dear Henry—no, you do not now,'") and he utters no objection. She becomes, instead, the recipient of the very different kind of passion pent up in his heart for his long-dead mother. Just how different it is, in fact, can be measured unmistakably by the genuine sexual attraction he feels for Beatrix in the famous staircase scene of the very next chapter.

It seems to be generally assumed, however, that even if Esmond's feeling for Rachel throughout most of the novel is filial or fraternal, it has somehow changed into an erotic one by the time he marries her at the end. J. Y. T. Greig asserts [in his *Thackeray: A Reconsideration* (1950)] that the "love that begins as filial on the one side [Esmond's] and maternal on the other [Rachel's] . . . is gradually transformed into sexual on both." Indeed, "the gradual transformation of Esmond's dutiful but indeterminate affection for Rachel into love of the same kind, though perhaps never of the same intensity, as hers for him" is for Greig the novel's main subject. As I have already pointed out, Rachel's feelings for Esmond, despite her efforts to conceal the fact, are strongly sexual, and never merely maternal, almost from the beginning. But, even leaving this aside, Greig's view seems to me mistaken. Not only can I find no positive evidence for such a "transformation" in Esmond's feelings as he posits (unless one adopts the question-begging-assumption that it is attested to by the mere fact of his mar-

rying), but the weight of the evidence is actually against it. If we consider, for example, Esmond's account of how he came to propose to Rachel a second time, we will surely be struck by his almost comic lack of eagerness: "We had been so accustomed to an extreme intimacy and confidence, and had lived so long and tenderly together, that we might have gone on to the end without thinking of a closer tie." The marriage is precipitated solely, as Esmond himself admits, when "circumstances" in the form of her father's death, Beatrix's flight with the Pretender to the Continent, and Frank's marriage and religious conversion, finally leave her wholly dependent on his concern and pity. Coming upon her one day after a quarrel with her daughter-in-law has left her "in tears," he simply beseeches her "to confide herself to the care and devotion of one who, by God's help, would never forsake her," and she, no longer having the pretexts for refusing him which she had at Walcote, tenderly yields. Esmond describes his proposal merely as "respectful importunity."

Moreover, his feelings for her do not change even after the marriage has been consummated. This is made perfectly clear in a key passage at the end of Book 2, chapter 8, occasioned by Esmond's memory of his departure from Walcote:

> . . . 'twas difficult to say with what a feeling he regarded her. 'Twas happiness to have seen her: 'twas no great pang to part; a filial tenderness, a love that was at once respect and protection, filled his mind as he thought of her; and near her or far from her, and from that day until now, and from now till death is past, and beyond it, he prays that sacred flame may ever burn.

Esmond is flatly telling us not only that he loved Rachel more as a son than as a lover at the time, but that he still loves her this way now in his old age after many years of marriage to her, and, moreover, that he even hopes he will continue to feel so beyond death itself. It is, indeed, a remarkable statement—so remarkable that John W. Dodds violently balks at it ("Come now, Esmond, *what* flame? Your 'filial tenderness,' long before this writing, must have been sublimated at the marriage altar"), and charges Thackeray with being "uncertain" about his protagonist's psychology [see excerpt dated 1941]. I would submit, however, that Thackeray knows quite well what he is doing, and that unless we accept Esmond's statement as the literal truth we shall fail to understand what the novel is about. For given the fact that from the very beginning, as we have seen, Esmond has needed to love a mother figure, that his "love" for Rachel has always been the result of gratitude rather than of passion, and that the split between these two emotions was widened even further as a result of the development of his violent sexual attraction to Beatrix (not to mention the fact, which I shall urge presently, that his passion for the latter long outlives her betrayal of it), the existence after his marriage of the state of mind he describes is, though unusual, not improbable in the least. To assume a priori that his filial feelings "must have been sublimated" into erotic ones at the marriage altar is to ignore not only the fact that the twentieth century has learned stranger things about human emotions than anything Esmond has to tell us, but to ignore also the unique particulars of his own psychic history which the novel has been at great pains to establish.

The passage at the end of Book 2, chapter 8, is, in fact, intimately related to what Esmond has just said two chapters earlier about the motives for his first proposal and to what he says in the novel's final chapter about the sources of his marital "happiness." . . . What will strike one first is the number of close verbal parallels. As in the earlier passage Esmond speaks of Rachel's devotion as filling "his heart with thanksgiving," so in the later he speaks of his heart as "full of thankfulness" and as being moved by "a transport of wonder and gratitude"; as in the earlier he calls her love "a treasure," a "great boon," and a "blessing," so in the later he calls it a "boon," "the one blessing in comparison of which all earthly joy is of no value," and a "gift which God hath bestowed upon me"; and as in the earlier he asks, "What is ambition to that [love] but selfish vanity? To be rich, to be famous? What do these profit a year hence [?]" so in the later he declares that such love "is immeasurably above all ambition, more precious than wealth, more noble than name." But to see these parallels is also to see one of the fundamental features of the novel's structure—its division into two almost equal parts, each climaxed by a proposal scene. The first, which runs from the beginning through Book 2, chapter 6, traces the development of Esmond's gratitude and "filial tenderness" from the time he first meets Rachel to the moment of his first proposal to her at Walcote; and the second, which runs from Book 2, chapter 7, to the end, traces the continuance of these emotions, alongside the development of his erotic passion for Beatrix, to the moment of his second proposal to Rachel in Brussels. In each part his feelings for Rachel remain essentially unchanged, and in both parts they are essentially the same. If it is gratitude which gives birth to the "filial tenderness" in the first, it is the persistence of that gratitude which assures the sustenance of the "filial tenderness" in the second.

But, granting that Esmond's love for Rachel, even long after their marriage, has always been primarily filial and not, like hers, erotic, are we entitled to conclude that this is a source of marital dissatisfaction for him—that his marriage, for this reason, has left him unfulfilled? It is true that as a result of the traumatic loss of his mother in infancy, he has always wanted a mother figure. It is also true that of all the mother surrogates he has known Rachel is the most devoted. But, although Esmond's quest has been *generated by* the loss of his mother, it has never been a quest *for* mother-love exclusively. It has been a quest for love in various forms. In boyhood, before he met Rachel, he was moved to devotion by the kindness of Father Holt; later, in young manhood, he responded in a similar way to the kindness of General Webb, and expressed, and sought requital of, sexual desire for Beatrix. His desire for erotic experience is, indeed, crucial. If he needs to be a son, he also needs to be a lover. To be a son alone can never suffice him, for it is essentially an infantile need bred of the emotional deprivations of his childhood and hence cannot be a substitute for mature passion. The pathos of Esmond's fate consists in the fact that both needs cannot be satisfied for him by the same woman. For the former he turns to Rachel; for the latter to Beatrix. He cannot bring both mother and sex-object together in the same person. The fact that Rachel becomes a mother figure for him so early in his life (we remember that he is only twelve when he first meets her) freezes her in that posture for him forever and thus precludes his ever loving her in any other way. Nor, of course, can he love Beatrix (who is eight years younger than himself) filially—though he seems to make a ludicrous attempt to do so (perhaps with wry self-irony) in his famous mock *Spectator* paper by calling her Jocasta and himself Oedipus.

Thus, Esmond's marriage to Rachel must inevitably frustrate him. He has no recourse but to expend his unsatisfied passion futilely on his hopeless memories of Beatrix. Here again, of course, there is a cover-up: in addition to celebrating his marriage in the extravagant terms I have already noted, he emphatically asserts that after Beatrix's betrayal he was filled with disgust and that his love for her completely died. He even affirms that he is "thankful" for his loss of Beatrix because it "hath caused the whole subsequent happiness of his life." But we can no more accept these statements at face value than we could accept those concerning his marriage, for contradictory remarks elsewhere in the text enable us to pierce the facade and see that Esmond's passion for Beatrix has remained a potent residue in his emotional life. In one place he tells us that the memory of her laughter still brings him pleasure: "I fancy I hear it now. Thirty years afterwards I hear that delightful music." . . . Madam Warrington also recalls in her preface how, after Beatrix's marriage to Tusher, Esmond came to her defense when Rachel and her daughter-in-law accused her of having become "old and ugly." Even more striking is his plea that her pride and cruelty—of which, of course, he has been one of the chief victims—be judged leniently, for the reason that in acting as she did she was only obeying the law of her nature. Above all, Esmond affirms the continued vitality of his passion for Beatrix in a remarkable passage at the beginning of Book 3, chapter 6—a passage which belongs with that in Book 1, chapter 11, concerning the disenchantments of marriage, as one of the two most essential glimpses into his buried life which the novel offers.

> Who, in the course of his life, hath not been so bewitched [as he has been by Beatrix], and worshipped some idol or another? Years after this passion hath been dead and buried, along with a thousand other worldly cares and ambitions, he who felt it can recall it out of its grave, and admire, almost as fondly as he did in his youth, that lovely queenly creature. I invoke that beautiful spirit from the shades and love her still; or rather I should say such a past is always present to a man; such a passion once felt forms a part of his whole being, and cannot be separated from it; it becomes a portion of the man to-day, just as any great faith or conviction, the discovery of poetry, the awakening of religion, ever afterward influence him. . . . Parting and forgetting! What faithful heart can do these? Our great thoughts, our great affections, the Truths of our life, never leave us. Surely, they cannot separate from our consciousness; shall follow it whithersoever that shall go; and are of their nature divine and immortal.

As in the earlier passage, what is so compelling here is the vigor, the "poetry," the authentic personal note struck by the language, which stands in such moving contrast to the "officialese" in which Esmond habitually describes Rachel's "goodness" or the "happiness" of his marriage. In such writing as this he transcends the measured prose of the eighteenth-century gentleman to become something close to a nineteenth-century Romantic, and in doing so reveals that, however sincere and however deeply felt it may be, the filial gratitude with which he repays his wife's devotion may coexist with such feelings as he here describes, but never replace them. They belong to incommensurate worlds.

We return, then, to that key passage from chapter 3 of *The Virginians* with which we began. For the sources of the final pathos and irony of Esmond's life—of that "tinge of melancholy" and that "bankruptcy of his heart, which his spirit never recovered"—are now clear. The dominant need of his life, rooted in the emotional deprivations of his childhood, has been to love and be loved. Yet the woman whom he loves with the greatest erotic passion (Beatrix) cannot love him in return and eventually betrays him; while the woman who does love him with erotic passion (Rachel) is the one he can love only filially, and who eventually even jeopardizes that love with the concomitant of her passion and devotion, her morbid jealousy. Thus, although the novel is about Esmond's discovery of vanities, as George J. Worth has said, these discoveries do not end when he has become an Anglican and a Whig, rejected Beatrix, and married Rachel. They go beyond these points to show him the vanity of his marriage itself, and hence of his whole life's quest. (pp. 305-15)

> John Hagan, " 'Bankruptcy of His Heart': The Unfulfilled Life of Henry Esmond," in Nineteenth-Century Fiction, *Vol. 27, No. 3, December, 1972, pp. 293-316.*

BARBARA HARDY   (essay date 1972)

[*Hardy explores two aspects of the love theme in* Henry Esmond, *analyzing how love is influenced by societal corruption and how past experiences of love can be reanimated through the act of memory.*]

Much has already been written about the love-story of *Esmond,* especially its subtleties of dramatic presentation and its possible psychological roots in Thackeray's experience; I will therefore confine myself to one or two aspects of his analysis of love.

The celebrated end of *Esmond,* in which we move violently and abruptly from the death of Esmond's love for Beatrix to his happy marriage with Rachel, is functionally and most eloquently abrupt, and neither clumsy nor evasive. In a way, it is unlike Thackeray's commonly muted happy endings and his refusal to show love as a climactic or conclusive prize. But as in *Vanity Fair,* there is a double ending: we have the end of a fictional construction made by the characters, which is followed by the ending of the whole story, the reader's fiction. In *Vanity Fair* Thackeray showed the end of Dobbin's desire, and in the margin beyond showed how living has to survive certain endings. In *Esmond,* he images the end of Esmond's life-fiction, and in the margin beyond shows how survival may sometimes bring new gains after all. The melancholy loss of Esmond's fiction about Beatrix, about his striking heroic and revolutionary role, about the Pretender, and about England, is succeeded by another story, and one, it is implied, which is less like a 'drama': 'With the sound of King George's trumpets, all the vain hopes of the weak and foolish young Pretender were blown away; and with that music, too, I may say, the drama of my own life was ended.'

If the images for his passions and illusions were 'music' and 'drama,' the new image for the happy-ever-after with Rachel is that of the American Indian summer, and its emphasis is quiet. There are two kinds of quiet here, that of the relationship itself, for which words like 'calmest', 'serene' and 'rest' are used, and that of the narrator's reticence:

> That happiness, which hath subsequently crowned it, cannot be written in words; 'tis of its nature sacred and secret, and not to be spoken of, though the heart be ever so full of thankfulness, save to Heaven and the One Ear alone—to one fond being, the truest and tenderest and purest wife ever man was blessed with.

The joining of 'secret' to 'sacred' makes the conclusion erotic as well as ideal, and its emotional particularization reminds me of Coventry Patmore's erotic joining of sacred and profane love, on which Gerard Manley Hopkins commented, 'That's telling secrets'. The ending is a kind of evasion, no doubt, but

it seems to be also a deliberately quiet way of describing happiness. In *Vanity Fair, Rowena and Rebecca* and *The Newcomes,* Thackeray declines to commit himself to more than a speculative and provisional fantasy of sober content. In *Esmond,* he does want to make high claims, and in the running title makes Esmond call his love 'My crowning happiness'. Esmond claims, 'Sure, love *vincit omnia;* is immeasurably above all ambition, more precious than wealth, more noble than name', and says 'he hath not felt the highest faculty of the soul who hath not enjoyed it'. The reticence suggests privacy and reverence.

In accord with this restraint, and perhaps accounting for it, is the surprising nature of the last 'crowning happiness', which does come unexpectedly upon Esmond, as a second attachment of a different and better kind. The word 'crowning' is not merely a traditional metaphor. In one sentence, quoted above, Thackeray speaks of the sound of King George's trumpets blowing away the vain hopes of the Pretender, and takes up the 'music' which ends the Pretender's hopes, to end also his hopes and 'drama'. In the same way the image of the lost crown surely recurs in the next sentence: '. . . and with that music, too, I may say, the drama of my own life was ended. That happiness, which hath subsequently crowned it. . . .' Both the image of the crown and the image of the conquest (*amor vincit omnia*) are revived and refreshed images in this novel, which is not only about real crowns and conquests, but about the contamination of love by crowns and conquests. When Esmond speaks of the highest faculty of the soul employed in love, when he esteems it above ambition, more precious than wealth, more noble than name, he is not indulging in hyperbole for conclusion and triumph, but consummating the moral action of the novel.

Thackeray joins most subtly many aspects of loving; its obsessions, its pangs, its snatched strong moments, its transports, its moderate contents and its possessiveness. He is a marvellous chronicler of jealousy, and his portrait of Rachel, for instance, is a brilliant and versatile rendering of repression and releases, sometimes rendered in silence, sometimes overcome in noble self-effacing generosity, sometimes insistently betrayed in the tapping of a foot, sometimes bursting out in hostility. Like her jealousy, too, is her passion for Esmond. It is a rational passion, like Dobbin's and Amelia's, in desiring an appropriate object after an inappropriate one, but it often shows itself irrationally, in anger, coldness and hostility. Thackeray's rendering of the *odi* in the *amo* is the more complex for being done implicitly and dramatically. It is sometimes shown without explanation, sometimes accompanied by ambiguous explanations, sometimes then slowly revealed and brought into a light which illuminates past darkness. The loves of Rachel, Beatrix and Esmond are more than studies in passion and jealousy; they are very carefully placed analyses of love in the environment of emulation, ambition, and acquisition. The explicit and radical theme of *Henry Esmond* is implicit but more subdued and subordinated than the social satire in the other novels. It is the theme of the corruptions of love in the corrupt society. Love exists, and is better than 'name', 'wealth' and 'ambition', but it cannot transcend them entirely. Working back from the end, then, we find a love which is not 'above all ambition', not 'more precious than wealth', and not 'more noble than name'. Esmond's ambitions were created by his attempts to win and buy love, through going to war, winning money and name, and making complicated sacrifice of legitimacy and name for love's sake.

The novel begins with Thackeray's insistence on its dehistoricizing aims: 'Why shall History go on kneeling to the end of time? I am for having her rise up off her knees, and take a natural posture. . . . In a word, I would have History familiar rather than heroic. . . .' His way of making history familiar is twofold. He shows historical events and characters in ordinary quotidian life, in so far as this is possible (with military events, for instance, it is less easy than with literature or politics), and he shows the private and personal motivation of historical events. In this respect, he is at first sight doing something bizarre in the history of the Victorian novel, which is on the whole engaged in the rather more modern enterprise of historicizing private events, showing the social and economic basis or background to the personal life, the public shaping of the individual story. But . . . in *Vanity Fair, Pendennis* and *The Newcomes* Thackeray is also doing what Dickens and George Eliot do in *Great Expectations* and *Middlemarch,* in attempting to show the public pressures that shape our personal dramas. But although *Esmond* does dehistoricize the public life, showing the pursuit of war, fame, literary glory and honour as enterprises undertaken for love, there is also, as in the social novels, the analysis of a determining public life. All the persons of the novel are shown as directed by acquisitiveness, ambition, reputation and emulation. Esmond is not set apart from the others; he is initially shown as loving and generous, and then as being contaminated by social ends. Afterwards he finds that the pursuit of title, crown, glory, honour and love end in a betrayal and disillusion: the Pretender cares more for a beautiful woman than for a crown, Beatrix cares more for money and rank than for love or politics, the Duke of Marlborough cares more for fame than honour. His own pursuits of the ideal are also vanities and he returns to the nearest thing to a free and unconditioned love, the devoted, suffering, unworldly constancy of Rachel.

That is only a crude outline of the novel's causality. Thackeray's full achievement is to dramatize the individual psychology of these intricate social and moral relations. In so doing, he shows a man in love with two women, something many of his contemporary readers found startling and even disgusting. (In this connection, it is interesting to see Thackeray himself, though perhaps not very seriously, criticizing Charlotte Brontë in *Villette* for showing a 'good woman' ready to love two men, and objecting that if he had done that Miss Brontë would have been the first to object—a fine example of the double standard in literary criticism.) From the beginning of *Esmond,* we see Esmond's obsessed and plainly sexual passion for Beatrix, which may well ironically show the pursuit of an ideal Beatrice. We also see his more muted, passive, grateful devotion to 'his mistress', Rachel Castlewood, eight years his elder. Thackeray blurs and prepares for the end by ambiguity of words such as 'love', 'devotion', 'dear', 'dearest', 'heart' and 'mistress'. ('Mistress' is a special case of ambiguity, carrying with it the connotation of actual service, remote adoration and amorous relationship.) The vagueness of emotional terminology stands Thackeray in good stead. But the early stages are also presented in ways which relate to Thackeray's feeling for Jane Brookfield, especially to his sense that she was a suffering and patient wife of an unworthy husband, a view coming more naturally than reliably from the unsatisfied lover. Thackeray also presents the ease and comfort of the moderate happiness, with no transports, but the undemanding pleasures of company and affinity. . . . Throughout the novel Thackeray shows Rachel's reticence, guilt and jealousy; and also Esmond's devotion, gratitude and contented companionship.

The interweaving of the two loves is presented from the very beginning, in the Preface to the 'memoirs' purporting to be written by the 'editor', his daughter Rachel. She is made to emphasize three aspects of feeling: the passionate and exclusive devotion of 'her mother' (unnamed) for Esmond; his affection for his wife, suggested with effective vagueness; and his feeling that Beatrix was peerless, flashing out in her defence, even though dishonoured. The sentence is loaded with the weight of an old attachment, fidelity to the past. The weight is heavily impressed on us in a reply to a jealous comment:

> . . . After visiting her, my poor mamma said she had lost all her good looks, and warned me not to set too much store by any such gifts which nature bestowed upon me. She grew exceedingly stout; and I remember my brother's wife, Lady Castlewood, saying 'No wonder she became a favourite, for the King likes them old and ugly, as his father did before him.' On which papa said—'All women were alike; that there was never one so beautiful as that one; and that we could forgive her everything but her beauty.' And hereupon my mamma looked vexed. . . .

The retrospects of Henry Esmond, like those of David Copperfield, form the medium of the narrative, shifting from foreground to background, past to present. From time to time we are reminded of the retrospect by the shifts from third person to first, from 'Henry Esmond' to 'Colonel Esmond' to 'the writer of this memoir' to 'I'. The 'I' is often used eloquently to mark moments of great depth of feeling, though it is by no means used for all those moments. The memorial reconstructions of *Esmond* differ from those of *David Copperfield* or *Jane Eyre* in having a much more pointed psychological purpose. Charlotte Brontë makes Jane revise her innocence in the light of her experience, softening criticism, summing up effort, marking the permanent damage, and so forth. Dickens makes David look with a special comic and pathetic nostalgia at innocence, seeing the sharp irony of a future-haunted past in retrospect, or of the strangeness and silliness of what at the time seemed profound or rational. Both novelists use memory constantly, but have surprisingly little to say about its nature. It is memory's content, not its form, that engages them as they remember and observe how different the past looks as we look back at it, through time, over time, in time. For Thackeray, the experience of remembering is much more analysed and analytic, much closer to Wordsworth's imaginative time-travelling in *The Prelude* through those 'spots of time' which are saturated with the values of deeply felt experience, and so saturated that memory revives and does not weaken them. Thackeray's sense of emotional memory is not involuntary as it is in Proust, and at times in George Eliot, nor is it part of a moral series of related visions, as in Wordsworth. It is perhaps closest of all to Thomas Hardy, for whom also memory is a means of loving, and at times, apparently, a means more reliable than others. *Esmond* is like some of Hardy's best love-lyrics, such as "Joys of Memory", "Before Knowledge" or "During Wind and Rain", in its appreciation and revival of the past passion in a present passion. Thackeray and Hardy both seem most lucid, steady and passionate when the loving is a looking back, a harking back, itself a retrospect, a loving memory. *Esmond* is actually a memorial act of love, secretly addressed to Jane Brookfield in lingering retrospect after the experience is finished, an affectionate fantasy of unacted possibilities. His insistence on love-in-memory may also derive point from the sharp contrast between past and present in the two strongest emotional ties that we know about, the tie to the memory of his young wife, after they were separated by her schizophrenia, as well as the tie to Jane Brookfield, after they 'separated'. But strong as the autobiographical roots must be, the retrospects are also consistent with the presentation of moderate content at the end of *Vanity Fair, Rowena and Rebecca* and *The Newcomes,* providing yet another way of showing the limits of love honestly and toughly, without cynicism or devaluation.

Esmond's story is about idolatry and vanity, about his love for one of the most attractive and most corrupt of Thackeray's heroines. Beatrix is corrupt: ambitious for money and rank, often *ennuyée*, self-disgusted, perhaps self-destructive, having a short-lived period of active virtue. In Rachel's Preface we have the first brief but strong flash of Esmond's passion (in the part already quoted) when he says 'there was never one so beautiful'. The retrospect is not an idealized selection by any means, its chronicles including recollections of thwarted desires, painful obsession, 'nights of rage . . . days of torment . . . passionate unfulfilled desire . . . sickening jealousy. . . .' Nevertheless, the key sentences draw our attention to the passionate act of memory, making it clear that the novel is about a man who may have found a faithful love, that '*amor vincit omnia*', but also that the man discovers in the act of writing his complex fidelity to the past. Beatrix is a much-criticized character, and so is Esmond as Don Quixote and 'The Faithful Fool'. But the memoir writer, knowing very well that in writing we discover thoughts we did not know we had, writes, remembers, and is restored to the past, which is not destroyed by the satirist or the comedian. It is the opposite of the memorial action in *Jane Eyre* and *David Copperfield*, for Thackeray shows his character penetrating the past experience with a reanimated passion. He does more, he insists that we are everything which we have been; it is not remarkable that our dead loves can rise up easily, never having died:

> How well all things were remembered! The ancient towers and gables of the Hall darkling against the east, the purple shadows on the green slopes, the quaint devices and carvings of the dial . . . all these were before us, along with a thousand memories of our youth, beautiful and sad, but as real and vivid in our minds as that fair and always-remembered scene our eyes behold once more. We forget nothing. The memory sleeps, but wakens again. . . .

and again:

> Years after this passion hath been dead and buried, along with a thousand other worldly cares and ambitions, he who felt it can recall it out of its grave, and admire, almost as fondly as he did in his youth, that lovely queenly creature. I invoke that beautiful spirit from the shades and love her still; or rather I should say that such a past is always present to a man; such a passion once felt forms a part of his whole being, and cannot be separated from it. . . .

He compares the imprint of passion to the influence of faith, poetry, religion, becoming a part of us even if we get over it. His image for what has marked us, healed, and still remained, is the scar he got at Blenheim. It is this constant insistence on the revival of passion that makes *Esmond* more than an act of memory. Like no other Victorian novel it is an act of invocation. We have to wait for Proust to get such another, though *La recherche du temps perdu* is more the finding of an aesthetic unity in life and art, than a celebration of love. *Esmond* is an invocation and an act of love.

The beginning and the end of the novel make heroic claims; one for the virtuous and distinguished Esmond, the other for the great and noble love of Rachel and Esmond. But in the centre, there is the story of a limited, unheroic and quotidian

love. In being unheroic, it is very like the unheroic stories of the 'two great men of the age', as Esmond calls them, Marlborough and Swift, corrupted, as Thackeray's rudely familiar History Muse insists, by ambition, ruthlessness, dishonesty and emulation. Esmond is like them, pursuing his vanity of love (as he admits to Lord Bolingbroke when they debate their preferences in vanity) with the other vanities of the age, military, literary and political. He tries to be a soldier, a wit and a Jacobite revolutionary, in order to do the most corrupt thing of all, to trade with love, barter for it, and buy it. The love is determined by its conditions, becomes two-faced or two-hearted, corrupt, private. The memoir itself is a most intimate record, happily and ironically misunderstood by its editor, who knows enough about her mother's passion for her father to call it 'so passionate and exclusive as to prevent her, I think, from loving any other person except with an inferior regard; her whole thoughts being centered on this one object of affection and worship'. The novel makes plain that this was not the case with Esmond. Esmond tell us that when he found Beatrix's intrigue with the Pretender his love fell down dead on the spot:

> But her keen words gave no wound to Mr Esmond; his heart was too hard. As he looked at her, he wondered that he could ever have loved her. His love of ten years was over; it fell down dead on the spot, at the Kensington Tavern, where Frank brought him the note out of Eikon Basilike. The Prince blushed and bowed low, as she gazed at him, and quitted the chamber. I have never seen her from that day.

The whole novel makes it plain that this is not so, that loves do not die, that the past is still alive.

What the novel achieves as fiction looks confused but is, I suggest, a consistent if complicated proof of what Thackeray so shrewdly sees as the discovery of experience in art: he speaks of finding our thoughts in writing them, and in the novel he finds passions too. He discovers something of their nature and their conditions; war, politics, religion, love, so the parallelisms of event, character and image argue, are similarly determined, and influence and pervert each other. Thackeray involves his hero in all the vanities of competition, acquisition and emulation, and all for love. That love was pain more than pleasure, resulting in what the ironic, but not wholly ironic, narrator calls a 'Diary of drivel', and of 'agonies'. In retrospect, the experience is crowned with the special glory of affectionate memory, still loved on this side—the right side—of idolatry. With irony, rapturous outburst, calm imagery, Thackeray writes his love-story. Its happinesses are either hidden, veiled like the sacred secret love for Rachel, or shown as most stable and joyful when revived in the appreciative acts of memory. The love suggests—though only in fits and starts—the possibility of triumph over Vanity Fair. It offers freedom and the conquest of time, but is still fleshed by vanity, its converse and action shaped by conquest, competition, honour, rank, money. The carefully eighteenth-century title, *The History of Henry Esmond, Esq., a Colonel in the Service of Her Majesty Queen Anne,* looks up first sight like a modest withdrawal from Vanity Fair, setting up the noble Esmond with a mere 'Esq.' and the name of Colonel. But the novel shows his sacrifice of title, rank and name as one of the subtlest perversions of honour and love. *Esmond* makes just as radical an act of social criticism as the other novels, but it does so from the inside, showing more passionately, and analytically, the difficulty of love in the great world. It is a great psychological and a great social novel, the greatness consisting in the unity of the public and the private worlds. (pp. 178-88)

Barbara Hardy, "Love," in her The Exposure of
Luxury: Radical Themes in Thackeray, *Peter Owen
Limited, London, 1972, pp. 161-88.*

A. O. J. COCKSHUT   (essay date 1977)

[*Cockshut interprets the ending of* Henry Esmond *as above all
realistic.*]

The first thing to notice about this extraordinary story [*Henry
Esmond*] is that it created a quite unusual flurry of disagreement
among contemporaries. The *Spectator* said:

> The relation between Esmond and Rachel Viscoun-
> tess Castlewood is of that sort that nothing short of
> consummate skill could have saved it from becoming
> ridiculous or offensive, or both. In Mr Thackeray's
> hands, the difficulty has become a triumph, and has
> given rise to beauties which a safer ambition would
> have not dared to attempt . . . [see excerpt by George
> Brimley dated 1852].

John Forster said simply: 'The thing is incredible, and there
an end on 't'. George Eliot called it the most 'uncomfortable
book you can imagine' [see excerpt dated 1852].

Here we have in germ the three conflicting views which have
persisted and developed ever since, that it is strange and surprising but beautiful and convincing, that it is impossible, and
that it is probable enough but aesthetically displeasing. This
will be enough to prevent more thoughtful critics from leaping
in with routine denunciations of the early Victorians for their
misfortune in not having read Freud. These can, in any case,
be answered on their own level, by pointing out that they *had*
read, more often than most of their successors today, the *Oedipus Rex* of Sophocles.

Esmond's feeling that Lady Castlewood is his second mother
is entirely credible and convincing. Esmond has been led to
believe (wrongly) that he is illegitimate; his mother died deserted by her husband when he was very young. With a tactful
restraint that he does not always show, Thackeray keeps this
tender spring of filial feeling for the dead in reserve until his
story is more than half told. Then as Esmond, already a man,
sees her grave in Flanders for the first time, he conveys the
hidden purity of feeling in one of the most eloquent passages
he ever wrote:

> A bird came down from a roof opposite, and lit first
> on a cross, and then on the grass below it, whence
> it flew away presently with a leaf in its mouth: then
> came a sound as of chanting, from the chapel of the
> sisters hard by; others had long since filled the place
> which poor Mary Magdalene once had there, were
> kneeling at the same stall and hearing the same hymns
> and prayers in which her stricken heart had found
> consolation. Might she sleep in peace; and we, too,
> when our struggles and pains are over! But the earth
> is the Lord's as the heaven is; we are alike his crea-
> tures here and yonder. I took a little flower off the
> hillock and kissed it, and went my way, like the bird
> that had just lighted on the cross by me, back into
> the world again. Silent receptacle of death; tranquil
> depth of calm, out of reach of tempest and trouble!
> I felt as one who had been walking below the sea
> and treading amidst the bones of shipwrecks.'

The long-delayed eloquence of this helps to convince us that
Esmond's feeling for Lady Castlewood will be ambivalent from
the first. When he says to Lord Mohun, in answer to the
taunting suggestion that he is in love with her, 'I never had a

mother but I love this lady as one' he partly means it. But not
wholly, because the hidden feeling for the real dead mother is
potentially so very powerful. It is natural that a lonely boy,
with no fixed home or position in the world, should respond
gratefully to feminine kindness. As she is older, and the kindness begins when he is very young, it is natural that his feeling
for her should be vaguely filial. She, who is in love with him
long before he knows it, has equally natural reasons for dressing
her passion in maternal guise. She is married, she is too old
for him, and before long she sees him infatuated with her
daughter.

The daughter, for all the elaborate rhetoric that is poured out
in her honour, is nothing more nor less than a sexy piece.
Esmond is a sober, serious young man, who might be expected
to delight in domesticity. Why does he remain so long at her
mercy? Once again, as so often, Thackeray's psychology is
suggestive and interesting rather than clear. Are we to think
that Esmond set his heart on a girl he was sensible enough
inwardly to despise, and one he had no hope of winning,
because he was unconsciously saving himself for her mother,
when she should finally become free? As the rightful heir to
the title, supposed to be illegitimate, and willingly surrendering
his honours to his young cousin, he might well think it imprudent to marry at all.

This seems a promising line of thought. But Thackeray does
not really endorse it. Indeed, by making Beatrix captivate the
Duke of Hamilton, presented as a sober man of middle age,
he seems rather to be overstressing to an almost absurd degree
the power of the sexy piece over sensible men. By doing so,
he removes the need for any subtle explanations for Esmond's
long slavery. He almost seems to say that no one could have
resisted her.

So we have a respectable hero who is a kind of double Oedipus,
since he not only marries the woman he has treated as his
mother, but transfers his love to her from her own daughter.
It is tempting and plausible to say that this was less shocking
to the book's first readers than to their successors because they
chose so largely to ignore the element of sexual satisfaction in
virtuous and happy marriage.

In their general celebration of the chaste, dutiful, affectionate
woman, the uniqueness of relationships became blurred. Mother,
wife, sister all appeared to have nearly the same function. Of
the many examples that could be quoted in support of this, the
ending of *Bleak House* is one almost exactly contemporary
with *Esmond*. Here a prospective bridegroom steps down almost at the altar steps to offer the bride to young Prince Charming, and to revert himself to the role of affectionate and confidential uncle.

Before we give too much weight to this, we must remind
ourselves that some contemporaries, like Forster, called the
ending of *Esmond* incredible. Moreover, we may well say that
in judging thus, he incautiously ignored the great skill with
which the catastrophe is prepared. The Lady Castlewoods of
this world are adept at concealing their true feelings most of
the time, and hers do break out plainly enough at times. As
for Esmond, would he not surrender eventually, out of gratitude, out of weariness, out of a gentlemanly disinclination to
give pain, out of fellow-feeling for unrequited love from which
he, too, has suffered so long through Beatrix's coquetry?

Are we then to agree with those who found it touching and
beautiful? Are we to take Esmond's paean of praise [to] his

mother-wife at the book's end as Thackeray's verdict and our own?

This will not do, because it is not really Thackeray's verdict. Lady Castlewood shows a jealousy of her daughter's power over Esmond that might well be called vicious. She even goes to the length of taunting her with her failure to capture the Duke in marriage before a violent death overtook him. She is repeatedly shown as conquering her jealousy only with a terrible effort. Nor is it true, as may be incautiously assumed, that Esmond himself can see no fault in her:

> 'Do you leave this too, Beatrix?' says her mother, taking the miniature [of her recently dead betrothed] out, and with a cruelty she did not very often show; but there are some moments when the tenderest women are cruel, and some triumphs which angels can't forgo. [In the text of **Henry Esmond,** an asterisk here refers the reader to a fictional footnote written by the daughter of Esmond and Rachel Castlewood: "This remark shows how unjustly and contemptuously even the best of men will sometimes judge of our sex. Lady Castlewood had no intention of triumphing over her daughter; but from a sense of duty alone pointed out her deplorable wrong."] . . . If my mistress was cruel, at least she never could be got to own as much. Her haughtiness quite overtopped Beatrix's; and, if the girl had a proud spirit, I very much fear it came to her by inheritance.

We have here mother and daughter fighting for a man's love, and the mother dead to all shame about the weapons she will use in the struggle. And we have the man over whom they are fighting aware of this. What then are we to make of the daughter's soothing note and of Esmond's own final judgement: 'To have such a love is the one blessing, in comparison of which all earthly joy is of no value; and to think of her is to praise God'?

What Thackeray seems to be doing here, with all his usual artfulness and indirection, is drawing attention to something we all know: that it is impossible to judge one's nearest and dearest. By making the daughter exonerate her mother, and the husband (momentarily) blame her and then praise her to the skies, he opens for the reader other possibilities. He makes us wonder, if the daughter could be so blind to her mother's clearly-revealed passions, perhaps the husband's moment of insight was a brief flash. Perhaps the picture of Lady Castlewood as cruel, designing and jealous was the true one after all? Does that mean we are to dismiss Esmond's final tribute of unlimited praise and adoration as part of the author's irony? The text will hardly support that, and it would in any case be uncharacteristic. Thackeray does not push his irony, or his satire, or his scepticism or his reforming zeal to the limit. One man who did so was Jonathan Swift; and Thackeray wrote in fiercer condemnation of him than of any other. No; Thackeray was a realist. A sensible man always tries to be more keenly aware of his wife's virtues than of her faults. Esmond was a sensible man. If his wife was not perfect, she really loved him; and she had been very patient and long-suffering. And she was infinitely preferable to her daughter.

There will never be universal agreement about the ending of **Esmond**. If everyone must stand up and be counted, I would say, first, that Thackeray convinces me completely that the marriage would really have occurred. I agree that the mingling of maternal, filial and sexual feelings is unpleasant, but it is the unpleasantness of truth. Thackeray's triumph here, and what makes the novel, for all its tedious 'period' trappings,

still of high interest, is that he showed how the normal and the abnormal, duty and egoism, truth and delusion meet and mingle. He refuses to show them rigidly separated as the world likes to think they are; but he also refused to show them almost indistinguishable, with respectability only a mask for appetite, as the cynical railers at the world like to think they are. The happy ending is of the mixed, flawed kind that the world really offers to some; and they are sensible if they give thanks, remembering how easily it could have been an unhappy ending.

Most important of all, he shows the adaptability, or what might be called the *hospitality,* of conventional marriage. It can absorb dangerous passions, Esmond's exhausted lust for Beatrix, Lady Castlewood's fierce jealousy and possessiveness. It is a very strange case, but what case is entirely ordinary? There is a kind of cautious boldness in Thackeray, or even a brave timidity. He shows us these disturbing things, which are also enlarging and heartening things, about Victorian marriage. But he is careful to pretend that he is only speaking about the reign of Queen Anne. (pp. 81-6)

> *A. O. J. Cockshut, "The Realists," in his* Man and Woman: A Study of Love and the Novel, 1740-1940, *1977. Reprint by Oxford University Press, 1978, pp. 72-99.*

H. M. DALESKI   (essay date 1985)

[*Daleski traces Esmond's process of maturation and discusses the quality of his love for the two women in his life.*]

The History of Henry Esmond, Esq., "A Colonel in the Service of Her Majesty Q. Anne," as the imitation eighteenth-century title page informs us, is "Written by Himself," but the novelist's narrative method ensures that Esmond's tale is subject to a number of refractions. For a start, it does not even begin with itself but with a preface by Esmond's daughter, Rachel Esmond Warrington, written some sixty years after the point at which her father chooses to end his story. Her introductory description of her father is fulsome in the extreme, strenuously evoking his nobility in a blast of superlatives and a refusal of all qualification. . . . This clearly is the suspect tone of hero-worship, if not of fixation; and Rachel Esmond Warrington's preface in effect invites us to register a discrepancy between her view of her father and that which will emerge in his own narrative, for we assume that the actual story of any man will not be amenable to such wholly uncritical adulation. Her preface, that is to say, at once establishes an ironic frame for what follows.

Nor is hers the only preface. Though not formally labeled as such, the narrator's introductory remarks (which precede chapter I of book I of his story) constitute a preface to the whole history which follows, and not inappropriately deal with the role of the historian:

> I have seen in his very old age and decrepitude the old French King Lewis the Fourteenth, the type and model of king-hood—who never moved but to measure, who lived and died according to the laws of his Court-marshal, persisting in enacting through life the part of Hero; and, divested of poetry, this was but a little wrinkled old man, pock-marked, and with a great periwig and red heels to make him look tall— a hero for a book if you like . . . but what more than a man for Madame Maintenon, or the barber who shaved him, or Monsieur Fagon, his surgeon? I wonder shall History ever pull off her periwig and cease to be court-ridden? . . . [Queen Anne] was neither

better bred nor wiser than you and me, though we knelt to hand her a letter or a washhand-basin. Why shall History go on kneeling to the end of time? I am for having her rise up off her knees, and take a natural posture.

The traditional historian, it appears, has much in common with Rachel Esmond Warrington, being "court-ridden" where she is father-struck, and kneeling obsequiously before a great personage in a manner that suggests her position in respect of her father. Esmond himself, however, wants the historian to get off his knees and "take a natural posture," to pull off the king's periwig and show the man beneath. And since Esmond, as his title insists, is himself writing a history, he is to be seen as dedicating himself to the attempt to show things as they are, having "taken truth for his motto." The juxtaposition of the two prefaces, with Esmond's coming after that of his daughter, collapses a possible distinction between a "history" of public personages and that of private lives; and in this historical novel we are invited to see *all* bald heads for what they are.

The prefatorial apparatus, therefore, is complex, suggesting that we will have to try to save Esmond's story not only from his daughter but also from himself, for an ironic frame is no respecter of persons and an intention is no guarantee of performance. Nor is it anyway clear who exactly "Esmond himself" is, as another narrative device indicates: Esmond tells his own story, but he habitually refers to himself in the third person; it is only in the titles of chapters and on comparatively few occasions in the text that he uses the first person. The use of the third person in this respect is in the tradition of eighteenth-century memoir writing; and may be regarded simply as part and parcel of Thackeray's magisterial attempt to produce a historical novel that should itself be the thing it is intended to evoke.... But the use of both the first and third persons to refer to Esmond also points to an important feature of the narrative.

In the text, as distinct from the chapter titles, the first person is used in two sharply different ways. On some rare occasions it is used to suggest a special stress that Esmond is subject to, as when he visits his mother's grave: "I felt as one who had been walking below the sea, and treading amidst the bones of shipwrecks." For the rest, the first person is used to refer to the older narrator as distinct from his younger self—though, when used in this manner, it sometimes slides slipperily between the two selves. "At this time," we are told, "Harry Esmond was a lad of sixteen" and strongly drawn to Nancy Sievewright's "bonny face": "'Tis surprising the magnetic attraction which draws people together from ever so far. I blush as I think of poor Nancy now . . . and that I . . . made speeches in my heart, which I seldom had courage to say . . . Poor Nancy! . . . I remember thy kind voice as if I had heard it yesterday." What the play of pronouns does, however, for all the slippage, is effectively to signal, in the difference between "he" and "I," one between Esmond's "experiencing self" and his "narrating self." Such a distinction is operative in all retrospective first-person narrative, but it is specially important in this novel because it is a further means of refracting Esmond's story. The experiencing self is presented to us in all the blindness and obtuseness of the moment; and sometimes the narrating self is at pains to point this out to us: "'Tis not to be imagined that Harry Esmond had all this experience at this early stage of his life, whereof he is now writing the history—many things here noted were but known to him in later days. Almost everything Beatrix did or undid seemed good, or at least pardonable, to him then, and years after-

wards." Even when the narrating self chooses (in an important instance) to keep silent, another piece of apparatus alerts us to what the experiencing self does not know. The history comes equipped too with sporadic footnotes, most of them supplied by the putative editor (the novelist), but some initialed by members of Esmond's family. Two such notes are initialed "R."—who can only be Rachel, Lady Castlewood—and they are inserted at that point in the narrative when Esmond is passionately declaring his love for Beatrix Esmond, her daughter. The mere presence of these footnotes, quite apart from their insignificant content, is indicative of the fact that Rachel is in a position to provide them—and so implies the outcome of Esmond's strange entanglement with mother and daughter. By such means, therefore, we become accustomed to forming our own judgments of the life of the experiencing self even when—or precisely when—the narrating self remains silent. For a feature of this narrative, which is so elaborately framed for ironic undercutting, is the silence of the narrator about some of the most crucial matters of his history. It becomes clear that he would prefer to keep quiet about certain things.

Esmond's silences are most marked in respect of his relations with Rachel and Beatrix, and his omissions or evasions in this regard leave a gap at the very center of his self-portrait, for the two women matter more than anything else to him. The very idea of the triangle that is constituted by his relations with them is so original, and its presentation so complex (encompassing one of the subtlest portrayals of a woman in English fiction), that perhaps we should not expect a smooth narrative surface. But the necessary critical response to the portrait the narrator gives us of himself, I believe, should not be an attempt to deconstruct it, but rather to fill in the gap. Only when Esmond's emotional life has been carefully pieced together, can we try to get at the heart of its mystery. That, indeed, is what we are tacitly invited to do: "So much and suddenly had grief, anger, and misfortune appeared to change [Rachel]. But fortune, good or ill, as I take it, does not change men and women. It but develops their characters. As there are a thousand thoughts lying within a man that he does not know till he takes up the pen to write, so the heart is a secret even to him (or her) who has it in his own breast." The last comparison is instructive. In life, it is intimated, we know nothing of our inmost selves. It is only in the act of writing that the secret heart is revealed to the man who writes. But it does not follow that he will disclose its secrets to others—directly, at any rate— or fully accept them himself. *The History of Henry Esmond* is at once the record, in respect of what is central to his life, of the narrator's discoveries and camouflages. Where his relations with Rachel and Beatrix are concerned, we have to refuse both to take him at his word and to let him escape into his silences.

A way of approaching Esmond's story is suggested by his insistence, in the passage in which he talks about the secret heart, that the characters of men and women do not so much change as develop. This view reflects that which he gives great prominence to in the Latin epigraph on his title page: "Servetur ad imum / Qualis ab incepto processerit, et sibi constet." The full quotation from Horace is: "[If you bring a new concept to the stage and boldly form a new character], let his development be subordinated to his initial personality, and remain self-consistent." It is as an English form of the *Bildungsroman* that *Henry Esmond* should first and foremost be read; and it is the nature of the protagonist's "initial personality"—a crucial feature of the form—that not only is the basis of his development but provides a clue to its mysteries. (pp. 151-55)

The opening discriminated occasion in a *Bildungsroman* is always important, for it sets the scene for what is to follow with more careful particularity than in an ordinary novel. In *Great Expectations,* that prototypical English *Bildungsroman,* for instance, the major lines of Pip's developing life lead straight from the opening scene in the churchyard. In ***Henry Esmond*** the beginning of the narrative is not only significant in much the same way but is given special emphasis by being displaced chronologically: it is the beginning of the *sjuzet* but not of the *fabula,* and after chapter I there is a lengthy flashback of some fifty pages (chapters 2-6) before the chronological order is resumed and then maintained throughout. Looking back on his life, the narrator clearly chooses to start his history at the point which constitutes its effective beginning for him, though he is twelve years old when the new Viscount and his family come to take possession of their house at Castlewood in 1691:

> The new and fair lady of Castlewood found the sad lonely little occupant of this gallery busy over his great book, which he laid down when he was aware that a stranger was at hand. And, knowing who that person must be, the lad stood up and bowed before her, performing a shy obeisance to the mistress of his house.
>
> She stretched out her hand—indeed when was it that that hand would not stretch out to do an act of kindness, or to protect grief and ill-fortune? "And this is our kinsman," she said; "and what is your name, kinsman?"
>
> "My name is Henry Esmond," said the lad, looking up at her in a sort of delight and wonder, for she had come upon him as a *Dea certè,* and appeared the most charming object he had ever looked on. Her golden hair was shining in the gold of the sun; her complexion was of a dazzling bloom; her lips smiling, and her eyes beaming with a kindness which made Harry Esmond's heart to beat with surprise.
>
> "His name is Henry Esmond, sure enough, my lady," says Mrs. Worksop the housekeeper . . . and the old gentlewoman looked significantly towards the late lord's picture.

All the needs that shape Esmond's life are encapsulated in this scene. Rachel's coming upon him "as a *Dea certè*" becomes for him a controlling image for many years, an image that springs from a complex combination of his own emotions and her appearance and attitude. To her the boy no doubt seems only sad and lonely, but he is in the grip of ravening anxiety; an orphan, he has just previously been feeling "quite alone in the world," and has awaited the arrival of the new occupants of the house with "terror and anxiety," wondering how they will "deal with him," and knowing that those to whom he has "formerly looked for protection" are "forgotten or dead." In his overwhelming insecurity, Esmond's most immediate need is for a protector; and when Rachel stretches out her hand to him, her eyes "beaming with . . . kindness," it is as such that she appears to him. (pp. 155-56)

Rachel's appearance when Esmond first sees her is supportive of the image he projects of her. With "her golden hair . . . shining in the gold of the sun," her complexion "a dazzling bloom," her "lips smiling," and her "eyes beaming," she comes into Esmond's life as an effulgence of light, an illumination, and the effect on him is as of an epiphany, for he sees her as a goddess certainly. The image is long-lived, and it has a compulsive force. . . . Worship is no doubt an appropriate response to a protective goddess, and its posture is one

that he either literally or figuratively continues to take in relation to Rachel for many years to come. But the posture is also that adopted by the historians Esmond reviles in his preface; and in life, no less than in history, a man needs to get off his knees and see people and things as they are. That Esmond—to the end—is not doing so in respect of Rachel is suggested in this opening scene by his parenthetic comment on the way she stretches out her hand to the boy, for it is the narrating self that speaks retrospectively here: "indeed when was it that that hand would not stretch out to do an act of kindness, or to protect grief and ill-fortune?" Esmond seems to have forgotten what he will later record so vividly, how in *his* grief and ill-fortune (as he lies wounded and in prison after the duel in which Lord Castlewood is killed) she proceeds to wound him again, cruelly and unjustly, with a wound that, he says, leaves its mark forever. Or is it, we wonder, that he is repressing the knowledge he has of her, seeking by means of such adulatory comments—from the start of his narrative and throughout—to make up to her, in his history if not in life, for what he knows the woman who becomes his wife has never had of him?

Nor is this all that the marvelously packed opening scene conveys. For in the *Aeneid* "*Dea certè*" registers Aeneas's response not only to a goddess but to his mother, Venus; and Rachel comes into Esmond's life in the figure of a mother as well as a goddess, even though she is only twenty. He cannot even remember his own mother, and Rachel clearly supplies a lack that has not hitherto been provided for. But the lack is not so much, as we might expect, a lack of love, the cross of all orphans, as a lack of someone to love. Esmond's suffering stems not from a desiccated heart but a full soul, as we are made to realize at a strategic moment—at the end of the long flashback that brings his story up to the night preceding the arrival of the new family at Castlewood: "The soul of the boy was full of love, and he longed as he lay in the darkness there for some one upon whom he could bestow it. He remembers, and must to his dying day, the thoughts and tears of that long night, the hours tolling through it." It is at this point in the narrative that Esmond asks the questions "Who was he and what?"—and one of the answers immediately suggested is that he is a person who must love somebody. As well as a full soul, he is said to have "a fond and affectionate heart, tender to weakness, that would fain attach itself to somebody"; and his feeling for Rachel speedily becomes "a devoted affection and passion of gratitude which entirely [fills] his young heart." The gratitude of "the orphan lad whom she [protects]" issues in a vow that "no power should separate him from his mistress," and he longs for a chance to "show his fidelity to her." That this boyhood vow of fidelity provides an important clue to the nature of Esmond's whole relationship with Rachel is suggested by his mature view of it: "Now, at the close of his life, as he sits and recalls in tranquillity the happy and busy scenes of it, he can think, not ungratefully, that he has been faithful to that early vow."

When Esmond is sixteen, having suddenly "grown from a boy to be a man," Rachel is led unwittingly to betray a change in her feeling toward him. He has been with Nancy Sievewright, holding her little brother on his lap, and when it is announced that the boy has the small-pox, Esmond tries to prevent Beatrix from coming to him, saying in French to Rachel, "Madam, the child must not approach me; I must tell you that I was at the blacksmith's to-day, and had his little boy upon my lap." Rachel's uncontrollable outbursts are a feature of her characterization, and the one that follows this admission of Esmond's is subtly evocative of her situation:

For once her mother took little heed of [Beatrix's] sobbing, and continued to speak eagerly—"My lord," she said, "this young man—your dependant—told me just now in French—he was ashamed to speak in his own language—that he had been at the alehouse all day, where he has had that little wretch who is now ill of the small-pox on his knee. And he comes home reeking from that place—yes, reeking from it— and takes my boy into his lap without shame, and sits down by me, yes, by *me*. He may have killed Frank for what I know—killed our child. Why was he brought in to disgrace our house? Why is he here? Let him go—let him go, I say, to-night, and pollute the place no more."

Rachel's staccato ejaculations indicate how her words are jerked out of her, as if against her will, and what they reveal to the reader—and to herself [though to no one who hears her] is the extent of her erotic feeling for Esmond. It is in a passion of sexual jealousy of Nancy Sievewright that she turns on Esmond, her willful misrepresentation of his speaking in French showing how she needs first of all to wound him for his association with the blacksmith's daughter. . . . The disowning, of course, is also a disowning of her illicit feeling, the protector now being concerned to protect herself. Her husband prevents the boy's expulsion, and Rachel is reconciled to him; but she insists that "at [his] age, and with [his] tastes, it is impossible that [he] can continue to stay upon the intimate footing" in which he has been in the family. When she comes into a legacy, she arranges for Esmond "to go to college," so that he can "make a name to [himself]." That this is not her only concern, however, is indicated in a neat tableau: "'By G——d, Rachel, you're a good woman!' says my lord, seizing my lady's hand, at which she blushed very much, and shrank back, putting her children before her." It is not from her husband's touch that she shrinks but from his praise, her blush revealing her own sense of how much she has compromised herself, if only in her own feelings and thoughts. But she is determined to put her marriage—as well as her children—before herself, and Esmond's being sent to the university is not only for his own good.

Though the narrator continues to hint at Rachel's hidden feeling for Esmond—we are told, for instance, that thereafter she "scarce ever [sees] him" without the company of her children—he (as experiencing self) remains quite unaware of it. It is not until he is twenty-two and becomes involved in Lord Mohun's pursuit of her that he seems to have a first glimmering of a possible complication of their relationship. The recognition is a concomitant of a newly demonstrated maturity on his part. When Frank Castlewood becomes suspicious of Mohun's attentions to his wife and it seems as if the outcome will be a duel between them, it is the young Esmond who, with as much aplomb as unwonted self-assertion, succeeds in stepping between them and smoothing over the quarrel. The change in Esmond is notable, and one measure of it is that, no longer in need of protection, he has himself become a protector—as Rachel, who has overheard the dispute, seems tacitly to grant: "Thank you, and God bless you, my dear brother Harry," she says. (pp. 156-59)

When Rachel visits Esmond in prison, however, she recoils from him: "Take back your hand—do not touch me with it!" she cries out. "Look! there's blood on it!" This sets the tone for the outburst that follows, and her wild denunciation of him now recalls her earlier fury over Nancy Sievewright. Once again she expresses physical revulsion from him, though this time because he reeks not of the alehouse but of the blood of her husband. Again she pours out unjust accusations on Esmond: we know that he has tried to forestall Castlewood by taking the quarrel with Mohun on himself, but she says, "Why did you stand by at midnight and see him murdered?" and she repeats this: "My husband lies in his blood—murdered for defending me, my kind, kind, generous lord—and you were by, and you let him die, Henry!" In effect she accuses Esmond of betraying her husband, and furthermore declares that he has brought the family only "grief and sorrow," has merely "pretended to love" them, and would have done better to have died when he "had the small-pox." Rachel, however, betrays that it is her own corrosive guilt she is projecting onto Esmond when she extravagantly praises Castlewood, from whom she had long been estranged, says she has lost "the husband of [her] youth" through Esmond, that young as he was she "knew there was evil" in keeping him, and that all that has happened is "a just judgment" on her "wicked jealous heart." (pp. 160-61)

Rachel's disowning of Esmond may be regarded as the crisis of his life—it is a "critical" malady that he suffers—and constitutes the most decisive test he ever has to face. "Ah! no man knows his strength or his weakness," says the narrator, in a statement that anticipates an essential concern of Joseph Conrad's, "till occasion proves them"; and in his response to the disowning Esmond really discovers what he is. It is a discovery that is more important than the earlier revelation of who he is in Castlewood's confession. The test (as in Conrad) first of all exposes his weakness, the "soft spot" that is in all of us. When he is "left . . . alone and friendless," it is as if all the intervening years are cancelled at a stroke and he is returned to the helpless dependence of his childhood. The "temptation" that he then faces is to give way to his despair, and what that would mean (again as in Conrad) would be to embrace the release of death, for it is death that is the danger— as the riding simile indicates. Esmond must also be presumed to face another temptation, the temptation of repaying Rachel in kind for her treatment of him, either by staking his claim to the title (for Atterbury too knows of the confession) or, at the least, by making her aware that it is by his bounty that she and hers continue to enjoy what is not theirs. He discovers, however, that if he has been left with nothing, he is endowed *"virtute sua,"* and he finds the inner strength to withstand both these temptations, and to vanquish his difficulties "by endurance."

Esmond comes through the test, but only by being made new. When "his cruel goddess" shakes her wings and flees, it is not only a desertion that is recorded but a liberation. From this point on, Rachel ceases to be a goddess for him, and though her blows lay him low, they also force him to get up off his knees and see her for what she is. At the same time, his previous sense of self has, as it were, been anchored in his worship of her; when he ceases to regard her as a goddess, there is apparently nothing left for him to hold to, and the self runs aground and shatters. But there is something left, his own strength and a readiness to start again: *"Reficimus rates quassas"*—we repair our shattered vessels, says the narrator, quoting Horace, and "try upon new ventures." For Esmond the experience both reveals what he is and serves as "an initiation": it is an initiation "into life" and into full manhood. . . . It is also a consummation of self, and we might well expect it to mark the conclusion of a *Bildungsroman*; but the experience described in fact takes place at the beginning of the second of three books, and it is clear that Esmond's new or reconstituted self is not complete. His self is now founded on its own independent strength—he is not only off his knees but standing on his own two feet—but he still needs someone to love. The rest of the narrative is primarily concerned with his quest for love, which ends nominally in his marriage at the close of his story. *Henry Esmond* is thus unique among *Bildungsromane* in charting the protagonist's development in two trajectories, from childhood to maturity, and then—as he "tries upon new ventures"—from young manhood to a purported further fulfillment in marriage. But, as we shall see, it is the way he copes with his experience in prison that remains the more significant "initiation . . . into life."

When Esmond leaves prison, he tells the truth about the title to his grandfather's widow, and my Lady Dowager shows a readiness to take him up; but he has "made up his mind to continue at no woman's apronstrings longer," and casting about "how he should distinguish himself, and make himself a name," he decides to go into the army. He takes part in the Vigo Bay expedition, and during the campaign "his energies [seem] to awaken and to expand." On his return the dowager "[pushes] his fortunes" to such effect that she gets the "promise of a company" for him, and has him "make his appearance at the Queen's drawing-room occasionally" and "frequent my Lord Marlborough's levees." In the midst of his activities, however, Esmond's "heart [often] fondly [reverts]" to Rachel and her family; and when he hears a rumor that she is likely to marry her chaplain, Tom Tusher, he hurries down to Walcote, where he is reconciled to her after "the year of grief and estrangement":

> She smiled an almost wild smile as she looked up at him. . . .
>
> "Do you know what day it is?" she continued. "It is the 29th of December—it is your birthday! But last year we did not drink it—no, no. My lord was cold, and my Harry was likely to die; and my brain was in a fever; and we had no wine. But now—now you are come again, bringing your sheaves with you, my dear." She burst into a wild flood of weeping as she spoke; she laughed and sobbed on the young man's heart, crying out wildly, "bringing your sheaves with you—your sheaves with you!"
>
> As he had sometimes felt, gazing up from the deck at midnight into the boundless starlit depths overhead, in a rapture of devout wonder at that endless brightness and beauty—in some such a way now, the depth of this pure devotion (which was, for the first time, revealed to him quite) smote upon him, and filled his heart with thanksgiving. Gracious God, who was he, weak and friendless creature, that such a love should be poured out upon him? Not in vain, not in vain has he lived . . . that has such a treasure given him. . . .
>
> "If—if 'tis so, dear lady," Mr. Esmond said, "why should I ever leave you? If God hath given me this great boon . . . let me have that blessing near me, nor ever part with it till life separate us. Come away—leave this Europe, this place which has so many sad recollections for you. Begin a new life in a new world. . . ."
>
> "And my children—and my duty—and my good father, Henry?" she broke out. . . .
>
> "I would leave all to follow you," said Mr. Esmond; "and can you not be as generous for me, dear lady?"
>
> "Hush, boy!" she said, and it was with a mother's sweet plaintive tone and look that she spoke.

This is one of the subtlest scenes in the novel, and the novelist's handling of his protagonists—and of their silences—is mas-

terly. Once again a major scene is initiated by an outburst on Rachel's part, but this time it is one of joy. Her wildness, referred to three times in the first ten lines, is the overt sign of the way she at last feels free to let herself go, to abandon herself to the passion for Esmond that she has sought for so long to repress. And her references to Psalm 126 (she has just previously repeated the lines sung that day in the church: "When the Lord turned the captivity of Zion, we were like them that dream") express both her own sense of liberation and—in her reiteration of his having brought his sheaves with him—her invitation to him to rejoice in his return and reap in joy. Esmond's response is curious in the extreme. The nature of her feeling is apparently clear to him . . . for the narrator parenthetically remarks that it is "for the first time, revealed to him quite"; but he at once proceeds to transform it into something other than it is, turning her obviously sexual passion into a "pure devotion" and losing himself "in a rapture of [carefully] devout wonder" at it. He transforms himself too, for the returning warrior, the captain with influential friends, is hardly a "weak and friendless creature," though his self-image certainly reflects, in its involuntary regression to his childhood, his own unreadiness for her love. The regression is evident too in his passivity before the love that is "poured out upon him": he clearly regards "such a love" as of great value—it is "a treasure" and a "great boon"—but he does not seem to feel called on to do much in order to secure it. It is notable that at no point does he actually say that he loves her, and the omission is so marked that it suggests he is silenced by a profound inhibition in relation to her. At the same time, Esmond still feels bound by his childhood vow of loyalty to Rachel; and though he cannot fake any enthusiasm for the project, he does rise to the occasion and propose that she come away with him to Virginia. Rachel, however, is swift to understand the significance of his response, and she then backs away, though she was not much concerned with her various duties to start with. She later says to him, "You never loved me, dear Henry—no, you do not now, and I thank Heaven for it." But by then she has reverted to their accustomed relationship, calling him "boy," and speaking with "a mother's sweet plaintive tone." Esmond is only too glad, it seems, to accept the reversion: "'I think the angels are not all in heaven,' Mr. Esmond said. And as a brother folds a sister to his heart; and as a mother cleaves to her son's breast—so for a few moments Esmond's beloved mistress came to him and blessed him." If he no longer regards Rachel as a goddess, he now has no difficulty in spiritualizing her into an angel.

Immediately following this encounter, Rachel and Esmond walk back to the house at Walcote. As they stand in the hall, Beatrix comes down the stairs, illuminated by the candle she carries. . . . Esmond's visit to Walcote certainly faces him with some troubling transformations. He has no sooner contended with Rachel's sea changes from mother figure to passionate woman and back again than he has to confront the metamorphosis of the child he has left into the lustrous beauty that Beatrix has become. She is now sixteen—his age when Rachel first woke to him as a man at the time of the Nancy Sievewright affair—and he is eight years her senior, as Rachel in turn is eight years older than he. Some parallels are clearly intended, and none is more significant than the description of Rachel's coming into his life as a *Dea certè* in comparison with that of Beatrix's irruption into it. He does not see Beatrix, he insists, as a goddess, for he grants that her mouth and chin might be considered "too large and full . . . for a goddess in marble," whereas such flaws are apparently becoming in "a woman." For a mere woman, however, she is seen as enjoying a large measure of perfection—her shape is "perfect symmetry, health, decision, activity," and her motion "always perfect grace"—and if she is not a goddess, there is no doubt about her being "a paragon."

Beatrix's appearance on the stairs is furthermore contrasted with Esmond's first view of Rachel by a repeated detail which, though apparently equating the effect of the two women on him, subtly differentiates it. Both are "dazzling," but whereas Rachel's dazzle is a radiance that obscures any human blemish in its strong light, Beatrix's is the brightness of a sexual brilliance that casts all round her into shadow—as she does "the great Duke . . . at the playhouse after Ramillies." The "irresistible attraction" that she exerts is pure sexual magnetism; it also, like fire, "melts" those on whom the brightness shines. At the same time her dazzle is associated with the whiteness of snow, a comparison that catches her essential coldness, for all her apparent fire. Esmond seems to register the fact of such coldness, but he remains oblivious to its implications. He is wholly given over to the recording of her beauty, with a loving particularity of physical detail that contrasts sharply with the few generalized features accorded the *Dea certè*. The "brown beauty" as dark temptress is set squarely against the fair (erstwhile) goddess, and it is clear where Esmond's eyes are fixed. Indeed, Rachel is "still hanging on his arm" as he looks at Beatrix, and when the older woman speaks, he turns "with a start and a blush": "He had forgotten her, rapt in admiration of the *filia pulcrior*." The close juxtaposition of the scenes of Esmond's response to Rachel's outburst and of his contemplation of Beatrix, together with his "forgetting" of the mother in his preoccupation with the daughter, makes it seem that the intensity of his feeling for Beatrix is generated by the force of his inhibition in relation to Rachel; it is as if a previously inhibited sexuality is now compulsively released. At all events, "rapt in admiration," he now falls as surely under the spell of the daughter—he later refers to her as "this Circe"—as he was formerly spellbound by the mother. Even though he is made well aware of her faults—she is "imperious," "light-minded," "flighty," "false," and has "no reverence in her

character"—and though he notes she is "in everything . . . the contrast of her mother," who is "the most devoted and the least selfish of women," he is nevertheless compelled to her: "Well, from the very first moment he saw her on the stairs at Walcote, Esmond knew he loved Beatrix. There might be better women—he wanted that one. He cared for none other." At Walcote, that is, Esmond's need to love someone centers itself in Beatrix, and his "passionate fidelity of temper" ensures that his feeling is concentrated there for a long time. (pp. 162-67)

A wiser and a better man in all things else, a man who has distinguished himself in the world, Colonel Esmond persists in his unrequited love for the ambitious and flirtatious Beatrix. She puts him off with all sorts of reasons, but it is clear why he fundamentally has no hope of winning her, and she eventually articulates this: "I feel as a sister to you," she says, "and can no more. Isn't that enough, sir?" In the relationships of Esmond and Rachel and of Beatrix and Esmond, it is in each case the younger of the two who is inhibited by the familial situation in which they grow up. Consequently Esmond's grand plan to win the throne for the Pretender, which he undertakes primarily as a last desperate effort to impress and so win Beatrix, is ironically beside the point. The episode, however, though quite unhistorical, neatly serves to link the tale of Esmond's life to its historical setting, for Esmond's story serves as a dramatic counterpart to that of the Pretender. Each man is dispossessed of a title which is his by right; but where the Pretender intrigues to regain his title only to forfeit it through his own ineptitude, Esmond magnanimously renounces the title he is offered and determines rather to make his own name. And it is of course in the (historical) battles in which he participates prior to the attempt to gain the throne for the Pretender that Esmond makes that name. The historical setting is thus more integral to Esmond's story than might at first appear; and it merges with it completely when Beatrix's flirtation with the Pretender is made the occasion of Esmond's breaking with her. At the same time, when he tells Rachel about his plan, she thinks the "Restoration [is] to be attributed under Heaven to the Castlewood family and to its chief, and she [worships] and [loves] Esmond . . . more than ever she [has] done."

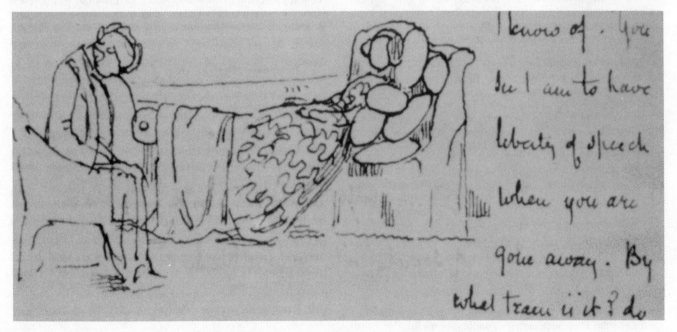

Thackeray's sketch of himself in chains at Jane Brookfield's feet.

The Pretender pursues Beatrix to Castlewood and so forfeits a crown; Beatrix, in enticing him and surrendering to him if only in "the treacherous heart within her," forfeits Esmond's love. Or so he says: "He sickened at [the] notion [of "the young Prince's lips . . . feeding on" her]. Her cheek was desecrated, her beauty tarnished; shame and honour stood between it and him. The love was dead within him." It is Beatrix's treachery—to their cause, to her family, and to him personally—that Esmond, whose whole life has been predicated on allegiance and fidelity, cannot stomach; and it is this that finally makes him give her up. But whether his love is as dead as he says in another matter. The very intensity of the physical revulsion from her bespeaks his desire (as analogously, on several occasions, does Rachel's in relation to him). And an earlier (retrospective) passage makes us view his break with Beatrix somewhat differently:

> Who, in the course of his life, hath not been so bewitched, and worshipped some idol or another? Years after this passion hath been dead and buried, along with a thousand other worldly cares and ambitions, he who felt it can recall it out of its grave, and admire, almost as fondly as he did in his youth, that lovely queenly creature. I invoke that beautiful spirit from the shades and love her still; or rather I should say such a past is always present to a man; such a passion once felt forms a part of his whole being, and cannot be separated from it; it becomes a portion of the man to-day, just as any great faith or conviction, the discovery of poetry, the awakening of religion, ever afterward influence him; just as the wound I had at Blenheim, and of which I wear the scar, hath become part of my frame and influenced my whole body, nay, spirit subsequently, though 'twas got and healed forty years ago.

It is a fine passage, and tells us more than Esmond would seem ready to grant. On the one hand, it records his liberation from Beatrix, his escape from bewitchment, from the Circean enchantment in which she has held him for so long. It also records how the image of Beatrix that is set up in his imagination at the foot of the stairs at Walcote, the image of her as a "lovely queenly creature," a "paragon," is tumbled down, and how he understands, seeing things as they are, that he has been worshipping an "idol." But at the same time, though he declares that his passion for her is "dead and buried," it is clear—by his own admission—that it will not stay in "its grave," and that he "loves her still." When the admission of his continuing love is made, the narrator quickly amends what he has said—"or rather I should say such a past is always present to a man"—but his elaboration of this idea in fact amounts to the same thing. If his passion "forms a part of his whole being," just like "the wound" he received at Blenheim, and so "becomes a portion of [him] to-day," then indeed he loves her still. Colonel Esmond has three major wounds in his life, wounds that permanently scar him: the wound he receives at Blenheim; the wound Rachel inflicts on him when he is in prison; and the wound he gets when he falls irretrievably in love with an unworthy Beatrix.

It is with such a love still alive in him that Esmond marries Rachel. This perhaps explains why he needs so strenuously and repeatedly to assert his happiness in his marriage, though he involuntarily betrays his feeling on a number of occasions. Looking back on the crisis of his relations with Beatrix, for instance, he cannot help regretting that he conceived his plan to restore the Pretender and so "undid" himself. The word slips out, and is hastily qualified, but a lot is revealed: "He

was not the first that has regretted his own act, or brought about his own undoing. Undoing? Should he write that word in his late years? No, on his knees before Heaven,—[that suspect position]—rather be thankful for what then he deemed his misfortune, and which hath caused the whole subsequent happiness of his life."

It is when Rachel feels "severed from her children and alone in the world" that she is ready to marry Esmond. Her need, it must be assumed, outweighs any doubt she may have as to the nature of his feeling for her; and the "duties" that nominally prevented her from accepting his earlier proposal have now fallen away. He finds her "one day in tears" and begs her "to confide herself to the care and devotion of one who, by God's help, [will] never forsake her." It is not indicated, however, how he overcomes his former inhibition. It is rather like the end of *Mansfield Park*, when Edmund Bertram, equally without explanation, is able to displace a long-held view of Fanny Price as a sister and happily to marry her. But in *Mansfield Park* that is the end of the story; whereas **Henry Esmond** is a retrospective narrative. What it tells us, consequently, is that Esmond never really overcomes his inhibition, and can never really give Rachel the love she is entitled to. But he is an honorable man, and he stands by her in her need, determined not to "forsake" her. It is a repeated motif: "Years ago, [as] a boy . . . , he had made a vow to be faithful and never desert her dear service. Had he kept that fond boyish promise? Yes, before Heaven; yes, praise be to God! His life had been hers; his blood, his fortune, his name, his whole heart ever since had been hers and her children's." But we know that his whole heart is not hers; and even in the final account he offers of the "happiness" which "crowns" his life—for he is a successful pretender—it is notable that he celebrates the joys of being loved rather than loving: Rachel is the "tenderest and purest wife ever man was blessed with"; the "depth and intensity" of her love "[blesses him]"; the love that is "bestowed" on him is "a boon," and a "gift"; and "to have such a love is the one blessing, in comparison of which all earthly joy is of no value." Gentlemen too may protest too much, and, in celebrating one thing, forget another—as Esmond, in his retrospective narrative, seems to do when he describes his departure from Rachel after the scene at Walcote:

> As for his mistress, 'twas difficult to say with what a feeling he regarded her. 'Twas happiness to have seen her: 'twas no great pang to part; a filial tenderness, a love that was at once respect and protection, filled his mind as he thought of her; and near her or far from her, and from that day until now, and from now till death is past, and beyond it, he prays that sacred flame may ever burn.

By the end of his story, Esmond has long been standing on his own feet, has made a name for himself, and has loyally served as a constant protector of the Castlewood family. He is also suitably disillusioned, having learned to see both men and women for what they are. His need to love is ostensibly met in his relationship with Rachel; but he is not satisfied in love, and though "filial tenderness" may be a "sacred flame," it is not what should burn in a marriage. But Esmond is not prepared to face all the implications of his own narrative, and its evasions and contradictions suggest that there is one head at least that remains in need of a stately periwig. (pp. 167-70)

H. M. Daleski, "A Secret Heart: 'The History of Henry Esmond'," in his Unities: Studies in the English Novel, The University of Georgia Press, 1985, *pp. 151-70.*

ADDITIONAL BIBLIOGRAPHY

Bledsoe, Robert. "*Sibi Constet*: The Goddess of Castlewood and the Goddess of Walcote." *Studies in the Novel* V, No. 2 (Summer 1973): 211-19.

    Argues that the progress of Esmond's love from Rachel to Beatrix to Rachel illustrates his "circular journey from paradise through experience back to paradise."

Colby, Robert A. "William Makepeace Thackeray." In *Victorian Fiction: A Second Guide to Research*, edited by George H. Ford, pp. 114-42. New York: Modern Language Association of America, 1978.

    A sequel to Lionel Stevenson's bibliographical study (see entry below), extending through 1974.

————. "*Henry Esmond*; or, The Complete Cavalier." In his *Thackeray's Canvass of Humanity: An Author and His Public*, pp. 313-55. Columbus: Ohio State University Press, 1979.

    Discusses Thackeray's concept of historiography, relating *Henry Esmond* to contemporary historical fiction.

Donnelly, Jerome. "Stendhal and Thackeray: The Source of *Henry Esmond*." *Revue de littérature comparée* XXXIX, No. 3 (1965): 372-81.

    Establishes parallels between *Henry Esmond* and Stendhal's *Le rouge et le noir* (1830), claiming that "the likelihood of a direct Stendhal influence" on Thackeray's novel "seems almost certain."

Donovan, Robert Alan. "*Redgauntlet, Henry Esmond,* and the Modes of Historical Fiction." In his *The Shaping Vision: Imagination in the English Novel from Defoe to Dickens*, pp. 173-205. Ithaca: Cornell University Press, 1966.

    Evaluates *Henry Esmond* as a historical novel, commenting that "the trappings of history . . . disguise the fact that *Esmond* is really a Victorian novel." Donovan also appraises the novel's narrative technique, arguing that *Henry Esmond* is in no sense a *Bildungsroman*, for "Esmond does not become; he is."

Edgar, Pelham. "Austen and Thackeray." In his *The Art of the Novel from 1700 to the Present Time*, pp. 102-16. New York: Macmillan Co., 1933.

    Offers general comments on Thackeray as a novelist, focusing on the implications of his choice of narrative style in *Henry Esmond*.

Ennis, Lambert. "Over the Crest." In his *Thackeray: The Sentimental Cynic*, pp. 173-92. Evanston, Ill.: Northwestern University Press, 1950.

    Examines the characters of *Henry Esmond* in the context of Thackeray's own life.

Flamm, Dudley. *Thackeray's Critics: An Annotated Bibliography of British and American Criticism, 1836-1901*. Chapel Hill: University of North Carolina Press, 1966, 184 p.

    A chronologically arranged annotated guide to criticism of Thackeray's works through 1901.

Fleishman, Avrom. "Thackeray: Beyond Whig History." In his *The English Historical Novel: Walter Scott to Virginia Woolf*, pp. 127-48. Baltimore: Johns Hopkins University Press, 1971.

    Alleges that in *Henry Esmond* Thackeray transcends historiography, approaching "the universal in [his] . . . conception of history."

Forsythe, Robert Stanley. *A Noble Rake: The Life of Charles, Fourth Lord Mohun, Being a Study in the Historical Background of Thackeray's "Henry Esmond."* Cambridge: Harvard University Press, 1928, 310 p.

    A biography of one of the historical characters in *Henry Esmond* that includes consideration of how Thackeray adapted the character for his novel.

Harden, Edgar F. "Esmond and the Search for Self." In *The Yearbook of English Studies*, Vol. 3, edited by T. J. B. Spencer and R. L. Smallwood, pp. 181-95. Cambridge, England: Modern Humanities Research Association, 1973.

    Reads the novel as Esmond's triumphant journey to self-knowledge, fulfillment, and "awareness that his identity is defined by the testimony given his worth by his own character and actions."

Hardy, Barbara. "Memory and Memories." In her *Tellers and Listeners: The Narrative Imagination*, pp. 56-101. London: Athlone Press, 1975.

    Includes an analysis of the role of memory in *Henry Esmond*.

Iser, Wolfgang. "Self-Reduction: The Self-Communication of Subjectivity in Autobiographical Fiction. W. M. Thackeray: *Henry Esmond*." In his *The Implied Reader: Patterns of Communication in Prose Fiction from Bunyan to Beckett*, pp. 123-35. Baltimore: Johns Hopkins University Press, 1974.

    Argues that in *Henry Esmond* "history is not interpreted . . . as the progressive fulfillment of an underlying purpose, but more as a reflection that gives the hero a greater chance of self scrutiny."

Millgate, Jane. "History *versus* Fiction: Thackeray's Response to Macaulay." *Costerus* n.s. II (1974): 43-58.

    Documents the influence of Thomas Babington Macaulay on Thackeray's view of history in *Henry Esmond*.

Olmsted, John Charles. *Thackeray and His Twentieth-Century Critics: An Annotated Bibliography, 1900-1975*. New York: Garland Publishing, 1977, 249 p.

    An annotated guide to twentieth-century criticism of Thackeray's works.

Phillipps, K. C. "The Language of *Henry Esmond*." In his *The Language of Thackeray*, pp. 148-75. London: Andre Deutsch, 1978.

    Analyzes the eighteenth-century style Thackeray employed in *Henry Esmond*, claiming that the novel is a "linguistic *tour de force*."

Rawlins, Jack P. "The Fiction That Is True: *Henry Esmond, The Virginians,* and *Philip*." In his *Thackeray's Novels: A Fiction That Is True*, pp. 187-233. Berkeley and Los Angeles: University of California Press, 1974.

    Characterizes *The Virginians* as a parody debunking the heroic idealism of *Henry Esmond*.

Ray, Gordon N. "*Esmond*." In his *The Buried Life: A Study of the Relation between Thackeray's Fiction and His Personal History*, pp. 78-96. London: Oxford University Press, 1952.

    Demonstrates the extent to which Thackeray modeled the characters and plot of *Henry Esmond* on his relationship with the Brookfields.

————. *Thackeray: The Uses of Adversity, 1811-1846*, Vol. I; *Thackeray: The Age of Wisdom, 1847-1863*, Vol. II. New York: McGraw-Hill Book Co., 1955, 1958.

    The definitive biography by a prominent scholar.

Sanders, Andrew. "Clio's Heroes and Thackeray's Heroes: *Henry Esmond* and *The Virginians*." In his *The Victorian Historical Novel: 1840-1880*, pp. 97-119. New York: St. Martin's Press, 1979.

    A close analysis of *Henry Esmond* as a historical novel and of Thackeray's attitude toward the presentation of history in fiction.

Scarry, Elaine. "*Henry Esmond*: The Rookery at Castlewood." In *Literary Monographs*. Vol. 7, *Thackeray, Hawthorne and Melville, and Dreiser*, edited by Eric Rothstein and Joseph Anthony Wittreich, Jr., pp. 1-43. Madison: University of Wisconsin Press, 1975.

    Suggests that Thackeray undermines Esmond's implicit belief in the validity of personal, subjective truth through manipulative techniques of language. Scarry argues that Esmond's narrative is systematically subverted by discredited metaphors, antithetical imagery, and factual discrepancies, all designed to illustrate Thackeray's theme that subjective truth is as elusive as objective reality.

Stevenson, Lionel. "William Makepeace Thackeray." In *Victorian Fiction: A Guide to Research*, edited by Lionel Stevenson, pp. 154-87. Cambridge: Harvard University Press, 1964.

    Provides bibliographical information on both primary and secondary sources in Thackeray studies. This essay reviews scholarship through 1963; Robert A. Colby's continuation of this work (see entry above) covers the next ten years.

Sutherland, John A. "Thackeray's Patchwork: A Note on the Composition of the Eleventh Chapter of *Henry Esmond*." In *The Yearbook of English Studies*, Vol. 1, edited by T. J. B. Spencer and R. L. Smallwood, pp. 141-48. Cambridge, England: Modern Humanities Research Association, 1971.

   Notes inconsistencies and errors in chapter eleven of *Henry Esmond*, speculating that Thackeray must have compiled the section by piecing together different drafts and fragments of his novel.

———. "Thackeray's Notebook for *Henry Esmond*." *Costerus* n.s. II (1974): 193-215.

   Reprints pages from and provides discussion of the notebook Thackeray kept while writing *Henry Esmond*. Sutherland concludes that the notebook, which consists mainly of historical research notes and miscellaneous sketches, "has, at best, a tangential relationship to *Esmond*."

———. "*Henry Esmond*: The Virtues of Carelessness." In his *Thackeray at Work*, pp. 56-73. London: Athlone Press, 1974.

   Posits that *Henry Esmond* is not, as is commonly believed, a carefully planned novel, but one that evolved during composition. Sutherland argues that the novel was written in the same manner as Thackeray's serially published novels, "at the serialist's creative gallop in which the ground could be covered only once." Thus the work's unity is attributable not to Thackeray's revisions, but to his genius for adapting and improvising. "Thackeray," notes Sutherland, "was prepared to make great creative efforts so as not to have to rewrite anything."

———. "*Henry Esmond*: The Shaping Power of Contract." In his *Victorian Novelists and Publishers*, pp. 101-16. Chicago: University of Chicago Press, 1976.

   Details circumstances of the composition and publication of *Henry Esmond*.

Talon, Henri-A. "Time and Memory in Thackeray's *Henry Esmond*." *The Review of English Studies* n.s. 13, No. 50 (May 1962): 147-56.

   An analysis of time in the novel. Talon contends that Esmond's narrative "is an attempt to understand the self through the rediscovery of his life and the reconstruction of time."

Tilford, John E. "The 'Unsavoury Plot' of *Henry Esmond*." *Nineteenth-Century Fiction* VI, No. 2 (September 1951): 121-30.

   Cites critical preoccupation with the incestuous implications of Esmond's relationship with Rachel.

Tillotson, Geoffrey, and Hawes, Donald, eds. *Thackeray: The Critical Heritage*. The Critical Heritage Series, edited by B. C. Southam. London: Routledge & Kegan Paul, 1968, 392 p.

   An annotated selection of nineteenth-century critical commentary on *Henry Esmond*.

Williams, Ioan. "*The History of Henry Esmond*: Thackeray's Anatomy of Sentimental Man." In his *The Realist Novel in England: A Study in Development*, pp. 156-68. Pittsburgh: University of Pittsburgh Press, 1975.

   Perceives *Henry Esmond* as the story of a man who discovers a great truth: that love, for all its pain, is the origin of all happiness and meaning in human life.

Williamson, Karina. "A Note on the Function of Castlewood in *Henry Esmond*." *Nineteenth-Century Fiction* 18, No. 1 (June 1963): 71-7.

   Observes that Thackeray's descriptions of the Castlewood estate reflect the emotional moods of the novel's characters and scenes.

Nineteenth-Century
Literature Criticism

Cumulative Indexes

This Index Includes References
to Entries in These Gale Series

Contemporary Literary Criticism

Presents excerpts of criticism on the works of novelists, poets, dramatists, short story writers, scriptwriters, and other creative writers who are now living or who have died since 1960. Cumulative indexes to authors and nationalities are included, as well as an index to titles discussed in the individual volume. Volumes 1-53 are in print.

Twentieth-Century Literary Criticism

Contains critical excerpts by the most significant commentators on poets, novelists, short story writers, dramatists, and philosophers who died between 1900 and 1960. Cumulative indexes to authors, nationalities, and titles discussed are included in each new volume. Volumes 1-32 are in print.

Nineteenth-Century Literature Criticism

Offers significant passages from criticism on authors who died between 1800 and 1899. Cumulative indexes to authors, nationalities, and titles discussed are included in each new volume. Volumes 1-21 are in print.

Literature Criticism from 1400 to 1800

Compiles significant passages from the most noteworthy criticism on authors of the fifteenth through eighteenth centuries. Cumulative indexes to authors, nationalities, and titles discussed are included in each new volume. Volumes 1-10 are in print.

Classical and Medieval Literature Criticism

Offers excerpts of criticism on the works of world authors from classical antiquity through the fourteenth century. Cumulative indexes to authors, titles, and critics are included in each volume. Volumes 1-2 are in print.

Short Story Criticism

Compiles excerpts of criticism on short fiction by writers of all eras and nationalities. Cumulative indexes to authors, nationalities, and titles discussed are included in each new volume. Volumes 1-2 are in print.

Children's Literature Review

Includes excerpts from reviews, criticism, and commentary on works of authors and illustrators who create books for children. Cumulative indexes to authors, nationalities, and titles discussed are included in each new volume. Volumes 1-17 are in print.

Contemporary Authors Series

Encompasses five related series. *Contemporary Authors* provides biographical and bibliographical information on more than 92,000 writers of fiction, nonfiction, poetry, journalism, drama, motion pictures, and other fields. Each new volume contains sketches on authors not previously covered in the series. Volumes 1-126 are in print. *Contemporary Authors New Revision Series* provides completely updated information on active authors covered in previously published volumes of *CA*. Only entries requiring significant change are revised for *CA New Revision Series*. Volumes 1-26 are in print. *Contemporary Authors Permanent Series* consists of updated listings for deceased and inactive authors removed from the original volumes 9-36 when these volumes were revised. Volumes 1-2 are in print. *Contemporary Authors Autobiography Series* presents specially commissioned autobiographies by leading contemporary writers. Volumes 1-8 are in print. *Contemporary Authors Bibliographical Series* contains primary and secondary bibliographies as well as analytical bibliographical essays by authorities on major modern authors. Volumes 1-2 are in print.

Dictionary of Literary Biography

Encompasses three related series. *Dictionary of Literary Biography* furnishes illustrated overviews of authors' lives and works and places them in the larger perspective of literary history. Volumes 1-78 are in print. *Dictionary of Literary Biography Documentary Series* illuminates the careers of major figures through a selection of literary documents, including letters, notebook and diary entries, interviews, book reviews, and photographs. Volumes 1-6 are in print. *Dictionary of Literary Biography Yearbook* summarizes the past year's literary activity with articles on genres, major prizes, conferences, and other timely subjects and includes updated and new entries on individual authors. Yearbooks for 1980-1988 are in print. A cumulative index to authors and articles is included in each new volume.

Concise Dictionary of American Literary Biography

A six-volume series that collects revised and updated sketches on major American authors that were originally presented in *Dictionary of Literary Biography*. Volumes 1-3 are in print.

Something about the Author Series

Encompasses two related series. *Something about the Author* contains heavily illustrated biographical sketches on juvenile and young adult authors and illustrators from all eras. Volumes 1-54 are in print. *Something about the Author Autobiography Series* presents specially commissioned autobiographies by prominent authors and illustrators of books for children and young adults. Volumes 1-7 are in print.

Yesterday's Authors of Books for Children

Contains heavily illustrated entries on children's writers who died before 1961. Complete in two volumes. Volumes 1-2 are in print.

Literary Criticism Series
Cumulative Author Index

This index lists all author entries in the Gale Literary Criticism Series and includes cross-references to other Gale sources. For the convenience of the reader, references to the *Yearbook* in the *Contemporary Literary Criticism* series include the page number (in parentheses) after the volume number. References in the index are identified as follows:

AAYA: *Authors & Artists for Young Adults*, Volume 1
CAAS: *Contemporary Authors Autobiography Series*, Volumes 1-8
CA: *Contemporary Authors* (original series), Volumes 1-126
CABS: *Contemporary Authors Bibliographical Series*, Volumes 1-2
CANR: *Contemporary Authors New Revision Series*, Volumes 1-26
CAP: *Contemporary Authors Permanent Series*, Volumes 1-2
CA-R: *Contemporary Authors* (revised editions), Volumes 1-44
CDALB: *Concise Dictionary of American Literary Biography*, Volumes 1-3
CLC: *Contemporary Literary Criticism*, Volumes 1-53
CLR: *Children's Literature Review*, Volumes 1-18
CMLC: *Classical and Medieval Literature Criticism*, Volumes 1-2
DLB: *Dictionary of Literary Biography*, Volumes 1-78
DLB-DS: *Dictionary of Literary Biography Documentary Series*, Volumes 1-6
DLB-Y: *Dictionary of Literary Biography Yearbook*, Volumes 1980-1987
LC: *Literature Criticism from 1400 to 1800*, Volumes 1-10
NCLC: *Nineteenth-Century Literature Criticism*, Volumes 1-22
SAAS: *Something about the Author Autobiography Series*, Volumes 1-7
SATA: *Something about the Author*, Volumes 1-53
SSC: *Short Story Criticism*, Volumes 1-2
TCLC: *Twentieth-Century Literary Criticism*, Volumes 1-32
YABC: *Yesterday's Authors of Books for Children*, Volumes 1-2

Author Index

Author Index

Birney (Alfred) Earle
  1904-..................CLC 1, 4, 6, 11
  See also CANR 5, 20
  See also CA 1-4R

Bishop, Elizabeth
  1911-1979...... CLC 1, 4, 9, 13, 15, 32
  See also CANR 26
  See also CA 5-8R
  See also obituary CA 89-92
  See also CABS 2
  See also obituary SATA 24
  See also DLB 5

Bishop, John 1935-...............CLC 10
  See also CA 105

Bissett, Bill 1939-................CLC 18
  See also CANR 15
  See also CA 69-72
  See also DLB 53

Biyidi, Alexandre 1932-
  See Beti, Mongo
  See also CA 114

Bjørnson, Bjørnstjerne (Martinius)
  1832-1910.................. TCLC 7
  See also CA 104

Blackburn, Paul 1926-1971 ..... CLC 9, 43
  See also CA 81-84
  See also obituary CA 33-36R
  See also DLB 16
  See also DLB-Y 81

Blackmore, R(ichard) D(oddridge)
  1825-1900.................. TCLC 27
  See also CA 120
  See also DLB 18

Blackmur, R(ichard) P(almer)
  1904-1965................. CLC 2, 24
  See also CAP 1
  See also CA 11-12
  See also obituary CA 25-28R
  See also DLB 63

Blackwood, Algernon (Henry)
  1869-1951.................. TCLC 5
  See also CA 105

Blackwood, Caroline 1931- ...... CLC 6, 9
  See also CA 85-88
  See also DLB 14

Blair, Eric Arthur 1903-1950
  See Orwell, George
  See also CA 104
  See also SATA 29

Blais, Marie-Claire
  1939-............. CLC 2, 4, 6, 13, 22
  See also CAAS 4
  See also CA 21-24R
  See also DLB 53

Blaise, Clark 1940- ....CLC 29
  See also CAAS 3
  See also CANR 5
  See also CA 53-56R
  See also DLB 53

Blake, Nicholas 1904-1972
  See Day Lewis, C(ecil)
  See also DLB 77

Blake, William 1757-1827 .... NCLC 13
  See also SATA 30

Blasco Ibáñez, Vicente
  1867-1928................. TCLC 12
  See also CA 110

Blatty, William Peter 1928-.........CLC 2
  See also CANR 9
  See also CA 5-8R

Blish, James (Benjamin)
  1921-1975.................CLC 14
  See also CANR 3
  See also CA 1-4R
  See also obituary CA 57-60
  See also DLB 8

Blixen, Karen (Christentze Dinesen)
  1885-1962
  See Dinesen, Isak
  See also CANR 22
  See also CAP 2
  See also CA 25-28
  See also SATA 44

Bloch, Robert (Albert) 1917-.......CLC 33
  See also CANR 5
  See also CA 5-8R
  See also DLB 44
  See also SATA 12

Blok, Aleksandr (Aleksandrovich)
  1880-1921.................. TCLC 5
  See also CA 104

Bloom, Harold 1930-..............CLC 24
  See also CA 13-16R
  See also DLB 67

Blount, Roy (Alton), Jr. 1941- .....CLC 38
  See also CANR 10
  See also CA 53-56

Bloy, Léon 1846-1917.......... TCLC 22
  See also CA 121

Blume, Judy (Sussman Kitchens)
  1938-................... CLC 12, 30
  See also CLR 2, 15
  See also CANR 13
  See also CA 29-32R
  See also SATA 2, 31
  See also DLB 52

Blunden, Edmund (Charles)
  1896-1974....................CLC 2
  See also CAP 2
  See also CA 17-18
  See also obituary CA 45-48
  See also DLB 20

Bly, Robert (Elwood)
  1926-.......... CLC 1, 2, 5, 10, 15, 38
  See also CA 5-8R
  See also DLB 5

Bochco, Steven 1944?-
  See Bochco, Steven and Kozoll, Michael

Bochco, Steven 1944?- and
  Kozoll, Michael 1940?- ....CLC 35

Bødker, Cecil 1927-...............CLC 21
  See also CANR 13
  See also CA 73-76
  See also SATA 14

Boell, Heinrich (Theodor) 1917-1985
  See Böll, Heinrich
  See also CANR 24
  See also CA 21-24R
  See also obituary CA 116

Bogan, Louise
  1897-1970........CLC 4, 39 (383), 46
  See also CA 73-76
  See also obituary CA 25-28R
  See also DLB 45

Bogarde, Dirk 1921-..............CLC 19
  See also Van Den Bogarde, Derek (Jules
    Gaspard Ulric) Niven
  See also DLB 14

Bogosian, Eric 1953-..............CLC 45

Bograd, Larry 1953-..............CLC 35
  See also CA 93-96
  See also SATA 33

Böhl de Faber, Cecilia 1796-1877
  See Caballero, Fernán

Boiardo, Matteo Maria
  1441-1494....................LC 6

Boileau-Despréaux, Nicolas
  1636-1711......................LC 3

Boland, Eavan (Aisling) 1944-......CLC 40
  See also DLB 40

Böll, Heinrich (Theodor)
  1917-1985...... CLC 2, 3, 6, 9, 11, 15,
                          27, 39 (291)
  See also Boell, Heinrich (Theodor)
  See also DLB 69
  See also DLB-Y 85

Bolt, Robert (Oxton) 1924- ....CLC 14
  See also CA 17-20R
  See also DLB 13

Bond, Edward 1934-......CLC 4, 6, 13, 23
  See also CA 25-28R
  See also DLB 13

Bonham, Frank 1914-.............CLC 12
  See also CANR 4
  See also CA 9-12R
  See also SAAS 3
  See also SATA 1, 49
  See also AAYA 1

Bonnefoy, Yves 1923- .... CLC 9, 15
  See also CA 85-88

Bontemps, Arna (Wendell)
  1902-1973................. CLC 1, 18
  See also CLR 6
  See also CANR 4
  See also CA 1-4R
  See also obituary CA 41-44R
  See also SATA 2, 44
  See also obituary SATA 24
  See also DLB 48, 51

Booth, Martin 1944-...............CLC 13
  See also CAAS 2
  See also CA 93-96

Booth, Philip 1925-...............CLC 23
  See also CANR 5
  See also CA 5-8R
  See also DLB-Y 82

Booth, Wayne C(layson) 1921- .....CLC 24
  See also CAAS 5
  See also CANR 3
  See also CA 1-4R
  See also DLB 67

Borchert, Wolfgang 1921-1947 .... TCLC 5
  See also CA 104
  See also DLB 69

Borges, Jorge Luis
  1899-1986......CLC 1, 2, 3, 4, 6, 8, 9,
                  10, 13, 19, 44 (352), 48
  See also CANR 19
  See also CA 21-24R
  See also DLB-Y 86

Brink, André (Philippus)
1935-.................... **CLC 18, 36**
See also CA 104

Brinsmead, H(esba) F(ay)
1922-.........................**CLC 21**
See also CANR 10
See also CA 21-24R
See also SAAS 5
See also SATA 18

Brittain, Vera (Mary)
1893?-1970....................**CLC 23**
See also CAP 1
See also CA 15-16
See also obituary CA 25-28R

Broch, Hermann 1886-1951...... **TCLC 20**
See also CA 117

Brock, Rose 1923-
See Hansen, Joseph

Brodsky, Iosif Alexandrovich 1940-
See Brodsky, Joseph (Alexandrovich)
See also CA 41-44R

Brodsky, Joseph (Alexandrovich)
1940-....... **CLC 4, 6, 13, 36, 50 (109)**
See also Brodsky, Iosif Alexandrovich

Brodsky, Michael (Mark)
1948-........................**CLC 19**
See also CANR 18
See also CA 102

Bromell, Henry 1947-..............**CLC 5**
See also CANR 9
See also CA 53-56

Bromfield, Louis (Brucker)
1896-1956................. **TCLC 11**
See also CA 107
See also DLB 4, 9

Broner, E(sther) M(asserman)
1930-.......................**CLC 19**
See also CANR 8, 25
See also CA 17-20R
See also DLB 28

Bronk, William 1918-.............**CLC 10**
See also CA 89-92

Brontë, Anne 1820-1849.......... **NCLC 4**
See also DLB 21

Brontë, Charlotte
1816-1855................**NCLC 3, 8**
See also DLB 21

Brontë, (Jane) Emily
1818-1848.................. **NCLC 16**
See also DLB 21, 32

Brooke, Frances 1724-1789 .... **LC 6**
See also DLB 39

Brooke, Henry 1703?-1783 .... **LC 1**
See also DLB 39

Brooke, Rupert (Chawner)
1887-1915................ **TCLC 2, 7**
See also CA 104
See also DLB 19

Brooke-Rose, Christine 1926- ......**CLC 40**
See also CA 13-16R
See also DLB 14

Brookner, Anita
1928-...........**CLC 32, 34 (136), 51**
See also CA 114, 120
See also DLB-Y 87

Brooks, Cleanth 1906- ....**CLC 24**
See also CA 17-20R
See also DLB 63

Brooks, Gwendolyn
1917-.......... **CLC 1, 2, 4, 5, 15, 49**
See also CANR 1
See also CA 1-4R
See also SATA 6
See also DLB 5, 76
See also CDALB 1941-1968

Brooks, Mel 1926-...............**CLC 12**
See also Kaminsky, Melvin
See also CA 65-68
See also DLB 26

Brooks, Peter 1938-......... **CLC 34 (519)**
See also CANR 1
See also CA 45-48

Brooks, Van Wyck 1886-1963......**CLC 29**
See also CANR 6
See also CA 1-4R
See also DLB 45, 63

Brophy, Brigid (Antonia)
1929-.................. **CLC 6, 11, 29**
See also CAAS 4
See also CANR 25
See also CA 5-8R
See also DLB 14

Brosman, Catharine Savage
1934-.......................**CLC 9**
See also CANR 21
See also CA 61-64

Broughton, T(homas) Alan
1936-......................**CLC 19**
See also CANR 2, 23
See also CA 45-48

Broumas, Olga 1949-.............**CLC 10**
See also CANR 20
See also CA 85-88

Brown, Charles Brockden
1771-1810.................. **NCLC 22**
See also DLB 37, 59
See also CDALB 1640-1865

Brown, Claude 1937- ....**CLC 30**
See also CA 73-76

Brown, Dee (Alexander)
1908-.................... **CLC 18, 47**
See also CAAS 6
See also CANR 11
See also CA 13-16R
See also SATA 5
See also DLB-Y 80

Brown, George Douglas 1869-1902
See Douglas, George

Brown, George Mackay
1921-..................... **CLC 5, 28**
See also CAAS 6
See also CANR 12
See also CA 21-24R
See also SATA 35
See also DLB 14, 27

Brown, Rita Mae 1944- .... **CLC 18, 43**
See also CANR 2, 11
See also CA 45-48

Brown, Rosellen 1939- ....**CLC 32**
See also CANR 14
See also CA 77-80

Brown, Sterling A(llen)
1901-...................... **CLC 1, 23**
See also CANR 26
See also CA 85-88
See also DLB 48, 51, 63

Brown, William Wells
1816?-1884.................. **NCLC 2**
See also DLB 3, 50

Browne, Jackson 1950-...........**CLC 21**

Browning, Elizabeth Barrett
1806-1861............... **NCLC 1, 16**
See also DLB 32

Browning, Robert 1812-1889..... **NCLC 19**
See also YABC 1
See also DLB 32

Browning, Tod 1882-1962 ....**CLC 16**
See also obituary CA 117

Bruccoli, Matthew J(oseph)
1931-................ **CLC 34 (416)**
See also CANR 7
See also CA 9-12R

Bruce, Lenny 1925-1966..........**CLC 21**
See also Schneider, Leonard Alfred

Brunner, John (Kilian Houston)
1934-..................... **CLC 8, 10**
See also CAAS 8
See also CANR 2
See also CA 1-4R

Brutus, Dennis 1924-.............**CLC 43**
See also CANR 2
See also CA 49-52

Bryan, C(ourtlandt) D(ixon) B(arnes)
1936-......................**CLC 29**
See also CANR 13
See also CA 73-76

Bryant, William Cullen
1794-1878.................. **NCLC 6**
See also DLB 3, 43, 59
See also CDALB 1640-1865

Bryusov, Valery (Yakovlevich)
1873-1924.................. **TCLC 10**
See also CA 107

Buchanan, George 1506-1582 .... **LC 4**

Buchheim, Lothar-Günther
1918-.......................**CLC 6**
See also CA 85-88

Buchwald, Art(hur) 1925- ....**CLC 33**
See also CANR 21
See also CA 5-8R
See also SATA 10

Buck, Pearl S(ydenstricker)
1892-1973.............. **CLC 7, 11, 18**
See also CANR 1
See also CA 1-4R
See also obituary CA 41-44R
See also SATA 1, 25
See also DLB 9

Buckler, Ernest 1908-1984........**CLC 13**
See also CAP 1
See also CA 11-12
See also obituary CA 114
See also SATA 47

Buckley, William F(rank), Jr.
1925-.................... **CLC 7, 18, 37**
See also CANR 1
See also CA 1-4R
See also DLB-Y 80

Evtushenko, Evgenii (Aleksandrovich) 1933-
See Yevtushenko, Yevgeny

Ewart, Gavin (Buchanan)
1916-...................**CLC 13, 46**
See also CANR 17
See also CA 89-92
See also DLB 40

Ewers, Hanns Heinz
1871-1943..................**TCLC 12**
See also CA 109

Ewing, Frederick R. 1918-
See Sturgeon, Theodore (Hamilton)

Exley, Frederick (Earl)
1929-................**CLC 6, 11**
See also CA 81-84
See also DLB-Y 81

Ezekiel, Tish O'Dowd
1943-..................**CLC 34** (46)

Fagen, Donald 1948-
See Becker, Walter and Fagen, Donald

Fagen, Donald 1948- and
Becker, Walter 1950-
See Becker, Walter and Fagen, Donald

Fair, Ronald L. 1932-.............**CLC 18**
See also CANR 25
See also CA 69-72
See also DLB 33

Fairbairns, Zoë (Ann) 1948-.......**CLC 32**
See also CANR 21
See also CA 103

Fairfield, Cicily Isabel 1892-1983
See West, Rebecca

Fallaci, Oriana 1930-.............**CLC 11**
See also CANR 15
See also CA 77-80

Faludy, George 1913-................**CLC 42**
See also CA 21-24R

Farah, Nuruddin 1945-............**CLC 53**
See also CA 106

Fargue, Léon-Paul 1876-1947 .... **TCLC 11**
See also CA 109

Farigoule, Louis 1885-1972
See Romains, Jules

Fariña, Richard 1937?-1966 ....**CLC 9**
See also CA 81-84
See also obituary CA 25-28R

Farley, Walter 1920-.............**CLC 17**
See also CANR 8
See also CA 17-20R
See also SATA 2, 43
See also DLB 22

Farmer, Philip José 1918- ...... **CLC 1, 19**
See also CANR 4
See also CA 1-4R
See also DLB 8

Farrell, J(ames) G(ordon)
1935-1979.....................**CLC 6**
See also CA 73-76
See also obituary CA 89-92
See also DLB 14

Farrell, James T(homas)
1904-1979............**CLC 1, 4, 8, 11**
See also CANR 9
See also CA 5-8R
See also obituary CA 89-92
See also DLB 4, 9
See also DLB-DS 2

Farrell, M. J. 1904-
See Keane, Molly

Fassbinder, Rainer Werner
1946-1982...................**CLC 20**
See also CA 93-96
See also obituary CA 106

Fast, Howard (Melvin) 1914-......**CLC 23**
See also CANR 1
See also CA 1-4R
See also SATA 7
See also DLB 9

Faulkner, William (Cuthbert)
1897-1962...... **CLC 1, 3, 6, 8, 9, 11,**
14, 18, 28, 52
.... **SSC 1**
See also CA 81-84
See also DLB 9, 11, 44
See also DLB-Y 86
See also DLB-DS 2

Fauset, Jessie Redmon
1884?-1961..................**CLC 19**
See also CA 109
See also DLB 51

Faust, Irvin 1924-.................**CLC 8**
See also CA 33-36R
See also DLB 2, 28
See also DLB-Y 80

Fearing, Kenneth (Flexner)
1902-1961....................**CLC 51**
See also CA 93-96
See also DLB 9

Federman, Raymond 1928- ..... **CLC 6, 47**
See also CAAS 8
See also CANR 10
See also CA 17-20R
See also DLB-Y 80

Federspiel, J(ürg) F. 1931-........**CLC 42**

Feiffer, Jules 1929- .... **CLC 2, 8**
See also CA 17-20R
See also SATA 8
See also DLB 7, 44

Feinstein, Elaine 1930- ....**CLC 36**
See also CA 69-72
See also CAAS 1
See also DLB 14, 40

Feldman, Irving (Mordecai)
1928-........................**CLC 7**
See also CANR 1
See also CA 1-4R

Fellini, Federico 1920- ....**CLC 16**
See also CA 65-68

Felsen, Gregor 1916-
See Felsen, Henry Gregor

Felsen, Henry Gregor 1916-........**CLC 17**
See also CANR 1
See also CA 1-4R
See also SAAS 2
See also SATA 1

Fenton, James (Martin) 1949-......**CLC 32**
See also CA 102
See also DLB 40

Ferber, Edna 1887-1968..........**CLC 18**
See also CA 5-8R
See also obituary CA 25-28R
See also SATA 7
See also DLB 9, 28

Ferlinghetti, Lawrence (Monsanto)
1919?-...............**CLC 2, 6, 10, 27**
See also CANR 3
See also CA 5-8R
See also DLB 5, 16
See also CDALB 1941-1968

Ferrier, Susan (Edmonstone)
1782-1854...................**NCLC 8**

Feuchtwanger, Lion
1884-1958...................**TCLC 3**
See also CA 104
See also DLB 66

Feydeau, Georges 1862-1921 ..... **TCLC 22**
See also CA 113

Fiedler, Leslie A(aron)
1917-...................**CLC 4, 13, 24**
See also CANR 7
See also CA 9-12R
See also DLB 28, 67

Field, Andrew 1938- .... **CLC 44** (463)
See also CANR 25
See also CA 97-100

Field, Eugene 1850-1895 .... **NCLC 3**
See also SATA 16
See also DLB 21, 23, 42

Fielding, Henry 1707-1754...........**LC 1**
See also DLB 39

Fielding, Sarah 1710-1768 ....**LC 1**
See also DLB 39

Fierstein, Harvey 1954-.............**CLC 33**
See also CA 123

Figes, Eva 1932-..................**CLC 31**
See also CANR 4
See also CA 53-56
See also DLB 14

Finch, Robert (Duer Claydon)
1900-........................**CLC 18**
See also CANR 9, 24
See also CA 57-60

Findley, Timothy 1930-............**CLC 27**
See also CANR 12
See also CA 25-28R
See also DLB 53

Fink, Janis 1951-
See Ian, Janis

Firbank, (Arthur Annesley) Ronald
1886-1926....................**TCLC 1**
See also CA 104
See also DLB 36

Firbank, Louis 1944-
See Reed, Lou

Fisher, Roy 1930- ....**CLC 25**
See also CANR 16
See also CA 81-84
See also DLB 40

Fisher, Rudolph 1897-1934 ...... **TCLC 11**
See also CA 107, 124
See also DLB 51

Fisher, Vardis (Alvero)
1895-1968....................**CLC 7**
See also CA 5-8R
See also obituary CA 25-28R
See also DLB 9

FitzGerald, Edward
1809-1883...................**NCLC 9**
See also DLB 32

Author Index

Author Index

Author Index

Author Index

Author Index

Author Index

Rawlings, Marjorie Kinnan
1896-1953 . . . . **TCLC 4**
See also CA 104
See also YABC 1
See also DLB 9, 22

Ray, Satyajit 1921- . . . . **CLC 16**
See also CA 114

Read, Herbert (Edward)
1893-1968 . . . . **CLC 4**
See also CA 85-88
See also obituary CA 25-28R
See also DLB 20

Read, Piers Paul 1941- . . . . . . **CLC 4, 10, 25**
See also CA 21-24R
See also SATA 21
See also DLB 14

Reade, Charles 1814-1884 . . . . **NCLC 2**
See also DLB 21

Reade, Hamish 1936-
See Gray, Simon (James Holliday)

Reading, Peter 1946- . . . . **CLC 47**
See also CA 103
See also DLB 40

Reaney, James 1926- . . . . **CLC 13**
See also CA 41-44R
See also SATA 43

Rebreanu, Liviu 1885-1944 . . . . . . **TCLC 28**

Rechy, John (Francisco)
1934- . . . . **CLC 1, 7, 14, 18**
See also CAAS 4
See also CANR 6
See also CA 5-8R
See also DLB-Y 82

Redcam, Tom 1870-1933 . . . . **TCLC 25**

Redgrove, Peter (William)
1932- . . . . **CLC 6, 41**
See also CANR 3
See also CA 1-4R
See also DLB 40

Redmon (Nightingale), Anne
1943- . . . . **CLC 22**
See also Nightingale, Anne Redmon
See also DLB-Y 86

Reed, Ishmael
1938- . . . . **CLC 2, 3, 5, 6, 13, 32**
See also CANR 25
See also CA 21-24R
See also DLB 2, 5, 33

Reed, John (Silas) 1887-1920 . . . . . . **TCLC 9**
See also CA 106

Reed, Lou 1944- . . . . **CLC 21**

Reeve, Clara 1729-1807 . . . . **NCLC 19**
See also DLB 39

Reid, Christopher 1949- . . . . **CLC 33**
See also DLB 40

Reid Banks, Lynne 1929-
See Banks, Lynne Reid
See also CANR 6, 22
See also CA 1-4R
See also SATA 22

Reiner, Max 1900-
See Caldwell, (Janet Miriam) Taylor
(Holland)

Reizenstein, Elmer Leopold 1892-1967
See Rice, Elmer

Remark, Erich Paul 1898-1970
See Remarque, Erich Maria

Remarque, Erich Maria
1898-1970 . . . . **CLC 21**
See also CA 77-80
See also obituary CA 29-32R
See also DLB 56

Remizov, Alexey (Mikhailovich)
1877-1957 . . . . **TCLC 27**

Renard, Jules 1864-1910 . . . . **TCLC 17**
See also CA 117

Renault, Mary
1905-1983 . . . . **CLC 3, 11, 17**
See also Challans, Mary
See also DLB-Y 83

Rendell, Ruth 1930- . . . . **CLC 28, 48**
See also Vine, Barbara
See also CA 109

Renoir, Jean 1894-1979 . . . . **CLC 20**
See also obituary CA 85-88

Resnais, Alain 1922- . . . . **CLC 16**

Reverdy, Pierre 1889-1960 . . . . **CLC 53**
See also CA 97-100
See also obituary CA 89-92

Rexroth, Kenneth
1905-1982 . . . . . . **CLC 1, 2, 6, 11, 22, 49**
See also CANR 14
See also CA 5-8R
See also obituary CA 107
See also DLB 16, 48
See also DLB-Y 82
See also CDALB 1941-1968

Reyes y Basoalto, Ricardo Eliecer Neftali
1904-1973
See Neruda, Pablo

Reymont, Władyslaw Stanisław
1867-1925 . . . . **TCLC 5**
See also CA 104

Reynolds, Jonathan 1942?- . . . . . **CLC 6, 38**
See also CA 65-68

Reynolds, Michael (Shane)
1937- . . . . **CLC 44 (514)**
See also CANR 9
See also CA 65-68

Reznikoff, Charles 1894-1976 . . . . . . **CLC 9**
See also CAP 2
See also CA 33-36
See also obituary CA 61-64
See also DLB 28, 45

Rezzori, Gregor von 1914- . . . . **CLC 25**
See also CA 122

Rhys, Jean
1890-1979 . . . . . . **CLC 2, 4, 6, 14, 19, 51**
See also CA 25-28R
See also obituary CA 85-88
See also DLB 36

Ribeiro, Darcy 1922- . . . . **CLC 34 (102)**
See also CA 33-36R

Ribeiro, João Ubaldo (Osorio Pimentel)
1941- . . . . **CLC 10**
See also CA 81-84

Ribman, Ronald (Burt) 1932- . . . . **CLC 7**
See also CA 21-24R

Rice, Anne 1941- . . . . **CLC 41**
See also CANR 12
See also CA 65-68

Rice, Elmer 1892-1967 . . . . **CLC 7, 49**
See also CAP 2
See also CA 21-22
See also obituary CA 25-28R
See also DLB 4, 7

Rice, Tim 1944-
See Rice, Tim and Webber, Andrew Lloyd
See also CA 103

Rice, Tim 1944- and
Webber, Andrew Lloyd
1948- . . . . **CLC 21**

Rich, Adrienne (Cecile)
1929- . . . . **CLC 3, 6, 7, 11, 18, 36**
See also CANR 20
See also CA 9-12R
See also DLB 5, 67

Richard, Keith 1943-
See Jagger, Mick and Richard, Keith

Richards, I(vor) A(rmstrong)
1893-1979 . . . . **CLC 14, 24**
See also CA 41-44R
See also obituary CA 89-92
See also DLB 27

Richards, Keith 1943-
See Richard, Keith
See also CA 107

Richardson, Dorothy (Miller)
1873-1957 . . . . **TCLC 3**
See also CA 104
See also DLB 36

Richardson, Ethel 1870-1946
See Richardson, Henry Handel
See also CA 105

Richardson, Henry Handel
1870-1946 . . . . **TCLC 4**
See also Richardson, Ethel

Richardson, Samuel 1689-1761 . . . . **LC 1**
See also DLB 39

Richler, Mordecai
1931- . . . . **CLC 3, 5, 9, 13, 18, 46**
See also CLR 17
See also CA 65-68
See also SATA 27, 44
See also DLB 53

Richter, Conrad (Michael)
1890-1968 . . . . **CLC 30**
See also CANR 23
See also CA 5-8R
See also obituary CA 25-28R
See also SATA 3
See also DLB 9

Richter, Johann Paul Friedrich 1763-1825
See Jean Paul

Riding, Laura 1901- . . . . **CLC 3, 7**
See also Jackson, Laura (Riding)

Riefenstahl, Berta Helene Amalia 1902-
See Riefenstahl, Leni
See also CA 108

Riefenstahl, Leni 1902- . . . . **CLC 16**
See also Riefenstahl, Berta Helene Amalia

Rilke, Rainer Maria
1875-1926 . . . . **TCLC 1, 6, 19**
See also CA 104

Rimbaud, (Jean Nicolas) Arthur
1854-1891 . . . . **NCLC 4**

Author Index

NCLC Cumulative Nationality Index

NCLC Cumulative Title Index

Title Index

Title Index

Title Index

Title Index

Title Index

Title Index

Title Index

Title Index

Title Index

Title Index

Title Index

Title Index

Title Index

Title Index